D1289157

NORDSTROM ON SALES & LEASES OF GOODS

SECOND EDITION

Gregory M. Travalio
Professor of Law, The Ohio State University College of Law

Robert J. Nordstrom
Partner, Porter, Wright, Morris and Arthur; Professor Emeritus,
The Ohio State University College of Law

Albert L. Clovis
Of Counsel, Porter, Wright, Morris and Arthur; Professor Emeritus,
The Ohio State University College of Law

ASPEN LAW & BUSINESS
A Division of Aspen Publishers, Inc.
Gaithersburg   New York

This publication is designed to provide accurate and authoritative information in regard to the subject matter covered. It is sold with the understanding that the publisher is not engaged in rendering legal, accounting, or other professional services. If legal advice or other professional assistance is required, the services of a competent professional person should be sought.

— From a *Declaration of Principles* jointly adopted by
a Committee of the American Bar Association and
a Committee of Publishers and Associations

Copyright © 2000 by Aspen Law and Business
A Division of Aspen Publishers, Inc.
A Wolters Kluwer Company
www.aspenpublishers.com

Printed in the United State of America.

1 2 3 4 5 6 7 8 9 0

Library of Congress Cataloging-in-Publication Data

Nordstrom, Robert J.
    Nordstrom on sales & leases of goods / Robert J. Nordstrom,
Gregory M. Travalio, Albert L. Clovis. — 2nd ed.
      p. cm.
    Includes bibliographical references and index.
    ISBN 0-7355-0684-1 (alk. paper)
    1. Sales—United States. 2. Leases—United States. I. Travalio,
Gregory M., 1947–   . II. Clovis, Albert L. III. Title.
KF915.N62   1999
346.7307'2—dc21
                                             99-36569
                                               CIP

About Aspen Law & Business

Aspen Law & Business—comprising the former Prentice Hall Law & Business, Little, Brown and Company's Professional Division, and Wiley Law Publications—is a leading publisher of authoritative treatises, practice manuals, services, and journals for attorneys, financial and tax advisors, corporate and bank directors, and other business professionals. Our mission is to provide practical solution-based how-to information keyed to the latest legislative, judicial, and regulatory developments.

We offer publications in the areas of banking and finance; bankruptcy; business and commercial law; construction law; corporate law; pensions, benefits, and labor; insurance law; securities; taxation; intellectual property; government and administrative law; real estate law; matrimonial and family law; environmental and health law; international law; legal practice and litigation; and criminal law.

Other Aspen Law & Business products treating contract law issues include:

Contemporary Corporation Forms
Contract Enforcement
Drafting Effective Contracts, Second Edition
Farnsworth on Contracts, Second Edition
Uniform Commercial Code

ASPEN LAW & BUSINESS
A Division of Aspen Publishers, Inc.
A Wolters Kluwer Company
www.aspenpublishers.com

SUBSCRIPTION NOTICE

This Aspen Law & Business product is updated on a periodic basis with supplements to reflect important changes in the subject matter. If you purchased this product directly from Aspen Law & Business, we have already recorded your subscription for the update service.

If, however, you purchased this product from a bookstore and wish to receive future updates and revised or related volumes billed separately with a 30-day examination review, please contact our Customer Service Department at 1-800-234-1660, or send your name, company name (if applicable), address, and the title of the product to:

ASPEN LAW & BUSINESS
A Division of Aspen Publishers, Inc.
7201 McKinney Circle
Frederick, MD 21704

ABOUT THE AUTHORS

Gregory M. Travalio is a graduate of the University of Pittsburgh (B.A. 1969; J.D. *magna cum laude* and Order of the Coif 1975) and Columbia University (L.L.M. 1979). He practiced in the areas of corporate and commercial law with the firm of Wolf, Block, Schorr & Solis-Cohen in Philadelphia prior to spending a year as an Associate-in-Law at Columbia University and then joining the faculty at The Ohio State University College of Law. During his time at Ohio State, Professor Travalio has served as the Associate Dean for Academic Affairs and has taught contracts, sales, consumer law, commercial paper, and other subjects. He is the author of numerous law review articles relating to commercial law and other topics, and is the Editorial Advisor to the Ohio Judicial Conference Jury Instruction Committee for whom he has drafted jury instructions on sales, secured transactions, and the Ohio Lemon Law.

Robert J. Nordstrom is a graduate of Western Michigan University (A.B. *summa cum laude*) and the University of Michigan (J.D. 1949; Order of the Coif). He was an associate in the Providence, Rhode Island firm of Hinckley, Allen, Salisbury and Parsons for approximately three years before joining the faculty of The Ohio State University College of Law. During his 25 years at Ohio State, and as a visitor at Duke University School of Law, Professor Nordstrom taught contracts, sales, and other commercial law courses. He is currently a partner in the Columbus, Ohio, firm of Porter, Wright, Morris & Arthur, LLP, specializing in national and international commercial law. He is the author or co-author of five text and case books on commercial law, including the first edition of this treatise.

Albert L. Clovis is a graduate of Yale College (B.A.), the University of Michigan (M.A.), and the Harvard Law School (LL.B. *cum laude*). He practiced business law with the firm of Day, Ketterer, Raley, Wright & Rybolt in Canton, Ohio, for three years, and, in 1965, joined the faculty of The Ohio State University College of Law. There, and as a visiting professor at the University of Virginia School of Law, the Notre Dame Law School, and the College of William and Mary School of Law, he has taught contracts, sales, secured transactions, bankruptcy, and other courses. Since 1972, he has been of counsel to the Columbus, Ohio, law firm of Porter, Wright, Morris & Arthur, LLP. He is the co-author of three casebooks on commercial law.

To my wife, Barbara, and to my daughters,
Sarah and Elisa, who are the lights of my life.
—G.M.T.

To Avis K.
—R.J.N.

To Judy.
—A.L.C.

CONTENTS

Chapter 5
PERFORMANCE OF THE SALES CONTRACT 567

I. PERFORMANCE OBLIGATIONS OF THE SELLER 570

Chapter 9
STATE REGULATION OF CONSUMER SALES **901**

Chapter 10
THE CONVENTION ON CONTRACTS FOR
INTERNATIONAL SALE OF GOODS **933**

Chapter 11
LEASES UNDER ARTICLE 2A **989**

PREFACE

This book focuses on Article 2 of the Uniform Commercial Code, as any book about the American law of sales and leases must do. The First Edition was written in Article 2's youth (1970). This Second Edition was written in Article 2's maturity and during the preparation of a revised Article 2.

The current Article 2, on which this book concentrates, is likely to remain in force in most states for the next several years. In time, it will probably be replaced by the new Article that, as of this writing, is, perhaps, two years away from completion and promulgation. The new Article contains more continuity than change, treating most matters in a manner substantially similar to the current Article. However, it treats a number of important issues differently and provides for some recent developments that are not covered in the current Article. This Second Edition identifies the instances in which the new Article departs significantly from the current Article and comments on its new and different provisions.

Legislative change of the kind that will be wrought by the eventual enactment of the new Article 2 is, of course, important. It is also important, however, to understand the fundamental problems—many of them perennial—with which the law of sales must cope. It is on these problems that we have concentrated our attention in drafting the Second Edition. We have tried to approach them thoughtfully and analytically, and we have tried to suggest what their legal treatment ought to be—under the current statute and generally. We hope and believe that this approach will be useful to lawyers, judges, and students of the law.

The coverage of this book is not limited to Article 2. Article 2A on leases of goods, the United Nations Convention on Contracts for the International Sale of Goods, and a number of statutes and regulations dealing with issues of consumer protection are also covered. Our goal here is to provide a comprehensive and analytical treatment of the law of sales and leases of goods, as that law exists and is developing at the turn of the millennium.

September 1999

G. M. T.
R. J. N.
A. L. C.

ACKNOWLEDGMENTS

We gratefully acknowledge the research assistance of Noel Alden, Jason Ritchey, Ted Taggart, Andrew Shaw, Colleen Libbey, Amanda Zibners, and Charles Clovis. Their help was essential to the completion of this book and significantly enhanced its quality. We also thank Pat Schirtzinger and Nancy Darling for their outstanding secretarial assistance.

CHAPTER 1

INTRODUCTION

---

§ 1.01   SCOPE OF THIS TEXT

This text outlines the basic law of the United States relating to the sale of goods. Like its predecessor,[1] the text deals primarily with Article 2 of the Uniform Commercial Code. However, when the *Law of Sales* was published in 1970, Professor Nordstrom had very little case law to work with. *The Uniform Commercial Code Reporting Service* had six volumes of published cases. At the time of this writing it has seventy-seven. As a result of this dearth of case law, the primary focus of the original work was analytical rather than descriptive. The *Law of Sales* was intended to guide judges, lawyers, and students in interpreting and applying Article 2 of the Code in a thoughtful and intelligent manner—to state what the law *should be* rather than what it is.

Stating what the law should be remains a primary goal of this book. The authors have made an effort to provide their analysis and perspective on most of the important issues raised by Article 2 of the Code. Despite the passage of years, many important problems remain unresolved, and one of the purposes of a work such as this is to assist in their resolution. In addition, as will be described shortly, a major effort is underway to revise Article 2. The authors hope that this book can assist in that effort.

Nonetheless, seventy-seven volumes of reported cases can hardly be ignored. As a result, there is a larger descriptive component to this work than was present in the original work. Some of the issues anticipated by Professor Nordstrom in the *Law of Sales* have largely been resolved, generally in a manner consistent with the analysis offered in the *Law of Sales*. In these cases, the authors have made an effort to provide ample case authority for the propositions stated in the book. Even on the important issues that remain open, we now have the benefit of many judicial opinions, and many of the leading cases are dealt with in detail. At the same time, we have consciously struggled to maintain the strong analytical component of the original work.

Although the focus of this work remains squarely on Article 2, unlike the *Law of Sales,* Article 2 is not the exclusive focus. In recognition of the growing global economy, a chapter has been added on the Convention on the International Sale of Goods. The consumer movement has spawned two chapters. The first of these (Chapter Eight) deals primarily with the Magnuson-Moss Federal Warranty Act, with a short section on the FTC Rule Concerning the Preservation of Consumer Defenses. The second (Chapter Nine) discusses the impact of state statutes regulating unfair and deceptive

---

[1] Robert J. Nordstrom, Law of Sales (West 1970).

practices, including the "lemon laws" that have been passed in virtually all jurisdictions. Finally, a chapter (Eleven) has been added dealing with Article 2A of the Code—leases of goods.

Much has been left out, however, that could have reasonably been included. There is little discussion of credit and the state and federal statutes that comprehensively regulate it. Yet the extension of credit is involved in millions (perhaps billions) of sales per day. Thus, the work does not discuss statutes such as the Truth-in-Lending Act, the Fair Credit Reporting Act or state Retail Installment Sales Acts. Despite the close relationship that products liability in tort has to warranty law under the Code, this work does not deal comprehensively with products liability in tort. Like the original work, this book deals with the history of commercial law only when necessary to interpret present law. All of this has been left out in order to keep the book focused and the project manageable. The goal of this book, however, ultimately remains the same as that of Professor Nordstrom's original work— to present in a textual fashion the current law of the United States applicable to the sale of goods.

§ 1.02   HISTORY OF THE CODE

The Uniform Commercial Code is a product of approximately twenty years of hard work by a number of dedicated people.[2] This work began around the mid-forties (although legal historians may select an earlier date)[3] and falls into two stages. First, there was the drafting followed by study, analysis, and more drafting. All of the drafting was sponsored by the National Conference of Commissioners on Uniform State Laws and the American Law Institute. The most comprehensive study was that of the New York Law Revision Commission, which concentrated its attention on the 1952 Official Text of the Code.[4] There were, in addition, many scholarly articles

---

[2] There is a concise history of the Code in Malcolm, "The Uniform Commercial Code in the United States," 12 Int'l & Comp. L.Q. 226 (1963). There is also a short history of the Code and a listing of those who worked on it in the Introductory Comment to the 1962 Official Text.

[3] One possible earlier date is 1938, when the Merchants Association of the City of New York sponsored a proposal for the drafting of a federal sales act to govern interstate sales. Responding to this proposal, the National Conference of Commissioners on Uniform State Laws undertook a revision of the Uniform Sales Act. Two years later the National Conference broadened the undertaking to include a complete commercial code. *See* Malcolm, *supra* note 2.

[4] The Report of the New York Law Revision Commission was made in 1956. The Commission concluded that codification of the major parts of commercial law was a good idea, but also concluded that the 1952 draft was "not satisfactory in its present form and cannot

written by both practitioners and teachers of the law. The result was the adoption of two further drafts: the 1958 and the 1962 drafts. While some of the other articles have undergone substantial revision since 1972,[5] the 1962 draft remains the basis for the present Article 2.

The next stage in the history of the Code is found in the Code's adoption in all fifty states, the District of Columbia, and the Virgin Islands. In the main, this stage was a product of the 1960s with the last state's Code having become effective in 1974.[6] Thus, in roughly twenty years the Uniform Commercial Code grew from little more than an idea to a comprehensive code enacted by all but one state in the United States. The two sponsoring organizations have established a Permanent Editorial Board for the Uniform Commercial Code. This Board reviews state changes in the Code's official text and recommends whether those changes should be uniformly adopted. In addition, the Board recommends amendments whenever new commercial practices have rendered provisions of the Code obsolete or new provisions desirable, court decisions have cast doubt on the intended interpretation of some section, some provision has proved unworkable, or for any other reason a provision "obviously requires amendment."

The third stage began over a decade ago, in 1985. In this year, the Editorial Board discussed the possibility of a review of Article 2.[7] This led to an analysis and review of Article 2 by a subcommittee of the Committee on Uniform Commercial Code, ABA Section of Corporation, Banking and Business Law. This subcommittee recommended that a possible revision of Article 2 should be studied by the National Conference and the ALI. Following this recommendation, the Permanent Editorial Board approved a study to consider whether Article 2 should be revised; the National Conference and the ALI approved the project and provided funding.[8]

A nine-member Study Group was appointed in March 1988, and they were given the task of identifying the "major problems of practical importance" in the "interpretation and application of Article 2."[9] In June 1988,

---

be made satisfactory without comprehensive reexamination and revision in the light of all critical comment obtainable." 1956 N.Y. Law Rev. Comm. Rep. 67–68. The Commission's hearings occupy two volumes, and its study three volumes.

[5] For example, Article 9 was revised in 1972; Article 3 was revised in 1990; and Article 5 was revised in 1995.

[6] Louisiana adopted the Code except for Articles 2 and 9 in 1974. It has since adopted Article 9, but has not adopted Article 2.

[7] Charles W. Mooney, "Proposed Revision of Article 2," C465 A.L.I.-A.B.A. 403, 405 (1989).

[8] PEB Study Group: Uniform Commercial Code, Article 2 Executive Summary, 46 Bus. Law. 1869, 1870 (1991).

[9] *Id.*

the Study Group had its first meeting, after which ten study topics were assigned. Between June 1988 and March 1990, the Study Group met five times. In March 1990, a Preliminary Report, in which the Study Group unanimously recommended that Article 2 should be revised, was distributed to the public for comments. Written responses to the Preliminary Report were considered by the Study Group, and after review, the Group revised their original recommendation. The appointment of a Drafting Committee followed the revised Preliminary Report.[10]

The first meeting of the Article 2 Drafting Committee took place in December 1991, and the drafting process continues as this book goes to press. There have been numerous drafts that have been considered by the NCCUSL and the ALI. The drafting process has considered the comments of the American Bar Association and its interested committee, and has received input from many interested organizations and parties. Completion of the drafting process and the promulgation of revisions by NCCUSL is unlikely to occur before 2001, and perhaps not until 2002 or 2003.

---

[10] The Drafting Committee was appointed by the NCCUSL and the ALI in the fall of 1991.

CHAPTER 2

COVERAGE OF ARTICLE 2

§ 2.01   UNIFORMITY AND CONSTRUCTION OF THE CODE

[A]   The Uniformity of Commercial Law

Commercial transactions are planned transactions in which the parties set certain terms for an exchange, usually an exchange of money for goods. According to classic economic theory, both parties are made better off by a voluntary exchange, and exchanges of goods and services increase the over-all welfare of those in society. People, however, will not invest in the planning and performance of transactions unless they can anticipate that the reasonable expectations created by the terms of the exchange will be fulfilled. Commercial law needs a substantial degree of predictability in order for the market to function effectively.

The nation-wide adoption of the Code has, for the most part, succeeded in providing this predictability. Although every state has included at least some nonuniform provisions in its version of the Code, the number of states that have modified any particular provision is usually small.[1] This means that interstate transactions can be planned with considerable certainty. Further, even with intrastate transactions, the uniform origin of the Code makes decisions from sister states relevant in construing the local Code, promoting uniformity among the states.

For at least three reasons, however, some of the uniformity which the drafters intended for the Code has been lost. As previously mentioned, every state version varies in some way from the Official Text. While most of the variations are minor in their impact on commercial transactions, their cumulative effect cannot be ignored. Also, a few of the variations are of considerable significance in their own right.

More important, during the thirty-six years since the promulgation of the 1962 Official Text, judges have frequently lost sight of the importance of uniformity among the states. Instances of substantial disagreement among the courts as to the proper interpretation of a Code provision occupy a substantial portion of this book. Although judges should not follow a clearly erroneous interpretation by sister courts for the sake of uniformity, too often the important goal of uniformity is simply not taken into account at all.

Finally, as mentioned earlier,[2] the Code does not comprehensively cover the law of sales. For example, the law does not regulate consumer credit, and even though a Uniform Consumer Credit Code has been prom-

---

[1] An exception to this is U.C.C. § 2-318 which, by providing three alternatives to the states, is inherently nonuniform. In addition, a number of states have adopted variations of section 2-318 that are different from any of the three alternatives.

[2] *See* § 1.01, *supra.*

ulgated and most states have passed Retail Installment Sales Acts, the law from state to state in this area is far less uniform than the Code. There were a variety of reasons for carving this and other areas out of the scope of the Code. In some instances, the drafters feared that local policies were so strong and so varied that an attempt to incorporate a uniform solution into the Code would jeopardize the chances of its adoption. In some instances, other groups were at work on uniform legislation and deference was given to their labors. Time, too, must have been a factor in determining what was to be covered. If every commercial problem had been covered and agreement reached among the drafters on all those problems, the drafting time would have been extended for many more years. The result is that there are several areas of the law affecting commercial transactions that are not touched by the Code.

[B]   Construing the Code

Construing the Code requires a strange kind of double-mindedness. The Code is a group of statutes, and all statutes must be read precisely. For example, section 2-703 begins: "Where the buyer wrongfully rejects or revokes acceptance of goods or fails to make a payment due on or before delivery or repudiates with respect to a part or the whole. . . ." It is not accurate to say that what this phrase really means is "When the buyer defaults." Section 2-703 does not use the word "default." Instead, it selects four events—each of which may be a default, but all of which do not add up to all of the possible defaults that a buyer may commit—and lists those events with precision. It is only when one of these events occurs that section 2-703 is applicable.

The Code, however, is more than a group of statutes; it is a code. As such, it expresses several discernable policies. Sometimes these policies are expressed in specific Code sections.[3] Other times they emerge only from a reading of several parts of the Code and from an understanding of the business background from which those parts were written. A search for Code policies sometimes results in a broad interpretation of the statute not apparent from a literal reading. It is this double-mindedness that is required in construing the Code.

Something must be said about role of the Code Comments in interpreting the Code. Each section of the Code is followed by one or more Comments. These Comments, which vary in length from a single sentence to several pages, contain information about prior uniform statutory provi-

---

[3] *See, e.g.*, U.C.C. §§ 1-102(2) and 1-106.

sions; the changes, if any, made in these prior provisions; and the purposes of the Code section.

The Comments were drafted by the committees that worked on the various Articles of the Code. They were not enacted by the legislatures that enacted the Code. Thus, they are not "law," nor are they legislative history in the sense of being a record of the committee deliberations at the time the Code was being considered in the state legislature.

Nonetheless, the Comments have frequently been accorded significant weight by courts in construing the Code. One reason for this is best summarized by the introductory comment to the Code:

> This comment and those which follow are the Comments of the National Conference of Commissioners on Uniform State Laws and the American Law Institute. Uniformity throughout American jurisdictions is one of the main objectives of this Code; and that objective cannot be obtained without substantial uniformity of construction. To aid in uniform construction these Comments set forth the purpose of various provisions of this Act to promote uniformity, to aid in viewing the Act as an integrated whole, and to safeguard against misconstruction.[4]

In addition to uniformity, there is another reason why courts have relied heavily upon the Comments in construing the Code. There is a wealth of material in the Comments; that material was before the legislatures when the Code was adopted and should not be overlooked as a source of Code construction. The Comments often explain why certain statutory language was chosen, what policies were sought to be adopted or rejected, and how the section under consideration harmonizes with other parts of the Code. The material is too valuable to be ignored by courts or lawyers.[5]

Nevertheless, it must be remembered that the Comments are not the legislation. They should not be relied upon in preference to a close study of the Code. The Comments may suggest a construction of the statutory language, form a basis for double-checking a construction already arrived at, and refer to other sections that might otherwise be overlooked. For these reasons, they are an extremely valuable aid in construing the Code. When the Code and the Comments conflict, however, the Comments must be rejected.

---

[4] Comment to the title of the Code.

[5] *See* Burchett v. Allied Concord Fin. Corp., 74 N.M. 575, 396 P.2d 186 (1964) (although the Comments are not direct authority for the construction of the Code, they are highly persuasive).

§ 2.02   THE CODE AND CHOICE OF LAW

When a suit is brought on a commercial transaction with multistate connections, a decision may have to be made as to what law should govern the transaction. Should it be the law of the forum, the law specified by the parties in the contract, the law of the place where the contract was made or where it was to be performed, or some other law?

To the extent that the states have taken the drafters' goal of uniformity seriously, in many cases it should not matter which state's law is applicable, because adoption of the Code by U.S. jurisdictions is universal, with the partial exception of Louisiana. As will become clear upon reading this text, however, some states have adopted nonuniform provisions in their versions of the Code. More frequently, courts in the various states have differed as to how to interpret many of the Code provisions. On many, if not most, of the most significant interpretive issues arising under Article 2, there are disparate views among the courts. Finally, courts will sometimes be required to choose between adopting the substantive law of a U.S. jurisdiction and that of a foreign jurisdiction.

The basic Code section designed to aid in the solution of these problems is section 1-105, which establishes three rules:

1. In eight situations, specific sections of the Code provide the law that is applicable to the transaction. These eight are: transactions dealing with the rights of creditors against goods sold (§ 2-402); issues involving the compliance or noncompliance with a certificate of title on leased goods and certain limitations on the choice of law in consumer leases (§§ 2A-105, 2A-106); bank deposits and collections (§ 4-102); funds transfers (§ 4A-507); letters of credit (§ 5-116); bulk transfers (§ 6-103); investment securities (§ 8-110); and secured transactions perfection provisions (§ 9-103).[6] Often, these are situations in which a third party is likely to become involved and for which a type of situs law can reasonably be selected as the controlling law.

2. Aside from these situations, the parties are free to choose the applicable law so long as their choice bears a reasonable relation to the transaction.[7]

3. If the parties fail to choose the applicable law and if the transaction is not one of the eight mentioned above, the Code of the forum state is to be applied to transactions bearing an "appropriate relation" to the forum state.[8]

---

[6] U.C.C. § 1-105(2).
[7] U.C.C. § 1-105(1).
[8] *Id.*

[A] Party Autonomy and the Choice of Law—The Reasonable Relation Test

The Code Comments recognize a distinction between a choice of law regarding the *interpretation* of a contract, and a choice of law regarding the *validity* of a contract. The parties to a contract ought to be free, with little restriction, to select the system of law that will be used to aid in the interpretation of the language that they use. After all, the parties could have written into their contract the detailed principles of interpretation used by the selected state, and the court would have honored these principles in construing the parties' language. The Comments to section 1-105 recognize this freedom:

> But an agreement as to choice of law may sometime take effect as a shorthand expression of the intent of the parties as to matters governed by their agreement, even though the transaction has no significant contact with the jurisdiction chosen.[9]

The privilege of the parties, however, to select the system of law governing matters other than interpretation, is subject to greater restriction, both traditionally[10] and under section 1-105. Nonetheless, it is clear that the drafters intended the parties to have wide latitude in selecting the law governing their rights and duties under the contract. All that is required is that the transaction bear a "reasonable relation" to the law chosen by the parties in order for that law to govern the transaction.[11]

Comment 1 to section 1-105 provides some guidance as to when the law chosen by the parties will bear a "reasonable relation" to the transaction:

> In general, the test of "reasonable relation" is similar to that laid down by the Supreme Court in *Seeman v. Philadelphia Warehouse Co.*, 274 U.S. 403, 47 S. Ct. 626, 71 L. Ed. 1123 (1927). Ordinarily the law

---

[9] U.C.C. § 1-105, Comment 1.

[10] *See, e.g.*, E. Geril & Co. v. Cunard S.S. Co., 48 F.2d 115 (2d Cir. 1931); Johnston v. Commercial Travelers Mut. Accident Ass'n, 242 S.C. 387, 131 S.E.2d 91 (1963); Russell J. Weintraub, "The Contracts Proposals of the Second Restatement of Conflict of Laws—A Critique," 46 Iowa L. Rev. 713 (1961).

[11] U.C.C. § 1-105(1) provides in part:

> Except as provided hereafter in this section, when a transaction bears a reasonable relation to this state and also to another state or nation the parties may agree that the law either of this state or of such other state or nation shall govern their rights and duties.

chosen must be that of a jurisdiction where a significant enough portion
of the making or performance of the contract is to occur or occurs.[12]

The *Seeman* case cited in the Comment involved the question of which
state's usury statute was to govern a loan transaction between a Pennsylvania
lender and a New York borrower. Although the contract contained no explicit
choice-of-law clause, the Court determined that the parties intended Pennsylvania law to apply to the transaction. In upholding the parties' choice of
Pennsylvania law, the Court said that the parties were free to choose the
applicable law unless the law chosen "has no normal relation to the transaction" and was chosen simply to evade the law that would otherwise be
applicable.[13] Thus, only when it is shown that the contact did not occur in
the normal course of the transaction, but was contrived to validate the parties' choice of governing law, should the relation be held unreasonable.[14]

The cases confirm the broad latitude given to the parties to choose the
applicable law. In the vast majority of cases, the parties' choice of law has
been upheld by the courts.[15] This is true even in cases where the courts
explicitly recognized that the transaction's most significant contacts were
with a state (or foreign country) other than the one whose law was chosen.[16]

---

[12] U.C.C. § 1-105, Official Comment 1.

[13] 274 U.S. at 408, 47 S. Ct. at 627.

[14] A number of cases have explicitly adopted the "normal relation" standard suggested
by Comment 1. *See, e.g.*, Woods-Tucker Leasing Corp. of Ga. v. Hutchinson-Ingram Dev.
Co., 642 F.2d 744, 30 UCCR 1505 (5th Cir. 1981); Superfos Invs. Ltd. v. Firstmiss Fertilizer,
Inc., 809 F. Supp. 450, 20 UCCR2d 4 (S.D. Miss. 1992); Admiral Ins. Co. v. Brinkcraft
Dev. Ltd., 921 F.2d 591, 14 UCCR2d 38 (5th Cir. 1991).

[15] *See, e.g.*, Tennessee Carolina Transp., Inc. v. Strick Corp., 16 N.C. App. 198, 692
S.E.2d 702, 11 UCCR 970 (1972); Mell v. Goldberg & Co., 10 Ill. App. 3d 809, 295 N.E.2d
97, 12 UCCR 172 (Ill. Ct. App. 1973); Calloway v. Manion, 572 F.2d 1033, 23 UCCR 1143
(5th Cir. 1978); Western Auto Supply Co. v. Craig, 30 UCCR 1206 (S.D. Ala. 1981); AMF,
Inc. v. Computer Aviation, Inc., 573 F. Supp. 924, 37 UCCR 1588 (S.D. Ohio 1983); As-
sociated Metals & Minerals Corp. v. Sharon Steel Corp., 590 F. Supp. 18, 39 UCCR 892
(S.D.N.Y. 1983); Mostek Corp. v. Chemetron Corp., 642 S.W.2d 20, 40 UCCR 840 (Tex.
Ct. App. 1982); Intamin, Inc. v. Figley-Wright Contractors, Inc., 595 F. Supp. 1350, 40
UCCR 766 (N.D. Ill. 1984); Besicorp Group, Inc. v. Thermo Electron Corp., 981 F. Supp.
86; 34 UCCR2d 1024 (N.D.N.Y. 1997).

[16] *See, e.g.*, Woods-Tucker Leasing Corp. of Ga. v. Hutchinson-Ingram Dev. Co., 642 F.2d
744, 30 UCCR 1505 (5th Cir. 1981) (court recognized that Texas contacts were most significant but upheld parties' choice of Massachusetts law); Fuller v. Compaigne Des Bauxites
de Guinee, 421 F. Supp. 938, 20 UCCR 629 (W.D. Pa. 1976) (court upheld parties' choice
of foreign law even though 97 percent of the contract was to be performed in the United
States); Triangle Underwriters, Inc. v. Honeywell, Inc., 457 F. Supp. 765, 24 UCCR 1088
(S.D.N.Y. 1978) (court upheld parties' choice of Massachusetts law while recognizing that
contacts with Massachusetts were "minimal").

Some courts have held that it is sufficient if the seller's principal place of business is in the state whose law is chosen, even though that is the only significant contact with the transaction.[17]

Occasionally, however, courts have not acceded to the parties' contractual choice of law. In a number of cases, this was because the transaction bore *no* relationship to the state chosen.[18] In a few cases, however, courts have not honored the parties' choice of law, despite the existence of some relationship between the transaction and the state whose law was agreed to by the parties. For example, in *Bank of Indiana, N.A. v. Holyfield*,[19] the court refused to apply Kentucky law to a lease of dairy cows, although the lessor was a Kentucky corporation and the lease had a provision making Kentucky law applicable. A year and a half after the cows were delivered, a tornado struck the lessee's farm killing 30 of 115 leased cows and destroying the lessee's farm. A provision in the lease placed the entire risk of loss on the lessee, requiring the lessee to continue to pay the rent for the term of the lease and to replace the lost cows. The insurance provided by the lessor through the lease was completely inadequate to compensate the lessees for the loss and to enable them to carry out their responsibilities under the lease.

Despite the provision in the lease applying Kentucky law to the contract, the court refused to do so. Instead, it applied Mississippi law, the law of the forum and the state of residence of the lessee. The court said that the contract was an adhesion contract, drafted by the lessor, and not subject to negotiation. The lessee, who had an eighth-grade education, had not read the entire 26-paragraph lease, which the court described as "so complex that a party with no training in the law could not hope to decipher all the potential disadvantageous terms therein."[20] It further found that the lessee had no idea that he was dealing with a Kentucky company; the agent that the lessee had dealt with had not disclosed this fact, and the lessee had no reason

---

[17] *See* Island Creek Coal Co. v. Lake Shore, Inc., 636 F. Supp. 285, 2 UCCR2d 59 (W.D. Va. 1986); Samuel Black Co. v. Burroughs Co., 33 UCCR 954 (D. Mass. 1981); Damin Aviation v. Sikorsky Aircraft, 705 F. Supp. 170, 9 UCCR2d 491 (S.D.N.Y. 1989); Triangle Underwriters, Inc. v. Honeywell, Inc., 957 F. Supp. 765, 24 UCCR 1088 (S.D.N.Y. 1978); Lafayette Stabilizer Repair, Inc. v. Machinery Wholesalers Corp., 750 F.2d 1290, 40 UCCR 122 (5th Cir. 1985).

[18] *See* Baker v. Gotz, 16 UCCR 26 (D. Del. 1975); WOCO v. Benjamin Franklin Corp., 20 UCCR 1015 (D.N.H. 1976); Duplan Corp. v. W.B. Davis Hosiery Mills, 442 F. Supp. 86, 23 UCCR 591 (S.D.N.Y. 1977); United Counties Trust Co. v. Mac Lum Inc., 31 UCCR 401 (5th Cir. 1981).

[19] 27 UCCR 635 (S.D. Miss. 1979).

[20] 27 UCCR at 642.

to know of it. The court concluded that, "[i]n light of the substantial contacts this state has with this lease, when contrasted with the lesser connection with Kentucky and the hidden nature of the contacts with that state, it is far more reasonable for Mississippi law to control this lawsuit."[21] The court found the contract unconscionable under Mississippi law.

The result in *Bank of Indiana* is justified. To the extent that a choice of law has been *agreed upon* by the parties, it should be the governing law. The court, however, must not abdicate its task of determining the *objective agreement* of the parties. A choice-of-law clause reproduced in the fine print of a take-it-or-leave-it document may, like other clauses in the same document, properly be held not to have been the product of the objective agreement of the parties. This does not mean that the clause must have been discussed or that the complaining party must actually have read the clause. It means only that the court must be convinced that the clause was fairly enough obtained so that it ought to become part of the total legal obligations of the parties.

The result of *Bank of Indiana* is also consistent with the suggestion in a number of cases that choice-of-law provisions in consumer contracts be subject to stricter standards for enforcement than contracts between commercial parties.[22] In these cases, the commercial sophistication of the parties was emphasized by the courts in allowing a contractual choice of law to stand. The difference between consumer and commercial contracts with regard to choice-of-law provisions has been recognized by commentators as well.[23] The provision governing choice of law in Article 2A makes the law of the lessee's place of residence the governing law in consumer leases regardless of a choice by the parties in the lease.[24] The lessee in *Bank of Indiana* was much more like a consumer than the typical commercial party.

---

[21] *Id.*

[22] *See* Delhomme Indus., Inc. v. Houston Beechcraft, Inc., 669 F.2d 1049, 33 UCCR 490 (5th Cir. 1982); Nantahala Village v. NCNB Nat'l Bank of Fla., 976 F.2d 876, 18 UCCR2d 1027 (4th Cir 1992); Providence & Worcester R.R. Co. v. Sargent & Greenleaf, Inc., 19 UCCR2d 21 (D.R.I. 1992).

[23] *See, e.g.*, Russell Weintraub, "Choice of Law in Contract," 54 Iowa L. Rev. 399, 426–429 (1968). *But see* William J. Woodward, Jr., " 'Sale' of Law and Forum and the Widening Gulf Between 'Consumer' and 'Nonconsumer' Contracts in the UCC," 75 Wash. U. L.Q. 243, 269–274 (1997) (criticizing the distinction between "consumer" and "nonconsumer" contracts in the enforcement of choice-of-law provisions).

[24] U.C.C. § 2A-106.

[B] Other Limits on Party Autonomy and Choice of Law

[1] Rights of Third Parties

Although the parties may agree as to the law that will govern their rights and duties, this choice may not bind third parties to the transaction.[25] This limitation on party autonomy is exemplified in some of the exceptions contained in subsection (2) of section 1-105. For example, section 2-402 provides that situs law determines the rights of creditors against sold goods. This "limit" on party autonomy is nothing more than an application of the general principle that parties to a contract cannot bind non-parties. There is no more reason that a non-party should be bound to a choice-of-law provision in a contract than any other provision in the contract.

[2] Public Policy

A few cases indicate that the public policy of the forum state might also impose a limitation on the application of foreign law chosen by the parties. In upholding the parties' choice of law in *Nederlands Draadindustrie NDI B.V. v. Grand Pre-Stressed Corp.*[26] the court said that the parties may consent to the law to be applied to the contract unless there is a strong countervailing public policy. The court in *Kathenes v. Quick Chek Food Stores*,[27] in enforcing the parties' choice of law where the harm resulting from breach of warranty was solely economic loss, indicated that the result might be different if personal injury had occurred. It said that the parties' choice of law would be honored under section 1-105 so long as there was a reasonable relationship between the law chosen and the transaction *and* the public policy of the forum would not be violated by enforcing the parties' choice. The Restatement (Second) of Conflict of Laws provides an even broader limitation, stating that the law chosen by the parties should not be applied if it "would be contrary to a fundamental policy of a state which has a materially greater interest than the chosen state in the determination of the particular issue and . . . would be the state of the applicable law in the absence of an effective choice of law by the parties."[28]

---

[25] *See* In re Automated Bookbinding Servs., Inc., 10 UCCR 209 (D. Md. 1972); Industrial Packaging Prods. Co. v. Fort Pitt Packaging Int'l, Inc., 399 Pa. 643, 161 A.2d 19 (1960). *See also* Cooper Power Sys. v. Union Carbide, 23 F.3d 675, 33 UCCR2d 803 (7th Cir. 1997) (dicta indicating that parties' choice of law would not bind third party beneficiary's tort claim).

[26] 466 F. Supp. 846, 26 UCCR 406 (E.D.N.Y. 1979).

[27] 596 F. Supp 713, 39 UCCR 1326 (D.N.J. 1984).

[28] Restatement (Second) of Conflict of Laws § 187 (1971).

Courts should be reluctant to read a public policy exception into section 1-105. It contains no express public policy exception to party autonomy and generally none is merited. Although local Code variations exist and courts in different jurisdictions have interpreted the same Code provision differently, these variations generally do not express a fundamental policy—some "deep-rooted tradition of the common weal."[29] While legislatures and judges will generally make their respective choices with public policy as a significant, if not paramount, concern, courts should refuse to enforce the parties' choice only when the competing policies involved are truly foundational.[30]

[C]   The "Appropriate Relation" Test

When the parties have not agreed as to the law that will govern their rights and duties, section 1-105 states that "this Act applies to transactions bearing an appropriate relation to this state."[31] Such a terse legislative command to the forum court attempting to solve a choice of law problem presents many difficulties. Those that will be dealt with in this section are:

1. What is an "appropriate relation"? Does it differ from the "reasonable relation" which has to be found before the parties can affirmatively select the applicable law?

2. Once some meaning is given to "appropriate relation," the court is told to apply the local Code. Suppose, however, the court finds that the transaction bears a minimal, although "appropriate," relation to the forum but is much more closely connected with another Code state and the Codes of the two states differ on the solution to the problem. Does the appropriate relation test require that the forum state nonetheless apply its own Code law?

3. What does the forum state do if it determines that the transaction does not bear an appropriate relation to the forum? Section 1-105 is silent

---

[29] Loucks v. Standard Oil Co., 224 N.Y. 99, 111, 120 N.E. 198, 202 (1918).

[30] *See* United Wholesale Liquor Co. v. Brown-Forman Distillers Corp., 108 N.M. 467, 775 P.2d 233, 9 UCCR2d 18 (N.M. 1989). In this case, the New Mexico Supreme Court upheld a provision in a distributorship contract which called for the application of Kentucky law. The court upheld the choice of law and refused to apply the New Mexico Franchise Act to the transaction. The court recognized that the New Mexico legislature had a legitimate public policy in attempting to balance the bargaining power between a wholesaler and a supplier, but held that freedom of the parties to choose the applicable law should nonetheless prevail.

[31] U.C.C. § 1-105(1).

as to what should be done if the forum (as judged by the appropriate relation test) is completely disinterested in the dispute?

The history of section 1-105 is crucial to resolving these problems. The drafters of the Uniform Commercial Code believed that it would take years, and perhaps decades, before there would be unanimous acceptance of the Code. At the same time, they firmly believed that the Code was a marked improvement over prior law and ought to be applied to as many transactions as possible. It appears that the primary goal of the drafters in devising section 1-105 was to secure the widespread application of adopted Codes.[32] In order to accomplish this purpose, the drafters selected a choice-of-law rule which provided that a forum with the Code should apply the Code to determine the rights and duties of the parties any time an "appropriate relation" to the Code state existed. Thus, the focus of the drafters in section 1-105 was on a situation in which the forum state had adopted the Code and the other state (or nation), whose law might apply, had not.[33]

With the virtually universal adoption of the Code, however, the cases arising today almost always involve situations in which the problem is not choosing between Code and non-Code law, but choosing which state's version of the Code should apply or, more frequently, which state's judicial gloss on the same Code provision will be applicable. How section 1-105 should apply in this context is unclear.[34] The Comments to section 1-105 do not address the situation at all; they focus on a conflict between a jurisdiction which has adopted the Code and one that has not.[35] There are at

---

[32] See Note, "Conflicts of Laws and the 'Appropriate Relation' Test of Section 1-105 of the Uniform Commercial Code," 40 Geo. Wash. L. Rev. 797, 801 (1972).

[33] This focus is made clear by Comment 3 to § 1-105:

Where a transaction has significant contacts with a state which has enacted the Act and also with other jurisdictions, the question what relation is "appropriate" is left to judicial decision. In deciding that question, the court is not strictly bound by precedents established in other contexts. Thus a conflict-of-laws decision refusing to apply a purely local statute or rule of law to a particular multi-state transaction may not be valid precedent for refusal to apply the Code in an analogous situation. Application of the Code in such circumstances may be justified by its comprehensiveness, by the policy of uniformity, and by the fact that it is in large part a reformulation and restatement of the law merchant and of the understanding of a business community which transcends state and even national boundaries.

[34] See David D. Siegel, "The U.C.C. and Choice of Law: Forum Choice or Forum Law," 21 Am. U. L. Rev. 494 (1972). The court in Alpert v. Thomas held that § 1-105 applies only where the choice of law at issue is between a state or entity that has enacted the U.C.C. and one that has not.

[35] See note 28, supra.

least three plausible interpretations of section 1-105, and each would resolve the problems posed above in a different way.

The first interpretation is that section 1-105 has no application when the choice of law is between two Code states. That is, the drafters, in drafting the Code, did not envision conflicting Code provisions or conflicting judicial interpretations of the Code. After all, one of the primary goals of the Code was uniformity, and it is reasonable to believe that section 1-105 was not intended to reach cases in which the Code would apply in some form whatever choice of law was made.[36] The court in *Alpert v. Thomas*[37] took this view and held that when the conflict was between two jurisdictions that had adopted the Code, the conflict was governed by other conflict rules of the forum, not section 1-105. While *Alpert* is one of the few cases explicitly adopting this view,[38] a number of other courts have seemed implicitly to accept it by ignoring section 1-105 in resolving conflicts between two Code states.[39]

There are two problems with this interpretation. First, it requires some stretching of the language of section 1-105. Section 1-105 mandates that "this Act" apply to transactions bearing an appropriate relation to the forum. Because the Code must be enacted by the forum state to be governing law, "this Act" logically refers to the *forum state's* Code. The language of section 1-105 admits of no exception when a non-forum state, whose law might be applicable, has also adopted the Code. Second, by its nature, it undercuts the Code's goal of uniformity. If the appropriate relation test of section 1-105 is simply ignored by states and their traditional conflict-of-laws rules applied, the conflict-of-laws rules in Code cases will be different from state to state to the extent that their traditional conflict-of-laws rules differ. If all states apply the "appropriate relation" test of section 1-105, at least the

---

[36] *See* David D. Siegel, "The U.C.C. and Choice of Law: Forum Choice or Forum Law," 21 Am. U. L. Rev. 494, 508 (1972).

[37] 643 F. Supp. 1406, 2 UCCR2d 99 (D. Vt. 1986).

[38] In a similar holding, the court in Madaus v. November Hill Farm, 1 UCCR2d 24 (W.D. Va. 1986) decided that U.C.C. § 1-105 should be interpreted to retain pre-Code choice-of-law rules. It held that section 1-105 must be read consistently with prior case law because the Comments to section 1-105 state that the "appropriate relation" is to be determined by the courts. *See also* Morgan v. Mar-bel, Inc., 614 F. Supp. 438, 41 UCCR 1271 (N.D. Ga. 1985) (court seems to interpret § 1-105 as calling for the application of the forum's choice of law rules rather than its substantive Code law).

[39] *See, e.g.,* Handy v. Uniroyal, Inc., 327 F. Supp. 596, 9 UCCR 629 (D. Del. 1971); Cohen v. Hathaway, 595 F. Supp. 579, 39 UCCR 857 (D. Mass. 1984); Long v. Sears Roebuck & Co., 877 F. Supp. 8, 26 UCCR2d 152 (D.D.C. 1995); Minnesota Mining & Mfg. Co. v. Mishika, Ltd., 953 S.W.2d 733, 33 UCCR2d 817 (Tex. 1996); Cox v. Lewiston Grain Growers, Inc., 86 Wash. App. 351, 936 P.2d 1191, 33 UCCR2d 443 (1997).

language of the conflict-of-laws rule in Code cases will be the same in all states.

If this interpretation of section 1-105 is adopted, however, the three questions posed above are easily resolved. As to the first question, there is no necessity for determining whether there is an appropriate relationship between the forum and the transaction—the test is irrelevant when the conflict is between two Code states. As to questions 2 and 3, the court simply refers to its traditional conflict rules, ignoring the appropriate relationship test, and applies the law of the state that is dictated by its traditional conflict rules.

The second, and most literal, interpretation of the "appropriate relation" test is that it establishes a threshold relation that the transaction must meet in order for the forum law to be applicable. Once an "appropriate relation" with the forum state is established, forum law applies even if the relationship of a non-forum state to the transaction is greater. The language of section 1-105 most strongly supports this interpretation. It requires only that the forum state have *an* appropriate relationship with the transaction for its law to apply, not *the* appropriate relationship, or *the most* appropriate relationship.

It is extremely difficult to determine the number of cases that have adopted this view. There are many cases in which the court simply recites the contacts that the transaction had with the forum state and concludes that an "appropriate relationship" exists.[40] In these cases, the courts do not discuss (1) what is required to establish an appropriate relationship; (2) whether the forum state had the most significant contacts with the transaction; and (3) what would occur if another state had more significant contacts than the forum state. Thus, it is not clear whether the "appropriate relation" test establishes a threshold after which forum law will apply, and, if this is true, what is necessary to meet this threshold.

A couple of cases, however, seem to have accepted this interpretation of section 1-105. In *Hope's Architectural Products, Inc. v. Lundy's Con-*

---

[40] *See, e.g.,* Skinner v. Tober Foreign Motors, Inc., 342 Mass. 429, 187 N.E.2d 669, 1 UCCR 1 (1963); Park County Implement Co. v. Craig, 397 P.2d 800, 2 UCCR 379 (Wyo. 1964); General Instrument Corp. v. Penn Pressed Metals, Inc., 366 F. Supp. 139, 13 UCCR 829 (M.D. Pa. 1973); Lloyd v. Classic Motor Coaches, Inc., 388 F. Supp. 785, 17 UCCR 761 (N.D. Ohio 1974); Aldon Indus., Inc. v. Don Myers & Assocs., Inc., 517 UCCR 1002 (7th Cir. 1975); Dart Indus., Inc. v. Adell Plastics, Inc., 517 F. Supp. 9, 31 UCCR 1397 (S.D. Ind. 1980); Cherry Creek Dodge, Inc. v. Carter, 733 P.2d 1024, 3 UCCR2d 1791 (Wyo. 1987); Optical Cable Corp. v. Mass Elec. Constr. Co., 35 UCCR2d 773 (W.D. Pa. 1998).

struction Co.[41] the court held that the "appropriate relation" test was satisfied and forum law applied under section 1-105 so long as the application of forum law was not arbitrary or unfair. The court in *Armstrong Cork Co. v. Drott Manufacturing Co.,*[42] in deciding whether to apply the law of the forum, stated that, "Essentially, the conflicts issue [under section 1-105] is whether the sale of a logger . . . was a transaction bearing an *appropriate enough* relationship to Pennsylvania to justify an application of the state's law."[43] The italicized language is indicative of a threshold test, although the court did not find the test to have been met with respect to the application of Pennsylvania law. Although the plaintiff was a Pennsylvania corporation and the plaintiff's check was signed and drawn in Pennsylvania, Georgia law was held to apply because the transaction took place in Georgia, the goods were received in Georgia, and the goods were used and serviced in Georgia.[44]

There are serious problems with interpreting the "appropriate relation" test as establishing a minimum threshold, the satisfaction of which will mandate the application of forum law. First, this interpretation carries the serious potential for forum shopping.[45] If the appropriate relation test requires only that the forum satisfy a threshold standard for the application of forum law, and this threshold does not require that the law of the forum be the *most appropriate* law, then a potential plaintiff will be able to choose the applicable law through its choice of forum. If both states *A* and *B* satisfy the threshold test, if the lawsuit is brought in state *A*, the law of state *A* will apply. If the lawsuit is brought in state *B*, the law of state *B* will apply. Second, as one commentator has pointed out,[46] this approach is likely to preclude more than a superficial inquiry into the relative significance or weight of the contacts that several related states may have with the transaction. If all that is required, for example, to satisfy the appropriate relation test is that a state have "substantial" or "significant" contacts with the forum, once these contacts have been established, it is unnecessary to consider whether the policies underlying the forum's law, as well as those underlying the law of competing jurisdictions, suggest a choice of law other than the forum's.

---

[41] 781 F. Supp. 711, 16 UCCR2d 1059 (D. Kan. 1991).

[42] 433 F. Supp. 413, 23 UCCR 338 (E.D. Pa. 1977).

[43] 433 F. Supp. at 418, 23 UCCR at 341 (emphasis added).

[44] *See also* Bernick v. Jurden, 293 S.E.2d 405, 34 UCCR 458 (N.C. 1982) (fact that injury occured in a state sufficient to satisfy the appropriate relation test).

[45] *See* David D. Siegel, "The U.C.C. and Choice of Law: Forum Choice or Forum Law," 21. Am. U. L. Rev. 494, 502 (1972).

[46] *Id.*

The third approach the courts have adopted is to interpret section 1-105 to require, at least when the conflict is between Code states, the application of the law of the state that has the *most significant* contacts with the transaction or the *most appropriate* relationship to the transaction. This is the approach adopted by almost all of the courts that have thoughtfully considered the issue, and represents the view of most of the more recent cases.[47]

The leading case is *Boudreau v. Baughman*,[48] decided by the Supreme Court of North Carolina. In this case the plaintiff sued the defendant for injuries sustained when the plaintiff cut his foot on a chrome-plated chair designed by the defendant. The plaintiff's complaints had counts in negligence, products liability, and breach of warranty. The defendant was a resident of North Carolina. The plaintiff was a resident of Massachusetts who had injured his foot on the metal surface of the chair while visiting friends in Florida. The chair was purchased in Florida by the friends of the plaintiff.

In deciding the applicable law for breach of warranty claims,[49] the court recognized that it must apply section 1-105 and the appropriate relation test contained therein. In its opinion, it considered and rejected the first two interpretations of section 1-105 considered above. As to an interpretation that would have the court simply apply the pre-Code choice-of-law rules, the court said that the North Carolina comments to section 1-105 indicated that the section was intended to change the earlier rigid choice-of-law rules. It also refused to adopt an interpretation that would apply forum law whenever the forum had significant contact with the transaction. The court said

---

[47] For cases adopting this view, *see, e.g.*, General Elec. Credit Corp. v. R.A. Heintz Constr. Co., 302 F. Supp. 958, 6 UCCR 1137 (D. Or. 1969); Simmons v. American Mut. Life Ins. Co., 20 UCCR 402 (S.D. Ala. 1976); Halstead v. United States, 535 F. Supp. 782, 34 UCCR 472 (D. Conn. 1982); P&E Elec., Inc. v. Utility Supply of Am., Inc., 655 F. Supp. 89, 3 UCCR 1310 (M.D. Tenn. 1986); Compliance Marine, Inc. v. Campbell, 839 F.2d 203, 5 UCCR2d 900 (4th Cir. 1988); Boudreau v. Baughman, 322 N.C. 331, 368 S.E.2d 849, 6 UCCR2d 1393 (1988); Terry v. Pullman Trailmobile, 92 N.C. App. 687, 376 S.E.2d 47, 8 UCCR2d 45 (1988); Thornton v. Cessna Aircraft Co., 886 F.2d 85, 10 UCCR2d 1183 (4th Cir. 1989); Morris v. SSE, Inc., 12 UCCR2d 628 (11th Cir. 1990); Dassault Falcon Jet Corp. v. Oberflex, Inc., 909 F. Supp. 345, 29 UCCR2d 406 (M.D.N.C. 1995); Cox v. Lewiston Grain Growers, Inc., 936 P.2d 1191, 33 UCCR2d 443 (Wash Ct. App. 1997); Minnesota Mining & Mfg. Co. v. Nishika Ltd., 33d UCCR2d 817 (Tex. 1997); Corsica Coop. Ass'n v. Behlen Mfg. Co., Inc., 967 F. Supp. 382, 35 UCCR2d 1116 (D.S.D. 1997). *See also* Bunge Corp. v. D.A. Biglane, 418 F. Supp. 1159, 20 UCCR 596 (1976) (adopting a similar approach described as the "center of gravity" approach).

[48] 322 N.C. 331, 368 S.E.2d 849, 6 UCCR2d 1393 (1988).

[49] The court determined that Florida law was applicable to the negligence and product liability claims on the basis of the forum's traditional choice-of-law rule in tort cases.

that this interpretation was a "very literal-minded" and "outmoded" reading of the Code, likely to induce forum shopping.[50]

The court said that it chose to interpret "appropriate relation" to mean the "most significant relationship." It found that Florida—the place of sale, distribution, delivery, and use of the product, as well as the place of injury—had the most significant relationship to the transaction and accordingly applied Florida law. In doing so, the court, in part, relied upon Florida's interest in protecting its citizens from the commercial movement of defective goods into the state.

In a later case the same year, the North Carolina Court of Appeals expanded upon the meaning of the most significant relationship test that the court had established in *Boudreau* and had applied in a somewhat conclusory manner. In *Terry v. Pullman Trailmobile*[51] the court said that the court in *Boudreau*, by focusing on the physical location of certain aspects of the transaction, had left it unclear "whether it fully embraced the integration of policy concerns with location factors."[52] Finding that it was the intention of *Boudreau* to fully integrate policy concerns in its interpretation of section 1-105's choice of law rule, the court referred to the Restatement (Second) of Conflict of Laws as establishing the guiding principles for understanding the "most significant relationship" test. The court relied primarily on section 6(2) of the Restatement (Second):

> In determining which state has the most significant relationship to the transaction and the parties, relevant factors to be considered include:
>
> (a)   the needs of the interstate and international systems,
> (b)   the relevant policies of the forum,
> (c)   the relevant policies of other interested states and the relative interests of those states in the determination of the particular issue,
> (d)   the protection of justified expectations,

---

[50] *See also* United Overseas Bank v. Veneers, Inc., 375 F. Supp. 596, 14 UCCR 1349 (D. Md. 1973) in which the court similarly rejected this approach in the context of a conflict between Code and non-Code jurisdictions:

> While § 1-105 may appear at first glance to compel the application of the UCC anytime a transaction has an 'appropriate relation' to the forum, even though another state or nation may have a more 'appropriate relation,' such a restrictive, forum-oriented interpretation is not warranted.

375 F. Supp. at 601, 14 UCCR at 1355, 1356.

[51] 92 N.C. App. 687, 376 S.E.2d 47, 8 UCCR2d 45 (1988).

[52] 92 N.C. App. at 691, 376 S.E.2d at 49, 8 UCCR2d at 48.

    (e)   the basic policies underlying the particular field of law,

    (f)   certainty, predictability and uniformity of result,

    (g)   ease in the determination and application of the law to be applied.[53]

Other cases interpreting the "appropriate relation" test of section 1-105 to mean the "most significant relationship" have also relied on the Restatement (Second) of Conflict of Laws in order to determine which state has the most significant relationship to the transaction.[54]

Of the three interpretations of the "appropriate relation" test adopted thus far by the courts, the third is clearly preferable. It avoids the forum-shopping objections of the more literal interpretation of section 1-105. Further, it allows the court to identify and evaluate the competing policies of the various states whose law might be applicable. Finally, it permits the court not only to determine whether forum law should or should not be applied, it also permits the court to choose what law *will* be applicable based upon whose policies will be promoted by the solution of the legal issue presented.

Fortunately, the appropriate relation test adopted by the drafters is sufficiently flexible to give the courts freedom to continue to develop rational choice-of-law rules and apply them to commercial transactions.[55] The advantages of this flexibility are apparent, for a relation that was *appropriate* when the problem was whether to apply a newly drafted comprehensive code or the law of a non-Code state does not necessarily continue to be *appropriate* when all states involved have the same basic legislation. The "appropriate relation" test is sufficiently broad to enable the courts of Code states to continue their development of choice-of-law principles in commercial cases, and not feel bound to apply forum law in a commercial transaction simply because they find a minimum contact between the facts of the transaction and the forum.

---

[53] Restatement (Second) of Conflict of Laws § 6(2) (1971).

[54] *See, e.g.*, P&E Elec., Inc. v. Utility Supply of Am., Inc., 655 F. Supp. 89, 3 UCCR2d 1310 (M.D. Tenn. 1986); Dassault Falcon Jet Corp. v. Oberflex, Inc., 909 F. Supp. 345, 29 UCCR2d 406 (M.D.N.C. 1995).

[55] Admittedly, this interpretation of the appropriate relation test of U.C.C. § 1-105(1) takes some liberty with the terse command of the section. However, section 1-105, as described earlier, was drafted for situations in which it was assumed that only a few states had the Code, and the drafters decided that its comprehensive restatement of the law merchant has the widest application. Now that this application has been obtained through wide adoption of the Code, the "appropriate relation" test can take on new meaning, lose its forum-oriented direction, and promote rational choice-of-law results.

§ 2.03   THE SCOPE OF ARTICLE 2

The basic scope section of Article 2 is found in section 2-102. The section is divided into two parts—the first is affirmative, indicating the reach of Article 2; the second is negative, listing transactions to which Article 2 has no application.

The affirmative portion is extremely short: "Unless the context otherwise requires, this Article applies to transactions in goods."[56] If section 2-102 stopped with only this affirmative statement, some transactions in goods would be brought into Article 2 that were not intended to be covered. For example, a loan of money secured by goods could be considered a *transaction* in goods. However, a negative portion was also included in section 2-102: Article 2 "does not apply to any transaction which although in the form of an unconditional contract to sell or present sale is intended to operate only as a security transaction nor does the Article impair or repeal any statute regulating sales to consumers, farmers or other specified classes of buyers."[57] Thus, a simple loan of money secured by goods would not be within the scope of Article 2, but would, instead, be governed by Article 9, because the transaction in goods would be intended to operate only as a security transaction. In construing the negative part of section 2-102, however, the word "only" needs to be underscored. A transaction in goods may be both a sale and the creation of a security interest—as when a seller sells goods to a buyer and reserves a security interest in those goods for the balance of the unpaid purchase price. Article 9 applies to the part of the transaction that involves the creation and perfection of the security interest, but Article 2 applies to the portion that involves the sale from the seller to the buyer.[58]

[A]   "Sales" Under Article 2

Although "transaction" is not defined in the Code, it is at least clear that Article 2 applies both to contracts for the sale of goods and to the actual sale of goods. A cursory reading of the sections of Article 2 makes it clear that the sale of goods lies at the core of the Article. Nearly every section contains some reference to a sale,[59] a contract for sale,[60] or to a seller[61] or

---

[56] U.C.C. § 2-102.

[57] *Id.*

[58] U.C.C. § 2-102, Comment.

[59] *See, e.g.,* U.C.C. § 2-402.

[60] *See, e.g.,* U.C.C. § 2-314.

[61] For example, the remedies given in U.C.C. § 2-703 are limited to *sellers.*

a buyer.[62] Further, section 2-101 states that this "Article shall be known and may be cited as Uniform Commercial Code—Sales."

The problem is not whether the word "transaction" includes sales and contracts for sale; the question is whether "transaction" is also broad enough to embrace relationships which fall short of a contract to sell or a sale—that is, relationships that do not result in the passing of title from a seller to a buyer for a price.[63] Does Article 2 reach transactions such as gifts, bailments, or leases of goods? Consider the following situations:

Case 1. Ben was visiting the local county fair. The day was hot; Ben was thirsty. Ben stopped at a local soft-drink stand and, when he was informed that the vendor had just run out of soft drinks, Ben asked for and was given a cup of water. Ben paid nothing for the water—which was polluted and caused Ben to become extremely ill. Are Ben's rights against the vendor determined by Article 2?

Case 2. Patient visited Dentist's office to have a tooth filled. While Dentist was administering a local anesthetic, the hypodermic needle broke just below Patient's gum line. A painful operation was required to remove the broken piece of metal. It has been determined that a defect in the needle (and not any negligence of Dentist) was the cause of the break. While Dentist *may* have sold the anesthetic to Patient,[64] it is more difficult to find that the Dentist sold the needle (which Dentist immediately discarded) to the patient. Are Patient's rights against the Dentist determined by Article 2?

Case 3. Instead of purchasing a new car, Sandra, an attorney, decided to lease a new car from Dealer for a five-year period. The automobile had a number of defects, including a defective transmission. Are Sandra's rights against Dealer determined by Article 2?

In each of these cases there appears to be no sale of goods involved. In the first there was a gift; in the second the goods were used only in conjunction with the delivery of other goods; in the third the goods were only leased. Nevertheless, in each case it is arguable that there was a *transaction* in goods and that Article 2 should apply to the relationship between the parties.

Even though "transaction" can be read broadly to include more than sales or contracts for sale, many Article 2 sections, including sections implicated in the cases described above, are limited by their terms to sales of

---

[62] *See* U.C.C. § 2-711 which outlines the remedies of a *buyer*. Both "buyer" and "seller" are defined in terms of either a sale or a contract for the sale of goods. U.C.C. § 2-103.

[63] This is the definition of "sale" in U.C.C. § 2-106(1).

[64] *See, e.g.,* Dorfman v. Austenal, Inc., 3 UCCR 856 (N.Y. Sup. Ct. 1966); Redwine v. Baptist Gen. Convention, 681 P.2d 1121, 34 UCCR 883 (Okla. Ct. App. 1982).

goods and to contracts for the sale of goods. For example, one of the sections that would be involved in each of the above cases is section 2-314—the implied warranty of merchantability. That section begins:

> Unless excluded or modified (Section 2-316), a warranty that the goods shall be merchantable is implied in a contract *for their sale* if the seller is a merchant with respect to goods of that kind.[65]

Therefore, even if "transaction" in section 2-102 is given a broad application reaching beyond sales and contracts for sale, there is no explicit basis in the Code for finding a warranty of merchantability in non-sale cases. This applies to many other sections of the Code as well.[66]

On the other hand, while a sizeable number of specific sections of Article 2 are expressly applicable only to sales and contracts for sale, it should not be concluded that these sections are inappropriate to shape the rights and duties of parties in non-sales cases. The Code is more than an isolated statute adopted by a few states; it is a comprehensive treatment of commercial law enacted by more than fifty legislatures. It expresses several discernable policies regarding commercial transactions. Although many sections are built on the concept of a contract for sale, the policies behind the sections may apply to transactions that do not fit the Code's definition of a "sale" or "contract for sale."

Many cases have resolved this difficulty by applying Article 2, or particular sections of Article 2, "by analogy" to transactions that do not fit the Article definition of a sale. Most of these cases involved leases of personal property and are now specifically governed by Article 2A.[67] Leases, however, are not the only situations in which the courts have applied Article 2 by analogy.[68] Furthermore, the lease cases are instructive of the various approaches courts have taken in applying Article 2 to non-sale cases.

Courts have often applied Article 2 by analogy when they are convinced that the transaction sufficiently resembles a sale of the goods to

---

[65] U.C.C. § 2-314 (emphasis added).

[66] *See, e.g.,* U.C.C. § 2-305(1)—"The parties if they so intend can conclude a contract for *sale* even though the price is not settled."; U.C.C. § 2-204(1)—"A contract for *sale* of goods may be made in any manner sufficient to show agreement."; U.C.C. § 2-609(1)—"A contract for *sale* imposes an obligation on each party that the other's expectation of receiving due performance will not be impaired."

[67] *See* Chapter 11, *infra.*

[68] *See, e.g.,* Buford v. Wilmington Trust Co., 841 F.2d 81, 5 UCCR2d 621 (3d Cir. 1988); Leiber v. Raynor Mfg. Co., 571 S.W.2d 640, 24 UCCR 40 (Ky. Ct. App. 1978); Zapatha v. Dairy Mart, Inc., 408 N.E.2d 1370, 29 UCCR 1121 (Mass. 1980); Herman v. Bonanza Bldgs., Inc., 390 N.W.2d 536, 2 UCCR2d 430 (Neb. 1986).

justify the application of Article 2. In cases involving leases, the courts have looked to such things as the relationship of the length of the lease to the useful life of the goods,[69] the existence of an option to purchase and the terms of the purchase option,[70] and the respective responsibilities of the lessor and lessee with respect to the goods.[71] A number of these courts have applied Article 2 as a whole without concern as to the particular section of Article 2 at issue in the case.[72] That is, once the transaction was sufficiently "close" to a sale, the court applied Article 2 to the transaction as if it were a sale. While this approach is appropriate when the "lease" is nothing more than a "disguised" sale,[73] it is more problematic in other circumstances because of the different policies behind the various sections of Article 2.

In response, a number of courts have adopted an approach which focuses more on whether the policy behind a particular section is applicable to the transaction. The leading case is *Glenn Dick Equipment Co. v. Galey Construction, Inc.*[74] In this case, the court had to decide whether the warranty and disclaimer provisions of Article 2 should be applied to a two-month lease of three "motor scraper units." In deciding to apply these sections of Article 2 to the lease "by analogy" the court was critical of those cases in which Article 2 was applied by the courts *in toto* with little regard for the specific provisions of the Code at issue and the policies behind them:

---

[69] *See, e.g.,* J.L. Teel Co. v. Houston United Sales, Inc., 1 UCCR2d 337 (Miss. 1986).

[70] *See, e.g.,* Glenn Dick Equip. Co. v. Galey Constr., Inc., 541 P.2d 1184, 18 UCCR 340 (Idaho 1975). *See also* Sawyer v. Pioneer Leasing Corp., 244 Ark. 943, 428 S.W.2d 46, 5 UCCR 453 (1968) (probable that ice machine would be offered for sale at the end of the lease).

[71] *See, e.g.,* Redfern Meats, Inc. v. Hertz Corp., 134 Ga. App. 381, 215 S.E.2d 10, 17 UCCR 82 (1975).

[72] *See* Harris Market Research, Inc. v. Marshall Mktg. Communications, Inc., 1988 U.S. Dist. Lexis 4066 (D. Kan. 1988); In re Vaillencourt, 7 UCCR 748 (Bankr. D. Me. 1970); Xerox Corp. v. Hawkes, 475 A.2d 7, 38 UCCR 159 (N.H. 1984); Owens v. Patent Scaffolding Co., 77 Misc. 2d 992, 354 N.Y.S.2d 778, 14 UCCR 610 (N.Y. Sup. Ct. 1974).

[73] In some cases, it is hard to discern whether the court is applying Article 2 "by analogy" or applying Article 2 directly because the court believes that the transaction is, in fact, a sale "disguised" as a lease. If the economic consequences of a transaction are indistinguishable from a sale, the transaction should be treated as a sale even if title is withheld by the "lessor" and the transaction is described by the parties as a "lease." In such cases, the court should find that a "sale" has occurred and apply Article 2 directly; there is no need in these cases to apply it "by analogy." U.C.C. § 1-201(37) sets out the criteria for determining whether a transaction is a true lease or a sale accompanied by a security interest. For a full discussion of the difference between "true" leases and sales "disguised" as leases, see §§ 11.01 and 11.02[A], *infra.*

[74] 541 P.2d 1184, 18 UCCR 340 (Idaho 1975).

Reasoning by analogy does not require us to apply Article 2 in toto to a lease; rather, we need apply only those provisions which are sufficiently analogous. In order to determine which provisions are applicable, we will look to the commercial setting in which the problem arises and contrast the relevant common law with Article 2—we will use Article 2 as a "premise for reasoning only when the case involves the same considerations that gave rise to the Code provisions and an analogy is not rebutted by additional antithetical circumstances" [citations omitted].

A number of other courts have explicitly approved of the approach taken in the *Glenn Dick* case.[75]

The approach of the *Glenn Dick* case is the proper way to determine whether the Code should be applied by analogy. Courts should search for the reasons behind the particular section or sections involved in the case and determine whether these reasons justify its application in the non-sales transaction. If they do, the Code should be used to shape the rights and duties of the parties.

There are cases, however, in which the courts have simply refused to apply the Code by analogy to non-sale transactions.[76] While in some cases this can be justified because the Code section was unsuitable for the particular transaction at issue,[77] in other cases the court appears to reject the *concept* of applying Article 2 to non-sales transactions.[78] Sometimes, the courts justify this conclusion on the basis that to apply Article 2 to a non-sale transaction would be judicial legislation because the legislature has limited Article 2 (or at least many of the most important sections) to the sale of goods.[79]

---

[75] *See* Knox v. North Am. Can Corp., 80 Ill. App. 3d 683, 399 N.E.2d 1355, 28 UCCR 336 (1980); Walter E. Heller & Co. v. Convalescent Home of the First Church of Deliverance, 49 Ill. App. 3d 283, 365 N.E.2d 1285, 22 UCCR 574 (1977); J.L. Teel Co. v. Houston United Sales, Inc., 1 UCCR2d 337 (Miss. 1986).

[76] Strong v. Retail Credit Co., 552 P.2d 1025, 19 UCCR 1322 (Colo. Ct. App. 1976); Jones v. Clark, 244 S.E.2d 183, 24 UCCR 605 (N.C. Ct. App. 1979); Union College v. Kennedy, Slomonson & Smith, 400 A.2d 850 (N.J. Sup. Ct. 1979); Labella v. Charlie Thomas, Inc., 942 S.W.2d 127, 34 UCCR2d 289 (Tex. Ct. App. 1997); Micro Data Base Sys., Inc. v. Dharma Sys., Inc. 35 UCCR2d 747 (7th Cir. 1998).

[77] *See, e.g.*, Carroll v. Grabavoy, 77 Ill. App. 3d 895, 396 N.E.2d 836, 27 UCCR 940 (1979); Ortiz v. Gas Co. of N.M., 636 P.2d 900, 32 UCCR 1329 (N.M. 1981); Redwine v. Baptist Gen. Convention, 681 P.2d 1121, 34 UCCR 883 (Okla. Ct. App. 1982).

[78] *See, e.g.*, Mashlan v. E.M. Trucks, Inc., 443 N.W.2d 226, 9 UCCR2d 444 (Minn. Ct. App. 1989); Mays v. Citizens & S. Nat'l Bank, 132 Ga. App. 602, 15 UCCR 579 (1974); DeKalb Agresearch, Inc. v. Abbott, 391 F. Supp. 152, 17 UCCR 65, *aff'd in opinion below*, 511 F.2d 1162 (4th Cir. 1975).

[79] *See* Mays v. Citizens & S. Nat'l Bank, 132 Ga. App. 602, 15 UCCR 579 (1974).

This reasoning should be rejected. In the absence of a governing statute, there is no reason why the courts should not use an existing statute to assist it in formulating an appropriate rule. In fact, to the extent that the policy behind legislation is clear and is applicable to the case before the court, it would be absurd for the court to ignore the existence of the legislation and the rule it embodies. Only if there is reason to believe that the legislature limited the statute in order to affirmatively exclude cases similar to the one before the court, should the court refuse to consider the statute in fashioning an appropriate rule.[80] These ideas were clearly and succinctly stated by the Mississippi Supreme Court:

> Our decision to apply Article 2 by analogy is wholly in keeping with this court's proper role as an interstitial lawmaker. Were our law of sales still in the form of common law rules, we would not hesitate to extend them to situations functionally analogous to those which gave rise to and fell within the coverage of those rules. Such is the nature of the common law process. That the rules are now in statutory form compels no change in the process. The only alteration is in the materials employed as the basis of deliberation and adjudication. Instead of precedent and case law analogies, the statutes are available. The statutory rules, like the former common law rules, remain only the points of departure, only analogies, although exceptionally informative and illuminating analogies.[81]

Thus, in fashioning rules to resolve the cases posed at the beginning of this section, the courts should examine the policies behind the Code sections that are relevant to the issues in the case, and determine whether these policies justify the application of the rules expressed in these sections. In each of the three cases, an issue is sure to be whether the transaction should contain a warranty analogous to the Code's implied warranty of merchantability. In each case, the inquiry should identify the policies behind the Code's warranty of merchantability and determine whether those policies will be furthered by its application to this transaction. In addition, the court

---

[80] There is evidence that, at least with respect to the warranty sections, the Code drafters intended the Code's rules to be extended by analogy to non-sale cases. Comment 2 to U.C.C. § 2-313 provides, in relevant part:

> Although this section [section 2-313] is limited in its scope and direct purpose to warranties made by the seller to the buyer as part of a contract for sale, the warranty sections of this Article are not designed in any way to disturb those lines of case law growth which have recognized that warranties need not be confined either to sales contracts or to the direct parties to such a contract.

[81] J.L. Teel Co. v. Houston United Sales, Inc., 1 UCCR2d 337, 346–347 (Miss. 1986).

should ask whether the application of the warranty of merchantability in this non-sales transaction will have consequences suggesting that its application would be inappropriate.

What are the policies behind the warranty of merchantability? In capsule form,[82] the policies behind the warranty of merchantability are: (1) a merchant in the business of selling particular goods is generally in a better position to detect and guard against product defects than is a buyer of those goods; (2) imposing liability on the seller will provide an incentive to the seller to produce and/or market safer or higher quality goods; (3) the seller is in a better position to spread the risk of the damage caused by defective products than is the buyer; and (4) buyers generally expect those who introduce products into the stream of commerce for a profit to stand behind their products—to provide a product suitable for its intended purpose.

Applying this analysis to *Case 3* is probably the easiest. In general, a person in the business of leasing a particular kind of good is in a better position to detect and guard against product defects than is a lessee.[83] This is especially true with respect to complex goods such as automobiles. Furthermore, to the extent that the lessor experiences problems with the goods that it leases, it can either change its supplier or threaten to do so, thus putting pressure on the supplier to produce better goods. Also, lessors in the business of leasing goods are generally able to efficiently spread the risk of product defects through insurance or through the price charged, just as sellers. Finally, most people in situations such as *Case 3* would expect the lessor to take responsibility for the quality of the product it has introduced into the stream of commerce and from which it will make a profit.[84] It should be no surprise that Article 2A, which would now govern *Case 3*, provides for a warranty of merchantability that is indistinguishable from section 2-314.

---

[82] The list is intended to be neither comprehensive nor detailed. It does, however, express some of the policies underlying the warranty of merchantability with sufficient clarity to permit the analysis that follows.

[83] This is not to say that this must always be the case in order to justify the application of the Code's warranty provisions by analogy. Even when goods are sold, occasionally the buyer will be in a better position to detect and guard against product defects, but nonetheless the merchantability warranty will be applicable. The fact that in some unusual circumstances the policies of a rule will not be furthered by its application does not necessarily mean that a general rule is inappropriate; some overinclusiveness is inherent in the concept of rules of general application. Furthermore, the warranty provisions of Article 2 give the parties the ability to modify or exclude the warranty protection that would otherwise result from the statute. *See* U.C.C. § 2-316.

[84] It is understood that this final policy—the expectations of the buyer—has its foundation, in part, in the other policies. However, the authors believe that it has independent significance as well.

Cases 1 and *2* are both more difficult. In *Case 2*, the dentist is probably in a better position to detect and guard against defects in the hypodermic needle than the patient, although generally not in as good a position to do so as someone in the business of selling or producing these items.[85] In addition, imposing liability on the dentist will provide an incentive to the dentist to deal only with reliable producers of hypodermic needles.[86] It is not clear, however, whether the dentist is in a better position to spread the risk of this accident through insurance or otherwise than the patient, given the unusual nature of the accident.[87] Finally, it is also not clear whether people would reasonably expect a dentist to assume responsibility for a broken needle to the same extent that they would expect persons in the business of selling a product to stand behind their goods.

Accordingly, the results are mixed in cases involving the provision or use of defective equipment in the course of professional treatment. In most cases, however, the courts have not imposed warranty liability or strict tort liability[88] on health care professionals when defective products have been used or administered by them in the course of treatment.[89] This is true even

---

[85] *See* Skelton v. Druid City Hosp. Bd., 459 So. 2d 818, 39 UCCR 369 (Ala. 1984) (liability imposed on hospital for defective suture needle because patients are completely dependent on hospital to choose fit products for their care).

[86] *See* Magrine v. Spector, 100 N.J. Super. 223, 232, 241 A.2d 637, 642 (App. Div. 1968) (Blotter, J. dissenting) (imposition of liability will encourage greater care on the part of dentist in purchasing equipment and examining for defects).

[87] It is no answer to say that the dentist can spread the loss through insurance. The patient can presumably also purchase first-party insurance to avoid catastrophic loss. The issue is who can best insure against this kind of event.

The manufacturer is probably in the best position to spread this risk. However, the manufacturer can be reached by allowing the dentist an indemnity action against the manufacturer or by allowing suit directly by the consumer against the manufacturer. In Great Britain, for example, retailers are generally not responsible for personal injury or property damage to consumers caused by defective products unless the retailer is unable or unwilling to identify his supplier. *See* Part I of the Consumer Protection Act of 1987, §§ 2(2) and 2(3) *reprinted in* Halsbury's Statutes of England and Wales, Volume 39 (4th ed. 1995). If, however, the patient is unable to sue the manufacturer because of the lack of privity of contract, see § 4.09, *infra*, then, in order to reach the best risk-spreader, it may be necessary to impose liability on the dentist and provide an action to the dentist against the manufacturer for indemnification.

[88] See § 4.06[B][5], *infra* for a discussion of strict products liability in tort and its relationship to warranty liability.

[89] *See, e.g.*, San Diego Hosp. Ass'n v. Superior Court, 30 Cal. App. 4th 8, 35 Cal. Rptr. 2d 489 (1994) (hospital not liable for injuries caused by defective laser); Carmichael v. Reitz, 17 Cal. App. 3d 958, 95 Cal. Rptr. 381 (1971) (doctor not liable for defective prescription drugs); Murphy v. Squibb & Sons, 156 Cal. App. 3d 589, 202 Cal. Rptr. 802 (1984) (pharmacist not liable for providing defective drugs); Probst v. Albert Einstein Med. Ctr., 82 A.D. 2d 739, 440 N.Y.S. 2d 2 (App. Div. 1981) (hospital not liable for defective spinal rod);

if the defective item was retained by the patient,[90] unlike *Case 2*. A number of cases have involved facts very similar to those in *Case 2*, and the majority of courts have declined to hold the dentist or physician responsible for defects in hypodermic needles or similar items.[91]

In a recent case, the Supreme Court of Pennsylvania adopted the policy-oriented approach suggested above to resolve these cases. In *Cafazzo v. Central Medical Health Services, Inc.*,[92] the plaintiff was injured when a mandibular prosthesis that had been implanted in his jaw proved defective. He sued both the hospital in which the prosthesis had been implanted and the attending physician, arguing that they were strictly liable for supplying a defective prosthesis.[93] The Pennsylvania Supreme Court upheld the dismissal of these claims. It reached its decision after reviewing the policies behind strict liability and determining that the policies were either not furthered, or only weakly furthered, by the application of strict liability to the doctor and hospital. The court said that imposing liability on the defendants

---

Cafazzo v. Cent. Medical Health Servs., Inc., 542 Pa. 526, 668 A.2d 521 (1995) (physician and hospital not liable for defective implants). *But see* Mauran v. Mary Fletcher Hosp., 318 F. Supp. 297, 8 UCCR 526 (D. Vt. 1970) (hospital administering anesthesia); Garcia v. Edgewater Hosp., 613 N.E.2d 1243, 21 UCCR2d 595 (Ill. App. Ct. 1993) (hospital liable for supplying defective heart valve); Providence Hosp. v. Truly, 611 S.W.2d 127, 30 UCCR 785 (Tex. App. 1980) (drug injected into patient's eye as part of cataract operation).

[90] *See, e.g.*, Murphy v. E.R. Squibb & Sons, Inc., 40 Cal. 3d 672, 710 P.2d 247, 221 Cal. Rptr. 447 (1985) (retail pharmacy not liable for defect in drug dispensed by licensed pharmacist); Caffazo v. Cent. Medical Health Servs., Inc., 542 Pa. 526, 668 A.2d 521 (1995) (defective implants).

[91] *See* Silverhart v. Mount Zion Hosp., 20 Cal. App. 3d 1022, 98 Cal. Rptr. 187 (1971) (defect in surgical needle used by physician); Magrine v. Krasnica, 94 N.J. Super. 228, 227 A.2d 539 (Law Div. 1967), *aff'd sub nom.* Krasnica v. Spector, 100 N.J. Super. 223, 241 A.2d 637 (App. Div. 1968), *aff'd per curiam* 53 N.J. 259, 250 A.2d 129 (1969) (defect in hypodermic needle used by dentist); Easterly v. HSP of Texas, Inc., 772 S.W.2d 211, 9 UCCR2d 530 (Tex. App. 1989) (defective needle and catheter); Ethicon, Inc. v. Parten, 520 S.W.2d 527 (Tex. App. 1975) (defective surgical needle).

A notable exception is the case of Skelton v. Druid City Hosp. Bd., 459 So. 2d 818, 39 UCCR 369 (Ala. 1984). In this case, the Alabama Supreme Court held a hospital liable for breach of the implied warranty of fitness (U.C.C. § 2-315) for damages caused by a suture needle that broke off in the patient's body. The court said that there was a transaction in goods under the Code sufficient to impose warranty liability. The court based its decision on the disparity in the ability of patients and hospitals to judge the quality of medical supplies provided to the patient.

[92] 542 Pa. 526, 668 A.2d 521 (1995).

[93] The suit was brought in tort as a strict products liability suit, not a warranty suit under the U.C.C. However, in deciding whether or not to extend strict products liability to cover the case, the court engaged in the same kind of analysis that this text advocates in deciding whether to apply the Code's warranty sections by analogy.

would have little effect on the safety of medical devices, because the safety of these devices primarily depends upon those connected with the research, development, manufacture, and marketing of the product.[94] Further, because the safety testing and licensing for medical devices is a responsibility of the FDA, imposing liability on physicians or hospitals is unlikely to affect their safety. In addition, the court said that a hospital is not in a good position to detect and guard against such defects; the list of medical devices employed by the modern hospital is so large that a hospital cannot exercise any effective control over the existence and detection of product defects.[95] Finally, the court said that although a hospital might be able to spread the costs of such injuries, imposing liability would result in increased costs to "an already beleaguered health care system" and would inhibit research and innovation in medical equipment and treatment.[96]

Even though some of the court's conclusions are subject to criticism,[97] the approach taken by the court was proper. Rather than focusing on the formalities of whether the hospital or the doctor engaged in a sale or were "suppliers,"[98] the court examined the policies inherent in strict liability and attempted to discern whether these policies were furthered by their application in this case. Although the specific issue in the case was the application of strict tort liability, the same approach should be adopted in deciding whether to apply the warranty provisions of the Code by analogy to a non-sale transaction.

In *Case 1* there are reasonable competing arguments for the imposition of warranty liability by analogy, despite the lack of a "sale." Although the vendor is in a better position than the "customer" to be aware of pollution occurring after the water has come into the vendor's possession, the vendor is probably in no better position than the customer to detect pollution caused

---

[94] 542 Pa. at 534, 668 A.2d at 525.

[95] The dissent justifiably questioned the court's conclusion that this justified a decision not to impose strict liability. Justice Cappy said that this would mean that department stores carrying a multitude of merchandise should not be subject to strict liability. 542 Pa. at 539, 668 A.2d at 528 (Cappy, J. dissenting).

[96] 542 Pa. at 537, 668 A.2d at 526; *see also* Murphy v. E.R. Squibb & Sons, Inc., 40 Cal. 3d 672, 221 Cal. Rptr. 447, 710 P.2d 247 (1985) (holding pharmacies strictly liable for the drugs they dispense might cause pharmacies to refuse to dispense drugs that pose even a remote risk of harm despite value of drugs to patients).

[97] In addition to the criticism of the dissent noted in note 95, *supra*, the court's conclusion that imposing liability on hospitals and physicians will inhibit research and innovation in medical equipment and treatment is unsupported by any analysis by the court. Also, even though hospitals and physicians are not well equipped to detect defects in medical equipment, they are arguably in a better position than are their patients.

[98] *See* Restatement (Second) of Torts § 402A (1965).

prior to the acquisition of the water by the vendor. In this regard, the case is probably no different from that of a non-vendor (for example, a friend) who provides a glass of water in response to a request. Further, if the water has been provided to the vendor by a public authority, the vendor is likely to have little influence over the quality of water provided. On the other hand, the vendor is providing the water in the course of conducting its business, and even if there is no direct charge to the individual requesting the water, there is likely to be an indirect charge imposed on customers generally for water provided as a convenience through the prices charged for other food and drinks.[99] In addition, the vendor may capture some good will as a result of its willingness to provide water. Whether the vendor is in a better position to spread the risk from this kind of event than the customer is far from self-evident.

Again, no effort has been made to provide a comprehensive policy analysis of each of these cases. Much more will be said later about the policies underlying warranty liability and strict products liability.[100] Rather, the purpose of this discussion is to illustrate how an analysis might proceed that focuses on underlying policies instead of on technical differences and formal definitions. Whether title to a good passes, thus satisfying the formal definition of a sale in section 2-106(1), is often irrelevant in deciding if it makes sense to impose warranty liability.

Rather than apply Code principles by analogy, some courts have stretched the concept of a "sale" beyond the breaking point in order to reach what was obviously a sensible result. For example, there are a number of cases in which customers picked up merchandise from a shelf or counter and were injured before they had actually purchased the product. For example, in *Gillespie v. Great Atlantic and Pacific Tea Co.*,[101] the plaintiff was injured by a soda bottle that exploded while he was carrying it to the check-out counter in the defendant's grocery store. The plaintiff's claim included an allegation that the defendant had breached the Code's implied warranty of merchantability. The defendant replied that because no sale or contract

---

[99] *See* Levondosky v. Marina Assocs., 731 F. Supp. 1210, 11 UCCR2d 487 (D.N.J. 1990) (court found "sale" for purposes of implied warranty of merchantability when casino patron was injured by chips on the rim of a glass containing a free cocktail; court said that by purchasing gambling tokens, drink received was part of sale even though there was no specific charge for it); Cain v. Sheraton Perimeter Park S. Hotel, 592 So. 2d 218, 16 UCCR2d 347 (Ala. 1991) (court held there was a "sale" of allegedly contaminated oysters by lounge when provision of oysters for "free" was implicitly conditioned on purchase of alcoholic beverages).

[100] *See* § 4.06, *infra.*

[101] 14 N.C. App. 1, 187 S.E.2d 441, 10 UCCR 754 (1972).

for sale had taken place at the time of the explosion, the warranty of merchantability was not applicable. The court found that the presence of the drinks on the shelves constituted an offer by the defendant, which was accepted by the customer's taking possession of the goods. According to the court, this resulted in a sale of the goods, including the passage of title to the customer, even though payment of the price was delayed until the customer passed through the checkout counter. If the customer decided to return the goods to the shelf before paying for them, title revested in the seller.

The court's analysis is thoroughly unconvincing. It would surprise many consumers to discover that by taking a box of cereal from the shelf and putting it in their cart they had bought the cereal; the court's conclusion that a sale results as soon as a buyer takes possession does not accord with the reasonable understanding of consumers. Furthermore, the court does not explain why customers cannot be sued for breach when they return items to the shelf before going through the checkout, or, if the customers have an unfettered right to return the goods prior to checkout, why the "sale" isn't illusory—that is, no sale at all.

In a similar decision,[102] the Maryland Court of Special Appeals also found that the presence of goods on the shelves of a self-service grocery store constituted an offer to sell that was accepted by the customer's taking possession. The court said that the customer's taking possession of the goods constituted a promise to take the goods to the checkout and pay for them, thus concluding a contract for sale. The court dealt with the fact that customers generally believe that they have a right to return goods to the shelf prior to checkout without liability by saying that there is an implied agreement between the retailer and the customer that the customer can terminate the contract without liability prior to checkout. The court did not deal with the question of why such an unfettered right of cancellation in one party would not, under traditional contract doctrine, make the "contract" illusory.[103]

There is no reason for these courts to play so fast and loose with the law of contracts in order to apply the Code's warranty provisions. The policy reasons for applying a warranty of merchantability by analogy in these circumstances are strong; the policies underlying warranty liability are largely unaffected by whether the customer has proceeded through the checkout counter. Manipulating established contract concepts to reach the desired result presents the danger of undermining the certainty of contract law gen-

---

[102] Sheeskin v. Giant Foods, 318 A.2d 874, 14 UCCR 892 (Md. Ct. Spec. App. 1974).

[103] For another case adopting identical reasoning and citing *Siegel* with approval, see Fender v. Colonial Stores, Inc., 225 S.E.2d 691, 19 UCCR 402 (Cal. Ct. App. 1976).

erally and invites its misapplication in other contexts. It would be more appropriate for the court to forthrightly acknowledge that it was applying the principles of the Code by analogy.[104]

[B] "Goods" Under Article 2

Article 2 applies to transactions in *goods*, and the Code defines a "sale" and "contract for sale" in terms of sales and contracts for the sale of *goods*.[105] The definition of goods is found in section 2-105(1):

> "Goods" means all things (including specially manufactured goods which are movable at the time of identification to the contract for sale other than the money in which the price is to be paid, investment securities (Article 8) and things in action. "Goods" also includes the unborn young of animals and growing crops and other identified things attached to realty as described in the section on goods to be severed from realty (Section 2-107).

The core of this definition is found in the opening phrase. To be goods, items must fall within a category called *things*; those things must be *movable*; and the movability must occur at the time those things are *identified to the contract*. The words chosen in section 2-105 are far from precise. There is no Code definition of "things," although the entire scope of Article 2 is dependent upon this concept. Also, what is movable and what is immovable may well depend on how hard someone is willing to work on the project of moving. Furthermore, to be "goods," a thing must be movable at a particular time—the time of "identification" to the contract, itself a somewhat ambiguous concept.[106] The question of whether something is "goods" (i.e., whether it is a "thing" that is movable at the time of identification to the contract) has most frequently arisen in cases of two types: (1) cases in

---

[104] In McQuiston v. K-Mart Corp., 796 F.2d 1346, 1 UCCR2d 1115 (11th Cir. 1986), the court refused to find a warranty of merchantability when a customer lifted a glass jar from the shelf to see if the price tag was inside because no sale had occurred. The court suggested, however, that the result might be different had she "formed [an] intent to purchase" the jar. For liability to depend on whether she had subjectively decided to purchase the jar is both unrelated to whether a contract for sale existed (because of the objective theory of contracts) and completely unrelated to any plausible policy underlying warranty liability. By not applying the Code by analogy the court lost the opportunity to further the policies underlying the relevant sections of the Code and made a clearly erroneous decision.

[105] U.C.C. § 2-106(1).

[106] The concept of "identification" is found in U.C.C. § 2-501. *See* § 6.03, *infra,* for a more detailed discussion.

which the contract calls for something to be constructed by the "seller" and attached to or installed on real property, and (2) cases involving computer software.[107]

An early case provided the basis for a broad construction of the term "goods," a construction that has generally been followed by later courts. In *Pittsburgh-Des Moines Steel Co. v. Brookhaven Manor Water Co.,*[108] the parties entered into a contract under which Pittsburgh-Des Moines Steel Co. (PDM) agreed to construct a one-million-gallon water tank for the Brookhaven Manor Water Co. (Brookhaven). PDM failed to construct the tank, and Brookhaven sued. In the ensuing litigation, the District Court determined that Article 2 was not applicable to the transaction because the contract was not for the sale of goods. On appeal, the Circuit Court of Appeals, while affirming the decision of the District Court, disagreed that Article 2 was not applicable. After reviewing some pre-Code law that indicated the term "goods" should be broadly construed, the court further said:

> We find ample support in the cases arising under the U.C.C. itself that the scope of coverage of "goods" is not to be given a narrow construction but instead should be viewed as being broad in scope so as to carry out the underlying purposes of the Code in achieving uniformity in commercial transactions. . . . In the present case, while the unfinished tank was scarcely one to be taken off the shelf, we are unaware of any authority that specially manufactured small dies should be goods and a very large tank not so classified. In the words of the U.C.C. this was a "movable thing" specially manufactured.[109]

A similar broad construction can be found in other cases. For example, the court held in *Cambridge Planting Co. v. Napco, Inc.*[110] that a contract for the construction of a wastewater treatment plant was a contract for the sale of goods. In response to a claim by the defendant that the plant was not movable, the court said that the components of the plant were movable at the time of identification to the contract. Similarly, the court in *Kline Iron & Steel Co. v. Gray Communications Consultants, Inc.*[111] found that a contract for the erection of a TV tower was a contract for the sale of goods. Citing the *Pittsburgh-Des Moines Steel* case, the court said that the U.C.C.

---

[107] Both of these cases also involve the question of whether the necessarily involved "service" component predominates such that Article 2 will not be applicable in any event, an issue to be discussed shortly. *See* § 2.03[B][1] and [2], *infra*.

[108] 532 F.2d 572, 18 UCCR 931 (1976).

[109] *Id.* at 580, 18 UCCR at 939–940.

[110] 991 F.2d 31, 20 UCCR2d 739 (1st Cir. 1993).

[111] 715 F. Supp. 135, 9 UCCR2d 858 (D.S.C. 1989).

definition of goods is very broad. Emphasizing that the tower was to be manufactured in advance and assembled and erected at the site, the court found that the tower was movable at the time of identification to the contract. In *Meeker v. Hamilton Grain Elevator Co.,*[112] the court held that a contract to supply and erect two large grain bins on a farm was a contract for the sale of goods. Like the court in *Kline,* the court in *Meeker* relied upon the fact that the components for the structure had been cut and shaped prior to transportation to the site, and that they needed only to be fitted together and erected. Thus, the bins were movable at the time of identification to the contract even though they were not yet assembled. The court specifically rejected the argument that the subject of the contract—grain bins—did not exist until assembly and erection. Finally, in a questionable decision, the U.S. District Court for the Southern District of New York in *Consolidated Edison Co. v. Westinghouse Electric Corp.,*[113] perhaps extended the concept of goods beyond the breaking point. It held that the Article 2 was not in-applicable as a matter of law to a contract for the construction of a nuclear power plant. Ignoring the language of section 2-105, the court said that the lack of movability of the plant was not crucial since (citing *Pittsburgh-Des Moines Steel*) the concept of movability had not been rigidly interpreted.[114]

Despite the broad reading given to the term "goods," the courts have not found Article 2 to be applicable to typical construction contracts.[115]

---

[112] 110 Ill. App. 3d 668, 442 N.E.2d 921, 35 UCCR 347 (1982).

[113] 567 F. Supp. 358, 36 UCCR 1496 (S.D.N.Y. 1983).

[114] For other cases giving an expansive meaning to the term "goods," *see* Republic Steel Corp. v. Pennsylvania Eng'g Corp., 785 F.2d 174, 42 UCCR 1319 (7th Cir. 1986) (contract for the design and assembly of two steel furnaces was contract for the sale of goods; no discussion of whether they were movable at the time of identification to the contract); Ritz-Craft Corp. v. Stanford Management Group, 800 F. Supp. 1312, 19 UCCR2d 987 (D. Md. 1992) (contract to manufacture prefabricated multifamily housing was contract for the sale of goods); Shirone, Inc. v. Tasco, Inc., 283 N.W.2d 280, 27 UCCR 421 (Iowa 1979) (large calf-confinement buildings are goods; they were movable when shipped to the site and needed merely to be erected); Holstad v. Southwestern Porcelain, Inc., 421 N.W.2d 371, 5 UCCR2d 912 (Minn. Ct. App. 1988) (sale and installation of farm silos; silos were movable at the time of identification to the contract because unassembled parts were movable); Little v. Grizzly Mfg., 636 P.2d 839, 32 UCCR 1087 (Mont. 1981) (specially constructed modular home is "goods"); Robertson Cos. v. Kenner, 311 N.W.2d 194, 32 UCCR 387 (N.D. 1981) (galvanized steel buildings are goods; fact that buildings were in existence only as dissembled materials did not change their status as goods).

[115] *See, e.g.,* Inhabitants of City of Saco v. General Elec. Co., 779 F. Supp. 186, 17 UCCR2d 1068 (D. Me. 1991); Boddie v. Litton Unit Handling Sys., 118 Ill. App. 3d 520, 455 N.E.2d 142, 37 UCCR 1116 (1983); DeMatteo v. White, 233 Pa. Super. 339, 336 A.2d 355, 16 UCCR 926 (1975).

While the reasoning of the courts in these cases is often based on the pre-dominance of services,[116] courts have also based their decisions on the fact that the subject matter of the contract was not movable. For example, the court in *Chlan v. KDI Sylvan Pools, Inc.,*[117] held that a poured concrete swimming pool was not movable at the time of identification to the contract. The court said that the pool had no existence until the concrete had been poured into the excavation site, and at that point, the pool was not movable. In *Osterholt v. St. Charles Drilling Co.,*[118] the court held that a contract to install a well and water system was not a contract for the sale of goods. It said that the component parts did not become identifiable as a "well and water system" until installed, at which time they were no longer movable. In another case, a contract to install an elevator system was held not to constitute the sale of goods.[119] Finally, in *Niagara Mohawk Power Corp. v. Graver Tank & Manufacturing Co.,*[120] the court held that a contract for the construction and erection of a primary containment liner for a nuclear power plant was not a contract for the sale of goods.[121]

The key to understanding these decisions and to understanding why, in most cases, the courts have gotten it right, is the concept of identification. Although the Code's definition of identification is confusing and largely self-referential,[122] the basic idea is that identification occurs when specific goods can be pointed to—"identified"—*as the subject matter of the contract.*[123] Thus, when a contract requires the subject matter of the contract to be constructed from component parts, identification does not occur until the component parts can reasonably be described in terms of the subject matter of the contract. For example, the bricks, mortar, and lumber sitting beside an excavated hole cannot reasonably be described as a "house," even though all of the components of the house might be present and movable.[124] Thus,

---

[116] *See* § 2.03[B][1], *infra.*

[117] 452 A.2d 1259, 35 UCCR 37 (Md. Ct. Spec. App. 1982).

[118] 500 F. Supp. 529, 30 UCCR 807 (E.D. Mo. 1980).

[119] Chestnut Hill Dev. Corp. v. Otis Elevator Co., 653 F. Supp. 927, 4 UCCR2d 1359 (D. Mass. 1987).

[120] 470 F. Supp. 1308, 26 UCCR 1060 (N.D.N.Y. 1979).

[121] *Cf.* McClanahan v. American Gilsonite Co., 494 F. Supp. 1334, 30 UCCR 21 (D. Colo. 1980) (sale of oil refinery not goods even assuming severability and movability of component parts when buyer had no intention of moving refinery).

[122] U.C.C. § 2-501(a) says that identification occurs "when the contract is made if it is for the sale of goods already existing *and identified*" (emphasis added).

[123] *See* § 6.02, *infra.*

[124] *See* GWL, Inc. v. Robichaux, 643 S.W.2d 392, 35 UCCR 342 (Tex. 1982). *See also* Corsica Coop. Ass'n v. Behlen Mfg. Co., Inc., 967 F. Supp. 382, 24 UCCR2d 1116 (D.S.D.

the court in *Chlan v. KDI Sylvan Pools, Inc.*[125] was correct when it held that a contract for an in-ground concrete pool was not a contract for the sale of goods. The concrete could not reasonably be described as a pool until it was poured; as the court pointed out, before the concrete was poured, it could have been put to innumerable uses. Likewise, the court was correct in *Meeker v. Hamilton Grain Elevator Co.,*[126] when it held that the grain bins called for by the contract were goods. Even before assembly and installation, the component parts could reasonably be described as "grain bins," the subject matter of the contract. The component parts had been cut and shaped prior to delivery and, presumably, could not readily be used for other purposes. While close cases will inevitably occur,[127] if it is kept in mind that if component parts are movable and they can reasonably be described in terms of the subject matter of the contract, then the contract is one for the sale of goods.[128]

The issue of whether something is "goods" has also surfaced in connection with computer software. While it is clear that the tape, disk, or CD-ROM containing a software program is "goods,"[129] it is also clear that the value of the disk, etc. is the information contained on it, not the disk itself. Consequently, it has been suggested that computer software is not a "thing" as contemplated by the Code, and therefore contracts for the purchase of computer software are not contracts for the sale of goods.[130] This argument was specifically rejected in *Advent Systems Ltd. v. Unisys Corp.*[131] In holding that a contract for computer software is covered by Article 2, the court said:

> That a computer program may be copyrightable as intellectual property does not alter the fact that once in the form of a floppy disc or other

---

1997) (holding that the U.C.C. governed a dispute where the underlying transaction was the construction of a grain elevator).

[125] 452 A.2d 1259, 35 UCCR 37 (Md. Spec. Ct. App. 1982).

[126] 110 Ill. App. 3d 668, 442 N.E.2d 921, 35 UCCR 347 (1982).

[127] The *Pittsburgh-Des Moines Steel Co.* case is probably such a case. It is debatable whether a 1,000,000 gallon water tower can come into existence—be identified—prior to construction.

[128] This does not, however, guarantee that Article 2 will be applicable to the contract. If the provision of services predominates over the goods aspect of the contract, Article 2 will still not be applicable. *See* § 2.03[B][1], *infra.*

[129] Marcus G. Larson, Comment, "Applying Uniform Sales Law to International Software Transactions: The Use of the CISG, Its Shortcomings, and a Comparative Look at How the Proposed U.C.C. Article 2G Would Remedy Them," 5 Tul. J. Int'l & Comp. L. 445 (1997).

[130] It is also argued that contracts for at least some computer software are not contracts for the sale of goods because the service component of the contract outweighs the goods component. This topic is dealt with in § 2.03[B][1], *infra.*

[131] 925 F.2d 670, 13 UCCR2d 669 (3d Cir. 1991).

medium, the program is tangible, movable and available in the market-place.[132]

The overwhelming majority of courts have held the Code applicable to contracts for the sale of computer software.[133]

A significant number of cases have dealt with the question of whether electricity constitutes goods for purposes of Article 2. In the majority of cases, the courts have said "no."[134] This conclusion has been based on a number of theories, including the heavy regulation to which utilities are subject;[135] the fact that there is no "individual product" but, instead, a flow of electrons;[136] and the fact that electricity cannot be packaged or labeled as other goods.[137] At least in some circumstances, a minority of courts have been willing to characterize the provision of electricity as the sale of goods. An appellate court in Indiana has held that electricity is both a "thing" and "movable" and therefore, qualifies as a "goods."[138]

---

[132] 925 F.2d at 975, 13 UCCR2d at 674. *See* Communications Groups, Inc. v. Warner Communications, Inc., 138 Misc. 2d 80, 827 N.Y.S.2d 341, 6 UCCR2d 636 (N.Y. Civ. Ct. 1988) (computer software is tangible and movable, not merely intangible idea or thought).

[133] *See, e.g.,* Micro Data Base Sys., Inc. v. Dharma Sys., Inc. 35 UCCR2d 7474 (7th Cir. 1998); RRX Indus., Inc. v. Lab-Con, Inc., 772 F.2d 543, 41 UCCR 1561 (9th Cir. 1985); Pro CD, Inc. v. Zeidenberg, 908 F. Supp. 640, 28 UCCR2d 1132 (W.D. Wis. 1996); Colonial Life Ins. Co. of Am. v. Electronic Data Sys. Corp., 817 F. Supp. 235, 20 UCCR2d 753 (D.N.H. 1993); In re Amica, Inc., 135 B.R. 534, 17 UCCR2d 11 (Bankr. N.D. Ill. 1992); Triangle Underwriters, Inc. v. Honeywell, Inc., 457 F. Supp. 765, 24 UCCR 1088 (E.D.N.Y. 1978); Schroders, Inc. v. Hogan Sys., Inc., 137 Misc. 2d 738, 522 N.Y.S.2d 404, 4 UCCR2d 1397 (Sup. Ct. 1987); W.R. Weaver Co. v. Burroughs Corp., 580 S.W.2d 76, 27 UCCR 64 (Tex. App. 1979). *But see* Micro-Managers, Inc. v. Gregory, 434 N.W.2d 97, 7 UCCR2d 1375 (Wis. 1988).

The American Law Institute and the National Conference of Commissioners on Uniform State Laws have instituted a project to deal with issues of computer software licensing. This project resulted in a draft Article 2B, which was abandoned in 1999 as a joint ALI-NCCUSL project. The fate of a uniform law dealing with software licensing is now uncertain.

[134] *See, e.g.,* Sterling Partners, L.P. v. Niagra Mohawk Power Corp., 657 N.Y.S.2d 407, 35 UCCR2d 814 (1997).

[135] New Balance Athletic Shoe, Inc. v. Boston Edison Co., 29 UCCR2d 397 (Mass. Super. 1996) (because public utilities are heavily regulated, they do not fall into the category of companies that require the imposition of product liability to adequately protect the consumer).

[136] Bowen v. Niagra Mohawk Power Corp., 183 A.2d 243, 590 N.Y.S.2d 628, 19 UCCR2d 716 (N.Y. App. Div. 1992).

[137] Navarro County Elec. Coop., Inc. v. Prince, 640 S.W.2d 398, 34 UCCR 1521 (Tex. App. 1982).

[138] *See* Helvey v. Wabash County REMC, 278 N.E.2d 608, 10 UCCR 333 (Ind. Ct. App. 1972). This holding was later limited to cases where the electricity has passed the customer's

Cases involving other utilities have been sparse. In a recent Pennsylvania case, the Pennsylvania Superior Court held that the provision of cable TV is not a sale of goods, in part because there was no quantity of goods that could be measured.[139] With regard to the delivery of water, however, which can be measured and moved, the courts have determined that there is a sale of goods.[140]

[1] The Goods/Services Dichotomy

Many contracts unquestionably involve the sale of goods but also require, in connection with the sale of goods, that the seller perform services as well. These services might consist of designing the goods,[141] applying the goods,[142] installing the goods,[143] erecting the goods,[144] or servicing the goods.[145] In some cases, separate charges are made for the goods and for the services,[146] but more frequently, the price is not broken down in this manner. To what extent, if at all, should Article 2 apply to these cases? The

---

meter. Petroski v. Northern Ind. Pub. Serv. Co., 171 Ind. App. 14, 354 N.E.2d 736 (1976). *See also* Buckeye Union Fire Ins. Co. v. Detroit Edison Co., 38 Mich. App. 325, 196 N.W.2d 316, 10 UCCR 977 (1972) (although electricity is not a "good," Code warranties apply by analogy); Ransome v. Wisconsin Elec. Power Co., 87 Wisc. 2d 605, 275 N.W.2d 641 (1979) (electricity is a "product" for purposes of strict products liability).

[139] Kaplan v. Cablevision of PA, Inc., 671 A.2d 716, 29 UCCR2d 425 (Pa. Super. Ct. 1996).

[140] Zepp v. Mayor & Council of Athens, 180 Ga. App. 72, 348 S.E.2d 673, 2 UCCR2d 1179; Gall v. Allegheny County Health Dept., 521 Pa. 68, 555 A.2d 786, 8 UCCR2d 379 (1989).

[141] *See, e.g.,* Neibarger v. Universal Coops., Inc., 486 N.W.2d 612, 18 UCCR2d 729 (Mich. 1992); Murphy v. Spelts-Schwartz, 240 Neb. 275, 481 N.W.2d 422, 17 UCCR2d 467 (1992).

[142] *See, e.g.,* Newark v. Gimbel's, Inc., 102 N.J. Super. 279, 246 A.2d 11, 5 UCCR 686 (1968).

[143] *See, e.g.,* Riffe v. Black, 548 S.W.2d 175, 21 UCCR 467 (Ky. Ct. App. 1977); O'Laughlin v. Minnesota Natural Gas Co., 253 N.W.2d 286, 21 UCCR 1258 (Minn. 1977); Inn Between, Inc. v. Remanco Metro., Inc., 33 UCCR2d 1110 (N.Y. Dist. Ct. 1997).

[144] *See, e.g.,* Standard Structural Steel Co. v. Debron Corp., 515 F. Supp. 803, 32 UCCR 393 (D. Conn. 1980); Cacace v. Morcald, 37 Conn. Supp. 735, 435 A.2d 1035, 32 UCCR 404 (1981); Corisca Coop. Ass'n v. Behlen Mfg. Co., Inc., 967 F. Supp. 382, 35 UCCR2d 1116 (D.S.D. 1997).

[145] *See, e.g.,* American Warehouse & Moving Serv., Inc. v. Floyd's Diesel Servs., 164 Ga. App. 106, 296 S.E.2d 64, 34 UCCR 1529 (1982); Perlmutter v. Don's Ford, Inc., 409 N.Y.S.2d 628, 25 UCCR 675 (1978).

[146] *See, e.g.,* Dehahn v. Innes, 356 A.2d 711, 19 UCCR 407 (Me. 1976); Micro-Managers, Inc. v. Gregory, 434 N.W.2d 97, 7 UCCR2d 1375 (Wis. 1988).

cases are legion, and the analysis employed in almost all of them derives from the 1974 case of *Bonebrake v. Cox*.[147] In this case, a bowling alley was gutted by a fire. The owners entered into a contract for reconstruction of the alley, including the provision and installation of ten bowling lanes, a cleaning machine, ball returns, chairs, tables, lockers, and other assorted items. Quoting from the predecessor to this text,[148] the court recognized that

> [services] always play an important role in the use of goods, whether it is the service of transforming the raw materials into some usable product or the service of distributing the usable product to a point where it can easily be obtained by the consumer. The [section 2-105(1)] definition should not be used to deny Code application simply because an added service is required to inject or apply the product.[149]

This analysis caused the court to reject the Special Master's conclusion that Article 2 was not meant to apply to nondivisible contracts involving both goods and services. Simply because services provided by the seller play a role in the ultimate use of the goods should not bar the application of Article 2 to the contract. Instead, the court said, this should be a function of which factor (i.e., goods or services) predominates in the contract:

> The test for inclusion or exclusion is not whether they are mixed, but, granting that they are mixed, whether their predominate factor, their thrust, their purpose, reasonably stated, is the rendition of service, with goods incidentally involved (e.g., contract with artist for painting) or is a transaction of sale, with labor incidentally involved (e.g., installation of a water heater in a bathroom).[150]

Courts have referred to the test established in *Bonebrake* in a number of ways: the "predominate-factor test,"[151] the "predominate-purpose test,"[152]

---

[147] 499 F.2d 951, 14 UCCR 1318 (8th Cir. 1974).

[148] Robert Nordstrom, Handbook of the Law of Sales (1970).

[149] 499 F.2d at 958–959, 14 UCCR at 1330.

[150] 499 F.2d 960, 14 UCCR at 1332–1333.

[151] *See, e.g.,* Conopco, Inc. v. McCreedie, 826 F. Supp. 855, 21 UCCR2d 889 (D.N.J. 1993); Executive Ctrs. of Am., Inc. v. Bannon, 62 Ill. App. 3d 738, 379 N.E.2d 364, 24 UCCR 1096 (1978).

[152] *See, e.g.,* DeFilippo v. Ford Motor Co., 516 F.2d 1313, 16 UCCR 1199 (3d Cir. 1975); St. Anne-Nackawic Pulp Co. v. Research-Cottrell, Inc., 788 F. Supp. 729, 18 UCCR2d 187 (S.D.N.Y. 1992); Micro Data Base Sys., Inc. v. Dharma Sys., Inc., 35 UCCR2d 747 (7th Cir. 1998); Princess Cruises, Inc. v. General Elec. Co., 35 UCCR2d 804 (4th Cir. 1998).

and the "essence of the contract."[153] Hundreds of cases have cited *Bonebrake* with approval and used the test recited by the court. A number of earlier cases, however, involving contaminated blood and other medical services, precursed the approach adopted by the court in *Bonebrake*.

The most notable of these cases is probably *Perlmutter v. Beth David Hospital*.[154] In this case, the plaintiff contracted hepatitis from a blood transfusion received while she was a patient in the hospital. She sued the hospital, claiming a breach of warranty under the Uniform Sales Act, the predecessor to Article 2, and the trial court upheld the claim as stating a cause of action. The New York Court of Appeals reversed the trial court's refusal to dismiss the complaint, saying that "when service predominates, and transfer of personal property is but an incidental feature of the transaction, the transaction is not deemed a sale within the Sales Act."[155] The court pointed out that (at that time) there was neither a means of detecting the presence of the jaundice-producing agent in the donor's blood nor a practical method of treating the blood to eliminate the danger.[156]

In the 1960s and 1970s, a large number of similar cases arose under the Code. The majority of those cases adopted the same analysis as the *Perlmutter* case and concluded that, because the service aspect of the relationship between the patient and the hospital predominated, the hospital was not liable under Code warranty law for the goods provided along with the services. These cases dealt not only with contaminated blood,[157] but with other goods, such as a pacemaker[158] and a surgical pin,[159] provided while the patient was in the hospital. In addition, on this basis Article 2 was generally held not to apply to other health care professionals who provided goods in conjunction with their services.[160] Although there were occasional

---

[153] *See, e.g.*, United States ex rel. Bartec Indus., Inc. v. Union Pacific Co., 976 F.2d 1274, 18 UCCR2d 696 (9th Cir. 1992); Embryo Progeny Assoc. v. Lavone Farms, Inc., 203 Ga. App. 447, 416 S.E.2d 833, 17 UCCR2d 1064 (1992).

[154] 308 N.Y. 100, 123 N.E.2d 792 (1954).

[155] 308 N.Y. at 104, 123 N.E.2d at 794.

[156] *Id.*

[157] *See, e.g.*, Sloneker v. St. Joseph's Hosp., 233 F. Supp. 105 (D. Colo. 1964); St. Luke's Hosp. v. Schmaltz, 188 Colo. 353, 534 P.2d 781, 17 UCCR 65 (1975); Fisher v. Sibley Memorial Hosp., 403 A.2d 1130, 26 UCCR 1128 (D.C. 1979); Lovett v. Emory Univ., Inc., 116 Ga. App. 277, 156 S.E.2d 923, 4 UCCR 688 (1967); Schuchman v. Johns Hopkins Hosp., 9 UCCR 637 (Md. Super. 1971). *But see* Mercy Hosp., Inc. v. Benitez, 257 So. 2d 51, 10 UCCR 340 (Fla. Dist. Ct. App. 1972).

[158] Cutler v. General Elec. Co., 4 UCCR 300 (N.Y. Sup. Ct. 1967).

[159] Dorfman v. Austena, Inc., 3 UCCR 856 (N.Y. Sup. Ct. 1966).

[160] *See, e.g.*, Osborn v. Kelley, 402 N.Y.S.2d 463, 23 UCCR 871 (N.Y. App. Div. 1978) (dispensing of prescription drugs by a physician); Makripodis v. Merrell-Dow Pharmaceu-

cases to the contrary,[161] the majority of cases, both before and after *Bonebrake*, refused to hold hospitals and other health care providers subject to warranty liability for goods provided incident to the rendering of medical services. This was true even when a separate charge was made for the goods involved.[162]

The "predominate-factor" test of the *Bonebrake* case and the medical treatment cases has become so well accepted that it has been frequently applied in cases not involving services at all. For example, the *Bonebrake* mode of analysis has been applied in cases involving contracts in which both goods and realty have been sold,[163] contracts for the sale of a business in which both goods and intangibles are sold,[164] and contracts for franchises or distributorships.[165] In most jurisdictions, whether goods or services predominate in a contract is a question of fact.[166]

Courts have relied on a large number of indicators to determine whether goods or services predominate in a contract. One of the most frequent in-

---

ticals, Inc., 523 A.2d 374, 3 UCCR2d 1362 (Pa. Super. Ct. 1987) (pharmacist not liable for breach of warranty for harmful effects of drug); Walden v. Jeffery, 907 S.W.2d 446, 26 UCCR2d 344 (Tex. 1995) (preparation of false teeth by dentist).

[161] *See, e.g.,* Hansen v. Mercy Hosp., 40 Colo. App. 17, 570 P.2d 1309, 23 UCCR 36 (1977) (blood bank found liable for contaminated blood although hospital not liable); Garcia v. Edgewater Hosp., 613 N.E.2d 1243, 21 UCCR2d 595 (Ill. App. Ct. 1993) (hospital subject to warranty liability for supplying defective heart valve); Providence Hosp. v. Truly, 611 S.W.2d 127, 30 UCCR 785 (Tex. App. 1980) (U.C.C. warranty provisions applicable to drug injected into plaintiff's eye).

[162] *See, e.g.,* Perlmutter v. Beth David Hosp., 308 N.Y. 100, 123 N.E.2d 792 (1954). *But see* Providence Hosp. v. Truly, 611 S.W.2d 127, 30 UCCR 785 (Tex. App. 1980).

[163] *See* Beaulieu of Am., Inc. v. Coronet Indus., Inc., 173 Ga. App. 556, 327 S.E.2d 508, 41 UCCR 20 (1985); Dehahn v. Innes, 356 A.2d 711, 19 UCCR 407 (Me. 1976).

[164] *See, e.g.,* Fink v. DeClassis, 745 F. Supp. 509, 13 UCCR2d 693 (N.D. Ill. 1990).

[165] *See, e.g.,* Corenswet, Inc. v. Amana Refrigeration, Inc., 594 F.2d 129, 26 UCCR 301 (5th Cir. 1979) (although distributorship agreements are more than sales contracts, Code applies to them); DeFillippo v. Ford Motor Co., 516 F.2d 1313, 16 UCCR 1199 (3d Cir. 1975); A. H. Capen's Co., Inc. v. American Trading & Prod. Corp., 973 F. Supp. 247, 33 UCCR2d 1009 (D.P.R. 1997). Whether relying on the *Bonebrake* test or not, a large majority of cases have held that Article 2 applies to franchise and distributorship agreements.

[166] *See, e.g.,* Conopco, Inc. v. McCreedie, 826 F. Supp. 855, 21 UCCR2d 883 (D.N.J. 1993); Prince v. Spive Corp., 584 S.W.2d 108, 27 UCCR 6 (Mo. Ct. App. 1979); Docteroff v. Barra Corp. of Am., Inc., 659 A.2d 948, 27 UCCR2d 1238 (N.J. Super. App. Div. 1995); Tacoma Athletic Club, Inc. v. Indoor Comfort Sys., Inc., 79 Wash. App. 250, 902 P.2d 175, 30 UCCR2d 219 (1995) (issue can be disposed of only as a matter of law if standard for summary judgment is met). *But see* Cleveland Lumber Co. v. Proctor & Schwartz, Inc., 397 F. Supp. 1088, 17 UCCR 1148 (N.D. Ga. 1975) (on motion for reconsideration, the court held that in the absence of fraud and on undisputed facts, issue was a question of law).

dicators is the language of the contract itself.[167] This gives the parties considerable control over whether the Code is applicable to the contract. For example, the court in *DeGroft v. Lancaster Silo Co.*[168] held that a contract to build a silo on a farmer's land was predominately a contract for services, despite the fact that the silo was completely prefabricated and sold as a kit and all of the parts were readily identifiable. The court emphasized that the contract authorized the defendant to "construct" the silo and contained repeated references to "construction" or "erection" of the silo. On the other hand, the contract had no reference to "sale" or "purchase."[169] Thus, if the contract uses language such as "contractor," "installation," or "improvement," it is more likely that the court will find services to predominate in the contract.[170] Use of language such as "sale," "seller," or "purchase," will likely influence the court to find that goods predominate in the transaction.[171] Cases are rare in which a court has found goods to predominate where the language of the contract is language of service, and vice versa.[172]

---

[167] *See, e.g.*, St. Anne-Nackawic Pulp Co. v. Research-Cottrell, Inc., 788 F. Supp. 729, 17 UCCR2d 6991 (S.D.N.Y. 1992); Ranger Constr. Co. v. Dixie Floor Co., 433 F. Supp. 442, 22 UCCR 567 (D.S.C. 1977); Bailey v. Montgomery Ward & Co., 690 P.2d 1280, 40 UCCR 90 (Colo. Ct. App. 1984); DeCroft v. Lancaster Silo Co., 527 A.2d 1316, 4 UCCR2d 20 (Md. Ct. Spec. App. 1987); Van Sistine v. Tollard, 291 N.W.2d 636, 28 UCCR 1274 (Wisc. Ct. App. 1980).

[168] 527 A.2d 1316, 4 UCCR2d 20 (Md. Ct. Spec. App. 1987).

[169] 527 A.2d at 1325, 4 UCCR2d at 30. On the other hand, in Holstad v. Southwestern Porcelain, Inc., 421 N.W.2d 371, 5 UCCR2d 912 (Minn Ct. App. 1988), the court found that a similar contract was a contract for the sale of goods. The court did not refer to the language of the contract in its analysis.

[170] *See, e.g.*, Inhabitants of City of Saco v. General Elec. Co., 779 F. Supp. 186, 17 UCCR2d 1068 (D. Me. 1991) ("design, equip, construct and start-up"); Filmservice Labs, Inc. v. Harvey Bernard Enters., Inc., 208 Cal. App. 3d 1297, 256 Cal. Rptr. 753, 8 UCCR 15 (1989) ("services and materials"); Frommert v. Bobson Constr. Co., 219 Mich. App. 735, 558 N.W.2d 239, 31 UCCR2d 676 (1996) ("home improvement and installation"); Higgins v. Lauritzen, 209 Mich. App. 266, 530 N.W.2d 171, 26 UCCR2d 679 (1995) ("contractor").

[171] *See, e.g.*, Bonebrake v. Cox, 499 F.2d 951, 14 UCCR 1318 (8th Cir. 1974) ("equipment"); Kline Iron & Steel Co. v. Gray Communications Consultants, Inc., 715 F. Supp. 135, 9 UCCR2d 858 (D.S.C. 1989) ("buyer"); Colorado Carpet Installation Inc. v. Palermo, 668 P.2d 1384, 36 UCCR 1516 (Colo. 1983) ("seller," "customer"); Bailey v. Montgomery Ward & Co., 690 P.2d 1280, 40 UCCR 90 (Colo. Ct. App. 1984) ("purchase," "merchandise"); B&B Refrigeration & Air Conditioning Serv., Inc. v. Haifley, 25 UCCR 635 (D.C. Super. 1978) ("purchaser," "seller"); Cober v. Corle, 416 Pa. Super. 191, 610 A.2d 1036, 18 UCCR2d 1041 (1992) ("purchase agreement").

[172] *See* Art Metal Prods. Co. of Chicago v. Royal Equip. Co., 670 S.W.2d 152, 38 UCCR 1202 (Mo. Ct. App. 1984). *See also* Intamin Inc. v. Figley-Wright Contractors, Inc., 393 F.

Other factors have also consistently played a role in determining whether goods or services predominate in a contract. If the contract allocates a portion of the contract price to goods and a portion to services, courts will rely heavily on whichever is the larger to determine the predominate factor.[173] Even when the contract itself does not allocate the price between goods and services, if the court can do so, the ratio will remain important.[174] Interestingly, courts have cited a failure to break down the price between goods and services to support both a finding of a sale of goods and a finding of a sale of services.[175]

Other factors that a number of courts have relied upon are the amount of expertise necessary to perform the services portion of the contract, and whether the seller's expertise in providing the services induced the buyer to choose the particular seller. For example, in *Pittsley v. Houser*,[176] the court determined that goods predominated in a contract for the sale and installation of carpet because installation played no part in the buyer's choice of the supplier of the carpet. Instead, the buyer had relied entirely on the price of the carpet in selecting the supplier.[177] In *Higgins v. Laurit-*

Supp. 1350, 40 UCCR 766 (N.D. Ill. 1984) (court held that contract for construction of a roller coaster was subject to the Code because the contract expressly provided that the Code would control).

[173] *See* In re L.B. Trucking, Inc., 163 B.R. 709, 23 UCCR2d 1092 (D. Del. 1994) (Article 2 applies when charge for herbicide is ten times greater than charge for spraying); Southern Tank Equip. Co. v. Zartic, Inc., 221 Ga. App. 503, 471 S.E.2d 587, 30 UCCR2d 54 (1996) (greater than one-half of the price allocated to goods; Article 2 applies); Navasso County Elec. Coop. Inc. v. Prince, 640 S.W.2d 398, 34 UCCR 1521 (Tex. App. 1982) (Article 2 applies to sale of irrigation system when only $2,000 of price of $92,000 allocated to installation).

[174] *See, e.g.,* St. Anne-Nackawic Pulp Co. v. Research-Cottrell, Inc., 788 F. Supp. 729, 17 UCCR2d 699 (S.D.N.Y. 1992) (court relied on internal memo of seller to determine that only a small percentage of the price charged related to services); J. Lee Gregory, Inc. v. Scandinavian House, L.P., 433 S.E.2d 687, 23 UCCR2d 373 (Ga. Ct. App. 1993) (although no separate charge for services, Article 2 applied because more than two-thirds of the price reflected the cost of windows).

[175] *See* Smith v. Urethane Installations, Inc., 492 A.2d 1266, 41 UCCR 733 (Me. 1985) (no separate charge for materials indicates services contract); DeGroft v. Lancaster Silo Co., 527 A.2d 1316, 4 UCCR2d 20 (Md. Spec. Ct. App. 1987) (court cites no breakdown in price as supporting service contract); Neibarger v. Universal Coops., Inc., 486 N.W.2d 612, 18 UCCR2d 779 (Mich. 1992) (goods predominate when there is no separate charge for services in contract for purchase, installation, and servicing of milking machine); Huyler Paper Stock Co. v. Information Supplies Corp., 117 N.J. Super. 353, 284 A.2d 568, 9 UCCR 1337 (Law Div. 1971) (no separate charge for services indicates contract for the sale of goods).

[176] 125 Idaho 820, 875 P.2d 232, 24 UCCR2d 792 (Idaho Ct. App. 1994).

[177] For similar decisions, *see* Bob Neiner Farms, Inc. v. Lendrix, 141 Ill. App. 3d 499,

zen,[178] however, the court found that a contract to drill a well and install piping and an electric pump was not a contract for the sale of goods, in part because the plaintiff had specifically sought out the supplier's expertise and knowledge in the method and manner of drilling wells. Similarly, in *Geotech Energy Corp. v. Gulf States Telecomms. & Info Systems, Inc.,*[179] the court held that because significant expertise was required for the design and installation of a telephone system, the contract was for the sale of services, not goods, despite the large amount of equipment involved.[180]

In a similar vein, the discretion allowed in the contract to the supplier to choose the materials supplied to the buyer and to determine the place, manner, and mode of installation have influenced the decision as to which factor predominates. The greater the discretion permitted the supplier in these choices, the more likely the contract will be for services rather than goods. In *Missouri Farmers Assoc. v. McBee,*[181] the court refused to find a contract for the sale of goods when the supplier agreed to spray the buyer's fields with herbicide when the contract gave the supplier complete discretion to select the herbicide and the method of application. Another court decided that a contract to install a well and water system was not governed by Article 2 when the contract permitted the supplier to choose the components of the system.[182]

In a couple of cases the courts have focused on which aspect of the transaction is treated in more detail in the contract. In *Kirkpatrick v. Introspect Healthcare Corp.,*[183] the court pointed to a detailed itemization of twenty-three services in deciding that a contract to create an interior design for a mental health facility was not a contract for the sale of goods. Conversely, the court in *Cambridge Planting Co. v. Napco, Inc.*[184] held that a

---

490 N.E.2d 257, 1 UCCR2d 634 (1986) (since construction of farm machinery shed required only "non-creative, formula-like" construction, contract was for the sale of goods); Gross Valentino Printing Co. v. Clarise, 120 Ill. App. 3d 907, 458 N.E.2d 1027, 37 UCCR 1460 (1982) (printing services were largely fungible to buyer).

[178] 209 Mich. App. 266, 530 N.W.2d 171, 26 UCCR2d 679 (1995).

[179] 788 S.W.2d 386, 12 UCCR2d 41 (Tex. App. 1990).

[180] *See also* Kirkpatrick v. Introspect Healthcare Corp., 845 P.2d 800, 21 UCCR2d 493 (N.M. 1992) (contract that required the supplier to develop an appropriate ambience and community image for mental health facility not covered by Article 2).

[181] 787 S.W.2d 756, 12 UCCR2d 32 (Mo. Ct. App. 1990).

[182] *See also* Higgins v. Lauritzen, 209 Mich. App. 266, 530 N.W.2d 171, 26 UCCR2d 679 (1995) (contract to drill a well and supply piping and electric motor was not for the sale of goods when supplier decided the location of the well and chose the equipment).

[183] 845 P.2d 804, 21 UCCR2d 493 (N.M. 1992).

[184] 991 F.2d 21, 20 UCCR2d 739 (1st Cir. 1993).

contract for the design and installation of a wastewater treatment facility was a contract for the sale of goods. The contract specifically listed 82,188 items of goods to be provided in connection with the contract. Other factors used by courts to determine whether goods or services predominate include the intent of the parties,[185] the general nature of the supplier's business,[186] whether the supplier charged sales tax,[187] the value of the goods absent installation,[188] and whether the buyer has supplied the seller with materials to make a product.[189]

One factor that appears to significantly influence the decision whether goods or services predominate is whether the cause of action arises from the goods or services portion of the transaction. Perhaps because the source of the cause of action is logically unrelated to whether goods or services predominate in a contract, courts only occasionally acknowledge its significance. Over the broad run of cases, however, it is clear that if the cause of action arose from a defect in the goods, courts have been more inclined to find the goods aspect to predominate. Conversely, if the cause of action arose from the service component, courts have been more likely to hold the service element to predominate. A few courts have been willing forthrightly to acknowledge the significance of this factor.[190]

---

[185] See Standard Structural Steel Co. v. Debron Corp., 515 F. Supp. 803, 32 UCCR 393 (D. Conn. 1980); Urban Indus. of Ohio, Inc. v. Tectum, Inc., 81 Ohio App. 3d 768, 612 N.E.2d 382, 20 UCCR2d 1193 (1992).

[186] See Abex Corp./Jetway Div. v. Controlled Sys. Corp., 93 F.2d 1055, 22 UCCR2d 166 (4th Cir. 1993); Cockley & Williams, Inc. v. Shatterproof Glass Corp., 706 F.2d 456, 36 UCCR 87 (4th Cir. 1983); Burton v. Artery Co., 367 A.2d 935, 20 UCCR 1207 (Md. Ct. App. 1977); In re Trailer & Plumbing Supplies, 578 A.2d 343, 12 UCCR2d 1029 (N.H. 1990). The nature of the supplier's business would seem to be logically unrelated to whether goods or services predominated in the particular contract under consideration. Certainly, a supplier can make a sale of goods in an individual contract even though services predominate in its business as a whole. For example, a shoe-repair business might sell shoe polish, brushes, and other accessories as a minor part of its business. Similarly, a barber might sell shampoo, shaving cream, and other such items, even though her predominate business is the provision of services.

[187] See Meeker v. Hamilton Grain Elevator Co., 110 Ill. App. 3d 668, 442 N.E.2d 921, 35 UCCR 347 (1982).

[188] See Frammert v. Bobson Constr. Co., 558 N.W.2d 239, 31 UCCR2d 676 (Mich. Ct. App. 1996).

[189] See Omac, Inc. v. Southwestern Mach. & Tool Works, Inc., 189 Ga. App. 42, 8 UCCR2d 616 (1988); McDowell v. Atco Rubber Prods. Inc., 221 A.D.2d 876, 634 N.Y.S.2d 554, 30 UCCR2d 459 (App. Div. 1995).

[190] See Baker v. Compton, 455 N.E.2d 382, 38 UCCR 10 (Ind. Ct. App. 1983) ("Further, if the cause of action on a mixed contract centers exclusively on the materials or the services

Contracts for repair[191] or alteration[192] of existing goods are virtually always classified as service contracts. This is true even if the repair might include providing a significant number of replacement parts,[193] or even when the cost of parts to the buyer exceeds the cost of labor.[194]

A difficult set of cases in which courts have reached somewhat inconsistent results are those in which the contracts contemplate only the delivery of goods but where the seller must engage in substantial development or production activities in order to produce the goods for the buyer. When the buyer purchases goods "off the shelf," the fact that the seller may have engaged in substantial research, development, and production activities to create the goods is recognized by the courts to be irrelevant. In this situation, courts do not ask which aspect of the contract predominates; they simply find an Article 2 contract. All goods require "services" to transform the raw materials into useful products, and many goods have been created only after substantial research-and-development work. In fact, for many items the cost of services performed on the goods far exceeds the value of the raw material. Were these activities to become a part of the *Bonebrake* calculus, there would be little room left for application of Article 2.

When the buyer does not purchase goods off the shelf, however, but employs the supplier to produce the goods specifically for it, courts have struggled to decide whether the Code is applicable. The problem was posed by an example used in the *Bonebrake* case itself: is it predominately a sale of goods or services when a person commissions an artist to paint a portrait?

---

portion of the contract, that fact may weigh heavily in the determination of the predominate aspect of the contract."); Montgomery Ward & Co. v. Dalton, 665 S.W.2d 507, 38 UCCR 428 (Tex. App. 1984) (where the complaint relates only to services, dominate factor was the furnishing of labor).

[191] *See, e.g.,* Stafford v. International Harvester Co., 668 F.2d 142, 32 UCCR 1331 (2d Cir. 1981) (contract to repair truck); Gentile v. MacGregor Mfg. Co., 493 A.2d 647, 41 UCCR 15 (N.J. Super. Ct. 1985) (contract to recondition football helmets); Mack Fin. Corp. v. Harnett Transfer, Inc., 42 N.C. App. 116, 256 S.E.2d 491, 27 UCCR 8 (1979).

[192] *See, e.g.,* Filmservice Lab., Inc. v. Harvey Bernhard Enters., Inc., 256 Cal. Rptr. 735, 8 UCCR2d 15 (Cal. Ct. App. 1989) (services predominated in contract to manufacture motion picture prints from negatives); OMAC, Inc. v. Southwestern Mach. & Tool Works, Inc., 189 Ga. App. 42, 374 S.E.2d 829, 8 UCCR2d 616 (1988) (contract to manufacture parts from materials supplied by buyer).

[193] *See* Gee v. Chattahoochee Tractor Sales, Inc., 172 Ga. App. 351, 323 S.E.2d 176, 40 UCCR 30 (1984) (rebuilding of engine including replacement of that portion of engine from the cylinder head down to, and including, the crankshaft).

[194] *See* Northwestern Equip., Inc. v. Cudmore, 312 N.W.2d 347, 33 UCCR 160 (N.D. 1981) (services predominate even though cost of parts exceeds cost of labor to repair bulldozer).

The court in *Bonebrake* thought that the answer was self-evident: such a contract is predominately for services, not goods.[195] The answer, however, is not nearly so clear as the court apparently believed.

First, the definition of goods in section 2-105 explicitly includes "specially manufactured goods." While "specially manufactured goods" is not defined in the Code, it is generally accepted to mean goods that are produced or manufactured for a specific buyer, normally pursuant to the buyer's specifications or to meet the buyer's particular needs.[196] Thus, the Code itself clearly contemplates that a contract for the sale of goods can exist even when the seller designs and manufactures goods to meet the needs or desires of a particular customer.[197]

Second, it is hardly self-evident what policy or policies support the application of the Code when the buyer agrees to purchase goods after the development and production activities have already occurred, but not when they are incurred as a result of the contract with the buyer. What legitimate reasons support not finding a sale of goods when an artist is commissioned to paint a picture and finding a sale of goods when the same painting is sold by a gallery?

A few examples illustrate the difficulties that these cases have posed. In *Care-Display, Inc. v. Didde-Glaser, Inc.*,[198] Didde-Glaser (D-G) contracted with Care-Display for Care-Display to design and construct a display booth for D-G to use at a trade show. The court held that the predominate factor in the contract was the provision of services rather than the sale of goods. In explaining its conclusion, the court said that "the major objective [of the parties] contemplated utilizing the knowledge and expertise of Care-Display to create a unique setting in which to exhibit and promote to best advantage the products of Didde-Glaser." Reliance upon the knowledge and expertise of the supplier to provide a suitable product, however, is virtually always present when a buyer chooses a seller to produce specially manufactured goods. Contrast this case with *Colonial Life Insurance Co. of America v. Electronic Data Systems Corp.*,[199] in which the court found goods to predominate despite the fact that the supplier spent four years developing

---

[195] Bonebrake v. Cox, 499 F.2d 951, 14 UCCR 1318 (8th Cir. 1974).

[196] *See* LTV Aerospace Corp. v. Bateman, 492 S.W.2d 703, 12 UCCR 1042 (Tex. App. 1973).

[197] *See* Valley Farmers' Elevator v. Lindsay Bros. Co., 398 N.W.2d 553, 2 UCCR2d 1495 (Minn. 1987) (specially designed grain storage system is contract for the sale of goods; Code applies to specially manufactured goods).

[198] 589 P.2d 599, 25 UCCR 1254 (Kan. 1979).

[199] 817 F. Supp. 235, 20 UCCR2d 753 (D.N.H. 1993).

53

and customizing a computer software package especially for the buyer.[200] In another case, a court held that a contract to take photographs at a wedding constituted a sale of goods.[201] Why this case should come out differently from a contract with an artist to do a painting is not obvious. Both require expertise and knowledge to produce, and the intrinsic value of the goods (i.e., paper, paint, etc.) is small compared to the effort required to produce the finished product.[202]

Cases involving printing contracts evidence similar confusion. In *Printing Center of Texas, Inc. v. Supermind Publishing Co.*,[203] a publisher entered into a contract with a printer to print 5,000 books. The books proved defective, which resulted in a lawsuit. The case was tried in the lower court on the assumption that Article 2 applied to the contract. On appeal, the court made it clear that, in its view, the Code was not applicable, even though it found any objection to application of the Code to have been waived. The court said that while the printer sells paper and ink, it also sells its binding, typesetting, and proofing services necessary to produce the finished product. Therefore, the essence of the contract was for services.[204] Just one year earlier, however, an appellate court in Illinois held that a contract to print a magazine for a publisher was predominately a sale of goods.[205] Any policy justification for distinguishing between a contract to print books and a con-

---

[200] *See also* Triangle Underwriters, Inc. v. Honeywell, Inc., 457 F. Supp. 765, 24 UCCR 1088 (E.D.N.Y. 1978) (goods predominated in contract for "turnkey" computer system even though system required effort to produce); W.R. Weaver Co. v. Burroughs Corp., 580 S.W.2d 76, 27 UCCR 64 (Tex. App. 1979) (contract for computer program designed to meet buyer's needs covered by Article 2).

[201] Carpel v. Saget Studios, Inc., 326 F. Supp. 1331, 9 UCCR 82 (E.D. Pa. 1971).

[202] *See also* Mayo v. Caldwell, 547 N.Y.S.2d 207, 11 UCCR2d 1153 (Just. Ct. 1989). In this case, the court held that a contract to produce a magnetic sign that would adhere to the buyer's truck and advertise the business name and telephone number of the buyer was predominately for the sale of goods. It said that while the supplier was to provide the layout and painting of the sign, this was incidental to the sign itself. Apparently, sign-painters produce goods, artists provide services.

[203] 669 S.W.2d 779, 39 UCCR 127 (Tex. App. 1984).

[204] *See also* North Am. Leisure Corp. v. A&B Duplicators, Ltd., 468 F.2d 695, 11 UCCR 518 (2d Cir. 1972). In this case, the buyer provided a master tape of music to the supplier. The supplier agreed to take the master tape and produce salable cassettes and 8-track cartridges, which it would sell to the buyer for resale. Despite the fact that the supplier was to supply all of the tape, cassettes, and cartridges, the court found that services predominated in the contract.

[205] Gross Valentino Printing Co. v. Clarke, 120 Ill. App. 3d 907, 458 N.E.2d 1027, 37 UCCR 1460 (1983).

tract to print magazines insofar as the application of Article 2 is concerned is not apparent.[206]

The confusion in these cases and the difficulty in resolving many goods/service cases is largely the result of a serious defect in the predominate factor test of *Bonebrake*. The great majority of the cases applying the predominate factor test take an "all or nothing" approach to the application of the Code. That is, if the court finds the goods aspect of the contract to predominate, it will apply Article 2 in its entirety, whether or not the cause of action has its genesis with the goods, the services, or both. In many cases, for example, where both goods and services were delivered to the buyer, courts have found Article 2 applicable even though the cause of action arose with the service component[207] or have found Article 2 inapplicable even though the cause of action arose with the goods.[208] Similarly, in the cases discussed in the immediately preceding paragraphs, if the court found services to predominate in the contract, the Code did not apply to any aspect of the contract even though the ultimate purpose of the contract was the production of goods for the buyer.

The *Bonebrake* approach is both superficial and sterile. It is superficial because it fails to recognize that all contracts for the sale of goods have services lurking somewhere in the background. The price of all goods contains a large percentage for services that were involved in creating, preparing, transporting, and distributing them. To include these services as part of the "predominate factor" calculus when they occur at one time (i.e., after

---

[206] For other cases hard to reconcile, *compare* Incomm, Inc. v. Thermo-Spa, Inc., 41 Conn. Supp. 566, 595 A.2d 954, 15 UCCR2d 427 (1991) (the "essence" of a contract to produce sixteen-page ad brochure was not the sale of goods, but labor and services) *with* Dessmone v. Sullivan, 25 UCCR2d 351 (Mass. Super. 1994) (contract in which buyer paid all seller's development costs except labor to develop "VIDEO MESSENGER" was predominately sale of goods).

[207] *See, e.g.,* Long Island Lighting Co. v. IMO Indus., 6 F.3d 876, 22 UCCR2d 205 (2d Cir. 1993) (Article 2 applied to promise to repair in contract in which goods predominated); Cambridge Planting Co., Inc. v. Napco, Inc., 991 F.2d 21, 20 UCCR2d 739 (1st Cir. 1993) (Article 2 statute of limitations applies to contract for wastewater treatment system because goods predominate even though allegations are of faulty installation); Riffe v. Black, 548 S.W.2d 175, 21 UCCR 467 (Ky. Ct. App. 1977) (Article 2 applies to improper installation of swimming pool). *See also* Lane Constr. Corp. v. Trading Merchandising Co., 24 UCCR2d 797 (Va. Cir. Ct. 1994) (if paving contract is primarily for sale of goods, U.C.C. applies to claims of defective goods *and* defective installation).

[208] *See, e.g.,* Coakley & Williams, Inc. v. Shatterproof Glass Corp., 778 F.2d 196, 42 UCCR 60 (4th Cir. 1985) (Article 2 did not apply to claimed defect in glass because contract was predominately for services).

the parties have contracted for the goods) and not include them when they occur at another time (i.e., before the parties contracted for the goods), without explanation or sound policy, is not careful analysis.

It is also a sterile mode of analysis because it fails to recognize the true problem involved in any individual case. The answer to the application of Article 2 to a contract should not be determined by trying to decide whether goods or services "predominate," but on the basis of the impact of the Code on the case and the policies relevant to the issues before the court. Fortunately, there is an alternative mode of analysis which some courts have adopted that—with a little tweaking—should provide more consistent and satisfactory results.

Two early cases laid the groundwork for a better approach: *Newmark v. Gimbel's, Inc.*[209] and *Foster v. Colorado Radio Corp.*[210] In *Newmark*, the plaintiff contracted a case of dermatitis from hair lotion applied by the defendant in the course of giving the plaintiff a permanent wave. As a result, the plaintiff suffered severe inflammation and hair loss. She sued the defendant for breach of warranty, and her claim was dismissed by the trial court because there was not a sale of goods as contemplated by the Code.

The Supreme Court of New Jersey reversed the trial court and allowed the cause of action to stand. The court recognized that the transaction was a "hybrid" involving the supplying of both goods and services. Instead of attempting to decide which of the two "predominated," the court proceeded on the basis that "the distinction between a sale and the rendition of a service is a highly artificial one."[211] As a result, the court's inquiry was whether the *policies* that make implied warranties appropriate in conventional sales were applicable to the provision of hair lotion by the beautician. The court decided that the policies behind warranty liability were applicable no less than if there had been a "straight sale" of the hair lotion. The primary policies, applicable in both cases, were the reliance on the skill and expertise of the seller to select sound and appropriate products and the inability of the patron to protect herself.[212] To the argument that the Code

---

[209] 258 A.2d 697, 6 UCCR 1205 (N.J. 1969).

[210] 381 F.2d 222, 4 UCCR 446 (10th Cir. 1967).

[211] 258 A.2d at 700, 6 UCCR at 1210.

[212] The court said:

> When a patron responds to the solicitation she does so confident that any product used in the shop has come from a reliable origin and can be trusted not to injure her. She places herself in the hands of the operator relying upon his or her expertise both in the selection of the products to be used on her and in the method of using them. The ministrations and the products employed on her are under the control and selection of the operator; the patron is a mere passive

is limited in application to sales of goods, the court responded that it was not the intention of the drafters to limit implied warranties to transactions "which technically meet its definition of a sale."[213]

The other early case did not deal with services at all. In *Foster v. Colorado Radio Corp.*,[214] the buyer repudiated a promise to buy a radio station as a going concern. The radio station's assets consisted of both goods and non-goods (real estate and improvements, good will, the station's broadcasting license). The issue was whether the seller was required to give notice of resale under section 2-706 when the seller sold the station to another purchaser.[215] The court rejected the idea that it should determine whether the sale of goods or "non-goods" was the contract's "main purpose" and apply the Code *in toto* or not at all based upon that conclusion. Instead, the court found no reason not to view the contract in separate parts and apply the Code to the goods portion, but not the non-goods portion. Consequently, it required notice of resale for the goods portion, but not for the non-goods portion.[216]

Although both of these cases preceded *Bonebrake,* the willingness of the courts to go beyond the simplistic approach later adopted in *Bonebrake* has not been widely followed. Instead, the "predominate factor" test has received nearly universal adoption and approval. There are, however, a few exceptions. In *Paint Products Co. v. AA-1 Steel Equipment Co.*,[217] the court, citing *Newmark* with approval, held that an implied warranty applied to a claim that shelving had been installed with "lags" and "molly bolts" of insufficient size and strength. The contract called for the supplier to both furnish and install shelving, which later collapsed. The court did not consider whether goods or services predominated in the contract. Instead, it made a policy decision that a warranty that the bolts would be of sufficient

---

recipient.

258 A.2d at 701, 6 UCCR at 1211.

[213] 258 A.2d at 701, 6 UCCR at 1211. In support of this argument, the court cited Comment 2 to U.C.C. § 2-313 (N.J.S.A. 12A:2-313) which suggests that the Code's waranty provisions may be appropriately applied to transactions that are not strictly sales.

[214] 381 F.2d 222, 4 UCCR 446 (10th Cir. 1967).

[215] U.C.C. § 2-706 requires that a seller give the breaching buyer notice that the seller intends to resell the goods by private resale. *See* U.C.C. § 2-706; § 7.08[A], *infra.*

[216] Because the undisputed testimony indicated that the maximum value of the goods portion was only 10 percent of the contract price, the court used this figure to decide how much of the resale price could be used to calculate damages. 381 F.2d at 226–227, 4 UCCR at 449.

[217] 393 A.2d 1317, 25 UCCR 677 (Conn. Super. Ct. 1977).

size and strength to support the shelving made sense in the context of the contract.[218]

The most thoroughly considered departure from the *Bonebrake* analysis is the case of *Anthony Pools v. Sheehan*.[219] The plaintiff was injured when he fell from the diving board of his new in-ground swimming pool. He sued the supplier who had constructed the pool, the construction of which included installing the diving board. One of the buyer's claims was that the diving board was defective in breach of implied warranties. The court concluded that the transaction was a hybrid of services and goods. (It found the diving board to be goods despite the fact that it was part of and attached to the pool.) The court said that if it applied the predominate factor test, there was no question that the diving board was incidental to the construction services and there would be no implied warranty. The court said, however, that it would take a "more policy-oriented approach to determining whether warranties of quality and fitness are implied with respect to goods sold as part of a hybrid transaction."[220] Quoting extensively from *Newmark*, the court adopted what it called the "gravamen" test: the gravamen of the complaint determines the applicable law. If the buyer's complaint relates to the goods, the Code will be applicable, whether or not goods predominate in the transaction.

A number of courts explicitly rejected the approach taken in the *Anthony Pools* case and adopted the *Bonebrake* test. In most of these cases, the courts provide little justification beyond the obvious fact that *Bonebrake* represents the majority rule.[221] In the case of *Insul-Mark Midwest, Inc. v. Modern Materials, Inc.*,[222] however, the Indiana Supreme Court attempted

---

[218] The court stated:

> There is no sound reason why a manufacturer who either incidentally or as an integral part of his operations renders services in the installation of his goods, who knows the use and purpose for which they are intended, and knows the user thereof is relying on his skill and judgment, should not be held liable under the theory of breach of warranty for each and every step of the process under his control, including services rendered by him, by which the goods are transferred to the ultimate user.

393 A.2d at 1317, 25 UCCR at 677.

[219] 455 A.2d 434, 35 UCCR 408 (Md. Ct. App. 1983).

[220] 455 A.2d at 439, 35 UCCR at 415.

[221] *See, e.g.,* Rajala v. Allied Corp., 66 B.R. 582, 2 UCCR2d 1203 (D. Kan. 1986); *In re* Trailer & Plumbing Supplies, 578 A.2d 343, 12 UCCR2d 1029 (N.H. 1990); Consolidated Edison Co. of N.Y., Inc. v. Westinghouse Elec. Corp., 567 F. Supp. 358, 36 UCCR 1496 (S.D.N.Y. 1983); Neibarger v. Universal Coops., Inc., 439 Mich. 512, 486 N.W.2d 612, 18 UCCR2d 729 (1992).

[222] 612 N.E.2d 550, 21 UCCR2d 219 (Ind. 1993).

a lengthy justification of the *Bonebrake* test. The case involved a contract by the supplier to coat the buyer's screws with a rust-resistant coating. The screws, which were later sold to third parties, failed to meet rust-resistance standards, and suit was brought for breach of warranty under the Code. The court described the contract as a hybrid contract, because both goods (the coating) and services (the application of the coating) were provided. The court then considered whether to adopt the *Bonebrake* approach or the "gravamen" approach of the *Anthony Pools* case.[223]

The court decided to adopt the *Bonebrake* test and refused to bifurcate the contract between goods and services. Relying heavily on an article in the Indiana Law Review,[224] the court justified its decision:

> The bifurcation approach seems less sensitive to the parties' expectations. Rather, the effect of such approach is to break an agreement into two contracts, with one governed by the U.C.C. and one by the common law. Such an outcome in some cases might drastically alter the legal effect of the agreement as intended by the parties [citation omitted]. Dean (now Chancellor) Bepko suggests that bifurcation could lead to difficulties when the substantive issue at trial is not related to performance, but is related to the enforceability of the agreement [citation omitted]. For example, when the issue is the Statute of Frauds, bifurcating an oral goods/services contract might lead to enforcement of only the services portion of the contract, with the goods portion held unenforceable. Such a result would defeat the intentions of the parties who sought to create a unitary contract [citation omitted].
>
> Moreover, the bifurcation test would be difficult to apply in cases where the goods and service components of a transaction are essentially intertwined [citation omitted]. Bifurcation would be unworkable where an agreement is not easily divisible, or where the transaction is not easily traced to solely the goods or services portion.[225]

The court made some good points. There may be cases where the "gravamen" test adopted by *Anthony Pools* will not provide the best result. The criticism, however, misses a number of crucial points. First, the question should not be whether the approach in *Anthony Pools* will *always* provide

---

[223] One district in the Indiana intermediate appeals court system had adopted the gravamen approach in an earlier case. *See* Data Processing Servs., Inc. v. L.H. Smith Oil Corp., 492 N.E.2d 314, 1 UCCR2d 29 (Ind. Ct. App. 1986); Stephenson v. Frazier, 399 N.E.2d 794, 28 UCCR 12 (Ind. Ct. App. 1980). The others had adopted the *Bonebrake* test.

[224] Gerald L. Bepko, "Contracts, Commercial Law, and Consumer Law," 14 Ind. L. Rev. 223 (1981).

[225] 612 N.E.2d at 554–555, 21 UCCR2d at 226.

a better result, but whether it will *generally* provide a better result than the predominate factor test. In large portion of the cases, the issue is simply whether the Code's warranty provisions should apply to the plaintiff's claim.[226] In such a case, there is little likelihood of the "parade of horribles" envisioned by the court. In fact, in the very case before it, none of the potential difficulties mentioned by the court were present. Another large percentage of the cases involve the appropriate statute of limitations to apply to the plaintiff's claim.[227] In these cases, applying the U.C.C. statute of limitations to claims arising from the goods and applying other applicable statutes of limitations to claims arising from the services generally does not create difficulties. Also, contrary to the court's suggestion, the claims relating to the goods and services are rarely so intertwined that they cannot be reasonably distinguished. The question is whether the *Bonebrake* test or something else will generally lead to fairer, more predictable, more sensible outcomes in the broad run of cases, not whether an alternative to *Bonebrake* may itself present occasional problems in application.

Second, there is no reason that any approach in these mixed goods/ services cases must be exclusive. In occasional cases, the approach of *Newmark* or *Anthony Pools* will not work well, such as the example cited by the court *Insul-Mack*: whether an oral contract that includes both goods and services is enforceable under the statute of frauds. In such a case, another solution—perhaps even the predominate factor test—might be adopted.[228] There is nothing that mandates that only one test be used, regardless of the issue or circumstances, to determine the applicable law in these mixed goods/services cases.[229] Because the legislation has not made clear how these cases are to be handled, the mixed goods/services cases provide the courts with an opportunity for creative, policy-oriented solutions.

---

[226] *See, e.g.*, Sawyer v. Methodist Hosp. of Memphis, 552 F.2d 1102, 17 UCCR 708 (6th Cir. 1975); Jandreau v. Sheesley Plumbing & Heating Co., Inc., 3245 N.W.2d 266, 34 UCCR 785 (S.D. 1982).

[227] *See, e.g.*, B&B Refrigeration & Air Conditioning Serv., Inc. v. Haifley, 25 UCCR 635 (D.C. Super. Ct. 1978); Perlmutter v. Don's Ford, Inc., 409 N.Y.S.2d 628, 25 UCCR 675 (City Ct. Utica 1978); Jandreau v. Sheesley Plumbing & Heating Co., Inc., 324 N.W.2d 266, 34 UCCR 785 (S.D. 1982).

[228] *See, e.g.*, In re Trailer & Plumbing Supplies, 578 A.2d 343, 12 UCCR2d 1029 (N.H. 1990) (court rejects gravamen approach because issue is simply who has title to the goods, but says that in a future case alleging defective goods or services, it will consider gravamen approach).

[229] Certainly with respect to warranties, the Code drafters themselves have clearly indicated that courts should not be constrained by a narrow interpretation of the scope of the Code and its principles. *See* U.C.C. § 2-313, Official Comment 2.

The nature of this choice can be seen by returning to where we began this section: the *Perlmutter* case, in which the court held that a hospital was not liable for contaminated blood. While "blood shield" laws have been passed in virtually every state, making this particular problem relatively unimportant from a Code standpoint,[230] *Perlmutter* illustrates the kind of hard choices the courts must make to properly resolve these issues. To resolve the question in *Perlmutter*, a policy choice had to be made: is it preferable to allow the hospital to use or experiment with life-saving processes without fear of legal liability unless there is negligence, thus making the individual bear the entire loss when the treatment proves unsuccessful, or to spread the risk to all those who use the hospital? Will liability lead to greater safety or, on the other hand, to a greater reluctance to use life-saving treatment? The answers to these, and other, relevant questions turn on many factors, including the availability and cost of insurance to the various parties, but it should not turn on the superficial question of whether goods or services "predominate." In making these different choices, the courts should make clear the policies they are weighing and how they are resolving the competing claims that the parties might have. This approach would make clear, for example, why the hospital should be exempt from warranty liability for contaminated blood but not for poisoned food served in its cafeteria. These cases, by their nature, will not go away, and the present methodology of the *Bonebrake* case for resolving them is not sufficient.

[2] Realty, Choses in Action, Etc.

The definition of "goods" excludes money in which the "price is to be paid."[231] This exclusion refers to the money used as a medium of payment. Thus, when money (such as foreign money or a coin collection) is the subject of the sale, the exception found in section 2-105 should not apply.[232]

---

[230] "Blood shield" laws generally insulate hospitals, and in some cases other providers such as blood banks, from warranty liability or strict liability in tort for contaminated blood, although negligence liability generally remains (assuming there is no other kind of immunity from suit available such as charitable or sovereign immunity). *See, e.g.*, Ariz. Rev. Stat. Ann. § 32-1481 (West 1992); Ark. Code Ann. § 20-9-802 (Michie 1991); 745 Ill. Comp. Stat. Ann. 40/2 (West 1993); Ohio Rev. Code Ann. § 1547.11 (Banks-Baldwin Supp. 1996); S.C. Code Ann. § 44-43-10 (Law Co-op. 1985); Wis. Stat. Ann. § 895.53 (West 1997).

[231] U.C.C. § 2-105.

[232] *See* U.C.C. § 2-105, Official Comment 2:

Goods is intended to cover the sale of money when money is being treated as

The exclusion from goods in section 2-105 also includes "things in action." Although the Code does not define "things in action," presumably it means such things as negotiable instruments, chattel paper, and other contract rights. Few cases have involved the interpretation of "things in action,"[233] and most cases that have dealt with such things have correctly held them to be non-goods. Such items as an insurance policy,[234] airline tickets,[235] safari tickets,[236] and a liquor license[237] have all been excluded from Article 2. There is, however, a group of cases holding shares in co-operative apartments to be "goods" under Article 2.[238] These cases are un-doubtedly wrong. A share in a cooperative apartment simply documents a contractual interest in real estate; it is the tangible evidence of a contract right and is not covered by Article 2. Although the courts may have been justified in applying Article 2 by analogy,[239] this is not what they did. In-stead, the cases appear to apply Article 2 by its terms to the transaction.

The definition of "goods" continues in section 2-107, a section in which the drafters were concerned about where realty ends and goods begin. Three principles form the basis of that section:

1. Under section 2-107(1), certain materials affixed to the real estate are to be considered goods only if they are to be severed by the seller. These include "minerals or the like (including oil and gas) or a structure or its materials to be removed from realty."[240] By implication, it is assumed that

---

a commodity but not to include it when money is the medium of payment.

See also Saboundjian v. Bank Audi (USA), 157 A.D.2d 278, 556 N.Y.S.2d 258, 11 UCCR2d 1165 (App. Div. 1990).

[233] First Am. Bank Valley v. George J. Hegstrom Co., 551 N.W.2d 288 (N.D. 1996) ("thing in action" is a comprehensive term including an infinite variety of contracts and promises that confer on one party a right to recover a personal chattel or a sum of money from another by action).

[234] Elrad v. United Life & Accident Ins. Co., 624 F. Supp. 742, 42 UCCR 849 (N.D. Ill. 1985).

[235] O'Keefe Elevator Co. v. Second Ave. Properties, Ltd., 343 N.W.2d 54, 37 UCCR 1103 (Neb. 1984).

[236] Rosen v. DePorter-Butterworth Tours, Inc., 62 Ill. App. 3d 762, 379 N.E.2d 407, 24 UCCR 1094 (1978).

[237] Tomb v. Lavalle, 298 Pa. Super. 75, 444 A.2d 666, 32 UCCR 677 (1982).

[238] *See, e.g.,* Friedman v. Sommer, 63 N.Y.2d 788, 471 N.E.2d 139, 40 UCCR 764 (1984) (court said that interest in co-op was "in reality" a sale of securities, but nonetheless applied Article 2); McLeod v. Cowles, 215 A.D.2d 460, 626 N.Y.S.2d 831, 28 UCCR2d 796 (App. Div. 1995).

[239] *See* U.C.C. § 2-105, Official Comment 1.

[240] U.C.C. § 2-107(1). Until severance, however, a purported present sale of goods to be severed by the seller acts only as a contract for sale, not as a present sale.

if the buyer is to remove these materials, the subject matter of the contract is not goods, but realty. There is good reason for requiring severance by the seller in the case of minerals or even structures. A lease of land ought not to be converted into a contract for the sale of goods even though the lessee in possession is given the privilege of removing a part of the realty. Such an arrangement has long been treated by the law as a lease with all the attendant duties of recording under applicable real estate laws. There simply was no good policy reason to change this.

2. Under section 2-107(2), certain other materials affixed to the real estate are to be considered goods irrespective of whether the seller or the buyer is to remove them from the realty.[241] These include (1) timber[242] and (2) growing crops or other things attached to the realty if (a) they are sold "apart" from the realty, (b) they are capable of severance without material harm to the realty, and (c) they do not fall within the kinds of material listed in section 2-107(1). Whether removal will result in material harm is a question of fact for the trier of fact.[243]

3. Rights of third parties are protected if they comply with the real estate laws of the jurisdiction involved. The Code also makes clear what otherwise ought to have been clear: contracts for the sale of things attached to the real estate—even though they may involve goods under the above discussions—may be executed and recorded as documents transferring an interest in land, thereby acquiring whatever protection is accorded to such transfers.[244]

---

[241] U.C.C. § 2-107(2).

[242] Prior to 1972, timber was included in U.C.C. § 2-107(1) and did not constitute goods unless it was to be severed by the seller. In 1972, a change was recommended by the Permanent Editorial Board to transfer timber to section 2-107(2) such that timber would be goods regardless of who severed it from the realty.

[243] Ames Contracting Co. v. City Univ. of N.Y., 120 Misc. 2d 358, 466 N.Y.S.2d 182, 36 UCCR 1511 (Ct. Cl. 1983).

[244] U.C.C. § 2-107(3).

CHAPTER 3

FORMATION AND INTERPRETATION OF A CONTRACT FOR SALE

I.   FORMALITIES

§ 3.01   THE STATUTE OF FRAUDS

[A]   The Basic Rule

The statute of frauds for Article 2 is contained in section 2-201. The section incorporates several principles common to prior statutes of frauds relating to the sale of goods, as well as containing some marked departures from prior statutes.

The statute must be satisfied only if goods are sold for a price of $500 or more.[1] The $500 limit is applicable, under section 2-201 to *a* contract for the sale of goods. This may require a determination that the goods involved were purchased under a single contract rather than a series of contracts. If there are a series of separate contracts, each with a price of less than $500, none must be in writing to be enforceable. The principle method of satisfying the statute is by a writing signed "by the party against whom enforcement is sought or by his authorized agent or broker."[2] The terms

---

[1] The Uniform Sales Act § 4 also established $500 as the minimum amount, but referred to *value* rather than *price*. This should make no difference, since under U.C.C. § 2-304 the price of goods can be payable in money or otherwise. Section 2-201 suggests, although it does not say directly, that if the price is payable in other than money, the value of the thing exchanged will control. *See* Country Wide Leasing Corp. v. Subaru of Am., Inc., 520 N.Y.S.2d 24, 4 UCCR2d 1362 (N.Y. Sup. Ct. App. Div. 1987); Smith v. Hudson, 48 N.C. App. 347, 269 S.E.2d 172, 30 UCCR 25 (1980); Nebraska Builders Prods. Co. v. The Indus. Erectors, Inc., 239 Neb. 744, 478 N.W.2d 257, 16 UCCR2d 568 (1992); In re MSR Exploration LTD, 147 B.R. 560, 20 UCCR2d 49 (D. Mont. 1992); Advent Syst. Ltd. v. Unisys Corp., 925 F.2d 670, 13 UCCR2d 669 (3d Cir. 1991); Kline v. Lorillard, 878 F.2d 791, 9 UCCR2d 61 (4th Cir. 1989); Roboserve v. Tom Foods Inc., 940 F.2d 1441,16 UCCR2d 987 (11th Cir. 1991); Songbird Jet Ltd. v. Alan Rosenfielde, 581 F. Supp. 912, 38 UCCR 431 (S.D.N.Y. 1984).

The $500 limit is applicable under U.C.C. § 2-201 to a "contract" for the sale of goods. This provision may require a determination that the goods involved were purchased under a single contract rather than a series of contracts. If there are a series of separate contracts, each with a price of less than $500, none must be in writing to be enforceable. The proposed revisions to Article 2 raise the price to $5,000 before the statute becomes applicable. *See* The American Law Institute, Uniform Commercial Code Revised Article 2, Sales, Council Draft No. 4, December 1, 1998, § 2-201 (hereinafter Council Draft No. 4).

[2] U.C.C. § 2-201. New Mexico v. Wilson, 112 N.M. 193, 787 P.2d 821 (1990); In re Atkins, 139 B.R. 39, 19 UCCR2d 18 (D. Fla. 1992); Monetti v. Anchor Hocking Corp., 931 F.2d 1178, 14 UCCR2d 706 (7th Cir. 1992); Carl Wagner & Sons v. Appendagez, 485 F. Supp. 762, 29 UCCR 752 (S.D.N.Y. 1980).

"writing" and "signed" are given broad meaning by the Code. A "writing" includes printing, typewriting, and any other reduction to tangible form.[3]

Similarly, "signing" is broadly defined; it includes any symbol executed or adopted by a party with the present intention to authenticate a writing.[4] The Official Comment to section 1-201(39) makes it clear that the required symbol can be printed, stamped, or written, and that it can consist of a billhead or letterhead. The crucial issue in all cases is whether the symbol was executed *or adopted* with the present intention to authenticate a writing.[5] The writing may, of course, be sufficient if signed by an agent of a party.[6]

[B]   The Contents of the Writing

The Code statute of frauds requires a bare minimum to satisfy the writing requirement. According to Official Comment 2:

> Only three definite and invariable requirements as to the memorandum are made by this subsection. First, it must evidence a contract for the sale of goods; second, it must be "signed" . . . ; and third, it must specify a quantity.[7]

This is a marked departure from much pre-Code law. Many pre-Code cases concluded that the memorandum must state the essential elements or ma-

---

[3] Newer forms of technology, like electronic mail and other computer communication systems, pose serious difficulties for section 2-201. Although computer services are designed to improve efficiency and reduce paperwork, computer transactions do not clearly fall within the U.C.C.'s definition of written and signed documents. *See* American Dredging Co. v. Plaza Petroleum Inc., 799 F. Supp. 1335, 18 UCCR2d 1101 (E.D.N.Y. 1992) (telex was valid contract although not signed; the letters "AdCo ˆCˆDN" at the bottom of the page referred to the company and were treated as a signature). *See generally* Deborah L. Wilkerson, "Are Electronic Messages Enforceable?," 41 UKSLR 403 (1993). Section 2-201 of the proposed revisions to Article 2 no longer requires a "signed writing"; it requires an "authenticated record" of the contract. A "record" includes information stored in an electronic or other medium that is retrievable in perceivable form. See Council Draft No. 4 §§ 2-201, 2-102(26).

[4] U.C.C. § 1-201(39).

[5] See Merrill, Lynch, Pierce, Fenner & Smith v. Cole, 189 Conn. 518, 457 A.2d 656, 35 UCCR 944 (1983) (letterhead or bill head sufficient); A.G. Constr. Co. v. Reid Bros. Logging Co., Inc., 547 P.2d 1207, 19 UCCR 37 (Alaska 1976) (typed name at end of letter sufficient to meet requirements).

[6] *See* Siam Numong Prod. Co. Ltd. v. Eastimpex, 866 F. Supp. 445, 27 UCCR2d 59 (N.D. Cal. 1994); A.M. Capen's Co., Inc. v. American Trading & Prod. Corp., 973 F. Supp. 247, 33 UCCR2d 1009 (D.P.R. 1997).

[7] U.C.C. § 2-201(1), Official Comment 2.

terial terms of the contract.[8] It is clear, for example, that the memorandum required by section 2-201 does not have to state the price,[9] the time of delivery,[10] or other terms of the contract. These skeletal requirements reflect the drafters' belief that the purpose of the statute of frauds is merely "that the writing afford a basis for believing that the offered oral evidence rests on a real transaction."[11] Satisfaction of the statute of frauds does not mean that a claimant who is relying on the existence of a contract will win. It means only that the statute of frauds has been removed as a bar; the claimant must still prove the existence of a contract, as well as a breach of the contract and resultant damages.[12]

Section 2-201(1) provides that a contract is not enforceable beyond the quantity of goods shown in the writing.[13] It should be sufficient, however, if the quantity can be reasonably inferred from other terms in the contract.[14] The quantity term may also be stated in terms of requirements or output.[15]

---

[8] R.H. Lindsay Co. v. Greager, 204 F.2d 129, 131 (10th Cir. 1953), *cert. denied*, 346 U.S. 828, 74 S. Ct. 50, 98 L. Ed. 353 (1953); Webster v. Harris, 189 Or. 671, 222 P.2d 644 (1950); S.T. Edwards & Co. v. Shawano Milk Prods. Co., 211 Wis. 378, 247 N.W. 465 (1933). *See* Walter Jeager, Williston on Contracts, Sec. 576A at 17–18 (3d ed. 1978); Arthur L. Corbin, Corbin on Contracts, § 499 at 684, § 500 p. 690 (1950); Restatement (First) of Contracts, § 207 (1932).

[9] Section 2-201, Official Comment 1; LRJ Ryan v. Wersi Elec. Gmlt and Co., 3 F.3d 174, 21 UCCR2d 523 (7th Cir. 1993); Barto v. United States, 823 F. Supp. 1369, 21 UCCR2d 924 (E.D. Mich. 1993); JoAnn Inc. v. Alfrin Fragrances Inc., 731 F. Supp. 149, 11 UCCR2d 782 (D.N.J. 1989).

[10] Barto v. United States, 283 F. Supp. 1369, 21 UCCR2d 924 (E.D. Mich. 1993); Nebraska Builders Prods. Co. v. The Indus. Erectors Inc., 259 Neb. 744, 478 N.W. 2d 257, 16 UCCR2d 568 (1992).

[11] U.C.C. § 2-201, Official Comment 1.

[12] Lorenz Supply Co. v. American Standard Inc., 358 N.W.2d 845, 39 UCCR 1169 (Mich. 1984); Perdue Farms Inc. v. Motts Inc. of Miss., 459 F. Supp. 7, 25 UCCR 9 (N.D. Miss. 1978); Bazak Int'l Corp. v. Mast Indus. Inc., 535 N.E.2d 633, 7 UCCR2d 1380 (N.Y. 1983).

[13] U.C.C. § 2-201(1). *See* Official Comment 1 to section 2-201; Omega Eng'g, Inc. v. Eastman Kodak Co., 908 F. Supp. 1084, 30 UCCR2d 194 (D. Conn. 1995); A.M. Capen's Co., Inc. v. American Trading & Prod. Corp., 973 F. Supp. 247, 33 UCCR2d 1009 (D.P.R. 1997) (noting that lack of quantity term was not fatal).

[14] *See* Regal Fiber Corp. v. Anderson Gin Co., 512 F.2d 784, 16 UCCR 1207 (5th Cir. 1975) (where contract provided for sale of cotton grown on certain number of acres and provided projected yield per acre, contract met statute of frauds and was not unenforceable for lack of definiteness); Upsher-Smith Laboratories, Inc. v. Mylan Labs., Inc., 944 F. Supp. 1411, 31 UCCR2d 698 (D. Minn. 1996).

[15] *See* Syrovy v. Alpine Resources Inc., 68 Wash. App. 35, 841 P.2d 1279, 19 UCCR2d 995 (Wash. Ct. App. 1992); Roboserve LTD v. Tom's Foods Inc., 940 F.2d 1441, 16 UCCR2d 987 (11th Cir. 1991); Zayre Corp. v. S.M.&R. Co. Inc., 882 F.2d 1145, 9 UCCR2d 465 (7th Cir. 1989).

The writing must also "be sufficient to indicate that a contract for sale has been made between the parties."[16] This requirement has engendered a significant amount of litigation. Most courts interpret this language to mean that the writing must indicate that a contract came into existence *either prior to or as a result of the writing*. Consequently, while signed acceptances will generally satisfy the statute,[17] purchase orders and other offers have generally not been held to do so.[18]

The language of the section does not demand this analysis; section 2-201 can be interpreted to mean that the writing must merely indicate that a contract was made *at some time*, not necessarily that it had been made at the time of the writing or as a result of the writing. In view of the limited purpose of the statute as expressed in Official Comment 1—that the writing affords a basis to believe that the offered oral evidence rests on a real transaction—and the necessity for the claimant to prove his case to the fact-finder,[19] the courts' reading of this requirement is too restrictive.

For example, the presence of a signed offer should be sufficient to permit evidence by the offeree of his oral acceptance of the offer. The offeree must prove that the offer was orally accepted before it was revoked or otherwise terminated, and the presence of the signed offer certainly indicates that the offeror was of a mind to contract. The argument for finding the statute satisfied is especially compelling in view of the fact that had the offeree sent a *written* acceptance, there is authority that both writings, taken together, would satisfy the statute against the offeror, even though he signed no document that created a contract or that indicated that a contract already existed.[20] Although most courts reject the proposition that a signed offer can satisfy the statute,[21] there are a number of cases to the contrary.[22]

---

[16] U.C.C. § 2-201(1).

[17] *See* Spinnerin Yarn Co. Inc. v. Apparel Retail Corp., 614 F. Supp. 1174, 42 UCCR 65 (S.D.N.Y. 1985); Axelson Inc. v. McElroy-Willis, 7 F.3d 1230, 22 UCCR2d 647 (5th Cir. 1993).

[18] *See* Bazak Int'l Corp. v. Mast Indus., Inc., 535 N.E.2d 633, 7 UCCR2d 633 (N.Y. 1989).; Harper Trucks Inc. v. Allied Welding Supply, 2 UCCR 2d 835 (D. Kan. 1986).

[19] It is too often forgotten that the presence of a sufficient writing does not establish a contract or its terms. The party asserting the contract still has the burden of proving the existence of a contract and its terms. *See* Perdue Farms, Inc. v. Motts, Inc. of Miss., 459 F. Supp 7, 25 UCCR 9 (N.D. Miss. 1978); General Matters, Inc. v. Penny Prods., Inc., 651 F.2d 1017, 31 UCCR 1556 (5th Cir. 1981).

[20] *See* Ore & Chem. Corp. v. Howard Butcher Trading Corp., 455 F. Supp 1150, 24 UCCR 823, 827 (E.D. Pa. 1978) and authorities cited therein. Of course, the offeree in this situation could also satisfy the statute through U.C.C. § 2-201(2) if the offeror failed to respond to the acceptance within ten days. *See* § 3.01[C][1], *infra*.

[21] *See, e.g.*, Micromedia v. Automated Broadcast Controls, 799 F.2d 230, 20 UCCR2d 48 (5th Cir. 1986); Alice v. Robett Mfg. Co., 328 F. Supp. 1377, 9 UCCR 854 (N.D. Ga. 1970)

In *Monetti, S.P.A. v. Anchor Hocking Corp.*,[23] Judge Richard Posner dealt with the issue of whether a writing made before the contract was formed can satisfy the statute of frauds. In *Monetti*, the parties entered into negotiations for an agreement giving the defendant exclusive distributorship rights for plaintiff's products in the United States. The plaintiff presented a draft agreement to the defendant. The defendant then prepared and signed a memorandum entitled "Topics of Discussion With Monetti," and attached to the signed memo was a copy of the draft agreement that had been submitted by plaintiff. Two additional minor paragraphs had been added to the agreement by defendant, and beside the paragraph relating to exclusivity, the defendant had written "We want Canada." Otherwise the agreement was identical to the draft submitted by plaintiff, and the defendant had written "Agree" beside each of the principal paragraphs of the agreement.

When the relationship broke down, and plaintiff sued for breach of contract, the defendant moved for summary judgment on the basis of the Code's statute of frauds. The plaintiff offered the memorandum with its attached agreement as a sufficient memorandum under section 2-201. Defendant argued that the "futuristic" nature of the memorandum disqualified it as a writing "sufficient to indicate that a contract for sale *"has been made.*"[24]

Judge Posner distinguished the case from one involving only an offer, which he acknowledged would not be sufficient under Illinois law.[25] He said that in this case, the signed writing gave some indication of the promisee's acceptance of the offer,[26] even though the actual acceptance (because of the minor disagreement over terms) may not have occurred until after the writing. He refused to find that the choice of tenses in section 2-201—that a contract "had" been made—was dispositive; in fact, he said it was "weak

---

aff'd per curiam, 445 F.2d 316 (5th Cir. 1971); Conaway v. 20th Century Corp., 491 Pa. 189, 420 A.2d 405, 29 UCCR 1387 (1980); Maderas Tropicales v. Southern Crate & Veneer Co., 588 F.2d 971, 25 UCCR 1259 (5th Cir. 1979).

[22] *See* Tymon v. Linoki, 16 N.Y.2d 293, 213 N.E.2d 661 (1965); Farrow v. Cahill, 663 F.2d 201 (D.C. Cir. 1980); General Matters v. Penny Prods., 651 F.2d 1017 (5th Cir. 1981); *see also* Architectural Metal Sys., Inc. v. Consolidated Sys., Inc., 58 F.3d 1227, 26 UCCR2d 1047 (7th Cir. 1995) (price quotations by seller and purchase order from buyer sufficient to satisfy the statute of frauds).

[23] 931 F.2d 1178, 14 UCCR2d 706 (7th Cir. 1991).

[24] *Id.* at 1181, 14 UCCR2d at 712–713.

[25] R.S. Bennett & Co. v. Economy Mechanical Indus., Inc. 606 F.2d 182 (7th Cir. 1979).

[26] It should be remembered, however, that the defendant did not indicate agreement with *all* of the terms of the offer. There was no indication in the writing that defendant would accept that agreement in the absence of plaintiff's agreement to its modifications, especially with regard to the exclusive distribution rights in Canada.

evidence" of the drafter's intent.[27] He added that it was "well settled" that a memorandum could satisfy the general statute of frauds even though it had been made before the contract was concluded, and should be sufficient under the circumstances present in this case to satisfy the Code's statute of frauds.[28]

Writings may be pieced together to satisfy the statute even though none, taken individually, would be sufficient.[29] For example, in *Migerobe, Inc. v. Certina USA, Inc.*,[30] the Fifth Circuit pieced together three documents to satisfy the statute, even though none made specific reference to the others, one was unsigned, and none was sufficient by itself to satisfy the statute. The documents consisted of (1) a memorandum signed by the seller indicating that one of its agents was authorized to sell watches to the buyer at a certain price; (2) an internal memorandum signed by the seller to several of the seller's employees announcing that "a new promotion code had been set up to cover a special order" from the buyer; and (3) an unsigned seller's order form listing the quantity, styles, and prices of watches ordered by the buyer.

The court found sufficient connection between these documents to treat them as an integrated whole for purposes of the statute, even though none

---

[27] *Id.*

[28] Judge Posner also cited Professor Farnsworth's treatise on Contracts in support of the proposition that a writing signed prior to the conclusion of a contract could satisfy the statute. Professor Farnsworth agrees with the authors of this text that an offer signed by the party to be charged should satisfy the Code's statute of frauds. *See* 2 E. Allan Farnsworth, II Farnsworth on Contracts § 6.7 at 132–133 n.16 (1990). For a case following *Monetti* and also finding that a writing made before the contract can satisfy § 2-201(1), see *Wells, Waters & Gases, Inc. v. Air Prods. & Chems., Inc.*, 19 F.3d 157, 23 UCCR2d 54 (4th Cir. 1994).

Perhaps the most liberal interpretation of the writing requirement can be found in Barber & Ross Co. v. Lifetime Doors, Inc., 810 F.2d 1276, 3 UCCR2d 41 (4th Cir. 1987). In this case the court permitted written sales brochures given by the seller to satisfy the statute where the buyer asserted that he had orally accepted the seller's offer of a requirements contract to supply doors to the buyer. The courts said that the sales brochures promised that the seller would meet the monthly needs of the buyer, and that this was sufficient to provide "a basis for believing that the offered oral evidence rests on a real transaction." The court further held that the writings met the signature requirement because the seller's trademark appeared on the brochures.

[29] *See, e.g.,* Nebraska Builders Prods. Co. v. The Indus. Erectors, Inc., 239 Neb. 744, 478 N.W.2d 257, 16 UCCR2d 568 (1992); Roboserve LTD v. Tom's Foods Inc., 940 F.2d 1441, 16 UCCR2d 987 (11th Cir. 1991); Vess Beverages v. The Padding Corp., 886 F.2d 208, 10 UCCR2d 209 (8th Cir. 1989); Bayless Materials Co. v. Peerless Land Co., 509 S.W.2d 206 (Mo. Ct. App. 1974); Mayer v. King Cola Mid Am. Inc., 660 S.W.2d 746 (Mo. Ct. App. 1983); Architectural Metal Sys., Inc. v. Consolidated Sys., Inc., 58 F.3d 1227, 26 UCCR2d 1047 (7th Cir. 1995); Fairley v. Turan-Foley Imports, Inc., 65 F.3d 475, 27 UCCR2d 723 (5th Cir. 1995).

[30] 924 F.2d 1330, 14 UCCR2d 59 (5th Cir. 1991).

made reference to the others. The unsigned order form contained the same promotion code referred to in the internal memorandum, as well as the buyer's name and the salesman's name referred to in the authorization memorandum. The court held that if a document contains an "implied reference" to another writing, no explicit reference is necessary.[31] This case is especially interesting because only the unsigned writing contained a quantity term.

[C] Exceptions to the Writing Requirement

The Code drafters recognized that exceptions to the writing requirement of section 2-201 were necessary to avoid the injustice of refusing to enforce oral contracts when there is strong evidence (apart from the mere assertions of a party) that a contract has been made. The last two subsections of section 2-201 respond to the concern that fixed adherence to a writing requirement might perpetrate more fraud than it prevents. In each of these cases, there is good reason to believe, outside the oral testimony of the party seeking to enforce the contract, that some agreement exists between the parties. The following sections discuss the application of sections 2-201(2) and 2-201(3).

[1] Exceptions to the Writing Requirement—Writings Signed by the Party Seeking to Enforce the Contract

Prior to the adoption of the Code, the only writing that would satisfy the statute of frauds was one signed by the party against whom enforcement was sought. When only one party signed an executory agreement, the nonsigner could sit back and await the day set for performance. If the agreement turned out to be profitable for the nonsigner, it could secure enforcement of the other's promise; if, however, the agreement turned out to be unprofitable, it could use the statute of frauds to shield itself from liability.

Section 2-201 does not entirely eliminate this possibility, but it does, under some circumstances, permit a writing signed by the party seeking to enforce the contract to satisfy the statute. Subsection (2) of section 2-201 provides:

> Between merchants if within a reasonable time a writing in confirmation of the contract and sufficient against the sender is received and the party receiving it has reason to know its contents, it satisfies the requirements

---

[31] 924 F.2d at 1333, 14 UCCR2d at 62. *See* American Plastics, Inc., v. CBS, 886 F.2d 521, 9 UCCR2d 848 (2d Cir. 1989).

of subsection (1) against such party unless written notice of objection
to its contents is given within ten days after it is received.

Although this provision has engendered a fair amount of litigation, most of
the cases have involved relatively simple and straightforward issues. There
are a number of requirements that must be met, however, before the section
will permit the party seeking enforcement of the contract to rely on his own
signature to satisfy the writing requirement.

First, the subsection applies only when the transaction is between merchants.[32] Both the seller and the buyer must be merchants; if either is a
nonmerchant, only a writing signed by the party against whom enforcement
is sought will suffice. The definition of the term "merchant" is discussed
elsewhere in this text,[33] but the term generally includes two classes of persons: a person who deals in goods of the kind involved in the transaction
and a person who holds himself out as having, or is chargeable with, knowledge or skill "peculiar to the practices or goods involved in the transaction."[34] The second portion of this definition makes section 2-201(2)
applicable to nearly everyone in business, because the relevant practices
involved appear to be those of reading and answering one's mail.[35]

---

[32] The term "between merchants" is defined in U.C.C. § 2-104(3). The proposed revisions
to Article 2 require only that the *recipient* of the confirmation be a merchant. *See* Council
Draft No. 4 § 2-201(b).

[33] *See* § 4.06[B][1], *infra*.

[34] U.C.C. § 2-104.

[35] U.C.C. § 2-104, Official Comment 2. This Comment suggests that many non-businesses
(such as universities) also fall within this definition of "merchant" because they hold themselves out as having knowledge of the practice of answering mail. Even a private person has
knowledge of the practice of answering mail, although it is true that U.C.C. § 2-104 requires
that a person, *by his occupation*, hold himself out as having this knowledge. Thus, Comment
2 to U.C.C. § 2-104 indicates that persons acting in their private capacity are not merchants,
even when they are clearly merchants when acting in their business or professional capacities
("A lawyer or bank president buying fishing tackle for his own use is not a merchant").

When not acting in a purely private capacity, however, it is not clear when a person
is a "merchant." This issue has surfaced primarily in a group of cases involving farmers. A
number of courts have held that a farmer is not a merchant for purposes of section 2-201(2)
when selling his farm products. Cook Grains, Inc. v. Fallis, 239 Ark. 962, 395 S.W.2d 555,
2 UCCR 1141 (1965); Loeb & Co., Inc. v. Schreiner, 294 Ala. 722, 321 So. 2d 199, 17
UCCR 897 (1975). On the other hand, the majority of the farm cases seem to go the other
way. Sierens v. Clawson, 60 Ill. 2d 585, 328 N.E.2d 559, 16 UCCR 1185 (1975); Ohio
Grain Co. v. Swisshelm, 40 Ohio App. 2d 203, 318 N.E.2d 428, 15 UCCR 305 (1974).
Although some of the cases are distinguishable on the facts, the decision often seems to turn
on whether the court focuses on the practice of answering mail or on the type of goods
involved in the transaction.

There have been a small number of cases in which the courts have discussed the

The subsection also requires that the writing (a) be in confirmation of the contract and (b) be sufficient against the sender. To be "sufficient against the sender" requires that the court refer back to subsection (1), assume that the sender was being sued, and determine whether the writing involved would prevent the sender from relying successfully on the statute of frauds.[36]

It could be argued that the first requirement of section 2-201(2) ("confirmation" of the contract) requires a more detailed writing than the minimum necessary to satisfy subsection (1), which uses the somewhat looser test of *indication* of a contract. While the courts do not seem to require a more *detailed* writing (in the sense of requiring additional terms of the contract be in the writing),[37] the writing must *confirm* an already existing oral contract.[38] A party cannot use a writing (such as a purchase order) that preceded contract formation to satisfy the writing requirement of 2-201(2).[39]

---

merchant requirement of section 2-201(2) outside of the context of farmers. Again, the results seem to depend on the focus of the court. For example, in Playboy Clubs Int'l, Inc. v. Loomskill, Inc., 13 UCCR 765 (N.Y. Sup. Ct. 1974), the court held that the buyer of costumes for a Playboy Club was not a merchant because the buyer was not in the textile business. Similarly, in Cudahy Foods Co. v. Holloway, 286 S.E.2d 606, 55 N.C. App. 626, 32 UCCR 1352 (1982), the court held that a real estate broker who allegedly guaranteed the purchase of cheese for a client was not a merchant because it was not in the pizza, cheese, or restaurant business. It said the focus should be on the occupation or type of business of the party as it relates to the subject matter of the transaction.

The District Court for the Southern District of New York has held, however, that a bank selling used microfilm equipment is a merchant for purposes of section 2-201(2), and quoted Comment 2 to section 2-104 to the effect that the relevant inquiry was whether the bank held itself out as having knowledge of the practice of answering mail. National Microsales v. Chase Manhattan Bank, 761 F. Supp. 304, 14 UCCR2d 995 (S.D.N.Y. 1991).

[36] *See* Perdue Farms, Inc. v. Motts, Inc. of Miss., 459 F. Supp. 7, 25 UCCR2d 9 (N.D. Miss. 1978); Bazak Int'l Corp. v. Mast Indus., Inc., 533 N.Y.S.2d 503, 535 N.E.2d 633, 7 UCCR2d 1380 (N.Y. Sup. Ct. 1989); Trilco Terminal v. Prebilt Corp., 400 A.2d 1237, 26 UCCR 616 (N.J. Super. 1979); Khoshnow v. Paine, Webber, Jackson & Curtis, Inc., 525 So. 2d 977, 6 UCCR2d 187 (Fla. Dist. Ct. App. 1988).

[37] *See* Perdue Farms, Inc. v. Motts, Inc. of Miss., 459 F. Supp. 7, 25 UCCR 9 (N.D. Miss. 1978).

[38] *See* Khoshnow v. Paine, Webber, Jackson & Curtis, Inc., 525 So. 2d 977, 6 UCCR2d 187 (Fla. Dist. Ct. App. 1988); Bazak Int'l Corp. v. Mast Indus., Inc., 533 N.Y.S.2d 503, 535 N.E.2d 633, 7 UCCR2d 1380 (1989); Perdue Farms, Inc. v. Motts, Inc. of Miss., 459 F. Supp. 7, 25 UCCR 9 (N.D. Miss. 1978); Reich v. Helen Harper, Inc., 3 UCCR 1048 (N.Y. Civ. Ct. 1966); Harry Rubin & Sons v. Consolidated Pipe Co. of Am., 153 A.2d 472, 1 UCCR 40 (Pa. Super. 1959).

[39] *See* Triangle Marketing v. Action Indus., 630 F. Supp. 1578, 1 UCCR2d 36 (N.D. Ill. 1986). *See also* Aircraft Inventory Corp. v. Falcon Jet Corp., 35 UCCR2d 815 (D.N.J. 1998) (when only writing is a letter from a prospective buyer, the assorted contract is unenforceable against the seller). *But see* Busby Inc. v. Smokey Valley Bean, Inc., 767 F. Supp. 235 (D.

Two related issues have surfaced with respect to the requirement that a document must *confirm* a contract to satisfy section 2-201(2). First, must the document *explicitly* refer to and confirm a preexisting oral contract, or will a more ambiguous reference nonetheless satisfy section 2-201(2)? Second, to what extent can a document, which does not appear on its face to confirm a preexisting oral contract, be supplemented or explained by extrinsic evidence? The courts' decisions have not been entirely consistent on these issues.

As to the first question, the courts have generally not required an explicit reference to a prior oral contract, so long as the document can reasonably be read as confirming a prior oral contract.[40] For example, in *Dura-Wood Treating Co. v. Century Forest Industries, Inc.*,[41] the court found a document sufficient that simply said "confirming our conversation, please enter our order."[42] In *Azevedo v. Minister*,[43] the court held that references to "approximately 16,000 bales of hay yet to be hauled on your purchase" and "approximately 14,000 bales remaining to be hauled" to be sufficient to satisfy section 2-201(2). The governing standard appears to be that if the language of the document permits a reasonable inference that it confirms an existing oral contract, the document will be sufficient to satisfy section 2-201(2).[44]

The second issue has arisen with some frequency when the document offered to satisfy section 2-201(2) is a purchase order sent by the buyer that, on its face, is nothing more than an offer. The buyer's argument is that the document, despite its appearance, actually confirms a preexisting oral contract,[45] and the buyer will offer extrinsic evidence (generally of the circumstances surrounding the making of the oral contract) to prove that the doc-

---

Kan. 1991) (document that appears to be offer or acceptance of offer sufficient to satisfy U.C.C. § 2-201(2)).

[40] *See, e.g.*, Perdue Farms, Inc. v. Motts, Inc. of Miss., 459 F. Supp. 7, 25 UCCR 9 (N.D. Miss. 1978); Dura-Wood Treating Co. v. Century Forest Indus., Inc., 675 F.2d 745, 33 UCCR 1201 (5th Cir. 1982); Cives Corp. v. Callier Steel Pipe and Tube, 482 A.2d 852, 39 UCCR 1705 (Me. 1980).

[41] 675 F.2d 745, 33 UCCR 1201 (5th Cir. 1982); *cert. denied*, 459 U.S. 865 (1982).

[42] *Id.* at 747, 33 UCCR 1202.

[43] 471 P.2d 661, 7 UCCR 1281 (Nev. 1970).

[44] *See* Howard Constr. Co. v. Jeff-Cole Quarries, Inc., 669 S.W.2d 221, 37 UCCR 1040 (Mo. Ct. App. 1983).

[45] It should be clear from the language of U.C.C. § 2-201(2) that the buyer cannot use a purchase order to satisfy section 2-201 unless the buyer argues that the purchase order was sent as a *confirmation* of an existing contract. *See* Ed Gilkey & Sons, Inc. v. A-E Architect Materials, Inc., 86 A.D.2d 970, 33 UCCR 472 (N.Y. Sup. Ct. App. Div. 1982); Triangle Marketing v. Action Indus., 630 F. Supp. 1578, 1 UCCR2d 36 (N.D. Ill. 1986).

ument is a confirmation. The courts have reached disparate results on whether such a document can satisfy section 2-201(2).

One group of courts takes the position that a purchase order, as a matter of law, cannot satisfy section 2-201(2).[46] These courts reason that because the purchase order is unambiguous on its face, extrinsic evidence should not be permitted to prove its confirmatory nature.[47] This is particularly true when the extrinsic evidence consists of proof of the very oral contract that the statute of frauds renders unenforceable.[48] In a number of cases, however, the courts have permitted a purchase order to satisfy section 2-201(2) even though the writing contains no language that would suggest that it is anything other than an offer.[49] In one case, the court referred to Official Comment 1 to section 2-201 to the effect that "all that is required is that the writing afford a basis for believing that the offered oral evidence rests on a real transaction."[50]

Assuming that the purpose of the statute of frauds is to prevent the assertion of claims based upon nonexistent contracts, it is the authors' belief that a document, *on its face*, must at least be sufficient to alert the reasonable person receiving it that the sender is claiming that he has a contract with the recipient. Unless the document, by the terms of the writing itself, reasonably conveys that the sender is asserting the existence of a contract, it should not be sufficient to satisfy the section 2-201(2) exception. The prem-

---

[46] *See, e.g.*, Adams v. Petgrande Int'l, Inc., 754 S.W.2d 696, 7 UCCR2d 369 (Tex. Ct. App. 1988) (document could not be confirmation as a matter of law where it has place for accepting party to sign, even though purchase order says "it confirms arrangements" between the parties); Bazak Int'l Corp. v. Mast Indus., Inc., 528 N.Y.S.2d 62 (App. Div. 1988); Great W. Sugar Co. v. Lone Star Donut Co. 567 F. Supp. 340, 37 UCCR 35 (N.D. Tex. 1983).

[47] *See* Adams v. Petgrande, 754 S.W.2d 696, 7 UCCR2d 369 (Tex. Ct. App. 1988). *See also* Ryan v. Wersi Elecs. 3 F.3d 174, 21 UCCR2d 523 (7th Cir. 1993); Western Sugar Co. v. White Stokes, 736 F.2d 428, 38 UCCR 1493 (7th Cir. 1984).

[48] *See* Bazak Int'l Corp. v. Mast Indus., Inc., 535 N.E.2d 633, 7 UCCR2d 1380 (N.Y. Sup. 1989); Smith Packing Co. v. Quality Pork Int'l, 167 A.D.2d 875, 13 UCCR2d 698 (N.Y. Sup. Ct. App. Div. 1990).

[49] *See* Cives Corp. v. Callier Steel Pipe and Tube, 482 A.2d 852, 39 UCCR 1705 (Me. 1984); Paramount Supply v. Sherlin, 16 Ohio App. 3d 176, 40 UCCR 447 (1984). *See also* M.K. Metals v. Container Recovery Corp., 645 F.2d 583, 31 UCCR 487 (8th Cir. 1981) (purchase order sufficient under U.C.C. § 2-201(2) because terms are geared toward satisfaction of seller rather than buyer and are so specific as to "desires" of seller that they reflect prior dealings); GPL Treatment, Ltd. v. Louisiana-Pacific Corp., 133 Or. App. 633, 894 P.2d 470, 26 UCCR2d 316 (1995) (court admitted parol evidence to determine whether document was confirmation).

[50] M.K. Metals, Inc. v. Container Recovery Corp., 645 F.2d 583, 31 UCCR 487 (8th Cir. 1981).

ise of section 2-201(2) is that people generally respond to assertions of nonexistent contracts. This premise is not valid, however, when the writing does not reasonably suggest that a contract exists.

Third, the writing must be received within a reasonable time. Although the Code does not state the point from which a reasonable time is to be measured, courts have assumed, probably correctly, that the drafters intended a reasonable time to be measured from the time of the purported oral agreement.[51] In many cases, whether the writing was received within a reasonable time will be a question of fact,[52] although courts have, in some cases, found the passage of periods of time reasonable[53] or unreasonable[54] as a matter of law. Course of dealing, course of performance and usage of trade, when present, are especially important in resolving these issues, because they represent the commercial context for the particular transaction as well as for similar transactions. Courts should remain focused on the rationale of the section: to permit satisfaction of the statute of frauds when a merchant would have normally responded to a communication asserting that a contract exists between the parties when none, in fact, exists. If a merchant would, because of staleness, have reasonably ignored such a communication, it should not satisfy section 2-201(2).[55]

Fourth, the writing must be received by the party against whom enforcement is sought. This requirement has spawned very little litigation.

---

[51] *See* Rockland Indus. v. Frank Kasmir Assocs., 470 F. Supp. 1176, 26 UCCR 852 (N.D. Tex. 1979); Serna v. Harmen, 742 F.2d 186, 39 UCCR 481 (5th Cir. 1984).

[52] *Seé* Rockland Indus. v. Frank Kasmir Assocs., 470 F. Supp. 1176, 26 UCCR 852 (N.D. Tex. 1979); Adams v. Petrade Int'l, 754 S.W.2d 696, 7 UCCR2d 369 (Tex. Ct. App. 1988). U.C.C. § 1-204, which courts have determined to be applicable, says that a reasonable time for taking any action "depends on the nature, purpose, and circumstances of such action."

[53] Tipton v. Woodberg, 616 F.2d 170, 28 UCCR 1473 (5th Cir. 1980).

[54] Starry Constr. v. Murphy Oil USA Inc., 785 F. Supp. 1356, 17 UCCR2d 353 (D. Minn. 1992).

[55] In Lish v. Compton, 547 P.2d 223, 18 UCCR 1174 (Utah 1976), the court held that a delay of twelve days was unreasonable as a matter of law because both parties knew that there was a fluctuating market, and the price, in fact, changed substantially between the time of the alleged oral contract and the confirmation. This case appears to be wrong, at least insofar as the rationale of U.C.C. § 2-201(2) is that a party's failure to respond to a confirmation provides a credible basis to believe that the oral contract exists. Assuming that the oral contract can be proved and that twelve days would not be unusual in the trade for the sending of a confirmation, the fact that the market for the goods is unstable should not affect the result. Although the section does permit a party to an oral contract to wait and see what the market will do before attempting to bind the other (and certainly himself) by the sending of a confirmation, this possibility is open to both parties at the time of contracting, and the adversely affected party can always object when the confirmation is received and thereby prevent the enforcement of the oral contract.

Although there is no separate definition of the word "received" in section 2-201, there is a related Code section that the drafters probably intended to apply to this situation. Section 1-201(26) provides that a person "receives" a notice or notification when it either comes to his attention or when it is duly delivered at the place of business through which the contract was made or at any other place held out by him as the place for receipt of such communications.[56] Although one court has expressed some doubt that section 1-201(26) applies to receipt of a confirmation under section 2-201(2),[57] section 1-201(26) provides the appropriate standard for section 2-201(2). Both concern correspondence that is necessary to preserve some right for the sending party or that will likely result in adverse consequences for the receiving party unless the receiving party acts upon the correspondence.[58]

An issue that has arisen in a number of cases is whether there must be direct proof of receipt, or whether receipt can sometimes be presumed for purposes of section 2-201(2). The cases are unanimous in holding that common-law or statutory presumptions of receipt apply for purposes of section 2-201(2).[59] For example, in *Perdue Farms, Inc. v. Motts, Inc. of Mississippi*,[60] the court held that affidavits stating that a confirmation was mailed, was correctly addressed, had proper postage and a return address, and was not returned to the sender gave rise to a presumption of receipt for purposes of section 2-201(2). Neither section 2-201(2) nor section 1-201(26) limits the manner in which receipt can be proved.[61]

Fifth, the recipient must have reason to know of the contents of the writing. Again, a provision of Article 1 should supply the governing standard. Section 1-201(27) provides that:

> Notice, knowledge or a notice or notification received by an organization is effective for a particular transaction from the time when it is brought to the attention of the individual conducting that transaction, and in any

---

[56] U.C.C. § 1-201(26).

[57] *See* Perdue Farms, Inc. v. Motts, Inc. of Miss., 459 F. Supp. 7, 25 UCCR 9 (N.D. Miss. 1978) (court expresses doubt that section 1-201(26) applies because "receipt" in that section applies, by its terms, only to "notice" or "notification").

[58] *See, e.g.*, U.C.C. § 2-607(3) requiring a buyer to notify the seller of breach within a reasonable time or be barred from any remedy.

[59] *See, e.g.*, Dawkins & Co. v. L&L Planting Co., 602 So. 2d 838, 19 UCCR2d 1013 (Miss. 1992); Tabor & Co. v. Gorenz, 356 N.E.2d 1150, 43 Ill. App. 3d 124, 20 UCCR 837 (1976); Pillsbury Co. v. Buchanan, 346 N.E.2d 386, 37 Ill. App. 3d 876, 19 UCCR 431 (1976).

[60] 459 F. Supp. 7, 18, 25 UCCR 9 (N.D. Miss. 1978).

[61] *Id.*

event from the time when it would have been brought to his attention
if the organization had exercised due diligence.

This section, like section 1-201(26), applies only to "notice, knowledge or
a notice or notification," and therefore it is not clear that it governs whether
a party has reason to know of the contents of a confirmation under section
2-201(2).[62] The rationale of the section, however, suggests it is the appropriate standard for section 2-201(2).

The requirement that the recipient have reason to know of the contents
of the confirmation has received its most thorough discussion in the case of
Thompson Printing Machinery Co. v. B.F. Goodrich.[63] In this case, representatives of Goodrich and Thompson met to discuss the sale by Goodrich
of used printing machinery. Four days later, Thompson sent Goodrich a
purchase order for the equipment, and a $1,000 check in part payment.
When Goodrich failed to perform and Thompson sued, Goodrich denied a
contract and also raised the statute of frauds as a defense. Thompson responded that the statute of frauds was satisfied through section 2-201(2).

Goodrich responded that the purchase order did not satisfy section 2-
201(2) because it was not received within a reasonable time by anyone at
Goodrich who had reason to know of its contents. Goodrich claimed that
neither the envelope, the check, nor the purchase order named the Goodrich
representative who had met with Thompson, nor did they indicate that the
items were intended for the surplus equipment department. Goodrich said
that by the time it was able to "find a home" for the items, the equipment
had already been sold to another.

The court first decided that the confirmation had been "received" by
Goodrich. It was sufficient, said the court, that the communication arrive at
the recipient's principal place of business, a place of business from which
negotiations were conducted, or a place from which the sender may have
transmitted previous communications. There is no requirement that the receipt be by a particular agent.

As to whether Goodrich had reason to know of its contents, the court
looked to section 1-201(27). The court held that, under this section, Goodrich would have reason to know of the confirmation at the time that it was,
or in the exercise of due diligence should have been, communicated to the
individual conducting the transaction. In this case, the documents clearly
referred to a purchase of used printing equipment, and Goodrich had only

---

[62] *See* Thompson Printing Mach. Co. v. B.F. Goodrich, 741 F.2d 744, 36 UCCR 737 (7th
Cir. 1983).

[63] 741 F.2d 744, 36 UCCR 737 (7th Cir. 1983).

one surplus machinery department. Also, Thompson's address and phone number were on the purchase order, and a simple phone call could have determined its proper destination. Thus, Goodrich did not use due diligence in locating the proper "home" for the communication, and had it done so, it could have located the proper person within a reasonable time.

If the five requirements have been met, the writing will satisfy the statute of frauds unless "written notice of objection to its [the writing's] contents is given within ten days after it is received."[64] Unlike the confirmation, the objection does not have to be received; posting a properly addressed and stamped letter is sufficient.[65] The right to object gives the recipient a chance to retain the statute of frauds defense even though he has received a confirmation that complies with section 2-201(2). This provision has generated relatively little litigation.

The contents of the objection have been the subject of a few cases. Although the language of the section requires only that the recipient object *to the contents* of the confirmation, the cases indicate that the intent of the section is that the objection, explicitly or implicitly, deny the existence of a contract. For example, in the *Perdue Farms* case discussed earlier, the court held that a response indicating that credit terms were not available and stating that "the previous proposed purchase was automatically canceled" was insufficient. While this response is plausibly characterized as an objection to the contents of the confirmation, the court said that the tenor of the communication was "that of disagreement over terms or an attempt to cancel a previous agreement," and was, therefore, insufficient as an objection.[66]

A problematic case is *M.K. Metals, Inc. v. Container Recovery Corp.*[67] In this case the buyer alleged the existence of an oral contract for the pur-

---

[64] U.C.C. § 2-201(2).

[65] *See* U.C.C. § 1-201(26); Sebasty v. Perschke, 404 N.E.2d 1200, 29 UCCR 39 (Ind. Ct. App. 1980); Tabor & Co. v. Gorenz, 356 N.E.2d 1150 (Ill. App. Ct. 1976); Tiffany, Inc. v. W.M.K Transit Mix, Inc., 493 P.2d 1220, 1223, 16 Ariz. App. 415, 418, 10 UCCR 393 (Ariz. Ct. App. 1972).

Although the Code does not indicate how the ten days is to be computed, it appears that the courts will use the traditional method of excluding the first day and including the last day of the relevant period. *See* Tiffany, Inc. v. W.M.K. Transit Mix, Inc., 16 Ariz. 415, 493 P.2d 1220, 10 UCCR 393 (Ariz. App. 1972) (applying Arizona statute).

[66] The court said that it believed that "if no oral transaction had occurred . . . Perdue would have sent a short note denying the existence of such a purchase." Perdue Farms, Inc. v. Motts, Inc. of Miss., 459 F. Supp. 7, 25 UCCR 9 (N.D. Miss. 1978). *Perdue* should not be read to indicate that a response that claims that no contract exists *because* there was no agreement on the terms of a contract is insufficient. *See* East Europe Domestic Int'l Sales Corp. v. Island Creek Coal Sales Co., 37 UCCR 1030, 572 F. Supp. 702 (S.D.N.Y. 1983).

[67] 645 F.2d 583, 31 UCCR 487 (8th Cir. 1981).

chase of steel scrap. The seller defended on the basis of the statute of frauds. The buyer presented a purchase order, which the court concluded was sufficient to constitute a confirmation for purposes of section 2-201(2) because it was sent subsequent to the asserted oral contract. The court then looked to the seller's response to the purchase order which said:

> At this time we regret that we cannot enter into an agreement with you for a six month period as defined in your enclosed purchase order . . . because of an offer of $140/G.T. for our flattened cans.[68]

The court said that this response was insufficient to qualify as an objection to the confirmation's contents under section 2-201(2):

> The language does not challenge the price stated in the purchase order as incorrect or something the parties never discussed. Rather, it simply indicates that there was someone who was willing to pay more than the amount stated in the purchase order.[69]

Looking solely at the writings, the court's decision was wrong. The clear implication of the language, "we cannot enter into an agreement" is to deny the present existence of a contract. This implication is especially strong in light of the fact that the "confirmation" relied upon by the buyer was nothing more than a purchase order. In fact, the seller's response is precisely what one would expect from a seller who turns down one offer in order to accept a higher offer, and the response in no way acknowledges the existence of a contract. The court's decision can be explained only by its apparently strong belief that an oral contract existed and a desire to avoid applying the statute of frauds.

The merchant confirmation rule has occasionally been misapplied to determine the *terms* of a contract,[70] or to establish conclusively the existence of a contract.[71] Satisfaction of the statute of frauds through section 2-201(2) does neither. Both the existence of an oral contract and the terms of the oral contract must be proved by the party asserting the contract.

[2]   Exceptions to the Writing Requirement—Specially Manufactured Goods

Three subsections of section 2-201(3) provide ways other than a writing to satisfy the Article 2 statute of frauds. The first relates to goods that are

---

[68] *Id.* at 591, 31 UCCR at 497.

[69] *Id.*

[70] Bazak Int'l Corp. v. Mast Indus., Inc., 535 N.E.2d 633, 7 UCCR 1380 (N.Y. 1989).

[71] Tidewater Lumber Co. Inc. v. Maryland Lumber Co., 3 UCCR 351 (N.Y Sup. Ct. 1966).

to be specially manufactured by a seller. If the seller is able to satisfy three requirements,[72] the seller will satisfy the statute of frauds.[73] First, the goods must be specially manufactured—that is, not suitable for sale to others in the ordinary course of the seller's business.[74] Second, the circumstances must reasonably indicate that the goods are for the buyer. Finally, before repudiation by the buyer,[75] the seller must have made a substantial beginning of their manufacture or commitments for their procurement. The justification for this exception is that the chances are good that a seller will not incur commitments for goods that are not readily resalable simply to fabricate a claim against a buyer.[76] In addition, because the goods are specially manufactured, the seller will probably be unable to recoup much of its loss through resale if the contract is not enforced.[77]

The first requirement has not given the courts much trouble. Some examples of situations in which the courts have found that the goods are specially manufactured involve the manufacture of shipping cartons built to specification,[78] cellophane wrapping material manufactured to size and imprinted with the buyer's name,[79] and specially cut mirrors for a hotel.[80] A number of cases involve contracts for goods, such as sales brochures, which contain the name of the company that ordered them.[81] On the other hand, apparently standard-sized cleats for the manufacture of wood crates were

---

[72] This exception is available only to sellers. *See* Global Truck & Equip. Co., Inc. v. Palmer Machine Works, Inc., 628 F. Supp. 641, 42 UCCR 1250 (N.D. Miss. 1986).

[73] The exception apparently applies as well to oral modifications of written contracts that fall within the statute of frauds under U.C.C. § 2-209. *See* S.C. Gray, Inc. v. Ford Motor Co., 92 Mich. App. 789, 29 UCCR 417 (1979).

[74] The statute requires that the goods are to be specially manufactured for the buyer. Thus, goods already manufactured at the time of the contract are not within the exception—no matter how special their purpose. *But see* Smith-Scarff Paper Co. v. P.N. Hirsch & Co., 754 S.W.2d 928, 7 UCCR2d 38 (Mo. Ct. App. 1988) (seller pre-purchased bags to have on hand when buyer gave purchase order—unclear whether seller was contractually liable to buyer at the time bags were purchased).

[75] The statutory language is "before notice of repudiation is received." U.C.C. § 2-201(3)(a).

[76] *See* Impossible Elec. Techniques, Inc. v Wackenhut Protective Sys., Inc., 669 F.2d 1026, 33 UCCR 806 (5th Cir. 1982).

[77] *Id.*

[78] LTV Aerospace Corp. v. Bateman, 492 S.W.2d 703, 12 UCCR 1042 (Tex. Ct. App. 1973).

[79] Flowers Baking Co. of Lynchburg, Inc. v. R.P. Packing, Inc., 329 S.E.2d 462, 40 UCCR 1631 (Va. 1985).

[80] Distribu-Dor, Inc. v. Karadamis, 11 Cal. App. 3d 463, 8 UCCR 36 (1970).

[81] *See, e.g.*, Associated Lithographers v. Stay Wood Prods., Inc., 279 N.W.2d 787, 26 UCCR 273 (Minn. 1979); Smith-Scharff Paper Co. v. P.N. Hirsch & Co. Stores, Inc., 754 S.W.2d 462, 7 UCCR2d 38 (Mo. Ct. App. 1988).

held not to be within the exception, even though temporary market conditions made their sale to others difficult.[82] The fact that the seller is in the *business* of producing custom-made goods does not preclude application of the exception.[83] If altering the goods will make them resalable in the ordinary course, the result will depend on whether the alteration is substantial.[84]

There is virtually no case law on the requirement that the circumstances reasonably indicate that the goods are for the buyer. In most cases, the nature of the goods has rather clearly indicated that they were for the particular buyer.[85] On the other hand, cases can be easily envisioned where this requirement might be troublesome.[86]

The prerequisite that the seller make a substantial beginning of the manufacture, or commitments for the procurement, of the goods has also generated little case law, and should not be difficult to apply in a routine case.[87] Potential trouble lurks in this provision, however, which the case law is beginning to encounter. What happens for example if the seller asserts a

---

[82] Maderas Tropicales S. de R.L. de C.V. v. Southern Crate and Veneer Co., 588 F.2d 971, 25 UCCR 1259 (5th Cir. 1979). *See* Colorado Carpet Installation, Inc. v. Palermo, 647 P.2d 686, 33 UCCR 473 (1982) (standard carpet, not specially cut to room dimension, was not within exception).

[83] *See* Impossible Elecs. Techniques, Inc. v. Wackenhut Protective Sys., Inc., 669 F.2d 1026, 33 UCCR 806 (5th Cir. 1982).

[84] Impossible Elecs. Techniques, Inc. v. Wackenhut Protective Sys., Inc., 669 F.2d 1026, 33 UCCR 806, 817–818 (5th Cir. 1982).

[85] *See* Flowers Baking Co. of Lynchburg v. R-P Packaging Inc., 329 S.E.2d 466, 40 UCCR 1631 (Va. 1985) (the nature of cellophane wrapping paper made to a certain size requested by the buyer and imprinted with the buyer's name indicated that the goods were intended for buyer); Smith-Scharff Paper Co. v. P.N. Hirsch & Co. Stores, 754 S.W.2d 928, 7 UCCR2d 38 (Mo. Ct. App. 1988) (the court determined that bags with the buyer's printed name on them and kept in stock by the seller were made for the buyer).

[86] For example, assume that plaintiff is a carpet manufacturer and defendant is the owner of a new store about to open. Defendant orally agrees to purchase 2,500 yards of a specially dyed and brightly colored carpeting. After the carpet has been manufactured, the buyer repudiates. The manufacturer cannot resell the carpet because of its color. Although the carpeting has clearly been specially manufactured for someone, what is it about the color to connect this carpeting with this buyer?

It is unclear whether this requirement must be satisfied without relying on the asserted oral agreement. There are arguments both ways. One can argue that it is unacceptable "bootstrapping" to permit the plaintiff to rely on the very agreement at issue to show that the plaintiff's evidence that the agreement was made is reliable. On the other hand, to the extent that the exception is based upon the premise that people do not manufacture goods that are not resalable in the ordinary course of business without a prior contract, permitting evidence of the alleged agreement to tie the goods to the defendant is not obviously improper.

[87] *See* Perlmuter Printing Co. v. Strome, Inc., 22 UCCR 1092, 436 F. Supp. 409 (N.D. Ohio 1976) (completion of 62 percent of printed flyers is a substantial beginning).

contract for 50,000 custom-made widgets and the seller has completed and delivered 7,000 of them, but has not begun the production of any others? The buyer denies that there was a contract for 50,000 widgets, although it acknowledges a contract for the 7,000. Can the seller argue that the manufacture of the 7,000 is a substantial beginning on the contract and therefore overcome the statute of frauds for the entire 50,000? Or is the seller limited to recovering for the 7,000 because he has not made a substantial (or any) beginning on the others.

This is the case of *Epprecht v. IBM Corp*,[88] except that the widgets were actually specially manufactured printhead assemblies. Without deciding whether 7,000 would be a "substantial" beginning on a contract for 50,000 items, the court held that the plaintiff was limited to recovery for 7,000. It allowed recovery for only those individual items that the seller had already substantially begun to manufacture. The court held that the exceptions to the statute of frauds were to be narrowly construed, and that it was "clearly illogical" to allow recovery for items on which manufacture had not begun.[89]

Other cases, however, take a more lenient approach. For example, in *LTV Aerospace Corp. v. Bateman*,[90] the court allowed the plaintiff to prove a contract for 8,000 custom-made shipping containers even though only 653 had been built. Similarly, the court in *Distribu-dor, Inc. v. Karadanis*[91] permitted the plaintiff to overcome the statute of frauds with respect to *non–*specially made shower and tub enclosures that were part of a contract for specially made mirrors.

The *Epprecht* decision is wrong for a number of reasons. First, unlike subsections (3)(b) and (3)(c) of section 2-201, which contain express limitations on the quantity that can be proved,[92] subsection (a) contains no such limitations. Had the drafters intended to limit the exception in subsection (a) in a manner similar to the exceptions in the other subsections, they could have easily done so. The introductory language of subsection (3) states that once the conditions of one of the subsections is met, the contract "is enforceable," and subsection (a) contains no further limitations on enforcement. The seller still has the burden of proving that the contract was for a larger amount than those which it has begun to manufacture.

---

[88] 36 UCCR 391 (E.D. Pa. 1983).

[89] *Id.* at 393, 394.

[90] 492 S.W.2d 703, 12 UCCR 1042 (Tex. Civ. App. 1973).

[91] 11 Cal. App. 3d 463, 90 Cal. Rptr. 231, 8 UCCR 36 (Cal. App. 1970).

[92] Subsection (3)(b) permits enforcement only up to the quantity of goods admitted and subsection (3)(c) permits enforcement only up to the quantity of goods accepted by the buyer or the quantity of goods for which payment has been made and accepted.

Second, there will often be cases in which it will be reasonably clear that the quantity of goods which the seller has manufactured or begun to manufacture is not the quantity contracted for. This might occur when the buyer would normally order more goods than the seller has begun to manufacture, suggesting that the contract is for a greater number of goods. More likely, in some cases the seller will have to incur significant start-up costs to be able to specially manufacture the goods, and would not have incurred these costs to fulfill a contract for the quantity that it has already begun to manufacture, again providing evidence that the contract is for a larger quantity.[93]

Finally, the likelihood of reliance losses is another strong justification for the specially manufactured goods exception to the statute of frauds. When the seller has incurred substantial "sunk costs" in preparing to produce the specially manufactured goods, the seller will suffer substantial reliance losses unless the seller is permitted to enforce the contract for an amount greater than the quantity that the seller has begun to manufacture. By permitting the seller to prove this larger quantity, the overall policy of subsection (a) of protecting reliance expenditures is furthered.

[3] Exceptions to the Writing Requirement—Admissions

Under section 2-201(3)(b), a party cannot admit in court the existence of a contract and also rely upon the statute of frauds to prevent its enforcement. This overrules some pre-Code case law,[94] which made little sense given the purpose of the statute.[95] There appears to be no requirement that the admission be in the action now pending; admission in some other suit should suffice.[96]

Two issues are of concern with respect to this exception: what constitutes an "admission" for purposes of the provision, and to what extent can

---

[93] This will not always be the case, of course. In some cases, the beginning of production of some number of divisible items will provide no reliable evidence that a contract for a greater number exists.

[94] Gogle v. Blazofsky 142 A.2d 313, 187 Pa. Super. 32 (1958); Cournett v. Clere, 193 Ky. 590 (1922).

[95] Comment 7 to U.C.C. § 2-201 says that if the existence of a contract is admitted in court, no additional writing is necessary for protection against fraud.

[96] *But see* International Commodities Export Co. v. Walfkill Feed & Fertilizer Corp., 32 UCCR 687 (9th Cir. 1981) (admission in different action with different plaintiff does not satisfy section 2-201(3)(b) exception to statute of frauds). This case does not appear to be correctly decided. There is nothing in section 2-201(3)(b) that limits admissions to any particular action. More important, the policy underlying the exception (reliability of plaintiff's claim that a contract exists) is furthered by permitting admission from other action to satisfy the exception.

the plaintiff, through the use of pre-trial procedure and discovery (and perhaps even at trial) attempt to elicit an admission from a reluctant defendant.

The cases establish that it is not necessary that the defendant[97] explicitly acknowledge that a contract exists.[98] A number of cases have held that if the defendant admits facts that *as a matter of law* constitute a contract, then the exception will be satisfied.[99] This conclusion is unobjectionable; there is no reason a defendant should have to use certain "magic words" in his admission in order to satisfy the exception when, assuming the admission is factually true,[100] there is no question that a contract exists.[101]

This reasoning should be extended to cases in which the defendant admits facts that would create a jury question as to whether a contract exists. For example, assume the seller admits in a court proceeding to statements made during negotiations that the buyer understood as indicating the seller's assent to a bargain. The defendant argues, however, that he believed that no contract existed as a result of these statements (i.e., that these statements did not objectively indicate his assent). Whether a contract exists as the result of these negotiations will be a question of fact for the jury so long as the judge determines that reasonable people could differ over whether the seller, by his statements, objectively indicated assent.

In this situation, the court should find the exception satisfied by the seller's admissions. The purpose of the statute of frauds is to prevent fraudulent assertions by a plaintiff that he had an agreement with the defendant. Through his admissions in a court proceeding, the seller has acknowledged that negotiations took place, and that he made statements that *could* be construed as creating a contract. The seller's admissions in this case certainly

---

[97] U.C.C. § 2-201 requires that the "party" against whom enforcement is sought admit the existence of a contract. In Esso Geometric v. Harvard Indus., 46 F.3d 718, 25 UCCR2d 661 (8th Cir. 1995), the court held that a person who was an employee at the time of the alleged oral contract but retired two years before his deposition was not a "party" for purposes of the admission exception.

[98] *See* Quaney v. Tobyne, 236 Kan. 201, 689 P.2d 844, 40 UCCR 37 (1974).

[99] *See* Lewis v. Hughes, 346 A.2d 231, 18 UCCR 52 (Md. Ct. App. 1975); Packwood Elevator Co. v. Heis Dorfer, 260 N.W.2d 543, 23 UCCR 293 (Iowa 1977). In fact, the defendant is not saved by an explicit denial that he believed a contract existed, so long as his admissions of fact conclusively establish one.

[100] The admission of the defendant does not conclusively establish a contract, it merely overcomes the statute of frauds. The admission, of course, is also evidence that a contract exists. Comment 7 to U.C.C. § 2-201.

[101] Despite the suggestion of some commentators, for example, J. White & R. Summers, 1 Uniform Commercial Code § 2-5 at 92–94 (3d ed. 1988)—a denial does not constitute an admission simply because it is not credible. *See* Cox v. Cox, 292 Ala. 106, 289 So. 2d 609, 14 UCCR 330 (1974); Starry Constr. Co. Inc. v. Murphy Oil U.S.A., Inc.,785 F. Supp. 1356, 17 UCCR2d 353 (D. Minn. 1992).

provide a basis for believing that buyer's oral evidence rests on a real trans-action, which is all that is required of a writing, and is all that should be required of the exceptions to the writing requirement as well.[102] The pro-posed revisions to Article 2 appear to adopt this analysis. The revised section 2-201 states that the statute of frauds is satisfied if "the party against whom enforcement is sought admits, in pleading or testimony in court or otherwise under oath, *facts from which an agreement can be found.*"[103]

The courts disagree as to the precise effect of a section 2-201(3)(b) admission. The text of section 2-201(3)(b) provides that an admission is effective only as to the quantity admitted,[104] but it contains no other limi-tations. What happens, for example, if the seller admits a contract, but at a different price than that asserted by the buyer?

A number of cases indicate that once the defendant admits in a court proceeding the existence of a contract, a dispute over terms—except perhaps quantity—is a question for trial.[105] However, in *Allen v. Harris Truck and Trailer Sales, Inc.*[106] the court held that a contract is enforceable under section 2-201(3)(b) only on the terms admitted, and it limited enforcement to the price admitted by the defendant but disputed by the plaintiff. In *Barton v. Tra-Mo, Inc.*,[107] the court held that a defendant who admits a contract for the amount already delivered cannot be held liable for breach of an asserted requirements contract. On the other hand, in *Oskey Gasoline and Oil Co., Inc. v. Continental Oil Co.*,[108] an admission that defendant believed he had "some" contract with plaintiff was sufficient to permit plaintiff to prove a one year contract for 50,000 tons, even though defendant stated he believed he had only a spot contract for a far lesser quantity. The court said that so long as a jury could reasonably find a contract on the terms asserted by the

---

[102] *See* Comment 1 to U.C.C. § 2-201. There are no cases that clearly hold in the manner suggested. There are some cases, however, that suggest this analysis. *See* Dangerfield v. Markel, 222 N.W.2d 373, 15 UCCR 765 (N.D. 1974) ("If a fair consideration of his testi-mony, and implications under the circumstances as established by the record, establishes the claimed agreement, it will be enforced"); Oskey v. Gasoline & Oil Co., Inc. v. Continental Oil Co., 534 F.2d 1281, 19 UCCR 61 (8th Cir. 1976); Quaney v. Tobyne, 236 Kan. 201, 689 P.2d 844, 40 UCCR 37 (1974); Gooch v. Farmers Marketing Ass'n, 519 So. 2d 1214, 5 UCCR2d 934 (Miss. 1988).

[103] *See* Council Draft No. 4 § 2-201(c)(3) (emphasis added).

[104] U.C.C. § 2-201(3)(b). This limitation is removed in the proposed revisions to Article 2. *See* Council Draft No. 4 § 2-201(c)(3).

[105] *See* Jackson v. Meadows, 153 Ga. App. 1, 264 S.E.2d 503, 28 UCCR 990 (1984); Dangerfield v. Markel, 252 N.W.2d 184, 21 UCCR 1239 (N.D. 1977).

[106] 490 F. Supp. 488, 29 UCCR 397 (E.D. Mo. 1980).

[107] 73 Or. App. 804, 41 UCCR 373 (1985).

[108] 534 F.2d 1281, 19 UCCR 61 (8th Cir. 1976).

plaintiff, the admission was sufficient under section 2-201(3)(b). While these latter two cases are not necessarily inconsistent,[109] they do indicate somewhat different attitudes toward the exception.[110]

An issue that has received a great deal of attention in the commentary[111] and cases[112] is the extent to which the plaintiff can "force" a defendant into an admission through discovery or trial, or conversely, the degree to which the defendant can avoid an admission through creative pleading. Because resolution of this issue depends upon strongly competing policy considerations and varying views of the efficacy of the statute of frauds, the cases are in disagreement.

The competing policies are obvious and have been well articulated by the cases[113] and commentary.[114] On the one hand, according to the terms of section 2-201(3)(b), admissions made in the pleadings, discovery, and at trial all satisfy the exception. Therefore, the party asserting the existence of the contract ought not to be prevented by the other party's pleadings from using these procedural devices to elicit an admission. This is particularly

---

[109] It might be that if the defendant in *Oskey* had been more categorical in his denial, the result would have been different.

[110] *See* Gestetner Corp. v. Case Equip. Co., 815 F.2d 806, 3 UCCR2d 1328 (1st Cir. 1987) (plaintiff permitted to prove requirements contract although there was no reference to quantity in admission evidence). *See also* Harper Plastics, Inc. v. AMOCO Chems. Corp., 617 F.2d 468, 28 UCCR 985 (7th Cir. 1980) (unpublished). For an interesting twist, *see* Songbird Jet Ltd. v. AMAX, Inc., 581 F. Supp. 912, 38 UCCR 431 (S.D.N.Y. 1984). In this case the plaintiff claimed a contract for the sale of a single jet. The defendant admitted that an oral agreement had been made for the sale of the jet, but asserted that it was part of a package deal involving the sale and lease of two other aircraft, which the plaintiff denied. Thus, the plaintiff was, in a sense, arguing for a *lesser* quantity than the defendant. The court held that the admission was not effective for purposes of overcoming the statute of frauds on the asserted contract for the sale of a single aircraft. Given the purpose of the limitation in U.C.C. § 2-201(3)(b)—to prevent fraudulent assertions of quantity—the court's decision is reasonable.

[111] *See, e.g.*, Michael Herbert, "Procedure & Promise: Rethinking the Admissions Exception to the Statute of Frauds Under U.C.C. Article 2, 2a, and 8," 47 Bus. Law. 1517 (1992); John C. Ward & Kim S. Dockstander, "Placing Article 2's Statute of Frauds in its Proper Prospective," 27 IDLR 507 (1991); Thomas D. Crandall, I Uniform Commercial Code, § 3.4.5, 3:54–3:55 (1993); James J. White & Robert S. Summers, 1 Uniform Commercial Code § 2-5 at 91 (3d ed. 1988).

[112] *See* Chrysler Corp. v. Majestic Marine Inc., 35 Mich. App. 403, 192 N.W.2d 507, 10 UCCR 130 (1971); Davis v. Aandeweil, 16 Ariz. App. 262, 10 UCCR 135 (Ariz. Ct. App. 1981); Oskey Gasoline & Oil Co. Inc., v. Continental Oil Co., 534 F.2d 1281, 19 UCCR 61 (8th Cir. 1967); Quad County Grain Inc. v. Poe, 202 N.W.2d 118, 11 UCCR 720 (Ia. 1972).

[113] *See, e.g.*, D.F. Activities Corp. v. Brown, 851 F.2d 920, 7 UCCR2d 1396 (7th Cir. 1988).

[114] *See* Crandall, *supra* note 111, § 3.4.5 at 3:54–3:55.

true because the party relying on the statute of frauds does not have to admit a contract, but only facts sufficient to constitute one, in order to satisfy the exception. Consequently, there are a number of cases in which a party has apparently denied a contract in the pleadings, but the other party has overcome the statute through discovery or cross-examination at trial.[115] On the other hand, allowing one party to force the other party to incur the costs of litigation all the way through trial in order to elicit an admission substantially undercuts the purpose of the statute—to avoid litigation as to the existence of a contract when there is no writing.

The cases can generally be grouped into four categories. The first, and least expansive, permits a defendant to assert the statute of frauds through a demurrer or motion to dismiss.[116] This approach does not even require the defendant to affirm or deny the existence of a contract.[117] Its premise is that unless the defendant voluntarily admits the existence of a contract at the outset of the litigation, he is entitled to its protection.[118]

While this approach prevents the defendant from potentially needless litigation, it does not afford a plaintiff much opportunity to satisfy the exception. As a result, a number of courts permit the proceeding to continue until the defendant affirmatively denies the existence of a contract in a responsive pleading.[119] This procedure has the advantage of requiring the defendant to assert in good faith that no contract exists.[120] If the defendant is

---

[115] See Nebraska Builders Prods. Co. v. The Indus. Erectors Inc., 239 Neb. 744, 478 N.W.2d 268, 16 UCCR2d 568 (1992); M&W Farm Serv. Co. v. Ken Callison, 285 N.W.2d 271, 27 UCCR 1239 (Iowa 1979).

[116] See, e.g., Simmons Oil Corp. v. Bulk Sales Corp., 498 F. Supp. 457, 31 UCCR 1236 (D.N.J. 1980); Triangle Marketing, Inc. v. Action Indus., Inc., 630 F. Supp. 1578, 1 UCCR2d 36 (N.D. Ill. 1986).

[117] A "technical" admission for purposes of a demurrer or motion to dismiss is not a 2-201(3)(b) admission. Anthony v. Tidwell, 560 S.W.2d 908, 23 UCCR 561 (Tenn. 1977). See In re Morristown Lincoln-Mercury, Inc., 25 B.R. 377, 35 UCCR 268 (E.D. Tenn. 1982) (not an admission when answer denies contract, but admits one in connection with alternative affirmative defense).

[118] The availability of this approach may depend upon local rules of procedure. See Triangle Marketing v. Action Indus., Inc., 630 F. Supp. 1578, 1 UCCR2d 36 (N.D. Ill. 1986).

[119] See D.F. Activities Corp. v. Brown, 851 F.2d 920, 7 UCCR2d 1396 (7th Cir. 1988); Presti v. Wilson, 11 UCCR 716 (E.D.N.Y. 1972).

[120] Under most rules of pleading, an assertion of fact in a pleading not made in good faith subjects both the attorney and client to sanctions. See the excellent discussion of the procedural aspects of this issue in Crandall et al, supra note 111, § 3.4.5 at 3:56. In addition, if the pleadings are sworn or are accompanied by a sworn affidavit, a false factual assertion opens up at least the theoretical possibility of perjury prosecution. D.F. Activities Corp. v. Brown, 851 F.2d 920, 7 UCCR 1396 (7th Cir. 1988). The proposed revisions to Article 2

unable to do so, the plaintiff's case may proceed. On the other hand, it affords no further opportunity to elicit an admission from a defendant who is willing to assert fraudulently that no contract exists, or to elicit an admission of facts that would establish a contract, and thus significantly limits the scope of the exception.

A third approach permits the plaintiff to elicit an admission through discovery, but if the defendant persists in denying a contract through discovery the plaintiff's case is dismissed prior to trial.[121] As a result, the plaintiff is permitted considerable opportunity to elicit an admission, but the proceeding is stopped short of trial. This technique does, however, deprive the plaintiff of cross-examination, a technique that has proved valuable in a number of cases to plaintiffs seeking admissions.[122] It also subjects the defendant who persists in denying a contract to the prospect of considerable delay, expense and inconvenience.[123]

The final group of cases permits the case to go to trial. A large number of cases exist in this category,[124] despite the lack of protection it affords the defendant.

Perhaps the best approach is one suggested by the dissenting judge in *D.F. Activities Corp. v. Brown.*[125] Judge Flaum concluded that the judge should have discretion to determine how far he or she should allow the case to proceed when the defendant denies the existence of a contract. If, for example, the defendant denies even the existence of any negotiations with the plaintiff and is willing to provide sworn testimony to that effect, and this testimony is credible, summary judgment based on the statute is probably appropriate. On the other hand, if negotiations are admitted or the

---

require a party to deny the existence of facts from which an agreement can be found before being accorded the benefit of the statute of frauds. *See* Council Draft No. 4 § 2-201(a). Thus, it appears that if the proposed revision is adopted, Article 2 will not permit raising the statute by way of demurrer or motion to dismiss. The proposed revisions do not, however, indicate what additional procedural devices the party asserting a contract is entitled to use to elicit an admission.

[121] *See* Reissman Int'l Corp. v. J.S.O. Wood Prods. Inc., 10 UCCR 1165 (N.Y. Civ. Ct. 1972).

[122] *See, e.g.* Hoffman v. Boone, 708 F. Supp. 78, 9 UCCR2d 474 (S.D.N.Y. 1989); D.F. Activities Corp. v. Brown, 851 F.2d 920, 7 UCCR2d 1396 (7th Cir. 1988).

[123] *See* Gaultney-Klineman Art v. Hughes, 227 A.D.2d 221, 642 N.Y.S.2d 265, 32 UCCR2d 421 (App. Div. 1996) (defendant subjected to "excessive badgering" in deposition).

[124] *See, e.g.,* Nebraska Builders Prods. Co. v. Industrial Erectors Inc., 478 N.W.2d 257, 16 UCCR2d 568 (Neb. 1992); Skyline Steel Corp. v. A.J. Dupuis Co., 648 F. Supp. 360, 3 UCCR2d 475 (E.D. Mich. 1986).

[125] 851 F.2d 920, 7 UCCR2d 1396 (7th Cir. 1988).

testimony of the defendant is questionable, the case should be allowed to proceed further, perhaps even to trial, to give the plaintiff an opportunity to seek an admission.

[4] Exceptions to the Writing Requirement—Partial or Full Performance

Under the Uniform Sales Act, part performance by either the seller or the buyer satisfied the statute of frauds.[126] The difficulty with this rule was that part performance provided no indication of the quantity involved in the alleged oral agreement. For example, delivery of four new stoves to an owner of an apartment complex did not indicate whether the oral agreement had been for four, four hundred, or some other number of stoves. However, once part performance was established, the parties were free to attempt to prove an oral contract for any amount.

The Code has partially changed this rule. The statute of frauds in Article 2 is satisfied under section 2-201(3)(c) "with respect to goods for which payment has been made and accepted or which have been received and accepted."[127] In the example above, the statute of frauds is satisfied with respect to four stoves, providing that they have been accepted by the buyer, and the parties[128] will be allowed to introduce evidence of the oral agreement. If the existence of the agreement is proved, recovery will be allowed for the four stoves—but no more. Unlike the Uniform Sales Act, neither party is permitted to establish an oral contract for a greater number.

Much of the litigation concerning this section deals with whether goods have been accepted.[129] The issue of acceptance arises in other contexts and is governed by section 2-606.[130] It is generally discussed in detail elsewhere,[131] although one comment is appropriate here. For purposes of section

---

[126] Uniform Sales Act § 4(1).

[127] U.C.C. § 2-201(3)(c).

[128] According to Comment 2 to U.C.C. § 2-201, part performance by either party satisfies the statute of frauds with respect to *both* of the parties. One court apparently misunderstood the intent of this section. *See* In re Flying W. Airway Inc., 341 F. Supp. 26 (E.D. Pa. 1972). The case of Nann v. Commissioner of Internal Revenue, 483 F.2d 673, 13 UCCR 630 (8th Cir. 1973) is correct.

[129] *See, e.g.* Buffaloe v. Hart, 441 S.E.2d 172, 23 UCCR2d 354 (N.C. Ct. App. 1994); Sjorgen v. Maybrooks Inc., 673 N.E.2d 1367, 15 UCCR2d 1160 (Ill. App. Ct. 1991); Uni Prods. v. Bearse, 153 B.R. 764, 20 UCCR2d 1233 (E.D. Mich. 1993).

[130] It is clear that mere delivery of the goods without acceptance, as defined in the Code, is not sufficient to satisfy this exception to the statute of frauds. Groeteke v. Nelsen, 311 N.W.2d 508, 32 UCCR 702 (Neb. 1981).

[131] *See* § 7.03[D], *infra.*

2-201(3)(c), acceptance of the goods by the *buyer* is not necessary. Acceptance by a third party who is not a party to the contract qualifies as an acceptance so long as delivery to the third party is authorized by the buyer.[132]

If all of the goods have been accepted, or if the entire price has been paid by the buyer and accepted by the seller, the contract is fully enforceable.[133] When, however, only a part of the goods called for by the oral agreement has been accepted or where only a part of the price has been accepted, Comment 2 to section 2-201 requires that the court make. a "just apportionment."[134] That is, if a part of the price has been paid, the contract will be enforceable to the extent of a proportionate quantity of goods. Conversely, if a quantity of goods has been accepted, the contract will be enforceable to a proportionate part of the price. In many cases, it will be easy for the court to make such an apportionment.[135]

In some cases, however, no just apportionment can be made between the full performance called for by the oral agreement and the partial performance that has occurred. This issue can arise in two different contexts. The first is when the oral agreement alleged by the buyer is for one item and the buyer has paid only a part of the total purchase price. While one early case decided that the contract could not be enforced under these circumstances,[136] the cases are now plentiful permitting enforcement of the contract.[137] This is clearly the proper result, given the fact that the buyer

---

[132] *See* Dairyman's Co-operative Creamery Ass'n v. Leipold, 34 Cal. App. 3d 184, 109 Cal. Rptr. 753, 13 UCCR 237 (1973); Dykes Restaurant Supply Inc. v. Grimes, 481 So. 2d 1149, 42 UCCR 1603 (Ala. Civ. Ct. App. 1985).

[133] *But cf.* Stanfield v. Grove, 924 S.W.2d 611, 32 UCCR2d 423 (Mo. Ct. App. 1996) (car not delivered and accepted since seller never gave buyer certificate of title).

[134] The requirement for a just apportionment is a function of the fact that U.C.C. § 2-201(3)(c) only permits enforcement up to the quantity of goods which have been accepted or for which payment has been made.

[135] *See, e.g.,* Bagby Land & Cattle Co. v. Calif. Livestock Comm'n, 439 F.2d 315, 8 UCCR 844 (5th Cir. 1971) (contract enforceable to the extent of 222 cattle delivered and accepted); Rio Trading Co. v. Fried, 33 UCCR2d 1067 (N.Y. Sup. Ct. 1997) (partial performance only validates the contract for goods that have been accepted or paid for).

[136] Williamson v. Martz, 11 Pa. D.&C. 2d 33 (Pa. C.P. 1956).

[137] *See* Starr v. Freeport Dodge, 282 N.Y.S.2d 58, 4 UCCR 644 (N.Y. Dist. Ct. 1967) (contract for car removed from statute of frauds by $25 deposit); Lockwood v. Smigel, 18 Cal. App. 3d 800, 96 Cal. Rptr., 9 UCCR 452 (Cal. Ct. App. 1971) (payment of $100 on $11,400 car); Paloukos v. Intermountain Chevrolet, 25 UCCR 655 (Idaho 1978) ($120 deposit on $3,650 car); Sedmak v. Charlie's Chevrolet, 622 S.W.2d 694, 31 UCCR 851 (Mo. Ct. App. 1981) ($500 payment on $15,000 Corvette); Songbird Jet Ltd., Inc. v. AMAX Inc., 581 F. Supp. 912, 38 UCCR 431 (S.D.N.Y. 1984) (payment of $250,000 on $8,850,000 airplane).

The amount of the downpayment makes no difference as to enforceability in these

cannot possibly be attempting to fraudulently inflate the quantity of the contract when the quantity is one.[138]

There are other cases in which "just apportionment" cannot be made. For example, the price set by the oral agreement may reflect a quantity discount that the seller is willing to give only because the buyer has agreed to purchase a large quantity of the goods but that the seller would not have been willing to give for the smaller number accepted by the buyer. In this case, the court has three alternatives: enforce the entire contract, not enforce the contract at all, or attempt to reach some other solution. The few cases that exist do not provide a clear answer. They do, however, indicate that the courts are unlikely to refuse enforcement altogether.[139] The law of restitution may provide a useful guide in difficult cases.

When part performance consists of payment, the courts have held that acceptance of a check will suffice.[140] Although there is some authority suggesting a contrary result,[141] it is not necessary that the check be indorsed, deposited, or cashed before acceptance of payment will be found.[142] This is

---

cases. *See* Songbird Jet Ltd. v. AMAX Inc., 581 F. Supp. 912, 992, 38 UCCR 431 (S.D.N.Y. 1984).

[138] *See also* Comment 1 to U.C.C. § 2-201 indicating that all that is required of a writing to satisfy the statute of frauds is that "it afford a basis to believe that the offered oral evidence rests on a real transaction." This is an appropriate standard to apply to the exceptions to the writing requirement as well, and is certainly satisfied under these circumstances.

[139] *See* The Press, Inc. v. Fins & Feathers Publishing Co., 361 N.W.2d 171, 40 UCCR 33 (Mo. Ct. App. 1985). In this case a partial payment was made on a contract for the publication of 2,000,000 newspaper ad inserts. The court found that the contract was indivisible and could be enforced in its entirety. The court noted, however, that there was no dispute over quantity. In W.I. Snyder Corp. v. Caracciolo, 373 Pa. Super. 486, 541 A.2d 775, 7 UCCR2d 993 (Pa. Super. 1988), the parties agreed to exchange construction equipment consisting of bulldozers, cranes, and bobcats for some loads of scrap metal, a portion of which were delivered and accepted. There was no apportionment in the oral contract. The court found the contract indivisible and enforced the entire agreement. *See also* Moretti S.P.A. v. Anchor Hocking Corp., 931 F.2d 1178, 14 UCCR2d 706 (7th Cir. 1991) (contract for distributorship can be shown by part performance).

[140] *See* Kaufman v. Solomon, 524 F.2d 501, 17 UCCR 1159 (3d Cir. 1975); Miller v. Wooters, 476 N.E.2d 11, 40 UCCR 1623 (Ill. App. Ct. 1985); Buffaloe v. Hart, 441 N.E.2d 172, 23 UCCR2d 354 (N.C. Ct. App. 1994). This is consistent with Comment 2 to U.C.C. § 2-201.

[141] *See* Presti v. Wilson, 348 F. Supp. 543, 11 UCCR 716 (E.D.N.Y. 1972).

[142] *See* Kaufman v. Solomon, *supra* note 140 (retention of check for thirty days is acceptance of payment for purposes of section 2-201(3)(c) despite the fact that it was never indorsed or cashed); Miller v. Wooters, *supra* note 140 (acceptance or payment occurred when buyer stopped payment on check before check indorsed or deposited).

true even though payment by check is conditional under section 2-511(3).[143] One court found an acceptance of payment when the seller accepted a negotiable promissory note.[144]

Most courts have held that the part performance under section 2-201(3)(c) does not have to be "exclusively referable" to the alleged oral contract.[145] That is, the payment or acceptance of the goods does not have to be inconsistent with other possible transactions in order to satisfy the exception. In *Gerner v. Vasby*,[146] the defendant argued that plaintiff's acceptance of the goods was as consistent with a "spot sale"—a type of transaction the parties had conducted on previous occasions—as with the contract alleged by the plaintiff. The Supreme Court of Wisconsin responded:

> When the parties' conduct is consistent with the contract, such conduct is sufficient to take the contract out of the statute of frauds even though it is not inconsistent with some other dealings arguably had between the parties; it is not necessary that the conduct be "exclusively referable" to the contract.[147]

One case, however, has held that to satisfy section 2-201(3)(c) the payment must be "unequivocally referable" to the contract.[148]

The proposed revisions to Article 2 will eliminate most of these problems in a curious way—by returning to the rule of the Uniform Sales Act. Section 2-201(c)(2) provides an exception to the statute of frauds when "the conduct of both parties in performing the agreement recognizes that a contract was formed."[149] Section 2-201 would no longer contain a quantity limitation in the exceptions to the writing requirement if the proposed revisions were adopted.[150] In fact, under the proposed revision, the conduct required to satisfy the exception does not necessarily have to consist of the

---

[143] Kaufman v. Solomon, *supra* note 140.

[144] Uni-Prods. Inc. v. Bearse, 153 B.R. 764, 20 UCCR2d 1233 (E.D. Mich. 1993).

[145] *See, e.g.,* Gerner v. Vasby, 75 Wis. 2d 660, 250 N.W.2d 319, 21 UCCR 44 (Wis. 1977); West Cent. Packing, Inc. v. A.F. Murch Co., 109 Mich. App. 493, 311 N.W.2d 404, 32 UCCR 1361 (1981); Hoffman v. Stoller, 320 N.W.2d 786, 33 UCCR 1622 (N.D. 1982).

[146] 75 Wis. 2d 660, 250 N.W.2d 319, 21 UCCR 44 (1977).

[147] *Id.* at 669, 250 N.W.2d at 325, 21 UCCR at 51.

[148] Songbird Jet Ltd. v. AMAX Inc., 581 F. Supp. 912, 38 UCCR 431 (S.D.N.Y. 1984). The court nonetheless found the exception was satisfied by a payment of $250,000 on an alleged contract for an airplane for a price of $8.5 million.

[149] Council Draft No. 4 § 2-201(3)(c).

[150] Council Draft No. 4, Note 3.

acceptance of goods or payment but may be any conduct that "recognizes a contract was formed." It must, however, be conduct of *both* parties.

[D] Estoppel and the Statute of Frauds

There are many situations when one party will have relied upon an oral contract but is unable to satisfy any of the statutory exceptions. This party will suffer substantial losses which cannot be recovered if the defaulting party is allowed to use the statute of frauds as a shield against liability. In the decades leading up to the adoption of the Code, some courts were beginning to allow recovery of such losses through the application of equitable or promissory estoppel.[151] Unfortunately, the Code drafters did not clearly indicate whether they intended this case law to survive the Code or to be preempted by it.

Strong arguments exist that the drafters did not intend to remove estoppel as a means of overcoming the statute of frauds. First, section 1-103 expressly mentions estoppel as a supplementary principle of law that survives the Code, except where displaced by a "particular provision."[152] The drafters of Article 2 had to be aware of the growing case law permitting recovery for reliance losses on oral contracts, and they could have easily explicitly preempted estoppel in section 2-201. In addition, the drafters made the concept of good faith pervasive in the Code, and the concepts of good faith and estoppel are closely related.[153] Also, the Code was intended to displace the excessive formalism extant in prior law and replace it with formulations based upon good faith and mercantile reasonability.[154]

The application of estoppel to the Code statute of frauds has now been considered by courts in most jurisdictions. A significant majority of the

---

[151] *See* Miller v. Lawlor, 245 Iowa 1144 (1954); Waugh v. Lennard, 69 Ariz. 214 (1949); Fruth v. Gaston, 187 S.W.2d 581 (Tex. Civ. Ct. App. 1945); Harris v. Backus, 212 Or. 695, 321 P.2d 315 (1958).

[152] U.C.C. § 1-103.

[153] *See* Allied Grape Growers v. Bronco Wine Co., 249 Cal. Rptr. 872, 6 UCCR 2d 1059 (Cal. Ct. App. 1988); Potter v. Hatter Farms, 56 Or. App. 254, 33 UCCR 819 (1982).

[154] *See* Karl N. Llewellyn, The Common Law Tradition: Deciding Appeals (1960); Zipporan B. Wiseman, "The Limits of Vision: Karl Llewellyn & the Merchant Rules," 100 Harv. L. Rev. 465 (1987); John E. Murray, Jr., "The Chaos of the 'Battle of The Forms': Solutions," 39 Vand. L. Rev. 1307 (1986).

courts have accepted an estoppel exception.[155] Although most pre-Code cases,[156] and some post-Code cases,[157] rely on equitable estoppel, most of the cases today use the doctrine of promissory estoppel.[158] Although formulations sometimes differ, many cases have relied upon the requirements of Section 139 of the Restatement (Second) of Contracts. These requirements are:

    (1) a promise;
    (2) which the promisor should reasonably expect to induce action or forbearance on the part of the promisee;
    (3) which does induce such action or forbearance; and
    (4) injustice can only be avoided by enforcement of the contract.[159]

Although cases permitting an estoppel exception abound, the case of *Hatter v. Potter Farms*[160] is representative. Potter operated a turkey hatchery, which hatched eggs and then sold "poults"[161] to turkey growers. Hatter was a turkey grower who raised and sold adult turkeys. Potter and Hatter entered into an oral contract in which Potter agreed to sell and Hatter agreed to buy 192,000 poults for eighty cents per poult. Transportation problems led to Potter's advising Hatter that he had another prospective buyer. Hatter made it clear that he wanted the poults. In reliance on the contract and Hatter's statements, Potter refused the other offer. Hatter then informed Potter that he would no longer be able to use the poults, and repudiated the contract.

---

[155] *See, e.g.,* Talkington v. Anchor Gasoline Corp., 821 F. Supp. 505 (M.D. Tenn. 1993); Hurwitz v. Prime Communications, Inc., 23 UCCR2d 1213 (Mass. Super. 1994); Siam Numhong Prods. Co., Ltd. v. Eastimpex, 866 F. Supp. 445, 27 UCCR2d 59 (N.D. Cal. 1994); Borsih v. Grahm, 655 A.2d 831 (Del. Super. Ct. 1994); Brookside Farms v. Mama Rizzo's, Inc., 873 F. Supp. 1029, 28 UCCR2d 1110 (S.D. Tex. 1995). *Contra* First Nat'l Bank in Staunton v. McBride Chevrolet, Inc., 642 N.E.2d 138, 267 Ill. App. 3d 367, 204 Ill. Dec. 676 (Ill. App. Ct. 1994) (court said promissory estoppel is not an exception to statute of frauds).

[156] *See, e.g.,* Gladville v. McDole, 247 Ill. 34 (1910); Seymour v. Oelrichs, 156 Cal. 782 (1910).

[157] Sayer v. Bowley, 243 Neb. 801 (1993); Esso Geometric v. Harvard Indus., 46 F.3d 718, 25 UCCR2d 661 (8th Cir. 1995); Siam Numhong Prods. Co., Ltd v. Eastimpex, 866 F. Supp. 495, 27 UCCR2d 59 (N.D. Cal. 1994).

[158] Although the distinction between equitable estoppel and promissory estoppel has become blurred, the primary historical distinction is that equitable estoppel requires proof of the misrepresentation of an existing fact, while promissory estoppel requires proof of a promise.

[159] Restatement (Second) of Contracts § 139 (1981).

[160] 641 P.2d 628, 56 Or. App. 254, 33 UCCR 819 (1982).

[161] "Poults" are young turkeys.

There was no writing to evidence the contract, and none of the exceptions in section 2-201 was applicable. The court held, however, that Hatter was barred by promissory estoppel from raising the statute of frauds. The court's opinion relied upon most of the reasons courts have used to justify an estoppel exception. It said that if the drafters had intended estoppel to be unavailable as a supplementary principle of law under section 1-103, they would have said so explicitly.[162] The court also analogized the estoppel exception to the Code's obligation of good faith, and reasoned that if estoppel was not permitted as an exception to the statute of frauds, a party would be allowed to enter into an oral contract, induce another to detrimentally rely, and then escape any liability.[163] Finally, the court said that allowing an estoppel exception would further the purpose of the statute of frauds by preventing the statute from itself being used as an instrument of fraud. Anticipating concerns about the unpredictable and discretionary nature of the estoppel exception, the court said that "the legislature did not intend to provide predictability and consistency at the expense of equitable principles."[164]

There is a strong minority position that refuses to acknowledge an estoppel exception to the Code's statute of frauds.[165] Both textual and policy rationales have been offered for this position. Some courts have relied on the introductory language of section 2-201 for support.[166] Others have suggested that an estoppel exception would eviscerate the statute of frauds.[167] Still others have suggested that an estoppel exception breeds unnecessary confusion and uncertainty.[168]

---

[162] 56 Or. App. at 260, 641 P.2d at 632, 33 UCCR at 823.

[163] *Id.* at 261, 641 P.2d at 632, 33 UCCR at 825.

[164] *Id.* at 263, 641 P.2d at 633, 33 UCCR at 826.

[165] *See, e.g.,* Thomas v. Prewitt, 355 So. 2d 657, 23 UCCR 1001 (Miss. 1978).

[166] *See, e.g.,* C.G. Campbell & Son Inc. v. Comdeq Corp., 586 S.W.2d 40, 27 UCCR 11 (Ky. Ct. App. 1979); B&W Glass v. Weathershield Mfg., 829 P.2d 809, 18 UCCR 2d 1 (Wyo. 1992). U.C.C. § 2-201 begins "*Except as otherwise provided in this section* a contract for the sale of goods for the price of $500 or more is not enforceable . . . unless there is some writing sufficient to indicate that a contract for sale has been made . . . and signed by the party against whom enforcement is sought." These courts interpret this as an unambiguous statement by the legislature that the only exceptions to the statute are to be found in the section itself.

[167] *See, e.g.,* Anderson Constr. Co., Inc. v. Lyon Metal Prods. Inc., 370 So. 2d 935 (Miss. 1979).

[168] *See, e.g.,* Lige Dickson Co. v. Union Oil Co. of Cal., 635 P.2d 103 (Wash. 1981); McDabco, Inc. v. Chet Adams Co., 548 F. Supp. 456, 34 UCCR 1101 (D.S.C. 1982).

[E]   The Future of the Statute of Frauds

The statute of frauds has been increasingly criticized as being relatively ineffective at preventing fraud while at the same time resulting in significant injustice.[169] This is reflected in both the breadth of the statutory exceptions and the widespread adoption of an estoppel exception. An earlier draft of the proposed Article 2 revisions completely eliminated the Article 2 statute of frauds.[170] The authors are generally skeptical of the efficacy of the statute of frauds, and seriously doubt that many persons conjure up nonexistent contracts in order to defraud their neighbors; nevertheless, it arguably serves some other salutary purposes.

Most important, it probably moves some people to commit their contracts to writing who might not otherwise do so. While it may be true that most business people are not even aware of the Code's statute of frauds, some are (and certainly their lawyers are), and it probably influences the conduct of at least a few. In addition, many people reduce their contracts to writing under the erroneous impression that *all* contracts require a writing to be enforced.[171] If the Code's statute were abolished, this number would surely decrease. A writing not only provides good evidence that a contract exists, but prompts the parties to recognize and resolve issues that they might not otherwise deal with explicitly. Also, the statute of frauds probably decreases the amount of litigation by allowing some cases to be disposed of on summary judgment or motions to dismiss. With the statutory exceptions, and restitution and estoppel principles in place, it is not clear that abolition of the statute would lead to an overall increase in justice.

II.   FORMATION OF A CONTRACT OF SALE

§ 3.02   APPLICATION OF GENERAL CONTRACT PRINCIPLES TO CODE CASES

The law of sales is a branch of the more general law of contracts. The Code confirms this principle by providing that the broad rules of law ap-

---

[169] *See* Michael Braunstein, "Remedy, Reason and the Statute of Frauds: A Critical Economic Analysis," 1989 Utah L. Rev. 383 (1989); Arthur L. Corbin, Corbin on Contracts, § 429 at 469–472 (1960).

[170] American Law Institute, Uniform Commercial Code Revised Article 2, Sales, Council Draft No. 2 (Nov. 1, 1996).

[171] The authors are all teachers or former teachers of the first-year Contracts course. It is our common experience that many brand-new law students believe that contracts generally are not enforceable unless in writing.

plicable to contracts generally are applicable to the sale of goods unless specifically displaced by the Code:

> Unless displaced by the particular provisions of this Act, the principles of law and equity, including the law merchant and the law relative to capacity to contract, principal and agent, estoppel, fraud, misrepresentation, duress, coercion, mistake, bankruptcy, or other validating or invalidating cause shall supplement its provisions.[172]

All principles of law and equity which validate or invalidate a transaction are brought into the Code by this section.[173] Although the Code rests firmly on a foundation of general contract law,[174] there have been significant changes in some common-law principles.[175]

§ 3.03   CONTRACT FORMATION UNDER THE U.C.C.: SECTIONS 2-204 AND 2-206

The Code contains only two requirements for the formation of a contract: the parties must have intended to make a contract, and there must be a reasonably certain basis for giving an appropriate remedy.[176] There is no requirement that the contract be formed in a particular manner, nor does the Code require that the time of contract formation be determinable. The Code's liberal approach to contract formation both reflects recent contract doctrine and has played a role in its development.[177]

Although the Code does not say so explicitly, the requisite intention of the parties to a contract is their *objective* intention, as manifested either

---

[172] U.C.C. § 1-103.

[173] The Official Comments indicate that the drafters intended this provision to have considerable breadth. Official Comment 1 to U.C.C. § 1-103 states that " 'validating' as used here in conjunction with 'invalidating' is not intended as a narrow word confined to original validation, but extends to cover any factor which at any time or in any manner renders or helps to render valid any right or transaction."

[174] There has been occasional controversy in specific contexts over whether a general principle of contract law has been displaced by a specific Code provision. This has been most evident with respect to whether courts are free to apply estoppel as an exception to the Code's statute of frauds. *See* § 3.01[D], *supra*.

[175] A far greater number of changes were made by the Code to the contract doctrine prevailing at the time of its promulgation than by the Uniform Sales Act.

[176] U.C.C. § 2-204(3).

[177] Comment b to Restatement (Second) of Contracts § 22 relies on U.C.C. § 2-204 and 2-207 for the propositions that it is unnecessary to determine the precise time of the making of a contract or which party made the offer or acceptance.

through their words or conduct.[178] This intention can be manifested in any manner sufficient to show agreement. If the existence of a contract is shown by the conduct of the parties, it is unnecessary to establish which party was the offeror and which was the offeree.[179]

Conduct establishing a contract has often been found in the shipment and acceptance of goods,[180] but other conduct has sufficed as well. For example, in *Caisson Corp. v. Ingersoll-Rand*,[181] when the seller assembled the goods for the buyer, monitored its operation, and responded to problems by sending people to the job site and replacing broken parts, the court found a contract through the conduct of the parties. In another case, a court held representations to a third party by a seller was conduct tending to establish a contract.[182] Another case found conduct creating a contract when a buyer remained silent after receiving an executed contract from a farmer who had contracted to sell his cotton crop.[183]

The Code cases follow the general principle that parties can conclude a contract even though they contemplate the execution of a formal instrument at some time in the future.[184] Although the Statute of Frauds can present enforcement problems when no writing is eventually signed, the issue of contract creation (as opposed to enforcement) is determined by whether the parties intended to be bound at the time of their oral understanding or only upon the execution of a writing.

Section 2-206 is an example of the Code's bias in favor of contract formation. Beginning with "unless otherwise *unambiguously* agreed by the language or circumstances," section 2-206 codifies a principle that has become the general law of contracts:[185]

---

[178] *See* Computer Network Ltd. v. Purcell Tire & Rubber Co., 747 S.W.2d 669, 6 UCCR2d 642 (Mo. Ct. App. 1988); Cohn v. Fisher, 118 N.J. Super. 286, 287 A.2d 22, 10 UCCR 372 (1972); U.C.C. § 2-204(1).

[179] *See* U.C.C. § 2-207, Official Comment 7.

[180] *See* Quaker State Mushroom Co. v. Dominick's Finer Foods, Inc., 635 F. Supp. 1281, 1 UCCR2d 365 (N.D. Ill. 1986).

[181] 622 F.2d 672, 29 UCCR 47 (3d Cir. 1980). *See also* Nebraska Builders Prods. Co. v. The Industrial Erectors, Inc., 239 Neb. 744, 478 N.W.2d 257, 16 UCCR2d 568 (1992) (sufficient conduct in preparation and submission of shop drawings by seller, reliance on contract by buyer in submitting bid, and visit by seller to buyer's office to discuss use of equipment).

[182] Apex Oil Co. v. Vanguard Oil & Serv. Co., 760 F.2d 417, 40 UCCR 1221 (2d Cir. 1985).

[183] Austin v. Montgomery, 336 So. 2d 745, 20 UCCR 265 (Miss. 1976).

[184] *See* H.B. Zachry Co. v. O'Brien, 378 F.2d 423 (10th Cir. 1967); Williams v. Fixdal, 6 Wash. App. 24, 491 P.2d 1309 (1971).

[185] *See* Restatement (Second) of Contracts § 30(2) (1981).

an offer to make a contract shall be construed as inviting acceptance in any manner and by any medium reasonable in the circumstances.[186]

Consider this situation: On November 1, Buyer mails Seller an offer to buy goods for a stated price "if Seller promises to have the goods delivered by December 1." Seller responds by a facsimile, which states that Seller will have the goods delivered by December 1. Early common law had difficulty in finding that the response was an acceptance because Seller used something other than the mails to convey the words of acceptance. This is no longer the law and probably has not been for quite some time. Such technical rules have been rejected in favor of the test of whether the medium was "reasonable under the circumstances."[187]

If, instead of sending any response, Seller had put the goods on a truck which arrived at Buyer's place of business on November 15, early common law had a different problem. Buyer asked for a promise; instead Buyer received an act. As a result no contract was formed.[188] The common law strained to rid itself of so demanding a rule.[189] The Code is more straightforward. First, the shipment is a "manner" of acceptance within the above quoted language[190] and becomes an acceptance if reasonable under the circumstances. Second, the Code goes on to provide that, unless the offer or circumstances unambiguously indicate to the contrary, an offer to buy goods for prompt or current shipment is to be construed as inviting acceptance

---

[186] U.C.C. § 2-206(a).

[187] U.C.C. § 2-206, Official Comment.

[188] Under the common law, there were two categories of offers: offers to form bilateral contracts and offers to form unilateral contracts. *See* Restatement (First) of Contracts § 12 (1932). Under the classical approach to contract formation, an offer sought *either* a promissory acceptance or acceptance by performance. If the offer proposed a unilateral contract, the offeree could not accept by promising to perform. Conversely, if the offer proposed a bilateral contract, performance would not suffice. *See* Davis v. Jacoby, 1 Cal. 2d 370, 34 P.2d 1026 (1934).

[189] For example, if a person made an offer to a bilateral contract, he could not simply stand by and watch the other party (who had not rendered a promissory acceptance) perform and then disavow the contract. Also, if an offeree to a bilateral contract performed within the time provided for a promissory acceptance and provided timely notice of performance to the offeror, a contract was formed. Restatement (First) of Contracts § 63 (1932). *See* Allied Steel & Conveyors, Inc. v. Ford Motor Co., 277 F.2d 907 (6th Cir. 1960).

[190] Although the official comments indicate that this portion of U.C.C. § 2-206 is meant primarily to eliminate the rule that an acceptance must be rendered through the same medium as the offer, section 2-206 refers to the "manner" of acceptance as well as the medium of acceptance.

either by a prompt promise or by the prompt or current shipment of the goods.[191]

Section 2-206(1)(b) goes further. An offer to buy goods invites acceptance by the shipment of either conforming or nonconforming goods. If Buyer had ordered goods classed as "X-A" and Seller shipped goods classed as "X-B," the shipment can be simultaneously an acceptance and a default. Seller may, however, prevent contract formation when the X-B goods are shipped if Seller notifies Buyer that the X-B goods are being shipped as an accommodation to Buyer.

There are two caveats to this discussion. First, the offeror may *unambiguously* require a response by mail, facsimile, telephone, or (to put the situation to the extreme) carrier pigeon. The offeror may also *unambiguously* require a promise and not an act, or an act and not a promise. If the offeror does either of these, the response must comply if the response is to be an acceptance.[192] Second, even if the seller does not unambiguously require a particular response, the response must be reasonable in the circumstances. If the circumstances known to the parties require that Buyer have knowledge of the seller's acceptance prior to the arrival of the goods on November 15, shipment is not an invited method of acceptance.

Subsection (2) of 2-206 provides:

> where the beginning of a requested performance is a reasonable mode of acceptance, an offeror who is not notified of acceptance within a reasonable time may treat the offer as having lapsed before acceptance.

This subsection is ambiguous and is intended either to create a contract immediately upon the beginning of performance, conditional upon the offeree's providing timely notice of acceptance, or to make an offer irrevocable for a reasonable period of time after the beginning of performance necessary to provide the notice of acceptance.[193] In either case, once performance has

---

[191] U.C.C. § 2-206(1)(b). *But see* Hill v. Gateway 2000, Inc., 105 F.3d 1147 (7th Cir. 1997) (court appears to ignore U.C.C. § 2-206(1)(b) in its analysis of contract formation). *See* the discussion of the *Hill* case at § 4.07[C][3], *infra*.

[192] The indication must be *unambiguous*. It is not enough to state "ship at once" or the like. U.C.C. § 2-206, Official Comment 2. There must be some expression or some circumstance that clearly makes the offer different from the usual or ordinary offer.

[193] It appears that the drafters intended the former interpretation. If the beginning of a requested performance is a reasonable mode of acceptance, then the beginning of that performance will necessarily create a contract. Further, the section says that if timely notice of acceptance is not provided, the offeror "may treat" the offer as having lapsed; it does not say that the offer *will* have lapsed. The proposed revisions to Article 2 make it clear that a contract is formed upon the beginning of performance, which is then discharged if timely notice is not provided. *See* Council Draft No. 4, § 2-206(b).

begun, the offeror no longer has the power to revoke the offer. Unless the offer stipulates otherwise, it is not necessary that the offeror receive notice of acceptance, so long as it is properly dispatched.[194]

The relationship between subsection (1)(b) and subsection (2) of section 2-206 is unclear. If there is an offer for prompt or current shipment, subsection (1)(b) says that acceptance occurs upon shipment of the goods. Comment 2 says that the term "shipment" is used in the same sense as it is in section 2-504; "shipment" apparently does not include preparations to ship the goods, nor delivery by the seller or his agent.[195] However, the same Comment indicates that under subsection (2), loading on the seller's own trucks "might" be a "beginning-of-performance" acceptance. Thus, an acceptance may occur to an offer for prompt or current shipment prior to the actual shipment of the goods, so long as the beginning of performance is a reasonable mode of acceptance.[196]

The primary effect of sections 2-204 and 2-206 is to enable courts to find a contract where commercial reality recognizes the existence of a contract. Although these sections have been cited in numerous cases, they have generated little controversy and largely remain unchanged in the proposed revisions to Article 2. The same can hardly be said about the next section of the Code.

§ 3.04   THE DEVIANT ACCEPTANCE

[A] Introduction

Probably no section of Article 2 has generated more controversy and resulted in more commentary than section 2-207. Law reviews continue to

---

[194] See U.C.C. § 1-201(26).

[195] See U.C.C. § 2-606, Official Comment 2 ("shipment" does not include the beginning of delivery by the seller's own truck or by messenger).

[196] See Barto v. United States, 823 F. Supp. 1369, 21 UCCR2d 924 (E.D. Mich. 1993) (dealer accepted buyer's offer to buy Mercedes by placing an order for the car and cashing buyer's check); Nasco, Inc. v. Dahltron Corp., 74 Ill. App. 3d 302, 392 N.E.2d 1110, 27 UCCR 360 (1979) (buyer's knowledge of seller's preparation to produce goods sufficient to constitute acceptance under U.C.C. § 2-206).

Under the Restatement (Second) of Contracts § 62, if the offer seeks *only* acceptance by performance (i.e., an offer to enter a "unilateral" contract) the beginning of performance renders the offer irrevocable but does not create a contract until performance is complete. Given the strong presumption in section 2-206, however, that offers for prompt or current shipment can be accepted either by promise or performance—they are not offers to unilateral contracts—the beginning of performance will often be sufficient to constitute acceptance under the Code. Even if the offer seeks acceptance only by performance, the rule of the Restatement (Second) § 62 should apply as a supplementary principle under section 1-103 to make the offer irrevocable.

print scholarly critiques of section 2-207[197] more than twenty-five years after the first such article appeared and after more than a hundred have intervened.[198] It is unlikely that any rule of law on which the fate of the Republic does not hinge justifies this degree of attention. The number of reported cases citing section 2-207, however, which now numbers close to 1,000, indicates that at least some of this scholarly dissection is deserved.

The following example offers a starting point to begin the analysis of section 2-207. Assume that a buyer wants to purchase widgets from a seller and sends the seller its purchase order form. The form, prepared by the buyer's attorney, contains a number of printed clauses, with several blank spaces in which the buyer has typed the name of the seller, a description of the goods, the quantity and price of the goods, and the date and method of delivery. The form contains no provision dealing with arbitration of disputes.

The seller receives the buyer's order, decides it can fill the order, and responds to the buyer with an acknowledgement form in which the description, quantity, and price of the goods, as well as the delivery provisions, all agree with those on the buyer's form. The seller's form, however, also contains many printed paragraphs, few of which agree with those on the buyer's form. One of these printed provisions requires that disputes be submitted to arbitration. Despite this disparity between the printed forms, the seller ships the goods, and the buyer accepts and pays for them.

Three questions immediately arise from this simple hypothetical. Has a contract been formed? If so, how was it formed? What are its terms?

Under pre-Code common law, the answer would probably be that a contract was formed when the buyer accepted the goods, and that the terms of the contract were those on the seller's form.[199] Pre-Code common law would treat the seller's acknowledgment—deviating as it did from the buyer's offer—not as an acceptance, but as a counteroffer. When the seller then shipped the goods, the acceptance of the goods by the buyer operated as an acceptance of the seller's counteroffer on the terms of the acknowledgment form, including the arbitration clause. It has been said that a response to an offer had to be the "mirror image" of the offer before it could act as an acceptance. Otherwise, it was a counteroffer or, perhaps, a rejection.

The common-law "mirrow-image" rule worked without serious difficulty at a time when parties individually and carefully negotiated most trans-

---

[197] *See, e.g.*, John D. Wladis, "Ending the 'Battle of the Forms': A Symposium on the Revision of Section 2-207 of the Uniform Commerical Code," 49 Bus. Law. 1029 (1994).

[198] One of the authors is guilty of contributing to this plethora. *See* Gregory M. Travalio, "Clearing the Air After the Battle: Reconciling Fairness and Efficiency in a Formal Approach to U.C.C. Section 2-207," 33 Case W. Res. L. Rev. 327 (1983).

[199] Much of the analysis in this section is taken from Travalio, *supra* note 198 at 329.

actions. As commercial actors increased in size and complexity, however, the assumptions underlying the mirror-image rule became increasingly unrealistic. As the size of firms increased, the number of their customers, transactions, and suppliers also increased. Clerks with neither the authority to negotiate on behalf of their employers, nor the time and training to analyze correspondence in detail, often were responsible for routine transactions.[200] Firms began using form documents in which each party included printed terms designed to operate in their favor. Thus was born the boilerplate of modern purchase and acknowledgment forms.

Differences in the forms were generally ignored. In the typical case, where the goods were shipped, the price was paid, and the goods functioned satisfactorily, the differences in the forms created no problem. Sometimes, however, these differences, in conjunction with the common-law mirror-image rule, led to unexpected results. For example, if the buyer sought to withdraw from the transaction prior to accepting the goods, the buyer merely had to find a variation in the two forms to avoid the deal, even though both parties had assumed that a binding contract already existed.[201] Or, if after accepting the goods, the buyer complained about their quality or performance, the buyer might find itself bound by a printed disclaimer of warranties on the seller's form.

The drafters of the Code believed that the common-law mirror-image rule did not reflect commercial reality and frustrated the reasonable expectations of the parties. The arbitrary preference for the party (usually the seller) sending the last document did not seem fair nor did it appear to reflect the understanding of parties transacting in the commercial arena. Despite the risks of surprise, however, people continued to transact business through their forms because of the efficiency benefits the forms provided. The drafters decided that the law needed to reflect this reality, and at the same time provide for a better result when problems arose.

[B] Section 2-207

Section 2-207 provides in full:

> (1) A definite and seasonable expression of acceptance or a written confirmation which is sent within a reasonable time operates as an acceptance even though it states terms additional to or different from those

---

[200] *See* Stewart Macaulay, "Non-Contractual Relations in Business: A Preliminary Study," 28 Am. Soc. Rev. 55, 59 (1963); Stewart Macaulay, "The Use and Non-Use of Contracts in the Manufacturing Industry," (Prac. Law, Nov. 1963 at 13, 22, 28–29).

[201] *See, e.g.*, Rugg v. Davis, 15 Ill. App. 647 (1885).

offered or agreed upon, unless acceptance is expressly made conditional on assent to the additional or different terms.

(2) The additional terms are to be construed as proposals for addition to the contract. Between merchants such terms become part of the contract unless:

    (a)   the offer expressly limits acceptance to the terms of the offer;

    (b)   they materially alter it; or

    (c)   notification of objection to them has already been given or is given within a reasonable time after notice of them is received.

(3) Conduct by both parties which recognizes the existence of a contract is sufficient to establish a contract for sale although the writings of the parties do not otherwise establish a contract. In such case the terms of the particular contract consist of those terms on which the writings of the parties agree, together with any supplementary terms incorporated under any other provisions of this Act.

In the simple example above, the seller's acknowledgment form would create a contract, despite the mirror-image rule, so long as it was a "definite and seasonable expression of acceptance." Section 2-207 allows a document to be a definite and seasonable expression of acceptance even though it states terms additional to or different from those offered.

Assuming that the acknowledgment is a definite and seasonable expression of acceptance, section 2-207(2) determines whether the arbitration provision becomes part of the contract. Because both parties are merchants, the arbitration provision will become part of the contract unless (1) the buyer's offer expressly limited acceptance to its terms; (2) the arbitration provision was a *material* alteration of the contract;[202] or (3) the buyer seasonably notified the seller of its objection to the arbitration provision.

---

[202] Courts have disagreed on whether arbitration provisions are material alterations. *Compare* Valmont Indus. Inc. v. Mitsui & Co. (U.S.A.) Inc., 419 F. Supp. 1238, 20 UCCR 662 (1976) (material alteration); Franes Hosiery Mills, Inc. v. Burlington Indus., Inc., 19 N.C. App. 678, 200 S.E.2d 668, 13 UCCR 759, *aff'd*, 285 N.C. 344, 204 S.E.2d 668, 14 UCCR 1110 (1974); Stanley-Bostick, Inc. v. Regenerative Envtl. Equip. Co., Inc., 697 A.2d 323, 35 UCCR2d 828 (R.I. 1997) (material alteration) *with* Dixie Aluminum Prods. Co. v. Mitsubishi Int'l Corp., 785 F. Supp. 157, 17 UCCR2d 1073 (N.D. Ga. 1992) (not material alteration); Polyclad Laminates, Inc. v. Vits Maschinenbau GmbH, 749 F. Supp. 342, 13 UCCR2d 721 (D.N.H. 1990) (not material alteration); Levy v. Gateway 2000, Inc., 33 UCCR2d 1060 (N.Y. Sup. Ct. 1997) (not material alteration). The decision as to whether an arbitration clause in one form is a material alteration will (and should) often depend upon the particular industry or trade in which the parties are operating. *See* Hatzlachh Supply, Inc. v. Moishe's Elecs., Inc., 828 F. Supp. 178, 22 UCCR2d 667 (S.D.N.Y. 1993) (rejects "per se" rule that arbitration clauses are material alternations).

The above hypothetical is the kind of situation the drafters had in mind when they created section 2-207. Unfortunately, real transactions do not always follow the paths of professors' hypotheticals, and problems have arisen which the drafters did not envision and which section 2-207 was not designed to solve. The remainder of this chapter deals with the most salient of these problems.

[C] Definite and Seasonable Expression of Acceptance

Is the response a "definite and seasonable expression of acceptance?" Although section 2-207 alters the mirror-image rule, it does not change the ability of a person to respond to an offer by a rejection or counteroffer. To form a contract under section 2-207, a response to an offer still must be a definite and seasonable expression of acceptance. Comment 2 provides the starting point: "Under this Article a proposed deal which in commercial understanding has in fact been closed is recognized as a contract." This comment directs attention to the particular commercial environment in which the parties are operating. In one commercial setting, a response would be a definite and seasonable expression of acceptance, while in another commercial setting, the same response would not satisfy the standard.[203] Consistent with the fundamental theme of Article 2, the law attempts to reflect commercial reality.

Within the specific commercial environment, the proper test is whether a reasonable offeror receiving the offeree's response would consider the deal to be closed.[204] The mere presence of terms in the offeree's form that are different from or additional to those in the offeror's form is, of course, not sufficient to preclude a contract; this would render section 2-207 meaningless. Even the presence of *material* differences in the two forms does not necessarily prevent the formation of a contract. Unfortunately, one of the first cases dealing with section 2-207 missed this crucial point.

In *Roto-Lith, Ltd. v. F.P. Bartlett & Co.,*[205] the buyer sent a purchase order for glue to the seller. The purchase order said nothing about warranties. The seller responded with an acknowledgment form that conspicuously dis-

---

[203] *See* Gardner Zemke Co. v. Dunham Bush, Inc., 115 N.M. 260, 850 P.2d 319, 324, 20 UCCR2d 842 (1993); Gryptal v. Englehard Corp., 801 F. Supp. 887, 893, 18 UCCR2d 1059 (D. Mass. 1992).

[204] *See* Gardner Zemke Co. v. Dunham Bush, Inc., 115 N.M. 260, 850 P.2d 319, 20 UCCR2d 842 (1993); John E. Murray Jr., "Section 2-207 of the Uniform Commercial Code: Another Word About Incipient Unconscionability," 39 U. Pitt. L. Rev. 597, 602 (1978).

[205] 297 F.2d 497, 1 UCCR 79 (1st Cir. 1962), *overruled* Ionics v. Elmwood Sensors, Inc., 32 UCCR2d 1 (1st Cir. 1997).

claimed implied warranties. When the glue failed to adhere, the buyer sued the seller for breach of warranty.

The court in *Roto-Lith* held that the acknowledgment form was a counteroffer that was accepted when the buyer accepted the goods. The court's reasoning was that any response that materially alters the offer to the disadvantage of the offeror must be considered to be a counteroffer, not an acceptance.[206] When the buyer accepted the goods, it accepted the seller's counteroffer, and thus the goods were sold without implied warranty.

This reasoning is assuredly incorrect, virtually all subsequent courts have rejected it,[207] and the case, after standing for thirty-five years, was recently overruled.[208] A careful reading of sections 2-207(1) and 2-207(2)(b) makes it clear that a response form, such as a seller's acknowledgment, may constitute a "definite and reasonable" expression of acceptance even though it contains a term or terms that "materially alter" the offer. Subsection 2-207(2)(b) plainly contemplates the formation of a contract in this circumstance, with the terms of the response which materially alter the contract dropping out. While this subsection does not permit terms that materially alter the terms of the offer to become part of the contract, it necessarily assumes that a contract has been formed by the response.

In deciding whether a response is a "definite and seasonable expression of acceptance" the courts have focused on whether the negotiated or "dickered" terms agree.[209] When the dickered terms agree, and the parties go ahead and perform, the response form will generally be found to be a definite and seasonable expression of acceptance, at least if it does not contain "conditional assent" language attempting to prevent contract formation.[210] When the dickered terms do not agree, a contract will not result from the exchange of forms, although a contract may result from the subsequent conduct of the parties.[211]

---

[206] *Id.* at 500.

[207] Although the reasoning in *Roto-Lith* was faulty, the *result* may be defensible. There is some indication in the case that the buyer was actually aware of the disclaimer and its importance to the seller. Thus, if the disclaimer was more in the nature of a dickered term, although not explicitly negotiated, it should be a part of the contract. *See* Thomas D. Crandall, et al., I Uniform Commercial Code § 4.3.5, at 4:18 (1993).

[208] Ionics v. Elmwood Sensors, Inc., 32 UCCR2d 1 (1st Cir. 1997).

[209] *See* United States Indus., Inc. v. Semco Mfg., Inc., 562 F.2d 1061, 22 UCCR 589 (8th Cir. 1977); Bergquist Co. Sunroc, 777 F. Supp. 1236, 16 UCCR2d 1013 (E.D. Pa. 1991).

[210] *See* § 3.04[C][1], *infra*.

[211] *See* Lambert v. Kysar, 983 F.2d 1110, 19 UCCR2d 979 (1st Cir. 1993) (difference in quantity between buyer's and seller's forms results in a counteroffer by offeree-buyer accepted by seller's shipment); Caribe BMW, Inc. v. Bayerishe Motoren Werke Aktiengesellschaft, 821 F. Supp. 802 (D.P.R. 1993).

[1] The "Conditional" Acceptance

Unfortunately, the drafters encumbered section 2-207(1) with a clause that has created immense difficulty. According to section 2-207(1), a definite and seasonable expression of acceptance "operates as an acceptance *unless* the acceptance is expressly made conditional on the offeror's assent to the additional or different terms."[212] The apparent consequence of this exception is that a response that is otherwise a definite and seasonable expression of acceptance[213] will not conclude a contract if the offeree has expressed an intention not to proceed unless the original offeror assents to the terms on the offeree's response. Two issues arise: first, what must the offeree do in order to make an effective "conditional acceptance?" Second, if the parties proceed with performance with no further communication, is there a contract, and what are its terms?

The leading case on the issue of the prerequisites of an effective "conditional acceptance" is *Dorton v. Collins & Aikman Corp.*[214] In this case, the seller responded to the buyer's oral purchase offers for carpet with printed acknowledgment forms. Each of the acknowledgment forms had a provision on the face of the form making the acceptance of the buyer's order "subject to" all of the terms and conditions on both sides of the acknowledgment form, and providing that the acknowledgment form would "supersede" terms of the buyer's order. The seller's acknowledgment form further provided that all claims arising under the contract would be submitted to arbitration. The buyer's oral purchase offer apparently did not include arbitration.[215]

After the seller delivered the goods, a dispute arose as to the quality of the carpet. When the buyer filed suit for breach of warranty, the seller moved for a stay pending arbitration based upon the clause in its acknowledgment. The district court refused to grant the stay, holding that, because of the divergence in terms, no contract was formed by the seller's response. Instead, the parties' conduct in shipping and accepting the goods established a contract under section 2-207(3).[216] Because, under section 2-207(3), arbitration is not a supplementary term supplied by the Code, the buyer was not bound to arbitrate.

---

[212] U.C.C. § 2-207(1).

[213] The clause in U.C.C. § 2-207 beginning with "unless" only applies to a response that is a "definite and seasonable expression of acceptance."

[214] 453 F.2d 1161, 10 UCCR 585 (6th Cir. 1972).

[215] The district court assumed that the buyer's offer was silent as to arbitration, without making a specific finding. 453 F.2d at 1165, 10 UCCR at 592.

[216] 453 F.2d at 1165, 10 UCCR at 592.

In reviewing the district court's decision, the Sixth Circuit recognized that under the common-law mirror-image rule, the buyer would have been obligated to arbitrate the dispute. Because the terms on the acknowledgment form were different from the offer, the seller's response to the offer would have been construed as a counteroffer. The buyer's acceptance of the goods without objection would have been an acceptance of the counteroffer, including the arbitration provision. The court, however, stated that "[u]nder § 2-207 the result is different."

The court then turned to the issue of whether the language in the seller's form making acceptance "subject to" the terms and conditions on the seller's form meant that the acceptance was "expressly made conditional on [the buyer's] assent to the additional or different terms," thus precluding the seller's response from forming a contract. The court decided that the language was insufficient to make the acceptance conditional, and found that a contract was created by the seller's response.[217]

The court noted that the language used in the seller's form deviated from the language of the statute; it did not make the acceptance *expressly* conditional on the buyer's *assent* to the seller's terms.[218] Using language quoted in many subsequent cases,[219] the court stated that the subsection (1) proviso was intended to apply only to an "acceptance" which clearly reveals that the offeree is unwilling to proceed with the transaction unless he is assured of the offeree's assent to the additional or different terms.[220] That the acceptance is conditional upon the offeror's assent must be "directly and distinctly stated."[221]

With a few exceptions,[222] the restrictive approach of the *Dorton* case to the section 2-207(1) proviso has been adopted by most other courts.[223]

---

[217] Actually, this holding was contingent upon a finding, upon remand, that the seller's acknowledgment was an acceptance rather than a confirmation of a preexisting oral contract.

[218] *Dorton*, at 1168, 10 UCCR at 593.

[219] *See, e.g.*, Idaho Power Co. v. Westinghouse Elec. Corp., 596 F.2d 924, 26 UCCR 538 (9th Cir. 1979); Air Masters Sales Co. v. Northridge Park Co-Op, Inc., 748 F. Supp. 1110, 13 UCCR 2d 726 (D.N.J. 1990); Argo Welded Prods., Inc. v. J.T. Ryerson Steel & Sons Inc., 528 F. Supp. 583, 33 UCCR 1349 (E.D. Pa. 1981); Mace Indus. v. Paddock Pool Equip. Co., 288 S.C. 65, 339 S.E.2d 527, 42 UCCR 825 (Ct. App. 1986).

[220] *Dorton*, at 1168, 10 UCCR at 593.

[221] *Id.* at 1168, 10 UCCR at 594.

[222] *See, e.g.*, Construction Aggregates Corp. v. Hewitt-Robins, Inc., 404 F.2d 505, 6 UCCR 112 (5th Cir. 1969) (dictum); Ionics, Inc. v. Elmwood Sensors, Inc., 110 F.3d 184 (1st Cir. 1997) (language stating response was a "counteroffer" which would be accepted unless rejected within ten days of receipt was a "conditional acceptance").

[223] *See* Gardner Zemke Co. v. Dunham Bush, Inc., 115 N.M. 260, 850 P.2d 319, 20 UCCR2d 842 (1993) (acceptance not expressly conditional that stated it was subject to terms

This is consistent with the basic assumption of section 2-207 that parties frequently intend to form contracts upon the exchange of forms even though the forms contain boilerplate languge that does not coincide and frequently goes unread by either party. The intent of section 2-207 is that responsive documents that look like acceptances (minus the boilerplate) should function as acceptances. To easily allow boilerplate language to create "conditional acceptances" would significantly frustrate this intent. Requiring strict adherence to the statutory language is more a result of this consideration than any real difference in meaning between the language used by the seller in *Dorton* and the statutory language.[224]

On the other hand, when the language of the form closely tracks the language of the section 2-207(1) proviso, most courts have given it effect, thus preventing contract formation upon the exchange of forms.[225] This has occurred even when the statute-tracking language was among other printed provisions and just as likely to go unread as the language in *Dorton*.[226]

---

and conditions on reverse side of acceptance form); McCarty v. Verson Allsteel Press Co., 89 Ill. App. 3d 498, 411 N.E.2d 936, 44 Ill. Dec. 570, 30 UCCR 440 (1980); Clifford-Jacobs Forging Co. v. Capital Eng'g Mfg. Co., 107 Ill. App. 3d 29, 437 N.E.2d 22, 62 Ill. Dec. 785, 34 UCCR 24 (1982) (acceptance stating it was accepted in accord with terms on reverse side held not expressly conditional); Boese-Hilburn Co. v. Dean Mach. Co., 616 S.W.2d 520; 31 UCCR 830 (Mo. Ct. App. 1981); Daitom, Inc. v. Pennwalt Corp., 741 F.2d 1569, 39 UCCR 1203 (10th Cir. 1984) (acceptance merely stating it was expressly limited to its terms is not expressly conditional because it does state unwillingness to form a contract); AEL Indus., Inc. v. Loral Fairchild Corp., 882 F. Supp. 1477, 27 UCCR2d 1171 (E.D. Pa. 1995).

[224] *See* Idaho Power Co. v. Westinghouse Elec. Corp., 596 F.2d 924, 26 UCCR 683 (9th Cir. 1979); Reaction Molding Technologies, Inc. v. General Elec. Co., 588 F. Supp. 1280, 38 UCCR 1537 (E.D. Pa. 1984); Lockheed Elecs. Co. v. Keronix, Inc., 114 Cal. App. 3d 304, 170 Cal. Rptr. 591, 30 UCCR 827 (Cal. Ct. of App. 1981); Clifford-Jacobs Forging Co. v. Capital Eng'g & Mfg. Co., 107 Ill. App. 3d 29, 437 N.E.2d 22, 62 Ill. Dec. 785, 34 UCCR 24 (1982); Gardner Zemke Co. v. Dunham Bush, Inc., 115 N.M. 260, 850 P.2d 319, 20 UCCR 842 (1993).

[225] *See, e.g.,* Luria Bros. & Co. v. Pielet Bros. Scrap Iron & Metal, 600 F.2d 103, 26 UCCR 1081 (7th Cir. 1979); Dresser Indus., Inc. v. The Gradall Co., 702 F. Supp. 725 (E.D. Wis. 1988); American Tempering, Inc. v. Craft Architectural Metals Corp., 107 A.D.2d 565, 483 N.Y.S.2d 304 (App. Div. 1984); Reaction Molding Technologies, Inc. v. General Elec. Co., 588 F. Supp. 1280, 38 UCCR 1537 (1984); Air Masters Sales Co. v. Northridge Park Co-Op, 784 F. Supp. 1110, 13 UCCR3d 711 (N.J. 1990). The proposed revisions to Article 2 provide that "Language which expressly conditions the intention to contract upon agreement by the other party to terms proposed prevents contract formation." Council Draft No. 4, § 2-203(d).

[226] The rigid adherence to the statutory language required by the court is justified by the ease with which lower level personnel can then be trained to look for and identify "conditional acceptance" language in responsive forms without having to confront difficult issues of interpretation, and the certainty it provides to commercial transactions. *See* Travalio, *supra*

Assume now that conditional language in the seller's (offeree's) form is effective to prevent contract formation, but the seller nevertheless ships the goods and the buyer accepts them. If a dispute as to terms arises, whose form (if anyone's) controls?

The seminal case on this issue is *C. Itoh & Co. v. Jordan International Co.*[227] *Itoh* was a classic battle of the forms, with the parties' disparate printed terms passing unnoticed like ships in the night. Itoh (the buyer) submitted a purchase order for steel coils to Jordan (the seller). The seller responded with an acknowledgment that included (on its front) a printed provision stating:

> Seller's acceptance is, however, expressly conditional on Buyer's assent to the additional or different terms and conditions set forth below and printed on the reverse side. If these terms and conditions are not acceptable, Buyer should notify Seller at once.

The reverse side of the acknowledgment form contained a provision for arbitration of disputes. The buyer neither expressly assented to nor objected to any terms on the acknowledgment form and the coils were delivered and accepted. When the coils were discovered to be defective, the buyer sued the seller, who sought to have the suit stayed pending arbitration.

The court concluded that the language in the acknowledgment was an acceptance that was expressly conditioned on the offeror's assent to the additional or different terms on the acknowledgment. Consequently, the acknowledgment was a counteroffer, not an acceptance. Contrary to common law, however, the court said that the acceptance of the goods by the buyer was not an acceptance of the counteroffer. Rather, a contract was created under section 2-207(3) by conduct of the parties that recognized the existence of a contract. As a result, the terms of the contract were those on which the writings agreed, together with terms supplied by the Code, which meant that the contract did not require arbitration of disputes.

While the result in *Itoh* is correct,[228] and has been consistently followed in subsequent cases,[229] the court did not provide a convincing rationale for

---

note 198 at 364–365 (1983). *See also* N&D Fashions, Inc. v. DHJ Indus., Inc., 548 F.2d 722, 20 UCCR 847 (8th Cir. 1977).

[227] 552 F.2d 1228, 21 UCCR 353 (7th Cir. 1977).

[228] *See* § 3.04[E], *infra*.

[229] *See, e.g.*, Transwestern Pipeline Co. v. Monsanto Co., 53 Cal. Rptr. 887, 29 UCCR2d 1178 (Cal. Ct. App. 1996); Arizona Retail Sys., Inc. v. Software Link, Inc., 831 F. Supp. 759, 22 UCCR2d 70 (D. Ariz. 1993); Diamond Fruit Growers, Inc. v. Krack Corp., 794 F.2d 1440, 1 UCCR2d 1073 (9th Cir. 1986); Luria Bros. & Co. v. Pielet Bros. Scrap Iron & Metal Inc., 600 F.2d 103, 26 UCCR 1081 (7th Cir. 1979); Idaho Power Co. v. Westinghouse Elec. Corp., 596 F.2d 924, 26 UCCR 638 (9th Cir. 1979); Frank M. Booth, Inc. v. Reynolds

its decision. While it described the seller's response as a counteroffer, it did not treat it as a counteroffer in the classical common-law manner. According to one author, the court treated the response as if the seller had simply *rejected* the buyer's offer and thus left nothing further on the table.[230] When the parties then proceeded to perform, the court treated the contract as having been created by their performance with no reference to the exchange of forms.

Even this analysis is not entirely satisfactory, however. If the seller's response was simply a rejection, the buyer would not have the power to conclude a contract by agreeing to the terms in the seller's form. Nowhere in the court's opinion, however, does the court suggest that Itoh's *express assent* to the terms on the seller's acknowledgment would not have sealed the deal. Had the buyer responded affirmatively to the proposals in the seller's form, there is little doubt that both parties (and undoubtedly the court) would have considered the deal to be closed. The court's characterization of the seller's response as a counteroffer was clearly correct. But, if so, then why wasn't the counteroffer accepted by the buyer's acceptance of the goods?

The simple explanation is that the court was unwilling to infer the buyer's assent to the counteroffer from the acceptance of the goods. To permit this inference would simply open the gate too wide for the return of the "last shot" doctrine that section 2-207 was designed to reverse. Because the underlying premise of section 2-207 is that the boilerplate generally goes unread or unheeded, it cannot be assumed that the buyer had read the conditional assent clause in the seller's form nor intended to be bound by the form's substantive terms.

The result in *Itoh,* and the cases which have followed it is proper. Given the assumption that *neither* side pays attention to the printed forms, other than to ensure that the "dickered terms" agree, the approach of the *Itoh* court avoids the unfairness of both a "first-shot" and a "last-shot" rule.[231]

Metal Co., 745 F. Supp. 1441, 13 UCCR2d 709 (E.D. Cal. 1991); Leonard Pevar Co. v. Evans Prods. Co., 524 F. Supp. 546, 32 UCCR 720 (D. Del. 1981); Scott Brass, Inc. v. C&C Metal Prods. Corp., 473 F. Supp. 1124, 27 UCCR 372 (D.R.I. 1979); Uniroyal, Inc. v. Chambers Gasket & Mfg. Co., 177 Ind. App. 508, 380 N.E.2d 571, 24 UCCR 1109 (1978); Ionics, Inc. v. Elmwood Sensors, Inc., 110 F.3d 184 (1st Cir. 1997). *Contra* Middletown Eng'g Co. v. Climate Conditioning Co., 810 S.W.2d 57, 15 UCCR2d 746 (Ky. Ct. App. 1991).

[230] Thomas D. Crandall et al., I Uniform Commercial Code 3:23 (1993).

[231] *See* Diamond Fruit Growers, Inc. v. Krack Corp., 794 F.2d 1440, 1449, 1 UCCR2d 1073, 1079 (9th Cir. 1986) (court applies U.C.C. § 2-207(3) despite offeree's refusal to alter its form to eliminate disclaimer because of section 2-207 principle of "neutrality").

By including a conditional assent clause, an offeree can efficiently avoid terms on the offeror's form that operate in a harsh, oppressive, or unexpected manner.[232] To accomplish this, the offeree must sacrifice the additional or different terms on its form, unless the offeror *expressly* assents to those terms, or they are otherwise included as supplementary terms under section 2-207(3).[233] Alternatively, the offeree can demand express assent before performing or simply choose not to contract through the use of printed forms.

This approach also protects the original offeror as well. The offeror may continue to operate with printed forms without fear of a hindsight determination that a response, because of a printed conditional assent clause, binds the offeror to the offeree's boilerplate. In addition, cases requiring that conditional assent clauses track the language of the statute provide a simple way of determining—should the offeror chose to examine the printed form—what legal consequences will follow if the parties proceed with performance without further negotiation.[234]

Section 2-207, however, should not be interpreted to preclude entirely the ability of an offeree to make a counteroffer that can be accepted on the terms proposed rather than those provided by section 2-207(3). If the offeree includes an effective conditional assent clause and the offeror *expressly assents* to the additional or different terms on the offeree's form, there is a contract on the offeree's terms. In addition, there are two other situations

---

[232] Travalio, *supra* note 198, at 370. Professor Murray has suggested that the doctrine of unconscionability should operate to prevent this result. John E. Murray, Jr., "Section 2-207 of the Uniform Commercial Code: Another Word About Incipient Unconscionability," 39 U. Pitt. L. Rev. 597 (1978); John E. Murray, Jr., "The Chaos of 'the Battle of the Forms': Solutions," 39 Vand. L. Rev. 1307 (1986); John E. Murray, Jr., "The Revision of Article 2: Romancing the Prism," 35 Wm. & Mary L. Rev. 1447 (1994). Given the development of the law of unconscionability, this solution is unsatisfactory. Unconscionability has rarely been applied in commercial contexts, and only then where there is a gross inequality of bargaining power. *See* U.C.C. § 2-302, Official Comment 2. *See also* Restatement (Second) of Contracts § 208, cmt. d; Ashland Oil, Inc. v. Donahue, 159 W. Va. 463, 223 S.E.2d 433 (Ct. App. 1976); John W. Lodge Distrib. Co. v. Texaco, Inc., 161 W. Va. 603, 245 S.E.2d 157 (1978); American Nursery Prods. Inc. v. Indian Wells Orchards, 115 Wash. 2d 217, 797 P.2d 477, 12 UCCR2d 928 (1990). In addition, many of the clauses, such as warranty disclaimers and broad liability for consequential damages that sellers and buyers routinely place in their forms are hardly unconscionable. U.C.C. § 2-718.

[233] *But see* Ralph Shrader, Inc. v. Diamond Int'l Corp., 833 F.2d 1210, 4 UCCR 2d 1362 (6th Cir. 1987) (whether offeror *assented* to additional or different terms by acceptance of and payment for the goods is a question of fact for the jury).

[234] Travalio, *supra* note 198, at 371. Further, because the conditional acceptance language must closely track the statute to be effective, this examination can be done by fairly low-level employees. *Id.*

where an offeree might be deemed to accept the terms on the offeree's form in the absence of express assent.

The first is when the parties do not communicate through printed forms[235] or their functional equivalent.[236] While the text of section 2-207 is not limited to communication by printed forms, there is substantial evidence that this is the problem that the drafters of section 2-207 intended to confront, and application of section 2-207 is sensibly limited to this context.[237] When the parties communicate in ways that make it likely that each party will actually read and heed all of the terms offered by the other party or contained in an acceptance, there is greater justification to apply the traditional common-law rules.

Suppose, for example, that a seller responds to a purchase order by sending a letter to an officer of the buyer stating that the buyer's terms are unacceptable.[238] The letter further states that the seller is nonetheless shipping the goods as an accommodation to the buyer and the buyer should accept them only if it is willing to contract on all of the offeree's terms. If the buyer later accepts the goods and pays for them, it is reasonable to hold the buyer to the seller's terms.[239]

---

[235] *See* Koehring Co. v. Glowacki, 253 N.W.2d 64, 21 UCCR 715, 77 Wis. 2d 497 (1977); Construction Aggregates Corp. v. Hewitt Robbins Inc., 404 F.2d 505, 6 UCCR 112 (7th Cir. 1969); West Penn Power Co. v. Bethlehem Steel Corp., 236 Pa. Super. 413, 348 A.2d 144 (1975); In re Earle Indus., Inc., 88 B.R. 52, 7 UCCR2d 691 (E.D. Pa. 1988), *appeal dismissed*, 86 B.R. 386 (E.D. Pa. 1988).

[236] In today's world of computers, word processing, and e-mail, the distinction between "printed" forms and other communications breaks down somewhat. The focus should be on whether the communication contains the functional equivalent of the "boilerplate" on a printed form—language that the drafter of the communication is likely to have taken "off the rack" and made applicable to all similar transactions, and that is likely to go unread or unheeded by the other party.

[237] Travalio, *supra* note 198, at 367–368; Caroline N. Brown, "Restoring Peace in the Battle of the Forms: A Framework for Making Uniform Commercial Code Section 2-207 Work," 69 N.C. L. Rev. 893, 901 (1991); Alexander M. Meiklejohn, "Castles in the Air: Blanket Assent and the Revision of Article 2," 51 Wash. & Lee L. Rev. 599, 605 n.28 (1994).

[238] Professors Crandall et al. suggest that might be accomplished by sending a telegram or a fax in response to an offer. Crandall et al., *supra* note 230 at 3:24.

[239] This is a simplified form of the example offered by Dean John Murray in articles strongly critical of the *Itoh* case and its progeny. John E. Murray, Jr., "The Revision of Article 2: Romancing the Prism," 35 Wm. & Mary L. Rev. 1447 (1994); John E. Murray, Jr., "An Essay on the Formation of Contracts and Related Matters Under the United Nations Convention on Contracts for the Int'l Sale of Goods," 8 J.L. & Com. 11 (1988); John E. Murray, Jr., "The Chaos of the 'Battle of the Forms': Solutions," 39 Vand. L. Rev. 1307 (1986). While the authors of this treatise agree with the result Murray reaches in his example, the analysis in this section differs markedly from Murray's analysis in other ways. In particular, the authors' analysis gives a much broader scope to the application of U.C.C. § 2-

Second, applying the last shot rule would sometimes be appropriate even when printed forms are exchanged so long as the printed form cannot reasonably be understood as closing the deal. For example, when the "dickered" terms on the forms disagree, it might be reasonable to treat an offeree's response as a counteroffer that can be accepted by acceptance of the goods.[240] A contract on the offeree's terms might even be defensible when the dickered terms agree, if the response makes it *clear* that the response is a counteroffer, not an acceptance, and that acceptance of the goods will be an acceptance of the counteroffer.[241] However, the presence of a conditional assent clause, or similar language, in the printed form should not be sufficient to conclude a contract on the offeree's terms if the offeror accepts the goods. At a minimum, there must be a conspicuous, clear, and unambiguous statement that the response is a counteroffer rather than an acceptance, and that acceptance of the goods will constitute acceptance of all of the offeree's terms.[242] This issue is further developed in § 3.04[E], *infra*.

[D] Terms of the Contract

Unfortunately, difficult problems remain with section 2-207 even if the offeree responds with a definite and seasonable acceptance not containing a

---

207(3) when the offeree responds in a form containing a conditional acceptance provision. Murray would treat these responses either as unconditional acceptances and proceed to subsection (2) of section 2-207, or treat them as counteroffers subject to the "last-shot" rule. John E. Murray, Jr., "An Essay on the Formation of Contracts and Related Matters Under the United Nations Convention on Contracts for the Int'l Sale of Goods," 8 J.L. & Com. 11 (1988); John E. Murray, Jr., "The Chaos of the 'Battle of the Forms': Solutions," 39 Vand. L. Rev. 1307 (1986); John E. Murray, Jr., "The Revision of Article 2: Romancing the Prism," 35 Wm. & Mary L. Rev. 1447 (1994). *Cf.* Alan Wood Steel Co. v. Capital Equip. Enters., Inc., 39 Ill. App. 3d 48, 349 N.E.2d 627, 19 UCCR 1310 (1976) (offeror sent letter to offeree objecting to some of offeree's additional terms and adding some of its own; offeree's subsequent performance constituted acceptance of offeror's additional terms).

[240] *See* 1 E. Allan Farnsworth, Farnsworth on Contracts § 3.21 at 271 (1990); Travalio, *supra* note 198, at 361. *But see* 1 James White & Robert J. Summers, Uniform Commercial Code 51 (3d ed. 1991). Even when the dickered terms on the forms disagree, it could be argued that by accepting the goods, the original offeror is accepting only the offeree's alteration in the dickered terms and not the boilerplate that may also have been on his response.

[241] Travalio, *supra* note 198 at 361–363.

[242] Even under these circumstances, others believe that U.C.C. § 2-207(3) should determine the terms of the contract. *See* James J. White & Robert S. Summers, *supra* note 93 at 51. An offeree always remains free to refuse to proceed in the absence of the offeror's *express* assent to the offeree's proposed terms, and therefore it is not unfair to deprive the offeree of its boilerplate terms when it proceeds to perform in the absence of express assent. In Ionics, Inc. v. Elmwood Sensors, Inc., 110 F.3d 184 (1st Cir. 1997), the court applied section 2-207(3) to determine the terms of the contract even though the offeree arguably conspicuously indicated a response was a counteroffer.

conditional assent clause. While section 2-207 makes it abundantly clear that a contract is created under these circumstances by the exchange of forms, determining the terms of the contract is often no easy task.

Under section 2-207(2), an additional term in a response will become part of the contract created by the exchange of forms only if four conditions are satisfied. First, the contract must be one *between* merchants[243] (i.e., both parties to the transaction must be merchants). Second, the offer must not expressly limit acceptance to the terms of the offer.[244] Third, the additional term cannot be a *material* addition to the contract.[245] Finally, the offeree must not object to the additional term within a reasonable time.[246]

A frequently litigated problem is that section 2-207(2) refers to only *additional* terms as proposals for addition to the contract; it says nothing about *different* terms. Comment 3 suggests, however, that *both* additional and different terms can become part of the contract under section 2-207(2).[247] Many cases and commentators have now considered this issue, and three approaches have emerged.

The first approach reads the statute literally and permits only additional, not different, terms in a response to become part of the contract under subsection (2). Different terms on the offeree's form simply drop out and the terms on the offeror's form prevail. This rule has been adopted by a number of courts.[248] One difficulty with this approach, recognized by the

---

[243] U.C.C. § 2-207(2). The definition of merchant is contained in section 2-104(1).

[244] *Id.*

[245] *Id.*

[246] *Id.* Few additional terms ever manage all of these hurdles. Lawyers have now become sufficiently familiar with the battle of the forms and U.C.C. § 2-207 that, in drafting purchase orders or similar forms, they almost always include language sufficient to limit the offer to its terms. In addition, the requirement that the additional term be immaterial keeps most additional terms from becoming part of the contract. *See* I Crandall et al., *supra* note 230, at § 4:7.

[247] Official Comment 3 states in part:

> Whether or not additional *or different* terms will become part of the agreement depends upon the provisions of subsection (2) (emphasis added).

[248] *See, e.g.*, Reaction Molding Technologies, Inc. v. General Elec. Co., 588 F. Supp. 1280, 38 UCCR 1537 (E.D. Pa. 1984); Valtrol, Inc. v. General Connectors Corp., 884 F.2d 149, 10 UCCR2d 165 (4th Cir. (1989); In re Earle Indus., Inc. v. Circuit Eng'g, Inc., 88 B.R. 52, 7 UCCR2d 691 (E.D. Pa. 1988); American Parts Co., Inc. v. American Arbitration Ass'n, 8 Mich. App. 156, 6 UCCR 119, 154 N.W.2d 5 (1968); Oskey Gasoline & Oil Co. v. OKC Refining, Inc., 364 F. Supp. 1137, 13 UCCR 767 (D. Minn. 1973).

courts, is that there is no easy way to distinguish a term that is "additional" from one that is "different."[249] A couple of examples are illustrative.

Assume that Walt sends Sarah an order for 100 hammers. The order form says nothing about consequential damages. Sarah responds with an acknowledgment that excludes liability for consequential damages. Delivery and payment ensue, and because the hammers are defective, Walt suffers consequential damages in the form of lost profits. Is the exclusion of consequential damages an "additional" term because Walt's form contained nothing about consequential damages, or is it a "different" term because it conflicts with the provisions of the Code that hold a seller liable for the foreseeable consequential damages suffered by a buyer?[250]

Or, suppose that usage of trade defines a relevant term in a particular way. The offeror's form says nothing about the definition of this term. The offeree's response varies the usage of trade definition in a minor way. Is the term in the offeree's form "different" because of the conflict with the usage of trade or is it an "additional" term because the offeror's form is silent?[251]

Most commentators suggest that a term is "different" only if it conflicts with an *express* term in the offeror's form.[252] The cases appear largely in accord.[253] This distinction, however, makes little commercial sense.[254] When the buyer's attorney in the first example prepared the order form, he or she understood (perhaps even consciously) that it was not necessary to include a term permitting recovery of consequential damages; the Code expressly

---

[249] *See, e.g.*, Northrop Corp. v. Litronic Indus., 29 F.3d 1173, 1175, 24 UCCR2d 407, 410 (7th Cir. 1994) ("It is hair splitting ('metaphysical,' 'casuistic,' 'semantic,' in the pejorative senses of these words) because all different terms are additional and all additional terms are different").

[250] *See* U.C.C. §§ 2-712, 2-713, 2-714, 2-715.

[251] A further variation assumes that the offeror's form contains a term contrary to the usage of trade. The offeree's form is silent on the issue. Can the offeree's form be viewed as impliedly containing a contrary term? It appears that courts do not interpret silence under these circumstances as implying a contrary term. *See* Idaho Power Co. v. Westinghouse Elec. Corp., 596 F.2d 924, 26 UCCR 638 (9th Cir. 1979) (acceptance silent on warranties does not conflict with disclaimer in offer).

[252] *See, e.g.*, 1 J. White & R. Summers, Uniform Commercial Code (3d ed. 1988) § 1-3 at 39; 1 Crandall et al., *supra* note 111 § 4.3.3.3.

[253] *See, e.g.*, Album Graphics, Inc. v. Beatrice Foods, 87 Ill. App. 3d 338, 408 N.E.2d 1041, 53 UCCR 53 (1980) (disclaimer on offeree's form treated as additional term); Wheaton Glass Co. v. Poly-Seal Corp., 548 F. Supp. 1242, 35 UCCR 65 (D.N.J. 1982) (limitation of remedy treated as additional term).

[254] *See* Ionics, Inc. v. Elmwood Sensors, Inc., 110 F.3d 184 (1st Cir. 1997). In *Ionics*, the court said that it would be "artificial and arbitrary" to distinguish between language that conflicts with express terms and language that conflicts with background legal rules.

provides for their recovery.[255] The recovery of consequential damages in the event of breach was *implied* in the buyer's order. Viewed this way, the term in the seller's form precluding their recovery is a "different" term, rather than an "additional" term. Similarly, in the second example, the usage of trade may have been so well recognized that the offeror thought to mention it would be unnecessary.[256]

In addition, this approach favors the offeror without justification. Because the assumption underlying section 2-207 is that *neither* party pays attention to the boilerplate, there is no reason to prefer the offeror's term over the conflicting term of the offeree.[257] This reading of section 2-207 would replace the "last-shot" rule with a "first-shot" rule.

Other courts adhere to the suggestion of Comment 3 and make no distinction between "additional" and "different" terms.[258] The semantic difficulties described above certainly recommend this approach. Furthermore, there is at least some evidence that the omission of "different" from the text of section 2-207(2) was not purposeful.[259]

While more defensible than the first interpretation,[260] this approach, too, has the effect of preferring the offeror's form. This rule does make it *theoretically* possible for a "different" term in the offeree's form to become part of the contract. When, however, both parties have regarded a particular matter as sufficiently important to warrant coverage by an express term, and when their express terms differ, it seems likely that courts will regard the offeree's term as a material alteration, and the offeror's terms will control.[261]

---

[255] This would also be true, for example, with respect to the implied warranty of merchantability.

[256] *See* Meiklejohn, *supra* note 237, at 626.

[257] *See* Gardner Zemke Co. v. Dunham Bush, Inc., 115 N.M. 260, 268, 850 P.2d 319, 326, 20 UCCR2d 842, 853 (1993).

[258] *See, e.g.*, Steiner v. Mobil Oil Corp., 20 Cal. 3d 90, 569 P.2d 751, 141 Cal. Rptr. 157, 22 UCCR 865 (1977); Boese-Hilburn Co. v. Dean Mach. Co., 616 S.W.2d 520, 31 UCCR 830 (Mo. Ct. App. 1981) (en banc). Air Prods. & Chems., Inc. v. Fairbanks Morse, Inc., 58 Wis. 2d 193, 206 N.W.2d 414, 12 UCCR 794 (1973).

[259] John L. Utz, "More on the Battle of the Forms: The Treatment of 'Different' Terms Under the Uniform Commercial Code," 16 UCC L.J. 103, 110–112 (1983).

[260] *See* Northrop Corp. v. Litronic Indus., 29 F.3d 1173, 1175, 24 UCCR2d 407, 415 (7th Cir. 1994) (court found this view to be the "most sensible" of the three interpretations of U.C.C. § 2-207(2)).

[261] It is true, however, that the materiality of the additional or different term is measured at the time of the *formation* of the contract. Thus, a difference that appeared immaterial at the time of contract formation, but later turned out to be important, would not prevent the offeree's term from becoming part of the contract.

The rule which has gained the widest acceptance is the so-called knock-out rule.[262] Under this view, when there is a conflict between the express terms in the offer and acceptance forms,[263] *both* terms fall out and are replaced by Code "gap-fillers." The basis for this approach is Comment 6 to section 2-207:

> If no answer is received within a reasonable time after additional terms are proposed, it is both fair and commercially sound to assume that their inclusion has been assented to. Where clauses on confirming forms sent by both parties conflict each party must be assumed to object to a clause of the other conflicting with one on the confirmation sent by himself. As a result the requirement that there be notice of objection which is found in subsection (2) is satisfied and the conflicting terms do not become a part of the contract. The contract then consists of the terms originally expressly agreed to, terms on which the confirmations agree, and terms supplied by this Act, including subsection (2). The written confirmation is also subject to Section 2-201. Under that section a failure to respond permits enforcement of a prior oral agreement; under this section a failure to respond permits additional terms to become part of the agreement. [Comment 6 was amended in 1966.]

The advantage of the knock-out rule is that it gives neither side the advantage in the battle of the forms. Where both parties make the effort (albeit on a printed form) to deal with a subject and their efforts are inconsistent, neither side prevails. Rather, the "neutral"[264] supplementary terms of the Code fill in the gaps left in the contract.[265]

The problem is that Comment 6 refers only to *confirmations*, not to documents that *create* the contract. When the offeree responds to an offer with a "definite and seasonable expression of acceptance," section 2-207 appears to create a contract on the offeror's terms, with the potential for

---

[262] *See, e.g.*, Northrop Corp. v. Litronic Indus., 29 F.3d 1173, 24 UCCR2d 407 (7th Cir. 1994); Daitom, Inc. v. Pennwalt Corp., 741 F.2d 1569, 39 UCCR 1203 (10th Cir. 1984); Pennsylvania Power & Light Co. v. Joslyn Corp., 7 UCCR 2d (E.D. Pa. 1988), *aff'd*, 875 F.2d 311 (3d Cir. 1989); Gardner Zemke Co. v. Dunham Bush, Inc., 115 N.M. 260, 850 P.2d 319, 20 UCCR2d 842 (1993); Challenge Mach. Co. v. Mattison Mach. Works, 138 Mich. App. 15, 359 N.W.2d 232, 39 UCCR 1578 (1984).

[263] Courts adopting the "knock-out" rule still distinguish between "different" and "additional" terms on the basis of whether there is an express contradiction between the two forms. *See* Daitom, Inc. v. Pennwalt Corp., 741 F.2d 1569, 39 UCCR 1203 (10th Cir. 1984).

[264] *See* Crandall et al., *supra* note 230 at 4:11; John E. Murray, Jr., "The Chaos of the 'Battle of the Forms': Solutions," 39 Vand. L. Rev. 1307, 1377 (1986).

[265] U.C.C. § 2-207, Official Comment 6.

123

additional (and perhaps different) terms in the offeree's form to become part of the contract under section 2-207(2). The language of section 2-207 does not suggest that the offeree's acceptance is anything but an acceptance *of the terms of the offeror's offer*. This is consistent with the limitation of the knock-out rule in Comment 6 to confirmations. There is nothing in the Code or Comments to indicate that the knock-out rule applies to the exchange of offer and acceptance documents.

Nonetheless, the courts seem impressed by the evenhandedness of the knock-out rule.[266] And although it is not supported by the text of the statute or the Comments, there is some historical support for applying the knock-out rule in this context. In an article,[267] Professor Wladis argues from the drafting history that the intention of the drafters of section 2-207 was to create a contract under section 2-207(1) on the joint terms of the parties' documents, with neither party getting the advantage of boilerplate that did not appear on the other's form.[268] Rather, they intended section 2-207(1) to deal only with the issue of contract *formation*, and to say nothing about contract terms.[269] As Professor Wladis admits, however, if this was the intent of the drafters, they did an exceedingly poor job expressing it.

However one resolves this issue, section 2-207(2) poses other difficulties as well. Under subsection (2)(a), additional terms in the offeree's form cannot become part of the contract if the offer "expressly limits acceptance to the terms of the offer." The apparent intent of this provision is to permit the offeror to object in advance to any additional terms in the offeree's form. The offeror may do so by using a clause such as: "Acceptance of this offer constitutes an acceptance of only the terms of the offer and any additional or different terms in the acceptance are hereby excluded."[270] Assuming that

---

[266] To the extent that the premise of the "knock-out" rule is evenhandedness, it should not be applied when *one* party sends a confirmation to an already existing contract. A party should not be able to "knock out" a term to which he has already agreed, either expressly or by conduct, by sending a confirmation. The knock-out rule should be limited to conflicting terms on offer and acceptance forms and conflicting terms on two confirmations.

[267] John D. Wladis, "U.C.C. Section 2-207: The Drafting History," 49 Bus. Law. 1029 (1994).

[268] *Id*. at 1042.

[269] *Id*. at 1043.

[270] One of the authors uses the following language:

> *Exclusivity of Terms*. Acceptance of this offer is limited to the terms contained herein. If acceptance has not occurred earlier, shipment of the goods covered hereunder is an acceptance of the terms stated herein, irrespective of any additional or different terms contained in any of seller's forms. Buyer hereby notifies seller that buyer objects to any additional or different terms contained in any form or forms supplied to buyer by seller.

the offeree responds with a definite and seasonable expression of acceptance, a contract is concluded on the offeror's terms.[271]

On the other hand, similar restrictive language in an offer might mean that unless the response precisely tracks the offer, it is not an acceptance. For example, the offer might say "Acceptance of this offer must be on the terms in this offer and only the terms in this offer." If the words of this clause are given their literal effect, a response that includes additional or different terms will not create a contract. If the parties nevertheless proceed to perform, the resulting contract should be governed by subsection (3) of 2-207. The offeror remains "master of the offer" and can require express agreement to all of its terms (and no others) before a contract is formed.[272] Lawyers must be careful and precise in drafting these clauses to ensure that their intentions are not later misinterpreted by courts.

Additional terms also cannot become part of a contract if they materially alter the contract. Comment 4 provides both a basic test for materiality and some illustrative examples. According to Comment 4, a term "materially alters" a contract if it results "in surprise or hardship if incorporated without express awareness by the other party."[273]

Numerous cases have considered the issue of material alteration. When the contract term is one that is mentioned as a material alteration in Comment 4, the courts have generally followed the direction of the Comment.[274] When the Comment does not provide illustrative assistance, the results are mixed.

---

[271] U.C.C. § 2-207(1).

[272] *See* Tecumseh Int'l Corp. v. City of Springfield, 70 Ill. App. 3d 101, 388 N.E.2d 460, 26 UCCR 645 (1979).

[273] In re Chateaugay Corp. v. LTV Energy Prods. Co., 162 B.R. 949, 22 UCCR2d 1012, (S.D.N.Y. 1994). It is not at all clear what Comment 4 means by the term "express awareness." Does the Comment require only that the offeror be *actually aware* of a term in the offeree's form before it becomes part of the contract despite the fact that it is a material alteration? Or, does it require that the offeree somehow manifest ("express") this awareness? Since additions in the offeree's form are considered to be proposals for addition to the contract, in order to accept these proposals, the original offeror should have to manifest this acceptance in some manner. This is consistent with the general principle of contract law that silence does not generally constitute an acceptance of an offer. *See* Restatement (Second) of Contracts § 53 cmt. a (1979). The issue becomes more problematic when the parties engage in repeated transactions in which the offeror is aware of the material additions in the offeree's form.

[274] *See, e.g.*, Shur-Value Stamps, Inc. v. Phillips Petroleum Co., 50 F.3d 592, 26 UCCR2d 27 (8th Cir. 1995); Step-Saver Data Sys., Inc. v. WYSE Technology & The Software Link, Inc., 939 F.2d 91, 15 UCCR2d 1 (3d Cir. 1991).

Perhaps the most litigated issue of materiality involves clauses requiring arbitration of disputes. The majority of cases holds that a clause requiring arbitration is a material alteration.[275] In cases where arbitration was not held to be a material alteration, it has often been because arbitration was common in the industry[276] or because the offeree had included the same arbitration provision in earlier similar transactions without objection by the offeror.[277]

A second materiality issue resulting in considerable litigation concerns terms that limit the buyer's available remedies, especially terms limiting the recovery of consequential damages. *LTV Energy Products Co. v. Northern States Contracting Co.*[278] provides a good review of the cases on this issue.

Northern States, a construction firm, sent LTV a purchase order for certain construction materials, contingent upon Northern States' receiving a contract to construct a bridge for the New York State Department of Transportation (NYSDOT). The Northern purchase order required delivery "ASAP" but contained no general terms or conditions of sale.[279] LTV responded with an acknowledgment containing a number of printed conditions of sale. These terms included a disclaimer of implied warranties, a limitation of remedies to repair and replacement, and an exclusion of liability for consequential damages.

Northern received the contract from NYSDOT and LTV shipped the goods. Testing revealed that some of these materials were unsatisfactory. Meetings were held between representatives of the interested parties, and LTV redesigned the product. The modified goods were tested and again rejected. After further design and manufacturing delays, satisfactory goods were produced and accepted. Eventually the whole problem ended up in

---

[275] *See* Valmount Indus., Inc. v. Mitsui & Co., 419 F. Supp 1238, 20 UCCR 626 (D. Neb. 1976); Lea Tai Textile Co. v. Manning Fabrics, Inc., 411 F. Supp 1404, 19 UCCR 1080 (S.D.N.Y. 1975); Album Graphics, Inc. v. Beatrice Foods Co., 87 Ill. App. 3d 338, 408 N.E.2d 1041, 30 UCCR 53 (1980); In re Doughboy Indus., Inc., 17 A.D.2d 216, 233 N.Y.S.2d 488, 1 UCCR 77 (App. Div. 1962); Stanley-Bostick, Inc. v. Regenerative Envtl. Equip. Co., Inc., 697 A.2d 323, 35 UCCR2d 828 (R.I. 1997).

[276] *See, e.g.*, Dixie Aluminum Prods. Co. v. Mitsubishi Int'l Corp., 785 F. Supp. 157, 17 UCCR2d 1073 (N.D. Ga. 1992); Schulze & Burch Biscuit Co. v. Tree Top, Inc., 831 F.2d 709, 4 UCCR2d 641 (7th Cir. 1987); Hatzlachh Supply Inc. v. Moishe's Elecs., Inc., 828 F. Supp. 178, 22 UCCR2d 667 (S.D.N.Y. 1993).

[277] *See* Dixie Aluminum Prods. Co. v. Mitsubishi Int'l Corp., 785 F. Supp. 157, 17 UCCR2d 1073 (N.D. Ga. 1992).

[278] 162 B.R. 949, 22 UCCR2d 1012 (S.D.N.Y. 1994).

[279] *Id.* at 952.

bankruptcy court, where LTV sought the unpaid purchase price for the materials and Northern sought damages for the delays caused by LTV.[280]

The parties conceded, and the court found, that a contract had been formed under section 2-207(1), despite the difference in the terms on the forms. The court then looked to subsection (2) to decide whether the disclaimer of implied warranties and the limitations on remedies and consequential damages became part of the contract. Because both parties were merchants, and Northern had neither limited the offer to the terms of the offer nor objected to the terms in LTV's form, the only issue was whether the additional terms were material alterations of the contract.

The court began its opinion by citing Comment 4's "surprise and hardship" test for materiality. It then noted that Comment 5 specifically mentions terms "otherwise limiting remedy in a reasonable manner (see Sections 2-718 and 2-719)" as examples of clauses that are not material alterations. The court said that a "straightforward" approach to the issue would be to determine if the remedy limitations were acceptable under sections 2-718 and 2-719 and, if they were, to treat them as incorporated into the contract as nonmaterial additions.[281]

The court said, however, that many courts have ignored the suggestion in Comment 5 and held that because exclusions of consequential damages significantly shift the allocation of risks, they are material alterations as a matter of law.[282] In a second set of cases, courts have analyzed the issue factually, case by case.[283] Under this approach, it is presumed that the remedy limitation is not material, but the party opposing its inclusion is given the opportunity to prove surprise or hardship. Adopting language from an earlier case,[284] the court adopted this reasoning that because a *per se* rule was "absolutely contrary to the UCC's special emphasis on the particular circumstances surrounding each contractual relationship."[285]

---

[280] Concurrently with this suit, Northern was pursuing a suit against NYSDOT in the N.Y. Court of Claims on the grounds that improper testing procedures by NYSDOT had caused its damages. *Id.* at 953.

[281] The court cited a number of cases that had adopted this approach. *Id.* at 955.

[282] *Id.* at 955.

[283] *Id.* at 955–956.

[284] Bergquist Co. v. Sunroc Corp., 777 F. Supp. 1236 at 1246, 16 UCCR2d 1013 (E.D. Pa. 1991).

[285] LTV Energy Prods. Co. at 956. *See* Wilson Fertilizer & Grain, Inc. v. ADM Milling Co., 654 N.E.2d 848, 27 UCCR2d 801 (Ind. Ct. App. 1995) (court refuses to adopt *per se* rule); Waukesha Foundry, Inc. v. Industrial Eng'g, Inc., 91 F.3d 1002, 30 UCCR2d 12 (7th Cir. 1996) (court rejects *per se* rule).

As to the elements of surprise and hardship, the court said that "surprise" has both subjective and objective elements: what did the assenting party know and what should it have known.[286] Factors bearing on this issue include the parties' prior course of dealing, the number of written confirmations that they exchanged, industry custom, and the conspicuousness of the term.[287]

The court recognized the "hardship" prong as more "problematic,"[288] because allowing consequential damages to be limited will almost always cause "substantial economic hardship." Adoption of this standard would mean that limitations on consequential damages will always be material alterations, contrary to the suggestion in Comment 5. Consequently, the court decided to ignore the "hardship" prong of the test and concluded that limitations on remedies or damages are not material additions unless (1) their inclusion consitutes unreasonable surprise in light of the parties' prior dealings, industry custom or inconspicuousness of the term, (2) the clause is unconscionable, or (3) the limited remedy fails of its essential purpose.[289] Because a limitation falling under (2) or (3) would be struck under sections 2-302 or 2-719 even if it became part of the contract under section 2-207, the heart of the inquiry under section 2-207(2)(b) is whether the limitation caused unreasonable surprise.[290]

The *LTV* case provides a thorough collection of the cases on this issue and is cogent in its analysis. The "hardship" prong of the Comment 4 inquiry is inapppropriate for the reasons cited by the court, at least if "hardship" is determined after contract formation. And, if "hardship" is measured at the time of contract formation, it is hard to see how the analysis would be different from the analysis of "surprise." Both would presumably focus on what the party might reasonably expect to be included in the contract. The proper focus of the inquiry is whether the party receiving the form that

---

[286] LTV Energy Prods. Co. at 957.

[287] *Id.* at 957.

[288] *Id.* at 957.

[289] *Id.* at 958.

[290] The court found that since Northern had introduced no evidence regarding surprise, Northern failed to show surprise as a matter of law. *Id.* at 958. The court said that its analysis was inapplicable to the warranty disclaimer since warranty disclaimers are universally viewed as material alterations. *Id.* at 960. This is consistent with the guidance in Official Comment 4.

excludes consequental damages would, in the total context of the transaction, reasonably anticipate the allocation of this risk to itself.[291]

[E]   Section 2-207(3) Contracts

Section 2-207(3) permits a court to find that a contract exists between the parties even when it cannot find one based upon the writings exchanged by the parties. In these cases, the terms of the contract are those "on which the writings of the parties agree, together with any supplementary terms incorporated under any other provisions of this Act."[292]

The writings might not establish a contract for at least three reasons: (1) the writings exchanged by the parties do not agree on the "dickered" terms, (2) the acceptance is made "expressly conditional" on the offeror's assent to additional or different terms,[293] or (3) the response is not otherwise a definite and seasonable expression of acceptance. The scope of section 2-207(3) in these situations has been a matter of almost endless debate.[294]

As discussed earlier,[295] when the writings do not establish a contract because the offeree's response is expressly made conditional on the offeror's assent, if the conduct of the parties evidences a contract, courts uniformly proceed to section 2-207(3) to determine its terms.[296] The other two situations have caused more difficulty.

---

[291] Courts have differed, however, on whether the presence of the term in forms exchanged in prior transactions is relevant. *Compare* Dixie Aluminum Prods. Co. v. Mitsubishi Int'l Corp., 785 F. Supp. 157, 17 UCCR2d 1073 (N.D. Ga. 1992) (arbitration clause was not material alteration when it had been present in seller's form in sixteen previous transactions without objection by buyer) *with* Maxon Corp. v. Tyler Pipe Indus., Inc., 497 N.E.2d 570, 3 UCCR2d 52 (Ind. Ct. App. 1986) (repeated use of forms not relevant to parties' awareness of their contents since assumption of U.C.C. § 2-207 is that forms are never read). *See also* Waukesha Foundry, Inc. v. Industrial Eng'g, Inc., 91 F.3d 1002, 30 UCCR2d 12 (7th Cir. 1996) (consent to warranty disclaimers and remedy limitations in seller's form can be inferred from silence over long course of dealing).

[292] U.C.C. § 2-207(3).

[293] *See* § 3.04[C][1], *supra.*

[294] *See, e.g.,* John E. Murray, Jr., "The Chaos of the 'Battle of the Forms': Solutions," 39 Vand. L. Rev. 1307 (1986); John E. Murray, Jr., "The Revision of Article 2: Romancing the Prism," 35 Wm. & Mary L. Rev. 1447 (1994); Travalio, *supra* note 198; David F. Megnin, "All Quiet on the 2-207 Front?," 35 U. Pitt L. Rev. 685 (1978).

[295] *See* § 3.04[C][1], *supra.*

[296] C. Itoh & Co. v. Jordon Int'l Co., 552 F.2d 1228, 21 UCCR 353 (7th Cir. 1977); Leonard Pevar Co. v. Evans Prods. Co., 524 F. Supp. 546, 32 UCCR 720 (D. Del. 1981); In re Barney Schogel, Inc., 12 B.R. 697, 34 UCCR 29 (S.D.N.Y. 1981); McCarty v. Verson Allsteel Press Co., 89 Ill. App. 3d 98, 411 N.E.2d 936, 30 UCCR 440 (1980). *Contra* Roto-Lith Ltd. v. F.P. Bartlett & Co., 297 F.2d 497, 1 UCCR 73 (1st Cir. 1962), *overruled* Ionics, Inc. v. Elmwood Sensors, Inc., 32 UCCR2d 1 (1st Cir. 1997).

When parties proceed despite the disagreement in the writings on a "dickered" term,[297] there are two possible approaches: (1) to rely on the "last-shot" doctrine, treat the last form as a counteroffer, and find that the counteroffer is accepted by performance (usually acceptance of the goods), or (2) to find a contract under section 2-207(3). Depending upon the facts, *either* approach may be appropriate, as the following cases illustrate.

The first approach was adopted in *Lambert v. Kysar*.[298] Kysar, the seller, owned a tree farm and Lambert, the buyer, owned a retail operation that sold Christmas trees during the holiday season. The buyer had purchased trees from the seller for a number of years using order forms supplied by the seller. The seller visited the buyer in July of 1989 to discuss the buyer's needs for the upcoming season. Upon returning to its Washington state farm, the seller sent the buyer an order form for the buyer to use in which the seller had inserted a quantity of 2,600 Christmas trees in 4 loads of 650 trees each. Using this order form, the buyer changed the quantity to *3* loads of *550* trees each, for a total of 1,650. The buyer inserted the new quantity in handwriting over the handwritten figures of the seller, and returned the form. The price of $11.60 per tree remained the same. In August, the buyer sent the seller a letter with a deposit of $4,785 on the tree order. The letter stated that "[t]here will be three loads of 1650 trees at $11.60 for a total cost of $19,140."[299]

In November, the seller sent the buyer 1,650 trees. Upon their arrival, the buyer claimed that the trees were defective and refused to pay the balance to the seller. The seller filed suit in Washington pursuant to a provision in the order form that established an agreed venue of Clark County, Washington. The buyer argued that he had not agreed to this venue. He said that the changes that he made in the order form constituted a rejection of the seller's offer, and that he made a new offer in his August letter which was accepted by the seller's performance in shipping the trees and accepting payment.

The court properly rejected the buyer's argument and found a contract which included the Washington venue. It stated that the change in quantity (a "dickered" term) did indeed prevent the buyer's order from being an acceptance. However, the buyer's response with the change in quantity was not a rejection, but a counteroffer that was accepted by the seller's delivery.

---

[297] This analysis assumes that the writings do not merely confirm a preexisting oral contract. *See* § 3.04[F], *infra*. It also assumes that the disagreement in the writings is not simply the result of a drafting error.

[298] 983 F.2d 1110, 19 UCCR2d 979 (1st Cir. 1993).

[299] *Id.* at 1112, 19 UCCR2d at 981.

Because the choice-of-venue provision was on the form used to make the counteroffer, it became part of the contract upon acceptance.

This result was correct. Under the circumstances, it would have been improper to find that no contract had been formed by the exchange of correspondence and to then use section 2-207(3) to supply the terms of the contract. The buyer's counteroffer was on the same form as the seller's offer, including the venue clause. Had the buyer not changed the quantity and simply accepted the offer, there is no doubt that the venue clause would have been part of the contract. There is no reason to change this result when it is the buyer's counteroffer that contains this term rather than an acceptance. Further, it was clear that the buyer's response was, in fact, a counteroffer,[300] and that the seller's delivery was an acceptance.[301]

In *Alliance Wall Corp. v. Ampat Midwest Corp.*[302] the buyer ordered approximately 200 aluminum panels. The seller sent an acknowledgment indicating a different shipment date from that specified on the buyer's purchase order. The parties corresponded over the next ten months stating different understandings as to the delivery date without resolving their differences. Ultimately, the goods were shipped and some were found to be defective. Although adjustments were made by the seller, the buyer refused to pay the remainder due on the purchase price and the seller sued. The buyer counterclaimed for damages, including damages for delay in delivery.

The court found that the delivery date was a "crucial term of the contract."[303] The parties' lack of agreement on this term prevented the formation of a contract on the basis of their correspondence. Nevertheless, they had proceeded to perform without agreement as to this term. To determine the delivery date, the court looked to section 2-207(3) and the "gap-filler" provisions. On this basis, it determined that the time of delivery was a "reasonable time," which happened to coincide with the time asserted by the seller.

The court could have treated the seller's final response as a counteroffer which was accepted by the buyer's acceptance of the goods. Under the circumstances, however, application of section 2-207(3) was more appro-

---

[300] Alternatively, one could argue that the buyer made an *offer* rather than a counteroffer. By providing the order form to the buyer with the quantity already supplied, the seller did not make an offer but merely supplied the proper form for the buyer to make *his* offer. Under either analysis, the result would be the same.

[301] *See* U.C.C. § 2-206: "[A]n order or other offer to buy goods for prompt or current shipment shall be construed as inviting acceptance either by a prompt promise to ship or by the prompt or current shipment of conforming or non-conforming goods."

[302] 17 Ohio App. 3d 59, 477 N.E.2d 1206, 41 UCCR 377 (1984).

[303] *Id.* at 62, 477 N.E.2d at 1210, 41 UCCR at 381.

priate. A number of letters had been exchanged concerning the delivery date, and the position of both parties became entrenched. Neither gave any indication in the correspondence that it would accede to the delivery date of the other. Under these circumstances, it would not have been proper to allow the seller to win simply because it had sent the "last shot."

The key to resolving these cases is whether it should be clear to the party receiving a response that the other party has made a counteroffer that can be accepted by performance.[304] When the response is clearly and unambiguously a counteroffer, and the original offeror should reasonably understand that his performance will be understood as accepting the counteroffer, the common-law "last-shot" rule is applicable. When, however, as in *Alliance Wall*, the situation remains ambiguous, even after the last shot has been fired, resort to section 2-207(3) is proper.

A similar analysis applies to a response in which the dickered terms (price, quantity, delivery) do not differ from the offer, but which nonetheless cannot be characterized as "a definite and seasonable expression of acceptance." For example, a seller might respond to an order for widgets with a letter that states that while the price, quantity, and delivery date are acceptable, the buyer's warranty provisions are not. Therefore, the seller can accept the buyer's order only on its own warranty terms. However, because the buyer needs the goods immediately, the seller is shipping them. If the buyer does not wish to accept the seller's warranty terms, it should return the goods.[305]

The "non-form" nature of the response, the unambiguous refusal to accept the buyer's terms, and the necessity to ship the goods before the disagreement can be resolved all suggest the application of the last-shot rule rather than section 2-207(3). The seller has made it clear that it will deal only on its terms and that the buyer should understand that acceptance of the goods will constitute acceptance of the counteroffer. If, however, one changes the facts, the case for applying section 2-207(3) becomes stronger. If, for example, the "counteroffer" language were contained in a printed form and did not expressly indicate that acceptance of the goods would constitute acceptance of the counteroffer and the seller had the ability to secure the buyer's express assent prior to proceeding, section 2-207(3) would properly apply to determine the terms of the contract.[306]

---

[304] Travalio, *supra* note 198 at 361.

[305] *See* John E. Murray, Jr., "Intention Over Terms: An Exploration of UCC 2-207 and New Section 60, Restatement of Contracts," 37 Fordham L. Rev. 317, 335–336 (1969) for a similar example.

[306] This assumes that such changes in the hypothetical are not sufficient to make the response a "definite and seasonable expression of acceptance."

As presently drafted, section 2-207 is not well suited to these cases; they are too factually distant from the classic "battle of the forms."[307] In fact, other Code sections may be available to better resolve at least some of these cases. For example, the court in *Alliance Wall* could have reached the same result by relying on section 2-204 rather than on section 2-207, and finding that the parties had intended to make a contract through their correspondence and left the delivery date to be agreed later. Upon their failure to agree, the court supplied the term. The language of section 2-207, however, was sufficiently flexible (or poorly drafted) to permit the courts to reach the right result in both the *Lambert* and *Alliance Wall* cases.

The other issue arising under section 2-207(3) that has troubled some courts is the proper interpretation of the phrase "supplementary terms incorporated under any other provisions of this Act." Some cases hold that the only permissible supplementary terms are the Code "gap-fillers."[308] Others interpret the provision more broadly, and allow course of dealing, usage of trade, and course of performance to supplement the terms on which the parties' writings agree.[309]

The latter position is correct, both as a result of the text of the statute and the principles underlying the Code. The language of section 2-207(3) is not limited to the gap-filler provisions of Article 2; it is not even limited to the provisions of Article 2. It permits supplementary terms "incorporated under *any* other provisions of this *Act*."[310] Section 1-201(3) defines the agreement of the parties to include any applicable course of dealing, usage of trade, or course of performance.[311] There is no suggestion that a contract formed by the conduct of the parties should be treated differently in this regard from one formed by an exchange of documents.

Further, the underlying assumption of section 2-207 is that, in the typical case, the parties do not pay attention to the boilerplate. If, for example, an offeror expects a relevant usage of trade such as arbitration to apply, this

---

[307] In fact, the court in Lambert v. Kysar viewed U.C.C. § 2-207 as "inapplicable" in determining the terms of the contract. Lambert v. Kysar, 983 F.2d 1110, 1115, 19 UCCR 979 (1st Cir. 1993).

[308] *See, e.g.*, Northrop Corp. v. Litronic Indus., 29 F.3d 1173, 24 UCCR2d 407 (7th Cir. 1994); Arizona Retail Sys., Inc. v. The Software Link, Inc., 831 F. Supp. 759, 22 UCCR2d 70 (D. Ariz. 1993); Phillips Petroleum Co. v. Bucyrus-Erie Co., 131 Wis. 2d 21, 388 N.W.3d 584, 1 UCCR2d 667 (1986).

[309] *See, e.g.*, Dresser Indus., Inc. v. Gradall Co., 965 F.2d 1442, 18 UCCR2d 43 (7th Cir. 1992); Daitom, Inc. v. Pennwalt Corp., 741 F.2d 1569, 39 UCCR 1203 (10 Cir. 1984); Anchor Fish Corp. v. Tony Harris, Inc., 135 F.3d 856, 34 UCCR2d 906 (2d Cir. 1998) (court looks at course of dealings).

[310] U.C.C. § 2-207(3) (emphasis added).

[311] U.C.C. § 1-201(3).

expectation should not be frustrated by boilerplate on the offeree's form containing conditional assent language and a boilerplate term negating arbitration. If the offeree is to overcome a practice that has risen to the level of a usage of trade, it should either make its demand clear in its responsive document,[312] or refuse to proceed unless its gets the offeror's express assent to the term negating the usage of trade.

[F]   Confirmations

The application of section 2-207 to confirmations of exisiting contracts is—thankfully—simple and more straightforward. The drafters recognized that in many cases, contracts were orally negotiated, with the parties later exchanging standardized forms. Each form contained terms that were not expressly negotiated and were not present in the other party's form or that conflicted with the boilerplate in the other's form.[313] Section 2-207 was designed to deal with this problem, and deals with it rather well.

Section 2-207(1) begins, however, with some unfortunate language:

> A definite and seasonable expression of acceptance or a written confirmation which is sent within a reasonable time *operates as an acceptance* even though it states terms additional to or different from those offered or agreed upon.[314]

The difficulty is immediately apparent: how can a confirmation of an already existing contract "operate as an acceptance"? A confirmation is just that; a confirmation of an already existing contract. What did the drafters mean in saying that a confirmation will *operate as an acceptance*?

What they meant was that additional or different terms in a confirmation would be tested under subsection (2) of section 2-207 to determine whether they become part of the contract. That is, these terms would be permitted to become part of the contract in the same manner as those additional or different terms contained in an actual acceptance. This is made clear by Comment 2:

> Therefore, any additional matter contained in the *confirmation or the acceptance* falls within subsection (2) and must be regarded as a proposal for an added term.[315]

---

[312] *See* § 3.04[C], *supra*.

[313] *See* John D. Wladis, "U.C.C. Section 2-207: The Drafting History," 49 Bus. Law. 1029, 1038 (1994).

[314] U.C.C. § 2-207(1) (emphasis added).

[315] U.C.C. § 2-207, Official Comment 2.

Thus, confirmations are not intended to operate literally as acceptances; rather, they are to be treated like acceptances to determine whether the additional terms contained in the confirmations become part of the contract.

For example, assume that the seller and the buyer orally agreed that the buyer would purchase 1,000 blankets from the seller. Shortly thereafter, the buyer sent its printed purchase order form to the seller. The form contained a printed provision permitting a specific time period during which the buyer would be permitted to reject the goods. Concurrently, seller also sent a confirmation which included a remedy limitation. Do the respective provisions become part of the contract?

One should consider each confirmation separately under subsection (2) of section 2-207. Assuming that the contract is between merchants,[316] subsection (2)(a) is irrelevant because we are dealing with confirmations and not offers. Under subsection (2)(b), each additional term is analyzed to determine whether it materially alters the contract.[317] For this purpose, the existing "contract" includes the terms orally agreed upon, Code "gap-fillers" that operate in the absence of express agreement, and terms implied from usage of trade, course of dealing, and course of performance. A material alteration of any of these terms does not become part of the contract. Finally, under subsection (2)(c) each party has a reasonable time in which to object to the additional terms in the other's confirmation.[318] If such objection is made, the term does not become part of the contract through section 2-207(2), although it may still be part of the original oral contract through usage of trade, course of dealing, or course of performance, or as a result of the Code's gap-filling provisions.

If there is a conflict between clauses on confirming forms, both clauses drop out.[319] According to Comment 6, when clauses on confirming forms conflict, the conflicting clause on each form is treated as an objection to the clause on the other's form under subsection (2)(c). The resulting gap is then

---

[316] If the contract is not between merchants, no additional terms can become part of the contract and the inquiry ends.

[317] *See* Hatzlachh Supply, Inc. v. Moishe's Elecs., Inc., 828 F. Supp. 178, 22 UCCR2d 667 (S.D.N.Y. 1993); Bergquist Co. v. Sunroc Corp., 777 F. Supp. 1236, 16 UCCR2d 1013 (E.D. Pa. 1991). Assuming the explicit time for rejection is reasonable under U.C.C. § 1-204, it is probably not a material alteration. As to the remedy limitation, *see* § 3.04[D], *supra*.

[318] It is not clear whether a confirmation can contain a "blanket" objection to additional terms in the confirmation of the other party.

[319] U.C.C. § 2-207, Official Comment 6.

filled by using usage of trade, course of dealing, course of performance, or the Code's gap-fillers.[320]

Finally, "conditional assent" language in a confirmation has no effect. Because the contract already exists prior to the confirmation, a conditional assent clause cannot have the normal effect of preventing contract formation.[321] If, however, the conditional assent clause can reasonably be interpreted as an objection to the additional terms on the other party's confirmation, it may preclude those additional terms from becoming part of the contract.

Many times the problems inherent in section 2-207 can be avoided through judicious application of section 2-206. Section 2-206 permits a seller who receives an offer for prompt or current shipment of the goods to accept either by a prompt promise to ship *or the prompt or current shipment* of the goods.[322] Thus, if a seller responds to an offer by shipping the goods and concurrently sending an acknowledgment, or includes the acknowledgment with the goods, the acknowledgment should be treated as a confirmation. The result will be that there is a contract on the offeror's terms with additional terms constituting proposals for addition to the contract.[323] Be-

---

[320] Comment 6 appears to be inapplicable when a clause on a confirming form conflicts with an *implied* term on the other party's confirmation. Comment 6 applies only when *clauses* (plural) on confirming forms conflict. For example, a disclaimer on a confirmation that conflicts with an implied warranty would not appear to be covered by Comment 6. Because of the materiality requirement of subsection (2)(b), however, such terms will rarely become part of the contract. For a different interpretation of Comment 6, *see* James J. White & Robert S. Summers, Uniform Commercial Code § 1-3, at 49 (3d ed. 1988).

[321] *See* Album Graphics, Inc. v. Beatrice Foods Co., 87 Ill. App. 3d 338, 408 N.E.2d 1041, 30 UCCR 53 (1980); Luria Bros. & Co. v. Pielet Bros. Scrap Iron & Metal, Inc., 600 F.2d 103, 26 UCCR 1081 (7th Cir. 1979); American Parts Co. v. American Arbitration Ass'n, 8 Mich. App. 156, 154 N.W.2d 5, 6 UCCR 119 (1967).

[322] U.C.C. § 2-206(1)(b).

[323] Comment 2 to U.C.C. § 2-206 indicates that "shipment" is used in the same sense as in section 2-504. Therefore, once the requirements of section 2-504 have been met, the offer has been accepted by shipment. If an acknowledgment is not mailed until after shipment has occurred, the acknowledgment is a confirmation, not an acceptance or counteroffer. Two recent cases, however, seem to suggest that determining whether section 2-206 or section 2-207 is applicable (i.e., whether the acknowledgment is a confirmation or an acceptance/counteroffer) is a function of whether the confirmation or the goods *arrives* first. *See* Winter Panel Corp. v. Reichold Chems., Inc., 823 F. Supp. 963, 970, 21 UCCR2d 533, 541–542 (D. Mass. 1993) (defendant's limitations clauses on acknowledgment form must be analyzed as mere proposals to already completed contract if acknowledgment arrived after the goods); Glyptal, Inc. v. Engelhard Corp., 801 F. Supp. 887, 893, 18 UCCR2d 1059, 1068–1069 (D. Mass. 1992) (genuine issue of fact as to whether goods or acknowledgment was received first). Where the two arrive concurrently, *Winter Panel* suggests that the acknowledgment is either an acceptance or a counteroffer. 823 F. Supp. at 970, 21 UCCR2d at 542. In Arizona Retail Sys., Inc. v. The Software Link, Inc., 831 F. Supp. 759, 22 UCCR2d 70 (D. Ariz.

cause the acknowledgment is a confirmation, any language of conditional assent will not prevent the formation of a contract.

[G] The Future of Section 2-207

[1] Introduction

The proposed revisions to Article 2 significantly change both the form and substance of the present section 2-207. Some concepts incorporated in the present section 2-207 have been moved elsewhere in Article 2, and what remains of section 2-207 is far different from the present section, although the results under the revised provisions appear to be generally consistent with those suggested in this book.

There is little assurance that the latest version of the proposed Article 2 revision of section 2-207 will eventually be recommended for adoption by the states by the National Conference of Commissioners on Uniform State Laws. The revision process to date has involved a number of very different variations on section 2-207.[324] Also, it is by no means clear how many states will adopt the proposed revisions to section 2-207 or how many will amend the revisions prior to adoption. The present Article 2 has been in effect, with little change, in most states for more than thirty years. A substantial body of case law has built up resolving many of the drafting problems in section 2-207, and it is problematic whether states will choose to abandon this body of law for a new set of uncertainties and ambiguities. As a result, the authors only highlight some of the most important aspects of the present proposed revisions rather than engaging in a detailed, line-by-line examination of them.

To begin the analysis, consider a simple hypothetical:

> Buyer sends the seller a purchase order for 1,000 widgets at $10 each, delivery not later than June 15. The purchase order contains a number of printed provisions, one of which calls for the arbitration of disputes arising under the contract. The seller responds with an acknowledgment which states that the seller will deliver 1,000 widgets at $10 each, de-

---

1993), however, the court concluded that a license agreement included with the goods was a proposal to modify an already existing contract formed by the shipment of the goods under section 2-206. *But see* Hill v. Gateway 2000, 105 F.3d 1147 (7th Cir. 1997) (arbitration clause contained in box containing computer enforceable when buyer has opportunity to return computer if dissatisfied with terms); ProCo, Inc. v. Zeidenberg, 86 F.3d 1447, 29 UCCR 1109 (7th Cir. 1996) ("shrinkwrap" license on computer software enforceable).

[324] *See* National Conference of Commissioners on Uniform State Laws, Revision of Uniform Commercial Code Article 2, Sales (Draft for Discussion Only). March 1, 1998, § 2-207, Note 1.

livery on or before June 15. Seller's acknowledgment also contains a number of printed provisions, one of which limits implied warranties and provides for an exclusive repair and replacement remedy.

[2]　Contract Formation

As with the old section 2-207, the revisions to Article 2 also permit a response to act as an acceptance even though it contains terms different from those contained in the offer. This is now accomplished, however, in section 2-206(a)(1) which states:

> An offer to make a contract shall be construed as inviting acceptance in any manner and by any medium reasonable under the circumstances. A definite and seasonable expression of acceptance operates as an acceptance even though it contains terms that add to or differ from the offer.[325]

As a result of this provision, so long as a response to an offer is a "definite and seasonable expression of acceptance" the response may contain standard terms that add to or differ from the offer. The revised section 2-207, like its predecessor, also rejects the "mirror-image rule." Thus, assuming in our hypothetical that Seller's acknowledgment is a definite expression of acceptance, a contract is formed despite the variant term in the offer and acknowledgment.

[3]　Terms of the Contract

Once a contract has been formed, what are its terms? It is here that the revisions dramatically change the present section 2-207. Section 2-207(b) of the proposed revisions states:

> If a contract is formed by offer and acceptance and the acceptance is by a record[326] containing terms additional to or different from the offer or by conduct of the parties that recognizes the existence of a contract but the records of the parties do not otherwise establish a contract for sale, the contract includes:

---

[325] Council Draft No. 4, § 2-205(a)(1).

[326] In light of developing technology, a central concept to the proposed revisions is that of a "record." This term is defined in proposed U.C.C. § 2-103(1)(c)(26) as:

> [I]nformation that is inscribed on a tangible medium, or that is stored in an electronic or other medium and is retrievable in perceivable form.

(1)   [standard] terms in the records of the parties to the extent that the records agree;

(2)   non-standard terms, whether or not in a record, to which the parties have agreed;

(3)   [standard] terms in a record supplied by a party to which the other party has expressly agreed; and

(4)   terms supplied or incorporated under any provision of this [Act].[327]

The proposed section completely eliminates the complicated formula in the present section 2-207(2) for determining the terms of a contract. Instead, the revised section adopts the same methodology for determining the terms of a contract when there is a definite and seasonable expression of acceptance which the present section 2-207(3) uses to determine a contract's terms when the contract is formed by the parties' conduct rather than by the exchange of forms. The revised section 2-207 does not distinguish between a contract formed by the exchange of forms and one formed by the conduct of the parties. It uses the same process to determine the terms of a contract whether a contract is formed by offer and acceptance or by the conduct of the parties that recognizes the existence of a contract.[328] Thus, in our hypothetical *neither* the standard terms in the buyer's or the seller's purchase order would become part of the contract unless the terms were found in the other's form, were expressly agreed to by both parties, or were otherwise supplied by the Code.

A number of things are noteworthy about the revised section. First, agreement to standard terms that are found on only one form must be express; it cannot be implied from acceptance of the goods. In other words, the revised section 2-207 makes it clear that there is no last-shot rule with regard to standard terms. While an offeree can still preclude a contract through the mechanism of a "conditional acceptance" so long as it is conspicuous,[329] the effect of such language does not create a counteroffer that

---

[327] Council Draft No. 4, §§ 2-207(b)(1)–2-207(b)(4).

[328] *Id.*

[329] Proposed U.C.C. § 2-204(d) provides:

Language which expressly conditions the intention to contract upon agreement by the other party to terms proposed prevents contract formation unless the required agreement is given or there is conduct by both parties that recognizes the existence of a contract. However, language of express condition in a record must be conspicuous.

Under this section an offeror can also make its offer conditional upon agreement to only the terms proposed in the offer. Under these circumstances, if the offeree's response does not agree with the terms of the offer, there is no contract formed at that point in time.

can be accepted by the performance of the original offeror. In this way, the revised section 2-207 is consistent with the *Itoh* case and the great majority of the cases that have been decided under the present section 2-207.

Second, the offeror loses the advantage of the "first-shot" rule that exists under the present section 2-207. Even if the offeree responds to an offer with a definite expression of acceptance, standard terms found in the offer become part of the contract only if the terms are also found in the response, if the offeree expressly agrees to them,[330] or if they would otherwise be implied by law. This is a major change from the present section 2-207. Under the revised section 2-207, an offeror has no means to ensure that the terms that it proposes will become part of the contract should the offeree accept the offer. While both the offeror and offeree can condition a contract upon agreement to all of its terms,[331] the mere fact that an offeree responds with a definite and seasonable expression of acceptance will not ensure that the offeror's terms are part of the contract if the response contains variant terms.

Third, the offeror appears to lose *all* of the terms in its form that are not also in the offeree's form so long as the offeree's form contains *any* terms that are different from those on the offeror's form. Subsection (b) of the revised section 2-207 applies whenever "acceptance is by a record containing terms additional to or different from the offer."[332] In fact, section 2-207(b) may be applicable to determine the contract's terms if the offeree's form merely omits a term not found on the offeror's form, since the offeree's acceptance must merely be by a record that contains terms "different from" the offer.

[4] The Counteroffer

As previously discussed,[333] one of the most difficult aspects of the present section 2-207 is determining the terms of the contract when the offeree makes a counteroffer. As described earlier,[334] a response might be a counteroffer for two reasons under the present section 2-207: (1) it cannot reasonably be understood as a definite and seasonable expression of acceptance, or (2) it appears to be a definite and seasonable expression of accep-

---

[330] Under proposed U.C.C. § 2-207(b)(2) *nonstandard* terms in a record become part of the contract if the parties have "agreed." Unlike standard terms, *express* agreement is not required. Thus, the last-shot rule may still apply to nonstandard terms.

[331] Council Draft No. 4, § 2-204(d).

[332] Council Draft No. 4, § 2-207(b).

[333] *See* §§ 3.04[C][1], 3.04[E], *supra.*

[334] *See* § 3.04[E], *supra.*

tance, except that it contains a "conditional assent" clause. As with the present section 2-207, it appears clear under the proposed revisions that if a response contains a "conditional assent" clause but otherwise appears to be an acceptance, section 2-207(b)(1)-(4) will determine the terms of the contract should the parties go ahead and perform despite the failure of the forms to create a contract. The last-shot rule will not apply.

It is not clear, however, what would occur under the revised section 2-207 if the offeree's response cannot be characterized as a definite and seasonable expression of acceptance and the parties nonetheless proceed to perform. As discussed earlier,[335] whether the terms of a contract created under these circumstances is governed by the "last-shot" rule or by section 2-207(3) is problematic. The same is true under the revised section 2-207. Section 2-207(b) of the revisions does not distinguish among cases in which the conduct of the parties creates a contract; it appears to govern all such cases. Consequently, one can infer that the revised section 2-207 does not permit a counteroffer that can be accepted by the performance of the original offeror (for example, by the acceptance of the goods by an offeror-buyer). However, the commentary to the revised section 2-207 does not indicate that the section extends this far.[336] The bottom line is that the revised section 2-207 still does not resolve one of the thorniest issues created by the battle of the forms—under what circumstances can an offeree make a counteroffer that can be accepted by the original offeror's performance. Or, stated another way, is there anything left of the "last-shot" rule?[337]

[5] Confirmations

When one or both parties has sent a form confirming a preexisting contract, the method for determining which terms on the confirmation(s) become part of the contract is similar to that of the present section 2-207. Proposed section 2-207(c) provides:

---

[335] *Id.*

[336] The commentary to the revised U.C.C. § 2-207 is not of much help in resolving this issue. It makes clear that if contract formation is precluded by a typical "conditional assent" clause, the terms of a contract created by conduct will be governed by section 2-207(b). *See* Council Draft No. 4, § 2-207, Note (f). The commentary does not, however, deal with a case in which the offeree's response is not a definite and seasonable expression of acceptance.

[337] Proposed U.C.C. § 2-207(b)(2) permits nonstandard terms in a party's form to become part of the contract so long as the parties have "agreed" to the term. Unlike a standard term, express agreement is not required. Therefore, it is possible that the last shot would apply if a response was not a definite and seasonable expression of acceptance because it varied a nonstandard term.

[I]f a contract is formed by any manner permitted under this article and either party or both parties confirms the agreement by a record, the contract includes:

(1) [standard] terms in the records, including the confirmations, of the parties to the extent that they agree;

(2) non-standard terms, whether or not in the confirming records, to which the parties have otherwise agreed;

(3) [standard] terms in a confirming record that add to or differ from the prior agreement to which the other party has expressly agreed; and

(4) terms supplied or incorporated under any provision of this [Act].[338]

If, for example, a buyer and seller orally agree to the sale of 100 widgets for $1,000 and the seller sends a confirmation form, any terms on the confirmation form to which the parties have not already agreed will not become part of the contract unless the other party "agrees" to the nonstandard terms or "expressly agrees" to standard terms. If both parties send confirmations, the terms of the contract will include the terms orally agreed upon, terms on the confirmations that agree, terms on the confirmations on which there is subsequent agreement, and terms supplied by the Code.

[6] The End Result

The new section 2-207 departs even further from the common law of offer and acceptance than the present section 2-207. As a general proposition, it says to both offerors and offerees that if you use boilerplate, don't expect the boilerplate to become part of the contract unless you get the other party's express agreement. Its rejection of both the last-shot and the first-shot advantages is laudable, as is its requirement that "conditional assent" clauses be conspicuous.

Questions, however, both large and small, remain. For example, does the revised section even further limit the last-shot rule? More significantly, to what extent will the unwillingness of the revisions to give effect to boilerplate terms increase transaction costs?[339] Also, to what extent will states be reluctant to adopt the new section 2-207 now that a substantial body of

---

[338] Council Draft No. 4, § 2-207(c).

[339] The economic benefits of "form" transactions have been recognized by commentators and catalogued elsewhere. *See, e.g.*, Karl Llewellyn, The Common Law Tradition—Deciding Appeals 362 (1960). Under the new section 2-207, sellers will probably have to get the express agreement of the buyer for warranty disclaimers and remedy limitations. This is true even though these limitations and disclaimers will ultimately be accepted by the buyer in the vast majority of contracts. In order to get the express assent of the buyer, however, transaction costs are bound to increase.

law has built up interpreting the present section and providing commercial lawyers with some degree of certainty as to its application? It is likely that the new section 2-207 will not create peace—or even a truce—in the battle of the forms. We can only hope that any revision ultimately adopted will simply reduce the level of the conflict.

[H]   Conclusion

Despite this lengthy sojourn, other issues surrounding 2-207 remain unexplored.[340] Forests of paper examine its intricacies, almost always critically.[341] It has been described as a "miserable, bungled, patched-up job."[342] As a result, section 2-207 will undoubtedly be revised.[343] Despite all of this, and the volume of litigation section 2-207 has engendered, it has generally worked well, given the almost infinite variety of transactional facts involved. The courts have usually reached fair results, even if their reasoning has not always been sound.[344] Furthermore, the law has had sufficient opportunity to develop that the cases have resolved most of the more troublesome issues.[345] Hopefully, the cure, in the form of the proposed revisions to Article 2, will not be worse than the illness.

§ 3.05   FIRM OFFERS

According to common-law dogma, an offer is revocable even though the offeror has stated that the offer is irrevocable or that the offer is to

---

[340] Examples include: the interplay between U.C.C. § 2-207 and U.C.C. § 2-201(2), *see* Crandall et al., *supra* note 230, § 4.3.5.3.; the relationship between section 2-209 and section 2-207, *see* James J. White & Robert S. Summers, Uniform Commercial Code § 1-3, at 36 (3d ed. 1988); the omission in section 2-207(3) of terms to which the parties expressly agreed but were not included in the writings, *see* Thomas J. McCarthy, "An Introduction: The Commercial Irrelevancy of the 'Battle of the Forms'," 49 Bus. Law. 1019, 1022–1023 (1994).

[341] One scholar has written *four* lengthy articles dealing entirely, or in large part, with section 2-207. John E. Murray, Jr., "Section 2-207 of the Uniform Commercial Code: Another Word About Incipient Unconscionability," 39 U. Pitt. L. Rev. 597 (1978); John E. Murray, Jr., "The Chaos of the 'Battle of the Forms': Solutions," 39 Vand. L. Rev. 1037 (1986); John E. Murray, Jr., "An Essay on the Formation of Contracts and Related Matters Under the United Nations Convention on Contracts for the Int'l Sale of Goods," 8 J.L. & Com. 11 (1988); John E. Murray, Jr., "The Revision of Article 2: Romancing the Prism," 35 Wm. & Mary L. Rev. 1447 (1994).

[342] Letter from Professor Grant Gilmore to Professor Robert Summers (Sept. 10, 1980) *reprinted in* Richard E. Speidel, Commercial and Consumer Law (1st ed. 1974).

[343] *See* § 3.04[G], *supra*.

[344] *See, e.g.*, Roto-Lith Ltd. v. F.P. Bartlett & Co., 297 F.2d 497, 1 UCCR 73 (1st Cir. 1962).

[345] For example, the question of whether a "conditional acceptance" is a counteroffer that can be accepted by performance. *See* § 3.04[C][1], *supra*.

remain open for a given period of time.[346] In compelling cases, the common law found ways around this dogma, but the exceptions produced cumbersome rules and artificial distinctions.[347] If promissory estoppel was available, a search was required for the necessary reliance.[348]

The Code's approach is much simpler. Merchants can make firm offers, subject to certain limitations. By a "firm" offer the Code means that during the period that the offeror assures the offeree that the offer will remain open, the offeror may not revoke the offer on the basis that the offer was not supported by consideration. During the stated period of time, the offeree has the power to accept the offer, notwithstanding attempts by the offeror to revoke prior to acceptance.[349] A Code firm offer is thus an option contract.[350]

Section 2-205 provides:

> An offer by a merchant to buy or sell goods in a signed writing which by its terms gives assurance that it will be held open is not revocable for lack of consideration, during the time stated or if no time is stated for a reasonable time, but in no event may such period of irrevocability exceed three months; but any such term of assurance on a form supplied by the offeree must be separately signed by the offeror.[351]

Five criteria must be met to satisfy section 2-205. First, the proposal must be one to buy or sell goods. Second, there must be an offer. Preliminary negotiation or the quotation of prices not rising to the level of an offer will not suffice.[352] Because "offer" is not defined by the Code, common-law

---

[346] *See, e.g.*, Petterson v. Pattberg, 248 N.Y. 86, 161 N.E. 428 (1928). *But see* Restatement (Second) of Contracts § 89 (1981). This result was based upon the idea that a promise to leave an offer open for a specified period was, like any other promise, unenforceable unless supported by consideration or some other validating device.

[347] *See* 1 Joseph Perillo, Corbin on Contracts, §§ 2.23, 2.24 (1993).

[348] *See* Franklin M. Schultz, "The Firm Offer Puzzle: A Study of Business Practice in the Construction Industry," 19 U. Chi. L. Rev. 237, 238 (1951); Michael B. Metzger & Michael J. Phillips, "Promissory Estoppel and Reliance on Illusory Promises," 44 Sw. L.J. 841, 842–848 (1990).

[349] IUE AFL-CIO Pension Fund v. Barker & Williamson, 788 F.2d 118, 1 UCCR2d 205 (3d Cir. 1986); Bethlehem Steel Corp. v. Litton Indus., Inc., 507 Pa. 88, 488 A.2d 581, 40 UCCR 1639 (1985); Lownenstern v. Stop & Shop Co., Inc., 1981 WL 13972, 32 UCCR 414 (Mass. Super. Ct. 1981).

[350] "An option contract is a promise which meets the requirements for the formation of a contract and limits the promisor's power to revoke an offer." Restatement (Second) of Contracts § 25 (1981).

[351] U.C.C. § 2-205.

[352] *See* Janke Constr. Co. v. Vulcan Materials Co., 386 F. Supp. 687, 16 UCCR 937 (E.D. Wis. 1974); Realty Dev., Inc. v. Kosydar, 322 N.E.2d 328, 17 UCCR 1178 (Ohio Ct. App. 1974).

cases remain relevant in determining whether the documents involved contain only a request for further negotiations or whether they indicate that the signer is willing to deal on the terms stated if they are accepted by the other party.[353]

Third, the offer must be made by a *merchant*. Nonmerchants are not covered by section 2-205; their offers remain subject to general contract law.[354] "Merchant" is a defined Code term,[355] and the definition is discussed elsewhere in the text.[356] It was pointed out previously that the Code includes two classes of persons as "merchants": (1) those who deal in goods of the kind involved in the transaction, and (2) those who hold themselves out by their occupations as having knowledge or skill peculiar to the practices or goods involved in the transaction or who employ such persons as agents, brokers, or intermediaries. The second category is broader than the first; it includes a person who does not deal in the kind of goods involved in the transaction, but who by his occupation holds himself out as having knowledge peculiar to the goods *or practices* involved in the transaction. Thus, under section 2-104, a person is a merchant with respect to section 2-205 if that person is familiar with the business practice of making offers (or perhaps firm offers).[357] While this broad concept of merchant applies to section 2-205, a firm offer will result only if the signer is acting in his or her mercantile capacity in making the offer.[358]

Fourth, the offer must be contained in a *signed writing*.[359] An oral offer will not suffice, even if the price of the goods involved is less than $500. There is no question but that the writing must be signed by the offeror, although the Code's language is only that there must be a "signed" writing—without indicating who must do the signing. Indeed, if the irrevocability clause is contained in a form that was prepared by the offeree, that clause must be separately signed by the offeror.[360]

---

[353] *See* Brown Mach. v. Hercules, Inc., 770 S.W.2d 416, 9 UCCR2d 480 (Mo. Ct. App. 1989).

[354] This limitation on section 2-205 was probably included because of a belief that merchants could be fairly held to a standard of reliability when they make firm offers even though the assurance that the offer would be left open was unsupported by consideration. Section 87 of the Restatement (Second) of Contracts, by permitting the parties to create an option through a false recital of consideration or through detrimental reliance, liberalizes the common law. *See* Peterson v. Pattberg, 248 N.Y. 86, 166 N.E. 428 (1928).

[355] U.C.C. § 2-104(1).

[356] *See* § 3.01[C][1], *supra*; § 4.06[B][1], *infra*.

[357] *See* U.C.C. § 2-104(1), Official Comment 2.

[358] U.C.C. § 2-104, Official Comment 2.

[359] As to the Code's definition of "signed," *see* § 3.01[B], *supra*. The proposed revisions to Article 2 require an "authenticated record." Council Draft No. 4, § 2-205.

[360] *See* U.C.C. § 2-205.

Finally, the writing must contain a term that gives *assurance* that the offer will be kept open. The term may be for a specified time period, or it may contain no stated time period. Thus, statements such as "this offer to be irrevocable until midnight of June 17," or "this offer to remain firm" comply with the assurance requirement of section 2-205. In the latter example, a reasonable time will be implied, but in no case can the period of irrevocability exceed three months.[361] Thus, a written assurance that an offer will remain open for one year is limited by section 2-205 to a three-month period of irrevocability.[362]

The statement in an offer, however, that the offeree "has ten days in which to accept the offer" or that the offeree "must accept this offer by July 10" does not satisfy 2-205. Such statements only establish when the offer will lapse by its own terms; they do not give assurance that the offer will not be revoked in the meantime.[363] Conversely, a statement in an offer that it will be irrevocable or a period of thirty days does not mean that the offer will lapse at the end of that period.[364]

If these five criteria are met, the offeror of a section 2-205 firm offer cannot withdraw that offer simply because the offeree did not give consideration to keep the offer open. Section 2-205 does not, however, make firm offers irrevocable against other invalidating causes. Thus, a firm offer obtained by fraud or duress will be revocable prior to acceptance, just as the completed contract arising out of the fraud or duress could be avoided later.

Section 2-205 also does not deal with the revocation of offers for which consideration has been given. In such a case, the consideration should make

---

[361] The Code does not say whether the three-month period is to be calculated from the time the offer is sent or from the time it is received. *See* Mid-South Packers, Inc. v. Shoneys Inc., 761 F.2d 1117, 41 UCCR 38 (5th Cir. 1985) (period began when the offeror tendered the letter containing the offer). According to general contract doctrine, an offer is not effective until it reaches the offeree. *See* E. Allan Farnsworth, Farnsworth on Contracts § 3.10, at 212 (1990). Therefore, the three-month period should not begin until receipt. Also, if the offer, even though received, is not to take effect until sometime in the future, the period of irrevocability should begin at the time the offer takes effect.

[362] *See* Paper Corp. of U.S. v. Schoeller Technical Papers, Inc., 773 F. Supp. 632, 17 UCCR 2d 365 (S.D.N.Y. 1991); Mid-South Packers, Inc. v. Shoneys Inc., 761 F.2d 1121, 41 UCCR 38 (5th Cir. 1985).

[363] *See* Friedman v. Sommer, 63 N.Y.2d 788, 471 N.E.2d 139, 40 UCCR 764 (1984) (offer granting tenant "non-exclusive right to purchase for a period of thirty days" does not give assurance that it will be held open for thirty days). The proposed revisions to Article 2 change this rule. Under proposed section 2-205, a firm offer is irrevocable "during the time stated." Also, the three-month limit on irrevocability applies only if no time is stated in the firm offer. Council Draft No. 4, § 2-205.

[364] Loranger Plastics Corp. v. Incoe Corp., 670 F. Supp 145, 5 UCCR2d 58 (W.D. Pa. 1987).

the offer irrevocable to the same extent that it would under the common law. In addition, section 2-205 does not preclude the application of promissory estoppel or some other substitute for consideration that would make an offer irrevocable.[365] While it can be argued that section 2-205 has provided the exclusive method by which merchants can make their offers firm, it should not be so interpreted. Comment 1 to section 1-103 indicates that supplementary bodies of law will continue to be applicable unless *explicitly* displaced by the Code. The Code does not deal with revocation of offers for which consideration has been given or for which a substitute for consideration is present. Section 2-205 is aimed at a different matter: the enforcement of merchant promises to hold offers open when there is no consideration to support the promise.

III. TERMS OF A CONTRACT FOR SALE

§ 3.06   INTRODUCTION

For an agreement to be enforceable at common law, the parties must have reached agreement on all material terms.[366] Even if the parties intended to contract, if they left a material term to be agreed upon in the future, the result was an unenforceable "agreement to agree."[367] The Code has substantially changed the common law and made it much easier for the parties to conclude a binding agreement, despite the intentional or unintentional omission of a material term from their agreement. The Code contains a number of "gap-filler" provisions designed to supply missing terms in the absence of the agreement of the parties. In addition, the Code reads into the parties' agreement usage of trade, course of dealing, and course of performance. Finally, it permits the parties to intentionally agree to defer agreement on some terms while at the same time concluding a binding contract.

§ 3.07   CONTRACT FORMATION AND OMITTED TERMS

Section 2-204(3) provides:

Even though one or more terms are left open a contract for sale does not fail for indefiniteness if the parties have intended to make a contract

---

[365] In E.A. Coronis Assocs. v. M. Gordon Constr. Co., 90 N.J. Super. 69, 80, 216 A.2d 246, 253, 3 UCCR 42, 45 (1966), the court remarked in a footnote that "[w]e do not consider whether the existence of section 2-205 of the Uniform Commercial Code precludes reliance on an offer not conforming to its provisions."

[366] John E. Murray, Jr., Murray on Contracts § 38 at 25 (3d ed. 1990).

[367] *Id.*

and there is a reasonably certain basis for giving an appropriate remedy.[368]

Thus, there are only two requirements for contract formation: (1) the parties must have manifested a present intention to be bound, and (2) there must be a reasonably certain basis for an appropriate remedy in the event of breach. The Official Comment to section 2-204 expands upon these ideas:

> If the parties intend to enter into a binding agreement, this subsection recognizes that agreement as valid in law, despite missing terms, if there is any reasonable basis for granting a remedy. The test is not certainty as to what the parties were to do nor as to the exact amount of damages due the plaintiff. Nor is the fact that one or more terms were left to be agreed upon enough of itself to defeat an otherwise adequate agreement.[369]

The cases generally recognize that the Code has made it significantly easier to form a contract.[370] Cases have found contracts to exist when the parties have omitted one or more material terms,[371] when they have explicitly left the terms to be decided later,[372] and when they have been unable to agree during the negotiation process but, nonetheless, evidence an intention to be bound despite the failure to agree.[373]

Under the relaxed Code standards, courts have been willing to supply many terms that would have been fatal if omitted at common law. These include terms for which Code "gap-fillers" are available as well as those

---

[368] U.C.C. § 2-204(3).

[369] Official Comment to U.C.C. § 2-204.

[370] *See, e.g.*, City of Louisville v. Rockwell Mfg. Co., 482 F.2d 159, 12 UCCR 840 (6th Cir. 1973) (U.C.C. is more liberal than prior Kentucky law in permitting open terms and not requiring complete certainty); Taunton v. Allenberg Cotton Co., Inc., 378 F. Supp. 34, 15 UCCR 311 (M.D. Ga. 1973) (U.C.C. is "extremely liberal" in its requirements for contract formation); Bethlehem Steel Corp. v. Litton Indus., 35 UCCR 1091 (Pa. Super. 1982), *disapproved on other grounds*, 468 A.2d 748 (Pa. Super. 1983) (unlike prior Pennsylvania law, U.C.C. specifically contemplates enforceable agreement to agree); Computer Network, Ltd. v. Purcell Tire & Rubber Co., 747 S.W.2d 669, UCCR2d 642 (Mo. Ct. App. 1988) (U.C.C. renders obsolete earlier cases in Missouri on indefiniteness).

[371] *See, e.g.*, J.W. Knapp Co. v. Sinas, 19 Mich. App. 427, 7 UCCR 176 (1969); Dick House, Inc. v. Scarborough, Sheffield & Gaston, Inc., 139 Ga. App. 173, 228 S.E.2d 142, 20 UCCR 278 (1976); Dura-Wood Treating Co. v. Century Forest Indus., Inc., 675 F.2d 745, 33 UCCR 1201 (5th Cir. 1982); Carolina Builders Corp. v. Howard-Vessey Homes, Inc., 324 S.E.2d 626, 40 UCCR 73 (N.C. Ct. App. 1985); H.C. Schmerdling Produce Co., Inc. v. Cagle, 529 So. 2d 243, 7 UCCR2d 676 (Ala. 1988).

[372] *See, e.g.*, Bernstein v. Somerson, 341 So. 2d 1043, 21 UCCR 36 (Fla. Dist. Ct. App. 1977); Potter v. Hatter Farms, 641 P.2d 628, 56 Or. App. 254, 33 UCCR 819 (1982).

[373] *See* Southwest Eng'g v. Martin Tractor, 205 Kan. 684, 7 UCCR 1288 (1970).

for which they are not. For example, courts have relied on gap-fillers to fill in price, delivery terms, time of payment, and time of performance.[374] When no Code gap-fillers were available, courts have supplied such terms as period of repayment on an installment sale,[375] the interest rate on an installment sale,[376] the means of transportation,[377] an index for cost escalation,[378] and a schedule of payments.[379]

Courts have found contracts to exist when few of the material terms have been expressed by the parties. For example, in *Deck House, Inc. v. Scarborough, Sheffield & Gaston, Inc.*[380] a contractor agreed to purchase a "basic package" of building supplies for a townhouse for $58,817. Using Code gap-fillers, the court supplied the time for payment, and the method, time, and place of delivery. Similarly, the court enforced a promise to "buy everything that [the other party] supplied so long as they would sell it to me and my company."[381] Based upon prior dealings and other circumstances, the court interpreted the promise as a requirements contract for building materials with open price and delivery terms.

The Comment to section 2-204, however, recognizes that the more terms the parties leave open, the less likely they are to have the requisite contractual intent.[382] The more terms that have not been agreed upon, the more likely it is that the parties reasonably understand that they have not yet reached the point where they have assumed a legal obligation. While relevant, however, neither the number of terms omitted, nor the nature of the terms omitted, should be *conclusive* on the issue of contractual intent.[383]

The objective theory of contracts is properly used by the courts to determine whether the parties intend to be bound by their agreement.[384]

---

[374] *See* § 3.07[B], *infra.*

[375] J.W. Knapp v. Sinas, 19 Mich. App. 427, 7 UCCR 176 (1969).

[376] *Id.*

[377] Potter v. Hatter Farms, Inc., 641 P.2d 628, 56 Or. App. 254, 33 UCCR 819 (1982).

[378] Bethlehem Steel Corp. v. Litton Indus., 35 UCCR 1091 (Pa. Super. 1982), *disapproved on other grounds*, 468 A.2d 748, 37 UCCR 1059 (Pa. Super. 1983).

[379] Nebraska Builders Prods. Co. v. The Industrial Erectors, Inc., 478 N.W.2d 257, 239 Neb. 744, 16 UCCR2d 568 (1992).

[380] 228 S.E.2d 142, 139 Ga. App. 173, 20 UCCR 278 (1976).

[381] *Id.* at 175.

[382] Official Comment to U.C.C. § 2-204.

[383] For example, partial or complete performance by one or both parties may be strong evidence of contractual intent. *See* Computer Network, Ltd. v. Purcell Tire & Rubber Co., 747 S.W.2d 669, 6 UCCR2d 642 (Mo. Ct. App. 1988) (part performance is a good indication of intent to contract).

[384] *See* Computer Network Ltd. v. Purcell Tire & Rubber Co., 747 S.W.2d 669, 6 UCCR2d 642 (Mo. Ct. App. 1988); Jo-Ann, Inc. v. Alfin Fragrances, Inc., 731 F. Supp. 149, 11 UCCR2d 782 (D.N.J. 1989).

While some cases continue to say that the parties must experience a "meeting of the minds,"[385] there is no reason to believe that the drafters intended a subjective standard to govern contractual intent. Certainly, such a dramatic change from the course of twentieth-century contract law would have been more clearly expressed if that had been the drafters' desire.

[A] Open Price Agreements

Of all of the agreements with open terms, perhaps those causing the most difficulty at common law were open price agreements.[386] In many cases, if nothing was said as to price, courts would refuse to enforce the contract because of indefiniteness.[387] If the parties agreed that one of them could fix the price, some courts concluded that the contract was illusory since any price could be set.[388] Although a few courts were willing to imply a reasonable price,[389] there are many examples of courts' refusing to enforce contracts without explicit agreement as to price.[390]

Although section 2-204 generally validates contracts with missing terms, the Code deals specifically with open price terms in section 2-305. This section provides that the parties, "if they so intend," can conclude a contract even though the price is not set by their agreement. Section 2-305 sets out rules for the determination of price, depending on whether the price was (1) left for future determination by one or both of the parties, (2) to be set by some third party or market standard, or (3) omitted altogether.

If the agreement allows one of the parties to set the price, that party must set the price *in good faith*.[391] In many instances, the "good faith"

---

[385] First Am. Farms, Inc. v. Marden Mfg. Co., 255 So. 2d 526, 10 UCCR 648 (Fla. Dist. Ct. App. 1971); Lakeside Pump & Equip., Inc. v. Austin Constr. Co., 576 P.2d 392, 89 Wash. 2d 839, 23 UCCR 886 (1978).

[386] William Prosser, "Open Price in Contracts for the Sale of Goods," 16 Minn. L. Rev. 733 (1932).

[387] *See, e.g.*, Sun Printing & Publishing Ass'n v. Remington Paper & Power Co., 235 N.Y. 338, 139 N.E. 470 (1923).

[388] *See* Weston Paper Mfg. Co. v. Downing Box Co., 293 F. 725 (7th Cir. 1923).

[389] *See, e.g.*, Boeving v. Vandover, 218 S.W.2d 175, 240 Mo. App. 117 (Mo. Ct. App. 1949); Fountain v. Fountain, 89 A.2d 8, 9 N.J. 558 (1952); Fuller v. Michigan Nat'l Bank, 68 N.W.2d 771, 342 Mich. 92 (1955).

[390] *See, e.g.*, Bride v. City of Slater, 263 S.W.2d 22 (Mo. 1953); Calcasiem Paper Co., Inc. v. Memphis Paper Co., 222 S.W.2d 617, 32 Tenn. App. 293 (1949); Montclair Distrib. Co., Inc. v. Arnold Bakers, Inc., 62 A.2d 491, 1 N.J. Super. 568 (N.J. Super. Ct. Ch. Div. 1948).

[391] In Columbus Milk Producers Coop. et al. v. Department of Agric. of the State of Wis. et al., 180 N.W.2d 617, 48 Wis. 2d 451, 8 UCCR 481 (1970), the court said that a price set in good faith is one in which the other party will not be deprived of its "reasonable expectations" under the contract. This analysis is appropriate, given the definition of good faith

requirement translates into the market price of the goods at the time specified in the contract, since this is the price the parties would normally expect. A price that deviates from the market, however, might nonetheless be set in good faith if other factors, such as a prior course of dealing or an accelerated delivery date, would cause the parties reasonably to expect a price that deviates from the market.[392]

If nothing is said as to price in the contract, the agreement is construed as setting a reasonable price at the time of delivery.[393] In most cases, a reasonable price will be established by reference to the market for the same or similar goods.[394] Courts must ensure, however, that contracts used to establish market prices are sufficiently similar to the contract in question.[395] Occasionally, a reasonable price will diverge from the market for other reasons such as usage of trade or course of dealing,[396] or when the terms of the contract themselves provide some evidence of a reasonable price.[397]

If the price is to be fixed by later agreement of the parties and they fail to agree, the price is a reasonable price at the time of delivery. Parties are obligated to bargain in good faith to reach agreement,[398] but if they are unable to agree on price, a binding contract nonetheless exists and the court

---

in U.C.C. § 2-103 as "the observance of reasonable commercial standards of fair dealing in the trade."

[392] *See* TCP Indus., Inc. v. Uniroyal, Inc., 661 F.2d 542, 32 UCCR 369 (6th Cir. 1981) (price set in good faith does not necessarily equate to fair market value).

[393] U.C.C. § 2-305(1)(a).

[394] *See, e.g.,* Pulprint, Inc. v. Louisiana-Pacific Corp., 477 N.Y.S.2d 540, 124 Misc. 2d 728, 39 UCCR 426 (N.Y. Sup. Ct. 1984).

[395] For example, in Spartan Grain & Mill Co. v. Ayers, 735 F.2d 1284 (11th Cir. 1984), the court properly rejected contracts for chicken feed offered by other sellers, which, unlike the contract in question, did not contain a guaranteed outlet for the buyer's eggs.

[396] *See, e.g.,* Weisberg v. Handy & Harman, 747 F.2d 416, 39 UCCR 1617 (7th Cir. 1984) (course of dealing indicated that reasonable price was market price at time of processing of silver).

[397] For example, the contract might set maximum or minimum prices that act as a guide for the court. *See, e.g.,* Sylvia Coal Co., Inc. v. Mercury Coal & Coke Co., 156 S.E.2d 1, 151 W. Va. 818, 4 UCCR 650 (1967) (contract set price of coal between $2.25 and $2.50); Schmieder v. Standard Oil Co. of Ind., 230 N.W.2d 732, 69 Wis. 2d 419, 17 UCCR 360 (1975) (price equal to seller's cost plus depreciation "as might be mutually agreed upon").

[398] Official Comment 6 to U.C.C. § 2-305 states that although the purpose of the entire section is to give effect to the agreement that has been made, that effect is always conditioned by the requirement of good faith inherent in all contracts. *See* Marquette Co. v. Norcem, Inc., 494 N.Y.S.2d 511, 114 A.D.2d 738, 42 UCCR 79 (N.Y. Sup. Ct. App. Div. 1985). In this case, the contract called for the sale of cement at a price to be agreed upon but not to exceed $38 per ton. The seller demanded $38 per ton for the cement and would take nothing less. On consideration of a motion to vacate a default judgment, the court said that the seller's unwillingness to consider anything less than the maximum price appeared to be a failure to negotiate in good faith.

will set a reasonable price. The parties can, however, expressly condition their duties under the contract upon reaching an agreement on price.[399] In this case, if the parties fail to agree, their duties under the contract are discharged and neither party is liable for nonperformance.

The parties may also choose to have the price fixed by some external standard. For example, an agreement might set the price as a certain percentage of the price recorded in a trade publication. There are surprisingly few cases,[400] however, and the most frequent example seems to be when a buyer contracts to purchase a limited edition automobile at the "sticker" or "list" price.[401] If, for some reason, the pricing mechanism established in the contract fails, the agreement is construed as setting a reasonable price at the time for delivery.

Comment 4 to section 2-305 suggests, however, that there will be cases where the failure of an agreed pricing mechanism will preclude the formation of an enforceable contract. The Comment says that there may be cases where "a particular person's judgment is not chosen as a barometer of a fair price, but is an essential condition to the parties' intent to make any contract at all."[402] An example mentioned in the Comment is the choice of an expert trusted by both parties to value a painting for which there is no market standard.

These cases should not be limited, however, to those requiring a "particular person's" judgment. Any time that it appears from the circumstances surrounding the contract that the parties intended to condition their obliga-

---

[399] Assuming that the parties are obligated to bargain in good faith to reach agreement on price, a contract formed on this basis should not fail on the ground that the promises exchanged are illusory and, therefore, the contract lacks consideration. *See, e.g.*, Wagner Excello Foods, Inc. v. Fearn Int'l, Inc., 601 N.E.2d 956, 235 Ill. App. 3d 224, 20 UCCR2d 1221 (1992) (price was to be periodically renegotiated; if parties were unable to agree on price, contract was to terminate thirty days after end of last period).

[400] *See, e.g.*, Board of Comm'rs v. Annadale Scrap Co., Inc. 398 N.E.2d 810, 60 Ohio App. 2d 415, 28 UCCR 52 (1978) (price based upon a percentage of the price for melting steel printed in leading trade magazine). The most notable case is North Cent. Airlines, Inc. v. Continental Oil Co., 574 F.2d 582, 23 UCCR 581 (D.C. Cir. 1978) where the parties entered into a long-term contract for the purchase of aviation fuel. The price of the fuel was tied to posted crude oil prices. As a result of the Arab oil embargo, the government introduced a two-tier pricing system that rendered the contractual index unworkable. The court found, despite the failure of the pricing mechanism, that the parties intended to be bound, and remanded the case to the District Court to determine a reasonable price.

[401] *See, e.g.*, Sedmack v. Charlie's Chevrolet, Inc., 622 S.W.2d 694, 31 UCCR 851 (Mo. Ct. App. 1981); Roy Buckner Chevrolet v. Cagle, 418 So. 2d 878, 34 UCCR 413 (Ala. 1982); Barto v. United States, 823 F. Supp. 1369, 21 UCCR2d 924 (E.D. Mich. 1993).

[402] U.C.C. § 2-305, Official Comment 4.

tions on the existence of a particular pricing mechanism,[403] they should be relieved of those obligations if the chosen standard is not available. This will usually be the case where there is no well-functioning market for the goods in question.

As with section 2-204, section 2-305 requires that the parties *intend* to conclude a contract for sale, despite the open price term, in order for the court to supply a price and enforce the contract.[404] Comment 2 to section 2-305 recognizes that under some circumstances, the absence of a price term will mean that the parties have not concluded a deal. Although the issue of contract formation will generally be a question for the trier of fact,[405] most open-price cases in which courts have found no contractual intent have also involved many other gaps in the agreement.[406] If no intent to contract is found, but there has nonetheless been partial performance, section 2-305(4) requires restitution by the buyer of goods received[407] and by the seller of any portion of the price paid by the buyer.[408]

[B]   Open Terms Other Than Price

There are a number of other Code sections that supply content to incomplete agreements. Many of these are discussed in other portions of the text.[409] Some, however, can be conveniently grouped under two hypothetical cases.

---

[403] Although Comment 4 to U.C.C. § 2-205 describes a situation in which the parties' intent *to contract at all* is conditioned upon the existence of a pricing standard, it is also possible, and probably more likely, that the parties will intend to conclude a contract, but to condition *their duties under the contract* on the existence of the pricing mechanism. The parties to such an agreement are bound at the time they conclude their agreement, but if the pricing mechanism fails, their duties are discharged.

[404] It should be emphasized again that we are talking about *manifested* or *objective* intent, not subjective intent. *See* § 3.07, *supra.*

[405] *See* Bethlehem Steel Corp. v. Litton Indus., 1982 WL 171058, 35 UCCR 1091 (Pa. Super. 1982), *rev'd on other grounds*, 40 UCCR 1639 (Pa. Super. 1985).

[406] *See, e.g.*, Board of Trustees of the Samaritan Hosp. Ass'n of Mich. v. American Hosp. Supply Corp., 221 N.W.2d 561, 49 Mich. App. 106, 13 UCCR 733 (1973); Flowers Baking Co. of Lynchburg, Inc. v. R-P Packaging, Inc., 329 S.E.2d 462, 229 Va. 370, 40 UCCR 1631 (1985); W.J. Schafer Assocs., Inc., v. Cordont, Inc., 493 S.E.2d 512, 33 UCCR2d 1073 (Va. 1997).

[407] If the buyer cannot return the goods, he must pay to the seller their reasonable value at the time of delivery. U.C.C. § 2-305(4).

[408] Quaker State Mushroom Co., Inc. v. Dominick's Finer Foods, Inc. of Ill., 635 F. Supp. 1281, 1 UCCR2d 365 (N.D. Ill. 1986); In re Glover Constr. Co. v. Peyton, 49 B.R. 581, 41 UCCR 32 (W.D. Ky. 1985).

[409] *See, e.g.*, §§ 5.02, 5.05, *infra.*

Case 1. Seller is a grower of grapes, and the buyer is a winery. Two weeks ago, the parties entered into a contract whereby the grower agreed to supply the winery with 3,000 tons of grapes of a particular variety at a specified price per ton from its early fall harvest. The parties signed a writing that was sufficient to satisfy the Code's statute of frauds but that contained only the terms set out above.[410]

Despite the absence in Case 1 of terms dealing with such things as delivery date, place of delivery, means of transportation, and whether the delivery must be made in a single lot, if the parties intend to be bound, the absence of these terms will not preclude the formation of a contract.[411] A number of Code sections assist in filling in these gaps in the contract.

Most of the Code sections applicable to Case 1 begin with the language "unless otherwise agreed." The Code leaves the parties free to work out their own agreement. The agreement need not be entirely in writing; to the extent that the parol evidence rule permits, evidence of oral agreements is admissible to supplement the writing.[412] Also, usage of trade, course of dealing, and course of performance can be used to fill in the gaps in a writing.[413] It is only when a term is not supplied by the agreement of the parties that the Code steps in to supply the term.[414] The solutions for the open terms in the hypothetical are discussed in the following paragraphs.

Single or Separate Lots. All of the goods are to be delivered at one time, not in several lots, unless circumstances give either party the right to make or demand delivery in lots.[415]

---

[410] *See* Allied Grape Growers v. Bronco Wine Co., 249 Cal. Rptr. 872, 6 UCCR2d 1059 (Cal. Ct. App. 1988) for a case with facts similar to the hypothetical.

[411] U.C.C. § 2-204. See § 3.07, *supra.*

[412] *See* Rajala v. Allied Corp., 66 B.R. 582, 2 UCCR2d 1203 (D. Kan. 1986); George v. Davoli, 91 Misc. 2d 246, 397 N.Y.S.2d 895, 22 UCCR 603 (Cal. Ct. App. 1977); § 3.15, *infra.*

[413] *See, e.g.,* Architectural Metal Sys., Inc. v. Consolidated Sys., Inc., 58 F.3d 1227, 26 UCCR2d 1047 (7th Cir. 1995) (allowing trade usage to supply terms of a contract that were not included in the writing); Mid-South Packers, Inc. v. Shoneys, Inc., 761 F.2d 1117, 41 UCCR 38 (5th Cir. 1985) (parties' course of performance supplied new price).

[414] Terms supplied through usage of trade, course of dealing, and course of performance are part of the "agreement" of the parties. U.C.C. § 1-201.

[415] U.C.C. § 2-307 provides:

> Unless otherwise agreed all goods called for by a contract for sale must be tendered in a single delivery and payment is due only on such tender but where the circumstances give either party the right to make or demand delivery in lots the price if it can be apportioned may be demanded for each lot.

See Luedtke Eng'g Co., Inc. v. Indiana Limestone Co., Inc., 740 F.2d 598, 39 UCCR 400 (7th Cir. 1984) (section 2-307 did not require delivery of 70,000 tons of limestone in a

Time of Delivery. The seller must make delivery within a reasonable time.[416] In determining a "reasonable time" for delivery, factors such as the nature of the goods, the extent of the seller's knowledge of the buyer's intentions,[417] the nature of the market for the goods, available methods of transportation, and other factors[418] should be taken into account.[419] Usage of trade, course of dealing, and course of performance may also be used to determine what is a reasonable time for delivery.[420]

Courts have relied on section 2-309 to supply a time for delivery in a variety of circumstances apart from simply filling in gaps in an express agreement. For example, in a number of cases courts have relied on section 2-309 to establish a time for delivery when the original contract contained a time for delivery, but the failure of the seller to deliver the goods at the time established by the contract was waived by the buyer and no further time for delivery was agreed upon.[421] The section has also been invoked where the parties have expressly left the time for delivery to be agreed upon in the future and they have failed to agree.[422]

---

single lot because circumstances indicated parties expected delivery in lots); Stinnes Interoil, Inc. v. Apex Oil Co., 604 F. Supp. 978 (S.D.N.Y. 1985) (question of fact whether circumstances called for delivery in lots of 500,000 barrels of oil).

[416] U.C.C. § 2-309.

[417] When the buyer has a particular need for the goods that the seller has no reason to know, that need is not relevant for the purpose of determining a reasonable time for delivery. *See* Beiriger & Sons Irrigation, Inc. v. Southwest Land Co., Inc., 705 P.2d 532, 41 UCCR 1621 (Colo. Ct. App. 1985); Mendelson-Zekker Co., Inc. v. Joseph Wedner & Son Co., 7 UCCR 1045 (USDA 1970).

[418] *See, e.g.*, Mendelson-Zeller Co., Inc. v. Joseph Wedner & Son Co., 7 UCCR 1045 (USDA 1970) (the weather).

[419] *See* Anderson & Nafinger v. G.T. Newcomb, Inc., 595 P.2d 704, 100 Idaho 175, 27 UCCR 21 (1979).

[420] *See* United States ex rel. Shankle-Clairday, Inc. v. Crow, 414 F. Supp. 160, 20 UCCR 47 (M.D. Tenn. 1976); Allied Grape Growers v. Bronco Wine Co., 249 Cal. Rptr. 872, 203 Cal. App. 3d 432, 6 UCCR2d 1059 (1988). There is, at least in theory, a difference between cases in which usage of trade, course of dealing, and course of performance are used to directly fill in the time for delivery (and other gaps in the express contract), and where they are used to help determine a reasonable time for purposes of U.C.C. § 2-309. If usage of trade, course of dealing, or course of performance can be used to supply directly the time of delivery, there is no need to resort to section 2-309. U.C.C. § 2-309, Official Comment 1.

[421] *See* United States ex rel. Shankle-Clairday, Inc. v. Crow, 414 F. Supp. 160, 20 UCCR 47 (M.D. Tenn. 1976); Farmers Union Grain Terminal Ass'n v. Hermanson, 549 F.2d 1177, 21 UCCR 61 (8th Cir. 1977); Taft-Pierce Mfg. Co. v. Seagate Technology, Inc., 789 F. Supp. 1220, 17 UCCR 711 (D.R.I. 1992).

[422] *See* Allied Grape Growers v. Bronco Wine Co., 249 Cal. Rptr. 872, 203 Cal. App. 3d 432, 6 UCCR2d 1059 (1988).

A couple of cases have relied upon section 2-309 to fill in gaps created by the "battle of the forms."[423] In *Southern Idaho Pipe & Steel Co. v. Cal-Cut Pipe and Supply, Inc.*,[424] documents exchanged by the parties contained different delivery dates; the seller's form contained a delivery date of October 15 and the buyer's form contained a delivery date of December 15. Despite this disagreement, the court found a binding contract was formed by the exchange of documents and held that the two delivery dates canceled each other.[425]

In *Alliance Wall Corp. v. Ampat Midwest Corp.*,[426] the court refused to find the creation of a binding contract where the documents exchanged by the parties disagreed as to delivery date.[427] Because the parties had partially performed, however, a contract was found under section 2-207(3), and section 2-309 was used to fill in the gap. Finally, in *Ward Transformer Co. v. Distrigas of Massachusetts Corp.*,[428] the written agreement for the purchase of a transformer was silent as to delivery date. The parties then exchanged confirmations with conflicting delivery dates. Pursuant to Comment 6 to section 2-207, the conflicting dates dropped out, and the gap was filled in using section 2-309.

Sometimes when the parties have not agreed on a delivery date, one party (assume the buyer) will later demand delivery by a particular date. The other party (assume the seller) will be unable or unwilling to meet that date. A number of questions might arise in this scenario. If the date by which the buyer demands delivery is unreasonable, has the buyer breached by making the demand? If the time demanded by the buyer is reasonable, is the seller's refusal to deliver on that date a breach?

Neither of these circumstances, without more, will result in a default under the Code. According to Comment 4 to section 2-309, "such demands are to be treated, in the first instance, as expressions of desire or intention, requesting the assent or acquiescence of the other party, not as final positions which may amount without more to breach or to create breach by the other side."[429] If a party suggests a time for performance, however, and the other

---

[423] *See* § 3.04[B], *supra*.

[424] 567 P.2d 1246, 98 Idaho 495, 22 UCCR 25 (1977).

[425] *See* the discussion of the "knock-out" rule in the battle of the forms at § 3.04[D], *supra*.

[426] 17 Ohio App. 3d 59, 477 N.E.2d 1206, 41 UCCR 377 (1984).

[427] *Id*. at 1210–1211. The court felt that a contract could not be formed under U.C.C. § 2-207(1) when the "dickered" terms did not agree.

[428] 1992 WL 316072, 18 UCCR2d 29 (E.D.N.C. 1992).

[429] U.C.C. § 2-309, Official Comment 4. *See* Southern Utils., Inc. v. Jerry Mandel Mach. Corp., 321 S.E.2d 508, 39 UCCR 1231 (N.C. Ct. App. 1984).

party fails to respond, the Code treats the failure as acquiescence in the suggestion.[430]

When both parties allow a reasonable time for performance to pass without communication, neither can place the other in default without providing reasonable notice. According to Comment 5 to section 2-309, this conduct can be viewed as enlarging the reasonable time permitted for performance.[431]

Place for Delivery. In the absence of agreement by the parties, the place for delivery of the goods is governed by section 2-308. If the contract is for the sale of identified goods[432] and if the parties know the location of those goods, that location is the place of delivery. Otherwise, the seller's place of business (or, if he has no place of business, his residence) is the place of delivery.[433] Neither of these rules is applicable if the agreement can be interpreted as authorizing or requiring the seller to ship the goods to the buyer. These contracts are governed by section 2-504 and are discussed later in this text.[434]

Payment. Payment of the price is due on receipt of the goods,[435] although the seller's tender of the goods to the buyer must be at a reasonable hour and the goods must be kept available for a sufficient time to enable the buyer to take possession.[436] Payment of the price is subject to the right of the buyer to inspect the goods prior to payment.[437] When the circumstances give either party the right to make or demand delivery in lots, the price, if it can be apportioned, may be demanded for each lot.[438] If delivery is made by way of documents of title, however, the above rules may not apply. Shipment under documents of title is discussed later in this text.[439]

Applying these rules to Case 1, the sale of 3,000 tons of grapes, the seller is obligated to deliver all of the grapes to the buyer within a reasonable

---

[430] U.C.C. § 2-309, Official Comment 6. *But see* Solitron Devices, Inc. v. Veeco Instruments, Inc., 492 So. 2d 1357, 1 UCCR2d 1437 (Fla. Dist. Ct. App. 1986) (statement in Comment 6 that a failure to reply is an acquiescence was not binding because comments have not been adopted as the law in Florida and are "at best persuasive only").

[431] U.C.C. § 2-309, Official Comment 5.

[432] "Identification" is discussed in §§ 2.03[B], *supra* and 6.02, *infra*.

[433] U.C.C. § 2-308.

[434] *See* § 5.02[A], *infra*.

[435] U.C.C. § 2-310(a).

[436] U.C.C. § 2-503(1)(a). "Tender" is defined in U.C.C. § 2-503(1).

[437] U.C.C. § 2-513.

[438] U.C.C. § 2-307. If the price cannot be apportioned, it is not due until all of the goods have been delivered unless the contract explicitly or implicitly, through usage of trade, course of dealing, or course of performance provides otherwise. *See* U.C.C. § 2-507.

[439] *See* § 5.02[B], *infra*.

time, and all of the grapes must be delivered at one time. Unless the agreement provides otherwise—either expressly or through usage of trade, course of dealing, or course of performance—or the contract authorizes the seller to ship the grapes, they must be delivered to the buyer at the seller's place of business. Payment must be made at the time the goods are delivered, and may be made by check unless the seller demands cash.[440]

Case 2. Assume the same basic factual pattern as in Case 1: a contract for the sale and purchase of 3,000 tons of grapes at a specified price. Assume further, however, that the contract requires delivery of a number of different variety of grapes and that the contract gives the buyer the option of selecting the quantity of each variety.

In addition to the Code's "gap-fillers," the Code gives content to a term that permits one of the parties to fill in the particulars of the agreement.[441] The specifications by that party (the buyer in Case 2) "must be made in good faith and within the limits set by commercial reasonableness."[442] If the specifications are not seasonably made by the buyer and materially affect the seller's performance, the seller may either proceed to perform in any reasonable manner or treat the failure to specify as a breach.[443] Furthermore, the failure to cooperate excuses the seller from any resulting delay in performance.[444]

---

[440] U.C.C. § 2-511. If the seller demands cash, the buyer has a reasonable time to procure the cash. U.C.C. § 2-511(2).

[441] U.C.C. § 2-311(1) provides:

> An agreement for sale which is otherwise sufficiently definite (subsection (3) of section 2-204) to be a contract is not made invalid by the fact that it leaves particulars of performance to be specified by one of the parties. Any such specification must be made in good faith and within limits set by commercial reasonableness.

See Ninth St. E., Ltd. v. Harrison, 259 A.2d 772, 7 UCCR 171 (Conn. Cir. Ct. 1968) (arrangements as to shipment at seller's option under § 2-311(2); Bethlehem Steel Corp. v. Litton Indus., Inc., 1982 WL 171058, 35 UCCR 1091 (Pa. Super. 1982) (time of performance left to buyer).

[442] U.C.C. § 2-311(1).

[443] *See* Jon-T Farms, Inc. v. Perryton Equity Exch., 567 S.W.2d 560, 23 UCCR 1130 (Tex. Ct. App. 1978) (failure of buyer to cooperate with seller to insure seller's presence at place of delivery excused seller's tender and constituted breach); Cole v. Melvin, 441 F. Supp. 193, 22 UCCR 1154 (D.S.D. 1977) (failure of buyer to notify seller as required by contract that he is ready to receive goods excuses seller's tender under U.C.C. § 2-311 and permits seller to resell and collect damages).

[444] *See* Precise Tool & Gage Co., Inc. v. Multiform Desiccants, Inc., 42 B.R. 677 (E.D. Tenn. 1984) (buyer's delay in providing revised, workable design excused seller's delay in performance).

[C] Duration

Occasionally, parties will make agreements calling for successive performances but which contain no express duration term.[445] This sometimes occur in franchise or distributorship arrangements,[446] which most courts have held are covered by the Code.[447] When no duration is prescribed, how long must the parties continue to deal with each other, and how may the agreement be terminated by one of the parties?[448]

The Code attempts to resolve these difficulties through subsections (2) and (3) of section 2-309. Subsection (2) of section 2-309 states that a contract that provides for successive performances, but which is indefinite in duration is "valid for a reasonable time." It adds, however, that "unless otherwise agreed [the contract] may be terminated at any time by either party." Finally, in subsection (3), the Code requires that termination of the contract by one party (except upon the happening of an agreed event) requires reasonable notification to the other party. For a number of reasons these Code provisions are not wholly satisfactory.

First, section 2-309(2) seems to create a contract lasting for "a reasonable time" while at the same time permitting either party to terminate "at any time." Further, Comment 2 indicates that when an arrangement has been carried on by the parties over the years, the reasonable time will continue indefinitely and the contract will not terminate until notice. As a result of this text and Comment, it is not clear that the "reasonable time" provision in section 2-309(2) has any effect. It does not set a minimum duration of

---

[445] *See, e.g.*, Lumber Enters., Inc. v. Hansen, 846 P.2d 1046, 257 Mont. 11, 20 UCCR2d 774 (1993); Michael Halebian, N.J., Inc. v. Roppe Rubber Corp., 718 F. Supp. 348, 10 UCCR2d 703 (D.N.J. 1989).

[446] *See, e.g.*, Pharo Distrib. Co. v. Stahl, 782 S.W.2d 635, 11 UCCR2d 814 (Ky. Ct. App. 1989); Jo-Ann, Inc. v. Alfin Fragrances, Inc., 731 F. Supp. 149, 11 UCCR2d 782 (D.N.J. 1989); Thermal Sys. of Ala. v. Sigafoose, 533 So. 2d 567, 7 UCCR2d 698 (Ala. 1988).

[447] *See, e.g.*, Weilerbacher v. Pittsburgh Brewing Co., 218 A.2d 806, 421 Pa. 118 (1966); Division of the Triple T Serv., Inc. v. Mobil Oil Corp., 304 N.Y.S.2d 191, 6 UCCR 1011 (N.Y. Sup. Ct. 1969); Artman v. Int'l Harvester Co., 355 F. 2482, 12 UCCR 87 (W.D. Pa. 1973); Newman v. West Loop Sav. Ass'n, 993 F.2d 90, 20 UCCR2d 1377 (5th Cir. 1993). *Contra* Kansas City Trailer Sales v. Holiday Rambler Corp., 1994 WL 49932 (W.D. Mo. 1994); Vigano v. Wylain, Inc., 633 F.2d 522 (8th Cir. 1980).

[448] At common law, such arrangements created problems of mutuality of obligation. *See, e.g.*, Velie Motor Car Co. v. Kopmeier Motor Car Co., 194 F. 324 (7th Cir. 1912); E.I. du Pont de Nemours Co. v. Clairborne-Reno Co., 64 F.2d 224 (8th Cir. 1933), *cert. denied,* 290 U.S. 646 (1933). It is now generally accepted, however, that they create enforceable contracts. *See, e.g.*, Artman v. Int'l Harvester Co., 355 F. Supp. 482 (W.D. Pa. 1973); In re Pennsylvania Tire Co., 26 B.R. 663, 37 UCCR 410 (N.D. Ohio 1982).

the contract because either party can terminate "at any time,"[449] and neither does it set a maximum duration, because if the parties continue the relationship without termination, the reasonable time becomes indefinite.

Second, although subsection (3) requires reasonable notification before termination of a contract without duration, it allows the parties to provide contractually for termination without notice unless the *operation* of such a provision would be unconscionable.[450] The problem with this language is that under section 2-302, unconscionability is determined from *the time that the contract is made.*[451] Contrary to the explicit direction of section 2-302, section 2-309(3) looks to the hardship created at the time of termination, not to the circumstances at the time of contracting.[452]

Despite these difficulties, most of the cases have focused on two issues: (1) whether the notice of termination was reasonable under section 2-309(3), and (2) whether the Code's obligation of good faith limits the right of a party under section 2-309(2) to terminate at any time.

Comment 8 to section 2-309 indicates that reasonable notice will generally give the other party a reasonable time to seek a substitute arrangement.[453] Courts have adhered to this standard,[454] although the circumstances

---

[449] *See* Jo-Ann, Inc. v. Alfin Fragrances, Inc., 731 F. Supp. 149, 11 UCCR2d 782 (D.N.J. 1989) (contract without duration may be terminated at any time without regard to whether a reasonable time has already expired). McCasland v. Prather, 585 P.2d 336, 92 N.M. 192, 25 UCCR 49 (N.M. Ct. App. 1978) (subsections 2 and 3 of U.C.C. § 2-309, when read together, set out a contract that is terminable at will upon reasonable notification). *But see* Superior Foods, Inc. v. Harris-Teeter Super Mkts., Inc., 217 S.E.2d 566, 288 N.C. 213, 17 UCCR 970 (1975) (court held that the right of either party to terminate does not begin until after the passage of a reasonable time).

[450] Similarly, Comment 8 provides that a term dispensing with reasonable notification is valid *unless the results of putting it into operation would be the creation of an unconscionable state of affairs.*

[451] U.C.C. § 2-302 states in part, "if the court as a matter of law finds the contract or any clause of the contract to have been unconscionable *at the time it was made.*"

[452] *But see* Sinkoff Beverage Co., Inc. v. Jos. Schlitz Brewing Co., 273 N.Y.S.2d 364, 51 Misc. 2d 446, 3 UCCR 733 (N.Y. Sup. Ct. 1966) (volume increase in business and subsequent expansion and development of its facilities and other expenditures in reliance upon continuing relationship *not* relevant in determining unconscionability; U.C.C. § 2-302 applies only at the time of contract).

[453] U.C.C. § 2-309, Official Comment 8.

[454] *See, e.g.,* Superior Foods, Inc. v. Harris-Teeter Super Mkts., Inc., 217 N.E.2d 566, 288 N.C. 213, 17 UCCR 970 (1975); Circo v. Spanish Gardens Food Mfg. Co., Inc., 643 F. Supp. 51, 2 UCCR2d 839 (W.D. Mo. 1985); City Builders Supply Co. v. National Gypsum Co., 39 UCCR 826 (D. Mass. 1984); Monarch Beverage Co., Inc. v. Tyfield Importers, Inc., 823 F.2d 1187, 4 UCCR2d 388 (7th Cir. 1987); Cherick Distrib., Inc. v. Polar Corp., 41 Mass. App. 125, 669 N.E.2d 218, 30 UCCR2d 464 (Mass. App. Ct. 1996).

of the contract may require consideration of other factors as well. For example, in *Hamilton Tailoring Co. v. Delta Airlines, Inc.*,[455] Delta terminated the contract with its supplier for flight attendant uniforms. The contract was an open-ended requirements contract, and in order to fulfill the contract the supplier had to keep a substantial number of uniforms in inventory. As a result of Delta's termination, the supplier was left with approximately $75,000 in inventory at the time the contract was terminated. Delta refused to take this inventory, and it could not be disposed of elsewhere. The court held that under these circumstances, a reasonable period of notification would be long enough to allow the supplier to sell Delta the inventory which it carried.[456]

Although the necessity for reasonable notice generally requires that a party give the other party time to find a substitute arrangement, an acceptable substitute may be something other than a replica of the terminated contract.[457] Furthermore, a supplier should not have to show that the substitute contract will be equally profitable for the other party. The time period, however, should be sufficient to allow the other party enough time to explore the market. The issue of reasonable notification will normally be a question of fact,[458] although a number of cases have held notifications in some circumstances sufficient (or insufficient) as a matter of law.[459]

The most contentious issue involving section 2-309 is whether the Code's provisions on good faith and unconscionability place limitations on the right to terminate the agreement at will, whether that right is found in section 2-309(2) or in the agreement itself. Courts have responded differ-

---

[455] 14 UCCR 1310, 1974 WL 21756 (S.D. Ohio 1974).

[456] *Id.* at 1315, 1316.

[457] In Monarch Beverage Co. v. Tyfield Importers, Inc., 823 F.2d 1187, 4 UCCR2d 388 (7th Cir. 1987), the court held that thirty days' notice of termination was sufficient when Monarch, a wholesaler of wine products, canceled its distributorship agreement with Tyfield for the distribution of Tosti Asti Spumante sparking wine. The court found that Tyfield could have contracted within this period for another brand of Asti Spumante, specifically Martini & Rossi, and therefore, the notice was reasonable.

[458] *See* Teitelbaum et al. v. Hallmark Cards, Inc., 520 N.E.2d 1333, 25 Mass. App. Ct. 555, 7 UCCR 2d 705 (1988); William H. White Co., Inc. v. B&A Mfg. Co., 794 P.2d 1099, 12 UCCR2d 28 (Colo. Ct. App. 1990).

[459] *See, e.g.,* Teitelbaum v. Hallmark Cards, Inc., 520 N.E.2d 1333, 25 Mass. App. Ct. 555, 7 UCCR2d 705 (1988) (period that allowed retailer to obtain full line of greeting cards from another supplier reasonable as a matter of law); Pharo Distrib. Co. v. Stahl, 782 S.W.2d 635, 11 UCCR2d 814 (Ky. Ct. App. 1989) (six days' notice insufficient as a matter of law to terminate beverage distributorship); Jo-Ann, Inc. v. Alfin Fragrances, Inc., 731 F. Supp. 149, 11 UCCR2d 782 (D.N.J. 1989) (no time between notice and termination unreasonable as a matter of law).

ently to this question, which reflects a clash of competing policies. On the one hand, there is a natural tendency to protect those who have invested considerable time and money in developing a business from the unexpected termination of a relationship upon which that business is based.[460] On the other hand there are policies permitting parties to fashion their own agreements and permitting easy termination of contracts that have become unsatisfactory for one of the parties.[461] These cases have been the subject of both scholarly comment[462] and legislation.[463]

A number of cases have held that termination at will under section 2-309 is limited by the Code's provisions on good faith,[464] although these cases provide little guidance as to the nature of these limitations. The majority of courts, however, have not applied the Code's good-faith standard to termination in cases when the contract either expressly permits termination at will or where it is silent as to termination.[465] Furthermore, in one

---

[460] *See, e.g.,* Burton v. Hitachi Am., Ltd., 504 F.2d 721 (7th Cir. 1974) (plaintiff, who had made considerable investments of time and money preparing for exclusive distributorship, entitled to damages when supplier terminates distributorship after four months); McGinnis Piano & Organ Co. v. Yamaha Int'l Corp., 480 F.2d 474, 12 UCCR 265 (8th Cir. 1973) (dealer entitled to sufficient period to recoup investment and recover reasonable profit).

[461] *See, e.g.,* Corenswet, Inc. v. Amana Refrigeration, Inc., 594 F.2d 129, 26 UCCR 301 (5th Cir. 1979) (clause permitting termination "without cause" or "for any reason" not in bad faith); Delta Servs. & Equip., Inc. v. RYKO Mfg. Co., 908 F.2d 7, 14 UCCR2d 414 (5th Cir. 1990) (goal of U.C.C. to promote mutually beneficial business dealings is undermined if parties are required to remain in relationship after it has served its purpose). *See also* Paulson, Inc. v. Bromar, Inc., 775 F. Supp. 1329, 17 UCCR2d 690 (D. Haw. 1991) (manufacturer may refuse to renew distributorship without good cause).

[462] *See, e.g.,* Anne L. Austin, "When Does a Franchisor Become a Fiduciary," 43 Case W. Res. L. Rev. 1151 (1993); Robert Hillman, "An Analysis of the Cessation of Contractual Relations," 68 Cornell L. Rev. 617 (1983); Thomas Diammond & Howard Foss, "Proposed Standards for Evaluating When the Covenant of Good Faith and Fair Dealing Has Been Violated: A Framework for Resolving the Mystery," 47 Hastings L.J. 585 (1996).

[463] *See, e.g.,* Ariz. Rev. Stat. Ann. § 28-1304.02 (1994) ("Notwithstanding the terms, provisions or conditions of any agreement or franchise, no franchisor shall cancel, terminate or refuse to continue any franchise unless the franchisor has good cause for termination or noncontinuance."); Calif. Bus. & Prof. Code, § 20021 (1994); Ohio Rev. Code § 4517.54 (1995).

[464] *See, e.g.,* Zapatha v. Dairy Mart, Inc., 408 N.E.2d 1370, 29 UCCR 1121 (Mass. 1980); Zidell Explorations, Inc. v. Conval Int'l, Ltd., 719 F.2d 1465, 37 UCCR 466 (9th Cir. 1983).

[465] *See, e.g.,* Sports & Travel Mktg., Inc. v. Chicago Cutlery Co., 811 F. Supp. 1372 (D. Minn. 1992); Highway Equip. Co. v. Caterpillar, Inc. 707 F. Supp. 954, 9 UCCR2d 29 (S.D. Ohio 1989); Blalock Mach. & Equip. Co., Inc. v. Iowa Mfg. Co. of Cedar Rapids, 576 F. Supp. 774, 36 UCCR 753 (N.D. Ga. 1983); Frank Lyon Co. v. Maytag Corp., 715 F. Supp. 922, 9 UCCR 2d 1222 (E.D. Ark. 1989); Amoco Oil Co. v. Burns, 437 A.2d 381, 496 Pa.

case where the court applied the Code's good-faith provisions, it held that the good-faith requirement in section 1-203 imposed only the obligation to act honestly and could not be used to import standards of decency, fairness, or reasonableness.[466]

The issue with respect to unconscionability under section 2-302, however, is more complex. Courts have been willing to subject *explicit* provisions permitting termination at will (or otherwise without cause)[467] to examination under the Code's unconscionability provision.[468] As previously discussed, section 2-309 appears to allow termination at will in a contract of indefinite duration even when the contract is silent on the issue.[469] Does section 2-302 apply to a term that is implied as a matter of law through section 2-309(2)?

There is no suggestion in the Code that its "gap-filler" provisions are subject to scrutiny under section 2-302. The language of section 2-302 provides that a court may find "the contract or any *clause* of the contract" to be unconscionable.[470] The use of the word "clause" suggests that the section was designed to deal with explicit provisions imposing surprise or undue hardship, not terms implied by the Code itself. Also, there appear to be no reported cases where a court has declared a term supplied by the Code to be unconscionable. Thus, the anomalous situation arises in which a explicit provision allowing termination at will may be determined by a court to be unconscionable, whereas the same term implied under section 2-309(2) is safe from scrutiny under section 2-302.

In refusing to apply section 2-302 to an express provision permitting termination at will, the court in *Artman v. International Harvester Co.*[471] said that subsection (2) of section 2-309 creates a policy favoring easy ter-

---

336 (1981). *But see* Hentze v. Unverfehrt, 604 N.E.2d 536, 237 Ill. App. 3d 606, 178 Ill. Dec. 280 (Ill. App. Ct. 1992) (at-will termination clause in dealership contract is not an express disavowal of implied obligation of good faith and fair dealing).

[466] Zapatha v. Dairy Mart, Inc., 408 N.E.2d 1370, 29 UCCR 1121 (Mass. 1980).

[467] Many franchise or distributorship contracts require a period of notice prior to termination and therefore are not literally terminable "at will." Generally, however, they are terminable without cause, and the notice periods are short. Functionally, therefore, provisions permitting termination "at will" and "without cause" are the same.

[468] *See, e.g.*, Corenswet, Inc., v. Amana Refrigeration, Inc., 594 F.2d 129, 26 UCCR 301 (5th Cir. 1979); Cardinal Stone Co., Inc. v. Rival Mfg., Co., 669 F.2d 395, 32 UCCR 1313 (6th Cir. 1982); Moridge Mfg. Co. v. Butler, 451 N.E.2d 677, 36 UCCR 1548 (Ind. Ct. App. 1983).

[469] *See* Weilersbacher v. Pittsburgh Brewing Co., 218 A.2d 806, 3 UCCR 309 (Pa. 1966).

[470] U.C.C. § 2-302 (emphasis added).

[471] 355 F. Supp. 482, 12 UCCR 87 (W.D. Penn. 1973).

mination of contracts of indefinite duration and the court should not use section 2-302 to emasculate these provisions. It indicated that even if it were to delete the express provision as unconscionable, section 2-309(2) itself would mandate the same result.

The reasoning of the Artman court is sound. In the absence of legislation, express provisions permitting termination "at will" or "without cause" in indefinite-duration contracts should not be subject to scrutiny under either section 1-203 or section 2-302. Nor should the right to terminate at will found in section 2-309(2), nor the exercise of that right, be subject to claims of bad faith or unconscionability. If there is evidence of fraud, duress, or mistake, section 1-103 provides a sufficient basis to prevent overreaching. Furthermore, if the conduct of one party has led the other reasonably to believe that termination would occur only for cause, the court can always find an implied term in the contract itself.[472]

§ 3.08 OUTPUT, REQUIREMENTS, AND EXCLUSIVE DEALING CONTRACTS

[A] Output and Requirements Contracts

Changing the fact pattern in the case above, assume now that our winery enters into a five-year contract with the grower in which the grower agrees to supply all of the winery's requirements for a particular kind of grape for a five-year period. No further quantity is stated, although the winery has purchased grapes in various quantities from the grower on a number of earlier occasions. The price for the grapes is to be established by a published market standard.[473]

Many pre-Code cases held such contracts unenforceable for two distinct reasons. First, the absence of a quantity term rendered the contract too indefinite for enforcement.[474] Second, the promise of the winery to purchase

---

[472] *See* McGinnis Piano & Organ Co. v. Yamaha Int'l Corp., 480 F.2d 474, 12 UCCR 265 (8th Cir. 1973) (where dealer has made substantial investment in reliance upon franchise agreement, court says jury should be instructed that they can find implied agreement that franchise shall continue for sufficient time to permit dealer to recoup investment, with prior termination permitted only for cause).

[473] *See* § 3.07[B], *supra.*

[474] *See, e.g.,* In re United Cigar Co. of Am., 72 F.2d 673 (2d Cir. 1934); Fort Wayne Corrugated Paper Co. v. Anchor Hocking Glass Corp., 130 F.2d 471 (3d Cir. 1942); Pessin v. Fox Head Waukesha Corp., 282 N.W. 582, 230 Wis. 277 (1938).

its requirements from the seller was illusory, and therefore did not provide consideration for the seller's promise to fill the buyer's requirements.[475]

The policy of the Code, however, clearly favors the enforcement of requirements and output[476] contracts, and they often make good commercial sense. Although the Code does not explicitly validate requirement and output contracts, the implication in section 2-306(1) is clear:

> A term which measures the quantity by the output of the seller or the requirements of the buyer means such actual output or requirements as may occur in good faith, except that no quantity unreasonably disproportionate to any stated estimate or in the absence of a stated estimate to any normal or otherwise comparable prior output or requirements may be tendered or demanded.

Comment 2 to section 2-306 states that output and requirements contracts do not lack consideration nor are they, by their nature, too indefinite to be enforceable.[477] These agreements do not lack consideration for at least two reasons. First, the buyer in a requirements contract or the seller in an output contract is not free, with unfettered discretion, to determine the quantity of goods that can be demanded or tendered under the agreement, and thus has not made an illusory promise. Unlike an agreement in which the buyer can order as much of a specified quantity of goods "as he wants,"[478] an agreement by which the seller will sell and the buyer will buy all (or a stated portion) of the buyer's requirements does not leave the buyer free to order or not order at his discretion. *If the buyer has requirements*, he must purchase them (or a stated portion of them) from the seller.[479] Similarly, *if a seller has output*, he must provide it (or a stated portion of it) to the buyer.

Second, section 2-306 requires that the parties exercise good faith in determining requirements or output. Furthermore, a requirements buyer may

---

[475] *See, e.g.*, Swindell & Co. v. First Nat'l Bank, 49 S.E. 673, 121 Ga. 714 (1905); Scar Schlegel Mfg. Co. v. Peter Cooper's Glue Factory, 132 N.E. 1481, 231 N.Y. 459 (1921); Crane v. C. Crane & Co., 105 F. 869 (7th Cir. 1901).

[476] An "output" contract is one in which a buyer agrees to buy all or a specified portion (e.g., one-half) of a seller's output.

[477] U.C.C. § 2-306, Official Comment 2.

[478] *See, e.g.*, Nat Nal Serv. Stations, Inc. v. Wolf, 107 N.E.2d 473, 304 N.Y. 332 (1952).

[479] Cases inevitably arise that present problems of interpreting the language of the agreement to determine whether the parties have limited their freedom to buy or sell from others. *See* Homestake Mining Co. v. Washington Public Power Supply Sys., 476 F. Supp. 1162, 26 UCCR 1113 (N.D. Cal. 1979); Century Ready-Mix Co. v. Lower & Co., 770 P.2d 692, 10 UCCR2d 705 (Wyo. 1989). *See also* Chemical Distribs. Inc. v. Exxon Corp., 1 F.3d 1478 (5th Cir. 1993) (court held that trial court correctly found contract was susceptible to more than one interpretation with respect to quantity and therefore was properly a jury issue).

not demand, nor an output seller tender, a quantity that is unreasonably disproportionate to stated estimates or, in the absence of a stated estimate, disproportionate to any normal or comparable prior output or requirement. These provisions act as further limitations on the freedom of action of the parties, as well as providing the courts with guidance for policing these agreements. It is this policing function, rather than the issue of validity, that has occupied the attention of the courts.

The duty of good faith imposed by section 2-306 includes both honesty in fact and the observance of reasonable commercial standards of fair dealing in the trade.[480] Because the issue of good faith is a question of fact,[481] it is difficult to define with precision, and the results of some cases cannot be easily reconciled.[482]

The requirement that quantities not be "unreasonably disproportionate" is not the equivalent of "good faith."[483] The requirement of proportionality is an independent limitation so that, for example, a buyer's demand in a requirements contract may be unreasonably disproportionate even though

---

[480] U.C.C. §§ 1-201(19), 2-103. *See* Sherrock v. Commercial Credit Corp., 2690 A.2d 407, 8 UCCR 123 (Del. Super. Ct. 1970). It is interesting that while Official Comment 2 to U.C.C. § 2-306 makes clear that the Article 2 definition of "good faith" is applicable to section 2-306, which includes the observance of reasonable standards of fair dealing in the trade, the definitional cross-reference to "good faith" is only to section 1-201, which defines "good faith" for purposes of the entire Code as "honesty in fact."

[481] *See* Bloor v. Falstaff Brewing Corp., 601 F.2d 609, 26 UCCR 281 (2d Cir. 1979); Gruschus v. C.R. Davis Contracting Co., 409 P.2d 500, 75 N.M. 649, 2 UCCR 1080 (1966). *See also* Feld v. Henry S. Levy & Sons, Inc., 335 N.E.2d 320, 373 N.Y.S.2d 102, 17 UCCR 365 (1975) (unresolved question of fact as to whether the cessation of manufacture of bread crumbs was in good faith prevented entry of summary judgment); Miami Packaging, Inc., v. Processing Sys., Inc., 792 F. Supp. 560 (S.D. Ohio 1991) (genuine issues of material fact precluded summary judgment on claim of breach for contract because a reasonable jury could differ on whether a breach of the obligation of good faith occurred).

[482] *Compare* Seaside Petroleum Co., Inc. v. Steve E. Rawl, Inc., 339 S.E.2d 601, 177 Ga. App. 341, 42 UCCR 1223 (1985) (buyer did not breach contract by purchasing no gasoline for three years and informing the seller that it would not be purchasing *any* gasoline, when the terms of their contract provided the seller to deliver "(buyer's) requirements of [gasoline]" for a ten-year period *with* United Serv. Auto Ass'n v. Schlang, 894 P.2d 967, 28 UCCR2d 151 (Nev. 1995) (a court may enforce a requirements contract by finding an "implied" promise on the part of the buyer when it is apparent that the parties intended to enter a binding requirements contract).

[483] *See* Empire Gas Corp. v. American Bakeries Co., 840 F.2d 1333, 5 UCCR2d 545 (7th Cir. 1988); Atlantic Track & Turnout Co. v. Perini Corp., 989 F.2d 541, 20 UCCR2d 426 (1st Cir. 1993); Orange & Rockland Utils., Inc. v. Amerada Hess Corp., 397 N.Y.S.2d 814, 59 A.D.2d 110, 22 UCCR 310 (N.Y. Sup. Ct. 1977).

made in good faith.[484] The proportionality requirement, however, has generally been applied only to cases involving an *increase* in the requirements or output of a party. The sole limitation applied by the courts to a *decrease* in requirements has been the obligation of good faith.[485]

A substantial majority of the cases deal with requirements contracts rather than output contracts. Consequently, the law surrounding section 2-306 has largely developed from cases in which a requirements buyer has (1) sought a large increase in the amount of goods demanded under the contract or (2) substantially decreased the amount of goods demanded or completely eliminated its demand for goods under the contract.

The opinion in *Orange & Rockland Utilities, Inc. v. Amerada Hess Corp.*[486] contains the most thorough explanation of the good-faith and proportionality limitations of section 2-306. In June of 1969, Amerada Hess (the seller) agreed to supply Orange & Rockland's (the buyer's) oil requirements for its Thompson's Cove, New York, plant at a fixed price of $2.14 a barrel for five years. The contract contained estimates prepared by the buyer as part of a five-year budget projection. Within five months of the execution of the contract, the price of oil began to climb rapidly, and by March 1971, the market price was at $4.30 per barrel. As the market price increased, the buyer began demanding larger amounts of oil. By mid-1970, the buyer told the seller that it estimated that its total demand for 1970 would be more than a million barrels greater than the contract estimate, an

---

[484] For example, a dramatic increase in a buyer's requirements caused by the discovery by the buyer of a revolutionary manufacturing process would not be in bad faith but would probably be unreasonably disproportionate. *See* Angelica Uniform Group, Inc. v. Ponderosa Sys., Inc., 487 F. Supp. 1374 (E.D. Mo. 1980); Empire Gas v. American Bakeries Co., 840 F.2d 1333, 5 UCCR2d 545 (7th Cir. 1988); Wilsonville Concrete Prods. v. Todd Bldg. Co., 574 P.2d 1112, 281 Or. 345, 23 UCCR 590 (1978). Brewster of Lynchburg, Inc. v. Dial Corp., 33 F.3d 355, 24 UCCR2d 738 (4th Cir. 1994).

[485] *See* Empire Gas Corp. v. American Bakeries Co., 840 F.2d 1333, 5 UCCR2d 545 (7th Cir. 1988) (court held that it was an error to read to the jury the "unreasonably disproportionate" proviso of U.C.C. § 2-306 because that provision applies only when buyer demands more than his requirements). Limiting application of the "unreasonably disproportionate" test to an increase in requirements is apparently the result of the fact that Comment 2 to section 2-306 contemplates that a complete shutdown by a requirements buyer may under some circumstances be permissible, and the cases have so held. *See, e.g.,* Empire Gas v. American Bakeries Co., 840 F.2d 1333, 5 UCCR2d 545 (7th Cir. 1988); Wilsonville Concrete Prods. v. Todd Bldg. Co., 574 P.2d 1112, 281 Or. 345, 23 UCCR 590 (1978). Brewster of Lynchburg Inc. v. Dial Corp., 33 F.3d 355, 24 UCCR2d 738 (4th Cir. 1994). A total lack of requirements would hardly seem to be a proportionate decrease to normal or comparable requirements.

[486] 397 N.Y.S.2d 814, 22 UCCR 310 (N.Y. Sup. Ct. 1977).

increase of about 63 percent. The seller refused to supply more than the estimate plus 10 percent for the remainder of the contract. During the period from 1971 until the contract terminated in 1973, the buyer used more than double the contract estimate in oil, some of which it purchased elsewhere because of the seller's refusal to fill the buyer's entire requirements. The buyer then sued the seller for the difference between its total cost for fuel oil during the period of the contract and the cost it would have incurred had the seller delivered the amount demanded at the contract price.

The trial court denied any recovery to the buyer. It reasoned that the increase in oil consumption was due primarily to (1) increases in sales of electricity by the buyer to other utilities and (2) a net shift by the buyer from other fuels, primarily gas, to fuel oil. The court found that these two factors did not provide a good-faith basis for increasing its requirements. In light of this conclusion, the trial court did not consider the issue of whether the requirements were "unreasonably disproportionate."[487]

The appeals court held that the trial court's decision that the buyer did not act in good faith was justified. It found that from 1969 to 1970, the buyer had used the favorable price of oil to increase its sale of electricity to other transmitters by a factor of six. Because of the price of oil in the contract with the seller, the buyer was able to "suddenly and dramatically propel itself into the position of a large seller of power to other utilities," a position it had not occupied at the time the contract was signed. The court found that the buyer was "reselling" the cheap fuel provided by the seller to other utilities through the sale to them of electricity at cheaper prices than they could themselves produce. These transactions were not foreseeable at the time of the contract, did not enter into the parties' estimates, and were, therefore, not in good faith.

The court also decided that the quantities demanded by the buyer were "unreasonably disproportionate" as a matter of law. The touchstone of the court's analysis was the reasonable expectations of the parties.[488] The court listed five factors to be considered in determining whether a quantity was "unreasonably disproportionate": (1) the amount by which the requirements exceeded any stated estimate; (2) whether the seller had any reasonable basis on which to forecast or anticipate the requested increase; (3) the amount, if any, by which the market price of the goods exceeded the contract price; (4) whether the increase in market price was itself fortuitous; and (5) the reason for the increase in requirements. The court found that on the basis

---

[487] 397 N.Y.S.2d at 818, 22 UCCR at 315.
[488] *Id.* at 819, 22 UCCR at 316.

of these factors, the amount demanded by the buyer was unreasonably disproportionate and denied it any relief.

The court's focus on the reasonable expectations of the parties in its analysis of both the good-faith and proportionality requirements was entirely proper. These expectations formed the basis of the parties' agreement. The seller reasonably understood that it would be responsible for supplying fuel requirements to the buyer for the production of electricity for its own "retail" customers. The estimates in the contract were based on this assumption and this assumption was the foundation for the seller's understanding of the buyer's "requirements." Therefore, the buyer's demands disproportionately exceeded its "requirements" as the seller had reasonably understood them.

Certainly the case for the seller would have been weaker if the buyer had been primarily engaged in the business of "wholeselling" electricity, and would have been weaker still if the increase in the market price of oil had been more foreseeable.[489] The *Orange & Rockland Utilities* case is consistent with other cases which have held that a buyer cannot increase its requirements to take advantage of a favorable market price to resell all or a portion of the goods, when resale was not reasonably contemplated at the time of the contract.[490]

Even more numerous are cases in which a requirements buyer has dramatically decreased its requirements, often to the point of having no requirements at all. Comment 2 to section 2-306 attempts to provide guidance in these cases, but it is, at best, ambiguous and, at worst, contradictory.[491] It indicates that if a requirements buyer suffers from decreased sales of a product for which the requirement goods are an input, a decrease in requirements—even to the point of shutdown—might be permissible. At the same time, the Comment suggests that a shutdown merely to curtail losses that the buyer is suffering on the sale of its products is not permissible. These situations, however, are probably two sides of the same coin, and result from the fact that the product of the requirements buyer has become less competitive in the market. If, for example, a requirements buyer can no longer sell its product profitably at $2.00 per unit but must now sell at $3.00 per unit, the quantity demanded of the product is likely to decrease.[492] As

---

[489] *See* Lakeland v. Union Oil Co., 352 F. Supp. 758 (M.D. Fla. 1973) (increasing wholesale sales were beyond the contemplation of the parties and the scope of the contract).

[490] *See, e.g.*, Crane v. C. Crane & Co., 105 F. 869 (7th Cir. 1901). *See also* Massachusetts Gas & Elec. Light Supply Corp. v. V-M Corp., 387 F.2d 605, 4 UCCR 897 (1st Cir. 1967).

[491] U.C.C. § 2-306, Official Comment 2.

[492] Assuming, of course, a downward sloping demand curve. *See* Paul A. Samuelson & William D. Nordhaus, Economics, at 48–50 (14th ed. 1992).

a result, fewer of the requirements goods will be needed. Is the resulting decrease in its requirements due to the avoidance of losses—and therefore apparently impermissible under Comment 2—or is it merely due to a decrease in orders?

Despite the apparent proscription of Comment 2, the cases indicate that economic loss can justify a significant decrease in requirements, even to the point of shutdown. The cases further attempt, with some difficulty, to provide some guidelines for determining whether such a decrease is in "good faith."

In *Empire Gas Corp. v. American Bakeries Co.,*[493] Judge Richard Posner provided a thorough examination of the good-faith requirement in the context of a decrease in requirements. In *Empire Gas,* American Bakeries (the buyer) signed a contract with Empire Gas Co. (the seller) to purchase approximately 3,000 conversion units[494] for its delivery vehicles, "more or less depending on the requirements of the Buyer." The buyer further agreed to purchase all of the propane required to run the converted vehicles for a period of four years. Within days of the contract signing, the buyer decided, for undisclosed reasons, not to convert its delivery fleet, and thus never ordered any conversion units or propane. The seller sued and recovered over $3,000,000.

On appeal, Judge Posner treated the entire contract as a requirements contract and concluded that "good faith" provided the relevant standard to determine whether the buyer had breached the contract.[495] Describing "good faith" as a "chameleon" with no settled meaning, Judge Posner quickly established the outside parameters of the meaning of "good faith":

> Clearly, American Bakeries was acting in bad faith if during the contract period it bought propane conversion units from anyone other than Empire Gas, or made its own units, or reduced its purchases because it wanted to hurt Empire Gas (for example because they were competitors in some other market). Equally clearly, it was not acting in bad faith if it had a business reason that was independent of the terms of the contract or any other aspect of the relationship with Empire Gas, such as a drop in the demand for its bakery products that led it to reduce or abandon its fleet of delivery trucks.[496]

---

[493] 840 F.2d 1333, 5 UCCR2d 545 (7th Cir. 1988).

[494] The conversion units enabled gas-powered vehicles to run on propane with a flick of a switch.

[495] 840 F.2d at 1336, 5 UCCR2d at 551. Judge Posner rejected the application of the "unreasonably disproportionate standard" to *decreases* in requirements.

[496] 840 F.2d at 1339, 5 UCCR2d at 553.

The "harder question," as Judge Posner recognized, was when, short of these extremes, economic factors permit a substantial decrease, or total elimination, of a buyer's requirements. Understandably, the best Judge Posner could do was to suggest in general terms that this question depends on the degree of economic hardship that prompts the buyer's actions:

> The seller assumes the risk of a change in the buyer's business that makes continuation of the contract *unduly* costly, but the buyer assumes the risk of a *less urgent* change in his circumstances.[497]

Judge Posner concluded his analysis by stating that it is a "nice question" how exigent the buyer's circumstances must be to allow him to scale down his requirements, and although "more than a whim is required . . . how much more is unclear."[498] In this case, however, Judge Posner found that no reasonable jury could have failed to find bad faith in that *American Bakeries* had not disposed of its fleet of trucks, had the financial wherewithal to go through with the conversion process, and introduced no evidence justifying its reduction in requirements to zero.

The New York Court of Appeals, in *Feld v. Henry S. Levy & Sons,*[499] took a similar quantitative approach to the problem of economic loss in the context of an *output* contract. Feld (the buyer) contracted to buy all bread crumbs produced by Levy & Sons (the seller) for successive one-year periods.[500] The contract contained a provision allowing termination on six-months notice. Without serving the notice, the seller stopped producing bread crumbs because the process had become "uneconomical," and agreed to resume production only if the buyer agreed to a price increase. When the buyer refused to pay more for the crumbs, the seller dismantled the oven, sold the equipment, and transformed the space into a computer room.

The seller defended its elimination of output on the basis of the "economic feasibility" of continuing to produce bread crumbs at the contract price. As evidenced by its subsequent actions, the seller had more economically valuable uses for the resources it used to produce bread crumbs for the buyer. To continue to produce bread crumbs was costly, if only in terms of opportunity cost, and therefore, according to the seller, there was a good-faith basis for ceasing production.

The court in *Feld* held that the fact that the resources could be more profitably employed, or even that the production of bread crumbs had be-

---

[497] *Id.* at 1340, 5 UCCR2d at 554 (emphasis added).
[498] *Id.* at 1340, 5 UCCR2d at 555.
[499] 335 N.E.2d 320, 373 N.Y.S.2d 102, 37 N.Y.2d 466, 17 UCCR 365 (1975).
[500] *Id.* at 321, 373 N.Y.S.2d 102, 37 N.Y.2d 466, 17 UCC Rep. Serv. at 365.

come unprofitable, was not sufficient under section 2-306 to permit the seller to cease production and escape damages. This was particularly true in view of a cancellation clause in the contract that allowed the parties to terminate the contract on relatively short notice if it became unprofitable. On the other hand, the court said that if continued production of bread genuinely imperiled the seller's stability or threatened bankruptcy, discontinuing production would not have been in bad faith.

A final case meriting discussion is *Brewster of Lynchburg Inc. v. Dial Corp.*[501] In June 1988, Dial and Brewster agreed that Brewster would supply plastic bottles for use in Dial's Salem, Virginia plant. A few months later, Dial notified Brewster that it was closing the Salem facility because of the continued unprofitability of the plant. Dial notified Brewster that the contract would terminate in ninety days pursuant to a ninety-day termination clause in the contract. Brewster disputed Dial's right to terminate under this clause, arguing that this right accrued only on the anniversary date of the contract. Shortly thereafter, Brewster filed suit against Dial, and the trial court granted summary judgment in favor of Dial.

On appeal, the Court of Appeals for the Fourth Circuit decided that Dial could not exercise the escape clause prior to the anniversary date, and therefore its termination was not proper under that clause. Because the contract was a requirements contract, however, the inquiry did not end there. Citing *Empire Gas*, the court said that a buyer in a requirements contract can reduce its requirements to zero without breach so long as it does so in good faith.[502]

Although the court stated that "there is no established standard for determining whether a buyer acted in good faith,"[503] it had no trouble determining that Dial acted in good faith in this case. Dial closed that plant as a result of a restructuring, which ultimately resulted in the closure of all but one plant in the division because of low profitability. Because the decision was "a legitimate business decision" that the Salem plant was unprofitable rather than "a desire to avoid its obligations to Brewster," the court concluded that the elimination of any requirements for plastic bottles was in good faith.[504]

The court's opinion suggests that so long as the decision to decrease or eliminate requirements is based upon factors apart from dissatisfaction

---

[501] 33 F.3d 355, 24 UCCR2d 738 (4th Cir. 1994).

[502] *Id.* at 364, 24 UCCR2d at 752.

[503] *Id.* at 365, 24 UCCR2d at 753.

[504] *Id.* at 365, 24 UCCR2d at 754.

with the terms of requirements contract itself, it would be in good faith.[505] The court did not seem concerned with the extent to which the Salem plant was unprofitable, nor the extent to which the plant's operation imperiled the operations of the entire company or affected its profitability. Nor did it consider the suggestion of Comment 2 that a shutdown merely to curtail losses would not be in good faith. The *Lynchburg* case appears to be a favorable omen for requirements buyers.

Courts have been liberal in permitting a severe reduction or elimination of requirements when an event occurs that is beyond the control of the requirements buyer and unrelated to the requirements contract. For example, in *Wisonville Concrete Products v. Todd Building Co.*,[506] a seller of concrete entered into a requirements contract with a contractor who was building a hospital for the state of Oregon. Although the contract contained an estimate of approximately 3,000 cubic yards of concrete, as a result of the state's cancellation of the contract, the contractor purchased only 245 cubic yards. The court held that the dramatic difference between the estimate and the actual requirements did not constitute bad faith.[507] Also, reduction or elimination of requirements due to strikes[508] or to standard industry practices of which the requirements seller should have been aware are not in bad faith.[509]

[1] Conclusion

The proper focus in deciding whether a party acted in good faith is risk allocation; who should bear the risk of an event that causes a dramatic decrease or elimination of a party's requirements or output. The analysis does not differ fundamentally from issues such as mistake or impracticabil-

---

[505] *Id.* at 336, 24 UCCR2d at 753. ("An essential ingredient of good faith in the case of the buyer's reducing his estimated requirements is that he not merely have had second thoughts about the terms of the contract and want to get out.")

[506] 574 P.2d 1112, 281 Or. 345, 23 UCCR 590 (1978).

[507] *Id.* at 1115, 281 Or. at 350, 23 UCCR at 594. *See* R.A. Weaver & Assocs., Inc. v. Asphalt Constr., Inc., 587 F.2d 1315, 25 UCCR 388 (D.C. Cir. 1978) (failure by contractor to order limestone under requirements contract not bad faith when the government decided limestone would not be needed on the project); Romine Inc. v. Savannah Steel Co., 117 Ga. App. 353, 160 S.E.2d 659, 5 UCCR 103 (1968) (purchase by contractor of only 10 percent of estimate not in bad faith when estimate resulted from erroneous government specifications on project).

[508] 574 P.2d at 115, 281 Or. at 351, 23 UCCR at 595 (dicta).

[509] *See* Eastern Air Lines, Inc. v. Gulf Oil Corp., 415 F. Supp. 429, 19 UCCR 721 (S.D. Fla. 1975) (reduction in fuel requirements resulted from standard industry practice of "fuel freighting").

ity. The resolution should depend upon such factors as the foreseeability of the event to one or both parties, the length of the contract, the existence of express "escape" mechanisms in the contract, the amount of investment or reliance by the seller required to perform the contract, and the amount of the reduction or decrease in requirements or output. Similar to the law of excuses, there is no magic formula for resolving these cases; judges will always have a broad range of discretion. To date, however, the courts have generally done a credible job.

[B]   Exclusive Dealing Contracts

The Code, in section 2-306(2), also deals with exclusive dealing contracts:

> A lawful agreement by either seller or the buyer for exclusive dealing in the kind of goods concerned imposes, unless otherwise agreed, an obligation by the seller to use best efforts to supply the goods and by the buyer to use best efforts to promote their sale.

This section codifies the rule of the famous Cardozo opinion in *Wood v. Lucy, Lady Duff-Gordon,*[510] familiar to generations of first-year law students. The section's "best-efforts" requirement imposes an obligation to use reasonable diligence on the part of the seller to supply the goods and the part of the buyer to promote their sale.[511] This obligation is intended primarily to protect the seller who depends *solely* upon the buyer to market the goods,[512] and is not generally imposed in nonexclusive agreements.[513]

Virtually no cases have litigated the content of the "best-efforts" standard. Parties to exclusive dealing contracts are probably unwilling to rely upon such a vague and uncertain standard; typically, they draft more explicit provisions specifying the parties' obligations.

§ 3.09   UNCONSCIONABLE CONTRACTS AND CONTRACT TERMS

Although freedom of contract is a cherished, fundamental, and immensely valuable idea, no thoughtful person would contend that all agreements should be enforced. Courts have long refused to enforce agreements on grounds such as want of consideration, fraud, duress, mistake, illegality,

---

[510] 118 N.E. 214, 222 N.Y. 88 (1917).

[511] U.C.C. § 2-306.

[512] *See* Wood v. Lucy, Lady Duff-Gordon, 118 N.E. at 214, 222 N.Y. at 91.

[513] *See* Tigg Corp. v. Dow Corning Corp., 962 F.2d 1119, 17 UCCR2d 730 (3d Cir. 1992).

and incapacity. The enactment of the Code has had little impact on these reasons to refuse enforcement.[514] It has had a much greater impact on a less established and more amorphous ground—unconscionability—or the idea that when enforcement of a contract shocks the conscience of the judge, it will be denied.

For more than two centuries before the enactment of the Code, courts of equity had from time to time refused to enforce agreements on unconscionability grounds.[515] Courts of law had also long ago found reasons for refusing to enforce agreements that they found oppressive or otherwise shocking to the conscience. They often did this without using "unconscionability," but rather indirectly by stretching or manipulating other (generally more well-established) legal doctrines.[516]

Operating against this background, the drafters of Article 2 made what at the time was a controversial decision: to grant courts the power to police sale-of-goods agreements on unconscionability grounds. The unconscionability section, section 2-302, was one of the more novel features of Article 2, and it generated considerable commentary, both during the drafting process[517] and after the adoption of the Code.[518] Its thrust, and often much of its language, has since been incorporated into a number of statutes and into the second Restatement of Contracts.[519] Section 2-302 has plainly worked a significant change in how lawyers think and talk about various agreement-enforcement problems. The extent to which it has changed the law and altered business practice is far less clear. Section 2-302(1) reads as follows:

---

[514] *See* U.C.C. § 1-103.

[515] *See, e.g.*, Earl of Chesterfeld v. Janssen, 2 Ves. Sr. 125, 28 Eng. Rep. 82 (1750) (court refused to enforce contract that "no man in his senses and not under delusion would make on the one hand, and as no honest and fair man would accept on the other").

[516] *See* U.C.C. § 2-302, Official Comment 1.

[517] *See* J.H.A., Note, "Unconscionable Contracts Under the Uniform Commercial Code," 109 U. Pa. L. Rev. 401 (1961). According to the author, U.C.C. § 2-302 sparked fears of "wildcat lawsuits by overly optimistic counsel" and lawsuits being settled for nuisance amounts. In addition, critics feared section 2-302 would have a disruptive effect on general business affairs that depend on the stability and predictability of contracts. Testimony of Mr. Mason O. Dannon in 1954, N.Y. Report of the Revision Commission Report on Hearings on the Uniform Commercial Code, 1231–1232.

[518] *Critical*: Arthur Allen Leff, "Unconscionability and the Code—The Emperor's New Clause," 115 U. Pa. L. Rev. 485 (1967); Richard W. Duesenberg, "Practitioner's View of Contract Unconscionability (U.C.C. § 2-302)," 8 UCC L.J. 237 (1976). *Supportive:* Paul M. Morley, Note, "Commercial Decency and the Code—The Doctrine of Unconscionability Vindicated," 9 Wm. & Mary L. Rev. 1143 (1968); M.P. Ellinghaus, "In Defense of Unconscionability," 78 Yale L.J. 757 (1969); Frank P. Darr, "Unconscionability and Price Fairness," 30 Hous. L. Rev. 1819 (1994).

[519] Restatement (Second) of Contracts § 208 (1981).

If the court as a matter of law finds the contract or any clause of the contract to have been unconscionable at the time it was made the court may refuse to enforce the contract, or it may enforce the remainder of the contract without the unconscionable clause, or may so limit the application of any unconscionable clause as to avoid an unconscionable result.

Summarizing the principal points in this provision: whether the contract or clause is unconscionable is to be determined as of the time the contract was made;[520] unconscionability is determined as a matter of law by the judge, not as a question of fact by the jury;[521] the court is not limited to the single remedy of refusal to enforce the entire agreement, but may in an appropriate case strike the clause that is unconscionable[522] or limit the application of the clause.[523] Thus, section 2-302 gives courts the express authority to remake, modify, or rescind sales agreements on unconscionability grounds. Although the Code is silent on the burden of proof, courts have

---

[520] Phillips Mach. Co. v. LeBlond, Inc., 494 F. Supp. 318, 31 UCCR 445 (N.D. Okla. 1980); Lecates v. Hertich Pontiac Buick Co., 515 A.2d 163, 2 UCCR2d 865 (Del. Super. Ct. 1986); Zapatha v. Dairy Mart, Inc., 381 Mass. 284, 408 N.E.2d 1370, 29 UCCR 1121 (1980). There is at least one instance, however, where the Code suggests that unconscionability is measured at some time after the contract. *See* U.C.C. § 2-309(3), discussed in § 3.07[C], *supra*.

[521] Evidence is admissible, however, to show the commercial setting, purpose, and effect of the contract or clause. U.C.C. § 2-302(2). This generally requires a hearing out of the presence of the jury, and discovery should be permitted for the purpose of eliciting evidence of unconscionability. *See* Gregory Lumber Co. v. United States, 9 Cl. Ct. 503 (1986). A number of cases have held that the failure to allow this opportunity is reversible error. *See, e.g.*, State v. Avco Fin. Serv. of N.Y., Inc., 50 N.Y.2d 383, 406 N.E.2d 1075, 429 N.Y.S.2d 181, 29 UCCR 60 (1980); Beckman v. Vassal-Dillworth Lincoln-Mercury, Inc., 321 Pa. Super. 428, 468 A.2d 784, 39 UCCR 69 (1983). The drafters appear to have made unconscionability an issue for the judge because they believed the jury would misuse the concept and allow people to escape their contractual obligations too easily. *See* Arthur Allen Leff, "Unconscionability and the Code—The Emperor's New Clause," 115 U. Pa. L. Rev. 485 (1967). It also serves, however, to ensure greater consistency in results and to allow for a more orderly development of the concept.

[522] *See, e.g.*, Frank's Maintenance & Eng'g, Inc. v. C.A. Roberts Co., 86 Ill. App. 3d 980, 408 N.E.2d 403, 42 Ill. Dec. 25, 30 UCCR 163 (1980); McCarty v. E.J. Korvette, Inc., 28 Md. App. 421, 347 A.2d 253, 18 UCCR 14 (Ct. Spec. App. 1975).

[523] *See* In re Hamby, 19 B.R. 776, 33 UCCR 1811 (N.D. Ala. 1982) (court did not limit contract clause pursuant to U.C.C. § 2-302 but to a state statute worded identically); Frostifresh Corp. v. Reynoso, 52 Misc. 2d 26, 274 N.Y.S.2d 757, 3 UCCR 1058 (Dist. Ct. 1966), *rev'd on issue of remedy*, 54 Misc. 2d 119, 281 N.Y.S.2d 964, 4 UCCR 300 (App. Div. 1967).

generally held that the party asserting unconscionability has the burden of proof.[524]

The Code does not define "unconscionability." Although Comment 1 to section 2-302 states both the "basic test" of unconscionability and describes the "principle" of unconscionability, the Comment is not very helpful. The "basic test" is:

> whether, in light of the general commercial background and the commercial needs of the particular trade or case, the clauses involved are so one-sided as to be unconscionable under the circumstances at the time of the making of the contract.[525]

The largely tautological nature of this "basic test" is readily apparent. Although the Comment draws attention to the necessity that an unconscionable contract or clause be "one-sided," it fails to answer the question of how one-sided the clause or contract must be before it becomes unconscionable, except in terms of the word itself.

The Comment expresses the principle of unconscionability as "the prevention of oppression and unfair surprise."[526] It goes on to say that the principle of unconscionability is *not* the "disturbance of allocation of risks because of superior bargaining power."[527] The essence of contract, however, is the allocation of risk; all contracts, even the most simple, distribute risks between the parties.[528] Were courts precluded from considering the effects of unequal bargaining power on the parties' allocation of risks, the concept of unconscionability would be largely bereft of content. It is not surprising that many courts have ignored this portion of Comment 1, focusing explicitly on the equality of bargaining power as a critical component of unconscionability.[529]

---

[524] *See, e.g.*, Emlee Equip. Leasing Corp. v. Waterbury Transmission, Inc., 31 Conn. App. 455, 626 A.2d 307, 23 UCCR2d 389 (1993); Rite Color Chem. Co. v. Velvet Textile Co., 105 N.C. App. 14, 411 S.E.2d 645, 18 UCCR2d 384 (1992).

[525] U.C.C. § 3-302, Official Comment 1.

[526] *Id.*

[527] *Id.*

[528] For example, even a simple fixed-price contract for an automobile to be delivered on a certain date distributes the risk that the value of the car might increase or decrease before the delivery date.

[529] *See, e.g.*, Johnson v. Mobil Oil Corp, 415 F. Supp. 264, 20 UCCR 637 (E.D. Mich. 1976); Construction Assocs., Inc. v. Fargo Water Equip. Co., 446 N.W.2d 237, 10 UCCR2d 821 (N.D. 1989).

The examples in Comment 1 are also not helpful. The majority of the illustrations are taken from older cases dealing with disclaimers of warranty, which are now specifically governed by other substantive provisions of the Code. Most of the examples also involve commercial contracts, which constitute only a portion of unconscionability claims and in which assertions of unconscionability are rarely successful.[530] Finally, it is not at all clear from the examples *why* the clause or contract is unconscionable under the circumstances of the case.

An early article by Professor Arthur Leff[531] provides a framework for examining unconscionability claims that has been accepted by both courts[532] and commentators.[533] The framework differentiates between conduct occurring during the bargaining process and the substantive fairness of the terms of the contract. Leff describes the former as presenting the issue of "procedural" unconscionability and the latter as raising concerns of "substantive" unconscionability. As we shall see,[534] however, the ingredients of procedural and substantive unconscionability are closely related and many of the factors relevant to one issue are important components of the other.

[A]   Procedural Unconscionability

Procedural unconscionability encompasses much conduct that would also be subject to attack under present-day doctrines of fraud, misrepresentation, mistake, undue influence, duress, and the like. The law in these areas has become sufficiently developed that a great deal of misconduct that occurs during the bargaining process is probably better dealt with by these doctrines than by unconscionability.[535] In addition, various kinds of con-

---

[530] *See* text at § 3.09[D], *infra.*

[531] Arthur Allen Leff, "Unconscionability and the Code—The Emperor's New Clause," 115 U. Pa. L. Rev. 485 (1967).

[532] *See, e.g.,* Johnson v. Mobil Oil Corp. 415 F. Supp. 264, 20 UCCR 637 (E.D. Mich. 1976); Missouri ex rel. State Highway Comm'n of Mo. v. City of St. Louis, 575 S.W.2d 712 (Mo. Ct. App. 1978); Schroeder v. Fageol Motors, Inc. 86 Wash. 2d 256, 544 P.2d 20, 18 UCCR 584 (Wash. 1975).

[533] *See* G. Richard Shell, "Arbitration and Corporate Governance," 67 N.C. L. Rev. 517 (1989); Robert A. Hillman, "Debunking Some Myths About Unconscionability: A New Framework for U.C.C. Section 2-302," 67 Cornell L. Rev. 1 (1981); David S. Miller, Note, "Insurance As Contract: The Argument for Abandoning the Ambiguity Doctrine," 88 Colum. L. Rev. 1849 (1988); Thomas D. Crandall et al., I Uniform Commercial Code, § 4.8.4 (1993).

[534] *See* §§ 3.09[A], 3.09[B], *infra.*

[535] It is important to remember that unconscionability is a *defensive* doctrine; it does not allow for compensatory or punitive damages, except to the extent that modification of the contract terms or concepts of restitution would permit such a recovery. *See* Abrams v. Two Wheel Corp., 71 N.Y.2d 693, 525 N.E.2d 692, 530 N.Y.S.2d 46 (1988).

sumer-protection statutes, such as Consumer Sales Practices Acts[536] or Deceptive Trade Practices Acts,[537] have gone beyond the common law in protecting consumers from seller misconduct.

There are two kinds of situations where procedural unconscionability retains some vitality outside common-law theories and consumer-protection legislation. The first involves the lack of opportunity for the consumer to understand the terms of the contract or the use of sharp sales practices falling short of common-law fraud. These cases probably represent what the drafters had in mind in their reference to "unfair surprise" in Comment 1. The second involves the so-called contract of adhesion where a party possesses a fair opportunity to understand the terms of the contract, and may, in fact, understand them, but where the terms are presented to the party on a "take-it-or-leave-it basis." Another way of describing these situations is that the first involves a lack of knowledge, while the second involves a lack of voluntariness.[538] Courts have frequently referred to both situations as involving a "lack of meaningful choice."[539] In the second situation, in particular, the line between procedural and substantive unconscionability becomes blurred.

[1] Opportunity to Understand the Contract

Findings of unconscionability in which a party has not had a reasonable opportunity to understand the terms of a contract have occurred in many different contexts. The well-known case of *Williams v. Walker-Thomas Furniture Co.*[540] is an excellent illustration of procedural unconscionability that also demonstrates the close connection between procedural and substantive unconscionability. The case arose in the District of Columbia shortly before the enactment of the Code, but the court nevertheless was influenced by the Code in reaching its decision.

---

[536] *See, e.g.,* Ohio Rev. Code Ann. § 1345.01 (1995); Utah Code Ann. § 13-11-1 (1994). *See* Chapter 9, *infra.*

[537] *See, e.g.,* Ga. Code Ann. § 10-1-430 (1995); Me. Rev. Stat. Ann. tit. 10, § 206 (West 1994).

[538] *See* Bank of Ind. v. Holyfield, 476 F. Supp. 104, 109–110 (S.D. Miss. 1979).

[539] *See* John Deere Leasing Co. v. Blubaugh, 636 F. Supp. 1569, 1 UCCR2d 658 (D. Kan. 1986) (defendant's agreement to terms of which he had no knowledge was not voluntary); Colonial Leasing Co. of New Eng., Inc. v. Best, 552 F. Supp. 605 (D. Or. 1982) (court said the lessee had no knowledge of the meaning of the clause embedded in a contract of adhesion); Henningsen v. Bloomfield Motors, Inc., 32 N.J. 358, 161 A.2d 69 (1960) (court described contract of adhesion as "not in reality involving any bargaining or freedom of consent").

[540] 350 F.2d 445, 121 U.S. App. D.C. 315 (D.C. Cir. 1965).

In *Williams,* a retailer sold approximately $1,800 worth of merchandise to a consumer over a five-year period. Each purchase was on credit, and in each case, the consumer signed an installment contract that contained a highly technical "cross-collateral" clause.[541] The effect of this provision was to consolidate all unpaid installment sales made to the customer so that a security interest was retained in all items sold until the entire account was paid in full. After Mrs. Williams had paid the store more than $1,400, she defaulted, and the retailer sought to replevy everything purchased during the previous five years, although the balance due was less than the purchase price of the last item purchased. The customer claimed that the contract was unconscionable. Although the trial court and intermediate appellate court upheld the replevin, the Circuit Court of Appeals for the D.C. Circuit remanded on the grounds that the trial court should have considered the conscionability of the contract. In doing so, the court established the lack of meaningful choice as the touchstone for procedural unconscionability:

> Unconscionability has generally been recognized to include an absence of meaningful choice on the part of one of the parties together with contract terms which are unreasonably favorable to the other party. Whether a meaningful choice is present can only be determined by consideration of all of the circumstances surrounding the transaction.[542]

The court then established the standard for determining whether there was an absence of meaningful choice in the bargaining process:

> Did each party to the contract, considering his obvious education or lack of it, have a reasonable opportunity to understand the terms of the contract, or were the important terms hidden in a maze of fine print and minimized by deceptive trade practices?[543]

---

[541] The portion of the clause quoted by the court is as follows:

> [T]he amount of each periodical installment payment to be made by [purchaser] to the company under this present lease shall be inclusive of and not in addition to the amount of each installment payment to be made by [purchaser] under such prior leases, bills or accounts; and all payments now and hereafter made by [purchaser] shall be credited pro rata on all outstanding leases, bills, and accountants due to the Company by [purchaser] at the time such payment is made.

350 F.2d at 447, 121 U.S. App. D.C. at 316 (alteration in original).

[542] 350 F.2d at 449, 121 U.S. App. D.C. at 319.

[543] *Id.* at 449, 121 U.S. App. D.C. at 319.

Although the court remanded the case for a determination of unconscionability, the contract, or at least the cross-collateral clause, was probably unconscionable under the standard that Judge Wright established. The cross-collateral clause was so complex and written in such stilted language that it was hard for law students, and even law professors,[544] to understand. In addition, Mrs. Williams received her monthly income of $218 from ADC on which she kept herself and seven children. She was apparently a woman of little formal education and the intermediate appellate court, while finding against her, stated that it could "not condemn too strongly" the conduct of the seller for its "sharp practice and irresponsible business dealings."[545]

The opinion in *Williams* also suggests the relationship between procedural and substantive unconscionability. Judge Wright did not hold that Mrs. Williams' failure to understand the effect of the cross-collateral clause was itself sufficient for a finding of unconscionability. To the contrary, the opinion suggests that the clause or contract also had to be one-sided or unfair:

> But when a party of little bargaining power, and hence little real choice, signs a *commercially unreasonable contract* with little or no knowledge of its terms, it is hardly likely that his consent, or even an objective manifestation of his consent, was ever given to all the terms. In such a case the usual rule that the terms of the agreement are not to be questioned should be abandoned and the court should consider whether the terms of the contract *are so unfair* that enforcement should be withheld.[546]

The relationship between procedural and substantive unconscionability will be further explored in a later section.[547]

Lack of education has played a part in a number of cases where unconscionability has been found, including some commercial cases.[548] For example, in *Johnson v. Mobil Oil Corp.*[549] the Indiana Supreme Court re-

---

[544] The first time one of the authors taught the case, he had to read the clause four or five times to even begin to understand it.

[545] 350 F.2d at 448, 121 U.S. App. D.C. at 318.

[546] *Id.* at 449, 121 U.S. App. D.C. at 319 (emphasis added).

[547] *See* § 3.09[C], *infra.*

[548] *See, e.g.*, Albert Merrill Sch. v. Goday, 78 Misc. 2d 647, 357 N.Y.S.2d 378 (Civ. Ct. 1974); Weaver v. American Oil Co., 257 Ind. 458, 276 N.E.2d 144 (1971); Kelly v. Widner, 236 Mont. 523, 771 P.2d 142 (1989); Johnson v. Mobil Oil Corp., 415 F. Supp. 264, 20 UCCR 637 (E.D. Mich. 1976).

[549] 415 F. Supp. 264, 20 UCCR 637 (E.D. Mich. 1976).

fused to enforce a clause exculpating Mobil Oil from liability for its own negligence when Johnson's gas station was destroyed by an explosion following Mobil's delivery of gasoline. The court emphasized that Johnson had dropped out of school in the eighth grade and was "practically illiterate."[550] Despite the fact that Johnson had never told Mobil's representative that he could not read, and, as the court acknowledged, Mobil had not engaged in "unfair or oppressive conduct, fraud, overreaching, misrepresentation or sharp practices," the court nonetheless found the clause to be unconscionable.[551] According to the court, because of the immense bargaining power of Mobil, it had an affirmative obligation to ensure that Johnson understood the import of the clause.[552]

Regardless of formal education, the consumer's ability to understand English is an important factor in determining conscionability.[553] This is particularly true where the clause in question is printed in "legalese" and the other party makes no effort to point the provision out and explain its consequences.[554] On the other hand, educated[555] experienced[556] and sophisticated[557] parties will have a much harder time convincing a court that a clause or contract should be struck because of procedural unconscionability.

---

[550] *Id.* at 268, 20 UCCR at 641.

[551] *Id.* at 269, 20 UCCR at 642.

[552] *Id.* at 269, 20 UCCR at 642. *See also* Weaver v. American Oil Co., 257 Ind. 458, 276 N.E.2d 144 (1971) (court refused to enforce exculpatory clause against plaintiff who dropped out of high school after one year); Kelly v. Widner, 236 Mont. 523, 771 P.2d 142 (Mont. 1989).

[553] *See, e.g.*, Universal Leasing Servs. v. Flushing Hae Kwan Restaurant, 169 A.D.2d 829, 565 N.Y.S.2d 199 (N.Y. Sup. Ct. 1991); Albert Merrill Sch. v. Godsy, 78 Misc. 2d 647, 357 N.Y.S.2d 378 (Civ. Ct. 1974); Jefferson Credit Corp. v. Marcano, 60 Misc. 2d 138, 302 N.Y.S.2d 390, 6 UCCR 602 (Civ. Ct. 1969).

[554] *See* Williams v. Walker Thomas Furniture Co., 350 F.2d 445, 121 U.S. App. D.C. 315 (D.C. Cir. 1965); John Deere Leasing Co. v. Blubaugh, 636 F. Supp. 1569, 1 UCCR2d 658 (D. Kan. 1986); Weaver v. American Oil Co., 257 Ind. 458, 276 N.E.2d 144 (1971); Discount Fabric House of Racine, Inc. v. Wisconsin Tel. Co., 113 Wis. 2d 958, 334 N.W.2d 922, 36 UCCR 1128 (Wis. Ct. App. 1983).

[555] *See* Dixon Contracting, Inc. Co. v. Amsted Indus., Inc., 20 UCCR2d 940 (W.D. Va. 1992); Smith v. Price's Creameries, 98 N.M. 541, 650 P.2d 825, 34 UCCR 1118 (1982).

[556] *See* Bailey Farms, Inc. v. Nor-Am Chem. Co., 27 F.3d 188, 24 UCCR2d 843 (6th Cir. 1994); Dixon Contracting, Inc. Co. v. Amsted Indus., Inc., 20 UCCR2d 940 (W.D. Va. 1992); Edart Truck Rental Corp. v. B. Swirsky & Co., 23 Conn. App. 137, 579 A.2d 133, 14 UCCR2d 75 (1990).

[557] *See* John Deere Leasing Co. v. Blubaugh, 636 F. Supp. 1569, 1 UCCR2d 658 (D. Kan. 1986); Buettner v. Supe. Laundry Mach., 857 F. Supp. 471, 23 UCCR2d 79 (E.D. Va. 1994); Dillman & Assocs., Inc. v. Capital Leasing Co., 110 Ill. App. 3d 335, 442 N.E.2d 311, 66 Ill. Dec. 39, 35 UCCR 369 (1982).

The greater the buyer's opportunity to understand and evaluate a contract's terms, the less likely a court will find unconscionable conduct. Where a party hires counsel[558] or takes a substantial amount of time deliberating over the terms of the contract,[559] a finding of unconscionability is highly unlikely. On the other hand, when a party, usually a consumer, is simply handed a form contract and expected to sign it on the spot, courts are likely to take a claim of unconscionability much more seriously.[560]

In commercial contracts, a clause that is routine to contracts in the industry will usually not be found unconscionable.[561] For example, in *Dixon Contracting, Inc. v. Amsted Industries, Inc.*,[562] the court held a limitation of remedies both procedurally and substantively conscionable despite the fact that the provision was not conspicuous and was not read by the purchaser. Because the buyer was an educated and experienced businessman[563] and had dealt with the seller before, and because a limitation of remedies is not uncommon in commercial contracting, there was no basis for striking the term as unconscionable.[564] However, clauses that are so prevalent that a buyer cannot bargain for different terms from other sellers may present a claim of unconscionability as a contract of adhesion.[565]

A comparison of *Williams* with another case, *McDonald v. Firstate Credit Alliance, Inc.*,[566] illustrates the importance of these factors. *Williams* involved a convoluted cross-collateral clause in a printed contract. *McDonald* also involved an inconspicuous cross-collateral clause inserted by a seller which the court acknowledged to have superior bargaining

---

[558] *See* Colonial Life Ins. Co. v. Electronic Data Sys. Corp., 817 F. Supp. 235, 20 UCCR2d 753 (D.N.H. 1993); K&C, Inc. v. Westinghouse Elec. Corp., 437 Pa. 303, 263 A.2d 390, 7 UCCR 679 (1970).

[559] *See, e.g.*, Siemens Credit Corp. v. Marvik Colour, Inc., 859 F. Supp. 686, 24 UCCR2d 705 (S.D.N.Y. 1994); American Tel. & Tel. Co. v. New York City Human Resources Admin., 833 F. Supp. 962, 23 UCCR2d 410 (S.D.N.Y. 1993); York v. Georgia Pac. Corp., 585 F. Supp. 1265 (N.D. Miss. 1984).

[560] *See, e.g.*, Weaver v. American Oil Co., 257 Ind. 458, 276 N.E.2d 144 (1971); Henningsen v. Bloomfield Motors, Inc., 32 N.J. 358, 161 A.2d 69 (1960).

[561] *See* Stirn v. E.I. du Pont de Nemours & Co., 21 UCCR2d 979 (S.D. Ind. 1993) (liability disclaimer was not procedurally unconscionable because experienced farmers are aware that herbicide manufacturers routinely include disclaimers on product labels); Southland Farms, Inc. v. Ciba-Geigy Corp., 575 So. 2d 1077, 14 UCCR2d 404 (Ala. 1991) (consequential damage exclusion clauses an accepted usage of trade and thus not unconscionable).

[562] 20 UCCR 2d 940 (W.D. Va. 1992).

[563] Dixon, the buyer, had an engineering degree and more than twenty-eight years in the pipe-laying business. 20 UCCR at 942, n.1.

[564] *Id.* at 941.

[565] *See* § 3.09[A][2], *infra*.

[566] 100 B.R. 714, 10 UCCR2d 1057 (D. Del. 1989).

power.[567] Mrs. Williams apparently did not have much formal education, and McDonald likewise hadn't finished the eleventh grade.[568] Yet the court in *McDonald* upheld the clause against an unconscionability attack. Unlike Mrs. Williams, McDonald was experienced in the trade and cross-collateral clauses were common in the industry. In addition, it was clear that Mc-Donald understood the concept of security interests.[569] Thus, despite the fact that the clause was "difficult to find in the small boilerplate,"[570] the court held it to be conscionable.[571]

Although the cases generally emphasize the understanding and expectations of the party claiming unconscionability, it is equally possible to view this branch of procedural unconscionability doctrine by looking at the expectations of the party resisting the claim of unconscionability: when the transaction was consummated and the names had been affixed to the writing, did the party who is now asserting that the clause is conscionable have a *reasonable* expectation that this clause was understood by the other party to be part of the agreement? If not, and the clause involves a substantial risk-shift from what would normally be expected under the circumstances, it should not be enforced.

[2] Contracts of Adhesion

The second branch of procedural unconscionability also involves an absence of meaningful choice, but it does not entail the lack of an opportunity to understand the terms of the contract. Rather, the lack of meaningful choice is a result of having no reasonable alternatives to the seller's terms—a contract of adhesion. Although most cases involving contracts of adhesion also contain elements of the first branch of procedural unconscionability—the lack of a reasonable opportunity to understand the terms of the contract—the concepts are different. A party may fully understand the risks and obligations that she is undertaking in a contract and nonetheless claim that she had no realistic choice because the terms demanded by the seller, in-

---

[567] *Id.* at 721, 10 UCCR2d at 1065.

[568] *Id.*

[569] McDonald even asked what was secured by the agreement and was erroneously told by the seller's representative that only the equipment being purchased was subject to a security interest. The court said that the fact that the representative gave him incorrect information was of "no consequence." *Id.* at 721, 10 UCCR2d at 1065.

[570] *Id.*

[571] The court did, however, strike as unconscionable an "omnibus" clause that made virtually *everything* owned by the debtor, including after-acquired property, subject to a security interest.

cluding the clause in question, were the only terms she could get. This branch of procedural unconscionability probably approximates the drafters' concept of "oppression" in Comment 1.

Much has been written about contracts of adhesion, beginning with the famous article of Professor Kessler that appeared in the Columbia Law Review in 1943.[572] Despite the amount of attention given to adhesion contracts, there remains considerable controversy over whether it is a viable concept.[573] The cases, however, have generally accepted the idea that the "take-it-or-leave-it" quality that characterizes a contract of adhesion can, under some circumstances, result in unconscionability.[574]

The fountainhead case is the pre-Code case of *Henningsen v. Bloomfield Motors, Inc.*[575] Mr. and Mrs. Henningsen purchased a new car with a standard warranty that excluded all consequential and incidental damages. Only ten days after taking delivery, an apparent malfunction in the steering column resulted in a crash that destroyed the car and injured Mrs. Hen-

---

[572] Frederick Kessler, "Contracts of Adhesion—Some Thoughts About Freedom of Contract," 43 Colum. L. Rev. 629 (1943). *See also* Steven A. Arbittier, "The Form 50 Lease: Judicial Treatment of an Adhesion Contract," 111 U. Pa. L. Rev. 1197 (1967); Michael Z. Green, "Preempting Justice Through Binding Arbitration of Future Disputes: Mere Adhesion Contract or a Trap for the Unwary Consumer?," 5 Loy. Consumer L. Rep. 112 (1993); Ronald L. Hebsbergen, "Contracts of Adhesion Under the Louisiana Civil Code," 43 La. L. Rev. 1 (1982); Charles A. Oldfather, "Toward a Usable Method of Judicial Review of the Adhesion Contractor's Lawmaking," 16 U. Kan. L. Rev. 303 (1968); Todd D. Rakoff, "Contracts of Adhesion: An Essay in Reconstruction," 96 Harv. L. Rev. 1173 (1983); W. David Slawson, "Standard Form Contracts and Democratic Control of Lawmaking Power," 84 Harv. L. Rev. 529 (1971); Gregory R. Kim, Note, "Graham v. Scissor Tail, Inc.: Unconscionability of Presumptively Biased Arbitration Clauses Within Adhesion Contracts," 70 Calif. L. Rev. 1014 (1982).

[573] For articles critical of the concept, see Randy E. Barnett, "The Sound of Silence: Default Rules and Contractual Consent," 78 Va. L. Rev. 821 (1992); Richard A. Epstein, "The Unintended Revolution in Product Liability Law," 10 Cardozo L. Rev. 2193 (1989); Alan Schwartz, "Seller Unequal Bargaining Power and the Judicial Process," 49 Ind. L.J. 367 (1974); Donald E. Schwartz, Comment, "In Praise of Derivative Suits: A Commentary on the Paper of Professors Fischel and Bradley," 71 Cornell L. Rev. 322 (1986). *But see* Victor P. Goldberg, "Institutional Change and the Quasi-Invisible Hand," 17 J. L. & Econ. 461 (1974); W. David Slawson, "The New Meaning of Contract: The Transformation of Contracts Law by Standard Forms," 46 U. Pitt. L. Rev. 21 (1984); W. David Slawson, "Standard Form Contracts and Democratic Control of Lawmaking Power," 84 Harv. L. Rev. 529 (1971).

[574] *See, e.g.*, Worldwide Ins. Group v. Klopp, 603 A.2d 788 (Del. 1992); Henningsen v. Bloomfield Motors, Inc., 32 N.J. 358, 161 A.2d 69 (1960); Wille v. Southwestern Bell Tel. Co., 219 Kan. 755, 549 P.2d 903, 19 UCCR 447 (1976); John Deere Leasing Co. v. Blubaugh, 636 F. Supp. 1569, 1 UCCR2d 658 (D. Kan. 1986).

[575] 32 N.J. 358, 161 A.2d 69 (1960).

ningsen. Mr. and Mrs. Henningsen sued both the seller and manufacturer for property damage to the car and for personal injury to Mrs. Henningsen. The defendants relied on the damage limitation contained in the warranty.[576]

The damage limitation appeared on the back of the sales contract among eight and one-half inches of fine print. The limitation was not read by the Henningsens nor was it called to their attention. Furthermore, the limitation did not mention liability for personal injury. These facts gave the court multiple avenues to grant relief to the Henningsens without the necessity of invoking the concept of adhesion contracts. The court could have relied on accepted interpretive principles and held that the remedy limitation applied only to recovery for consequential damages other than personal injury.[577] Somewhat more boldly, it could have said that the remedy limitation had not been objectively agreed to by the Henningsens because of its location and effect.[578] Instead, the court invalidated both the remedy limitation and the accompanying disclaimer of implied warranties as contrary to public policy.

The court's rationale was premised on what it called the grossly unequal bargaining positions of the manufacturer and the customer. This unequal bargaining power resulted from the fact that there were only three automobile manufacturers and they all had the same warranty. The court described the situation as it saw it:

> The warranty before us is a standardized form designed for mass use. It is imposed upon the automobile consumer. He takes it or leaves it, and he must take it to buy an automobile. No bargaining is engaged in with respect to it.[579]

Under the court's analysis, because the consumer had no choice but to accept the remedy limitation, it would not matter whether the consumer was aware and understood the provision prior to contracting. Therefore, in the court's view, the more limited bases available to it to assist the Henningsens would not solve the underlying problem. The real problem was the oligopolistic

---

[576] The contract also disclaimed implied warranties arising under the Uniform Sales Act as well as limiting the recoverable damages for breach of express warranty. 32 N.J. at 367, 161 A.2d at 74.

[577] The court said that, in the context in which the limitation appeared, a reasonable conclusion would be that the limitation referred only to remedies for physical deficiencies in the car and was not intended to limit liability for personal injuries. 32 N.J. at 377, 161 A.2d at 79.

[578] *See* Restatement (Second) of Contracts § 211 (1981).

[579] 32 N.J. at 390, 161 A.2d at 87.

behavior of the automobile industry.[580] More drastic means were necessary to deal with that phenomenon, and the court adopted those means.

The ideas embodied in the *Henningsen* case have become well established in the unconscionability cases. While most of the cases in which this "market-failure" branch of procedural unconscionability occurs also involve elements of unfair surprise as well,[581] there are occasional cases in which the party asserting unconscionability is successful despite fully comprehending the effect of the contract or clause at issue.[582]

The lack of available alternatives to the objectionable provision has appeared frequently in unconscionability cases. For example, in *Adams v. American Cyanamid Co.*[583] Adams sued American Cyanamid for the value of his lost bean crop, approximately $183,000. Adams claimed that the use of Cyanamid's herbicide, Prowl, had destroyed his crop. Cyanamid defended on the basis of an exclusion of consequential damages placed on the herbicide label.

The court found that the clause was substantively unconscionable because it left the buyer "without any substantial recourse for its loss."[584] Before a finding of unconscionability could be found in a commercial contract, however, the court said that there also had to be indicia of procedural unconscionability as well.[585] Although the court indicated that the language of the exclusion may not have been readily understandable to a layman, the court relied primarily on the lack of alternatives in finding the exclusion procedurally unconscionable:

> This is a situation where the Adamses had no alternative other than to accept the manufacturer's exclusion. The undisputed evidence is that Adams could not purchase any manufacturer's herbicide without such an exclusion. The Adamses were not in a position to bargain with the

---

[580] *Id.* at 391, 161 A.2d at 87.

[581] *See, e.g.*, John Deere Leasing Co. v. Blubaugh, 636 F. Supp. 1569, 1 UCCR2d 658 (D. Kan. 1986); Weaver v. American Oil, 257 Ind. 458, 276 N.E.2d 144 (1971); Adams v. American Cyanamid Co., 498 N.W.2d 577, 21 UCCR2d 962 (Neb. Ct. App. 1992).

[582] *See, e.g.*, Carboni v. Arrospide, 2 Cal. Rptr. 2d 845, 16 UCCR2d 584 (1991); A&M Produce Co. v. FMC Corp., 135 Cal. App. 3d 473, 186 Cal. Rptr. 114, 34 UCCR 1129 (1982). *See also* Pittsfield Weaving Co. v. Grove Textiles, Inc., 121 N.H. 344, 430 A.2d 638, 32 UCCR 421 (1981) (plaintiff was unsuccessful in negotiating elimination of arbitration provision with other sellers in the industry; arbitration provision was part of contract that was unconscionable as a whole).

[583] 498 N.W.2d 577, 21 UCCR2d 962 (Neb. Ct. App. 1992).

[584] 498 N.W.2d at 590, 21 UCCR2d at 977.

[585] *See* § 3.09[C], *infra*.

defendant for more favorable terms than those set out in the pre-printed label. Nor were they in position to test the effectiveness of the herbicide prior to purchase.[586]

While other courts have relied on the lack of alternatives to justify a finding of unconscionability,[587] most assertions of unconscionability based on contracts of adhesion are not successful.[588] A number of factors account for the lack of success.

First, courts recognize that parties faced with contracts of adhesion always have one alternative, even if all sellers are offering the same non-negotiable terms[589]—not to contract at all. Should enough people choose this path, sellers will inevitably alter their contracts more to consumers' liking in order to better their competitive position. The fact that all sellers of particular goods offer similar warranty terms may represent a competitive equilibrium rather than collusion; consumers as a whole may simply be unwilling to pay the increased cost a more desirable term might entail.[590]

---

[586] 498 N.W.2d at 591, 21 UCCR2d at 978.

[587] *See, e.g.*, John Deere Leasing Co. v. Blubaugh, 636 F. Supp. 1569, 1 UCCR2d 658 (D. Kan. 1986) (lease agreement did not leave room for negotiation; if farmer wanted to lease combine, he had to "take it or leave it"); Allen v. Michigan Bell Tel. Co., 18 Mich. App. 632, 171 N.W.2d 689 (1969); Art's Flower Shop, Inc. v. Chesapeake & Potomac Tel. Co. of W. Va., Inc., 186 W. Va. 613, 413 S.E.2d 670 (1991).

[588] *See, e.g.*, Dillard v. Merrill Lynch, Pierce, Fenner & Smith, Inc., 961 F.2d 1148 (5th Cir. 1992) (arbitration provision in brokerage contract not unconscionable); Cayuga Harvester, Inc. v. Allis-Chalmers Corp., 95 A.D. 205, 465 N.Y.S.2d 606, 37 UCCR 1147 (1983) (exclusion of consequential damages conscionable despite the fact that all farm equipment manufacturers required the execution of similar contracts); Levy v. Gateway 2000, Inc., 33 UCCR2d 1060 (N.Y. Sup. Ct. 1997) (where consumer had the option of making a purchase from other retailers, it cannot be said consumer had no choice).

[589] Courts often seem to assume that because a term appears in a form, it is therefore nonnegotiable. If the price is right, probably very little is truly "nonnegotiable." In addition, as others have recognized, there are definite efficiencies, which ultimately benefit the consumer, in contracting with preprinted forms. *See* Karl N. Llewellyn, The Common Law Tradition 362, 363 (1966).

[590] *See* Armen Alchain & William R. Allen, Exchange and Production: Competition, Coordination & Control 276 (3d ed. 1983). Even when sellers behave oligopolistically, rather than competitively, they are nonetheless responsive to consumer preferences. As Professor Schwartz has shown, a rational monopolist will exploit its market power fully. If the "insurance of a warranty or remedy is worth more to the consumer than it costs the seller to provide, even monopolist sellers will offer the desired protection." Alan Schwartz, "Seller Unequal Bargaining Power and the Judicial Process," 49 Ind. L.J. 367, 379–382 (1974). In addition, if the culprit, as *Henningsen* suggests, is oligopoly, courts are rarely able to engage in the sort of sophisticated economic analysis that would enable them to deal rationally with

Second, courts are not inclined to find unconscionability under the "adhesion branch" where the goods do not involve "necessities." To the courts, "leaving it"—refusing to contract—is a meaningful choice when the goods are not of significant value or are otherwise not essential. In *Westlye v. Look Sports, Inc.*,[591] a skier was injured when his rental bindings failed to release his skis from his boots. He sued for breach of warranty, despite the fact that he had signed an "as is" agreement with respect to the equipment. The court held that the rental of ski equipment was not a matter of practical necessity and refused to find the agreement unconscionable.

Finally, and most important, courts will not relieve a party on unconscionability grounds solely because the contract is one of adhesion. The term must also unfairly favor the stronger party (i.e., it must be substantively unconscionable as well).[592]

[B] Substantive Unconscionability

Substantive unconscionability refers to the fairness of the clause or contract, without regard to the process by which it was created.[593] In virtually all cases, when a contract or one of its terms is unfair—substantively unconscionable—procedural unconscionability will be present as well.[594] In fact, as will be discussed shortly,[595] there is some question as to whether a term can ever be unconscionable under section 2-302 without at least a modicum of procedural unconscionability. Moreover, the cases rarely deal

---

these issues. The behavior of suppliers in a market with a small number of firms is highly unpredictable. It is far from clear under what circumstances oligopolies behave in ways similar to competitive markets and in what circumstances their behavior mirrors that of a monopoly. *See* Alchain & Allen at 272; Paul A. Samuelson & William D. Nordhaus, Economics 184, 185 (14th ed. 1992).

[591] 17 Cal. App. 4th 1715, 22 Cal. Rptr. 781 (1993).

[592] *See* Graham v. State Farm Mut. Auto. Ins. Co., 565 A.2d 908 (Del. 1989); Benoay v. E.F. Hutton & Co., 699 F. Supp. 1523 (S.D. Fla. 1988); Bishop v. Washington, 331 Pa. Super. 387, 480 A.2d 1088, 39 UCCR 825 (1984); Arkoosh v. Dean Witter & Co., 415 F. Supp. 535 (D. Neb. 1976); Hornberger v. General Motors Corp., 929 F. Supp. 484, 30 UCCR2d 483 (E.D. Pa. 1996).

[593] Arthur Allen Neff, "Unconscionability and the Code—The Emperor's New Clause," 115 U. Pa. L. Rev. 485, 487 (1967).

[594] *See, e.g.*, John Deere Leasing Co. v. Blubaugh, 636 F. Supp. 1569, 1 UCCR2d 658 (D. Kan. 1986); Carboni v. Arrospide, 2 Cal. App. 4th 76, 2 Cal. Rptr. 2d 845, 16 UCCR2d 584 (1991); Weaver v. American Oil Co., 257 Ind. 458, 276 N.E.2d 144 (1971); Adams v. American Cyanamid Co., 498 N.W.2d 577, 21 UCCR2d 962 (Neb. Ct. App. 1992); Ryan v. Weiner, 610 A.2d 1377 (Del. Ch. 1992).

[595] *See* § 3.09[C], *infra*.

with provisions that are *per se* unfair or unconscionable;[596] thus, the context in which the term or contract arises is generally important.[597] In fact, many cases deal with remedy limitations or warranty disclaimers, terms specifically sanctioned by other sections of the Code.[598]

Claims of substantive unconscionability have been made in a large number of contexts, although the largest number of cases, by far, involve various limitations on remedies or warranties. Terms attacked as substantively unconscionable have included excessive price,[599] provisions for attorney's fees,[600] bank charges for NSF checks,[601] terms requiring arbitration,[602] waiver of jury trial,[603] excessive interest rates,[604] and others.[605]

---

[596] *See* Thomas A. Crandall et al., I Uniform Commerce Code, § 4.8.4 at 4:77 (1993).

[597] *See* A&M Produce Co. v. FMC Corp., 135 Cal. App. 3d 473, 487, 34 UCCR 1129, 1141 (1982) (substantive unconscionability "turns not only on a 'one-sided' result, but also on an absence of 'justification' for it").

[598] *See, e.g.*, Stirn v. E.I. du Pont de Nemours & Co., 21 UCCR2d 979 (S.D. Ind. 1993); Andover Air Ltd. Partnership v. Piper Aircraft Corp., 7 UCCR2d 1494 (D. Mass. 1989); Southland Farms, Inc. v. Ciba-Geigy Corp., 575 So. 2d 1077, 14 UCCR2d 404 (Ala. 1991); Henningsen v. Bloomfield Motors, 32 N.J. 358, 161 A.2d 69 (1960). Remedy limitations are permitted by U.C.C. § 2-719(1)(a), and warranty disclaimers are sanctioned by section 2-316.

[599] *See, e.g.*, Murphy v. McNamara, 36 Conn. Supp. 183, 416 A.2d 170, 27 UCCR 911 (1979); American Home Improvement v. McIver, 105 N.H. 435, 201 A.2d 886, 2 UCCR 235 (1964); Jones v. Star Credit, 59 Misc. 2d 189, 298 N.Y.S.2d 1264, 6 UCCR 76 (N.Y. Sup. Ct. 1969); In re Lefkowitz, 52 Misc. 2d 39, 275 N.Y.S.2d 774, 3 UCCR 775 (N.Y. Sup. Ct. 1966).

[600] *See, e.g.*, Leasing Serv. Corp. v. Carbonex, Inc., 512 F. Supp. 253, 31 UCCR 1789 (S.D.N.Y. 1981); Gen. Elec. Credit Corp. v. Castiglione, 142 N.J. Super. 90, 360 A.2d 418, 19 UCCR 705 (1976); Weidman v. Tomaselli, 81 Misc. 2d 328, 365 N.Y.S.2d 681 (1975).

[601] *See, e.g.*, Perdue v. Crocker Nat'l Bank, 141 Cal. App. 3d 200, 190 Cal. Rptr. 204 (1983); Best v. United States Nat'l Bank of Or., 78 Or. App. 1, 714 P.2d 1049, 1 UCCR2d 6 (1986).

[602] *See* Worldwide Ins. Group v. Klopp, 603 A.2d 788 (Del. 1992); Copen Assocs., Inc. v. Dan River, Inc., 18 UCCR 62 (N.Y. Sup. Ct. 1975); Board of Educ. v. W. Harley Miller, Inc., 160 W. Va. 473, 236 S.E.2d 439 (1977).

[603] *See* All-States Leasing Co. v. Top Hat Lounge, Inc., 198 Mont. 1, 649 P.2d 1250, 33 UCCR 152 (1982); Fairfield Leasing Corp. v. Techni-Graphics, Inc., 256 N.J. Super. 538, 607 A.2d 703, 18 UCCR2d 713 (1992); Greenberg v. Schefler, 100 Misc. 2d 502, 419 N.Y.S.2d 810 (N.Y. Civ. Ct. 1979).

[604] *See* English Whipple Sailyard, Ltd. v. Yawl Ardent, 459 F. Supp. 866 (W.D. Pa. 1978); Carboni v. Arrospide, 2 Cal. App. 4th 76, 2 Cal. Rptr. 2d 845, 16 UCCR2d 584 (1991).

[605] *See, e.g.*, Resources Invest. Corp. v. Enron Corp., 669 F. Supp. 1038, 5 UCCR2d 616 (D. Colo. 1987) ("take or pay" clause); Jamestown Farmers Elevator, Inc. v. Gen. Mills, Inc., 413 F. Supp. 764, 9 UCCR 745 (D.N.D. 1976) (clause allowing extension of delivery date).

The excessive price cases are interesting for a number of reasons. First, they concern a term of which the buyer always has at least some awareness; claims of unconscionability in excessive price cases do not arise from unread fine print.[606] Second, the price term is at the core of a free-market system. In a market economy, if any term should be the result of bargaining between the parties rather than imposition by a third party, it should be the price. Finally, the price cases provide the best illustration of the relationship between substantive and procedural unconscionability.

Claims of unconscionability arising from excessive price have been relatively infrequent.[607] This rarity may be the result of excessive price cases being tried under other statutes,[608] or perhaps because people who contract to pay excessive prices are too embarrassed by their apparent gullibility to press the issue. A surprising number of plaintiffs in the reported cases, however, have been successful.[609]

The first excessive price case under the Code was *American Home Improvement, Inc. v. McIver*.[610] McIver contracted for home improvements, including the installation of fourteen windows, a door, and some siding for a total cost of $2,568.60. Of this amount, $800 was immediately payable as a "sales commission" with the remainder payable over five years at $42.81 per month. The court accepted McIver's assertion that the value of the improvements was only $959. After paying the commission, McIver had second thoughts and notified the seller to stop work shortly after it had begun. The seller then sued McIver on the contract.

The court found the contract was unenforceable because the seller had failed to comply with a state disclosure statute. Alternatively, in an exceptionally cursory opinion, it held that the price was unconscionable. The court simply noted that it had the power under section 2-302 to declare the contract unconscionable, and stated that "[i]nasmuch as the defendants have received little or nothing of value and under the transaction they entered into they were paying $1609 [the $800 sales commission plus the interest

---

[606] *But cf.* In re Lefkowitz, 52 Misc. 2d 39, 275 N.Y.S.2d 774, 3 UCCR 775 (N.Y. Sup. Ct. 1966) (buyers were told that because of referral plan, they would not have to pay anything for merchandise, when, in fact, "referral plan" was nothing more than pyramid scheme).

[607] As of the end of 1998, there were slightly less than thirty cases reported in the Uniform Commercial Code Reporting Service in which claims of excessive price have been made.

[608] *See, e.g.*, Ohio Rev. Code Ann. § 1345.03(B)(2) (1994). *See* Jarrell v. Carter, 577 So. 2d 120 (La. Ct. App. 1991).

[609] Plaintiffs are successful about two-thirds of the time in the reported cases.

[610] 105 N.H. 435, 201 A.2d 886, 2 UCCR 235 (1964).

charges] for goods and services valued at far less, the contract should not be enforced because of its unconscionable features."[611]

In addition to being the first excessive price case, *McIver* is noteworthy for a number of reasons, all of which cast doubt upon the opinion. First, the court gave no indication, if the price was so excessive, *why* McIver agreed to the purchase. Although it is true that the seller did not comply with the installment sales disclosure law, there is no indication that McIver was misled by this failure. The court made no reference to the circumstances surrounding the agreement, such as whether it was a door-to-door sale, whether McIver understood the terms of the contract, whether he had been subjected to high pressure salesmanship, or whether McIver was well-educated or was experienced in business.

Second, the court did not indicate where the value it accepted for the goods came from (other than from McIver's counsel) and why that figure was appropriate for comparison to the contract price. It is impossible to determine whether the court's basis for comparison was appropriate and, therefore, whether the court's decision was defensible.

Third, the court paid no attention to the fact that the price was to be paid over a five-year period. Even if one accepts the value of the contract as $959, and counts all of the other charges as interest, the annual interest rate is about 21 percent. High to be sure, but even in 1964 it was problematic as to whether such a price, if freely and voluntarily accepted, was such as "no man in his senses and not under delusion would make."[612]

McIver remains one of the more questionable excessive price cases. Fortunately, subsequent cases have been clearer both as to the facts and the basis for finding (or refusing to find) a price to be unconscionable. The questions raised by the *McIver* case provide a foundation for exploring subsequent cases and some remaining broader issues.

[C] The Necessity for Procedural Unconscionability

As mentioned, the court in *McIver* gave no suggestion, apart from the incomplete installment sales contract, of any defects in the bargaining process. This raises the question of whether excessive price *alone* can ever be sufficient for a contract to be unconscionable, and, more broadly, whether *any* contract or contract term can be unconscionable solely on the basis of substantive unfairness, with no procedural irregularities.

---

[611] *Id.* at 439, 201 A.2d at 888, 2 UCCR at 238.

[612] Earl of Chesterfield v. Janssen, 2 Ves. Sr. 125, 28 Eng. Rep. 82 (1750).

There are very few excessive-price cases in which a claim of unconscionability has been upheld that does not involve at least some evidence of substantial procedural unconscionability. For example, in both *Frostifresh Corp. v. Reynoso*[613] and *In re Lefkowitz,*[614] the sales involved referral schemes in which it was made to appear that the buyer would ultimately have to pay little or nothing for the product after referring other names to the seller. Further, in *Frostifresh* the buyer was Spanish-speaking and the contract was neither translated nor explained to him.[615] The sales techniques used in the *Lefkowitz* case involved visits to the customers' homes in which poor customers were subjected to high pressure sales pitches lasting up to *five hours.*[616] Other cases contain similar evidence of procedural unconscionability.[617] One case has *explicitly* held that excessive price alone is insufficient for a finding of unconscionability without some procedural irregularity,[618] and another suggests this result.[619]

Even among the few cases which do not clearly evidence procedural unconscionability, there are usually circumstances present suggesting a high likelihood of its presence. Of the three cases, other than *McIver,* that do not contain explicit indicia of procedural unconscionability, two involved welfare recipients[620] and the third buyer went on welfare one month after signing the contract.[621] Also, two of the three involved door-to-door sales,[622] an

---

[613] 52 Misc. 2d 26, 274 N.Y.S.2d 757, 3 UCCR 1058 (Dist. Ct. 1966), *rev'd on issue of remedy,* 54 Misc. 2d 119, 281 N.Y.S.2d 964, 4 UCCR 300 (Sup. Ct. 1967).

[614] 52 Misc. 2d 39, 275 N.Y.S.2d 303, 3 UCCR 775 (Sup. Ct. 1966).

[615] 281 N.Y.S.2d at 758, 3 UCCR at 1058.

[616] 275 N.Y.S.2d at 313; 3 UCCR at 782.

[617] *See, e.g.,* Sho-Pro of Ind., Inc. v. Brown, 585 N.E.2d 1357, 17 UCCR2d 56 (Ind. Ct. App. 1992) (seller misrepresented to buyer that he had "no obligation" to buy windows when in fact he had signed contract represented by seller to be something else); Toker v. Perl, 103 N.J. Super. 500, 247 A.2d 701, 5 UCCR 1171 (1968) (buyers were led to believe that they were buying only food when, in fact, they contracted to buy freezer); Vom Lehn v. Astor Art Galleries, Ltd., 86 Misc. 2d 1, 380 N.Y.S.2d 532, 18 UCCR 861 (Sup. Ct. 1976) (seller fraudulently represented value of jade pieces and stated that they were from Ming Dynasty). *See also* Davis v. Kolb, 263 Ark. 158, 563 S.W.2d 458, 23 UCCR 887 (1978) (buyer misrepresented both his experience and the value of the goods to inexperienced seller and received unconscionably *low* price).

[618] In re Colin, 136 B.R. 856, 17 UCCR2d 873 (D. Or. 1991) (court said that "it is not appropriate for the court to substitute its judgment for that of the buyers in a free market").

[619] Patterson v. Walker-Thomas Furniture Co., 277 A.2d 111, 9 UCCR 27 (D.C. 1971).

[620] Murphy v. McNamara, 36 Conn. Supp. 183, 416 A.2d 170, 27 UCCR 911 (1979); Jones v. Star Credit, 59 Misc. 2d 189, 298 N.Y.S.2d 1264, 6 UCCR 76 (Sup. Ct. 1969).

[621] Toker v. Westerman, 113 N.J. Super. 452, 274 A.2d 78, 8 UCCR 798 (Dist. Ct. 1970).

[622] *Id.;* Jones v. Star Credit, 59 Misc. 2d 189, 298 N.Y.S.2d 1264, 6 UCCR 76 (Sup. Ct. 1969).

environment especially susceptible to abuse and the subject of protective legislation.[623] The third, *Murphy v. McNamara*,[624] involved a rent-to-own operation, a subject that has also been addressed by legislation.[625] In addition, the court in *Murphy* emphasized the inability of the consumer to obtain credit and further mentioned that the "renter" never disclosed the full amount that the "lessee" would pay before she would acquire ownership of the goods.[626]

Although *McIver* and a couple of other excessive price cases suggest that substantive unconscionability alone may be sufficient, only one case has clearly so held,[627] and a number of cases *outside* the excessive-price arena have explicitly stated that *both* procedural and substantive unconscionability are necessary before relief under section 2-302 is available.[628] Whether this would be true in the case of truly outrageous terms is not clear,[629] although in such a case, there is likely to be procedural unconscionability or relief is likely to be present under some other legal theory such as duress or undue influence, or the contract will be void against public policy. In addition, most courts have adopted a sliding scale, some explicitly,[630] in which the greater the amount of one kind of unconscionability that

---

[623] The Federal Trade Commission has promulgated a Rule that requires a cooling-off period in cases involving a sale or lease of consumer goods over $25 where the sale is solicited and the contract made at a place other than the seller's place of business. 16 C.F.R. § 429.1 (1994). Most states have similar provisions. *See, e.g.*, Ohio Rev. Code Ann. § 1345.22 (Anderson 1998).

[624] 36 Conn. Supp. 183, 416 A.2d 170, 27 UCCR 911 (1979).

[625] *See, e.g.*, Ohio Rev. Code Ann. §§ 1351.01–1351.09 (Anderson 1998).

[626] *Murphy*, 416 A.2d at 173, 27 UCCR at 912.

[627] Maxwell v. Fidelity Fin. Servs., 907 P.2d 51, 28 UCCR2d 806 (Ariz. 1995) (claim of unconscionability can be established with a showing of substantive unconscionability alone, especially in cases involving price-cost disparity or limitations of remedies).

[628] *See, e.g.*, Siemens Credit Corp. v. Marvik Colour, Inc., 859 F. Supp. 686, 24 UCCR2d 705 (S.D.N.Y. 1994); Construction Assocs., Inc. v. Fargo Water Equip. Co., 446 N.W.2d 237, 10 UCCR2d (N.D. 1989); Gillman v. Chase Manhattan Bank, 534 N.E.2d 824, 73 N.Y.2d 1, 537 N.Y.S.2d 787, 7 UCCR2d 945 (1988); Rite Color Chem. Co. v. Velvet Textile Co., 105 N.C. App. 14, 411 S.E.2d 645, 18 UCCR2d 384 (1992). *But see* Jones v. Asgrow Seed Co., 749 F. Supp. 836, 13 UCCR2d 1032 (N.D. Ohio 1990) (unconscionability can be *either* procedural or substantive).

[629] *See* Master Lease Corp. v. Manhattan Limousine Ltd., 177 A.D.2d 85, 580 N.Y.S.2d 952, 16 UCCR2d 1039 (App. Div. 1992) (court says, *in dicta*, that in rare and extreme cases unconscionability can be found irrespective of the contract formation process).

[630] *See* Ellis v. McKinnon Broadcasting Co., 18 Cal. App. 4th 1796, 23 Cal. Rptr. 2d 80, (1993); Carboni v. Arrospide, 2 Cal. Rptr. 2d 845, 2 Cal. App. 4th 76, 16 UCCR2d 584 (1991); Liberty Fin. Management Corp. v. Beneficial Data Processing Corp., 670 S.W.2d 40, 38 UCCR 1471 (Mo. Ct. App. 1984); Master Lease Corp. v. Manhattan Limousine Ltd., 177 A.D.2d 85, 580 N.Y.S.2d 952, 16 UCCR2d 1039 (N.Y. Sup. Ct. App. Div. 1992); Friedman v. Egan, 64 A.D.2d 70, 407 N.Y.S.2d 999 (N.Y. Sup. Ct. App. Div. 1978).

exists (i.e., procedural or substantive), the less of the other that will be required to be shown.[631]

[D] Commercial Versus Consumer Unconscionability

Although unconscionability is generally associated with consumer contracts, there are a surprisingly large number of cases in which assertions of unconscionability have been made in a commercial context. In fact, the majority of recent unconscionability cases involve commercial rather than consumer contexts.[632] A number of conclusions can be drawn from examining these cases.

The first conclusion is that most commercial parties who claim that a contract or term is unconscionable lose.[633] The second conclusion is that, surprisingly, a fair number do not.[634] Since most business transactions involve fairly knowledgeable and sophisticated parties, active negotiation, commonly accepted and acknowledged trade practices, and repeated transactions, it is not unexpected to find most claimants are unsuccessful. In fact, a number of courts have explicitly stated that there is a presumption of conscionability in commercial contracts.[635] Others have indicated that it will

---

[631] *See* Tacoma Boatbuilding Co. v. Delta Fishing Co., 28 UCCR 26 (W.D. Wash. 1980); Ciba-Geigy Corp. v. Alter, 309 Ark. 426, 834 S.W.2d 136, 20 UCCR2d 448 (1992).

[632] This is undoubtedly the result of consumer protection legislation that contain much more liberal remedial provisions than the Code. *See* § 9.02[C], *infra*.

[633] *See, e.g.*, Earman Oil Co. v. Burroughs Corp., 625 F.2d 1291, 30 UCCR 849 (5th Cir. 1980); Am. Dredging Co. v. Plaza Petroleum, Inc., 799 F. Supp. 1335, 18 UCCR2d 1101 (E.D.N.Y. 1992); LTV Energy Prods. Co. v. Northern States Contracting Co., 162 B.R. 949, 22 UCCR2d 1012 (S.D.N.Y. 1994); Emlee Equip. Leasing Corp. v. Waterbury Transmission, Inc., 31 Conn. App. 455, 626 A.2d 307, 23 UCCR2d 389 (1993); Borden Inc. v. Advent Ink Co., 701 A.2d 255, 33 UCCR2d 975 (Pa. Super. Ct. 1997).

[634] *See, e.g.*, John Deere Leasing Co. v. Blubaugh, 636 F. Supp. 2569, 1 UCCR2d 658, 665 (D. Kan. 1986); Weaver v. American Oil Co., 257 Ind. 458, 276 N.E.2d 144 (1971); Fairfield Leasing Corp. v. Techni-Graphics, Inc., 256 N.J. Super. 538, 607 A.2d 703, 18 UCCR2d 713 (1992); Construction Assocs., Inc. v. Fargo Water Equip. Co., 446 N.W.2d 237, 10 UCCR2d 821 (N.D. 1989); Moscatiello v. Pittsburgh Contractors Equip. Co., 407 Pa. Super. 363, 595 A.2d 1190, 16 UCCR2d 71 (1991); Art's Flower Shop, Inc. v. Chesapeake & Potomac Tel. Co. of W. Va., Inc., 186 W. Va. 613, 413 S.E.2d 670 (1991).

[635] *See* Aquascence, Inc. v. Noritsu Am. Corp., 831 F. Supp. 602, 22 UCCR2d 746 (M.D. Tenn. 1993); American Dredging Co. v. Plaza Petroleum, Inc., 799 F. Supp. 1335, 18 UCCR2d 1101 (E.D.N.Y. 1992). *See also* Emlee Equip. Leasing Corp. v. Waterbury Transmission, Inc., 31 Conn. App. 455, 626 A.2d 307, 23 UCCR2d 389 (1993) (court stated that courts generally do not find contracts between business people unconscionable).

be difficult to show unconscionability in commercial settings,[636] or that courts will be "reluctant" to apply unconscionability principles in a commercial setting.[637]

Many of the examples in which unconscionability claims were successful were cases in which the party asserting unconscionability was more like a consumer than a typical commercial party.[638] In many cases the successful party was a small farmer[639] or a sole proprietor running a small business.[640] He had none of the institutional backup or experience available to larger businesses and was generally unrepresented by counsel. Furthermore, he tended to be relatively uneducated[641] and unsophisticated. Although he may have had some significant experience in his small business, he often had a narrow range of business experience and did not possess a broad understanding of business practices or was inexperienced and unfamiliar in the particular business.[642]

A few cases do not fit this pattern,[643] and some of the results are questionable. In *Maxon Corp. v. Tyler Pipe Industries*[644] the court struck as unconscionable an indemnification clause between commercial parties. In May 1973, Maxon (the seller) submitted a price quotation to Tyler Pipe (the

---

[636] *See* Stanley A. Klopp, Inc. v. John Deere Co., 510 F. Supp. 807, 31 UCCR 454 (E.D. Pa. 1981); A&M Produce Co. v. FMC Corp., 135 Cal. App. 3d 473, 186 Cal. Rptr. 114, 34 UCCR 1129 (1982) (despite recognizing the difficulty in proving unconscionability between business persons, the court did so in this case); Cayuga Harvester, Inc. v. Allis-Chalmers Corp., 95 A.D.2d 5, 465 N.Y.S.2d 606, 37 UCCR 1147 (1983).

[637] *See* Ohio Sav. Bank v. H.L. Vokes Co., 54 Ohio App. 3d 68, 560 N.E.2d 1328, 13 UCCR2d 92 (1989).

[638] *See* Eugene Jetvig, Inc. v. Monsanto Co., 18 UCCR 2d 1111 (D. Minn. 1992) ("commercial transaction" is one in which the good is used in an income generating activity and the purchaser has "some bargaining power").

[639] *See* A&M Produce Co. v. FMC Corp., 135 Cal. App. 3d 473, 186 Cal. Rptr. 114, 34 UCCR 1129 (1982); John Deere Leasing Co. v. Blubaugh, 636 F. Supp 1569, 1 UCCR2d 658 (D. Kan. 1986); Martin v. Joseph Harris Co., 767 F.2d 296, 41 UCCR 315 (6th Cir. 1985).

[640] *See, e.g.,* Weaver v. American Oil Co., 257 Ind. 458, 276 N.E.2d 144 (1971); Art's Flower Shop, Inc. v. Chesapeake & Potomac Tel. Co. of W. Va., Inc., 186 W. Va. 613, 413 S.E.2d 670 (1991); Discount Fabric House of Racine, Inc. v. Wisconsin Tel. Co., 113 Wis. 2d 858, 334 N.W.2d 922, 36 UCCR 1128 (1983).

[641] *See, e.g.,* Johnson v. Mobil Oil Corp., 415 F. Supp. 264, 20 UCCR 637 (E.D. Mich. 1976); Weaver v. American Oil Co., 257 Ind. 458, 276 N.E.2d 144 (1971).

[642] *See* Langemeier v. Nat'l Oats Co., 775 F.2d 975, 41 UCCR 1616 (8th Cir. 1985) (although an agronomist, plaintiff was new at growing popcorn).

[643] *See, e.g.,* Andover Air Ltd. Partnership v. Piper Aircraft Corp., 7 UCCR2d 1494 (D. Mass. 1989); Construction Assocs., Inc. v. Fargo Water Equip. Co., 446 N.W.2d 237, 10 UCCR2d 821 (N.D. 1989); Moscatiello v. Pittsburgh Contractors Equip. Co., 407 Pa. Super. 363, 595 A.2d 1190, 16 UCCR2d 71 (1991).

[644] 497 N.E.2d 570, 3 UCCR2d 52 (Ind. Ct. App. 1986).

buyer) for the sale of two "pre-mix blower-mixer" units. The buyer responded with a purchase order and the seller shipped the two units. The invoice contained a mass of printed material, which included the indemnification clause. The printed material was in the same type as the indemnification clause, and the indemnification clause was toward the end of a large untitled paragraph dealing generally with installation and maintenance. After the buyer installed the two units, one of them exploded, injuring one of the buyer's employees. The seller sought indemnification for a settlement reached with the employee.

The court held that the indemnification provision was not part of the contract under section 2-207. As an alternative holding, it held the indemnification provision unconscionable and against public policy. The court first dispensed with the argument that unconscionability is inappropriate in a commercial context by noting that while most unconscionability cases involve disadvantaged consumers, unconscionability under the Code "is by no means limited to unsophisticated consumers."[645] The court said that the indemnity provision was comparable to the one in *Weaver v. American Oil*,[646] a case involving two commercial parties, that had been found unconscionable by the Indiana Supreme Court in 1971. While noting that the court in *Weaver* had found a great disparity in bargaining power between the two parties, the court specifically held that the lack of disparity in bargaining power between the seller and the buyer was not controlling.[647]

The expressed willingness of the *Maxon* court to find unconscionability in a commercial setting, particularly one involving two parties of acknowledged equal bargaining power, is unusual. The result is probably explained by the nature of the clause involved, the type of injury that occurred, and the manner in which the clause appeared in the seller's invoice. Because the underlying cause of action was a products-liability suit for personal injury, the court said that public-policy concerns were implicated by the indemnification clause. Allowing the manufacturer to shift responsibility for product defects undermined the deterrent effect of the products-liability statute. Also, the clause appeared in an *invoice* sent to the buyer after the contract had been created, rather than in a contract document. The buyer would have no reason to expect to find such a significant risk-shifting clause in an invoice accompanying the goods.[648]

---

[645] *Id.* at 577, 3 UCCR2d at 62.

[646] *Id.* at 577, 3 UCCR2d at 62, 63.

[647] *Id.* at 578, 3 UCCR2d at 63.

[648] For a somewhat similar case, *see* Construction Assocs., Inc. v. Fargo Water Equip. Co., 446 N.W.2d 237, 10 UCCR2d 821 (N.D. 1989) (limitation of remedy unconscionable when the limitation is included as part of preprinted installation guide that arrives with pipe). *See also* Moscatiello v. Pittsburgh Contractors Equip. Co., 407 Pa. Super. 363, 595 A.2d

Less defensible is the decision in *Andover Air Ltd. Partnership v. Piper Aircraft Corp.*[649] In this case, the buyer purchased an airplane manufactured by the seller. A defective landing gear resulted in a crash landing in which over $100,000 in damage resulted to the plane. The contract contained a provision limiting the buyer's remedy to the repair and replacement of defective parts, and excluded liability for all consequential and general damages. The court interpreted this provision as excluding liability for damage to the aircraft.[650]

In deciding that the exclusion was unconscionable, the court acknowledged the absence of procedural unconscionability. The buyer, *who was both an attorney and a pilot*, actively negotiated the contract in which the exclusion appeared. The court further said that, as such, he was presumably aware of both the complexity of the aircraft and the legal significance of the warranty limitations. Nonetheless, the court held that the exclusions were substantively unconscionable, and further held that Andover could recover for *all* of its consequential damages.

This decision is wrong. An exclusive remedy of repair and replacement of defective parts is specifically sanctioned in section 2-719 of the Code.[651] Thus, the clause cannot be *per se* unconscionable. If, as the court assumes, the buyer understood, or should have understood, the exclusions in the contract, the parties have merely allocated the risks of product performance, and there is no reason to believe that the court's allocation is preferable to that of the parties.

A final case deserves mention. *Adams v. American Cyanamid Co.*[652] is noteworthy because its holding is so much at odds with similar cases. Adams was a farmer who lost his bean crop after applying the herbicide "Prowl," manufactured by the defendant, American Cyanamid. After a jury trial, Adams was awarded $193,000. On appeal, American Cyanamid argued that it had excluded liability for consequential damages through a notice on the herbicide label. Despite finding that the remedy limitation was conspicuous, the court found it to be unconscionable. It held that the limitation was substantively unconscionable because its enforcement would "leave the herbicide user without any substantial recourse for his loss."[653] It found the

---

1190, 16 UCCR2d 71 (1991) (court found unconscionable remedy limitations on the reverse side of contract buried in fine print one-quarter as large as print on the front of the contract).

[649] 7 UCCR2d 1494 (D. Mass. 1989).

[650] The court's decision was on a motion *in limine* to exclude evidence of incidental and consequential damages. 7 UCCR2d at 1506.

[651] U.C.C. § 2-719(1)(a).

[652] 498 N.W.2d 577, 21 UCCR2d 962 (Neb. Ct. App. 1992).

[653] *Id.* at 590, 21 UCCR2d at 977.

existence of procedural unconscionability largely on the basis that all her-bicide manufacturers included the same exclusion and therefore Adams could not bargain for more favorable terms.[654]

A substantial number of similar cases have been decided contrary to *Adams*,[655] and the decision in the case can be criticized on a number of points. First, the court seemed to rely on the reasoning that the clause was substantively unconscionable because it failed to provide a remedy for Adams's severe consequential damages.[656] Under this reasoning, of course, no exclusion of consequential damages would ever survive, because the whole purpose of the exclusion is to shift the risk of these losses to the product user. Yet, section 2-719 clearly contemplates that exclusions of consequential damages, other than for personal injury, are generally conscionable. Second, the court said that upholding the exclusion would leave Adams remediless, without ever discussing whether Adams could have secured *first-party* insurance for his crop loss, and, if such insurance was available, why Adams did not secure it. Finally, the court never asked what the consequences would have been if Adams had simply chosen not to use the herbicide in the face of the exclusion. Other courts have recognized the sound business reasons for which manufacturers might include such exclusions,[657] and it is not evident why such exclusions, upheld in most other commercial contexts, should not be upheld in this one as well.

---

[654] *Id.* In addition, the court suggested that the language of the exclusion may not have been immediately understandable by a layperson to exclude the kind of damage suffered. *Id.*

[655] *See, e.g.*, Lindemann v. Eli Lilly & Co., 816 F.2d 199, 4 UCCR2d 395 (5th Cir. 1987); Muzzy v. E.I. du Pont de Nemours & Co., 24 UCCR2d 917 (D. Minn. 1993); Jim Dan, Inc. v. O.M. Scott & Sons Co., 785 F. Supp. 1196, 17 UCCR2d 788 (W.D. Pa. 1992); Stirn v. E.I. du Pont de Nemours & Co., 21 UCCR2d 979 (S.D. Ind. 979); Bruce v. ICI Ams., Inc., 29 UCCR2d 796 (S.D. Iowa 1996); Southland Farms, Inc. v. Ciba-Geigy Corp., 575 So. 2d 1077, 14 UCCR2d 404 (Ala. 1991); Martin Rispens & Son v. Hall Farms, Inc., 601 N.E.2d 429, 19 UCCR2d 1021 (Ind. Ct. App. 1992); Arena v. Abbott & Cobb, Inc., 158 A.D.2d 926, 551 N.Y.S.2d 715, 11 UCCR2d 476 (1990); Cox v. Lewiston Grain Growers, Inc., 936 P.2d 1191, 33 UCCR2d 443 (Wash. Ct. App. 1997); Ronicker v. Kenworth Truck Co., 944 F. Supp. 179, 33 UCCR2d 479 (W.D.N.Y. 1996); Borden Inc. v. Advent Ink Co., 701 A.2d 255, 33 UCCR2d 975 (Pa. Super. Ct. 1997). *But see* A&M Produce Co. v. FMC Corp., 135 Cal. App. 3d 473, 186 Cal. Rptr. 114, 34 UCCR 1129 (1982) (court struck exclusion of consequential damages as unconscionable when weight-sizing machine failed).

[656] "The limitation would leave the herbicide user without any substantial recourse for his loss." 498 N.W.2d at 590, 21 UCCR2d at 977.

[657] *See, e.g.*, Stirn v. E.I. du Pont de Nemours & Co., 21 UCCR2d 979, 987 (S.D. Ind. 1979) (herbicide performance may be adversely affected by many factors outside the control of the manufacturer).

[E] Conclusion

The adoption of section 2-302 engendered fear that freedom of contract was at serious risk.[658] It is evident that these fears were largely unfounded. Judges have generally used the power bestowed by section 2-302 "judiciously." Consumer cases decided under section 2-302 have often involved flagrant abuses of the bargaining process and the results are, for the most part, reasonable and supportable, even under common law principles. During the past few years, consumer cases have dwindled considerably, almost certainly because of the passage of consumer-protection legislation during the 1970s and the 1980s. Much of this legislation regulates consumer contracts and restricts sales practices far beyond anything envisioned in section 2-302.[659]

A fair number of commercial cases are still brought under section 2-302 and, in the authors' view, the courts continue to be appropriately hesitant to apply unconscionability doctrine in commercial contexts. For the most part, those cases in which unconscionability has been found have been situations on the cusp of the consumer-commercial dichotomy.

Section 2-302 did not attempt to define unconscionability; the section embodies a principle rather than a rule. Fundamentally, it assumes that our consciences are subject to similar shocks, and to the extent that this is true, the concept needs no further definition. To the extent that it is not true, it offers insufficient guidance to attorneys and their clients, and creates the potential for inconsistent results. While some inconsistency has occurred, the principle of unconscionability is no more vague than many others, such as "reasonability," which permeate our law. As time passes, section 2-302 will undoubtedly decrease in importance. Its adoption, however, was a bold experiment and, on balance, was probably a success.

---

[658] *See, e.g.,* Richard W. Duesenberg, "Practitioner's View of Contract Unconscionability (U.C.C. § 2-302)," 8 UCC L.J. 237 (1976). In discussing American Home Improvement v. McIver, Professor Duesenberg had this to say:

> [McIver] aptly illustrates the danger lurking in a statute standing in the wings for a judge to call on stage at will. Without any basis, it simply decreed that a time-price yielding an annual interest rate of about 18 percent was unconscionable. In one fell swoop, the whole small loan industry was hanging by a judge's gastric pathos.

Id. at 241.

[659] *See* Chapters 8 and 9, *infra.*

§ 3.10 MODIFICATION AND WAIVER

[A] Introduction

Although the Code does not require that the exact moment of contract formation be ascertainable,[660] nevertheless there is some point in time when the bargain has been struck. Frequently, however, after a contract has been formed, the parties will find reason to modify the terms of their contract. In most cases, the modified contract will be performed without problems.

In some cases, however, things do not proceed so smoothly. Perhaps only one party's obligations were modified. At common law this created a problem, because of the preexisting duty rule that required contract modifications to be supported by consideration.[661] Perhaps the asserted modification was oral, creating potential problems under the statute of frauds.[662] Or, perhaps the parties had inserted an express provision in the written contract prohibiting oral modifications—a "no oral modifications" or "NOM" clause—but had nonetheless orally modified the contract.[663] Or, one of the parties may have relied upon an oral modification that the other now denies. The Code attempts to deal with each of these matters in section 2-209.

Subsection (1) of section 2-209 deals with the problem of the preexisting duty rule by flatly eliminating it in contracts for the sale of goods: "An agreement modifying a contract within this Article needs no consideration to be binding."[664] Although the scope of the preexisting duty rule has diminished[665] and has been subject to criticism,[666] the rule retained considerable vitality at the time the Code was adopted.[667] Thus, the drafters

---

[660] U.C.C. § 2-204(2).

[661] *See* Alaska Packers Ass'n v. Domenico, 117 F. 99 (9th Cir. 1902); Lingenfelder v. Wainwright Brewing Co., 103 Mo. 578, 15 S.W. 844 (1891).

[662] *See* § 3.10[C], *infra.*

[663] *See* § 3.10[D], *infra.*

[664] U.C.C. § 2-209(1).

[665] *See, e.g.,* Watkins & Son, Inc. v. Carrig, 91 N.H. 459, 21 A.2d 591 (1941); Schwartzreich v. Bauman-Basch, Inc., 231 N.Y. 196, 131 N.E. 887 (1921); Central London Property Trust, Ltd. v. High Trees House, Ltd., [1947] 1 K.B. 130; Restatement (Second) of Contracts § 89 (1981).

[666] E. Allan Farnsworth, Farnsworth on Contracts § 4.22 (2d ed. 1990); B.J. Reiter, "Courts, Consideration, and Common Sense," 27 U. Toronto L.J. 439 (1977); Patterson, "An Apology for Consideration," 58 Colum. L. Rev. 929 (1958).

[667] *See, e.g.,* Denny v. Reppert, 432 S.W.2d 647 (Ky. Ct. App. 1968); Tri-City Concrete Co. v. A.L.A. Constr. Co., 343 Mass. 425, 179 N.E.2d 319 (1962); Rexite Casting Co. v. Midwest Mower Corp., 267 S.W.2d 327 (Mo. Ct. App. 1954); Walden v. Backus, 81 Nev. 634, 408 P.2d 712 (1961).

made a significant change when they recognized that modifications and adjustments to existing contracts were common and that such standard practices deserved protection from the sometimes surprising consequences of the preexisting duty rule.[668] So far, the courts have had little trouble dealing with this aspect of section 2-209.[669]

There is good reason to relax the consideration requirement for modifications. Consideration is a tool to distinguish those promises that ought to be enforced from those that do not merit intervention of the legal system—to separate those promises that rest on an exchange from those that are no more than promises to make a gift. The requirement for consideration may perform this function, but once an enforceable promise clearly exists, consideration has served its purpose. Promises to forgo a right or modify a duty are normally made with an understanding of the consequences. Enforcement of the modified contract by the courts is not apt to create surprise or leave either party thinking that someone has received something for nothing.

Elimination of the requirement of consideration does not, however, remove the need to police carefully agreements modifying contracts. A contract will often foreclose other opportunities to one of the parties, and the other party may use the resulting increase in bargaining power to extract a new, more favorable, agreement.[670] For example, a buyer who has concluded a long-term requirements contract may have so rearranged the operation of its business in reliance on the contract that it would be very costly for the buyer to secure goods from another source if the seller refuses to supply the buyer's requirements. The seller may then be tempted to refuse to perform unless the buyer is willing to increase the price. The preexisting duty rule was frequently used to police such "extorted" modifications.[671] Now they must be policed more directly.

[B] Good Faith

The Code performs this policing function through the obligation of good faith. Comment 2 to section 2-209 provides that although modifications

---

[668] *See, e.g.*, Levine v. Blumenthal, 117 N.J.L. 23, 186 A. 457 (1936), *aff'd*, 117 N.J.L. 426, 189 A. 54 (1937).

[669] *See, e.g.*, Wisconsin Knife Works v. National Metal Crafters, 781 F.2d 1280, 42 UCCR 830 (7th Cir. 1986); Etheridge Oil Co. v. Panciera, 818 F. Supp. 480, 22 UCCR2d 82 (D.R.I. 1993); A&G Constr. Co. Inc. v. Reid Brothers Logging Co., 547 P.2d 1207, 19 UCCR 37 (Alaska 1976); Mulberry-Fairplans Water Ass'n, Inc. v. Town of North Wilkesboro, 105 N.C. App. 258, 412 S.E.2d 910, 17 UCCR2d 48 (1992).

[670] *See, e.g.*, Austin Instrument, Inc. v. Loral Corp., 29 N.Y.2d 124, 272 N.E.2d 533, 324 N.Y.S.2d 22 (1971).

[671] *See, e.g.*, Alaska Packers Ass'n v. Domenico, 117 F. 99 (9th Cir. 1902).

need no consideration to be binding, they must meet the test of good faith, and "the extortion of a 'modification' without legitimate commercial reason is ineffective."[672]

It is not clear whether the application of the Code's concept of good faith has added much to the law in this context. By the time the Code was drafted, and certainly today, the concept of "economic duress" had progressed far enough to render a modification unenforceable in most cases in which a party had "extorted" the modification via a threat of nonperformance.[673] Furthermore, the Code's unconscionability section might also be applicable to the modified term. Nonetheless, the Code drafters explicitly relied on the concept of good faith to police modifications.

There is no doubt under the Code that a party has acted in bad faith when its motivation in seeking a modification is solely to take advantage of its increased bargaining power.[674] On the other hand, when as a result of unexpected contingencies, both parties agree without coercion to modify their contract, the modification is in good faith and enforceable.

The statement in Comment 2 that "extortion of a modification without legitimate commercial reason is ineffective" is, nonetheless, somewhat puzzling. Does it mean that the extortion of a modification *with* legitimate commercial reason *is* effective? In other words, does the existence of a legitimate commercial reason make it acceptable to secure a modification through the threat of nonperformance? Conversely, is a modification unenforceable if a party seeks the modification without "legitimate commercial reason," even though there is no threat of nonperformance and the other party willingly agrees to the modification?

Although the case law is sparse, good faith seems to require *both* a legitimate commercial reason and an absence of coercion. The leading case on the issue of good faith is *Roth Steel Products v. Sharon Steel Corp.*[675] In

---

[672] U.C.C. § 2-209, Official Comment 2.

[673] *See, e.g.*, Urban Plumbing & Heating Co. v. United States, 187 Ct. Cl. 15, 408 F.2d 382 (1969); Austin Instrument, Inc. v. Loral Corp., 272 N.E.2d at 130. *See also* Wolf v. Marlton Corp., 57 N.J. Super. 278, 154 A.2d 625 (1959) (court remanded proceedings back to trial court to determine whether the threatened party actually believed the threat); King Constr. Co. v. W.M. Smith Elec. Co., 350 S.W.2d 940 (Tex. Ct. App. 1961).

[674] *See* Erie County Water Auth. for the Use and Benefit of Price Bros. Co. v. Hen-Gar Constr. Corp., 473 F. Supp. 1310, 27 UCCR 49 (W.D.N.Y. 1979) (seller acted in bad faith by demanding price increase or rescission when buyer reasonably believed no other source was available to supply pipe); Tonka Tours, Inc. v. Chadima, 354 N.W.2d 519, 39 UCCR 122 (Minn. Ct. App. 1984) (seller obtained concessions on repair obligations because it had buyer "over a barrel"), *rev'd*, 372 N.W.2d 723, 42 UCCR 430 (Minn. 1985) (buyer did not assert lack of good faith at trial and intermediate appellate court not authorized to make factual findings as to good faith on appeal).

[675] 705 F.2d 134, 35 UCCR 1435 (6th Cir. 1983).

Roth, the seller agreed to sell steel to the buyer at discount prices because the seller had excess manufacturing capacity. The imposition of federal price controls and increased steel exports, however, changed the market dramatically and soon the seller was using 100 percent of its capacity. As a result, it notified the buyer that it was withdrawing the price concessions in the contract. When the buyer immediately protested, the parties met and the seller agreed to sell steel at the contract price until June 30, 1973. It would, however, only sell at higher prices for the remainder of the contract period. The buyer reluctantly agreed because it could not procure sufficient steel elsewhere to meet its obligations, and the seller had threatened to stop deliveries unless the buyer agreed to the price concessions. When the seller failed to make deliveries, the buyer sued, claiming the difference between the original contract price and its cover price as damages. Among other things, the seller claimed that the contract price had been modified by the parties' agreement.

To determine whether the modification of the contract price had been made in good faith, Judge Celebreeze said that two requirements had to be met:

> In determining whether a particular modification was obtained in good faith, a court must make two distinct inquiries: whether the party's conduct is consistent with reasonable commercial standards of fair dealing in the trade [citations omitted] and whether the parties were in fact motivated to seek modification by an honest desire to compensate for commercial exigencies.[676]

As to the first prerequisite, Judge Celebreeze concluded that the seller had sought the modification because of "a factor that would cause an ordinary merchant to seek modification,"[677] and therefore the modification was sought for a legitimate commercial reason. The court found that if the seller had performed at the contract price, it would have suffered a loss on the contract and therefore was justified in seeking the modification.

As to the second part of the test, however, the seller's threat of nonperformance constituted bad faith. Despite the fact that the seller had a legitimate basis for *seeking* a modification, the use of coercive conduct—the threat of nonperformance—was bad faith. Although the court said that the inference of bad faith from coercive conduct could be rebutted by a showing that the seller had a *right* (contractual or otherwise) to refuse per-

---

[676] *Id.* at 145, 35 UCCR at 1451.
[677] *Id.* at 146, 35 UCCR at 1452.

formance, the seller had established no such right.[678] Thus, even if there is a legitimate commercial reason for seeking a modification, the threat of nonperformance is not a legitimate means to secure the modification unless there is a contractual right to the modification or the circumstances give rise to a legal excuse from the duty of performance.[679]

Conversely, the *Roth* case, Comment 2 to section 2-209, and other cases suggest that a party seeking a modification will, at least in some circumstances, have to possess a legitimate commercial reason for the modification, even if there is no threat of nonperformance.[680] This is probably a salutary

---

[678] *Id.* at 148, 35 UCCR at 1455.

[679] *See also* American Exploration Co. v. Columbia Gas Transmission Corp., 1095 WL 18668; 40 UCCR 1647 (S.D. Ohio 1985), *aff'd*, 779 F.2d 310, 42 UCCR 1218 (6th Cir. 1985) (threat of nonperformance if modification not accepted not in bad faith if contract permits modification).

The case of United States for the Use and Benefit of Crane Co. v. Progressive Enters., Inc., 418 F. Supp. 662, 19 UCCR 1306 (E.D. Va. 1976), however, suggests caution to those who would assume that all modifications made under the threat of nonperformance and without legal right are invalid. In *Crane*, the seller sought a modification in the price because of rapidly escalating material costs. In pressing for the modification, the seller indicated that it would ship the goods only at the price in effect at the time of shipment, not at the contract price. The buyer agreed to the modification without objection. Later the buyer refused to pay the higher price for the goods.

The court upheld the modification. It said that there was a good-faith basis for seeking the modification and, therefore, the buyer had an obligation to protest the demand for a higher price:

> If a seller in this situation cannot enforce such a modification, sought in good faith and objectively agreed to, the provisions of UCC § 2-209(1) would be hollow indeed. To avoid this predicament, the buyer must at least display some protest against the higher price in order to put the seller on notice that the modification is not freely entered into.

Id. at 664, 19 UCCR at 1309. In fact, the court said that the *buyer* had acted in bad faith by failing to tell the seller that it never intended to pay the higher price. The lesson of *Crane* is that a party should protest vigorously before acceding to a modification demanded by the other party, or risk losing its rights. In a later case, however, the Fourth Circuit refused to enforce a modification agreed to by the buyer without protest. *See* T&S Brass & Bronze Works, Inc. v. Pic-Air, Inc., 790 F.2d 1098, 1 UCCR2d 433 (4th Cir. 1986). The court in *T&S Brass* distinguished *Crane* by observing that, unlike the seller in *Crane*, the seller in *T&S Brass* had no legitimate commercial reason for seeking the modification. Therefore, it was irrelevant whether the buyer protested.

[680] Official Comment 2 provides:

> The test of "good faith" between merchants or as against merchants includes "observance of reasonable commercial standards of fair dealing in the trade" (Section 2-103), and may, in some situations require an objectively demonstrable reason for seeking a modification. But such matters as a market shift which

rule since "requests" for modification will often come with implicit threats of nonperformance.

In general, section 2-209(1) has created few problems. Unfortunately, the same cannot be said for the remainder of section 2-209. Recognized by numerous scholars as poorly drafted,[681] the section has spawned considerable litigation and a great deal of academic commentary.[682] Subsections (2) through (5) of section 2-209 attempt to deal with the remaining issues posed at the beginning of this section, but the language chosen by the drafters is, at best, inartful and confusing. At worst, it is incomprehensible and contradictory.

[C] The Statute of Frauds

Section 2-209 struggles with the same problem described in the discussion of section 2-201,[683] the Code's statute of frauds: to separate fabricators from those who rely on a handshake, a telephone call, or a face-to-face deal without reducing the agreement to writing. Like section 2-201, section 2-209 tries to provide a structure to resolve this problem. It requires certain modifications to satisfy the Code's statute of frauds and allows the parties to create their own statute of frauds through no oral modification (NOM) clauses. At the same time, it recognizes that NOM clauses frequently become part of the contract boilerplate and that the parties often ignore NOM clauses and the Code's statute of frauds in the course of their relationship. Balancing these opposing concerns has proved difficult.

Subsection (3) of section 2-209 provides:

---

makes performance come to involve a loss may provide such a reason even though there is no such unforeseen difficulty as would make out a legal excuse from performance under Section 2-615 and 2-616.

See Ralston Purina v. McNabb, 381 F. Supp. 181, 15 UCCR 390 (W.D. Tenn. 1974) (modification agreed to by farmer/seller not in good faith because buyer had no legitimate commercial reason to seek modification).

[681] *See, e.g.,* Robert A. Hillman, "Standards for Revising Article 2 of the U.C.C.: The NOM Clause Model," 35 Wm. & Mary L. Rev. 1509, 1524–1525 (1994); John E. Murray, Jr., "The Modification Mystery: Section 2-209 of the Uniform Commercial Code," 32 Vill. L. Rev. 1, 2 (1987); Douglas K. Newell, "Cleaning Up U.C.C. Section 2-209," 27 Idaho L. Rev. 487, 487 (1990).

[682] In addition to those sources cited in the previous note, *see* Beth A. Eisler, "Oral Modifications of Sales Contracts Under the Uniform Commercial Code: The Statute of Frauds Problem," 58 Wash U. L.Q. 277 (1980); Robert A. Hillman, "A Study of Uniform Commercial Code Methodology: Contract Modification Under Article Two," 59 N.C. L. Rev. 335 (1981).

[683] *See* § 3.01, *supra.*

The requirements of the statute of frauds section of this Article (Section 2-201) must be satisfied if the contract as modified is within its provisions.

In the easy case, this section operates without a hitch. If the parties had an oral contract to sell goods for $400 and then modified the price to $600, section 2-209(3) requires compliance with the Code's statute of frauds. Because the contract, *as modified,* has a price of greater than $500, section 2-201 would have to be satisfied before the contract could be enforced. Similarly, if the original agreement was for $600 and the parties orally modified the price to $450, the contract *as modified* would not be within the Code's statute of frauds and could be proved by oral evidence. This is true even if the original contract would have required a writing (or an exception to the writing requirement) to be enforceable.

Unfortunately, the application of section 2-209(3) is not nearly this simple, as a few additional examples will illustrate.

Example 1. The parties have a written contract signed by both parties for the sale of 100 cameras for $5,000. They orally modify the contract to change the quantity to 120 cameras for $6,000. Does the modification have to be in writing?

Example 2. Does the result change in **Example 1** if the oral modification *reduces* the quantity to 80 cameras for a price of $4,000?

Example 3. The parties have a written contract signed by both parties for the sale of 100 cameras for $5,000. They orally modify the contract to change the price of the 100 cameras to $5,500. Does the modification have to be in writing?

Example 4. The parties have a written contract signed by both parties for the sale of 100 cameras for $5,000, delivery to take place on November 15, 1995. The parties orally modify the contract to change the delivery date to November 30, 1995. Does the modification have to be in writing?

Example 1 is easily resolved. In this case the contract, as modified, has a price of $500 or more and therefore falls within the Article 2 statute of frauds. Section 2-201(1) specifically states that a contract is not enforceable beyond the quantity of goods shown in the writing. Therefore, unless an exception to the writing requirement is satisfied, the contract for 120 cameras cannot be enforced.

Example 2, however, is not so easily resolved. Again, the contract, as modified, has a price of $500 or more and must therefore comply with the statute of frauds. However, there *is* a writing that complies with the requirements of section 2-201: it is signed by both parties, it indicates that a contract has been made, and it contains a quantity term. Although the writing does not *accurately* state the quantity of the modified contract, section 2-201 states that "a writing is not insufficient because it omits or incorrectly states a term agreed upon but the contract is not enforceable . . . beyond the quantity of goods shown in the writing."[684] In this case there is no attempt to enforce a contract for a quantity *beyond* that shown in the writing; rather, the attempt is to show a quantity less than that stated in the writing. Although the Code does not clearly resolve the problem, the implication of section 2-201 is that the modification does not have to be in writing to be enforceable.

In **Example 3,** the case is even less compelling than Example 2 for requiring the modification to be in writing. In order for a writing to satisfy section 2-201(1), the writing *must* include a quantity term.[685] The *price*, however, does not have to be included in the writing to satisfy the statute.[686] Thus, had the original contract not included a price term, the contract nonetheless would have been enforceable. It would be anomalous to require the modification of a term to be in writing when the term would not have been required to be present in the original writing.

Example 4 represents the least justification for requiring that the modification be evidenced by a writing. Not only does the delivery date not have to be in a writing to satisfy section 2-201, the delivery date, unlike the price term, would not have been considered so essential as to be required to be in the writing under pre-Code law.[687]

Comment 3 to section 2-209(3) seems to indicate, however, that our tentative conclusions in Examples 2, 3 and 4 are wrong. In two separate places, Comment 3 suggests that *all* modifications to contracts that fall, after modification, within the Code's statute of frauds must be in writing. The first sentence of the comment states that "Subsections (2) and (3) are intended to protect against false allegations of oral modifications."[688] Thereafter, the Comment states that "[m]odification for the future cannot therefore be conjured up by oral testimony if the price involved is $500.00 or more since such modification must be shown by at least an authenticated memo."[689] Nowhere does Comment 3 or the text of section 2-209 indicate

---

[684] U.C.C. § 2-201(1).

[685] U.C.C. § 2-201(1), Official Comment 1: "The only term which must appear [in the writing] is the quantity term."

[686] *Id.* Official Comment 1 further states: "The price, time and place of payment or delivery, the general quality of the goods, or any particular warranties all may be omitted [from the writing]."

[687] *See* Consolidated Coiler Corp. v. Bogue Elec. Co., 141 N.J. Eg., 58 A.2d 759 (1948).

[688] U.C.C. § 2-201, Official Comment 3.

[689] *Id.*

that the modifications to which the Comment refers are modifications only to the quantity term.

The cases generally follow the apparent[690] direction of Comment 3 and require modifications of both the quantity term and terms other than the quantity term to be in writing. The vast majority of the cases simply *assume,* with no discussion, that section 2-209(3) requires modifications of terms other than the quantity term to be in writing. So long as the price of the modified contract is $500 or more, courts have taken for granted that modifications to a wide variety of terms must be in writing. These include modifications in the price,[691] responsibility for product defects,[692] financing or credit terms,[693] warranty terms,[694] delivery date,[695] time for payment,[696] and others.[697] Only one case has suggested that only modifications to the quantity term must be in writing.[698] In light of the ambiguity of section 2-209 and its comments, it is surprising that the courts have so readily assumed that section 2-209 requires all modifications of contracts falling within the statute of frauds to be in writing, and that counsel have not more frequently

---

[690] "Apparent" because U.C.C. § 2-209(3) requires only that the requirements of *section 2-201* be satisfied with respect to modified contracts. Since section 2-201 requires only that the quantity term be in writing, the argument exists that Comment 3 *implicitly* limits the modifications to which it refers to modifications of the quantity term.

[691] *See* Crosby-Mississippi Resources, Ltd. v. Florida Gas Transmission Co., 815 F. Supp. 977, 21 UCCR2d 257 (S.D. Miss. 1993); Mulberry-Fairplains Water Assocs., Inc. v. Town of North Wilkesboro, 105 N.C. App. 258, 412 S.E.2d 910, 17 UCCR2d 48 (1992); La Rosa v. Fortier, 492 So. 2d 425, 1 UCCR2d 1094 (Fla. Dist. Ct. App. 1986); Varnell v. Henry M. Milgrom, Inc., 78 N.C. App. 451, 337 S.E.2d 616, 42 UCCR 814 (1985); Monroc, Inc. v. Jack B. Parson Constr. Co., 604 P.2d 901, 28 UCCR 18 (Utah 1979).

[692] Akrosil Division of Int'l Paper Co. v. Ritrama Duramark, Inc., 847 F. Supp. 623, 23 UCCR2d 46 (E.D. Wis. 1994).

[693] In re Atkins, 139 B.R. 39, 19 UCCR2d 18 (M.D. Fla. 1992); Dangerfield v. Markel, 252 N.W.2d 184, 21 UCCR 1239 (N.D. 1977).

[694] Cooley v. Big Stone Harvestore Sys., Inc., 767 P.2d 740, 7 UCCR2d 1051 (Colo. Ct. App. 1989).

[695] Green Constr. Co. v. E.S.C. Stone Prods., Inc., 735 F. Supp. 1254, 12 UCCR2d 1034 (D.N.J. 1990); Trad Indus., Ltd. v. Brogan, 246 Mont. 439, 805 P.2d 54, 14 UCCR2d 718 (1991); Farmers Elevator Co. of Reserve v. Anderson, 170 Mont. 175, 552 P.2d 63, 19 UCCR 1084 (1976).

[696] Asco Mining Co. v. Gross Contracting Co., 3 UCCR 293 (Pa. Com. Pl. 1965).

[697] Tonka Tours, Inc. v. Chadima, 372 N.W.2d 723, 42 UCCR 430 (Minn. 1985) (repair of boat); Bone Int'l, Inc. v. Johnson, 74 N.C. App. 703, 329 S.E.2d 714, 41 UCCR 29 (1985) (repair of car).

[698] Starry Constr. Co. v. Murphy Oil U.S.A., Inc., 785 F. Supp. 1356, 1363, 17 UCCR2d 353, 363 (D. Minn. 1992) (in considering letter purportedly modifying quantity term of contract, the court said "Starry correctly argues that so long as a quantity term is included, the form of writing is unimportant.").

made the arguments raised by John Murray[699] and others[700] that there is no sound reason to expand the requirements of section 2-201 when oral modifications to existing contracts are involved. Despite the dearth of analysis by the courts, given the number of cases that have applied section 2-209(3) to modifications of terms other than quantity, it would be folly to rely on the enforceability of *any* oral modification of a contract that falls within the Article 2 statute of frauds.

The cases establish that the statutory exceptions to section 2-201 also apply to modifications. Each of the exceptions in subsection (3) of section 2-201 has been held to be applicable to a modification,[701] as has the "merchants" exception of section 2-201(2).[702] Some cases have applied the estoppel exception to the statute of frauds to oral modifications as well.[703] The primary method for modifications to overcome the obstacle of the statute of frauds, however, is dealt with in subsections (4) and (5) of section 2-209, and is discussed subsequently.[704]

[D] "No Oral Modification" (NOM) Clauses

Section 2-209(2) provides:

A signed agreement which excludes modification or recision except by a signed writing cannot be otherwise modified or rescinded, but except as between merchants such a requirement on a form supplied by a merchant must be separately signed by the other party.[705]

---

[699] John F. Murray, Jr., "The Modification Mystery: Section 2-209 of the Uniform Commercial Code," 32 Vill. L. Rev. 1, 21-22 (1987).

[700] Thomas A. Crandall et al., I Uniform Commercial Code, § 3.5.3 at 3-69 (1993).

[701] *See* Starry Constr. Co. v. Murphy Oil U.S.A., Inc., 785 F. Supp. 1356, 17 UCCR2d 363 (D. Minn. 1992); In re MSR Exploration, Ltd., 147 B.R. 560, 20 UCCR2d 49 (D. Mont. 1992); Hoff Cos., Inc. v. Danner, 822 P.2d 558, 121 Idaho 39, 16 UCCR2d 974 (Idaho Ct. App. 1992) (section 2-201(3)(c) exception); S.C. Gray, Inc. v. Ford Motor Co., 92 Mich. App. 789, 286 N.W.2d 34, 29 UCCR 417 (1979) (specially manufactured goods exception); Dangerfield v. Markel, 252 N.W.2d 184, 21 UCCR 1239 (N.D. 1977) (admissions exception).

[702] *See, e.g.,* Starry Constr. Co. v. Murphy Oil U.S.A., Inc., 785 F. Supp. 1356, 17 UCCR2d 363 (D. Minn. 1992); Mulberry-Fairplains Water Assoc., Inc. v. Town of North Wilkesboro, 105 N.C. App. 258, 412 S.E.2d 910, 17 UCCR2d 48 (1992).

[703] Starry Constr. Co. v. Murphy Oil U.S.A., Inc., 785 F. Supp. 1356, 17 UCCR2d 363 (D. Minn. 1992); Mulberry-Fairplains Water Assocs., Inc. v. Town of North Wilkesboro, 105 N.C. App. 258, 412 S.E.2d 910, 17 UCCR2d 48 (1992); Dixon v. Roberts, 853 P.2d 235, 21 UCCR2d 513 (Okla. Ct. App. 1993). *See* § 3.01[D], *supra.*

[704] *See* § 3.10[E], *infra.*

[705] U.C.C. § 2-209(2).

This section approves the use of clauses that require a writing to modify (or to rescind) a written contract. These clauses are intended to prevent mistaken or fraudulent assertions of modifications and are sometimes referred to as "private statutes of frauds."

NOM clauses were not generally enforced at common law.[706] The theory was that a contract, including the NOM clause itself, is always subject to subsequent agreement and that subsequent agreements can be oral or implied from conduct.[707] The Code, however, permits enforcement of NOM clauses, subject to the requirement that if one of the parties is a merchant and the other a consumer, a NOM clause on a form supplied by the merchant must be *separately* signed by the consumer.[708]

In two ways, NOM clauses apply more broadly than the "public" statute of frauds of section 2-201. First, there is no monetary floor to the applicability of a NOM clause; the parties can insert a NOM clause in a contract with a price of less than $500. More important, the statutory exceptions in section 2-201 may not be applicable to a NOM clause. Subsection (2) of section 2-209 explicitly says that if a contract contains a NOM clause, it cannot be modified "except by a signed writing," and the NOM clauses themselves usually provide for modification only by a signed writing. There is no indication in section 2-209 that sections 2-201(2) and 2-201(3) apply to NOM clauses, although there are good arguments that these exceptions to the requirement of a writing should apply.[709]

[E] Waiver of Writing Requirements

The danger, of course, in enforcing NOM clauses is that parties often disregard them and orally modify their contracts. Before the modification, one party may explicitly (albeit orally) waive the application of the NOM clause, but more frequently, both parties will simply ignore the clause and orally modify their contract.[710] As a result, a party may, in good faith, rely

---

[706] *See* John E. Murray, Jr., Murray on Contracts, § 64 at 260–261 (3d ed. 1990).

[707] *See* Teer v. George A. Filler Co., 30 F.2d 30 (4th Cir. 1929); Bartlett v. Stanchfield, 148 Mass. 394, 19 N.E. 549 (1889); Restatement (Second) of Contracts § 148, cmt. b (1981).

[708] *See* Wayman v. Amoco Oil Co., 932 F. Supp. 1322, 30 UCCR2d 58 (D. Kan. 1996) (NOM clause precludes enforcement of alleged subsequent modification).

[709] *See* Crandall et al., *supra* note 700, § 3.5.2 at 3:66 (suggesting that the Code concept of good faith would make the exceptions applicable); Murray, *supra* note 706, § 64 at 267 (not applying the admission exception to section 2-209(3) would subvert the essential philosophy of Article 2).

[710] *See, e.g.*, Park v. Dealers Transit, Inc., 596 F.2d 203 (7th Cir. 1979); Brookside Farms v. Mama Rizzo's, Inc., 873 F. Supp. 1029 (S.D. Tex. 1995); Linear Corp. v. Standard Hardware Co., 423 So. 2d 966, 35 UCCR 1141 (Fla. Dist. Ct. App. 1982); Universal Builders, Inc. v. Moon Motor Lodge, Inc., 244 A.2d 10, 430 Pa. 550 (1968).

on the modification and the failure to enforce it might result in serious injustice.

In the last two subsections of section 2-209, the drafters attempted to accommodate these conflicting concerns: to avoid injustice and maximize freedom of contract, while at the same time protecting against fraudulent allegations of contract modifications. Unfortunately, this attempt to balance competing concerns resulted in provisions that are vague and obscure. Subsections 2-209(4) and (5) provide:

> (4) Although an attempt at modification or recession does not satisfy the requirements of subsection (2) or (3) it can operate as a waiver.
> (5) A party who has made a waiver affecting an executory portion of the contract may retract the waiver by reasonable notification received by the other party that strict performance will be required of any term waived, unless the retraction would be unjust in view of a material change of position in reliance on the waiver.

The import of subsection (4) is that even though an attempt at modification does not satisfy the statute of frauds or NOM clause—that is, it is not in writing—the attempted modification may nonetheless operate as a waiver. Three crucial questions are (1) What does the term "waiver" mean? (2) *What* precisely is waived—the substantive contract term or the NOM clause? (3) *When* does the attempted modification operate as a waiver?

The Code provides little insight into the meaning of "waiver" and the term has no well-defined meaning in the law. It has often been described as "the voluntary relinquishment of a known right,"[711] but this definition is of little help. It suggests that a person "waiving" a right must have actual knowledge that he is giving up a legal right and intend to do so, which is not the case.[712] In addition, the definition can be read as suggesting that a waiver must be express, although there are cases that find waiver on the basis of conduct.[713] Further, it is not clear whether a waiver, once made, can

---

[711] *See* Clark v. West, 193 N.Y. 349, 86 N.E. 1 (1908); Bank v. Truck Ins. Exch., 51 F.3d 736 (7th Cir. 1995); Federal Deposit Ins. Corp. v. Attayi, 745 S.W.2d 939 (Tex. Ct. App. 1988).

[712] *See* McKenna v. Vernon, 259 Pa. 18, 101 A. 919 (1917); Pabst Brewing Co. v. Milwaukee, 126 Wis. 100, 125 N.W. 563 (1905).

[713] *See, e.g.,* Middletown Concrete Prods. Inc. v. Black Clawson Co., 802 F. Supp. 1135, 20 UCCR2d 1135 (D. Del. 1992); Southwest Wash. Prod. Credit Ass'n v. Seattle-First Nat'l Bank, 577 P.2d 589, 19 Wash. App. 397, 23 UCCR 1040 (1978).

be retracted.[714] Finally, courts are split on the necessity of consideration for a waiver, and most indicate that only some kinds of "rights" may be waived.[715] An early work concluded that, if the cases involving "waiver" are thoroughly analyzed, the concept could largely be "distributed" among other legal concepts such as estoppel and release.[716] The Code's only explanatory material is located in Comment 4, which states that subsection (4) is intended to "prevent contractual provisions excluding modification except by a signed writing from limiting in other respects the legal effect of the parties' actual later conduct."[717] This Comment suggests that the *conduct* of the parties may somehow affect the operation of a NOM clause, but does not say what sort of conduct is contemplated or *how* conduct might limit the effect of the clause. It makes no mention at all of how waiver might apply to the statute of frauds.

Section 2-209 also fails to answer the question: waiver of *what*? Does "waiver" refer to (1) a waiver of the application of the statute of frauds or the NOM clause to the contract? (2) a waiver of the term that the parties are attempting to modify? (3) a waiver of *certain* terms that the parties might attempt to modify orally but not others? (4) something else?

An early case addressing these issues is *Double-E Sportswear Corp. v. Girard Trust Bank*.[718] On March 24, 1971, Girard Bank (the seller) contracted to sell a quantity of knitted shirts and sweaters to Double-E Sports-

---

[714] *Compare* Tri-City Jewish Ctr. v. Blass Riddick Chilcote, 159 Ill. App. 3d 436, 512 N.E.2d 363, 111 Ill. Dec. 24 (1987) (a waiver, once made, is irrevocable); Gilbert v. Globe & Rutgers Fire Ins. Co., 91 Or. 59, 174 P. 1161, 178 P. 358 (1918) (unlike estoppel, waiver may not be retracted) *with* Computer Strategies, Inc. v. Commodore Business Mach., Inc., 105 A.D.2d 167, 483 N.Y.S.2d 716, 40 UCCR 1240 (1984) (waiver can be retracted upon reasonable notice).

[715] Some courts require consideration for waiver. *See* Smith v. Threshing Minneapolis Mach. Co., 89 Okla. 156, 214 P. 178 (1923). Others, however, do not. Champion Spark Plug Co. v. Automobile Sundries Co., 273 F. 74 (2d Cir. 1921). In any event, most authorities agree that only *conditions* may be waived without consideration, not contract obligations. Arthur L. Corbin, Corbin on Contracts § 753 (1952). Further, only conditions that do not constitute a material part of the agreed exchange may be waived without consideration. Restatement (Second) of Contracts § 84 (1981); Arthur L. Corbin, Corbin on Contracts § 753 at 710 (1952). Finally, waiver without consideration has sometimes been limited to situations in which a party abandons a contractual right, not where the other party's duties are changed or modified. *See* Quigley v. Wilson, 474 N.W.2d 277 (Iowa Ct. App. 1991), *aff'd,* 474 N.W.2d 277 (1991).

[716] J. Ewart, Waiver Distributed Among the Departments: Election, Estoppel, Contract, Release (1917).

[717] U.C.C. § 2-209, Official Comment 4.

[718] 488 F.2d 292, 13 UCCR 577 (3d Cir. 1973).

wear (the buyer) for the price of $11.75 per dozen. The arrangement gave the seller the right to terminate the agreement on or before April 1, 1971, by sending written notice. On March 31, the seller's attorney telephoned the buyer's attorney and related that the seller had received an offer for the goods of $14.00 per dozen, and asked the buyer if it would be willing to meet the offer. The buyer agreed to meet the price. After some further discussion, the parties agreed to a sealed-bid arrangement, whereby if the buyer's bid was the highest, the seller would unconditionally agree to sell the goods to the buyer for the amount of the bid. If the buyer's bid was not the highest, the March 24 agreement would be canceled.

On April 1, the buyer submitted a $15.50-per-dozen sealed bid. The seller informed the buyer that the goods had been sold on the previous evening for $14.00 per dozen and refused to accept the buyer's bid. The buyer sued, claiming that the parties had entered into an agreement in which the seller had agreed not to terminate the contract except in accordance with the sealed-bid procedure. The seller defended, in part, on the basis that the statute of frauds made the oral agreement unenforceable.

The Court of Appeals for the Third Circuit said that the seller's argument overlooked the fact that section 2-209(4) "explicitly provide[s] for an oral waiver of the operation of the statute of frauds."[719] According to the court, "once the statute of frauds is waived, there is no barrier to an oral modification of the terms of a written contract under § 2-209(1)."[720] The court noted, however, that a waiver is subject to retraction if the criteria of section 2-209(5) are met. The court then remanded to the lower court to determine: (1) whether there was a waiver of the statute of frauds;[721] (2) whether there was an oral modification of the March 24 agreement; and (3) whether there was a retraction of the waiver under section 2-209(5).

Judge Garth, in his concurrence, disagreed with the majority's analysis. According to Judge Garth, an essential, but erroneous, predicate of the majority's decision was that the "waiver" referred to in section 2-209(4) meant a waiver of the statute of frauds. Judge Garth believed the waiver contemplated by the section was much more limited:

---

[719] *Id.* at 296, 13 UCCR at 582.

[720] *Id.* at 296, 13 UCCR at 582–583.

[721] Although it is not clear, the court's opinion suggests that the attempted oral modification does not *itself* act as a waiver of the statute of frauds. It required the lower court to decide *both* whether there was a waiver and whether there was an oral modification. Also, the court says, "[w]hile we may fault, for incompleteness, the district court's explicit language which found an 'oral modification' of a written agreement, implicit in its analysis also was a finding of an oral agreement to waive the statute of frauds." *Id.* at 296, 13 UCCR 583.

> Rather, it is my view that the "waiver" to which 2-209(4) refers is a waiver limited to the particular condition, term or portion of the written contract sought to be waived by a party entitled to waive it. It does not constitute nor operate as a wholesale waiver of the statute of frauds. . . . Under my interpretation of § 2-209(4), after there has been an unsuccessful oral modification, a party entitled to waive a provision can waive that provision by agreeing to an oral modification, but obviously no new or affirmative term can be substituted therefor without satisfaction of the statute of frauds.[722]

Judge Garth cited the language of section 2-209(5) to support his position. This subsection refers to "a waiver affecting an executory *portion of the contract*" and "strict performance will be required of any *term* waived."[723] The language of subsections (4) and (5) made it clear to Judge Garth that the term "waiver" was used not to refer to a waiver of the statute of frauds but to permit only a waiver of conditions that were traditionally subject to waiver.[724]

The majority and concurring opinions in *Double-E Sportswear* take very different approaches to the scope of subsection (4). To illustrate, suppose that the parties orally agree to modify the price in a contract from $600 to $700. Under the majority's analysis, this modification would be enforceable as a subsection (4) waiver, as would any other oral modifications made by the parties. Under Judge Garth's analysis, because the oral change to the contract is a *change or modification* of a term, rather than a *waiver* of a term, it would not be enforceable. A similar issue exists with respect to NOM clauses—does a waiver entirely eliminate the prohibition on oral modifications or merely permit certain kinds of conditions to be waived?

Few other cases contain a helpful discussion of what is waived in the event of a "waiver." In the context of the statute of frauds, most cases seem to indicate, like the majority in *Double-E Sportswear,* that the waiver is of the statute of frauds.[725] As a result, once a waiver occurs, any oral modification becomes enforceable unless the waiver is properly retracted. Most cases reach similar results with respect to NOM clauses: the waiver permitted by section 2-209(4) is a waiver of the NOM clause rather than of a

---

[722] 488 F.2d at 298, 13 UCCR at 586 (Garth, J., concurring).

[723] *Id.* at 299, 13 UCCR at 587 (Garth, J., concurring).

[724] *Id.* at 300, 13 UCCR at 587 n.5 (Garth, J., concurring).

[725] *See, e.g.,* Green Constr. Co. v. First Indem. of Am. Ins. Co., 735 F. Supp. 1254, 12 UCCR2d 1034 (D.N.J. 1990); Farmers Elevator Co. of Reserve v. Anderson, 552 P.2d 63, 170 Mont. 175, 19 UCCR 1084 (1976); SonFast Corp. v. York Int'l Corp., 875 F. Supp. 1099, 27 UCCR2d 814 (M.D. Pa. 1995) (approving *Double-E Sportswear*); Smyers v. Quartz Works Corp., 880 F. Supp. 1424, 27 UCCR2d 142 (D. Kan. 1995).

particular term,[726] although some cases reach a contrary result.[727] Consequently, most courts have allowed oral changes to contract terms beyond the simple waiver of contract conditions or the removal of contract duties.[728]

Some agreements (no doubt drafted by lawyers) contain NOM clauses that by their terms exclude all but written waivers, as well as oral modifications. Without delving into the metaphysics of whether it is possible to draft a "no oral waiver" clause that cannot itself be orally waived, courts have reached different results on the issue, generally with little discussion. Some have permitted oral waivers to be shown under section 2-209(4) despite the presence of such clauses,[729] while others have not.[730]

Section 2-209(4) provides that an attempt at modification which does not satisfy the statute of frauds or a NOM clause *may* operate as a waiver. The use of the word "may" implies that a failed modification will not

---

[726] *See, e.g.*, Stinnes Interoil, Inc. v. Apex Oil Co., 604 F. Supp. 978, 41 UCCR 1293 (S.D.N.Y. 1985); Linear Corp. v. Standard Hardware Co., 423 So. 2d 966, 35 UCCR 1141 (Fla. Dist. Ct. App. 1983).

[727] *See* Marlowe v. Argentine Naval Comm'n, 808 F.2d 120, 257 U.S. App. D.C. 225, 2 UCCR2d 1226 (1986) (waiver extends only to specific terms); South Hampton Co. v. Stinnes Corp., 733 F.2d 1108, 38 UCCR 1137 (5th Cir. 1984) (oral "waiver" changing place of weighing of goods was really modification and barred by NOM clause). *See also* Knoxville Rod & Bearing, Inc. v. Bettis Corp. of Knoxville, Inc., 672 S.W.2d 203, 39 UCCR 415 (Tenn. Ct. App. 1984) (while NOM clause and U.C.C. § 2-209(2) prevent nonwritten modifications, party can waive right to enforce anticompetition clause).

[728] *See, e.g.*, Whitney Bros. Co. v. Sprafkin, 3 F.3d 530, 23 UCCR2d 1058 (1st Cir. 1993) (oral modification to permit prepayment); Etheridge Oil Co. v. Panciera, 818 F. Supp. 480, 22 UCCR2d 82 (D.R.I. 1993) (changes to time of payment, extension of credit, and other terms); Stinnes Interoil, Inc. v. Apex Oil Co., 604 F. Supp. 978, 41 UCCR 415 (S.D.N.Y. 1985) (oral modification of delivery date); Linear Corp. v. Standard Hardware Co., 423 So. 2d 966, 35 UCCR 1141 (Fla. Dist. Ct. App. 1983) (oral agreement that seller would repurchase on demand); Wisconsin Knife Works v. National Metal Crafters, 781 F.2d 1280, 1786, 42 UCCR 830, 836 (7th Cir. 1986) (it is "unsatisfactory" to distinguish between a modification that substitutes a new term for an old, and a waiver, which merely removes an old term).

[729] *See* Crosby-Mississippi Resources, Ltd. v. Florida Gas Transmission Co., 815 F. Supp. 977, 21 UCCR2d 257 (S.D. Miss. 1993); Battista v. Savings Bank of Baltimore, 507 A.2d 203, 67 Md. App. 257, 1 UCCR2d 1040 (Ct. Spec. App. 1986); Westinghouse Credit Corp. v. Shelton, 645 F.2d 689, 31 UCCR 410 (10th Cir. 1981).

[730] *See* Marlowe v. Argentine Naval Comm'n, 808 F.2d 120, 257 U.S. App. D.C. 225, 2 UCCR2d 1226 (1986); South Hampton Co. v. Stinnes Corp., 733 F.2d 1108, 38 UCCR 1137 (5th Cir. 1984). *See also* Cassidy Podell Lynch, Inc. v. Snydergeneral Corp., 944 F.2d 1131, 15 UCCR2d 1225 (3d Cir. 1991) (NOM clause has no effect on waiver established by course of performance); Brookside Farms v. Mama Rizzo's, Inc., 873 F. Supp. 1029, 28 UCCR2d 1110 (S.D. Tex. 1995) ("no-waiver" clause protects party from nonwritten waiver of NOM clause; however, exceptions in U.C.C. § 2-201(3) also govern NOM clauses).

always act as a waiver—that something more might be necessary. The Code gives no clue as to what this "something else" might be, and the cases contain little helpful discussion. The only case to make more than a superficial effort at analysis is *Wisconsin Knife Works v. National Metal Crafters*,[731] a case in which two jurisprudential soulmates, Judge Richard Posner and Judge Frank Easterbrook, ended up on opposite sides.

The case involved a contract for the sale by the seller of "spade bit blanks."[732] The spade bit blanks were not delivered on the dates specified in the various purchase orders. The buyer eventually terminated the contract after about half of the bits had been delivered and sued for damages for late delivery. The seller responded that the parties had orally modified the delivery dates in the contract. The buyer denied the modifications and relied upon a NOM clause in the contract.

Judge Posner began a detailed analysis of section 2-209 by recognizing that subsection (2) of section 2-209 validates NOM clauses and that it was improper for the trial court to have instructed the jury that it could find that the contract had been orally modified despite the NOM clause.[733] Immediately thereafter, however, Judge Posner said that this instruction may have been harmless error as a result of section 2-209(4) and the potential availability of waiver. Despite the trial judge's failure to use the term "waiver" in his instruction, Judge Posner said that if his instruction incorporated the concept of waiver, it might nonetheless be satisfactory.[734]

In making this determination, Judge Posner dismissed the idea that section 2-209(4) should be interpreted so broadly that *any* oral modification is immediately effective as a waiver. This interpretation would render section

---

[731] 781 F.2d 1280, 42 UCCR 830 (7th Cir. 1986).

[732] A "spade bit blank" is "a chunk of metal" out of which a spade bit is made. 781 F.2d at 1282, 42 UCCR at 831.

[733] 781 F.2d at 1284, 42 UCCR at 834.

[734] The judge's instruction was as follows:

> Did the parties modify the contract? The defendant bears the burden of proof on this one. You shall answer this question yes only if you are convinced to a reasonable certainty that the parties modified the contract.
>
> If you determine that the defendant had performed in a manner different from the strict obligations imposed on it by the contract, and the plaintiff by conduct or other means of expression induced a reasonable belief by the defendant that strict enforcement was not insisted upon, but that the modified performance was satisfactory and acceptable as equivalent, then you may conclude that the parties have assented to a modification of the original terms of the contract and that the parties have agreed that the different mode of performance will satisfy the obligations imposed on the parties by the contract.

Id.

2-209(2) superfluous. He further rejected an analysis that distinguished between a "waiver" and "modification" saying that, "[w]hether the party claiming modification is seeking to impose an onerous new term on the other party or to wiggle out of an onerous term that the original contract imposed on it is a distinction without a difference."[735] Instead, the path to reconciling sections 2-209(2) and 2-209(4) was reliance:

> The main purpose of forbidding oral modifications is to prevent the promisor from fabricating a modification that will let him escape his obligations under the contract; and the danger of successful fabrication is less if the promisor has actually incurred a cost, has relied.[736]

While recognizing that this analysis of section 2-209(4) creates some tension between subsections (4) and (5) of section 2-209,[737] Judge Posner said that his analysis was not inconsistent with section 2-209(5). To Judge Posner, a waiver occurs when there is an oral modification *and* the party benefited relies on it. Judge Easterbrook, on the other hand, felt that the term "waiver" should be given its classic meaning of the voluntary relinquishment of a known right, and that such a waiver may result from the failed attempt at oral modification,[738] without the necessity of reliance.

As Judge Easterbrook pointed out,[739] it does not matter in many cases which interpretation is adopted. Because section 2-209(5) often allows a waiver to be retracted in the absence of reliance, reliance is usually necessary for an enforceable waiver under either approach. In one case, however, it may make a difference whether one follows Posner or Easterbrook. Section 2-209(5) permits a waiver to be retracted only with respect to *executory* portions of the contract, and only then if there is no reliance.[740] If Easter-

---

[735] 781 F.2d at 1286, 42 UCCR at 837.

[736] *Id.*

[737] U.C.C. § 2-209(5) permits a waiver to be withdrawn *unless* there has been reliance; this seems to assume that a waiver already exists at the time of the reliance, which then acts to make the waiver irrevocable.

[738] 781 F.2d at 1290, 42 UCCR at 845 (Easterbrook, J., dissenting). Judge Easterbrook also suggested that it might be sensible to require more than simply evidence of the oral modification, such as evidence of a course of performance consistent with the modification. *Id.*

[739] 781 F.2d at 1292, 42 UCCR at 848 (Easterbrook, J., dissenting).

[740] U.C.C. § 2-209(5) provides:

> A party who has made a waiver affecting an executory portion of the contract may retract the waiver by reasonable notification received by the other party that strict performance will be required of any term waived, unless retraction would be unjust in view of a material change of position in reliance on the waiver.

brook's position is adopted, once a portion of the contract has been performed, the issue of reliance is irrelevant. Reliance is not required to establish a waiver, and reliance is not necessary to prevent retraction of a waiver with respect to *executed* portions of the contract. If reliance is required to establish a waiver in the first instance, however, as Judge Posner contends, a waiver may not be found even with respect to *executed* portions of the contract if there is no reliance.[741]

Other cases are split on whether the statute of frauds or a NOM clause can, without more, be orally waived. A couple of cases have said that a waiver requires more than evidence of an oral agreement and have required evidence of course of performance or other conduct evidencing the waiver.[742] At least one other case, however, indicates that an oral modification alone is sufficient to act as a waiver under section 2-209(4).[743]

Even when a NOM clause is waived, the modification of a term made pursuant to the waiver is not permanent unless supported by consideration or reliance.[744] A retraction of a waiver under section 2-209(5) reinstates the original term that has been modified, as well as retracting the waiver of the NOM clause. This is true despite the fact that under section 2-209(1) a modification needs no consideration to binding. The result is that if a modification occurs under section 2-209(4), it may be retracted unless supported by consideration or reliance.[745]

[F] Conclusion

Despite its obvious problems, section 2-209 has worked reasonably well. It has extricated sale-of-goods contracts from the technicalities of the

---

[741] Of course, if execution of a portion of the contract is itself sufficient reliance to create a waiver, then Posner's and Easterbrook's positions become, for practical purposes, indistinguishable.

[742] *See* Middletown Concrete Prods., Inc. v. Black Clawson Co., 802 F. Supp. 1135, 20 UCCR2d 815 (D. Del. 1992); Green Constr. Co. v. First Indem. of Am. Ins. Co., 735 F. Supp. 1254, 12 UCCR2d 1034 (D.N.J. 1990). *See also* J. W. Goodlife & Son v. Odzer, 283 Pa. Super. 148, 423 A.2d 1032, 31 UCCR 845 (1980) (attempt at oral modification is a waiver when combined with course of performance); Central Ill. Pub. Serv. Co. v. Atlas Minerals, 33 UCCR2d 386 (D. Ill. 1997) (only evidence of intentional waiver will suffice).

[743] *See* Linear Corp. v. Standard Hardware Corp., 423 So. 2d 966, 35 UCCR 1141 (Fla. Dist. Ct. App. 1982).

[744] *See* Exxon Corp. v. Crosby-Mississippi Resources, Ltd., 40 F.3d 1474, 25 UCCR2d 1103 (5th Cir. 1995) (oral agreement to forgo enforcement of price floor not effective as modification although it acted as waiver of the term when relied upon).

[745] It may be that if the modification is oral when the contract requires it to be written, the modification can be retracted even if supported by consideration, assuming no reliance. If courts so hold, principles of restitution would require the return of the consideration.

preexisting duty rule. Moreover, it has enabled courts to balance a concern about the ease with which an oral modification may be fabricated with the fact that oral modifications do occur, despite the presence of the statute of frauds and NOM clauses. The drafters have concluded that when such modifications occur and are justifiably relied upon, they should be enforced.

[G] Proposed Revisions to Section 2-209

In the proposed revisions to Article 2, section 2-209 has been significantly recast. The proposed revision is generally laudable, clearing up some of the ambiguities in the present section. The thrust of the section, however, remains the same and continues the drafters' attempt to balance the competing policies described earlier. The proposed section 2-209 provides:

> (a) An agreement made in good faith modifying a contract under this article needs no consideration to be binding.
> (b) Except in a consumer contract, an authenticated record containing a term that excludes modification or rescission except by an authenticated record may not be otherwise modified or rescinded. Such a term in a form record supplied by a merchant to a non-resident must be conspicuous. However, a party whose language or conduct is inconsistent with the exclusion term is precluded from asserting it if the language or conduct induced the other party to change its position reasonably and in good faith.
> (c) Except as provided in subsection (b), a condition in a contract may be waived by the party for whose benefit it was included. Language or conduct, including a course of performance between the parties, is relevant to show a waiver. A waiver affecting an executory portion of a contract, however, may be retracted by seasonable notification received by the other party that strict performance will be required of any term waived, unless the waiver induced the other party to change its position reasonably and in good faith.[746]

Subsection (a) restates the rule of the present section 2-209 that consideration is not necessary to modify a contract. Unlike the existing section 2-209, however, the requirement that modifications be in good faith is made

---

[746] The American Law Institute, Uniform Commercial Code Revised Article 2, Sales, Council Draft No. 4, December 1, 1998, § 2-209 (Council Draft No. 4). Subsection (3) of former U.C.C. § 2-209 has been deleted. That subsection stated that the requirements of the statute of frauds "must be satisfied if the contract as modified is within its provisions." After the deletion it is clear that if the original agreement satisfies the statute the modification is enforceable even though the resulting contract is within the statute and the modification is not in writing.

explicit in the section itself. Neither the revised section nor the commentary following it provides any additional guidance on the requirement of good faith, and the extant case law, discussed earlier,[747] should continue to apply.

Section 2-209 no longer contains any reference to the Code's statute of frauds. The commentary to the revised section 2-209 suggests that the statute of frauds is irrelevant to modifications unless the modification brings a contract within the statute of frauds that was not originally within it.[748] If a contract was originally within the statute and was evidenced by a sufficient writing, however, under the proposed revisions, it may be modified without a writing. This apparently extends to a modification of the quantity term as well as a modification of any other terms. Under section 2-201, if the modification *increases* the quantity, however, the contract is not enforceable beyond the amount stated in the writing.[749]

The revised section continues to enforce NOM clauses, except in consumer contracts, but provides more explicit guidance than the present section 2-209 on what is required in order to preclude their enforcement. The ambiguous language of the present subsection (4) has been replaced by subsection (b) of section 2-209. This provision provides that a term may be modified or rescinded despite a NOM clause, if the "language or conduct" of one party is inconsistent with the NOM clause and "induce[s] the other party to change its position reasonably and in good faith."[750] Unlike the present section, the revision makes it clear that reliance is the *sine qua non* of enforcing a modification or rescission despite a NOM clause. Language or conduct inconsistent with a NOM clause will result in the enforcement of the modification or rescission only if there is good faith and reasonable reliance.[751]

Subsection (b) also makes it clear that these principles apply to the modification of *any* term that is subject to the NOM clause, not simply a waiver of conditions or other terms which were subject to waiver at common law.[752] In fact, subsection (b) does not use the term "waiver" at all.[753] Thus, so long as a party relies reasonably and in good faith on an oral modification,

---

[747] *See* § 3.10[B], *supra*.

[748] Council Draft No. 4, § 2-209, Note 2.

[749] Council Draft No. 4, § 2-201(a).

[750] Council Draft No. 4, § 2-209(b).

[751] Subsection(b) vindicates Judge Posner's analysis in Wisconsin Knife Works v. National Metalcrafters. *See* §3.10[E], *supra*.

[752] *See* Judge Easterbrook's opinion in Wisconsin Knife Works v. National Metalcrafters discussed in § 3.10[E], *supra*.

[753] However, the Notes to U.C.C. § 2-209 do use the term "waiver" in connection with subsection(b). *See* Council Draft No. 4, § 2-209, Note 3.

the modification can be to any term of the contract, such as price, quantity, delivery date, or any other term.

The revised section itself does not indicate when language or conduct is "inconsistent" with a NOM clause, but the commentary and illustrations following the revised section are helpful. A waiver can occur from an express statement by a party that it will not rely on a NOM clause with respect to the modification of a term or terms. Thus, if a seller relies upon the assurance of the buyer in orally extending a delivery date that the buyer will not insist on the NOM clause, a waiver will occur.[754] The commentary also makes it clear, however, that the NOM clause does not have to be *explicitly* waived. If, for example, the buyer orally agrees to the extension and the seller proceeds under the revised delivery date, the modification will be effective despite the NOM clause.[755]

Subsection (c) deals with waiver of conditions in the absence of a NOM clause. Again, the concept of reliance plays a pivotal role. The subsection provides generally that a condition in a contract may be waived by the party for whose benefit it was included. Language, conduct, or a course of performance is relevant (although apparently not conclusive) in establishing a waiver. Unlike subsection (b), a waiver of a condition under subsection (c) can occur prior to any reliance.[756] Subsection (c) applies only to conditions, not to any term of the contract, however, and under subsection (c), the seller may retract the waiver as to any *executory* portion of the contract by reasonable notification received by the other party[757] prior to a reasonable and good-faith change in position in reliance upon the waiver.

Neither subsections (b) or (c) describe what kind of reliance or how much reliance is required to create an enforceable modification or rescission under subsection (b) or to make a waiver of a condition irrevocable under subsection (c). It is not clear whether the change in position will have to be substantial or whether any change in position, however small, in reliance on the waiver will be sufficient. Furthermore, it is not certain what the drafters mean by a "good faith" change of position. Is it sufficient, for example, to establish bad faith that the party benefiting from the waiver knew of an NOM clause in the contract at the time he changed position in reliance on an oral modification, and further knew that the other party was unaware of the NOM clause in the contract? Is it sufficient for bad faith if the party benefiting from an oral modification changes his position solely to establish

---

[754] *See* Council Draft No. 4, § 2-209, Note 3.

[755] *Id.*

[756] *See* Council Draft No. 4, § 2-209, Note 3.

[757] Note that the notification of retraction must be *received*, not simply sent.

waiver under subsection (b) or to make a waiver irrevocable under subsection (c), even when the change in position is not otherwise necessary? Only time will provide answers to these questions.

Overall, the revisions are an improvement to the present section 2-209. They do not substantially change the law under the present section, but they do clear up a number of interpretive difficulties discussed earlier.

IV. INTERPRETATION OF A CONTRACT FOR SALE

§ 3.11   THE GENERAL PROBLEM OF INTERPRETATION

Thousands of pages of judicial opinion have been devoted to the task of interpreting the words the parties used in reaching their agreement. That this task is difficult cannot be denied.[758] Many words lack precision, and many sales agreements result from an exchange of forms that contain broadly drafted clauses couched in vague and general language.[759] The court must, if possible, extract a meaning from these words so that it can determine the scope of the promises exchanged.

Interpretation is the process of determining the meaning of words. Yet even well into the twentieth century it was not established *whose* meaning governed the interpretation of an agreement. This uncertainty was created by the ascendancy of the objective theory of contract *formation*, which supplanted the older theory that a subjective "meeting of the minds" was necessary to form a contract. By the first few decades of the twentieth century, it had become widely accepted that contracts were created not on the basis of the concurrence of mutual subjective intention, but on the basis of the external manifestations of the parties. When the contracting parties disagreed as to subjective intention, the question of contract formation was determined by whether one party had been led to reasonably believe that a contract had been formed by the objective manifestations of the other.[760]

The extent to which the objective theory of contract formation rendered subjective intention irrelevant was a matter of controversy. Some, such as

---

[758] *See, e.g.*, Chastain & Blass Real Estate & Ins., Inc. v. Davis, 280 Ala. 489, 195 So. 2d 782 (1967); Daman v. Walton Lumber Co., 53 Wash. 2d 747, 337 P.2d 37 (1959). Of the many books discussing the "softness" of the English language, one of the best in still C. Ogden & I. Richards, The Meaning of Meaning (10th ed. 1952).

[759] Mead Corp. v. McNally-Pittsburgh Mfg. Corp., 654 F.2d 1197, 35 UCCR 368 (6th Cir. 1981); Homestake Mining Co. v. Washington Public Power Supply Sys., 476 F. Supp. 1162, 26 UCCR 1113 (N.D. Cal. 1979); First State Bank v. Keilman, 851 S.W.2d 914, 22 UCCR2d 282 (Tex. Ct. App. 1993).

[760] *See, e.g.*, Embry v. Hargadine, McKittrick Dry Goods Co., 127 Mo. App. 383, 105 S.W. 777 (1907); Samuel L. Williston, Williston on Contracts, § 4:1 at 241 (4th ed. 1990).

Professor Williston,[761] suggested that the objective theory of contracts rendered evidence of the subjective intentions of the parties entirely irrelevant. Thus, even when a mutual subjective understanding did exist, it was not material to the issue of whether a contract had been formed. The underlying notion was that words have an objective, or usual, meaning to a disinterested third party. In deciding whether a contract has been formed, the law imposes that meaning on the parties irrespective of their understanding when they used those words.[762]

Professor Corbin, on the other hand, took the position that it was absurd to carry the objective theory of contracts to this extreme.[763] Corbin believed that the objective theory should come into play only when the subjective understandings of the parties varied. If neither party understood that a contract had been created, the courts should not create one for them.[764]

The debate surrounding the objective and subjective theories of contract formation necessarily carried over into the law of contract interpretation as well.[765] The view of the objective theorists was embodied in the "plain meaning" rule.[766] This doctrine required judges to refuse to consider extrinsic evidence of the parties' understanding of a term unless the term was vague or ambiguous. The most famous dictum expressing this idea comes from an early opinion by Mr. Justice Holmes: "It would open too great risks if evidence were admissible to show that when they said five hundred feet they agreed it should mean one hundred inches or that Bunker Hill Monument should signify the Old South Church."[767] This view was endorsed by Professor Williston[768] and was incorporated into the First Restatement of

---

[761] Williston, *supra* note 3, § 4:1, at 237.

[762] *See* American Sumatra Tobacco Corp. v. Willis, 170 F.2d 215 (5th Cir. 1948). *See also* the majority opinion and Justice Traynor's answer in Laux v. Freed, 53 Cal. 2d 512, 348 P.2d 873 (1960). Judge Learned Hand appeared to express Williston's view in Hotchkiss v. National City Bank, 200 F. 287, 293 (S.D.N.Y. 1911), *aff'd*, 201 F. 664 (2d Cir. 1912), *aff'd*, 231 U.S. 50 (1913):

> A contract has, strictly speaking, nothing to do with the personal, or individual, intent of the parties. . . . If . . . it were proved by twenty bishops that either party, when he used the words, intended something else than the usual meaning which the law imposes upon them, he would still be held, unless there was some mutual mistake, or something else of that sort.

[763] Arthur L. Corbin, Corbin on Contracts, § 106 at 157 (one-volume edition 1952).

[764] Corbin, *supra* note 763, § 541 at 506.

[765] *See* A. Farnsworth & W. Young, Contracts: Cases and Materials 591 (5th ed. 1995).

[766] E. Allan Farnsworth, Contracts, § 7.12 at 520 (2d ed. 1990); In re Continental Airlines, Inc., 932 F.2d 282, 21 Bankr. Ct. Dec. 1111 (3d Cir. 1991); Roe v. Miles Labs., Inc., 740 F. Supp. 740, 10 UCCR2d 1191 (D. Alaska 1989).

[767] Goode v. Riley, 153 Mass. 585, 586, 28 N.E. 228 (1891).

[768] Samuel L. Williston, Williston on Contracts, § 95 (4th ed. 1990).

Contracts.[769] To Corbin, the meaning of words is never so clear as to exclude proof of the circumstances surrounding their use.[770] Parties should be free to choose their own usage and definitions.[771] To Corbin, "[w]hite can be made to mean black, five can be made to mean ten, 500 feet can be made to mean 100 inches, and Bunker Hill can be made to signify Old South Church."[772] Professor Corbin's views of both contract formation and contract interpretation are embodied in the Restatement (Second) of Contracts.[773]

This brief introduction is intended to provide background for understanding the Code's provisions. The following sections will discuss the problems of interpreting contractual language under the Code, including the Code's parol evidence rule. The reader should keep in mind, however, that the rules of fraud,[774] mistake,[775] equitable reformation,[776] custom,[777] and other contract doctrines also play a part in contract interpretation, and will generally remain applicable under the Code, although they are not discussed in detail in this text.[778]

§ 3.12 DISTINCTION BETWEEN "AGREEMENT" AND "CONTRACT"

The Code's approach to contract interpretation begins with its distinction between the *fact* of agreement and the *concept* of contract. "Agreement" is defined as follows:

> "Agreement" means the bargain of the parties in fact as found in their language or by implication from other circumstances including course of dealing or usage of trade or course of performance.[779]

On the other hand, "contract" is defined as:

---

[769] *See* Restatement (First) of Contracts, § 231, illus. 2 (1932).

[770] Corbin, *supra* note 763, § 542 at 514–516.

[771] Corbin, *supra* note 763, § 544 at 519–521.

[772] *Id.*

[773] Restatement (Second) of Contracts, §§ 20, 201 (1981).

[774] *See* Wagner v. Rao, 885 P.2d 174, 180 Ariz. 486 (Ariz. Ct. App. 1994); Herzog Contracting Corp. v. McGowen Corp., 976 F.2d 1062, 18 UCCR2d 1170 (7th Cir. 1992); Wood v. R.R. Donnelley & Sons Co., 888 F.2d 313, 10 UCCR2d 468 (3d Cir. 1989).

[775] *See* Bell v. Carroll, 212 Ky. 231, 278 S.W. 541 (1925).

[776] Cases are discussed in Palmer, "Reformation and the Parol Evidence Rule," 65 Mich. L. Rev. 833 (1967).

[777] *See* Walker v. Sims, 118 Mich. 183, 76 N.W. 320 (1898); Soutier v. Kellerman, 18 Mo. 509 (1853); Hurst v. W.J. Lake & Co., 141 Or. 306, 16 P.2d 627 (1932).

[778] U.C.C. § 1-103.

[779] U.C.C. § 1-203(3).

the total legal obligation which results from the parties' agreement as affected by this Act and any other applicable rules of law.[780]

Agreement is the word used by the Code to describe what the parties do; *contract* is the word used by the Code to describe what the law does about what the parties have done. The parties negotiate through oral conversations, printed forms, exchanged memoranda, inflections of the voice, a wave of the hand, or a nod of the head. Their words or acts may have special meaning to them because they have used them before or because the trade to which they belong attaches a special meaning to them. The parties do not enter into a contract; they reach a bargain. The bargain is the Code's "agreement." The next step is to decide what legal obligations arose from their agreement. If the agreement lacks consideration, results from fraud or unconscionability, or is the product of a mistake, a court may conclude that there are no legal obligations—that there is no contract despite the "agreement." Or, it may conclude that there is a contract, but with terms different from those of the agreement.[781] Finally, it may decide that a contract exists, the terms of which are reflected in the agreement of the parties.

The distinction between "agreement" and "contract" is important to the Code's approach to interpretation. Each of the Code sections that creates principles of interpretation refers in some manner to the agreement of the parties.[782] These references focus attention on what the parties *did*—on the meaning they gave their words and acts—not on some meaning forced on them because the words they chose have a "usual" dictionary meaning.[783]

Any doubts about this are resolved by a careful reading of the Code's definition of "agreement."[784] It is the *bargain in fact* of the parties that is important. Although "bargain" is not defined, it carries with it the notion of coming to terms, of reaching a deal. Furthermore, it is the bargain *of the parties* that is essential. If they understood that their words (or their actions or silence) have a certain meaning, that understanding is their agreement.

---

[780] U.C.C. § 1-203(11).

[781] *See* U.C.C. § 2-302, which permits a court to refuse to enforce an unconscionable provision of a contract or limit the application of an unconscionable provision. For an example, *see* American Home Improvement, Inc. v. MacIver, 105 N.H. 435, 201 A.2d 886, 2 UCCR 235 (1964) (court reduced the price of the goods to a conscionable price).

[782] U.C.C. §§ 1-205, 2-202, 2-208, 2-209.

[783] *See* Stewart-Decatur Sec. Sys., Inc. v. Von Weise Gear Co., 517 F.2d 1136, 1140, 17 UCCR 24, 30 nn.11 & 12 (8th Cir. 1975) (concept of construing a commercial transaction in accordance with the parties' intent pervades the Code; application of the rules of U.C.C. § 2-317 not appropriate when inconsistent with the intent of the parties).

[784] Agreement is defined in U.C.C. § 1-201(3) as "the bargain of the parties in fact as found in their language or by implication from other circumstances including course of dealing or usage of trade or course of performance."

The fact that some third person would interpret what they did or said differently does not change the bargain of these parties.[785] Language, course of dealing, course of performance, and usage of trade are part of the totality of experience that gives meaning to the parties' bargain.[786]

§ 3.13   MEANING UNDER THE CODE

Two problems are important to the process of interpretation under the Code. The first has already been introduced in the preceding section: *whose meaning is important for interpreting the agreement*. This text has already suggested how this question ought to be answered: *if the parties meant the same thing by a word or an act, that common meaning is their agreement and ought to be enforced by a court*. This is true for two reasons. The first is the Code's focus on the factual bargain of the parties.[787] It is the bargain of the *parties* that is critical in interpreting their contract. Second, this position, espoused by Corbin[788] and embodied in the Restatement (Second) of Contracts,[789] now represents fundamental contract law.[790] The Code incorporates the general law of contracts.[791] To this extent, the focus is on the subjective understanding of the parties.

If the parties did not have a common meaning, the approach is "objective," and the principle of "relative fault" embodied in the second Restatement of Contracts governs interpretation. When two parties (*A* and *B*) have ascribed different meanings to the same word or act, to the extent that *A* knows or has reason to know of *B*'s meaning, and *B* neither knows nor has reason to know of *A*'s meaning, then *B*'s meaning will prevail.[792] Even if *B* has reason to know of *A*'s meaning, if *A* has *actual knowledge* of *B*'s

---

[785] *See* Stewart-Decatur Sec. Sys., Inc. v. Van Weise Gear Co., 517 F.2d 1136, 1139, 17 UCCR 24, 31.

[786] *See* Printing Ctr. of Tex., Inc. v. Supermind Publishing Co., Inc., 669 S.W.2d 779, 39 UCCR 127 (Tex. Ct. App. 1984) (contract of the parties includes more than their words; it extends to the bargain between them as shown by their language and implications from other circumstances, course of dealing, usage of trade, or course of performance).

[787] *See* § 3.04[B], *supra*.

[788] Arthur L. Corbin, Corbin on Contracts, § 538 (one-volume edition 1952).

[789] Section 201 (1) of the Restatement (Second) of Contracts provides:

(1)   Where the parties have attached the same meaning to a promise or agreement or a term thereof, it is interpreted in accordance with that meaning.

[790] *See* American Casualty Co. v. Baker, 22 F.3d 880, 887 (9th Cir. 1994); Beladevon, Inc. v. Assott Labs., Inc., 871 F. Supp. 89, 98 (D. Mass. 1994).

[791] According to the Code, "[c]ontract" means "the total legal obligation which results from the parties' agreement as affected by this Act *and any other applicable rules of law*." U.C.C. § 1-201(11) (emphasis added).

[792] Restatement (Second) of Contracts, §§ 20, 201 (1979).

meaning, *B*'s meaning will still be protected.[793] If the fault of the parties is equal—neither party knows or has reason to know of the other's meaning, or both have reason to know or both know of the other's meaning—the contract will fail because of misunderstanding[794] or the term may be supplied by the court.[795]

The second problem is what evidence is relevant to determine the meaning of the parties. Some types of evidence are clearly admissible. For example, a writing that purports to set forth some or all of the terms of the parties' agreement will be considered by a court in interpreting that agreement. Words chosen by the parties and deliberately reduced to writing are excellent evidence of what they intended. The more difficult issue is what *other* evidence is admissible and under what circumstances will it be admitted.

As a general matter, *any* evidence that aids the court in determining the meaning of the parties should be admitted. There are, however, three sources of extrinsic evidence specifically recognized by the Code as relevant to interpretation: usage of trade, course of dealing, and course of performance. The Code sections applicable to these sources are considered in the following sections.

§ 3.14   PRINCIPLES OF INTERPRETATION

The Code establishes a hierarchy of probative values for various types of evidence used to interpret agreements. First, the express terms of the agreement and any course of performance, course of dealing, and usage of trade are to be construed as consistent with each other whenever such a construction is "reasonable."[796] This is the Code's mandate to consider *all* of the relevant evidence of the parties' meaning and to attempt to construe this evidence as consistent. The reason is clear: most of the time the parties have in fact bargained from the background of their trade, their prior dealings, and their prior performance, and have selected the terms of their agreement in light of this background.

Second, there will be times when the parties intend to change the obligations that would otherwise arise from the way they have been performing

---

[793] *Id.*

[794] *See* Raffles v. Wichelhaus, 159 Eng. Rep. 375 (1864); Restatement (Second) of Contracts, § 20 (1979).

[795] Restatement (Second) of Contracts, § 201, cmt. d (1979).

[796] This conclusion is drawn from two Code sections: U.C.C. § 1-205(4) dealing with course of dealing and usage of trade, and U.C.C. § 2-208(2) dealing with course of performance.

their contract, from the way they have dealt with each other in the past, or from those obligations suggested by the usages of their trade. The Code makes it clear that they may do so; whenever it is unreasonable to construe the express terms of the writing as consistent with course of performance, course of dealing, and usage of trade, the terms of the writing shall control.[797]

Reading sections 1-205(4) and 2-208(2) together, the Code's interpretive hierarchy of extrinsic evidence makes course of performance controlling over both course of dealing and usage of trade, and makes course of dealing controlling over usage of trade. Whenever these produce conflicting meanings, this hierarchy presumptively controls.

These "rules" of interpretation should not, however, be read inflexibly or applied simplistically. Determining the meaning of a contract is not simply a matter of mechanically applying a set of rules. A course of dealing may be "strong" (that is, it may have occurred over many months under agreements very similar to the one involved),[798] or it may be extremely "weak" (that is, the prior conduct may consist of but a few acts and, as compared to the terms of the present writing, may be on the edge of being ambiguous).[799] On the other hand, the usage of trade may be ancient and well-known,[800] perhaps even privately codified in industry standards,[801] or it may be only emerging and still bordering on the amorphous.[802] Should the Code be read to mean that a clear trade usage must bow to a doubtful course of performance? Only if these "rules" of interpretation are read with a rigidity they were never intended to have.

---

[797] *See* U.C.C. §§ 1-205(4), 2-208(2).

[798] *See, e.g.*, Gindy Mfg. Corp. v. Cardinale Trucking Corp., 268 A.2d 345, 111 N.J. Super. 383, 7 UCCR 1257 (1970); Earl M. Jorgensen Co. v. Mark Constr., Inc., 540 P.2d 978, 56 Haw. 466, 17 UCCR 1126 (1975); Walker v. Walker, 854 F. Supp. 1443 (D. Neb. 1994).

[799] *See, e.g.*, Lake Ontario Prod. Credit Ass'n of Rochester v. Grove et al., 526 N.Y.S.2d 985, 138 A.D.2d 930, 6 UCCR2d 1597 (N.Y. Sup. Ct. 1988); Kern Oil & Ref. Co. v. Tenneco Oil Co., 792 F.2d 1380, 1 UCCR2d 651 (9th Cir. 1986).

[800] *See, e.g.*, Moe v. John Deere Co., 516 N.W.2d 332, 25 UCCR2d 997 (S.D. 1993); Schulze & Burch Biscuit Co. v. Tree Top, Inc., 831 F.2d 709, 4 UCCR2d 641 (7th Cir. 1987); Lincoln Pulp & Paper Co., Inc. v. Dravo Corp., 445 F. Supp. 507, 25 UCCR 400 (D. Me. 1977).

[801] *See, e.g.*, Martin Rispens & Sons v. Hall Farms, Inc., 601 N.E.2d 429, 19 UCCR2d 1021 (Ind. Ct. App. 1992); A.J. Cunningham Packing Corp. v. Florence Beef Co., 785 F.2d 348, 42 UCCR 1196 (1st Cir. 1986); Foxco Indus., Ltd. v. Fabric World, Inc., 595 F.2d 976, 26 UCCR 694 (5th Cir. 1979).

[802] *See, e.g.*, Marion Coal Co. v. Marc Rich & Co. Int'l, Ltd., 539 F. Supp. 903, 34 UCCR 12 (S.D.N.Y. 1982); Franklin Computer Corp. v. Wolsten's Projector House, Inc., 57 B.R. 155, 42 UCCR 1264 (E.D. Pa. 1986).

The Code ought not to be read this inflexibly. The principles in sections 1-205 and 2-208 should not be understood as rigid rules, because the slightest change in the background of a particular agreement can have a profound impact on the meaning of the words used. In general, course of performance is more apt to point toward the parties' meaning than is a more general course of dealing;[803] in turn, a course of dealing will usually be of greater impact than a usage of trade.[804] The court, however, should not use the interpretive *presumptions* in sections 1-205 and 2-208 to avoid the balancing or weighing necessary to arrive at the true bargain of the parties.[805]

Unfortunately, the cases do not always evidence this thoughtful balancing.[806] Some courts are quick to find that an express term is inconsistent with a usage of trade or course of dealing, simply because "on their face" the words appear so.[807] Other courts, however, have been more willing to permit evidence of usage of trade, course of dealing, or course of performance, even when it is apparently inconsistent with an express term.[808]

[A] Course of Performance

Course of performance is the "closest" to the contract of the various forms of extrinsic evidence mentioned by the Code.[809] It provides the clearest picture of how the parties themselves understood their rights and obli-

---

[803] *See* Marlowe v. Argentine Naval Comm'n, 808 F.2d 120, 2 UCCR2d 1226 (D.C. Cir. 1986) (course of dealing has "weaker effects" than course of performance).

[804] *See* Capital Converting Equip., Inc. v. LEP Transport, Inc., 750 F. Supp. 862, 14 UCCR2d 51 (N.D. Ill., E.D. 1990) (course of dealing is more important than usage of trade because it involves specific usages between the two parties).

[805] *Cf.* Nanakuli Paving & Rock Co. v. Shell Oil Co., Inc., 664 F.2d 772, 780, 32 UCCR 1025, 1032 (9th Cir. 1981) ("The Code would have us look beyond the printed pages of . . . the agreement in order to reach the 'true understanding' of the parties.").

[806] *See, e.g.*, Marlowe v. Argentine Naval Comm'n, 808 F.2d 120, 2 UCCR2d 1226 (D.C. Cir. 1986).

[807] *See, e.g.*, Seattle-First Nat'l Bank v. Westwood Lumber Co., 65 Wash. App. 811, 829 P.2d 1152, 18 UCCR2d 351 (1992); Aberdeen Prod. Credit Ass'n v. Redfield Livestock Auction, Inc., 379 N.W.2d 829, 42 UCCR 1481 (S.D. 1986); Indian Harbor Citrus, Inc. v. Poppell, 658 So. 2d 605, 27 UCCR2d 55 (Fla. Dist. Ct. App. 1995). *See also* Smith v. Penbridge Assocs., Inc., 655 A.2d 1015, 26 UCCR2d 273 (Pa. Super. Ct. 1995); Echo, Inc. v. Whitson Co., Inc., 121 F.3d 1099, 33 UCCR2d 40 (7th Cir. 1997).

[808] *See* Nanakuli Paving & Rock Co. v. Shell Oil Co., Inc., 664 F.2d 772, 32 UCCR 1025 (9th Cir. 1981) for an extraordinarily thorough discussion of the issue of inconsistency of trade usage and course of performance with express terms.

[809] *See* Nanakuli Paving & Rock Co. v. Shell Oil Co., Inc., 664 F.2d 772, 32 UCCR 1025 (9th Cir. 1981); In re Dakota Country Store Foods, Inc. v. Red Owl Stores, Inc., 107 B.R. 977, 10 UCCR2d 361 (D.S.D. 1989); Estate of Frost v. Frost, 344 N.W.2d 331, 130 Mich. App. 556, 37 UCCR 1476 (Mich. Ct. App. 1983).

gations under the contract.[810] Course of performance is relevant in determining the terms of a contract in four separate ways: (1) to interpret the meaning of a term or terms; (2) to show a waiver of a term; (3) to establish a modification of a term; and (4) to fill in a "gap" in a contract. The Code both defines course of performance and states its relevance to determine the meaning of the written terms of the contract in section 2-208(1):

> Where the contract for sale involves repeated occasions for performance by either party with knowledge of the nature of the performance and opportunity for objection to it by the other, any course of performance accepted or acquiesced in without objection shall be relevant to determine the meaning of the agreement.[811]

Before this section is applicable, the contract must call for more than one performance—"repeated occasions for performance" is the Code language.[812] No specific number of performances greater than one is required; one court has held that under some circumstances, as few as two are sufficient.[813] So long as the actions of the parties in performing the contract are sufficient to provide some indication of the meaning of the agreement, they should be sufficient to constitute a course of performance. The weight of the evidence should be a matter for the trier of fact; the longer the course of performance, the better are the chances that the trier of fact will find that the words meant what the parties "did."[814]

Sometimes what the parties have done appears inconsistent with what they wrote. For example, the writing may call for several deliveries at a price "FOB Buyer's City." For the first ten deliveries the seller charged, and the buyer paid, the price "FOB *Seller's* City." What is the price that must be paid for the eleventh delivery?[815]

---

[810] Official Comment 1 to U.C.C. § 2-208 provides:

> The parties themselves know best what they have meant by their words of agreement and their action under that agreement is the best indication of what that meaning was.

[811] U.C.C. § 2-208(1).

[812] U.C.C. § 2-208, Official Comment 4.

[813] Nanakuli Paving & Rock Co. v. Shell Oil Co., Inc., 664 F.2d 772, 32 UCCR 1025 (9th Cir. 1981) (where parties acted in a particular way on the only two relevant occasions, a sufficient course of performance was established).

[814] *See* Southwest Concrete Prods. v. Gosh Constr. Corp., 263 Cal. Rptr. 387, 10 UCCR2d 73 (Cal. Ct. App. 1989); Ramsey Prods. Corp. v. Morbark Indus., Inc., 823 F.2d 798, 4 UCCR2d 428 (4th Cir. 1987).

[815] For a similar fact situation, *see* Brunswick Box Co., Inc. v. Coutinho, Caro, & Co., Inc., 617 F.2d 355, 28 UCCR 616 (4th Cir. 1980).

The buyer might first argue that it paid the "FOB Seller's City" price (which, therefore, included shipping charges) by mistake, that both parties intended the price to be "FOB Buyer's City," and that the buyer should be required to pay only "FOB Buyer's City" price for future deliveries and be reimbursed shipping charges for the prior deliveries. If the buyer is able to prove the existence of a mistake by the requisite standard of proof, its argument should succeed because mistake remains available under the Code.[816]

The seller, however, might argue that, despite the usual meaning given to the term "FOB Buyer's City,"[817] the parties *intended* that the buyer would be responsible for shipping charges. To support the seller's argument, the seller would offer evidence of the parties' course of performance over the prior ten contracts, and cite section 2-208(1) of the Code, which provides that "any course of performance accepted or acquiesced in without objection shall be relevant to determine the meaning of the agreement."[818]

The buyer's response would undoubtedly be that the writing is unambiguous because the Code itself supplies a definite meaning to the term "FOB Buyer's City."[819] Furthermore, the second subsection of section 2-208 states that whenever it is unreasonable to construe the express terms of an agreement as consistent with the course of performance, "express terms shall control the course of performance."[820] Finally, the buyer can argue that while the Code's parol evidence rule permits course of performance evidence to explain or supplement a writing without a showing of ambiguity, it does not permit evidence that *contradicts* the writing.[821]

---

[816] U.C.C. § 1-103. *See* Kern Oil & Ref. Co. v. Tenneco Oil Co., 792 F.2d 1380, 1 UCCR2d 651 (9th Cir. 1986) (payments made under mistake of fact do not constitute course of performance).

[817] *See* U.C.C. § 2-319(1)(b): "when the term is F.O.B. the place of destination, the seller must *at his own expense* and risk transport the goods to that place and there tender delivery of them in the manner provided in this Article." (section 2-503) (emphasis added).

[818] U.C.C. § 2-208(1).

[819] *See* U.C.C. § 2-319(1)(b). Many pre-Code cases have stated that the course of performance—or "practical construction," as it was often called—was admissible only if the writing was ambiguous. *See, e.g.*, Fowler v. Pennsylvania Tire Co., 326 F.2d 526 (5th Cir. 1964); Pekovich v. Coughlin, 258 F.2d 191 (9th Cir. 1958). Interestingly, some courts have allowed the conduct of the parties itself to show the ambiguity, thus reaching sensible results while clinging to the old case language. *See, e.g.*, Crestview Cemetery Ass'n v. Dieden, 54 Cal. 2d 744, 8 Cal. Rptr. 427, 356 P.2d 171 (1960); Bullough v. Sims, 16 Utah 2d 304, 400 P.2d 20 (1965).

[820] U.C.C. § 2-208(2).

[821] *See* U.C.C. § 2-202.

The Code provides answers to each of the buyer's arguments. First, it is not a condition to the admissibility of course of performance evidence that there be an ambiguity in the writing.[822] Second, although section 2-208 elevates express terms over a contradictory course of performance, a court first must determine what the parties *meant* by their express terms before it can decide whether the evidence of course of performance contradicts the express term. *All* relevant evidence, including the actions of the parties in carrying out the terms of the contract, should be considered for this purpose.[823] Comment 2 to Section 2-208 provides that "a course of performance is *always* relevant to determine the meaning of an agreement."[824] If the judge decides that a factfinder could reasonably believe that the parties intended to give their words a meaning consistent with the course of performance (despite an apparent contradictory "plain meaning"), the course-of-performance evidence should be admitted. Once that evidence has been admitted (and believed), the words written by the parties are not inconsistent with the course of performance. The standard for admission should be whether the judge believes that there is sufficient credible evidence to sustain a finding that the parties intended the words of their agreement to have a meaning consistent with the course of performance.

In *Brunswick Box Co., Inc. v. Coutinho, Caro & Co., Inc.*,[825] a case similar to the foregoing hypothetical, the Fourth Circuit correctly analyzed the issue of the consistency of course-of-performance evidence with the express terms of the contract. Brunswick (the seller) agreed to supply 95,000 stevedoring pallets to Coutinho (the buyer) for $9.95 each. The delivery term of the contract was "F.A.S. Port, Norfolk, Virginia area." Under section 2-319(2) of the Code, this term would ordinarily make the seller responsible for the payment of unloading and transfer charges once the goods arrived

---

[822] U.C.C. § 2-202, Official Comment 1; U.C.C. § 2-208, Official Comment 2. *See* Carter Baron Drilling v. Badger Oil Corp., 581 F. Supp. 592, 38 UCCR 1498 (D. Colo. 1984); Nanaluki Paving & Rock Co. v. Shell Oil Co., Inc., 664 F.2d 772, 32 UCCR 1025 (9th Cir. 1981); Cibro Petroleum Prods., Inc. v. Sohio Alaska Petroleum Co., 602 F. Supp. 1520, 40 UCCR 1220 (N.D.N.Y. 1985); Board of Trade of San Francisco v. Swiss Credit Bank, 597 F.2d 146, 25 UCCR 1132 (9th Cir. 1979).

[823] This is not to say, however, that this process should be solely the function of the factfinder. The judge should make an initial determination as to whether, in light of *all* available evidence, the course of performance can be *reasonably* read as consistent with the interpretation suggested by the course of performance.

[824] U.C.C. § 2-208, Official Comment 2 (emphasis added).

[825] 617 F.2d 355, 28 UCCR 616 (4th Cir. 1980).

at the port in Norfolk.[826] When the first load of pallets was delivered, Lambert's Point Docks, Inc. was employed by the seller to unload and transfer the goods. When the seller received the bill from Lambert for these services, it contacted Lambert and told Lambert that the buyer was responsible for the unloading and transfer charges. Lambert then forwarded the bill to the buyer who paid it. Thereafter, the buyer paid all unloading, storage, and transfer charges for subsequent deliveries.

After all of the pallets had been delivered, the buyer made a claim for $52,237.50 upon a letter of credit given by the seller as a performance bond. This figure represented all of the unloading, transfer, and storage charges relating to the contract. The bank paid the buyer, and the seller sued the buyer for breach. At trial, the court directed a verdict for the buyer and refused to admit evidence proffered by the seller that the parties had intended that the buyer be responsible for these charges, despite the use of the term "F.A.S. Norfolk." The trial court held that this evidence was inconsistent with the written term and was, therefore, barred.

Although the seller argued that the delivery term was ambiguous, and therefore extrinsic evidence should be permitted, the Fourth Circuit conceded that the term was not ambiguous on its face.[827] Nonetheless, the court decided that the trial judge had erred in refusing to admit the evidence of the parties' course of performance. The court said that this evidence, along with other extrinsic evidence, indicated that the parties intended the buyer to be responsible for the unloading and transfer charges. According to the court, the evidence was not offered to contradict the express terms, but to ascertain "the parties' intentions in using the term in controversy."[828] It was for the factfinder to determine, based on this evidence, what these parties in these circumstances meant by the language they had used.[829]

---

[826] U.C.C. § 2-319(2)(a) provides that:

> Unless otherwise agreed the term F.A.S. vessel (which means "free along-side") at a named port . . . is a delivery term under which the seller must (a) at his own expense and risk deliver the goods alongside the vessel in the manner usual in that port or on a dock designated and provided by the buyer.

[827] 617 F.2d at 359, 28 UCCR at 622.

[828] *Id.* at 360, 28 UCCR at 624.

[829] *See also* Nanakuli Paving & Rock Co. v. Shell Oil Co, Inc., 664 F.2d 772, 780, 32 UCCR 1025, 1032 (9th Cir. 1981) (in allowing evidence of trade usage, course of dealing, and course of performance to show that oil company had agreed to provide "price protection" despite apparently inconsistent term, the court said, "[t]he Code would have us look beyond the printed pages of the contract to usages and the entire commercial context of the agreement in order to reach the 'true understanding' of the parties." *But cf.* Lemnah v. American Breeders Serv., Inc., 144 Vt. 568, 482 A.2d 700, 38 UCCR 1558, 1562, n.2 (1984) (U.C.C. § 2-208 not relevant where there is no question as to the plain meaning of a term).

Even when the parties' course of performance cannot be read consistently with the express terms after considering all of the evidence, the course of performance may constitute a waiver or modification of the written terms.[830] The Code provides that "[s]ubject to the provisions of the next section on modification and waiver, such course of performance shall be relevant to show a waiver or modification of any term inconsistent with such course of performance."[831] Modification and waiver are discussed in an earlier section of this text,[832] and that discussion is generally applicable to waivers and modifications by course of performance.

Course-of-performance evidence has been permitted to establish a waiver, even in the face of a "no waiver" clause in the contract,[833] and is given a broad scope by the Code. Course of performance can add a term to a contract where the contract is silent;[834] it is always relevant to determine the meaning the parties attach to a written term;[835] it can be used to show that the parties have modified their contract;[836] and it is relevant to show a waiver of a term by a party.[837] This emphasis is consistent with the philos-

---

[830] *See* Radiation Sys., Inc. v. Amplicon, Inc., 882 F. Supp. 1101, 26 UCCR2d 695 (D.D.C. 1995).

[831] U.C.C. § 2-208(3).

[832] *See* § 3.10, *supra*.

[833] *See, e.g.*, Exxon Corp. v. Crosby-Mississippi Resources, Ltd., 40 F.3d 1474, 25 UCCR2d 1103 (5th Cir. 1995); Westinghouse Credit Corp. v. Shelton, 645 F.2d 869, 31 UCCR 410 (10th Cir. 1981) and cases cited therein. *Contra* Hale v. Ford Motor Credit Co., 374 So. 2d 849, 26 UCCR 383 (Ala. 1979); Universal C.I.T. Credit Corp. v. Middlesboro Motor Sales, Inc., 424 S.W.2d 409, 4 UCCR 1126 (Ky. Ct. App. 1968).

[834] U.C.C. § 1-201(3). *See* Dresser Indus., Inc. v. Gradall Co., 965 F.2d 1442, 18 UCCR2d 43 (7th Cir. 1992) (court stated that in determining applicable terms of contract for sale of engines, jury could consider, among other things, course of performance.). *See also* Alpert v. Thomas, 643 F. Supp. 1406, 2 UCCR2d 99 (D. Vt. 1986) (despite "as is" clause in the contract for a sale of Arabian horse, the parties' course of dealing and course of performance and the usage of trade all indicated that the implied warranty of breeding soundness was part of the parties' contract).

[835] U.C.C. § 2-208, Official Comment 2.

[836] U.C.C. § 2-209(3). *See* CT Chems. Inc. v. Vinmar Impex, Inc., 81 N.Y.2d 174, 613 N.E.2d 159, 597 N.Y.S.2d 284, 20 UCCR2d 853 (1993); Exxon Corp. v. Crosby-Mississippi Resources, Ltd., 40 F.3d 1474, 25 UCCR2d 1103 (5th Cir. 1995); Mulberry-Fairplans Water Assocs., Inc. v. Town of North Wilkesboro, 412 S.E.2d 910, 105 N.C. App. 258, 17 UCCR2d 48 (1992); Radiation Sys., Inc. v. Amplicon, Inc., 882 F. Supp. 1101, 26 UCCR2d 695 (D.D.C. 1995); General Elec. Capital Commercial Automotive Fin., Inc. v. Spartan Motors, Ltd., 36 UCCR2d 19 (1998).

[837] *See* Farmers State Bank v. Farmland Foods, Inc., 225 Neb. 1, 402 N.W.2d 277, 3 UCCR2d 902 (1987); Southwest Indus. Import & Export, Inc. v. Borneo Sumatra Trading Co., Inc., 666 S.W.2d 625, 38 UCCR 445 (Tex. Ct. App. 1984); J.W. Goodlife & Son v. Odzer, 423 A.2d 1032, 283 Pa. Super. 148, 31 UCCR 854 (1980); Central Ill. Pub. Serv. Co. v. Atlas Minerals, 965 F. Supp. 1162, 33 UCCR2d 386 (C.D. Ill. 1997). As Judge

ophy of the Code that the agreement that ought to be enforced is the agreement the parties in fact entered into. The writing is evidence of that agreement, but so is what the parties did under the words of the writing. Neither is conclusive. While it may sometimes be difficult to determine the content of their bargain in fact, this is the duty with which the Code charges the courts.

[B] Course of Dealing

In addition to evidence of course of performance, evidence of course of dealing is also admissible to interpret an agreement. "Course of dealing" is defined by the Code in section 1-205(1): "A course of dealing is a sequence of previous conduct between the parties to a particular transaction which is fairly to be regarded as establishing a common basis of understanding for interpreting their expressions and other conduct."[838]

The difference between course of performance and course of dealing centers on the time that the conduct occurs. A sequence of conduct occurring *prior to* a particular agreement is a "course of dealing," while a sequence of conduct occurring *pursuant to* an agreement is a course of performance. Both rest on the notion that how parties have acted is relevant in determining what they meant when they used the words of the agreement. Because course of dealing is more remote to the particular agreement involved than is course of performance, course of performance is stronger evidence of the parties' intent,[839] and where the two are inconsistent, course of performance controls under the Code.[840]

A sequence of previous conduct is a "course of dealing" if it "is fairly to be regarded as establishing a common basis of understanding for interpreting the expression of the parties."[841] There must be a *sequence* of pre-

---

Easterbrook recognized in Sethness-Greenleaf, Inc. v. Green River Corp., 65 F.3d 64, 27 UCCR2d 360 (7th Cir. 1995), courts should not be too eager to interpret a course of performance as a waiver or modification. In doing so, they may provide a disincentive to a party to "cut [the other party] some slack" in their performance obligation, thus reducing contract flexibility. 65 F.3d at 67, 27 UCCR2d at 365. *See also* Simpson Properties, Inc. v. Oexco, Inc., 916 P.2d 853, 29 UCCR2d 748 (Okla. Ct. App. 1996) (seven-year practice of accepting late payments not sufficient to establish waiver).

[838] U.C.C. § 1-205(1).

[839] *See* Marlowe v. Argentine Naval Comm'n, 808 F.2d 120, 2 UCCR2d 1226 (D.C. Cir. 1986).

[840] U.C.C. § 2-208(2).

[841] U.C.C. § 1-205(1).

vious conduct before there can be a course of dealing; a single occasion will not suffice.[842] Whether a course of dealing exists is a question of fact.[843]

The definition of "agreement" in the Code indicates that course of dealing, as well as usage of trade and course of performance, can be used to provide supplementary terms when the parties' agreement is silent on an issue.[844] Most cases are consistent with this direction and have allowed course of dealing, if established, to add terms to an agreement.[845] This is true even when one of the Code "gap-fillers" would otherwise supply the term.[846] One case, however, suggests that such evidence cannot be used to create additional obligations on a party.[847]

Course of dealing has also emerged as a player in the "battle of the forms." In a number of cases, a litigant has argued that a term was part of a contract through course of dealing because it had been included in that party's invoice or acknowledgment form on repeated prior occasions without

---

[842] *See* Kern Oil & Ref. Co. v. Tenneco Oil Co., 792 F.2d 1380, 1 UCCR2d 651 (9th Cir. 1986); Unique Designs, Inc. v. Pittard Mach. Co., 409 S.E.2d 241, 200 Ga. App. 647, 16 UCCR2d 116 (1991). *But see* Steinmetz v. Bradbury Co., Inc. 618 F.2d 21, 28 UCCR 961 (8th Cir. 1980) (court in dicta suggests that course of dealing could possibly arise from one instance of conduct).

[843] Capitol Converting Equip., Inc. v. LEP Transp., Inc., 965 F.2d 391, 18 UCCR2d 363 (7th Cir. 1992); Kessel v. Western Savs. Credit Union, 463 N.W.2d 629, 15 UCCR2d 319 (N.D. 1990).

[844] U.C.C. § 1-201(3) provides: " 'Agreement' means the bargain of the parties in fact as found in their language *or by implication* from other circumstances including course of dealing or usage of trade or course of performance." (emphasis added).

[845] *See, e.g.*, Columbia Nitrogen Corp. v. Royster Co., 451 F.2d 3, 9 UCCR 977 (4th Cir. 1971); Koener v. Royal Buick Co., 783 P.2d 822, 11 UCCR2d 1096 (Ariz. Ct. App. 1989) (allowing parties' prior course of dealing to provide the price when it was excluded from the contract); Reisman & Sons v. Snyder's Potato Chips, 20 UCCR 856 (Pa. C.P. 1976) (course of dealing may furnish a reasonably certain basis for filling gaps in a sales contract). *But see* Southern Concrete Servs., Inc. v. Mableton Contractors, Inc., 407 F. Supp. 581, 19 UCCR 79 (N.D. Ga. 1975) (court restricted ability of "course of dealing" to alter written contract).

[846] *See* Tolmic Forms, Inc. v. Stauffer Chem. Co., Inc., 862 P.2d 305, 20 UCCR2d 859 (Idaho Ct. App. 1992) (finding parties' course of dealing was sufficient to establish the seller's intent to exclude implied warranties after a sale even though the general rule is that disclaimers to exclude warranties that are presented after a sale are ineffective).

[847] *See* Latex Glove Co., Inc. v. Gruen, 146 Ill. App. 3d 868, 497 N.E.2d 466, 2 UCCR2d 424 (1986) (court refused to allow usage of trade to impose term for sale of by-products, although court would allow usage of trade to act as "gap-filler." *See also* Seattle-First Nat'l Bank v. Westwood Lumber, Inc., 65 Wash. App. 811, 829 P.2d 1152, 18 UCCR2d 351 (Wash. Ct. App. 1992) (court stated that a course of dealing does not override express terms of a contract or add additional obligations but rather is a tool for interpreting the provisions of a contract).

objection by the other party. The responses of courts to this argument have been varied and interesting.

One end of the spectrum is represented by *Step-Saver Data Systems, Inc. v. Wyse Technology*.[848] Pursuant to an oral agreement, the seller shipped software to the buyer. The box in which the software was shipped had on it a provision that excluded all warranties, except a warranty that the disks contained in the box were free of physical defects. The language on the box further provided that the sole remedy for breach was replacement of a defective disk. Simplifying the facts somewhat, when the software failed to perform adequately, the buyer attempted to recover damages from the seller caused by defects in the software. The seller relied upon the disclaimer and remedy limitation, while the buyer argued that these were unilateral terms to which it had not agreed and which were, therefore, not part of the contract.

Although the case did not deal with the typical acceptance or acknowledgment form, the court determined section 2-207 to be the appropriate section of the Code to resolve the case.[849] It decided that, under section 2-207, the disclaimer and remedy limitations were material alterations to an existing oral contract and, therefore, could not become part of the contract under section 2-207(2).[850] The seller also argued that the limitations had become part of the contract through a prior course of dealing because these terms had appeared on other boxes of software accepted by the buyer without objection. The court rejected the seller's argument, stating that, "the repeated sending of a writing which contains certain standard terms, without any action with respect to the issues addressed by those terms, cannot constitute a course of dealing which would incorporate a term of the writing otherwise excluded under § 2-207."[851] The court reached this conclusion for two reasons. First, it said that although the terms on the box might alert the buyer to the fact that the seller *desired* these terms, they did not indicate to the buyer that the seller intended the contract to be *conditioned* upon acceptance of these terms. Second the seller had the opportunity to negotiate these terms and was either unable or unwilling to do so. Consequently, the seller should not be given these terms simply as a result of including them on its box.[852]

---

[848] 939 F.2d 91, 15 UCCR2d 1 (3d Cir. 1991).

[849] *But see* ProCD, Inc. v. Zeidenberg, 86 F.3d 1447, 29 UCCR2d 1109 (7th Cir. 1996). In this case the court held, under similar facts, that U.C.C. § 2-207 was not applicable.

[850] 939 F.2d at 104, 15 UCCR2d at 22. *See* § 3.04[D], *supra*.

[851] *Id.* at 104, 15 UCCR2d at 19.

[852] *Id.* at 104, 15 UCCR2d at 19–20. For cases reaching a similar result, *see* Tuck Indus. v. Reichhold Chems., Inc., 10 UCCR2d 1170, 542 N.Y.S.2d 676, 151 A.D.2d 566 (N.Y. App. Div. 1989); Transwestern Pipeline Co. v. Monsanto Co., 53 Rptr. 2d 887, 29 UCCR2d 1178 (Cal. Ct. App. 1996).

The other end of the spectrum is represented by *Capitol Converting Equipment, Inc. v. LEP Transport, Inc.*[853] This case also dealt with a remedy limitation. LEP agreed to arrange for the transportation of goods from Genoa to Chicago. The goods arrived from Genoa in Norfolk, Virginia. For reasons that are unclear, the goods never made it to Chicago but were sold by the U.S. Customs Service. Capitol sought to hold LEP responsible for the loss.

LEP relied upon a provision contained in its invoice that limited its liability to $50 per container, in this case a total of $150. The parties, however, had never discussed this limitation, and Capitol's president submitted an affidavit that neither he nor anyone else at Capitol was aware of the limitation or had ever agreed to it. Nonetheless, the court upheld the grant of summary judgment for LEP limiting its liability to $150.

The court based its decision on a course of dealing resulting from hundreds of transactions in which the parties had engaged over the prior ten years. For each of these transactions LEP had submitted an invoice containing the liability limitation. This was sufficient for the court to find a course of dealing, sufficient as a matter of law, to incorporate the limitation into the parties' agreement, despite the lack of knowledge of Capitol. The court did not even mention section 2-207 in its analysis.

Another Seventh Circuit case represents an intermediate approach to the issue. In *Schulze & Burch Biscuit Co. v. Tree Top, Inc.*,[854] the buyer purchased dehydrated apple powder from the seller, which the buyer used in making "toastettes," which it then sold to Nabisco. When the buyer attempted to use the apple powder, the buyer claimed that it was so full of apple stems and wood splinters that it clogged the buyer's machinery and required the closing of the assembly line. The buyer sued for damages for breach. The seller filed a motion to stay the suit pending arbitration, relying on an arbitration clause in the confirmation form that it had sent to the buyer. Because the parties had not expressly agreed to arbitration, the court had to decide whether the arbitration clause on the seller's form became part of the contract.

The court used section 2-207(2) to determine whether the arbitration clause was part of the contract. This required the court to determine whether the arbitration term materially altered the contract. Under Illinois law, this depended upon whether it caused unreasonable surprise.[855] The court decided that the arbitration clause did not create unreasonable surprise in this case because there was a prior course of dealing involving nine prior transactions in which the same arbitration clause had been included in the seller's

---

[853] 965 F.2d 391, 18 UCCR2d 363 (7th Cir. 1992).
[854] 831 F.2d 709, 4 UCCR2d 641 (7th Cir. 1987).
[855] *Id.* at 712, 4 UCCR2d at 646. *See* § 3.04[D], *supra.*

239

confirmation. Thus the buyer had ample notice that an arbitration clause would be included in the tenth transaction. The buyer had only to give objection to the clause within a reasonable time under section 2-207(2) to prevent it from becoming part of the contract, which it did not do. As a result, the buyer was stuck with arbitrating its claim.[856]

Implicit in the court's decision is the understanding that a clause in an acknowledgment or confirmation form must pass through section 2-207 to become part of the contract. This distinguishes the opinion in *Schulze* from that in *Capitol Converting,* which held that a course of dealing that consists of including the same clause on prior confirmations can *directly* result in that clause becoming part of the contract without passing through section 2-207.[857] The case is also different from *Step-Saver,* which refused to even consider course of dealing relevant to the issue of whether a term on a confirmation became part of the contract.[858]

Of the three cases, *Step-Saver* represents the best approach. The Code drafters probably envisioned a course of dealing as the manner in which the parties actually *carried out* their contractual obligations under prior similar contracts in order to determine better what their obligations are under the present contract.[859] Sending confirmations does not involve conduct by the

---

[856] *See also* Barliant v. Follett Corp., 138 Ill. App. 3d, 756, 483 N.E.2d 1312, 42 UCCR 1206 (1985) (term in invoice providing for additional charges for transportation and insurance does not create unfair surprise when same term appeared in twenty-four prior invoices).

[857] The opinion of the district court in *Capitol Converting* also relies on U.C.C. § 1-205, rather than U.C.C. § 2-207 in holding that the liability limitation became part of the contract. The district court viewed sections 1-205 and 2-207 as *alternative* means by which a term on a confirmation might become part of a contract. Under section 2-207 such a term could become part of the contract only if it was not a material alteration; no such limitation exists with respect to section 1-205. *See* 750 F. Supp. at 866, 14 UCCR2d at 55.

[858] The court in *Step-Saver* explicitly disapproved of the decision in *Schulze. See* 939 F.2d at 104, 15 UCCR2d at 19 n.42. In yet another Seventh Circuit decision, the court in Trans-Aire Int'l, Inc. v. Northern Adhesive Co., Inc., 882 F.2d 1254, 9 UCCR2d 878 (7th Cir. 1989) held that an exchange of twelve forms containing an indemnification clause did not create a course of dealing since the plaintiff sought to impose liability from one of the earliest shipments, before a course of dealing could have arisen. The court further suggested, without deciding, that since there were a relatively small number of forms exchanged over a short period of time, a course of dealing might not have arisen in any event. 882 F.2d at 1262, 9 UCCR2d at 889 n.9.

[859] *See* U.C.C. § 1-205. A "course of dealing" is a sequence of previous conduct between the parties to a particular transaction which is fairly to be regarded as establishing a common basis of understanding for *interpreting their expressions and other conduct* (emphasis added). *See* Olathe Mfg., Inc. v. Browning Mfg., 259 Kan. 735, 915 P.2d 86, 30 UCCR2d 495 (1996) (although *X* had frequently purchased goods from a third party manufactured by *Y*, there was no prior course of dealing between *X* and *Y* such that would impose remedy limitations in *Y*'s catalog on *X*).

parties *in the performance of their contractual obligations*; it merely confirms the existence of a contract and attempts to reflect one party's version of the contract's terms. The opinion in *Step-Saver* is most consistent with this understanding of course of dealing. Moreover, section 2-207 was drafted specifically to deal with the issue of additional terms on confirming forms, and there is no indication in the Code that section 1-205 was intended to supplant section 2-207 when repeated transactions are involved. Finally, section 2-207 was premised on the assumption that the parties do not read the fine print on each other's form. There is no more reason to believe that a party would read the fine print on the tenth (or hundredth) form than on the first. In fact, if earlier transactions have proceeded without a hitch, the parties are likely to pay even less attention to the boilerplate in later transactions.

A course of dealing may be found to exist, but may not control the issue presented. For example, in *Kunststoffwerk Alfred Huber v. R.J. Dick, Inc.*,[860] the court held that a course of dealing in which the buyer accepted credits or replacements for defective goods did not establish an agreement on the part of the buyer to forgo consequential damages. The court suggested that in prior transactions, the defective goods might have been replaced before any damages accrued, or the buyer's customers may have been willing to accept replacement goods. Thus, even though a course of dealing existed in which the buyer agreed to accept replacement goods, the course of dealing did not provide a "common basis of understanding" that the buyer had agreed to forgo consequential damages.

According to section 2-208, a course of performance can serve not only as a basis for interpretation, but also, in a proper case, as a basis for modification or waiver.[861] There is no similar provision for a course of dealing. This is logical because, by definition, a course of dealing occurs *prior to* the transaction involving the asserted waiver. Nonetheless, in a number of cases dealing with the sale of collateral without consent, courts have found a prior course of dealing to constitute a waiver of a contractual provision requiring a creditor's consent to the sale of collateral.[862] Other cases have refused to find a waiver under these circumstances.[863]

---

[860] 621 F.2d 560, 28 UCCR 1371 (3d Cir. 1980).

[861] U.C.C. § 2-208(3).

[862] *See, e.g.*, State Bank v. Scoular-Bishop Grain Co., 217 Neb. 379, 38 UCCR 1368 (1984); Planters Prod. Credit Ass'n v. Bowles, 256 Ark. 1063, 14 UCCR 1435 (1974). Other cases have reached similar results without explicitly relying on the concept of waiver. *See, e.g.*, Hedrick Savs. Bank v. Myers, 229 N.W.2d 252, 16 UCCR 1412 (Iowa 1975).

[863] *See, e.g.*, Aberdeen Prod. Credit Ass'n v. Redfield Livestock Auction, Inc., 379 N.W.2d 829, 42 UCCR 1481 (S.D. 1986); Erlandson Implement, Inc. v. First State Bank of Brownsdale, 400 N.W.2d 421, 3 UCCR2d 349 (Minn. Ct. App. 1987); Farmers State Bank v. Farmland Foods, Inc., 225 Neb. 1, 402 N.W.2d 277, 3 UCCR2d 902 (1987).

[C]   Usage of Trade

The third type of extrinsic evidence the Code specifically makes admissible is evidence of usage of trade. This term is defined as follows: "A usage of trade is any practice or method of dealing having such regularity of observance in a place, vocation, or trade as to justify an expectation that it will be observed with respect to the transaction in question."[864] The basic idea is the same as it is for course of dealing. Words of agreement are not to be read out of context. Like a course of dealing, a usage of trade can give content and meaning to the words that the parties have used.

Perhaps the most important part of the definition is the emphasis placed on the justified expectations of the parties.[865] One of the primary reasons for enforcing promises is to protect the justified expectations of those to whom the promises were made. To the extent that a particular trade has a practice that is so regularly observed and followed as to create a justified expectation that the parties had it in mind when they exchanged their promises, the trade practice becomes part of their agreement under the Code.[866]

The definition of usage of trade is broader than the merchant notion of "trade usage" (i.e., practices in a vocation or trade). Usage of trade also includes any practice or method of dealing *in a place* so as to create justified expectations that those practices or methods of dealing will be followed in this particular transaction. Thus, merchants engaged in different trades who are dealing *at a particular place* may be bound by a usage of trade if the parties "are or should be aware" of these common practices or methods of

---

[864] U.C.C. § 1-205(2).

[865] *See also* Official Comment 4 to U.C.C. § 1-205 which provides:

> This Act deals with "usage of trade" as a factor in reaching the commercial meaning of the agreement which the parties have made. The language used is to be interpreted as meaning what it may fairly be expected to mean to parties involved in the particular commercial transaction in a given locality or in a given vocation or trade.

[866] *See* Advent Sys. Ltd. v. Unisys Corp., 925 F.2d 670, 13 UCCR2d 669 (3d Cir. 1991); North Dakota Pub. Serv. Comm'n v. Central States Grain, Inc., 371 N.W.2d 767, 42 UCCR 59 (N.D. 1985); Peck v. Augustin Bros. Co., 203 Neb. 574, 279 N.W.2d 397, 26 UCCR 889 (1979).

dealing.[867] Even non-merchants can be bound by trade usages if they "are or should have been aware of the practice."[868]

The parties are bound by a usage of trade if they are or should be aware of the usage *or* if it is a usage of trade in the vocation or trade in which they are engaged. The use of the disjunctive *"or"* indicates that so long as a party is engaged in a trade, that party is bound by the usages of that trade, whether or not the party is aware of the usage, or even whether it should be aware of it.[869]

Subsection 1-205(3) provides that a usage of trade can serve three purposes: (1) it may give a particular meaning to the terms of an agreement;[870] (2) it may supplement the terms of the agreement;[871] (3) or it may qualify the terms of the agreement.[872] Once established, a usage of trade may always be used to explain or supplement a writing, regardless of the Code's parol

---

[867] *See* Nanakuli Paving & Rock Co. v. Shell Oil Co., 664 F.2d 772, 32 UCCR 1025 (9th Cir. 1981) (parties can be bound to common usage in place where they are in business, even if it is not a usage specific to their particular vocation or trade, if it is so commonly practiced in a locality that they should be aware of it); Brunswick Box Co., Inc. v. Coutinho, Caro & Co., Inc., 617 F.2d 355, 28 UCCR 616, 621 (4th Cir. 1980) (trade practice of the port of Norfolk, Virginia is to unload freight for transport at the dock rather than at the ship's berth).

[868] *See* Zappanti v. Berge Serv. Ctr., 549 P.2d 178, 19 UCCR 96 (Ariz. Ct. App. 1976) (consumer purchaser of "dune buggy" bound by usage of trade that treated the year of reconstruction as the model year of the dune buggy).

[869] *See* Marion Coal Co. v. Marc Rich & Co. Int'l, Ltd., 539 F. Supp. 903, 34 UCCR 12 (S.D.N.Y. 1982) (court refused to submit issue to jury of whether party knew or should have known of usage since it did not deny it was engaged in the applicable trade); Heggblade-Marguleas-Tenneco, Inc. v. Sunshine Biscuit Co., 131 Cal. Rptr. 183, 19 UCCR 1067 (Cal. Ct. App. 1976) (persons carrying on a trade are deemed to be aware of prominent trade customs applicable to their industry regardless of the length of time in the industry). In U.S. ex rel. Union Bldg. Materials Corp. v. Haas & Haynie Corp., 577 F.2d 568, 27 UCCR 32 (9th Cir. 1978), the court refused to apply a trade usage to a subcontractor who was a newcomer to the industry. However, the other party to the contract had reason to know that the subcontractor attached a meaning to the term contrary to the usage. Thus, the case should not be viewed as authority for the proposition that a trade usage, once established, does not apply to newcomers in the industry.

[870] *See, e.g.,* Banca Del Sempione v. Suriel Fin., 852 F. Supp. 417, 24 UCCR2d 1196 (D. Md. 1994); New West Fruit Corp. v. Coastal Berry Corp., 1 Cal. Rptr. 2d 664, 1 Cal. App. 4th 92, 16 UCCR2d 25 (1991).

[871] *See, e.g.,* Bib Audio-Video Prods. v. Herold Mktg. Assocs., Inc., 517 N.W.2d 68, 24 UCCR2d 455 (Minn. Ct. App. 1994); Petroleo Brasileiro, S.A., Petrobras v. NALCO Chem. Co., 784 F. Supp. 160, 18 UCCR2d 61 (D.N.J. 1992).

[872] *See* Nanakuli Paving & Rock Co. v. Shell Oil Co., 664 F.2d 772, 32 UCCR 1025 (9th Cir. 1981); Posttape Assocs. v. Eastman Kodak Co., 537 F.2d 751, 19 UCCR 832 (3d Cir. 1976).

evidence rule.[873] Usage of trade is available for this purpose, whether or not the writing is ambiguous[874] or whether it constitutes a "complete integration."[875] Only if a usage is determined to be "inconsistent" with an express term of the writing might evidence of the usage be excluded in determining the agreement of the parties. This issue is considered in the following section.[876]

The existence and scope of a trade usage are to be proved as facts.[877] If a written trade code is offered as evidence of the usage, its interpretation is a matter for the court.[878] The usage of trade at the place of performance is to be used in interpreting the agreement relating to that part of performance.[879]

The burden of proof is on the person who asserts the existence of a usage of trade,[880] and presumably expert testimony will be necessary to establish a trade usage. The Code guards against unfair surprise by providing that evidence of trade usage is not admissible unless and until sufficient notice has been given to the other party.[881]

In liberally permitting evidence of course of performance, course of dealing, and usage of trade, the Code has rejected any notion that words have but one meaning and that meaning is to be imposed upon the parties irrespective of how they meant those words. While this may marginally increase uncertainty—and only then in the sense that a lawyer cannot take a written agreement and a copy of a new unabridged dictionary, lay them side-by-side, and tell the client just what the agreement "means"—the

---

[873] U.C.C. § 2-202. *See* § 3.15[B][2], *infra.*

[874] U.C.C. § 2-202, Official Comment 1. *See* C-Thru Container Corp. v. Midland Mfg. Co., 533 N.W.2d 542 (Iowa 1995); Magallanes Inv., Inc. v. Circuit Sys., Inc., 994 F.2d 1214, 20 UCCR2d 765 (7th Cir. 1993); Tigg Corp. v. Dow Corning Corp., 822 F.2d 358, 4 UCCR2d 44 (3d Cir. 1987).

[875] U.C.C. § 2-202(a) permits evidence of usage of trade, course of dealing, or course of performance to explain or supplement a writing even if the court finds the writing to be the complete and exclusive statement of the terms of the agreement. *See* C-Thru Container Corp. v. Midland Mfg. Co., *supra* note 874 at 545; Middletown Concrete Prods. Inc. v. Black Clawson Co., 802 F. Supp. 1135, 20 UCCR2d 815 (D. Del. 1992); Ralph's Distrib. Co. v. AMF, Inc., 667 F.2d 670, 32 UCCR 1111 (8th Cir. 1981).

[876] *See* § 3.15, *infra.*

[877] U.C.C. § 1-205(2).

[878] *Id.*

[879] U.C.C. § 1-205(5).

[880] Century Ready-Mix Co. v. Lower & Co., 770 P.2d 692, 10 UCCR2d 705 (Wyo. 1989); Wright v. Commercial & Savs. Bank, 464 A.2d 1080, 297 Md. 148, 36 UCCR 1687 (Md. Ct. App. 1983).

[881] U.C.C. § 1-205(6); Paymaster Oil Mill Co. v. Mitchell, 319 So. 2d 652, 17 UCCR 1173 (Miss. 1975).

Code's approach is eminently sound. If a primary goal of contract law is to enforce the justified expectations of the parties to a contract, the Code's approach is much preferable to the "plain meaning" rule of old.[882]

§ 3.15 THE CODE'S PAROL EVIDENCE RULE

[A] Introduction

Each of the authors of this book has taught Contracts for many years. We agree that one of the most difficult and frustrating aspects of this endeavor is teaching the parol evidence rule. The confusion and inconsistency among court decisions understandably leads to frustration among law students (as well as practitioners and judges). Unfortunately, the Code's parol evidence rule has not proved to be much of an improvement over the common-law parol evidence rule. The same issues that have confounded courts in the past—what is the relationship of the rule to contract interpretation; how does one determine whether a writing is integrated, completely integrated, or not integrated at all; when is an asserted parol agreement "inconsistent" with a writing; what are the respective roles of the court and jury—continue to produce muddled opinions and inconsistent decisions. It is not an exaggeration to suggest that the rule hardly functions as a rule at all and that judges are free to apply it to reach any result they choose. Nonetheless, the question of the degree of sanctity that we accord to a writing continues to plague us, as we are reminded by the hundreds of decisions under the Code.

To the extent that the parol evidence rule gives preference to a writing,[883] it does so for two reasons: certainty and perjury. Undoubtedly certainty is a desirable goal in commercial transactions. Opening a writing to evidence of other agreements (especially oral ones) creates uncertainty in the enforcement of contracts. How can a party rely on a writing to reflect the agreement if that writing is subject to being changed through oral testimony? This uncertainty is compounded by the fear that such testimony will be fabricated. By perjured testimony a party may be able to convince the trier of fact that a prior agreement was made by the parties and was intended to survive the writing even though this was not, in fact, the case. Strict application of a rule that prevents consideration of testimony of prior understandings will both increase the certainty of transactions and prevent a perjurer from winning his case.

---

[882] *But see* cases cited in the following section indicating that the plain-meaning rule is far from dead.

[883] *See* discussion in this section, *infra*.

On the other hand, the purpose of contract law is not to obtain certainty as such, but to enforce the justified expectations of the parties. It is always possible that the prior agreement was, in fact, entered into and that the parties did not intend to extinguish that prior agreement when they signed the writing. In such a case, the agreement between the parties is a combination of what is contained in the writing and what was orally agreed upon before they signed the writing. A blanket prohibition against admission of testimony relating to that prior agreement would frustrate the legitimate expectations of the parties and preclude enforcement of their true "agreement"—their "bargain in fact."[884]

These are the concerns the parol evidence rule seeks to balance. As we shall see, courts have struck this balance in a multitude of ways. Some courts have made a real effort to determine the intention of the parties, and when their intention appeared to be to incorporate a prior understanding into their agreement, these courts have liberally allowed evidence of the prior agreement to reach the factfinder.[885] Other courts, however, have approached the parol evidence rule as a formal exercise with little concern about the parties' intentions, and have rigorously excluded evidence of prior agreements, even when it has been clear that such agreements were made by the parties and expected to survive the writing.[886]

Lest there be any mistake, the authors are firmly in the first camp. Certainty and the prevention of perjury are legitimate goals, but they should not be purchased at the expense of the fundamental goal of contract law—to determine the actual agreement of the parties and enforce it. To the extent that the parties *intended* their writing to displace prior understandings, those prior understandings are no longer material to the dispute before the court and form no part of the parties' agreement. To the extent, however, that the parties *intended* their agreement to consist of both the writing and their prior understandings, the prior understandings are material, and evidence of them should be admitted. Furthermore, the search for the parties' intention should not be a formal exercise in which only limited evidence is considered—for

---

[884] *See* U.C.C. § 1-201(3).

[885] *See, e.g.*, Sierra Diesel Injection Serv., Inc. v. Burroughs Corp., Inc., 874 F.2d 653, 8 UCCR2d 617 (9th Cir. 1989); L.S. Heath & Sons, Inc. v. AT&T Info. Sys., Inc., 9 F.3d 561, 22 UCCR2d 27 (7th Cir. 1993); Central Jersey Dodge Truck Ctr., Inc. v. Sightseer Corp., 608 F.2d 1106, 27 UCCR 1256 (6th Cir. 1979).

[886] *See, e.g.*, Noble v. Logan Dees-Chevrolet-Buick, Inc., 293 So. 2d 14, 14 UCCR 1107 (Miss. 1974); In re Tom Woods Used Cars, Inc. v. Woods, 23 B.R. 563, 35 UCCR 52 (U.S. Bankr. E.D. Tenn. 1981); FMC Corp. v. Seal Tape Ltd., Inc., 396 N.Y.S.2d 993, 22 UCCR 297 (N.Y. Sup. Ct. 1977).

example, whether a merger clause is present,[887] or whether a hypothetical "reasonable person," divorced from the context of the contract, would have included the prior agreement in the writing.[888] Rather, the judge should, in the first instance, consider *all* evidence relevant to the question of the parties' actual understanding.[889] This inquiry should include the nature of the parties, the subject matter and scope of the asserted prior agreement, the circumstances under which it was made, and possible explanations for its omission from the writing. Issues of weight and credibility should largely be left to the jury.[890]

[B]   The Rule

Section 2-202, the Code's parol evidence rule, provides in full:

Terms with respect to which the confirmatory memoranda of the parties agree or which are otherwise set forth in a writing intended by the parties as a final expression of their agreement with respect to such terms as are included therein may not be contradicted by evidence of any prior agreement or of a contemporaneous oral agreement but may be explained or supplemented

(a) by course of dealing or usage of trade (Section 1-205) or by course of performance (Section 2-208); and

(b) by evidence of consistent additional terms unless the court finds the writing to have been intended also as a complete and exclusive statement of the terms of the agreement.

The section contains three rather simple ideas. The first is that if the parties have exchanged memoranda confirming a contract, of which both contain the same term, or if the parties intend a writing to be the final expression of their agreement, the writing(s) cannot be contradicted by evidence of prior agreements. That is, if the parties intend the writing to represent their agree-

---

[887] *See, e.g.,* Franz Chem. Corp. v. Philadelphia Quartz Co., 594 F.2d 146, 26 UCCR 276 (5th Cir. 1979); Jordan v. Doonan Truck & Equip., 220 Kan. 431, 552 P.2d 881, 19 UCCR 1297 (1976); Earman Oil Co., Inc. v. Burroughs Corp., 625 F.2d 1291, 30 UCCR 849 (5th Cir. 1980).

[888] *See, e.g.,* Mitchell v. Lath, 247 N.Y. 377, 160 N.E. 646 (1928).

[889] Our references to the "true" or "actual" intention of the parties should not mislead the reader into thinking that we are talking about the parties' subjective state of mind. As discussed in an earlier section, intention is determined by the *objective* manifestations of the parties, at least when their subjective intentions do not coincide. *See* § 3.13, *supra.*

[890] Evidence of the prior oral understanding should be kept from the factfinder only if the evidence is such that reasonable people could not believe it.

ment as to those terms that are in the writing, that intention will be honored. Second, writings may be explained or supplemented by consistent additional terms, unless the parties intended the writing to embody *all* of the terms of their agreement. In other words, if the parties intend that no prior understandings or agreements should survive the writing, even those that are consistent with the writing, that intention will likewise be honored. Otherwise, prior agreements consistent with the writing can be proved. Finally, course-of-dealing, usage-of-trade, and course-of-performance evidence can always be used to explain or supplement a writing.

Stated in this manner, the parol evidence rule is not only simple, it is absolutely necessary if we are to accomplish the fundamental purpose of contract law: to enforce the objective intent of the parties. *It is nothing more than a statement that the law will give a writing the effect the parties intended it to have.* If this were all that there was to the parol evidence rule, generations of law students (and lawyers) would be a much happier lot. Unfortunately, this was not the case prior to the Code and has not been the case under the Code as well.

[1] The Negative Rule

Evidence extrinsic to a writing[891] will be admitted unless the court finds that three conditions exist:

1. *The writing is made up of either (a) confirmatory memoranda that agree as to the term in dispute or (b) a writing intended by the parties as a final expression of agreement as to the term in dispute.* Thus, not all writings prevent the introduction of evidence of prior agreements or contemporaneous oral agreements. A confirmation sent by one party or a proposed formulation of the agreement does not exclude this evidence.[892]

If a party relies on the "confirmatory memoranda" portion of the rule, there must be more than one memorandum,[893] and each party must have

---

[891] That is, evidence of *prior agreements* or *prior or contemporaneous oral agreements.* Evidence of fraud or mistake is generally not precluded by the parol evidence rule either at common law or under the Code. *See* Agri Tec, Inc. v. Brewster Heights Packing, Inc., 7 F.3d 222, 24 UCCR2d 440 (4th Cir. 1994); Dominion Bank of Richmond v. Star Five Assocs., Inc., 16 UCCR2d 688 (Va. Cir. Ct. 1991); Latham & Assocs., Inc. v. William Raveis Real Estate, Inc., 589 A.2d 337, 218 Conn. 297, 14 UCCR2d 394 (1991).

[892] *See* Sutton v. Stacey's Fuel Mart, Inc., 431 A.2d 1319, 33 UCCR 1632 (Me. 1981); B.N.E. Swedbank, S.A. v. Banker, 794 F. Supp. 1291, 20 UCCR2d 35 (S.D.N.Y. 1992) (writing was preliminary to the contract).

[893] *See* Album Graphics, Inc. v. Beatrice Foods Co., 408 N.E.2d 1041, 87 Ill. App. 3d 338, 30 UCCR 53 (Ill. Ct. App. 1980).

sent at least one memorandum.[894] Further, these memoranda must agree on the term that is now in dispute. The memoranda may agree on many points but if neither (or only one) contains the term being challenged, the writings do not satisfy the memoranda requirement.[895] Finally, the memoranda must confirm a prior agreement. The requirement of confirmatory memoranda cannot be satisfied by documents that constitute offers and acceptances.[896]

Generally, however, parties do not rely on confirmatory memoranda to prevent evidence of parol agreements from being admitted. Rather, they rely upon a writing that is "intended by the parties as a final expression of their agreement with respect to the terms that are included therein."[897] Although the Code speaks in terms of a "writing," it need not be a single document; several documents may be pieced together to satisfy the need for a writing.[898]

The crucial aspect of the Code's parol evidence rule is that to exclude extrinsic evidence, the parties must have *intended* the writing to be final on the terms contained in the writing.[899] This prerequisite is the same as the

---

[894] U.C.C. § 2-202 refers to "memoranda of the *parties*."

[895] *See* Airstream, Inc. v. CIT Fin. Servs., Inc., 111 Idaho 307, 723 P.2d 851, 2 UCCR2d 816 (1986).

[896] *See* Nations Enters., Inc. v. Process Equip. Co., 579 P.2d 655, 24 UCCR 828 (Colo. Ct. App. 1978) (purchase order did not constitute a confirmatory memorandum in the absence of a valid contract entered into previously); Triangle Mktg., Inc. v. Action Indus., Inc., 630 F. Supp. 1578, 1 UCCR2d 36 (N.D. Ill. 1986) (confirmatory memorandum must follow the formation of an agreement and must indicate that the parties have already made a deal or reached an agreement). A document accepting an offer may, however, satisfy the other prong of the parol evidence rule—a writing intended by the parties as a final expression of their agreement.

[897] U.C.C. § 2-202.

[898] *See* Empire Gas Corp. v. UPG, Inc., 781 S.W.2d 148, 11 UCCR2d 453 (Mo. Ct. App. 1989); Stern & Co. v. State Loan & Fin. Corp., 238 F. Supp. 901, 2 UCCR 721 (D. Del. 1965).

[899] Numerous cases have expressly referred to the intention of the parties as the touchstone of integration. *See, e.g.*, Sierra Diesel Injection Serv., Inc. v. Burroughs Corp., Inc., 874 F.2d 653, 8 UCCR2d 617 (9th Cir. 1989); Middletown Concrete Prods., Inc. v. Black Clawson Co., 802 F. Supp. 1135, 20 UCCR2d 1135 (D. Del. 1992); Camargo Cadillac Co. v. Garfield Enters., Inc., 3 Ohio App. 3d 435, 445 N.E.2d 1141, 35 UCCR 749 (1982); Betaco, Inc. v. Cessna Aircraft Co., 32 F.3d 1126, 24 UCCR2d 718 (7th Cir. 1994); Transamerica Oil Corp. v. Lynes, Inc., 723 F.2d 758, 37 UCCR 1076 (10th Cir. 1983); Besicorp Group, Inc. v. Thermo Electron Corp., 981 F. Supp. 86, 34 UCCR2d 1024 (S.D.N.Y. 1997). *But see* Mid-State Elec., Inc. v. H.L. Libby Corp., 787 F. Supp. 494, 18 UCCR2d 372 (W.D. Pa. 1992) (court invoked parol evidence rule based on contract's clarity without mentioning the intent of the parties); Apple Valley Red-E-Mix, Inc. v. Mills Winfield Eng'g Sales, Inc., 436 N.W.2d 121, 8 UCCR2d 21 (Minn. Ct. App. 1989) (only if term is ambiguous will parol evidence be permitted to reach the intent of the parties).

common-law concept of "integration." Although the Code does not use that term, courts nonetheless continue to use it.[900] It is, of course, possible to treat the issue of intention in parol evidence cases as any other question of fact: to be turned over to the factfinder unless there is insufficient credible evidence to support a finding for one side or the other.[901] Were this the case, there would be little, if anything, left of the parol evidence rule.[902] As one might expect, this is not the case. Although courts have recognized that the inquiry called for by the parol evidence rule is essentially factual;[903] its application is always treated as a function of the court.[904] Furthermore, the ways in which the courts have determined the parties' intention vary dramatically. One notable scholar, in his treatise on contract law, has identified six basic approaches to discovering the parties' intention, with many variations and permutations.[905] In addition, courts often decide the question of integration with little discussion of the process by which they gleaned the parties' intent.[906] This inconsistency continues under the Code, although a number of courts have suggested that section 2-202 was intended to liberalize the parol evidence rule.[907]

---

[900] Alaska N. Dev., Inc. v. Alyeska Pipeline Serv. Co., 666 P.2d 33, 36 UCCR 1527 (Alaska 1983); Bettaco, Inc. v. Cessna Aircraft Co., 32 F.3d 1126, 24 UCCR2d 718 (7th Cir. 1994); Anderson & Nafziger v. G.T. Newcomb, Inc., 100 Idaho 175, 27 UCCR 21, 595 P.2d 709 (1979).

[901] In fact, Professor Corbin seems to come close to adopting this position. Corbin insisted that the parol evidence rule was nothing more than the "ordinary substantive law of contracts." Arthur L. Corbin, Corbin on Contracts, § 574 (1961). *See* John E. Murray, Jr., Murray on Contracts (3d ed. 1990) § 82 at 378–379, § 84 at 389.

[902] *See* Thomas D. Crandall, et al., I Uniform Commercial Code, § 4.4 at 4:25 (1993); Murray, *supra* note 901, § 84.

[903] *See* Providence & Worcester R.R. Co. v. Sargent & Greenleaf, Inc., 802 F. Supp. 680, 19 UCCR2d 21 (D.R.I. 1992); Sho-Pro of Ind., Inc. v. Brown, 585 N.E.2d 1357, 17 UCCR2d 56 (Ind. Ct. App. 1992); Sierra Diesel Injection Serv., Inc., 890 F.2d 108, 9 UCCR2d 1236 (9th Cir. 1989).

[904] *See, e.g.*, FMC Corp. v. Seal Tape Limited, Inc., 396 N.Y.S.2d 993, 22 UCCR 297 (N.Y. Sup. Ct. 1977); Camargo Cadillac Co. v. Garfield Enters., Inc., 3 Ohio App. 3d 435, 445 N.E.2d 1141, 35 UCCR 749 (1982); Bib Audio Video Prods. v. Herold Mktg. Assocs., Inc., 517 N.W.2d 68, 24 UCCR2d 455 (Minn. Ct. App. 1994).

[905] Murray, *supra* note 901, § 84, at 385–399.

[906] *See* Middletown Concrete Prods., Inc. v. Black Clawson Co., 802 F. Supp. 1135, 1142, 20 UCCR2d 815, 826 (D. Del. 1992) ("Case law explaining how courts actually determine the intent of the parties is scant. Often courts simply assume a contract is integrated and move on to determine whether that contract is merely final as to the terms it contains or is the complete and exclusive final agreement of the parties").

[907] *See* Barbara Oil Co. v. Kansas Gas & Supply Co., 250 Kan. 438, 827 P.2d 24, 17 UCCR2d 1078 (1992). *See also* Burnham, "The Parol Evidence Rule: Don't Be Afraid of the Dark," 55 Mont. L. Rev. 93, 101 (1994); Greenberg, "Oral Warranties and Written Disclaimers in Consumer Transactions: Indiana's End Run Around the U.C.C. Parol Evi-

Professor Arthur Corbin believed that the court should consider *all* relevant evidence in determining whether the parties intended the writing to be the final repository of the terms of their agreement, including evidence of the parties' prior negotiations and agreements.[908] Although by no means universal, the trend in Code cases is generally consistent with Professor Corbin's approach,[909] with the exception of cases in which the contract contains a clear merger clause.[910] Among the factors that courts have examined in order to determine the intent of the parties are the relative sophistication of the parties,[911] whether one or both parties was represented by counsel,[912] the scope and atmosphere of negotiations,[913] whether the parties' behavior after the contract was inconsistent with an intent to integrate,[914] and other reasons why the proffered prior agreement was not included in the writing.[915]

Courts have become increasingly solicitous of consumers in applying the parol evidence rule. Usually, these cases involve oral representations made by salespersons to induce the consumer to purchase the product. Once

---

dence Rule," 23 Ind. L. Rev. 199, 209 (1990). Comment 1 to U.C.C. § 2-202 expressly rejects three ways in which some courts applying the common-law parol evidence rule made the admission of parol evidence more difficult: (1) it rejects the presumption that an integrated writing represents a *total* integration; (2) it requires that language be interpreted in its commercial context rather than by rules of construction; (3) it permits course-of-dealing and usage-of-trade evidence without a prior showing of ambiguity.

[908] Arthur L. Corbin, Corbin on Contracts § 533 (1952).

[909] *See, e.g.*, Sierra Diesel Injection Serv. v. Burroughs Corp., Inc. 890 F.2d 108, 9 UCCR2d 1236 (9th Cir. 1989); Betaco, Inc. v. Cessna Aircraft Co., 32 F.3d 1126 (7th Cir. 1994); Session v. Chartrand Equip. Co., 133 Ill. App. 3d 719, 479 N.E.2d 376, 41 UCCR 749 (1985). *See also* Anderson & Nafziger v. G.T. Newcomb, Inc., 100 Idaho 175, 595 P.2d 709, 27 UCCR 21 (1979) (court should examine all extrinsic evidence relevant to the issue of whether the parties intended the written agreement to be a complete integration although the writing itself has superior probative value).

[910] *See* § 3.15[C], *infra*.

[911] *See* Middletown Concrete Prods. v. Black Clawson Co., 802 F. Supp. 1135, 20 UCCR2d 815 (D. Del. 1992); Sierra Diesel Injection Serv. v. Burroughs Corp., 890 F.2d 108, 9 UCCR2d 1236 (9th Cir. 1989); Betaco, Inc. v. Cessna Aircraft Co., 32 F.3d 1126 (7th Cir. 1994).

[912] *See* Binks Mfg. Co. v. National Presto Indus., Inc., 709 F.2d 1109, 36 UCCR 14 (7th Cir. 1983).

[913] *See* Central Jersey Dodge Truck Ctr., Inc. v. Sightseer Corp., 608 F.2d 1106, 27 UCCR 1256 (6th Cir. 1979) (informal atmosphere of negotiations suggested that parties did not intend the written agreement to supersede an earlier agreement); Betaco, Inc. v. Cessna Aircraft Co., 32 F.3d 1126 (7th Cir. 1994); MPM Hawaiian, Inc. v. World Square, 4 Haw. App. 341, 666 P.2d 622, 36 UCCR 1543 (Haw. Ct. App. 1983).

[914] Central Jersey Dodge Truck Ctr., Inc. v. Sightseer Corp., 608 F.2d 1106 (6th Cir. 1979).

[915] *See* Hardin v. Cliff Pettit Motors, Inc., 407 F. Supp. 297, 19 UCCR 421 (E.D. Tenn. 1976) (finding parties intended oral agreement to extend credit to survive writing because it was an inducement for the entire bargain).

the consumer has decided to buy the product, he or she is then presented with a printed form contract that contains a statement in the fine print that the writing is the final and complete agreement of the parties and there have been no oral representations or promises beyond those contained in the writing. The buyer signs the contract, usually paying no attention to the fine print, and later the representations that induced the contract turn out to be false.

Courts are correct in these cases not to bar evidence of the prior representations even though a term in the writing is being contradicted by the proffered evidence. In most cases, the seller has reason to know that the buyer does not intend the writing to supersede the oral representations that induced the sale. The seller will also usually know that the buyer has not even *read* the fine print, let alone understood its significance. Thus, the *objective* intent of the parties (i.e., the understanding of a reasonable person under the circumstances) is that the oral representations were intended to survive the writing.

Representative of these cases is *Carpetland, U.S.A. v. Payne.*[916] In November 1986, the buyer went to Carpetland to purchase carpet for the house she owned with her husband. The buyer was assisted by a salesman who told her that the carpet she was considering was guaranteed for a year. Upon selecting the carpet, she signed an agreement disclaiming all express and implied warranties. Within three or four weeks the nap of the carpet began coming loose, creating bald spots. The buyer complained a number of times and was advised to cut the loose strings off the carpet. The condition of the carpet, however, continued to deteriorate, and when Carpetland refused to replace it, the buyer sued.

The court first determined that the salesman's statement was an express warranty under the Code. As such, it was inconsistent with the disclaimer and, therefore, the express warranty prevailed under section 2-316(1).[917] Then, in a lengthy footnote, the court considered the effect of the parol evidence rule. The court recognized a split of authority as to whether the parol evidence rule should bar the admission of evidence of a prior oral express warranty. The court aligned itself with the "pro-consumer" faction and held that whenever a prior oral express warranty is contradicted by a written disclaimer, the parol evidence rule is ineffective and evidence of the oral warranty is admissible. The court believed this result was consistent with earlier Indiana law.[918]

---

[916] 536 N.E.2d 306, 8 UCCR2d 942 (Ind. Ct. App. 1989).

[917] *See* § 4.07[B], *infra.*

[918] *But see* Greenberg, "Oral Warranties and Written Disclaimers in Consumer Transactions: Indiana's End Run Around the U.C.C. Parol Evidence Rule," 23 Ind. L. Rev. 199, 202–203 (1990) (concluding that none of the cases cited by the court supported its holding).

While the judgment of the court in the case was undoubtedly correct, its opinion in the case went too far. The court's language suggests that evidence of an oral warranty should *always* be admissible despite a written disclaimer, at least in consumer transactions. Instead of an ironclad rule in favor of consumers, however, the court should have focused on the *objective intent* of the parties and asked whether it was reasonable for the buyer to believe that the oral representations survived the writing and whether the seller had reason to know of the buyer's understanding. If the answer to these questions is "yes," the parties did not objectively intend the writing to be their final expression on warranties, and the evidence should be admitted.

The proposed analysis is preferable because it is possible, even in consumer transactions, for the parties to intend to exclude prior oral understandings from their contract. For example, the salesman in *Carpetland U.S.A.* could have explained the effect of the disclaimer and that his representations were not part of the final deal. If this explanation and the buyer's response to it were sufficient to give the salesman reason to believe that the buyer understood that his representations were not part of the contract, evidence of them would be precluded by the parol evidence rule.[919] This approach continues to give effect to the Code's parol evidence rule, while allowing consumers to prove the existence of oral warranties when it is justified.[920]

A nonconsumer case epitomizing a liberal approach to integration is *Sierra Diesel Injection Service v. Burroughs Corp., Inc.*[921] In *Sierra Diesel*, Sierra Diesel Injection Service wanted to improve its bookkeeping equipment. It contacted Burroughs, which suggested that instead of an improved bookkeeping machine, Sierra should purchase a computer. Convinced by this advice, Cathey, Sierra's president, decided to purchase a computer and related software from Burroughs. The contract contained an integration clause[922] stating that the written agreement constituted the entire agreement of the parties and superseded all prior communications between the parties.

---

[919] The representations would also not be express warranties under these circumstances because they would not be part of the basis of the bargain. *See* § 4.05[F], *infra*.

[920] It also gives effect to Official Comment 2 to U.C.C. § 2-316, which suggests that the parol evidence rule is intended to protect the seller against false allegations of oral warranties. Courts have also refused to apply the parol evidence rule in cases brought under Consumer Sales Practices Acts or Deceptive Trade Practices Acts. *See, e.g.*, Weitzel v. Barnes, 691 S.W.2d (Tex. 1985); Love v. Keith, 383 S.E.2d 674 (N.C. Ct. App. 1989). This topic is more fully considered in a later section of this book. *See* § 9.02[B], *infra*.

[921] 656 F. Supp. 426, 3 UCCR2d 1378 (D. Nev. 1987).

[922] *See* § 3.15[C], *infra*.

The equipment apparently[923] failed to conform to Burroughs's oral representations, and Sierra sued.

The court began its opinion by stating that the fundamental test of integration was whether the parties intended the writing to be the final expression of their agreement with respect to the terms included in the writing.[924] Although the integration clause in the writing was some evidence of this intent, it was not conclusive. Instead, to determine the parties' intent, the court looked at the circumstances surrounding the contract. While acknowledging that Cathey was an experienced businessman, he was not particularly versed in contract law or computer science. Further, he read only those portions of the agreement describing the equipment, its price, and the delivery date, and merely scanned the remainder. The court said that he did not understand the integration clause to mean that the representations of Burroughs's salespersons about computer's capabilities were nullified, especially since the computer's capabilities were an essential part of the agreement. According to the court, the equipment and software were "just so much useless metal, plastic and paper if they would not do the job required for plaintiff's business."[925] Although the defendant "may have believed or hoped that the integration clause would protect it from responsibility or liability for the representations of its salespersons," from the standpoint of the buyer there could be no agreement absent the representations.[926] The court concluded, because integration requires the mutual intent of the parties that the writing should bar reliance on prior representations or agreements, that the contract was not integrated.[927]

The reasoning of the court in *Sierra* was generally sound. The only basis for criticism is the court's suggestion that integration requires that both parties *subjectively* intend that the writing be the final expression of their agreement.[928] The intent to integrate should be treated like all other questions of intent in contract law; it should be a function of the *objective* intent of the parties.[929] If the subjective intentions of both parties coincide as to the issue of integration, then their subjective intention should decide the issue. If, however, their subjective intentions are different, then the issue

---

[923] The opinion in the case does not describe what oral representations were made and how the computer hardware and software failed to live up to them.

[924] 656 F. Supp. at 429, 3 UCCR2d at 1380.

[925] *Id.* at 428, 3 UCCR2d at 1381.

[926] *Id.*

[927] *Id.*

[928] *See* Crandall et al., *supra* note 902, at 4:29.

[929] *See* the discussion of contract formation in § 3.02, *supra* and the general discussion of contract interpretation in § 3.11, *supra*.

should be whether, in view of all the surrounding circumstances, it is reasonable for the person proffering the evidence to believe that the representations survived the writing and whether the other party had reason to know of this belief. In *Sierra,* the answer to these questions appears to be "yes," and the court's decision that the contract was not integrated was, therefore, correct.[930]

Despite the attitude represented by these cases, some courts still give little or no consideration to extrinsic evidence in determining whether the parties intended the contract to be integrated in a writing. This is most frequently true in cases in which a merger clause is present in the writing, a situation that will be discussed subsequently,[931] and is even true in some consumer cases. A graphic illustration is *In re Tom Woods Used Cars, Inc. (McCloud v. Woods).*[932] The buyers bought a used car from the seller. The buyers claimed that the seller had orally promised to hold the contract open while the buyers looked for cheaper financing, a promise the seller denied. After finding cheaper financing, the buyers discovered that the contract had not been held open, and, consequently, they owed the purchase price to two different banks. In a suit by the buyers, the court held that although the evidence supported the buyers' version of the facts, the evidence was barred by the parol evidence rule. The court held that the contract was complete on its face and that under Tennessee law, this raised a conclusive presumption of integration.[933]

2. *The extrinsic evidence contradicts a term of the writing.* The parol evidence rule protects against evidence of parol terms that *contradict* the writing. Unless the court also finds the writing to be a *complete and exclusive* statement of the agreement,[934] there is no prohibition against the introduction of evidence of prior agreements or contemporaneous oral agreements to *supplement* or *explain* a writing. Also, a usage of trade, course of dealing, or course of performance is always admissible to explain or sup-

---

[930] For cases in which the court used similar reasoning but reached a different conclusion as to integration, *see* Middletown Concrete Prods., Inc. v. Black Clawson Co., 802 F. Supp. 1135, 20 UCCR2d 815 (D. Del. 1992); Betaco, Inc. v. Cessna Aircraft Co., 103 F.3d 1281, 31 UCCR2d 1 (7th Cir. 1996).

[931] *See* § 3.15[C], *infra.*

[932] 23 B.R. 563, 35 UCCR 52 (Bankr. E.D. Tenn. 1981).

[933] *Id.* at 567. *See also* Noble v. Logan-Dees Chevrolet-Buick, Inc., 293 So. 2d 14, 14 UCCR 1107 (Miss. 1974) ("where parties, without fraud or mistake, have deliberately put their contract in writing, the writing is not only the best, *but the only*, evidence of their agreement") (emphasis added).

[934] *See* § 3.15[B][2], *infra.*

plement a writing, so long as it does not contradict the writing.[935] The line between contradiction and explanation or supplementation is not easy to draw, however, as the disparity in the cases makes evident.

The difficulty is evidenced by the following hypothetical and a variation. Suppose that Buyer and Seller exchange memoranda confirming a telephone conversation in which Seller agreed to sell Buyer certain goods for "$35.00 per hundredweight." The memoranda agreed as to the price. Buyer is now claiming that Seller agreed, during the telephone conversation, to give Buyer a 2 percent discount for payments made within ten days of the invoice date. Seller claims that the parol evidence rule prevents this statement from being considered.[936] A variation on the hypothetical assumes that the Buyer wants to introduce evidence of a usage of trade in which sellers provide a discount to buyers for payments made within ten days or a course of dealing between the two parties in which such discounts were given.

In the hypothetical, there is a price term, but there is no term dealing with discounts. Are we to imply from this omission and the statement of a specific price that the price is not discounted and, therefore, the proffered evidence contradicts a term of the writing? Or, should we conclude that, because the subject of discounts is not dealt with in the writing, the oral evidence does not contradict a term of the writing and, therefore, is admissible to supplement the writing?

The cases are far from consistent in dealing with this problem. Two basic approaches have emerged to determine whether proffered oral evidence "contradicts" a "term" of the writing.[937] The first requires that the oral evidence *negate* or *directly contradict* an express term before the evidence will be precluded by section 2-202. Representative of this line of cases is *Hunt Foods & Industries v. Doliner*.[938] Doliner and Hunt engaged in negotiations for the sale to Hunt of Doliner's stock in the Eastern Can Company. The parties agreed on a price for the sale of the stock, but the negotiations adjourned before agreement was reached on other items relating to the sale. Because Hunt was concerned that Doliner would use the price to leverage a higher bid from a third party, Hunt demanded and received a written unconditional option to purchase the stock at the agreed-upon price. Doliner claimed that when he learned of the implications of the unconditional option, he obtained an oral agreement from Hunt that the option would be exercised

---

[935] *See* Middletown Concrete Prods., Inc. v. Black Clawson Co., 802 F. Supp. 1135, 20 UCCR2d 815 (D. Del. 1992); Dakota Country Store Foods, Inc. v. Red Owl Stores, Inc., 107 B.R. 977, 10 UCCR2d 361 (Bankr. D.S.D. 1989).

[936] Assume at this point that the evidence will not be precluded because the memoranda constitute a complete and exclusive statement of the agreement. *See* § 3.15[B][2], *infra*.

[937] As usual, such generalizations oversimplify the true richness of the case law.

[938] 270 N.Y.S.2d 937, 26 A.D.2d 41, 3 UCCR 597 (N.Y. App. Div. 1966).

only if Doliner solicited another offer. When subsequent negotiations failed to produce an agreement, Hunt attempted to exercise the option and Doliner refused to deliver the stock.

In the lawsuit that ensued, Hunt moved for summary judgment, arguing that Doliner's evidence of the oral condition to the option was barred by the parol evidence rule. The court denied the motion using the following language:

> We believe the proffered evidence to be inadmissible only where the writing contradicts the existence of the claimed additional term. [Citations omitted.] The conversations in this case, some of which are not disputed, and the expectation of all the parties for further negotiations, suggest that the alleged oral condition precedent cannot be precluded as a matter of law or as factually impossible. *It is not sufficient that the existence of the condition is implausible. It must be impossible.*[939]

Hunt Foods has come to stand for the proposition that nothing less than a *direct contradiction* of the written language of the agreement will suffice to bar evidence of a parol agreement.

A number of cases following *Hunt Foods* evidence a similar willingness to admit parol agreements, and a number of these cases cite *Hunt Foods* with approval.[940] For example, in *Michael Schiavone & Sons, Inc. v. Securalloy Co., Inc.*,[941] the court permitted a seller to introduce evidence of an oral understanding that a quantity term of "500 tons" in a contract for the delivery of steel solids meant "up to 500 tons" depending on the amount that the seller could secure. Citing *Hunt Foods*, the court said that, "it must be borne in mind that to be inconsistent the terms [of the oral agreement] must contradict or negate a term of the written agreement; and a term which has a lesser effect is deemed a consistent term."[942]

---

[939] Id. at 940, 26 A.D.2d at 43, 3 UCCR at 599 (emphasis added).

[940] *See, e.g.*, Computerized Radiological Servs., Inc. v. Syntex Corp., 595 F. Supp. 1495, 40 UCCR 49 (E.D.N.Y. 1984); Tropical Leasing, Inc. v. Fiermonte Chevrolet, Inc., 439 N.Y.S.2d 566, 80 A.D.2d 467, 31 UCCR 827 (N.Y. Sup. Ct. 1981); In re W.T. Grant Co. v. N&A Goldman Co., Inc., 1 B.R. 516, 28 UCCR 1283 (S.D.N.Y. 1979).

[941] 312 F. Supp. 801, 7 UCCR 674 (D. Conn. 1970).

[942] *Id.* at 804, 7 UCCR at 678. *See also* Brunswick Box Co., Inc. v. Coutinho, Caro & Co., Inc., 617 F.2d 355, 28 UCCR 616 (4th Cir. 1980) (court permitted the introduction of parol evidence to show that parties intended term "F.A.S. Norfolk" to mean other than Code definition of "F.A.S." term despite finding that term was unambiguous); Hawaii Leasing v. Klein, 658 P.2d 343, 35 UCCR 1365 (Haw. Ct. App. 1983) (oral option to purchase consistent with lease making no mention of option to purchase); Hoff Cos., Inc. v. Danner, 822 P.2d 558, 16 UCCR2d 974 (Iowa Ct. App. 1991).

Several courts have explicitly rejected the approach of *Hunt Foods*. In *Snyder v. Herbert Greenbaum & Associates, Inc.*,[943] the buyer and seller entered into a contract in which the seller agreed to supply and install carpeting for apartments being built by the buyer. During negotiations leading up to the contract, the seller estimated that approximately 19,000 to 20,000 yards of carpet would be needed. After signing the contract the buyer purchased large amounts of carpet to be used in its apartments from another supplier. Shortly thereafter, the buyer canceled the contract.

When the seller sued for breach, the buyer alleged that the parties had orally agreed that either party could unilaterally rescind the contract. The court refused to permit evidence of this agreement, and specifically rejected the approach of *Hunt Foods*:

> Rather [than the *Hunt Foods* approach] we believe "inconsistency" as used in § 2-202(b) means the absence of reasonable harmony in terms of the language *and* respective obligations of the parties. [Citations omitted.] In terms of the obligations of the appellee, which required appellee to make extensive preparations in order to perform, unqualified unilateral cancellation by appellants is not reasonably harmonious.[944]

Despite its rejection of *Hunt Foods,* the court in *Snyder* did not restrict its analysis to a facial examination of the writing. The court was willing to consider the circumstances surrounding the contract and its formation before deciding that there was an absence of reasonable harmony between the writing and the proffered oral evidence. Thus, even the more restrictive approach to consistency in *Snyder* represents welcome progress over the "four corners" approach of the Willistonians.[945]

---

[943] 380 A.2d 618, 38 Md. App. 144, 22 UCCR 1104 (Md. Ct. Spec. App. 1977).

[944] *Id.* at 623, 38 Md. App. at 152, 22 UCCR at 1111.

[945] The "four corners" approach looks solely at the writing to determine the question of integration. *See* Samuel L. Williston, Williston on Contracts, § 631 (1961).

A second case rejecting the approach of *Hunt Foods* is Luria Bros. & Co., Inc. v. Pielet Bros. Scrap Iron & Metal, Inc., 600 F.2d 103, 26 UCCR 1081 (7th Cir. 1979). In this case, the seller orally agreed to sell the buyer 35,000 tons of scrap metal from old barges that were to be cut into sections. Subsequent to the oral agreement, the parties exchanged written confirmations. The confirmations agreed on all terms except the delivery date, which was incorrectly stated on the buyer's confirmation. After receiving Luria's confirmation, Pielet's representative (Bloom) called Luria's representative (Forlani) about the error. Forlani agreed that Luria's confirmation was incorrect, and that Pielet's confirmation stated the correct delivery date. There was no dispute as to these facts. When the seller failed the deliver the scrap steel, the buyer sued. The seller said that its obligation to deliver the steel was subject to an oral condition that the seller be able to obtain the steel from a specific supplier. The seller argued that it had informed the buyer that this supplier was new to the seller, that

The authors believe that so long as the factfinder could reasonably find that a prior oral agreement was made and the parties objectively intended that agreement to survive the writing, the evidence should be admitted. If the "absence of reasonable harmony" test means that, in order to bar the evidence of a prior agreement, the judge must conclude, *after examining all of the evidence*, that no reasonable factfinder could find that the parties objectively intended a prior agreement to survive the writing, then the authors approve of the test. A judge reaching this conclusion has determined that the proffered evidence is not material to the parties' bargain-in-fact and acts properly in excluding it.

The same division in the case law exists with respect to the admission of evidence of usage of trade, course of dealing, or course of performance. Section 2-202(a) permits the introduction of evidence of course-of-dealing, usage-of-trade, or course-of-performance evidence to explain or supplement a writing, whether or not the writing is integrated or even fully integrated.[946] Courts, however, have generally held that this evidence is not admissible if it *contradicts* an integrated writing. While courts have probably been more willing to admit evidence of course-of-dealing, usage-of-trade, and course-of-performance evidence than express prior oral agreements, courts have again split along the lines of the *Hunt Foods* and *Snyder* cases.

Courts could (and probably should) have taken the approach that evidence of course of dealing, usage of trade, and course of performance is not subject to the parol evidence rule at all. Section 2-202 says that the terms of an integrated writing may not be contradicted by "evidence of any *prior agreement* or *contemporaneous oral agreement*."[947] While usage of trade, etc. may be an implicit part of the parties' overall bargain under section 1-201(3), it is not really an agreement of the parties as this phrase would be normally understood. In addition, course-of-dealing, usage-of-trade, and course-of-performance evidence requires proof of objective facts independent of the expressions of the parties, and is therefore less subject to falsification. Furthermore, Comment 1 rejects any requirement of ambiguity for the admission of evidence of usage of trade, course of dealing, or course of performance, a requirement that the Code does not reject with respect to other kinds of extrinsic evidence. Finally, Comment 2 specifically states that

---

the seller was worried about the supplier's reliability, and that the seller was promising delivery of the scrap only if it received it from the supplier. At trial, the court ruled that the parol evidence rule barred the seller from introducing evidence of these conversations and the oral agreement. Relying on the *Snyder* test of "absence of reasonable harmony" between the oral evidence and the written contract, the trial court's ruling was upheld on appeal.

[946] *See* § 3.15[B][2], *infra.*

[947] U.C.C. § 2-202 (emphasis added).

such evidence becomes an element of the meaning of the words used "unless carefully negated."[948]

Were courts to reject application of the parol evidence rule to evidence of usage of trade, course of dealing, and course of performance, any conflict between this evidence and the express terms would be resolved by the fact-finder according to sections 1-205 and 2-208.[949] So long as there is sufficient evidence to establish a factual question as to the existence of a usage of trade, course of dealing, or course of performance, determining whether this evidence is consistent or inconsistent with the express terms is an issue for the factfinder rather than the judge.

Unfortunately, courts have not adopted this analysis. By and large, the courts have applied the parol evidence rule to evidence of course of dealing, usage of trade and course of performance in the same manner as they have applied the rule to evidence of asserted prior express agreements. Courts have subjected evidence of usage of trade, course of dealing, and course of performance to the parol evidence rule and excluded this evidence from the factfinder when they have considered it to be inconsistent with the express terms.[950]

Despite the near universal application of the parol evidence rule to evidence of usage of trade, course of dealing, and course of performance, most courts have been generous in finding that they do not contradict the terms in the writing and are, therefore, admissable. Representative of this line of cases is *Provident Tradesmens Bank & Trust Co. v. Pemberton.*[951] In this case, the Pennsylvania Superior Court permitted evidence of a usage of trade requiring the giving of notice prior to cancellation of insurance, despite a provision in the contract that waived "all notices whatsoever in respect of this agreement" and which further provided that the defendant's liability was "absolute and unconditional."[952] The court said that the evidence of a well-established custom is not "carefully negated" by the use of a printed form that makes no reference to custom or usage.

The most noted case examining the admission of evidence of trade usage and course of dealing is *Columbia Nitrogen Corp. v. Royster Co.*[953]

---

[948] U.C.C. § 2-202, Official Comment 2.

[949] *See* § 3.14, *supra.*

[950] *See* Warrick Beverage Corp. v. Miller Brewing Co., 352 N.E.2d 496, 170 Ind. App. 114, 20 UCCR 46 (Ind. Ct. App. 1976); Bib Audio-Video Prods. v. Herold Mktg. Assocs., Inc., 517 N.W.2d 68, 24 UCCR2d 455 (Minn. Ct. App. 1994); Middletown Concrete Prods. v. Black Clawson Co., 802 F. Supp. 1135, 20 UCCR2d 815 (D. Del. 1992); H&W Indus., Inc. v. Occidental Chem. Corp., 911 F.2d 1118, 12 UCCR2d 921 (5th Cir. 1990).

[951] 196 Pa. Super. 180, 173 A.2d 780, 1 UCCR 57 (1961).

[952] *Id.* at 182, 173 A.2d at 781, 1 UCCR at 62 (Flood, J., dissenting).

[953] 451 F.2d 3, 9 UCCR 977 (4th Cir. 1971).

In a written contract, the seller agreed to sell the buyer excess phosphate that the seller did not need for its own operations. The writing provided for a minimum tonnage at a fixed price, with a price escalation clause depending upon the seller's production costs. Subsequent to the agreement, phosphate prices plunged, and the buyer ordered only a portion of the scheduled tonnage. When the buyer refused to take more, even after the seller made some temporary price concessions, the seller sued for breach. At trial, the buyer offered evidence of a usage of trade in the industry that price and quantity terms are only projections, depending upon the state of the market. It offered further evidence of a course of dealing between the two parties in which the seller had agreed to substantial changes in price and quantity under similar contracts. The trial court excluded this evidence.

On appeal, the court agreed that evidence of usage of trade or course of dealing should be excluded if it is inconsistent with the writing. The court, however, found that the evidence was not inconsistent with the written agreement, and held that the trial court had improperly refused to admit it. The court held that the evidence was not inconsistent with the writing for four reasons: (1) the contract did not expressly state that course of dealing and usage of trade could not be used to explain or supplement the contract; (2) the contract was silent about adjusting prices in a declining market—it neither permitted nor prohibited adjustment; (3) minimum tonnages were expressed in terms of "Products Supplied Under Contract" rather than "Products" or "Products Purchased Under Contract"; and (4) the default clause of the contract referred only to the buyer's failure to pay for delivered phosphate.

The heart of the court's analysis is in its first two reasons; the last two are largely make-weights.[954] By relying on the fact that the contract neither expressly excluded usage of trade and course of dealing evidence nor expressly prohibited price and quantity adjustment, the court adopted an approach to inconsistency similar to *Hunt Foods*. Evidence of anything less than a direct contradiction of an express term of the writing was admissible.

Nanakuli Paving & Rock v. Shell Oil Co., Inc.,[955] contains the most extensive discussion of the admissibility of usage of trade and course of dealing found in the cases. After a comprehensive review of the prior cases and scholarly literature, the court ultimately adopted an analysis similar to *Columbia Nitrogen*. Nanakuli Paving was a paving contractor in Honolulu,

---

[954] The difference in language mentioned by the court appears inconsequential, and the failure of the default clause to mention a failure to take the minimum tonnage should be irrelevant in light of the Code's presumption that remedies are cumulative rather than exclusive. *See* U.C.C. § 2-719(1)(b) and Official Comment 2.

[955] 664 F.2d 772, 32 UCCR 1025 (9th Cir. 1980).

Hawaii, attempting to establish a place in the asphalt paving market that had been occupied by only one company. Nanakuli entered into a long-term contract with Shell to provide Nanakuli with asphalt for its operations. The contract provided that the price for asphalt would be Shell's "Posted Price" at the time of delivery. During the term of the contract with Shell, Nanakuli entered into paving contracts using Shell's current "Posted Price" to calculate its bids. When Shell raised its posted price prior to delivery, Nanakuli objected. When Shell refused to provide Nanakuli with asphalt at the earlier posted price, Nanakuli sued.

Nanakuli argued that there was both a usage of trade and course of dealing which obligated Shell to provide "price protection" to Nanakuli, such that Nanakuli would only be charged the posted price at the time that Nanakuli entered into paving contracts rather than the posted price at the time of delivery. Shell responded that this evidence was inconsistent with the express terms of the contract, which expressly provided for the posted price at the time of delivery. The Ninth Circuit agreed with Nanakuli. It held that course-of-dealing and usage-of-trade evidence occupies a "unique and important" role under the Code[956] and that the Code requires that it be "carefully negated" before evidence of it is barred.[957] The court said that the federal courts had been lenient in permitting such evidence and cited with approval the test for consistency in *Hunt Foods*. The court held that usage-of-trade and course-of-dealing evidence was admissible so long as it was not a "total negation" of an express term.[958] As long as the proffered evidence merely constitutes a partial exception to an express term or "cuts down" the express term rather than negates it entirely, the evidence is admissible.[959]

Other cases are similar to *Nanakuli* and *Columbia Nitrogen*. For example, in *Michael Schiavone & Sons, Inc. v. Securalloy Co., Inc.*,[960] the court admitted usage-of-trade evidence that the term "500 Gross Tons" was merely a maximum quantity, dependent upon how much steel the seller could secure.[961] In *Modine Manufacturing Co. v. North East Independent School District*,[962] evidence of a usage of trade allowing reasonable variations in cooling capacity was admitted despite specifications that provided

---

[956] *Id.* at 797, 32 UCCR at 1059.

[957] *Id.* at 783, 32 UCCR at 1065.

[958] *Id.* at 803, 32 UCCR at 1068.

[959] *Id.*, 32 UCCR at 1068.

[960] 312 F. Supp. 801, 7 UCCR 674 (D. Conn. 1970).

[961] The court cited *Hunt Foods* and said that to be inconsistent, the evidence must contradict or negate an express term; a term that has a lesser effect is deemed consistent. 312 F.2d at 804, 7 UCCR at 678.

[962] 503 S.W.2d 833, 14 UCCR 317 (Tex. Civ. App. 1974).

that "capacities shall not be less than indicated."[963] Citing *Columbia Nitrogen*, the court said that usage of trade must be carefully negated to be barred.[964]

There are, however, cases contrary to *Nanakuli* and *Columbia Nitrogen* in their analysis, if not in result. One of the most cited and best reasoned is *Southern Concrete Services, Inc. v. Mableton Contractors, Inc.*[965] A written contract between the parties provided that the seller was to supply "approximately 70,000 cubic yards of concrete to the buyer." The contract also stipulated that "no conditions that are not incorporated in the contract will be recognized."[966] The buyer ordered only 12,500 cubic yards and refused to take more. When the seller sued, the buyer attempted to introduce evidence of a usage of trade that the quantity stated in the contract was not obligatory on either party but was simply an estimate. The court phrased the issue:

> The question then becomes what is meant by the term "explained or supplemented"; does defendant's evidence "explain" the contract or does it attempt to "contradict" it?[967]

The court decided that the evidence contradicted the express terms and therefore was inadmissible. In so doing, it provided the most thoroughly reasoned justification of any case for a more restrictive approach to the admission of parol evidence of usage of trade and course of dealing. The court first turned to the traditional certainty function of the parol evidence rule discussed earlier:[968]

> To allow such specific contracts to be challenged by extrinsic evidence might jeopardize the certainties of contractual duties which parties have a right to rely on. This court does not believe that § 2-202 was meant to invite a frontal assault on the terms of a clear and explicit contract.[969]

---

[963] *Id.* at 838, 14 UCCR at 322.

[964] *Id.* at 839, 14 UCCR at 324. *See also* Heggblade-Marguleas-Tenneco, Inc. v. Sunshine Biscuit, Inc., 59 Cal. App. 3d 948, 131 Cal. Rptr. 183, 19 UCCR 1067 (1976) (usage of trade admissible to show amount stated in contract was merely estimate); Paragon Resources, Inc. v. National Fuel Gas Distrib. Corp., 695 F.2d 991, 35 UCCR 352 (5th Cir. 1983) (usage of trade permissible to show ambiguity not apparent on the face of the contract). The court also said that section 1-205 of the Code did not result in the exclusion of evidence of usage of trade but merely permits inconsistent express terms to control.

[965] 407 F. Supp. 581, 19 UCCR 79 (N.D. Ga. 1975).

[966] *Id.* at 582, 19 UCCR at 80.

[967] *Id.* at 584, 19 UCCR at 81.

[968] *See generally* § 3.04, *supra.*

[969] 407 F. Supp. at 584, 19 UCCR at 83.

Furthermore, while recognizing that usage of trade was a important tool of interpretation, the court said that an excessively liberal approach to its admissibility would encourage parties to explicitly negate reference to it, probably through boilerplate exclusions. This practice would paradoxically make usage of trade less, rather than more, able to serve its interpretive function.[970] Finally, if a mere willingness to be flexible in renegotiating prior contracts was to become admissible as evidence of a course of dealing, despite the express terms of a contract, parties would forego this flexibility, an unfortunate result.[971]

Another early case restricting the admission of usage-of-trade evidence is *Division of Triple T Service, Inc. v. Mobil Oil Corp.*[972] In this case, a franchisee, whose service station franchise had been terminated by Mobil, sought to introduce parol evidence of a usage of trade that franchises in the industry were terminated only for cause. The contract language provided that the franchise could be terminated by either party on "not less than 90 days notice."[973] The evidence of the usage of trade was not admitted. The court said that only evidence "consistent with the tenor of the agreement" should be admitted. Since the express terms covered the entire area of termination, evidence of an implicit limitation was inconsistent and inadmissible.

Southern Concrete and *Division of Triple T* have developed their following as have *Columbia Nitrogen* and *Nanakuli*. For example, in *State ex rel Conley Lott Nichols Machinery Co. v. SAFECO Insurance Co. of America*[974] the court refused to admit evidence of a usage of trade allowing lessees of heavy equipment to return the equipment prior to the end of the lease if it was no longer needed. The lease was for a period of eight months with no mention of early termination. The court said that evidence of usage of trade would not be admitted if it changed the basic meaning of the contract and "produced an agreement wholly different from and wholly inconsistent with the written agreement."[975] In *Golden Peanut Co. v. Hunt*,[976] the Georgia Court of Appeals refused to admit evidence of a usage of trade that a "bona fide offer from a third party" in a peanut contract was limited to an offer from a federally registered peanut broker. The court cited *Southern*

---

[970] *Id.* at 584, 19 UCCR at 84.

[971] *Id.*, 19 UCCR at 84. The court, however, attempted to distinguish *Columbia Nitrogen* rather than explicitly disagree with the decision. Its attempt is unconvincing.

[972] 304 N.Y.S.2d 191, 6 UCCR 1011 (N.Y. Sup. Ct. 1969).

[973] *Id.* at 194, 6 UCCR at 1014.

[974] 100 N.M. 440, 671 P.2d 1151, 38 UCCR 423 (N.M. Ct. App. 1983).

[975] *Id.* at 444, 671 P.2d at 1155, 38 UCCR at 427.

[976] 203 Ga. App. 469, 416 S.E.2d 896, 18 UCCR2d 26 (1992).

Concrete with approval and held that evidence of the usage contradicted the express terms of the contract.[977]

Courts applying the "absence of reasonable harmony" approach of *Snyder v. Herbert Greenbaum* have broad discretion whether to admit extrinsic evidence. Whether there is "reasonable harmony" between the proffered evidence and the express term will undoubtedly often turn on the court's assessment of the credibility of the evidence, as do many parol evidence rule decisions. The more likely the court believes the prior agreement to have actually been made the more likely it will find that there is "reasonable harmony" between the extrinsic evidence and the writing. It is the authors' view that the parol evidence rule should never bar evidence of usage of trade, course of dealing, or course of performance so long as that evidence is material to the parties' bargain-in-fact.

3. *The proffered evidence is of a prior agreement or of a contemporaneous oral agreement. Prior* agreements, *whether written or oral*, are excluded if the requirements of the Code's parol evidence rule are met. A prior written agreement, like a prior oral agreement, may be integrated into a later writing. However, only *oral* contemporaneous agreements, not written contemporaneous agreements, are excluded. The reason is that if a number of documents are signed contemporaneously, the factfinder should consider all of these documents in determining the agreement of the parties.

Under no interpretation of the parol evidence rule is evidence of *subsequent* agreements inadmissible. If a subsequent agreement is oral, it may fail to comply with the statute of frauds,[978] but the parol evidence rule is inapplicable.[979] The parol evidence rule seeks only to determine the parties' agreement at the time of the writing. Parties may later change this agreement without involving the parol evidence rule.

The parol evidence rule should also not bar parol evidence relevant to the *interpretation* of a term that the parties have used on their writing. The evidence should be barred only if, after hearing *all* of the evidence, including the proffered parol evidence, the judge determines that the meaning supported by the parol evidence is not one to which the writing is reasonably

---

[977] For other cases in which a court applied a more restrictive view to the admission of usage-of-trade and course-of-dealing evidence, *see* Advance Process Supply Co. v. Litton Indus. Credit Corp., 745 F.2d 1076, 39 UCCR 565 (7th Cir. 1984); Warnaco, Inc. v. Farkas, 664 F. Supp. 738, 4 UCCR2d 1651 (S.D.N.Y. 1987).

[978] *See* § 3.01, *supra.*

[979] *See* EPN-Delaval, S.A. v. Inter-Equip, Inc., 542 F. Supp. 238, 34 UCCR 130 (S.D. Tex. 1982); Gold Kist, Inc. v. Pillow, 582 S.W.2d 77, 26 UCCR 1078 (Tenn. Ct. App. 1979).

susceptible.[980] Thus, the "plain-meaning" rule, which bars parol evidence relevant to interpretation if the writing is "unambiguous on its face," should be rejected. Despite the criticism to which the plain-meaning rule has been subjected,[981] a significant number of Code cases continue to apply it.[982] Further discussion of this issue is presented in the next section.

[2] The Positive Rule

Evidence of consistent additional terms is admissible. Because the writing is final as to some terms of the agreement (for example, price, subject matter, and warranties), this does not mean that it is final as to all matters agreed upon. Therefore, terms that add to the agreement expressed in the writing are admissible so long as they are "consistent"—that is, they do not contradict the writing. The Code, however, adds a significant condition to the admissibility of consistent additional terms: they will be admitted "unless the court finds the writing to have been intended also as a complete and exclusive statement of the terms of the agreement."[983] This limitation *does not* apply to evidence of usage of trade, course of dealing, or course of performance. The fact that the writing was intended as complete and exclusive does not prevent the admission of extrinsic evidence of this sort.[984]

Excluding consistent additional terms when the parties intend the writing to be the complete and exclusive statement of their agreement is consistent with the common-law parol evidence rule and with the general theory that the parties' intention should determine the content of their agreement. If the parties intend a writing to be the final embodiment of all they have agreed upon, and intend that all prior understandings are rescinded if not contained in the writing, then all of their prior agreements—whether consistent or contradictory—are inadmissible because they show nothing that is material to a determination of the contract of these parties.

---

[980] *See* Restatement (Second) of Contracts §§ 212, 215, cmt b.

[981] *See, e.g.*, Arthur L. Corbin, Corbin on Contracts, § 543 (1960).

[982] *See, e.g.*, O'Neill v. United States, 50 F.3d 677, 26 UCCR2d 1 (9th Cir. 1995); Moncrief v. Williston Basin Interstate Pipeline Co., 880 F. Supp. 1495, 27 UCCR2d 195 (D. Wyo. 1995). Courts that are willing to consider extrinsic evidence to "create" an ambiguity, which then permits introduction of the parol evidence to the factfinder, are not "plain-meaning" jurisdictions as the term is used here. *See* Vogel v. W.A. Sandri, Inc., 27 UCCR2d 1167 (D. Vt. 1995).

[983] U.C.C. § 2-202(b).

[984] *See* C-Thru Container Corp. v. Midland Mfg. Co., 533 N.W.2d 542 (Iowa 1995); Middletown Concrete Prods., Inc. v. Black Clawson Co., 802 F. Supp. 1135, 20 UCCR2d 815 (D. Del. 1992).

As with the issue of integration,[985] the issue of *how* a court determines whether a writing is a complete and exclusive statement of the parties' agreement—a *"complete* integration"[986]—is the subject of considerable disagreement in both the pre-Code and Code cases. One possible approach, already discussed with respect to integration, is for the judge to consider *all* relevant evidence of the parties' objective intention, including evidence of their negotiations and of the alleged prior agreement. This is the position of Professor Corbin[987] and appears to be the position of the Restatement (Second) of Contracts.[988] While some courts adopt this approach,[989] the focus of most pre-Code and Code cases in resolving this issue is considerably more narrow.

Some pre-Code cases decided the question of whether the parties intended to incorporate all of the terms of the contract by simply looking at the document itself; if it appeared on its face to be complete, that was the end of the inquiry.[990] Despite the strong criticism that this approach has received,[991] it unfortunately appears to survive in a few Code cases.[992] In other pre-Code cases, the issue was determined by ascertaining whether the particular subject involved in the suit was dealt with by the writing,[993] or

---

[985] *See* discussion at § 3.15[B][1], *supra.*

[986] *See* Restatement (Second) of Contracts, § 210 (1981).

[987] Arthur L. Corbin, Corbin on Contracts, § 573 (1960). *See* Interform Co. v. Mitchell, 575 F.2d 1270 (9th Cir. 1978).

[988] Restatement (Second) of Contracts, § 210, cmt. b (1981).

[989] *See, e.g.,* Middletown Concrete Prods., Inc. v. Black Clawson Co., 802 F. Supp. 1135, 20 UCCR2d 815 (D. Del. 1992); Alaska N. Dev., Inc. v. Alyeska Pipeline Serv. Co., 666 P.2d 33, 36 UCCR 1527 (Alaska 1983); H.T. Richeson and Others v. Ben Wood, 163 S.E. 339, 158 Va. 269 (Va. 1932).

[990] *See, e.g.,* Spurgeon v. Buthcher, 192 Cal. App. 2d 198, 13 Cal. Rptr. 354 (1961); Thompson v. Libby, 34 Minn. 374, 26 N.W. 1 (1885). This approach is often called the "four corners" test.

[991] *See, e.g.,* Corbin, *supra* note 901, § 581 (1961); John E. Murray, Jr., Murray on Contracts § 84 (3d ed. 1990) ("such a rule borders on the absurd"); James J. White & Robert Summers, Uniform Commercial Code, § 2-10 (3d ed. 1988) (rule is "ostrich-like" and "question-begging").

[992] *See* Dave Markley Ford, Inc. v. Lair, 565 P.2d 671, 22 UCCR 21 (Okla. 1977) (if examination of "four corners" of document demonstrates writing was intended to be complete and exclusive, parol evidence of consistent terms will not be admitted); In re Tom Woods Used Cars, Inc., (McCloud v. Woods), 23 B.R. 563, 35 UCCR 52 (Bankr. E.D. Tenn. 1982); Philipp Bros. Div. of Englehard Minerals & Chem. Corp. v. El Salto, S.A., 28 UCCR 1280 (S.D.N.Y. 1980). Comment 1 to U.C.C. § 2-202, however, explicitly rejects any presumption that an integrated writing is completely integrated.

[993] *See* Shelton Yacht & Cabana Club, Inc. v. Suto, 150 Conn. 251, 188 A.2d 493 (1963); Salzman v. Maldaver, 315 Mich. 403, 24 N.W.2d 161 (1946); Rogers v. Zielinski, 92 R.I. 479, 170 A.2d 294 (1961).

whether the parol agreement was "collateral" to the writing.[994] These tests also seem to have retained some following in Code cases.[995] Another approach, which conclusively demonstrated completeness to Professor Williston,[996] is to examine the writing for a clause saying that the writing is complete, a so-called merger clause.[997] A final test is whether the parties normally and naturally would have included the prior agreement in the writing.[998] These final two tests appear, in various forms, to have the most vitality in the Code cases and are discussed in the following two sections.

[C]   The Effect of a Merger Clause

The purpose of merger clauses is for the writing to establish its own completeness. A typically worded merger clause might be as follows:

> This contract signed by both parties is intended to be the complete and exclusive agreement of the parties. The parties agree that there are no promises, representations or agreements not included in this contract, and that they are relying solely on the terms set forth in this contract.

Virtually all courts agree that merger clauses are relevant evidence of the parties' intention to completely integrate their agreement.[999] The disputed issue is whether merger clauses are *conclusive* on the question, and, if not, how much weight they should be accorded. Professor Williston took the view that in the absence of fraud or mistake, the parties' statement that the

---

[994] *See* Lefforge v. Rogers, 419 P.2d 625 (Wyo. 1966).

[995] *See, e.g.*, J.W. Birsner v. Bolles, 97 Cal. Rptr. 846, 20 Cal. App. 3d 365, 9 UCCR 1220 (Cal. Ct. App. 1971).

[996] Williston, *supra* note 945, § 633.

[997] *See, e.g.*, J.B. Colt & Co. v. Clay, 216 Ky. 782, 288 S.W. 745 (1926); Valley Refrigeration Co. v. Lange Co., 242 Wis. 466, 8 N.W.2d 294 (1943). Although the presence of such a clause was often *sufficient* for a finding of completeness, its inclusion was generally not *necessary* for a writing to be complete.

[998] *See, e.g.*, Mitchill v. Lath, 247 N.Y. 377, 160 N.E. 646 (1928); O'Brien v. O'Brien, 362 Pa. 66, 66 A.2d 309 (1949).

[999] *See, e.g.*, L.S. Heath & Sons v. AT&T Info. Sys., Inc., 9 F.3d 561, 22 UCCR2d 27 (7th Cir. 1993); Sierra Diesel Injection Servs., Inc. v. Burroughs, Inc., 874 F.2d 653, 8 UCCR2d 617 (9th Cir. 1989); Betaco, Inc. v. Cessna Aircraft Co., 32 F.3d 1126, 24 UCCR2d 718 (7th Cir. 1994).

writing was complete and exclusive barred the introduction of parol evidence.[1000] One can easily find numerous cases adhering to this position.[1001]

A more liberal view, championed by Professor Corbin, argues against reflexive enforcement of merger clauses. Corbin urged judges to look beyond the writing to determine the intent of the parties.[1002] In Corbin's words, since "paper and ink possess no magic power to cause statements of fact to be true when they are actually untrue,"[1003] merger clauses should not automatically be dispositive of the issue of completeness. Although, as with most issues surrounding the parol evidence rule, generalizations are dangerous, Corbin's view seems to have taken hold. Most Code cases consider circumstances in addition to the presence of a merger clause in deciding whether a writing is complete and exclusive,[1004] and a number have explicitly held that although merger clauses are evidence of complete integration, they are not dispositive of the issue.[1005]

Assuming merger clauses are not given conclusive effect, to how much weight are they entitled? Although courts have varied significantly in the weight they attach to merger clauses under apparently similar circumstances,[1006] they generally examine the context surrounding contract formation and the execution of the writing in deciding how much effect to give to the clause. For example, if the parties are of relatively equal bargaining power, the courts are likely to give substantial, and sometimes conclusive,

---

[1000] Williston, *supra* note 945, §§ 631–632.

[1001] *See, e.g.*, Colafrancesco v. Crown Pontiac-GMC, Inc., 485 So. 2d 1131 (Ala. 1986); Mellon Bank Corp. v. First Union Real Estate Equity & Mortgage Invs., 750 F. Supp. 711 (W.D. Pa. 1990); Noble v. Logan Dees-Chevrolet-Buick, Inc., 293 So. 2d 14, 14 UCCR 1107 (Miss. 1974); Wayman v. Amoco Oil Co., 932 F. Supp. 1322, 30 UCCR2d 58 (D. Kan. 1996).

[1002] 3 Corbin, *supra* note 981, § 573–596 (1963).

[1003] Arthur L. Corbin, The Parol Evidence Rule, 53 Yale L.J. 603 (1944).

[1004] *See, e.g.*, Betaco, Inc. v. Cessna Aircraft Co., 32 F.3d 1126, 24 UCCR2d 455 (7th Cir. 1994); Bib Audio-Video Prods. v. Herold Mktg. Assocs., Inc., 517 N.W.2d 68, 24 UCCR2d 455 (Minn. Ct. App. 1995); Sicor Ltd. v. Cetus Corp., 51 F.3d 848, 26 UCCR2d 686 (9th Cir. 1994); Lakeside Bridge & Steel Co. v. Mountain State Constr. Co., Inc., 400 F. Supp. 273, 17 UCCR 917 (E.D. Wis. 1975).

[1005] L.S. Heath & Sons v. AT&T Info. Sys., Inc., 9 F.3d 561, 22 UCCR2d 27 (7th Cir. 1993); Enrico Farms Inc. v. H.J. Heinz Co., 629 F.2d 1304 (9th Cir. 1980); Sierra Diesel Injection Serv., Inc. v. Burroughs Corp., Inc., 874 F.2d 653, 8 UCCR2d 617 (9th Cir. 1989); ARB, Inc. v. E-Sys., Inc., 663 F.2d 189, 30 UCCR 949 (D.C. Cir. 1980).

[1006] *Compare* Franz Chem. Corp. v. Philadelphia Quartz Co., 594 F.2d 146, 26 UCCR 276 (5th Cir. 1979) *with* Sunbury Textile Mills v. Commissioner of Internal Revenue Serv., 585 F.2d 1190, 25 UCCR 642 (3d Cir. 1978).

effect to the merger clause.[1007] If the integration clause is present on a pre-printed form, it is likely to be given less weight than if the terms of the contract are individually negotiated.[1008] Similarly, the conspicuousness of the clause is important in deciding the weight accorded to a merger clause.[1009]

Merger clauses are less likely to be given substantial weight in consumer transactions, especially when the clauses are preprinted and their effect is not explained to the consumer.[1010] In fact, the use of such clauses in consumer transactions may in some cases be unconscionable[1011] or in violation of a state consumer-protection statute.[1012] Conversely, courts are more likely to give weight to a merger clause when large commercial entities are involved.[1013]

[1007] *See, e.g.*, Ray Martin Painting, Inc. v. Ameron, Inc., 638 F. Supp. 768, 1 UCCR2d 713 (D. Kan. 1986) (integration clause was effective to prevent parol evidence since both parties were merchants with equal bargaining power and were aware of clause's significance); Jaskey Fin. & Leasing v. Display Data Corp., 564 F. Supp. 160, 36 UCCR 26 (E.D. Pa. 1983) (parties were of equal bargaining power, and there was no suggestion that plaintiff was unaware of the significance of integration clause); Betaco, Inc. v. Cessna Aircraft, 103 F.3d 1281, 31 UCCR2d 1 (7th Cir. 1996) (integration clause is "strong evidence" of integration between sophisticated parties).

[1008] *See* TransAmerica Oil Corp. v. Lynes, Inc., 723 F.2d 758, 37 UCCR 1076 (10th Cir. 1983); Middletown Concrete Prods. v. Black Clawson Co., 802 F. Supp. 1135, 20 UCCR2d 815 (D. Del. 1992) (preprinted integration clause supported finding that integration clause not controlling); Seibel v. Layne & Bowler, Inc., 56 Or. App. 387, 641 P.2d 668, 33 UCCR 893 (1982); American Research Bureau, Inc. v. E-Sys., Inc., 663 F.2d 189, 30 UCCR 949 (D.D.C. 1980) (court found that contract's exhaustive detail, settled upon after prolonged negotiations, supported giving merger clause effect).

[1009] *See, e.g.*, Seibel v. Layne & Bowler, Inc., 56 Or. App. 387, 641 P.2d 668, 33 UCCR 893 (1982) (merger clause ineffective because its inconspicuousness provided little or no evidence of the parties' intentions).

[1010] *See, e.g.*, Carpetland, U.S.A. v. Payne, 536 N.E.2d 306, 8 UCCR2d 942 (Ind. Ct. App. 1989); Bob Robertson, Inc. v. Webster, 679 S.W.2d 683, 40 UCCR 810 (Tex. Ct. App. 1984); Seibel v. Layne & Bowler, Inc., 56 Or. App. 387, 641 P.2d 668, 33 UCCR 893 (1982). *Contra*, Jordan v. Doonan Truck & Equip., Inc., 552 P.2d 881, 220 Kan. 431, 19 UCCR 1297 (Kan. 1976); In re Tom Woods Used Cars, Inc., 23 B.R. 563, 35 UCCR 52 (Bankr. E.D. Tenn. 1981).

[1011] *See* Macintosh, "When Are Merger Clauses Unconscionable?," 64 Den. L. Rev. 529 (1988); Seibel v. Layne & Bowler, 56 Or. App. 387, 641 P.2d 668, 33 UCCR 893 (1982) (unconscionable to permit inconspicuous merger clause to exclude evidence of express oral warranty).

[1012] *See* § 9.02[B], *infra*.

[1013] *See, e.g.*, Binks Mfg. Co. v. National Presto Indus., Inc., 709 F.2d 1109, 36 UCCR 14 (7th Cir. 1983); Empire Gas Corp. v. UPG, Inc., 781 S.W.2d 148, 11 UCCR2d 453 (Mo. Ct. App. 1989). A recent case in which many of these factors came into play is Betaco, Inc. v. Cessna Aircraft Co., 32 F.3d 1126, 24 UCCR2d 718 (7th Cir. 1994). In this case, the

Courts unwilling to give a merger clause conclusive effect will often attempt to determine whether the document's content is consistent with the merger clause's declaration of completeness and exclusivity. Thus, if a writing containing a merger clause omits important terms that are usually present in similar contracts, the court may find that the document is not a complete and exclusive statement of the agreement, despite the merger clause.[1014] For example, in *L.S. Heath & Sons v. AT&T Information Systems*,[1015] the Seventh Circuit found that AT&T's "Master Agreement" disclaiming all warranties was not complete simply because it contained a merger clause. The omission of important terms such as prices, products, services, and software configurations was sufficient to reverse a trial court's summary judgment excluding evidence of additional warranty terms. Likewise, when a contract consisted of three concurrently executed writings, each of which contained a merger clause, none of the writings could be the entire agreement of the parties.[1016]

Behavior subsequent to contract formation that is inconsistent with a merger clause's statement of completeness and exclusivity can influence the weight the court accords to the clause. In *Sierra Diesel Injection Services, Inc. v. Burroughs Corp., Inc.*,[1017] the court, in refusing to give summary judgment on the basis of a disclaimer of warranties and a merger clause, noted that plaintiff's assertions of prior oral warranties was consistent with defendant's numerous efforts to remedy alleged defects in the goods.

There are Code cases, however, in which merger clauses are accorded very heavy, if not conclusive, weight despite the presence of other factors.[1018] For example, in *Franz Chemical Corp. v. Philadelphia Quartz Co.*,[1019] the Fifth Circuit considered only the presence of a merger clause in holding that the parties intended the writing to be a completely integrated agreement. Similarly, in *General Aviation, Inc. v. Cessna Aircraft Co.*,[1020] the Sixth

---

Seventh Circuit gave effect to a merger clause, despite the fact that it was preprinted, because it was clearly written and conspicuous and both parties were sophisticated in business matters, especially in the field of aviation.

[1014] *See* Rajala v. Allied Corp., 66 B.R. 582, 2 UCCR2d 203 (D. Kan. 1986).

[1015] 9 F.3d 561, 22 UCCR2d 27 (7th Cir. 1993).

[1016] Middletown Concrete Prods. v. Black Clawson Co., 802 F. Supp. 1135, 20 UCCR2d 815 (D. Del. 1992). This does not mean, however, that an operative merger clause cannot encompass writings other than the one containing the merger clause.

[1017] 651 F. Supp. 1371, 3 UCCR2d 538 (D. Nev. 1987).

[1018] *See, e.g.*, General Aviation, Inc. v. Cessna Aircraft Co., 915 F.2d 1038, 14 UCCR2d 73 (6th Cir. 1990); MPM Hawaiian, Inc. v. World Square, 666 P.2d 622, 4 Haw. App. 341, 36 UCCR 1543 (Haw. Ct. App. 1983); RedFern Meats, Inc. v. Hertz Corp., 215 S.E.2d 10, 134 Ga. App. 381, 17 UCCR 82 (Ga. Ct. App. 1975).

[1019] 594 F.2d 146, 26 UCCR 276 (5th Cir. 1979).

[1020] 915 F.2d 1038, 14 UCCR2d 73 (6th Cir. 1990).

Circuit looked only to the presence of a merger clause in affirming summary judgment for a manufacturer and excluding evidence that manufacturer had orally agreed to continue supplying planes under a distributorship contract.[1021]

Although the absence of a merger clause does not prevent a finding that a writing is complete and exclusive,[1022] a number of courts have cited the absence of a merger clause as a factor weighing against a finding of complete integration.[1023] As a result, it is always advisable to include a well-drafted and conspicuous merger clause to prevent assertions of parol agreements.

[D]   The "Comment 3" Test

In deciding the issue of a writing's completeness, courts at common law often considered whether the parties would have naturally included the asserted parol agreement in the writing.[1024] A variant of this test appears at Comment 3 to section 2-202:

> Under paragraph (b) [to section 2-202] consistent additional terms, not reduced to writing, may be proved unless the court finds that the writing was intended by the parties as a complete and exclusive statement of the terms. If the additional terms are such that, if agreed upon, they would certainly have been included in the document in the view of the court, then evidence of their alleged making must be kept from the trier of fact.[1025]

[1021] *See also* Earman Oil Co., Inc. v. Burroughs Corp., 625 F.2d 1291, 30 UCCR 849 (5th Cir 1980) (because other courts had ruled identical merger clause operative to exclude parol evidence, court was bound to do so without consideration of particular circumstances of contract).

[1022] *See* Lee v. Joseph E. Seagram & Sons, Inc., 413 F. Supp. 693, 19 UCCR 1043 (S.D.N.Y. 1976); Empire Gas Corp. v. UPG, Inc., 781 S.W.2d 148, 11 UCCR2d 453 (Mo. Ct. App. 1989).

[1023] *See* Rajala v. Allied Corp., 66 B.R. 582, 2 UCCR2d 203 (D. Kan. 1986); Computerized Radiological Servs., Inc. v. Syntex Corp., 595 F. Supp. 1495, 40 UCCR 49 (E.D.N.Y. 1984); Industrial Plants Corp. v. Sicherman, 156 B.R. 988, 22 UCCR2d 675 (Bankr. N.D. Ohio 1993); Hawaii Leasing v. Klein, 658 P.2d 343, 35 UCCR 1365 (Haw. Ct. App. 1983); Sandlun v. Shoemaker, 617 A.2d 1330, 421 Pa. Super. 353, 20 UCCR2d 432 (Pa. Super. Ct. 1992).

[1024] *See* E. Allan Farnsworth, II Farnsworth on Contracts, § 7.3 at 208 (1990).

[1025] U.C.C. § 2-202, Official Comment 3.

Numerous courts have referred to this test in deciding whether to admit evidence of consistent additional terms under section 2-202.[1026]

A few comments about the test are necessary. First, the test appears to adopt a higher standard for the exclusion of evidence than the common-law test.[1027] The common-law test is stated in terms of whether the parties would "normally and naturally" have included the asserted parol agreement in the writing;[1028] the test under Comment 3 is whether the parties would *certainly* have done so. Second, the Code does not describe the method by which a judge is to determine whether the parties would "certainly" have included the oral agreement in the writing. At common law, deciding whether the parties would have naturally included the parol agreement in the writing was often a very constrained exercise. It frequently consisted of comparing the subject matter of the writing to the subject matter of the oral agreement to determine if they were sufficiently closely related that the oral agreement would ordinarily be found in the writing.[1029] Given the Code's emphasis on the bargain of the parties *in fact*, the inquiry should not be so limited. The judge should consider all of the circumstances surrounding the contract to decide if *these parties, situated as they were at the time of the writing,* would certainly have included the parol agreement in the writing. This would include, for example, consideration of evidence of possible explanations as to why the parol agreement was omitted. The judge should not simply ask whether such terms would ordinarily be in the writing or whether reasonable people would include them in the writing, but whether he or she believes that the parties to *this contract* under *these circumstances* would certainly have done so. The test is essentially one of credibility.

Courts have varied in their application of the Comment 3 test. Some have concluded, with little or no analysis, that a parol agreement would have certainly been included in the writing.[1030] In a number of cases, however,

---

[1026] *See, e.g.*, Middletown Concrete Prods. v. Black Clawson Co., 802 F. Supp. 1135, 20 UCCR2d 835 (D. Del. 1992); Betaco, Inc. v. Cessna Aircraft Co., 32 F.3d 1126, 24 UCCR2d 718 (7th. Cir. 1994); Camargo Cadillac Co. v. Garfield Enters., Inc., 445 N.E.2d 1141, 35 UCCR 749 (Ohio Ct. App. 1982); American Research Bureau, Inc. v. E-Sys., 663 F.2d 189, 30 UCCR 949 (D.D.C. 1980); Rajala v. Allied Corp., 66 B.R. 582, 2 UCCR2d 203 (D. Kan. 1986).

[1027] *See* John E. Murray, Jr., Murray on Contracts § 84 at 395 (3d ed. 1990).

[1028] Samuel L. Williston, 4 Williston on Contracts § 638 (1961).

[1029] *See* Mitchill v. Lath, 247 N.Y. 377, 160 N.E. 646 (1928); John E. Murray, Jr., Murray on Contracts § 84 at 391 (3d ed. 1990).

[1030] *See, e.g.*, Southern Concrete Servs., Inc. v. Mableton Contractors, Inc., 407 F. Supp. 581, 19 UCCR 79 (N.D. Ga. 1975) (cursory reference to Comment 3 in footnote); Dave Markley Ford, Inc. v. Lair, 565 P.2d 671, 22 UCCR 21 (Okla. 1977); Sky Acres Auction Servs., Inc. v. Wearever-Proctor-Silex Corp., 1987 U.S. Dist. LEXIS 5328 (S.D.N.Y. 1987).

courts have gone beyond simply concluding that the Comment 3 test is (or is not) satisfied, and have examined the individual circumstances surrounding the transaction.[1031] A few cases have engaged in thorough discussions of the circumstances surrounding the contract in deciding whether the Comment 3 test was satisfied. For example, in *ARB, Inc. v. E-Systems*,[1032] the court, in deciding that an alleged oral agreement limiting the buyer's remedy of cover would certainly have been put in the writing, considered the prolonged negotiations, the importance of the cover remedy, the length of the writing, and the detail present in the writing. Similarly, in *Betaco, Inc. v. Cessna Aircraft Co.*,[1033] the Seventh Circuit refused to allow evidence of an alleged oral agreement as to the range of an airplane. In concluding that the oral agreement would certainly have been put in the writing, the court discussed the prolonged negotiations leading up to the contract, the importance of the term to the buyer, and the specificity of the writing on the subject of range.[1034] These latter cases represent the proper approach in applying the Comment 3 test for complete integration.[1035]

Traditional exceptions to the parol evidence rule continue to apply under the Code.[1036] Reformation of a writing for mistake can be obtained despite the parol evidence rule.[1037] A typical case for reformation is when

---

[1031] *See, e.g.*, Snyder v. Herbert Greenbaum & Assocs., Inc., 380 A.2d 618, 38 Md. App. 144, 22 UCCR 1104 (Md. Ct. App. 1977) (because seller had to engage in substantial preparatory conduct prior to performance, parties certainly would have included unilateral cancellation right in writing); Luria Bros. & Co., Inc. v. Pielet Bros. Scrap Iron & Metal, Inc., 600 F.2d 103, 26 UCCR 1081 (7th Cir. 1979) (size of contract makes it unlikely that parties would not have put condition in contract making seller's performance conditional upon receipt of goods from supplier); Norwest Bank Billings v. Murnion, 684 P.2d 1067, 210 Mont. 417, 38 UCCR 1509 (Mont. 1984) (nature of promise and past dealings between the parties make it likely term would have been included in the writing).

[1032] 663 F.2d 189, 30 UCCR 949 (D.C. Cir. 1980).

[1033] 32 F.3d 1126, 24 UCCR2d 718 (7th Cir. 1994).

[1034] *See also* Mid Continent Cabinetry v. George Koch, 1991 U.S. Dist. LEXIS 10644 (D. Kan. 1991) (court considered the nature of the parties and their relationship, the detailed nature of the writing, the cautious and prudent nature of the negotiations, and the fact that one party continually insisted that terms be put in writing).

[1035] It was suggested in the first edition of this book that the Comment 3 test was intended to be a test of credibility rather than a test of whether a document was completely integrated. R. Nordstrom, Law of Sales, § 53 at 168 (1970). This is an appropriate use of the Comment 3 test, and perhaps of the parol evidence rule as a whole. However, because of its similarity to a common-law test for complete integration ("normally and naturally included in the writing") and because the test immediately follows a discussion of completeness and exclusivity in Comment 3, it appears that the drafters intended it to be a test of complete integration. This is the manner in which it has been used by the courts.

[1036] Norwest Bank Billings v. Murnion, 684 P.2d 1067, 210 Mont. 417, 38 UCCR 1509 (Mont. 1984).

[1037] *Luria Bros. & Co., Inc., supra* note 1031.

the parties have reached agreement, but the writing does not accurately reflect that agreement. For example, assume the parties orally agreed to sell, and buy, a horse for $500. The writing that followed, however, substituted "cow" for "horse." The parol evidence rule ought not to prevent one party from proving the actual bargain, and most courts agree.[1038] The problem becomes more difficult when the prior agreement was intended by one of the parties to attain an objective known to the other party, but performance of the terms of the writing will not accomplish the objective. Suppose, for example, a buyer was constructing a building and believed that fifteen tons of steel beams would be sufficient to complete construction, and the parties entered into a writing calling for the purchase and sale of fifteen tons of steel beams. When it turns out that twenty tons were needed, reformation would not be granted even if the seller knew of the buyer's belief. The *agreement* was for fifteen tons of steel; the buyer's *objective* was not part of that agreement. Relief in this case, if it were granted at all, would be based on grounds of mutual or unilateral mistake or frustration of purpose, not reformation.[1039] In other situations, the answer is not that easy; objectives blur into the bargaining process and arguably become part of the agreement. We leave any attempt to expand these ideas to others, in part because they would result in a treatise, as they did for Professor Palmer.[1040]

Proof of fraud is generally not subject to the parol evidence rule.[1041] There is some authority, however, that a sufficiently detailed and conspicuous merger clause stating that there have been no prior representations and that none are being relied upon will bar evidence of even fraudulent oral representations.[1042] Finally, proof of oral conditions precedent to contract formation are not affected by the parol evidence rule.[1043]

[1038] Not all reformation cases deal with a mistake by the scrivener. Reformation has been allowed when there was no error in the writing, but the parties believed the words they used had a different meaning—as, for example, when a writing contains a legal description that the parties believed was correct but that did not describe the property that was the subject of the contract. For an excellent discussion, *see* George Palmer, The Law of Restitution, Chapter 13 (1978).

[1039] *See* discussion in E. Allan Farnsworth, II Farnsworth on Contracts, § 7.5 at 219–220 (1990); Restatement (Second) of Contracts, § 153 (1981).

[1040] George Palmer, The Law of Restitution (1978).

[1041] Latham & Assocs., Inc. v. William Raveis Real Estate, Inc., 589 A.2d 337, 218 Conn. 297, 14 UCCR2d 394 (1991); King Indus., Inc. v. Worlco Data Sys., Inc., 736 F. Supp. 114, 11 UCCR2d 1146 (E.D. Va. 1989).

[1042] *See* Danann Realty Corp. v. Harris, 5 N.Y.2d 317, 157 N.E.2d 597 (N.Y. 1959); Grumman Allied Indus., Inc. v. Rohr Indus., 748 F.2d 729 (2d Cir. 1984).

[1043] Tropical Leasing, Inc. v. Fiermonte Chevrolet, Inc., 439 N.Y.S.2d 566, 80 A.D.2d 467, 31 UCCR 827 (N.Y. App. Div. 1981); InfoComp, Inc. v. Electra Prods., Inc., 103 F.3d 267, 31 UCCR2d 413 (3d Cir. 1996), *remanded on issue of damages*, 109 F.3d 902, 32

[E] Proposed Revisions and the Parol Evidence Rule

The proposed revisions to Article 2 make a number of changes to section 2-202. Despite the changes, however, many of the difficulties discussed in the preceding sections remain unresolved. The revised section 2-202 reads as follows:

> (a) Terms on which confirmatory records of the parties agree, or which are otherwise set forth in a record intended by the parties as a final expression of their agreement with respect to the included terms, may not be contradicted by evidence of any prior agreement or of a contemporaneous oral agreement. However, terms in such a record may be supplemented by evidence of:

> (1) noncontradictory [consistent] additional terms unless the court finds that:
> (A) The record was intended as a complete and exclusive statement of the terms of the agreement, or
> (B) The terms if agreed upon by the parties would certainly have been included in the record; and
> (2) course of performance, usage of trade, or course of dealing.

> (b) Terms in a record may be explained by evidence from course of performance, usage of trade, or course of performance without a preliminary determination by the court that the language used is ambiguous. Terms in a record may also be explained by evidence from the surrounding circumstances and other sources as determined by a court.[1044]

The proposed section 2-202(b) states that terms may be explained by evidence from the surrounding circumstances and other sources "as determined by a court." An earlier draft stated explicitly that terms may be explained by *"credible* evidence."[1045] The prior draft was a welcome change and would have made clear that the parol evidence rule is irrelevant to issues

---

UCCR2d 97 (3d Cir. 1997). This exception does not apply, however, where the evidence is offered to show that a party's *duties* under an already existing contract are conditional. *See* Luria Bros. & Co., Inc. v. Pielet Bros. Scrap Iron & Metal, Inc., 600 F.2d 103, 26 UCCR 1081 (7th Cir. 1979). It also may not apply where the asserted condition to the effectiveness of the writing *contradicts* a term of the writing. *See* discussion in E. Allan Farnsworth, II Farnsworth on Contracts, § 7.4 at 215.

[1044] The American Law Institute, Uniform Commercial Code, Revised Article 2, Sales, Council Draft No. 4, December 1, 1998, § 2-202.

[1045] National Conference of Commissioners on Uniform State Laws, Revision of Uniform Commercial Code, Article 2 Sales (Draft for Discussion Only), March 1, 1998, § 2-202.

of interpretation so long as the evidence offered meets the foundational test of credibility.[1046] It cannot be determined whether proffered oral evidence contradicts a term in a writing unless it is first determined what the term *means*, and all relevant credible evidence should be considered on this issue. The present draft would permit judges to continue to apply discredited doctrine such as the "plain-meaning" rule, and is an unfortunate change from the earlier draft.

Another change, of uncertain effect, is the alteration of the present subsection (b) which now permits the introduction of "consistent additional terms" unless the court finds the writing to be complete and exclusive. The proposed revisions would replace the word "consistent" with the word "noncontradictory." How "consistent" differs from "noncontradictory" is not made clear by either the text or the commentary. Furthermore, the proposed revision to section 2-202 incorporates the Comment 3 test, discussed previously, into the text of the section itself. More important, it does so as an *alternative* method by which evidence of a noncontradictory additional term can be excluded. That is, under the revised section 2-202, evidence of a noncontradictory additional term is barred if *either* (1) the court finds that the parties intended a record as a complete and exclusive statement of the terms of the agreement, or (2) the additional term would certainly have been included in the record. As discussed earlier,[1047] the Comment 3 test has heretofore been understood as simply *one* way of determining whether the parties intended the writing to be complete and exclusive, not as a separate hurdle which the evidence must overcome to be admitted. If the proposed revision is adopted, the admission of consistent additional terms may actually become marginally more difficult than under the present section.[1048]

[F] Conclusion

The Code's parol evidence rule, while clearly intended to make the introduction of extrinsic evidence easier,[1049] has not swept away the con-

---

[1046] *Id.* § 2-202, Note 2. ("If both parties intend the record to be a final and exclusive statement of all terms evidence of non-contradictory terms will be excluded but credible evidence relevant to interpretation will not").

[1047] *See* § 3.15[D], *supra*.

[1048] This is because a judge could find that although the writing was not intended by the parties as a complete and exclusive statement of the terms of their agreement, the oral term would certainly have been included in the writing if made.

[1049] Anderson & Nafziger v. G.T. Newcomb, Inc., 100 Idaho 175, 595 P.2d 709, 27 UCCR 21 (1979); Killion v. Buran Equip. Co., 1979 WL 30096, 27 UCCR 970 (Cal. Ct. App. 1979).

fusion and inconsistency that accompanied the common-law rule. Many of the controversies surrounding the common-law rule have survived and flourished under the Code. The ability of some judges to manipulate the rule to reach whatever result they choose also remains, while at the same time other judges feel constrained by the rule to reach results they recognize are unfair. The rule will continue to confound law students and test the mettle of hardened practitioners. Nonetheless, it provides a framework for resolving the clash of the values of certainty and predictability, on one hand, and the search for the bargain *in fact* of the parties on the other.

CHAPTER 4

WARRANTIES OF THE SELLER

§ 4.01   OVERVIEW OF THE CODE'S WARRANTY PROVISIONS

Article 2 of the Code contains several sections dealing with the warranties of a seller. These sections are central to the Code and the seller's obligations with respect to the goods. A brief overview introduces detailed discussions of each of these sections.

First, the seller warrants certain things about the title to the goods sold. He warrants that the title is good, that the transfer is rightful, and that there are no outstanding security interests or liens unknown to the buyer.[1] This assures the buyer that if title does fail, either wholly or partially, there is a cause of action against the seller.

Second, there are three sections defining the scope of warranties of quality. The first section provides for express warranties arising from affirmations of fact, promises, descriptions, samples, or models.[2] The next two establish implied warranties—warranties that accompany a sale just because it is a sale of goods. The first, the implied warranty of merchantability,[3] applies only to merchants who deal in goods of the kind involved in the transaction. The second, the implied warranty of fitness for a particular purpose,[4] applies both to merchants and nonmerchants, but only if the seller has reason to know the particular purpose for which the goods will be used and that the buyer is relying on the seller's skill or judgment to select or furnish suitable goods. These sections assure the buyer that if the goods are below the contractual standard of quality, the buyer will have an action against the seller for breach of warranty.

Third, these warranties are not limited to the immediate buyer. The Code provides to the states three increasingly inclusive alternatives that permit third parties to benefit from a seller's warranties.[5] Some states have further modified these alternatives.[6]

Fourth, warranties can be disclaimed or excluded by the seller. Express warranties are excluded by not making them; implied warranties may be excluded by certain specific language which, if in writing, must be conspicuous.[7] It is, therefore, possible under the Code for sellers to limit their contractual liability—but they must do so under conditions that make it

---

[1] U.C.C. § 2-312.

[2] U.C.C. § 2-313

[3] U.C.C. § 2-314.

[4] U.C.C. § 2-315.

[5] U.C.C. § 2-318.

[6] *See* § 4.09, *infra.*

[7] U.C.C. § 2-316.

reasonable for the court to conclude that the exclusion or modification was understood by the buyer.

Fifth, the parties may agree, under certain circumstances, to expand or limit the remedies available under the Code for default.[8] The Code requires, however, that the buyer be provided with a fair quantum of remedy, and limitations that do not do so will be struck as unconscionable.[9] Further, if a limited remedy "fails of its essential purpose," the general remedy provisions of the Code again become available.[10] Although these sections generally support freedom of contract by allowing the parties to craft their own bargain, cutting across these provisions are the Code concepts of good faith and unconscionability, which act to limit this freedom.

I. THE WARRANTY OF TITLE

§ 4.02   THE BASIC CODE SECTION

The basic title warranty of the Code is contained in section 2-312(1). This section provides:

> (1) Subject to subsection (2) there is in a contract for sale a warranty by the seller that
>   (a) the title conveyed shall be good, and its transfer rightful; and
>   (b) the goods shall be delivered free from any security interest or other lien or encumbrance of which the buyer at the time of contracting has no knowledge.[11]

Subsection (2) provides for the exclusion or modification of the warranty of title, and subsection (3) requires merchants to sell goods free from the claims of third persons. Both are discussed later in the text.[12]

Section 2-312(1) is the Code section most often relied on to determine the existence and scope of the warranty of title.[13] The section need not, however, be the exclusive subsection for these determinations. Section 2-313—dealing with express warranties—may also be the basis for a warranty

---

[8] U.C.C. § 2-719.

[9] U.C.C. § 2-719, Official Comment 1.

[10] U.C.C. § 2-719(1)(a).

[11] U.C.C. § 2-312.

[12] See §§ 4.02[B], 4.02[C] infra.

[13] See, e.g., First Valley Leasing, Inc. v. Goushy, 795 F. Supp. 693, 19 UCCR2d 1002 (D.N.J. 1992); Maroone Chevrolet, Inc. v. Nordstrom, 587 So. 2d 514, 15 UCCR2d 759 (Fla. Dist. Ct. App. 1991); Camara v. Hill, 157 Vt. 156, 596 A.2d 349, 15 UCCR2d 1216 (1991).

of title.[14] Section 2-313 provides that promises or affirmations of fact relating to the goods or descriptions of the goods create express warranties that the goods shall conform to the promises, affirmations, or descriptions. If the seller affirms her ownership and promises that she is, or will at the time of sale be, the owner, or if she describes the goods as belonging to her, she has made an express warranty under section 2-313. In most instances it will not be necessary to rely upon section 2-313; section 2-312 will suffice for the buyer. Nevertheless, the two sections can be used to buttress each other and to support the buyer's claims of breach.[15]

The section 2-312 warranty is given by the "seller." Occasionally, cases have arisen in which the court has had to determine the meaning of "seller." In one unusual case, FBI agents, who sold Vehicle Identification Numbers and blank motor vehicle titles to suspects in a sting operation, were not liable as sellers when the suspects used these same items to sell stolen cars to innocent purchasers.[16] Another court held that a bank that retained title for security purposes when financing a sale from *A* to *B* was not a seller when it turned out later that *A*'s title was defective.[17] In another case, however, a person who provided funds to the buyer for the purchase of a car, and received a portion of the profit when the car was resold, was determined to be a seller for purposes of the title warranty.[18]

The majority of courts have held that section 2-312(1) permits recovery only against the buyer's *immediate* seller.[19] In doing so, they have ignored

---

[14] For cases recognizing an express warranty of title, see In re West Side Community Hosp., Inc., 112 B.R. 243, 12 UCCR2d 674 (N.D. Ill. 1990); Hudson v. Gaines, 199 Ga. App. 70, 403 S.E.2d 852, 14 UCCR2d 726 (1991); Goosic Constr. Co. v. City Nat'l Bank of Crete, 196 Neb. 86, 241 N.W.2d 251, 19 UCCR 117 (1976); Itoh v. Kimi Sales, Ltd., 74 Misc. 2d 402, 345 N.Y.S.2d 416, 13 UCCR 64 (Civ. Ct. 1973).

[15] See CIT Fin. Servs., Inc. v. Gott, 5 Kan. App. 2d, 615 P.2d 774, 29 UCCR 1395 (1980); Jefferson v. Jones, 286 Md. 544, 408 A.2d 1036, 27 UCCR 1174 (Md. Ct. App. 1979).

[16] Farmers Coop. Elevator Co. v. Union State Bank, 409 N.W.2d 178, 4 UCCR2d 1 (Iowa 1987).

[17] Bank of Nova Scotia v. Equitable Fin. Management, Inc., 882 F.2d 81, 9 UCCR2d 1 (3d Cir. 1989).

[18] Mercer v. Braziel, 746 P.2d 702, 4 UCCR2d 1370 (Okla. Ct. App. 1987).

[19] Crook Motor Co. v. Goolsby, 703 F. Supp. 511, 8 UCCR2d 363 (N.D. Miss. 1988); Universal C.I.T. Credit Corp. v. State Farm Mut. Ins. Co., 493 S.W.2d 385, 12 UCCR 648 (Mo. Ct. App. 1973); First State Bank & Trust Co. of Shawnee v. Wholesale Enter., Inc., 883 P.2d 207, 25 UCCR2d 677 (Okla. Ct. App. 1994). *But see* Hicks v. Thomas, 516 So. 2d 1344, 6 UCCR2d 105 (Miss. 1987); Mitchell v. Webb, 591 S.W.2d 547, 28 UCCR 58 (Tex. Ct. App. 1979). This result has been criticized as prompting duplicative litigation. Thomas D. Crandall et al., I Uniform Commercial Code § 7.28 (1993). With modern joinder rules, however, it is unlikely that more than one lawsuit would be necessary. *See* De Wit v. Firstar Corp., 879 F. Supp. 947 (N.D. Iowa 1995). It is true, however, that it would be more

section 2-318, the Code section dealing with third-party beneficiaries of warranties. Section 2-318 does not distinguish between the warranty of title and other warranties. Even if section 2-318 were applied, however, in most states the title warranty would not extend beyond the immediate buyer because most states have adopted Alternative A of section 2-318.[20] In one case, a bank that had acquired a car after foreclosing on a security interest tried unsuccessfully to overcome the lack of contractual privity with the seller by arguing a theory of subrogation to the warranty rights of the buyer (who was the debtor from whom the bank acquired the car in foreclosure).[21]

[A]   Warranty That Title Is Good and the Transfer Is Rightful

The first Code warranty of title is that "title shall be good and its transfer rightful."[22] The meaning of "and its transfer rightful" is obscure, and there are virtually no cases that discuss its scope. It appears from both the section's language and the Comments that "rightful transfer" is a requirement imposed on the seller *in addition to* the obligation to deliver good title, but the nature of the requirement is not clear. Evidently, the drafters had in mind a situation in which the title was good but where the seller had some agreement with a third party that made a transfer of the title wrongful and that, as a result, exposed the buyer to potential litigation to protect his title. This reading is confirmed by *Sumner v. Fel-Air, Inc.*,[23] the only case discussing the applicability of the "rightful transfer" portion of the statute.

In *Sumner*, the seller sold an airplane to the buyer. The seller was not the owner of the plane; rather, at the time of the sale, he was a lessee with an option to purchase and had no authorization from the true owner to sell the plane. However, under section 2-403 of the Code, the seller had been "entrusted" with the goods by the true owner and, therefore, had the ability

---

efficient to simply permit the buyer to sue the person first responsible for the breach of the warranty of title.

   [20] Alternative A of U.C.C. § 2-318 extends a seller's warranty to anyone who is in the family or household of his buyer and who is injured in person by a breach of warranty. Only if the chain of title could be considered part of the "distributive chain" might recovery against a remote seller be available under Comment 3 to section 2-318. *See* §§ 4.09[A], 4.09[B] *infra*. Obviously, personal injury will rarely, if ever, result in personal injury. The proposed revisions to Article 2 explicitly provide that the warranty of title extends to any remote buyer or transferee that may reasonably be expected to buy the goods and that suffers damage from breach of the warranty.

   [21] First State Bank & Trust Co. of Shawnee v. Wholesale Enter., Inc., 883 P.2d 207, 25 UCCR2d 677 (Okla. Ct. App. 1994).

   [22] U.C.C. § 2-312(1)(a).

   [23] 680 P.2d 1109, 38 UCCR 91 (Alaska 1984).

to transfer good title to a buyer in the ordinary course of business.[24] When the buyer found out that the seller was not the true owner, the buyer sued the seller for breach of the section 2-312 warranty. The seller argued that as a result of section 2-403, he had transferred good title to the buyer and could not be held liable for breach.

The court held that the seller had transferred good title as a result of section 2-403, but the transfer was not rightful and therefore there was a breach of the warranty of title. The court said that even though the buyer had received good title, the true owner's interest in the airplane was sufficient to cast a substantial shadow on the title, which was enough for a breach of the warranty that the transfer of the goods was rightful. To the argument that section 2-403 resulted in good title in the buyer as a matter of law, the court responded that to dispel the shadow on title created by the seller's lack of ownership, the buyer would have had to "become an expert on the UCC" and determine (1) that the seller had been "entrusted" with the airplane; (2) that the seller was a merchant who deals in airplanes; and (3) that the buyer qualified as a buyer in the ordinary course of business.[25]

The decision of the court is correct. While it may turn out, after protracted litigation, that the buyer received good title, this may be far from clear at the time that the buyer discovers the potential adverse interest in the goods. Furthermore, the ultimate determination of good title may be months, or even years, away. The buyer should, in this situation, be able to cancel the sale immediately and receive a return of his money.

Sumner held that a violation of section 2-312 does not require that the title ultimately prove to be defective, so long as there is a "substantial shadow" on the title created by a wrongful transfer. In other contexts, a similar standard has been adopted by courts to determine whether the title that has been delivered is, in fact, "good."[26] The factual patterns differ

---

[24] Section 2-403 provides:

> Any entrusting of possession of goods to a merchant who deals in goods of that kind gives him the power to transfer all rights of the entruster to a buyer in the ordinary course of business.

[25] 680 P.2d at 1113, 38 UCCR at 99.

[26] In fact, the court in *Sumner* suggested that it could have ignored the "rightful transfer" portion of the statute and nonetheless found a violation of good title:

> Even if we decide to ignore AS 45.02.0312's [2-312's] intimation that a "wrongful" transfer of title breaches the warranty which that section contains, we would be loath to conclude that a breach did not occur in this case.

680 P.2d at 1114, 38 UCCR at 100. This raises the issue as to whether the "rightful transfer"

considerably, but the issue is the same. A third party has presented a claim to the goods, and there is a genuine dispute as to its validity. Under these circumstances, what must a buyer show to recover for a breach of the good title warranty?

A leading case on this issue is *Jefferson v. Jones*.[27] In this case, the buyer purchased a motorcycle from the seller, which the police seized as stolen when the serial number did not match the certificate of title. The buyer sued the police in replevin and conversion and recovered the motorcycle. The buyer then sued the seller for breach of the warranty of good title to recover his expenses in regaining possession of the motorcycle.

The seller defended the action on the basis that there had been no proof of title paramount to the buyer and, therefore, there was no breach of the warranty of good title. The court rejected this argument. It emphasized the language of Comment 1—that a buyer should have assurance that he will not be exposed to a lawsuit in order to protect his title—and held that a breach of the warranty of title did not require proof that a buyer's title was subject to a superior or paramount title in a third person.[28] Whether or not a buyer is ultimately successful in defending his title after protracted litigation should not be the standard for breach.[29]

The court also recognized that the seller should not be a guarantor against spurious or frivolous claims. According to the court, "[a]ll that a purchaser should expect from a seller of property is that he be protected from colorable claims against his title and not from all claims."[30] For the seller to be liable for a claim made against the buyer's title, the claim must be "colorable, nonspurious, and of such a nature as to produce a reasonable

---

portion of the section is simply surplusage. As mentioned in the text, the language of the statute suggests otherwise. It may be that the idea of "rightful transfer" was meant to capture situations, like *Sumner*, where the transfer itself, rather than extrinsic facts, creates a cloud on title. *See* U.C.C. § 2-312, Official Comment 1 ("transferred to him also in a rightful manner so that he will not be exposed to a lawsuit in order to protect it"). The "rightful transfer" portion of the warranty may also cover situations where the seller knows of a frivolous claim on the property prior to sale, but does not disclose it to the buyer, and the buyer is later forced to defend against the frivolous claim.

[27] 408 A.2d 1036, 27 UCCR 1174 (Md. Ct. App. 1979).

[28] *Id.* at 1039, 27 UCCR at 1178.

[29] This is made explicit in the text or the proposed revisions to Article 2. U.C.C. Section 2-402(1) provides that the seller warrants that "the title conveyed is good and its transfer is rightful and does not, because of any colorable claim to or interest in the goods, unreasonably expose the buyer to litigation." The American Law Institute, Uniform Commercial Code Revised Article 2, Sales, Council Draft No. 4 (December 1, 1998) (hereinafter Council Draft).

[30] 408 A.2d at 1040, 27 UCCR at 1179.

doubt as to the title's validity."[31] A "colorable" claim, said the court, is one which is "of [such] a substantial nature that it may subject the buyer to serious litigation."[32] Based on this standard, the court found for the buyer in *Jefferson.*

The approach of the *Jefferson* court has been adopted in a multitude of cases,[33] and it is now clear that the warranty of good title can be breached without proof of paramount title in a third party.[34] A breach of the warranty of good title has been found when vehicles have been seized by the police,[35] the Department of Public Safety,[36] and an insurance company.[37] In *Trial v. McCoy,*[38] the court found a breach by the seller when police seized an antique gun as stolen, even though the buyer did not prove that a third party actually possessed paramount title to the gun. Even if the goods are returned to the buyer or good title is ultimately established in the buyer, a breach will still occur so long as the claim against which the buyer had to defend

---

[31] *Id.* at 1041, 27 UCCR at 1181.

[32] The court said that this issue was a mixed question of law and fact. If a factual dispute as to the claim exists, or if reasonable minds could differ as to whether the claim is colorable, the issue is for the jury. Otherwise, it is a question for the court. *Id.* at 1041, 27 UCCR at 1181.

[33] *See, e.g.,* Maroone Chevrolet, Inc. v. Nordstrom, 587 So. 2d 514, 15 UCCR2d 759 (Fla. Ct. App. 1991) (casting of substantial cloud is sufficient for breach; cloud must be predicated on some objective factor, not on the baseless anxiety of a hypersensitive purchaser); Ricklefts v. Clemens, 216 Kan. 128, 531 P.2d 94, 16 UCCR 322 (1975) (casting of substantial shadow over buyer's title is sufficient for breach); American Container Corp. v. Hanley Trucking Corp., 111 N.J. Super. 322, 268 A.2d 313, 7 UCCR 1301 (1970) (casting of a substantial shadow on title, regardless of ultimate outcome, is sufficient for breach); Saenz Motors v. Big H. Auto Auction, Inc., 653 S.W.2d 521, 37 UCCR 696 (Tex. Ct. App. 1983) (disturbance of quiet possession is sufficient for breach without proof of paramount title); Colton v. Decker, 540 N.W.2d 172, 30 UCCR2d 206 (S.D. 1995) (colorable challenge to title based on contradictory VINs sufficient for breach).

[34] *But see* Cochran v. Horner, 121 Ga. App. 297, 173 S.E.2d 448, 7 UCCR 707 (1970) (court upheld trial judge's charge that issue for jury to determine under U.C.C. § 2-312 is who had good title to the goods—not clear whether plaintiff objected to this aspect of charge); C.F. Sales, Inc. v. Amfert, Inc., 344 N.W.2d 543, 38 UCCR 844 (Iowa 1983) (no breach of warranty of title when manufacturer's claim to title is unfounded).

[35] *See* Jefferson v. Jones, 286 Md. 544, 408 A.2d 1036, 27 UCCR 1174 (Ct. App. 1979); American Container Corp. v. Hanley Trucking Corp., 111 N.J. Super. 322, 268 A.2d 313, 7 UCCR 1301 (N.J. Super. Ct. 1970); Itoh v. Kimi Sales, Ltd., 74 Misc. 2d 402, 345 N.Y.S.2d 416, 13 UCCR 64 (Civ. Ct. 1973); Horta v. Tennison, 671 S.W.2d 720, 38 UCCR 1576 (Tex. Ct. App. 1984).

[36] Saenz Motors v. Big H. Auto Auction, Inc., 653 S.W.2d 521, 37 UCCR 696 (Tex. Ct. App. 1983).

[37] City Car Sales, Inc. v. McAlpin, 380 So. 2d 865, 28 UCCR 993 (Ala. Ct. App. 1979).

[38] 553 S.W.2d 199, 22 UCCR 48 (Tex Ct. App. 1977).

was colorable.[39] A number of cases have held that the violation of the warranty of good title in a consumer context is actionable under a Deceptive Trade Practices Act.[40]

[B]   Warranty Against Security Interests, Liens, and Encumbrances

The second Code warranty of title provides that "the goods shall be delivered free from any security interest or other lien or encumbrance of which the buyer at the time of contracting has no knowledge."[41] This title warranty extends only to those security interests, liens, and encumbrances[42] that were not *actually known* by the buyer at the time of contracting. A security interest is not excluded from the warranty simply because the buyer has constructive knowledge of the security interest[43] or reason to know of the security interest. The buyer must be actually aware of the security interest, lien, or encumbrance at the time of contracting.[44] The warranty, however, is that the goods be *delivered* free from these claims, not that there are no outstanding interests at the time of contracting.

---

[39] *See* Jefferson v. Jones, *supra* note 15 (plaintiff successfully sued police for return of seized vehicle); Wright v. Vickaryous, 611 P.2d 20, 28 UCCR 1177 (Alaska 1980) (breach of warranty against encumbrances occurred by failure to remove security interests from record, even though they would be discharged as a matter of law); Frank Arnold Contractors, Inc. v. Vilsmer Auction Co., Inc., 806 F.2d 462, 2 UCCR2d 845 (3d Cir. 1986) (court upheld directed verdict for buyer when seller failed to remove security interests from record even though seller was not given the opportunity at trial to show that security interests had been waived as a matter of law by consent of holder of security interest to sale); Ricklefts v. Clemens, 216 Kan. 128, 531 P.2d 94, 16 UCCR 322 (1975) (breach occurred at time FBI warned buyer that car he purchased was stolen and he might be arrested for driving it). *See also* Jeanneret v. Vichey, 693 F.2d 259, 35 UCCR 75 (2d Cir. 1982) (court refused to decide on the state of the record the "serious question" of whether failure to get proper export license from Italian government for painting is a breach of title warranty despite fact that there was no reasonable prospect that possession of painting would be disturbed unless it was taken from the United States back to Italy).

[40] *See, e.g.,* Horta v. Tennison, 671 S.W.2d 720, 38 UCCR 1576 (Tex. Ct. App. 1984); Saenz Motors v. Big H. Auto Auction, Inc., 653 S.W.2d 521, 37 UCCR 696 (Tex. Ct. App. 1983). *See generally* section 9.02[B], *infra*.

[41] U.C.C. § 2-312(1)(b).

[42] Because the term "security interest" covers all contractual agreements which, prior to the Code, would have created a lien or encumbrance on goods to secure the payment of an obligation, the reference in section 2-312(1)(b) to "lien or encumbrance" applies only to noncontractual arrangements. Examples would include an outstanding levy or attachment, a mechanic's lien, or a lien arising from the operation of law.

[43] For example, through proper filing of a financing statement.

[44] Elias v. Dobrowolski, 120 N.H. 212, 412 A.2d 1035, 33 UCCR 1261 (1980). See the definition of "knowledge" in U.C.C. § 1-201(25).

The same general problem, discussed in the prior section, may also occur with respect to security interests, liens, or other encumbrances. There may be times in which a claim of an outstanding security interest, lien, or encumbrance is made against the buyer, but it is not clear whether the claim is actually enforceable against the buyer. If it should turn out, perhaps after costly litigation, that there is no enforceable interest, has the warranty been breached?

As with the warranty of good title, the Code does not provide a definitive answer. Comment 1, however, relied upon by the court in *Jefferson v. Jones*, is applicable to all of subsection (1) of section 2-312.[45] This Comment supports a similar approach to liens and encumbrances as was adopted in the *Jefferson* case with respect to title. Although litigation is sparse, this appears to be the direction of the cases. For example, in *Standing v. Midgett*,[46] the court held that the failure by the seller of a fishing boat to disclose to a buyer that the boat was subject to an outstanding recorded lien breached the warranty against security interests, liens, and encumbrances even though a bankruptcy court later agreed with the seller that the lien was unenforceable. The existence of the recorded interest was a sufficient cloud on title to breach the warranty despite the later holding of the bankruptcy court.[47]

A couple of cases deal with the issue of a secured party's consent to the sale of collateral which, under section 9-306 of the Code, releases the security interest as a matter of law.[48] In *Frank Arnold Contractors, Inc. v.*

---

[45] The first paragraph of Comment 1 to U.C.C. §‍ 2-312 provides:

> *Subsection 1* makes provision for a buyer's basic needs in respect to a title which he in good faith expects to acquire by his purchase, namely that he receive a good, clean title transferred to him also in a rightful manner so that he will not be exposed to a lawsuit in order to protect it.

(Emphasis added.)

[46] Standing v. Midgett, 850 F. Supp. 396, 22 UCCR2d 472 (E.D.N.C. 1993).

[47] *See also* Catlin Aviation Co. v. Equilease Corp., 626 P.2d 857, 31 UCCR 1581 (Okla. 1981) (burden was on seller to remove recorded airplane repairman's lien regardless of lien's questionable validity; "purchaser should have a title which shall enable him not only to hold his property but to hold it in peace"). *But see* Cochran v. Horner, 121 Ga. App. 297, 173 S.E.2d 448, 7 UCCR 707 (1970) (breach of warranty depends upon whether third party's attachment of goods was lawful).

[48] U.C.C. §‍ 9-306(2) provides in relevant part:

> Except where this Article otherwise provides, a security interest continues in collateral notwithstanding sale, exchange, or other disposition thereof unless the disposition was authorized by the secured party in the security agreement or otherwise.

Vilsmeier Auction Co.,[49] the Court of Appeals for the Third Circuit refused to overturn a directed verdict against a seller in favor of a buyer who had been sued by the holder of a security interest in the property. The seller argued that the trial court's refusal to permit him to show that the holder of the security interest had consented to the sale was in error. The court responded that the recorded lien was a sufficient cloud on title to make the seller's evidence of consent to the sale irrelevant.[50] Similarly, the court in *Wright v. Vickaryous*[51] permitted a buyer to refuse to complete the purchase of cattle when perfected security interests were held by a number of parties, each of whom had consented to the sale. The court said that the existence of the recorded liens was sufficient to constitute a breach of the warranty against encumbrances and to excuse the buyer from going forward with the sale even though the security interests would not have been enforceable against the buyer.

The result in *Wright* may appear questionable, because unlike *Frank Arnold Contractors*, there was no question that the lienholders had consented and the buyer was not subjected to threatened or actual litigation. The seller in *Wright*, however, had inexplicably refused to explain to the buyer that the holders had consented to the sale when the buyer notified the seller of his intention not to proceed. Had the seller explained to the buyer that the holders of the security interests had consented, the court said the seller could have saved the transaction.[52]

[C] Modification or Exclusion of Title Warranties

The Code warranties of title can be modified or excluded in only one of two ways:

---

[49] 806 F.2d 462, 2 UCCR2d 845 (3d Cir. 1986).

[50] *But see* Johnson v. Simpson, 621 P.2d 688, 30 UCCR 1212 (Utah 1980). In *Johnson,* the court refused to find a breach and allow a buyer to rescind a contract where an airplane was subject to an *unrecorded* security interest of which the buyer was unaware at the time of contracting. As a result the security interest was unenforceable against the buyer under both state *and* federal law. The case also involved no threat of litigation by the holder of the security interest, and the buyer's desire to rescind was probably not prompted by the existence of the unrecorded interest.

[51] Wright v. Vickaryous, 611 P.2d 70, 28 UCCR 1177 (Alaska 1980).

[52] It is the view of the authors that the buyer might also have justifiably demanded some proof of the consent of the holders of the security interests or a specific promise by the seller to hold the buyer harmless in the event of a suit by one or more of the holders of the security interests.

1. *By specific language.* The warranty of title may be modified or excluded from the sale by specific language which gives the buyer reason to know that the seller does not claim title in himself or that he is only selling such right or title as he or a third person may have. This is the Code's functional equivalent of a "quitclaim" deed in real property law.[53] The Code requires that the exclusion or modification be by "specific language." A general exclusion of "all warranties" from the sale is not sufficient to exclude the title warranty.[54] The reason for the Code's insistence on a specific reference to title rests on the assumption that language that only generally excludes warranties is apt to be understood by the buyer as referring to the quality of—not the title to—the goods purchased. Before language in the contract for sale negates a warranty of title, language must be specific enough to call the buyer's attention to the fact that the buyer is losing all or part of his title warranty. Most buyers assume (generally without thinking about it) that the seller owns the goods that she is selling, or otherwise has authority to dispose of them, and specific language is required to disabuse buyers of this notion.[55] The cases, although small in number, that deal with express exclusions of the warranty of title are consistent with this analysis and require very precise language for an effective disclaimer.

Sunseri v. RKO-Stanley Warner Theatres, Inc.[56] indicates how difficult it is to exclude the warranty of title, although it is arguable that the court made it *too* difficult in this particular case. The case involved the foreclosure sale of recreational equipment by the assignee of the holder of a security

---

[53] However a seller using language sufficient for a real property quitclaim deed may not satisfy U.C.C. § 2-312. *See* Sunseri v. RKO-Stanley Warner Theaters, Inc., 374 A.2d 1342, 22 UCCR 41 (Pa. Super. Ct. 1977) (language in which seller conveyed "any right title and interest Seller may have" insufficient for disclaimer of title warranty).

[54] *See* In re West Side Community Hosp., Inc., 112 B.R. 243, 12 UCCR2d 674 (N.D. Ill. 1990) ("as is" disclaimer ineffective; U.C.C. § 2-312 is not "implied" warranty for purposes of section 2-316); Brokke v. Williams, 235 Mont. 305, 766 P.2d 1311, 7 UCCR2d 1404 (1989) ("as is" disclaimer ineffective to exclude title warranty).

[55] Care must be taken not to misread a part of this exclusionary section. It can be argued that every seller purports to sell only the title which *he*—not some third party—has. This reading of the Code would virtually eliminate the warranty of title which, of course, was not the intention of the drafters. A more accurate understanding of the Code's language can be obtained by emphasizing the word "purporting"—there is no warranty of title when the buyer has reason to know that the seller is *purporting* to sell only such title as he has. The idea is that the seller has told the buyer that the seller does not know whether she is the owner of the goods but that she is willing to transfer whatever title it turns out that she possessed at the time of sale.

[56] 374 A.2d 1342, 22 UCCR 41 (Pa. Super. Ct. 1977).

interest in the equipment. The bill of sale from the seller to the buyer contained the following provisions as quoted by the court:

> [Seller] . . . does hereby sell, assign, convey, transfer and deliver to Buyer any right, title and interest Seller may have in the following goods and chattels. . . .
>
> It is expressly understood and agreed that the Seller shall in nowise be deemed or held to be obligated, liable, or accountable upon or under guaranties [sic] or warranties, in any manner or form including, but not limited to, the implied warranties of title, merchantability, fitness for use or quality.[57]

When the original owner recovered the goods in a replevin action against the buyer, the buyer sued the seller for breach of the warranty of title. The seller claimed that the warranty had been excluded by the language in the bill of sale. The trial court held the language ineffective as a matter of law to disclaim the warranty of title, and the seller appealed.

The Superior Court affirmed the trial court's decision. It said that the provision quoted above did not disclaim the warranty of title in the "specific" language the statute requires. As to the first provision, the court said that the sale of "any right title and interest Seller may have" was not a "positive warning" and would be unlikely to "even catch the eye" of an unsophisticated buyer.[58] To this point, the opinion is unobjectionable; most people would not reasonably understand this language to disclaim the warranty of title. As to the second provision, however, the court's analysis is somewhat disingenuous. The court quotes the provision as follows: "Seller shall in nowise be deemed or held to be obligated, liable or accountable upon or under any guaranties [sic] or warranties," omitting from its quotation the language of the provision *which specifically mentions the warranty of title as one of the warranties disclaimed.* In fact, the court nowhere mentions that the disclaimer explicitly referred to the warranty of title. Rather, the court said that the disclaimer was couched in "negative terminology" expressing what the seller would not be liable for rather than what the buyer is or is not receiving.[59] It offered the following language as an example of a successful disclaimer of the title warranty: "The seller does not warrant that he has any right to convey the title to the goods." The court did not discuss why the language in the contract that referred specifically to the

---

[57] *Id.* at 1344, 22 UCCR at 43.

[58] *Id.* at 1344, 22 UCCR at 44.

[59] *Id.* at 1344, 22 UCCR at 46.

warranty of title was sufficiently different from its suggested language as to be ineffective as a matter of law.

Despite the flaws in the court's opinion, the result is defensible. The contract did not call the buyer's attention to the exclusion of the title warranty—the exclusion was included in a boilerplate disclaimer dealing primarily with warranties of quality. Furthermore, while the second provision specifically excludes the warranty of title, it provides no further explanation as to what this means (i.e., that the seller is making no claim as to title). It is not clear that most people would understand a single reference to the "implied warranty of title" in a general disclaimer to exclude any liability on the part of the seller for the state of title.

It is clear from cases like *Sunseri* and others[60] that sellers desiring to exclude the warranty of title must be careful. Although the Code does not specifically require a disclaimer of the warranty of title to be conspicuous, courts are unlikely to find an exclusion that is buried in fine print to be effective even if it is stated in sufficiently "specific" language.[61] Furthermore, *Sunseri* indicates that it will be insufficient to use language that simply "disclaims the warranty of title." Rather, the language must make the buyer aware that the buyer is assuming the risk that the goods may be subject to the interests of a third party.[62]

2. By certain circumstances. Title warranties can also be excluded or modified by "circumstances which give the buyer reason to know that the person selling does not claim title in himself or that he is purporting to sell only such right or title as he or a third person may have."[63] Whether these circumstances exist is a question of fact,[64] but the Comments state that sales by sheriffs, executors, foreclosing lienors "and persons similarly situated"

---

[60] *See, e.g.*, Lawson v. Turner, 404 So. 2d 424, 32 UCCR 744 (Fla. Dist. Ct. App. 1981); Rockdale Cable T.V. Co. v. Spadora, 97 Ill. App. 3d 754, 423 N.E.2d 555, 53 Ill. Dec. 171, 33 UCCR 167 (1981); Jones v. Linebaugh, 34 Mich. App. 305, 191 N.W.2d 142, 9 UCCR 1187 (1971). *But see* Landmark Motors, Inc. v. Chrysler Credit Corp., 662 N.E.2d 971, 31 UCCR2d 1026 (Ind. Ct. App. 1996) (statement at auction that sale was "without warranties express or implied" sufficient to disclaim warranty of title).

[61] Such a disclaimer could be attacked as unconscionable under U.C.C. § 2-302.

[62] Certainly the following language should suffice:

> Seller does not claim title to these goods, and provides no warranty or guarantee of title to buyer. Seller only conveys whatever title or interest, if any, that seller may have in the goods conveyed.

[63] U.C.C. § 2-312(1)(b).

[64] Shelly Motors, Inc. v. Bortnick, 4 Haw. App. 265, 664 P.2d 755, 36 UCCR 39 (1983).

do not give rise to personal obligations if title fails.[65] These people purport to sell only the rights of some third person (the judgment debtor or the decedent), and a buyer at such a sale has reason to know this. Of course, the buyer must have notice that the sale is, in fact, a foreclosure sale or an estate sale. If the buyer is not given this notice, a warranty of title should attach.

Again the case law is sparse. There are cases holding that insurance companies that have acquired the rights to stolen cars from their insured owners are not analogous to those persons described in the Comment, and therefore there must be an express exclusion of the warranty of title when the insurance company sells the cars it has recovered.[66] An auctioneer, however, so long as he discloses that he is selling goods on behalf of another, does not give a warranty of title.[67] However, an auctioneer who fails to disclose his principal gives a warranty of title, despite the fact that the goods are sold at auction.[68] Likewise, one case holds that selling goods as a pawnbroker is not sufficient to give a buyer reason to know that the seller does not warrant title.[69] Other circumstances that courts have held insufficient to exclude the warranty of title include the seller's failure to sign a certificate of title,[70] the knowledge of the buyer that his seller had purchased goods at a judicial sale,[71] and the fact that the buyer had conducted a title search.[72] On the other hand, where a dealer purchased a car from a third party solely for the purpose of reselling to the buyer (who had located the car) and to

---

[65] U.C.C. § 2-312, Official Comment 5. *See* Marino v. Perna, 165 Misc. 2d 504, 629 N.Y.S.2d 669, 28 UCCR2d 1250 (N.Y. Civ. Ct. 1995) (sale of impounded automobile by city marshal does not include warranty of title).

[66] *See* Spillane v. Liberty Mut. Ins. Co., 65 Misc. 2d 290, 317 N.Y.S.2d 203, 8 UCCR 332 (Civ. Ct. 1970), *aff'd*, 68 Misc. 2d 783, 327 N.Y.S.2d 701 (1971); John St. Auto Wrecking v. Motors Ins. Co., 56 Misc. 2d 232, 288 N.Y.S.2d 281, 5 UCCR 112 (Dist. Ct. 1968).

[67] Universal C.I.T. Credit Corp. v. State Farm Mut. Auto. Ins. Co., 493 S.W.2d 385, 12 UCCR 648 (Mo. Ct. App. 1973).

[68] *See* Jones v. Ballard, Inc., 573 So. 2d 783, 14 UCCR2d 731 (Miss. 1990). *See also* Gordon v. Northwest Auto Auction, 97 N.C. App. 88, 387 S.E.2d 227, 11 UCCR2d 10 (1990), *rev'd*, 328 N.C. 268, 400 S.E.2d 13 UCCR2d 994 (1991) (appeals court decision holding auctioneer liable reversed on the basis of express exclusion of warranty of title in contract of sale).

[69] *See* Brokke v. Williams, 235 Mont. 305, 766 P.2d 1311, 7 UCCR2d 1404 (1989) (even with "as is" disclaimer, pawnbroker held liable for breach of warranty of title).

[70] Rockdale Cable T.V. Co. v. Spadora, 97 Ill. App. 3d 754, 423 N.E.2d 555, 53 Ill. Dec. 171, 33 UCCR 167 (1981).

[71] Marvin v. Connelly, 272 S.C. 425, 252 S.E.2d 562, 26 UCCR 370 (1979).

[72] Kirby Forest Indus., Inc. v. Dobbs, 743 S.W.2d 348, 5 UCCR2d 1321 (Tex. Ct. App. 1987).

enable the buyer to obtain financing, the seller was entitled to have the jury determine whether circumstances gave the buyer reason to know the seller was not warranting title.[73]

[D] Remedy for Breach of Title Warranty

The remedy problem for breach of the warranty of title can be illustrated through a simple hypothetical. Suppose a seller sold a buyer a painting for a price of $5,000. At the time of the sale, the market value of the painting was $7,000. Some time later, the buyer is dispossessed by a third party with superior title. At that time, the painting is worth $10,000. A variant of the hypothetical (which would be more applicable to automobiles!) would have the painting decline in value and be worth only $4,000 at the time of dispossession. What is the buyer's measure of recovery?

Three possible measures of recovery are immediately apparent: (1) the price paid by the buyer; (2) the value of the painting at the time the buyer accepted it; and (3) the value of the painting at the time the buyer was dispossessed. Prior to enactment of the Code, the buyer could, if she desired, rescind the sale and recover the purchase price.[74] In the hypothetical, this measure would award the buyer a minimum of $5,000, even though the goods might have depreciated in value.[75] The division among the courts in pre-Code cases occurred when the buyer sought to recover more than the price she had paid. Some courts limited the buyer to the price paid; others allowed her the value of the goods at the time of the sale; and still others granted the buyer the value of the goods at the time she was dispossessed.

Faced with this division, the drafters could have been expected to choose a uniform rule of damages for breach of the title warranty. However, they either ignored the issue or left the problem to be solved by the Code's general damage sections. Unfortunately, these sections were drafted for the situation in which the breach was one of tender or a warranty of quality and

---

[73] Maroone Chevrolet, Inc. v. Nordstrom, 587 So. 2d 514, 15 UCCR 759 (Fla. Dist. Ct. App. 1991). *See also* Rockdale Cable T.V. Co. v. Spadora, 97 Ill. App. 3d 754, 423 N.E.2d 555, 53 Ill. Dec. 171, 33 UCCR 167 (1981) (conversation to the effect that seller was selling only equipment that earlier buyer had left behind put present buyer on notice that seller was selling only such rights as it had after sale to previous buyer).

[74] *See, e.g.,* Mann v. Rafferty, 100 Pa. Super. 228 (1930); Crittenden v. Posley, 1 Head 311 (Tenn. 1858).

[75] For cases involving a claimed deduction for the value of the use of the goods, see Park Circle Motor Co. v. Wills, 201 Md. 104, 94 A.2d 443 (Md. Ct. App. 1953); Peregrine v. West Seattle State Bank, 120 Wash. 653, 208 P. 35 (1922).

do not fit neatly the problem of measuring recovery when the defect is in title. The courts have had to adapt them to the situation.

In place of the common-law remedy of rescission, which allowed the buyer to recover the purchase price upon dispossession, the Code has provided for the remedies of rejection and revocation of acceptance.[76] Both of these sections permit a buyer, under proper circumstances, to cancel the transaction and recover the purchase price of the goods.[77] Because rejection of the goods must take place before they have been accepted by the buyer,[78] and it is unlikely that breach of the warranty of title will be discovered before acceptance, rejection of the goods will rarely be applicable.[79] Courts, however, have permitted buyers to use the remedy of revocation of acceptance to secure the return of their purchase price when the warranty of title has been breached,[80] although courts often persist in using the common-law terminology of rescission.[81]

A buyer who has successfully rejected the goods or revoked his acceptance of them is also permitted to recover damages in addition to the purchase price. These damages are cataloged in section 2-711(3). This section provides the basis for recovering damages greater than the purchase price when the value of the goods at the time of purchase exceeds the purchase price, or when the goods have appreciated in value above the purchase price. First, a buyer can "cover"[82] (i.e., secure a reasonable replacement) and have damages measured by the cost of cover less the contract price. Thus, if the buyer replaces goods at a cost of $10,000 that originally cost him $7,000,

---

[76] *See* U.C.C. § 2-608, Official Comment 1; §§ 7.03[C], 7.03[E], *infra.*

[77] *See* U.C.C. § 2-711(1). Under section 2-601, a buyer can reject goods "if the goods or tender of delivery fail in any respect to conform to the contract." Under section 2-608, a buyer can revoke acceptance of goods "whose nonconformity substantially impairs its value to him." An argument can be made that the nonconformity must relate to the goods themselves or to the manner of delivery. This argument should be rejected. No matter how high the quality of the goods and no matter how formal the delivery, the buyer does not have goods that *conform* to the contract if he receives less than the warranted title. The court in *Sumner v. Fel-Air, Inc.,* 680 P.2d 1109, 38 UCCR 91 (Alaska 1984), explicitly held that a breach of the warranty of title was a nonconformity for purposes of section 2-608.

[78] U.C.C. § 2-606 describes when acceptance occurs. *See* §§ 5.03[A][1], 7.03[D], *infra.*

[79] *But see* Cochran v. Horner, 121 Ga. App. 297, 173 S.E.2d 448, 7 UCCR 707 (1970).

[80] *See, e.g.,* Sumner v. Fel-Air, Inc., 680 P.2d 1109, 38 UCCR 91 (Alaska 1984); Gilson v. Twin Trailer Sales of Sharon, Inc., 53 Pa. D. & C.2d 311, 10 UCCR 120 (C.P. Ct. 1971).

[81] *See* American Container Corp. v. Hanley Trucking Corp., 111 N.J. Super. 322, 268 A.2d 313, 7 UCCR 1301 (1970); Martin-Kahill Ford Lincoln Mercury, Inc. v. Skidmore, 62 N.C. App. 736, 303 S.E.2d 392, 36 UCCR 779 (1983); Insurance Co. of N. A. v. Cliff Petit Motors, Inc., 513 S.W.2d 785, 15 UCCR 816 (Tenn. 1974).

[82] *See* § 7.04[B], *infra,* for a discussion of the cover remedy.

he should be able to recover the entire $10,000 (return of the purchase price of $7000, plus the difference between the contract price and cost of cover of $3,000). Although the buyer is required to cover without unreasonable delay,[83] this time is measured from the time the buyer learns of the breach.[84]

Second, the buyer can elect not to cover and have damages measured under section 2-713 by the difference between the market price at the time the buyer learned of the breach and the contract price. Again, if the market price of the goods has increased above the contract price, this remedy should permit the buyer to recover the appreciation, since the market price is measured at the time that the buyer learns of the breach.[85]

The section generally relied upon by the courts to resolve damage problems, however, has been section 2-714:

> (1) Where the buyer has accepted goods and given notification . . . [the buyer] may recover as damages for any non-conformity of tender the loss resulting in the ordinary course of events from the seller's breach as determined in any manner which is reasonable.
>
> (2) The measure of damages for breach of warranty is the difference at the time and place of acceptance between the value of the goods accepted and the value they would have had if they had been as warranted, unless special circumstances show proximate damages of a different amount.
>
> (3) In a proper case any incidental and consequential damages under the next section may also be recovered.

This section is applicable when the buyer has accepted the goods and does not desire to revoke acceptance or is unable to satisfy the criteria for revocation.[86]

---

[83] U.C.C. § 2-712.

[84] *See* Oloffson v. Coomer, 11 Ill. App. 3d 918, 296 N.E.2d 871, 12 UCCR 1082 (1973).

[85] U.C.C. § 2-713.

[86] For example, the buyer may be unable to revoke acceptance because more than a reasonable time has passed since the buyer discovered or should have discovered the defect in the goods or because of a substantial change in the goods not caused by their own defects. *See* Sumner v. Fel-Air, Inc., 680 P.2d 1109, 38 UCCR 91 (Alaska 1984) (whether revocation occurred within a reasonable time and whether revocation occurred before a substantial change in the goods are issues of fact to be determined by the trial court). *See* § 7.03[E], *infra*. In a few cases courts have categorically refused to permit the buyer to recover the purchase price for breach of the warranty of title and relegated the buyer to U.C.C. § 2-714. In these cases, however, the remedy of revocation of acceptance appears not to have been argued by the buyer. *See* Itoh v. Kimi Sales, Ltd., 74 Misc. 2d 402, 345 N.Y.S.2d 416, 13 UCCR 64 (Civ. Ct. 1973); Ricklefts v. Clemens, 216 Kan. 128, 531 P.2d 94, 16 UCCR 322 (1975). In *Ricklefts*, the court did consider the theory of rescission. It said that the theory

Section 2-714(2) provides that damages for breach of warranty will generally be the difference at the time and place of acceptance between the value of the goods as warranted and the value of the goods as accepted. When the buyer is dispossessed as a result of the lack of title, the value of the goods as accepted should be zero,[87] and thus the buyer will be entitled to the full value of the goods. Measuring the value of the goods at the time of acceptance, however, does not take into account any appreciation or depreciation in the value of the goods between the time of acceptance and the time the buyer is dispossessed. Thus, under section 2-714(2), the buyer might receive either more or less than the actual value lost at the time of dispossession.

An early case recognized this difficulty and relied upon the portion of section 2-714(2) that permits a different measure of damages where "special circumstances show proximate damages of a different amount."[88] The court in *Itoh v. Kimi Sales, Ltd.*,[89] held that dispossession resulting from breach of the warranty of title is a special circumstance requiring measurement of value at the time of dispossession rather than at the time of acceptance. This measure, said the court, will ensure that the buyer will benefit from the effects of appreciation and not be unduly enriched if the property has depreciated in value.[90]

This holding has been followed by other cases,[91] although two cases have held that where the buyer obtained no use value from the goods be-

---

had not been properly pled by the plaintiff, and the trial court's refusal to consider it was not an abuse of discretion. *See also* City Car Sales, Inc. v. McAlpin, 380 So. 2d 865, 28 UCCR 993 (Ala. Ct. App. 1979) (value, not purchase price, is proper measure of damages); Schneidt v. Absey Motors, Inc., 248 N.W.2d 792, 21 UCCR 536 (N.D. 1976) (court held that return of purchase price is "erroneous measure of damages"; unclear what measure was requested by plaintiff). *But see* Martin-Kahill Ford Lincoln Mercury, Inc. v. Skidmore, 62 N.C. App. 736, 303 S.E.2d 392, 36 UCCR 779 (1983) (court says plaintiff has right to either rescind transaction and recover purchase price or waive rescission and sue for damages).

[87] *See* Crook Motor Co. v. Goolsby, 703 F. Supp. 511, 8 UCCR2d 363 (N.D. Miss. 1988). In applying U.C.C. § 2-714(2), courts should not use *market* value when determining the value of the goods as accepted. While this measure is often appropriate for breaches of quality warranties, it is not proper for measuring damages for breach of the warranty of title. Instead, courts should consider the value of the goods to a buyer who does not have title and faces dispossession. This value is normally zero.

[88] U.C.C. § 2-712(2).

[89] 345 N.Y.S.2d 416, 13 UCCR 64 (Civ. Ct. 1973).

[90] *Id.* at 419, 13 UCCR at 70.

[91] *See* City Car Sales, Inc. v. McAlpin, 380 So. 2d 865, 28 UCCR 993 (Ala. Ct. App. 1979); Schneidt v. Absey Motors, Inc., 248 N.W.2d 792, 21 UCCR 536 (N.D. 1976). *See also* Jeanneret v. Vichey, 541 F. Supp. 80, 34 UCCR 56 (S.D.N.Y. 1982), *rev'd on other grounds*, 693 F.2d 259, 35 UCCR 75 (2d Cir. 1982) (buyer is entitled to value of property

tween the time of acceptance and the time of dispossession, the "special circumstances" exception to section 2-714(2) does not apply, and the value of the goods was measured at the time of acceptance.[92] Simply because a buyer does not use the goods, however, should not preclude him from benefiting from their appreciation in value while they are in his possession. If the object of the Code's damage provisions is to put the buyer in the same position as performance,[93] the buyer should not lose the benefit of any appreciation in the value of the goods when she loses them to a person with superior title simply because he has not used them.[94]

Although section 2-714(2) measures damages by the *value* of the goods rather than the purchase price paid by the buyer, the purchase price is admissible evidence of the value of the goods.[95] Beyond this, a number of courts have simply awarded a dispossessed buyer the purchase price of the goods under section 2-714 without discussing whether the purchase price represented the value at the time of dispossession.[96]

Incidental and consequential damages are also available under section 2-714.[97] For example, in one case a buyer was permitted to recover, as

---

at time of *trial*); Ricklefts v. Clemens, 216 Kan. 128, 531 P.2d 94, 16 UCCR 322 (1975) (value measured at the time buyer was unable to make further use of vehicle even though actual dispossession occurred later).

[92] Steele v. Cofer, 612 So. 2d 1220, 20 UCCR2d 438 (Ala. Ct. App. 1992) (special circumstances rule does not apply when vehicle proves unsaleable by dealer who purchased it for resale); Canterra Petroleum, Inc. v. Western Drilling & Mining Supply, 418 N.W.2d 267, 5 UCCR2d 1002 (N.D. 1987) (pipe remained in possession of entrustee during period of ownership).

[93] *See* U.C.C. § 1-106.

[94] In both cases cited in *supra* note 94, *appreciation* in the value of the goods was not at issue. Rather, both courts viewed the special-circumstances rule, measuring damages at the time of dispossession, as intended to give the seller the benefit of the use that the buyer has made of the goods between the time of their acceptance and their loss to the buyer. Even when the buyer receives no use value from the goods, however, it is not apparent why the buyer should not be responsible for the decline in the value of the goods during his possession. Had he received good title to the goods as promised, the goods would be worth only their diminished value to him. *See* Itoh v. Kimi Sales, Ltd, 345 N.Y.S.2d 416, 13 UCCR 64 (Civ. Ct. 1973) (buyer should get benefit of appreciation and suffer burden of depreciation); Marino v. Perna, 165 Misc. 2d 504, 629 N.Y.S.2d 669, 28 UCCR2d 1250 (Civ. Ct. 1995) (damages adjusted downward to reflect depreciation and upward to reflect improvements).

[95] *See* Ricklefts v. Clemens, 216 Kan. 1281, 531 P.2d 94, 16 UCCR 322 (1975). *See also* Landmark Motors, Inc. v. Chrysler Credit Corp., 662 N.E.2d 971, 31 UCCR2d 1026 (Ind. Ct. App. 1996) (court awarded purchase price under U.C.C. § 2-714).

[96] *See* Jerry Parks Equip. Co. v. Southeast Equip. Co., Inc., 817 F.2d 340, 3 UCCR2d 1354 (5th Cir. 1987); Crook Motor Co., Inc. v. Goolsby, 703 F. Supp. 511, 8 UCCR2d 363 (N.D. Miss. 1988); First Valley Leasing, Inc. v. Goushy, 795 F. Supp. 693 (D.N.J. 1992).

[97] U.C.C. § 2-714(3).

consequential damages, the cost (including attorney's fees) of extricating himself from prison when arrested for possessing stolen property.[98] In granting attorney's fees, the court said that although attorney's fees are generally not recoverable, attorney's fees that are expended in litigation with a *third person* made necessary by the defendant's wrongdoing are recoverable.[99] Other incidental and consequential damages that are recoverable include lost wages resulting from defending the title;[100] lost business when a vehicle could not be used;[101] lost profits from anticipated resale of a dispossessed vehicle;[102] and interest, storage, and insurance expenses incurred when a cloud on the title prevented a buyer from reselling a boat.[103] Assuming that the buyer is given the benefit of appreciation in value, repairs and improvements to the goods are generally not recoverable as consequential damages because their cost will be reflected in an increase in the value of the goods.[104] However, recovery of consequential damages is limited by the contract doctrines of foreseeability and mitigation,[105] and punitive damages are not available, at least in the absence of fraud.[106]

---

[98] De La Hoya v. Slim's Gun Shop, 146 Cal. Rptr. 68, 24 UCCR 45 (Cal. App. Dept. Super. Ct. 1978).

[99] *See also* Schneidt v. Absey Motors, Inc., 248 N.W.2d 792, 21 UCCR 536 (N.D. 1976) (court allowed buyer attorney's fees incurred in action by owner against buyer).

[100] Bill Branch Chevrolet, Inc. v. Redmond, 378 So. 2d 319, 28 UCCR 56 (Fla. Dist. Ct. App. 1980).

[101] U-J Chevrolet Co. v. Marcus, 460 So. 2d 1341, 40 UCCR 485 (Ala. Ct. App. 1984).

[102] Crook Motor Co. v. Goolsby, 703 F. Supp. 511, 8 UCCR2d 363 (N.D. Miss. 1988).

[103] Standing v. Midgett, 850 F. Supp. 396, 22 UCCR2d 472 (E.D.N.C. 1993).

[104] *See* Schneidt v. Absey Motors, 248 N.W.2d 792, 21 UCCR 536 (N.D. 1976); Ricklefts v. Clemens, 716 Kan. 1281, 531 P.2d 94, 16 UCCR 322 (1975). *But see* Crook Motor Co. v. Goolsby, 703 F. Supp. 511, 8 UCCR2d 363 (N.D. Miss. 1988) (court allowed recovery of price paid for goods and further permitted recovery of expenses of putting automobile in condition for resale as consequential damage).

[105] *See* Standing v. Midgett, 850 F. Supp. 396, 22 UCCR2d 472 (E.D.N.C. 1993) (amount of consequential damages for interest, storage, and insurance reduced because of buyer's delay in petitioning court to clear title); De La Hoya v. Slim's Gun Shop, 146 Cal. Rptr. 68, 24 UCCR 45 (Cal. App. Dept. Super. Ct. 1978) (expenses in defending against criminal charge foreseeable); Catlin Aviation Co. v. Equilease Corp., 31 UCCR 1581 (Okla. 1981) (buyer's failure to mitigate by paying lien precluded buyer from recovering $17,000 in incidental and consequential damages in interest, insurance, hangar rental, and lost profits); U.C.C. § 2-715(2).

[106] Crook Motor Co. v. Goolsby, 703 F. Supp. 511, 8 UCCR2d 363 (N.D. Miss. 1988); Bill Branch Chevrolet, Inc. v. Redmond, 378 So. 2d 319, 28 UCCR 56 (Fla. Ct. App. 1980). *See also* First Valley Leasing, Inc. v. Goushy, 795 F. Supp. 693, 19 UCCR2d 1002, (D.N.J. 1992) (action for fraudulent sale of goods knowing sale of goods without title not displaced by Code).

No single Code section deals specifically with damages recoverable when title fails. Written from the background of damages for inferior quality or defective tender, none is directly applicable to damages for a breach of the warranty of title. However, the Code sections and the cases previously discussed support the following conclusions:

1. A *dispossessed* buyer will generally recover *at least* the purchase price either under section 2-608 or section 2-714(2). Courts have permitted revocation of acceptance in those cases where the buyer has demanded it, sometimes under the guise of rescission. In those cases in which the court has refused to permit recovery of the purchase price, the buyer does not appear to have requested the remedy of revocation of acceptance. The fact that the buyer is often unable to return the goods to the seller should not preclude revocation of acceptance.[107] So long as the buyer has been dispossessed and can otherwise satisfy the requirements of section 2-608, he should receive a return of the purchase price.[108]

2. In addition, a buyer is generally able to recover appreciation in the value of the goods between the time of acceptance and the time of dispossession. Courts have used the "special circumstances" clause of section 2-714(2) to accomplish this result. In the context of revocation of acceptance, it can also be done through sections 2-712 and 2-713.

3. In cases not involving dispossession, the measure of damages is the amount required to defend or clear the title.[109]

§ 4.03   WARRANTIES AGAINST INFRINGEMENT

Section 2-213 contains a separate subsection dealing with warranties against infringement.[110] The warranties are of two kinds. First, there is the warranty of the seller-merchant. If the seller is a merchant who deals in goods of the kind involved in the transaction and selects them from his normal stock, he warrants that the goods are delivered free from any rightful claim by a third person "by way of infringement or the like." A rightful claim of a trademark or patent against the buyer would amount to a default

---

[107] *See* American Container Corp. v. Hanley Trucking Corp., 111 N.J. Super. 322, 268 A.2d 313, 7 UCCR 1301 (1970).

[108] For a discussion of an offset for the value of the use of the goods prior to revocation of acceptance, see § 7.03[E], *infra*.

[109] *See* Gaito v. Huffman, 5 UCCR 1056 (N.Y. Sup. Ct. 1968); Catlin Aviation Co. v. Equilease Corp., 626 P.2d 857, 31 UCCR 1581 (Okla. 1981).

[110] U.C.C. § 2-312(3).

in this warranty,[111] and the section has been held to apply to copyright infringement as well.[112] Similar to the warranty of title, a "colorable" claim of violation, even if the buyer is ultimately successful in defending against the alleged infringement, should be sufficient to hold the seller liable for breach.[113] However, the goods themselves must cause the infringement; section 2-312 does not cover a claim that a seller induced the buyer to use the goods in such a way as to violate the "process patent" of another.[114]

Second, there is the warranty of the buyer. On some occasions the buyer furnishes the seller with plans and specifications for goods the buyer has contracted to have the seller manufacture. In these situations, the seller is not warranting that the final product will be free from infringement claims. To the contrary, the buyer is obligated to hold his seller harmless against any claim arising out of compliance with the furnished specifications.

II.   WARRANTIES OF QUALITY

§ 4.04   THE SELLER'S RESPONSIBILITY FOR PRODUCT QUALITY— AN OVERVIEW

The seller has many obligations under a contract for the sale of goods: the obligation to deliver the goods the buyer ordered, the obligation to deliver the correct quantity, and the obligation to ensure that delivery is timely. The seller's responsibility for product quality, however, is the obligation that has most engaged lawyers and the law. *Caveat emptor* notwithstanding, sellers have always had some responsibility for the quality of the products

---

[111] U.C.C. § 2-312, Official Comment 3 ("When the goods are part of the seller's normal stock and are sold in his normal course of business, it is his duty to see that no claim of infringement of a patent or trademark by a third party will mar the buyer's title.").

[112] Dolori Fabrics, Inc. v. Limited, Inc., 662 F. Supp. 1347, 4 UCCR2d 393 (S.D.N.Y. 1987).

[113] *See* Official Comment 4 to U.C.C. 2-312, which provides:

This section rejects the cases which recognize the principle that infringements violate the warranty of title but deny a buyer a remedy unless he has been expressly prevented from using the goods. Under this Article "eviction" is not a necessary condition to the buyer's remedy *since the buyer's remedy arises immediately upon receipt of notice of infringement; it is merely one way of establishing the fact of breach* (emphasis added).

[114] Motorola, Inc. v. Varo, Inc., v. Philip A. Hunt Chem. Corp., 656 F. Supp. 716, 2 UCCR2d 437 (N.D. Tex. 1986). *See* Chemtron, Inc. v. Aqua Prods., Inc., 830 F. Supp. 314, 21 UCCR2d 550 (E.D. Va. 1993) (section does not require seller to warrant that buyer will not use goods in some manner that will result in an infringement).

they sell. The nature of this responsibility has varied over the centuries,[115] but no century has seen a more dramatic change in the nature of a seller's responsibility for the quality of its products than the twentieth century. A short look at history will enable the reader to place this change in context and understand the current state of the law relating to product quality.

Cases holding sellers responsible for representations of product quality begin as early as the fourteenth century, and these cases have their origin in forms of action that today lawyers would classify as tort.[116] These actions were based on deceit rather than promise, although a promise or representation often formed the basis for the seller's deceit. In fact, the beginnings of assumpsit (contract) were only vaguely emerging at this time, and more than a hundred years passed before assumpsit split from the common-law writ of trespass on the case that forms the basis of modern tort law.[117]

When assumpsit became a recognized form of action, a promise or representation could be the gist of the cause of action. To be actionable, however, the promise of product quality—the *warranty*—had to be in very specific form. Thus, in a famous seventeenth century case, a seller's "affirmation" that a stone he sold to the buyer was a "bezoar"[118] stone provided no basis for recovery.[119] Unless the words "warrant" or "guarantee" were part of the seller's representation, the seller gave no warranty, and the buyer, unless he could prove deceit, was without recovery. It necessarily followed that, if a seller's "affirmation" was an insufficient basis for recovery, the seller's silence carried with it no implied warranties of product quality.

This history provided the backdrop for the development of the law in the United States, and the nineteenth-century tradition of *caveat emptor*— let the buyer beware. The presence of a sprawling country with vast resources and a faith in rugged individualism both advanced the idea that society as a whole would benefit if each person was left alone to make his own advantage or disadvantage. Furthermore, the capitalist ideology prevailing at the time required that markets be as free from interference as possible.[120] In any event, the English tradition continued in which the buyer

---

[115] *See* W. Page Keeton, et. al., Prosser and Keeton on the Law of Torts § 9.54A 679 (1984).

[116] F. R. Ames, "The History of Assumpsit," 2 Harv. L. Rev. 1, 8 (1888).

[117] Theodore F.T. Plucknett, A Concise History of the Common Law, 7-46 (5th ed. 1956).

[118] A "bezoar" is defined as "any of various concretions found chiefly in the alimentary organs of ruminants and formerly believed to possess magical properties." Webster's Ninth New Collegiate Dictionary 147 (1983).

[119] Chandelor v. Lopus, 3 Cro. Jac. 4, 79 Eng. Rep. 3 (Ex. 1603).

[120] *See* Morton J. Horwitz, The Transformation of American Law, 1870–1960: The Crisis of Legal Orthodoxy, 262–263 (1992).

was largely left to his own devices in the absence of the "magic words" of warranty.[121]

Historically, the principal tort remedies also provided little protection against product defects. To recover for deceit, the seller had to be aware of the falsity of his representation at the time it was made.[122] Also, the buyer had to rely on the representation, the reliance had to be reasonable, and the representation had to be material.[123] These requirements made deceit an imperfect tool, at best, for ensuring product quality.

The second tort theory—negligence—was hardly better. First, to recover in negligence, a plaintiff had to prove that the seller failed to use reasonable care, which led to the buyer's injury. Even with the doctrine of *res ipsa loquitur*, proving the seller's negligence was often not an easy matter. Second, the doctrine of negligence was, and largely remains today, applicable only to personal injury and property damage claims.[124] If the loss was purely economic—for example, if the seller's negligence merely caused the goods to be worth less than they would otherwise be worth, or caused the buyer to lose profits—negligence was inapplicable.

Much has changed during the last hundred years. Both the Uniform Commercial Code[125] and its predecessor, the Uniform Sales Act,[126] provide that affirmations of fact, promises, and descriptions can all give rise to express warranties. The Code explicitly states that it is not necessary for the seller to use words such as "warrant" or "guarantee" to create an express warranty.[127] Further, the Code provides an implied warranty that products will be "merchantable"—fit for their ordinary purpose—in every sale by a merchant.[128] Beyond the Code, both federal and state law provide additional protections of product quality to consumers.[129]

---

[121] *See* Bradford v. Manly, 13 Mass. 139 (1816); Seixas v. Woods, 2 Caines (N.Y.) 48 (1804).

[122] *See* First Nat'l Bank of Louisville v. Brooks Farms, 821 S.W.2d 925 (Tenn. 1991).

[123] *Id.*

[124] *See* Dundee Cement Co. v. Chemical Labs, Inc., 712 F.2d 1166 (7th Cir. 1983); Palah Int'l Tranders, Inc. v. Norcam Aircraft, Inc., 653 So. 2d 412 (Fla. Dist. Ct. App. 1995); Aikens v. Baltimore & Ohio R.R. Co., 348 Pa. Super. 17, 501 A.2d 277 (1985).

[125] U.C.C. § 2-313(1).

[126] Uniform Sales Act, §§ 12, 14.

[127] U.C.C. § 2-313(2).

[128] U.C.C. § 2-314. *See* § 4.06[B], *infra.*

[129] *See, e.g.*, Magnuson-Moss Federal Warranty Act, § 108, 15 U.S.C. § 2308 (1996) (restricting a seller's ability to disclaim or limit implied warranties); Ohio Consumer Sales Practices Act, Ohio Rev. Code Ann. § 1345.02(B)(2) (Baldwin 1998) (making it an unfair or deceptive consumer sales practice to represent that the subject of a consumer transaction is of a particular standard, quality, grade, style, prescription, or model, if it is not). *See* Chapters 8 and 9, *infra.*

Changes in tort law have been equally revolutionary. In the landmark case of *Greenman v. Yuba Power Products, Inc.*[130] the California Supreme Court established the principle of strict liability in tort for injuries caused by defective products. No longer would a buyer be required to prove negligence in order to recover in tort; according to the court in *Greenman*, a manufacturer was "strictly liable in tort when an article he places on the market, knowing that it is to be used without inspection for defects, proves to have a defect that causes injury to a human being."[131] The doctrine of strict liability became embodied shortly thereafter in the Restatement (Second) of Torts.[132]

Despite these extraordinary changes, issues remain that form a large part of the substance of the subsequent sections in this chapter:

1. Which parties in the chain of distribution ought to be liable for product defects and to whom? Can a bystander who is injured when the brakes fail on a automobile recover directly against the manufacturer of the brakes? Can a company that loses profits when a computer fails to function recover against the computer's manufacturer, or must the company sue its immediate seller?

2. For what kinds of defects ought the parties be liable? The broken brake rivet and poisoned food present easy cases, but what about the harm caused by cigarettes?[133] By handguns?[134] Are these products in any sense "defective" because of the injury they cause? Is a product defective when it is safe for a large percentage of the population but harmful to a few who are allergic to it?[135]

3. To what extent can the parties alter the seller's obligations by agreement? For what defects or what injuries can sellers escape liability? To what extent can a seller limit the remedies available to a buyer when the product fails to perform as promised? If a seller is permitted to limit her obligations, how must she do so?

This text examines these problems and others, largely from the perspective of the Code. With respect to strict products liability in tort, in particular, the reader will be left to other sources for a comprehensive analysis. Nonetheless, we will try to provide an overview of all of the significant

---

[130] 59 Cal. 2d 57, 377 P.2d 897, 27 Cal. Rptr. 697 (1963).

[131] 59 Cal. 2d at 62, 377 P.2d at 900; 27 Cal. Rptr. at 700.

[132] Restatement (Second) of Torts § 402A (1975).

[133] *See* Cipollone v. Liggett Group, Inc., 893 F.2d 541, 10 UCCR2d 625 (3d Cir. 1990).

[134] *See* Kelley v. R.G. Indus., Inc., 304 Md. 124, 497 A.2d 1143 (Ct. App. 1985).

[135] *See* Bennett v. Pilot Prods. Co., 170 Utah 474, 235 P.2d 525 (1951).

ways, including tort liability, in which modern society regulates product quality.

§ 4.05   EXPRESS WARRANTIES

[A]   Overview of Express Warranties

Section 2-313 states that express warranties can be created in any one of four ways: by the affirmation of a fact, by a promise, by a description, or by a sample or model. Before there is an express warranty, two other conditions must be met:

1. In cases of an affirmation of fact or the making of a promise, the affirmation or promise must be made by the seller to the buyer and must relate to the goods. No such condition is stated for the other two methods of making an express warranty; by their nature they relate to the goods.[136]

2. In all instances, the affirmation, promise, description, or sample or model must be "a part of the basis of the bargain."[137]

The full text of section 2-313 is set out below:

(1)   Express warranties by the seller are created as follows:
  (A)   Any affirmation of fact or promise made by the seller to the buyer which relates to the goods and becomes part of the basis of the bargain creates an express warranty that the goods shall conform to the affirmation or promise.
  (B)   Any description of the goods which is made part of the basis of the bargain creates an express warranty that the goods shall conform to the description.
  (C)   Any sample or model which is made part of the basis of the bargain creates an express warranty that the whole of the goods shall conform to the sample or model.
(2)   It is not necessary to the creation of an express warranty that the seller use formal words such as "warrant" or "guarantee" or that he have a specific intention to make a warranty, but an affirmation merely of the value of the goods or a statement purporting to be merely the seller's opinion or commendation of the goods does not create a warranty.

---

[136] Only a description "of the goods" creates a warranty as to those goods, and a sample or model is one to which "the goods" shall conform. U.C.C. § 2-313(1).

[137] U.C.C. § 2-313(1).

[B] Affirmation of Fact or Promise

An express warranty may be created by either an affirmation of fact or a promise. Because both an affirmation of fact or a promise can create an express warranty, it makes no difference whether the seller says, "I promise you that this coal contains no more than 10 percent ash," or if the seller says, "This coal contains no more than 10 percent ash." If either of these statements becomes part of the basis of the bargain between the parties, an express warranty that the coal contains 10 percent ash, or less, has been created.[138] Although the meaning of the warranty is open to interpretation (if the delivered coal contains 10.05 percent ash, has the warranty been breached?),[139] the form in which the seller made his statement—whether as an affirmation of fact or a promise—makes no difference as far as express warranties are concerned.

It is sometimes difficult, however, to determine when a statement constitutes an "affirmation of fact." Under early warranty law, as previously described,[140] sellers could make almost any assertion about their goods without risking warranty liability so long as the assertion was not fraudulent or did not contain the words "warrant" or "guarantee." The history of warranty law has been a continual expansion of the number of situations in which statements made by the seller amount to an affirmation of fact or promise.[141] Nonetheless, not all statements about the goods, even today, give rise to express warranties. The Code, like the Uniform Sales Act preceding it,[142] allows some level of sales talk, or "puffing." Section 2-313(2) attempts to distinguish mere puffery from affirmations of fact: "an affirmation merely of the value of the goods or a statement purporting merely to be the seller's opinion or commendation of the goods does not create a warranty."[143]

The line between warranty and puffing evades specific rules. Although there have been hundreds of cases involving this issue, and courts and commentators have identified a number of factors relevant to whether a statement is one of fact or opinion, a test that can be applied easily or mechanically remains elusive for a number of reasons. First, the issue is generally a ques-

---

[138] See Moore v. Beary, 217 Ga. App. 697, 458 S.E.2d 879, 27 UCCR2d 1219 (1995).

[139] See § 3.11, supra.

[140] See § 4.04, supra.

[141] See Michael J. Ezer, "The Impact of the Uniform Commercial Code on the California Law of Sales Warranties," 8 U.C.L.A. L. Rev. 281, 286–87 (1961).

[142] Uniform Sales Act § 12.

[143] U.C.C. § 2-313(2).

tion of fact for the jury to decide.[144] As a result, decisions made by courts as a matter of law occur only at the margins. More important, however, the issue of fact versus opinion is inextricably intertwined with another criterion for the creation of an express warranty—the requirement that a statement be part of the basis of the bargain between the parties.[145] Comment 8 makes this relationship explicit:

> Concerning affirmations of value or a seller's commendation under subsection (2), the basic question remains the same: What statements of the seller have in the circumstances and in objective judgment become part of the basis of the bargain? . . . The provisions of subsection (2) are included, however, since common experience discloses that some statements or predictions cannot fairly be viewed as entering into the bargain.[146]

Although a full discussion of the basis of the bargain requirement must await a subsequent section,[147] at the core of the concept are the reasonable expectations of the parties to the contract. Because the parties' reasonable expectations depend upon the context in which the words are spoken, the focus cannot be on the words alone. All of the circumstances surrounding the contract affect what expectations are created and whether those expectations are reasonable.[148] Thus, two decisions in which similar language is at issue and which nonetheless reach opposite results are not necessarily inconsistent.[149] In one situation, the words may be reasonably understood as an affirmation of fact and in another situation reasonably understood as "puffing."

---

[144] *See* Royal Business Mach., Inc. v. Lorraine Corp., 633 F.2d 34, 30 UCCR 462 (7th Cir. 1980); Yuzwak v. Dygert, 144 A.D.2d 938, 534 N.Y.S.2d 35, 35, 7 UCCR2d 731 (1988).

[145] *See* Downs v. Shouse, 18 Ariz. App. 225, 501 P.2d 401, 11 UCCR 481 (1972).

[146] U.C.C. § 2-313, Official Comment 8.

[147] *See* § 4.05[F], *infra.*

[148] *See* Voelkel v. General Motors Corp., 846 F. Supp. 1482, 1485, 23 UCCR2d 676, 678 (D. Kan. 1994) ("'Great road cars' offering 'innovative styling and engineering' is nonspecific language *used in a context and manner* that this court believes would qualify it as a seller's opinion or commendation") (emphasis added); Ruffin v. Shaw Indus., Inc., 36 UCCR2d 341 (4th Cir. 1998) (statement by store manager that carpet was "higher quality" was only seller's opinion).

[149] *Compare* Curry Motor Co. v. Itasty, 505 So. 2d 367, 3 UCCR2d 1373 (Ala. 1987) (description as "1979 Ford Truck" created warranty that engine was of that year) *with* Szajna v. Gen. Motors Corp., 30 Ill. App. 3d 173, 474 N.E.2d 397, 85 Ill. Dec. 669, 40 UCCR 77 (1985) (description as "1976 Pontiac Ventura" did not expressly warrant that car's transmission would be a certain type or quality).

The relative expertise of the buyer and the seller has been explicitly recognized as an important factor in distinguishing statements of fact from opinion. In language that has been quoted in numerous Code cases,[150] the court in the pre-Code case of *Keller v. Flynn*[151] put it this way:

> To determine whether or not there is a warranty, the decisive test is whether the vendor assumes to assert a fact of which the buyer is ignorant, or merely states an opinion or judgment on a matter of which the vendor has no special knowledge, and on which the buyer may be expected also to have an opinion and to exercise his judgment. In the former case there is a warranty and in the latter there is not.[152]

Courts have frequently found an express warranty to exist despite vague or general language used by the seller when there was a great disparity between the knowledge or expertise of the buyer and seller.[153] For example, in *Valley Datsun v. Martinez*[154] the court found a statement by a seller that a VW camper was in "excellent condition" to be an express warranty when two days after the sale the camper threw a rod and the clutch burned out. The court said that under the circumstances, the seller's statement was more than "puffing" or "dealer's talk" because the superior knowledge of the seller coupled with the buyer's relative ignorance "operates to make the slightest divergence from mere praise into representations of fact."[155]

Other courts have found express warranties created in similar circumstances. In *Balog v. Center Art Gallery-Hawaii, Inc.*[156] the court held that representations by an art dealer that paintings were done by Salvador Dali were express warranties rather than expressions of the dealer's opinion. The court emphasized that the purchaser had little choice but to rely on the seller's statement because of the prohibitive cost of independent verification. In *Goldman v. Barnett*,[157] the court refused summary judgment for an art dealer, saying that a reasonable jury could find that representations of the

---

[150] *See, e.g.*, Weiss v. Rockwell Mfg. Co., 9 Ill. App. 3d 906, 293 N.E.2d 375, 12 UCCR 429 (1973); Interco Inc. v. Randustrial Corp., 533 S.W.2d 257, 19 UCCR 464 (Mo. Ct. App. 1976); Valley Datsun v. Martinez, 578 S.W.2d 485, 26 UCCR 331 (Tex. Ct. App. 1979); Royal Business Mach., Inc. v. Lorraine Corp., 633 F.2d 34, 30 UCCR 462 (7th Cir. 1980).

[151] 346 Ill. App. 499, 105 N.E.2d 532 (1952).

[152] 346 Ill. App. at 508, 105 N.E.2d at 536.

[153] *See, e.g.*, Cagney v. Cohn, 13 UCCR 998 (D.C. Super. 1973) ("excellent condition"); Pake v. Byrd, 58 N.C. App. 551, 286 S.E.2d 588, 33 UCCR 835 (1982) ("good condition").

[154] 578 S.W.2d 485, 26 UCCR 331 (Tex. Ct. App. 1979).

[155] *Id.* at 490, 26 UCCR at 341.

[156] 745 F. Supp. 1556, 12 UCCR2d 962 (D. Haw. 1990).

[157] 793 F. Supp. 28, 18 UCCR2d 55 (D. Mass. 1992).

value of certain paintings were express warranties, despite the direction of section 2-313(2) that mere representations of value are not express warranties. The court held that under the circumstances, the seller's statements could be found by a jury to be more than *mere* statements of value.

Conversely, there are a number of cases in which courts have pointed to the relative equality of the parties' access to information in finding expressions not to be affirmations of fact. In *Conner v. Bogrett*[158] a seller's comments about a Labrador Retriever's competition potential was held to be merely the seller's opinion. The court pointed out that the buyer was an afficionada of Labrador Retrievers, was knowledgeable about them, and had even won a national championship. Similarly, in *Euroworld of California, Inc. v. Blakely,*[159] the court held that statements by a seller about the condition of aircraft engines were not express warranties when the buyer knew that the seller was relying solely on documentation rather than personal knowledge in making the statements. The court said that the buyer was in a better position than the seller, as a result of twenty-five years in the business of buying, overhauling, and selling airplane engines, to determine the likely condition of the engines.[160] Cases reaching different results even though the seller's language is similar can often be explained by the relative expertise of the parties.[161]

The degree to which the expression is subject to quantification or objective measurement is understandably important in determining whether a statement is an affirmation of fact. This makes sense for a number of reasons. The more general the statement, the more unlikely it is that a buyer

---

[158] 596 P.2d 683, 26 UCCR 902 (Wyo. 1979).

[159] 613 F. Supp. 129, 41 UCCR 403 (S.D. Fla. 1985).

[160] *See also* Thursby v. Reynolds Metal Co., 466 So. 2d 245, 39 UCCR 1625 (Fla. Dist. Ct. App. 1984) (seller's statement will be construed as opinion or commendation where, other things equal, buyer and seller have equal knowledge of the facts and are in equal positions to express an opinion); Miller v. Lentine, 495 A.2d 1229, 41 UCCR 1228 (Me. 1985) (knowledge of parties should be considered in determining whether statement is warranty—representation that outboard motor was "in perfect running condition" not express warranty).

[161] *Compare* Cagney v. Cohn, 13 UCCR 998 (D.C. Super. 1973) (statement that motorcycle was in "excellent condition" was express warranty when seller had substantially more knowledge about motorcycles than buyer and held himself out as "quasi-mechanic") *with* Guess v. Lorenz, 612 S.W.2d 831, 30 UCCR 1529 (Mo. Ct. App. 1981) (statement by seller that car is in "good shape" not express warranty when seller gave no impression of knowing anything about cars).

will rely on the statement in making the purchase.[162] Also, the more specific the claim, the easier it is to determine whether the alleged defect was included within the warranty.[163] On the one hand, there is the kind of general statement that is always puffing and not a warranty. For example, the representation in an ad that "Chevy's business is providing the right truck for your business" is puffing,[164] as is the representation that "You meet the nicest people on a Honda."[165] At the other extreme are those representations that are specifically quantitative.[166] In between are numerous cases where there is arguably some objective content to the seller's statements, but they are far from precise. Prediction is more difficult for statements in this category, and context becomes very important. There are many cases in which courts have treated similar terms differently. For example, statements that a car is in "mint condition,"[167] explosives are of "good quality,"[168] a motorcycle is "in good condition,"[169] a camper is "in excellent condition,"[170] a

---

[162] *See* Jordan v. Paccar, Inc., 37 F.3d 1181, 24 UCCR2d 1106 (6th Cir. 1994) (statements that truck is "rock-solid" and "strong" are the kind of "subjective" statements "to which ordinary consumers are inured"). *But see* Alcan Aluminum Corp. v. Carlton Aluminum of New Eng., Inc., 617 N.E.2d 1005, 24 UCCR2d 66 (Mass. App. Ct. 1993) (statement that seller "would back up its materials one hundred per cent" was express warranty).

[163] *See* Chase Resorts, Inc. v. Johns-Manville Corp., 476 F. Supp. 633, 27 UCCR 1287 (E.D. Mo. 1979) ("years of trouble-free service" not express warranty—not susceptible of exact knowledge). Statements that refer to matters of taste or aesthetics will generally not be express warranties. *See* Carpenter v. Alberto Culver Co., 28 Mich. App. 399, 184 N.W.2d 547, 8 UCCR 1234 (1970) (statement by clerk that she had used hair-dying product and it had come out "very nice" and "very natural" not express warranties); Baughn v. Honda Motor Co., 107 Wash. 2d 127, 727 P.2d 655, 2 UCCR2d 445 (1986) ("You meet the nicest people on a Honda" not an express warranty).

[164] Shaw v. General Motors Corp., 727 P.2d 387, 1 UCCR2d 76 (Colo. Ct. App. 1986).

[165] Braughn v. Honda Motor Co., Ltd., 107 Wash. 2d 127, 2 UCCR2d 445 (1986). *See also* Rock v. Oster Corp., 810 F. Supp. 665, 19 UCCR2d 720 (D. Md. 1991) (statement that fondue pot is "finest product of its kind available" not express warranty); Ruffin v. Shaw Indus. Inc., 36 UCCR2d 341 (4th Cir. 1998) (statement that product is "high quality" is not an express warranty).

[166] *See, e.g.*, Capital Equip. Enters., Inc. v. North Pier Terminal Co., 117 Ill. App. 2d 264, 254 N.E.2d 562, 7 UCCR 290 (1969) (description of crane as "30-ton" crane); Drier v. Perfection, Inc., 259 N.W.2d 496, 23 UCCR 323 (S.D. 1977) (representation that printing press would produce 8,500 copies impressions per hour); Cox v. Lewiston Grain Growers, Inc., 936 P.2d 1191, 33 UCCR2d 443 (Wash. App. 1997) (representation that seed had 85 percent or better germination).

[167] Taylor v. Alfama, 145 Vt. 6, 481 A.2d 1059, 39 UCCR 1235 (1984).

[168] Olin Mathieson Chem. Co. v. Moushan, 93 Ill. App. 2d 280, 235 N.E.2d 263, 5 UCCR 363 (1968).

[169] Cagney v. Cohn, 13 UCCR 998 (D.C. Super. 1973).

[170] Valley Datsun v. Martinez, 578 S.W.2d 485, 26 UCCR 331 (Tex. Ct. App. 1979).

tractor is "in good condition,"[171] a truck is "road ready,"[172] a refrigerator is in "good condition,"[173] and a car is in "A-1 condition,"[174] all were held to create express warranties. On the other hand, statements that a trailer is in "perfect condition"[175]; a copier is of "high quality"[176]; a car is in "good shape,"[177] "good condition,"[178] or "excellent condition"[179]; a horse is an "exceptional stallion"[180]; and a piece of jewelry is of "excellent quality"[181] were all held not to be express warranties.

While some of these decisions may simply be inconsistent, a detailed factual examination frequently explains apparently contrary results. For example, the court in *Uganski v. Little Giant Crane & Shovel, Inc.*[182] found a statement by a seller that its crane was "as good as or better" than the buyer's present crane to be an express warranty, whereas the court in *Ingram River Equipment, Inc. v. Pott Industries, Inc.*[183] held that a statement by a seller that its furnace weld pipe was "just as good as" seamless pipe was not an express warranty. In the *Uganski* case, however, the seller had observed the buyer's crane in operation and had engaged in a discussion with the buyer concerning its features. In *Ingram*, on the other hand, the statement had been made by one of the seller's officers *after* the contract had been made and construction begun.[184]

The extent to which the seller has explicitly or implicitly qualified its representation by other statements is also important. Additional statements by the seller provide a context to determine whether a representation has sufficient content to be an express warranty and whether the buyer is entitled

---

[171] Pake v. Byrd, 55 N.C. App. 551, 286 S.E.2d 588, 33 UCCR 835 (1982).

[172] Wiseman v. Wolfe's Terre Haute Auto Auction, Inc., 459 N.E.2d 736, 37 UCCR 1486 (Ind. Ct. App. 1984).

[173] Eddington v. Dick, 87 Misc. 2d 793, 386 N.Y.S.2d 180, 20 UCCR 50 (N.Y. City Ct. 1976).

[174] Jones v. Kellner, 5 Ohio App. 3d 242, 451 N.E.2d 548, 36 UCCR 784 (1982).

[175] Performance Motors, Inc. v. Allen, 280 N.C. 385, 186 S.E.2d 161, 10 UCCR 568 (1972).

[176] Royal Business Machs., Inc. v. Lorraine Corp., 633 F.2d 34, 30 UCCR 462 (7th Cir. 1980).

[177] Guess v. Lorenz, 612 S.W.2d 831, 30 UCCR 1529 (Mo. Ct. App. 1981).

[178] Wood v. Secord, 122 N.H. 323, 444 A.2d 539, 33 UCCR 1313 (1982).

[179] Scaringe v. Holstein, 103 A.D.2d 880, 477 N.Y.S.2d 903, 38 UCCR 1595 (1984).

[180] Vanier v. Ponsoldt, 251 Kan. 88, 833 P.2d 949, 19 UCCR2d 90 (1992).

[181] Hall v. T.L. Kemp Jewelry, Inc., 71 N.C. App. 101, 322 S.E.2d 7, 39 UCCR 1648 (1984).

[182] 35 Mich. App. 88, 192 N.W.2d 580, 10 UCCR 57 (1971).

[183] 573 F. Supp. 896, 37 UCCR 88 (E.D. Mo. 1983).

[184] This is not to say, however, that statements made after the contract is made cannot be express warranties under the Code. *See* § 4.05[F][2], *infra*.

to consider it a part of the basis of the bargain. For example, if the seller prefaces a statement with language such as "I think," a representation will likely be determined to be opinion.[185] In *Petroleo Brasileiro, S.A. Petrobras v. Nalco Chemical Co.*,[186] the court held a statement that an emulsifier would reduce the water content of fuel oil to 0.5 percent was not an express warranty, because the seller had elsewhere categorically refused to give any warranties or guarantees as to the performance of its product. The court in *Flynn v. Biomet*[187] held language that a composite replacement hip would last twenty years not to be an express warranty when the doctor had fully explained to the patient the experimental nature of hip replacement prosthesis and the patient understood that the operation and prosthesis posed "unknown risks."[188]

The importance of context is also apparent from a number of cases in which statements that might not otherwise be express warranties were found to qualify because they were in response to specific inquiries by the buyer. In *Cagney v. Cohn*,[189] the court found an express warranty when the seller responded to the buyer's inquiry about a metallic noise in the engine of a motorcycle by saying the motorcycle was in "good condition."[190] A statement by the seller that a truck was "road ready" was an express warranty when made in response to the buyer's expression of concern about the condition of the truck.[191] A seller's statement that its paving material was "equal to or better" than a competitor's was an express warranty when the statement

---

[185] *See* Wendt v. Beardmore Suburban Chevrolet, Inc., 219 Neb. 775, 366 N.W.2d 424, 40 UCCR 1659 (1985) ("to his knowledge" seller "didn't think" car had been previously wrecked); Hupp Corp. v. Metered Washer Serv., 256 Or. 245, 472 P.2d 816, 8 UCCR 42 (Or. 1970) ("we think"); Roberts v. Robert V. Rohrman, Inc., 909 F. Supp. 545, 29 UCCR2d 1208 (N.D. Ill. 1995).

[186] 784 F. Supp. 160, 18 UCCR2d 61 (D.N.J. 1992).

[187] 21 UCCR2d 580 (E.D. Va. 1993).

[188] *Id.* at 591.

[189] 13 UCCR 998 (D.C. Super. 1973).

[190] *Id.* at 1005. In response to the buyer's inquiry, the seller also said that the motorcycle needed no major repairs. This statement was also found to be an express warranty.

[191] Wiseman v. Wolfe's Terre Haute Auto Auction, Inc., 459 N.E.2d 736, 37 UCCR 1486 (Ind. Ct. App. 1984). The seller made the representation after the buyer had stated "I don't want to buy this truck if there is anything wrong with it mechanically. I'm buying it to put it on the road." 459 N.E.2d 736, 37 UCCR 1486, 1488. *See* Stuck v. Pioneer Logging Mach., Inc., 301 S.E.2d 552, 36 UCCR 74 (S.C. 1983) (description of truck and harvesting equipment by seller as "roadworthy" is express warranty when made in response to being told by buyer the specific purpose for which buyer was purchasing goods).

was made in response to the buyer's inquiry about the application rate of the product.[192]

A number of courts have explicitly connected the warranty/puffing distinction to the basis of the bargain requirement for express warranties. Generally, this is done through an analysis of the extent and reasonableness of the buyer's reliance on the seller's statements.[193] In *Price Bros. Co. v. Philadelphia Gear Corp.*,[194] the buyer manufactured reinforced concrete pipe. For many years, it had wrapped its concrete pipe in wire by using a machine of its own design. When the buyer decided to expand its operations, it contacted the seller about replacing certain components in the buyer's pipe-wrapping machine. After receiving brochures from the seller and engaging in discussions with its representatives, the buyer purchased a number of components from the seller. When the buyer experienced difficulty with its machine, it sued the seller for breach of express and implied warranties.

The buyer's assertion of breach of express warranties was based upon statements made by the seller in a trade journal article and in sales literature as well as assurances by the seller's representatives. Although the court did not elaborate on these statements and assurances, the statements in the advertising literature and trade journal apparently dealt in a general way with product characteristics and performance.[195] The assurances of the salespeople appear to be that components designed according to the buyer's specifications would perform in a certain manner.[196] Subsequent to receiving these statements and assurances, the buyer contracted with the seller to manufacture the components according to very detailed specifications provided by the buyer. There was no allegation that the components did not conform to the specifications provided by the buyer.

The court said that whether the statements were warranties or mere "puffing" depended upon "the circumstances surrounding the transaction,

---

[192] Figueroa v. Kit-San Co., 845 P.2d 567, 20 UCCR2d 799 (Ind. App. 1992). *See also* Mercedes-Benz of N. Am., Inc. v. Garten, 94 Md. App. 547, 618 A.2d 233, 21 UCCR2d 937 (1993) (statement that 1986 model year was "identical" to 1990 model year was express warranty when made in response to buyer's request to enumerate all differences between model years).

[193] *See* Thursby v. Reynolds Metals Co., 466 So. 2d 245, 39 UCCR 1625 (Fla. Dist. Ct. App. 1984); Balog v. Center Art Gallery-Haw., Inc., 745 F. Supp. 1556, 12 UCCR2d 962 (D. Haw. 1990); Pake v. Byrd, 55 N.C. App. 551, 286 N.E.2d 588, 33 UCCR 835 (1982); Scaringe v. Holstein, 103 A.D.2d 880, 477 N.Y.S.2d 903, 38 UCCR 1595 (1984); Eddington v. Dick, 87 Misc. 2d 793, 386 N.Y.S.2d 180, 20 UCCR 50 (N.Y. City Ct. 1976).

[194] 649 F.2d 416, 31 UCCR 469 (6th Cir. 1981).

[195] The court describes the journal article as containing "nonspecific, pre-contract statements." 649 F.2d at 422, 31 UCCR at 478.

[196] 649 F.2d at 421, 31 UCCR at 474–475.

the reasonableness of the buyer in believing the seller, and the reliance placed on the seller's statements."[197] In analyzing the circumstances surrounding the transaction, the court said that the representatives of the buyer who participated in the negotiations were engineers who were, or should have been, intimately familiar with the complicated pipe-wrapping machines that had been designed by the buyer itself. The buyer was in at least as good a position as the seller's representatives to judge whether components, which met the buyer's own specifications would do the job the buyer intended them to do. The court said that the expertise of the buyer's representatives enabled them to make an independent assessment of the adequacy of the components. In light of this, the buyer should have recognized the assurances of the seller's representatives as either puffing or false. As to the statements in the literature, the court said that the detailed specifications belied any contention that the buyer had relied upon nonspecific writings intended for unspecified general audiences. The court concluded that "it would stretch reason beyond limits" to find that the buyer relied upon these assurances and statements, and held as a matter of law that the seller had made no express warranties.

Although the court's apparent equation of reliance with the basis of the bargain test of the Code[198] is questionable,[199] the opinion focuses on the proper issue: given the entire context of the transaction, were the statements such that they would be objectively understood as part of the basis of the bargain? The relative expertise of the parties, the general nature of the oral statements in contrast to the detailed specifications, and the timing and circumstances of the statements were all factors bearing on this question and thus properly considered by the court.

Other courts have focused on reliance as well. In *Scaringe v. Holstein,*[200] the court found a statement that a car was in "excellent condition" to be puffing, in part because the buyer was on notice that the car had a transmission problem and could not have reasonably relied on the seller's statement. In *Thursby v. Reynolds Metals Co.,*[201] the court held statements by a seller to be puffing because at the time they were made, the buyer had already made up his mind to buy the product for other reasons.

---

[197] 649 F.2d at 422, 31 UCCR at 478.

[198] The court's equivalence of reliance with the basis of the bargain test is evident in such language as, "[I]t would stretch reason beyond its limits to find that the buyer *relied* on verbal assurances by salesmen and writings intended for unspecified general audiences *as a part of the basis of the bargain.*" 649 F.2d at 422–423, 31 UCCR at 475.

[199] *See* § 4.05[F][1], *infra.*

[200] 103 A.D.2d 880, 477 N.Y.S.2d 903, 38 UCCR 1595 (Div. 1984).

[201] 466 So. 2d 245, 39 UCCR 1625 (Fla. Ct. App. 1984).

Other factors, both stated and unstated, also play a role in determining whether a statement is an affirmation of fact or puffing.[202] The extent of the buyer's damages, while logically unrelated to the issue, appears to play a part.[203] Whether the statement or assurance is in writing or oral may also be a factor.[204] At least one case has indicated that representations regarding the safety of the product will be closely scrutinized.[205] Whether the performance or condition of the goods is inherently unpredictable is also a factor; the greater the inherent uncertainty, the more likely a statement will be puffing.[206]

Notwithstanding the variety of factors that come into play, some cases are simply wrongly decided. One such case is *Hall v. T.L. Kemp Jewelry,*

---

[202] In Federal Signal Corp. v. Safety Factors, Inc., 125 Wash. 2d, 886 P.2d 172, 25 UCCR2d 765 (1994) the Washington Supreme Court listed the following: whether any "hedging" occurred by the seller, the experimental nature of the good, the buyer's knowledge or imputed knowledge of the defect, and the nature of the defect.

[203] *See, e.g.,* Wiseman v. Wolfe's Terre Haute Auto Auction, Inc., 459 N.E.2d 736, 37 UCCR 1486 (Ind. Ct. App. 1984) (statement that truck was "road ready" was warranty where truck turned out to have cracked engine block); Crothers v. Cohen, 384 N.W.2d 562, 1 UCCR2d 72 (Minn. Ct. App. 1986) (jury finding that assurance that car was a "good runner" was express warranty upheld where plaintiff seriously injured when car hit tree); McGregor v. Dimou, 101 Misc. 2d 756, 422 N.Y.S.2d 806, 28 UCCR 66 (N.Y. Civ. Ct. 1979) (advertisement of car as in "very good condition" was warranty where car had previously been totaled); Eddington v. Dick, 89 Misc. 2d 793, 386 N.Y.S.2d 180, 20 UCCR 50 (N.Y. Ct. 1976) (statement that a used refrigerator was in "good condition" was a warranty where cost of repair was more than 100 percent of purchase price); Jones v. Kellner, 5 Ohio App. 3d 548, 36 UCCR 784 (1982) (statement that car was in "A-1 condition" was warranty where cost of repair exceeded value of vehicle); Valley Datsun v. Martinez, 578 S.W.2d 485, 26 UCCR 331 (Tex. Ct. Civ. App. 1979) ("excellent condition" is express warranty where automobile threw a rod and clutch burned out two days after purchase).

[204] *See* Price Bros. Co. v. Philadelphia Gear Corp., 649 F.2d 416, 31 UCCR 469 (6th Cir. 1981) (where sales agreement is reduced to writing specifying technical requirements, verbal statements by salesmen not express warranties); James J. White & Robert S. Summers, Uniform Commercial Code § 9-4, at 489 (4th ed. 1995).

[205] Hauter v. Zogarts, 14 Cal. 3d 104, 534 P.2d 377, 120 Cal. Rptr. 16 UCCR 938 (1975). *See also* Moore v. Berry, 217 Ga. App. 697, 458 S.E.2d 879 (1995) (seller's representation that tree-climbing stand was "probably the safest one on the market" sufficient to raise jury question).

[206] *See* Sessa v. Riegle, 427 F. Supp. 760, 21 UCCR 745 (E.D. Pa. 1977), *aff'd,* 568 F.2d 770 (3d Cir. 1977) (statement that a racehorse was "sound" is opinion rather than express warranty); Axion Corp. v. G.D.C. Leasing Corp., 359 Mass. 474, 269 N.E.2d 664, 9 UCCR 17 (1971) (prototype machine); Connor v. Bogreth, 596 P.2d 683, 26 UCCR 902 (Wyo. 1979) (statements regarding potential of dog). *But see* Simpson v. Widger, 709 A.2d 1366, 35 UCCR2d 837 (N.J. Super. 1998) (representation that horse was "sound" created express warranty).

Inc.,[207] which involved a husband searching for an anniversary present for his wife. He visited the seller's jewelry shop and liked a diamond bracelet. After some negotiation concerning the price, the buyer decided to purchase the bracelet for $1,900. He asked the seller about the quality of the gems, and the seller replied that they were of "excellent quality." The buyer then said to the seller, "If I have $2,000 worth of jewelry, let's wrap it up." The seller then gave the buyer an appraisal form which indicated the value of the bracelet to be $2,650. After he gave the bracelet to his wife, she later had the bracelet appraised by two other jewelers. One appraised the bracelet at $900 and the other at $550. When the buyer sued, the court found none of the seller's representations to be express warranties. Instead, it found the seller's representations to be statements of value which it said are not express warranties in the absence of special circumstances. The court found no special circumstances.

The court made the wrong decision by ignoring the circumstances surrounding the transaction. First, there is a great disparity in the ability of the parties to judge the worth of the goods. Only an expert can discern whether gems are of high quality and were cut properly. Second, the seller's representations came in response to the buyer's expressed concerns about the quality of the gems and their value. Finally, the insurance appraisal form, although stating that it was for insurance purposes only, described the gems, without qualification, as having a value of $2,650. The authors believe the court should have found a breach of express warranty in this case.

Although an attempt has been made to isolate some of the factors relevant to the puffing/warranty decision, the necessity of examining the total context cannot be avoided.[208] Although section 2-313 prevents a statement that is *merely* the seller's opinion from being warranty, only by examining the context in which a statement is made can it be determined whether the statement is one *merely* of opinion or whether *more* than the seller's opinion is involved. This brings us back to the requirement that statements must be part of the basis of the bargain and the test of Comment

---

[207] 71 N.C. App. 101, 322 S.E.2d 7, 39 UCCR 1648 (1984).

[208] *See* Trumpey Tire Sales & Serv., Inc. v. Stine, 266 Pa. Super. 9, 403 A.2d 108, 27 UCCR 92 (1979) (statement that retread tires would have a 5 to 7 percent failure rate mere opinion in the context of "no adjustments" clause in contract); Alcan Aluminum Corp. v. Carlton Aluminum of New Eng., Inc., 35 Mass. App. Ct. 161, 617 N.E.2d 1005, 24 UCCR2d 66 (1993) (statement that manufacturer would "back up its materials 100%" is express warranty where manufacturer knows buyer has given its own buyers long-term unconditional warranty).

8 to section 2-313: "What statements of the seller have in the circumstances and in objective judgment become a part of the basis of the bargain?"[209]

[C]　Description of the Goods

There were cases in both England[210] and the United States[211] holding that descriptions of the goods did not constitute warranties. These cases, however, were firmly rejected by the Uniform Sales Act, which provided that descriptions of the goods created *implied* warranties. The Code has continued the idea that warranties may be created by descriptions, but descriptions are now *express* warranties. Section 2-313(1)(b) provides:

> Any description of the goods which is made part of the basis of the bargain creates an express warranty that the goods shall conform to the description.[212]

There were good reasons for changing the description warranty from "implied" to "express," although the seller's liability for breach is fundamentally the same whether the warranty is express or implied. First, the factual background which produces the description warranty is similar to that which produces an affirmation-of-fact warranty. For example, when a seller states that she has a certain brand of goods for sale,[213] she is affirming a fact about those goods (that they are of the brand stated) and she is, at the same time, describing them.

Second, express warranties cannot be disclaimed.[214] A disclaimer of implied warranties will not affect a warranty by description, and a general disclaimer of express warranties that is inconsistent with a warranty by de-

---

[209] U.C.C. § 2-313, Official Comment 8.

[210] *See, e.g.*, Chandelor v. Lopus, 3 Cro. Jac. 4, 79 Eng. Rep. 3 (Ex. 1603); Budd v. Fairmaener, 8 Bing. 48 52, 131 Eng. Rep. 318, 320 (C.P. 1831) ("grey four year old colt" held not to be a warranty but a "matter of description only").

[211] *See, e.g.*, Seixas v. Woods, 3 Caines (N.Y.) 48 (1804); Shambaugh v. Current, 111 Iowa 121, 82 N.W. 497 (1900); Willard v. Stevens, 24 N.H. 271 (1851); Rollins v. Northern Land & Logging Co., 134 Wis. 447, 114 N.W. 819 (1908).

[212] U.C.C. § 2-313(1)(b).

[213] *See, e.g.*, Preiser v. Jim Letts Oldsmobile, Inc., 160 Ga. App. 658, 288 S.E.2d 219 (Ga. Ct. App. 1981); Riggs v. Peach State Ford Truck Sales, Inc., 503 F. Supp. 190 (N.D. Ga. 1980); Gour v. Daray Motor Co., Inc., 373 So. 2d 571 (La. Ct. App. 1979).

[214] *See* U.C.C. § 2-316(1); § 4.07[B], *infra*.

scription will not be given effect.[215] A buyer can quite properly assume that a general warranty disclaimer does not mean that the buyer will not receive the goods he ordered. It is reasonable for the buyer to believe that he is entitled to the described goods and that the seller cannot perform his agreement by shipping something different—even though there is a general disclaimer of express warranties.[216]

Warranties of description exist in virtually every contract for the sale of goods. Apart from the rare case in which a seller sells an unopened box and the buyer takes the complete risk as to its contents, sometime during the negotiation, the seller will have in some way described the product he or she intends to sell (or the product will have described itself).[217] For example, the seller will have called the item a car, a bottle of aspirin, a calculator, a computer, or whatever it is. The description may be contained in an acknowledgment,[218] in an advertisement,[219] in the contract itself,[220] on a label,[221] or made orally by the seller.[222]

Descriptions may also be very detailed. A seller's description of a machine may have included detailed specifications of the machine's size, power, tolerances, and speed.[223] In such cases, it is easy to determine the

---

[215] U.C.C. § 2-316(1). An attempted disclaimer, however, may prevent a description from becoming a part of the basis of the bargain, and therefore from becoming a warranty. *See* § 4.05[F], *infra*. *See also* Murray v. D&J Motor Co., 35 UCCR2d 1117 (Okla. Civ. App. 1998) (warranty by description survives disclaimer of "all warranties").

[216] *See* U.C.C. § 2-313, Official Comment 4:

[A] contract is normally a contract for a sale of something describable and described. A clause generally disclaiming "all warranties, express or implied" cannot reduce the seller's obligation with respect to such description and therefore cannot be given literal effect under Section 2-316.

[217] *See* Roth v. Ray-Stel's Hair Stylists, Inc., 470 N.E.2d 137, 39 UCCR 1239 (Mass. Ct. App. 1984).

[218] Northern States Power Co. v. ITT Meyer Indus., 777 F.2d 405, 42 UCCR 1 (8th Cir. 1985). *But see* Witherspoon v. Phillip Morris, Inc., 964 F. Supp. 455, 35 UCCR2d 850 (D.D.C. 1997) (cigarette ad did not create an express warranty).

[219] Mennonite Deaconess Home & Hosp., Inc. v. Gates Eng'g Co., Inc., 363 N.W.2d 155, 40 UCCR 396 (Neb. 1985).

[220] Ricwil, Inc. v. S.L. Pappas & Co., Inc., 599 So. 2d 1126, 18 UCCR2d 88 (Ala. 1992).

[221] Agricultural Servs. Ass'n, Inc. v. Ferry-Morse Seed Co., Inc., 551 F.2d 1057, 21 UCCR 443 (6th Cir. 1977); Swenson v. Chevron Chem. Co., 234 N.W.2d 38, 18 UCCR 67 (S.D. 1975).

[222] Transamerica Oil Corp. v. Lynes, Inc., 723 F.2d 758, 37 UCCR 1076 (10th Cir. 1983).

[223] *See, e.g.*, Betaco, Inc. v. Cessna Aircraft Co., 32 F.3d 1126, 24 UCCR2d 718 (7th Cir. 1994); Fournier Furniture, Inc. v. Waltz-Holst Blow Pipe Co., 980 F. Supp. 187, 36 UCCR2d 347 (W.D. Va. 1997) (reference to specifications for a furnace created express warranties).

scope and content of the description, and thus easy to determine whether the description was accurate.[224] When the description is more general, however, the task is more difficult. Calling an item of goods a "car" describes the item of goods. It is thus an express warranty if it is a part of the basis of the bargain. But what has the seller warranted by this description? If it turns out that the item delivered by the seller has no engine, has the express warranty been breached? Certainly it would seem so; a car without an engine is more apt to be described as a "car body" than a car. On the other hand, if everything is in working order except the windshield wipers, no one would be offended at the description of the item as a "car." At some point between an automobile without an engine and an automobile with everything except windshield wipers, the item has become a "car." But what is that point?

This interpretive problem—determining the "implied content" of express warranties[225]—is complicated by the fact that the content of the Code's *implied* warranty of merchantability is, to a significant degree, a function of the *description* of the goods.[226] This reliance on the contract description to provide content to the merchantability warranty is explicit in Comment 3 to section 2-314:

> A specific designation of goods by the buyer does not exclude the seller's obligation that they be fit for the general purposes appropriate to such goods. A contract for the sale of second-hand goods, however, involves only such obligation as is appropriate to such goods *for that is their contract description.*[227]

Thus, the contract description provides the framework for determining what qualities are *implied* for purposes of the merchantability warranty: a description of a car as "used" will imply certain qualities different from a description of a car as "new." It is possible that certain express warranties by

---

[224] *See* Sullivan v. Young Bros. & Co., Inc., 893 F. Supp. 1148, 30 UCCR2d 106 (D. Me. 1995) (product would attain "near maximum hoop and longitudinal strengths"), *aff'd in part and reversed in part*, 91 F.3d 242, 30 UCCR2d 121 (1st Cir. 1996).

[225] *See* Herbert, "What's in a Name?: The Implied Content of Express Warranties," 12 U. Dayton L. Rev. 297 (1986).

[226] *See* U.C.C. § 2-314(2):

> Goods to be merchantable must be at least as such as
> (a) pass without objection in the trade under the contract *description*;
> (b) in the case of fungible goods, are of fair average quality within the *description*;
> (c) are fit for the ordinary purposes for which *such goods* are used;

[227] U.C.C. § 2-314, Official Comment 3 (emphasis added).

description—called by one author "generic" descriptions[228]—and the implied warranty of merchantability are simply mirror images of each other; the express warranty given by the description "car" guarantees precisely those same qualities necessary to make the car merchantable.

If true, this duplication would not be a problem except that the Code treats express and implied warranties differently in a number of respects. As previously mentioned, express warranties cannot be disclaimed. On the other hand, while there are certain procedural hoops that a seller must first jump through, implied warranties can be disclaimed with relative ease. If the implied warranty of merchantability has been disclaimed, can the buyer do an "end-run" around the disclaimer through a claimed warranty by description? In addition, the statute of limitations for implied warranties can extend no longer than four years from the date tender of delivery of the goods.[229] The statute of limitations extends beyond this period only if a warranty *explicitly* extends to future performance, something implied warranties, by their nature, cannot do.[230] Express warranties, however, can explicitly extend to future performance. Thus, it may be that the statute of limitations has run on the implied warranty of merchantability but not on express warranties.[231] Can the buyer, by arguing that the seller's general description of the goods implies the same characteristics about product quality or performance as the implied warranty of merchantability, overcome the statute of limitations?

On the other hand it is possible that the generic description "car," while implying certain qualities about the item, does not imply the same qualities as "merchantable car." The contract description of the goods can be *relevant* to determine the content of the warranty of merchantability without implying the same content. Nonetheless, the relationship between express warranties by description and the implied warranty of merchantability remains obscure.

Few cases have dealt with this problem in its starkest form—determining the implied content of a simple description of the broad category to which the good belongs, such as "car," "boat," "engine," etc.—and they have reached dramatically different results. In *Tacoma Boatbuilding*

---

[228] Barkley Clark & Christopher Smith, The Law of Product Warranties, § 4.02(2)(b) at 4-16 (1984).

[229] U.C.C. § 2-725(2).

[230] *See* Rutland v. Swift Chem. Co., 351 So. 2d 324, 22 UCCR 1180 (Miss. 1977); Safeway Stores, Inc. v. Certainteed Corp., 710 S.W.2d 544, 1 UCCR2d 1237 (Tex. 1986); Nationwide Ins. Co. v. General Motors Corp., 625 A.2d 1172, 21 UCCR2d 277 (Pa. 1993).

[231] *See* Moore v. Puget Sound Plywood, Inc., 214 Neb. 14, 332 N.W.2d 212, 36 UCCR 82 (1983); Anderson v. Crestliner, 564 N.W.2d 218, 33 UCCR2d 99 (Minn. Ct. App. 1997).

Co., Inc. v. Delta Fishing Co., Inc.,[232] the court was unwilling to read more than the bare essentials into a generic description. Tacoma built four fishing vessels for four Greek fishing companies (the "buyers") that were engaged in deep sea purse seine fishing for tuna. The engines developed mechanical problems, and, as a result, the buyers withheld a portion of the purchase price. Eventually, Tacoma sued, and the buyers counterclaimed for damages for breach of warranty against Tacoma and also sued General Electric and Western Gear, which had manufactured some component parts. Unfortunately for the buyers, the contracts between Tacoma and both General Electric and Western Gear contained disclaimers of implied warranties.[233]

The buyers attempted to overcome these disclaimers by arguing that the generic description "engine" was an express warranty that was breached by the defects present in the engines. The court agreed that an express warranty had been created by this description, but drew a distinction between the description of an item and its performance:

> The [buyers] liken the [defective] marine engine to a "wooden box," but their analogy is made of straw. GE delivered what the contracts called for: marine engines. Each functioned for a time after installation and, with one exception, each of the engines is still being used by the [buyers] to catch fish.
>
> Had GE in fact delivered a wooden box instead of an engine, the GFCs would be entitled to relief. . . . Most likely, the contract's description of the goods as an "engine" created an express warranty, under § 2-313, that GE would deliver something *of that general nature and function*.[234]

A similar case is *Universal Drilling Co. v. Camay Drilling Co.*[235] The case involved the sale of used oil-drilling equipment. Both parties were sophisticated businesspeople, experienced in the oil-drilling business. The sale was made on an "as is" basis, effectively disclaiming implied warranties. When the equipment failed to function properly, the buyers claimed that the description of the goods had created an express warranty that they would perform the function goods of that description were intended to perform. In rejecting this argument, the court said that if the seller had delivered

---

[232] 28 UCCR 26 (W.D. Wash. 1980).

[233] The court determined that to the extent that the disclaimers were effective against Tacoma, they would also be effective against the buyers. 28 UCCR at 29–30.

[234] 28 UCCR at 29 (emphasis added).

[235] 737 F.2d 869, 38 UCCR 1576 (10th Cir. 1984). See also Colton v. Decker, 540 N.W.2d 172, 30 UCCR2d 206 (S.D. 1995) (description as "1975 Peterbilt Model 359 Tractor" was not breached by defects in truck).

junk metal that in no way resembled drilling equipment, there would indeed be a breach of express warranty, despite the disclaimer. The description, however, did not carry with it a promise that the goods would function properly.

At the other end of the spectrum is *Moore v. Puget Sound Plywood, Inc.*[236] In this case, Mr. and Mrs. Moore purchased siding for their house in 1971. Within a few years the siding had deteriorated significantly, but suit was not brought by the Moores until 1981. The statute of limitations on implied warranties had expired in 1975[237] and, on this basis, the suit was not timely. Although it had not been pleaded, the court was willing to consider the complaint as incorporating a claim for breach of express warranty as well. If an express warranty extending to future performance could be shown, the suit would not be barred by the statute of limitations.

The court found that the contract had described the goods as "siding" and that this language had created an express warranty by description. The court noted that the trial court, with the consent of the parties, had taken judicial notice that "generally siding, when it's put on, is supposed to last the life of the house."[238] From this general expectation that siding should last for the life of a house, the court found that the description carried with it a representation that it would, in fact, do so.[239]

The court's decision effectively obliterated any distinction between a warranty by description and the implied warranty of merchantability. The touchstone of the implied warranty of merchantability is the characteristics of quality and performance that buyers reasonably expect goods of a particular description to have.[240] The court read all of these expectations into the description itself. [241]

---

[236] 214 Neb. 14, 332 N.W.2d 212, 36 UCCR 82 (1983).

[237] *See* U.C.C. § 2-725(1).

[238] 214 Neb. at 16, 332 N.W.2d at 214, 36 UCCR at 83.

[239] "Therefore, the requisite elements of § 2-313(1)(b) are present; that is, the description of the goods became a part of the bargain and created in the minds of the parties the expectation that the siding would last the lifetime of the house." 214 Neb. at 16, 332 N.W.2d at 214, 36 UCCR at 84.

[240] *See* § 4.06[B][4], *infra.*

[241] Relying on *Moore*, the Court of Appeals for the Eighth Circuit, in Economy Housing Co., Inc. v. Continental Forest Prods., 757 F.2d 200, 40 UCCR 823 (8th Cir. 1985), said that a defendant was not entitled to summary judgment on a buyer's express warranty claim when the paint peeled on siding that the buyer had purchased from the defendant. The court said that the product had been described as "exterior siding" which, under *Moore*, created a sufficient issue of fact on the express warranty claim to preclude summary judgment. *But see* Murphy v. Spelts-Schultz Lumber Co. of Grand Island, 240 Neb. 275, 17 UCCR2d 467 (1992), another Nebraska case seemingly at odds with *Moore*. In this case, the court held

Most of the cases appear to follow the approach of *Tacoma Boatbuilding* rather than *Moore*. For example, in *Stephens v. Crittenden Tractor Co.*,[242] plaintiff had been promised a "floating grain head" in the contract. The court held that it was a question of fact whether a warranty by description had been breached. The court said that if the defendant had delivered a "fixed grain head" instead of a floating grain head there was a breach; if, however, defendant had delivered a floating grain head that did not work, there was no breach of the warranty by description.[243] In *Alan Wood Steel Co. v. Capital Equipment Enterprises*,[244] the description of a crane as a "75 ton, 40 foot boom Brownhoist Steam Locomotive Crane" was held not to be a warranty that the crane could actually lift 75 tons. And, in *Szajna v. General Motors Corp.*,[245] the Illinois Supreme Court said that the description of a car as a "1976 Pontiac Ventura" identified the manufacturer and model, but did not imply anything about the nature and quality of the transmission.[246] There are, however, a number of cases in addition to those already mentioned that have more of the flavor of *Moore*, although their holdings do not extend as far.[247]

A number of cases have dealt with the content of the description "new" in the context of the sale of automobiles. The case of *Blankenship v. Northtown Ford, Inc.*[248] appears to take an approach more like *Moore* than *Tacoma Boatbuilding*, although the opinion is somewhat confused. In this case, the buyers bought a "new" 1979 Ford Bronco. Within four months of purchase, the car had been in the shop eleven times for various defects.[249] At the end

---

that the mere representation of goods as "roofing trusses" does not create warranty extending to future performance.

[242] 187 Ga. App. 545, 370 S.E.2d 757, 7 UCCR2d 724 (Ga. Ct. App. 1988).

[243] *Id.* at 370 S.E.2d at 757, 7 UCCR2d 724.

[244] 39 Ill. App. 3d 48, 349 N.E.2d 627, 19 UCCR 1310 (Ill. Ct. App. 1976).

[245] 503 N.E.2d 760, 115 Ill. 2d 294, 2 UCCR2d 1268 (Ill. 1986).

[246] *See also* Davis v. Siloo, Inc., 267 S.E.2d 354, 29 UCCR 492 (N.C. Ct. App. 1980) (statement that "product permits the immersion of hands; some dryness of the skin may result after prolonged exposure" did not give rise to express warranty that product would not be harmful when spilled all over plaintiff's arms).

[247] *See, e.g.*, Poter v. MCP Facilities Corp., 471 F. Supp. 1344, 26 UCCR 651 (E.D.N.Y. 1979) (brochure describing paint as "underwater paint" could create express warranty that paint would adhere under water); Pau v. Yosemite Park and Curry Co., 928 F.2d 880, 14 UCCR2d 79 (9th Cir. 1991) (statement that bike trail was "safe and enjoyable cycling area" constituted express warranty that rental bicycles were safe for the trail when company that made statement in brochure was also sole renter of bikes).

[248] 420 N.E.2d 167, 95 Ill. App. 3d 303, 31 UCCR 480 (Ill. Ct. App. 1981).

[249] These included oil leaks, a broken alternator belt, a maladjusted clutch, a broken drive shaft, a broken U-joint, and other problems. 420 N.E.2d at 170, 95 Ill. App. 3d at 305, 31 UCCR at 483.

of this period, the buyer attempted to give the Bronco back to the seller for a refund, an offer that the seller refused. When the buyer sued on the basis of the implied warranty of merchantability, the seller pointed to a disclaimer of the warranty of merchantability. In an opinion in which it is unclear whether the court found the disclaimer of implied warranties ineffective or relied on an express warranty,[250] the court upheld the plaintiff's claim. Focusing on the description of the Bronco as "new," the court said:

> Defendants were purportedly selling plaintiffs a "new" car. The logical extension of the dealer's argument in this case is that delivery by the dealer of anything which it referred to as a "new car," even an automobile without an engine would bar plaintiff's action for rescission.[251]

Thus, the court relied upon the description of the car as "new" to permit the return of a "lemon" despite the disclaimer of the merchantability warranty.

In *Horne v. Claude Ray Ford Sales, Inc.*,[252] the court adopted a more restrictive definition of "new." It said that the "intrinsic quality" of a new car is only that it has neither been damaged nor used to a significant extent. The court in *General Motors Corp. v. Green*[253] agreed with this general definition of "new," but permitted the manufacturer to restrict this definition even further in its new car warranty to allow for repair of damage occurring at the factory during the manufacturing process.[254]

---

[250] The disclaimer of the warranty of merchantability in the case appears to comply with U.C.C. § 2-316; at least, there is no indication that it does not. Furthermore, the court makes no finding that the disclaimer is unconscionable or otherwise ineffective. It also quotes in its entirety Comment 4 to section 2-313 dealing with express warranties. All of this would suggest the basis for the court's decision is breach of express warranty. Other language in the opinion, however, casts doubt on this conclusion.

[251] 420 N.E.2d at 170, 95 Ill. App. 3d at 307, 31 UCCR at 485.

[252] 290 S.E.2d 497, 34 UCCR 880 (Ga. Ct. App. 1982).

[253] 173 Ga. App. 188, 325 S.E.2d 794, 40 UCCR 828 (Ga. Ct. App. 1984).

[254] *Id.* at 189, 325 S.E.2d at 795, 40 UCCR at 829. The court in Harris v. Ford Motor Co., Inc., 845 F. Supp. 1511, 25 UCCR2d 53 (M.D. Ala. 1994) reached the same result as the court in the *Green* case. The court allowed the definition of "new" to be limited in the New Car Warranty despite the fact that the warranty was located in the glove compartment and had not been delivered to the plaintiff prior to the contract. Because the plaintiff knew the New Car Warranty was in the glove compartment at the time of the purchase, it held the limitation effective. Other cases have held limitations of remedies and warranty disclaimers located in the glove compartments of new cars to be ineffective. Koellmer v. Chrysler Motors Corp., 276 A.2d 807, 8 UCCR 668 (Conn. Cir. Ct. 1970) (finding warranty disclaimer placed in glove compartment and including small type did not meet UCC requirements that disclaimers be conspicuous); Hahn v. Ford Motor Co., Inc., 434 N.E.2d 943, 33 UCCR 1277

The problem of the "generic" description has no easy solution. The drafters almost certainly did not intend a generic description of an item to incorporate all of the aspects of merchantability (i.e., to warrant against run-of-the-mill defects). On the other hand, there is a limit beyond which a term no longer accurately describes an item without explicit qualification.[255] The answer will turn on the facts of each case, but statements and descriptions should always be interpreted as a reasonable buyer would have understood them under the circumstances.

[D]   Sample or Model

The final method of creating an express warranty is through the use of samples or models. The basic framework of this warranty is the same as the others:

> Any sample or model which is made part of the basis of the bargain creates an express warranty that the whole of the goods shall conform to the sample or model.[256]

Although the Code does not contain definitions for either "sample" or "model," the Comments describe what was intended by the drafters. Comment 6 states that:

> The section includes both a 'sample' drawn from the bulk of goods which is the subject matter of the sale, and a 'model' which is offered for inspection when the subject matter is not at hand and which has not been drawn from the bulk of the goods. Thus, a model may exist even though there is yet no bulk of goods, as where the seller has exhibited an item which has yet to be produced or acquired by the seller.[257]

(Ind. Ct. App. 1982) (finding modification of implied warranties and limitation of remedies contained in the automobile manufacturer's booklet in car's glove compartment ineffective unless evidence was shown that the buyer asserted to the modified terms prior to the sale). *See also* Century Dodge, Inc. v. Mobley, 155 Ga. App. 712, 272 S.E.2d 502, 30 UCCR 844 (Ga. Ct. App. 1980) (whether car that had been allegedly involved in an accident is "new" is question of fact for the jury); American Honda Motor Co., Inc. v. Boyd, 475 So. 2d 835, 41 UCCR 410 (Ala. 1985) (car which suffers major damage en route to U.S. and is repaired before delivery is not "new").

[255] *See* Warner v. Reagan Buick, Inc., 483 N.W.2d 764, 240 Neb. 668, 17 UCCR2d 746 (Neb. 1992) (warranty created by description "1983 Buick Riviera" breached when car was skeleton of 1983 Buick Riviera with mishmash of parts from other years and models).

[256] U.C.C. § 2-313(1)(c).

[257] U.C.C. § 2-313, Official Comment 6.

This Comment suggests that a prototype, even though intended to be a replica of the goods to be produced for the buyer, would be a "model" rather than a "sample," because the subject matter of the contract is not yet at hand. In the cases involving prototypes, however, courts have referred to the prototypes as both "samples" and "models."[258]

The fact that a seller shows a buyer either a sample or a model does not necessarily create an express warranty. The sample or model must be made part of the "basis of the bargain" before a warranty is created.[259] A seller may show a buyer a "sample" or "model" intending to suggest to the buyer the nature and quality of the seller's goods, but not intending to promise that the goods delivered will have those (or any particular) qualities. To create a warranty, the seller must present the sample or model in such a way and under such circumstances as to reasonably represent to the buyer the seller's *assurance* that the goods delivered to the buyer will have certain qualities or characteristics.

In *Kopper Glo Fuel, Inc. v. Island Lake Coal Co.*,[260] the buyer, a coal broker, was interested in purchasing coal to provide to General Motors, one of the buyer's customers. The buyer and seller discussed the qualities of the seller's coal, and the buyer was permitted to examine samples of the coal. In addition, the buyer was given laboratory analyses of the seller's coal. Thereafter, the buyer agreed to purchase coal from the seller. When it turned out that the coal that was delivered had higher ash and sulphur contents than the samples and the laboratory results, the buyer refused to pay for a portion of the coal delivered.[261] The seller then sued the buyer for the price, and the buyer counterclaimed for breach of warranty.

The buyer argued that the samples and the lab analyses had created express warranties that the coal would have a certain content of ash and

---

[258] *Compare* Baltimore Mach. and Equip., Inc. v. Holtite Mfg. Co., Inc., 215 A.2d 458, 3 UCCR 36 (Md. 1965) (warranty by sample can exist of goods manufactured in the future); Automated Controls, Inc. v. MIC Enters., Inc., 27 UCCR 661 (D. Neb. 1978) ("in-house" test of prototype sale by "sample") *with* Barton v. Tra-Mo, Inc., 69 Or. App. 295, 38 UCCR 1601 (Or. Ct. App. 1984) (preproduction model of storage tank created express warranty by model); Pacific Marine Schwabacher, Inc. v. Hydroswift Corp., 525 P.2d 615, 15 UCCR 354 (Utah 1974) (sample must be drawn from bulk of goods that are the subject of the sale— piece of acrylic of the type to be used in goods is not sample).

[259] *See* Furlong v. Alpha Chi Omega Sorority, 73 Ohio Misc. 2d 26, 657 N.E.2d 866, 28 UCCR2d 1194 (Mun. Ct. 1993).

[260] 436 F. Supp. 91, 22 UCCR 1117 (E.D. Tenn. 1977).

[261] The buyer refused to pay for a portion of the coal even though it had been paid in full by General Motors. The buyer argued that as a result of the quality of the coal provided by the seller, the buyer lost future business and profits. 436 F. Supp. at 93, 22 UCCR at 1120.

sulphur. The court, however, agreed with the seller that express warranties had not been created. Instead, the samples and analyses had merely been provided as information the buyer could use to arrive at its own judgment about the seller's coal. The court said that the quality of coal differs substantially within a given mine, and the buyer's representative was a highly educated man who was well-versed in the chemistry of coal. Although the court called the issue of a warranty by sample in the case a "close question," it held that under these circumstances, the seller intended only to provide the samples to the buyer "for what they were worth," and the buyer's representative should have understood this.[262]

Kopper Glo is a close case, and the court would have been justified in finding for the buyer. Simply because both parties understood that the quality of the coal within a mine varies significantly does not *necessarily* mean that the parties intended the buyer to bear the risk if the coal did not meet the quality of the sample and lab analyses. Further, while under these circumstances the sample may not have created a warranty that none of the coal would vary from the sample, it may have created a warranty that a variation as large as occurred would not take place. The court's analysis (as opposed to its conclusion), however, is unassailable. Its focus on the surrounding circumstances to determine whether the buyer reasonably understood the sample as *promising* certain characteristics or as merely provided to the buyer "for what it's worth" is correct.[263]

Dormont Manufacturing Co., Inc. v. ITT Grinnell Corp.[264] presented the interesting question of whether a warranty by sample was created by goods provided in prior sales. From 1973 to 1977, Dormont bought fittings from Grinnell for use in manufacturing hose connectors. Dormont used the fittings to make connectors for hoses that transmitted both liquids and gases. In 1977, Grinnell changed the material from which it made the fittings from brass to copper. While copper provided a satisfactory fitting for a connector when liquid was transmitted in the hose, it proved unsatisfactory for the transmission of gas. When Dormont's connectors were rejected by some of its customers who transmitted natural gas, it sued Grinnell. Among other things, Dormont argued that Grinell's shipments of brass fittings during the prior four years had created a warranty by sample.

---

[262] *Id.* at 96, 22 UCCR at 1122.

[263] For a very similar case, *see* Sylvia Coal Co., Inc. v. Mercury Coal & Coke Co., 156 S.E.2d 1, 4 UCCR 650 (W. Va. 1967).

[264] 469 A.2d 1138, 323 Pa. Super. 17, 37 UCCR 1087 (Pa. Super. Ct. 1983).

Relying on an earlier case,[265] the court rejected this argument, saying that satisfactory prior sales alone do not create a warranty by sample or model. The brass fittings sold earlier had not been drawn from the bulk of goods and therefore were not samples. Also, because they had not been offered for inspection prior to the sale, they were also not models. The court said that a sample or a model is something exhibited as such by the seller, not simply the subject of a prior sale.

The court's analysis is correct; goods delivered under prior sales do not conform to our common understanding of the meanings of "sample" and "model." The problem is better analyzed by asking whether the seller had created an implied warranty as to the composition of the goods under section 2-314(3), which permits implied warranties to be created by course of dealing.[266]

In a couple of cases, the circumstances under which goods were shown to the buyer were sufficient to preclude a warranty by sample or model. In *Logan Equipment Corp. v. Simon Aerials, Inc.*,[267] the demonstration of a 42-foot full hydraulic boomlift did not create a warranty by model with respect to the operation of an 80-foot hydraulic boomlift. The court said that the physical differences between the two machines, as well as the buyer's own knowledge that a boomlift's design varies greatly with such characteristics as its boom length and weight, were sufficient to prevent the formation of an express warranty. Similarly, in *Flynn v. Biomet, Inc.*,[268] a doctor slamming a hip prosthesis on a table to demonstrate its strength did not create a warranty as to its durability when used within the human body.

These last two cases suggest an important point. A "sample" or "model" may create an express warranty as to some characteristics, but not others. For example, in the *Logan Equipment* case above, the demonstration may not have created a warranty as to the performance characteristics of the 80-foot boom, but it may have created an express warranty as to its general design or style. In the same manner, the physician's actions in *Flynn* may not have created a warranty that the hip prosthesis would not deteriorate over time in the human body, but may have created a warranty that it would not shatter abruptly.

---

[265] Agricultural Servs. Ass'n, Inc., v. Ferry-Morse Seed Co., 551 F.2d 1057, 21 UCCR 443 (6th Cir. 1977).

[266] The court did consider whether the seller breached the implied warranty of merchantability (U.C.C. § 2-314) or the implied warranty of fitness for a particular purpose (U.C.C. § 2-315). *See* § 4.06, *infra*.

[267] 736 F. Supp. 1188, 12 UCCR2d 387 (D. Mass. 1990).

[268] 21 UCCR2d 580 (E.D. Va. 1993).

In addition to *whether* a warranty has been created with respect to a particular quality or characteristic, the precise *content* of any warranty must be considered. For example, a buyer who purchases 10,000 bricks after examining one that had been shown to him by the seller would not reasonably understand that all of the bricks delivered by the seller would conform exactly to the size, shape, and color of the sample brick. Nevertheless, the exhibited brick would probably create a warranty by sample of the *general* characteristics of the bricks to be purchased—that is, of their general size, shape, color, and hardness. On the other hand, the nature of the goods and the circumstances of the contract sometimes requires that the goods delivered conform *precisely* to the sample delivered.[269]

This problem is illustrated by the early case of *Washington Fruit & Produce Co. v. Ted Mirski Co.*[270] The contract in this case called for the seller to deliver cherries that were "12 row larger." The seller sent the buyer a card with a hole that was precisely 56/64" in diameter. The buyer claimed that the contract description and the sizing card created a warranty that the cherries would have a *minimum* diameter of 56/64". The seller, on the other hand, asserted that it needed only to deliver cherries that had an *average* size of 56/64". The court agreed with the seller, finding that the sizing card was an indication of the average size to be expected.[271] The court referred to an understanding in the trade, as exemplified by the Washington Cherry Marketing Committee standard, to reach its conclusion as to the meaning of the sizing card.

The problem of interpretation is exacerbated when a model is shown rather than a sample. As Comment 6 to section 2-313 states, the presumption that a model is a literal description of the subject matter of the sale is not as strong when a model, rather than a sample, is offered for the buyer's inspection.[272] A small-scale model or a model made from different materials than the product itself may cause special problems in determining the scope of the warranty. Two cases, involving similar products, are illustrative. In

---

[269] *See, e.g.*, Rock Creek Ginger Ale Co., Inc. v. Thermice Corp., 352 F. Supp. 522, 12 UCCR 810 (D.D.C. 1971) (carbon dioxide for use in preparation of soft drinks).

[270] 3 UCCR 175 (U.S.D.A. 1965).

[271] It is not clear from the case whether the court found the sizing card to constitute an express warranty by sample or model. It apparently did not, erroneously believing that to do so would require that *every* cherry would have to be *exactly* 56/64" in diameter. 3 UCCR at 177. As the foregoing text argues, however, a warranty by sample does not necessarily require exact conformity with the sample.

[272] U.C.C. § 2-313, Official Comment 6.

one case,[273] the buyer purchased storm windows after examining a smaller model of the windows. The model windows fit their frame relatively tightly, even though there was no inside support. When the full-scale windows were installed, however, the fit was quite different. On the full-size window, the lack of an inside support became critical, and the windows rattled—letting in the wind, snow, and rain. Because of the small size of the model, the lack of an inside support seemingly made little difference in the tightness of the fit of the window. In the full-size window, however, the loss of contact between the sash and the window increased proportionately, causing the elements to enter. Did the windows conform to the model?

In one sense, they did. The product contained the same number of pieces arranged in exactly the same manner as found on the model. In another sense, however, the product did not conform: the model windows fit relatively snugly within the frame, the actual windows did not. What does the language "conform to the sample or model" in section 2-313 mean? Does it mean that the larger product must operate in the same fashion as the smaller model, or is it sufficient if the larger product has the same physical features?

A later case presented another court with a similar problem. In *Mileham & King, Inc. v. Fitzgerald,*[274] a buyer was shown a model of inside shutters for her windows. The shutters used in the model fit tightly into the window frames. When the actual shutters were installed, however, there were small gaps between the shutters and the frames that allowed light to enter when the shutters were closed. The court found that the buyer was told that her windows were not perfectly rectangular, but that the shutters would be custom made. On these facts, the court held that the model had become part of the basis of the bargain and, therefore, had created an express warranty that the shutters would fit tightly against the windows.

The court recognized, however, that its decision that a warranty had been created that the shutters would fit tightly did not end the inquiry. The court had to determine what "tightly" meant in this context. Citing the earlier edition of this text, the court concluded that it could not answer this question without inquiring into the purposes a buyer might have in purchasing the shutters, and whether those purposes were frustrated by the divergence between the model and the actual windows. The court concluded that the shutters should serve three purposes: to enhance the appearance of the interior, to provide privacy, and to keep out the light. While the shutters

---

[273] Loomis Bros. Corp. v. Queen, 17 Pa. D. & C. 2d 482, 1 UCCR 107 (Pa. Ct. C.P. 1958).

[274] 33 UCCR 208 (D.C. Super. 1982).

fulfilled the first two purposes, the gaps were sufficient to allow light to enter, and thus the shutters did not accomplish the third goal. Therefore, there was a breach of the warranty created by the model.

The case is an example of a proper analysis of a warranty by model. It is not enough to find that a warranty has been created by the model and that the actual product diverges in some way from the model. When a model is used, this will almost inevitably be the case. Instead, the court must determine the *scope* of the warranty. The problem is ultimately one of interpretation. When the model was exhibited, what was its meaning to a *reasonable* buyer under the circumstances? Like any problem of contract interpretation, the answer requires that all of the circumstances surrounding the contract be considered, including the nature of the goods, the purposes for which the buyer is purchasing the goods, and the words used by the parties that accompanied the demonstration of the model. A model or sample should never be considered in isolation.

[E] Consistency of Warranties

Affirmations of fact, promises, and descriptions often accompany a model or sample. On occasion, there is an inconsistency between what is shown and what is said. The delivered goods may conform to the sample or model, but not to the statements the seller made about the goods—or the delivered goods may conform to the statements, but not to the sample or model.

Section 2-317 suggests three principles to be used to resolve these issues:

1. Whenever reasonable, warranties are to be construed as consistent with each other and as cumulative. If the sample creates a warranty of strength and the affirmation of fact creates a warranty of durability, these warranties are to be accumulated. The buyer has an express warranty of strength *and* durability.[275]
2. If "such construction is unreasonable the intention of the parties shall determine which warranty is dominant."
3. In determining intent, "the following rules apply:

---

[275] *See* Salt Lake City Corp. v. Kasler Corp., 855 F. Supp. 1560, 24 UCCR2d 518 (D. Utah 1994); Beck v. Plastic Prod. Corp., 412 N.W.2d 315, 5 UCCR2d 292 (Minn. Ct. App. 1987).

(a) Exact or technical specifications displace an inconsistent sample or model or general language of description.[276]

(b) A sample from an existing bulk displaces inconsistent general language of description."

Again, the issue is fundamentally one of contract interpretation, and the second principle—the intention of the parties—is the touchstone of the analysis. The first principle—that warranties are to be cumulative—applies only when such a reading is "reasonable." Whether cumulation is "reasonable" will depend upon what the parties *intended* the language they used to mean under the circumstances. Similarly, the "rules" of principle number three are not cast in stone; they are merely presumptions that should guide courts in determining the intentions of the parties in the absence of stronger evidence to the contrary.

A case which may cause difficulty is when the seller has made statements or promises relating to the quality of a product, but has allowed the buyer to examine a sample or model that does not measure up to the warranted quality. If the buyer fails to discover the discrepancy between the statements or promises and the operation of the sample or model, does the examination negate the express warranties that were made?

No single answer is possible, but the general principles discussed previously remain applicable, along with additional guides contained in the Code. First, the examination does not automatically negate *express* warranties. The Code provides that an examination (or a refusal to examine) a sample or model prevents the creation of *implied* warranties as to any defects "which an examination ought in the circumstances to have revealed" to the buyer.[277] Nothing is said in this subsection as to the effect of examination on express warranties.

Second, the words relevant to the creation of an express warranty are to be construed as consistent with conduct (examination) tending to negate the warranty; but if such a construction is unreasonable, the negation is inoperative.[278] The objective intention of the parties, however, is central in determining whether or not the two can be interpreted consistently and

---

[276] *See* Logan Equip. Corp. v. Simon Aerials, Inc., 736 F. Supp. 1188, 12 UCCR2d 387 (D. Mass. 1990) (subsequent technical specifications supersede possible warranty by sample). *See also* Neville Chem. Co. v. Union Carbide Corp., 294 F. Supp. 649, 5 UCCR 1219 (W.D. Pa. 1968) (appendix to contract listing four qualities are not "exact specifications" displacing warranty by sample).

[277] U.C.C. § 2-316(1).

[278] U.C.C. § 2-316(1). *See* § 4.07[B], *infra*.

whether the seller's words were a part of the basis of the bargain.[279] If, as a result of the examination, the seller's words cannot be reasonably understood to be a part of the basis of the bargain, no express warranty is created by the words.

Third, the warranty created by the words is to be construed as consistent and cumulative with any warranty created by the sample, if reasonable; otherwise, the intention of the parties is to determine the dominant warranty. The examination may or may not create a warranty. If it does, section 2-317, discussed previously, is applicable.

An example of the application of these ideas is found in *General Electric Co. v. United States Dynamics, Inc.*[280] The seller in this case sold a gas-purifying machine that had been designed to remove oxygen from nitrogen in a pipe line. Before the sale, the buyer had tested a small-scale model for over a year and had found that the model did, in fact, remove the oxygen. The advertisements of the model also stated that, "No hydrogen mixes with the main gas stream." When the buyer purchased the large machine, its purchase order required in part that, "No other impurities should be introduced into the effluent nitrogen," and the seller's letter of acceptance guaranteed that the apparatus would "purify the quantity of gas specified to the level required." Thus, there were affirmations of fact, a description, and a promise that the nitrogen would be pure; there was also an examination of a model that satisfied the buyer that no *oxygen* remained with the nitrogen.

When the machine began operation the buyer discovered that *hydrogen* remained in the main stream of gas. This defect could not be cured, and a further test of the model indicated that it, too, had allowed hydrogen in the main stream. The court had, therefore, a case in which there was apparently an express warranty of purity, combined with a lengthy examination of a model that did not completely purify. The case was made even more difficult because the seller had no test facilities and had relied upon the buyer's reports of satisfaction with the model.

Nevertheless, the court granted summary judgment for the buyer. Evidencing doubts about "whether a small-scale model can be considered a 'sample' of a much larger device," the court further stated that "inspection could not offset express warranties."[281] As statements of general law, these statements are too broad. In some cases, an examination may either limit the scope of an express warranty or prevent a statement from becoming part

---

[279] *See* § 4.05[F], *infra*.
[280] 403 F.2d 933, 5 UCCR 1053 (1st Cir. 1958).
[281] *Id.* at 934, 5 UCCR at 1053.

of the basis of the bargain.[282] In the context of the facts of this case, however, the statement is unobjectionable. The buyer reasonably relied on both his inspection (for oxygen removal) and the statements of the seller (for the removal of other gases). Under these circumstances, the examination and the words creating the warranty could be read consistently with each other, and the express warranty was operative.

[F] Basis of the Bargain

An express warranty is not created simply because the seller has affirmed a fact or made a promise about the goods. That affirmation or promise (as well as any description, sample, or model) must become "part of the basis of the bargain" before an express warranty is created. This requirement has been referred to briefly in preceding sections, and now will be dealt with in detail.

The "basis of the bargain" requirement has engendered much controversy and commentary.[283] The focal point has been the extent to which, if at all, the reliance requirement of the Uniform Sales Act has been retained by the Code.[284] The cases are in conflict, and many are muddled and confused. Suggestions to revise the requirement have varied,[285] and an earlier

---

[282] See Cagney v. Cohn, 13 UCCR 998 (D.C. Super. Ct. 1973) (purchaser may not be able to recover on a breach of express warranty cause of action if their presale inspection reveals the seller made false assertions of fact); Belvision, Inc. v. General Elec. Co., 2 UCCR 942, 260 N.Y.S.2d 579 (N.Y. Sup. Ct. 1965) (explicit exclusion of all warranties remains in effect when the buyer has inspected and approved of only a single sample of the goods).

[283] See, e.g., John E. Murray, Jr., " 'Basis of the Bargain': Transcending Classical Concepts," 66 Minn. L. Rev. 283 (1982) (Murray I); Heckman, " 'Reliance' " or 'Common Honesty of Speech': The History and Interpretation of Section 2-313 of the Uniform Commercial Code," 38 Case W. Res. L. Rev. 1 (1987); Hodaszy, "Express Warranties Under the Uniform Commercial Code: Is There a Reliance Requirement?," 66 N.Y.U. L. Rev. 468 (1991); Adler, "The Last Best Argument for Eliminating Reliance From Express Warranties: 'Real World' Consumers Don't Read Warranties," 45 S.C. L. Rev. 429 (1994); John E. Murray, Jr., "The Revision of Article 2: Romancing the Prism," 35 Wm. & Mary L. Rev. 1447 (1994) (Murray II).

[284] The full text of the Uniform Sales Act was as follows:

Any affirmation of fact or any promise by the seller relating to the goods is an express warranty if the natural tendency of such affirmation or promise is to induce the buyer to purchase the goods, and if the buyer purchases the goods relying thereon. Uniform Sales Act § 12.

[285] Compare Murray I, supra note 285 and Heckman, supra note 285, (both arguing that no reliance should be required) with Hodaszy, supra note 285 (arguing that reliance requirement of Uniform Sales Act should be retained in the Code).

draft of the proposed revisions to Article 2 eliminated the basis of the bargain test.[286] The "basis of the bargain" requirement remains one of the great mysteries of the Code.

First, the easy case: if a buyer proves that he or she has reasonably relied on a seller's promise, description, or affirmation of fact—or on a sample or model—there is no doubt that the basis of the bargain test is satisfied.[287] Furthermore, it is clear that where reliance is required to satisfy the basis of the bargain test, the seller's statement does not have to be the *sole* inducement for the purchase.[288]

The cases that have confounded judges and commentators, however, are those in which the buyer is unable to demonstrate affirmatively that he or she relied on the seller's representations. The issue is made more difficult by the myriad factual patterns in which this can occur. For example, the seller's statements may come after the sale has been made;[289] the seller's statements may have come before the sale, but the buyer may not have seen or heard them until after the sale[290]—or even after an injury—has occurred;[291] the buyer may have heard the seller's statements but examined the goods to ascertain whether the statements were true;[292] or the seller's representations may have been made through mass advertising.[293] And, of

---

[286] *See* National Conference of Commissioners on Uniform State Laws, Revision of Uniform Commercial Code Article 2, Sales (Draft for Discussion Only), March 1, 1998, § 2-403(a). *See* § 4.05[F][4], *infra*.

[287] *See* Brunner v. Jensen, 524 P.2d 1175, 215 Kan. 416, 15 UCCR 64 (1974); Overstreet v. Norden Labs., Inc., 669 F.2d 1286, 33 UCCR 174 (6th Cir. 1982); Bernick v. Jurden, 293 S.E.2d 405, 306 N.C. 435, 34 UCCR 458 (1982).

[288] *See, e.g.,* Ewers v. Eisenzopf, 88 Wis. 2d 482, 276 N.W.2d 802, 26 UCCR 315 (1979); Royal Business Mach., Inc. v. Lorraine Corp., 633 F.2d 34, 30 UCCR 462 (7th Cir. 1980).

[289] *See, e.g.,* Autzen v. John C. Taylor Lumber Sales, Inc., 280 Or. 783, 572 P.2d 1322, 23 UCCR 304 (1977); Bigelow v. Agway, Inc., 506 F.2d 551, 15 UCCR 769 (2d Cir. 1974); Flory v. Silvercrest Indus., Inc., 633 P.2d 383, 129 Ariz. 574, 31 UCCR 1256 (1981); Hrosik v. J. Keim Builders, 345 N.E.2d 514, 37 Ill. App. 3d 352, 19 UCCR 472 (Ill. App. Ct. 1976); Glyptal, Inc. v. Englehard Corp., 801 F. Supp. 887, 18 UCCR2d 1059 (D. Mass. 1992).

[290] *See* Global Truck & Equip. Co., Inc., v. Palmer Mach. Works, Inc., 628 F. Supp. 641, 42 UCCR 1250 (N.D. Miss. 1986); Harris v. Ford Motor Co., Inc., 845 F. Supp. 1511, 25 UCCR2d 53 (M.D. Ala. 1994); Keith v. Buchanan, 220 Cal. Rptr. 392, 173 Cal. App. 3d 13, 42 UCCR 386 (Cal. Ct. App. 1985).

[291] *See* Lowe v. Sporicidin Int'l, 47 F.3d 124, 26 UCCR2d 87 (4th Cir. 1995).

[292] *See* Cagney v. Cohn, 13 UCCR 998, 173 WL 21368 (D.C. Super. 1973); Keith v. Buchanan, 220 Cal. Rptr. 392, 42 UCCR 386 (Cal. Ct. App. 1985).

[293] *See* Garthwait v. Burgio, 153 Conn. 284, 216 A.2d 189, 3 UCCR 171 (1965); Royal Business Mach., Inc., v. Lorraine Corp., 633 F.2d 34, 30 UCCR 462 (7th Cir. 1980); Whitaker v. Farmhand, Inc., 567 P.2d 916, 173 Mont. 345, 22 UCCR 375 (1977); Drayton v. Jiffee Chem. Corp., 591 F.2d 352, 26 UCCR 865 (6th Cir. 1978).

course, these factual patterns may occur in various combinations. Each of them presents a potential obstacle to satisfying the "basis of the bargain" test of the Code.

The factual patterns described above suggest a number of ways in which the discussion of the basis of the bargain test might be organized. Cases and commentators have sometimes identified three approaches to the basis of the bargain test.[294] The first requires a showing of reliance, the second creates a rebuttable presumption of reliance, and the third dispenses altogether with the reliance requirement. The authors of this text, however, believe that this division, while useful, is oversimplified, and have decided to divide the cases into two general categories: (1) cases dealing with statements made before the closing of the deal and, (2) cases involving statements made after the sale or not seen by the buyer until after the sale. These categories will be further subdivided on the basis of the nature of the representation; in particular, whether the representation was made directly to the buyer or was directed toward the general public.

[1]   Statements Made Prior to the Sale

There is strong evidence, both historical[295] and textual, that the drafters intended to alter the reliance requirement of the Uniform Sales Act. Foremost among the textual evidence is that there is no mention of reliance in the text of section 2-313; a clear departure from the explicit requirement of reliance in the Uniform Sales Act. Moreover, the Comments to section 2-313 strongly suggest that a buyer may recover on an express warranty without affirmative proof of reliance. Comment 3 provides, in part:

> In actual practice affirmations of fact made by the seller about the goods during a bargain are regarded as part of the description of those goods; hence no particular reliance on such statements need be shown in order to weave them into the fabric of the agreement. Rather, any fact which is to take such affirmations, once made, out of the agreement requires clear affirmative proof. The issue is normally one of fact.[296]

Furthermore, Comment 7 permits at least some representations made after the closing of a deal to be express warranties:

---

[294] *See* Thomas D. Crandall, et al., I Uniform Commercial Code § 7.2.2 (1993); John E. Murray, Jr., Murray on Contracts, § 100 at 545 (3d ed. 1990).

[295] *See* Heckman, *supra* note 285 at 7-16.

[296] U.C.C. § 2-313, Official Comment 3.

> The precise time when words of description or affirmation are made or samples shown is not material. The sole question is whether the language or samples are fairly to be regarded as part of the contract. If language is used after the closing of the deal (as when the buyer taking delivery asks and receives an additional assurance), the warranty becomes a modification and need not be supported by consideration if it is otherwise reasonable and in order (Section 2-209).

Obviously, a buyer could not possibly rely on the seller's representations in deciding whether to enter into a contract if those representations are not made until after the deal is closed. Comment 7 creates a strong inference that reliance is no longer required by the Code to create an express warranty.[297]

The majority of recent cases agree that the Code has modified or eliminated the reliance requirement of the Uniform Sales Act.[298] The extent, however, to which the courts have modified or dispensed with the reliance requirement is, to a large extent, dependent upon which factual variation described above is involved. When a statement is made by the seller directly to the buyer and is heard by the buyer prior to the sale, most courts do not require the buyer to affirmatively prove reliance to satisfy the basis of the bargain test. When representations are made to the public generally, however, and especially when they are not seen heard by the buyer until after the sale, the reliance requirement retains great vitality.

1. *Statements made directly to the buyer and seen or heard by the buyer prior to the sale.* When statements or assurances have been made by the seller directly to the buyer in the course of the bargaining process, relatively few cases have demanded that the buyer affirmatively prove reliance in order to recover on an express warranty.[299] Although there are a number of cases in which the courts allude to a reliance requirement, the courts almost always find the requirement satisfied in these cases, generally with little discussion.[300] Most of the cases in which the courts explicitly

---

[297] *But see* Hodaszy, *supra* note 285 at 492.

[298] *See, e.g.*, Neff v. Kehoe, 708 F.2d 639, 36 UCCR 445 (11th Cir. 1983); Daughtrey v. Ashe, 413 S.E.2d 336, 243 Va. 73, 16 UCCR2d 294 (1992); Unified Sch. Dist. No. 500 v. United States Gypsum Co., 788 F. Supp. 1173, 18 UCCR2d 97 (D. Kan. 1992) Keith v. Buchanan, 220 Cal. Rptr. 392, 173 Cal. App. 3d 13, 42 UCCR 386 (Cal. Ct. App. 1985).

[299] *See, e.g.*, Carpetland U.S.A. v. Payne, 536 N.E.2d 306, 8 UCCR2d 942 (Ind. Ct. App. 1989); Mattingly, Inc. v. Beatrice Foods Co., 835 F.2d 1547, 5 UCCR2d 1329 (10th Cir. 1987).

[300] *See* Hillcrest Country Club v. N.D. Judds Co., 461 N.W.2d 55, 236 Neb. 233, 12 UCCR2d 990 (1990).

dispense with a reliance requirement are in this category,[301] and those that suggest that the buyer must show reliance are often older.[302] There are also a considerable number of cases in this category in which the courts expressly adopt a "rebuttable presumption" of reliance and require that the seller introduce clear, affirmative proof to the contrary before the presumption of reliance will be rebutted.[303] There are virtually no cases involving face-to-face, pre-contract, statements in which courts have precluded recovery for express warranty solely because the buyer has not affirmatively demonstrated reliance.[304] In the large majority of jurisdictions today, a buyer is not required to affirmatively prove reliance as an element of recovery in express warranty where the seller has made an affirmation of fact or promise directly to the buyer prior to the contract.

2. *Advertisements seen by the buyer prior to the sale.* In deciding whether reliance is necessary, the courts usually do not *explicitly* distinguish between advertisements made to the public and statements made directly by the seller to the individual buyer.[305] Further, there is little doubt, as a general matter, that an advertisement can create an express warranty.[306] When the buyer uses an advertisement, catalog, or other material distributed to the public as a basis for an express warranty claim, however, courts have been

---

[301] *See, e.g.,* Massey-Ferguson v. Laird, 432 So. 2d 1259, 36 UCCR 437 (Ala. 1983); Cagney v. Cohn, 13 UCCR 998, 1973 WL 21368 (D.C. Super. 1973); Jensen v. Siegel Mobile Homes Group, 668 P.2d 65, 105 Idaho 189, 35 UCCR 804 (1983).

[302] *See* Hrosik v. J. Keim Builders, 345 N.E.2d 514, 37 Ill. App. 3d 352, 19 UCCR 472 (Ill. App. Ct. 1976); Fogo v. Cutter Labs., Inc., 137 Cal. Rptr. 417, 68 Cal. App. 3d 744, 21 UCCR 986 (Cal. Ct. App. 1977); Hagenbuch v. Snap-On Tools Corp., 339 F. Supp. 676, 10 UCCR 1005 (D.N.H. 1972).

[303] *See, e.g.,* Cipollone v. Liggett Group, Inc., 893 F.2d 541, 10 UCCR2d 625 (3d Cir. 1990); Connick v. Suzuki Motor Co. Ltd., 275 Ill. App. 3d 705, 656 N.E.2d 170, 28 UCCR2d 1152 (1995); Weng v. Allison, 678 N.E.2d 1254, 32 UCCR2d 755 (Ill. App. Ct. 1997).

[304] *But see* Thursby v. Reynolds Metals Co., 466 So. 2d 245, 39 UCCR 1625 (Fla. Ct. App. 1984) (refusing recovery under express warranty because there was no evidence that the buyer relied on the seller's affirmations of fact).

[305] One commentator, however, has forcefully argued for this distinction. *See* Hodaszy, "Express Warranties Under the Uniform Commercial Code: Is There a Reliance Requirement?," 66 N.Y.U. L. Rev. 468 (1991). In this article the author argues that if a seller makes an affirmation directly to the buyer in the course of bargaining reliance should be presumed. If the affirmations are made to the public, however, the buyer cannot reasonably be presumed to have relied upon them and should have the burden of showing reliance. *Id.* at 470.

[306] *See, e.g.,* Tochet Valley Grain Growers, Inc., v. Opp & Seibold General Constr., Inc., 831 P.2d 724, 119 Wash. 2d 334, 19 UCCR2d 1041 (1992); Scheuler v. Aamco Transmissions, Inc., 1 Kan. App. 2d 525, 571 P.2d 48, 23 UCCR 30 (1977); Hannon v. Original Gunite Aquatech Pools, Inc., 434 N.E.2d 611, 385 Mass. 813, 33 UCCR 840 (1982); Schlenz v. John Deere Co., 511 F. Supp. 224, 31 UCCR 1020 (D. Mont. 1981).

more demanding than when the seller makes a face-to-face representation to the buyer, and a greater proportion of the cases have required a showing of reliance.

For example, the court in the early case of *Speed Fasteners, Inc. v. Newsom*[307] denied recovery to an injured employee on the basis of representations in an advertising pamphlet. Although privity problems were involved in the case, the court said that the employee had not shown that the buyer (his employer) had relied on the statements in the advertising material, and therefore the statements had not created express warranties. Similarly, in *Hagenbuch v. Snap-on Tools Corp.*,[308] the court refused recovery to a buyer who purchased a hammer that broke and injured his eye. The buyer had seen a catalog advertising the hammer and attempted to characterize statements in the catalog as express warranties. The court denied the buyer's claim because he had not introduced evidence that he relied upon the representations in the catalogue in making his purchase. In *Overstreet v. Norden Laboratories, Inc.*,[309] the appellate court disapproved of a judge's instruction to the jury on express warranty because it did not require a finding of reliance. The case involved a veterinarian who sought to prove an express warranty through statements as to the efficacy of a drug in advertisements and promotional literature.[310]

A number of cases in this category have adopted a rebuttable presumption of reliance.[311] In *Keith v. Buchanan*[312] the buyer purchased a sailboat. Prior to the purchase, the buyer examined sales literature that described the boat as, among other things, "very seaworthy." Before buying the boat, however, the buyer also had an expert examine the boat, who pronounced it satisfactory for the buyer's purposes. When the vessel turned out not to

---

[307] 382 F.2d 395, 4 UCCR 681 (10th Cir. 1967).

[308] 339 F. Supp. 676, 10 UCCR 1005 (D.N.H. 1972).

[309] 669 F.2d 1286, 33 UCCR 174 (6th Cir. 1982).

[310] *See also* Adolphson v. Gardener-Denver Co., 553 N.E.2d 793, 12 UCCR 2d 651 (Ill. App. Ct. 1990) (representations in sales brochure for well-drilling rig not warranty where buyer testified he didn't rely on it and didn't remember whether he saw it before or after the sale); Smith v. Anheuser-Busch, Inc., 599 A.2d 320, 16 UCCR2d 595 (R.I. 1991) (claim on express warranty dismissed where plaintiff failed to prove any reliance on advertising); Wisconsin Elec. Power Co. v. Zallea Bros., Inc., 606 F.2d 697, 27 UCCR 923 (7th Cir. 1979) (court refused to permit buyer to establish express warranty saying catalogue was "not among documents constituting the contract"); American Tobacco Co., Inc. v. Grinnel, 951 S.W.2d 420, 33 UCCR2d 331 (Tex. 1997) (claim on express warranty dismissed where plaintiff failed to show reliance on cigarette advertisements).

[311] *See, e.g.*, Keith v. Buchanan, 220 Cal. Rptr. 392, 42 UCCR 386 (Cal. Ct. App. 1985); Cipollone v. Liggett Group, Inc., 893 F.2d 541, 10 UCCR2d 625 (3d Cir. 1990).

[312] 220 Cal. Rptr. 392, 42 UCCR 386 (Cal. Ct. App. 1985).

be seaworthy, the buyer sued on grounds of express warranty. The trial court dismissed the complaint at the end of the case.

One of the issues on appeal was whether the buyer was required to prove that he had relied on the sales literature in making the purchase. The court concluded that the Code had clearly changed the requirement for reliance established by the Uniform Sales Act, at one point stating that "the concept of reliance has been purposefully abandoned."[313] In the next paragraph, however, despite the quoted language, the court did not entirely abandon the concept of reliance:

> The change of the language in § 2-313 . . . modified both the degree of reliance and the burden of proof in express warranties under the Code. The representation need only be part of the basis of the bargain, *or merely a factor or consideration inducing the buyer to enter into the bargain.* A warranty statement made by a seller is *presumptively* part of the basis of the bargain, and the burden is on the seller to prove that the resulting bargain does not rest at all on the representation.[314]

The quoted language suggests that while reliance will be presumed, if the seller can show that the representation played no part in inducing the buyer to make the purchase, there is no warranty.

One of the most thorough discussions of the basis of the bargain test is in the opinion in *Cipollone v. Liggett Group, Inc.*[315] The case involved a suit by Ms. Rose Cipollone against three manufacturers of cigarettes. Ms. Cipollone was diagnosed with lung cancer in 1981, having smoked between one and two packs of cigarettes per day since 1942. She brought suit in 1983 against the manufacturers for damages based upon theories of fraud, strict liability in tort, and express warranty. She died in 1984 and her husband continued the litigation as her executor and on his own behalf. Upon trial of the case,[316] the only claim upon which she recovered was the claim for breach of express warranty, for which she received $400,000 in damages.[317] Both parties appealed.

Ms. Cipollone's express-warranty claims were based on allegations that during the period in which she had smoked, she had seen numerous adver-

---

[313] *Id.* at 398, 42 UCCR at 393.

[314] *Id.* at 398, 42 UCCR at 393 (emphasis added).

[315] 893 F.2d 541, 10 UCCR2d 625 (3d Cir. 1990).

[316] 693 F. Supp. 208, 6 UCCR2d 1408 (D.N.J. 1988).

[317] The jury rejected Ms. Cipollone's fraud claims. It also found that she was more than 50 percent responsible for her injury on the tort claim of failure to warn. Under New Jersey's comparative fault law, this precluded her from recovering any damages on the tort claim.

tisements of the defendant's products on television, radio, and in print, indicating that cigarettes would not cause adverse health effects. During the same period, however, there was evidence that she had expressed concern about the possible health effects of cigarettes and indicated that she did not believe the claims of the manufacturers that cigarettes were not harmful. Thus, there was evidence that she may not have relied on the advertisements of the manufacturers in continuing to purchase and use cigarettes. At trial, the judge instructed the jury that reliance was unnecessary for recovery for breach of express warranty; it was sufficient if the representation "would naturally induce the purchase of the product."

The Circuit Court of Appeals recognized the conflict in the decisions and the lack of clarity in the "basis of the bargain" test. It wasted little time, however, in disapproving the trial judges's charge:

> The District Court instructed the jury that a statement could be considered part of the basis of the bargain if it "would naturally induce the purchase of the products." This instruction is completely objective and would permit a buyer to sue for breach of express warranty even if the seller's warranties were advertisements made in another state or country, and even if the buyer did not hear of the claims in the advertisements until the day she walked into an attorney's office to bring suit for personal injury. It strains the language to say that a statement is part of the buyer's "bargain" when the buyer had no knowledge of the statement's existence.[318]

The court was convinced, however, that the drafters intended to change the reliance requirement of the Uniform Sales Act. It suggested that the statement in Comment 4 to section 2-313 that "the whole purpose of the law of warranty is to determine what it is that the seller has in essence agreed to sell" indicates that reliance is irrelevant to warranty law.[319] The court also

---

[318] 893 F.2d 566, 10 UCCR2d at 647.

[319] *Id.* at 567, n.28, 10 UCCR2d at 648 n.28. The court provided an imaginative example to illustrate its point:

> For example, imagine a tire merchant describing a tire to three different prospective purchasers, each listening to his sales talk at the same time. The seller guarantees that the tire will: (1) be safe for use even in heavily loaded vehicles; (2) last at least 20,000 miles; and (3) be the same style tire sold with a Rolls Royce. The first purchaser buys the tire relying on the seller's safety warranty. The second buys the tire relying on the seller's durability warranty. The third buys the tire relying on the seller's style warranty. None of the purchasers communicates to the seller the reason why he or she is purchasing one of the tires, although the reason for the purchase is communicated to the buyer's spouse, who will later come forward to testify truthfully regarding what the buyer relied

indicated that a reliance requirement does not comport well with Comment 7, which suggests that warranties can arise subsequent to the closing of the deal. In light of what the court called "inconsistent mandates" on the reliance question, it came up with an approach similar to, but not quite the same as, the rebuttable presumption test suggested in the *Keith* case.

The court held that a buyer can satisfy the basis of the bargain test by proving that "she read, heard, saw, or knew of the advertisement containing the affirmation or promise."[320] These statements are then presumed to be part of the basis of the bargain. The defendant is then permitted to show that the plaintiff knew that the representations were untrue or did not believe the representation of the seller. Even if the defendant proves that the buyer did not believe the representations to be true, however, the buyer still has the opportunity to show that she relied upon them in purchasing the product.[321]

The court explained in a footnote the difference between its test and the "rebuttable presumption" test of earlier cases. It said that a seller cannot overcome the presumption that a statement is part of the basis of the bargain by merely showing non-reliance; the seller must show that the buyer did not believe the representation. Reliance comes into play only when the seller is able to establish the buyer's disbelief. Even then, if the buyer can show she nonetheless relied on the representation, she can still collect economic damages for breach of warranty.

The *Cipollone* case contains the most comprehensive discussion of the "basis of the bargain" test found in the case law. The opinion is an admirable effort to reconcile the conflicting strands found in the cases and the Code. Certainly, the court's view is correct that a buyer should not have to affirmatively demonstrate reliance to establish a cause of action, whether the representation is made in a face-to-face statement or is contained in an advertisement, brochure, or catalog. Moreover, the court is correct that a buyer usually expects the seller's representations to be part of his or her contract, whether or not the representations induced the purchase. Buyers are not required to prove that they relied on "non-warranty" terms of a contract—such as a promise to deliver the goods within two days—in order to enforce the obligation. There is no reason that representations of product

---

on when making the purchase. It is implausible that each buyer has a different warranty, and that the second buyer, but not the first or third buyers, can sue if the tire wears out before 20,000 miles.

[320] *Id.* at 567, 10 UCCR2d at 648.

[321] The court said, however, that consequential damages would not be recoverable in this case. 893 F.2d at 568, 10 UCCR2d at 649.

quality should be treated differently. On the other hand, the cases and the Code Comments support the idea that a seller's statements that a buyer knows are false should not create warranty liability.[322] Furthermore, as is discussed subsequently,[323] there is little support for the proposition that an advertisement of which the buyer is unaware at the time of purchase, and on which she does not otherwise rely, can give rise to liability for breach of warranty.

As the court in *Cipollone* noted, there are cases involving advertisements, catalogs, brochures, etc. which state that reliance is not an element of express warranty.[324] For example, in *Interco v. Randustrial Corp.*,[325] the court permitted the buyer to sue on the basis of language in a catalog that a floor-covering product "would absorb considerable flex without cracking." In addition to deciding that the quoted statement was not "puffing," the court said that so long as the catalog was read by the buyer, it was not necessary for the buyer to plead and prove reliance. In another case,[326] the court held that statements in a brochure, which was given by the seller to the buyer of scaffolding, became part of the basis of the bargain without proof of reliance. The court held that because the representations in the brochure concerning the scaffolding had been given by the seller to the buyer in order to induce the purchase, it was not necessary for the buyer to show that he had actually relied upon them.

[2] Statements Made (or Seen) After the Sale

The cases causing the most difficulty are those involving representations not seen by the buyer until after the contract has been concluded. In some cases, these representations precede the sale—such as brochures or manuals given to the buyer before or at the time of the sale or advertisements published prior to the sale—but are not seen or read by the buyer until after the sale.[327] In other cases, the representations, whether in the form of advertisements or otherwise, are not made until after the sale.

---

[322] *See* § 4.05[F][3], *infra.*

[323] *See* § 4.05[F][2], *infra.*

[324] *See, e.g.*, Hawkins Constr. Co. v. Matthews Co., Inc., 209 N.W.2d 643, 190 Neb. 546, 12 UCCR 1013 (1973).

[325] 533 S.W.2d 257, 19 UCCR 464 (Mo. Ct. App. 1976).

[326] Hawkins Constr. Co. v. Matthews Co., Inc., 209 N.W.2d 643, 190 Neb. 546, 12 UCCR 1013 (Neb. 1973).

[327] *See, e.g.*, State of Idaho v. Mitchell Constr. Co., 699 P.2d 1349, 108 Idaho 335, 39 UCCR 90 (1985); Worm v. American Cynamid Co., 20 UCCR2d 441, 1992 WL 368062 (D. Md. 1992).

1. *Statements Made Directly to the Buyer.* Comment 7 to section 2-313, quoted previously, makes it clear that at least some post-contract representations are warranties. The example in Comment 7, however, involves an additional assurance about the product asked for and received by the buyer at the time the goods are delivered and shortly after the contract has been made. It is possible that the drafters intended to limit post-contract warranties to situations where the seller makes some representation about product quality or performance shortly after the deal has been closed in response to some expression of concern by the buyer. In many cases, even though the deal has been closed, the buyer can realistically expect the seller to allow the buyer to exchange or return the product if the seller is unable to provide the assurances sought by the buyer about the product. When the buyer retains the product as a result of the seller's assurances, the bargain does, in fact, rest on the seller's representations, and they can reasonably be characterized as part of the basis of the bargain.

Even if the seller's statement is made at a time when the buyer does not have the option of exchange or return, the seller's statements may still be part of the basis of the parties' bargain. A "bargain" is not something that occurs at a particular moment in time, and is forever fixed as to its content; instead, it describes the commercial relationship between the parties in regard to the product. A "contract" under the Code incorporates the "bargain of the parties in fact,"[328] and the Code has expanded the notion that a contract comes into existence at some precise moment in time.[329] The Code's word is "bargain"—a process that can extend beyond the moment in time that the offeree utters the magic words, "I accept."

Courts have generally followed this reasoning and permitted post-contract statements made directly to the buyer to be express warranties. The most notable case is *Autzen v. John C. Taylor Lumber Sales, Inc.*[330] In this case, the buyer was interested in purchasing a boat from the seller. On September 5, the parties met to discuss the sale of the boat. At this meeting, they agreed that the total price would be $100,000, and the buyer would pay a downpayment of $20,000 at the time of transfer of possession of the boat. At a subsequent meeting on September 8, the seller told the buyer that he believed the boat was in good shape, but that he wanted to have the boat

---

[328] U.C.C. § 1-201(11) defines "contract" to include both the parties agreement and applicable rules of law. Section 1-201(3) defines "agreement" as the bargain of the parties in fact.

[329] *See* U.C.C. § 2-204(2) (an agreement sufficient to constitute a contract may be found even though the moment of its making is undetermined); section 2-209(1) (an agreement modifying a contract needs no consideration to be binding).

[330] 280 Or. 783, 572 P.2d 1322, 23 UCCR 304 (1977).

surveyed (examined by an expert for conditions such as dry rot and insect infestation) prior to transferring possession to the buyer. The buyer said that a survey was not necessary, but the seller said he would have one done at his own expense. The survey was performed the following day, and the surveyor pronounced the boat "very sound." The buyer then gave the seller a check for $20,000 and took possession of the boat. About two months later, it was discovered that the boat was heavily damaged by dry rot and insect infestation. The buyer notified the seller that he was revoking acceptance of the boat. When the seller refused to return the purchase price, the buyer sued on the basis that the seller had breached express warranties, including those contained in the survey, and recovered the purchase price of the boat.

On appeal, the seller argued that the representations in the survey were not express warranties because they were not part of the basis of the bargain.[331] The seller first argued the survey could not be a part of the basis of the bargain because the contract for sale had already taken place before the seller decided to have the boat surveyed. In response, quoting from the predecessor to this text,[332] the court said that the seller's argument confused "contract" with "bargain." Although the parties had agreed on a price, and the contract had already been formed, they had not yet decided upon many other specifics, such as the time of payment and transfer of possession. According to the court, the "bargain" was still in process even though a contract may have been formed. Also, the court said that the jury could have found that the survey was intended to induce and did, in fact, induce the buyer's satisfaction with the agreement and lessened the buyer's vigilance in inspecting the boat prior to acceptance.

The seller also argued that the survey could not be a part of the basis of the bargain because the buyer was indifferent to it. According to the seller, there was nothing to indicate that the buyer had bargained for the survey and, therefore, it was not part of the basis of the bargain. The court rejected this argument, saying that the basis of the bargain requirement does not mean that the representation must have been *bargained for*, only that it go *to the essence of the contract*.[333]

---

[331] The seller also argued that the representations in the survey could not be express warranties because they were not made by the seller. The court characterized the survey as a "description" and said that there was nothing in U.C.C. § 2-313 requiring that a description be made by the seller—the seller need only introduce the description into the bargaining process. 280 Or. at 789, 572 P.2d at 1325, 23 UCCR at 309.

[332] Robert J. Nordstrom, Law of Sales, § 67 (1971).

[333] 280 Or. 790, 572 P.2d at 1326, 23 UCCR at 309.

Although it is unclear what the *Autzen* court meant by the "essence of the contract,"[334] there is no doubt that the court's holding departs substantially from the reliance requirement of the Uniform Sales Act. The *Autzen* court was the first to recognize an expanded concept of bargain continuing after the contract. Although some aspects of the opinion are less than clear,[335] the case represents a significant advance from earlier conceptions of warranty.

Like *Autzen*, most cases in which a seller makes a direct post-contract representation to a buyer permit the representation to be an express warranty, even when the representation occurs a considerable time after the formation of the contract. This is particularly true if the buyer can show some post-contract reliance upon the seller's representations.[336] For example, in *Bigelow v. Agway, Inc.*,[337] decided before *Autzen*, a salesman represented to a farmer that the product the farmer had previously purchased would permit the farmer to bale hay with a high moisture content. The farmer, relying on these representations, baled his hay while it was wet and, as a result, the barn in which the hay was stored burned down. The court allowed the farmer to recover on the basis of an express warranty. Relying upon Comment 7, it reasoned that the statements were designed to promote future sales and constituted a modification of the contract.

In *Downie v. Abex Corp.*,[338] the court permitted the buyer to recover for breach of express warranty when a seller made post-contract representations that its ball-screw assemblies were "fail-safe." The assemblies later caused the collapse of an airplane passenger loading bridge, and the court permitted the recovery because the buyer had relied on the representations by not making safety modifications to the assemblies.

---

[334] *See* John E. Murray, Jr., " 'Basis of the Bargain': Transcending Classical Concepts," 66 Minn. L. Rev. 283 (1982).

[335] For example, it is not clear whether it is critical to the court's conclusion that the jury could have found that the survey induced the buyer's satisfaction with the agreement and lessened the degree of vigilance in his examination prior to acceptance. Given the court's expanded notion of bargain and its rejection of the traditional reliance requirement, this inducement to the buyer's post-contract behavior should not be necessary to the result.

[336] For additional cases in which courts have permitted face-to-face post-contract statements to be express warranties, see Glyptal Inc. v. Engelhard Corp., 801 F. Supp. 887, 18 UCCR2d 1059 (D. Mass. 1992); Roxalana Hills, Ltd. v. Masonite Corp., 627 F. Supp. 1194, 42 UCCR 1330 (S.D. W. Va. 1986); Bailey Farms, Inc. v. Nor-Am Chem. Co., 27 F.3d 188, 24 UCCR2d 843 (6th Cir. 1994). *But see* Byrd Motor Lines, Inc. v. Dunlop Tire & Rubber Corp., 304 S.E.2d 773, 36 UCCR 1169 (N.C. Ct. App. 1983) (representation made two years after purchase not express warranty).

[337] 506 F.2d 551, 15 UCCR 769 (2d Cir. 1974).

[338] 741 F.2d 1235, 39 UCCR 427 (10th Cir. 1984).

In *Daugherty v. Ashe,*[339] the Supreme Court of Virginia decided that a post-contract description gave rise to an express warranty even in the absence of post-contract reliance. The buyer in *Daugherty* agreed to purchase a diamond bracelet from the seller. When the buyer picked up the bracelet, the seller gave the buyer an appraisal form that listed the quality of the diamonds as "v.v.s."—diamonds of very high quality. When the diamonds turned out to be of lesser quality, the buyer sued for breach of express warranty. The seller's defense was that the "v.v.s." description was not part of the basis of the bargain, because the buyer had not relied upon the description in making the purchase. The court, however, agreed with the buyer and held that the basis of the bargain test does not require reliance. Citing Comments 3, 5, and 7 to section 2-313, the court said that the Code had adopted a broad definition of "agreement" and required only that the parties consider a statement or description as part of their bargain.

2. *Brochures, pamphlets, warranties, etc. directed to the buyer but not seen until after the contract.* There are a significant number of cases in which a document, directed to the particular buyer and arguably containing an express warranty, was not seen until after the sale. This category does not include face-to-face representations nor does it include advertisements, brochures, etc., directed at the general public. Rather, we are talking about cases where, for example, the packaging contains certain representations not read by the buyer until after the contract, or where a pamphlet is contained with a sealed package. In this category, the results are more mixed than a post-contract statement is made face-to-face.

Representative of those cases in which recovery on an express warranty theory has been permitted is *Winston Industries, Inc. v. Stuyvesant Ins. Co., Inc.*[340] In this case, a mobile home was severely damaged when a loose waterline flooded the mobile home. The buyer's insurance company (after a lawsuit) paid the buyer for the damage and, as subrogee of the buyer, brought suit against the manufacturer claiming that the mobile home was defective. The suit was based upon both express and implied warranties.

The problem with the express-warranty claim was that the buyer had never received the manufacturer's warranty which usually accompanied its mobile homes, nor was the buyer aware that one existed. Although the bill of sale from the retailer indicated that the mobile home came with the "usual factory warranty," there was no indication that the buyer had relied on, or even seen, this language in the bill of sale. Only after the damage occurred

---

[339] 413 S.E.2d 336, 243 Va. 73, 16 UCCR2d 294 (1992).
[340] 317 So. 2d 493, 17 UCCR 924 (Ala. Civ. App. 1975).

did the purchaser find out about the existence of the manufacturer's warranty. The manufacturer claimed that under these circumstances, its warranty could not possibly have been part of the basis of the bargain.

The court would have none of the seller's argument. It first pointed to an admission by the manufacturer during discovery that a written warranty existed at the time of the sale. Further, the court said that the manufacturer's course of conduct after being informed of the damage was consistent with the existence of a warranty. Finally, the court, stated that no particular reliance is necessary to give rise to an express warranty, and held that the mention of the warranty in the bill of sale established the warranty as part of the basis of the bargain, despite the fact that the purchaser had neither seen it nor knew about it at the time of the sale.

The result in this case is correct. Buyers reasonably expect and understand that manufacturers' warranties are part of their deal, whether or not they know the contents of the warranties at the time of sale, or even know that the warranty exists. It is very likely that many buyers, upon finding a warranty inside a sealed box after they have purchased the goods, simply file it away without reading the specifics, and refer to its contents only if something goes wrong with the goods. Nonetheless, buyers in these circumstances would be astonished to be told that because they were not aware of the warranty or its contents at the time they purchased the goods, they are not entitled to its benefits. Both sellers and buyers consider "warranties" made by the seller—whether or not seen by the buyer—to be part of the deal.[341]

Not all courts have adopted this reasoning, however. In *Stang v. Hertz Corp.*,[342] two nuns rented a car from Hertz Corp. The rental agreement provided that the car was in good mechanical condition. In addition, subsequent to the rental, the rental agent told the nuns that the car had "good tires." One of the tires blew out, causing an accident that killed one of the

---

[341] *See also* Perfetti v. McGhan Medical, 662 P.2d 646, 99 N.M. 645, 35 UCCR 1472 (N.M. Ct. App. 1983) (statements contained in package insert and flyer enforceable as express warranties without reliance); Harris v. Ford Motor Co., Inc, 845 F. Supp. 1511, 25 UCCR2d 53 (M.D. Ala. 1994) (warranty in glove compartment enforceable where buyer knew at time of sale that new car came with warranty); Flory v. Silvercrest Indus., 633 P.2d 383, 129 Ariz. 574, 31 UCCR 1256 (Ariz. 1981) (manufacturer's warranty given to buyer after the sale was not a U.C.C. express warranty because buyer was not in privity with manufacturer and delivery was after the sale, but may create an enforceable "non-UCC express warranty"). *Cf.* Martin v. American Medical Sys., Inc., 32 UCCR2d 1101 (4th Cir. 1997) (buyer could enforce express warranty as third-party beneficiary given by manufacturer to surgeon even though buyer did not become aware of warranty until litigation).

[342] Stang v. Hertz Corp., 490 P.2d 475, 83 N.M. 217, 9 UCCR 794 (N.M. Ct. App. 1971).

nuns. In a wrongful death action against Hertz, it was argued that the forgoing statements were express warranties. The court found against the plaintiffs and held that neither statement created an express warranty. As to the language in the rental agreement, the court said that it did not create an express warranty because "[t]here is no evidence that the nuns relied on, or in any way considered, the terms of the rental agreement before agreeing to the rental."[343] It also found the comment by the rental agent that the car had "good tires" not to be an express warranty because it had been made after the car had been rented.

The *Stang* decision is wrong on both counts. The statement by the agent is precisely the kind of situation contemplated by Comment 7. The statement was made shortly after the rental agreement was signed by the nuns, perhaps in response to some concern expressed by them about the condition of the tires. The "bargain" was still in process; certainly they would have been permitted to back out of the deal had they not been assured about the quality of the tires. It is hard to imagine a clearer case for the application of Comment 7's validation of post-contract warranties.

The statement that the car was in good operating condition also should have been found to be an express warranty. Under modern contract law, terms in a standardized agreement are enforceable whenever they are reasonably expected and do not operate unconscionably.[344] It has never been true that a party cannot *benefit* from a provision in a contract of which he was unaware at the time of signing.[345] For example, an insurer would certainly have to pay for the loss of jewelry if it was included in an insurance contract, even if the buyer erroneously believed jewelry was not covered. The result should be no different when the contract form relates to product quality. Unfortunately, a number of other courts have reached decisions similar to *Stang*.[346]

---

[343] 490 P.2d at 477, 83 N.M. at 219, 9 UCCR at 795.

[344] *See* Restatement (Second) of Contracts § 211(1):

> Except as stated in Subsection (3), where a party to a agreement signs or otherwise manifests assent to a writing and has reason to believe that like writings are regularly used to embody terms of agreements of the same type, he adopts the writing as an integrated agreement with respect to the terms included in the writing.

[345] *See, e.g.*, Vizcaino v. Microsoft Corp., 97 F.3d 1187 (9th Cir. 1996) (holding that employees' lack of knowledge that they were eligible for certain benefits under their employment contract did not permit employer to deny benefits).

[346] *See, e.g.*, Schmaltz v. Nissen, 431 N.W.2d 657, 7 UCCR2d 1061 (S.D. 1988) (language on bag regarding quality of seed not express warranty when buyer admitted purchasing seed prior to seeing the language on the bag); Cuthbertson v. Clark Equip. Co., 448 A.2d 315,

3. *Advertisements, etc., not directed to the buyer and not seen until after the contract.* Although there are cases in this category which recovery has been permitted, the category in which a buyer has the least chance for success involves those cases in which the buyer asserts that a statement made in an advertisement not seen by the buyer until after the sale constitutes an express warranty. Most of the cases in this category deny recovery to the buyer, especially when the buyer is unable to show any reliance on the advertisement.

For example, a statement in a brochure that a truck had the necessary design strength for all types of material hauling was not an express warranty where the brochure containing the statement was not seen until after the contract.[347] The court contrasted the case with a post-contract statement made directly by the seller to the buyer, which the court said had "the usual contractual prerequisite of mutual assent" required for a contract modification. In *DiIenno v. Libbey Glass Division, Owens-Ill., Inc.,*[348] a glass jar shattered, severely injuring the buyer's wrist when she attempted to open it. The court refused to permit a buyer to recover for breach of express warranty on the basis of a statement made in a catalog that a glass jar would open and close properly when there was no evidence that the buyer saw the catalog or relied upon it when purchasing the jar. In *Adolphson v. Gardner-Denver Co.,*[349] the court refused to consider representations in a sales brochure for a well-drilling rig to be express warranties when the buyer could not recall whether he first saw the brochure before or after the sale. There are many other examples of similar rulings with respect to advertisements and promotional materials not seen until after the purchase of the goods.[350]

---

34 UCCR 71 (Me. 1982) (language in manual accompanying loader was not express warranty when there was no indication that the buyer saw the language prior to the contract or relied upon it).

[347] Global Truck & Equip. Co., Inc. v. Palmer Mach. Works, Inc., 628 F. Supp. 641, 42 UCCR 1250 (N.D. Miss. 1986).

[348] 668 F. Supp. 373, 4 UCCR2d 706 (D. Del. 1987).

[349] 553 N.E.2d 793, 12 UCCR2d 651 (Ill. Ct. App. 1990).

[350] *See, e.g.,* Ciba-Geigy Corp. v. Alter, 309 Ark. 426, 834 S.W.2d 136, 20 UCCR 2d 448 (1992) (statement in advertising literature that farmers need not worry about crop damage from herbicide is not express warranty where buyer could not recall reading ad prior to purchase); Worm v. American Cyanamid Co., 20 UCCR2d 441, 1992 WL 368062 (D. Md. 1992) (advertising and promotional material stating that it was safe to plant corn eleven months after use of herbicide did not influence purchase and was therefore not an express warranty; general statements not made in connection with a particular sale cannot be express warranties when they do not induce purchase); Anderson v. Heron Eng'g Co., 198 Colo. 391, 604 P.2d 674 (1979) (statement in sales brochure that chair lift was "safe" was not express warranty where buyer had not seen or relied upon sales brochure); State of Idaho v.

Only if a buyer is able to demonstrate specific reliance on an advertisement not seen until after the purchase might recovery be available for breach of express warranty.[351]

The lesson of the cases is that the state of the law cannot simply be described as a split of authority between those courts which require reliance and those that do not. Although court decisions often speak in these simplistic terms, the actual results of the cases are much more complex. Statements made in advertisements and other promotional literature not directed toward the individual buyer are less likely to create express warranties than face-to-face statements, and advertisements not seen until after the sale are almost never treated as express warranties. The rule appears to be that the more the statement is detached from the individual transaction and the less it is a function of direct communication between the buyer and the seller, the more difficult it will be to establish the statement as an express warranty.

Some commentators, including one of the authors of this text, have argued elsewhere that unread advertisements should be considered to be express warranties,[352] despite the extant case law to the contrary. Statements made in advertisements about product quality or performance are made by sellers to induce buyers to purchase the seller's goods. Buyers expect sellers to stand behind their representations, whether or not these representations are made directly to the buyer, and whether or not the buyer purchases the goods in reliance upon them. The seller's willingness to make good on these representations is considered by the public to be part of the overall deal that they have with society's sellers. In this sense, they are part of the "basis of the bargain."

Mitchell Constr. Co., 699 P.2d 1349, 39 UCCR 90 (Idaho 1985) (statement in ad brochure cannot be express warranty since nothing in record showed buyer was aware of the brochure when it entered into contract for sale of roofing system). *See also* Voelkel v. General Motors Corp., 846 F. Supp. 1482, 23 UCCR2d 676 (D. Kan. 1994) (statement in sales manual did not create express warranty where there was nothing in the record to indicate that buyer was aware of the manual prior to the sale); Lowe v. Sporicidin Int'l, 47 F.3d 124, 26 UCCR2d 287 (4th Cir. 1995) (no causation exists where no allegation that buyer did not read seller's ads prior to injury); Board of Directors of Providence Village Townhome Condominium Ass'n v. Allied Plywood Corp., 27 UCCR2d 884 (Va. Cir. Ct. 1995) (statement in sales literature cannot be express warranty when plaintiff had never received the literature).

[351] *See* Downie v. Abex Corp., 741 F.2d 1235, 39 UCCR 427 (10th Cir. 1984).

[352] *See* Robert J. Nordstrom, Law of Sales, § 68 at 209 (1970); Heckman, " 'Reliance' or 'Common Honesty of Speech': The History and Interpretation of Section 2-313 of the Uniform Commercial Code," 38 Case W. Res. L. Rev. 1, 36 (1987); John E. Murray, Jr., "The Revision of Article 2: Romancing the Prism," 35 Wm. and Mary L. Rev. 1447, 1487–1488 (1994). *See also* John E. Murray, Jr., " 'Basis of the Bargain': Transcending Classical Concepts," 66 Minn L. Rev. 283, 322 (1982).

[3] Conclusion

In deciding whether a statement is "part of the basis of the bargain" a number of related principles and considerations should be kept in mind. First, the affirmation of fact, promise, or description must be *interpreted* before it can be decided whether a warranty has been given covering the particular defect. The words used by the seller must be read in the way in which the buyer would reasonably understand them. Thus, if a seller asserts that a second-hand automobile is in "excellent shape," the meaning of those words, including whether they are mere "puffing," must be considered in the entire context of the contract. If the automobile involved had an obviously rusted fender and door panel, the words "excellent shape" made to the buyer who was examining the automobile should be limited to the mechanical condition of the engine, so that if something was faulty with the engine, there would be a default—but the existence of obvious rust would not amount to a breach. An examination of the goods prior to the contract provides a backdrop for interpreting the seller's statements as well as determining whether they are part of the basis of the bargain.

Furthermore, the Code requires only that the statements of the seller become a *part* of the basis of the bargain; it is not necessary that they be the sole basis of the bargain.[353] If a buyer has examined the goods prior to the purchase and did not discover the defect, a seller's statement that no such defect exists will be part of the basis of the bargain. Even if the buyer discovered the defect—but bought anyway—the purchase still often rests upon both what the buyer discovered and what the seller said. The buyer's discovery may have caused doubts, but those doubts may have been at least partially removed by the seller's representations.[354]

If, however, the resulting bargain does not rest *at all* on the representations of the seller, those representations are not part of the basis of the bargain and are not express warranties. That is, if a buyer cannot reasonably

---

[353] *See* C.E. Alexander & Sons, Inc. v. DEC Int'l, Inc., 811 P.2d 899, 112 N.M. 89, 15 UCCR2d 464 (1991).

[354] For example, in City Mach. & Mfg. Co. v. A.&A. Mach. Corp, 4 UCCR 461, 1967 WL 8832 (E.D.N.Y. 1967), the seller represented that a mill had a spindle speed of up to 1,300 revolutions per minute. The buyer, however, had inspected the mill and noticed that the instruction sheet indicated that its maximum speed was only 358 revolutions per minute. Nonetheless, the buyer purchased the mill. On these facts, the court held that the representations of the seller were a *part* of the basis of the bargain. The buyer had purchased the goods both on the basis of what he saw and what he was told by the seller. Thus, an inspection of the goods—even an inspection that discovers that the seller's statements might be false—does not *necessarily* bar recovery for breach of express warranty.

consider the seller's statements to be *part of his deal*, those statements are not express warranties. This determination may come from an express understanding—as where the seller, before the deal is concluded, tells the buyer that he is withdrawing a specific statement that he made about the goods. It may also come from the conduct of the parties. When the buyer's examination discovers a defect and it is clear that the seller's representations to the contrary play no part in the buyer's decision to purchase the goods, no express warranty should be found. The price the buyer agreed to pay may also indicate whether a statement was part of the basis of the bargain. If the price paid by the buyer did not reflect the existence of a defect, the probabilities are that the seller's statements formed at least part of the basis of the bargain. If, however, the price paid indicates that the parties were placing the risk that the goods might be faulty on the buyer, there is evidence that the seller's prior statements did not form part of the basis of the bargain.

In the final analysis, the best approach is simply to ask whether the buyer *reasonably considers the seller's statements to be part of the deal that he made with the seller*. Such a test would not require a showing of reliance; it would require only that a reasonable buyer consider the seller's statements to be part of his deal. Thus, post-contract statements could be express warranties, so long as a buyer would consider them to be part of his deal with the seller. Similarly, unread documentation accompanying a product—such as a package insert or flyer in a sealed package or language on the package itself—would also qualify as an express warranty. Advertisements read prior to the sale, although somewhat more problematic, should also be considered to be express warranties under this standard. Buyers generally consider a seller's statements that are intended to induce them to purchase a product to be part of their deal; most buyers would not distinguish between pre-contract statements of a seller in an advertisement and other pre-contract statements of the seller. In both cases, the sellers have made the statements for the same purpose—to induce the buyer to purchase the product.

The case that may not satisfy this standard is the advertisement which is not read until after the contract, or perhaps not until after the injury occurs. Although a buyer may feel that the seller should be held responsible for products which do not live up to those representations, it is not clear that most buyers would consider such ads to be part of *their* deal with the seller. Courts have generally not found such statements to be part of the basis of the bargain. It may be, as one court has suggested,[355] that it simply stretches

---

[355] Cipollone v. Liggett Group, Inc., 893 F.2d 541, 10 UCCR2d 625 (3d Cir. 1990).

the concept of "bargain" beyond the breaking point to permit advertisements to be express warranties under these circumstances.

[4] Proposed Revisions

The proposed revisions to section 2-313 are substantial and complex. They are generally, although not entirely, consistent with the expansive approach to express warranties suggested in this text. They reflect much of the existing case law discussed previously, and apply different requirements to two broad categories of representations, depending upon the relationship between the seller making the representations and the buyer. The proposed revisions to Article 2 distinguish between "immediate" buyers and "remote" buyers. An "immediate buyer" is a buyer "in a contractual relationship with the seller,"[356] while a "remote buyer" is a buyer "from a person other than the seller against which a claim for breach of warranty is asserted."[357]

Section 2-403 of the proposed revisions is the analog to the present section 2-313. It covers, however, only "immediate" buyers.[358] A separate section, section 2-408, deals with express warranties and remote buyers. According to section 2-403(c), a representation or promise made by the seller to an immediate buyer becomes part of the agreement "unless a reasonable person in the position of the immediate buyer would not believe that the representation or promise was part of the agreement."[359]

The approach of this subsection is in accord with the objective theory of contracts and with the methodology suggested in this text. It asks simply whether a reasonable buyer would assume under the circumstances that a representation made by the seller was part of the deal. It does not matter when the statement is made or whether the buyer relies upon it; if the buyer reasonably believes that the seller intends the representation to be part of the agreement, it *is* part of the agreement. Furthermore, it is not up to the buyer to prove that the buyer's understanding was reasonable; it is up to the seller to prove that it was unreasonable.

Section 2-403 has a provision that deals explicitly with representations and promises made to the public generally. Section 2-403(c)(3) states that a representation becomes part of the basis of the bargain unless:

---

[356] Council Draft § 2-401(3).

[357] Council Draft § 2-401(4).

[358] Council Draft § 2-403.

[359] Council Draft § 2-403(c).

in case of a representation made in any medium of communication to the public, including advertising, the immediate buyer did not know of the representation at the time of the sale.

Thus, under the proposed revisions, representations made to the public are treated the same as representations to individual buyers, with the crucial exception that the buyer must be aware of the representation at the time of his agreement with the seller.

As previously mentioned, "remote" buyers[360] are dealt with in section 2-408. As presently written, this section is cumbersome and poorly drafted. The intent of the section, however, appears to be to make it clear that representations by a seller (for example, a manufacturer) explicitly directed toward the remote buyer are enforceable by the remote buyer as warranties. Section 2-408(b) provides:

> If a seller makes a representation in a record packaged with or accompanying the goods and the seller reasonably expects the record to be furnished to a remote buyer and the record is so furnished, the following rules apply:
>
> (1) The seller has an obligation to the remote buyer that the goods will conform to the representation unless:
>
> (A) A reasonable person in the position of the remote buyer would not believe that the representation created an obligation; or
>
> (B) The representation is merely of the value of the goods or is an affirmation purporting to be merely the seller's opinion or commendation of the goods.
>
> (2) A seller's obligation to a remote buyer created under subsection (b)(1) and any remedial promise also extends to:
>
> (A) any member of the family or household unit or any invitee of a remote consumer buyer;
>
> (B) a transferee from the remote consumer buyer and any subsequent transferee. However, for purposes of subsection (b)(2), the seller may limit its obligation to the remote consumer buyer or may limit extension to a particular person or transferee or a class of persons or transferees, provided that the limitation is furnished to the remote consumer buyer with the record that makes the representation or at the time of sale, whichever is later.[361]

---

[360] "Remote buyers" are defined as "a buyer from a person other than the seller against which a claim for breach of warranty is asserted." Council Draft § 2-401(4).

[361] Council Draft § 2-408(b).

This provision makes it clear that the fact that there is no privity of contract between a manufacturer and a buyer does not prevent representations made by the manufacturer directly to the remote buyer from becoming express warranties. As a subsequent section of this text explains, cases interpreting the present law have almost unanimously reached the same conclusion.[362] The proposed section also indicates that a representation can be an express warranty even if it is not made until after the contract for sale has been made. Again, this has already been generally established by existing case law when a representation is made directly by the seller to a remote buyer on a container, label, etc.[363]

The proposed revision also extends the same protection to a transferee of the remote buyer as is enjoyed by the remote buyer, although the seller is able explicitly to limit coverage of an express warranty to the first remote buyer.[364] The section also extends coverage to any member of the family or household unit of a remote consumer buyer, or an invitee of the consumer buyer. This is a clear extension of the present law, which extends coverage to such persons only in very limited circumstances.[365]

Section 2-408(b) states that a representation will not be a warranty if "a reasonable person in the position of the remote buyer would not believe that the representation created an obligation."[366] This is the proper standard for determining whether a representation is an express warranty. A seller should be bound by a representation that a buyer would reasonably consider to be part of his deal with the sellers.

Section 2-408(c) adopts a similar rule to section 2-403 with respect to representations made to the public. So long as the remote purchaser has knowledge of the representation at the time of the agreement, purchased the goods in the normal chain of distribution, and reasonably believed the goods would conform to the representation, the representation can be an express warranty. The remaining subsections of section 2-408 deal primarily with damages recoverable by remote buyers for breach of express warranty. The only significant aspect of these subsections is that a remote buyer cannot recover consequential damages in the form of lost profits for breach of an express warranty.[367]

---

[362] *See* § 4.09[E], *infra.*

[363] *See* § 4.05[F][2], *supra.*

[364] Council Draft § 2-408(b)(2)(B).

[365] *See* U.C.C. § 2-318; § 4.09[A], *infra.*

[366] Council Draft § 2-408(b)(1)(A).

[367] Council Draft § 2-408(f)(3).

§ 4.06   IMPLIED WARRANTIES

[A]   Overview of Implied Warranties

There are two implied warranties under the Code: that of merchantability and that of fitness for a particular purpose. These warranties are *implied*, rather than *express*. With the express warranty, some affirmation of fact or promise has been made by the seller, or the goods have been described, or some sample or model has been shown. It is against these words or acts that the conformity of the delivered goods is measured. On the other hand, implied warranties arise from the nature of the sale itself—the warranty of merchantability if the seller is a merchant with respect to goods of the kind involved in the transaction, and the warranty of fitness for a particular purpose if the seller (merchant or not) has reason to know of the buyer's particular purpose and that the buyer is relying on the seller's skill or judgment in selecting or furnishing suitable goods.

Quite naturally, in a particular sale these warranties can shade into each other, and they may exist simultaneously.[368] For example, the buyer may have told the seller the purpose for which he needs certain goods and that he is relying upon the seller to furnish goods that will meet that purpose. In discussing the goods with the buyer, the seller may well have made affirmations of fact about the goods and, in writing out the sales slip, will probably have described the goods she is selling. If the seller is a merchant, this example provides the factual background for the existence of express warranties and both of the implied warranties. It is difficult to determine the point at which words and conduct giving rise to an express warranty cease and words and conduct giving rise to implied warranties begin. Fortunately, there is usually no reason to try to discover such a point. Once a court has found that a warranty exists, the liability of the seller is not diminished just because the default pertains to an implied warranty. The words, conduct, writings, trade usages, course of performance, and course of dealing—all of these go into the parties' bargain, and it is from this bargain that warranties emerge.

The Code nonetheless has drawn a distinction between express and implied warranties. Part of the reason for this may simply be historical— the Uniform Sales Act drew the same distinction, and the drafters of the Code may have simply accepted the prior terminology. In addition, however, implied warranties do not rest on some specific affirmation of fact or prom-

---

[368] *See, e.g.,* C.E. Alexander & Sons, Inc. v. DEC Int'l, Inc., 811 P.2d 899, 15 UCCR2d 464 (N.M. 1991).

ise made by the seller; they do not arise out of a description of the goods; and they do not owe their existence to a sample or model that was exhibited. Implied warranties are created against a much less specific background; they arise because the seller is a merchant with respect to the goods or has knowledge about the buyer's purpose and reliance. In short, Article 2 assumes that implied warranties are less apt to create specific impressions in the mind of the buyer than are express warranties. Consequently, the disclaimer of an implied warranty does not generally require language as specific as would be necessary to avoid representations about the goods from becoming express warranties.[369]

[B] Implied Warranty of Merchantability

[1] Introduction

The implied warranty of merchantability is established by the Code in one sentence: "Unless excluded or modified (Section 2-316), a warranty that the goods shall be merchantable is implied in a contract for their sale if the seller is a merchant with respect to goods of that kind."[370]

The warranty of merchantability is implied only if the seller is a "merchant with respect to goods of that kind." "Merchant" is a defined Code term,[371] which includes three groups of people (although the last two can easily be grouped together):

1. Persons who deal in goods of the kind involved in the transaction;
2. Persons who hold themselves out as having knowledge or skill peculiar to the practices or goods involved in the transaction; or
3. Persons to whom this knowledge or skill may be attributed because of their employment of someone who, by his occupation, holds himself out as having this knowledge or skill.

---

[369] Although U.C.C. § 2-316(2) requires that a disclaimer of the implied warranty of merchantability mention "merchantability," section 2-316(3)(a) permits *all* implied warranties to be disclaimed by any language which in common understanding calls the buyer's attention to the exclusion of warranties and makes plain that there is no implied warranty. *See* § 4.07[C][2], *infra.*

[370] U.C.C. § 2-314(1).

[371] U.C.C. § 2-104(1) defines a "merchant" as a "[p]erson who deals in the goods of the kind or otherwise by his occupation holds himself out as having knowledge or skill peculiar to the practices or goods involved in the transaction or to whom such knowledge or skill may be attributed by his employment of an agent or broker or other intermediary who by his occupation holds himself out as having such knowledge or skill."

The last two categories are broader than the first and include persons having knowledge or skill peculiar to "practices" as well as goods. For example, under section 2-205, the relevant practice is that of making offers (or perhaps firm offers).[372] If section 2-205 is at issue, the person making the offer may be a merchant even if he does not deal in goods of the kind involved in the transaction. In addition, a person who does not *deal* in a particular kind of goods may nevertheless be a merchant because he holds himself out as having knowledge regarding those goods—or he may have hired someone who represents that he has such knowledge.[373]

The warranty of merchantability is limited to persons who have a merchant status with respect to *goods* of the kind involved in the transaction— a seller does not make a warranty of merchantability because he holds himself out as having skill or knowledge of the *practices* involved. There is some dispute, however, as to whether a seller must *deal* in the kind of goods involved in the transaction to make a warranty of merchantability, or whether a seller who has *skill or knowledge* about the goods also makes a merchantability warranty. That is, is the class of merchants who make the section 2-314 warranty limited to category 1 above, or does it also include a portion of those in categories 2 and 3—those who have skill or knowledge concerning the goods (but not the practices) involved in the transaction?

Some cases hold that a person is a merchant for purposes of section 2-314 who *either* deals in goods of the kind involved in the transaction or who holds himself out as having skill and knowledge about those goods. *Fay v. O'Connell*[374] is illustrative. In 1987, the buyer purchased a 1973 Dodge truck from the seller, who had used the truck in his daily business of selling and installing automotive parts. The truck's odometer proved to be defective, and the buyer sued for breach of the implied warranty of merchantability. The defendant argued that he had only sold two trucks during 1987 and was, therefore, not a merchant with respect to selling trucks. The court rejected this argument and held that, through his occupation as a specialist in auto repair, the seller had held himself out as having special knowledge or skills peculiar to motor vehicles so as to make him a merchant for purposes of section 2-314.[375]

---

[372] *See* § 3.05, *supra.*

[373] *See* County of Milwaukee v. Northrop Data Sys., Inc., 602 F.2d 767 (7th Cir. 1979).

[374] 1990 WL 251666, 12 UCCR2d 987 (Mass. Dist. Ct. 1990).

[375] *See also* Skelton v. Druid City Hosp. Bd., 459 So. 2d 818, 39 UCCR 369 (Ala. 1984) (although hospitals are not dealers in suturing needles, they are merchants with respect to such items because they hold themselves out to the public as having special knowledge regarding the provision of medical services to patients); Essex Crane Rental Corp. v. Weyher/ Livsey Constructors, Inc., 713 F. Supp 1350, 10 UCCR2d 314 (D. Idaho 1989); Neilson Business Equip. Ctr. v. Monteleone, 524 A.2d 1172, 3 UCCR2d 1721 (Del. 1987).

Representative of a more restrictive reading of "merchant" for purposes of section 2-314 is *Fred J. Moore, Inc. v. Schinman.*[376] The buyers contracted to buy from the seller scotch mint roots grown on eighteen acres of the seller's land. Although the seller had been raising mint oil for over twenty years, this contract was his first for the sale of roots. The roots that he delivered were contaminated with peppermint, and the buyers sued to revoke their acceptance of the roots, relying upon the implied warranty of merchantability. The buyers claimed that the seller, because of his occupation and experience as a mint farmer, held himself out as having skill and knowledge concerning mint roots and was, therefore, a merchant under section 2-314. The court rejected this argument and upheld summary judgment against the buyers. The court said that "to be liable for an implied warranty of merchantability, a merchant must *deal* in goods of the kind involved" in the transaction.[377]

Siemen v. Alden[378] also construed the "merchant" requirement of section 2-314 narrowly. Siemen purchased a used automated saw from Alden, a person engaged in the sawmill business. After suffering injuries while operating the saw, Siemen sued Alden under section 2-314, arguing that Alden was a merchant under section 2-314; that is, by his occupation and experience, Alden held himself out as having knowledge or skill peculiar to the goods (i.e., the automated saw). The court rejected the argument, holding that the warranty of merchantability is given only by those who, in a professional status, sell the kind of goods involved in the transaction. Since Alden was engaged in the sawmill business, not in selling saws, he was not liable for a breach of the warranty of merchantability.[379]

The approach of the *Fay* court is preferable. There is nothing in section 2-314 or the comments to the section that requires that the seller deal in the goods; the section requires only that the seller be a merchant *with respect to* the goods. Had the drafters wanted the section limited to those who deal in the particular goods, the language was readily available from section 2-104.[380] Moreover, Comment 2 to section 2-104, in discussing the merchant requirement, says only that section 2-314 requires "a professional status as to particular kinds of goods," not that the seller must *deal* in those goods.[381]

---

[376] 700 P.2d 754, 41 UCCR 741 (Wash. Ct. App. 1985).

[377] 700 P.2d at 757, 41 UCCR at 743 (emphasis added).

[378] 341 N.E.2d 713, 34 Ill. App. 3d 961, 18 UCCR 884 (Ill. App. Ct. 1975).

[379] *See also* Bagel v. American Honda Motor Co., 132 Ill. App. 3d 82, 41 UCCR 50 (Ill. App. Ct. 1985); Vince v. Broome, 443 So. 2d 23, 37 UCCR 1498 (Miss. 1983).

[380] *See also* U.C.C. § 2-403(2) on entrusting possession to a merchant "who deals in goods of that kind."

[381] U.C.C. § 2-104, Official Comment 2.

More important, the policy behind section 2-314 suggests its application in cases like *Fay*. The merchantability warranty is given, at least in part, by those who deal in goods *because* they are assumed to have skill and knowledge with respect to those goods that is greater than that of the buyer. Whether this skill or knowledge (or its appearance) exists because the person sells the goods or because of some other aspect of his or her profession should be irrelevant; the seller's presumed advantage over the buyer with respect to the goods nonetheless exists. If the seller chooses to disclaim this warranty, he is free to do so under the Code.

Apart from this ambiguity, there is little else in the merchant requirement that should create difficulty.[382] Because the concept of merchant has its roots in the concept of a professional in business,[383] the fact that one purchases goods regularly for personal or family use does not make the buyer a merchant.[384] Also, those making isolated or casual sales, whether or not engaged in business, are not merchants.[385]

The Code comments make it clear that simply because a person is a merchant in one context does not mean that she is a merchant for all purposes. A person may be an experienced and sophisticated businessperson, and even deal regularly in related goods, and still not be a merchant for purposes of section 2-314. A good example is *Rock Creek Ginger Ale Co. v. Themice Corp.*[386] In July 1969, Themice, a seller of liquid carbon dioxide,

---

[382] Perhaps the most litigated issue is the question of whether farmers are merchants. This issue has also engendered a fair amount of scholarly commentary. *See, e.g.*, Vivica Pierce, "What Do Farmers Impliedly Warrant When They Sell Their Livestock," 19 S.U. L. Rev. 357 (1992). The results of the cases are not entirely consistent, although there is no apparent reason to treat farmers who sell their produce differently from other sellers. In any event there is no justification for excluding farmers as a class from the definition of merchant; the inquiry should be fact specific. *See* Hupich v. Bitto, 667 So. 2d 615, 28 UCCR2d 526 (Ala. 1995) (farmer who did not advertise crop, did not solicit sales, and relied mainly on word of mouth was not merchant.) For a concise discussion of the issue, see Crandall et al., I Uniform Commercial Code § 2.6 (1993).

[383] U.C.C. § 2-104, Official Comment 2.

[384] *Id.* (person must be acting in mercantile capacity to be a merchant; lawyer or bank president buying goods for own use is not a merchant). *See* Allen v. Nicole, Inc., 172 N.J. Super. 442, 412 A.2d 824, 28 UCCR 982 (1980); North Carolina Nat'l Bank v. Robinson, 78 N.C. App. 1, 42 UCCR 579 (N.C. Ct. App. 1985).

[385] U.C.C. § 2-314, Official Comment 3. *See* Schuchman v. Johns Hopkins Hosp., 1971 WL 17892, 9 UCCR 637 (Md. Super. 1971); Bevard v. Ajax Mfg. Co., 473 F. Supp. 35, 27 UCCR 684 (E.D. Mich. 1979); In re Jackson Television, 121 B.R. 790, 13 UCCR2d 737 (E.D. Tenn. 1990). Under the view of the *Fay* case discussed previously, however, a person may be a merchant for purposes of U.C.C. § 2-314, even though making a casual or isolated sale, if the seller holds himself out as having skill or knowledge with respect to the goods.

[386] 352 F. Supp. 522, 12 UCCR 810 (D.D.C. 1971).

sold 20,000 pounds of the material to Rock Creek. Themice had purchased the carbon dioxide from the Schaffer Brewing Company, a brewer of beer. Soon after taking delivery, Rock Creek discovered that the liquid carbon dioxide was defective and sued Themice. Themice filed a third-party complaint against Schaffer, claiming a breach of the implied warranty of merchantability. The court held, however, that the sale from Schaffer to Themice was not accompanied by a warranty of merchantability because Schaffer, although a merchant of beer, was not a merchant of liquid carbon dioxide.

[2] Minimum Standards of Merchantability

The Code does not *define* merchantability. What it does in section 2-314 is set minimum standards of merchantability. The statutory language is that goods "to be merchantable must be *at least* such as . . . ."[387] More may be required by the parties' agreement, course of dealing, or usage of trade,[388] but the minimum standards assure the buyer that if he does not receive goods that conform at least to normal commercial expectations, he will have a cause of action to recover compensation for losses suffered.

Even though a seller has been careful not to make an assertion of fact or promise about the goods, the ordinary buyer in the normal commercial transaction expects that the goods he has just purchased will not turn out to be worthless. As Lord Ellenborough colorfully said in one case: "The purchaser cannot be supposed to buy goods to lay them on a dunghill."[389] On the other hand, a buyer who has purchased goods without obtaining an express warranty as to their quality cannot reasonably expect that those goods will be the best possible goods of that kind. The implied warranty of merchantability does not promise perfection, and a number of courts have said so.[390] The Code's protection lies between these extremes:

Goods to be merchantable must be at least such as:

> (a) pass without objection in the trade under the contract description; and
>
> (b) in the case of fungible goods, are of fair average quality within the description; and

---

[387] U.C.C. § 2-314(2) (emphasis added).

[388] U.C.C.§ 2-314, Official Comment 6.

[389] Gardiner v. Gray, 4 Camp. 144, 145, 171 Eng. Rep. 46, 47 (K.B. 1815).

[390] *See, e.g.,* Sessa v. Reigle, 427 F. Supp. 760, 21 UCCR 745 (E.D. Pa. 1977); Taterka v. Ford Motor Co., 271 N.W.2d 653, 25 UCCR 680 (Wis. 1978); Gross v. Systems Eng'g Corp., 1983 WL 160568, 36 UCCR 42 (E.D. Pa. 1983); Saratoga Spa & Bath Inc. v. Beeche Sys. Corp., 656 N.Y.S.2d 787, 35 UCCR2d 478 (1997).

(c) are fit for the ordinary purposes for which such goods are used; and

(d) run, within the variations permitted by the agreement, of even kind, quality and quantity within each unit and among all units involved; and

(e) are adequately contained, packaged, and labeled as the agreement may require; and

(f) conform to the promises or affirmations of fact made on the container or label, if any.[391]

Each of these subsections is connected with an "and." There is, therefore, a breach of the implied warranty of merchantability if the goods fail to meet any one of these minimum standards. Even though the goods would pass without objection, the warranty of merchantability is breached if those goods are not adequately packaged; conversely, adequate packaging is not sufficient to satisfy this warranty if the goods would not pass without objection in the trade.

Thus, section 2-314 contains six independent criteria by which merchantability is judged. Each is discussed in the text, but the key to merchantability—its heart—is section 2-314 (2)(c): the goods must be fit for the ordinary purpose for which such goods are used. When a merchant sells goods, there is a warranty that the goods purchased will be fit for their ordinary purpose.

There are hundreds, if not thousands, of cases in which it has been asserted that goods are not fit for their ordinary purpose. Although the fact patterns are of almost infinite variety, two issues inevitably arise in deciding whether an item is fit for the ordinary purpose for which such goods are made: what is the ordinary purpose of the goods, and how do we determine whether a good is fit for that purpose?

[3] Ordinary Purpose

Under section 2-314(2)(c), goods must only be fit for the *ordinary* purposes for which such goods are used. Most goods can be used for a multitude of purposes, especially if "purpose" is broadly defined. For example, a "steak knife" might routinely be used to cut chicken, ham, and turkey as well as steak, and might less frequently be used to cut other foods as well. Less frequently still, a steak knife might be used to cut string or twine. And, hopefully very rarely, it might even be used to stab someone. Which, among these, are the "ordinary" purposes for a steak knife?

---

[391] U.C.C. § 2-314(2).

The Code does not define "ordinary," and the Code Comments provide little helpful guidance. Certainly, the purpose for which the goods are designed and the manner in which they are marketed are central in determining the ordinary purpose of the goods.[392] However, goods are usually not sold with an explicit catalog of all of the purposes to which they can be put. One can think of many synonyms for the word "ordinary"—"common," "normal," "customary," "routine," to name a few[393]—but this effort is of little help in defining the scope of the warranty. A number of cases have focused on the idea of "foreseeability,"[394] but foreseeability largely represents a conclusion rather than a means of analysis. The issue is for what uses of a product should a seller be responsible beyond those for which the product is specifically designed?

An early case from Pennsylvania indicates the problem. In that case,[395] the buyer purchased a "log chain" from the seller who was engaged in the business of selling farm equipment and hardware. At the request of the buyer, the seller welded hooks on one end of the chain. The buyer used the chain to haul a truck up a dirt road, the chain broke, and the truck was damaged. The buyer sued, claiming a breach of the implied warranty of merchantability; the seller demurred to the complaint, arguing that the ordinary purpose of a log chain is to haul logs—not trucks. The court properly overruled the demurrer. The problem was to determine the ordinary purpose of a log chain with hooks welded on one end. In this case, the ordinary purpose of the goods, so described, could only be determined through further evidence of the circumstances of the particular sale and the uses to which others put similar goods. It may be, for example, that it was common practice in the vicinity to use "log chains with hooks" in this manner, and the seller was aware of the practice.[396] Perhaps the seller had even used the chain for similar purposes himself. This evidence would be important in

---

[392] *See* Gilmer v. Buena Vista Home Video, Inc., 939 F. Supp. 665, 31 UCCR2d 366 (W.D. Ark. 1996).

[393] Laurence Urdang, The Oxford Thesaurus (Oxford Univ. Press 1992).

[394] *See, e.g.,* Hayes, et al v. Ariens Co., 391 Mass. 407, 38 UCCR 48 (1984); Bernick v. Jurden, 306 N.C. 435, 34 UCCR 458 (1982).

[395] Robert H. Carr & Sons, Inc. v. Yearsley, 31 Pa. D.&C. 2d 262, 1 UCCR 97 (Pa. C.P. 1963).

[396] *See* Pisano v. American Leasing, 194 Cal. Rptr. 77, 36 UCCR 1153 (Cal. Ct. App. 1983) (determination of whether item is fit for ordinary purpose might depend on testimony of persons familiar with the industry standards and local practices).

determining whether pulling a truck was an ordinary purpose of a log chain with hook, and should not be precluded by demurrer.[397]

A seller should not be held responsible for any use to which a buyer decides to put the seller's product, even if the use is in some general sense foreseeable. For example, in *Olson v. Village of Babbitt*,[398] the court properly denied recovery for breach of the implied warranty of merchantability when a boy was injured by an unexploded firework. The boy had removed the powder from the firework and the powder had exploded when the boy ignited it.[399] On the other hand, sellers should not escape responsibility if the product fails to perform a function for which the goods are normally used by significant segments of the population, even if the goods were not specifically designed for that purpose.[400] Likewise, a seller should not avoid responsibility if the product is used in a *manner* that the seller should reasonably expect, but for which the product was not necessarily designed, when the manner in which it was used caused injury or causes the product to fail to perform properly.

A good case illustrating these principles is *Brickman-Joy Corp. v. National Annealing Box Co.*[401] In this case, the buyer ordered a "galvanizing kettle" from the seller for use in the buyer's operations. A galvanizing kettle is a tub that holds molten zinc, into which steel is then dipped during the galvanizing process.[402] During the first use of the kettle, it cracked and badly leaked molten zinc, causing more than $80,000 in damage. The buyer sued on the basis that the galvanizing kettle was not merchantable. The trial judge found a breach of the implied warranty of merchantability as a matter of law.

On appeal, the seller argued that galvanizing kettles are used in galvanizing operations employing a variety of components and design variables over which it has no control. In addition, the buyer's galvanizing process

---

[397] *See* T.J. Stevenson & Co., Inc. v. 81,193 Bags of Flour, 629 F.2d 338, 351, 30 UCCR 865, 881 (5th Cir. 1980) (term "fit for ordinary purpose for which such goods are used" has little meaning unless trade usage and other extrinsic evidence is considered).

[398] 189 N.W.2d 701, 9 UCCR 1041 (Minn. 1971).

[399] *See also* Venezia v. Miller Brewing Co., 626 F.2d 188, 29 UCCR 487 (1st Cir. 1980) (jury could not reasonably find that an ordinary purpose of bottle was to intentionally throw it against a telephone pole).

[400] *See, e.g.*, Glyptal, Inc. v. Engelhard Corp., 801 F. Supp 887, 18 UCCR2d 1059 (D. Mass. 1992) (warranty of merchantability includes not only intended uses but reasonably foreseeable uses).

[401] 459 F.2d 133, 10 UCCR 539 (2d Cir. 1972).

[402] As described by the court, galvanizing is a process in which steel, after being subjected to treatment with acid to remove impurities, is then coated with molten zinc to inhibit rust. *Id.* at 134 n.1, 10 UCCR at 540 n.1.

did not use side supports to brace the kettle which, the seller argued, caused the kettle to fail. In deciding whether the method in which the buyer had employed the kettle constituted an "ordinary use," the appeals court approved the following instruction of the trial judge:

> If the manner in which the plaintiff used the kettle was *in accord with practices employed by an appreciable number of galvanizers* . . . you may then find that the plaintiff is entitled to the benefit of the warranty of merchantability and is entitled to recover, even if not all galvanizers would have used the kettle as plaintiffs did.
>   . . . That does not mean that in order to avoid being charged with misuse he would have to use the kettle in the best way that galvanizers use it. He wouldn't have to use it the way that most galvanizers use it. He wouldn't have to use it in the way that it's regarded as the best practice. If he used it in a way that's used by an appreciable number of galvanizers, people in the industry, then that warranty stands.[403]

According to the court, so long as an appreciable number of people in the industry would use the galvanizing kettle in a manner similar to the buyer, then it was "not unfair to put the onus on the manufacturer" to disclaim liability when the product is used in that way.[404] Thus, if a seller would reasonably expect an appreciable number of people to use its product in a particular way or for a particular purpose, it is up to the seller to inform the buyer that the product is not appropriate for that purpose or to be used in that manner.

When, however, it is well known that a product is unsuited for a particular purpose, the purpose is not an ordinary one. For example, in *Lindy Homes, Inc. v. Evans Supply Co., Inc.*,[405] a contractor used electrogalvanized nails in exterior cedar siding. When the nails rusted, the contractor sued the seller. The issue was whether this use of electrogalvanized nails was an ordinary purpose. The question, said the court, was "premised in large part on the use of an item as recognized in the trade," and the court found that it was common knowledge in the trade that use of electrogalvanized nails for this purpose was not proper.[406] So far, the approach of the courts in these cases seems generally correct.

---

[403] *Id.* at 136, 10 UCCR at 543.

[404] *Id.* at 137, 10 UCCR at 544.

[405] 357 So. 2d 996, 24 UCCR 109 (Ala. Civ. App. 1978).

[406] In addition, *see* Guaranteed Constr. Co. v. Gold Bond Prods., 153 Mich. App. 385, 3 UCCR2d 74 (1986) (well known in industry that use of product in highly humid environment was not ordinary purpose when use was not accompanied with special precautions against corrosion).

When use of the product results in personal injury, the courts have generally employed a standard of reasonable foreseeability to determine whether the purpose or manner in which the goods were used falls within the ambit of section 2-314.[407] This coincides with the manner in which courts determine whether the "product misuse" defense is applicable in cases brought under strict products liability.[408]

The extent to which the "ordinary purpose" of a product extends beyond performing its basic function is a matter of some dispute, although most courts hold that the ordinary purpose of most items goes beyond *minimal* performance of their basic function. Courts generally agree that a product must perform its function with reasonable safety[409] and without unreasonable "collateral damage" to other goods.[410] Courts have often stated that, with respect to safety, the standards of merchantability under section 2-314 and the "unreasonably dangerous standard" of section 402A of the Restatement (Second) of Torts are the same.[411] A large number of cases have now held that a car is not fit for its ordinary purpose when it is not reasonably crashworthy,[412] although there remains some authority to the contrary.[413]

Under the standard of reasonable foreseeability, the results in some early cases are questionable. For example, in *Myers v. Montgomery Ward & Co.,*[414] the Maryland Supreme Court found that a lawn mower was not being used for an ordinary purpose when the owner slipped while cutting grass on a slope and was injured when his foot went under the lawn mower. The

---

[407] *See, e.g.,* Back v. Wickes Corp., 378 N.E.2d 964, 24 UCCR 1164 (Mass. 1978); Allen v. Chance Mfg. Co., Inc., 398 Mass. 32, 494 N.E.2d 1324, 1 UCCR2d 1124 (1986); Turner v. Manning, Maxwell & Moore, Inc., 217 S.E.2d 863, 17 UCCR 1200 (Va. 1975) (product must be reasonably safe for its intended purpose or some other reasonably foreseeable purpose).

[408] Restatement of Torts (Second), § 402A cmt. n. *See* § 4.12[C], *infra.*

[409] Federal Signal Corp. v. Safety Factors Inc., 886 P.2d 172, 25 UCCR2d 765 (Wash. 1994).

[410] *See, e.g.,* Holowka v. York Farm Bureau Coop. Ass'n, 1963 WL 8528, 2 UCCR 445 (insecticide that succeeds in eliminating boll weevils but also injures livestock not fit for ordinary purpose); R. Clinton Constr. Co. v. Bryant & Reaves, Inc., 442 F. Supp. 838, 23 UCCR 310 (N.D. Miss. 1977) (antifreeze that corrodes radiator not fit for ordinary purpose).

[411] *See* Olson v. U.S. Indus., Inc., 649 F. Supp. 1511, 1 UCCR2d 416 (D. Kan. 1986); Gumbs v. International Harvester Inc., 718 F.2d 88, 36 UCCR 1579 (3d Cir. 1983).

[412] *See, e.g.,* Back v. Wickes Corp., 378 N.E.2d 964, 24 UCCR 1164 (Mass. 1978); Smith v. Fiat-Roosevelt Motors, Inc., 402 F. Supp. 116, 18 UCCR 337 (M.D. Fla. 1975); Nicolodi v. Harley-Davidson Motor Co., 370 So. 2d 68 (Fla. Dist. Ct. App. 1979).

[413] *See* Frericks v. General Motors Corp., 317 A.2d 494, 20 Md. App. 518 (Md. Ct. Spec. App. 1974); Commonwealth v. Johnson Insulation, 683 N.E.2d 1328, 33 UCCR2d 426 (Mass. 1997).

[414] 253 Md. 282, 252 A.2d 855, 6 UCCR 493 (1969).

court characterized using the lawn mower to cut grass on a slope as an abnormal use of the mower. This conclusion is dubious, given the large number of residential yards that are likely to have significant slopes.[415]

In a couple of cases, courts have said that the ordinary purpose of a mobile home goes beyond its being minimally habitable. In *Jones v. Abriani*,[416] the court found a breach of the warranty of merchantability even though the buyers occupied the home for well over a year before attempting to reject it or revoke their acceptance. The court said that the ordinary purpose of a mobile home was "to serve as a modern comfortable dwelling where the purchasers could live and entertain guests without discomfort and embarrassment."[417] In a later case involving similar facts, the Virginia Supreme Court explicitly held that the ordinary purpose of a mobile home extends beyond mere habitability. In that case,[418] a mobile home was held to breach the implied warranty of merchantability, despite having been certified by a local official as meeting safety and sanitary standards.[419]

On the other hand, a number of cases have made it clear that the implied warranty of merchantability does not cover *all* imperfections that an item may have. In *Taterka v. Ford Motor Co.*,[420] the court held that a minor rust problem caused by improper taillight installation did not constitute a breach of the warranty of merchantability. The court said that the ordinary purpose of an automobile was to provide safe, reliable transportation, and the car had been driven for over 75,000 miles without serious incident.[421] In *Pronti v. DML of Elmira, Inc.*,[422] the court held that the or-

---

[415] *See also* Rupee v. Mobile Home Brokers, Inc., 124 Ga. App. 86, 9 UCCR 678 (1971) (the court, citing *Myers*, held that seller was not liable for breach of warranty of merchantability when owner of mobile home was injured by sharp metal object when he slipped in shower). Apparently, the *Myers* case has been superseded by the Maryland products-liability statute. *See* Hartford Ins. Co. v. Manor Inn of Bethesda, Inc., 335 Md. 135, 642 A.2d 219 (1994).

[416] 350 N.E.2d 635, 19 UCCR 1102 (Ind. Ct. App. 1976).

[417] *Id.* at 645, 19 UCCR at 120.

[418] Twin Lakes Mfg. v. Coffey, 281 S.E.2d 864, 32 UCCR 770 (Va. 1981).

[419] *See also* Mindell v. Raleigh Rug Co., 14 UCCR 1124 (Mass. Housing Ct. 1974) (rug must not only be durable but must hold its pattern and color for a reasonable length of time consistent with quality of rug).

[420] 86 Wis. 2d 140, 271 N.W.2d 653, 25 UCCR 680 (1978).

[421] *See also* Horne v. Claude Ray Ford Sales, Inc., 162 Ga. App. 329, 34 UCCR 880 (1982) (fact that "new" car had been damaged and repaired did not breach warranty of merchantability because it did not affect car's usefulness and driveability; defects did, however, breach express warranty that car was "new"); American Suzuki Motor Corp. v. Superior Court of Los Angeles County, 37 Cal. App. 4th 1291, 44 Cal. Rptr. 2d 526, 27 UCCR2d 392 (1995) (warranty of merchantability can be breached only if vehicle manifests a defect so basic that it renders the vehicle unfit for providing transportation); Lee v. General

dinary purpose of dining-room furniture was to hold food and provide seating and storage. Therefore, minor defects in the furniture did not make it unmerchantable.[423] In *Kaplan v. Cablevision of Pa., Inc.*,[424] the court held that periods of cable interruption did not make the cable service unfit for its ordinary purpose. A number of courts have held that prototype or experimental goods do not have an "ordinary purpose."[425] In such cases, if the goods fail to perform as expected, buyers must rely upon express warranties, or the implied warranty of fitness for a particular purpose.

An interesting case with far reaching potential implications is *Lancaster Glass Corp. v. Philips ECG, Inc.*[426] The facts of the case are rather complicated but can be distilled as follows. During the 1970s, the buyer purchased large numbers of glass bulbs from the seller for use in manufacturing cathode ray tubes. Before the buyer filled an order for its cathode ray tubes, it would treat the tubes with "implosion protection" to minimize the risk of violent explosion if the tube was broken. There were two implosion protection systems in existence at the time. The traditional method, "shell-bonding," involved placing a seal over the face of the tube. "T-banding," a more recent innovation, involved placing a steel strip around the perimeter of the glass and tightening the strip. It is critical to the T-banding process that the band not slip or move on the tube once it is tightened. If it does, the implosion protection is compromised.

In early 1980, the buyer placed a very large order for bulbs, in anticipation of a favorable sales year. The seller began sending completed bulbs to the buyer pursuant to the contract in March 1980. In April 1980, however, the buyer was notified by one of its customers that the T-bands on a shipment of tubes had slipped. Nonetheless, the buyer continued to accept bulbs from the seller and did not mention the slippage problem until August 1980, at which time it had accepted about 15,000 bulbs. At the same time, the

---

Motors Corp., 950 F. Supp. 170, 34 UCCR2d 315 (S.D. Miss. 1996) (fact that vehicles were used for ordinary purpose for significant amount of time without problems negated breach of implied warranty of merchantability). *But see* Nelson v. Wilkins Dodge, 256 N.W.2d 472, 21 UCCR 1001 (Minn. 1977) (new vehicle that had paint bubbles, inverted tail covers, loose wiper blades, and loose shift lever was not merchantable).

[422] 478 N.Y.S.2d 156, 39 UCCR 455 (N.Y. App. Div. 1984).

[423] It is probably significant to the court's conclusion, however, that the seller offered to cure the defects and was refused by the buyer.

[424] 671 A.2d 716, 29 UCCR3d 425 (Pa. Super. Ct. 1996) (an alternative holding).

[425] *See* Axion Corp. v. G.D.C. Leasing Corp., 269 N.E.2d 664, 474, 9 UCCR 17 (Mass. 1971) ("semi-experimental" valve-setting machine had no ordinary purpose); Binks Mfg. Co. v. National Presto Indus., Inc., 709 F.2d 1109, 36 UCCR 14 (7th Cir. 1983) (unique processing system has no ordinary purpose).

[426] 835 F.2d 652, 5 UCCR2d 1306 (6th Cir. 1987).

buyer discovered that its projections for a banner year were proving to be excessively optimistic. During the fall of 1980, there were a number of discussions about the price that the buyer was to be charged for the remaining bulbs, but the slippage issue did not resurface until January 1981. Despite the slippage problem, the parties reached apparent agreement in late January 1981 as to the delivery of the remaining bulbs. At a meeting in March 1981, however, the buyer asked for concessions on delivery dates, citing its poor market situation, and even asked the seller what the cancellation charges would be on the rest of the order. The buyer did not mention the T-band problem at this meeting. At a meeting about a month later, however, the buyer raised the T-band issue, and suggested that it resulted from the seller's failure to comply with the contract specifications. Shortly thereafter, the buyer demanded return credit for all of the bulbs that it had in inventory and refused to take any more. The seller then sued and won in the trial court.

The buyer made two arguments to justify its actions. The first argument was that the bulbs did not conform to the contract specifications. On this issue, the appeals court upheld the trial court's determination that the seller's bulbs conformed to the specifications that the buyer had provided. The buyer's second argument was that the bulbs were not merchantable because one of the ordinary purposes for which the bulbs were used was the production of T-banded cathode ray tubes, and the bulbs provided by the seller were not fit for this purpose. At the time that the bulbs were provided by the seller, the seller was aware of the T-banding process and the buyer argued that the seller should have provided bulbs that were capable of being successfully T-banded.

The court disagreed. It said that the seller did not breach the warranty of merchantability by tendering bulbs that were not perfectly suitable for the new technology. Because the buyer had shifted in 1980 from primarily using the shellbonding process to protect from implosion to the T-banding process, shellbonding was the "customary" process while T-banding was a "noncustomary use." The seller's duty, therefore, was to merely provide the kind of bulbs that it had normally provided. If the buyer wanted something different from that which it typically received, it had an obligation to inform the seller.

The court's decision was probably correct in the particular context of the case. There was evidence that the buyer was simply using the T-banding problem as a pretext for avoiding the contract. In addition, the buyer delayed in bringing up the T-banding problem and then did so only intermittently during 1980. The case, however, raises interesting questions about the obligation of sellers to keep up with advancing technology. What obligations, for example, do sellers of computer software have to ensure that it is compatible with the latest computer hardware that has just hit the market? Or, alternatively, to what extent can purchasers assume that new software they purchase will be useable on their hardware? In many cases, this problem can be avoided by specific warnings or instructions on the hardware or software, but the general issue is broader. Often, goods are used in conjunction with a variety of goods manufactured by other sellers, or used in a variety of processes. Sellers should have some obligation to ensure that when the use of its goods in conjunction with other goods or processes becomes sufficiently widespread as to become "ordinary," their goods are compatible with the other good or process. At what point this occurs (e.g., when T-banding is used by 2 percent of the industry?) cannot be stated with certainty. It should depend on such factors as the level of expertise of the seller about the industry in which its goods are used, the past dealings between the seller and the buyer, the length of time the buyer's use of the goods has been present in the industry, what warnings or limitations the seller has placed on the use of the goods, and other factors as well.[427]

A case in which the buyers went too far in attempting to extend the warranty of merchantability is *Schwartz v. Michigan Power Management Co.*[428] Pursuant to an agreement to be a "distributor" of "electrical power management systems" produced by Michigan Power, Schwartz purchased the systems from Michigan Power for resale in the Chicago area. After a very lengthy process, Michigan Power was unable to secure the seal of approval of Underwriters Laboratories (UL), an independent testing laboratory. This failure made the systems either unmarketable or much more difficult to market in the designated area. Schwartz sued, claiming, among other things, that a system that did not have UL approval was not fit for the "ordinary purpose" of resale.

The court rejected Schwartz's "impoverished"[429] argument. The court confined the "purpose" of a product to its end use. According to the court,

---

[427] *See also* Hollingsworth v. Queen Carpet, Inc., 827 S.W.2d 306, 17 UCCR2d 1125 (Tenn. Ct. App. 1991). In this case, carpet supplied by the seller came loose from the padding and became wrinkled in a relatively short time after installation. There was evidence that the buyer cleaned the carpet with a "Rinse-O-Vac" system, which may have caused the problem. The court found for the seller on the grounds that the buyer had not proved that moisture from the Rinse-O-Vac system had not caused the breakdown of the carpet. The court did not discuss whether the Rinse-O-Vac system was a generally accepted method of cleaning carpets of this sort. If it was, it seems that the seller should bear the responsibility for making carpet that can withstand cleaning by such a system or provide a warning to the buyer that it should clean the carpet in some other manner.

[428] 564 F. Supp. 125, 36 UCCR 1595 (N.D. Ill. 1983).

[429] *Id.* at 129, 36 UCCR at 1602.

the merchantability warranty (as well as the fitness warranty) applies only to the good's intrinsic qualities, not extrinsic conditions. While Schwartz intended to resell the product, and Michigan Power knew this, resale was not the purpose of an energy-management system—energy management was the purpose of an energy-management system. Because Schwartz had not alleged that the system was in any way deficient for this purpose, his merchantability claim failed. This result seems correct so far as it goes. At the time Michigan Power was attempting to gain UL approval, no energy-management system had received UL's approval. In fact, UL did not have standards in place by which to evaluate such systems. In different circumstances, however, a court could legitimately find that a system that fails to receive the approval of an outside agency might not "pass without objection in the trade" and thereby breach the merchantability warranty.[430]

[4]   Fitness

To be merchantable, a product must be "fit" for the ordinary purpose for which such goods are used. As discussed, a product can be fit for its ordinary purpose without being perfect or the best. To a large extent, whether a product is fit for its ordinary purpose is a function of reasonable buyer expectations and the contract description.[431] As will be discussed in greater detail, the standards of fitness for used goods are different from the standard for new goods,[432] and the price that is paid for the goods can be an important factor in determining the qualities that the goods must have in order to satisfy the standard of merchantability. Furthermore, whether goods are fit for their ordinary purpose is integrally related to the description of the ordinary purpose of the goods. A product may be fit if its ordinary purpose is defined one way, and not fit if its ordinary purpose is defined differently. To the extent that the ordinary purpose of a product is also a function of the contract description and buyer expectations,[433] the issues of "fitness" and "ordinary purpose" are even more closely connected.

---

[430] *See also* Skelton v. General Motors, 500 F. Supp. 1181, 30 UCCR 846 (N.D. Ill. 1980) (not a breach of the warranty of merchantability for a manufacturer to substitute a transmission of lesser quality in a new car—the auto and transmission were fit for driving which is the ordinary purpose of a car).

[431] This is explicitly recognized in the proposed revisions to Article 2. Under section 2-404 of the proposed revisions, to be merchantable, goods must "be fit for the ordinary purpose for which goods *of that description* are used." Council Draft, § 2-404.

[432] U.C.C. § 2-314, Official Comment 3.

[433] *See* § 4.06[B][3], *supra.*

There are three ways in which goods might fail to perform their ordinary purpose. The first is when there is a flaw in the manufacturing process, or the goods are otherwise defective when compared with other goods of the same description sold by the seller and, as a result of the defect, the goods do not perform as expected. An automobile may have been produced with faulty brakes,[434] food may be contaminated,[435] a mobile home may have a variety of production line defects.[436] These cases are usually not problematic; there is generally little difficulty in finding that such items are not fit for their ordinary purpose.[437]

The second type of case is often more difficult—the "design defect" case. In these cases, there is no manufacturing defect; the goods are produced exactly as intended. The contention of the buyer, however, is that the basic design of the goods is flawed; as designed they are simply unfit for the purpose for which they were created. These cases may or may not involve products that pose a safety hazard. Those that do not pose safety risks present far fewer analytical problems. They include such items as an automatic car washer that knocked parts from the cars that it washed,[438] paint that peeled shortly after it was applied,[439] a galvanizing tank that leaked molten zinc,[440] and a clamp that separated when used to straighten auto bodies.[441] Cases in which the product poses a threat to safety are discussed at length subsequently.

The third type of case in which a product might not be fit for its ordinary purpose is when the manufacturer has failed to provide adequate warnings or instructions concerning the product. As with the design defect problem, this issue also arises in both safety-related and nonsafety-related contexts, although it is far more frequently found when goods have caused

---

[434] *See* Henningsen v. Bloomfield Motors, Inc., 161 A.2d 69, 32 N.J. 358 (N.J. 1960).

[435] Blommer Chocolate Co. v. Bongards Creameries Inc., 635 F. Supp. 919 (N.D. Ill. 1986); Cain v. Sheraton Perimeter Park S. Hotel, 592 So. 2d 218, 16 UCCR2d 347 (Ala. 1991).

[436] Jones v. Abriani, 169 Ind. App. 556, 19 UCCR 1102 (Ind. Ct. App. 1976); Long v. Quality Mobile Home Brokers, Inc., 248 S.E.2d 311, 25 UCCR 470 (S.C. 1978).

[437] Or, if tort liability for personal injury or property damage is involved, there should be little problem in finding goods to be "defective" and "unreasonably dangerous." *See* Restatement (Second) of Torts § 402A. Such goods are also be unlikely to "pass without objection in the trade" and would, therefore, also be unmerchantable under U.C.C. § 2-314 (2)(a).

[438] Auto-Teria, Inc. v. Ahern, 352 N.E.2d 774, 20 UCCR 336 (Ind. Ct. App. 1976).

[439] Glyptal, Inc. v. Engelhard Corp., 801 F. Supp. 887, 18 UCCR2d 1059 (D. Mass. 1992).

[440] Brickman-Joy Corp. v. National Annealing Box Co., 459 F.2d 133, 10 UCCR 539 (2d Cir. 1972).

[441] Mattos, Inc. v. Hash, 368 A.2d 993, 21 UCCR 473 (Md. Ct. App. 1977).

personal injury.[442] In these cases, the goods have been reasonably designed but require instructions or warnings to be operated safely or properly.[443] Often these cases involve products that cannot accomplish their purpose without some danger to the user.[444]

[a] Food Cases

The warranty of merchantability applies to the consumption of food, whether it is to be consumed on or off the premises.[445] There are two limitations on the implied warranty of merchantability of food or drink. First, the warranty is made only by the person who is a merchant with respect to food. Thus, the warranty is implied in the case of a restaurant,[446] hotel,[447] and other establishments that routinely serve food for value. It is not, however, implied when friends have guests over for dinner, or when persons each bring a dish to a "pot-luck" dinner. There are some difficult cases between these extremes. For example, in *Samson v. Riesing*,[448] the Wauwatosa Band Mothers sponsored an annual fund-raiser in which food was sold. When the plaintiff became ill from the turkey salad served by the band mothers, apparently as a result of food poisoning, he sued eleven of the band mothers for negligence and breach of warranty. In summary fashion, the court dismissed the implied warranty claim, stating that the Wauwatosa Band Mothers were not merchants as contemplated by the statute. These

---

[442] For a prominent case not involving personal injury (at least not to people), see Kassab v. Central Soya, 246 A.2d 848, 5 UCCR 925 (Pa. 1968) (failure to warn that ingredient in cattle feed might cause abortions).

[443] *See, e.g.*, Duford v. Sears, Roebuck & Co., 833 F.2d 407, 4 UCCR2d 1374 (1st Cir. 1987) (failure to instruct on proper installation of chimney pipe caused fire); Wolfe v. Ford Motor Co., 376 N.E.2d 143, 24 UCCR 94 (Mass. Ct. App. 1978) (failure to warn of the dangers of underinflation of tires and overloading of vehicle caused blowout); Hayes v. Ariens Co., 391 Mass. 407, 462 N.E.2d 273 (1984); Reid v. Eckerd Drugs, Inc., 40 N.C. App. 476, 253 S.E.2d 344 (1979).

[444] *See* Wolfe v. Ford Motor Co., 376 N.E.2d 143, 24 UCCR 94 (Mass. Ct. App. 1978).

[445] U.C.C. § 2-314, Official Comment 5. Some pre-Code cases held that the purchase of food to be eaten on the premises was a service rather than a sale, and therefore warranties did not attach. *See, e.g.*, Lynch v. Hotel Bond Co., 117 Conn. 128, 167 A. 99 (1933); Nisky v. Childs Co., 135 A. 805 (N.J. Ct. Err. & App. 1927). *But see* Friend v. Childs Dining Hall Co., 231 Mass. 65, 120 N.E. 407 (1918). The Code definitively resolves this issue in its section 2-314(1): "Under this section, the serving for value of food or drink to be consumed either on the premises or elsewhere is a sale."

[446] Koster v. Scotch Assocs., 640 A.2d 1225, 23 UCCR2d 679 (N.J. Super. Ct. 1993); Kilpatrick v. Superior Court, 11 Cal. Rptr. 2d 323, 19 UCCR2d 72 (Cal. Ct. App. 1992).

[447] *See* Title v. Pontchertrain Hotel, 449 So. 2d 677 (La. Ct. App. 1984).

[448] 62 Wisc. 2d 698, 215 N.W.2d 662 (1974).

cases turn on their specific facts, and the same considerations that generally determine whether a seller is a merchant for purposes of section 2-314 are applicable in this context as well.[449]

Second, the food must be served "for value."[450] In most cases this will be easy to determine, but some cases may be difficult. For example, what about the water, salt and pepper, and condiments that are served gratuitously by most restaurants? Are they served "for value?" These should be included within the implied warranty of merchantability.[451] Restrauteurs and the like must cover all of their expenses, including the cost of water, condiments, etc., in the price they charge for meals.[452] Although the owner does not charge directly for these services (neither does it charge for the decor, the furniture, and other overhead expenses), they are paid by the owner from its receipts and, therefore, should be considered as given "for value" for purposes of section 2-314.[453]

The primary issue in these cases has been the applicable standard for determining whether a food product is fit for consumption. Courts applied two different standards prior to enactment of the Code, and because the Code provides no definitive solution, the battle has been waged largely along the pre-Code lines. A large number of cases coming from virtually every jurisdiction have now confronted the issue, and the battle has a pretty clear winner.

One test for merchantability is the "foreign/natural test." Under this test, if the object is one that occurs naturally in the food (such as bones in chicken), the food is not unfit for consumption.[454] A recent application of the foreign/natural test is in *Mexicali Rose v. Superior Court*.[455] In this case, the plaintiff ordered a chicken enchilada at defendant restaurant and sustained throat injuries when he swallowed a one-inch chicken bone contained in the enchilada. He alleged that the enchilada was unfit for consumption

---

[449] *See* § 4.06[B][1], *supra*.

[450] The Code's definition of "value" is in section 1-201(44).

[451] *See* Yochem v. Gloria, Inc., 134 Ohio St. 427, 17 N.E.2d 731 (1938).

[452] *See* Cain v. Sheraton Perimeter Park S. Hotel, 592 So. 2d 218, 16 UCCR2d 347 (Ala. 1991). In this case the plaintiff became ill from raw oysters that were served "free" in the defendant's lounge. The court held that the oysters were "sold" within the meaning of the Code and cited the fact that the plaintiff had spent $38.00 on drinks for himself and his associates to go with the oysters.

[453] *See* Shaffer v. Victoria Station, Inc., 91 Wash. 2d 295, 588 P.2d 233 (1978) (patron injured when glass broke in his hand; court held that drink sold includes both the wine and the glass in which it is served).

[454] *See* Goodwin v. Country Club of Peoria, 323 Ill. App. 1, 54 N.E.2d 612 (1944); Mix v. Ingersoll Candy Co., 6 Cal. 2d 674, 59 P.2d 144 (1936).

[455] 822 P.2d 1292, 16 UCCR2d 607 (Cal. 1992).

and, therefore, the defendant breached the merchantability warranty. After an extensive review of the cases, the court held that if the injury-producing substance is natural to the preparation of the food served, it is to be reasonably expected, and the food is not defective or unfit for human consumption. Therefore, there is no cause of action for breach of the implied warranty or merchantability.[456] In an important qualification, however, the court also held that the "naturalness" of the substance does not preclude an action in negligence for the preparation and service of the food. If the presence of the natural substance that causes the injury is due to a defendant's failure to exercise reasonable care, the injured plaintiff may bring an action in negligence.

The other test focuses on the reasonable expectations of the consumer, and does not differentiate between "foreign" and "natural" substances, except as they relate to the consumer's reasonable expectations.[457] The recent trend has been for courts to reject almost unanimously the "foreign/natural" test in favor of the reasonable expectations test.[458] The reasons for this trend are well stated in a case from Wisconsin that was based on a "warranty of fitness for consumption" rather than the Code's merchantability warranty (the Code was not yet in effect in Wisconsin at the time of the case):

> The "foreign-natural" test applied as a matter of law does not recommend itself to us as being logical or desirable. It is true one can expect a T-bone in T-bone steak, chicken bones in roast chicken, pork bone in a pork chop . . . and fish bones in a whole baked or fried fish, but the expectation is based not on the naturalness of the particular bone to the meat, fowl, or fish, but on the type of dish served containing the meat, fowl, or fish. There is a distinction between what a consumer expects to find in a fish stick and in a baked or fried fish, or in a chicken sandwich made from sliced white meat and in a roast chicken. The test should be what is reasonably expected by the consumer in the food as served, not what might be natural to the ingredients of that food prior to preparation.[459]

---

[456] 882 P.2d at 1301, 16 UCCR2d 620–621.

[457] *See* Zabner v. Howard Johnson's, Inc., 201 So. 2d 824 (Fla. Dist. Ct. App. 1967) (naturalness is important only in determining whether the consumer may reasonably be expected to find the substance in the food).

[458] *See, e.g.*, Jackson v. Nestle-Beich, Inc., 147 Ill. 2d 408, 589 N.E.2d 547 (1992); Goldman v. Food Lion, Inc., 879 F. Supp. 33, 26 UCCR2d 340 (E.D. Va. 1995); Langiulli v. Bumble Bee Seafood, Inc., 604 N.Y.S.2d 1020, 23 UCCR2d 71 (N.Y. Sup. Ct. 1993); Clime v. Dewey Beach Enters., Inc., 831 F. Supp. 341, 21 UCCR2d 559 (D. Del. 1993).

[459] Betehia v. Cape Cod Corp., 10 Wis. 2d 323, 331–332, 103 N.W.2d 64, 68–69 (1960).

In this day of highly processed foods, the court's rationale is even more convincing than when it was written.[460]

A number of conceptual problems, however, lurk in the reasonable expectations test. First, *whose* reasonable-expectations are we talking about? The average consumer? Those consumers with the experience, intelligence, and maturity of the plaintiff? Stated another way, to what extent should the reasonable expectations vary (if at all) with the characteristics of the individual plaintiff? Further, to what extent, if at all, should the expectations of the seller play a role in determining whether a breach has occurred? Should it matter, for example, whether the seller caters to a wide variety of people from a broad geographical area (e.g., The Four Seasons in New York City) or whether the restaurant is an out-of-the-way place catering only to locals?

An early Code case illustrates the problem. In *Webster v. Blue Ship Tea Room*,[461] the plaintiff was injured when a fish bone in her fish chowder lodged in her throat. She brought suit for her injuries claiming a breach of the implied warranty of merchantability. After an entertaining excursion into the culinary traditions of post-colonial New England, the court concluded that "we should be prepared to cope with the hazards of fish bones, the occasional presence of which in chowders is, it seems to us, to be anticipated."[462] But, anticipated *by whom*? Earlier in the opinion, the court had described as "a fact of some consequence" that the plaintiff had been born and brought up in New England. In addition, the restaurant was described as "quaint," apparently catering largely to natives.[463] Would the result have been different if the plaintiff had been a visitor from Nebraska, and the Blue Ship Tea Room had been a restaurant in a large downtown hotel?

The cases are by no means clear as to how reasonable expectations are to be determined. In many cases, this is a question of fact for the jury,[464]

---

[460] *See* O'Dell v. DeJean's Packing Co., Inc., 585 P.2d 399, 401–402, 24 UCCR 311, 313 (Okla. Ct. App. 1978):

> In the fast moving world today all aspects of life and law are continually transforming to keep in step with our rapidly changing manner of living. That is to say, more prepared food is bought than ever before in history. Complete meals are prepared from frozen or canned products and consumed. With such changes in demand for prepared foods so must the laws protecting the consumers change.

[461] 198 N.E.2d 309, 2 UCCR 161 (Mass. 1964).

[462] *Id.* at 312, 2 UCCR at 167.

[463] Plaintiff had apparently been in the Blue Ship Tea Room before. 198 N.E.2d at 310, 2 UCCR at 163.

[464] *See, e.g.,* Williams v. Braum Ice Cream Stores, Inc., 15 UCCR 1019 (Okla. Ct. App. 1974); Nadeau v. Bostonian Fishery, Inc., 1980 WL 98400, 30 UCCR 119 (Conn. Super. 1980); Kneibel v. RPM Enters., 506 N.W. 664, 22 UCCR 119 (Minn. Ct. App. 1993).

but food cases are often decided as a matter of law as well,[465] and, in any event juries must be given instructions on the applicable law. In most cases, courts talk simply of the reasonable expectations of "the consumer."[466] At least one case, however, suggests that reasonable expectations may be measured in light of the buyer's expected knowledge and maturity. In *Phillips v. Town of West Springfield*, [467] the plaintiff, a high school senior, was injured when a bone in a "bite-size" cube of white turkey meat lacerated his esophagus. In remanding for further clarification, the Massachusetts Supreme Judicial Court—the same court that decided *Webster*—said that the case should be decided based upon the reasonable expectations of an ordinary high school student. In a footnote, without further clarification, the court said that "[i]n particular circumstances, the special knowledge and expertise of a plaintiff may have a bearing on the reasonableness of his expectations and his right to recover."[468] There is no discussion in the cases of the bearing, if any, of the reasonable expectations of the seller as to who its clientele is likely to be.

Recent cases involving poisoning or infections caused by eating raw oysters or clams have raised further difficulties. The cases generally involve the presence of bacteria that cause little discomfort in healthy persons, but are potentially deadly to those with compromised immune systems. Further, detecting the presence of the bacteria is impossible without cooking or destroying the shellfish. The first issue raised by these cases is precisely *what* must a reasonable consumer expect before the defendant is off the hook? Must the consumer be aware of the precise nature and scope of the risk or will something less than full understanding relieve the defendant of liability? In *Clime v. Dewey Beach Enterprises, Inc.*,[469] the plaintiff became seriously ill from the bacterium *vibrio vulnificus* after eating raw clams at defendant's restaurant. The court applied the reasonable expectations test and held that consumers cannot reasonably expect raw clams to be free from *vibrio vul-*

---

[465] *See, e.g.*, Webster v. Blue Ship Tea Room, 198 N.E.2d 309, 2 UCCR 161 (Mass. 1964); Morrison's Cafeteria of Montgomery, Inc. v. Haddox, 431 So. 2d 975, 35 UCCR 1074 (Ala. 1983); Koperwas v. Publix Supermarkets, Inc., 534 So. 2d 872, 7 UCCR2d 733 (Fla. Ct. App. 1988).

[466] *See* Yong Cha Hong v. Marriott Corp., 656 F. Supp. 445, 3 UCCR2d 83 (D. Md. 1987) (jury should be instructed that "the consumer's" reasonable expectations form a part of the merchantability concept).

[467] 405 Mass. 411, 540 N.E.2d 1331, 9 UCCR2d 535 (1989).

[468] 540 N.E. at 1333, 9 UCCR2d at 539. *But see* Morrison's Cafeteria of Montgomery, Inc. v. Haddox, 431 So. 2d 975, 35 UCCR 1074 (Ala. 1983) in which a three-year-old injured by a bone in a piece of fried fish was held unable to recover as a matter of law.

[469] 831 F. Supp. 341, 21 UCCR2d 559 (D. Del. 1993).

nificus. As a result, summary judgment was granted to the defendant. As to those who might respond that most consumers have never even heard of *vibrio vulnificus,* the court had an answer:

> The inquiry is not whether a consumer should reasonably expect to suffer from exposure to a particular bacterium, i.e., vibrio vulnificus, but whether he or she should reasonably expect the intrinsic nature of clams in their raw, natural state to pose some risk of illness.[470]

Thus, so long as consumers should reasonably expect that raw clams pose *some* risk of illness (and the court, in effect, takes judicial notice that of this expectation), the defendant is off the hook.

In a similar case, however, summary judgment for a defendant was overturned. In *Cain v. Sheraton Perimeter Park South Hotel,*[471] the plaintiff had an allergic reaction and developed hepatitis after eating three dozen raw oysters. The trial court granted summary judgment for the defendant, using the reasonable expectations test. The Alabama Supreme Court reversed and remanded, holding that whether the "average consumer knows that raw oysters may be contaminated should be a question of fact for the jury."[472] In a Louisiana case not decided under the Code,[473] the court held, contrary to *Cline,* that the danger of *vibrio vulnificus* in raw oysters was *not* to be reasonably anticipated by the ordinary consumer. It answered the question of what the consumer must reasonably anticipate much more favorably to the consumer than the court in *Cline.* It held that for the seller to avoid liability, consumers would have to anticipate "that people with certain underlying conditions may become seriously ill or die as a result of eating raw oysters."[474]

A second issue (really two issues) raised by these cases is the responsibility of a seller to provide a warning, and the effect of a warning if one is provided. At least one case has explicitly stated that if the danger is one that is reasonably anticipated, no warning is necessary.[475] In another case,

---

[470] *Id.* at 350 n.6, 21 UCCR2d at 577 n.6.

[471] 592 So. 2d 218, 16 UCCR2d 347 (Ala. 1991).

[472] *Id.* at 221, 16 UCCR2d at 353. *See also* Battiste v. St. Thomas Diving Club, Inc., 26 UCCR 324 (D.V.I. 1979) (jury question whether poisoning resulting from algae ingested by local fish was to be reasonably expected).

[473] Simeon v. Doe, 618 So. 2d 948, 21 UCCR2d 948 (La. 1993). Louisiana has not adopted Article 2 of the Code.

[474] 618 So. 2d at 852, 21 UCCR2d at 956.

[475] Popour v. Holiday Ford Ctr., Inc., 364 N.W.2d 764, 40 UCCR 1671 (Mich. Ct. App. 1985) (where danger is apparent, failure to provide warning is inconsequential).

Jackson v. Nestle-Beich, Inc.,[476] the court indicated that strict liability was appropriate in food cases because it was so easy to preclude liability through a warning. In *Jackson,* the plaintiff was injured when she broke her tooth on a pecan shell contained in chocolate covered pecan caramel candy. Adopting the reasonable expectations test, the court said that even if a danger could not be reasonably anticipated by the consumer, such as the pecan shell in this case, the seller could nonetheless avoid liability via a warning:

> Even under the reasonable expectations test of strict liability . . . manufacturers, such as Nestle, of products posing the risk involved in this case can take one simple and relatively inexpensive step to make their products safe and to avoid liability for injuries caused thereby. Specifically, they can place an *adequate* warning to the consumer on their product's container of the possibility of risk of injury posed thereby. The relative ease with which such a measure may be taken also militates in favor of holding manufacturers of such products subject to strict liability in the absence thereof.[477]

Other cases also suggest that when the danger is one that a consumer would not reasonably anticipate, a warning relieves the seller from liability.[478] Care must be taken, however, not to extend this reasoning too far. Certainly, a manufacturer ought not to be allowed to escape liability for a defective automobile on the basis of a warning that a small percentage of the cars coming off the assembly line have brake defects. The manufacturer is in a better position to prevent such defects; it would be very costly for the buyer to discover them; and an automobile is a virtual necessity in today's world. Thus, there is little choice for the consumer but to purchase the car and take the risk. The food cases are generally distinguishable from this situation: often *neither* the buyer nor the seller is in a position to discover the "defect," and certainly the decision to assume the risk is more "voluntary" when the object is a particular food rather than an automobile. Nonetheless, one of the purposes of products liability law (and warranty law) is to spread the cost of product defects by making liability simply one of the costs of doing business.[479] In which cases a warning should cause us to disregard this fundamental assumption will remain a matter of continued controversy.

---

[476] 589 N.E.2d 547, 17 UCCR2d 396 (Ill. 1992).

[477] *Id.* at 552, 17 UCCR2d at 404.

[478] *See* Battiste v. St. Thomas Diving Club, Inc., 26 UCCR 324 (D.V.I. 1979); Simeon v. Doe, 618 So. 2d 848, 21 UCCR2d 948 (La. 1993).

[479] Greenman v. Yuba Power Prods., Inc., 49 Cal. 2d 57, 377 P.2d 897 (1963).

[5] Warranty and Products Liability

The food cases discussed in the preceding section are a subcategory of cases in which it is contended that a product is not merchantable because it does not perform its function "safely." Although the food cases have posed some special problems (such as the "foreign/natural" test versus the reasonable expectations test), many other issues carry over from the food cases into other goods that pose a danger to persons or their property. The widespread adoption of Section 402A of the Restatement (Second) of Torts, and the passage by most states of legislation dealing specifically with products liability,[480] has caused many of these cases no longer to be decided under the Code. The cases and literature on strict products liability in tort are voluminous, and there are many sources that deal comprehensively with products liability in tort.[481] It is neither possible nor desirable to do so in this volume. Because a large number of "products-liability" cases continue to be brought as warranty cases,[482] however, and because most courts have held that the standards by which the product is judged are the same whether the case is brought in tort or contract,[483] it is important to highlight and discuss the major issues that continue to plague the courts in this very difficult area.

Cases in which assembly-line defects cause injury are rarely problematic. The brakes that fail or the steering assembly that malfunctions rarely create any difficulty for the courts. So long as (1) the defect caused the harm; (2) the injury that resulted from the defect was foreseeable; (3) the defect was scientifically discoverable; and (4) the buyer was not aware of the danger, the seller is liable. The difficulties are almost exclusively confined to design defects and failure-to-warn cases.

As mentioned previously, courts have generally held that products must not only perform the function for which they were designed, but they must

---

[480] See, e.g., Me. Rev. Stat. Ann. tit. 14, § 221 (West 1980); Ind. Code § 33-1-1.5-3 (1993).

[481] See, e.g., W. Page Keeton, Prosser & Keeton on Torts § 679 et seq. (4th ed. 1984); Stuart Speiser, The American Law of Torts § 18.1 et seq. (1993).

[482] See, e.g., Carlin v. Superior Court, 38 Cal. Rptr. 2d 576, 26 UCCR2d 79 (Cal. Ct. App. 1995); Hadar v. Concordia Yacht Builders, Inc., 886 F. Supp. 1082 (S.D.N.Y. 1995); Sullivan v. Young Bros. & Co., 893 F. Supp. 1148, 30 UCCR2d 106 (D. Me. 1995).

[483] See, e.g., First Nat'l Bank of Dwight v. Regent Sports Corp., 803 F.2d 1431, 2 UCCR2d 458 (7th Cir. 1986); Grinnel v. Charles Pfizer & Co., 274 Cal. App. 3d 424, 79 Cal Rptr. 369 (1969). But see Denny v. Ford Motor Co., 87 N.Y.2d 248, 662 N.E.2d 730, 639 N.Y.S.2d 250, 28 UCCR2d 15 (1995) (tort was "risk/utility" test while warranty was "reasonable consumer expectation" test).

do so "safely."[484] Of course, there is no such thing as a totally safe product. An otherwise wholesome candy bar can produce serious illness when eaten by a diabetic, and even a nondiabetic can become ill by eating too many candy bars. Similarly, a person can drill a hole in his hand with an electric drill or suffer a severe electrical shock while trying to repair his plugged-in television set. Are these goods "safe" even though it is possible to manufacture an electric drill that will operate only when both hands are on the handle or to construct a television set so that the electrical contact is broken when the back is removed?

The cases have made it clear that sellers are not insurers of their products.[485] Simply because a product causes an injury does not make the seller liable for the costs the injury imposes.[486] Instead, both the warranty of merchantability and section 402A of the Restatement, (Second) of Torts require only a product not be *unreasonably* dangerous.[487] The Comments to the Restatement provide some guidance as to when a product is unreasonably dangerous: "The article sold must be dangerous to an extent beyond which would be contemplated by the ordinary consumer who purchases it, with the ordinary knowledge common to the community as to its characteristics."[488] Consequently, simply because one might cut oneself on a knife or be injured with a circular saw does not make the product defective or unmerchantable. The idea is that if the product contains a defect (either man-

---

[484] *See* § 4.06[B][4], *supra.*

[485] *See* Koster v. Scotch Assocs., 640 A.2d 1225, 23 UCCR2d 679 (N.J. Super. Ct. 1993); Goodman v. Wenco Foods, Inc., 423 S.E.2d 444, 19 UCCR2d 369 (N.C. 1992).

[486] *See, e.g.*, Keirs v. Weber Nat'l Stores, Inc., 507 A.2d 406, 1 UCCR2d 387 (Pa. Super. Ct. 1986) (jacket is not unmerchantable when it catches fire and injures plaintiff after being doused in a flammable liquid and set afire).

[487] *But see* Malawy v. Richards Mfg. Co., 150 Ill. App. 3d 549, 501 N.E.2d 376 (1986). The court held in this case that a plaintiff could recover for breach of implied warranty from a manufacturer of a metal bone plate for personal injuries caused when the bone plate allegedly malfunctioned without a showing that the bone plate was "unreasonably dangerous."

In Shell v. Union Oil Co., 489 So. 2d 569, 1 UCCR2d 692 (Ala. 1986), the plaintiff sued the defendant, alleging that a carcinogenic compound present in a naphtha product produced by defendant had given him leukemia. The plaintiff relied, in part, on a breach of the implied warranty of merchantability to establish his claim. The court dismissed this theory on the basis that the product performed the job that it was intended to do and that the warnings accompanying the product were consistent with the manufacturer's knowledge of the product's dangers. The court said that the U.C.C. warranty was one of *commercial* fitness and that liability for personal injury caused by products that are commercially fit is the province of tort law.

[488] Restatement (Second) of Torts § 402A, cmt. i.

ufacturing or design) that makes it more dangerous than the consumer would reasonably expect, the seller will be liable.

The simplicity of this standard, however, conceals some potential difficulties. First, what if the product does not contain a "hidden" danger— the danger presented is apparent to the ordinary consumer— but the product could have easily been made safer? This is of special concern because the "ordinary consumer" is a hypothetical construct; what is apparent to one consumer might not be apparent to another. If a manufacturer could have easily and cheaply provided a safety device to protect the "less vigilant than normal" consumer, which would not have interfered with the operation of the product, shouldn't it be required to do so?

Second, what about products that impose great costs upon society even though everyone is aware of their dangers? The most obvious example is cigarettes, which continue to be the active subject of much litigation under both Restatement section 402A and the Code.[489] Is it the proper province of the merchantability warranty or tort law to provide relief to those who are injured by these products?

Finally, what about those situations in which scientific knowledge was not far enough advanced at the time the goods were produced to predict that the goods might be harmful? Again, cigarettes may provide an example. The manufacturers claim that during the first half of the century scientific knowledge had not advanced to the point to clearly link cigarettes to lung cancer and other serious diseases. If the manufacturers are able to sustain this claim,[490] should they be able to avoid liability, even though medical science has now conclusively established the link? Similarly, a drug that has been carefully tested according to current test standards and federal regulations may show no harmful side effects. If medical evidence later proves that the drug was harmful, was the drug defective when it was sold?

None of these questions can be answered definitively. The case law of the various states is divergent, and the states that have passed product liability legislation have dealt with these issues differently. The best this treatise can hope to do is to highlight some of the more significant cases and summarize the general approaches that states have taken to these important and controversial problems.

---

[489] *See, e.g.,* Kotler v. American Tobacco Co., 926 F.2d 1217 (5th Cir. 1990). *See* section 4.06[B][5][b], *infra.*

[490] In light of recent developments, this seems unlikely.

[a] Unreasonably Dangerous

As previously stated, the Comments to the *Restatement (Second) of Torts* § 402A indicate that a product is unreasonably dangerous only when it is more dangerous than the ordinary consumer would expect. Both courts and legislatures have modified this standard. One standard that has been adopted by both courts[491] and legislatures[492] is the "risk/utility" test. This test determines whether a product is unreasonably dangerous by balancing the risk presented by the product against its utility. In practice, however, this test involves a much broader balance than the simple costs and benefits of the present design. In addition to the nature and magnitude of the risk presented by the product and the product's benefits, the test also considers such factors as the technical feasibility of alternative designs, the costs of alternative designs (including any decrease in the utility of the product under an alternative design), the risks associated with alternative designs, and the obviousness and foreseeability of the danger presented.

It is apparent that the risk/utility test is heavily laden with negligence concepts, despite its purported "strict liability."[493] In fact, a number of courts have explicitly stated that negligence theory and merchantability are indistinguishable with respect to design defects.[494] Under the risk/utility test, goods can be found unmerchantable even though they contain no hidden dangers. Rather, the issue is whether the manufacturer could *reasonably*

---

[491] *See, e.g.*, Klein v. Sears, Roebuck & Co., 608 A.2d 1276, 92 Md. App. 477 (1992); Barker v. Lull Eng'g Co., 20 Cal. 3d 413, 573 P.2d 443 (1978); Sutkowski v. Universal Marion Corp., 5 Ill. App. 3d 313, 281 N.E.2d 749 (1972).

[492] *See, e.g.*, Ohio Rev. Code Ann. § 2307.75(A)(1) (Baldwin 1993).

[493] In *Nacci v. Volkswagen of Am., Inc.*, 15 UCCR 378 (Del. Super. Ct. 1974) the court said that the proper test for liability under U.C.C. § 2-314 and strict liability in tort is "whether the design has created a risk of harm which is so probable that an ordinarily prudent person, acting as manufacturer, would pursue a different available design which would substantially lessen the probability of harm." This test would seem indistinguishable from the test for ordinary negligence, especially in light of the fact that the court stated that foreseeability of injury is inherent in the test. 15 UCCR at 383. *See* Frericks v. General Motors Corp., 336 A.2d 118, 16 UCCR 1232 (Md. Ct. App. 1975) (elements of duty under U.C.C. § 2-314 to provide reasonably safe vehicle are essentially the same as negligence action); Dreisonstok v. Volkswagenwerk, A.G., 489 F.2d 1066 (4th Cir. 1974) (makes little or no real difference whether liability is asserted on grounds of negligence, warranty, or strict liability against manufacturer for failure to design reasonably safe car).

[494] *See, e.g.*, Piatrowski v. Southworth Prods. Corp., 15 F.3d 748, 22 UCCR2d 723 (8th Cir. 1994); Denny v. Ford Motor Co., 87 N.Y.2d 248, 662 N.E.2d 730, 639 N.Y.S.2d 250, 28 UCCR2d 15 (1995); Buettner v. R.W. Martin & Sons, Inc., 47 F.3d 116 (4th Cir. 1995), *aff'd*, Buettner v. Super Laundry Mach., 857 F. Supp. 471 (E.D. Va. 1994); Hull v. Eaton Corp., 825 F.2d 448 (D.C. Cir. 1987).

have made them safer, given the state of technology and the costs and risks involved. Some courts[495] and legislatures[496] have combined the risk/utility test and the "unreasonably dangerous" test and made them alternative bases for liability.

[b]   Cigarettes, Handguns, Alcohol, Etc.

There are certain products that exact substantial costs from the public at large. The health care costs alone from smoking and alcohol have been estimated to be as high as $7 to $8 billion per year.[497] Thousands of Americans are killed each year by handguns,[498] and alcohol-related deaths, on the highway alone, are estimated to be over 17,000.[499] Despite the fact that virtually everyone is aware of the risks associated with these items, are they nonetheless unreasonably dangerous or unmerchantable because of the death and devastation that they cause?

An economic argument can be made that the price of these goods should reflect the costs that they impose upon society. At present, these costs are born by those who are killed or injured by these articles (who are often not users or purchasers of them) or by their families,[500] or by society at large. Risk-spreading is a recurrent theme throughout products liability, and it is certainly a defensible position that those who create the risk through the purchase and use of these items should bear the costs through higher prices for the goods rather than the victims, their relatives, or all of the members of society. It is not at all obvious that a simple cost/benefit calculus would conclude that the benefits of these items exceed their costs, and re-

---

[495] *See, e.g.,* Barker v. Lull Eng'g Corp., 20 Cal. 3d 413, 573 P.2d 443 (1978). In the recent case of Denny v. Ford Motor Co., *supra* note 496, the New York Court of Appeals held that the "risk/utility" test was the proper test for strict products liability while the "consumer expectation" test was appropriate for warranty liability. There was a strong dissent in the case arguing that there was no justification for two different tests of liability.

[496] *See, e.g.,* Ohio Rev. Code Ann. §§ 2307.7(A)(1) and 2307.7(A)(2) (Baldwin 1994).

[497] *See* David H. Jernigan, et al., Alcohol Related Problems and Public Hospitals: Defining a New Role in Prevention (1989).

[498] Eric Larson, 3 J. Pub. Health Policy 324; The Story of a Gun, The Atlantic, at 48–49 (1993).

[499] The Columbus Dispatch, November 27, 1996.

[500] For example, the family of a person who smokes cigarettes may suffer immense economic and emotional harm when a close relative dies of lung cancer caused by the cigarette smoking. These same family members may not have smoked themselves and may have earnestly attempted to get the dead family member to quit. Or, someone purposely or accidentally shot by a handgun may have not purchased the gun, and may even have been a vigorous advocate of gun control.

quiring the sellers of these items to "internalize" the costs would provide a practical test in the marketplace of their benefits versus their costs.

On the other hand, we do not make manufacturers of many other items that impose costs on society pay for these costs. People are killed with knives, or while scuba-diving, hang-gliding, mountain climbing, or engaging in other activities, and we do not look to the sellers of items necessary for these activities to bear the costs. Precisely where should the line be drawn? Should sellers of butter be responsible for heart attacks caused by high cholesterol? Furthermore, at least with respect to handguns and alcohol, there is little danger if the item is used properly. Why should the manufacturers and sellers of goods be held responsible for the misuse of the goods they produce?

Somewhat oversimplified, these are the terms of the debate. Although the battle continues, those who argue for an interpretation of the implied warranty of merchantability or strict liability in tort that holds sellers responsible for injuries caused by these items have, until recently, generally been unsuccessful. For example, a number of cases have been brought seeking damages from manufacturers caused by the ingestion of alcoholic beverages.[501] Among other theories, plaintiffs in these cases have asserted that alcohol is unmerchantable and unreasonably dangerous. These claims have been uniformly unsuccessful. The courts have said, relying on Comments i and j to the Restatement (Second) of Torts,[502] that the dangers of alcohol

---

[501] *See, e.g.*, Morris v. Adolph Coors Co., 735 S.W.2d 578, 5 UCCR2d 288 (Tex. Civ. App. 1987); Gawloski v. Miller Brewing Co., 96 Ohio App. 3d 160, 644 N.E.2d 731 (Ohio Ct. App. 1994).

[502] Comment i to the Restatement (Second) of Torts § 402A provides:

> *Unreasonably dangerous.* The rule stated in this Section applies only where the defective condition of the product makes it unreasonably dangerous to the user or consumer. Many products cannot possibly be made entirely safe for all consumption, and any food or drug necessarily involves some risk of harm, if only from over-consumption. Ordinary sugar is a deadly poison to diabetics, and castor oil found use under Mussolini as an instrument of torture. That is not what is meant by "unreasonably dangerous" in this section. The article sold must be dangerous to an extent beyond that which would be contemplated by the ordinary consumer who purchases it, with the ordinary knowledge common to the community as to its characteristics. Good whiskey is not unreasonably dangerous merely because it will make some people drunk, and is especially dangerous to alcoholics; but bad whiskey, containing a dangerous amount of fuel oil, is unreasonably dangerous. Good tobacco is not unreasonably dangerous merely because the effect of smoking may be harmful; but tobacco containing something like marijuana may be unreasonably dangerous. Good butter is not unreasonably dangerous merely because, if such be the case, it deposits cholesterol in the arteries and leads to heart attack; but bad butter, contaminated

overconsumption are within the common knowledge of the community and, therefore, no more dangerous than the ordinary consumer would expect. Similarly, so long as the beverage was untainted, courts have not considered alcoholic beverages to be unmerchantable under section 2-314.

A similar fate awaited the plaintiff in the case of *Rhodes v. R.G. Industries, Inc.*[503] In this tragic case, a handgun kept in the house was found by a child. The child removed the gun, cocked the hammer, and placed it in the basket of a bicycle. Another child found the gun, pulled the trigger, and accidentally killed a third child. The mother of the dead child brought suit against the manufacturer claiming that the handgun was unmerchantable because of the danger it presented. The court responded:

> [T]he evidence showed that the gun performed exactly as expected: when the hammer was cocked and the trigger was pulled, it fired. . . . The weapon clearly satisfied the purpose for which it was manufactured

---

with poisonous fish oil, is unreasonably dangerous.

Comment j provides:

> *Directions or warning.* In order to prevent the product from being unreasonably dangerous, the seller may be required to give directions or warning, on the container, as to its use. The seller may reasonably assume that those with common allergies, as for example to eggs or strawberries, will be aware of them, and he is not required to warn against them. Where however, the product contains an ingredient to which a substantial number of the population are allergic, and the ingredient is one whose danger is not generally known, or if known is one which the consumer would reasonably not expect to find in the product, the seller is required to give warning against it, if he had knowledge, or by the application of reasonable, developed human skill and foresight should have knowledge of the presence of the ingredient and the danger. Likewise in the case of poisonous drugs, or those unduly dangerous for other reasons, warning as to use may be required.
>
> But a seller is not required to warn with respect to products, or ingredients in them, which are only dangerous, or potentially so, when consumed in excessive quantity, or over a long period of time, when the danger, or potentiality of danger, is generally known and recognized. Again the dangers of alcoholic beverages are an example, as are also those of foods containing such substances as saturated fats, which may over a period of time have deleterious effect upon the human heart.
>
> Where warning is given, the seller may reasonably assume that it will be read and heeded; and a product bearing such a warning, which is safe for use if it is followed, is not in defective condition, nor is it unreasonably dangerous.

[503] 325 S.E.2d 465, 40 UCCR 1668 (Ga. Ct. App. 1984).

and purchased, and there was no evidence that the weapon was defective.[504]

The court further held as a matter of law that the failure of the gun to have a safety device did not make it unmerchantable. It said that the gun had been accompanied by warnings concerning its storage and use, which had been ignored by the buyer. Furthermore, had the older child not cocked the hammer, the child who discharged the weapon would not have had the strength to do so. Although additional safety devices might have been desirable, it was not, in the view of the court, its responsibility to mandate such requirements.[505]

The greatest number of cases of this genre, however, deal with cigarettes. Plaintiffs have generally made two claims under the warranty of merchantability: (1) that the cancer-causing aspect of cigarettes makes them unreasonably dangerous *per se*, and (2) even if cigarettes are not inherently unmerchantable, the manufacturers have not given adequate warning of their dangers. While the cigarette litigation persists[506] and the larger controversy continues,[507] the merchantability issues have been clarified, if not resolved.

---

[504] *Id.* at 467, 40 UCCR at 1672. *But see* Mason v. K-Mart Corp., 769 P.2d 682 (Kan. App. 1989) (error to direct verdict for defendant on whether air rifle not equipped with safety device was unreasonably dangerous for purposes of strict tort liability and breach of the warranty of merchantability).

[505] The court's decision on the issue of the safety device is subject to criticism. Many weapons do come equipped with safety devices, and these devices do not interfere with the basic operation or functioning of the weapon. They are also relatively inexpensive. At least under the cost/benefit test, the issue could justifiably have gone to the jury under a manufacturer's obligation to make the gun *reasonably* safe. The court's decision can be justified, however, on the grounds that most people are aware that guns are not always equipped with safety devices, and that those that are not so equipped present a greater danger than those that are.

The city of New Orleans, Louisiana, has filed suit against a number of handgun manufacturers alleging that manufacturers have failed to develop and employ safety devices necessary to prevent unauthorized users such as criminals and children from using them. Other cities, such as Philadelphia and Chicago, are suing handgun manufacturers on this and other theories.

[506] *See* American Tobacco Co., Inc. v. Grinnel, 951 S.W.2d 420, 33 UCCR2d 331 (Tex. 1997); Allgood v. R.J. Reynolds Tobacco Co., 80 F.3d 168 (4th Cir. 1996).

[507] For example, the Food and Drug Administration, with the backing of the Clinton administration, is asserting authority to regulate tobacco as a drug. In addition, the major tobacco companies have agreed to pay $206 billion over twenty-five years to forty-six states to settle claims by state attorneys general seeking to recover health costs relating to tobacco use. Florida, Mississippi, Texas and Minnesota have reached separate multibillion-dollar settlements. The tobacco companies also agreed to sweeping restrictions on marketing and advertising. *See* Antitrust Litigation Rptr. 13 (Andrews 1998).

The claim that cigarettes are *per se* unmerchantable because of the inherent risks they present has been rejected by most,[508] but not all,[509] courts. The court gave thorough consideration to this claim in *Kotler v. American Tobacco Co.*[510] The plaintiff argued that a balancing of the risk and utility of cigarettes made them unmerchantable under state law. The court responded that merely showing that the risks inherent in the consumption of cigarettes was greater than their social utility was insufficient to establish a breach of the implied warranty of merchantability. Because the standard of merchantability for design defects was essentially a negligence standard, all that was required was "reasonable" safety. Because the plaintiff had not shown that there was a feasible safer alternative design, a *sine qua non* for proof of negligence, the claim was dismissed. By allowing a plaintiff to prove a case by showing a feasible alternative design, however, the court left the door open for future claims.

The claim that cigarettes are unmerchantable because of inadequate warnings was at least partially resolved by the U.S. Supreme Court in 1992. Prior to 1992, the courts had been badly split on the effect of the Federal Cigarette Labeling and Advertising Act of 1965[511] and the Public Health Cigarette Smoking Act of 1969[512] on merchantability claims, especially on claims based upon inadequate warnings. Some courts had held that these claims were preempted by the federal legislation, which required specified warnings in cigarette advertising and on cigarette packages and cartons.[513] Other courts held, to the contrary, that state tort and merchantability claims were not preempted by the federal law.[514] In *Cipollone v. Liggett Group, Inc.*,[515] the U.S. Supreme Court, in a fractured decision, held that the 1969 Act preempted state claims after 1969 based upon a failure to warn. It further held, however, that claims prior to 1969 based upon a failure to warn were

---

[508] Kotler v. American Tobacco Co., 926 F.2d 1217 (1st Cir. 1990); Roysdon v. R.J. Reynolds Tobacco Co., 849 F.2d 230 (6th Cir. 1988); Pennington v. Vistron Corp., 876 F.2d 414 (5th Cir. 1989).

[509] *See* Kyte v. Philip Morris Co., 408 Mass. 162, 556 N.E.2d 1025 (1990) (court refused summary judgment on claim that Marlboro and Parliament cigarettes are defective because they are inherently carcinogenic and addictive); Rogers v. R.J. Reynolds Tobacco Co., 557 N.E.2d 1045 (Ind. Ct. App. 1990).

[510] 926 F.2d 1217 (1st Cir. 1990).

[511] 15 U.S.C.A. § 1331 *et seq.* (West 1982).

[512] *Id.*

[513] *See* Kotler v. American Tobacco Co., 926 F.2d 1217 (1st Cir. 1990); Palmer v. Liggett Group, 825 F.2d 620 (1st Cir. 1987).

[514] *See* Pennington v. Vistron Corp., 876 F.2d 414 (5th Cir. 1989); Roydson v. R.J. Reynolds Tobacco Co., 849 F.2d 230 (6th Cir. 1988).

[515] 505 U.S. 504, 112 S. Ct. 2608, 17 UCCR2d 1087 (1992).

not preempted, nor were claims based upon express warranty, fraud, conspiracy, or implied warranty not based upon a failure to warn.

Cippollone has caused the battleground to shift somewhat. Plaintiffs, after *Cipollone*, will rely more on the claims which the court determined were not preempted, rather than the failure-to-warn claims that at one time seemed to offer the best chance for success. Even implied warranty claims retain some vitality to the extent that they are based on a showing of a feasible alternative design[516] or are otherwise unrelated to the failure to warn.[517] Also, recent evidence suggests that tobacco companies were aware of the addictive nature of tobacco and actively concealed this information. This evidence is giving renewed vigor to the claims of those harmed by tobacco and appear, in part, to have prompted the recent settlement between the tobacco companies and the states' attorneys general.[518] The issue has political and economic ramifications as well as emotional and moral overtones. To a significant degree, it represents the division in the country today over the proper role of government and the responsibility of the citizenry for its own decisions. It will not be easily or quickly resolved.

[c] The Foreseeability of Harm—The State-of-the-Art Defense

Despite the "strict" liability of warranty, the preceding discussion has shown that liability, at least in the case of design defects, is laden with negligence concepts. Another challenge to strict liability—really the reverse of the problem of the preceding section—is the state-of-the-art defense. This is a claim by the seller or the manufacturer that at the time of sale and distribution, there were no scientific means available to determine that the product would produce a harmful side effect. At the time that the goods were manufactured and sold they appeared to be "safe." However, at the time of the injury, perhaps many years later, scientific knowledge has advanced to the point that a causal link between the use of the product and the resulting injury is clear.

Both cases and legislation have responded differently to this issue. Some cases have held that liability for defective products, whether in tort or under a theory of implied warranty, is not subject to a state-of-the-art

---

[516] *See* Grinnell v. American Tobacco Co., 883 S.W.2d 791 (Tex. Ct. App. 1994).

[517] *See, e.g.*, Castano v. American Tobacco Co., 870 F. Supp. 1425 (E.D. La. 1994) (court refused to dismiss claim that presence of addictive nicotine makes cigarettes unmerchantable).

[518] *See supra* note 509. *See also* Milo Geyelin, "Smokers Suit Tries New Approach: The Industry Made Them Do It," Wall St. J., March 21, 1995, at B1.

defense,[519] while others have allowed it.[520] Similarly, some product liability legislation contains a state-of-the-art defense.[521] The difficulty of the problem is illustrated by two cases from the state of New Jersey.

In *Beshada v. Johns-Manville Products Corp.*,[522] six plaintiffs brought suit against the manufacturers of asbestos. All of the plaintiffs were workers (or their survivors) who claimed to have been exposed to asbestos in their work for varying periods of time and, as a result, to have contracted a number of serious asbestos-related illnesses.[523] These cases involved exposures dating back as far as the 1930s. Although the plaintiffs raised a number of legal theories, the case focused on the claim that the manufacturers had breached a duty to warn those exposed to the asbestos of the dangerous propensities of the product. The manufacturers responded that they could not, at the times relevant to plaintiffs' exposure, have provided a warning because no one knew or could have known of the danger of asbestos at that time. Although the court acknowledged a substantial factual dispute over what the defendants knew about the dangers of asbestos and when they knew it, those factual issues were not relevant on appeal. The only issue was whether the trial judge had erroneously refused to strike the state-of-the-art defense as a matter of law.

Plaintiffs based their motion to strike the state-of-the-art defense on an earlier case, *Freund v. Cellofilm Properties, Inc.*[524] In this case, the court had said that in strict liability cases, knowledge of the dangerousness of the product is to be imputed to the defendant; the plaintiff need not prove that the defendant knew or should have known of its dangerousness. The plaintiffs argued that *Freund* made the state-of-the-art defense irrelevant. The defendants responded that *Freund* imputed to the defendants only the scientific knowledge available at the time; it did not apply to dangers that were scientifically "unknowable."

---

[519] *See, e.g.*, Hayes v. Ariens Co., 462 N.E.2d 273, 38 UCCR 48 (Mass. 1984); Spartanburg County Sch. Dist. Seven v. National Gypsum Co., 805 F.2d 1148, 2 UCCR2d 850 (4th Cir. 1986).

[520] *See* Brooks v. Beech Aircraft Corp., 902 P.2d 54 (N.M. 1995); Greenwood v. Eastman-Kodak Co., 1994 WL 133464 (Conn. Super. Ct. 1994); Anderson v. Owens-Ill., Inc., 799 F.2d 1 (1st Cir. 1986).

[521] *See, e.g.*, Ohio Rev. Code § 2307.75(A)(1) (risk/benefit test calculated according to *foreseeable* risks at the time product left manufacturer's control); Mo. Rev. Stat. § 537.760 (legislature defined products-liability claim in relation to state-of-the-art defense); Iowa Code § 668.12 (provides state-of-the-art defense).

[522] 90 N.J. 191, 447 A.2d 539 (N.J. 1982).

[523] These included asbestosis, mesothelioma, and other diseases.

[524] 87 N.J. 229, 432 A.2d 925 (1981).

The court began its analysis by describing the test for a defective product under New Jersey law. First, a product can fail the test if its risks outweigh its utility. When the risk of a product outweighs its utility, liability can be imposed without determining whether the product could have been made safer. Second, even a product that passes the risk/utility test is not reasonably safe if it could have been made or marketed more safely.[525] The court placed failure-to-warn cases in this second category, saying that the argument of the plaintiffs in such cases was that regardless of the overall cost/benefit calculation, the product is unsafe because a warning could make it safer at virtually no added cost and without limiting its utility.

The defendants' response to this was predictable: how could they have possibly warned of a danger that was scientifically unknowable? To impose a "retroactive" obligation to warn the plaintiffs about a danger that the manufacturers could not have scientifically discovered was both unfair and unreasonable. The court responded that the defendants misunderstood the nature of strict liability; its purpose was not to find fault but to impose liability upon sellers without regard to fault. According to the court, the question was whether imposition of liability for failure to warn of dangers which were undiscoverable will advance the goals and policies of strict liability, not whether it was unfair to impose liability upon a "faultless" defendant. The court discussed three policies behind strict liability and decided that imposition of liability on the defendants in this case would further all three.

The first policy was one that has been fundamental to strict liability from the beginning: the spreading of risks. Manufacturers can include the costs of product defects in the price of the goods and thereby distribute these costs among all of those who purchase the product, rather than impose catastrophic costs on those who are injured. The court dismissed the argument of the defendants that the price of the goods could not be adjusted to reflect unknowable risks, by responding that the same could be said for "unknown," as well as "unknowable," risks. The court also restated the premise that imposing liability on those who manufacture, distribute, and purchase a product is preferable to imposing liability on the victims.

The second policy mentioned by the court was accident avoidance. The court concluded that this policy was furthered as well by refusing to rec-

---

[525] 447 A.2d at 545. Although the court states that a product is not reasonably safe if the same product could have been made or marketed more safely, it is clear from the opinion that the court does not literally mean this. Rather the court would weigh the benefits of increased safety in an alternative design against the loss of utility caused by the design change. *Id.* at 545 n.4.

ognize the state-of-the-art defense. According to the court, the state of the art is partly determined by the level of investment in safety research. By imposing the costs on sellers of failing to discover hazards, an incentive is created for them to invest more actively in safety research. Finally, the court concluded that rejecting the state-of-the-art defense would also simplify the fact-finding process.

For better or worse, *Beshada* went a long way toward making producers insurers of their products. As the court itself acknowledged, it costs very little to provide a warning and generally does not detract from the product's utility. Consequently, whenever a product is discovered at some later time to present a danger of any significance, liability is virtually assured.

Two years later, the court was faced with a case which, under the rules of *Beshada*, seemed to be "open and shut."[526] Between 1960 and 1963, Carol Ann Feldman had been given the drug Declomycin as a small child by her father, a physician, to control upper respiratory and other infections. As a result, when her permanent teeth came in, they were badly discolored. The literature accompanying the drug at the time it was given to her gave no warning of the possible side effect of tooth discoloration. By 1965 or 1966, however, the literature included a warning of this side effect. Carol Ann sued the manufacturer of the drug, Lederle Labs, on the basis that it had failed to warn of the possible side effect of tooth discoloration. In response to Lederle's claim that the state of scientific knowledge between 1960 and 1963 made such a warning impossible, Feldman said that *Beshada* precluded this defense. The trial court nonetheless held for the defendants, a judgment which was upheld by the intermediate appellate court. The plaintiffs appealed to the New Jersey Supreme Court.

The opinion of the court, written two years after *Beshada*, is remarkable. If one follows the reasoning of *Beshada*, the case is easy: *assume* that Lederle knew of the side effects at the time that Feldman took the drug, and given this knowledge, the only question is whether Lederele should reasonably have provided a warning. Instead, the court's approach was a radical departure from *Beshada*. It began its analysis with a statement that sounds as if *Beshada* had been decided by the Supreme Court of Mars, not by the same court just two years earlier:

> Generally, the state-of-the-art in design defect cases and available knowledge in defect warning situations are relevant factors in measuring reasonableness of conduct.[527]

---

[526] Feldman v. Lederle Labs., 97 N.J. 429, 479 A.2d 374 (1984).
[527] *Id.* at 451, 479 A.2d at 386.

This statement is astonishing in light of the fact that the same court in *Beshada* had unequivocally stated that the reasonableness of the defendant's conduct in discovering a danger was not relevant to products liability, and had explicitly rejected any state-of-the-art defense. To assure that there was no misunderstanding the court continued:

> Similarly, as to warnings, generally conduct should be measured by knowledge at the time the manufacturer distributed the product. Did the manufacturer know, or should he have known, of the danger, given the scientific, technological, and other information available when the product was distributed; or, in other words, did he have actual or constructive knowledge of the danger?[528]

A clearer repudiation of the holding in *Beshada* is hard to imagine, yet the court refused to overrule the case. In view of the language quoted, one would expect that the court labored long and hard to explain its refusal to overrule *Beshada*. Remarkably, however, in two brief sentences the court lamely abdicated its judicial function to explain the law it had established:

> The rationale of *Beshada* is not applicable to this case. We do not overrule *Beshada*, but restrict *Beshada* to the circumstances giving rise to its holding.[529]

As to what those circumstances were, and what makes them sufficiently different from *Lederle* as to justify such a radically different approach, the opinion is completely silent.

Both decisions deserve criticism. In *Beshada*, the court's response to a fundamental point raised by the defendants—how can an unknowable risk be efficiently spread—was both unresponsive and inadequate. More profound was its failure in *Lederle* either to justify its dramatic reversal or to explain how *Beshada* and *Lederle* can continue to co-exist. In spite of these criticisms, the court deserves our sympathy. Its confusion reflects the uncertainty and competing values and policies inherent in this important issue. The defendants were clearly correct in *Beshada* in their argument that the spreading of unknown or unknowable risks is quite different from the typical manufacturing defect case. To the extent that a statistical number of injuries from foreseeable defects can be anticipated, the seller can adjust the price either to self-insure against the costs of injuries or purchase third-party insurance. To the extent, however, that the injuries are scientifically unfore-

---

[528] *Id.* at 452, 479 A.2d at 386.
[529] *Id.* at 455, 479 A.2d at 388.

seeable they cannot be spread in this way; a seller faced with liability has no idea how much insurance, if any, to purchase or how large a liability fund to create. The risks are not distributed; they are merely shifted from the consumer to the seller and manufacturer. To the extent that the manufacturer has secured too little insurance, it faces potential bankruptcy. In addition, it is not clear why the consumer cannot insure equally efficiently in these circumstances through first-party insurance.

Also, imposing liability on manufacturers may cause some products or sellers to disappear from the market, even though their products are socially desirable. Faced with unknown potential liability, sellers may prefer to make and distribute products whose dangers are known, rather than to produce products that the scientific evidence indicates are safe, but may present unknown dangers. The costs of unknowable risks cannot, by definition, be calculated, and some might prefer to avoid products that appear to present *any* significant risk.

This is not to say that the decision in *Beshada* and similar cases is not defensible. The court's suggestion that liability provides an incentive for enhanced product safety is probably true, although a company would be hard pressed to decide *how much more* to invest in safety research because of potential liability for unknowable risks. In addition, if someone has to bear the risk of potential catastrophe, a case can be made that it should be the party that profits from the good's distribution, regardless of fault.

Much more could be said about this issue. For those who are interested, there are many good articles and texts discussing the issue from many vantage points.[530] The preceding discussion is primarily intended to demonstrate the difficulty and complexity of a problem that seems a long way from resolution.

[d]   The Unforeseeable Plaintiff

There are some goods that are "safe" for use by most of the population but cause harm when used by a smaller segment that is allergic to the goods or one of its ingredients. If one of those who has such an allergy uses the goods and is injured, are the goods "nonconforming"? Does the warranty of merchantability extend not only to persons whose reactions are "normal" but to those whose reactions are "abnormal"?

---

[530] *See, e.g.*, John Vargo, "Caveat Emptor: Will the ALI Erode Strict Liability in the Restatement (Third) for Product Liability," 10 Touro L. Rev. 21 (1993); Ellen Wertheimer, "Azzarello Agonists: Bucking the Strict Products Liability Tide," 66 Temp. L. Rev. 419 (1993); William A. Worthington, "The 'Citadel' Revisited: Strict Liability and the Policy of Law," 365 Tex. L. Rev. 227 (1995).

There were many pre-Code cases dealing with this problem. One group of cases stated that implied warranties are limited to injuries that would have been caused to persons whose reactions are normal; goods are not defective simply because a person with abnormal reactions was injured through their use.[531] The cases rarely defined "normal" with any degree of precision. A second group of cases required an "appreciable number" of people who were adversely affected by the product before liability would be imposed.[532] This test was generally viewed as more favorable to plaintiffs because it unambiguously provided that a reaction by less than a majority would be sufficient to impose liability.[533] Despite these different formulations, the two tests do not appear to have produced significantly different results.[534]

Cases under the Code continue to use these different formulations,[535] although the majority appears to have adopted the "appreciable number" test. As with the pre-Code cases, the courts generally do not define "appreciable number" precisely, and at least one court has made it clear that the issue is a question of fact. In *Robbins v. Alberto Culver Co.*,[536] the court reversed a directed verdict on behalf of the defendant where there was evidence that the defendants had received ten complaints of allergic reaction during the preceding ten years (approximately 1 complaint per 2,000,000 bottles sold) and that distributors and retail establishments may have re-

---

[531] *See, e.g.*, Ross v. Porteous, Mitchell & Braun Co., 136 Me. 118, 3 A.2d 650 (1939); Bonowski v. Revlon, Inc., 251 Iowa 141, 100 N.W.2d 5 (1959); Bradt v. Hollaway, 242 Mass. 446, 136 N.E. 254 (1922).

[532] *See, e.g.*, Crotty v. Shartenberg's-New Haven, Inc., 147 Conn. 460, 162 A.2d 513 (1960); Reynolds v. Sun Ray Drug Co., 52 A.2d 666, 135 N.J.L. 475 (N.J. Ct. Err. & App. 1947).

[533] *See* Crotty v. Shartenberg's New Haven, 147 Conn. at 467, 62 A.2d at 517 (ingredient must affect appreciable number of people, though fewer in number than the number of normal buyers).

[534] *See* Esborg v. Bailey Drug Co., 61 Wash. 2d 347, 357, 378 P.2d 298, 304 (1963) (critical analysis of cases indicates two views are reconcilable); Robbins v. Alberto-Culver Co., 499 P.2d 1080, 1084–1085, 11 UCCR 1, 7 (Kan. 1972) (cleavage between two views not as broad or irreconcilable as first appears).

[535] *See* Corneliuson v. Arthur Drug Stores, Inc., 214 A.2d 676, 2 UCCR 1144 (Conn. 1965) (product must affect "appreciable number" of people); Robbins v. Alberto-Culver, 499 P.2d 1080, 11 UCCR 1 (Kan. 1972) (must be foreseeable that an "appreciable number" of people will be affected by product); Tiderman v. Fleetwood Homes of Wash., 684 P.2d 1302, 39 UCCR 442 (1983) ("appreciable number" of persons must suffer some ill effects); Graham v. Jordan Marsh Co., 319 Mass. 690, 67 N.E.2d 404 (1946) (plaintiff must have susceptibility of a "normal person" to recover); Peterson v. Bendix Home Sys., Inc., 318 N.W.2d 50, 33 UCCR 876 (Minn. 1982) (court applies test of "ordinary" user).

[536] 499 P.2d 1080, 11 UCCR 1 (Kan. 1972).

ceived additional complaints. This evidence was sufficient to permit the jury to decide whether it was foreseeable that the product would affect an appreciable number of people.

The relationship between foreseeability and the requirement that an appreciable number of people be affected by the product is not clear from the cases. One view is that foreseeability is irrelevant to the "appreciable number" test.[538] This view is suggested by a number of cases that discuss the issue of whether the product affects an appreciable class of persons with no mention of foreseeability.[538] Under this analysis, so long as the product adversely affects an appreciable number of persons, liability is present even if the danger or the number of persons affected was unforeseeable. Conversely, if an appreciable number of persons is not affected, it does not matter if the danger was foreseeable.

An alternative approach, suggested by the *Robbins* case, is that the plaintiff must reasonably foresee injury to an appreciable number of persons before there is liability. The court in *Robbins* stated that the concept of foreseeability was "key" and that the test to be applied by the factfinder was whether it was foreseeable that injury would occur to an appreciable class of persons. Under this view, the plaintiff would have to prove both that injury occurred to an appreciable class *and* that injury to this appreciable class was reasonably foreseeable. This appears to be the approach of the Restatement (Second) of Torts.[539]

A third alternative, most favorable to plaintiffs, is that the requirements of an appreciable class and the foreseeability of the danger are *alternative* bases for liability. That is, if the harm occurs to an appreciable class of persons, there is no requirement that the plaintiff demonstrate that the harm

---

[537] The "appreciable-number" test may, however, be a surrogate for foreseeability in that so long as the number of persons susceptible to injury is extremely small, the manufacturer cannot reasonably be expected to foresee the existence of these persons, nor uncover their susceptibility through testing and research.

[538] *See, e.g.*, Corneluison v. Arthur Drug Stores, Inc., 214 A.2d 676, 2 UCCR 1144 (1965); Graham v. Jordan Marsh Co., 67 N.E.2d 404 (Mass. 1946); Chambers v. G.D. Searle, 441 F. Supp. 377, 23 UCCR 598 (D. Md. 1975).

[539] Restatement (Second) of Torts § 402A, cmt. i provides:

Where . . . the product contains an ingredient to which a substantial number of the population are allergic, *and* the ingredient is one whose danger is not generally known, or if known, is one which the consumer would reasonably not expect to find in the product, the seller is required to give warning against it, *if he has knowledge, or by the application of reasonable, developed human skill and foresight should have knowledge, of the presence of the ingredient and the danger* (emphasis added).

was foreseeable. Conversely, if the harm was foreseeable to *some* persons, although they do not constitute an appreciable class, there is nonetheless liability, at least if the defendant did not provide a warning. Although no case has explicitly adopted this approach, language in one case suggests it. In *Gordon v. Procter & Gamble Distributing Co.*,[540] the court said that the "unusual susceptibility of the consumer is generally recognized as a complete defense *where the manufacturer did not know and had no reason to know that a very few users of his product might be injured.*"[541] This language suggests that if the manufacturer did have reason to know that even "a very few" persons might be injured, he would be liable, at least for failure to warn, despite the small number of those affected.[542]

Each of these approaches involves potential difficulties. The first is the most consistent with the concept of strict liability—liability without fault. It is not clear, however, why a distinction should be made between injury that occurs only to a few persons and injury that occurs to an "appreciable class," given the risk-distribution purposes of strict liability. Also, if the "appreciable class" requirement is merely a surrogate for foreseeability, why introduce a surrogate? Why not directly ask whether or not the injury was reasonably foreseeable by the defendant?

The problems of the second approach are somewhat different. Most significantly, it would appear to remove liability in some cases in which liability ought to exist. For example, if a manufacturer is aware (perhaps because of past experience) that a product will cause an allergic reaction that will seriously injure, or perhaps even kill, a very small number of consumers, shouldn't the manufacturer at least have a duty to warn the consumer about the danger?[543] To require that the product *both* affect an appreciable class *and* be foreseeable would seem to be too lenient a standard.

The final approach, which makes the appreciable class and foreseeability requirements alternative, also has an inherent difficulty—the amorphous nature of foreseeability. Even the unique consumer can be "foreseen"

---

[540] 789 F. Supp. 1384, 18 UCCR2d 426 (W.D. Ky. 1992).

[541] *Id.* at 1385, 18 UCCR2d at 427 (emphasis added).

[542] *See also* Griggs v. Combe, Inc., 456 So. 2d 790, 39 UCCR 446 (Ala. 1984). In this case, the court appeared to establish different standards for tort liability than for liability for breach of the merchantability warranty. For purposes of tort liability, the issue was foreseeability: "whether the defendant had a duty to warn of a possible reaction which it had no reason to suspect might occur." For purposes of merchantability, the sole issue appeared to be whether injury occurred to a significant number of persons.

[543] *See* Simeon v. Doe, 618 So. 2d 848, 21 UCCR2d 948 (La. 1993) (even though only fourteen cases of septemia resulted from eating raw oysters in nine years and therefore "defect" was in plaintiff rather than food, seller may nonetheless have had duty to warn).

in the sense that medical science can predict his or her existence. There are few ingredients for which there is not someone, somewhere, with an allergic reaction to them. If we impose liability simply because an injury is foreseeable in this sense, the manufacturer becomes an insurer against allergic reactions, regardless of how rare or unusual.

The best approach would be to impose strict liability when greater than an appreciable class is affected, and apply a standard of reasonability when less than an appreciable class is affected. To the extent that a greater than appreciable class is affected, the normal rules of strict liability should apply.[544] After all, there is no reason to apply a different rule of liability when an appreciable class is affected than when the defect would cause injury to *anyone* who uses it. When something less than an appreciable class is affected, the standard should be the reasonability of the defendant's conduct—negligence. Factors relevant to the reasonability of the defendant's conduct would include the likelihood of the injury to *some* person, whether the defendant was on notice that the product had caused adverse reactions in the past, the number of people affected, the potential efficacy of a warning, the seriousness of potential injury, and the likelihood that plaintiffs themselves would be aware of their susceptibility to injury through use of the product. Thus, for example, if a seller is aware that serving raw oysters causes harm to a very small number of persons with liver deficiencies, the seller might be liable for failing to provide a warning even though the number affected falls far below an "appreciable class."[545]

[6] Pass Without Objection in the Trade

To be merchantable, goods must also "pass without objection in the trade under the contract description."[546] Two aspects of this standard are important. The first is the centrality of the contract description. Only after it is clear *what* has been purchased and sold is it possible to determine whether it would pass without objection in the trade. The importance of the contract description is clearest with respect to second-hand goods. Both Comment 3 to section 2-314[547] and the cases[548] make it clear that the "sec-

---

[544] As discussed in prior sections, courts differ as to the extent, if at all, that foreseeability plays a part in strict liability. *See* §§ 4.06[B][3], 4.06[B][5][a], *supra.*

[545] *See* Simeon v. Doe, 618 So. 2d 848, 21 UCCR2d 948 (La. 1993).

[546] U.C.C. § 2-314(2)(a).

[547] U.C.C. § 2-314, Official Comment 3.

[548] *See* Whittle v. Timesavers Inc., 614 F. Supp. 115, 42 UCCR 126 (W.D. Va. 1985); McCormick Mach., Inc. v. Julian E. Johnson & Sons, Inc., 523 So. 2d 651, 7 UCCR2d 51 (Fla. Dist. Ct. App. 1988); Dickerson v. Mountain View Equip. Co., 109 Idaho 711, 710

ond-handedness" of goods is part of their contract description and affects the applicable standards of merchantability.

To the extent that courts are willing to find express warranties in generic descriptions,[549] the requirement of the implied warranty of merchantability that goods pass without objection in the trade significantly overlaps the express warranty by description. The contract description gives rise to an express warranty; the contract description is also important in determining the content of the implied warranty of merchantability. So long as implied warranties are not disclaimed, it makes no difference whether the resulting warranty is express or implied; if, however, implied warranties are disclaimed, the "pass without objection" test can be used to give content to express warranties by description.

There is also much overlap between the requirement that goods must pass without objection in the trade and the requirement that they be fit for their ordinary purpose.[550] Generally, goods that are fit for their ordinary purposes will pass without objection in the trade, while those that are not fit for their ordinary purposes will not pass without objection in the trade. The two standards, however, are not coextensive. For example, where an entire category of goods is defectively designed, or where the goods are produced by only one seller, they may pass without objection in the trade but nonetheless not be fit for ordinary purposes. Conversely, to the extent that all that is required for goods to be fit for their ordinary purpose is that they perform their basic function,[551] the goods may satisfy this standard and yet not pass without objection in the trade under the contract description.[552]

The second part of the test that is important is found in the language, "pass without objection *in the trade*." The standards are set by "the trade," not by the buyer or the buyer's particular needs.[553] Difficulties may be en-

---

P.2d 621, 42 UCCR 114 (Ct. App. 1985); Regan Purchase & Sales Corp. v. Primavera, 68 Misc. 2d 858, 328 N.Y.S.2d 490, 10 UCCR 300 (Civ. Ct. 1972).

[549] *See* § 4.05[C], *supra*.

[550] *See* Ambassador Steel Co. v. Ewald Steel Co., 33 Mich. App. 495, 190 N.W.2d 275, 9 UCCR 1019 (1971) (steel was not fit for its ordinary purpose when it was of a different quality than ordinarily sold in the custom and usage of the steel business).

[551] *See* § 4.06[B][4], *supra*; Taterka v. Ford Motor Co., 86 Wis. 2d 140, 271 N.W.2d 653, 25 UCCR 680 (1978).

[552] *See* Skelton v. General Motors Corp., 500 F. Supp. 1181, 30 UCCR 846 (N.D. Ill. 1980) *rev'd*, 660 F.2d 311, 32 UCCR 1118 (7th Cir. 1981), *cert. denied*, 456 U.S. 974, 102 S. Ct. 2238, 72 L. Ed. 2d 848 (1982).

[553] *See* Comark Merchandising, Inc. v. Highland Group, Inc., 932 F.2d 1196, 14 UCCR2d 999 (7th Cir. 1991) (customer's complaint about brochures "bleeding" when packed with freshly baked, greasy pizza does not mean the goods failed to pass without objection in the trade; "trade" refers to larger group than a single client).

countered in determining the scope of "the trade," but the purpose of the drafters was to seek out a group that dealt with the product on a routine basis. The product need not be the best the trade has to offer; it is only necessary that the goods pass without objection.[554]

Goods have failed to pass without objection in the trade for a variety of reasons. In *Delan Growers' Cooperative Winery v. Supreme Wine Co.*,[555] wine that contained sediment and a "cottony" substance would not pass without objection in the trade, and was therefore unmerchantable. In another case, books that were printed off-center, had wrinkled pages, and inadequate perforations would not pass without objection in the trade, despite the fact that the books could otherwise be used.[556] The plaintiff in *Dempsey v. Rosenthal*[557] recovered for breach of the warranty of merchantability on the basis that a pedigreed dog with an undescended testicle would not pass without objection in the trade. In *George Byers Sons, Inc. v. East Europe Import Export, Inc.*[558] the court held that goods can fail to pass without objection in the trade even though there is no defect in the goods themselves. The case involved motorcycles imported by the seller without certificates of compliance with federal safety standards, and that, therefore, could not legally be resold by the buyer. Although compliance or lack of compliance with regulations is relevant as to whether goods can pass without objection in the trade,[559] compliance with government regulations is not conclusive.[560]

[7]   In the Case of Fungible Goods, Are of Fair Average Quality Within the Description

This section applies to fungible goods the same basic tests that were applied in the prior subsection. "Fair average" is a term appropriate to agricultural bulk products and means goods centering around the middle belt of quality, not the least or worst that would pass without objection under the contract description. A fair percentage of the least passable is permis-

---

[554] *See* Royal Typewriter Co. v. Xerographic Supplies Corp., 719 F.2d 1092, 37 UCCR 429 (11th Cir. 1983).

[555] 393 Mass. 666, 473 N.E.2d 1066, 40 UCCR 93 (1985).

[556] Printing Ctr. of Tex., Inc. v. Supermind Publishing Co., 669 S.W.2d 779, 39 UCCR 127 (Tex. Ct. App. 1984).

[557] 121 Misc. 2d 612, 468 N.Y.S.2d 441, 37 UCCR 1091 (Civ. Ct. 1983).

[558] 488 F. Supp. 574, 28 UCCR 1293 (D. Md. 1980).

[559] Coffer v. Standard Brands, Inc., 30 N.C. App. 134, 226 S.E.2d 534, 20 UCCR 321 (1976).

[560] *See* Reid v. Eckerds Drugs, Inc., 40 N.C. App. 476, 253 S.E.2d 344, 26 UCCR 20 (1979).

sible, but the goods are not "fair average" if they are all of the least or worst possible under the contract description.[561]

Both this and the preceding subsection use the contract description to determine the merchantability of the goods. For example, a contract for "grade A eggs, large" sets the baseline from which the fair average quality is to be measured. It is also the standard which the eggs must meet to pass "without objection in the trade." Change the contract description to "Grade B eggs, large" or "Grade A eggs, medium" and a different measure will be applied to determine the merchantability of the delivered eggs.

[8] Are Adequately Contained, Packaged, and Labeled as the Agreement May Require

The meaning of this requirement is not entirely clear. Do the last five words ("as the agreement may require") modify "contained" and "packaged" as well as "labeled" or do they modify only "labeled"? If these words modify only "labeled," the subsection means that the goods must be adequately contained and adequately packaged, and must also be adequately labeled "as the agreement may require." Alternatively, the "requirements of the agreement" may also refer to the container and the package, as well as the labels. While no case has explicitly faced the issue, the decisions appear to suggest both interpretations.[562]

More importantly, the words "as the agreement may require" could be read to mean that the parties must have thought about the containers, packages, and labels (or perhaps just the labels if the former interpretation described above is adopted) and have entered into a specific agreement about them before a warranty of merchantability will arise under this section. This interpretation would make the subsection inapplicable when there was no specific agreement regarding the containers, packages, or labels—as, for example, when a consumer purchases bottled goods from a local grocery store. If the bottle is defective and if that defect causes injury, a restrictive

---

[561] U.C.C. § 2-314, Official Comment 7.

[562] *Compare* Standard Brands Chem. Indus., Inc. v. Pilot Freight Carriers, Inc., 65 Misc. 2d 1029, 319 N.Y.S.2d 457, 9 UCCR 422 (Sup. Ct. 1971) (Code creates warranty that "the goods were adequately contained or packaged as the agreement required.") *with* Indiana Farm Bureau Coop. Ass'n, Inc. v. S.S. Sovereign Faylenne, 24 UCCR 74 (S.D.N.Y. 1977) (warranty of merchantability includes warranty that "the goods are adequately contained and packaged.") *and* Schussler v. Coca-Cola Bottling Co. of Miami, 279 So. 2d 901, 12 UCCR 1050 (Fla. Ct. App. 1973) (statute imposes a warranty of merchantability which covers not only the goods but "the adequacy of the container and its packaging").

reading of "as the agreement may require" would make this subsection of section 2-314 inapplicable to the defect.

This language should not be read this narrowly. First, if the parties have expressly dealt with the requirements, for example, of the containers, an express warranty has been created; the seller has made affirmations of fact or promises about the containers. It should be assumed that the drafters intended section 2-314(2)(e) to do more than simply duplicate section 2-313. Furthermore, Comment 10 to section 2-314 indicates that the parties do not have to have *explicitly* agreed on the nature of the container, packaging, or labeling. This Comment states that: "Paragraph (e) applies where the *nature of the goods and of the transaction* require a certain type of container, package or label."[563] The Comment gives no indication that an explicit agreement on these matters is necessary. Finally, the Code definition of "agreement" is sufficiently broad to encompass implicit requirements as to the container. "Agreement" is defined in section 1-201(3) as "the bargain of the parties in fact as found in their language *or by implication from other circumstances* including course of dealing or usage of trade or course of performance."[564] Thus, the "requirements" of the agreement may be implicit as well as express.[565]

The cases under this subsection are consistent with this broader interpretation. There are a number of "exploding-bottle" cases in which courts have relied, at least in part, on subsection (e) in finding a breach of the warranty of merchantability.[566] In none of these cases have the courts required an explicit agreement as to the nature or adequacy of the container. In two other cases,[567] glasses from which consumers were drinking beverages broke, causing injury; one while a customer was drinking a glass of wine in a restaurant, the other while a customer was consuming a mixed drink in a casino. In both cases the courts said that the drinks were not adequately contained under section 2-314(2)(e) and, as a result, there was a breach of the warranty of merchantability. In neither case, of course, was there an explicit agreement as to the container.

---

[563] U.C.C. § 2-314, Official Comment 10 (emphasis added).

[564] U.C.C. § 1-204(3).

[565] The proposed revisions to Article 2 make this explicit. *See* Council Draft § 2-404.

[566] *See* Sheekin v. Giant Food, Inc., 20 Md. App. 611, 318 A.2d 874, 14 UCCR 892 (Ct. Spec. App. 1974); Lucchesi v. H.C. Bohack Co., 8 UCCR 326 (N.Y. Sup. Ct. 1970); Gillispie v. Great Atl. & Pac. Tea Co., 14 N.C. App. 1, 187 S.E.2d 441, 10 UCCR 754 (1972); Barker v. Allied Supermarket, 596 P.2d 870, 26 UCCR 597 (Okla. 1979).

[567] Levondosky v. Marina Assocs., 731 F. Supp. 1210, 11 UCCR2d 487 (D.N.J. 1990); Schaffer v. Victoria Station, Inc., 588 P.2d 233, 25 UCCR 427 (Wash. 1978).

Only a few other cases have dealt with this subsection of section 2-314. In *Pugh v. J.C. Whitney & Co.*,[568] an employee was injured when he removed automobile parts with sharp projections from the cardboard carton in which they had been sent by the seller. The items were shipped in the carton without any covering or sheathing, and the package contained no warning that the parts presented a danger. The court said that the seller had impliedly warranted that the package was reasonably safe to open. The buyer in another case[569] purchased a reactor for the mixing of chemicals. It arrived at the buyer's place of business with the glass lining broken. The court said that the seller, under section 2-314, impliedly warranted that the goods would be adequately packaged to prevent breakage during normal transportation.[570] In the one case of improper labeling, the court in *Reid v. Eckerds Drugs, Inc.*[571] held that an inadequate warning of a product's flammability on the label breached the warranty of merchantability.

[9] Conform to the Promises or Affirmations of Fact Made on the Container or Label If Any

Generally, promises and affirmations of fact made on labels or containers create express warranties.[572] This section makes it clear that they are also implied warranties. In the few cases in which courts have explicitly discussed this subsection, the buyer has also claimed a breach of express warranty. When recovery has been allowed under one theory, it has generally been allowed under the other as well.[573] This overlap, however, has two important consequences. First, if the implied warranty of merchantability is successfully disclaimed, a buyer may still be able to prove breach of express warranty. On the other hand, if the merchantability warranty is not disclaimed, the buyer can rely on section 2-314(2)(f) whenever representations do not conform to the label or container without having to prove reliance

---

[568] 9 UCCR 229 (E.D.N.Y. 1971).

[569] Standard Brands Chem. Indus., Inc. v. Pilot Freight Carriers, Inc., 65 Misc. 2d 1029, 319 N.Y.S.2d 457, 9 UCCR 422 (Sup. Ct. 1971).

[570] *See also* Indiana Farm Bureau Coop. Ass'n, Inc. v. S.S. Sovereign Faylenne, 24 UCCR 74 (S.D.N.Y. 1977).

[571] 40 N.C. App. 476, 253 S.E.2d 344, 26 UCCR 20 (1979).

[572] *See* § 4.05[B], *supra*.

[573] *See, e.g.*, Hauter v. Zogarts, 534 P.2d 377, 14 Cal. 3d 104, 120 Cal. Rptr. 681, 16 UCCR 938 (1975); Farmers Union Coop. Gin v. Smith, 9 UCCR 823 (Okla. Ct. App. 1971).

or that the representations were part of the basis of the bargain.[574] This subsection applies only to representations made on the product's label or container, however, so that representations made in an instruction manual are not subject to the warranty.[575]

[10] Conclusion

Section 2-314 establishes the baseline standard for merchantability. More may be required in a specific case, depending on the prior course of dealing between the parties and on the usages in the trade in which the parties are engaged.[576] In some circumstances, *less* may be required as well, as when the warranty is excluded or modified by the parties' course of dealing or a usage of trade.[577] Nevertheless, these standards ensure that the reasonable expectations of buyers are met with respect to the goods. In determining the content and scope of these warranties, the contract description is central. Only after it has been determined *what* the seller agreed to sell and the buyer agreed to buy can we decide what the buyer could reasonably expect by way of product quality and what risks the buyer assumed. Other circumstances of the transaction are important as well in giving content to the merchantability warranty. For example, as Comment 7 to section 2-314 points out, the price at which an item is sold is often an excellent indicator of the nature and scope of the warranty.[578] The thrust of the Code is to enforce the *bargain of the parties*—both express and implied terms. While section 2-314 provides a baseline, that bargain cannot be divorced from the surrounding circumstances.

---

[574] *But see* Fischbach v. Moore Int'l Corp. v. Crane Barge R-14, 476 F. Supp. 282, 27 UCCR 961 (D. Md. 1979). In this case, the court found that the weight stenciled on a transformer constituted an implied warranty under U.C.C. § 2-314(f). The transformer weighed more than the stenciled weight, causing a crane barge that was lifting it to partially capsize. Nonetheless, because the plaintiff either knew that the weight was inaccurate or "had knowledge of facts so obvious that they must have known," the court held that the implied warranty "was no longer applicable" to the plaintiffs. If the court meant that the implied warranty had to be relied upon or be otherwise part of the basis of the bargain, the case is surely wrong. If the court meant, however, that the warranty had been excluded by the circumstances of the transaction or that the breach was not the proximate cause of the damage, the decision is defensible. *See* U.C.C. §§ 2-316(3)(a), 2-316(3)(c) and 2-715(2)(b).

[575] Reddick v. White Consol. Indus., Inc., 295 F. Supp. 243, 6 UCCR 303 (S.D. Ga. 1968).

[576] *See* U.C.C. § 2-314(3).

[577] U.C.C. § 2-316(3)(c). *See* § 4.07[C][5], *infra*.

[578] U.C.C. § 2-314, Official Comment 7.

[C] The Implied Warranty of Fitness for a Particular Purpose

The second implied warranty of quality is that of fitness for a particular purpose. The Code provides in section 2-315:

> Where the seller at the time of contracting has reason to know any particular purpose for which the goods are required and that the buyer is relying on the seller's skill or judgment to select or furnish suitable goods, there is unless excluded or modified under the next section an implied warranty that the goods shall be fit for such purpose.

The warranty of fitness for a particular purpose rests on three requirements.[579] First, the seller must have reason to know of the particular purpose for which the buyer requires the goods. Actual knowledge is not required; reason to know will suffice.[580] Second, the seller must also have reason to know that the buyer is relying on the seller's skill or judgment to select or furnish suitable goods.[581] Finally, the buyer must actually rely on the seller's expertise in selecting the goods.[582]

The general application of the fitness warranty is well illustrated in two early cases. In the first,[583] the stucco walls of the buyer's house were chalky and powdery. The buyer took this problem to the seller—a retail paint merchant—who recommended a certain brand of paint. The buyer applied the paint, carefully following the directions that had been given to him by the seller. Less than five months later, the paint began to peel, flake, and blister. In a suit by the buyer, the court found that the necessary elements of an implied warranty of fitness existed: the seller had reason to know of the particular purpose for which the buyer wanted the paint and that the buyer was relying on the seller's judgment in selecting the proper paint. The

---

[579] *But see* Surface v. Kelly, 912 S.W.2d 646, 28 UCCR2d 162 (Mo. Ct. App. 1995) (Missouri variation of U.C.C. § 2-615 requires warranty of fitness to be in writing).

[580] *See* Lewis v. Mobil Oil Corp., 438 F.2d 500, 8 UCCR 625 (8th Cir. 1971); C.E. Alexander & Sons, Inc. v. DEC Int'l, Inc., 112 N.M. 89, 811 P.2d 899, 15 UCCR2d 464 (1991) (court found that there was enough evidence that seller should have known of buyer's particular purpose to submit issue to jury on retrial); Cohen v. Hathaway, 595 F. Supp. 579, 39 UCCR 857 (D. Mass. 1984); Jones, Inc. v. W.A. Wiedebusch Plumbing & Heating Co., 157 W. Va. 257, 201 S.E.2d 248, 13 UCCR 818 (Ct. App. 1973).

[581] *See* Jacobs v. E.I. du Pont de Nemours & Co., 67 F.3d 1219, 27 UCCR2d 1198 (6th Cir. 1995); Duffin v. Idaho Crop. Improvement Ass'n, 126 Idaho 1002, 895 P.2d 1195, 28 UCCR2d 133 (1995).

[582] *See* Berquist v. Mackay Engines, Inc., 538 N.W.2d 655, 28 UCCR2d 1168 (Iowa Ct. App. 1995); Presto v. Mackay Engines, Inc., 487 S.E.2d 70, 33 UCCR2d 418 (Ga. Ct. App. 1997).

[583] Catania v. Brown, 4 Conn. Cir. Ct., 344, 231 A.2d 668, 4 UCCR 470 (1967).

paint selected may well have been "merchantable"—that is, fit for its ordinary purpose.[584] This buyer, however, had not merely asked for "paint," but had made his particular purpose known to the seller. When the buyer, in fact, relied upon the seller's judgment in selecting a paint that would fulfill this purpose, a warranty was made under section 2-315, which the seller breached.

In the second case,[585] the buyer ordered boxes from the seller for packaging liquor bottles; he also ordered acetate bands to encircle the boxes. The seller furnished boxes and bands, both of which the court found to be merchantable. When the buyer attempted to insert the boxes into shipping cases, however, the fit was so tight that the acetate bands tore off on the sides of the boxes. The buyer had to insert the liquor boxes into glassine bags to reduce the contact between the bands and the sides of the cases. When the seller sued the buyer for the price of the boxes, the buyer claimed that the warranty of fitness had been breached, and counterclaimed for damages. The court, however, found that the seller did not have reason to know that the goods (the boxes and bands) were required for the particular purpose of fitting into shipping cases of undisclosed dimensions, nor did the seller have reason to know that the buyer was relying on the seller's skill and judgment to select goods that would do so.

A seller may have reason to know of the buyer's particular purpose in using the goods because the buyer has expressed this purpose directly to the seller.[586] An explicit statement of the buyer's purpose is not required, however; any facts that give the seller reason to know of the buyer's purpose are sufficient.[587] This knowledge may come from a course of dealing,[588] or

---

[584] As discussed in previous sections, the paint's merchantability would depend upon the reasonable expectations of a buyer in light of the contract description, price, and other circumstances of the transaction. *See* § 4.06[B][4], *supra*. As to the relationship between a "particular" purpose and "ordinary" purpose, see § 4.06[C][1], *infra*.

[585] Standard Packaging Corp. v. Continental Distilleries Corp., 378 F.2d 505, 4 UCCR 292 (3d Cir. 1967).

[586] *See, e.g.*, Cantania v. Brown, 231 A.2d 668, 4 UCCR 470 (Conn. Cir. Ct. 1967); Circle Land & Cattle Corp. v. Amoco Oil Co., 657 P.2d 532, 232 Kan. 482, 35 UCCR 403 (1983); First New Eng. Fin. Corp. v. Woffard, 421 So. 2d 590, 35 UCCR 650 (5th Cir. 1982); Agri-Business Supply Co., Inc., 447 So. 2d 769, 38 UCCR 738 (Ala. Ct. App. 1984); Gates v. Abernathy, 11 UCCR 491 (Okla. Ct. App. 1972); Jerry Alderman Ford Sales, Inc. v. Bailey, 291 N.E.2d 92, 12 UCCR 47 (Ind. Ct. App. 1972); Boeing Airplane Co. v. O'Malley, 329 F.2d 585, 2 UCCR 110 (8th Cir. 1964).

[587] *See* Official Comment 1 to U.C.C. § 2-315, which states in part:

Under this section the buyer need not bring home to the seller actual knowledge of the particular purpose for which the goods are intended . . . if the circum-

when the nature of the transaction necessarily discloses the buyer's purpose—as, for example, when the rendition of services accompanies the sales transaction.[589] Information sufficient to give the seller reason to know of the buyer's particular purpose can come from third parties as well.[590]

An interesting case suggesting that in some cases a seller has a duty to inquire into the buyer's purpose is *Lewis v. Mobil Oil Corp.*[591] In this case, Lewis, a sawmill operator, purchased a new hydraulic system. Because he was a longtime customer of Mobil, Lewis called Mobil's representative, Frank Rowe, and asked for a recommendation for hydraulic fluid for the new system. Lewis did not describe the system to Rowe in detail, saying only that it had a "gear type pump." Rowe told Lewis that he didn't know what the proper lubricant was, but that he would find out. Without asking for additional information from Lewis, Rowe later recommended Ambrex 810. Lewis immediately had trouble with the new system. Serious difficulties continued until a different representative from Mobil came to the sawmill and recommended a new oil, which functioned properly. Lewis then sued Mobil for breach of the warranty of fitness.

Mobil argued that it did not have reason to know of the particular purpose for which Lewis wanted the oil, because Lewis had given Mobil only sketchy information about the hydraulic system. The court held that despite the inadequate information, Mobil still had reason to know of Lewis' particular purpose. The court said that in light of Lewis' clear indication that he was relying on Mobil to supply the proper oil, if further information was needed, it was incumbent upon Mobil to secure the necessary information. *Lewis* suggests that when a buyer makes it clear that the buyer is relying upon skill and expertise of the seller to select suitable goods, and the seller does not indicate to the buyer that the information the buyer has supplied is inadequate, the seller will be deemed to have reason to know of the buyer's particular purpose. A court is particularly likely to impose this

---

stances are such that the seller has reason to realize the purpose intended.

[588] *See* AFA Corp. v. Phoenix Closures, Inc., 501 F. Supp. 224, 30 UCCR 81 (N.D. Ill. 1980); Utah Coop. Ass'n v. Egbert-Haderlie Hog Farms, Inc., 550 P.2d 196, 19 UCCR 1095 (Utah 1976).

[589] *See, e.g.*, Caldwell v. Brown Serv. Funeral Home, 345 So. 2d 1341, 21 UCCR 999 (Ala. 1979) (funeral director had reason to know of buyer's purchase of casket and vault for eight-year-old son, and U.C.C. § 2-315 warranty was breached when vault was too small).

[590] *See* Renze Hybrids, Inc. v. Shell Oil Co., 418 N.W.2d 634, 5 UCCR2d 1331 (Iowa 1988) (retail seller gave manufacturer reason to know of buyer's purpose when retailer requested that manufacturer provide insecticide to kill client's corn-borer larvae).

[591] 438 F.2d 500, 8 UCCR 625 (8th Cir. 1971).

duty on the seller when there is a significant disparity in expertise between the buyer and the seller.

The seller must also have reason to know of the buyer's reliance on the seller's skill and judgment in selecting suitable goods. In many cases, the buyer makes his needs explicit to the seller and asks the seller to provide goods suitable for those needs.[592] Unless there are facts indicating that the buyer is not relying on the seller's skill or expertise in selecting the goods, the buyer's disclosure of his particular purpose and his request to the seller to supply suitable goods will be sufficient to give the seller reason to know of the buyer's reliance. Generally, the greater the seller's expertise relative to that of the buyer, the easier it will be to find that the seller had reason to know of the buyer's reliance.[593]

The requirement that the seller have reason to know of the buyer's reliance on the seller's skill or judgment usually precludes a suit for breach of the warranty of fitness by the buyer against a manufacturer who has not sold the goods directly to the buyer.[594] In some cases, however, the manufacturer will have sufficient direct involvement with the buyer to satisfy this requirement,[595] or information about the buyer's needs may be conveyed to the manufacturer by a third party.[596] In addition, as is discussed in greater

---

[592] *See, e.g.*, Gyptal Inc. v. Engelhard Corp., 801 F. Supp. 887, 18 UCCR2d 1059 (D. Mass. 1992); Agri-Business Supply Co., Inc. v. Hodge, 447 So. 2d 769, 38 UCCR 738 (Ala. Civ. App. 1984); Circle Land & Cattle Corp. v. Amoco Oil Co., 232 Kan. 482, 657 P.2d 532, 35 UCCR 403 (1983).

[593] *See* Price Brothers v. Philadelphia Gear Corp., 649 F.2d 416, 31 UCCR 469 (6th Cir. 1981); Jetero Constr. Co., Inc. v. South Memphis Lumber Co., 531 F.2d 1348, 19 UCCR 478 (6th Cir. 1976); KLPR TV, Inc. v. Visual Elecs. Corp., 327 F. Supp. 315, 9 UCCR 649 (W.D. Ark. 1971), *rev'd in part on other grounds*, 465 F.2d 1382, 11 UCCR 50 (8th Cir. 1972); Neilson Business Equip. Ctr., Inc. v. Monteleone, 524 A.2d 1172, 3 UCCR2d 1721 (Del. 1987).

[594] *See, e.g.*, Bob Rigby, Inc. v. Eagle Crusher, Inc., 62 B.R. 900, 3 UCCR2d 954 (M.D. Fla. 1986); Hite v. Ed Smith Lumber Mill, Inc., 309 S.C. 185, 420 S.E.2d 860, 20 UCCR2d 438 (Ct. App. 1992). *See also* Dalton v. Stanley Solar & Stove, Inc., 137 N.H. 467, 629 A.2d 794, 21 UCCR2d 957 (1993) (distributor not liable when only dealer, not distributor, knew of buyer's particular purpose).

[595] *See* C.E. Alexander & Sons, Inc. v. DEC Intl., Inc., 112 N.M. 89, 811 P.2d 899, 15 UCCR2d 464 (1991).

[596] *See* Renze Hybrids, Inc. v. Shell Oil Co., 418 N.W.2d 634, 5 UCCR2d 1331 (Iowa 1988).

detail subsequently,[597] some states "merge" the warranties of merchantability and fitness when the buyer's particular purpose is also the ordinary purpose of the goods, and allow the buyer to recover on either warranty theory.[598] In these states, the courts seem to assume that the seller has reason to know of the buyer's reliance on the seller's skill and judgment when the buyer's particular purpose is also an ordinary purpose of the goods.[599]

Many cases have refused recovery because the buyer did not *in fact* rely on the seller's skill or judgment in choosing suitable goods. Evidence that the buyer's expertise is equivalent to, or greater than, the seller's is important to demonstrate that the buyer did not rely on the seller's skill or expertise.[600] On the other hand, evidence of a significant disparity in the other direction is a strong signal that reliance is present.[601] Reliance has also not been found when the buyer has engaged the services of a third-party expert to examine or evaluate the goods.[602] Courts almost never find that the buyer has relied on the seller's skill or judgment when the buyer provides

---

[597] *See* § 4.06[C][1], *infra.*

[598] *See* Great Dane Trailer Sales, Inc. v. Malvern Pulpwood, Inc., 301 Ark. 436, 785 S.W.2d 13, 11 UCCR2d 875 (1990); F.L. Davis Builders Supply, Inc. v. Knapp, 42 Ark. App. 52, 853 S.W.2d 288, 22 UCCR2d 113 (1993); Tennessee Carolina Transp., Inc. v. Strick Corp., 283 N.C. 423, 196 S.E.2d 711, 12 UCCR 1055 (1973); Soaper v. Hope Indus., Inc., 309 S.C. 438, 424 S.E.2d 493, 20 UCCR2d 101 (1992).

[599] *See* F.L. Davis Builders Supply, Inc. v. Knapp, 42 Ark. App. 52, 853 S.W.2d 288, 22 UCCR2d 113 (1993) (where buyer's particular purpose and ordinary purpose of the goods "merge," buyer can show that seller has reason to know of buyer's reliance on seller's skill or judgment by showing that buyer could reasonably have been expected to use the goods); Tennessee Carolina Transp., Inc. v. Strick Corp., 283 N.C. 423, 196 S.E.2d 711, 12 UCCR 1055 (1973).

[600] *See, e.g.*, Price Bros. Co. v. Philadelphia Gear Corp., 649 F.2d 416, 31 UCCR 469 (6th Cir. 1981). *See also* Valiga v. National Food Co., 58 Wisc. 2d 232, 206 N.W.2d 377, 12 UCCR 830 (1973) (in indemnity claim against seller by buyer who later resold defective salmon for mink food, court found no reliance when seller knew nothing about the use of salmon as mink food and buyer had been in the business of producing and selling mink food for many years).

[601] *See, e.g.*, Ingram River Equip., Inc. v. Pott Indus., Inc., 816 F.2d 1231, 3 UCCR2d 977 (8th Cir. 1987); KLPR TV, Inc. v. Visual Elecs. Corp., 327 F. Supp. 315, 9 UCCR 649 (W.D. Ark. 1971), *rev'd in part on other grounds,* 465 F.2d 1382, 11 UCCR 50 (8th Cir. 1972); Morrision v. DeVore Trucking, Inc., 68 Ohio App. 2d 140, 428 N.E.2d 438, 32 UCCR 779 (1980).

[602] *See* Sessa v. Riegle, 427 F. Supp. 760, 21 UCCR 745 (E.D. Pa. 1977) (expert examined horse); Donald v. City Nat'l Bank of Dothan, 295 Ala. 320, 329 So. 2d 92, 18 UCCR 891 (1976) (buyer hired experts to examine and survey boat).

technical specifications to the seller[603] or when the goods are built to the specifications of a third party.[604]

[1] The Relationship Between the Warranty of Merchantability and the Warranty of Fitness for a Particular Purpose

The relationship between the merchantability warranty of section 2-314 and the warranty of fitness for a particular purpose is puzzling and has been the subject of considerable litigation. The Code comments make clear that the warranties are not mutually exclusive; both warranties may arise in a particular transaction.[605] Thus, for example, in the absence of a valid disclaimer, a merchant selling an air conditioner to a consumer will give the buyer an implied warranty of merchantability that the air conditioner is fit for its ordinary purpose (i.e., to provide cool air). At the same time, the buyer may have communicated to the seller the size of the room to be cooled and requested a recommendation from the seller. If the seller provides a recommendation and the buyer relies upon it, a warranty of fitness has probably arisen that the air conditioner is suitable for a room the size of the buyer's. If a defect in the air conditioner causes it to throw out only warm air, there is clearly a breach of the merchantability warranty. If, on the other hand, the air conditioner functions perfectly but is too small for the buyer's room, there is a breach of the fitness warranty.

The issue, however, is not the extent to which the two warranties may coexist, but rather the extent to which they overlap. For example, if the seller recommends an air conditioner suitable for the buyer's room, but a defect causes it to emit only warm air, and the defect (rather than the capacity of the air conditioner) is the reason that it cannot cool the buyer's room, is there a breach of the warranty of merchantability, the warranty of fitness, or both? Or, if the buyer conveys to the seller no information about the size of the room, but the air conditioner, because of the defect, produces no cool air at all, can the buyer sue for breach of the fitness warranty?

The issue of the scope of the fitness warranty and its relationship to the warranty of merchantability is generally framed as whether the "ordi-

---

[603] *See, e.g.,* Ramsey Prods. Corp. v. Morbark Indus., Inc., 823 F.2d 798, 4 UCCR2d 428 (4th Cir. 1987); Hickham v. Chronister, 792 S.W.2d 631, 13 UCCR2d 132 (Mo. Ct. App. 1989); Controltek, Inc. v. Kwikee Enters., Inc., 284 Or. 123, 585 P.2d 670, 25 UCCR 421 (1978).

[604] *See, e.g.,* Klipfel v. Neill, 30 Colo. App. 428, 494 P.2d 115, 10 UCCR 582 (1972); Vacuum Concrete Corp. of Am. v. Berlanti Constr. Co., 206 Pa. Super. 548, 214 A.2d 729, 3 UCCR 30 (1965).

[605] U.C.C. § 2-315, Official Comment 2.

nary" purpose of an item can also be a "particular" purpose. That is, if the buyer seeks only to use the goods for their ordinary purpose, is the buyer relegated solely to the merchantability warranty, or can the buyer attempt to show a breach of the fitness warranty as well? This question cannot be resolved, however, by simply asking whether the buyer's particular purpose can also be an ordinary purpose. This inquiry fails to focus on the *reason* that the goods have failed to satisfy the buyer, which, as we will see, is the critical component of the analysis. Also, the attempt by courts to differentiate between the buyer's "particular" purpose and the "ordinary" purpose of the goods has often led to arbitrary results and confusing opinions.

In many cases, of course, it will make no difference whether the warranties overlap. If a buyer using the goods for their ordinary purpose can recover damages using the merchantability warranty, it will generally matter little that the buyer can recover under the fitness warranty as well. There are circumstances, however, where the extent of overlap may make a difference. For example, the buyer may fail to plead the warranty of merchantability.[606] Or, the warranty of merchantability may have been disclaimed, while the warranty of fitness was not. Finally, the seller may not be a merchant, and the warranty of merchantability may, for that reason, not be available.

Some courts have resolved the issue by explicitly "merging" the two warranties when the goods are used by the buyer for their ordinary purpose.[607] Other courts reach similar results by assuming, without analysis or discussion, that the buyer's particular purpose can be an ordinary purpose for the goods.[608] For these two groups of courts, if the goods are unfit for

---

[606] *See* Tennessee Carolina Transp., Inc. v. Strick Corp., 283 N.C. 423, 196 S.E.2d 711, 12 UCCR 1055 (1973). Of course, it seems likely that courts would permit such erroneous pleadings to be amended.

[607] *See, e.g.*, Great Dane Trailer Sales, Inc. v. Malvern Pulpwood, Inc., 301 Ark. 436, 785 S.W.2d 13, 11 UCCR2d 875 (1990); F.L. Davis Builders Supply, Inc. v. Knapp, 42 Ark. App. 52, 853 S.W.2d 288, 22 UCCR2d 113 (1993); Tennessee Carolina Transp., Inc. v. Strick Corp., 196 S.E.2d 711, 12 UCCR 1055 (1973); Soaper v. Hope Indus., Inc., 309 S.C. 438, 424 S.E.2d 493, 20 UCCR2d 101 (1992).

[608] *See, e.g.*, Sauers v. Tibbs, 48 Ill. App. 3d 805, 363 N.E.2d 444, 6 Ill. Dec. 762, 22 UCCR 363 (1977); Auto-Teria, Inc. v. Ahern, 170 Ind. App. 84, 352 N.E.2d 774, 20 UCCR 336 (1976); Tennessee Carolina Transp., Inc. v. Strick Corp., 283 N.C. 423, 196 S.E.2d 711, 12 UCCR 1055 (1973); Whitehouse v. Lange, 910 P.2d 801, 31 UCCR2d 78 (Idaho Ct. App. 1996); Maritime Co. v. Holiday Mansion, 983 F. Supp. 977, 33 UCCR2d 108 (D. Kan. 1997).

their ordinary purpose, they will be also unfit for the buyer's particular purpose. Furthermore, because the buyer's purpose is an ordinary purpose, these courts have had little trouble finding that the seller has reason to know of the buyer's purpose and reason to know that the buyer is relying on the seller's skill and judgment.[609]

Although a substantial number of courts take this approach, the majority attempt to distinguish between an item's ordinary purpose and the particular purpose of the buyer, and have held that the particular purpose of section 2-315 cannot be the ordinary purpose of the goods.[610] This effort has lead to a substantial amount of confusion and uncertainty, and the creation of various tests to distinguish a particular purpose from the ordinary purpose of the goods. The starting point for most of these courts is Comment 2 to section 2-315:

> A "particular purpose" differs from the ordinary purpose for which the goods are used in that it envisages a specific use by the buyer which is peculiar to the nature of his business whereas the ordinary purpose for which goods are used are those envisioned in the concept of merchantability and go to uses which are customarily made of the goods in question. For example, shoes are generally used for the purpose of walking upon ordinary ground, but a seller may know that a particular pair was selected to be used for climbing mountains.

---

[609] *See, e.g.*, Filler v. Rayex Corp., 435 F.2d 336, 8 UCCR 323 (7th Cir. 1970); Great Dane Trailer Sales, Inc. v. Malvern Pulpwood, Inc., 301 Ark. 436, 785 S.W.2d 13, 11 UCCR2d 875 (1990);

[610] There are a host of cases. *See, e.g.*, Crysco Oilfield Servs., Inc. v. Hutchison-Hayes Int'l, Inc., 913 F.2d 850, 12 UCCR2d 1019 (10th Cir. 1990); Duffee v. Murray Ohio Mfg. Co., 866 F. Supp. 1321, 25 UCCR2d 706 (D. Kan 1994); Unified Sch. Dist. No. 500 v. United States Gypsum Co., 788 F. Supp. 1173, 18 UCCR2d 97 (D. Kan. 1992); Porter v. Pfizer Hosp. Prods. Group, Inc., 783 F. Supp. 1466, 17 UCCR2d 1112 (D. Mo. 1992); DiIenno v. Libby Glass Div., Owens-Illinois, Inc., 778 F. Supp. 373, 4 UCCR2d 706 (D. Del. 1987); Fiat Auto U.S.A., Inc. v. Hollums, 185 Ga. App. 113, 363 S.E.2d 312, 5 UCCR2d 969 (1987); Van Wyk v. Norden Labs., Inc., 345 N.W.2d 81, 37 UCCR 1489 (Iowa 1984); Smith v. Stewart, 233 Kan. 904, 667 P.2d 358, 36 UCCR 1141 (1983); International Petroleum Servs., Inc. v. S&N Well Serv., Inc., 639 P.2d 29, 33 UCCR 217 (1982); Gall v. Allegheny County Health Dept., 521 Pa. 68, 555 A.2d 786, 8 UCCR2d 379 (1989); Lariviere v. Dayton Safety Ladder Co., 525 A.2d 892, 4 UCCR2d 433 (R.I. 1987); Stover v. Eagle Prods., 896 F. Supp. 1085, 29 UCCR2d 789 (D. Kan. 1995); Miles v. Ford Motor Co., 922 S.W.2d 572, 30 UCCR2d 1097 (Tex. Ct. App. 1996).

A number of courts have seized upon this comment, and said that a particular purpose must be unusual,[611] peculiar,[612] or one not normally expected to be made of the goods.[613] If the courts mean by these various formulations that to be a "particular purpose" the buyer's purpose had to fall outside the "ordinary" purpose of the goods as envisioned by the merchantability warranty, the analysis would, at least, be easy, if not sound. If the buyer's use of the product was sufficiently unexpected or unforeseeable to fall outside the parameters of the section 2-314 warranty, it would be a "particular use" for purposes of section 2-315; otherwise, the buyer would be relegated to the merchantability warranty.[614] This, however, is often not what the courts have meant. To the contrary, in many cases in which the courts have sought to distinguish an "ordinary" purpose from a "particular" purpose and have found a "particular" purpose to exist, the buyer's intended use is nonetheless sufficiently "ordinary" to fall within the merchantability warranty. For example, in one case the court found that an insecticide used by the buyer to kill corn borer larvae was purchased for a particular purpose, even though it was one of only three insecticides on the market designed to kill the larvae of the corn borer. The court said that since the insecticide was also designed to kill many other bugs as well, killing the corn borer was a particular purpose.[615] In an even more striking case, a farmer was permitted to recover under section 2-315 when a milking machine gave his cows mastitis even though the machine was being used for the precise purpose for which it was designed.[616] Other examples exist of similar holdings.[617] The point at which a use becomes sufficiently unusual to become a "particular" use is inevitably left vague and uncertain by the courts.

In addition, whether a use of goods is "non-ordinary" or "unusual" will often depend upon how the goods are described or characterized. The

---

[611] See Crysco Oilfield Servs., Inc. v. Hutchison-Hayes Int'l, Inc., 913 F.2d 850, 12 UCCR2d 1019 (10th Cir. 1990); Unified Sch. Dist. No. 500 v. United States Gypsum Co., 788 F. Supp. 1173, 18 UCCR2d 97 (D. Kan. 1992); Agristor Leasing v. Meuli, 634 F. Supp. 1208, 1 UCCR2d 1102 (D. Kan. 1986).

[612] Duford v. Sears, Roebuck & Co., 833 F.2d 407, 4 UCCR2d 1374 (1st Cir. 1987); Durfee v. Murray Ohio Mfg. Co., 866 F. Supp. 1321, 25 UCCR2d 706 (D. Kan. 1994).

[613] Van Wyk v. Norden Labs., Inc., 345 N.W.2d 81, 37 UCCR 1489 (Iowa 1984).

[614] See Lowe v. Sporicidin Int'l, 47 F.3d 124, 26 UCCR2d 87 (4th Cir. 1995).

[615] Renze Hybrids, Inc. v. Shell Oil Co., 418 N.W.2d 634, 5 UCCR2d 1331 (Iowa 1988).

[616] C.E. Alexander & Sons, Inc. v. DEC Int'l, Inc., 811 P.2d 899 (N.M. 1991).

[617] See, e.g., Ingram River Equip., Inc. v. Pott Indus., Inc., 816 F.2d 1231, 3 UCCR2d 977 (8th Cir. 1987); Cohen v. Hathaway, 595 F. Supp. 579, 39 UCCR 857 (D. Mass. 1984); see also Van Wyk v. Norden Labs., Inc., 345 N.W.2d 81, 37 UCCR 1489 (Iowa 1984) (although particular purpose is one that is not normally expected to be made of the goods, in some cases the particular purpose will overlap with the ordinary purpose).

case of *Ingram River Equipment, Inc. v. Pott Industries, Inc.*[618] illustrates the problem. In this case, the buyer contracted with the seller to supply four barges for a total price of over $2,000,000. The contract provided that the barges would be fitted with steam coil systems for heating heavy liquid cargo. The barges were delivered, and shortly thereafter, splits, cracks, and leaks were discovered in all four barges. Eventually, the steam coils in all four barges had to be replaced. The buyer sued for damages using theories of strict liability in tort and breach of express warranty, the implied warranty of merchantability, and the implied warranty of fitness.[619] The trial court held that strict liability in tort was not available to the plaintiff and that the implied warranty of merchantability had been displaced by the express warranty in the contract that the barges would conform to the specifications in the contract documents. The court, however, found that the implied warranty of fitness was available to the buyer and had been breached, and awarded damages of $361,757.

On appeal, the seller argued that the use of the barges to heat and carry heavy petroleum (the buyer's specific use) was an ordinary use of the goods. Characterizing the barges as "heating-oil-equipped tank barges," the seller argued that others used comparably constructed barges in a similar manner. In fact, the seller had constructed some thirty similar barges that were being used to heat and haul heavy petroleum. The seller also argued that since the defect was in the pipe, "pipe" was the relevant description of the goods. Since the use of pipe in steam coil heating systems was an ordinary purpose of pipe, the warranty of fitness did not apply. The buyer, however, characterized the goods as simply "tank barges" and argued that the use of "tank barges" to heat and haul heavy petroleum was sufficiently unusual to be a particular, rather than an ordinary, purpose.

The court struggled mightily with the problem. It first attempted to distinguish an "ordinary" from a "particular' purpose. It said that the buyer's use did not have to be "one-of-a-kind" to be a particular purpose. Rather the inquiry was "whether the buyer's use is sufficiently different from the customary use of the goods to make it not an ordinary use of the goods; because a buyer's use is not entirely idiosyncratic does not mean that it is ordinary."[620] The court agreed with the parties, however, that this determination depended upon how the goods were characterized: if the goods were simply "tank barges," heating and hauling heavy petroleum was a

---

[618] 816 F.2d 1231, 3 UCCR2d 977 (8th Cir. 1987).

[619] Ingram River Equip., Inc. v. Pott Indus., Inc., 573 F. Supp. 896, 37 UCCR 88 (E.D. Mo. 1983).

[620] 816 F.2d at 1233, 3 UCCR2d at 981.

"particular use." On the other hand, if the goods were described as "heating-coil-equipped tank barges," then heating and hauling heavy petroleum was an "ordinary use." Referring to the Code Comments, the court said that the issue is whether the case is more like one in which a buyer goes to a general shoe store to buy mountain-climbing shoes or like one in which the buyer seeks mountain-climbing shoes in a mountain-climbing gear store. The best the court could do, however, to provide further guidance was to say that the line between an ordinary and a particular purpose was "uncertain" and had to be resolved on a case-by-case basis as a question of fact.[621]

The key to understanding and resolving the confusion concerning the scope of the fitness warranty is that the fitness warranty does not apply to *defective* goods. Rather, the fitness warranty applies only when the goods are *inappropriate* or *unsuitable*. Goods are "defective" when they are not reasonably fit for the purposes for which they were designed or for which they can reasonably be expected to be used.[622] Goods are "inappropriate" or "unsuitable" when they are fit for the purposes for which they were designed or would normally be used (i.e., they are merchantable), but they are *not suited* for the buyer's specific purpose. It is only the latter case that is within the scope of section 2-315.

Although this interpretation of section 2-315 has not been explicitly adopted by the cases, it is strongly suggested by the language of section 2-315 and by the Comments to the section. Section 2-315 requires that the buyer rely on the seller's skill and judgment to furnish *suitable* goods. While one might argue that goods can be unsuitable because they are defective, the normal understanding of the term "suitable" is "appropriate," rather than "non-defective."[623] Neither the text nor the Comments of section 2-315 give any indication that the section is intended to apply in cases of product defects. Furthermore, interpreting section 2-315 in this manner provides a clear and understandable conceptual distinction between the two warranties. Product defects are governed by the warranty of merchantability; product suitability is the province of the fitness warranty. Finally, there is no good reason that the fitness warranty should overlap the merchantability warranty with regard to product defects. If the warranty of merchantability has been successfully disclaimed, it is improper to permit the buyer to "end-

---

[621] 816 F.2d at 1234, 3 UCCR2d at 981.

[622] *See* § 4.06[B][3], *supra*.

[623] Webster's Ninth New Collegiate Dictionary 1180 (1983) defines "suitable" as "adapted to a use or purpose." It further defines the verb "suit" as "to be appropriate or satisfactory." These definitions support the interpretation of U.C.C. § 2-315 suggested in the text.

run" the disclaimer by relying on the fitness warranty.[624] Finally, there is no reason to expand warranty liability for product defects to nonmerchants through section 2-315. The drafters made a reasoned decision that the merchantability warranty was to be limited to merchants, as defined by the Code, and that liability of nonmerchants for product defects should be either through express warranty[625] or common-law theories, such as nondisclosure.[626]

Under this approach, the buyer in *Ingram* would not be permitted to recover under section 2-315. The goods were designed for the purpose to which they were put by the buyer. They failed to suit the buyer's purpose because they were *defective*, not unsuitable. The buyer should have been relegated to either an express warranty theory or the implied warranty of merchantability.[627]

A number of cases illustrate the proper application of section 2-315. In *O'Shea v. Hatch*,[628] the buyer desired to purchase a horse for his young daughter. He informed the seller that he wanted a horse with a suitable temperament and disposition for riding by children. The horse turned out to be aggressive and unsuitable for riding by children, and the court permitted a recovery on the basis of section 2-315.[629] The court's reliance on section 2-315 was proper. The horse was not defective; it was healthy and apparently could be ridden by adults. Rather, the horse was *inappropriate* for the particular use conveyed to the seller by the buyer. In *Lewis v. Mobil Oil Corp.*,[630] discussed previously,[631] the Ambrex 810 oil was not defective. Rather, because the buyer's hydraulic pump required a detergent oil and

---

[624] *See* Ingram River Equip., Inc. v. Pott Indus., Inc., 816 F.2d 1231, 3 UCCR2d 977 (8th Cir. 1987) (court permitted recovery for defective pipes under section 2-315 when merchantability warranty had been limited by express language of contract).

[625] *See* U.C.C. § 2-314, Official Comment 4.

[626] *See* U.C.C. § 2-314, Official Comment 3.

[627] The proposed revisions to Article 2 have not cleared up this difficulty. In fact, the Comments to proposed section 2-405 continue to mischaracterize the issue as whether a buyer's particular purpose can be an ordinary purpose for the goods. *See* Council Draft § 2-405.

[628] 97 N.M. 409, 640 P.2d 515, 33 UCCR 561 (Ct. App. 1982).

[629] The court could also have permitted recovery on the basis of express warranty as well. According to the court's opinion, the seller verbally assured the buyer that the horse was suitable for children. Also, the seller described the horse as a "gelding" when, in fact, it was a "ridgeling." A ridgeling is a horse from which only one testicle has been removed, whereas a gelding has had both testicles removed. This difference apparently accounted for the horse's aggressiveness.

[630] 438 F.2d 500, 8 UCCR 625 (8th Cir. 1971).

[631] *See* § 7.04[F][2].

Ambrex 810 was a nondetergent oil, it was *unsuitable*, and the court's application of section 2-315 was proper. In *Caldwell v. Brown Service Funeral Home*[632] a nondefective burial vault was, nonetheless, too small for the body of the buyer's son, and therefore, breached the section 2-315 warranty. Although close cases will remain,[633] if section 2-315 is confined to circumstances similar to these, the confusion over the scope of the warranty of fitness will largely disappear.

[2] Conclusion

All warranties require a close look at the facts of the bargain; the warranty of fitness requires an especially close look at those facts. Before the seller can be held liable, each of the prerequisites for the fitness warranty must be found: (1) the seller must have had reason to know of the buyer's particular purpose—the seller must have notice of the *specific* use to which the buyer intends to put the goods; (2) the seller must have reason to know that the buyer is relying on the seller's skill or judgment to furnish suitable goods; (3) the buyer must in fact rely upon the seller's skill and judgment to select suitable goods. If these conditions are met, but only if they are met, is there a warranty for the buyer's particular purpose.

III. WARRANTY DEFENSES

§ 4.07 LIMITATIONS ON AND THE EXCLUSION OF WARRANTIES

[A] Disclaimers—General

The law of sales is usually viewed as a specialized branch of the law of contracts. The law of contracts forms both a backdrop to the Code,[634] and many of the principles of contract law are embodied in the provisions

---

[632] 345 So. 2d 1341, 21 UCCR 999 (Ala. 1977). *See also* House v. Armour of Am., Inc., 886 P.2d 542, 26 UCCR2d 721 (Utah Ct. App. 1994) (bulletproof vest alleged to be unsuitable for SWAT team duties).

[633] Courts still have to determine the ordinary purpose of the goods, which is sometimes difficult. If the goods cannot perform their ordinary purpose, they are "defective," whether this failure to perform the purpose is due to a manufacturing defect or a design defect. *See* § 4.06[B][3], *supra*. If the defect is the reason the goods fail to satisfy the buyer, the U.C.C. § 2-315 warranty does not apply.

[634] *See* U.C.C. § 1-103 (supplementary general principles of law remain applicable unless displaced by particular provisions of the Code).

of Article 2.[635] Conversely, in a number of instances, Code concepts have been expanded to apply to the law of contracts generally,[636] and citations to the Code in the Restatement (Second) of Contracts abound.[637]

The traditional view of contract is that parties are free, within certain broad bounds, to work out the terms of their agreement, and the courts will do their best to give effect to the agreement. This approach explains the warranties in sales agreements. Express warranties rest on the dickered terms of the parties' "deal," and implied warranties rest on the reasonable expectations of the buyer about product quality and performance.

Warranty disclaimers spring from the same idea. Parties to an agreement should be free to allocate the risk of product quality and performance. They should be free to provide that the buyer is purchasing the goods in their present condition without any promises—express or implied—from the seller as to the quality of the goods. The parties should also be free to define the scope of any express or implied promises that are made. Consistent with this thesis, the Code includes a section permitting warranties to be excluded or modified.[638] This section (2-316) is divided into four subsections but is discussed in the text under three headings:

1. The disclaiming of express warranties.[639]
2. The disclaiming of implied warranties.[640]
3. The limitation of remedies for breach of warranty.[641]

[B]   Disclaimers—Express Warranties

Subsection (1) of section 2-316 provides:

> Words or conduct relevant to the creation of an express warranty and words or conduct tending to negate or limit warranty shall be construed wherever reasonable as consistent with each other; but subject to the provisions of this Article on parol or extrinsic evidence (Section 2-202)

---

[635] *See, e.g.*, U.C.C. §§ 2-204 (formation of contract in general); 2-206 (offer and acceptance in formation of contract); 2-302 (unconscionability); 2-615 (commercial impracticability).

[636] *See, e.g.*, Restatement of Contracts (Second) § 59 (incorporating principles of U.C.C. § 2-207).

[637] *See, e.g.*, Restatement of Contracts (Second) §§ 6, 18, 90, 209, 305 (1981).

[638] U.C.C. § 2-316.

[639] *See* § 4.07[B], *infra.*

[640] *See* § 4.07[C], *infra.*

[641] *See* § 4.08, *infra.*

negation or limitation is inoperative to the extent that such construction is unreasonable.

This subsection serves two principal functions. First, it provides a rule of interpretation for agreements which contain words (or conduct) that both create and negate or limit express warranties. The Code's command, not surprisingly, is to interpret these words as consistent whenever one can reasonably do so. For example, in *Paulson v. Olson Implement Co., Inc.,*[642] a general disclaimer of express and implied warranties printed on an unsigned proposal of the seller was held to apply only to standard items, not to the specially manufactured items ordered by the buyer; therefore, the disclaimer was not inconsistent with the seller's express warranties. The court in *Harris v. Ford Motor Co., Inc.*[643] found a provision permitting the manufacturer of automobiles to repair minor damage incurred in shipment to be consistent with an express warranty by description that the car was "new."[644] In a couple of cases, the courts have properly found "as is" disclaimers to apply only to implied, not express warranties.[645] The lesson is that disclaimers, as with other contract language, should be read in the context of the entire agreement and should be given the meaning that would be ascribed to them by reasonable people in light of that context.

The second function of section 2-316(1) is to state a rule of construction when attempts to interpret the agreement as consistent have failed. When such an impasse has been reached, the express warranty is given precedence over the disclaimer.[646] The effect of this provision is that if an express warranty is found, a conflicting disclaimer will be ineffective—express warranties, unlike implied warranties, cannot be disclaimed.[647]

---

[642] 107 Wisc. 2d 510, 319 N.W.2d 855, 34 UCCR 146 (1982).

[643] 845 F. Supp. 1511, 25 UCCR2d (M.D. Ala. 1994).

[644] *See also* Curry Motor Co., Inc. v. Hasty, 505 So. 2d 347, 3 UCCR2d 1373 (Ala. 1987) (description in bill of sale constitutes a warranty "specifically set forth in writing by an authorized representative of seller" as permitted by disclaimer and therefore consistent with the disclaimer); Ciba-Geigy Corp. v. Alter, 309 Ark. 426, 834 S.W.2d 136, 20 UCCR2d 448 (1992) (disclaimer not inconsistent with express warranty by advertising materials when buyer never saw ads); Pig Improvement Co., Inc. v. Middle States Holding Co., 943 F. Supp. 392, 31 UCCR2d 422 (D. Del. 1996) (express warranty "fit for breeding" limited by disclaimer provisions).

[645] Killion v. Buran Equip. Co., 27 UCCR 970 (Cal. Ct. App. 1979); Limited Flying Club, Inc. v. Wood, 632 F.2d 51, 29 UCCR 1497 (8th Cir. 1980).

[646] *See* Giarratano v. Midas Muffler, 630 N.Y.S.2d 656, 27 UCCR2d 87 (City Ct. 1995).

[647] *See* Tacoma Boatbuilding Co., Inc. v. Delta Fishing Co., Inc., 28 UCCR 26 (W.D. Wash. 1980); Providence & Worcester R.R. Co. v. Sargent & Greenleaf, Inc., 802 F. Supp. 680, 19 UCCR2d 21 (D.R.I. 1992); Murray v. D&J Motor Co., Inc., 35 UCCR2d 1177 (Okla. Civ. App. 1998).

The Code Comments make clear that a primary purpose of section 2-316(1) is to render ineffective those ubiquitous clauses in form contracts that attempt to disclaim "all warranties, express or implied." Comment 1 to section 2-316 says this explicitly:

> This section is designed principally to deal with those frequent clauses in sales contracts which seek to exclude "all warranties, express or implied." It seeks to protect a buyer from unexpected and unbargained language of disclaimer by denying effect to such language when inconsistent with language of express warranty and permitting the exclusion of implied warranties only by conspicuous language or other circumstances which protect the buyer from surprise.[648]

The idea expressed in this Comment is consistent with the Code's emphasis on the parties' bargain in fact. To be an express warranty, a promise, description, or affirmation of fact has to be part of the basis of the bargain— a buyer must have a reasonable expectation that the representation of the seller is part of the buyer's *deal* with the seller.[649] To allow a general disclaimer of "all warranties, express or implied" to negate these representations would be necessarily inconsistent with the understanding and expectations of the buyer that the representations are part of his bargain.

Many cases have applied this section in precisely the circumstances envisioned by the Comment.[650] An excellent example of the operation of

---

[648] U.C.C. § 2-316, Official Comment 1. Comment 1 to U.C.C. § 2-313 similarly provides:

> "Express" warranties rest on "dickered" aspects of the individual bargain, and go so clearly to the essence of that bargain that words of disclaimer in a form are repugnant to the basic dickered terms.

[649] *See* § 4.05[F], *supra.*

[650] *See, e.g.,* Berk v. Gordon Johnson Co., 232 F. Supp. 682, 2 UCCR 240 (E.D. Mich. 1964) (promise of "kosher operation" not negated by boilerplate disclaimer of express warranties); Realmuto v. Straub Motors, Inc., 65 N.J. 336, 322 A.2d 440, 15 UCCR 105 (1974) (printed boilerplate disclaimer of express warranties ineffective against language on face of contract providing thirty-day warranty); Fargo Mach. & Tool Co. v. Kearney & Trecker Corp., 428 F. Supp. 364, 21 UCCR 80 (E.D. Mich. 1977) (boilerplate disclaimer ineffective to negate express warranties made in promotional literature regarding performance of machine); Werner v. Gulf Oil Corp., 264 N.W.2d 374, 23 UCCR 603 (Minn. 1978) (printed disclaimer does not negate express warranty on label that herbicide would not "carry over" to subsequent years); Murray v. Holiday Rambler, 83 Wisc. 2d 406, 265 N.W.2d 513, 24 UCCR 52 (1978) (printed language that there are "no warranties express or implied" ineffective to disclaim language in same contract that motor home is free of defects in material and workmanship); Century Dodge, Inc. v. Mobley, 272 S.E.2d 502, 155 Ga. App. 712, 30

section 2-316(1) is *Mobile Housing Inc. v. Stone.*[651] In this case, the buyers of a mobile home visited the seller's sales lot numerous times before deciding on a purchase. On each occasion the salesman used a mobile home on the lot as a model of the one that he was trying to sell to the buyers, and represented that the home they would receive would be precisely like the model. After the buyers decided to purchase the home, the purchase contract described the home as the same model that had been shown to them on the lot and provided that it would be furnished "as displayed on lot as Ser. #103."

When the home arrived it was, to say the least, an unmitigated disaster and bore little resemblance to the model the buyers had been shown. Among many other things, the carpet was different from the model and of poor quality, the windows were configured differently from the model, the hardware was mismatched, the doors didn't fit, the draperies didn't fit, the roof leaked, and there was no furniture in the home! When the buyer sought to reject the home, the seller attempted to cure some of the defects, but refused to take the home back. The buyers sued for breach of warranty, relying on the model that had been shown to them and the representations of the salesman. The seller argued that any express warranties had been disclaimed by printed provisions in the Purchase Agreement that said:

> It is mutually agreed the buyer takes the new mobile home, trailer or other described unit, "as is" and that there are no warranties, either

---

UCCR 844 (Ga. Ct. App. 1980) (description of car as "new" prevails over disclaimer of express warranties in same document); Schlenz v. John Deere, 511 F. Supp. 224, 31 UCCR 1020 (D. Mont. 1981) (disclaimer in purchase order insufficient to overcome express safety representations in operator's manual); Deaton, Inc. v. Aeroglide Corp., 657 P.2d 109, 35 UCCR 130 (N.M. 1982) (representations made by sales literature, demonstration model, and contract itself not overcome by general disclaimer); Consolidated Data Terminals v. Applied Digital Data Sys., Inc., 708 F.2d 385, 36 UCCR 59 (9th Cir. 1983) (general disclaimer of express and implied warranties ineffective to overcome representations that computer would operate at a particular speed); Fundin v. Chicago Pneumatic Tool Co., 199 Cal. Rptr. 789, 38 UCCR 55 (Ca. Ct. App. 1984) (statements in sales brochure that drilling rig would dig to a certain depth not negated by general disclaimer in same brochure); Muther-Ballenger v. Griffin Elec. Consultants, Inc., 387 S.E.2d 297, 100 N.C. App. 505 (1990) (representation that CT scanner would perform quality diagnostic scanning not negated by printed general disclaimer on second page of contract); Providence & Worcester R.R. Co. v. Sargent & Greenleaf, Inc., 802 F. Supp. 780, 19 UCCR2d 21 (D.R.I. 1992) (representations made in promotional literature about performance of "switchlocks" not negated by general disclaimer on preprinted invoice); Snelten v. Schmidt Implement Co., 26 UCCR2d 1092 (Ill. App. Ct. 1995) (printed "as is" disclaimer ineffective to overcome specific, written, affirmative representation).

[651] 490 S.W.2d 611, 12 UCCR 235 (Tex. Civ. App. 1973).

express or implied, made by the dealer. The seller specifically makes no warranty as to its merchantability or its fitness for any purpose. . . .

It is further agreed that there have been no descriptions, samples or models used or regarded as part of this contract.[652]

Quoting extensively from section 2-316 and the Comments to sections 2-316 and 2-313, the court refused to give effect to the disclaimer. It said that the conclusion was "inescapable" that the buyer's decision to buy the home was induced by and based upon the inspection of the model, and the representations of the salesman that their home would be just like the model. According to the court, these were the "dickered" aspects of the bargain and could not be overcome by a printed disclaimer.[653]

Although express warranties cannot be disclaimed, a representation by the seller must *be* an express warranty before section 2-316(1) is applicable: that is, it must be (1) an affirmation of fact, promise, or description (or be a sample or model), and (2) part of the basis of the bargain. Language of disclaimer may be relevant to whether either of these criteria has been met.[654]

In a number of cases, language in the contract was material to determine whether a representation was a promise or affirmation of fact, or whether it was merely opinion or puffing, or otherwise aspirational in nature. In *U.S. Fibres, Inc. v. Proctor & Schwartz, Inc.*,[655] a conveyor was described in the purchase contract as "especially designed with a deflection tolerance of [plus or minus] 1/32" across each conveyor plate." When the conveyor failed to operate within this deflection tolerance, the buyer sued for breach of warranty. Despite the quoted language, the court found that no express warranty had been created by the quoted language. In addition to the language describing the deflection tolerance, the contract also contained two other provisions. The first stated that "in view of the variables present effecting (sic) the capacity of the machine, no guarantees can be extended." The second was a disclaimer of express and implied warranties except where the word "guarantee" was used. The court found that the buyer had scrutinized the contract with care and was familiar with its provisions. Further,

---

[652] *Id.* at 612, 12 UCCR at 237.

[653] *Id.* at 614, 12 UCCR at 238. For similar cases involving mobile homes *see* Bowen v. Young, 14 UCCR 403 (Tex. Civ. App. 1974); Jones v. Abriani, 350 N.E.2d 635, 19 UCCR 1102 (Ind. Ct. App. 1976); Jensen v. Seigel Mobile Homes Group, 668 P.2d 65, 35 UCCR 804 (Idaho 1983).

[654] *See* Tacoma Boatbuilding Co., Inc. v. Delta Fishing Co., 28 UCCR 26, 32 n.9 (W.D. Wash. 1980).

[655] 509 F.2d 1043, 16 UCCR 1 (6th Cir. 1975).

because the goods were experimental in nature, the court found that the buyer was fully aware of the nature of the "variables" referred to in the disclaimer. The court concluded that, as a result of the two disclaimer provisions the "language of description referred only to the expectations of the designer's and in no way guaranteed that these expectations would be met."[656]

The Code and Comments are clear that general or "form" disclaimers of express warranties will not prevent express warranties from arising from the seller's representations.[657] It is possible, however, for the parties to agree during the negotiating process that prior representations of the seller will not become part of the parties' final deal—will not be part of the basis of the bargain. In *Ray Martin Painting, Inc. v. Ameron, Inc.*,[658] a purchaser of paint sued the seller on the basis of representations made by the seller's agent and statements contained in advertising brochures. The seller's initial price quotation, however, had contained a large-print, conspicuous disclaimer of all warranties, except for a warranty against defects in material and workmanship.[659] More important, the buyer signed a specific "warranty agreement" proposed by the seller. In two different places in this warranty agreement there were prominent provisions stating that there were no warranties other than those in the agreement itself. Prior drafts of this agreement had been sent to the buyer, and the buyer had requested two wording changes that were agreed to by the seller.

The court properly found for the seller on the buyer's express warranty claims. Relying on Comment 1 to 2-316, the court said that the purpose of section 2-316(1) was to protect the buyer from unexpected and unbargained language of disclaimer, not to prevent him from making the bargain he

---

[656] 509 F.2d at 1046, 16 UCCR at 5. In a similar case, a physician's representation that an artificial hip prosthesis would last twenty years did not create an express warranty where the patient was aware of the experimental nature of the item. Furthermore, the patient had signed a consent form which described the prosthesis as experimental and stated that no assurances or guarantees could be made as to its benefits or long range durability. Flynn v. Biomet, Inc., 21 UCCR2d 580 (E.D. Va. 1993).

[657] U.C.C. § 2-316(1) and Official Comment 1; Official Comments 1 and 4 to U.C.C. § 2-313.

[658] 638 F. Supp. 768, 1 UCCR2d 713 (D. Kan. 1986).

[659] The seller's proposal also contained a provision—undoubtedly suggested by the seller's lawyer—that the buyer waived "the benefit of any rule that disclaimers of warranty or limitation of liability shall be construed against Seller" and further agreed "that the disclaimers and limitations applicable to this transaction shall be construed liberally in favor of Seller." This provision was not in the same large print as the disclaimer, and the court did not rely on the provision in its opinion. It is doubtful that such a provision would be given effect in a printed form contract.

wished to make. Where there is no great disparity in bargaining power, parties can make any deal with respect to warranties that they "consciously desire." Although the court did not say it in so many words, the language in the proposal and the warranty agreement had effectively precluded any representations, other than those contained in the documents, from becoming part of the basis of the bargain.[660]

The court in *Ray Martin* also relied upon the Code's parol evidence rule in holding for the seller. When a disclaimer and an express warranty are inconsistent, for purposes of section 2-316(1) it should not matter whether the express warranty is oral or written, or whether it preceded or was contemporaneous with the disclaimer.[661] If an express warranty is found to exist, the disclaimer is "inoperative under section 2-316." The section, however, also states that this result is subject to the Code's parol evidence rule. There is no difficulty when the disclaimer and the warranty are in the same documents or in contemporaneous documents;[662] in these cases the parol evidence rule is inapplicable. When the alleged warranty consists of a prior oral representation, however, the same problems in applying the parol evidence rule in other contexts, discussed in detail earlier,[663] are present in the warranty context as well.

As others have recognized,[664] there is a close connection between the requirements for the creation of an express warranty and the parol evidence rule.[665] Express warranties must be part of the basis of the bargain. This

---

[660] In Tacoma Boatbuilding Co., Inc. v. Duluth Fishing Co., 28 UCCR 26 (W.D. Wash. 1980) the court succinctly stated the same idea: "Although a seller cannot disclaim express warranties, a disclaimer may prevent an express warranty from arising in the first place. By making it unreasonable for the buyer to rely upon contrary quality representations, a disclaimer may keep those representations from becoming part of the basis of the bargain." 28 UCCR at 32 n.9. *See also* Middletown Concrete Prods., Inc. v. Black Clawson Co., 802 F. Supp. 1135, 1143, 20 UCCR2d 815, 827 n.8 (D. Del. 1992) (language in contract precluded representations in prior letter from becoming part of the basis of the bargain); Hauter v. Zogarts, 534 P.2d 377, 14 Cal. 3d 104, 16 UCCR 938 (Cal. 1975) (words of disclaimer give way to words of warranty unless some clear agreement between the parties dictates a contrary relationship; buyer must be put on fair notice and fairly agree to the seller's terms); Cuthbertson v. Clark Equip. Co., 448 A.2d 315, 34 UCCR 71 (Me. 1982) (disclaimer in combination with evidence that representation in owner's manual was not read by buyer precluded representation from becoming part of the basis of the bargain).

[661] Miller v. Hubbard-Wray Co., Inc., 52 Or. App. 897, 630 P.2d 880, 32 UCCR 1378 (Or. Ct. App. 1981).

[662] *See* Harris v. Ford Motor Co., 845 F. Supp. 1511, 25 UCCR2d 53 (M.D. Ala. 1994); Fleming Farms v. Dixie AG Supply, Inc., 631 So. 2d 922, 22 UCCR2d 1039 (Ala. 1994).

[663] *See* § 3.15, *supra.*

[664] *See* Thomas A. Crandall et al., I Uniform Commercial Code, 7:87–7:89 (1993).

[665] *See* Betaco, Inc. v. Cessna Aircraft Co., 103 F.3d 1281, 31 UCCR2d 1 (7th Cir. 1996).

means that the buyer must reasonably understand the seller's representations to be part of the final deal struck by the parties.[666] Otherwise, they are not part of the basis of the bargain. Similarly, with respect to oral representations, the parol evidence rule asks whether the parties intended the writing (which presumably contains a disclaimer) to be their final expression on the question of warranties. If they did, the disclaimer will be effective and the evidence of the oral representations will precluded by the rule.[667] One could say, however, that if the parties intended the writing containing the disclaimer to be their final expression on the question of warranties, the disclaimer has removed any prior representations from the bargain, and as a result, these representations are not warranties. Thus, where the issue is whether a prior oral representation can be the basis for recovery by a buyer, the inquiries under sections 2-313 and 2-202 converge.[668]

Unfortunately, most courts have not treated these two issues as involving the same fundamental inquiry. First, most courts treat the question of whether a warranty exists as an issue of fact,[669] while the issue of integration under the parol evidence rule has normally been treated as an issue for the court.[670] As a result, to recover on the basis of an oral representation in the face of a written disclaimer, a buyer must first convince the court that the writing was not intended as the final expression of the parties on the issue of warranties, and then (assuming the buyer is successful in overcoming the parol evidence rule) convince the factfinder that the representations were part of the basis of the bargain despite the disclaimer. Second, and more important, all of the differences and inconsistencies among courts in their application of the parol evidence rule, discussed in detail previously in the text,[671] are evident in the context of warranties as well.[672] As a result, some

---

[666] See § 4.05[F], *supra.*

[667] In an interesting twist, the court in O'Neill v. United States, 50 F.3d 677, 26 UCCR2d 1 (9th Cir. 1994) held that the parol-evidence rule barred evidence of an oral disclaimer to a warranty contained in the writing.

[668] See O'Neil v. International Harvester Co., 40 Colo. App. 369, 575 P.2d 862, 23 UCCR 1152 (Colo. Ct. App. 1978) (issue of fact whether oral warranties were made and whether a written contract was the final expression of the parties' agreement).

[669] Martin Rispens & Son v. Hall Farms, Inc., 621 N.E.2d 1078, 22 UCCR2d 89 (Ind. 1993); Providence & Worcester R.R. Co. v. Sargent & Greenleaf, Inc., 802 F. Supp. 680, 19 UCCR2d 21 (D.R.I. 1992); Husky Spray Serv., Inc. v. Patzer, 471 N.W.2d 146, 15 UCCR2d 772 (S.D. 1991).

[670] See § 3.15, *supra.*

[671] See § 3.15[B], *supra.*

[672] For example, the same tendency of some courts to give near conclusive effect to merger clauses is evident in warranty cases as well. *See, e.g.,* St. Croix Printing Equip., Inc. v. Rockwell Int'l Corp., 428 N.W.2d 877, 8 UCCR2d 1009 (Minn. Ct. App. 1988); King Indus.,

courts allow proof of oral warranties with relative ease,[673] while other cases have more stringently excluded proof of oral warranties.[674]

It would be better, as a few courts appear to have done,[675] simply to ask the question: has the seller made a promise, affirmation of fact, or description that the buyer would reasonably expect, under all of the circumstances—including perhaps the execution of a writing with a disclaimer—to be part of the buyer's deal? If a reasonable buyer would understand the deal to include the representation of the seller, then the representation is a part of the basis of the bargain. At the same time, because the buyer's reasonable understanding is that the representation survives the writing, the writing is not integrated, and the parol evidence rule does not prevent the introduction into evidence. On the other hand, if the buyer should not reasonably expect the representations to survive the writing, then the representations are not warranties—because they are not part of the basis of the bargain—and the writing is integrated with respect to the subject of warranties. This singular inquiry should resolve both the issue of parol evidence and the existence of an express warranty. It should normally be an issue of fact, unless there is insufficient credible evidence that the representation was made or that a reasonable buyer would expect it to survive the writing.

[C]   Disclaimers—Implied Warranties

The Code provides three methods by which implied warranties may be modified or excluded: (1) by explicit disclaimer language; (2) by the buyer's examining the goods or refusing to examine them; and (3) by a course of dealing, course of performance, or usage of trade.

Inc. v. Worlco Data Sys., Inc., 736 F. Supp. 114, 11 UCCR2d 1146 (E.D. Va. 1989); Quality Acceptance Corp. v. Million & Albers, Inc., 367 F. Supp. 771, 14 UCCR 78 (D. Wyo. 1973); FMC Corp. v. Seal Tape Ltd., Inc., 396 N.Y.S.2d 993, 22 UCCR 297 (N.Y. Sup. Ct. 1977).

[673] *See, e.g.,* Killion v. Buran Equip. Co., 970 UCCR 90 (Cal. Ct. App. 1979) (oral statements that truck engine was original equipment and had been overhauled admitted); Society Nat'l Bank v. Pemberton, 409 N.E.2d 1073, 30 UCCR 76 (Mun. Ct. Akron, Ohio); Art Hill, Inc. v. Heckler, 457 N.E.2d 242, 37 UCCR 697 (Ind. Ct. App. 1983); Husky Spray Serv., Inc. v. Patzer, 471 N.W.2d 146, 15 UCCR2d 772 (S.D. 1991) (applying North Dakota law).

[674] *See, e.g.,* Stephens v. Crittenden Tractor Co., 187 Ga. App. 545, 370 S.E.2d 757, 7 UCCR2d 724 (Ga. Ct. App. 1988); Travel Craft, Inc. v. Wilhelm Mende GMBH & Co., 534 N.E.2d 238, 9 UCCR2d 871 (Ind. Ct. App. 1989); King Indus., Inc. v. Worlco Data Sys., Inc., 736 F. Supp. 114, 11 UCCR2d 1146 (E.D. Va. 1989)

[675] *See, e.g.,* O'Neil v. International Harvester Co., 40 Colo. App. 369, 575 P.2d 862, 23 UCCR 1152 (Colo. Ct. App. 1978); Transamerica Oil Corp. v. Lynes, Inc., 723 F.2d 758, 37 UCCR 1076 (10th Cir. 1983).

[1] Explicit Disclaimer Language: Section 2-316(2)

Unlike express warranties, implied warranties can be excluded or disclaimed. That is, implied warranties can be excluded by appropriate contract language. Although express representations by the seller may be removed from the bargain by language of disclaimer, removal is a rare occurrence.[676] As described in the preceding section, when a buyer reasonably understands a seller's express representation to be part of his bargain, a disclaimer is ineffective.

The approach of the Code to implied warranties is considerably more formal. With the exception of a few cases discussed later, so long as the seller complies with the formal prerequisites of section 2-316, the court will not conduct a factual inquiry into the actual objective intent of the parties (i.e., whether the buyer, under all of the circumstances, reasonably understood the disclaimer to eliminate implied warranties). The Code drafters have taken this issue from the factfinder and *presumed* that if the seller complies with the requirements of section 2-316, a reasonable buyer will understand that implied warranties are excluded from the sale.

Subsections (2) and (3) of section 2-316 provide methods by which the seller can exclude implied warranties by explicit language. Subsection (2) provides:

> Subject to subsection (3), to exclude or modify the implied warranty of merchantability or any part of it the language must mention merchantability and in case of a writing must be conspicuous, and to exclude or modify any implied warranty of fitness the exclusion must be by a writing and conspicuous. Language to exclude all implied warranties of fitness is sufficient if it states, for example, that "There are no warranties which extend beyond the description on the face hereof."[677]

The first point to notice is that the implied warranty of merchantability cannot be excluded by the ubiquitous language disclaiming "all warranties express or implied," or similar general language.[678] To disclaim the implied

---

[676] *See* § 4.07[B], *supra*.

[677] U.C.C. § 2-316(2).

[678] *See* Providence & Worcester R.R. v. Sargent & Greenleaf, Inc., 802 F. Supp. 680, 19 UCCR2d 21 (D.R.I. 1992); Richard O'Brien Co. v. Challenge-Cook Bros., Inc., 672 F. Supp. 466, 5 UCCR2d 73 (D. Colo. 1987); S-C Indus. v. American Hydroponics Sys., Inc., 468 F.2d 852, 11 UCCR 937 (5th Cir. 1972); Lecates v. Hertrich Pontiac Buick Co., 515 A.2d 163, 2 UCCR2d 865 (Del. Super. 1986); McCormick Mach., Inc. v. Julian E. Johnson & Sons, Inc., 523 So. 2d 651, 7 UCCR2d 51 (Fla. Dist. Ct. App. 1988). *But see* Recreatives, Inc. v. Myers, 67 Wis. 2d 255, 226 N.W.2d 474, 16 UCCR 1258 (Wis. Super. 1975) (holding,

warranty of merchantability under section 2-316(2), the word "merchantability" must be used, and courts have adhered to this requirement.[679] Further, to exclude the merchantability warranty through a writing,[680] the exclusion must be conspicuous. The warranty of fitness must be disclaimed in writing but, unlike the merchantability warranty, may be disclaimed through the use of general language of disclaimer;[681] it is not necessary to mention "fitness" or "the warranty of fitness." To exclude the warranty of fitness, however, even general language should make clear that *implied warranties* are being disclaimed. For example, in the case of *Auto-Teria, Inc. v. Ahern*,[682] the court found the language "THERE IS NO MAGIC implied" insufficient to disclaim the fitness warranty.[683] In addition, whenever there is an implied warranty of fitness, there are likely to be express warranties as well. Express warranties, as we have seen,[684] cannot be disclaimed by general disclaimers.

---

without discussion, that phrase "no other warranty, whether express or implied, shall exist" sufficient to disclaim warranty of merchantability).

[679] *See* Soo Line R.R. v. Fruehauf Corp., 547 F.2d 1365, 20 UCCR 1181 (8th Cir. 1977) (disclaimer must mention "merchantability" even in contract between two large commercial entities); Potler v. MCP Facilities Corp., 471 F. Supp. 1344, 26 UCCR 651 (E.D.N.Y. 1979); Curtis v. Murphy Elevator Co., 407 F. Supp. 940, 19 UCCR 145 (E.D. Tenn. 1976); Orrox Corp. v. Rexnord, Inc., 389 F. Supp. 441, 16 UCCR 354 (M.D. Ala. 1975); Brunsman v. DeKalb Swine Breeders, Inc., 138 F.3d 358, 35 UCCR2d 69 (8th Cir. 1998). *But see* Roto-Lith, Ltd. v. F.P. Bartlett & Co., 297 F.2d 497, 1 UCCR 73 (1st Cir. 1962) (court permitted language "all goods sold without warranties, express or implied," to disclaim warranty of merchantability). It is possible that the court in *Roto-Lith* believed the disclaimer language was effective under U.C.C. § 2-316(3)(a), rather than section 2-316(2). *See* § 4.07[C][2], *infra*. However, to permit such general language to exclude the implied warranty of merchantability under section 2-316(3)(a) would severely undercut, if not completely emasculate, the requirement of section 2-316(2) that a disclaimer of the implied warranty of merchantability mention the term "merchantability."

[680] Unlike the U.C.C. § 2-315 warranty of fitness, the warranty of merchantability can be orally disclaimed. The authors have found no cases involving an alleged oral disclaimer of the implied warranty of merchantability under section 2-316(2). There are rare cases of asserted oral disclaimers under section 2-316(3). *See* Regan Purchase & Sales Corp. v. Primavera, 68 Misc. 2d 858, 328 N.Y.S.2d 490, 10 UCCR 300 (Civ. Ct. 1972).

[681] *See* McDermott, Inc. v. Clyde Iron, 979 F.2d 1068, 19 UCCR2d 465 (5th Cir. 1992); Richard O'Brien Co. v. Challenge-Cook Bros., Inc., 672 F. Supp. 466, 5 UCCR2d 73 (D. Colo. 1987). Under the proposed revisions to Article 2, to disclaim the implied warranty of fitness in nonconsumer contracts the disclaimer must state that "the goods are not warranted to be fit for any particular purpose" or words of "similar import." Council Draft § 2-406(d) (2).

[682] 170 Ind. App. 84, 352 N.E.2d 774, 20 UCCR 336 (1976).

[683] *See also* Clements Farms, Inc. v. Ben Fish & Son, 120 Idaho 209, 814 P.2d 941, 15 UCCR 2d 785 (Ct. App. 1990).

[684] *See* § 4.07[B], *supra*.

Section 2-316(2) makes it relatively easy for sellers to disclaim the implied warranties of merchantability and fitness. There is, however, a limitation built into the section: the written disclaimer must be "conspicuous." This word is defined in section 1-201(10):

> "Conspicuous": A term or clause is conspicuous when it is so written that a reasonable person against whom it is to operate ought to have noticed it. A printed heading in capitals (as: NON-NEGOTIABLE BILL OF LADING) is conspicuous. Language in the body of a form is "conspicuous" if it is in larger or other contrasting type or color. But in a telegram any stated term is "conspicuous." Whether a term or clause is "conspicuous" or not is for decision by the court.[685]

The conspicuousness of disclaimers has been an issue in hundreds of reported cases. This undoubtedly results from sellers trying to make the disclaimer just conspicuous enough to satisfy section 2-316, but not sufficiently conspicuous so that the buyer's attention will actually be drawn to it.[686] Courts have generally focused on the examples in section 1-201(10), and provisions that are in larger type than surrounding material or in a different color usually pass muster,[687] while those that are in the same type and same color do not.[688] Contrasting color or type, however, are not absolute require-

---

[685] U.C.C. § 1-201(10).

[686] *See* Pestigiacomo v. Crane & Clark Lumber Corp., 9 UCCR 1367 (N.Y. Sup. Ct. 1971) (printing the word "NOTE" in large letters attempts to meet letter of the law while circumventing its intent).

[687] *See, e.g.*, Myrtle Beach Pipeline Corp. v. Emerson Elec. Co., 843 F. Supp. 1027, 23 UCCR2d 683 (D.S.C. 1993); Investors Premium Corp. v. Burroughs Corp., 389 F. Supp. 39, 17 UCCR 115 (D.S.C. 1974); Fleming Farms v. Dixie AG Supply, Inc., 631 So. 2d 922, 22 UCCR2d 1039 (Ala. 1994); Fincher v. Robinson Bros. Lincoln-Mercury Inc., 583 So. 2d 256, 15 UCCR2d 1197 (Ala. 1991); Willis v. West Ky. Feeder Pig Co., 132 Ill. App. 2d 266, 265 N.E.2d 899, 8 UCCR 1010 (1971); Bakal v. Burroughs Corp., 74 Misc. 2d 202, 343 N.Y.S.2d 541, 13 UCCR 60 (Sup. Ct. 1972). B*ut see* Lutz Farms v. Asgrow Seed Co., 948 F.2d 638, 15 UCCR2d 1167 (10th Cir. 1991) (disclaimer in different color not conspicuous where size of print is "minute").

[688] *See, e.g.*, Holcomb v. Cessna Aircraft Co., 439 F.2d 1150, 8 UCCR 992 (5th Cir. 1971); Boeing Airplane Co. v. O'Malley, 329 F.2d 585, 2 UCCR 110 (8th Cir. 1964); Office Supply Co. v. Basic/Four Corp., 538 F. Supp. 776, 34 UCCR 857 (E.D. Wis. 1982) (disclaimer on reverse side of document not conspicuous even though italicized); Neville Chem. Co. v. Union Carbide Corp., 5 UCCR 1219 (W.D. Pa. 1968); Sawyer v. Pioneer Leasing Corp., 244 Ark. 943, 428 S.W.2d 46, 5 UCCR 453 (1968); Tennessee Carolina Transp., Inc. v. Strick Corp., 16 N.C. App. 498, 192 S.E.2d 702, 11 UCCR 970 (1972) (applying Pennsylvania law); Lacks v. Bottled Gas Corp. of Va., 215 Va. 94, 205 S.E.2d 671, 14 UCCR 1275 (1974) (disclaimer not conspicuous, even though underlined, when in same size and color print as rest of document). *But see* Richard O'Brien Co. v. Challenge-Cook Bros., Inc.,

ments for conspicuousness, and there are occasional cases in which courts have determined disclaimers to be conspicuous when not in contrasting color or type.[689] Although courts have usually determined that a disclaimer that is *smaller* or *lighter* than the other provisions is not conspicuous,[690] this should not be a hard-and-fast rule.[691]

---

672 F. Supp. 466, 5 UCCR2d 73 (D. Colo. 1987) (fact that disclaimer was indented sufficient to make it conspicuous between commercial buyer and commercial seller).

[689] *See, e.g.*, Richard O'Brien Co. v. Challenge-Cook Bros., Inc., 672 F. Supp. 466, 5 UCCR2d 73 (D. Colo. 1984); Clements Farms, Inc. v. Ben Fish & Son, 123 Idaho 185, 814 P.2d 917, 15 UCCR2d 799 ((Idaho 1991) (disclaimer conspicuous when located in middle of front page immediately below letterhead and set off by indentation); Houck v. DeBonis, 38 Md. App. 85, 379 A.2d 765, 23 UCCR 60 (1977) (disclaimer only provision underscored); Ventura v. Ford Motor Co., 180 N.J. Super. 45, 433 A.2d 801, 32 UCCR 57 (1981) (court assumes that disclaimer set off in rectangular block with lined borders is conspicuous); Zicar v. Joseph Harris Co., 33 A.D.2d 17, 304 N.Y.S.2d 918, 6 UCCR 1246 (App. Div. 1969) (disclaimer is only print in paragraph form and placed immediately before handwritten order); Sherman v. Manhattan Ford Lincoln-Mercury, Inc., 104 Misc. 2d 1, 431 N.Y.S.2d 949, 30 UCCR 479 (Sup. Ct. 1980) (disclaimer set off in separate box directly above signature line).

[690] *See* DeLamar Motor Co. v. White, 249 Ark. 708, 460 S.W.2d 802, 8 UCCR 437 (1970) (smaller and lighter print not conspicuous even though italicized); Geo. C. Christopher & Son, Inc. v. Kansas Paint & Color Co., 215 Kan. 185, 523 P.2d 709, 14 UCCR 1256 (1974); Basic Adhesives, Inc. v. Robert Matzkin Co., Inc., 29 UCCR 499 (N.Y. App. Term 1980); Stauffer Chem. Co. v. Curry, 778 P.2d 1083, 10 UCCR2d 342 (Wyo. 1989). *But see* Clements Farms, Inc. v. Ben Fish & Son, 120 Idaho 185, 814 P.2d 917, 15 UCCR2d 799 (1991) (disclaimer in smaller type conspicuous).

[691] Consider the following warranty:

> 1. *Limited Warranty*. Seller warrants that the goods supplied hereunder will conform to the description herein, that it will convey good title to such goods free from any security interest unknown to Customer, and that such goods will be free from defects in material or workmanship when delivered to Customer.

> *SELLER MAKES NO WARRANTIES, EXPRESS OR IMPLIED (INCLUDING, WITHOUT LIMITATION, MERCHANTABILITY, FITNESS FOR PARTICULAR PURPOSE, OR AGAINST INFRINGEMENT OF ANY PATENT), EXCEPT AS EXPRESSLY PROVIDED HEREIN. THIS LIMITED WARRANTY CONSTITUTES CUSTOMER'S SOLE AND EXCLUSIVE REMEDY UNDER THIS CONTRACT, OR OTHERWISE, AND SELLER DISCLAIMS ALL LIABILITY IN TORT OR IN STRICT LIABILITY.*

> 2. If the goods supplied to Customer do not conform to the limited warranty set out above, Seller will, at its option, (a) repair the defective goods, (b) replace the defective goods, or (c) refund so much of the purchase price as Customer has paid for the defective goods, provided that written notice of the defect and its nature is given to Seller as soon as practical after discovery of

The conspicuous print must indicate that the provision is a *disclaimer* or *limitation* on warranties.[692] It is not sufficient, for example, that the word "WARRANTY" is capitalized, if the remainder of the provision disclaiming implied warranties is in regular print,[693] or, as International Harvester learned the hard way, if only the term "MERCHANTABILITY" or "FITNESS FOR A PARTICULAR PURPOSE" is highlighted.[694] The placement of the disclaimer near the signature line has been cited by a number of courts as relevant to the conspicuousness of a disclaimer,[695] although placing the dis-

---

the defect, but in no even later than 90 days from the date of shipment by Seller.

The attention of most people would probably be drawn first to the boxed, capitalized, italicized print even though it is in smaller type. The illustration in section 1-201(10) that larger or contrasting type makes the language conspicuous is an example—not a requirement. A disclaimer in the same size type, not capitalized or contrasting, might be conspicuous in a negotiated agreement. The test is whether a reasonable person against whom it is to operate would have noticed the provision.

[692] *See* U.S. Steel Corp. v. Fiberex, Inc., 751 S.W.2d 628, 6 UCCR2d 1438 (Tex. Ct. App. 1988) (capitalization of "IMPORTANT NOTICE TO PURCHASER" insufficient to make disclaimer in small print conspicuous).

[693] *See* Greenspun v. Amercian Adhesives, Inc., 8 UCCR 439 (E.D. Pa. 1970) (word "WARRANTIES" capitalized); Mack Trucks of Ark., Inc. v. Jet Asphalt & Rock Co., 246 Ark. 101, 437 S.W.2d 459, 6 UCCR 93 (Ark. 1969) (conspicuous titles that do not suggest exclusions or modifications of implied warranties do not satisfy U.C.C. § 1-201(10); Blankenship v. Northtown Ford, Inc., 95 Ill. App. 3d 303, 420 N.E.2d 167, 50 Ill. Dec. 850, 31 UCCR 480 (1981) (disclaimer titled "Factory Warranty" misleading and therefore not in compliance with section 2-316); Massey-Ferguson, Inc. v. Utley, 439 S.W.2d 57, 6 UCCR 51 (Ky. Ct. App. 1969) (capitalization of the words "WARRANTY AND AGREEMENT" not sufficient to meet requirement of conspicuousness); Latimer v. William Mueller & Son, Inc., 868 P.2d 21, 386 N.W.2d 618, 1 UCCR2d 1128 (capitalized word "WARRANTY" not sufficient for conspicuous disclaimer); Gindy Mfg. Corp. v. Cardinale Trucking Corp., 111 N.J. Super. 383, 268 A.2d 345, 7 UCCR 1257 (1970) (single word "WARRANTIES" printed in capital letters insufficient to satisfy section 1-201(10); Victor v. Mammana, 101 Misc. 2d 954, 422 N.Y.S.2d 350, 27 UCCR 1295 (Sup. Ct. 1979) (word "WARRANTY" printed in capital letters insufficient); Northwest Pine Prods., Inc. v. Cummins Northwest, Inc., 126 Or. App. 219, 22 UCCR2d 996 (1994) (disclaimer entitled "WARRANTY" not conspicuous). *But see* Marion Audiovisual Prods., Inc. v. Eastman Kodak Co., 487 F. Supp. 371, 28 UCCR 1020 (N.D. Ohio 1980) (small-print disclaimer conspicuous when introduced by conspicuous language stating "READ THIS NOTICE").

[694] *See* International Harvester Co. v. Pike, 249 Ark. 1026, 466 S.W.2d 901, 10 UCCR 1164 (1971); Dorman v. International Harvester Co., 46 Cal. App. 3d 11, 120 Cal. Rptr. 516, 16 UCCR 952 (1975); Adams Van Serv., Inc. v. International Harvester Corp., 14 UCCR 1142 (Pa. C.P. 1973).

[695] *See, e.g.,* King Indus., Inc. v. Worldco Data Sys., Inc., 736 F. Supp. 114, 11 UCCR2d 1146 (E.D. Va. 1989); United Van Lines v. Hertze Penske Truck Leasing, Inc., 710 F. Supp. 283, 8 UCCR2d 1024 (W.D. Wash. 1989); J&W Equip., Inc. v. Weingartner, 5 Kan. App.

claimer close to the signature line is probably not enough, by itself, to satisfy the conspicuousness requirement.[696]

A substantial number of cases have dealt with the issue of a disclaimer on the *back* of a form, and the holdings are not entirely compatible. A number of courts have cited the placement of a disclaimer on the reverse side of a form as a factor militating against conspicuousness.[697] The courts have also said, however, that placement on the reverse side of a document does not *per se* make a disclaimer inconspicuous.[698] A typical case is *Childers & Venters, Inc. v. Sowards*.[699] In this case, the seller sold a used truck to the buyer on an installment basis. The buyer ceased making payments on the note (which had been negotiated by the seller to a bank) and the seller, after paying the bank, sued the buyer. The buyer defended and counterclaimed on the basis that the truck was defective and the seller had breached the implied warranty of merchantability. The seller argued that the warranty of merchantability was disclaimed on the reverse side of the conditional sales contract. The disclaimer was in larger and heavier type and would clearly have been conspicuous had it been on the face of the contract. On the face of the contract, however, in regular print, was the language "The undersigned seller hereby sells, and the undersigned buyer or buyers, jointly and severally, hereby purchase(s), subject to the terms and conditions set forth below and upon the reverse side hereof, the following property." The words "upon the reverse side hereof" were in darker print than the remainder of the sentence.

2d 466, 618 P.2d 862, 31 UCCR 866 (1980); Lytle v. Roto Lincoln Mercury & Subaru, Inc., 167 Ill. App. 3d 508, 521 N.E.2d 201, 118 Ill. Dec. 133, 7 UCCR2d 1091 (1988).

[696] *See* Agristor Leasing v. Guggisberg, 617 F. Supp. 902, 41 UCCR 1671 (D. Minn. 1985); Lupa v. Jock's, 131 Misc. 2d 536, 500 N.Y.S.2d 962, 1 UCCR2d 724 (City Ct. 1986).

[697] *See, e.g.*, Jaskey Fin. & Leasing v. Display Data Corp., 564 F. Supp. 160, 36 UCCR 26 (E.D. Pa. 1983); Massey-Ferguson, Inc. v. Utley, 439 S.W.2d 57, 6 UCCR 51 (Ky. Ct. App. 1969); P.E.A.C.E. Corp. v. Oklahoma Natural Gas Co., 568 P.2d 1273, 22 UCCR 654 (Okla. 1977); Salov v. Don Allen Chevrolet Co., 10 UCCR 996 (Pa. C.P. 1971).

[698] *See* Winter Panel Corp. v. Reichhold Chems., Inc., 823 F. Supp. 963, 21 UCCR2d 533 (D. Mass. 1993); Cline v. Allis-Chalmers Corp., 690 S.W.2d 764, 41 UCCR 430 (Ky. Ct. App. 1985); Bartelt Aviation, Inc., v. Dry Lake Coal Co., 682 S.W.2d 796, 40 UCCR 112 (Ky. Ct. App. 1985); Childers & Venters, Inc. v. Sowards, 460 S.W.2d 343, 8 UCCR 433 (Ky. Ct. App. 1970); McJunkin v. Kaufman & Broad Home Sys., Inc., 229 Mont. 432, 748 P.2d 910, 5 UCCR2d 1341 (1987); Brown v. Range Rover of N. Am., Inc., 24 UCCR2d 418 (Va. Cir. Ct. 1993). *But see* Borden, Inc. v. Advent Ink. Co., 701 A.2d 255, 33 UCCR2d 975 (Pa. Super. Ct. 1997) (as a matter of law disclaimer on the back of invoice not conspicuous).

[699] 460 S.W.2d 343, 8 UCCR 433 (Ky. Ct. App. 1970).

Despite the fact that the notation on the front of the contract may not have been conspicuous, the court held that the disclaimer nonetheless satisfied section 1-201(10). It said that the drafters of the Code knew that commercial institutions customarily use both sides of the paper for form contracts. If they had intended that a disclaimer must appear on the face of the contract or the same page as the signature line, they could have so provided. The court distinguished an earlier case from the same court[700] on the basis that not only was the disclaimer in the earlier case on the reverse side, but it was in the same size print and type face as the rest of the contract.[701]

There are a number of cases, similar to *Childers*, in which a conspicuous disclaimer on the reverse side of a contract is accompanied by nonconspicuous language on the front of the contract directing the buyer to terms and conditions on the back. The results of these cases are mixed, with some courts upholding the disclaimer,[702] while other courts do not.[703] To

---

[700] Massey-Ferguson, Inc. v. Utley, 439 S.W.2d 57, 6 UCCR 51 (Ky. Ct. App. 1969).

[701] The court did not mention that the disclaimer in the earlier case did have a heading in all capital letters entitled "WARRANTY AND AGREEMENT." *See* 439 S.W.2d at 58, 6 UCCR at 53.

[702] *See, e.g.*, Winter Panel Corp. v. Reichhold Chems., Inc., 823 F. Supp. 963, 21 UCCR2d 533 (D. Mass. 1993) (conspicuous disclaimer on back upheld; reference on face of contract to terms on reverse side in normal print); Jaskey Fin. & Leasing v. Display Data Corp., 564 F. Supp. 160, 36 UCCR 26 (E.D. Pa. 1983) (conspicuous disclaimer on reverse side upheld where reference on the front of the contract to terms on reverse side was immediately above signature line); Thermo King Corp. v. Strick Corp., 467 F. Supp. 75, 26 UCCR 50 (W.D. Pa. 1979) (conspicuous disclaimer on back upheld in view of language on front stating "see reverse side for warranty"); Bowers Mfg., Inc. v. Chicago Mach. Tool Co., 117 Ill. App. 3d 226, 453 N.E.2d 61, 72 Ill. Dec. 756, 37 UCCR 103 (1983) (conspicuous disclaimer on reverse side OK where front of contract has provision saying "complete warranty terms on reverse"); Houck v. DeBonis, 38 Md. App. 85, 379 A.2d 765, 23 UCCR 60 (1977) (conspicuous disclaimer on reverse side upheld where reference on front to additional terms and conditions was above signature line); Wagaman v. Don Warner Chevrolet-Buick, Inc., 17 Pa. D.&C. 3d 572, 31 UCCR 1604 (Pa. C.P. 1981) (conspicuous disclaimer on back upheld although reference on face of contract to terms on reverse side was in ordinary print).

There are also a number of cases where disclaimers on the reverse side of forms were upheld even though there apparently was *no* reference on the front to terms on the reverse side, or at least the court made no reference to such language. *See* H.B. Fuller Co. v. Kenetic Sys., Inc., 932 F.2d 681, 14 UCCR2d 1080 (7th Cir. 1991); Beal v. General Motors Corp., 12 UCCR 78 (D. Del. 1972); Web Press Servs. Corp. v. New London Motors, Inc., 203 Conn. 342, 525 A.2d 57, 3 UCCR2d 1386 (1987); Nordberg, Inc. v. Sylvester Material Co., 101 Ohio App. 3d 89, 654 N.E.2d 1358 (1995).

[703] *See* Agristor Leasing v. Guggisberg, 617 F. Supp. 902, 41 UCCR 1671 (D. Minn. 1985) (conspicuous disclaimer on reverse side insufficient where front of contract does not refer to disclaimers and merely says that conditions of sale are on reverse side); Bodine

some extent, these results are case specific, turning on such things as the location of the reference to the terms on the reverse side (e.g., whether it is near the signature line),[704] or the specific language of the reference to the reverse side (e.g., whether it specifically mentions warranties or disclaimers).[705] Some generalizations, however, can be made when disclaimers appear on the reverse side of forms. First, simply placing a disclaimer on the reverse side creates a risk of having that disclaimer declared ineffective by a court, even though it is clearly conspicuous standing by itself (i.e., it is in larger print or a different color). Second, when a place for the buyer to sign the agreement is also located on the reverse side, courts treat the disclaimers as if they were on the front of the contract.[706] Third, placing the disclaimer on the reverse side of the contract or other document will almost always cause the court to examine more closely the conspicuousness of the disclaimer. Even courts which have upheld such disclaimers have repeatedly said that location on the reverse side is a factor in determining whether a disclaimer is conspicuous.[707] Finally, a substantial number of courts have stated that the standards for conspicuousness are higher when the buyer is

---

Sewer, Inc. v. Eastern Ill. Precast, Inc., 143 Ill. App. 3d 920, 493 N.E.2d 705, 97 Ill. Sec. 898, 1 UCCR2d 1480 (1986) (disclaimer on reverse side not conspicuous where small print on front says contract is subject to "standard conditions of sale"); Anderson v. Farmers Hybrid Co., Inc., 87 Ill. App. 3d 493, 408 N.E.2d 1194, 42 Ill. Dec. 485, 29 UCCR 1264 (1980) (disclaimer on reverse side of order confirmation slip not sufficient where small print on front said merely that contract was subject to terms and conditions on back); Krupp PM Eng'g, Inc. v. Honeywell, Inc., 209 Mich. App. 104, 530 N.W.2d 146, 26 UCCR2d 742 (1995) (disclaimer on reverse side not conspicuous when reference on front to conditions on back of form in small italicized print). *See also* Salov v. Don Allen Chevrolet Co., 10 UCCR 996 (Pa. C.P. 1971) (disclaimer on reverse side in only slightly larger print and only a shade darker not conspicuous where front of form is in small print and refers only generally to terms on back); Williams v. College Dodge, Inc., 11 UCCR 958 (Mich. Dist. Ct. 1972) (conspicuous disclaimer on reverse side does not satisfy U.C.C. § 1-201(10) where reference on front not conspicuous).

[704] *See, e.g.,* Rudy's Glass Constr. Co. v. E. F. Johnson Co., 404 So. 2d 1087, 32 UCCR 1373 (Fla. Dist. Ct. App. 1981); Houck v. DeBonis, 38 Md. App. 85, 379 A.2d 765, 23 UCCR 60 (1977).

[705] *See, e.g.,* Bowers Mfg. Co. v. Chicago Mach. Tool Co., 117 Ill. App. 3d 226, 453 N.E.2d 61, 72 Ill. Dec. 756, 37 UCCR 103 (1983) (reference on front was to "complete warranty contract" on reverse side).

[706] *See* Myers v. A.O. Smith Harvestone Prods., Inc., 114 Idaho 432, 757 P.2d 695, 6 UCCR2d 1467 (Ct. App. 1988).

[707] *See* cases cited at *supra* note 705.

a consumer than when the buyer is a commercial entity.[708] Consequently, a disclaimer on the reverse side is more likely to be effective against a business buyer than a consumer.[709] This distinction is entirely proper, because section 1-201(10) defines conspicuousness as "so written that a reasonable person *against whom it is to operate* ought to have noticed it."[710]

The reverse situation—where the reference on the front of the form is conspicuous but the disclaimer on the reverse side is not—has also generated some litigation. For example, in *Deaton, Inc. v. Aeroglide Corp.*,[711] the court held that a disclaimer was conspicuous when a statement in all capitals on the front of the form stated that the contract was "SUBJECT TO ALL THE CONDITIONS PRINTED ON THE BACK" despite the fact that the disclaimer on the back was in the same type and size as nine other printed paragraphs on the reverse side.[712] In contrast, in *Norman Gerghman's Things*

---

[708] *See, e.g.*, L.S. Heath & Son, Inc. v. AT&T Info. Sys., Inc., 9 F.3d 561, 22 UCCR2d 27 (7th Cir. 1993); R&L Grain Co. v. Chicago E. Corp., 531 F. Supp. 201, 33 UCCR 532 (N.D. Ill. 1981); Tribble Trucking Co. v. General Motors Corp., 14 UCCR 63 (N.D. Ga. 1973); Avenell v. Westinghouse Elec. Corp., 41 Ohio App. 2d 150, 324 N.E.2d 583, 16 UCCR 671 (1974).

[709] *See, e.g.*, H.B. Fuller Co. v. Kinetic Sys., Inc., 932 F.2d 681, 14 UCCR2d 1080 (7th Cir. 1991); Myrtle Beach Pipeline Corp. v. Emerson Elec. Co., 843 F. Supp. 1027, 23 UCCR2d 683 (D.S.C. 1993); Logan Equip. Corp. v. Simon Aerials, Inc., 736 F. Supp. 1188, 12 UCCR2d 387 (D. Mass. 1990).

One court has even gone so far as to suggest in dicta that where commercial parties are involved, it is irrelevant whether a disclaimer is conspicuous. Ray Martin Printing, Inc. v. Ameron, Inc., 638 F. Supp. 768, 1 UCCR2d 713 (D. Kan. 1986). In Sierra Diesel Injection Serv., Inc. v. Burroughs Corp., 874 F.2d 653, 8 UCCR2d 617 (9th Cir. 1989), the court found that a disclaimer located on the reverse side of a document did not satisfy U.C.C. § 1-201(10) even though it was printed in bold type in all capital letters and a conspicuous reference on the front indicated that the terms on the back contained a limitation of liability and warranty terms. The court emphasized that the buyer, although an experienced businessman, was not an expert in computers (the subject matter of the contract) or contracts.

[710] U.C.C. § 1-201(10) (emphasis added).

[711] 99 N.M. 253, 657 P.2d 109, 35 UCCR 130 (1982).

[712] *See* Logan Equip. Corp. v. Simon Aerials, Inc., 736 F. Supp. 1188, 12 UCCR2d 387 (D. Mass. 1990) (disclaimer on reverse side satisfies section 1-201(10) where front of form states "SUBJECT TO THE CONDITIONS ON BACK" in all capital letters even though disclaimer on reverse reverse side is in regular print except for title "LIMITED WARRANTY"). *See also* Rye v. International Harvester Co., 16 UCCR 966 (Tenn. Ct. App. 1975). Although the facts relating to the disclaimer in *Rye* are very sketchy, the court found that a disclaimer on the reverse side of a form was conspicuous even though it was apparently in the same type as the other provisions on the back of the form. The front of the form contained a statement that there were "ADDITIONAL PROVISIONS on the reverse side," as well as a statement in apparently non-distinguishable type that the regular warranty of International Harvester was the only warranty that accompanied the sale.

to Wear, Inc. v. Mercedes-Benz of North America, Inc., [713] the court refused to give effect to a disclaimer on the reverse side of a contract where the disclaimer itself was not in larger or contrasting print, even though the front of the form stated in all capitals "DISCLAIMER OF WARANTIES—SEE REVERSE SIDE."

Both cases are problematic. Although the reference on the front of the form in *Deaton* was in all capitals, it made no reference to warranties or disclaimers. The disclaimer on the reverse side was indistinguishable in type from nine other apparently unrelated provisions appearing there. Placing a conspicuous statement on the front of the form stating only that there are additional terms and conditions on the back should not transform an inconspicuous disclaimer into a conspicuous one. Even in *Deaton*, however, there may have been other factors, not mentioned by the court, which should have brought the disclaimer to the attention of a reasonable person in the position of the buyer. On the other hand, in *Norman Gerghman's Things to Wear, Inc.*, the notice on the front of the form conspicuously indicated that a disclaimer of warranties could be found on the back. In many cases, this should be sufficient to draw the attention of a reasonable person to the disclaimer.

Where *neither* the reference on the front to additional terms and conditions nor the disclaimer itself are conspicuous, the courts, as one might expect, do not enforce the disclaimer.[714] Conversely, when *both* the reference on the front of the form to additional terms and the disclaimer itself are conspicuous, the courts generally enforce the disclaimer.[715]

---

[713] 558 A.2d 1066, 9 UCCR2d 541 (Del. Super. Ct. 1989).

[714] *See, e.g.*, Bodine Sewer, Inc. v. Eastern Ill. Precast, Inc., 143 Ill. App. 3d 920, 493 N.E.2d 705, 1 UCCR2d 1480 (1986); Moscatiello v. Pittsburgh Contractors Equip. Co., 407 Pa. Super. 363, 595 A.2d 1190, 16 UCCR2d 71 (Pa. 1991); Borden, Inc. v. Advent Ink Co., 701 A.2d 255, 33 UCCR2d 975 (Pa. Super. Ct. 1997). *But see* Wagaman v. Don Warner Chevrolet-Buick, Inc., 17 Pa. D.&C. 3d 572, 31 UCCR 1604 (Pa. C.P. 1981) (disclaimer enforced although reference on front not conspicuous and disclaimer on back long and complicated although in bold type).

[715] *See, e.g.*, American Computer Trust Leasing v. Jack Farrell Instrument Co., 763 F. Supp. 1473, 15 UCCR2d 118 (D. Minn. 1991); Carpenter v. Mobile World, Inc., 194 Ill. App. 3d 830, 551 N.E.2d 724, 141 Ill. Dec. 537, 14 UCCR2d 1048 (1990); Cline v. Allis-Chalmers Corp., 690 S.W.2d 764, 41 UCCR 430 (Ky. Ct. App. 1985); Todd Equip. Leasing Co. v. Milligan, 395 A.2d 818, 25 UCCR 704 (Me. 1978); Brown v. Range Rover of N. Am., Inc., 24 UCCR2d 418 (Va. Cir. Ct. 1993). *See also* Rudy's Glass Constr. Co. v. E.F. Johnson Co., 404 So. 2d 1087, 32 UCCR 1373 (Fla. Dist. Ct. App. 1981) (conspicuous disclaimer on reverse side of contract sufficient where reference on front to additional terms located immediately above signature line).

Whether a disclaimer is conspicuous should be determined from the entire document[716] as well as the circumstances under which it was executed. While it is appropriate to consider the location of a disclaimer in deciding whether it is conspicuous, the placement of a disclaimer on the reverse side of a form should not, by itself, render the disclaimer inconspicuous. Language on the front of a form may be sufficient to draw the buyer's attention to a disclaimer located on the back, particularly if the notice on the front prominently mentions that a disclaimer is present on the reverse side. A disclaimer might also be conspicuous if, for example, the language on the front of the form prominently states that there are important terms on the reverse side, and the warranty disclaimer on the reverse side is itself conspicuous. On the other hand, if the language on the front of the form, even though conspicuous, merely notes that the terms continue on the reverse side, and the disclaimer itself is indistinguishable from a maze of fine print, then the disclaimer is unlikely to be conspicuous. Each case must be decided on its own facts, and no one factor—even larger or contrasting type or color—should be conclusive.

A number of cases have dealt with the situation where the disclaimer is not conspicuous, but the buyer has *actual knowledge* of its terms. Some of these cases hold that actual knowledge is irrelevant; under the terms of section 2-316(2), implied warranties cannot be disclaimed in other than conspicuous language.[717] The majority of cases, however, hold that the buyer's actual knowledge of the disclaimer eliminates the need for the disclaimer to be conspicuous.[718] It is significant that the cases in which courts have strictly held the seller to the requirements of section 2-316(2) generally involved consumer buyers, whereas cases holding that actual knowledge of a dis-

---

[716] *See* J&W Equip., Inc. v. Weingartner, 5 Kan. App. 2d 466, 618 P.2d 862, 31 UCCR 826 (1980).

[717] *See, e.g.*, Rehurek v. Chrysler Credit Corp., 262 So. 2d 452, 10 UCCR 988 (Fla. Ct. App. 1972) (inconspicuous disclaimer invalid even though consumer had read disclaimer clause); Smith v. Sharpensteen, 13 UCCR 609 (Okla. Ct. App. 1973) (fact that lessee read and knew of disclaimer irrelevant when disclaimer not conspicuous; only when there is some doubt as to the conspicuousness of a provision is the question of knowledge important).

[718] *See, e.g.*, Fargo Mach. & Tool Co. v. Kearney & Trecker Corp., 428 F. Supp. 364, 21 UCCR 80 (E.D. Mich. 1977) (between two sophisticated commercial entities actual knowledge obviates need for conspicuousness); O'Neil v. International Harvester Co., 40 Colo. App. 309, 575 P.2d 862, 23 UCCR 1152 (1978); Imperial Stamp & Engraving Co., Inc. v. Barley, 82 Ill. App. 3d 835, 403 N.E.2d 294, 28 UCCR 1307 (1980); Office Supply Co., Inc. v. Basic/Four Corp., 538 F. Supp. 776, 34 UCCR 857 (E.D. Wis. 1982); Ray Martin Painting, Inc. v. Ameron, Inc., 638 F. Supp. 768, 1 UCCR2d 713 (D. Kan. 1986); Twin Disc, Inc. v. Big Bud Tractor, Inc., 772 F.2d 1329, 41 UCCR 1627 (7th Cir. 1985).

claimer obviates the conspicuousness requirement usually involve commercial buyers.

This distinction between consumer and commercial buyers, while not specifically sanctioned by the Code, is defensible. Commercial buyers having actual knowledge of a disclaimer are more likely to understand its significance (or have the means to understand it) despite its lack of conspicuousness. For commercial buyers, the conspicuousness requirement serves exclusively to guard against surprise, and, if there is actual knowledge of the disclaimer, there can be no surprise. The conspicuousness requirement, however, arguably serves an additional purpose with respect to consumer buyers—to highlight the importance of the disclaimer provision. When a provision is highlighted, consumers are more likely to read it carefully and ask questions about it because its relative importance to other terms has been suggested by its conspicuousness. On the other hand, when the disclaimer is not conspicuous, consumers are likely to read it more superficially and casually. Courts can effectively distinguish between commercial and consumer buyers without doing violence to the statute by making actual knowledge of the disclaimer simply one factor to consider under section 1-201(10).[719]

A distinction between consumer and commercial buyers has also occurred in the converse situation—when a disclaimer is conspicuous under section 1-201(10) but the buyer does not have actual knowledge of the disclaimer. When the buyer is a commercial entity, courts uniformly hold that actual knowledge is irrelevant; if the disclaimer is objectively conspicuous, it is upheld. When the buyer is a consumer, however, a small number of courts have held that a disclaimer is ineffective unless the buyer has actual knowledge of it.[720] A number of states have also passed statutes[721] or

---

[719] If the consumer buyer, in addition to having actual knowledge of the disclaimer, gives the seller reason to believe that the buyer understands the *effect* of the disclaimer, the disclaimer should be effective not withstanding its lack of conspicuousness.

[720] *See, e.g.,* Zabriskie Chevrolet, Inc. v. Smith, 240 A.2d 195, 5 UCCR 30 (N.J. Super. Ct. 1968); Higel v. General Motors Corp., 544 P.2d 983, 18 UCCR 901 (Colo. 1975); Berg v. Stromme, 79 Wash. 2d 184, 484 P.2d 380, 8 UCCR 1185 (1971); Husky Spray Serv., Inc. v. Patzer, 471 N.W.2d 146, 15 UCCR2d 772 (S.D. 1991) (applying North Dakota law). *See also* Williams v. College Dodge, Inc., 11 UCCR 958 (Mich. Dist. Ct. 1972) (seller must specifically point out disclaimer to buyer if not on face of document).

The proposed revisions to Article 2 make it more difficult to disclaim implied warranties in consumer contracts. It is not sufficient in a consumer contract simply to mention merchantability. The disclaimer must conspicuously state "The seller makes no representations about and is not responsible for the quality of the goods, except as otherwise provided in this contract." Council Draft § 2-406(c)(1) [Alternative A].

[721] *See, e.g.,* W. Va. Code § 46A-6-107 (1996).

amended the Code[722] to preclude or limit disclaimers of the implied warranty of merchantability in consumer transactions. In addition, the Magnuson-Moss Federal Warranty Act, discussed in detail subsequently in the text,[723] limits the ability of sellers of consumer goods who make written warranties to disclaim implied warranties.

A couple of courts have forgotten the lesson that the conspicuousness of a provision should be determined in the context of the entire document. These cases deal with disclaimers found in manuals or catalogs that are conspicuous when viewed in isolation, but are arguably not conspicuous when considered in the context of the entire document in which they appear. For example, in *Adams v. American Cyanamid*[724] the court found a disclaimer of the warranties of merchantability and fitness located on the 17th page of a 107-page manual to be conspicuous. The disclaimer itself was arguably conspicuous,[725] but the court gave no reason why the buyer would be expected to read the entire manual or otherwise be drawn to the page containing the disclaimer. In another case, *LWT, Inc. v. Childers,*[726] the court found a disclaimer located in a catalog sufficient to satisfy section 1-201(10) when the buyer claimed a breach of the implied warranty of merchantability for a defective oil heater. Although the disclaimer itself was clearly conspicuous, the court never discussed the placement of the disclaimer within the catalog, the size of the catalog, or why the buyer might otherwise reasonably be expected to see the disclaimer.[727] These cases are not necessarily wrong—there should be no *per se* rule disqualifying disclaimers in manuals or catalogs. In fact, given the nature of the products involved in the preceding cases—herbicides and oil heaters—a buyer might have been expected to examine the manual or catalog rather carefully.[728]

---

[722] *See, e.g.*, Mass. Gen. L. ch. 106, § 2-316(A) (1990 & 1996 Supp.); Ala. Code § 7-2-316(5) (1993).

[723] *See* § 8.02[G][3], *infra*.

[724] 498 N.W.2d 577, 21 UCCR2d 962 (Neb. Ct. App. 1992).

[725] Although the disclaimer itself was in normal size print, the heading "DISCLAIMER" was prominently displayed in capital letters and the disclaimer was set off from other material. 498 N.W.2d at 585, 21 UCCR2d at 970.

[726] 19 F.3d 539, 23 UCCR2d 73 (10th Cir. 1994).

[727] In Earl Brace & Sons v. Ciba-Geigy Corp., 708 F. Supp. 708, 8 UCCR2d 690 (W.D. Pa. 1989), a warranty disclaimer on page 5 of a 32-page booklet attached to a product was held to be conspicuous. In this case, however, the buyer had admitted reading the instructional booklet on prior occasions.

[728] *See* Hornberger v. General Motors Corp., 929 F. Supp. 884, 30 UCCR2d 483 (E.D. Pa. 1996). In this case, the court upheld a disclaimer located in the middle of a 35-page warranty booklet. The disclaimer language was clearly conspicuous when compared to the other language in the booklet, and the fact that it was located in the warranty booklet rather than in the more voluminous owner's manual probably played a part in the court's decision.

The courts in these cases, however, should have considered the context more inclusively rather than focusing solely on the conspicuousness of the disclaimer provision itself.

[2]   Section 2-316(3)(a)

Subsection (3) of 2-316 provides several additional ways in which a seller can disclaim implied warranties. The most important of these is subsection (3)(a) which provides:

> (a) unless the circumstances indicate otherwise, all implied warranties are excluded by expressions like "as is," "with all faults" or other language which in common understanding calls the buyer's attention to the exclusion of warranties and makes plain that there is no implied warranty.[729]

Three issues meriting discussion have arisen in connection with this subsection: (1) what specific language will suffice under this subsection to disclaim implied warranties?; (2) does a disclaimer under this subsection have to be conspicuous?; (3) what is meant by the phrase "unless the circumstances indicate otherwise"?

The subsection itself provides two examples of language that "in common understanding" makes plain that there is no implied warranty: "as is" and "with all faults."[730] Comment 7 to section 2-316 provides another: "as they stand." At least when they are conspicuous, these phrases should be effective to disclaim implied warranties under section 2-316(3)(a).[731] Difficulty arises, however, when unwary sellers (or their incompetent attorneys) use other language and later assert that the purported disclaimer is valid under subsection (3)(a). For example, a number of cases have dealt with language that provides that an express warranty is provided "in lieu of" implied warranties. These disclaimers are not sufficient to disclaim the implied warranty of merchantability under section 2-316(2)—because they do not mention "merchantability"—so sellers, with mixed results, have tried to bring them within the purview of subsection (3)(a).

---

[729] U.C.C. § 2-316(3)(a).

[730] U.C.C. § 2-316(2)(a).

[731] For cases that uphold the validity of "as is" disclaimers, *see, e.g.*, Frank Griffin Volkswagen, Inc. v. Smith, 610 So. 2d 597, 19 UCCR2d 410 (Fla. Ct. App. 1993); Pelc v. Simmons, 249 Ill. App. 3d 852, 620 N.E.2d 12, 189 Ill. Dec. 353, 23 UCCR2d 1113 (1993).

In *Logan Equipment Corp. v. Simon Aerials, Inc.,*[732] the U.S. District Court in Massachusetts held that language stating that a limited express warranty was "in lieu of any warranty or condition implied by law as to the quality or fitness for any particular purpose" satisfied subsection (3)(a). In *Cox Motor Car Co. v Castle,*[733] the court assumed, without discussion, that an express warranty that was provided "in lieu of all other warranties, expressed or implied" successfully disclaimed implied warranties. On the other hand, the Ohio Supreme Court, in *Insurance Co. of North America v. Automatic Sprinkler Corp. of America,*[734] strongly disapproved of these cases and held that an express warranty provided "in lieu of all other warranties express or implied" did not satisfy subsection (3)(a). The court reasoned that for language to effectively disclaim implied warranties under subsection (3)(a), the language must describe *the quality of the goods.* Quoting Comment 7 to section 2-316, the court said that satisfactory language under subsection (3)(a) must be understood in ordinary commercial usage to mean that the buyer takes the entire risk as to the quality of the goods, and the language "in lieu of" does not satisfy this standard. The result in this case is correct. To permit a seller to disclaim implied warranties by merely providing that any express warranties are "in lieu of" implied warranties without mentioning "merchantability" emasculates section 2-316(2) by allowing general language to disclaim the implied warranty of merchantability.[735]

Sellers have also had mixed success in convincing courts that the language "in its present condition" satisfies subsection (3)(a). A number of courts have upheld disclaimers containing this or similar language,[736] but the majority of courts have held otherwise.[737] Courts have generally been

---

[732] 736 F. Supp. 1188, 12 UCCR2d 387 (D. Mass. 1990).

[733] 402 S.W.2d 429, 3 UCCR 397 (Ky. Ct. App. 1966).

[734] 67 Ohio St. 2d 91, 423 N.E.2d 151, 31 UCCR 1595 (1981).

[735] *See* Lecates v. Hertrich Pontiac Buick Co., 515 A.2d 163, 2 UCCR2d 865 (Del. Super. Ct. 1986) (general disclaimer that there were "no other guaranties, responsibilities or agreements, express or implied" fails under both subsections (2) and (3)(a) of U.C.C. § 2-316). *But see* Avery v. Aladdin Prods. Div., Nat'l Serv. Indus., Inc., 128 Ga. App. 266, 196 S.E.2d 357, 12 UCCR 628 (1973) (statement that "no representations or warranties of any sort, express or implied, except warranty of title, have been made by seller" sufficient to disclaim implied warranties under section 2-316(3)(a)).

[736] *See* Avery v. Aladdin Prods. Div., Nat'l Serv. Indus., Inc., 196 S.E.2d 357, 128 Ga. App. 266, 12 UCCR 628 (Ga. Ct. App. 1973); First Nat'l Bank of Elgin v. Husted, 205 N.E.2d 780, 2 UCCR 777 (Ill. Ct. App. 1965).

[737] Miller v. Badgley, 753 P.2d 530, 51 Wash. App. 285, 6 UCCR2d 1082 (Wash. Ct. App. 1988); McDonald v. Mobley, 555 S.W.2d 916, 23 UCCR 65 (Tex. Civ. App. 1977); Hull-Dobbs, Inc. v. Mallicoot, 3 UCCR 1032 (Tenn. Ct. App. 1966).

unwilling to permit substitutes for the phrases mentioned in the subsection and Comment 7.[738] Thus, they have rejected language under subsection (3)(a) in which the lessee of a grain bin accepted "full responsibility" and in which the lessor did "not guarantee any part hereof,"[739] and held a disclaimer ineffective which stated that the seller "accept[s] no responsibility for the results obtained following [the product's] use."[740] If alternative language is common in a particular industry to disclaim implied warranties, however, courts will give it effect under subsection (3)(a).[741] Further, if language makes it obvious in the context of the transaction that the buyer bears the risk of the quality of the goods, the disclaimer should be upheld.[742]

Cases are divided over whether subsection 3(a) disclaimers must be conspicuous. Unlike subsection (2), subsection (3)(a) contains no requirement of conspicuousness. A substantial number of cases have considered the issue, and although the decisions are split, the majority of cases require that a subsection 3(a) disclaimer be conspicuous. Those that do not require the disclaimer to be conspicuous[743] rely on the absence of any requirement in the section itself.[744] These courts suggest that had the drafters intended a conspicuousness requirement in subsection (3)(a), they could have easily provided for one, as they did in the immediately preceding subsection.[745]

---

[738] *See* Lecates v. Hertrich Pontiac Buick Co., 515 A.2d 163, 2 UCCR2d 865 (Del. Super. Ct. 1986) ("courts so far have not been eager to expand the list of acceptable phrases").

[739] Agrarian Grain Co. v. Meeker, 526 N.E.2d 1189, 7 UCCR2d 786 (Ind. Ct. App. 1988).

[740] Pearson v. Franklin Labs., Inc., 254 N.W.2d 133, 22 UCCR 351 (S.D. 1977). *See also* Overland Bond & Inv. Corp. v. Howard, 9 Ill. App. 3d 348, 292 N.E.2d 168, 11 UCCR 945 (Ill. Ct. App. 1972) ("acceptance in good condition" ineffective under U.C.C. § 2-316(3)(a)); Gaylord v. Lawler Mobile Homes, 477 So. 2d 382, 42 UCCR 131 (Ala. 1985) ("except as required under . . . state law the dealer makes no warranties" not equivalent to "as is"); Davis Indus. Sales, Inc., v. Workman Constr. Co., Inc., 856 S.W.2d 355, 21 UCCR2d 607 (Miss. Ct. App. 1993) ("sold as used equipment . . . no warranties or liability express or implied" not sufficient under U.C.C. § 2-316(3)(a)).

[741] *See, e.g.,* Trimpley Tire Sales & Serv., Inc. v. Stine, 266 Pa. Super. 91, 403 A.2d 108, 27 UCCR 92 (1979) ("no adjustments" the equivalent of "as is" in used tire industry).

[742] *See* Jacobs v. E.I. du Pont de Nemours & Co., 67 F.3d 1219, 27 UCCR2d 1198 (6th Cir. 1995).

[743] *See, e.g.,* Gilliam v. Indiana Nat'l Bank, 337 So. 2d 352, 20 UCCR 307 (Ct. Civ. App. 1976); Gindy Mfg. Corp. v. Cardinale Trucking Corp., 268 A.2d 345, 111 N.J. Super. 383, 7 UCCR 1257 (N.J. Super. Ct. 1970).

[744] Lumber Mut. Ins. Co. v. Clarklift of Detroit, Inc., 569 N.W.2d 681, 33 UCCR2d 1105 (Mich. Ct. App. 1997).

[745] *See, e.g.,* Patton v. McHone, 822 S.W.2d 608, 17 UCCR2d 404 (Tenn. Ct. App. 1991); Leland Indus., Inc. v. Suntec Indus., Inc., 362 S.E.2d 441, 184 Ga. App. 635, 5 UCCR2d 981 (Ga. Ct. App. 1987); Fernandez v. Western R.R. Builders, Inc., 112 Idaho 907, 736 P.2d 1361, 5 UCCR2d 347 (Idaho Ct. App. 1987); Alpert v. Thomas, 643 F. Supp. 1406, 2

An early case from New Jersey contains an exhaustive treatment of this issue. In *Gindy Manufacturing Corp. v. Cardinale Trucking Corp.*,[746] the court accepted the buyer's argument that an "as is" disclaimer must be conspicuous. The court reasoned that the intention of subsection (3)(a) was to allow sellers to substitute some commonly understood terms for the term "merchantability," without eliminating the requirement of subsection (2) that a disclaimer be conspicuous. Relying on the drafting history of the section, the court noted that at one time, the present provisions of subsection (3)(a) were contained in subsection (2), which included its requirement of conspicuousness. When subsection (3) was separated from subsection (2), it was done so for reasons unrelated to conspicuousness. There is no indication in the drafting history that the drafters intended to remove the conspicuousness requirement when subsection (3) was carved out from subsection (2).

The court also relied on convincing policy arguments to support a requirement of conspicuousness. To quote the court:

> It does not make sense to require conspicuous language when a warranty is disclaimed by use of the words "merchantability" or "fitness" and not when a term like "as is" is used to accomplish the same result. It serves no intelligible design to protect buyers by conspicuous language when the term "merchantability" is used, but to allow an effective disclaimer when the term "as is" is buried in fine print. . . . The expectations of the buyer need as much protection in one case as in another.[747]

Other courts have relied upon similar reasoning.[748] Further, Comment 1 to section 2-316 indicates that the purpose of section 2-316 is to protect the buyer against "unexpected and unbargained language of disclaimer," which would suggest that the disclaimer must be conspicuous. Most courts have held, however, that when the buyer is actually aware of the "as is" disclaimer, there is no requirement that it be conspicuous.[749]

UCCR2d 99 (D. Vt. 1986); Koperski v. Husker Dodge, Inc., 302 N.W.2d 655, 208 Neb. 29, 31 UCCR 113 (Neb. 1986); Fairchild Indus. v. Maritime Air Serv., Ltd., 333 A.2d 313, 274 Md. 181, 16 UCCR 663 (Md. Ct. App. 1975).

[746] 268 A.2d 345, 7 UCCR 1257 (N.J. Super. Ct. 1970).

[747] 268 A.2d at 352–353, 7 UCCR at 1267.

[748] *See* Fairchild Indus. v. Maritime Air Serv., Ltd., 333 A.2d 313, 274 Md. 181, 16 UCCR 663 (Md. Ct. App. 1975); Hartwig Farms, Inc. v. Pacific Gamble Robinson Co., 625 P.2d 171, 28 Wash. App. 539, 30 UCCR 1552 (Wash. Ct. App. 1981); Osborne v. Genevie, 289 So. 2d 21, 14 UCCR 85 (Dist. Ct. App. Fla. 1974).

[749] *See* St. Croix Printing Equip., Inc. v. Rockwell Int'l Corp., 428 N.W.2d 877, 8 UCCR2d 1009 (Minn. Ct. App. 1988).

Subsection (3)(a) is qualified by an introductory phrase that makes "as is" disclaimers effective *"unless the circumstances indicate otherwise."* The scope of this qualification is not clear. There are at least three plausible interpretations. The first is that a seller claiming the benefit of a subsection (3)(a) disclaimer must establish that the words of the disclaimer are commonly understood to disclaim implied warranties by the buyers in the particular industry or trade. Under this interpretation, a seller must establish that the language was equivalent to a usage of trade. Thus, even though "as is" is explicitly mentioned in subsection 3(a), a consumer buyer might be able to avoid the effect of an "as is" disclaimer by proving that most (or at least many) consumers would not understand "as is" as disclaiming all implied warranties.[750] This interpretation is supported by Comment 7 to section 2-316, which states that "the terms covered by paragraph (a) are in fact merely a particularization of paragraph (c) which provides for the exclusion or modification of implied warranties by usage of trade."[751] This interpretation would often make the effectiveness of a disclaimer under subsection (3)(a) a question of fact because the existence and scope of a usage of trade are issues of fact.[752]

The second interpretation presumes that the phrases used in subsection 3(a) and Comment 7 are generally effective to disclaim implied warranties, but a buyer in an individual case should have the opportunity to show that the parties, through the use of "as is" language, objectively intended something other than a disclaimer of all implied warranties. Under this interpretation, if the buyer could show that he reasonably understood the "as is" language as doing something other than disclaiming implied warranties, and if the seller had reason to know of this understanding, the buyer's interpretation would prevail.[753] A couple of cases support this interpretation. In *Knipp v. Weinbaum,*[754] the buyer purchased a customized "trike" (three-

---

[750] *See* Gindy Mfg. Corp. v. Cardinale Trucking Corp., 111 N.J. Super. 383, 268 A.2d 345, 7 UCCR 1257 (1970). In this case, the court held that the use of "as is" in a form contract was not effective to disclaim implied warranties. The court found that a usage of trade existed in which "as is" disclaimers were expected in sales of used vehicles, but not new goods. Since the form contract could be used for either new or used goods, the buyer could reasonably expect that the clause was applicable only when the form contract was employed in the sale of used vehicles. *See also* Maritime Mfrs., Inc. v. Hi-Skipper Marina, 19 Ohio St. 3d 93, 41 UCCR 1262 (1985) (Sweeney, J., dissenting) (usage of trade in the new boat industry that "where is, as is" means that the dealer will do minor cleaning to the boat being sold).

[751] U.C.C. § 2-316, Official Comment 7.

[752] U.C.C. § 1-205(2).

[753] *See* § 3.11, *supra.*

[754] 351 So. 2d 1081, 22 UCCR 1141 (Fla. Dist. Ct. App. 1977).

wheeled motorcycle) from the seller. The buyer signed a bill of sale which included the prominent statement: "CYCLE SOLD AS IS—ONE CUSTOM TRIKE HONDA THREE WHEELER." Several hours after the purchase, the buyer was severely injured when a defective weld gave way causing the "trike" to crash. When the buyer sued the seller, the court granted summary judgment on the buyer's implied warranty count, relying on the conspicuous "as is" language.

The appeals court reversed the grant of summary judgment. The court rejected the seller's argument that the use of the words "as is" constituted an *automatic* disclaimer of implied warranties. According to the court, the clause "unless the circumstances indicate otherwise" precludes a finding that "automatic absolution can be achieved in the sale of used consumer goods merely by the inclusion in a bill of sale of the magic words 'as is.' "[755] Because there was conflicting evidence as to what the buyer reasonably understood—there was evidence that the term was intended only to disclaim liability for minor defects which would preclude the trike from passing a motor vehicle inspection—summary judgment was inappropriate.

The final interpretation is that the language "unless circumstances indicate otherwise" is applicable only when the seller does not use the "magic words" specifically mentioned in subsection (3)(a) and Comment 7 to disclaim implied warranties. Under this interpretation, the court should examine the practices of the trade and the circumstances of the transaction to determine whether the buyer should reasonably have understood the words the seller used to be a disclaimer of implied warranties. If the seller used the magic words "as is," "with all faults," or "as they stand," however, it will be conclusively presumed that implied warranties are disclaimed.[756]

The Code's focus on the parties' bargain-in-fact and the breadth of the language "unless the circumstances indicate otherwise" suggests that the *Knipp* case is correct. If the most reasonable interpretation of the language, in light of all of the circumstances, is that it is intended to do something other than disclaim all implied warranties, that interpretation should be given effect. There is no reason that the parties should not be permitted to give this language any meaning that they choose. In addition, subsection (3)(a) does not confine the qualifying language "unless the circumstances indicate otherwise" to cases where the "magic words" explicitly mentioned in the subsection and Comment 7 are not used; the language qualifies *all* of sub-

---

[755] 351 So. 2d at 1084, 22 UCCR at 1144.

[756] One prominent treatise on warranties has adopted this position. *See* Barkley Clark and Christopher Smith, The Law of Product Warranties, at 8-24 and 8-25 (1984). *See also* Keeneland Ass'n, Inc. v. Hollendorfer, 986 F. Supp. 1070, 36 UCCR2d 373 (1997).

section (3)(a). Consequently, if a buyer can show that he reasonably understood "as is" or "with all faults" in some manner other than to disclaim all implied warranties, and the seller had reason to know of the buyer's understanding, the buyer's interpretation should be given effect.[757] Most courts, however, have presumed the Code's magic words effective to disclaim implied warranties, with little consideration of the circumstances of the individual transaction. Certainly, there is no indication that courts would be willing to apply the qualification "unless the circumstances indicate otherwise" to broad categories of transactions—such as consumer sales—when the seller uses the magic words explicitly contained in subsection 3(a).

[3]   The Timing of the Disclaimer

Sometimes disclaimers are present in documents that the buyer does not receive or are not reasonably available to the buyer until after a contract has been created. The disclaimer may be in an owner's manual that is not given to the buyer until after the contract has been signed,[758] it may be inside the package or carton containing the goods,[759] it may be on an invoice accompanying the goods,[760] or it may be in a written warranty or other document not delivered until after the sale.[761] Are these disclaimers effective?

---

[757] *See* K&M Joint Venture v. Smith Int'l, Inc., 669 F.2d 1106, 33 UCCR 1 (6th Cir. 1981) ("as is" language as used by the parties intended only to indicate that seller refused to incur further expense to consummate sale).

[758] *See, e.g.,* Marion Power Shovel Co. v. Huntsman, 437 S.W.2d 784, 6 UCCR 100 (Ark. 1969); Jensen v. Seigel Mobile Homes Group, 668 P.2d 65, 35 UCCR 804 (Idaho 1983); Dougall v. Brown Bay Boat Works & Sales, Inc., 178 N.W.2d 217, 7 UCCR 1160 (Minn. 1970).

[759] *See, e.g.,* Midland Supply Co., Inc. v. Ehret Plumbing & Heating Co., 108 Ill. App. 3d 1120, 440 N.E.2d 153 (1982); Adams v. American Cyanamid Co., 498 N.W.2d 577, 1 Neb. App. 337, 21 UCCR2d 962 (Neb. Ct. App. 1992); Step-Saver Data Sys., Inc. v. WYSE Technology, 939 F.2d 91, 15 UCCR2d 1 (3d Cir. 1991); Billings v. Joseph Harris Co., Inc., 290 N.C. 502, 226 S.E.2d 321, 19 UCCR 1326 (1976).

[760] *See, e.g.,* First Sec. Mortgage Co. v. Goldmark Plastics Compounds, Inc., 862 F. Supp. 918, 25 UCCR2d 66 (E.D.N.Y. 1994); Singleton v. LaCoure, 712 S.W.2d 757, 2 UCCR2d 121 (Tex. Ct. App. 1986); Tolmie Farms, Inc. v. J.R. Simplot Co., Inc., 124 Idaho 607, 862 P.2d 299, 23 UCCR2d 65 (1993).

[761] *See, e.g.,* Ford Motor Co. v. Taylor, 446 S.W.2d 521, 6 UCCR 798 (Tenn. Ct. App. 1969); Van Den Broeke v. Bellanca Aircraft Corp., 576 F.2d 582, 24 UCCR 594 (5th Cir. 1978); Taterka v. Ford Motor Co., 86 Wis. 2d 140, 271 N.W.2d 653, 25 UCCR 680 (1978); Wilson v. Marquette Elecs., Inc., 630 F.2d 575, 29 UCCR 399 (8th Cir. 1980); Horizons, Inc. v. AVCO Corp., 551 F. Supp. 771, 35 UCCR 102 (D.S.D. 1982) (limited warranty attached to engine of airplane delivered after contract); Hemmert Agric. Aviation, Inc. v. Mid-Continent Aircraft Corp., 663 F. Supp. 1546, 4 UCCR2d 726 (D. Kan. 1987).

Courts generally refuse to enforce these disclaimers on one of two grounds: (1) they are attempts by the seller to modify unilaterally a contract to which the buyer has not agreed or (2) they are not conspicuous.[762] It is a tenet of elementary contract law that a contract, once made, cannot be unilaterally modified by one party.[763] When the buyer does not receive a disclaimer until after the contract has been concluded, most courts hold that the disclaimer is merely an attempt by the seller to modify unilaterally the contract, which is ineffective without the buyer's concurrence.[764] Consistent with general contract law, courts do not find the buyer's silence to constitute assent to the modification, nor does the buyer consent to the modification by retaining and using the goods.[765]

---

[762] *See, e.g.*, Flory v. Silvercrest Indus., Inc., 633 P.2d 424, 29 UCCR 832 (Ariz. Ct. App. 1980); Bowdoin v. Showell Growers, Inc., 817 F.2d 1543, 3 UCCR2d 1366 (11th Cir. 1987).

[763] *But see* U.C.C. § 2-207. Under this provision, a definite and seasonable expression of acceptance containing terms additional to or different from those offered is nonetheless effective to accept the offer. The additional terms are then considered proposals for additions to the contract and between merchants and become part of the contract unless (1) the offer expressly limits acceptance to the terms of the offer; (2) they materially alter the offer; (3) notification of objection has been given or is given within a reasonable time. Under this provision, additional terms in written confirmations are treated similarly. For a thorough discussion of section 2-207, *see* § 3.04[B], *supra.*

[764] *See, e.g.*, Tiger Motor Co., Inc. v. McMurtry, 224 So. 2d 638, 6 UCCR 608 (Ala. 1969); Wright v. Dow Chem. USA, 845 F. Supp. 503, 24 UCCR2d 507 (M.D. Tenn. 1993); Fleck v. Jacques Seed Co., 445 N.W.2d 649, 9 UCCR2d 1232 (N.D. 1989); Flory v. Silvercrest Indus., Inc., 633 P.2d 424, 29 UCCR 832 (Ariz. Ct. App. 1980); Horizons, Inc. v. Avco Corp., 35 UCCR 102 (D.S.D. 1982); Hortwig Farms, Inc. v. Pacific Gamble Robinson Co., 625 P.2d 171, 30 UCCR 1552 (Wash. Ct. App. 1981); Woodword v. Naylor Motor Sales, 14 UCCR 1269 (Mich. Ct. App. 1974); International Harvester Co. v. Pike, 466 S.W.2d 901, 10 UCCR 1164 (Ark. 1971); Duffin v. Idaho Crop Improvement Ass'n, 126 Idaho 1002, 895 P.2d 1195, 28 UCCR2d 133 (1995).

[765] *See, e.g.*, Arizona Retail Sys., Inc. v. The Software Link, Inc., 831 F. Supp. 759, 22 UCCR2d 70 (D. Ariz. 1993); Wolf Bros. Oil Co., Inc. v. International Surplus Lines Ins. Co., 718 F. Supp. 839 (W.D. Wash. 1989); Grand Island Prod. Credit Ass'n v. Humphrey, 388 N.W.2d 807, 2 UCCR2d 193 (Neb. 1986). Additional support for this conclusion can be found in Comment 3 to U.C.C. § 9-206(2). According to the text of section 9-206(2), warranty disclaimers and limitations found in security agreements are governed by Article 2. Comment 3 to section 9-206 further elaborates on this provision:

> It [section 9-206(2)] also prevents a buyer from inadvertently abandoning his warranties by a "no warranties" term in the security agreement when warranties have already been created under the sales agreement.

But cf. Monsanto Agric. Prods., Inc. v. Edenfield, 35 UCCR 781 (Fla. Ct. App. 1982) (limitation of warranty on label effective where buyer read label before using product; assent occurred when buyer opened and used product with knowledge of limitation); Hill v. BASF Wyandotte Corp., 696 F.2d 287, 35 UCCR 91 (4th Cir. 1982) (remedy limitation on label

This conclusion is subject to four qualifications. First, if the buyer is made aware of the disclaimer prior to the contract, the disclaimer will not be ineffective solely because the writing containing the disclaimer was not delivered until after the contract was formed. Thus, in *Sanco, Inc. v. Ford Motor Co.,*[766] a buyer of thirty trucks argued that warranty limitations contained in booklets accompanying the trucks were post-contract disclaimers and, therefore, ineffective. The court rejected this argument because the buyer, a truck dealer, fully expected the booklets, including the limitations and disclaimers, to be part of the deal.[767]

The second caveat involves section 2-207. Under this section, additional terms contained in a written confirmation of a preexisting contract can become part of the contract.[768] This can occur, however, only if the additional terms do not materially alter the contract.[769] The vast majority of courts, consistent with Comment 4 to section 2-207, have determined that warranty disclaimers materially alter the contract.[770]

---

of can of herbicide effective when buyer admitted he used the herbicide after having read the label). In both of these cases, however, the product was delivered to the buyer at the time of sale with the label attached, and thus neither involved post-contract disclaimers.

[766] 771 F.2d 1081, 41 UCCR 766 (7th Cir. 1985).

[767] *See also* Hahn v. Ford Motor Co., Inc., 434 N.E.2d 943, 33 UCCR 1277 (Ind. Ct. App. 1982) (disclaimer in owner's manual located in glove compartment discussed with buyer prior to contract). In Harris v. Ford Motor Co., Inc., 845 F. Supp. 1511, 25 UCCR2d 53 (M.D. Ala. 1994), the court said that because truck buyers were aware at the time of purchase that a "New Car Warranty" was in the glove compartment, the buyers were bound by warranty limitations contained in the New Car Warranty. The court rejected the contention of the buyers that they did not receive the vehicle containing the "New Car Warranty" until after they had contracted to purchase the vehicle. The limitation at issue was a definition of the term "new" that included vehicles that had suffered minor damage during shipment from the factory and had been repaired.

[768] *See* § 3.04[D], *supra.*

[769] Also, for additional terms to become part of the contract under U.C.C. § 2-207, the contract must be between merchants, the offer must not limit acceptance to the terms of the offer, and the offeror must not object to the additional terms within a reasonable time. U.C.C. § 2-207(2).

[770] *See, e.g.,* Glyptal Inc. v. Engelhard Corp., 801 F. Supp. 887, 18 UCCR2d 1059 (D. Mass. 1992); Step-Saver Data Sys., Inc. v. WYSE Technology, 939 F.2d 91, 15 UCCR2d 1 (3d Cir. 1991); Graham Hyrdraulic Power, Inc., v. Stewart & Stevenson Power, Inc., 797 P.2d 835, 12 UCCR2d 658 (Colo. Ct. App. 1990); Southeastern Adhesives Co. v. Funder Am., Inc., 366 S.E.2d 505, 6 UCCR2d 403 (N.C. Ct. App. 1988); Twin Disc, Inc. v. Big Bud Tractor, Inc., 772 F.2d 1329, 41 UCCR 1627 (7th Cir. 1985); Album Graphics, Inc. v. Beatrice Foods Co., 408 N.E.2d 1041, 87 Ill. App. 3d 338, 30 UCCR 53 (Ill. Ct. App. 1980); Great Am. Lines, Inc. v. Global Petroleum Corp., 34 UCCR2d 37 (D.N.J. 1997). *But see* Old Albany Estates, Ltd. v. Highland Carpet Co., Inc., 24 UCCR 114 (Okla. 1978) (court held that although warranty disclaimer would normally materially alter a contract, it should

The third qualification is that some courts have permitted post-contract disclaimers to become part of the contract through course of dealing. For example, in *Tolmie Farms, Inc. v. Stauffer Chemical Co., Inc.,*[771] the buyer purchased Vapam, a soil fumigant, from the seller from 1982 to 1985. After each sale, the seller sent the buyer an invoice containing a conspicuous disclaimer of implied warranties. The buyer sued for breach of the warranty of merchantability when the product failed to prevent a root-eating worm from destroying the buyer's crop, and the seller pointed to the disclaimer on the invoices. The buyer responded that, in each case, the invoices had been delivered after the sale. The court, however, held that repeated trans-actions[772] over a three-year period were sufficient to establish a course of dealing that included the disclaimer. Similarly, in *Bickett v. W.R. Grace & Co.,*[773] the court found a course of dealing that incorporated a disclaimer located on bags of seed when seed purchased in the preceding two years also contained a similar disclaimer.

Other courts have been far more reluctant to find a post-contract dis-claimer effective solely as a result of prior transactions involving similar post-contract disclaimers. The fact that the buyer had accepted invoices con-taining warranty disclaimers for a period of *fifteen* years did not convince the court in *Hartwig Farms, Inc. v. Pacific Gamble Robinson Co.*[774] that a course of dealing incorporated the disclaimer. The court said that there was nothing about the parties' dealings over this period that would give rise to an inference of assent to the disclaimer by the buyer.[775] Similarly, in *Lutz Farms v. Asgrow Seed Co.,*[776] the appearance of a disclaimer on invoices in many prior transactions did not establish a course of dealing disclaiming implied warranties. The court said that the parties had never acted during their dealings in a manner indicating that warranties were disclaimed; in fact, to the contrary, the seller had always adjusted minor problems with the goods without reference to the disclaimer.

The final caveat is that a few decisions indicate, without directly de-ciding, that if the buyer becomes aware of the disclaimer prior to using the goods, and is afforded the opportunity by the terms of the disclaimer to

---

be incorporated as a new term into the contract when the purchaser was unquestionably aware of the disclaimer prior to receiving the first shipment of goods without objecting).

[771] 862 P.2d 305, 20 UCCR2d 859 (Idaho Ct. App. 1992).

[772] The opinion does not say how many individual sales were involved.

[773] 12 UCCR 629 (W.D. Ky. 1972).

[774] 625 P.2d 171, 30 UCCR 1552 (Wash. Ct. App. 1991).

[775] It should be noted, however, that Washington, where the case arose, has particularly strict standards for enforcing disclaimers.

[776] 948 F.2d 638, 15 UCCR2d 1167 (10th Cir. 1991).

return the product unused for a full refund, the buyer will be bound by the disclaimer if he then goes ahead and uses the goods. The cases generally involve disclaimers located on labels or on the packages containing the goods. In *Gold Kist, Inc. v. Citizens & Southern National Bank of South Carolina*,[777] the court held a post-contract disclaimer ineffective where there was no evidence that the buyer was aware of the disclaimer. In dicta, however, the court said that "an agreement to modify [the contract] can only be found . . . if the evidence reveals that the buyer acquired knowledge of the offered modification and had the opportunity to object to it."

The court in *Monsanto Agricultural Products Co. v. Edenfield*[778] said that even if a buyer was not aware of a limitation on implied warranties at the time of purchase, the limitation became part of the bargain when, with knowledge of the limitation, the buyer subsequently used the product. *Monsanto*, however, did not strictly involve a post-contract disclaimer; the label containing the disclaimer was on the outside of the cans containing the product, which were delivered at the time of purchase. As discussed earlier, courts have generally enforced disclaimers printed on the outside of a product when the product was delivered at the time of sale. In a final case indicating that assent to a disclaimer might be inferred from use of the product with knowledge of the disclaimer,[779] the court explicitly stated that the facts of its case did not involve a post-contract disclaimer.[780] Two other courts have expressly refused to decide the question, because the facts of the cases did not involve knowledge of the disclaimer by the buyer.[781]

Four recent cases have dealt with this issue in the context of computer software. The ultimate resolution of the issue will have potentially profound implications for the computer software industry. In the first case, *Step-Saver Data Systems, Inc. v. Wyse Technology*,[782] the court considered, and rejected, all four of the potential exceptions to the unenforceability of post-contract disclaimers. The buyer, Step-Saver, was a company that combined computer hardware and software to create custom designed computer systems for its customers. One of the software products it included in its systems was a program sold by TSL and designed as an operating system for a multiuser system. Combining this program with several other off-the-shelf programs,

---

[777] 286 S.C. 272, 333 S.E.2d 67, 41 UCCR 327 (S.C. Ct. App. 1985).

[778] 426 So. 2d 574, 35 UCCR 781 (Fla. Dist. Ct. App. 1982).

[779] Hill v. BASF Wyandotte Corp., 696 F.2d 287, 35 UCCR 91 (4th Cir. 1982).

[780] *Id.* at 291, 35 UCCR at 97.

[781] Pennington Grain & Seed, Inc. v. Tuten, 422 So. 2d 948, 36 UCCR 458 (Fla. Dist. Ct. App. 1982); Bowdoin v. Showell Growers, Inc., 817 F.2d 1543, 3 UCCR2d 1366 (11th Cir. 1987).

[782] 939 F.2d 91, 15 UCCR2d 1 (3d Cir. 1991).

Step-Saver marketed a system that it sold to over 140 customers. Severe problems developed with these systems almost immediately, which Step-Saver alleged were due, at least in part, to the operating system software purchased from TSL.

Unable to resolve the problems, Step-Saver sued TSL for breach of express and implied warranties. TSL defended against the implied warranty claims, relying on the terms of a "Limited Use License Agreement" printed on each package containing the computer program. The "box-top" license contained a disclaimer of all express and implied warranties except a warranty that the disks containing the program were free from physical defects. It further provided that the buyer's opening of the package indicated the buyer's assent to the box-top license, and that if the buyer did not assent the buyer could return the package unopened for a full refund. Step-Saver argued, however, that because its purchases (usually twenty at a time) of the program were concluded by telephone, before delivery, the license agreement on the package was a post-contract disclaimer and, therefore, ineffective.

The court began by discussing whether section 2-207 was applicable to the problem. It decided that section 2-207 applied because the policy of protecting an offeree from the "last-shot" rule[783] was equally applicable in these circumstances as in the classic battle of the forms.[784] After concluding that a contract had been formed between the parties and that TSL's package did not constitute a "conditional acceptance,"[785] the court found that TSL's

---

[783] See § 3.04[C], supra.

[784] The court's application of U.C.C. § 2-207 is intriguing. By its terms, section 2-207 applies only to "definite and seasonable expression[s] of acceptance" and "written confirmation[s]." Strictly speaking, the license agreement was neither of these. See Pawelec v. Digitcom, Inc., 192 N.J. Super. 474, 471 A.2d 60, 38 UCCR 31 (1984) (limitation of warranty in envelope strapped to machine that was not delivered until after contract was formed not governed by section 2-207). Because one premise of section 2-207 is that no one reads the fine print on preprinted forms, the application of the section under these circumstances is questionable. The license agreement was not a form invoice or acknowledgment; it was printed on each package. It was apparently conspicuous, and, in fact, was actually seen by the buyer. On the other hand, the court is correct in suggesting that one purpose of section 2-207 is to prevent the offeree from getting the "last shot" when it does not care sufficiently about a term to specifically negotiate for it prior to contracting.

[785] In discussing this issue, the court considered the language on the package stating that if the buyer did not want to accept the terms of the license, it could return the package unopened for a full refund. It concluded that this language was not sufficient to make TSL's acceptance conditional. The court could have avoided the issue of a conditional acceptance by holding that the various contracts were formed at the time that Step-Saver ordered the programs by telephone. Under this analysis, the terms on the package could not constitute a "conditional acceptance" because terms on a confirmation cannot "conditionally accept"

disclaimers were a material alteration of the contract. As a result, they did not become part of the contract.

The court also considered the argument of TSL that the disclaimer was included through a course of dealing that had been established by the repeated expression of the license agreement in multiple transactions. The court rejected this argument for two reasons. First, it held that simply repeating terms with no further action did not constitute a course of dealing incorporating the terms. The repetition of the disclaimer on each package merely indicated that TSL *desired* the term, not that Step-Saver had assented to it.[786] Second, the court said that the seller in a multiple transaction case typically has the opportunity to negotiate a desired term. The seller's decision not to do so is an indication that the term is not part of the parties' agreement. The court summarily rejected the seller's policy argument that an unfavorable decision would "destroy the software industry."[787]

In another case, involving the same software, in which TSL was also a defendant, the U.S. District Court in Arizona concurred with the decision in *Step-Saver*. Under very similar facts, the court in *Arizona Retail Systems, Inc. v. The Software Link, Inc.*[788] held that the license agreement on the software package constituted a "confirmation" containing additional terms. As such, under section 2-207, the additional terms were proposals to modify the contract. Because they materially altered the contract, they could not become part of the contract without the consent of the buyer, and mere silence did not constitute assent to the proposed modification.

Two decisions from the U.S. Court of Appeals for the Seventh Circuit are at odds with the decisions in *Step-Saver* and *Arizona Retail Systems*. Although neither case involved a disclaimer, the rationale of both cases is as applicable to disclaimers as it is to the provisions that were actually at issue. In both cases, the Seventh Circuit was much more protective of the computer software industry and its practices than the courts in *Step-Saver* and *Arizona Retail Systems*.

In *ProCD v. Zeidenberg*,[789] ProCD compiled information from more than 3,000 telephone directories into a computer database. The database cost ProCD more than $10 million to develop, and could be searched in various ways. ProCD marketed the program to manufacturers and retailers as well

---

an already existing contract. *See* § 3.04[C][1], *supra*. The court, however, had decided earlier that it was unnecessary to determine when the contract was formed.

[786] 939 F.2d at 104, 15 UCCR2d at 19.

[787] *Id.* at 104, 15 UCCR2d at 20.

[788] 831 F. Supp. 759, 22 UCCR2d 70 (D. Ariz. 1993).

[789] 86 F.3d 1447, 29 UCCR2d 1109 (7th Cir. 1996).

as consumers. The price charged to commercial users was considerably higher than that charged to consumers. In order to prevent commercial users from simply purchasing the cheaper consumer version, ProCD enclosed a license agreement with each copy of the program sold to consumers which prohibited the use of the program for commercial purposes. Although the license was enclosed inside the box containing the program, the outside of the box had a statement that the software came with restrictions stated in the enclosed license. The license itself stated that if the purchaser was unwilling to abide by the terms of the license, the purchaser could return the software unused for a full refund. The terms of the license also appeared every time the software was run.

Zeidenberg bought a consumer package of the software in a retail store. He then formed a corporation which resold information in the database over the Internet for a fee. Upon learning of Zeidenberg's enterprise, ProCD sued for injunctive relief. The District Court held the license to be ineffective because it was an attempt at post-contract modification to which Zeidenberg had not agreed.

The Seventh Circuit reversed the District Court and upheld the license. The Circuit Court agreed with the District Court that one party cannot unilaterally modify the terms of an existing contract, but said that the case did not involve an attempt to modify an existing contract. Instead, the court held that the terms of the license were included in the contract at the time of its formation. Zeidenberg had argued that the contract was formed by his payment of the price and leaving the store with the goods. Because the license agreement itself was contained unseen within the box, he argued (and the District Court agreed) that the license was not part of the contract. To this argument, Judge Easterbrook responded:

> One cannot agree to hidden terms, the [trial] judge concluded. So far, so good—but one of the terms to which Zeidenberg agreed by purchasing the software is that the transaction was subject to a license. Zeidenberg's position therefore must be that the printed terms on the outside of the box are the parties' contract—except for the printed terms that refer to or incorporate other terms. But why would Wisconsin fetter the parties' choice in this way? Vendors can put the entire terms of a contract on the outside of a box only by using microscopic type, removing other information that buyers might find more useful (such as what the software does) or both.[790]

---

[790] *Id.* at 1451–1452, 29 UCCR2d at 1113.

Judge Easterbrook could have stopped at this point in the opinion and reached a decision reasonably supportable by existing contract law. As the quoted language suggests, he could have found that the contract was formed at the time of purchase, and that the notice on the outside of the box was sufficient to incorporate the standard terms of the license into the contract. There is no reason why a party cannot agree in advance to be bound by terms of which he is specifically unaware at the time of contracting, at least if the terms are reasonable.[791]

Judge Easterbrook recognized, however, that in many cases the price of the goods is paid well before the buyer has had an opportunity to examine even the outside of the container in which the goods are packaged. In fact, as Judge Easterbrook recognized, only a minority of software sales take place over the counter; most sales take place by mail order, telephone, or over the Internet. Were the contract formed at the time of the payment of the purchase price, or the shipment of the goods,[792] the buyer would not have had the opportunity to examine the box, and therefore would not be bound by the license, a result Judge Easterbrook clearly did not favor. In order to subject the buyer to the license in even these cases, Judge Easterbrook returned to the fundamental principle of first-year contracts that an offeror is master of the offer:

> A vendor, as master of the offer, may invite acceptance by conduct, and may propose limitations on the kind of conduct that constitutes acceptance. . . . ProCD proposed a contract that a buyer would accept by using the software after having an opportunity to read the license at leisure. This Zeidenberg did.[793]

Because the notice on the box indicated that the software could be returned for a full refund if the buyer was unwilling to use it in accordance with the license, Judge Easterbrook found that a contract was formed, not by the buyer's payment of the price and the seller's delivery of the goods, but by

---

[791] Section 211 of the Restatement (Second) of Contracts allows a party to be bound by the terms of a standardized agreement even though both parties know that they have not been read by the party against whom the terms operate. *See* Restatement (Second) of Contracts § 211 (1981) and especially Comment b. However, the unread terms do not become part of the contract if the party seeking to enforce the terms has reason to believe that the other party would not have agreed to them had he been actually aware of their content. *See also* U.C.C. § 2-311(1) permitting the parties to agree in a contract to leave some particulars of performance to be specified by one of the parties. The specification, however, must be in good faith.

[792] *See* U.C.C. § 2-206(1)(b).

[793] 86 F.3d at 1452, 29 UCCR2d at 1115–1116.

the buyer's retention and use of the goods after having the opportunity to learn of the terms of the license.

A little more than six months later, Judge Easterbrook affirmed his opinion in *ProCD*, this time in a case involving the computer *hardware* industry. In *Hill v. Gateway 2000*,[794] the buyers purchased a Gateway 2000 computer over the phone using a credit card. When the computer arrived, a list of terms were included in the box, which were said to govern the contract if the buyer did not return the computer within thirty days for a full refund. One of the terms was an agreement to arbitrate disputes. The buyer kept the computer more than thirty days, a dispute arose over the quality of the computer, and the buyer filed suit. Gateway 2000 asked the court to enforce the arbitration clause and dismiss the case. The trial judge refused, and Gateway 2000 appealed.

Judge Easterbrook held the arbitration clause to be binding. He said that because of the "accept or return" provision, *ProCD* was applicable. Consequently, the contract was not formed when the buyer provided a credit-card authorization or when the seller shipped the goods. Rather, the contract was formed by the buyer's retaining the computer for more than thirty days following receipt. The court rejected arguments that *ProCD* applied only to computer software or to licenses, stating that *ProCD* was "about the law of contracts, not the law of software."[795]

Judge Easterbrook also rejected the distinction offered by plaintiffs that the buyer in *ProCD* had been alerted by the box before he purchased the software that there were license terms inside the box, whereas there was no such notice before the Hills had purchased the Gateway 2000. Judge Easterbrook said that "the Hills knew before they ordered the computer that the carton would include some important terms, and they did not seek to discover them in advance."[796]

The implications of the *ProCD* and *Gateway 2000* cases for contract disclaimers, as well as contract formation generally, are significant. While Judge Easterbrook does suggest in *ProCD* that warranty disclaimers would probably have to be conspicuous,[797] there is nothing in either case to indicate that warranty disclaimers are not otherwise subject to the rules laid down in those cases. There is no reason to believe, for example, that the warranty disclaimers and remedy limitations that undoubtedly accompanied the Hills' Gateway 2000 computer would not be enforceable under Judge Easter-

---

[794] 105 F.3d 1147, 31 UCCR2d 303 (7th Cir. 1997).
[795] *Id.* at 1149, 31 UCCR2d at 306.
[796] *Id.* at 1150, 31 UCCR2d at 308.
[797] 86 F.3d at 1453, 29 UCCR2d 1116.

brook's rationale in the same manner as the arbitration clause. It was sufficient for Judge Easterbrook that the buyers knew before ordering the computer that the carton would include some important terms. He required no notice that among those terms was an arbitration clause.[798]

In both opinions, Judge Easterbrook offers some sound efficiency reasons for his decision. If sellers such as Gateway 2000 were required to disclose all terms before shipping merchandise and collecting the price, transaction costs would undoubtedly increase. For example, advertising costs would probably be higher, and order forms supplied by the seller would be more voluminous. On the other hand, the *ProCD* and *Gateway 2000* cases contain some conceptual flaws and make it too easy for sellers to impose unilaterally terms on buyers. There is no indication in *Gateway 2000* that the buyer was informed at the time it paid the price through a credit authorization that no contract had been formed (or would not be formed upon shipment). While the offerer is master of the offer, as Judge Easterbrook affirms, contract formation remains *objective*—if a reasonable offeree believes from the offeror's objective manifestations that a contract has been formed, then a contract has been formed. Most buyers in the position of the Hills would be surprised to learn that no contract had been formed even after they had paid the price and Gateway 2000 had shipped the computer. To the contrary, most buyers would assume that a contract had been formed when the Hills authorized payment or at the latest, when Gateway 2000 shipped the computer. Judge Easterbrook's opinion in *Gateway 2000* never considered the question of contract formation from the standpoint of a reasonable offeree. If a contract, from the standpoint of a reasonable person, was formed at the time of payment or shipment, it is of no consequence that Gateway 2000 gave the Hills the right to return the computer for a full refund if they did not like the enclosed terms.

Further, the opinion in *Gateway 2000* requires only that the buyers know prior to paying the price that *some* important terms are contained in the carton. There appears to be no requirement that they have notice of even the general nature of those terms in order to be bound by them if they do not return the goods. Surely, the first thing on the Hills' mind after receiving their new computer was not to look for an arbitration clause. Modern computers arrive with massive amounts of documentation, much of which can

---

[798] According to Judge Easterbrook, the Hills were aware that the carton included important terms because Gateway 2000's advertisements stated that their products came with limited warranties and lifetime support. 105 F.3d at 1150, 31 UCCR2d at 308–309.

go unexamined for lengthy periods.[799] The Hills were probably much more interested in getting the computer "up and running" than in seeing whether there were any terms in the documents that they found sufficiently objectionable to cause them to return the computer. Also, by the time that a buyer has paid the price and received the goods, the buyer is probably much more committed to the sale than during the search process. Terms that the buyer learns about after receiving the goods that may have caused the buyer to consider an alternative if he had become aware of them during the search process, may not be sufficient to cause the buyer to go to the trouble of repackaging and returning the goods and beginning the search all over again.

If a seller desires to prevent contract formation until the buyer forgoes the opportunity to return the goods, the seller should have to provide clear and unambiguous notice to the buyer that the buyer's payment of the price and the seller's shipment of the goods does not create a contract; that a contract is created only after the buyer has retained the goods for a specified period of time sufficient to decide whether to accept the seller's terms. Otherwise, a contract is created when a reasonable buyer would expect one to be created—at the time the buyer pays the price and the seller ships or agrees to ship the goods.[800]

If the seller does not provide clear and unambiguous notice that the seller's shipment or agreement to ship does not create a contract, then the seller should not be able to impose a post-contract disclaimer upon the buyer simply by allowing the buyer to return the goods for a refund. A party cannot unilaterally impose a post-contract modification on the other party simply by giving that party the opportunity to rescind the contract if he doesn't like the modification.

What if the seller provides *pre-contract* notice to the buyer that by entering into the contract the buyer is agreeing to terms that will accompany the goods? For example, the seller's order form might clearly state that additional terms will accompany the goods, to which the buyer is bound unless he returns the goods. Is this sufficient to bind the buyer to the additional terms even if (contrary to Judge Easterbrook's analysis) a contract is created by payment of the price or shipment of the goods?

The answer should be "yes," providing four criteria are met. First, the seller must inform the buyer before the contract is formal that the contract

---

[799] One of the authors of this text has still not examined some of the documentation received with a computer he purchased more than four years ago.

[800] *See* U.C.C. § 2-204, which states that unless an offer unambiguously indicates to the contrary, an offer for prompt or current shipment is accepted by either a prompt promise to ship the goods or the prompt shipment of the goods.

includes additional terms that will accompany the goods. Second, the seller must provide the buyer with notice of the specific nature of the terms; for example, that they contain disclaimers of implied warranties, limitations on remedies, agreements to arbitrate, etc. Third, the terms must be reasonable; they cannot be terms that would be unexpected or such, had they been presented to the buyer before the contract, would likely have caused the buyer to reject the offer. Fourth, the buyer must have been offered the opportunity to examine the terms before the contract. That is, the seller must have said, in effect, that additional terms will accompany the goods and if you would like to see them before you pay the price and we ship the goods, here is how you can do so.

These criteria are consistent with the modern objective theory of contracts and with the manner in which the Restatement (Second) of Contracts deals with standard form agreements.[801] The buyer's agreement to be bound by terms arriving with the goods is, in effect, the same as the buyer's agreement to a standard form contract. Although the buyer has the opportunity to review the detailed terms before entering into the contract, both parties understand that buyers will generally not do so. The buyer's assent to the unseen terms that arrive with the goods is really an agreement to be bound by terms that are not oppressive or unreasonable, in the same manner as the buyer's agreement to a standard form contract.[802] The two situations should be treated similarly.

[4] Warranty Disclaimers and Unconscionability

Section 2-302 (unconscionability) has been discussed in detail elsewhere in this text.[803] A minor controversy has arisen concerning the applicability of this section to warranty disclaimers. It has been suggested by some commentators,[804] and cases have held,[805] that a disclaimer that satisfies the requirements of section 2-316 is *per se* conscionable; it is not subject to scrutiny under section 2-302.

---

[801] *See* Restatement (Second) of Contracts § 211 (1981).

[802] *See* Karl Llewellyn, The Common Law Tradition, 362–363 (1960).

[803] *See* § 3.09, *supra*.

[804] *See* James White & Robert Summers, Uniform Commercial Code § 12-11 at 615–616 (3d ed. 1988); Arthur Leff, "Unconscionability and the Code—The Emperor's New Clause," 115 U. Pa. L. Rev. 485 (1967).

[805] *See, e.g.*, Marshall v. Murray Oldsmobile Co., 207 Va. 972, 154 S.E.2d 140, 4 UCCR 172 (1967). *See also* Hinding v. Vline-Volvo, Inc., 29 UCCR2d 793 (Minn. Ct. App. 1996) (unpublished) (disclaimer of warranties not unconscionable in part because disclaimer is authorized under U.C.C. § 2-316).

The arguments advanced in support of this position are formidable.[806] Section 2-316 does not refer to section 2-302, nor is there a cross-reference to section 2-302 in the Comments to section 2-316. In contrast, section 2-719, dealing with remedy limitations, expressly incorporates unconscionability into section 2-719(3) and contains an explicit cross-reference to section 2-302. Had the drafters intended to subject warranty disclaimers to scrutiny under section 2-302, they could have easily done so in a manner similar to remedy limitations.

Further, according to Comment 1 to section 2-302, the principle of unconscionability is the prevention of oppression and unfair surprise, not the disturbance of the allocation of risks because of superior bargaining power.[807] Comment 1 to section 2-316 states that the section seeks, through its requirements, to protect a buyer from "unexpected and unbargained language of disclaimer."[808] If the drafters felt that compliance with section 2-316 protected the buyer from unexpected and unbargained language of disclaimer, how can the buyer nonetheless be subject to "oppression and unfair surprise" by a disclaimer that complies with its terms? Arguably, sections 2-316 and 2-302 were aimed at preventing the same evil, and the drafters felt that in the interests of certainty, they would provide a specific set of instructions for avoiding this evil in the case of disclaimers. Again, this is in contrast to section 2-719, which does not provide specific means for avoiding "unfair surprise" with respect to remedy limitations.

The majority of courts, however, have decided that warranty disclaimers are subject to scrutiny under section 2-302.[809] Arguments on this side are also impressive. First, section 2-302 applies, by its terms, to *any* clause of a contract.[810] Second, and perhaps more convincing, many of the examples of unconscionable clauses described in the comments to section 2-302 deal with warranty disclaimers. Third, Comment 1 to section 2-302

---

[806] These arguments are largely, although not entirely, developed from Professor Leff's article cited in *supra* note 807.

[807] U.C.C. § 2-302, Official Comment 1.

[808] U.C.C. § 2-316, Official Comment 1.

[809] *See, e.g.,* Hahn v. Ford Motor Co. Inc., 434 N.E.2d 943, 33 UCCR 1277 (Ind. Ct. App. 1982); FMC Fin. Corp. v. Murphree, 632 F.2d 413, 30 UCCR 496 (5th Cir. 1980); Rynders v. E.I. du Pont de Nemours & Co., 21 F.3d 835, 23 UCCR2d 333 (8th Cir. 1994); Martin v. Joseph Harris Co., Inc., 767 F.2d 296, 41 UCCR 315 (6th Cir. 1985). *See also* Potomac Plaza Terraces, Inc. v. QSC Prods., Inc., 868 F. Supp. 346, 26 UCCR2d 1069 (D.D.C. 1994) (disclaimer of implied warranties invalid if its inclusion was a violation of the obligation of good faith); Antz v. GAF Materials Corp., 36 UCCR2d 726 (Pa. Super. Ct. 1998).

[810] U.C.C. § 2-302 (emphasis added).

also refers to "oppression" as well as "unfair surprise." As we have seen,[811] courts have incorporated into their analysis of unconscionability concepts like "adhesion contracts" and "inequality of bargaining power" which go beyond terms that merely take the buyer by surprise. Terms can be "oppressive" because they are substantively unfair and the seller refuses to bargain over them, even if the buyer is aware of the disclaimer and understands its effects.

Despite their willingness to subject warranty disclaimers to section 2-302, courts rarely find a disclaimer that satisfies section 2-316 to be unconscionable.[812] This is consistent with the prevailing view that both substantive and procedural unconscionability are required before a provision will be unconscionable under section 2-302. Once a provision has met the requirements of section 2-316, it is a difficult task to show that it is nonetheless procedurally unconscionable.

This issue, while prompting lively classroom discussion, is becoming increasingly unimportant. The ability of a seller to disclaim implied warranties in consumer transactions is increasingly restricted or prohibited by state consumer-protection legislation[813] and by state variations to the Code itself.[814] In addition, state consumer-protection legislation, even when it does not explicitly prohibit or restrict disclaimers, provides an avenue to attack a disclaimer as unfair or unconscionable that is not subject to the preemption argument to which section 2-302 is vulnerable.[815] The Magnuson-Moss Federal Warranty Act also significantly restricts the ability of sellers in consumer transactions to disclaim implied warranties.[816] All of these developments have substantially diminished the number of cases in which

---

[811] See § 3.09[A][2], supra.

[812] See, e.g., Seekings v. Jimmy GMC of Tucson, Inc., 638 P.2d 223, 131 Ariz. 1, 31 UCCR 501 (Ariz. Ct. App. 1981); Buettner v. R.W. Martin & Sons, Inc., 47 F.3d 116, 25 UCCR2d 1086 (4th Cir. 1995); Siemens Credit Corp. v. Marvik Colour, Inc., 859 F. Supp. 686, 24 UCCR2d 705 (S.D.N.Y. 1994); Buettner v. Super Laundry Mach., 857 F. Supp. 471, 23 UCCR2d 79 (E.D. Va. 1994); Keeneland Ass'n, Inc. v. Eamer, 830 F. Supp. 974, 22 UCCR2d 130 (E.D. Ky. 1993). But see Hahn v. Ford Motor Co. Inc., 434 N.E.2d 943, 33 UCCR 1277 (Ind. Ct. App. 1982); FMC Fin. Corp. v. Murphree, 632 F.2d 413, 30 UCCR 496 (5th Cir. 1980); Rynders v. E.I. du Pont de Nemours & Co., 21 F.3d 835, 23 UCCR2d 333 (8th Cir. 1994); Martin v. Joseph Harris Co., Inc., 767 F.2d 296, 41 UCCR 315 (6th Cir. 1985).

[813] See, e.g., W. Va. Code Ann. § 46A-6-107 (1996).

[814] See Kan. Stat. Ann. § 84-2-316 (1983); Md. Code Ann., Commercial Law, § 2-316 (1992).

[815] See Metro Ford Truck Sales, Inc. v. Davis, 709 S.W.2d 785 (Tex. Ct. App. 1986); A.W. Attaway v. Tom's Auto Sales, Inc., 242 S.E.2d 740 (Ga. Ct. App. 1978).

[816] See § 8.02[G][3], infra.

consumers argue that disclaimers are unconscionable under section 2-302. With respect to nonconsumer buyers, the relationship of sections 2-302 and 2-316 has never been a significant issue, because nonconsumer buyers are almost never successful in arguing that warranty disclaimers are unconscionable even when they are permitted by the courts to make the argument.

[5] Disclaimer by Course of Dealing, Course of Performance, and Usage of Trade

The meaning of "course of dealing," "course of performance," and "usage of trade" is discussed elsewhere in this text.[817] The application of these concepts to disclaimers rests on the notion that each of them aids in determining the meaning of the parties' agreement. The language that the parties used in expressing their agreement has been chosen against the background of any usage of trade in which they are engaged or any prior course of dealing between them. Further, course of dealing, usage of trade, and course of performance may supply implied terms about subjects on which the express terms of the contract are silent. To the extent that they indicate that the parties intended to limit or exclude implied warranties, that intention will be given effect.

The most frequent argument that course of dealing has resulted in the disclaimer of implied warranties is that a disclaimer has appeared repeatedly in documents such as invoices, order forms, or acknowledgments without objection by the affected party. As discussed previously,[818] courts are divided on this question. Some courts have taken the position that the mere repetition of a disclaimer is insufficient to create a course of dealing in the absence of some affirmative assent by the affected party. Other courts have held that as few as two repetitions of a disclaimer without objection may be sufficient to create a course of dealing that includes the disclaimer.[819]

Disclaimers have also been found as a result of course of dealing under somewhat different circumstances. In a recent case, *Standard Structural Steel Co. v. Bethlehem Steel Corp.*,[820] the parties entered into an oral contract for the purchase of steel cable, which later proved to be defective. The buyer sued on the basis of the implied warranty of merchantability. The court held that the implied warranty had been successfully disclaimed by a course of dealing over the prior sixty-two years; the purchasing agent for the buyer

---

[817] *See* § 3.14, *supra.*

[818] *See* § 4.07[C][4], *supra.*

[819] *Id.*

[820] 597 F. Supp. 164, 40 UCCR 1245 (D. Conn. 1984).

was well aware that the seller would not sell its products without excluding implied warranties.[821] Generally speaking, the exclusion of implied warranties by course of dealing or course of performance will depend upon the length of the parties' association and the frequency of their interactions,[822] the extent of their business sophistication,[823] and the consistency and clarity of the exclusion or modification.[824]

A number of sellers have successfully argued that implied warranties have been excluded through trade usage,[825] although probably an equal number have been unsuccessful.[826] Among the lucky sellers was the seller in *Spurgeon v. Jamieson Motors*.[827] In 1970, Spurgeon contracted to buy a ten-year-old combine from Jamieson Motors for $1,700. After driving the combine home and harvesting only five acres, it broke down. Both parties attempted several repairs, but the combine broke down again after harvesting only fifteen additional acres. After further repairs, it broke down again the following spring, and Spurgeon then hired others to complete his harvest. Spurgeon sued for breach of the implied warranty of merchantability and recovered at trial. On appeal, Jamieson argued that trade usage had excluded

---

[821] *See also* J.D. Pavlak, Ltd. v. William Davies Co., Inc., 40 Ill. App. 3d 1, 351 N.E.2d 243, 20 UCCR 394 (1976) (contract language and past willingness of buyer to accept reduced price when meat had greater than 15 percent fat content established a disclaimer of implied warranty that fat content would not be greater than 15 percent); Country Clubs, Inc. v. Allis-Chalmers Mfg. Co., 430 F.2d 1394, 7 UCCR 1253 (6th Cir. 1970) (warranty of merchantability on golf carts disclaimed by course of dealing and course of performance).

[822] *See* Standard Structural Steel Co. v. Bethlehem Steel Corp., 597 F. Supp. 164, 40 UCCR 1245 (D. Conn. 1984); Tolmie Farms, Inc. v. J.R. Simplot Co., Inc., 124 Idaho 607, 862 P.2d 299, 23 UCCR2d 65 (1993); Allied Indus. Serv. Corp. v. Kasle Iron & Metals, Inc., 62 Ohio App. 2d 144, 405 N.E.2d 307, 29 UCCR 439 (1977); Ramsey Prods. Corp. v. Morbark Indus., Inc., 823 F.2d 798, 4 UCCR2d 428 (4th Cir. 1987).

[823] *See, e.g.*, Country Club, Inc. v. Allis-Chalmers Mfg. Co., 430 F.2d 1394, 7 UCCR 1253 (6th Cir. 1970); Commonwealth v. Johnson Insulation, 682 N.E.2d 1323, 33 UCCR2d 426 (Mass. 1997).

[824] *See, e.g.*, Ramsey Prods. Corp. v. Morbark Indus., Inc., 823 F.2d 798, 4 UCCR2d 428 (4th Cir. 1987).

[825] *See, e.g.*, Martin Rispens & Son v. Hall Farms, Inc., 601 N.E.2d 429, 19 UCCR2d 1021 (Ind. Ct. App. 1992); Hartwig Farms, Inc. v. Pacific Gamble Robinson Co., 625 P.2d 171, 28 Wash. App. 539, 30 UCCR 1552 (Wash. Ct. App. 1981); Lincoln Pulp & Paper Co. v. Dravo Corp., 445 F. Supp. 507, 25 UCCR 400 (D. Me. 1977).

[826] *See, e.g.*, Mallory v. Conida Warehouses, Inc., 350 N.W.2d 825, 134 Mich. App. 28 (Mich. Ct. App. 1984); Maru Shipping Co., Inc. v. Burmeister & Wain Am. Corp., 528 F. Supp. 210, 33 UCCR 230 (S.D.N.Y. 1981); Wilson v. Marquette Elecs., Inc., 630 F.2d 575, 29 UCCR 399 (8th Cir. 1980); Basic Adhesives, Inc. v. Robert Matzkin Co., Inc., 29 UCCR 499 (N.Y. Sup. Ct. 1980).

[827] 521 P.2d 924, 14 UCCR 651 (Mont. 1974).

implied warranties. The appellate court agreed. There was undisputed testimony of a usage of trade in farm machinery sales, especially used combines, that there was no warranty beyond a 50-50 warranty,[828] and that the buyer was aware of the usage, as adduced by payment of half of the repairs without objection.[829]

The seller was not so successful in *Certain-Teed Products Corp. v. Goslee Roofing & Sheet Metal, Inc.*[830] The buyer was a roofing contractor who used the seller's roofing material. It later leaked after installation. The seller argued that a usage of trade existed that a seller of roofing products warrants only that the roof is bondable, not that the roof will not leak. The appeals court found that the record did not establish such a usage of trade and that roofing materials that leaked breached the warranty of merchantability.

The seller's case will ultimately turn on the strength of the seller's evidence that an exclusion or modification of implied warranties has "such regularity of observance . . . as to justify an expectation that it will be observed with respect to the transaction in question,"[831] or, as another court has put it, the proof of the existence and acceptance of a dominant, industrywide pattern excluding or modifying an implied warranty.[832] It is, of course, not necessary that a party have actual knowledge of a trade usage before it can be applied against the party. The usage must be sufficiently well established that it can be reasonably be expected that those engaging in the trade *should* be aware of it.[833]

[6] Disclaimer by Examination

Defendants in warranty disputes often argue that implied warranties were disclaimed by a buyer's inspection of the goods which put the buyer

---

[828] A "50-50" warranty is one where each party pays half of the repair cost.

[829] For another case in which a usage of trade was found to exclude implied warranties on used goods, *see* Hummel v. Skyline Dodge, Inc., 589 P.2d 73, 26 UCCR 46 (Colo. Ct. App. 1978).

[830] 26 Md. App. 452, 339 A.2d 302, 18 UCCR 80 (Md. Ct. Spec. App. 1975).

[831] U.C.C. § 1-205(2).

[832] Hartwig Farms, Inc. v. Pacific Gamble Robinson Co., 625 P.2d 171, 175, 30 UCCR 1552, 1556 (Wash. Ct. App. 1981).

[833] The court in Zicari v. Joseph Harris Co., 33 A.D.2d 17, 304 N.Y.S.2d 918, 6 UCCR 1246 (N.Y. App. Div. 1969), concluded that the seller had failed to establish an exclusion of implied warranties by a usage of trade "understood by all persons in the seed business and farming." To the extent that this implies that all members of a trade must have actual knowledge of the usage before a usage of trade is established, the case is wrong.

on notice of any defects present in the goods. The Code recognizes this method of excluding warranties in section 2-316(3)(b) which provides:

> [W]hen the buyer before entering into the contract has examined the goods or the sample or model as fully as he desired or has refused to examine the goods there is no implied warranty with regard to defects which an examination ought in the circumstances to have revealed to him.[834]

Several points in this subsection deserve mention. First, the subsection does not purport to provide a method by which express warranties can be limited or excluded; it refers only to implied warranties. Nevertheless, an examination might prevent an express warranty from arising. As discussed in a previous section of this work,[835] a representation must be "part of the basis of the bargain" before an express warranty can exist. An examination may, in a particular case, indicate that no part of the bargain rested on any representation made by the seller. For example, in *Alan Wood Steel Co. v. Capital Equipment Enterprises, Inc.*,[836] the plaintiff purchased a old, used "75 ton" crane that was able to only lift 50 tons. Because the buyer relied upon an examination of the crane by two skilled agents, which should have revealed that the crane would not lift 75 tons, the description was held not to create an express warranty. If, however, a buyer purchases goods on the strength of both an examination and on statements made by the seller (or on descriptions, samples, or models), the statements will be *part* of the basis of the bargain, and will create express warranties.

Second, only those defects which an examination ought in the circumstances to have revealed to the buyer will be excluded from implied warranty coverage. Warranties are not excluded or modified by examinations that fail to discover latent or undetectable defects,[837] and examinations must only be reasonable under the circumstances.[838] Comment 8 to section 2-316, how-

---

[834] U.C.C. § 2-316(3)(b).

[835] *See* § 4.05[F], *supra*.

[836] 349 N.E.2d 627, 19 UCCR 1310 (Ill. Ct. App. 1976).

[837] *See* U.C.C. § 2-316, Official Comment 8. *See also* Lafayette Stabilizer Repair, Inc. v. Machinery Wholesalers Corp., 750 F.2d 1290, 40 UCCR 122 (5th Cir. 1985); Overland Bond & Inv. Corp. v. Howard, 9 Ill. App. 3d 348, 292 N.E.2d 168, 11 UCCR 945 (1972); Young & Cooper, Inc. v. Vestring, 214 Kan. 311, 521 P.2d 281, 14 UCCR 916 (1974); Controltek, Inc. v. Kwikee Enters., Inc., 284 Or. 123, 585 P.2d 670, 25 UCCR 421 (1978); Mountaineer Contractors, Inc. v. Mountain State Mack, Inc., 268 S.E.2d 886, 30 UCCR 134 (W. Va. 1980).

[838] *See* Henry Heide, Inc. v. WRH Prods. Co., Inc., 766 F.2d 105, 41 UCCR 419 (3d Cir. 1985). Comment 8 states that the normal method of examining goods in the circumstances determines what defects are excluded by the examination.

ever, makes it clear that a professional buyer will be held to a higher inspection standard than a layperson.[839] Whether an inspection ought to have
revealed a defect is normally a question of fact.[840] Examples of defects not
sufficiently apparent to exclude implied warranties include infected cattle,[841]
disease-ridden pigs,[842] internal engine and internal mechanical defects,[843]
microscopic fabric defects,[844] salt water damage to a yacht,[845] and misspe-
cified concrete strength.[846] Moreover, even if an examination reveals some
defects, implied warranties are not excluded for other defects, unless the
defects that were uncovered should have led to discovery of the others.[847]

Implied warranties, however, will be excluded for defects[848] that were
discovered or *should have been* discovered on reasonable inspection. Examples of defects for which implied warranties were excluded by examination include oversize tires and an improper steering wheel on a vehicle,[849]
defective handles on wiglet cases,[850] and a misdrilled hole on a garage door
track.[851] It is rare for the courts to find a warranty disclaimed by examination

---

[839] U.C.C. § 2-316, Official Comment 8.

[840] *See* Southeastern Adhesives Co. v. Funder Am., Inc., 366 S.E.2d 505, 6 UCCR2d 403
(N.C. Ct. App. 1988); Henry Heide Inc. v. WRH Prods. Co., Inc., 766 F.2d 105, 41 UCCR
419 (3d Cir. 1985).

[841] Young & Cooper, Inc., v. Vestring, 521 P.2d 281, 14 UCCR 916 (Kan. 1974).

[842] Murray v. Kleen, Inc., 354 N.E.2d 415, 20 UCCR 298 (Ill. Ct. App. 1976).

[843] Overland Bond & Inv. Corp. v. Howard, 292 N.E.2d 168, 11 UCCR 945 (Ill. App.
1976); Lafayette Stabilizer Repair, Inc. v. Mach. Wholesalers Corp., 750 F.2d 1290, 40
UCCR 122 (5th Cir. 1985).

[844] Wullschleger & Co., Inc. v. Jenny Fashions, Inc., 618 F. Supp. 373, 41 UCCR 1213
(S.D.N.Y. 1985).

[845] Barr v. S-2 Yachts, Inc., 7 UCCR2d 1431 (E.D. Va. 1988).

[846] Bevard v. Howat Concrete Co., Inc., 433 F.2d 1202, 7 UCCR 966 (D.C. Cir. 1970).

[847] *See, e.g.*, Barr v. S-2 Yachts, Inc., 7 UCCR2d 1431 (E.D. Va. 1988) (buyer's observance of rusty screws on trial run did not exclude implied warranty of merchantability since
defects discovered would not reveal extensive damage caused by previous sinking); Richards
v. Goerg Boat & Motors, Inc., 384 N.E.2d 1084, 179 Ind. App. 102, 25 UCCR 1002 (Ind.
Ct. App. 1979) (discovery of some cracks in the hull and cabins did not exclude implied
warranties as to structural defects and water damage).

[848] As in other contexts, "defects" include both design and manufacturing defects. *See*
Light v. Weldarc Co., 569 So. 2d 1302, 14 UCCR2d 431 (Fla. Dist. Ct. App. 1990) (safety
glasses lacking headstrap).

[849] Harison-Gulley Chevrolet, Inc. v. Carr, 134 Ga. App. 449, 214 S.E.2d 712, 16 UCCR
962 (1975).

[850] Blockhead, Inc. v. Plastic Forming Co., Inc., 402 F. Supp. 1017, 18 UCCR 636 (D.
Conn. 1975).

[851] Rhodes v. Lodi Door, Inc., 1 UCCR2d 63 (Utah 1986).

for an undiscovered defect when the buyer is a layperson with no special expertise in the goods.[852]

Third, it is only an *examination* of the goods or a refusal to *examine* the goods that limits or excludes implied warranties.[853] An examination must be distinguished from the Code's concept of inspection. Inspection generally occurs after the goods have been delivered to the buyer pursuant to an earlier contract for their sale. The Code gives the buyer a reasonable opportunity to inspect the goods after their delivery to determine whether they conform to the contract.[854] An examination, on the other hand, occurs (if at all) before the contract has been entered into, and its purpose is to assist the buyer in deciding whether to purchase the goods and on what terms.

Fourth, implied warranties may be excluded pursuant to section 2-316(3)(b) even if the buyer fails to examine the goods. If the buyer *refuses* the seller's request to examine the goods, he will have assumed the risk of any defects a reasonable examination would have detected. A "refusal" to examine the goods, however, is not the same as an opportunity to examine them. The buyer's failure to take advantage of an opportunity to examine the goods does not constitute a refusal to examine them.[855] The seller must demand that the buyer examine the goods (or a sample of the goods) and the buyer must refuse to do so.[856]

§ 4.08 LIMITATION OF REMEDIES

[A] Introduction

When a warranty has been successfully disclaimed, the buyer has no cause of action for a supposed breach of that warranty. The disclaimer has

---

[852] *See, e.g.*, Michael-Regan Co., Inc. v. Lindell, 527 F.2d 653, 17 UCCR 958 (9th Cir. 1975) (court emphasized buyer's experience in the wood industry).

[853] Banco Del Estado v. Navistar Int'l Transp. Corp., 954 F. Supp. 1275, 34 UCCR2d (N.D. Ill. 1997) ("fully examined goods precludes breach of implied warranty claim").

[854] U.C.C. § 2-606.

[855] *See, e.g.*, Austin Lee Corp. v. Cascades Motel, Inc., 182 S.E.2d 173, 9 UCCR 462 (Ga. Ct. App. 1971); Ambassador Steel Co. v. Ewald Steel Co., 33 Mich. App. 495, 190 N.W.2d 275, 9 UCCR 1019 (1971); Holm v. Hansen, 248 N.W.2d 503, 20 UCCR 879 (Iowa 1970).

[856] A couple of courts have failed to grasp the distinction between forgoing an opportunity to examine the goods and refusing to do so. *See* Michael-Regan, Co. Inc. v. Lindell, 527 F.2d 653, 17 UCCR 958 (9th Cir. 1975); Richards Mfg. Co. v. Gamel, 5 Wash. App. 549, 489 P.2d 366, 9 UCCR 1199 (1971). *See also* Taralli v. Birds in Paradise, 417 N.Y.S.2d 854, 26 UCCR 872 (N.Y. Civ. Ct. 1979) (seller *urged* buyer to have bird examined by a veterinarian).

removed the warranty and the seller is not in default. In this sense, the successful warranty disclaimer also removes all remedies which the buyer would have without the disclaimer, but this exclusion of remedies is only an indirect consequence of the removal of any cause of action for breach of warranty. Sellers frequently do not disclaim all warranties but seek to limit directly the buyer's remedies in the event that a warranty is breached. Section 2-719 deals exclusively with remedy limitations and has no applicability to disclaimers of warranty.[857] Some cases have incorrectly subjected warranty disclaimers to scrutiny under section 2-719.[858]

There are many instances in which the seller is willing to make express or implied warranties, but would like to limit the remedies otherwise available to the buyer under the Code. The most frequent manifestation of this are the common "repair or replacement" clauses found in many contracts—clauses in which the seller limits the buyer's remedy to the repair or replacement of goods found to be defective. Section 2-719 permits the parties to limit remedy for breach, subject to specific requirements and qualifications. This section provides:

(1) Subject to the provisions of subsections (2) and (3) of this section and of the preceding section on liquidation and limitation if damages,

    (a) the agreement may provide for remedies in addition to or in substitution for those provided in this Article and may limit or alter the measure of damages recoverable under this Article as by limiting the buyer's remedies to return of the goods and repayment of the price or to repair and replacement of nonconforming goods or parts; and

    (b) resort to a remedy as provided is optional unless the remedy is expressly agreed to be exclusive, in which case it is the sole remedy.

(2) Where circumstances cause an exclusive or limited remedy to fail of its essential purpose, remedy may be had as provided in this Act.

(3) Consequential damages may be limited or excluded unless the limitation or exclusion is unconscionable. Limitation of consequential

---

[857] *See* U.C.C. § 2-719, Official Comment 3. Comment 2 to section 2-316 makes it explicit that if warranties are successfully disclaimed, there is no issue under section 2-719 of a limitation of remedies: "If no warranty exists, there is of course no problem of limiting remedies for breach of warranty."

[858] *See, e.g.,* Ford Motor Co. v. Tritt, 244 Ark. 883, 430 S.W.2d 778, 5 UCCR 312 (1968); Walsh v. Ford Motor Co., 59 Misc. 2d 241, 298 N.Y.S.2d 538, 6 UCCR 56 (N.Y. Sup. Ct. 1969).

damages for injury to the person in the case of consumer goods is prima facie unconscionable but limitation of damages where the loss is commercial is not.

Section 2-719 allows parties to increase or decrease available remedies providing three conditions are met. These are (1) the variation in remedies must be contained in the parties' agreement and must provide at least a "fair quantum of remedy"; (2) an exclusive or limited remedy must not have failed of its essential purpose; and (3) attempt to limit or exclude consequential damages must not be unconscionable.

Litigation has focused on three issues: (1) what language is necessary to limit remedies and must that language be conspicuous or otherwise brought to the buyer's attention; (2) when has a remedy "failed of its essential purpose" and what remedies are available to the buyer in the event that this failure occurs; and (3) when is a limitation on remedies unconscionable. These issues will be considered in order.

[B] Requisite Language

The Code presumes that remedies provided in a contract are in addition to those provided in the Code unless the contract expressly states otherwise,[859] and a number of cases have held that the intention to make a remedy exclusive must be clearly expressed.[860] Comment 2 to section 2-719 makes this explicit:

> Subsection (1)(b) creates a presumption that clauses prescribing remedies are cumulative rather than exclusive. If the parties intend the term

---

[859] U.C.C. § 2-719(1)(b). *See* Herbstman v. Eastman Kodak Co., 131 N.J. Super. 439, 330 A.2d 384 (1974) *rev'd on other grounds*, 68 N.J. 1, 342 A.2d 181, 17 UCCR 39 (1975) (offer of free repairs does not exclude other remedies); Kelley Metal Trading Co. v. Al-Jon/United, Inc., 812 F. Supp. 185, 21 UCCR2d 993 (D. Kan. 1993) (requirement that seller repurchase equipment under certain circumstances insufficient to create exclusive remedy); JOC Oil USA, Inc. v. Consolidated Edison Co. of N.Y., Inc., 107 Misc. 2d 376, 434 N.Y.S.2d 623, 30 UCCR 426 (N.Y. Sup. Ct. 1980) (provision permitting buyer to withhold part of purchase price not exclusive); Foley v. L&L Int'l, Inc., 88 N.C. App. 710, 364 S.E.2d 733, 6 UCCR2d 53 (1988) (provision in contract that seller would refund buyer's downpayment if car were not delivered in ninety days not exclusive); McKenzie v. Alla-Ohio Valley Coals, Inc., 610 F.2d 1000, (D.C. Cir. 1979) (price reduction mechanism in contract not exclusive remedy for excessive ash content in the absence of express indication of exclusivity).

[860] *See, e.g.*, Parsons v. Motor Homes of Am., Inc., 465 So. 2d 1285, 40 UCCR 1264 (1st Cir. 1985); Council Bros., Inc. v. Ray Burner Co., 473 F.2d 400, 11 UCCR 1126 (5th Cir. 1973); McCarty v. E.J. Korvette, Inc., 28 Md. App. 421, 347 A.2d 253, 18 UCCR 14 (Md. Ct. Spec. App. 1975).

to describe the sole remedy under the contract, this must be *clearly* expressed.[861]

A number of sellers have run into trouble when they have not clearly expressed this exclusivity. A leading case is *Ford Motor Co v. Reid*.[862] The buyer in this case sued when his new car caught fire after approximately 1,800 miles. Damages included substantial consequential damages. Ford's new car express warranty provided a repair-and-replacement remedy for breach, and further provided that this obligations was "IN LIEU OF any other express or implied warranty . . . and of any other obligation on the part of the Company or the Selling Dealer."[863] The court held that this language was insufficient to create an exclusive repair-and-replacement remedy. Referring to the presumption that remedies are cumulative, the court said that the language of Ford's warranty referred only to "warranties" and "obligations," not to remedies. According to the court, "obligations" are not remedies; remedies arise from the failure to perform obligations. Therefore, all Code remedies were available to the buyers in addition to the express repair-and-replace remedy. Other cases have found similar language to be ineffective to create exclusive remedies.[864]

In *Clark v. International Harvester Co.*,[865] however, the court held language nearly identical to that in *Reid* created an exclusive remedy. International Harvester's New Equipment Warranty provided an express warranty and a repair-and-replacement remedy followed by this following language:

> THIS WARRANTY AND THE COMPANY'S OBLIGATION THEREUNDER IS IN LIEU OF ALL WARRANTIES, EXPRESS OR IMPLIED . . . and all other obligations or liabilities, including liability for incidental and consequential damages.

The court said that while it was disposed to strictly construe contractual provisions purporting to limit a party's remedies, it would "torture the plain meaning of the language" to interpret it other than providing for an exclusive

---

[861] U.C.C. § 2-719, Official Comment 2 (emphasis added).

[862] 465 S.W.2d 80, 8 UCCR 985 (Ark. 1971).

[863] *Id.* at 82, 8 UCCR at 988.

[864] *See, e.g.*, Gaynor Elec. Co., Inc. v. Hollander, 29 Conn. App. 865, 618 A.2d 532, 19 UCCR2d 791 (1993) (provision that the seller's liability "shall not exceed the cost of correcting defects in the goods" does not create an exclusive remedy); Stream v. Sportscar Salon, Ltd., 397 N.Y.S.2d 677, 22 UCCR 631 (N.Y. Civ. Ct. 1977) (remedy not exclusive where seller's "liability" limited to repair and replacement).

[865] 99 Idaho 326, 581 P.2d 784 (1978).

repair-and-replacement remedy.[866] The only way to reconcile these two cases is that the buyer in *Reid* was a consumer while the buyer in *International Harvester* was in the business of "custom farming."[867]

It is clear that the mere presence of a repair-and-replacement remedy in the contract should not overcome the presumption that remedies are cumulative.[868] A number of cases have further held that providing explicit alternative remedies in the contract does not create an implication that the remedies are exclusive.[869] For example, in *Council Bros., Inc. v. Ray Burner Co.,*[870] a provision in an express warranty that the seller would repair or replace defective parts or, at its option, refund the price was not sufficient to make the two remedies exclusive. In addition, where the seller provides a written warranty in a contract along with a remedy limitation, the seller must take care to insure that the exclusive remedy cannot be interpreted to apply only to the written warranty, thus permitting other remedies for breach of implied warranties and other express warranties.[871]

A case from the Seventh Circuit, *Cognitest Corp. v. Riverside Pub. Co.,*[872] correctly holds, however, that while a presumption exists that remedies are cumulative, the test is whether a reasonable construction of the

---

[866] *See also* Fredonia Broadcasting Corp. v. RCA Corp., 481 F.2d 781, 12 UCCR 1088 (5th Cir. 1973) (remedy of repair and replacement exclusive when contract provides that repair and replacement constitutes "the fulfillment of all RCA's obligations").

[867] According to the court, "custom farmers" contract to plow or preplant farmland for others.

[868] *See* Williams v. Hyatt Chrysler-Plymouth, Inc., 48 N.C. App. 308, 269 S.E.2d 184, 30 UCCR 90 (1980); In re Franklin Computer Corp., 55 B.R. 599, 42 UCCR 210 (Bankr. E.D. Pa. 1985). *But see* Goddard v. General Motors Corp., 27 UCCR 973 (1979) (provision that manufacturer would repair defects for a specified period and disclaimer of liability for consequential damages are an adequate expression of intent to create exclusive repair-and-replace remedy).

Occasionally, a court will hold that the nature of the remedy impliedly indicates that the remedy is exclusive, despite the lack of express language of exclusivity. *See* Veath v. Specialty Grains, Inc., 190 Ill. App. 3d 787, 546 N.E.2d 1005, 10 UCCR2d 771 (1989) (court held pricing formula for breach exclusive where any other interpretation would render formula meaningless).

[869] *See* Ralston Purina Co. v. Hartford Accident & Indem. Co., 540 F.2d 915, 19 UCCR 1348 (8th Cir. 1976).

[870] 473 F.2d 400, 11 UCCR 1126 (5th Cir. 1973).

[871] *See* Northern States Power Co. v. ITT Meyer Indus., 777 F.2d 405, 42 UCCR 1 (8th Cir. 1985) (limitation or remedy applies only to written warranty in contract, not to other express warranties). *See also* Falcon Tankers, Inc. v. Litton Sys., Inc., 300 A.2d 231, 11 UCCR 963 (Del. Super. Ct. 1972) (remedy limitation applies only to defects in material and workmanship, not other defects).

[872] 107 F.3d 493, 32 UCCR2d 11 (7th Cir. 1997).

contract indicates that the parties intended a limited remedy to be exclusive. Thus, the court found that the failure of the contract to expressly provide that a remedy is exclusive, or to use the word "exclusive" is not necessarily fatal to an exclusive remedy. In this case, the contract provided a detailed and specific remedy for precisely the kind of breach that occurred (the decision by a publisher not to go forward with the publication of a computer software program because of market conditions). The court held that, with respect to this particular kind of breach, a reasonable reading of the contract indicated that the parties had intended an exclusive remedy.

The distinction between consumer and commercial cases suggested by the different results in *Reid* and *International Harvester* is well justified. Consumers are less likely to read such limitations carefully and less likely to understand their effect (and sellers should know this). Contractual language establishing an exclusive remedy should leave no question, even in the mind of an unsophisticated consumer, that a remedy is their exclusive recourse in the event of a product defect.

[C] Conspicuousness

In contrast to section 2-316 dealing with warranty disclaimers, section 2-719 dealing with remedy limitations does not expressly require remedy limitations to be conspicuous. A number of courts have inferred from this that remedy limitations do not have to be conspicuous and have so held.[873] Others, however, have held that remedy limitations must be conspicuous, at least when the buyer is not commercially sophisticated.[874] In addition, other cases indicate that the conspicuousness of a remedy limitation will be relevant to the assent of the buyer to the limitation[875] or the conscionability of the limitation.[876]

---

[873] *See, e.g.,* Boone Valley Coop. Processing Ass'n v. French Oil Mill Mach. Co., 383 F. Supp. 606, 15 UCCR 650 (N.D. Iowa 1974); McCrimmon v. Tandy Corp., 414 S.E.2d 15, 17 UCCR2d 1134 (Ga. Ct. App. 1991); Webster v. Sensormatic Elec. Corp., 389 S.E.2d 15, 11 UCCR2d 499 (Ga. Ct. App. 1989).

[874] *See, e.g.,* Stauffer Chem. Co. v. Curry, 778 P.2d 1083, 10 UCCR2d 342 (Wyo. 1989); Adams v. American Cyanamid Co., 498 N.W.2d 577, 21 UCCR2d 962 (Neb. Ct. App. 1992).

[875] *See* Step-Saver Data Sys., Inc. v. WYSE Technology, 939 F.2d 91, 15 UCCR2d 1 (3d Cir. 1991); Dorman v. International Harvester Co., 120 Cal. Rptr. 516, 46 Cal. App. 3d 11, 16 UCCR 952 (Cal. Ct. App. 1975). *See also* Herbstman v. Eastman Kodak Co., 330 A.2d 384, 16 UCCR 133 (N.J. Super. Ct. 1974).

[876] *See* Stirn v. E.I. du Pont de Nemours & Co., Inc., 21 UCCR2d 979 (S.D. Ind. 1993); Keeneland Ass'n, Inc. v. Eamer, 830 F. Supp. 974, 22 UCCR2d 130 (E.D. Ky 1993); Emlee Equip. Leasing Corp. v. Waterbury Transmission, Inc., 626 A.2d 307, 23 UCCR2d 389 (Conn. Ct. App. 1993); Cox v. Lewiston Grain Growers, Inc., 936 P.2d 1191, 33 UCCR2d 443 (Wash. App. 1997).

Cases establishing an inviolate obligation to make remedy limitations conspicuous are surely wrong.[877] The drafters established a clear requirement for conspicuousness in section 2-316, and could have easily done so in section 2-719 had that been their intention. The conspicuousness of a remedy limitation, however, is unquestionably relevant to issues of buyer assent and unconscionability, and accounts for the fact that remedy limitations are much more likely to be struck because of lack of conspicuousness in cases where the buyer is a consumer.[878]

For a remedy limitation—or any other contractual provision for that matter—to be effective the buyer must objectively assent to it; it must be part of the parties' bargain in fact. If the limitation is contained in a printed clause which is not conspicuous or was not brought to the buyer's attention, the seller may have no reasonable expectation that the buyer understands that its remedies are restricted. To the contrary, the seller would have reason to know that the buyer believes that all remedies are available to him under the contract despite the printed clause.[879] As such, the clause cannot be said to be a part of the bargain because the buyer has not objectively assented to it. This result is far less likely in commercial transactions than consumer transactions, because in commercial transactions it is often reasonable for the seller to believe that the buyer has read and understood even an inconspicuous limitation of remedies.

The conspicuousness of contract provisions generally is a factor in assessing their conscionability,[880] and this should be no less true with respect to remedy limitations. Given their often dramatic effects on the buyer's rights,[881] remedy limitations should be subject to particular scrutiny for un-

---

[877] *See* Metalized Ceramics for Elecs., Inc. v. National Ammonia Co., 663 A.2d 762, 27 UCCR2d 1271 (Pa. Super. Ct. 1995) (even though remedy limitation was not in larger print or highlighted or emphasized in any other way, it was nonetheless enforceable when both parties were experienced business entities).

[878] As discussed in § 3.09[D], *supra*, contract clauses in transactions between commercial parties are rarely deemed to be unconscionable by the courts.

[879] *See* § 3.03, *supra*. *See also* Restatement (Second) of Contracts § 20 (1981) (if one party has reason to know of the other party's understanding of a contract, and the second party has no reason to know of the first party's understanding, the understanding of the second party prevails).

[880] *See* § 3.09[A], *supra*.

[881] An exclusive repair-and-replacement remedy, for example, generally has the effect of precluding virtually all of the buyer's remedies available under the Code. *See* Chapter 7, *infra*. If the exclusive repair-and-replacement remedy is effective, it will preclude the remedies of rejection (U.C.C. § 2-601) and revocation of acceptance (section 2-608), as well as limiting any damages to the cost of repairing or replacing the defective goods (sections 2-712, 2-713, 2-715). Only if the exclusive remedy fails of its essential purpose do these remedies become available. *See* § 4.08[D], *infra*.

conscionability. A more detailed discussion of remedy limitations and un-conscionability follows in a later section.[882]

[D] Failure of Essential Purpose

Subsection (2) of section 2-719 reads as follows:

> Where circumstances cause an exclusive or limited remedy to fail of its essential purpose, remedy may be had as provided in this Act.[883]

The meaning of this subsection is not apparent from the text of the provision. The "purpose" of a limited remedy depends on whether the buyer's or the seller's purpose is being considered. If the seller prepared the form in which the remedy limitation appears or otherwise insisted upon the limitation in the contract, it is reasonable to assume that the seller's "purpose" was to do exactly that which is spelled out in the clause: to limit his liability for defects in the goods. Therefore, from the seller's standpoint the only way the essential purpose of a limited remedy provision can fail is if the court refuses to enforce it. From the buyer's viewpoint, it is almost nonsensical to speak of the buyer's purpose for the limited remedy clause; the buyer has no interest *per se*—and therefore no purpose—in limiting its own reme-dies.[884] To speak of a purpose—as the Code does—for a provision limiting remedies merely confuses the question of whether a court should enforce the remedy limitation. The Comments indicate that what the drafters had in mind in this unfortunate choice of words was: "where an apparently fair and reasonable clause because of circumstances fails in its purpose *or op-erates to deprive either party of the substantial value of the bargain*, it must give way to the general remedy provisions of this Article."[885] The italicized portion of the quoted section is the proper focus of subsection (2) of section 2-719.

The remedy limitation must first be fair and reasonable at the time it was agreed upon by the parties; it must provide a "fair quantum" of rem-

---

[882] *See* § 4.08[E], *infra.*

[883] U.C.C. § 2-719(2).

[884] Although the buyer has no purpose *per se* in limiting his remedies, he is likely to be able to obtain the goods more cheaply from the seller if the seller does not have to bear the costs of broadly insuring product quality. This is true in individual cases, as where the seller and buyer explicitly bargain over alternative pricing schemes, and also with respect to certain categories of goods in general. *See* Priest, "A Theory of the Consumer Product Warranty," 90 Yale L.J. 1297 (1981). In this article, Professor Priest argues that limited warranties and remedies often represent the cheapest distribution of risks of product defects.

[885] U.C.C. § 2-719, Official Comment 1 (emphasis added).

edy.[886] If the clause does not meet this test it is unconscionable.[887] This issue will be discussed shortly. If it meets this test, however, the limitation of remedies still will not be effective if later circumstances indicate that the limitation will operate to deprive either party of the substantial value of its bargain. The value to the buyer of the bargain is the value of nondefective, functional goods. This expectation of receiving such goods is the reason, under normal circumstances, that the buyer has agreed to part with her hard-earned cash. A repair-and-replacement remedy normally fulfills this expectation if defective goods are satisfactorily repaired or replaced; the buyer will receive the value of her bargain. Although the limited remedy may prevent the buyer from recovering for additional inconvenience or loss in the form of incidental or consequential damages, she will nonetheless receive the substantial value of her bargain. Where, however, the remedy limitation makes it impossible to recover the substantial value of her bargain, the remedy fails, and the buyer has access to the remedies of Article 2.[888]

The primary effect of this provision has been to create—in conjunction with the Code's revocation remedy—a "lemon law" for defective goods, especially vehicles. Courts have interpreted a limited repair-and-replacement remedy to "fail of its essential purpose" whenever the seller is unable or unwilling to provide the buyer with conforming goods within a reasonable time. When this occurs, the buyer is generally entitled to revoke its acceptance of the goods under section 2-608—thrust them back on the seller—and recover its purchase price as well as other damages.[889] A representative case is *Ford Motor Co. v. Mayes.*[890] In this case, the buyer purchased a new 1976 Ford truck. A number of minor defects occurred almost immediately. These were repaired by the dealer under the manufacturer's warranty, which

---

[886] U.C.C. § 2-719, Official Comment 2.

[887] *Id.*

[888] This is not to say that a buyer, at least a nonconsumer buyer, should not be permitted to consciously bargain away even this right. A buyer might agree, as, for example, when the goods are experimental or the seller gives a steep price discount, that the seller's only obligation is to *try* in good faith to repair or redesign the goods to accomplish the buyer's purposes if, as delivered, they are unable to do so. In this case, however, the buyer will have received the substantial value of its bargain; the buyer's bargain was that the buyer would, except to a very limited extent, assume the risk of product failure. *See* Champlain Enters., Inc. v. United States, 957 F. Supp. 26, 34 UCCR2d 1058 (N.D.N.Y. 1997).

[889] *See* Mercedes Benz of N. Am., Inc. v. Norman Gershman's Things to Wear, Inc., 596 A.2d 1358, 16 UCCR2d 1076 (Del. 1991); Kelynack v. Yamaha Motor Corp., USA, 394 N.W.2d 17, 152 Mich. App. 105, 2 UCCR2d 166 (Mich. Ct. App. 1986); Durfee v. Rod Baxter Imports, Inc., 262 N.W.2d 349, 22 UCCR 945 (Minn. 1978); Bishop Logging Co. v. John Deere Indus. Equip. Co., 455 S.E.2d 183, 28 UCCR2d 190 (S.C. Ct. App. 1995).

[890] 575 S.W.2d 480, 24 UCCR 1057 (Ky. Ct. App. 1978).

contained an exclusive remedy that Ford would repair or replace defective parts. Approximately five weeks after the purchase, the buyer noticed an unusual noise and vibration in the truck. The problem was diagnosed as worn clutches in the rear end, which were replaced, but problems with the vehicle continued. The buyer returned the truck to the dealer on seven or eight more occasions, and the dealer made futile attempts to eliminate the problems. It was finally determined that the truck's frame was twisted, and the buyer returned the truck to the dealer and demanded a refund. Neither the dealer nor the manufacturer would agree to refund the buyer's money. Ford, however, offered to attempt to make further "corrective repairs."[891] The buyer refused further attempts at repair and the litigation ensued.

Ford argued that it had validly limited the buyer's remedies and the court agreed, stating that the Code permitted a seller to limit remedies to the repair and replacement of nonconforming goods or parts. The court, however, said that if an exclusive remedy fails of its essential purpose the buyer is entitled to the remedies that would otherwise be available under the Code. Quoting from an earlier case,[892] the court described the purpose of an exclusive remedy to repair or replace defective parts:

> The purpose of an exclusive remedy of replacement or repair of defective parts . . . is to give the seller an opportunity to make the goods conforming while limiting the risks to which he is subject by excluding direct and consequential damages that might otherwise arise. From the point of view of the buyer the purpose of the exclusive remedy is to give him goods that conform to the contract within a reasonable time after a defect is discovered.

As a result, the court concluded that an exclusive remedy fails of its essential purpose whenever the seller fails to correct a defect within a reasonable time. Because the seller had failed to correct the vehicle's defects within a reasonable time, the remedy failed of its essential purpose, and the buyer was entitled to revoke his acceptance of the goods and obtain a refund.

Mayes is typical of many cases in which the claim has been made that a remedy has failed of its essential purpose. Most of the cases involve similar "repair-and-replacement" limitations and numerous attempts at repair over a lengthy period of time. In some cases, like *Mayes*, the seller is unable or unwilling to repair a single major defect. In other cases, there are numerous defects that continue to crop up—no sooner has the seller corrected one

---

[891] *Id.* at 482, 24 UCCR at 1060.

[892] Beal v. General Motors Corp., F. Supp. 423, 12 UCCR 105 (D. Del. 1973).

problem than another becomes apparent.[893] In neither of these cases has the seller given the buyer what the buyer has bargained for—a conforming item within a reasonable period of time after the purchase.[894]

Another kind of case involves a situation when the exclusive remedy fails to provide the buyer with the value of his bargain because of the circumstances surrounding the breach. For example, suppose a buyer has purchased an automobile and has signed a standard form contract containing a clause limiting his remedies to the repair or replacement of defective parts. If the car's brakes later fail but the driver brings the automobile to a stop without a collision, the exclusive remedy will operate fairly and reasonably to give the buyer the benefit of his bargain. New brakes can be installed (or the old brakes repaired), and the buyer will have the conforming goods for which he bargained. However, if the brakes fail causing the automobile to be destroyed, repairing the old brakes or installing new brakes will not give the buyer the value of his bargain. The circumstances of the collision have made what appeared to be a fair and reasonable remedy wholly unfair and unreasonable.[895]

It is important to note that a remedy fails of its essential purpose only when events *subsequent* to the contract unexpectedly prevent the buyer from receiving what was expected from the contract. Courts have occasionally

---

[893] *See, e.g.*, Murray v. Holiday Rambler, Inc., 83 Wis. 2d 406, 265 N.W.2d 513 (1978); Lankford v. Rogers Ford Sales, 478 S.W.2d 248, 10 UCCR 777 (Tex. Ct. App. 1972); Osburn v. Bendix Home Sys., Inc., 613 P.2d 445, 29 UCCR 119 (Okla. 1980); Miller v. Pettibone Corp., 32 UCCR2d 839 (Ala. 1997). In a somewhat unusual case, Tampa Farm Serv., Inc. v. Cargill, Inc., 356 So. 2d 347, 24 UCCR 147 (Fla. Ct. App. 1978), the contract required the buyer of corn to accept a discount or replacement for defective shipments, and also required the buyer to go through an elaborate notification procedure. The court found that there was a material question of fact whether a remedy failed of its essential purpose when twenty-five of the first twenty-six shipments were defective. In the authors' view, this decision is correct, even though in each case the seller replaced the corn with nondefective corn. This case is analogous to one in which the buyer must continually return the goods to the seller for repair as new defects crop up.

[894] The buyer has the burden of proving that the exclusive remedy has failed of its essential purpose. *See* Tareyton Elec. Composition, Inc. v. Eltra Corp., 21 UCCR 1064 (M.D.N.C. 1977).

[895] *See* Russo v. Hilltop Lincoln-Mercury, Inc., 479 S.W.2d 211, 10 UCCR 768 (Mo. Ct. App. 1972) (buyer permitted to recover purchase price of car despite provision limiting remedy to repair or replacement of defective parts when car was destroyed by fire). *See also* Myrtle Beach Pipeline Corp. v. Emerson Elec. Co., 843 F. Supp. 1027, 23 UCCR2d 683 (D.S.C. 1993) (courts lists six factors relevant to determining when a remedy fails of its essential purpose: (1) surrounding circumstances; (2) nature of the parties' basic obligations; (3) nature of the goods; (4) uniqueness or experimental nature of the items; (5) general availability of the items; and (6) good faith and reasonableness of the provision).

misunderstood the necessary sequence and applied section 2-719(2) improperly. The most noted case is *Wilson Trading Corp. v. David Ferguson Ltd.*[896] In this case, the buyer purchased yarn from the seller. The contract provided that no claim for defects could be made after the yarn had been processed or more than ten days after receipt of shipment. Because the earliest possible time that some kinds of defects could reasonably be discovered was *after* processing, the court found that the remedy provided in the contract failed of its essential purpose. The court also considered the issue of whether the provision was unconscionable, but said that it was unnecessary to decide that question.

The court should have determined the conscionability of the limitation. To the extent the provision was a remedy limitation at all,[897] it did not fail of its essential purpose. It could be determined in advance of the contract whether defects were reasonably discoverable within the time limits established by the provision; subsequent events did not cause an apparently effective remedy to become ineffective. The court should have examined the conscionability of the provision at the time the contract was created rather than invalidating it under section 2-719(2). Unfortunately, other courts have repeated the mistake of *Wilson Trading*.[898] A number of courts, however, have subsequently recognized the error of *Wilson Trading* and have refused to apply section 2-719(2) to similar limitations.[899]

---

[896] 23 N.Y.2d 398, 297 N.Y.S.2d 108, 244 N.E.2d 685, 5 UCCR 1213 (1968).

[897] The provision can probably best be understood as a limitation on the *express warranty* in the contract, rather than a limitation on the remedy. If a defect was discovered within the time period and before processing, all remedies were apparently available to the buyer. If a defect was discovered after ten days, or after processing, no remedies were available. Thus, the provision did not limit remedies, it limited the duration of the express warranty.

[898] *See* Neville Chem. Co. v. Union Carbide Corp., 294 F. Supp. 649, 5 UCCR 1219 (W.D. Pa. 1968), *vacated on other grounds*, 422 F.2d 1205, 7 UCCR 81 (3d Cir. 1968) (remedy of return of purchase price fails of its essential purpose where defect could not reasonably be discovered until after buyer had suffered substantial consequential damages); Leprino v. Intermountain Brick Co., 759 P.2d 835, 6 UCCR2d 377 (Colo. Ct. App. 1988) (remedy of return of purchase price fails when staining in bricks cannot be discovered until after installation); Lutz Farms v. Asgrow Seed Co., 948 F.2d 638, 15 UCCR2d 1167 (10th Cir. 1981) (remedy of return of purchase price failed when defects in onion seed not discovered until after planting); Comind, Companhia de Seguros v. Sikorsky Aircraft Div. of United Technologies Corp., 116 F.R.D. 397, 5 UCCR2d 575 (D. Conn. 1987) (exclusive remedy fails when defect cannot be discovered in ninety-day contract period). *See also* Metalized Ceramics for Elecs., Inc. v. Ammonia Co., 663 A.2d 762, 27 UCCR2d 1271 (Pa. Super. Ct. 1995) (court applied U.C.C. § 2-719 to clause requiring buyer to test anhydrous ammonia before accepting it or waive any claim for defects).

[899] *See, e.g.*, Clark v. International Harvester Co., 99 Idaho 326, 581 P.2d 784, 25 UCCR 91 (1978); Hart Eng'g Co. v. FMC Corp., 593 F. Supp. 1471, 39 UCCR 1313 (D.R.I. 1984);

Furthermore, a limited remedy should not fail merely because it does not permit recovery of all of the buyer's damages.[900] Simply because the buyer suffers significant consequential damages that are noncompensable under the limited remedy should not alone cause the limited remedy to fail, so long as the limitation was conscionable at the time of inception. For example, in *Providence & Worcester Railroad Co. v. Sargent & Greenleaf, Inc.*,[901] a $20 lock on a railroad switch was "picked" by a vandal in under two minutes, causing a derailment resulting in almost $1 million in consequential damages. The court nonetheless refused to hold that a limited remedy providing solely for refund of purchase price failed of its essential purpose.[902]

The good faith of the seller in attempting to effect the limited remedy is, and should be, irrelevant to whether the remedy has failed of its essential purpose.[903] There are a few cases, however, that suggest that a remedy might not fail so long as the seller has attempted in good faith to effectuate the remedy.[904] Although the good faith of the seller might legitimately affect

---

Wisconsin Power & Light Co. v. Westinghouse Elec. Corp., 830 F.2d 1405, 4 UCCR2d 1381 (7th Cir. 1987); Arkwright-Boston Manufacturers Mut. Ins. Co. v. Westinghouse Elec. Corp., 844 F.2d 1174, 6 UCCR2d 73 (5th Cir. 1988).

[900] *See* Ritchie Enters. v. Honeywell Bull, Inc., 730 F. Supp. 1041, 11 UCCR2d 1170 (D. Kan. 1990); JOM, Inc. v. Adell Plastics, Inc., 36 UCCR2d 1 (1st Cir. 1998).

[901] 802 F. Supp. 680, 19 UCCR2d 21 (D.R.I. 1992).

[902] *But see* Phillips Petroleum Co. v. Bucyrus-Erie Co., 388 N.W.2d 584, 131 Wis. 2d 21, 1 UCCR2d 667 (Wis. 1986). In this case, an adapter for cranes used in North Sea oil drilling failed. The crane fell into the sea, and as a result, the adapters on thirteen other cranes were replaced. The resulting consequential damages exceeded $1,600,000. The contract provided that the exclusive remedy was the replacement of defective parts at the manufacturer's plant. The court determined that because the remedy failed to compensate the buyer for the huge consequential losses, the remedy failed of its essential purpose, even though the damages resulting from the defective adapter could reasonably be anticipated. The court said that a remedy fails of its essential purpose when it fails to make the innocent party whole.

The court's decision is clearly incorrect. Simply because the remedy failed to provide for the huge consequential damages does not mean that it has failed of its essential purpose. If a remedy failed of its essential purpose whenever it failed to make the innocent party whole, no exclusion of consequential damages could ever be upheld because, by definition, it excludes damages that the buyer has suffered. The exclusion of consequential damages may have been unconscionable, but it did not fail of its essential purpose.

[903] *See, e.g.*, Custom Automated Mach. v. Penda Corp., 537 F. Supp. 77, 33 UCCR 856 (N.D. Ill. 1982); Kelynack v. Yamaha Motor Corp., 394 N.W.2d 17, 152 Mich. App. 105, 2 UCCR2d 166 (Mich. Ct. App. 1986).

[904] *See* American Elec. Power Co. v. Westinghouse Elec. Corp., 418 F. Supp. 435, 19 UCCR 1009 (S.D.N.Y. 1976); Myrtle Beach Pipeline Corp. v. Emerson Elec. Co., 843 F. Supp. 1027, 23 UCCR2d 683 (D.S.C. 1993) (availability and willingness of the seller to

the length of the "reasonable time" in which the seller must provide a conforming product under an exclusive repair or replacement remedy,[905] a seller's good faith cannot indefinitely prevent a limited remedy from failing in its essential purpose. There is no support in the Code or the Comments for the idea that the availability of section 2-719(2) is dependent on the good faith of the seller.

How much time a seller can take to make the goods conform to the contract is normally a question of fact.[906] Some examples where courts have upheld determinations that the seller was unable to repair the goods within a reasonable time include the failure of the seller to repair a motorcycle while it was in the shop for three full months;[907] eight attempts to repair numerous defects in a new car within a nine-month period;[908] three engine replacements within an eight-month period;[909] numerous unsuccessful attempts to repair logging equipment over more than a year;[910] a pizza oven that remained defective after several years of attempted repairs;[911] the failure to repair a complex machine after more than two and one-half years;[912] and three attempts within a five-month period to repair a faulty plumbing system that caused a motor home to flood.[913]

Section 2-719(2) is roughly analogous to the excuse of impracticability.[914] In the typical case of a limited remedy, it is a basic assumption of

---

effectuate the exclusive remedy was a factor in determining that it did not fail of its essential purpose).

[905] A reasonable time should be shorter when the seller is not making a good-faith effort to effectuate the remedy. It would make little sense, for example, for the buyer to have to wait the same amount of time to avail himself of other remedies when the seller refuses to repair or replace defective goods as when the seller is making a good-faith effort to do so.

[906] Hightower v. General Motors Corp., 332 S.E.2d 336, 41 UCCR 1312 (Ga. Ct. App. 1985); Esquire Mobile Homes, Inc. v. Arrendale, 356 S.E.2d 250, 3 UCCR2d 1798 (Ga. Ct. App. 1987).

[907] Kelynack v. Yamaha Motor Corp., 394 N.W.2d 17, 152 Mich. App. 105, 2 UCCR2d 166 (Mich. Ct. App. 1986).

[908] King v. Taylor Chrysler-Plymouth, Inc., 457 N.W.2d 42, 184 Mich. App. 204, 12 UCCR2d 686 (Mich. Ct. App. 1990).

[909] Volkswagen of Am., Inc. v. Novak, 418 So. 2d 801, 34 UCCR 1150 (Miss. 1982).

[910] Young v. Hessel Tractor & Equip. Co., 782 P.2d 164, 99 Or. App. 262, 10 UCCR2d 1257 (Or. Ct. App. 1989).

[911] Nation Enters., Inc. v. Enersyst, Inc., 749 F. Supp. 1506, 13 UCCR2d 1116 (N.D. Ill. 1990).

[912] Milgard Tempering, Inc. v. Selas Corp. of Am., 902 F.2d 703, 11 UCCR2d 558 (9th Cir. 1990).

[913] Murphy v. Mallard Coach Co., 582 N.Y.S.2d 528, 179 A.D.2d 187, 19 UCCR2d 395 (N.Y. App. Div. 1992).

[914] See U.C.C. § 2-615.

the parties that the remedy will provide the buyer with the benefit of his bargain.[915] When unanticipated events cause the remedy to fail, the buyer (in most cases the party affected by the remedy limitation will be the buyer) will be "excused" from the limitation on remedies to which he earlier agreed. Similar to the excuse of impracticability, when the event that causes the remedy to fail is anticipated by the parties, it cannot be said that the effectiveness of the remedy was a basic assumption of the contract, and relief under section 2-719(2) should not be available.[916] The remedy limitation may, however, be unconscionable because it fails to provide a "fair quantum" of remedy.

[1] The Special Case of Consequential Damages

Once an exclusive or limited remedy fails of its essential purpose, the Code provides that "remedy may be had as provided in this Act."[917] Comment 1 amplifies this direction by stating that when an exclusive remedy

---

[915] The idea that the effectiveness of a limited remedy must be a basic assumption of the contract before it can fail of its essential purpose explains the distinction that some courts have drawn between commercial and consumer buyers in the application of U.C.C. § 2-719(2). *See, e.g.*, Reigel Power Corp. v. Voith Hydro, 888 F.2d 1043, 11 UCCR2d 552 (4th Cir. 1989); AES Technology Sys., Inc. v. Coherent Radiation, 583 F.2d 933, 24 UCCR 861 (7th Cir. 1978). Consumers are unlikely to expect that the seller or manufacturer will be unable to make the item conforming through repair or replacement of defective parts.

[916] *See* Price Bros. Co. v. Charles J. Rogers Constr. Co., 304 N.W.2d 584, 31 UCCR 579 (Mich. Ct. App. 1981). In this case, the contract limited the seller's remedy for defects in sewer pipe to above-ground replacement. When defects occurred in underground pipe, the seller refused to replace the defective pipe. The court found that defects in the underground pipe could be anticipated, and therefore the limited remedy was the result of a conscious allocation of risks between the parties.

In Coastal Modular Corp. v. Laminators, Inc., 635 F.2d 1102, 30 UCCR 103 (4th Cir. 1980), the buyer purchased panels from the seller for use in constructing air traffic control towers for the Navy. The panels had a latent defect that required their replacement. Because they had already been incorporated into the structure when the defect was discovered, they could be replaced only at great cost. The contract contained a remedy in which the seller agreed to provide (but not install) replacement panels in the event of defects. The court said that even if the remedy was exclusive, it failed in its essential purpose. The court said that the remedy was meant to deal with panels that were identified as defective before installation. If it is true that the parties would not have reasonably anticipated latent defects when the contract was created, the court's decision is correct; what was believed to be an adequate remedy turned out to be wholly inadequate because of the subsequent events. If the parties would have reasonably anticipated latent defects at the time they entered into the contract, however, U.C.C. § 2-719(2) was inapplicable, and the court should have determined whether the remedy was conscionable, not whether it failed of its essential purpose.

[917] U.C.C. § 2-719(2).

fails "it must give way to the general remedy provisions of this Article."[918] Consequently, when an exclusive remedy fails, the buyer's right to revoke acceptance of the goods is revived.[919] If the buyer revokes acceptance, the buyer may recover damages for cover[920] or damages based on the difference between the contract price and market price of the goods.[921] If the buyer does not revoke acceptance, but instead elects to keep the goods, she may recover damages for breach of warranty under section 2-714.[922]

Under the Code the buyer is also entitled to recover consequential damages.[923] Recovery of consequential damages, however, is excluded by implication when the contract provides for an exclusive repair and replacement remedy. When the exclusive remedy fails, and there is no mention of consequential damages in the contract, courts have permitted buyers to recover consequential damages under the "general remedy provisions" of Article 2.[924] Frequently, however, the exclusive repair and replacement remedy will be accompanied by a separate explicit exclusion of consequential damages. Whether the failure of an exclusive repair and replacement remedy also vitiates a *separate* exclusion of consequential damages is a much-litigated issue on which the courts are badly fragmented.

Some courts take the approach that once an exclusive remedy fails of its essential purpose, consequential damages may be recovered despite a separate exclusion.[925] A number of these cases simply cite to the language of section 2-719(2) and Comment 1, indicating that once a limited or ex-

---

[918] U.C.C. § 2-719(2), Official Comment 1.

[919] *See, e.g.*, Murray v. Holiday Rambler, Inc., 265 N.W.2d 513, 24 UCCR 52 (Wis. 1978); Universal Mach. Co. v. Rickburn Enters., 1992 WL 180128 (E.D. Pa. 1992); Computerized Radiological Servs., Inc. v. Syntex Corp., 595 F. Supp. 1495, 40 UCCR 49 (E.D.N.Y. 1984).

[920] U.C.C. § 2-712; In re Chateaugay Corp., 162 B.R. 949, 22 UCCR2d 1012 (Bankr. S.D.N.Y. 1994). *See* § 7.04[B], *infra*.

[921] U.C.C. § 2-712; American Nursery Prods., Inc. v. Indian Wells Orchards, 115 Wash. 217, 797 P.2d 477, 12 UCCR2d 928 (1990). *See* § 7.04[C], *infra*.

[922] *See* Gast v. Rogers-Dingus Chevrolet, 585 So. 2d 725, 16 UCCR2d 338 (Miss. 1991); Lidstrand v. Silvercrest Indus., 623 P.2d 710, 28 Wash. App. 359, 31 UCCR 978 (Wash. Ct. App. 1981). *See* § 7.04[E], *infra*.

[923] *See* U.C.C. §§ 2-712, 2-713, 2-715.

[924] *See* Caterpiller Tractor Co. v. Waterson, 679 S.W.2d 814, 40 UCCR 1721 (Ark. 1984); Adams v. J.I. Case Co., 261 N.E.2d 1, 7 UCCR 1270 (Ill. App. Ct. 1970).

[925] *See, e.g.*, Soo Line R.R. Co. v. Fruehauf Corp., 547 F.2d 1365, 20 UCCR 1181 (8th Cir. 1977); R.W. Murray Co. v. Shatterproof Glass Corp., 758 F.2d 266, 40 UCCR 1283 (8th Cir. 1985); Great Dane Trailer Sales, Inc. v. Malvern Pulpwood, Inc., 785 S.W.2d 13, 301 Ark. 436, 11 UCCR2d 875 (Ark. 1990); Severn v. Sperry Corp., 212 Mich. App. 406, 538 N.W.2d 50, 28 UCCR2d 204 (1995).

clusive remedy fails, all Article 2 remedies become available.[926] Other cases, more thoughtfully reasoned, reach the same result on the grounds that the buyer's willingness to forgo consequential damages is inextricably tied to the seller's obligation to repair or replace defective parts or goods within a reasonable time.[927] When the seller is unable or unwilling to perform this obligation, the willingness of the buyer to forgo consequential damages can no longer be assumed.

One court has applied this reasoning to *warranty disclaimers* as well as remedy limitations, striking down a disclaimer of implied warranties that was otherwise effective under section 2-316.[928] Most courts, however, properly take the position that a satisfactory warranty disclaimer is unaffected by the failure of an exclusive remedy.[929] It is hard to see why a warranty disclaimer should be invalidated by the failure of an exclusive remedy. Additional warranty coverage, apart from that which was bargained for, should not be provided simply because the remedy fails for the warranty that *was* given by the seller. When an exclusive remedy fails, the buyer should be given a *remedy* for breach of the seller's warranty—which is the purpose of section 2-719(2). That is all the buyer has bargained for and the buyer is entitled to no more.

Other courts hold that separate limitations on consequential damages remain effective despite the failure of an exclusive remedy.[930] These courts generally take the position that subsections (2) and (3) of section 2-719 function independently. That is, a separate exclusion of consequential damages remains effective, despite the failure of an exclusive remedy, unless the

---

[926] *See, e.g.,* King v. Taylor Chrysler-Plymouth, Inc., 457 N.W.2d 42, 12 UCCR2d 686 (Mich. Ct. App. 1990); Hibbs v. Jeep Corp., 666 S.W.2d 692, 38 UCCR 1257 (Mo. 1983).

[927] *See e.g.,* Clark v. International Harvester, 99 Idaho 326, 581 P.2d 784, 25 UCCR 91 (1978); Kelynack v. Yamaha Motor Corp., 394 N.W.2d 17, 152 Mich. App. 105, 2 UCCR2d 166 (Mich. Ct. App. 1986).

[928] Clark v. International Harvester Co., 99 Idaho 326, 581 P.2d 784, 25 UCCR 91 (1978).

[929] *See* Koehring Co. v. A.P.I., Inc., 369 F. Supp. 882, 14 UCCR 368 (E.D. Mich. 1974); Ritchie Enters. v. Honeywell Bull, Inc., 730 F. Supp. 1041, 11 UCCR2d 1170 (D. Kan. 1990).

[930] *See, e.g.,* Middletown Concrete Prods., Inc., v. Black Clawson Co., 802 F. Supp. 1135, 20 UCCR2d 815 (D. Del. 1992); McNally Wellman Co. v. New York State Elec. & Gas Corp., 63 F.3d 1188, 27 UCCR2d 289 (2d Cir. 1995); Fidelity & Deposit Co. of Md. v. Krebs Engineers, 859 F.2d 501, 7 UCCR2d 89 (7th Cir. 1988); Great Dane Trailer Sales, Inc. v. Malvern Pulpwood, Inc., 785 S.W.2d 13, 11 UCCR2d 875 (Ark. 1990); Board of Directors of City of Harriman Sch. Dist. v. Southwestern Petroleum Corp., 757 S.W.2d 669, 7 UCCR2d 386 (Tenn. Ct. App. 1988). *See also* Carboline v. Oxmoor Ctr., 40 UCCR 1728 (Ky. Ct. App. 1985) (court permits exclusion of consequential damages to stand when exclusive remedy fails, but refuses to enforce exclusion of incidental damages).

exclusion of consequential damages is unconscionable under section 2-719(3). To these courts, the exclusion of consequential damages is part of the agreed allocation of risk and should not be invalidated even if an exclusive remedy fails.[931]

The commercial sophistication of the buyer will weigh heavily in the decision as to whether a separate exclusion of consequential damages will remain effective when an exclusive remedy fails. Most of the cases that permit an exclusion to stand despite the failure of an exclusive remedy involve commercial parties,[932] and many judicial opinions emphasize the commercial nature of the parties and their business sophistication.[933] On the other hand, exclusions of consequential damages have been struck down in a much larger proportion of the cases involving consumers.[934] There are also a number of cases that hold that an exclusion of consequential damages will be effective so long as the seller has attempted in good faith to implement the remedy, but if the seller repudiates its obligations or otherwise acts in bad faith, the limitation on consequential damages will fail.[935]

A large number of cases have refused to draw categorical lines and have determined that whether a separate exclusion of consequential damages

---

[931] *See* Kearney & Trecker Corp. v. Master Engraving Co., Inc., 527 A.2d 429, 107 N.J. 584, 3 UCCR2d 1684 (N.J. 1987); American Elec. Power Co., Inc. v. Westinghouse Elec. Corp., 418 F. Supp. 435, 19 UCCR 1009 (S.D.N.Y. 1976); Lefebvre Intergraphics v. Sanden Mach. Ltd., 946 F. Supp. 1358, 34 UCCR2d 385 (N.D. Ill. 1996).

[932] *See, e.g.,* Myrtle Beach Pipeline Corp. v. Emerson Elec. Co., 843 F. Supp. 1027, 23 UCCR2d 683 (D.S.C. 1993); Damin Aviation Corp. v. Sikorsky Aircraft, 705 F. Supp. 170, 9 UCCR2d 491 (S.D.N.Y. 1989).

[933] *See, e.g.,* Damin Aviation Corp. v. Sikorsky Aircraft, 705 F. Supp. 170, 9 UCCR2d 491 (S.D.N.Y. 1989); Moscatiello v. Pittsburgh Contractors Equip. Co., 595 A.2d 1190, 407 Pa. Super. 363, 16 UCCR2d 71 (1991).

[934] *See, e.g.,* Waters v. Massey-Ferguson, Inc., 775 F.2d 587, 41 UCCR 1553 (4th Cir. 1985); Ford Motor Co. v. Mayes, 575 S.W.2d 480, 24 UCCR 1057 (Ky. Ct. App. 1978). This division has been explicitly noted in Canal Elec. Co. v. Westinghouse Elec. Corp., 406 Mass. 369, 10 UCCR2d 664 (1990) and Schurtz v. BMW of N. Am., Inc., 814 P.2d 1108, 15 UCCR2d 878 (Utah 1991). In fact, the proposed revisions to Article 2 codify this distinction between consumer and commercial contracts. If the contract is commercial, a separate exclusion of consequential damages is enforceable despite the failure of an exclusive remedy. In a consumer contract, the buyer may pursue all Code remedies despite a separate exclusion of consequential damages. *See* Council Draft, § 2-810(b)(1).

[935] *See* United States Fibres, Inc. v. Proctor & Schwartz, Inc., 358 F. Supp. 449, 13 UCCR 254 (E.D. Mich. 1972); Koehring Co. v. A.P.I., Inc., 369 F. Supp. 882, 14 UCCR 368 (E.D. Mich. 1974); Tareyton Elec. Composition, Inc. v. Eltra Corp., 21 UCCR 1064 (M.D.N.C. 1977); Cayuga Harvester, Inc. v. Allis-Chalmers Corp., 95 A.D.2d 5, 465 N.Y.S.2d 606, 37 UCCR 1147 (N.Y. App. Div. 1983); Employers Ins. of Wausau v. Suwannee River Spa Lines, Inc., 866 F.2d 752, 8 UCCR2d 659 (5th Cir. 1989).

will remain enforceable when an exclusive remedy fails can be decided only on a case-by-case basis.[936] These courts have considered such factors as the language of the contract, the bargaining power of the parties,[937] the good faith of the seller in attempting to effectuate the remedy,[938] the complexity of the goods,[939] and the particular language of the contract.[940] For example, in *Smith v. Navistar International Transportation Corp.,*[941] the buyer, an independent owner-operator of long-distance trucks, decided to purchase a new truck. The buyer requested a list of sixteen options and components on the truck and negotiated with a number of dealers before deciding to buy the truck manufactured by the seller. The purchase order signed by the buyer contained a disclaimer of implied warranties, as did the Owner's Limited Warranty booklet received by the buyer. In addition, the warranty booklet contained an exclusive repair-and-replacement remedy and a separate exclusion of liability for incidental and consequential damages. When a number of defects occurred in the truck, causing it to be out of service for forty-five days, the buyer revoked its acceptance and sought to recover consequential damages as well. The seller responded that liability for consequential damages had been excluded by the warranty booklet.

The court rejected a categorical analysis of the issue and adopted a case-by-case approach. It said that this approach allowed "some measure of certainty" to the parties that their allocation of risk will be respected, while at the same time permitting the court to deal with those cases in which the parties are of unequal bargaining power and the remedy fails to provide the

---

[936] *See, e.g.,* AES Technology Sys., Inc. v. Coherent Radiation, 583 F.2d 933, 24 UCCR 861 (7th Cir. 1978); Fiorito Bros., Inc. v. Fruehauf Corp., 747 F.2d 1309, 39 UCCR 1298 (9th Cir. 1984); Milgard Tempering, Inc. v. Selas Corp. of Am., 761 F.2d 553, 40 UCCR 1714 (9th Cir. 1985); Agristor Credit Corp. v. Schmidlin, 601 F. Supp. 1307, 41 UCCR 1653 (D. Or. 1985); RRX Indus., Inc. v. Lab-Con, Inc., 772 F.2d 543, 41 UCCR 1561 (9th Cir. 1985); Ritchie Enters. v. Honeywell Bull, Inc., 730 F. Supp. 1041, 11 UCCR2d 1170 (D. Kan. 1990).

[937] *See, e.g.,* Chatlos Sys., Inc. v. Nat'l Cash Register Corp., 635 F.2d 1081, 30 UCCR 416 (3d Cir. 1980); Ritchie Enters. v. Honeywell Bull, Inc., 730 F. Supp. 1041, 11 UCCR2d 1170 (D. Kan. 1980).

[938] *See, e.g.,* Kearney & Trecker Corp. v. Master Engraving Co., Inc., 527 A.2d 429, 107 N.J. 584, 3 UCCR2d 1684 (N.J. 1987); John Deere Co., Inc. v. Hand, 319 N.W.2d 434, 33 UCCR 1369 (Neb. 1982); Jacobs v. Rosemount Dodge-Winnebago S., 310 N.W.2d 71, 32 UCCR 456 (Minn. 1981).

[939] *See, e.g.,* Employers Ins. of Wausau v. Sawannee River Spa Lines, Inc., 866 F.2d 752, 8 UCCR2d 659 (5th Cir. 1989).

[940] *See* Cooley v. Big Horn Harvestore Sys., Inc., 813 P.2d 736, 14 UCCR2d 977 (Colo. 1991); Colonial Life Ins. Co. of Am. v. Electronic Data Sys. Corp., 817 F. Supp. 235, 20 UCCR2d 753 (D.N.H. 1993).

[941] 957 F.2d 1439, 17 UCCR2d 84 (7th Cir. 1992).

benefits the buyer expected. In this case, the buyer was an experienced purchaser of long-distance trucks, had visited six different dealers, had drawn up a detailed list of specifications, and had read the terms and conditions of the warranty without asking any questions or voicing any objections. The court let the exclusion of consequential damages stand.

The "case-by-case" analysis seems to be gaining momentum and is certainly defensible. A few courts, however, have applied an even more sophisticated analysis that distinguishes between consequential damages caused by the breach of warranty and consequential damages caused by the failure of the remedy. In *Waters v. Massey-Ferguson, Inc.*,[942] a farmer purchased a tractor for $31,000. The tractor soon developed hydraulic problems that caused serious planting delays while repairs were attempted. As a result, the farmer had to hire his neighbors to help plant his fields and he missed the optimal planting time, causing a less than normal yield. During the winter, repairs were again attempted, but the same problems surfaced the following spring. The farmer then sued the seller, claiming that the exclusive repair-and-replacement remedy had failed. The suit included a claim for consequential damages for lost profits on his crops. The seller defended against the farmer's claim for consequential damages on the basis of an explicit exclusion of consequential damages.

The court found that the exclusion of consequential damages did not deprive the farmer of *all* consequential damages suffered as a result of the defective tractor. It said that the contract really consisted of two promises: a promise to deliver conforming goods and a promise to correct any nonconformities that did appear. Both of these promises were breached and both created potential liability for consequential damages. According to the court, it had to determine whether the exclusion of consequential damages applied not only to damages flowing from the breach of the obligation to deliver conforming goods, but also to damages resulting from the breach of the obligation to repair them.[943] The court held that the contract language was ambiguous in this regard, but that it should be construed against the drafter, the seller. Further, because the tractor was a familiar, massed-produced good, the buyer would reasonably expect that it would be repaired in routine fashion. The court, therefore, allowed recovery for consequential damages caused by the failure of the seller to repair the goods.[944]

---

[942] 775 F.2d 587, 41 UCCR 1553 (4th Cir. 1985).

[943] *Id.* at 591, 41 UCCR at 1557.

[944] The court reached a similar result in Cooley v. Big Horn Harvestore Sys., Inc., 813 P.2d 736, 14 UCCR2d 977 (Colo. 1991). It found that the language "neither the manufacturer nor the seller shall be liable by virtue of this warranty, or otherwise, for any special or consequential loss or damages" to be insufficient to preclude recovery of consequential damages resulting from the failure of the seller to effectuate the limited remedy.

The reasoning of the *Waters* court should be applauded.[945] The failure of an exclusive remedy often causes consequential damages in addition to those caused by the initial breach of warranty. To the extent that the effectiveness of the remedy is a basic assumption of the contract, consequential damages from its failure are not contemplated by the buyer when the buyer agrees to the exclusion of consequential damages. In order to exclude these damages, as well as those consequential damages resulting from the seller's initial failure to deliver nonconforming goods, the contract should have clear language to this effect.

[E]   Unconscionability

The discussion of unconscionability earlier in this text[946] is applicable to remedy limitations and will not be repeated. Two issues, however, deserve brief discussion: the requirement in Comment 1 to section 2-719 that a contract that does not contain a "fair quantum" of remedy will be unconscionable, and the conscionability of limitations on consequential damages under section 2-719(3).

Comment 1 to section 2-719 provides, in part:

> However, it is of the very essence of a sales contract that at least minimum adequate remedies be available. If the parties intend to conclude a contract . . . they must accept the legal consequence that there be at least a fair quantum of remedy for breach of the obligations and duties outlined in the contract. Thus any clause purporting to modify or limit the remedial provisions of this Article in an unconscionable manner is subject to deletion.[947]

What is a "fair quantum" of remedy? The case law is sparse and unhelpful. It is clear that an agreement to refund the purchase price, or to repair or replace defective goods or parts, can be a "fair quantum" of remedy—these limited remedies are validated by the section itself.[948] Whether a fair quan-

---

[945] *See* Bishop Logging Co. v. John Deere Indus. Equip. Co., 455 S.E.2d 183, 28 UCCR2d 190 (S.C. Ct. App. 1995), a particularly well-reasoned case that expressly follows *Waters*. The proposed revisions to Article 2 provide that an agreed remedy creates a "remedial promise" for which there is independent liability for breach. *See* Council Draft, §§ 2-810(a)(3), 2-408.

[946] *See* § 3.09, *supra.*

[947] U.C.C. § 2-719, Official Comment 1.

[948] U.C.C. § 2-719(1)(a) provides that "the agreement . . . may limit or alter the measure of damages recoverable under this Article, as by limiting the buyer's remedies to return of the goods and repayment of the price or to repair and replacement of non-conforming goods or parts."

tum of remedy exists cannot be divorced from the particular facts surrounding the transaction; what might be a fair quantum of remedy in one context may be insufficient in a different context. As with unconscionability generally, the bargaining power of the parties is an important component in whether the contract provides a fair quantum of remedy. A limited remedy in a carefully negotiated contract between two commercial parties of relatively equal bargaining power should almost always be upheld as providing a fair quantum of remedy.[949] On the other hand, a consumer buyer presented with a form contract on a take-it-or-leave-it basis is in an entirely different position.[950] The same limitations on remedy in this context may be unconscionable.

The cases support this conclusion. In *Cayuga Harvester, Inc. v. Allis-Chalmers Corp.*,[951] the seller of a combine provided an exclusive repair-and-replacement remedy and expressly excluded consequential damages. The court first determined that the exclusive remedy had failed of its essential purpose because the seller did not deliver a conforming combine within a reasonable time. It also decided, however, that this failure did not negate the separate exclusion of consequential damages. The court then considered whether the exclusive repair-and-replacement remedy, combined with the exclusion of consequential damages, had failed to provide the buyer with a fair quantum of remedy. The court held that it did provide a fair quantum of remedy and cited a number of factors leading to this conclusion. First, the buyer was a large commercial grower, whose president had twenty-seven years of experience in the industry and was familiar with similar exclusion clauses. In addition, the transaction was substantial in size, which suggested that care was, or should have been, taken in negotiating the contract. Finally, the buyer had other available sources for purchasing similar equipment, and therefore was in a position to bargain. The court's analysis suggests, however, that these same remedy limitations might be unconscionable in another context, such as a consumer presented with a contract of adhesion.

A rare case in which a remedy limitation among commercial giants was held to be unconscionable is *Phillips Petroleum Co., Norway v. Bucyrus-Erie Co.*[952] In this case, the buyer purchased from the seller thirteen cranes

---

[949] *But cf.* Phillips Petroleum Co. v. Bucyrus-Erie Co., 388 N.W.2d 584, 1 UCCR2d 667 (Wis. 1986).

[950] *But cf.* Hornberger v. General Motors Corp., 929 F. Supp. 884, 30 UCCR2d 483 (E.D. Pa. 1996) (even though consumer plaintiffs lacked meaningful choice in their dealings with manufacturer, exclusive repair and replace remedy was not unconscionable because it did not "unreasonably favor" manufacturer).

[951] 95 A.D.2d 5, 465 N.Y.S.2d 606, 37 UCCR 1147 (N.Y. App. Div. 1983).

[952] 388 N.W.2d 584, 1 UCCR2d 667 (Wis. 1986).

and adapters to fit the cranes for off-shore drilling. During the negotiations, the buyer disapproved of the type of steel that the seller intended to use for the adapters, and a provision was inserted in the contract requiring that the seller fabricate the adapters from one of three specific qualities of steel. Despite this provision, the seller used a different type of steel for the adapters. The steel failed, causing one crane to fall into the ocean and rendering the others unusable until the adapters could be replaced. As a result, the buyer suffered approximately $1.6 million in consequential damages. The contract, however, contained an exclusive remedy providing that the seller would be liable only for the replacement of the defective part at the seller's plant in Erie, Pennsylvania.

The court first held that this limited remedy had failed of its essential purpose because it left the buyer with huge uncompensated consequential damages. This conclusion was erroneous. The circumstances surrounding the loss were not unusual or unanticipated; in fact, the court explicitly stated that the events could have been anticipated by the parties.[953] This was not a case where an apparently fair remedy failed because the parties could not reasonably anticipate the circumstances under which the remedy would be called to duty. Therefore, section 2-719(2) was inapplicable.

The court went on, however, and held that the remedy was also unconscionable. Although the contract was one between "giants in their areas of enterprise"[954] the remedy limitation was, according to the court, "concealed or masked in the warranty section."[955] Further, the agreed remedy only minusculely compensated the buyer for what were foreseeable damages. Therefore, the damage provision was "unconscionably low" and "unreasonable" and the buyer was permitted to recover the consequential losses. Although not specifically cited by the court, it was also important that the breach was of an explicitly negotiated promise that a very specific type of steel would be used, for which the buyer paid an additional price of $800 per adapter.

[1] Unconscionability and Exclusions of Consequential Damages

Section 2-719(3) deals with express exclusions of consequential damages and provides:

> Consequential damages may be limited or excluded unless the limitation or exclusion is unconscionable. Limitation of consequential damages for

---

[953] *Id.* at 592, 1 UCCR2d at 676.
[954] *Id.*, 1 UCCR2d at 676.
[955] *Id.*

injury to the person in the case of consumer goods is prima facie unconscionable but limitation of damages where the loss is commercial is
not.[956]

Although the section itself is straightforward, Comment 3 is a potential
source of confusion. It provides that "Subsection (3) recognizes the validity
of clauses limiting or excluding consequential damages but makes it clear
that they may not operate in an unconscionable manner."[957] A possible
interpretation of this language is that an exclusion of consequential damages
may be valid at the inception of the contract, but may be rendered unconscionable by *subsequent* events, depending upon how the exclusion "operates" in particular circumstances. This interpretation is contrary to the general law of unconscionability,[958] and is not supported by the text of section
2-302 or 2-719. The conscionability of a provision is determined from the
time of the contract. The suggestion in Comment 3 that unconscionability
be measured at some time subsequent to contract formation has not been
adopted by the cases and should be rejected.

The *prima facie* unconscionability of exclusions of consequential damages for personal injuries in the case of consumer goods is virtually impossible to overcome.[959] There are many cases in which courts have struck down
exclusions of consequential damages as they applied to personal injuries.[960]
In addition, liability in tort generally cannot be waived by a consumer. Consequently, it is extremely unlikely that sellers can escape liability for personal injuries through contractual exclusions caused by defective products.

---

[956] U.C.C. § 2-719(3).

[957] U.C.C. § 2-719, Official Comment 3.

[958] *See* § 3.09, *supra.*

[959] One case in which a seller was able to overcome this presumption of unconscionability
is Mullan v. Quickie Aircraft Corp., 797 F.2d 845, 1 UCCR2d 1540 (10th Cir. 1986). In this
case, the buyer purchased a home-built airplane kit from the seller. As a result of a defect,
the plane crashed upon takeoff. The sales contract and owner's manual contained an exclusion of consequential damages for personal injury. The court held that the exclusion was
conscionable despite the presumption of U.C.C. § 2-719(3), because (1) the plaintiff was an
experienced FAA certified pilot; (2) he was an expert woodmaker who made airplane pro-
pellers commercially; (3) he had thoroughly read and studied literature on the aircraft; (4)
he had thoroughly examined the contract and demanded a number of changes to it; (5) other
alternative sellers were available to the buyer; and (6) the exclusion was conspicuous and
unambiguous.

[960] *See, e.g.,* Martin v. American Medical Sys., Inc., 32 UCCR2d 1101 (4th Cir. 1997);
Werner & Pfleiderer Corp. v. Gary Chem. Corp., 697 F. Supp. 808, 8 UCCR2d 1064 (D.N.J.
1988); Illinois Cent. Gulf R.R. Corp. v. Pargas, Inc., 722 F.2d 253, 37 UCCR 1162 (5th Cir.
1984); Trinkle v. Schumacher Co., 301 N.W.2d 255, 31 UCCR 39 (Wis. Ct. App. 1980).

In many cases an exclusion of consequential damages will exclude *all* consequential damages without distinguishing between personal injury, property damage, and economic loss.[961] An argument could be made that because these provisions necessarily exclude liability for personal injury, the entire exclusion should be prima facie unconscionable, and consequential damages should be available for all types of harm. This is not the approach courts have generally taken. When an exclusion of consequential damages does not distinguish between various categories of injury, it will be prima facie unconscionable only *as applied* to personal injury. The exclusions will not be prima facie unconscionable with respect to economic injury.[962]

Holdings that exclusions of consequential damages are unconscionable are rare when the only harm is economic and the actors are commercial. While there are exceptions,[963] they often tend to have facts that make them distinguishable from the typical commercial transaction,[964] and the vast majority of consequential damages exclusions in a commercial context are upheld.[965] When a loss is solely economic, even consumers will have a difficult

---

[961] *See, e.g.*, Bishop Logging Co. v. John Deere Indus. Equip. Co., 455 S.E.2d 183, 28 UCCR2d 190 (S.C. Ct. App. 1995); Elite Professionals, Inc. v. Carrier Corp., 827 P.2d 1195, 16 Kan. App. 2d 625 (Kan. Ct. App. 1992); New York State Elec. & Gas Corp. v. Westinghouse Elec. Corp., 564 A.2d 919, 387 Pa. Super. 537, 10 UCCR2d 831 (1989).

[962] *See, e.g.*, Larsen v. Pacesetter Sys., Inc., 837 P.2d 1273, 20 UCCR2d 877 (Haw. 1992); Keblish v. Thomas Equip., Ltd., 21 UCCR2d 41 (Pa. Super. Ct. 1993); Collins v. Uniroyal, Inc., 315 A.2d 16, 14 UCCR 294 (N.J. 1974).

[963] *See, e.g.*, Constr. Assocs., Inc. v. Fargo Water Equip. Co., 446 N.W.2d 237, 10 UCCR2d 821 (N.D. 1989); Moscatiello v. Pittsburgh Contractors Equip. Co., 595 A.2d 1190, 16 UCCR2d 71 (Pa. Super. Ct. 1991).

[964] *See, e.g.*, Johnson v. Mobil Oil Corp., 415 F. Supp. 264, 20 UCCR 637 (E.D. Mich. 1976) (buyer was service station franchisee of limited education and business experience); Moscatiello v. Pittsburgh Contractors Equip. Co., 595 A.2d 1190, 16 UCCR2d 71 (Pa. Super. Ct. 1991) (buyer had no experience purchasing heavy equipment).

[965] *See, e.g.*, International Fin. Servs., Inc. v. Fronz, 534 N.W.2d 261, 26 UCCR2d 1137 (Minn. 1995); Wilk Paving, Inc. v. Southworth-Milton, Inc., 649 A.2d 778, 27 UCCR2d 130 (Vt. 1994); Farm Family Mut. Ins. Co. v. Moore Business Forms, Inc., 625 N.Y.S.2d 798, 164 Misc. 2d 656 (N.Y. Sup. Ct. 1995); Martin Rispens & Son v. Hall Farms, Inc., 601 N.E.2d 429, 19 UCCR2d 1021 (Ind. Ct. App. 1992); Southland Farms, Inc. v. Ciba-Geigy Corp., 575 So. 2d 1077, 14 UCCR2d 404 (Ala. 1991); American Nursery Prods., Inc. v. Indian Wells Orchards, 797 P.2d 477, 115 Wash. 2d 217, 12 UCCR2d 928 (1990); Stan D. Bowles Distrib. Co. v. Pabst Brewing Co., 317 S.E.2d 684, 69 N.C. App. 341, 39 UCCR 500 (1984); McNally, Wellman Co. v. New York State Elec. & Gas Corp., 63 F.3d 1188, 27 UCCR2d 289 (2d Cir. 1995); PIG Improvement Co., Inc. v. Middle States Holding Co., 943 F. Supp. 392, 31 UCCR2d 422 (D. Del. 1996); PC COM, Inc. v. Proteon, Inc., 946 F. Supp. 1125, 32 UCCR2d 663 (S.D.N.Y. 1996); Consolidated Edison Co. of N.Y., Inc. v. Westinghouse Elec. Corp., 567 F. Supp. 358, 36 UCCR 1496 (S.D.N.Y 1983); Fibematics, Inc. v.

time proving a conspicuous exclusion of consequential damages was unconscionable.[966]

There are two categories of cases, however, where commercial buyers have enjoyed somewhat greater protection. The first is when the buyer is a farmer. A number of cases have held exclusions of consequential damages on seed or other farm products unconscionable when the products proved defective and caused a lost or diminished crop,[967] although there is case law to the contrary.[968] The second category is a line of cases in which latent defects appear in the products, causing substantial consequential damages. In *Wilson Trading Corp. v. David Ferguson,*[969] the New York Court of Appeals suggested[970] that a provision requiring that all claims for defective goods be made within ten days was unconscionable under section 2-719.[971] In *Majors v. Kalo Labs, Inc.,*[972] the court held that an exclusion of consequential damages was unconscionable where a latent defect in a soybean inoculant could not be discovered until the crop had been developed, and where the defect caused large consequential damages.[973]

There is no justification, however, for exempting farmers or cases involving latent defects from the general rule that exclusions of consequential damages are not unconscionable in commercial settings. The Code contains no "farmer" exception, and farms may range from small family farms run

---

Web Sys., Inc., 34 UCCR 1600 (E.D. Pa. 1982); Tacoma Boatbuilding Co., Inc. v. Delta Fishing Co., Inc., 28 UCCR 26 (W.D. Wash. 1980).

[966] *See* NEC Technologies, Inc. v. Nelson, 267 Ga. 390, 478 S.E.2d 769, 31 UCCR2d 992 (1996).

[967] *See, e.g.,* Hanson v. Funk Seeds Int'l, 373 N.W.2d 30, 41 UCCR 1244 (S.D. 1985) (defective seed); Schmaltz v. Nissen, 431 N.W.2d 657, 7 UCCR2d 1061 (S.D. 1988) (defective seed); Majors v. Kalo Labs, Inc., 407 F. Supp. 20, 18 UCCR 592 (M.D. Ala. 1975) (defective soybean treatment); Adams v. American Cyanamid Co., 498 N.W.2d 577, 21 UCCR2d 962 (Neb. Ct. App. 1992) (defective herbicide).

[968] Stirn v. E.I. du Pont de Nemours & Co., Inc., 21 UCCR2d 979 (S.D. Ind. 1993); Southland Farms, Inc. v. Ciba-Geigy Corp., 575 So. 2d 1077, 14 UCCR2d 404 (Ala. 1991); Hill v. BASF Wyandotte Corp., 696 F.2d 287, 35 UCCR 91 (4th Cir. 1982). *But see* Paul W. Riesenbach Enters., Inc. v. Ciba-Geigy Corp., 34 UCCR2d 688 (Ind. Super. Ct. 1997).

[969] 23 N.Y.2d 398, 297 N.Y.S.2d 108, 244 N.E.2d 685, 5 UCCR 1213 (1968).

[970] Because the court held that the remedy failed of its essential purpose, it found it unnecessary to ultimately decide whether the provision was unconscionable.

[971] Although the court discussed the provision under section U.C.C. § 2-719, the provision was really a limitation on the duration of the warranty rather than an exclusion of damages. *See* § 4.08[D][1], *supra.*

[972] 407 F. Supp. 20, 18 UCCR 592 (M.D. Ala. 1975).

[973] *See also* Ciba-Geigy Corp. v. Alter, 309 Ark. 426, 834 S.W.2d 136 (1992) (suggesting, without deciding, that an exclusion of liability for consequential damages on herbicide was unconscionable).

by unsophisticated farmers to giant agribusinesses. Each case should be examined on its particular facts, and farmers, as a category, deserve no special treatment. Similarly, there is no basis in the Code for the categorical exemption of cases involving latent defects that are not likely to be discovered until substantial consequential damages have occurred. In fact, consequential damages are generally excluded by sellers to avoid liability in precisely these circumstances. So long as the exclusion is otherwise conscionable, the fact that the defect is latent should not, by itself, change the result.[974]

Two recent cases provide some useful guidance in analyzing exclusions of consequential damages under section 2-719(3). In *Myrtle Beach Pipeline Corp. v. Emerson Electric Co.*,[975] the buyer purchased an air eliminator from the seller for $1,145. Approximately ten months after its installation, the air eliminator ruptured, causing roughly 123,000 gallons of fuel to be spilled. The cost of the lost fuel and the subsequent clean-up apparently ran into hundreds of thousands of dollars.[976] The court upheld the exclusion of consequential damages and described six (overlapping) factors that should be considered in determining whether an exclusion is unconscionable: (1) the nature of the injuries (i.e., whether personal injuries are involved); (2) whether the plaintiff is a "substantial business concern"; (3) whether there is a disparity in the bargaining power of the parties; (4) the relative sophistication of the parties; (5) whether there is an element of surprise (i.e., whether such an exclusion would be reasonably expected); and (6) the conspicuousness of the exclusion. While not exhaustive, these factors provide a useful roadmap for the attorney.

The court in *Siemens Credit Corp. v. Marvik Colour, Inc.*[977] cited some of these same factors and suggested a few others. In upholding an exclusion of consequential damages caused by the failure of a computer system, the court said there is a "presumption of conscionability when the contract is between businessmen in a commercial setting."[978] Because the contract was actively negotiated, the exclusion was clearly visible, and there was no "at-

---

[974] *See* Cyclops Corp. v. Home Ins. Co., 389 F. Supp. 476, 16 UCCR 415 (W.D. Pa. 1975) *aff'd,* 523 F.2d 1050 (3d Cir. 1975) (irrelevant to conscionability of exclusion of consequential damages whether defect was latent).

[975] 843 F. Supp. 1027, 23 UCCR2d 683 (D.S.C. 1993).

[976] The court does not give a total damage figure in its opinion. It does say, however, that the cost of the lost fuel was $80,000 and that the costs of the cleanup exceeded the cost of the lost fuel. 843 F. Supp. at 1060, 23 UCCR2d at 690.

[977] 859 F. Supp. 686, 24 UCCR2d 705 (1994).

[978] *Id.* at 695, 24 UCCR2d at 715, *quoting* American Dredging Co. v. Plaza Petroleum, Inc., 799 F. Supp. 1335, 1399, 18 UCCR2d 1101 (E.D.N.Y. 1992).

mosphere of haste and pressure," there was nothing unconscionable about the exclusion.

[F] Conclusion

The courts have generally used section 2-719 well. In consumer transactions, courts have been rightfully suspicious of remedy limitations and damage exclusions. These provisions are often presented to consumers in circumstances in which they have little understanding of the consequences of the limitations and little choice in whether to accept them. Because the Magnuson-Moss Federal Warranty Act has significantly limited the ability of sellers to disclaim limited warranties,[979] remedy limitations and damage exclusions have even greater significance to consumers. In consumer transactions, courts must focus closely on the bargain-in-fact of the parties; what would a reasonable consumer believe she was receiving in the way of rights and remedies? If a seller has reason to know that the consumer does not understand that she is giving up substantial and important rights, the limitations and exclusions should not be enforced.

In commercial transactions, the heavy presumption that damage exclusions and remedy limitations are conscionable is also justified. Commercial parties have both the experience and expertise to understand these provisions and the bargaining power to negotiate an optimal result. At least in theory, whoever can most cheaply insure against product defects and particular elements of damage will bear that risk. The cheaper insurer often is not the seller. Frequently, the buyer has a better understanding of how a product defect will affect its business and can take measures through insurance or precautions to account for this risk. In exchange for assuming this risk (cost) the buyer should be able to secure a lower price. Sellers in this context generally have reason to believe that a buyer that does not object to a remedy limitation or damage exclusion has chosen to bear that risk willingly. While each case must be decided on its own facts, and there are even commercial cases where a finding of unconscionability is justified, the courts' reluctance to find these provisions unconscionable in a commercial context is appropriate.

---

[979] The Magnuson-Moss Federal Warranty Act prohibits a seller that makes a written warranty from disclaiming implied warranties. 15 U.S.C. § 2308 (1995). *See* § 8.02[G][3], *infra*.

§ 4.09   WARRANTY DEFENSES: LACK OF PRIVITY

[A]   Privity of Contract—Vertical and Horizontal Privity

This section deals with three questions:

1. Which parties in the chain of distribution ought to be liable for breach of warranty?
2. Who should be entitled to recover for breach of warranty?[980]
3. For what kinds of injuries should a party be liable?

Until the middle of the twentieth century, the answer to these questions turned, in large measure, on the legal classification of the factual pattern of the case. If the factual pattern was characterized as a contract action, only parties to the contract were permitted to recover. A non-party was not in "privity of contract" and thus (to the lawyerly mind) had no contractual rights against the seller who sold defective goods. If, however, the fact pattern could be classified as a tort, the plaintiff no longer had to be a contractual party, although the plaintiff had to be reasonably foreseeable as a user of the goods. For suit to be brought in tort, however, the buyer had to prove negligence on the part of the person the buyer sought to hold liable. Further, if the harm was solely economic—that is, involving no personal injury or property damage—recovery in tort was generally not available.

Two events in 1960 dramatically altered this landscape. The first was an article published in the Yale Law Journal by Dean William Prosser. Entitled *The Assault Upon the Citadel (Strict Liability to the Consumer)*,[981] this seminal article argued forcefully that sellers should be liable to consumers in tort for injuries caused by product defects without proof of negligence and without privity of contract. In fact, Dean Prosser argued, the assault on these roadblocks to recovery by injured consumers was already underway in the courts.

The second event was the decision of the New Jersey Supreme Court in *Henningsen v. Bloomfield Motors, Inc.*[982] The facts of the case were routine. Mr. Claus Henningsen decided to purchase a new automobile for his wife as a Mother's Day gift. Ten days after receiving the new car, Mrs. Henningsen was driving about twenty miles per hour when something

---

[980] Obviously, questions 1 and 2 are related. A person in the chain of distribution is not liable if liability does not extend to the party bringing the action. The discussion of vertical and horizontal privity that follows in the text should make clear why the questions are posed in this manner.

[981] 69 Yale L.J. 1099 (1960).

[982] 32 N.J. 358, 161 A.2d 69 (1960).

cracked under the hood, the steering wheel spun in her hands, and the automobile veered to the right and crashed into a brick wall. Mrs. Henningsen sued Bloomfield Motors (the dealer) and Chrysler Corporation (the manufacturer) for injuries received, and Claus Henningsen joined in the action. The complaint was based on negligence and on breach of express and implied warranties, but the negligence count was dismissed by the court. The jury returned a verdict against both defendants, who appealed.

Chrysler argued that its only sale was to Bloomfield Motors; there was no sale between Chrysler and either of the Henningsens to which implied warranties could attach (i.e., no privity of contract). The court's revolutionary answer was that privity was unnecessary:

> The limitations of privity in contracts for the sale of goods developed their place in the law when marketing conditions were simple, when maker and buyer frequently met face to face on an equal bargaining plane and when many of the products were relatively uncomplicated and conducive to inspection by a buyer competent to evaluate their quality. . . . With the advent of mass marketing, the manufacturer became remote from the purchase, sales were accomplished through intermediaries, and the demand for the product was created by advertising media. . . . Thus, where the commodities sold are such that if defectively manufactured they will be dangerous to life or limb, then society's interest can only be protected by eliminating the requirement of privity between the maker and his dealers and the reasonably expected ultimate consumer. In that way the burden of losses consequent upon the use of defective articles is borne by those who are in a position to either control the danger or make an equitable distribution of the losses when they do occur.[983]

Chrysler was joined by Bloomfield Motors in further arguing that whatever their liability to Claus Henningsen, that liability did not extend to Mrs. Henningsen. She had not purchased the car and had no contractual relationship with *either* Chrysler or Bloomfield Motors. The court likewise rejected this argument, stating that liability extended to anyone who might be expected to use or consume the product.

The two issues in the *Henningsen* case present two different kinds of privity problems. The first has come to be called *vertical* privity and deals with the relationships among persons as the goods move down the distributive chain from manufacturer to ultimate consumer—in this case, the relationship between Mr. Henningsen and Chrysler. The second problem is

---

[983] *Id.* at 378, 161 A.2d at 80–81.

that of *horizontal* privity and deals with the relationship between the ultimate consumer and the person who is injured by the goods; for example, the relationship between Mr. and Mrs. Henningsen. Although the Code never uses the terms "vertical" and "horizontal" privity, they have been used in countless cases,[984] and the concepts are essential to the analytical framework that the courts have adopted in privity cases.

The 1962 Official Text of the Code took a step in the direction of expanding the group of persons who could recover for breach of the seller's warranty, and provided in section 2-318:

> A seller's warranty whether express or implied extends to any natural person who is in the family or household of his buyer or who is a guest in his home if it is reasonable to expect that such person may use, consume or be affected by the goods and who is injured in person by breach of the warranty. A seller may not exclude or limit the operation of this section.

Almost immediately, a disagreement arose in the courts. Some courts read the provision as establishing the maximum boundaries for the group of third parties who could recover for breach of warranty when injured by defective goods. These courts read the provision as implicitly *excluding* from recovery those not specifically mentioned in section 2-318.[985] Other courts read the provision as *inclusive*, defining who was entitled to recover but not, by implication, excluding others the courts might feel were also entitled to recovery.[986]

In addition, it was not clear to what extent the section dealt with issues of vertical privity. The section did not directly state how far back the distributive chain liability might extend. The section, however, suggested that only the immediate seller was included as a potential defendant. This is because, under the section, liability extended only from the seller to *that seller's* buyer ("his buyer"), not to subsequent buyers. Under this reading, for example, a manufacturer's warranty would extend only to the wholesaler

---

[984] *See, e.g.,* Touchet Valley Grain Growers, Inc. v. Opp & Seibold Gen. Constr., Inc., 119 Wash. 2d 334, 831 P.2d 724, 19 UCCR2d 1041 (1992); Morris v. Osmose Wood Preserving, 340 Md. 519, 667 A.2d 624, 29 UCCR2d 170 (Ct. App. 1995); Dalton v. Stanley Solar & Stove, Inc., 137 N.H. 467, 629 A.2d 794, 21 UCCR2d 957 (1993).

[985] *See, e.g.,* Meyers v. Council Mfg. Corp., 276 F. Supp. 541, 4 UCCR 923 (W.D. Ark. 1967); State ex rel. Western Seed Corp. v. Campbell, 250 Or. 262, 442 P.2d 215, 5 UCCR 584 (1968), *cert. denied,* 393 U.S. 1093, 89 S. Ct. 862, 21 L. Ed. 784 (1969).

[986] *See, e.g.,* Speed Fasteners, Inc. v. Newsom, 382 F.2d 395, 4 UCCR 681 (10th Cir. 1967); Dealers Transp. Co. v. Battery Distrib. Co., 402 S.W.2d 441, 2 UCCR 896 (Ky. Ct. App. 1965); Dippel v. Sciano, 37 Wis. 2d 443, 155 N.W.2d 55, 4 UCCR 1053 (1967).

(*his* buyer) and to those who are guests in "his"—the wholesaler's—home. Because the person ultimately injured is unlikely to be either the wholesaler or a guest in the wholesaler's home, that person is not included as a beneficiary of a warranty.[987]

In 1966, the Permanent Editorial Board recognized the growing case law in the area, and recommended two optional amendments to the 1962 version set out above. The original section became Alternative A of section 2-318, and the two optional amendments became Alternatives B and C. The other alternatives are:

Alternative B:

A sellers' warranty whether express or implied extends to any natural person who may reasonably be expected to use, consume or be affected by the goods and who is injured in person by breach of the warranty. A seller may not exclude the operation of this section.

Alternative C:

A seller's warranty whether express or implied extends to any person who may reasonably be expected to use, consume or be affected by the goods and who is injured by breach of the warranty. A seller may not exclude or limit the operation of this section with respect to injury to the person of an individual to whom the warranty extends.

Alternative B clearly expanded horizontal privity, requiring only that the plaintiff be someone who might reasonably be expected to use, consume, or be affected by the goods. In addition, it appeared to expand vertical privity as well, deleting the restrictive "his buyer" language described above. By its terms, however, Alternative B, like Alternative A, only included within the category of third-party beneficiaries those who suffered personal injury, not other sorts of harm, such as property damage or economic harm. Alternative C was even more expansive, dropping the requirement of personal injury and requiring only that the person be reasonably expected to use, consume, or be affected by the goods and "be injured" by a breach of warranty. Different states have adopted each of the alternatives,

---

[987] *See* Denton v. Sam Blount, Inc., 669 So. 2d 951, 29 UCCR2d 1224 (Ala. Ct. Civ. App. 1995) (person injured when he sat on display chair in department store could not bring implied warranty action against manufacturer because he did not qualify as member of department store's "household" or "family" nor was he a guest in the store's "home") (applying North Carolina law); Barnett v. Leiserv, Inc., 968 F. Supp. 690, 24 UCCR2d 972 (N.D. Ga. 1997).

with Alternative A adopted in the majority of jurisdictions.[988] Seven states have adopted nonuniform provisions.[989]

Perhaps more important, the Editorial Board added an additional Comment to section 2-318 making it clear that, at least with respect to vertical privity, Alternative A should be read inclusively rather than exclusively:

> The first alternative [Alternative A] expressly includes as beneficiaries within its provisions the family, household and guests of the purchaser. Beyond this, the section in this form is neutral and is not intended to enlarge or restrict the developing case law on whether the seller's warranties, given to his buyer who resells, extend to other persons in the distributive chain.

This comment made it clear that Alternative A should not be read implicitly to exclude as third-party beneficiaries those not expressly mentioned in the section, at least insofar as vertical privity (suits against those in the distributive chain) is concerned.

The law that has developed around the issue of privity is immensely more complex than merely the choice of one of three alternatives. For example, some courts in Alternative A jurisdictions have expanded both vertical and horizontal privity beyond that included in the Alternative,[990] others have expanded only vertical privity,[991] and still others have refused to expand either.[992] In addition, many cases have drawn distinctions based on the nature of the plaintiff's injury, and others have different privity rules for express

---

[988] As of January 1, 1999, the following jurisdictions have adopted Alternative A: Alaska, Arizona, Arkansas, Connecticut, District of Columbia, Florida, Georgia, Indiana, Kentucky, Maryland, Michigan, Mississippi, Missouri, Montana, Nebraska, Nevada, New Jersey, New Mexico, North Carolina, Ohio, Oklahoma, Oregon, Pennsylvania, Tennessee, Washington, West Virginia, and Wisconsin. Five states and one U.S. territory have adopted Alternative B: Alabama, Colorado, Delaware, Kansas, New York, Vermont, and Virgin Islands. Eight states have adopted Alternative C: Hawaii, Iowa, Minnesota, North Dakota, Rhode Island, South Dakota, Utah, and Wyoming.

[989] These states are Maine, New Hampshire, Virginia, South Carolina, Texas, California, and Louisiana.

[990] See Whitaker v. Lian Feng Mach. Co., 156 Ill. App. 3d 316, 509 N.E.2d 591, 108 Ill. Dec. 895, 4 UCCR2d 444 (1987); Minnesota Mining & Mfg. Co. v. Nishika Ltd., 565 N.W.2d 16, 33 UCCR2d 58 (Minn. 1997).

[991] See Spring Motors Dist. Inc. v. Ford Motor Co., 98 N.J. 555, 489 A.2d 660, 40 UCCR 1184 (1985).

[992] See Oats v. Nissan Motor Corp., 126 Idaho 162, 879 P.2d 1095, 26 UCCR2d 1080 (1994); Brans v. Cooper Indus., Inc., 78 Ohio App. 3d 428, 605 N.E.2d 395, 20 UCCR2d 127 (1992); Denton v. Sam Blount, Inc., 669 So. 2d 951, 29 UCCR2d 1224 (Ala. Ct. Civ. App. 1995).

and implied warranties, despite the fact that all of the alternatives in section 2-318 treat express and implied warranties without distinction.[993] It would be fair to say that there are almost as many permutations to the privity rules as there are jurisdictions. The following discussion, therefore, will explain in only general terms how the courts have approached questions of privity.

[B] Personal Injury

Cases that marked the beginning of the privity revolution dealt primarily with personal injury.[994] The almost universal adoption of strict products liability in tort, however, has made personal injury cases a far less important aspect of warranty law. Section 402A of the Restatement (Second) of Torts makes any "seller" of a product liable for product defects, whether or not the ultimate user or consumer purchased the product from the seller or has any other contractual relation with the seller.[995] Strict products liability is thus unconcerned with vertical privity. Further, liability extends to any "user or consumer" of the product, so horizontal privity is also not a problem so long as the person injured is a "user" or "consumer." Only if the person injured is not a user or consumer is there an issue of horizontal privity, a question on which the Restatement explicitly takes no position.[996]

There are situations, however, in which personal injury cases are still brought in warranty. For example, the statute of limitations may have expired in tort,[997] or suit may be brought in one of the rare jurisdictions in which strict liability does not exist.[998] As a result, the rules that have developed with respect to privity in warranty actions for personal injury retain some importance.

Horizontal privity. Under Alternatives B and C, horizontal privity in the case of personal injury is coextensive with strict tort liability.[999] Therefore, issues of horizontal privity arise only under Alternative A.

---

[993] The proposed revisions to Article 2 do draw such a distinction. *See* Council Draft, §§ 408, 409; § 4.09[G], *infra.*

[994] *See, e.g.*, Patargias v. Coca-Cola Bottling Co., 332 Ill. App. 117, 74 N.E.2d 162 (1947); Valdez v. Gonzales, 50 N.M. 281, 176 P.2d 173 (1946).

[995] Restatement (Second) of Torts, § 402A(2)(b), cmts. b, c (1965).

[996] Restatement (Second) of Torts, § 402A(2)(b), cmt. i (1965).

[997] *See, e.g.*, Johnson v. Hockessin Tractor, Inc., 420 A.2d 154, 29 UCCR 477 (Del. 1980).

[998] This appears to be the case in only two jurisdictions: Delaware and Massachusetts. *See* Cline v. Prowler Indus. of Md., Inc., 418 A.2d 968, 29 UCCR 461 (Del. 1980); Swartz v. General Motors Corp., 375 Mass. 628, 378 N.E.2d 61, 24 UCCR 1161 (1978).

[999] *See* Official Comment 3 to U.C.C. § 2-318.

The primary issue concerning horizontal privity is whether Alternative A impliedly limits liability to those explicitly mentioned in the statute or whether courts are permitted to expand the class of horizontal privity beneficiaries. On this question the courts are divided. The majority of courts have read the provision narrowly and strictly confined warranty beneficiaries to those expressly mentioned in the statute.[1000] Others, however, have been willing to expand the class to include those not mentioned in the section.[1001] In addition, a few courts have accomplished similar results by liberally construing the terms of the statute.[1002]

[1000] *See, e.g.,* Boscarino v. Convenience Marine Prods., Inc., 817 F. Supp. 116, 22 UCCR2d 1048 (S.D. Fla. 1993); Hemphill v. Sayers, 552 F. Supp. 685 (S.D. Ill. 1982) (U.C.C. § 2-318 is neutral only as to vertical privity; horizontal privity limited to those specified in section); Verddier v. Neal Blun Co., 128 Ga. App. 321, 196 S.E.2d 469, 12 UCCR 243 (1973) (warranty runs only to those specified in section); Miller v. Sears, Roebuck & Co., 148 Ill. App. 3d 1022, 500 N.E.2d 557, 2 UCCR2d 1288 (1986) (U.C.C. § 2-318 limits third-party warranty protection to those enumerated in section); Williams v. Fulmer, 695 S.W.2d 411, 41 UCCR 795 (Ky. 1985) (horizontal privity limited to those stated in Alternative A); Crews v. W.A. Brown & Son, Inc., 106 N.C. App. 324, 416 S.E.2d 924, 18 UCCR2d 112 (1992) (horizontal privity limited to those specified in U.C.C. § 2-318); Bruns v. Cooper Indus., Inc, 78 Ohio App. 3d 428, 605 N.E.2d 395, 20 UCCR2d 127 (1992) (legislature declined to enlarge class of those in horizontal privity beyond those stated in section); Redwine v. Baptist Gen. Convention, 681 P.2d 1121, 34 UCCR 883 (Okla. Ct. App. 1982) (legislature deliberately declined to extend horizontal privity beyond that stated in Alternative A).

[1001] *See, e.g.,* Quadrini v. Sikorsky Aircraft Div., United Aircraft Corp., 425 F. Supp. 81, 21 UCCR 457 (D. Conn. 1977) *aff'd on reh'g,* 30 UCCR 1264 (D. Conn. 1981); Haragan v. Union Oil Co., 312 F. Supp. 1392, 8 UCCR 45 (D. Alaska 1970); Morrow v. New Moon Homes, Inc., 548 P.2d 279, 19 UCCR 1 (Alaska 1976) (dicta); Milbank Mut. Ins. Co. v. Proksch, 309 Minn. 106, 244 N.W.2d 105, 19 UCCR 774 (1976) (decided under Alternative A; legislature later adopted Alternative C).

[1002] *See, e.g.,* Roberto v. Firestone Tire & Rubber Co., 29 UCCR 1280 (Conn. Super. 1980) (employee was within "work family" of buyer/employer); McNally v. Nicholson Mfg. Co., 313 A.2d 913, 14 UCCR 381 (Me. 1973) (plaintiff/employee might be said to be in "family" of corporate buyer). *See also* Chastain v. Fuqua Indus., Inc., 156 Ga. App. 719, 275 S.E.2d 679, 31 UCCR 79 (1980) (court construes "family" in U.C.C. § 2-318, Alternative A, to include grandson who lives next door); Wolfe v. Ford Motor Co., 6 Mass. App. Ct. 346, 376 N.E.2d 143, 24 UCCR 94 (Mass. App. 1978) (court construes "family" to include niece of buyer, living elsewhere, who was injured when riding in truck with buyer); Miller v. Preitz, 422 Pa. 383, 221 A.2d 320, 3 UCCR 557 (1966) (member of "family" does not have to reside with buyer). *But see* Bobbin v. Dinger Chevrolet, Inc., 7 UCCR 470 (Pa. C.P. 1970) ("family" does not include fiancé).

Courts, however, have generally not been as liberal in their interpretation of the portion of the statute extending protection to "guests in the home, " as they have with respect to the category of "family." *See, e.g.,* Curlee v. Mock Enters., 173 Ga. App. 594, 327 S.E.2d

Vertical privity. The availability of strict tort liability in cases of personal injury has greatly decreased the significance of vertical privity in personal injury cases. As a result of liability in tort, it is fair to say that in most jurisdictions today, plaintiffs will have little trouble suing defendants back up the distributive chain. Even when the plaintiff is suing in warranty, many states have adopted Alternatives B and C[1003] or nonuniform provisions[1004] that make vertical privity unnecessary in personal injury actions. Further, a large number of courts in Alternative A jurisdictions have seized upon Comment 3 to section 2-318 and disposed of the requirement for vertical privity in personal injury cases,[1005] although there are a few cases to the contrary.[1006] Thus, it is a rare case where a plaintiff's personal injury suit is dismissed because vertical privity is not present.[1007]

[C] Property Damage

Warranty cases involving property damage without personal injury are relatively rare.[1008] "Property damage" is damage caused to the buyer's property by the breach of warranty, but does not include the loss in value because the defective goods are worth less than they would be if they had been as

---

736, 41 UCCR 63 (1985) (guest in buyer's boat); Bobbin v. Dinger Chevrolet, Inc., 7 UCCR 470 (Pa. C.P. 1970) (privity does not extend to guest in buyer's car not covered).

[1003] *See, e.g.,* Vermont Plastics, Inc. v. New Eng. Plastic Servs. Co., 824 F. Supp. 444, 22 UCCR2d 700 (D. Vt. 1993); Jacobs v. Yahama Motor Corp., 420 Mass. 323, 649 N.E.2d 758, 26 UCCR2d 747 (1995); Dalton v. Stanley Solar & Stove, Inc., 629 A.2d 794, 21 UCCR2d 957 (1993); Heller v. United States Suzuki Motor Corp., 477 N.E.2d 434, 64 N.Y.2d 407, 40 UCCR 917, 488 N.Y.S.2d 132 (1985).

[1004] *See, e.g.,* Me. Rev. Stat. Ann. tit. 14, § 161 (West 1980).

[1005] *See, e.g.,* Reid v. Volkswagen of Am., Inc., 512 F.2d 1294, 16 UCCR 743 (6th Cir 1975) (applying Michigan law); Berry v. G.D. Searle & Co., 56 Ill. 2d 548, 309 N.E.2d 550, 14 UCCR 346 (1974); Perfetti v. McGhan Medical, 99 N.M. 645, 662 P.2d 646, 35 UCCR 1472 (1983); Old Albany Estates, Ltd. v. Highland Carpet Mills, Inc., 604 P.2d 849, 28 UCCR 368 (Okla. 1979); Kassab v. Central Soya, 432 Pa. 217, 246 A.2d 848, 5 UCCR 925 (1968).

[1006] *See, e.g.,* Corbin v. Coleco Indus., Inc., 748 F.2d 411, 39 UCCR 1242 (7th Cir. 1984); Flory v. Silvercrest Indus., Inc., 129 Ariz. 574, 633 P.2d 383, 31 UCCR 1256 (1981).

[1007] *But see* Horne v. Armstrong Prods. Corp., 416 F.2d 1329 (5th Cir. 1969); Stovall & Co. v. Tate, 124 Ga. App. 605, 184 S.E.2d 834, 9 UCCR 1365 (1971).

[1008] When property damage is accompanied by personal injury and there is privity because of the personal injury, the property damage should be recoverable whether or not it would have been recoverable in the absence of the personal injury. Alternative A requires that a non-buyer plaintiff be injured in person before he or she receives the benefit of the seller's warranty. Once personal injury occurs, however, and establishes the requisite privity, then all damages resulting from the breach that would be recoverable under the Code should be available to the plaintiff.

warranted. For example, if defective brakes cause a buyer to crash into his garage, damage to the garage would be "property damage."[1009] If, however, the car glides harmlessly to a stop when the brakes fail rather than crashing into the garage, the cost of replacing the brakes is not property damage, but rather "economic loss," which is discussed in the following section.

As with cases of personal injury, strict products liability also governs most of these cases.[1010] The Restatement (Second) of Torts creates liability for physical harm caused to the "user or consumer, *or to his property.*"[1011] In those infrequent cases where strict products liability is for some reason not available, the lack of privity may be a problem. Under Alternatives A and B, a non-buyer plaintiff must suffer personal injury to be included as a third-party beneficiary of the seller's warranty. Unless a court is willing to read section 2-318 *inclusively* rather than *exclusively*,[1012] a non-buyer plaintiff in these jurisdictions who suffers only property damage as a result of the breach will be precluded from recovery. Only Alternative C does not require personal injury.

As to vertical privity, the analysis for property damage is the same as for personal injury. Courts willing to dispense with vertical privity in cases of personal injury should be equally willing to do so in the event of property damage. Although the breakdown of privity began with personal injury cases, the same policy reasons supporting the extension of liability throughout the distributive chain when the plaintiff suffers personal injury are applicable when he or she suffers only property damage.[1013] The cases are

---

[1009] There is a division in the cases as to whether physical damage to the goods themselves constitutes property damage. Some courts hold that it does, while others consider damage to the defective goods to be economic loss, even if the damage occurs catastrophically. *Compare, e.g.,* Sterner AERO AB v. Page Airmotive, Inc., 499 F.2d 709, 14 UCCR 1080 (10th Cir. 1974) (violent damage to goods themselves caused by defect is property damage) *with* S.J. Groves & Sons Co. v. Aerospatiale Helicopter Corp., 374 N.W.2d 431, 42 UCCR 100 (Minn. 1985) (damage to goods themselves caused by defect, even if traumatic, is economic loss). The U.S. Supreme Court, in the exercise of its admiralty jurisdiction, decided in a lengthy and well-reasoned opinion that damage to the goods themselves, even if it occurs in a catastrophic manner, is not property damage, but economic loss. East River S.S. Corp. v. Transamerica Delaval, Inc., 476 U.S. 858, 1 UCCR2d 609 (1986). The trend in recent cases seems to clearly follow the *East River* case. *See, e.g.,* Wellcraft Marine v. Zarzour, 577 So. 2d 414 (Ala. 1991).

[1010] *See* Rossignol v. Danbury Sch. of Aeronautics, Inc., 154 Conn. 549, 227 A.2d 418, 4 UCCR 305 (1967).

[1011] Restatement (Second) of Torts § 402A (1965).

[1012] *See* the discussion in § 4.09[B], *supra.*

[1013] This is, of course, implicitly recognized in the Restatement (Second) of Torts § 402A, which draws no distinction between the personal injury and property damage.

generally in accord with this analysis, and draw no distinctions between personal injury and property damage.[1014]

[D]   Economic Loss

As a result of the development of strict tort liability, the most active battleground recently has been where the sole harm suffered by the plaintiff is economic in nature. Both courts[1015] and commentators[1016] distinguish between two types of economic harm—direct and consequential. Direct economic harm is the benefit of the buyer's bargain; the difference in value between the goods promised by the seller and the goods actually delivered. Consequential economic harm consists of other damages (e.g., lost profits or lost wages suffered as a result of the breach of warranty).[1017] Returning to the earlier hypothetical, the difference in value between a car with defective brakes and a car with nondefective brakes is direct economic harm. It is frequently measured by the cost of repairing or correcting the defect.[1018] Consequential economic harm consists of wages or profits lost as a result of the unavailability of the vehicle while its brakes are being repaired or the cost of a substitute vehicle during this period.

Section 402A of the Restatement (Second) of Torts applies only to "physical . . . harm . . . caused to the ultimate user or consumer, or to his property."[1019] Virtually all courts have rejected application of section 402A to economic loss. The leading case is *Seely v. White Motor Co.*[1020] decided by the Supreme Court of California. In *Seely,* Justice Traynor took the position that a manufacturer should not be held responsible for the risk that its goods will not match the economic expectations of the buyer. Only if the manufacturer agrees that the product will match the consumer's economic expectations should recovery be available, and thus a tort recovery

---

[1014] *See, e.g.,* Tamura, Inc. v. Sanyo Elec., Inc., 636 F. Supp. 1065, 1 UCCR2d 416 (N.D. Ill. 1986); Kassab v. Central Soya, 432 Pa. 848, 246 A.2d 848, 5 UCCR 925 (1968).

[1015] *See* Oklahoma Gas & Elec. Co. v. McGraw-Edision Co., 834 P.2d 980, 18 UCCR2d 77 (Okla. 1992).

[1016] James J. White & Robert S. Summers, Uniform Commercial Code §§ 11-5 and 11-6, at 536–540 (4th ed. 1995).

[1017] Out-of-pocket losses resulting from personal injury are considered part of the personal injury damages and not economic harm.

[1018] *See, e.g.,* Hahn v. Ford Motor Co., Inc., 434 N.E.2d 943, 33 UCCR 1277 (Ind. Ct. App. 1982); Jones v. Abriani, 169 Ind. App. 556, 350 N.E.2d 635, 19 UCCR 1102 (Ind. Ct. App. 1976); Albert v. Boatsmith Marine Serv. & Storage, Inc., 65 Ohio App. 3d 38, 582 N.E.2d 1023 (1989).

[1019] Restatement (Second) of Torts § 402A (1965).

[1020] 63 Cal. 2d 9, 403 P.2d 145, 2 UCCR 915 (1965).

(as opposed to warranty) is inappropriate for solely economic loss.[1021] In a second notable case, *Morrow v. New Moon Homes, Inc.,*[1022] the Alaska Supreme Court reached the same result in a slightly different manner. The court refused to permit recovery in tort for economic harm because strict liability is unrestrained by disclaimers and remedy limitations. If strict liability were imposed, manufacturers could not limit their responsibility for product quality and could not effectively predict potential liability. In the court's view, this result would be contrary to the legislative intent behind the enactment of Article 2 and its provisions on warranty disclaimers and remedy limitations.[1023] With rare exceptions,[1024] other cases have followed the lead of *Seely* and *Morrow.* As a result, warranty is the only basis for recovery for nonprivity plaintiffs when the loss is solely economic.

With respect to warranty, Alternatives A and B of section 2-318 do not expressly include remote buyers who have suffered only economic harm. Both alternatives require that remote plaintiffs suffer personal injury before they are included as third-party beneficiaries of warranties. Alternative C, however, makes recovery available to "any person who may reasonably be expected to use, consume, or be affected by the goods and who *is injured* by breach of the warranty."[1025] Whether Alternative C extends to purely economic harm is a matter of disagreement. Certainly, it can be plausibly argued that a person who has suffered economic harm has been *injured.* On the other hand, Comment 3 to section 3-218 states that "[t]he third alternative [Alternative C] goes further [than Alternatives A and B], following the trend of modern decisions as indicated by the Restatement of Torts 2d § 402A." This Comment indicates that Alternative C was only intended to extend so far as strict products liability which, as previously discussed, covers only plaintiffs who suffer personal injury or property damage, not economic harm. Although there is some disagreement, the cases in Alternative C jurisdictions, however, generally extend privity to those who suffer only economic harm.[1026]

[1021] *Id.* at 23, 403 P.2d at 151, 2 UCCR at 921.

[1022] 548 P.2d 279, 19 UCCR 1 (Alaska 1976).

[1023] *Id.* at 285, 19 UCCR at 11.

[1024] *See, e.g.,* Santor v. A&M Karagheusian, Inc., 44 N.J. 52, 207 A.2d 305, 2 UCCR 599 (1965).

[1025] U.C.C. § 2-318 (Alternative C) (emphasis added).

[1026] *See, e.g.,* Horizons, Inc. v. AVCO Corp., 551 F. Supp. 771, 35 UCCR 102 (D.S.D. 1982); Industrial Graphics, Inc. v. Asahi Corp., 485 F. Supp. 793, 28 UCCR 647 (D. Minn. 1980); Western Equip. Co. v. Sheridan Iron Works, Inc., 605 P.2d 806, 28 UCCR 356 (Wyo. 1980). For a contrary decision, *see* Nebraska Innkeepers, Inc. v. Pittsburgh-Des Moines Corp., 345 N.W.2d 124, 38 UCCR 1177 (Iowa 1984).

In Alternative A and B jurisdictions, plaintiffs again have argued that section 2-318 should be interpreted *inclusively* and courts should be free to expand the class of plaintiffs, at least within the distributive chain (vertical privity). Defendants, of course, argue that recovery should be limited to those explicitly described in the statute. Many cases in Alternative A and B jurisdictions have now confronted this question, and there are roughly an equivalent number of decisions on each side. One text suggests that a distinction exists between direct economic loss and consequential economic loss, with recovery being more readily available to a remote purchaser in the former case than the latter.[1027] It is true that more cases have dispensed with the privity requirement when the economic harm is direct rather than consequential, but this distinction has not been explicitly drawn in most cases, and has been roundly criticized in one leading case.[1028]

The leading case abolishing vertical privity in the case of economic loss is probably *Morrow v. New Moon Homes, Inc.,*[1029] the case mentioned previously, in which the court refused to apply strict tort liability to economic harm. The plaintiffs in the case purchased a new mobile home that had been manufactured by the defendant, New Moon Homes. The mobile home soon developed a surfeit of problems,[1030] and while the buyers were still living in the home, the retailer from whom they had purchased it went out of business. The buyers then sued the manufacturer both in tort and for breach of the implied warranty of merchantability.

After rejecting the application of strict tort liability, the court considered whether a remote buyer could sue a manufacturer in warranty for economic loss. It acknowledged that a substantial number of courts had answered the question in the negative, but found their reasoning "unpersuasive." The court rejected the view that allowing recovery by nonprivity plaintiffs for economic losses created the potential for unforeseeable and catastrophic liability, and stated that manufacturers are free to disclaim or limit liability so long as they remain within the bounds of conscionabil-

---

[1027] White & Summers, *supra* note 1019, § 11-6 at 939.

[1028] *See* Szjana v. General Motors Corp., 115 Ill. 2d 294, 503 N.E.2d 760, 2 UCCR2d 1268 (1986).

[1029] 548 P.2d 279, 19 UCCR 1 (Alaska 1976).

[1030] The problems were so serious and so extensive that the mobile home hardly deserved the appellation "home." The defects included a malfunctioning furnace, doors that did not close, windows that were cracked, a leaking bathtub, a leaking roof, a short circuit in the electrical system, water coming through a light fixture when it rained, interior walls that did not fit together, paneling that came off the walls, door frames that fell off, closet doors that would not close properly, glue on the curtains, and a defective finish on the cabinet doors.

ity.[1031] Further, in the court's view, economic harm was no less deserving of protection than other kinds of injury. The buyer is equally unable to protect himself from defects that cause economic loss as he is from those that cause other kinds of injury. In addition, permitting buyers to sue manufacturers directly would preclude circularity of litigation and thus conserve judicial resources. The court concluded that there was no reason to distinguish between economic harm and other kinds of harm, and permitted the buyers' claim to stand. A number of other courts have followed *Morrow* and permitted warranty recovery for economic loss by a remote buyer.[1032]

Representative of those cases that have rejected warranty recovery for economic loss against remote sellers is *Szajna v. General Motors Corp.*[1033] In this case, the buyer sued General Motors for breach of implied warranty because his Pontiac Ventura had been equipped with an "inferior" Chevette transmission without his knowledge. The court refused to permit the suit, because the only harm was economic and the buyer was not in contractual privity with General Motors. The court reasoned that buyers, except in rare instances, have an available remedy against their immediate sellers for breach of implied warranty. The court further noted the fact that the Illinois legislature had retained Alternative A to section 2-318, despite the opportunity to adopt the more liberal Alternatives B or C. Also, the court was wary of the additional burden that liability would place upon manufacturers, and the undesirability of imposing additional costs upon the consuming public so that manufacturers "can insure against the possibility that some of his products will not meet the business needs of some of his customers."[1034] Finally, the court referred to both state and federal legislation protecting consumers who purchase automobiles, such as the Illinois New Car Buyer Protection Act. While the Act was not applicable to the transaction

---

[1031] 548 P.2d at 285, 19 UCCR at 11.

[1032] *See, e.g.*, Spring Motors Distrib., Inc. v. Ford Motor Co., 98 N.J. 555, 489 A.2d 660, 40 UCCR 1184 (1985); Koellmer v. Chrysler Motors Corp., 6 Conn. Cir. Ct. 478, 276 A.2d 807, 8 UCCR 668 (1970); Salmon Rivers Sportsman Camps, Inc. v. Cessna Aircraft Co., 97 Idaho 348, 544 P.2d 306 (1975); Groppel Co. v. United States Gypsum Co., 616 S.W.2d 49, 32 UCCR 35 (Mo. Ct. App. 1981); Hiles Co. v. Johnston Pump Co. of Pasadena, Cal., 93 Nev. 73, 560 P.2d 154, 21 UCCR 568 (1977); Kassab v. Central Soya, 432 Pa. 848, 246 A.2d 848, 5 UCCR 925 (1968); Gasque v. Eagle Mach. Co., 270 S.C. 499, 243 S.E.2d 831 (1978); City of La Crosse v. Schubert, Schroeder & Assocs., Inc., 72 Wis. 2d 38, 240 N.W.2d 124, 19 UCCR 490 (1976); Western Equip. Co. v. Sheridan Iron Works, Inc., 605 P.2d 806, 28 UCCR 356 (Wyo. 1980); Dualt Bldg. Restoration, Inc. v. 1143 East Jersey Ave. Assocs., Inc., 279 N.J. Super. 346, 652 A.2d 1225, 27 UCCR2d 884 (1995); Walter Oil & Gas Corp. v. NS Group, Inc., 867 F. Supp. 549, 27 UCCR2d 377 (S.D. Tex. 1994).

[1033] 115 Ill. 2d 294, 503 N.E.2d 760, 2 UCCR2d 1268 (1986).

[1034] *Id.* at 309, 503 N.E.2d at 766, 2 UCCR2d at 1278.

in the case because of the act's effective date, it evidenced "a legislative concern with and a pattern of remedies . . . for defective consumer products with which there is no compelling reason to judicially interfere."[1035] Other courts have similarly refused to allow recovery for economic harm by remote purchasers.[1036]

On balance, those cases permitting warranty recovery by remote purchasers for economic harm are more persuasive. The dangers of unknown and unlimited liability cited by some courts to justify their refusal to extend vertical privity are grossly exaggerated. First, as the *Morrow* court points out, sellers remain free to disclaim liability and limit remedies consistent with other provisions of the Code. Because remote buyers are considered *third-party beneficiaries* of warranties given by the seller to the immediate buyer, remote buyers receive only that warranty coverage that is given to the immediate buyer and no more. If the seller has successfully limited remedies in his contract with the immediate buyer, the remedies are also

---

[1035] 2 UCCR2d at 1279, 503 N.E.2d at 767, 115 Ill. 2d at 311.

[1036] *See, e.g.,* Hininger v. Case Corp., 23 F.3d 124, 24 UCCR2d 58 (5th Cir. 1994); Bruce v. ICI Am., Inc., 29 UCCR2d 796 (S.D. Iowa 1996); Hadar v. Concordia Yacht Builders, Inc., 886 F. Supp. 1082 (S.D.N.Y. 1995); Vermont Plastics, Inc. v. Brine, Inc., 824 F. Supp. 444, 22 UCCR2d 700 (D. Vt. 1993); Rhodes v. General Motors Corp., 621 So. 2d 945, 21 UCCR2d 34 (Ala. 1993); Beyond the Garden Gate, Inc. v. Northstar Freeze-Dry Mfg., Inc., 526 N.W.2d 305, 26 UCCR2d 140 (Iowa 1995); Connick v. Suzuki Motor Co., 275 Ill. App. 3d 705, 656 N.E.2d 170, 212 Ill. Dec. 17, 28 UCCR2d 1152 (1995); Professional Lens Plan, Inc. v. Polaris Leasing Corp., 234 Kan. 742, 675 P.2d 887, 38 UCCR 69 (1984); Fieldstone Co. v. Briggs Plumbing Prods., Inc., 62 Cal. Rptr. 2d 701, 32 UCCR2d 445 (Cal. Ct. App. 1997); Sharrad, McGee & Co. v. Suz's Software, Inc., 100 N.C. App. 428, 396 S.E.2d 815, 12 UCCR2d 1006 (1990). Even courts that require contractual privity when the loss is solely economic permit recovery by buyers in so-called tripartite leasing arrangements. In these transactions a seller sells the goods to a bank or other financial institution, or to a related entity established solely to lease the goods to the ultimate user. The lessee often deals directly with the manufacturer, the goods are delivered directly from the manufacturer to the lessee, and the parties' intention is that the lessee will, at the end of the lease or earlier, acquire title to the goods. In these cases, the courts do not hesitate to treat the lessee as being in privity with the seller. *See, e.g.,* Cline v. Allis-Chalmers Corp., 690 S.W.2d 764, 41 UCCR 430 (Ky. Ct. App. 1985); Werber v. Mercedes-Benz of N. Am., Inc., 38 UCCR 62 (Cal. Ct. App. 1984); Citicorp Leasing, Inc. v. Allied Institutional Distrib., Inc., 454 F. Supp. 511, 24 UCCR 1290 (W.D. Okla. 1977). *See also* Sanco, Inc. v. Ford Motor Co., 579 F. Supp. 893, 199 Cal. Rptr. 765, 38 UCCR 455 (S.D. Ind. 1984) (where manufacturer has direct contact with buyer in the purchase negotiations and financing, buyer may recover for breach of warranty against manufacturer in the absence of privity); NAEF v. Masonite Corp., 923 F. Supp. 1504, 31 UCCR2d 370 (S.D. Ala. 1996) (privity under U.C.C. § 2-318 not required when buyer is an intended third-party beneficiary under state contract law). *But see* Cooper Power Sys. Inc. v. Union Carbide Chem. & Plastics Co., 123 F.3d 675, 33 UCCR2d 803 (4th Cir. 1997).

limited with respect to a remote buyer.[1037] Comment 1 to section 2-318 makes this explicit:

> To the extent that the contract of sale contains provisions under which warranties are excluded or modified, or remedies for breach are limited, such provisions are equally operative against beneficiaries of warranties under this section.[1038]

Because remote buyers, under section 2-318, are only beneficiaries of warranties given to others, it should also not be necessary for sellers to provide notice to them that warranties have been disclaimed or remedies limited.[1039]

Allowing recovery for economic harm by remote purchasers does not create the potential for unforeseeable harm, even in the absence of warranty disclaimers or remedy limitations. Section 2-715 expressly limits recovery for consequential damages to those which the seller (in this case the manufacturer) had reason to know.[1040] Although section 2-715 does not apply to direct economic harm (loss of bargain), a similar limitation would attach to these damages through section 2-314. As we have seen, a seller impliedly warrants only that a product is fit for its *ordinary* use.[1041] An unforeseeable

---

[1037] *See, e.g.*, Western Equip. Co., Inc. v. Sheridan Iron Works, Inc., 605 P.2d 806, 28 UCCR 356 (Wyo. 1980); Moore v. Coachmen Indus., Inc., 499 S.E.2d 722, 35 UCCR2d 758 (N.C. Ct. App. 1998).

[1038] U.C.C. § 2-318, Official Comment 1.

[1039] It has been suggested that a warranty disclaimer or remedy limitation that does not make its way through the chain of distribution to a remote buyer will not be effective against the remote buyer where vertical privity has been abolished. *See* 1 B. Clark and C. Smith, The Law of Product Warranties ¶10.03[3][e], at 10-26 and 10-27 (1991). The case law is unclear. In Spagnol Enters., Inc. v. Digital Equip. Corp., 568 A.2d 948, 11 UCCR2d 49 (1989) the court held that because vertical privity had been abolished in Pennsylvania, the warranty disclaimers and remedy limitations in the contract between the manufacturer and the seller were ineffective against the ultimate purchaser who had never received them. *See also* Peterson v. North Am. Plant Breeders, 218 Neb. 258, 265, 354 N.W.2d 625, 631, 39 UCCR 1637, 1644 (1984) ("there is no reason that the defendant cannot disclaim its warranty liability by policing its dealers and making sure that its disclaimer reaches the ultimate user of its product during the negotiations for the product's sale"). In Wood Prods., Inc. v. CMI Corp., 651 F. Supp. 641, 651, 4 UCCR2d 407, 420 (D. Md. 1986), however, the court stated that a manufacturer who wishes to exclude warranties need only place the disclaiming language in the contract with his immediate buyer and that it would be commercially unreasonable to expect the manufacturer to notify the ultimate purchaser. *See also* Western Equip. Co. v. Sheridan Iron Works, Inc., 605 P.2d 806, 28 UCCR 356 (Wyo. 1980) (remote buyer can proceed against manufacturer only on the basis of the manufacturer's contract with its immediate buyer).

[1040] U.C.C. § 2-715(2)(a).

[1041] *See* § 4.06[B][3], *supra*.

use is not an ordinary use, and therefore a manufacturer does not impliedly warrant that its products will fulfill all of the purposes to which it might be put by a remote buyer. In addition, even if remote sellers were not held *directly* liable to remote buyers for economic harm, they would, in most cases, bear ultimate responsibility for damages suffered by remote buyers. Manufacturers will generally be liable to their immediate buyers (distributors or retailers) for breach of warranty or on indemnification principles for damages paid by the immediate buyer to the ultimate consumer.

Finally, at least in consumer cases, it is the manufacturer upon whom the consumer usually relies for assurances of product quality. Consumers realize that retail sellers are, in many circumstances, simply conduits through whom the goods pass on their way to the ultimate consumer—conduits that often have little direct control over the quality of the product they sell.[1042] Today consumers often can sue manufacturers for breach of warranty directly under Consumer Sales Practices Acts or Deceptive Trade Practices Acts without regard to privity,[1043] and there seems little harm in permitting these suits to proceed under the Code as well.

[E] Vertical Privity and Express Warranty

By its terms, section 2-318 makes no distinction between express and implied warranties. In practice, however, express and implied warranties are treated far differently with respect to issues of vertical privity. To the extent that an express warranty by a remote seller is *intended* for the ultimate consumer, lack of privity rarely poses a problem. In fact, it is reasonable to argue that section 2-318 does not apply at all.

If the manufacturer's express warranty is directed toward its immediate buyer (e.g., a distributor, wholesaler, or retailer), it is reasonable to treat express and implied warranties similarly under section 2-318. It is commonplace, however, for manufacturers to provide express warranties that are unquestionably directed to the ultimate consumer rather than the manufacturer's immediate buyer. Buyers understand that these representations are directed to them and reasonably expect to encounter no problem in enforcing them against the manufacturer. In the vast majority of cases, the courts permit such buyers to recover against the manufacturer any damages for

---

[1042] Of course, retailers may have a great deal of indirect control over product quality. To the extent that poor quality products generate customer returns and complaints and eventually diminish sales, dealers prefer to purchase and sell higher quality products.

[1043] *See* § 9.02[B], *infra.*

breach of warranty (including solely economic loss), except to the extent that the warranty itself limits available remedies.[1044]

This result can be justified on two separate theoretical bases. First, there is an argument that the ultimate buyer is an *intended* beneficiary of the seller's warranty rather than a third-party beneficiary whose status arises as a matter of law under section 2-318.[1045] To the extent that both the manufacturer and the retailer benefit from the manufacturer's warranty (in terms of increased consumer satisfaction, product desirability, etc.), one can argue that the consumer is entitled to enforce the warranty under traditional contract law, as an intended third-party beneficiary of the contract between the manufacturer and the retailer not subject to the limitations in section 2-318. The difficulty with this argument is that the manufacturer's warranty may not even be part of the contract between the manufacturer and the retailer and therefore does not fit neatly into the traditional conception of a third-party beneficiary contract. The second, and more satisfactory, solution is simply to say that a warranty can be made directly to the buyer by a manufacturer without regard to traditional contract notions. Comment 2 to section 2-313 addresses this idea directly:

> Although this section is limited in its scope and direct purpose to warranties made by the seller to the buyer as a part of a contract for sale, the warranty sections of this Article are not designed in any way to disturb those lines of case law growth which have recognized that warranties need not be confined either to sales contracts or to the direct parties to such a contract.[1046]

[1044] *See, e.g.*, Mainline Tractor & Equip. Co., Inc. v. Nutrite Corp., 937 F. Supp. 1095, 32 UCCR2d 763 (D. Va. 1996); Pegasus Helicopters, Inc. v. United Technologies Corp., 35 F.3d 507, 24 UCCR2d 835 (10th Cir. 1994); Crews v. W.A. Brown & Son, Inc., 106 N.C. App. 324, 416 S.E.2d 924, 18 UCCR2d 112 (1992). The only jurisdiction where the law is to the contrary appears to be Arizona. *See* Seekings v. Jimmy GMC of Tucson, Inc., 130 Ariz. 596, 638 P.2d 210, 32 UCCR 1450 (1981); Flory v. Silvercrest Indus., Inc., 129 Ariz. 574, 633 P.2d 383, 31 UCCR 1256 (1981). The Arizona Supreme Court, however, has created a *non-Code* warranty that can run from a manufacturer to a remote purchaser. *See* Rocky Mountain Fire & Cas. Co. v. Biddulph Oldsmobile, 131 Ariz. 289, 640 P.2d 851, 33 UCCR 546 (1982). In Stewart v. Gainesville Glass Co., 233 Ga. 578, 212 S.E.2d 377, 16 UCCR 687 (1975) the Georgia Supreme Court held that privity is required for an express warranty unless the warranty extends to "some identifiable third person." The requirement for "an identifiable third person" seems to have been liberally interpreted in later cases. *See, e.g.*, U.S. Indus., Inc. v. Mitchell, 148 Ga. App. 770, 252 S.E.2d 672, 26 UCCR 90 (1979).

[1045] *See* I Thomas Crandall et al., Uniform Commercial Code § 7.10.3, at 7:75 (1993).

[1046] U.C.C. § 2-313, Official Comment 2.

Requiring parties to have a direct contractual relationship before an explicit promise or representation from one to the other can be enforced is reminiscent of the worst kind of formalism and the rigid categorization of forms of action.

[F] Privity and Assignment

A small number of cases have dealt with the issue of the assignment of warranty rights to parties not in privity with the seller. On this issue, a distinction must be drawn between the assignment of a buyer's right to damages for a breach that has occurred (or perhaps will occur), and the assignment of the warranty itself to, for example, a subsequent purchaser. As to the former, there should be no problem; the right to damages for breach of contract has traditionally been an assignable right.[1047] In fact, section 2-210(2) makes a right to damages for breach of the whole contract assignable despite an agreement to the contrary.[1048] The assignment of this right, however, gives the assignee only the right to recover the damages suffered by the assignor, not the right to recover damages suffered independently by the assignee.

The more difficult issue is whether an assignor can transfer the *coverage* provided by an express or implied warranty given by the seller. For example, the seller of a used car may execute an express assignment at the time of sale of all of the seller's rights under express and implied warranties. In this manner, the class of both vertical and horizontal beneficiaries might be expanded beyond those included in section 2-318.

The cases have reached a variety of results. In *Kaiser Aluminum & Chemical Corp. v. Ingersoll-Rand Co.,*[1049] the District Court held that, under Georgia law, neither an express nor implied warranty could be expressly assigned to a person that was not included within the Code's categories of third-party beneficiaries. The court concluded that Georgia courts had decided that any assignment of warranties materially changed the risks and burdens of the original seller and therefore was precluded by section 2-210(2) of the Code.

In *Dravo Equipment Co. v. German,*[1050] the Oregon Court of Appeals held that express warranties were assignable, but that implied warranties

---

[1047] *See* E. Allan Farnsworth, Farnsworth on Contracts §§ 11.2–11.4 (3d ed. 1999).

[1048] U.C.C. § 2-210(2). *See* Kaiser Alumimun & Chem. Corp. v. Ingersoll-Rand Co., 519 F. Supp. 60, 32 UCCR 1369 (S.D. Ga. 1981) (court allows transfer of buyer's claim for damages to transferee).

[1049] 519 F. Supp. 60, 32 UCCR 1369 (S.D. Ga. 1981).

[1050] 73 Or. App. 165, 698 P.2d 63, 40 UCCR 1240 (1985).

were not. The court reasoned that express warranties were completely within the control of the seller; the seller could make them as broad or as narrow as the seller chose, and could limit their coverage in any way that the seller desired,[1051] to include making the warranty nontransferrable. Because the seller chose not to limit the warranty to the original buyer, the warranty should be freely assignable, notwithstanding the lack of privity. In contrast, said the court, implied warranties were imposed upon the seller as a matter of law, and therefore recovery for economic loss for breach of implied warranties should be limited to those in privity with the seller. In a footnote, however, the court suggested that there may be cases where the purposes for which the goods are used by a subsequent purchaser are so different from those of the original purchaser as to change the nature and character of the seller's obligation, and in these cases, even an express warranty would not be assignable.[1052]

Using identical reasoning, the Illinois Supreme Court in *Collins Co. v. Carboline Co.*[1053] held that whether the seller's obligations under an express warranty are assignable should be decided on the facts of the particular case under section 2-210(2). If an assignment of an express warranty is valid under this section, the assignee succeeds to all of the assignee's rights and may recover for economic harm even though contractual privity is absent. Because implied warranties arise as a matter of law, however, the court found rights under implied warranties to be nonassignable.

The courts' distinction between express and implied warranties is unpersuasive. It ignores a seller's ability under section 2-316 of the Code to modify or disclaim implied warranties, so long as the requirements of that section are met.[1054] There is no suggestion in the Code that this ability is limited in any way except, perhaps, by the constraints imposed by section 2-302.[1055] While the Magnuson-Moss Act imposes certain limitations on the

---

[1051] With respect to consumer transactions, as a consequence of the Magnuson-Moss Federal Warranty Act, the seller is not free to limit warranties in any way that the seller chooses. For example, section 108 of the Act prohibits a supplier that makes a written warranty from disclaiming implied warranties. In addition, a supplier that designates a warranty as "full" must provide the coverage designated in section 104, and may not include a provision that prematurely terminates warranty coverage in the event the product is transferred. *See* § 8.02, *infra*.

[1052] 73 Or. App. at 167 n.4, 698 P.2d at 66 n.4, 40 UCCR at 1244 n.4. The court used as an example a case where the original purchaser of a tractor had been a nonindustrial consumer who then sold the tractor to a buyer who used the tractor in a rock-crushing business.

[1053] 125 Ill. 2d 498, 532 N.E.2d 834, 7 UCCR2d 616 (1988).

[1054] U.C.C. §§ 2-316(2) and 2-316(3).

[1055] *See* § 4.07[C], *supra*.

disclaimer and limitation of implied warranties in consumer contracts,[1056] the seller is otherwise in as complete control of implied warranties as express warranties.

There are a number of cases indicating that rights under both express and implied warranties are assignable, at least so long as the requirements of section 2-210(2) are met. In *Ashley Square, Ltd. v. Contractors Supply of Orlando, Inc.,*[1057] the court held that even though a cause of action for breach of implied warranties normally requires privity, the existence of an express assignment creates the necessary privity.[1058] The court made no effort to distinguish express warranties, so presumably they are assignable as well. In two other cases,[1059] the courts indicated that warranties may be assigned, but in both cases the courts found that there was no express assignment, and contractual privity was therefore required.

With some qualification, the cases permitting the assignment of warranties are correct for a number of reasons. First, there is no indication in section 2-210 that warranty rights are to be treated differently from any other contract rights for purposes of assignment. Second, Comment 1 to section 2-210 states that both delegation of performance and assignability are "normal and permissible incidents of a contract for the sale of goods."[1060] Finally, assignability of warranty rights should not be held to conflict with section 2-318, because section 2-318 addresses the issue of *third-party beneficiaries* of warranties. An assignee of a contract right is not a third-party beneficiary; an assignee is a *successor* to the buyer's contract rights, not a third-party beneficiary.

Assignment of warranties should only be permitted in conjunction with the transfer of a substantial interest in the goods. Warranties are in the nature of insurance, and an asignee should not get the benefit of a warranty without the equivalent of an insurable interest. Also, the seller should not be held liable for consequential damages suffered by an assignee unless the damages were reasonably foreseeable at the inception of the contract.[1061]

[1056] *See* § 8.02[G][3], *infra.*

[1057] 532 So. 2d 710, 6 UCCR2d 1100 (Fla. Dist. Ct. App. 1988).

[1058] *Id.* at 711, 6 UCCR2d at 1101–1102 n.1.

[1059] Gold'n Plump Poultry, Inc. v. Simmons Eng'g Co., 805 F.2d 1312, 2 UCCR2d 1232 (8th Cir. 1986) (applying Minnesota law); Johnson v. General Motors Corp., 349 Pa. Super. 147, 502 A.2d 1317, 42 UCCR 851 (1986) (mere succession to title does not make one an "assignee" of express or implied warranties).

[1061] *See* U.C.C. section 2-715(2)(a).

[G] Proposed Revisions

The proposed revisions to Article 2 make substantial changes in the privity rules.[1062] Section 2-408 of the proposed changes deals solely with express warranties that are directed to remote buyers or their transferees and applies only to new goods or goods that are sold as new. Section 2-408(b) dispenses with any requirement of vertical privity, and, in addition, expands horizontal privity beyond that currently present in most versions of section 2-318.[1063] If (1) the seller makes a representation packaged with or accompanying the goods, (2) the seller reasonably expects the representation to be furnished to the remote buyer and it is so furnished, and (3) a reasonable person in the position of the buyer would believe that the representation creates an obligation, then vertical privity is irrelevant.[1064] The length of the distributive chain is irrelevant; the remote buyer is entitled to enforce the express warranty. While this result is also likely under the present law,[1065] the proposed revision leaves no room for doubt.

The proposed section also expands horizontal privity to include all transferees.[1066] Although some cases under the present law have held that an express assignment of an express warranty to a transferee is effective, other cases have held that they are not.[1067] The proposed section goes even further than merely to permit an express assignment of a warranty to a transferee—it provides that a transferee is automatically covered by the express warranty. A seller, however, can expressly limit warranty coverage to the first remote buyer. For example, a remote seller might provide a warranty on a product that is effective "for as long as you own your car." Such warranties are currently effective under the Code, and section 2-408 explicitly validates these warranties.

The section further expands horizontal privity by imposing liability for breach of the express warranty upon the seller for injury to those in the family or household of the remote buyer or to any invitee without regard to the type of injury suffered.[1068] Alternatives A and B of the present section 2-318 extend coverage only to those in the family or household of the buyer,

---

[1062] *See* Council Draft, *supra* note 29.

[1063] For a discussion of vertical and horizontal privity, *see* § 4.09[A], *supra*.

[1064] Similar privity rules apply under subsection (c) to U.C.C. § 2-408 to representations or promises that are made in a medium for communication to the public. A substantive analysis of this section can be found at § 4.05[F][4], *supra*.

[1065] *See* § 4.09[E], *supra*.

[1066] Council Draft, § 2-408(b)(2)(B).

[1067] *See* § 4.09[F], *supra*.

[1068] Council Draft, § 2-408(b)(2).

or guests in the buyer's home, and only if they suffer personal injury. It does not cover other invitees at all.

Subsection (f) of section 2-408 establishes rules applicable to the remedies for a breach of express warranty made to a remote purchaser. First, a seller may modify or limit the remedies available to a remote buyer, but the modification or limitation is not effective unless communicated to the remote buyer with the representation or promise. Second, unless special circumstances show proximate damages of a different amount, damages are measured by the difference between the value of the goods as represented and the value of the goods as delivered. This measure is the standard measure of damages for breach of warranty under the present law.[1069] Third, a seller is liable to a remote buyer for incidental and consequential damages, except that there is no liability to a remote buyer for lost profits. This last rule will expand the damages recoverable by a remote buyer in those jurisdictions that presently do not allow the recovery of *any* economic harm by a remote buyer.[1070]

Section 2-409 establishes privity rules with respect to implied warranties and express warranties that are made to immediate, rather than remote, buyers. The proposed section applies only to consumer buyers, and like the present section 2-319, provides some alternatives:

(a) In a consumer contract, a seller's express warranty or implied warranty made to an immediate consumer extends to any member of the family or household or to an invitee of the immediate consumer buyer or a transferee from the immediate consumer buyer that may reasonably be expected to use or be affected by the goods and that suffers damage other than injury to the person resulting from a breach of warranty. As to damages other than injury to person, the operation of this section may not be excluded, modified, or limited unless the seller has a substantial interest based on the nature of the goods in having a warranty *or a remedial promise* extend only to the immediate consumer buyer.

(b) Damages for personal injury to an individual other than the immediate buyer that proximately result from any breach of warranty may be recovered by: [States to choose an Alternative]

Alternative A

Any individual [natural person] who is the family or household of the immediate buyer or who is a guest in the immediate buyer's home if it is reasonable for the seller to expect that such person may use,

---

[1069] *See* U.C.C. § 2-714(2).
[1070] *See* § 4.09[D], *supra*.

consume or be affected by the goods. A seller may not exclude or limit the operation of this section.

Alternative B

Any individual [natural person] who may reasonably be expected to use, consume or be affected by the goods. A seller may not exclude or limit the operation of this section.

(c) The scope of any warranty extended under this section to other than the immediate buyer and the remedies for breach may be limited by the enforceable terms of the contract between the seller and the immediate buyer. To the extent not limited, the scope of the warranty is determined by Sections 2-402, 2-403, 2-404 and 2-405 and the remedies for breach of warranty or a remedial promise for other than the immediate buyer are determined by Section 2-408(f)(2) and (3).

(d) Nothing in this section diminishes the rights and remedies of any third party beneficiary or assignee under the law of contracts or of persons to which goods are transferred by operation of law or displaces any other law that extends a warranty to or for the benefit of any other remote buyer, transferee or person.

(e) A right of action for breach of warranty *or a remedial promise* under this section accrues as provided under Section 2-814.

This section changes much of the present law described earlier in this chapter for consumer buyers. Under section 2-409, if an express or implied warranty is made to an immediate consumer buyer, coverage extends to any buyer or transferee that may reasonably be expected to use or be affected by the goods. The warranty also extends to any member of the family or household or to an invitee. The proposed section is similar to Alternative C of the present section 2-318, the most encompassing of the existing alternatives, and substantially expands vertical and horizontal privity in many jurisdictions.[1071] In one way, however, it is slightly narrower than Alternative C. Alternative C extends a seller's warranty to *any person* who may reasonably be expected to use, consume, or be affected by the goods. Section 2-409, on the other hand, extends the warranty only to transferees, members of the buyer's family or household, and invitees who may be expected to use or be affected by the goods. In most cases, this will matter little. Most people who might be reasonably expected to use the goods will be subsequent transferees, invitees, or members of a consumer buyer's household or family. In an unusual case, however, such as where a bystander or a by-

---

[1071] *Id.*

stander's property is damaged, warranty liability will not attach under the proposed revisions.[1072]

As with present law, the rights and remedies of the beneficiaries under section 2-409 are determined by the contract between the immediate buyer and the seller. Thus, if the contract between the immediate buyer and the seller successfully disclaims the implied warranty of merchantability, then the beneficiaries under the section do not get the benefit of the warranty, regardless of whether they are aware of the disclaimer. Similarly, if the seller has limited the available remedies to repair or replacement of the goods, the remedies are limited in a similar manner to persons entitled to enforce the warranty under section 2-409. Subsection (d) makes it clear that the section does not displace the rights and remedies of third-party beneficiaries or assignees under the law of contracts.

Unlike section 2-408, section 2-409 generally prevents the seller from limiting coverage of a warranty to the immediate buyer. Thus, if a warranty is made to an immediate buyer, the seller cannot, by contract with the immediate buyer, limit the operation of section 2-409 by giving a beneficiary fewer rights than the immediate buyer, or no rights, under the warranty. There is an exception, however, where personal injury is not involved, if the seller can show a "substantial interest" based on the nature of the goods in having a warranty extend only to the immediate buyer.[1073]

[H] Conclusion

To a great degree, although not entirely, the citadel of privity has crumbled. Where strict tort liability is available, privity presents no problem. Even where strict tort is not available, if personal injury or property damages occurs, lack of contractual privity is unlikely to preclude recovery. The only remnants of privity left standing are cases in which the harm is solely economic,[1074] and some cases have concluded that privity is unnecessary even in these cases. The siege of the remaining outposts is bound to continue.

[1072] Of course, such cases are likely to be covered by strict tort liability. *See* Restatement (Second) of Torts § 402A (1969).

[1073] Council Draft, § 2-409(a).

[1074] The word *solely* in this phrase deserves emphasis. If a person suffers personal injury or property damage that results in his or her being a third-party beneficiary under Alternatives A or B of U.C.C. § 2-318, that person may also recover for any economic harm he or she may have suffered. Section 2-318 defines *to whom* warranty coverage extends; it does not limit the damages a person may recover once that person has the benefit of the seller's warranty. *But see* Kenney v. Sears, Roebuck & Co., 355 Mass. 604, 608, 246 N.E.2d 649, 653, 6 UCCR 313, 317 (1968) (section 2-318, Alternative A, limits seller's liability to injuries to the person).

§ 4.10   WARRANTY DEFENSES: NOTICE OF BREACH

Section 2-607(3) requires a buyer who has accepted[1075] goods to give the seller notice of any breach:

> Where a tender has been accepted
> (a) the buyer must within a reasonable time after he discovers or should have discovered any breach notify the seller or be barred from any remedy.

There are two significant aspects to this provision. First, it bars the buyer from "any remedy" if the buyer fails to give the proper notice. Thus, the buyer is not only barred from remedies such as rejection or revocation of acceptance, which permit the buyer to return the goods to the seller, but the buyer is also unable to recover any damages for breach.[1076] Second, the buyer is barred from any remedy if the buyer fails to give notice within a reasonable time after the buyer *should have discovered* the breach even if the buyer does not *actually* discover the breach until some later time. A buyer who does not promptly notify the seller if goods are nonconforming potentially bears the entire risk of their defects.[1077]

Much litigation has surrounded this simple provision because the consequences of the buyer's failure to comply with its requirements are so draconian. The section creates a potentially devastating defense for sellers, and sellers attempt to take advantage of it whenever there is any possibility of success. Thus, for example, sellers argue that the notice was not given,[1078]

[1075] U.C.C. § 2-606 defines when goods have been "accepted" under the Code. *See* § 5.03[A][1], *infra.*

[1076] *But cf.* Gulf Trading Corp. v. National Enters. of St. Croix, Inc., 912 F. Supp 177, 29 UCCR2d 478 (D.V.I. 1996) (although buyer failed to provide notice, buyer was entitled to offset damages against price due to seller when seller acted in bad faith by using buyer as a "dumping receptacle" for unmarketable goods).

[1077] The cases also indicate that the buyer has an affirmative obligation to plead and prove proper notice of breach. *See, e.g.*, Royal Typewriter Co. v. Xerographic Supplies Corp., 719 F.2d 1092, 37 UCCR 429 (11th Cir. 1983); Greenfield Seed Co. v. Bland, 18 Ark. App. 48, 710 S.W.2d 833, 1 UCCR2d 733 (1986); Dold v. Sherow, 220 Kan. 350, 552 P.2d 945, 19 UCCR 1356 (1976). *Cf.* Rich's Restaurant, Inc. v. McFann Enters., Inc., 39 Colo. App. 545, 570 P.2d 1305, 23 UCCR 93 (1977) (buyer's allegation that it had performed all conditions precedent to recovery sufficient to satisfy requirement that notice of breach be pleaded).

[1078] *See, e.g.*, Texpor Traders v. Trust Co. Bank, 720 F. Supp. 1100, 10 UCCR2d 1227 (S.D.N.Y. 1989); Kansas City v. Keene Corp., 855 S.W.2d 360 (Mo. 1993); Delorise Brown M.D., Inc., v. Allio, 86 Ohio App. 3d 359, 20 N.E.2d 1020, 22 UCCR2d 485 (1993).

that it was not given in a timely manner,[1079] that it did not properly apprise the seller of breach,[1080] and that it should have preceded the initiation of litigation.[1081] The defense applies to all warranties, including the warranty of title.[1082] In fact, the requirement of notice applies to *any* breach of a sales contract, such as late delivery of the goods.[1083] Comment 4 to section 2-607 suggests one reason behind the notice requirement:

> The notification which saves the buyer's rights under this Article need only be such as informs the seller that the transaction is claimed to involve a breach, and thus opens the way for normal settlement through negotiation.[1084]

The idea is that a seller, once notified of a breach, can begin the process of negotiating an agreed solution with the buyer and avoid litigation. In addition, early notice enhances the seller's ability to cure the defect,[1085] and mitigate damages caused by the breach.[1086] Finally, notice of breach permits the seller access to information concerning the alleged breach before memories have faded or evidence has been lost or destroyed, thus affording the seller a reasonable opportunity to defend against the allegations of breach. This section deals with four issues: the contents of the notice, the timeliness of the notice, the persons *to whom* notice is due, and the persons *from whom* notice is due.

[1079] *See, e.g.,* Buford v. Toys R' Us, Inc., 217 Ga. App. 565, 458 S.E.2d 373, 27 UCCR2d 123 (1995); Softa Group, Inc. v. Scarsdale Dev., 260 Ill. App. 3d 450, 632 N.E.2d 13, 197 Ill. Dec. 944, 24 UCCR2d 1128 (1993); Harry J. Whelchel Co. v. Ripley Tractor Co., 900 S.W.2d 691, 27 UCCR2d 879 (Tenn. Ct. App. 1995).

[1080] *See* Southeastern Steel Co. v. W.A. Hunt Constr. Co., 301 S.C. 140, 390 S.E.2d 475, 12 UCCR2d 103 (S.C. Ct. App. 1990); Agway v. Teitscheid, 144 Vt. 76, 472 A.2d 1250, 38 UCCR 818 (1984).

[1081] *See* M.K. Assocs. v. Stowell Prods., Inc. 697 F. Supp. 20, 7 UCCR2d 775 (D. Me. 1988); Voboril v. Namco Leisure World, Inc., 24 UCCR 614 (Super. Ct. Conn. 1978).

[1082] *See* Odgen & Sims Used Cars, Inc. v. Thurman, 165 Ga. App. 500, 301 S.E.2d 673, 36 UCCR 144 (1983); Mullins v. Wyatt, 887 S.W.2d 356, 25 UCCR2d 715 (Ky. 1994).

[1083] *See, e.g.,* Eastern Air Lines, Inc. v. McDonnell Douglas Corp., 532 F.2d 957, 19 UCCR 353 (5th Cir. 1976); Aqualon Co. v. MAC Equip. Co., 32 UCCR2d 818 (E.D. Va. 1997).

[1084] U.C.C. § 2-607, Official Comment 4.

[1085] *See* U.C.C. § 2-508; § 5.03[B], *infra.*

[1086] *See, e.g.,* Parker v. Bell Ford, Inc., 425 So. 2d 1101, 35 UCCR 1171 (Ala. 1983) (notice is required to enable the seller to make adjustments or replacements, or to suggest opportunities for cure, with the goal of minimizing the buyer's loss); Atwood v. Southeast Bedding Co., 485 S.E.2d 217, 33 UCCR2d 73 (Ga. App. 1997) (notice is required to allow seller to inspect goods and cure defects).

[A] Contents of the Notice

Official Comment 4 provides some guidance as to the contents of the required notice and makes it clear that no particular form or content is required:

> The content of the notification need merely be sufficient to let the seller know that the transaction is still troublesome and must be watched. There is no reason to require that the notification which saves the buyer's rights under this section must include a clear statement of all the objections that will be relied on by the buyer, as under the section covering statements of defects upon rejection (Section 2-605). Nor is there reason for requiring the notification to be a claim for damages or of any threatened litigation or other resort to a remedy. The notification which saves the buyer's rights under this Article need only be such as informs the seller that the transaction is claimed to involve a breach, and thus opens the way for normal settlement through negotiation.

As one might expect, courts have emphasized the policies behind the requirement of notice in deciding whether proper notice has been given,[1087] and the results of the cases are not entirely consistent. There are some situations, however, in which the cases are in agreement. The cases are unanimous in permitting notice to be oral as well as written,[1088] unless the contract explicitly requires that notice be in writing.[1089] Further, the mere refusal to pay for the goods when the price is due does not, by itself, constitute notice of breach.[1090] Finally, it is clear that courts, relying upon Comment 4 to section 2-607,[1091] have imposed less stringent notice requirements

---

[1087] *See* T.J. Stevenson & Co. v. 81,193 Bags of Flour, 629 F.2d 338, 30 UCCR 865 (5th Cir. 1980) (sufficiency of notice must be evaluated from the perspective of the policies which it seeks to encourage).

[1088] *See, e.g.*, Delano Growers' Coop. Winery v. Supreme Wine Co., 393 Mass. 666, 473 N.E.2d 1066, 40 UCCR 93 (1985); Church of the Nativity of Our Lord v. Watpro, 491 N.W.2d 1, 18 UCCR 2d 1017 (Minn. 1992); Chemtrol Adhesives, Inc. v. American Mfrs. Mut. Ins. Co., 42 Ohio St. 3d 40, 537 N.E.2d 624, 9 UCCR2d 88 (1989); Besicorp Group Inc. v. Thermo Electron Corp., 981 F. Supp. 86, 34 UCCR2d 1024 (N.D.N.Y. 1997).

[1089] *See* Prompt Elec. Supply Co. v. Allen-Bradley Co., 492 F. Supp. 344, 29 UCCR 1287 (E.D.N.Y. 1980) (oral notice insufficient as a matter of law where contract requires that notice of breach be in writing).

[1090] *See, e.g.*, Courtesy Enters., Inc. v. Richards Lab., 457 N.E.2d 572, 37 UCCR 765 (Ind. Ct. App. 1983); Fleet Maintenance, Inc. v. Burke Energy Midwest Corp., 11 Kan. App. 2d 523, 728 P.2d 408, 2 UCCR2d 905 (1986); M.K. Assocs. v. Stowell Prods., Inc., 697 F. Supp. 20, 7 UCCR2d 775 (D. Me. 1988).

[1091] U.C.C. § 2-607, Official Comment 4.

on consumer buyers than on commercial buyers.[1092] This difference is generally justified by reference to the more rigorous standard of good faith applicable to merchants under Article 2.[1093]

Most courts have held that the sufficiency of the notice of breach under section 2-607 is a question of fact.[1094] As a result, most appellate cases are decided in the context of whether a finding of fact at the trial level that notice was adequate (or inadequate) was proper,[1095] or whether a decision on a motion for summary judgment was justified.[1096] Because the issue is one of fact, a finding will be upheld unless there is only one conclusion that can be drawn from undisputed facts.[1097]

Because the issue of the content of proper notice of breach is a question of fact, it is somewhat difficult to generalize from the cases. Courts, however, are roughly divided between those taking a "lenient" approach and those taking a "strict" approach.[1098] To some extent, which approach a court adopts depends on which portion of Comment 4 the court focuses its attention. If the court emphasizes that part of Comment 4 indicating notice is sufficient if it simply apprises the seller that the transaction is "troublesome," the court is likely to uphold a problematic notice.[1099] On the other

---

[1092] *See, e.g.*, Eastern Air Lines, Inc. v. McDonnell Douglas Corp., 532 F.2d 957, 19 UCCR 353 (5th Cir. 1976); Perona v. Volkswagen of Am., Inc., 27 UCCR2d 890 (Ill. Ct. App. 1995); Maybank v. S.S. Kresge Co., 302 N.C. 129, 273 S.E.2d 681, 30 UCCR 985 (1981).

[1093] *See, e.g.*, Kopper Glo Fuel, Inc. v. Island Lake Coal Co., 436 F. Supp. 91, 22 UCCR 1117 (E.D. Tenn. 1977). Under U.C.C. § 2-103(b), "good faith" in the case of merchants requires the observance of reasonable commercial standards of fair dealing in the trade as well as "honesty in fact." In the case of consumer buyers, only "honesty in fact" is required.

[1094] Dudley v. Business Express, 882 F. Supp. 199, 26 UCCR2d 1113 (D.N.H. 1994); P&F Constr. Corp. v. Friend Lumber Corp. of Medford, 31 Mass. App. Ct. 57, 575 N.E.2d 61, 16 UCCR2d 377 (1991); Chemtrol Adhesives, Inc. v. American Mfrs. Mut. Ins. Co., 42 Ohio St. 3d 40, 537 N.E.2d 624, 9 UCCR2d 88 (1989). *But see* K&M Joint Venture v. Smith Int'l, Inc., 669 F.2d 1106, 33 UCCR 1 (6th Cir. 1984) (applying California law). In the *K&M* case, the court said that whether notice was given and the content of the notice were questions of fact. Whether the notice was sufficient under the statute, however, was a question of law.

[1095] Williams v. Mozark Fire Extinguisher Co., 318 Ark. 792, 888 S.W.2d 303, 26 UCCR2d 1116 (1994); Mullins v. Wyatt, 887 S.W.2d 356, 25 UCCR2d 715 (Ky. 1994).

[1096] Smith v. Stewart, 233 Kan. 904, 667 P.2d 358, 36 UCCR 1141 (1983).

[1097] Moldex, Inc. v. Ogden Eng'g Corp., 652 F. Supp. 584, 3 UCCR2d 572 (D. Conn. 1987); Mariner Water Renaturalizer of Wash., Inc. v. Aqua Purification Sys., Inc., 665 F.2d 1066, 214 U.S. App. D.C. 248, 34 UCCR 1180 (D.D.C. 1981).

[1098] *See* Southwestern Steel Co. v. W.A. Hunt Constr. Co., 301 S.C. 140, 390 S.E.2d 475, 12 UCCR2d 103 (1990) (surveying the cases and dividing them between those taking a "lenient" approach and those taking a "strict" approach).

[1099] *See, e.g.*, Chemtrol Adhesives, Inc. v. American Mfrs. Mut. Ins. Co., 42 Ohio St. 3d 40, 537 N.E.2d 624, 9 UCCR2d 88 (1989).

hand, if the court focuses on the final sentence of Comment 4, which suggests that a notice must claim a breach by the seller, a marginal notice is likely to be insufficient.

Illustrative of the former category of cases is *Oregon Lumber Co. v. Dwyer Overseas Timber Products Co.*[1100] In this case, the seller agreed to sell lumber processed in Ecuador. In November 1973, after delivery had begun, the buyer complained to the seller that the lumber was not running to the expected grade. The initial complaints were, according to the seller, "nothing of a substantial nature," but by late November they became more significant. At no time during this period, however, did the buyer specifically claim a breach or make a demand for damages. In December 1973, the buyer refused to pay the remainder of the purchase price, complaining that the lumber did not meet the standard required by the contract. While this final notice was clearly sufficient under section 2-607, the seller argued that it was not timely.

The court held that the complaint in November was sufficient to satisfy section 2-607. Focusing on the portion of Comment 4 that requires only that the buyer notify the seller that the transaction is troublesome, the court said that there is no requirement in section 2-607 that the buyer assert a claim for damages or declare an intent to pursue any other remedy for the notice to be sufficient. According to the court, the notice must merely apprise the seller that there are some problems with the transaction, and the notice can be given in any manner or form.[1101]

The leading case adopting a strict interpretation of section 2-607 is *Eastern Airlines, Inc. v. McDonnell Douglas Corp.*[1102] The case involved a series of contracts for the purchase of 100 jet aircraft to be delivered over a lengthy period of time at a cost of half a billion dollars. For a number of reasons, ninety of the aircraft were delivered a total of 7,426 days late. During the delivery process, the buyer (Eastern) complained continuously about the delays. Perhaps because of an "excusable delay" clause in the contracts and McDonnell Douglas' commitments to provide aircraft to the government for the Vietnam War, Eastern never explicitly claimed that the delays were a breach of contract. The trial court concluded, however, that Eastern's complaints, coupled with McDonnell Douglas' knowledge of

---

[1100] 280 Or. 437, 571 P.2d 884, 23 UCCR 87 (1977).

[1101] *See also* Arcor, Inc. v. Textron, Inc., 960 F.2d 710, 17 UCCR2d 475 (7th Cir. 1992) (buyer not required to notify seller that it considers deficiencies to be a breach of contract); Chemtrol Adhesives, Inc. v. American Mfrs. Mut. Ins. Co., 42 Ohio St. 3d 40, 37 N.E.2d 624, 9 UCCR2d 88 (1989) (notice does not have to allege breach of contract).

[1102] 532 F.2d 957, 19 UCCR 353 (5th Cir. 1976).

the delays, were sufficient as a matter of law to constitute adequate notice of breach.

The Court of Appeals for the Fifth Circuit disagreed and remanded the case for a finding of fact as to whether notice was adequate. The court said that it was not enough, given the policies of section 2-607, for the seller to have knowledge of the facts constituting a breach.[1103] Rather, the buyer is required to inform the seller that the buyer considers the seller to be in breach of the contract.[1104] The court said that the buyer's expressions of disappointment and concern as a result of the delays were insufficient to constitute notice under section 2-607. In addition, the court said that even if adequate notice had been given at one point, subsequent actions of the buyer may have dissipated its effect. The buyer's conduct as a whole must be examined, based upon commercial standards of good faith, to determine whether adequate notice was given. The court stated that commercial buyers were held to a higher standard of notice than consumer buyers.

Other cases have followed the lead of *Eastern*. In *Kopper Glo Fuel, Inc. v. Island Lake Coal Co.,*[1105] the buyer complained to the seller, both orally and in writing, that several of the carloads of coal that had been delivered to the buyer's customers were of substandard quality. One of the letters stated that the buyer would reject future shipments that did not satisfy the contract specifications. On the other hand, the buyer had also indicated on a number of occasions that its customers were happy with the coal, and it continued to order coal from the seller after it had complained about the quality of some shipments. Under these circumstances, the court held that the buyer had not given the seller sufficient notice under section 2-607. It said that "[a]t a minimum, it must be apparent from the written notice that the buyer, in fact, is claiming a breach of the particular contract involved,"[1106] which the buyer had not done. Similarly, in *Cotner v. Interna-*

[1103] Other courts have disagreed on this point. *Compare* Perona v. Volkswagen of Am., Inc., 276 Ill. App. 3d 609, 658 N.E.2d 1349, 28 UCCR2d (1995) (knowledge of manufacturer of defect sufficient notice) *with* Aqualon Co. v. MAC Equip., Inc., 32 UCCR2d 818 (E.D. Va. 1997).

[1104] *See* Thomas G. Faria Corp. v. Dana Jewelry Technology, Inc., 31 UCCR2d 115 (D.R.I. 1996) (merchant buyer must inform seller that buyer considers there to be a "breach of the contract").

[1105] 436 F. Supp. 91, 22 UCCR 1117 (E.D. Tenn. 1977).

[1106] *Id.* at 96, 22 UCCR at 1122. *See also* Connicle v. Suzuki Motor Co., Ltd., 30 UCCR2d 709 (Ill. 1996) (seller's knowledge that one of its model cars may have defect insufficient; U.C.C. § 2-607 requires that seller be apprised of the trouble with a particular product purchased by a particular buyer).

tional Harvester Co.,[1107] the court held that the fact that the buyer of a truck had described a problem with the truck to the seller's mechanics and talked with the seller's salesperson about trading the truck in did not constitute notice of breach. The court said that the requisite notice had to be more than a mere complaint and must inform the seller that the buyer demands damages upon an asserted breach of warranty. Part of the problem in *Cotner*, however, appears to be that the buyer dealt only with nonmanagement employees; the court strongly suggested that a phone call to the seller's headquarters would have done the trick.[1108]

Although it is probably unnecessary in the "lenient" jurisdictions, attorneys advising clients should ensure that a notice of breach indicates that the buyer considers the seller to be in "breach" of the contract, using that term. The notice does not have to demand damages or any particular relief and can be otherwise conciliatory, but to be certain that the notice is sufficient, it should be clear that the buyer does not consider the seller's performance to conform to the contract. In addition, if the buyer continues to deal with the seller after the buyer has complained about some aspect of the seller's performance, the buyer may be held to a higher standard under section 2-607. As both *Eastern Airlines* and *Kopper Glo* suggest, subsequent conduct may "dissipate" the effect of an ambiguous prior notice. A buyer should make it clear that its continued relationship with the seller is not intended to negate the effect of a prior notice of breach.

[B] Timeliness of Notice

Section 2-607(3)(a) requires that the buyer's notice be given "within a reasonable time" after the buyer discovers or should have discovered the defect. The timeliness requirement serves at least three purposes: (1) to give the seller the opportunity to minimize damages by curing the defect;[1109] (2)

[1107] 260 Ark. 885, 545 S.W.2d 627, 20 UCCR 1169 (1977).

[1108] For another case adopting a strict standard, see Standard Alliance Indus., Inc. v. Black Clawson Co., 587 F.2d 813, 25 UCCR 65 (6th Cir. 1978). The Sixth Circuit's interpretation of Ohio law in this case is probably no longer good, however, after the *Chemtrol* case. *See* Chemtrol Adhesives, Inc. v. American Mfrs. Mut. Ins. Co., 42 Ohio St. 3d 40, 37 N.E.2d 624, 9 UCCR2d 88 (1989).

[1109] *See* L.B. Trucking, Inc. v. Townsend Grain & Feed Co., 163 B.R. 709, 23 UCCR2d 1092 (D. Del. 1994); Williams v. Mozark Fire Extinguisher Co., 318 Ark. 792, 888 S.W.2d 303, 26 UCCR2d 1116 (1994); Atwood v. Southeast Bedding Co., Inc., 485 S.E.2d 217, 33 UCCR2d 73 (Ga. App. 1997).

to protect sellers from stale claims;[1110] and (3) to promote settlement without litigation.[1111]

Whether notice is timely depends heavily on the particular facts and circumstances of each case.[1112] For example, the buyer of perishable goods will have a shorter time to notify the seller of the breach than a buyer of more durable goods.[1113]

Courts have uniformly distinguished between commercial and consumer buyers with regard to the timeliness of notice as well as the contents of the notice. The distinction between consumers and other buyers is made explicit in Comment 4 to section 2-607:

> "A reasonable time" for notification from a retail consumer is to be judged by different standards [than a merchant buyer] so that in his case it will be extended, for the rule requiring notification is designed to defeat commercial bad faith, not to deprive a good faith consumer of his remedy.[1114]

The implication of this Comment is that consumers who act in good faith will rarely be deprived of their cause of action by section 2-607; many consumers are unaware until they consult an attorney that a notice requirement even exists.[1115] Commercial buyers, on the other hand, are held to an objective standard of good faith that requires conformity to reasonable standards of fair dealing in the trade.[1116] Notice that is inconsistent with established industry practices or standards invariably is ruled untimely.[1117]

[1110] See Courtesy Enters., Inc. v. Richards Lab., 457 N.E.2d 572, 37 UCCR 765 (Ind. Ct. App. 1983); Dowling v. Southwestern Porcelain, Inc., 237 Kan. 536, 701 P.2d 954, 41 UCCR 127 (1985).

[1111] See Roth Steel Prods. v. Sharon Steel Corp., 705 F.2d 134, 35 UCCR 1435 (6th Cir. 1983); P&F Constr. Corp. v. Friend Lumber Corp. of Medford, 31 Mass. App. Ct. 57, 575 N.E.2d 61, 16 UCCR2d 377 (1991).

[1112] See Palmer v. A.H. Robbins Co., 684 P.2d 187, 38 UCCR 1150 (Colo. 1984); Maybank v. S.S. Kresge Co., 302 N.C. 129, 273 S.E.2d 681, 30 UCCR 985 (1981).

[1113] See Allen Food Prods., Inc. v. Block Bros., Inc., 507 F. Supp. 392, 31 UCCR 553 (S.D. Ohio 1980).

[1114] U.C.C. § 2-607, Official Comment 4.

[1115] See Maybank v. S.S. Kresge Co., 302 N.C. 129, 273 S.E.2d 681, 30 UCCR 985 (1981); W. Prosser, Law of Torts § 97 at 655 (4th ed. 1971). But see Perona v. Volkswagen of Am., Inc., 684 N.E.2d 859, 34 UCCR2d 1001 (Ill. App. Ct. 1997).

[1116] U.C.C. § 2-103(b). See Steel & Wire Corp. v. Thyssen, Inc., 20 UCCR2d 892 (E.D. Mich. 1976); Hydronic Enters., Inc. v. Danal Jewelry Co., 2 UCCR2d 1537 (R.I. Super. Ct. 1986).

[1117] See, e.g., Smith-Moore Body Co. v. Heil Co., 603 F. Supp. 354, 40 UCCR 898 (E.D. Va. 1985); Steel & Wire Corp. v. Thyssen, Inc., 20 UCCR 892 (E.D. Mich. 1976).

Where prejudice to the seller results from a delay in notification, the courts apply the notice requirement more strictly. Late notices that have deprived sellers of the ability to investigate fully the buyer's allegations, interview or depose witnesses, or mitigate damages will generally be found wanting.[1118] Notice given after the buyer has disposed of the goods will often be held untimely.[1119] Despite prejudice to the seller, however, the notice is not due until the buyer *discovers or should have discovered the defect*. Therefore, notice given long after purchase may still be timely if the defect was difficult to discover.[1120] If discovery occurs long after purchase, however, the buyer should notify the seller immediately, since a reasonable time for notice after discovery of the defect may be short because of the length of time that has passed since the goods were purchased.

If the buyer provides some notice that the product is causing difficulty, even though the notice falls short of notice of breach under section 2-607(3),[1121] courts may be inclined to allow a longer time for an eventually effective notice of breach than would otherwise be the case.[1122] Even if the buyer's complaints fall short of notifying the seller that the buyer is claiming a breach, as some courts have required to satisfy section 2-607(3),[1123] the complaints put the seller on notice that there may be a problem with the goods.

An issue related to the timeliness of notice is whether the filing of a lawsuit or counterclaim can satisfy the notice requirement of section 2-607. Some courts have taken a hard line and have held that failing to give section 2-607(3) notice before filing a lawsuit or counterclaim bars the buyer from any remedy as a matter of law because it defeats a primary purpose of section 2-607(3): encouraging compromise and the mitigation of dam-

---

[1118] *See, e.g.*, Smith-Moore Body Co. v. Heil Co., 603 F. Supp. 354, 40 UCCR 898 (E.D. Va. 1985) (seller was deprived of opportunity to investigate lawyer's claim in a timely manner because of seven-month delay in giving notice; court found notice unreasonable as a matter of law).

[1119] *See, e.g.*, Hebron v. American Isuzu Motors, Inc., 60 F.3d 1095, 27 UCCR2d 125 (4th Cir. 1995) (notice unreasonable as a matter of law when buyer had waited two years to provide notice of breach and had disposed of supposedly defective vehicle at the time notice was provided).

[1120] *See, e.g.*, Greenfield Seed Co. v. Bland, 18 Ark. App. 48, 710 S.W.2d 833, 1 UCCR2d 733 (1986) (court held that because defect in red rice cannot be detected until time of harvest, buyer's notice was not untimely when notice was given months after purchase).

[1121] *See* § 4.10[A], *supra*.

[1122] *See* Delano Growers' Coop. Winery v. Supreme Wine Co., 393 Mass. 666, 473 N.E.2d 1066, 40 UCCR 93 (1985).

[1123] *See* § 4.10[A], *supra*.

ages.[1124] Other courts have taken a more lenient position, at least in some circumstances. If notice prior to filing a lawsuit is unlikely itself to have accomplished the purposes underlying section 2-607, some courts will find the filing of the lawsuit to be timely notice.[1125] In addition, notice by lawsuit is more likely to be sufficient when the buyer is a consumer, especially one who suffers personal injury.[1126] Courts, however, are inclined to find notice untimely when it occurs through the filing of a counterclaim or an answer rather than through the filing of a complaint.[1127]

Under the proposed revisions to Article 2, failure to give timely notice of breach bars the buyer from a remedy only to the extent that the party entitled to notice establishes that it was prejudiced by the failure.[1128] The authors applaud this change, although it is unlikely to change the result in many cases. Either silently or explicitly, courts have frequently taken into account the prejudice to the seller in deciding whether notice was timely. The proposed revisions do not indicate whether the burden of proving prejudice if notice is untimely will be on the buyer or the seller, although the authors believe that the seller, as the party with access to the facts concerning prejudice, should have the burden.

[1124] See M.K. Assocs. v. Stowell Prods., Inc. 697 F. Supp. 20, 7 UCCR2d 775 (D. Me. 1988); Voboril v. Namco Leisure World, Inc., 24 UCCR 614 (Conn. Super. 1978); see also Perona v. Volkswagen of Am., Inc., 27 UCCR2d 890 (Ill. Ct. App. 1995) (filing of lawsuit insufficient notice when no personal injury involved); Northwest Truck & Trailer Sales, Inc. v. Dvorak, 269 Mont. 150, 887 P.2d 260, 25 UCCR2d 1124 (1994) (filing of lawsuit insufficient notice).

[1125] See City of Wichita v. United States Gypsum Co., 828 F. Supp. 851, 23 UCCR2d 96 (D. Kan. 1993) (unlikely that earlier notice would have led to cure or settlement).

[1126] See, e.g., Simmons v. Clemco Indus., 368 So. 2d 569, 25 UCCR 1088 (Ala. 1979); Shooshanian v. Wagner, 672 P.2d 455, 37 UCCR 55 (Alaska 1983); Smith v. Steward, 233 Kan. 904, 667 P.2d 358, 36 UCCR 1141 (1983). See also Perona v. Volkswagen of Am., Inc., 276 Ill. App. 3d 609, 658 N.E.2d 1349, 28 UCCR2d 1231 (1995) (filing of lawsuit not timely notice in absence of personal injury); Connick v. Suzuki Motor Co., Ltd., 30 UCCR2d 709 (Ill. 1996) (only consumers who suffer personal injury satisfy notice requirement by filing complaint).

[1127] See Northwest Truck & Trailer Sales, Inc. v. Dvorak, 269 Mont. 150, 887 P.2d 260, 25 UCCR2d 1124 (1994) (notice by counterclaim untimely); Harry J. Whelchel Co., Inc. v. Ripley Tractor Co., 900 S.W.2d 691, 27 UCCR2d 879 (Tenn. Ct. App. 1995) (notice given through amendment to answer untimely); Fleet Maintenance, Inc. v. Burke Energy Midwest Corp., 11 Kan. App. 2d 523, 728 P.2d 408, 2 UCCR2d 905 (1986) (notice given only after seller files lawsuit for the price untimely).

[1128] Council Draft, § 2-707.

[C]   From Whom Notice Is Due

The text of section 2-607(3)(a) requires only that the "buyer" give notice of breach. As discussed previously, however, warranties may extend those who are not buyers.[1129] There are "horizontal privity" plaintiffs such as family members, guests in the home, and others that are given the right to sue for breach of warranty under section 2-318, or by judicial decision, even though they are not buyers.[1130] Comment 5 recognizes that the terms of section 2-607 apply only to "buyers," but then creates an undefined duty of notification for third-party beneficiaries under the rubric of good faith. The Comment reads:

> Under this Article various beneficiaries are given rights for injuries sustained by them because of the seller's breach of warranty. Such a beneficiary does not fall within the reason of the present section in regard to discovery of defects and the giving of notice within a reasonable time after acceptance, since he has nothing to do with acceptance. However, the reason of the section does extend to requiring the beneficiary to notify the seller that an injury has occurred. What is said above, with regard to the extended time for reasonable notification from the lay consumer is also applicable here; but even a beneficiary can be properly held to the use of good faith in notifying, once he has had time to become aware of the legal situation.[1131]

Thus, the Comment appears to impose at least some notice obligations on beneficiaries who become aware that they have been injured by a breach.

In many cases, the third-party beneficiary of a warranty will have suffered personal injury[1132] and will be suing in strict tort under section 402A of the Restatement of Torts or under a state products-liability statute.[1133] In cases involving state statutes, plaintiffs will only be required to give such notice, if any, as the statute requires. If the plaintiff is suing under section

---

[1129] See § 4.09, *supra.*

[1130] See § 4.09[A], *supra.*

[1131] U.C.C. § 2-607, Official Comment 5.

[1132] As previously discussed, Alternatives A & B of U.C.C. § 2-318 extend warranty protection only to third-party beneficiaries who suffer personal injury. See § 4.09[B], *supra.*

[1133] *See, e.g.,* Ohio Rev. Code Ann. § 2307.71 *et seq.* (Baldwin 1995).

402A, there is no requirement that the plaintiff provide notice of breach.[1134] Only when strict liability is not available must consumer beneficiaries who suffer personal injury be concerned with the section 2-607 notice requirement.

The existing warranty cases deal almost exclusively with personal injury and, with a few exceptions, have held that no notice of breach is required under section 2-607 for third-party beneficiaries who suffer personal injury.[1135] The leading case is *Frericks v. General Motors Corp.*,[1136] a case in which a passenger in a car was injured when the driver fell asleep and the car overturned. The passenger was severely injured, and alleged that his injuries were aggravated by the failure of a seat locking mechanism on the automobile. General Motors contended that the plaintiff had failed to give the required notice of breach under section 2-607(3)(a) and that the suit should be dismissed.

The court held that the notice requirement was inapplicable to third-party beneficiaries. The court noted that section 2-607, by its terms, applies only to "buyers," a term defined in section 2-103 of the Code as "a person who buys or contracts to buy goods."[1137] Although Comment 5 suggests that notice of breach is required even of nonbuyer beneficiaries, the court said that the Comments have not been enacted by the legislature and cannot vary the plain language of the statute. Further, requiring notice by third-party beneficiaries who suffer personal injury does not serve the policies of section 2-607. Because the injuries have already occurred in personal injury cases, notice cannot further the policies of cure or mitigation of damages. As to the defendant's argument that notice is necessary to guard against stale claims, the court responded that the Code's statute of limitations in section 2-725 is adequate for that purpose. The court concluded that the statute was clear and unambiguous in requiring notice of breach.

[1134] Restatement (Second) of Torts § 402A, cmt. m (1965). *See* Fischer v. Mead Johnson Lab., 41 A.D.2d 737, 341 N.Y.S.2d 257, 12 UCCR 68 (1973) (no notice required where tortious elements are involved); Garcia v. Texas Instruments, Inc., 598 S.W.2d 24, 29 UCCR 883 (Tex. Ct. App. 1980) (requirement of notice inconsistent with strict liability). *See also* Perona v. Volkswagen of Am., Inc., 684 N.E.2d 859, 34 UCCR2d 1001 (Ill. App. Ct. 1997) (commencement of lawsuit satisfies notice when personal injuries are alleged).

[1135] *See, e.g.*, Morgan v. Sears, Roebuck & Co., 693 F. Supp. 1154, 7 UCCR2d 464 (N.D. Ga. 1988) (applying Ga. law) (family member of buyer); Hansen v. F.M.C. Corp., 32 UCCR 828 (D. Kan. 1981) (employee of buyer); Simmons v. Clemco Indus., 368 So. 2d 509, 25 UCCR 1088 (Ala. 1979) (employee of buyer); Chaffin v. Atlantic Coca Cola Bottling Co., 127 Ga. App. 619, 194 S.E.2d 513, 11 UCCR 737 (1972) (family member of buyer).

[1136] 278 Md. 304, 20 UCCR 371 (Ct. App. 1976).

[1137] U.C.C. § 2-103(1)(a).

Only a few cases are contrary to *Frericks,* and none is as thoroughly reasoned. In *Parillo v. Giroux Co.,*[1138] the Rhode Island Supreme Court, with a simple citation to section 2-607(3)(a) and no discussion, required notice of breach by a bartender injured by an exploding bottle of grenadine, apparently purchased by his employer. In a subsequent case, again with no discussion of the issue, the same court followed *Parillo.*[1139] In a more recent case, the District Court for the Northern District of Illinois adopted a similar rule when the buyer's mother was injured as a result of ingesting a prescription drug.[1140] The court merely cited to Comment 5 to section 2-607, stating that the Comment made it "quite clear" that the drafters intended the notice provision to extend to third-party beneficiaries.

The decision in *Frericks* is correct and should be followed. As the court stated, the policies behind the notice provision of section 2-607 are furthered only marginally in personal-injury cases. After the injury has occurred there is no opportunity for the seller to cure the defective tender, nor do circumstances permit the seller the opportunity to mitigate damages. Also, personal injury cases do not present the same opportunities for compromise and settlement that may be furthered by early notice when the parties are involved in an ongoing commercial relationship. Finally, there is merit in making the Code consistent with tort liability for product defects that cause personal injury.

The situation is different, however, when a third-party beneficiary who is not a buyer suffers only economic harm. In this case, there is probably little difference between the position of a buyer and that of the beneficiary, and notice under section 2-607 should generally be required. Opportunities for cure and mitigation of damages may be present in these cases just as when the injured party is the buyer. The argument that the language of the statute precludes a notice requirement can be avoided by grounding the requirement in the Code's good-faith obligation, as Comment 5 suggests.[1141]

[D]   To Whom Must Notice Be Given

Section 2-607(3)(a) requires that notice of breach be given to "the seller." As discussed in detail previously in this text, many states no longer require "vertical privity" in many circumstances.[1142] Buyers are often enti-

---

[1138] 426 A.2d 1313, 31 UCCR 108 (R.I. 1981).

[1139] Lariviere v. Dayton Safety Ladder Co., 525 A.2d 892, 4 UCCR2d 433 (R.I. 1987).

[1140] Ratkovich v. Smithkline, 711 F. Supp. 436, 9 UCCR2d 118 (N.D. Ill. 1989).

[1141] This may not suffice with respect to consumer buyers, however, inasmuch as their only obligation of good faith is "honesty in fact." *See* U.C.C. § 1-203.

[1142] *See* § 4.09[A], *supra.*

tled to sue those remote in the chain of distribution such as manufacturers or intermediate distributors. The issue is whether a defendant, who has not sold the goods directly to the buyer is a "seller" within the language of section 2-607 and is entitled to notice of breach from the buyer.

The cases are divided on this question, although the majority view is that a buyer need notify only its immediate seller in order to satisfy the statute. The view that no notice to remote sellers is required clearly predominates when personal injury or property damage results from the breach.[1143] Although there are a few cases to the contrary,[1144] these cases tend to be largely devoid of reasoning or discussion of the issue. Thus, it appears that when personal injury is involved, notice of breach to a remote seller is not generally required.

When the damage is solely economic, the courts are more evenly divided.[1145] In these cases the policies of mitigation of damages and cure are more apparent than in personal injury cases, and the consequences of leaving the plaintiff without a remedy are probably less serious. In addition, consistency with tort law is not an issue when personal injury is not involved. As a result, it is not unsurprising that the cases are not in harmony.

A case in which the court refused to distinguish between personal injury and economic harm is *Cooley v. Big Horn Harvestore Systems, Inc.*[1146] In this case, the buyer purchased a grain storage and distribution system for use in his dairy farm operation. After the system was installed, the buyer's

---

[1143] *See, e.g.*, Cipollone v. Liggett Group, Inc., 683 F. Supp. 1487, 6 UCCR2d 683 (D.N.J. 1988); Snell v. G.D. Searle & Co., 595 F. Supp. 654, 40 UCCR 129 (N.D. Ala. 1984); Owen v. Glendale Optical Co, 590 F. Supp. 32, 39 UCCR 903 (S.D. Ill. 1984); Palmer v. A.H. Robbins Co., 38 UCCR 1150 (Colo. 1984); Tomczuk v. Town of Cheshire, 26 Conn. Supp. 219, 217 A.2d 71, 3 UCCR 147 (Conn. Super. 1965); Ragland Mills, Inc. v. General Motors Corp., 763 S.W.2d 357, 9 UCCR2d 893 (Mo. Ct. App. 1989) (property damage); Goldstein v. G.D. Searle & Co., 62 Ill. App. 3d 344, 378 N.E.2d 1083, 19 Ill. Dec. 208, 24 UCCR 888 (1978).

[1144] *See, e.g.*, McCure v. F. Alioto Fish Co., 597 F.2d 1244, 26 UCCR 912 (9th Cir. 1979) (applying California law); Branden v. Gerbie, 62 Ill. App. 3d 138, 379 N.E.2d 7, 9 Ill. Dec. 492, 24 UCCR 152 (1978).

[1145] *Compare* Wilcox v. Hillcrest Memorial Park of Dallas, 696 S.W.2d 423, 42 UCCR 169 (Tex. Ct. App. 1985) (notice required) *and* Western Equip. Co. v. Sheridan Iron Works, Inc., 605 P.2d 806, 28 UCCR 356 (Wyo. 1980) (notice of breach required) *with* Cooley v. Big Horn Harvestore Sys., Inc., 813 P.2d 736, 14 UCCR2d 977 (Colo. 1991) (no notice required) *and* Firestone Tire & Rubber Co. v. Cannon, 53 Md. App. 106, 452 A.2d 192, 34 UCCR 1564 (1982) *and* Vintage Homes, Inc. v. Coldiron, 585 S.W.2d 886, 27 UCCR (Tex. Ct. App. 1979) (no notice of breach to manufacturer required). The *Firestone* case provides a detailed discussion of the arguments on both sides of the issue and collects the cases prior to 1982.

[1146] 813 P.2d 736, 14 UCCR2d 977 (Colo. 1991).

cattle, which were fed with grain stored in the system, began to get sick and some later died. The buyer sued the manufacturer, but did not provide notice of breach. The manufacturer argued that notice was necessary, and attempted to distinguish an earlier Colorado case in which the court had determined that notice to a remote seller was not required. The manufacturer urged that the earlier case involved personal injury rather than economic harm and that notice should be required when solely economic harm was involved. The court refused to adopt this distinction, and refused to require notice to a remote seller. The court identified three policies behind notice of breach: to correct defects, to undertake negotiations, and to prevent stale claims. It said that filing a lawsuit against the manufacturer was sufficient to begin the negotiation process and that the statute of limitations was sufficient protection against stale claims. The court did not address the justification that notice of breach facilitates cure and the mitigation of damages.

In *Carson v. Chevron Chemical Co.,*[1147] the court distinguished between consumers and commercial buyers, requiring notice by commercial buyers to manufacturers, at least when the commercial buyer has had direct contact with the manufacturer. The buyer in this case was a farmer who worked with both the dealer and the manufacturer in purchasing and applying herbicide to a farming project. In fact, the manufacturer had even employed the buyer as a consultant. The court said that in the context of a relatively unsophisticated consumer and a "remote, inaccessible" manufacturer, the immediate seller is in a better position to determine whether the manufacturer or the immediate seller is responsible for the defect and which of the two is in a better position to remedy it. Therefore, in the "ordinary" buyer-seller relationship, the buyer is required to give notice of breach only to the immediate seller. When, however, the buyer is a sophisticated businessperson and deals directly with the manufacturer as well as the immediate seller, notice of breach to the manufacturer is necessary before the manufacturer can be held liable for breach.[1148]

One court has said that the notice requirement is satisfied as to a remote seller when that seller has actual knowledge of the defect, despite the buyer's failure to give notice.[1149] In addition, when the manufacturer's express war-

---

[1147] 6 Kan. App. 2d 776, 635 P.2d 1248, 32 UCCR 834 (1981).

[1148] *See* Fieldstone Co. v. Briggs Plumbing Prods., Inc., 62 Cal. Rptr. 2d 701, 32 UCCR2d 445 (Cal. Ct. App. 1997).

[1149] Prutch v. Ford Motor Co., 618 P.2d 657, 29 UCCR 1507 (Colo. 1980). The court in *Prutch*, however, did not indicate whether notice would be required in the absence of this knowledge. The *Cooley* case, discussed previously, determined that notice to a remote seller was not required in Colorado, even when the remote seller did not have actual knowledge of the breach. *See also* Seaside Resorts, Inc. v. Club Car, Inc., 308 S.C. 47, 416 S.E.2d 655,

ranty explicitly makes the immediate seller the manufacturer's agent for warranty service, there is no necessity to give the manufacturer notice of breach, so long as notice is given to the immediate seller.[1150] On the other hand, it appears that the remote seller is entitled to use the buyer's failure to notify the *immediate* seller of the breach as a defense, even when the buyer is under no obligation to notify the remote seller.[1151]

Although there are cogent arguments on both sides, the cases that have not required notice to remote manufacturers are the better reasoned. In most cases, buyers should be entitled to assume that notice of product defects will be passed "upstream" once the buyer has notified the immediate seller.[1152] The immediate seller will, in most cases, seek assistance or indemnification from the manufacturer when confronted with a claim for a defective product, and the buyer should be able to count on this communication occurring. In fact, a number of cases have held that the immediate seller will lose an indemnity claim against a remote seller unless the immediate seller provides his seller with notice of breach.[1153] Further, the seller is in a much better position than the buyer to know who in the distributive chain is likely to be responsible for the defect and how to best communicate with this party or parties. Only when the buyer has dealt directly with the manufacturer (or other remote seller) to such an extent that it would be unfair not to require notice of breach to the manufacturer should it be required. In this case, the court could couch the obligation in the Code's requirement of good faith, or find that, because of the direct contact, the manufacturer occupies the position of a "seller" under section 2-607.

---

19 UCCR2d 60 (Ct. App. 1992) (court stated in dicta that when remote manufacturer has actual knowledge of breach notice is unnecessary).

[1150] *See* Halprin v. Ford Motor Co., 107 N.C. App. 423, 420 S.E.2d 686, 19 UCCR2d 53 (1992). *See also* Church of the Nativity of Our Lord v. Watpro, 491 N.W.2d 1, 18 UCCR2d 1017 (Minn. 1992) (notice sufficient where given to seller who was identified in contract as manufacturer's "exclusive agent" in the United States).

[1151] *See* Snell v. G.D. Searle & Co., 595 F. Supp. 654, 40 UCCR 129 (N.D. Ala. 1984); Goldstein v. G.D. Searle & Co., 62 Ill. App. 3d 344, 378 N.E.2d 1083, 19 Ill. Dec. 208, 24 UCCR 888 (1978). *See also* Owen v. Glendale Optical, 590 F. Supp. 32, 39 UCCR 903 (S.D. Ill. 1984) (court implies that manufacturer would have benefit of buyer's failure to notify immediate seller of breach).

[1152] *See* Goldstein v. G.D. Searle & Co., 62 Ill. App. 3d 344, 378 N.E.2d 1083, 19 Ill. Dec. 208, 24 UCCR 888 (1978).

[1153] *See* Steel & Wire Corp. v. Thyssen, Inc., 20 UCCR 892 (E.D. Mich. 1976); Armco Steel Corp. v. Isaacson Structural Steel Co., 611 P.2d 507, 28 UCCR 1249 (Alaska 1980).

§ 4.11   STATUTE OF LIMITATIONS

Section 2-725 of the Code attempts to provide a uniform period of time within which actions must be brought on a contract for the sale of goods:

> An action for breach of any contract for sale must be commenced within four years after the cause of action has accrued. By the original agreement the parties may reduce the period of limitations to not less than one year but may not extend it.

The purpose of the drafters in including a specific statute of limitations in the Code was to remove contracts for the sale of goods from the periods of limitations for contracts generally, which varied greatly from state to state.[1154] Sellers who did business on a nationwide scale were often subject to many different statutes of limitations.[1155] Unfortunately, a lack of clarity in the section itself, and the uncertain relationship between warranty liability under the Code and strict tort liability, have given courts the opportunity to reintroduce the variation among the states that existed prior to the Code. Two issues predominate in the cases and illustrate the danger in assuming that the Code has accomplished its purpose of national uniformity.

[A]   Accrual of the Cause of Action

By far the most litigated issue concerning the Code's statute of limitations is when the cause of action begins to run. Subsection (2) of section 2-725 provides:

> A cause of action accrues when the breach occurs, regardless of the aggrieved party's lack of knowledge of the breach. A breach of warranty occurs when tender of delivery is made, except where a warranty explicitly extends to future performance of the goods and discovery of the breach must await the time of such performance the cause of action accrues when the breach is or should have been discovered.

If the cause of action is based upon a breach other than breach of warranty, the limitations period begins to run when the breaching party fails to perform as the contract requires.[1156] If a party anticipatorily repudiates the contract,

---

[1154] U.C.C. § 2-725, Official Comment.

[1155] *Id.*

[1156] *See* Rivers Mach. Co., Inc. v. Barclay Int'l, Inc., 553 So. 2d 579, 11 UCCR2d 890 (Ala. 1989); Deluxe Sales & Serv., Inc. v. Hyundai Eng'g & Constr. Co., Ltd., 254 N.J. Super. 370, 603 A.2d 552, 18 UCCR2d 1145 (1992); Westrock Ice Cream Corp. v. General Motors Corp., 20 UCCR2d 957 (N.Y. Sup. Ct. 1993).

the statute begins to run at the time of the repudiation.[1157] If multiple breaches occur, the limitations period for recovery for each breach begins at the time of that particular breach.[1158] The cause of action accrues at the time of the breach regardless of the buyer's knowledge of the breach.

Most cases, however, deal with the accrual of the cause of action for breach of warranty. The cause of action for breach of warranty generally arises on tender of delivery of the goods[1159] and, as with other breaches, the buyer's knowledge of the breach at the time of tender of delivery is irrelevant.[1160] Even when the buyer could not reasonably have discovered the breach upon tender of delivery, perhaps because the defect had not yet become apparent,[1161] the cause of action accrues upon tender of delivery.[1162]

[1157] *See* American Cyanamid Co. v. Mississippi Chem. Corp., 817 F.2d 91, 3 UCCR2d 1411 (11th Cir. 1987).

[1158] *See* Long Island Lighting Co. v. IMO Indus., Inc., 6 F.3d 876, 22 UCCR2d 205 (2d Cir. 1993); Montana Millwork, Inc. v. Caradco Corp., 648 F. Supp. 88, 2 UCCR2d 921 (D. Mont. 1986); Moncrief v. Williston Bason Interstate Pipeline Co., 880 F. Supp. 1495, 27 UCCR2d 195 (D. Wyo. 1995).

[1159] Under U.C.C. § 2-503 "tender of delivery" generally requires that the seller "put and hold conforming goods at the buyer's disposition and give the buyer any notification reasonably necessary to enable him to take delivery." U.C.C. § 2-503(1). For a full discussion of tender of delivery, *see* § 5.02, *infra*. Under the proposed revisions to Article 2, a cause of action for breach of warranty accrues when the seller *completes* tender of delivery. *See* Council Draft, § 2-814(c)(1).

[1160] *See* United Cal. Bank v. Eastern Mountain Sports, Inc., 546 F. Supp. 945, 34 UCCR 849 (D. Mass. 1982); Cumberland Valley Joint Sch. Autho. v. Haldeman, Inc., 23 Pa. D.&C.3d 616, 35 UCCR 1185 (Pa. C.P. 1982); Southerland v. Northeast Datsun, Inc., 659 S.W.2d 889, 38 UCCR 78 (Tex. Ct. App. 1983).

[1161] *See, e.g.,* Weiner v. Armstrong Cork Co., 25 UCCR 1362 (Pa. C.P. 1978) (floor did not discolor until years after delivery; statute of limitations nonetheless began to run at tender of delivery); Coakley & Williams, Inc. v. Shatterproof Glass Corp., 706 F.2d 456, 36 UCCR 87 (4th Cir. 1983) (replacement glass did not discolor until years after delivery).

[1162] The proposed revisions to Article 2 modify this somewhat. The present section 2-725 provides that an action must be brought within four years after a cause of action accrues. Under section 2-725, a cause of action for breach of warranty accrues upon tender of delivery unless the warranty extends to future performance of the goods. Section 2-814 of the proposed revisions extends the four-year limitations period by allowing an action to be brought during the *later* of four years after the cause of action accrued or within one year after the breach was or should have been discovered, with an outside limit of five years from the accrual of the cause of action. Thus, for example, if a buyer discovers a breach of implied warranty after three years and eight months following tender of delivery, the buyer (assuming that the defect should not have been discovered earlier) would have four years and eight months from tender of delivery to bring its action. Proposed section 2-814 also prohibits the contractual shortening of the limitations period in consumer contracts. Council Draft, § 2-814.

Had the drafters stopped with the simple rule that a breach of warranty occurs upon tender of delivery, there would be little to litigate in section 2-725. Perhaps unwilling to impose such a potentially harsh rule upon buyers without qualification, the drafters created an exception in subsection (2): if the warranty "explicitly extends to future performance of the goods" the cause of action accrues when the breach is or should have been discovered. Determining when a warranty "explicitly extends to future performance," however, has been extremely difficult for courts and, unfortunately, the Code provides virtually no guidance. The decisions have undermined the drafters' desire for a uniform statute of limitations and have permitted some courts to extend dramatically the limitations period in cases where the four-year limitations period from tender of delivery should, on the face of it, clearly apply.[1163]

With respect to implied warranties, there is little disagreement: implied warranties do not extend to future performance.[1164] Because section 2-725(2) requires that the warranty "explicitly" extend to future performance, courts have uniformly held that the cause of action for breach of the implied warranties of merchantability and fitness for a particular purpose begins to run at the time of tender of delivery.[1165]

A rare exception is *Moore v. Puget Sound Plywood*,[1166] although *Moore* is not so much an exception to the general rule as a circumvention of it. The Moores purchased siding for their home in 1971. Roughly six years later, the siding began developing defects, although suit was not filed until 1981, approximately ten years after the delivery of the goods. In their com-

---

[1163] *See, e.g.,* Balog v. Center Art Gallery-Haw., Inc., 745 F. Supp., 12 UCCR2d 962 (D. Haw. 1990) (warranty of authenticity of art work extends to future performance); Moore v. Puget Sound Plywood, Inc., 332 N.W.2d 212, 36 UCCR 82 (Neb. 1983) (oral statement that a product was "siding" extends to future performance since "siding" is ordinarily supposed to last for the life of a house).

[1164] *See* Nelson v. International Harvester Corp., 394 N.W.2d 578, 2 UCCR2d 855 (Minn. Ct. App. 1986); Wilson v. Massey-Ferguson, Inc., 21 Ill. App. 3d 867, 315 N.E.2d 580, 15 UCCR 654 (Ill. App. Ct. 1974); Stumler v. Ferry-Morse Seed Co., 644 F.2d 667, 30 UCCR 1590 (7th Cir. 1981); Snyder v. Boston Whaler, Inc., 892 F. Supp. 955, 27 UCCR2d 898 (W.D. Mich. 1994).

[1165] *See* Clark v. Delaval Separator Corp., 639 F.2d 1320, 30 UCCR 1542 (5th Cir. 1981) (Section 2-314); Long Island Lighting Co. v. Transamerica Delaval, Inc., 646 F. Supp. 1442, 2 UCCR2d 1333 (S.D.N.Y. 1986) (section 2-314); Dickerson v. Mountain View Equip. Co., 109 Idaho. 711, 710 P.2d 621, 42 UCCR 114 (Idaho Ct. App. 1985) (section 2-314); Grand Island Sch. Dist. #2 v. Celotex Corp., 203 Neb. 559, 279 N.W.2d 603, 26 UCCR 939 (1979) (section 2-315); Wright v. Cutler-Hammer, Inc., 358 So. 2d 444, 24 UCCR 161 (Ala. 1978) (section 2-315).

[1166] 214 Neb. 14, 332 N.W.2d 212, 36 UCCR 82 (1983).

plaint, the Moores pleaded only breach of implied warranty. The seller argued that implied warranties, by their nature, could not "explicitly" extend to future performance and, therefore, the suit was time-barred.

The Nebraska Supreme Court, however, held that the seller had made an express warranty that extended to future performance when it described the product it sold the Moores as "siding." According to the court, the description of the goods as "siding" carried with it an expectation that the goods would last the lifetime of the house. This expectation was sufficient for the warranty to extend explicitly to future performance. As a result, the limitations period did not begin running until 1977, the time the defects were discovered, rather than 1971, the time of delivery.[1167]

The court's opinion completely abrogates the requirement that the extension of a warranty to future performance must be *explicit*. The decision would extend the statute of limitations in every case in which the goods could be expected to remain defect-free for any period after delivery. This would leave very few, if any situations, where the statute of limitations would begin to run at the time of tender of delivery. The decision in *Moore* has been soundly, and justifiably, criticized by the commentators.[1168]

Deciding when a warranty explicitly extends to future performance is much more difficult when an express warranty is involved. There is a wide variation among courts, with some courts requiring a clear and unambiguous statement that the warranty extends to the future performance of the goods,[1169] while others are satisfied with far less.[1170] Furthermore, the precise

---

[1167] The court permitted recovery under this theory despite the fact that the Moores had not even pleaded a breach of express warranty. The court held that the facts pleaded and the evidence adduced were sufficient to put the seller on notice of the claim. 214 Neb. at 18, 332 N.W.2d at 215, 36 UCCR at 85 (1983). This conclusion is very problematic considering the court's "creative" determination that an express warranty existed that could explicitly extend to future performance. It is hard to see in light of the pleadings how the seller could have anticipated the theory relied upon by the court.

[1168] *See, e.g.,* I Thomas D. Crandall et al., Uniform Commercial Code § 8.20 at 119 (1993) (describing the decision as "peculiar"); B. Clark & C. Smith, The Law of Product Warranties, 1995 Cumulative Supp. ¶11.01[2][b] at S11-11.

[1169] *See, e.g.,* Patton v. Mack Trucks, Inc., 360 Pa. Super. 1, 519 A.2d 959, 3 UCCR2d 147 (1986); R.W. Murray Co. v. Shatterproof Glass Corp., 697 F.2d 818, 35 UCCR 477 (8th Cir. 1983); Standard Alliance Indus., Inc. v. Black Clawson Co., 587 F.2d 813, 25 UCCR 65 (6th Cir. 1978), Sudenga Indus., Inc. v. Fulton Performance Prods., Inc., 894 F. Supp. 1235, 29 UCCR2d 140 (N.D. Iowa 1995) (future performance exception requires clear and express statement; any ambiguity precludes the extension of a warranty to future performance).

[1170] *See, e.g.,* Mittasch v. Seal Lock Burial Vault, Inc., 42 A.D.2d 573, 344 N.Y.S.2d 101, 12 UCCR 665 (N.Y. Sup. Ct. App. Div. 1973); Rempe v. General Elec. Co., 28 Conn. Supp. 160, 254 A.2d 577, 6 UCCR 647 (Conn. Super. Ct. 1969).

manner in which the warranty is drafted is crucial in determining whether it explicitly extends to future performance.

The majority of cases strictly construe the exception, requiring a clear statement that the warranty extends to future performance of the goods.[1171] A number of cases require that the warranty mention a specific time period during which the product will perform at a particular standard or during which it remain defect free. Thus, a statement that roofing materials would last "as long as the built up roof would last" did not explicitly extend to future performance,[1172] nor did a promise that an IUD would perform satisfactorily for a period of "several years."[1173] Similarly, a description of a boat as "unsinkable" is not a warranty extending to future performance because it did not provide that the boat would be free from defects for a specified period of time.[1174]

There are a number of cases, however, where the courts have not construed section 2-725(2) so strictly. For example, the court in *Mittasch v. Seal Lock Burial Vault, Inc.*[1175] held a representation that a burial vault would "give satisfactory service at all times" to be a warranty that explicitly extended to future performance, despite the lack of a specified time period. In *Iowa Manufacturing Co. v. Joy Manufacturing Co.*,[1176] the court held that a warranty that emissions would not exceed 38 lbs. per hour when a machine

---

[1171] *See, e.g.*, Binkley Co. v. Teledyne Mid-Am. Corp., 333 F. Supp. 1183, 10 UCCR 111, (E.D. Mo. 1971) *aff'd*, 460 F.2d 276, 11 UCCR 69 (8th Cir. 1972); Anderson v. Crestliner Inc., 33 UCCR2d 99, 564 N.W.2d 218 (Minn. Ct. App. 1997) (warranty for future performance requires guarantee of performance for a specified period).

[1172] South Burlington Sch. Dist. v. Calcagni-Frazier-Zajchowski Architects, Inc., 138 Vt. 33, 48, 410 A.2d 1359, 1366, 28 UCCR 1382, 1386 (1980).

[1173] Tolen v. A.H. Robins Co., 570 F. Supp. 1146, 1154, 37 UCCR 790, 794 (N.D. Ind. 1983). *See also* Parrino v. 21st Century Scientific Inc., 648 N.Y.S.2d 702, 32 UCCR2d 148 (App. Div. 1996) (statement that wheelchair would serve buyer for "many years to come" did not create warranty extending to future performance); Cooper Power Sys., Inc. v. Union Carbide Chem. & Plastics Co., 123 F.3d 675, 33 UCCR2d 803 (7th Cir. 1997) (statement that product would maintain its appearance for "many years" did not create warranty for future performance).

[1174] Snyder v. Boston Whaler, Inc., 892 F. Supp. 955, 27 UCCR2d 898 (W.D. Mich. 1994). In some cases, the courts clearly go too far in refusing to find that a warranty explicitly extends to future performance. In Voth v. Chrysler Motor Corp., 545 P.2d 371, 18 UCCR 954 (Kan. 1976), the Kansas Supreme Court refused to find that a new car warranty "against defects in material and workmanship in normal use . . . for 12 months or 12,000 miles" was not a warranty that explicitly extended to future performance.

[1175] 42 A.D.2d 573, 344 N.Y.S.2d 101, 12 UCCR 665 (N.Y. Sup. Ct. App. Div. 1973).

[1176] 206 Mont. 26, 669 P.2d 1057, 36 UCCR 1636 (1983).

was operated "in accordance with specified design conditions" extended to future performance.[1177] These cases remain, however, a distinct minority.

The most difficult cases are those frequent situations in which the seller provides both a warranty and a limited remedy. In these cases, one must pay close attention to both the attitude of the court and the precise wording of the provision. Many pitfalls await the unwary or uninformed drafter. A typical warranty may be worded something like this:

ONE YEAR LIMITED WARRANTY

The CRA Corporation warrants that for a period of one year it will repair or replace, free of any charge for parts or labor, any part of this CRA television which is defective in material or workmanship. This warranty is in lieu of all other warranties, express or implied, including the IMPLIED WARRANTY OF MERCHANTABILITY and the remedy of repair and replacement is the exclusive remedy provided by this warranty.

It would appear, at first glance, that this is unquestionably a warranty that explicitly extends to future performance. The CRA Corporation appears to warrant that the product will be free from defects in material and workmanship for a period of one year. Therefore, the discovery rule of section 2-715(2) applies, and the limitations period of four years does not begin to run until the defect is discovered or reasonably should have been discovered—assuming that discovery of the defect occurs within a year. As a result, the four-year statute of limitations may be extended up to a year from the time of tender, depending upon when the defect is, or should have been, discovered.

Surprisingly, however, many courts would not find this warranty to extend to future performance, and a few may not find a warranty to exist at all. This is because courts have generally distinguished between promises that relate to *the future performance of the goods* and those which relate to

---

[1177] *Id.* at 33, 669 P.2d at 1060, 36 UCCR at 1639. *See also* Black Leaf Prods. Co. v. Chemsico, Inc., 39 UCCR 508 (Mo. Ct. App. 1984) (warranty that a product is "free from defects in quality and workmanship" extends to future performance despite lack of a specified time period); Rempe v. General Elec. Co., 28 Conn. 160, 254 A.2d 577, 6 UCCR 647 (1969) (warranty that a disposal would "work properly during its lifetime" extended to future performance); In re Lone Star Indus., Inc., 776 F. Supp. 206, 16 UCCR2d 301 (D. Md. 1991) (statement that "the intent of this specification is to obtain uniform quality, durability, and performance throughout the design service life of 50 years" created a warranty extending to future performance).

the *remedy* provided by the seller. Accordingly, under this view, the seller in the forgoing example is not promising that the goods will be defect-free for a year. Rather, the seller is merely guaranteeing that, if a defect *does* occur within this period, the seller will repair it free of charge. Because the time period relates to the period in which the remedy is available rather than the condition of the goods, the statute of limitations begins to run at tender of delivery.

If we were to change the language in the previous warranty just slightly, we would get a different result:

> The CRA Corporation warrants this television against defects in material and workmanship for a period of one year. The CRA Corporation will repair or replace, free of any charge for parts and labor, any part of this CRA television which proves defective within one year from the date of purchase. [Rest of warranty.]

With the language so modified, virtually all courts would now find that the seller has made a warranty that extends to the future performance of the goods, and the discovery rule of subsection (2) would be applied.[1178]

The problem is well illustrated by *Poppenheimer v. Bluff City Motor Homes*.[1179] In this case, the buyer purchased a motor home in June 1973. The buyer received a written warranty from GMC stating that GMC "warrants to the owner . . . that for a period of 12 months or 12,000 miles, whichever occurs first, it will repair any defective or malfunctioning part." When the motor home proved defective, and attempts at repair failed, the buyer finally sued, more than four years after delivery. In dismissing the buyer's suit, the court said that the seller had made no warranty extending to the future performance of the goods. The only promise relating to the

---

[1178] *See, e.g.*, Paskill v. Nobility Homes, Inc., 871 S.W.2d 481, 24 UCCR2d 537 (Tenn. 1994) ("guarantee of your roof and rafter system unconditionally for five year period" extends to future performance); Grand Island Express v. Trimpte Indus., Inc., 28 F.3d 73, 24 UCCR2d 920 (8th Cir. 1994) (promise that trailers would be "free from defects in materials and workmanship for a period of five years" explicitly extends to future performance); Alcan Aluminum Corp. v. Carlton Aluminum of New Eng., Inc., 35 Mass. App. Ct. 161, 617 N.E.2d 1005, 24 UCCR2d 66 (1993) (twenty-year unconditional guarantee on all aluminum siding that it installed explicitly extends to future performance); Church of the Nativity of Our Lord v. Watpro, Inc., 491 N.W.2d 1, 18 UCCR2d 1017 (Minn. 1992) (guarantee to maintain roof "in a watertight condition at its own expense for a period of five years" extends to future performance).

[1179] 658 S.W.2d 106, 38 UCCR 167 (Tenn. App. 1983).

future was the promise to repair. Because this promise, however, did not relate to the *goods*, it did not fall within subsection (2) of section 2-725 and could not, therefore, extend the statute of limitations beyond four years from tender of delivery. Many other courts have employed similar reasoning.[1180]

Some courts, however, have avoided this result, either directly or indirectly. They have held that a seller's promise to repair or replace defects within a specified period extends to future performance, even if the warranty of the goods does not.[1181] For example, in *Long Island Lighting Co. v. IMO Industries, Inc.*,[1182] generators delivered by the seller in 1976 and 1977 proved defective. Suit, however, was not brought until 1985, well after four years from the time of tender. The court held that the promise by the manufacturer to repair any defects occurring after the generators were "in place" extended to future performance. Also, the statute of limitations did not begin to run on *this promise* until the seller was either unable or unwilling to effect repairs, not when the buyer discovered or should have discovered the defect. Therefore, the buyer's suit was timely since the manufacturer refused to make repairs only in 1981, long after the generators were "in place."

The holdings of the *Long Island Lighting* case and a few other cases,[1183] provide at least partial relief to buyers who cannot be expected to scrutinize the language of warranties in the manner suggested by the majority of courts. Although buyers may not be able to receive damages caused by the defect itself—either because the goods themselves are not warranted at all or because suit is brought more than four years from the date of tender—

[1180] *See, e.g.*, Tittle v. Steel City Oldsmobile GMC Truck, Inc., 544 So. 2d 883, 8 UCCR2d 701 (Ala. 1989); Wilson v. Class, 605 A.2d 907, 17 UCCR2d 1166 (Del. Super. 1992); Muss v. Mercedes-Benz of N. Am., Inc., 734 S.W.2d 155, 4 UCCR2d 1459 (Tex. Ct. App. 1987); New Eng. Power Co. v. Riley Stoker Corp., 20 Mass. 25, 477 N.E.2d 1054, 40 UCCR 1735 (1985); Stoltzner v. American Motors Jeep Corp., Inc., 127 Ill. App. 3d 816, 39 UCCR 907 (Ill. App. Ct. 1984); Ontario Hydro v. Zallea Sys., Inc., 569 F. Supp. 1261, 36 UCCR 1222 (D. Del. 1983); Crouch v. General Elec., 699 F. Supp. 585 (S.D. Miss. 1988); Boyd v. A.O. Smith Harvestone Prods., Inc., 776 P.2d 1125, 9 UCCR2d 571 (Colo. Ct. App. 1989); Shapiro v. Long Island Lighting Co., 418 N.Y.S.2d 948, 27 UCCR 445 (N.Y. Sup. Ct. App. Div. 1979); Allis-Chalmers Credit Corp. v. Herbolt, 17 Ohio App. 3d 230, 479 N.E.2d 293, 41 UCCR 485 (1984); The Dreier Co., Inc. v. Unitronix Corp., 3 UCCR2d 1728 (N.J. Super. Ct. 1987); Kline v. U.S. Marine Corp., 882 S.W.2d 597, 27 UCCR2d 158 (Tex. Ct. App. 1994); Dynaco Corp. v. KLA Instruments Corp., 200 B.R. 750 (Bankr. D.N.H. 1996).

[1181] *See, e.g.*, Kreiger v. Nick Alexander Imports, Inc., 234 Cal. App. 3d 205, 285 Cal. Rptr. 717, 15 UCCR2d 895 (Cal. Ct. App. 1991); Space Leasing Assocs. v. Atlantic Bldg. Sys., Inc., 144 Ga. App. 320, 23 UCCR 642 (Ga. Ct. App. 1977).

[1182] 6 F.3d 876, 22 UCCR2d 205 (2d Cir. 1993).

[1183] *See* cases cited in *supra* note 1182.

the buyer can recover damages for the seller's failure to live up to its promise to repair.[1184]

A decision of the Supreme Court of Pennsylvania takes a more direct approach and refuses to distinguish between warranties that guarantee against defects for a specified period of time and promises to repair or replace a defective product within a specified time. In *Nationwide Insurance Co. v. General Motors Corp.,*[1185] the buyer purchased a new car and received a "New Car Limited Warranty" when the car was delivered. The relevant provisions of the warranty stated:

DEFECTS

This exclusive warranty covers any repairs and needed adjustments to correct defects in material and workmanship.

REPAIRS

Your Chevrolet dealer will make the repairs or adjustments, using new or remanufactured parts.

WHICHEVER COMES FIRST

The warranty is for 12 months or 12,000 miles, whichever comes first.

WARRANTY BEGINS

The warranty period begins on the date the car is first delivered or put in use.

The car was purchased and delivered on January 5, 1982. On November 22, 1982, the car (a Chevrolet Corvette) malfunctioned, caught fire, and was destroyed. On June 20, 1986, the buyer's insurance carrier instituted suit against the manufacturer. The suit was dismissed by the trial court on a motion for summary judgment on the basis that it was barred by the four-year statute of limitations in section 2-725.

The Supreme Court conceded that courts in other states have generally taken the position that promises to "repair and replace" were not covered by the subsection (2) exception to section 2-725 because they did not promise that the goods would be defect-free in the future. The court commented

---

[1184] The buyer, however, cannot argue that the seller's failure to repair caused the remedy to fail of its essential purpose and, therefore, all Code remedies should be available. This is because there is no underlying warranty for which other remedies could be used. The only "warranty" the seller has made or that remains in force is its promise of repair.

[1185] 533 Pa. 423, 625 A.2d 1172, 21 UCCR2d 277 (1993).

that many of these cases were distinguishable on their facts,[1186] and gave three reasons why it should interpret the warranty explicitly to extend to future performance. First, it said that the focus of section 2-725 is not on the precise nature of the promise but on the duration of the promise. Because a promise to repair or replace within twelve months or 12,000 miles cannot be breached until the vehicle requires repair or adjustment, the warranty must necessarily extend to future performance.

More convincingly,[1187] the court said that the provision could plausibly be interpreted in three ways: (1) as a warranty extending for twelve months or 12,000 miles accompanied by a limited repair and adjustment remedy; (2) as creating an "unextended" warranty against defects with a limited remedy of repair and adjustment if the breach is reported within twelve months; or (3) as no warranty at all with regard to defects, but a promise that, should defects occur within twelve months or 12,000 miles, GMC would make repairs or adjustments. In deciding to adopt the first interpretation, the court noted that the document the buyer received was labeled a "warranty" and it included the statement that General Motors "warrants each new 1982 car." The document further said that "This *warranty* is for 12 months or 12,000 miles, whichever comes first."[1188] Because documents should be construed against the drafter—and General Motors had obviously prepared the warranty document—a clearer statement was necessary to keep the warranty from extending to future performance under section 2-725.

Finally, the court said that any other interpretation would mislead consumers. Consumers would be unlikely to understand that if they were given a four-year warranty drafted in a manner similar to the GMC warranty, they might have a very short period of time in which to sue if the breach occurred late in the warranty period. Further, if the period of the "warranty" was greater than four years, any period beyond four years would be illusory because the statute of limitations would have already expired.[1189]

The *Nationwide* case should be applauded. To a buyer, it is irrelevant whether the seller has (1) made a promise that the goods will be defect-free for a specified period and, if the promise is breached, the buyer's exclusive

---

[1186] *Id.* at 430 n.7, 625 A.2d at 1173 n.7, 21 UCCR2d at 283 n.7. One case discussed by the court, however, Tittle v. Steel City Oldsmobile GMC Truck, Inc., 544 So. 2d 883, 8 UCCR2d 701 (Ala. 1989), construed the very language at issue in the *Nationwide* case.

[1187] The court's first argument is not very convincing because it completely ignores the language of U.C.C. § 2-725(2) that requires that the warranty explicitly extend to future performance "*of the goods.*"

[1188] 533 Pa. at 429, 625 A.2d at 1173, 21 UCCR2d at 284.

[1189] For a case relying on similar reasoning, *see* Doctaroff v. Barra Corp. of Am., Inc., 282 N.J. Super. 230, 659 A.2d 948, 27 UCCR2d 1238 (1995).

remedy is free repair or replacement; or (2) made no promise that the goods will be defect-free for the period, but if a defect appears within a specified period the buyer is entitled to free repair or replacement. In either case, the buyer is entitled to precisely the same relief if the goods prove defective within the specified period. To have an important issue such as the length of the statute of limitations turn on which of these promises the seller has made is absurd when most buyers are unlikely to recognize the difference between the two and, in any event, are justifiably indifferent to them.

If a seller makes a promise to "repair or replace" within a specified period, that promise should generally be treated no differently for purposes of section 2-725 from a promise that the goods would be defect-free for a similar period—both should be considered as warranties extending to future performance and treated as breached, at the earliest, when a defect is discovered or should have been discovered.[1190] If courts do not want to

---

[1190] *See* Weinberg v. Independence Lincoln-Mercury, Inc., 32 UCCR 2d 851 (Mo. Ct. App. 1997).

Even under the reasoning of the *Nationwide* case, however, a seller can still create a warranty containing an exclusive repair and replacement remedy in which the statute of limitations begins to run at tender of delivery. Consider the following provisions:

> **1. Limited Warranty.** Seller warrants that the goods supplied hereunder ("the Goods") will be free from defects in material or workmanship at the time they are shipped to the customer.
>
> **2. Limitation of Remedies.** If the Goods supplied do not conform to the limited warranty set out above, Seller will, at its option (a) repair or replace the Goods which are defective or (b) refund so much of the purchase price as Customer has paid for the defective goods, provided that written notice of the defect and its nature is given to Seller as soon as practicable after discovery of the defect, but in no event later than one year from the date of shipment by Seller. This remedy is the sole and exclusive remedy available to buyer for a defect in the Goods.
>
> **3.** **Limitation of Actions.** Any legal action against Seller for a default in any of its obligations to Customer must be commenced within two years from the date of shipment of the Goods to the Customer.

Under the above provision, if a defect is discovered after six months, the buyer will have only eighteen months in which to bring suit. Despite the fact that the buyer has up to one year to discover the defect and provide the required notice, the contract makes it clear that the limitations period runs from the time of shipment. The problem with the warranty in *Nationwide*, and with many similar warranties, is that the terms of the warranty did not make it sufficiently clear that the time period in which to discover the defects related solely to the *remedy*, not to the warranty.

treat them interchangeably because of the language of section 2-725(2) requiring that the warranty explicitly extend to the future perform-ance of the *goods*, they should treat the promise of repair or replacement as a separate obligation of the seller not involving a warranty at all.[1191] Breach occurs under section 2-725(2) at tender of delivery only with respect to *warranties*; with respect to all other contract obligations, breach occurs when then seller fails to meet those obligations. As some courts have already noted, a seller does not fail to meet its "repair or replace" obligations until a defect appears *and* the seller is either unwilling or unable to repair or replace the defective part. At this point, the statute of limitations begins to run and the buyer has four years in which to bring suit.[1192]

[B] Suit Against the Manufacturer: The Privity Problem

The Code says that the limitations period begins to run for breach of warranty at the time of tender of delivery, unless the warranty explicitly extends to future performance of the goods. When the buyer, however, as a third party beneficiary under section 2-318, sues a manufacturer for breach of warranty, what is the date of tender of delivery: the date the goods were tendered to the retail seller or the date that they were tendered to the buyer who is suing for breach? Because the goods may remain in the hands of the retail seller for quite some time before sale to the ultimate buyer, this issue has important implications for the time a buyer must sue under section 2-725.

The policies implicated in this question are conflicting, and this conflict has resulted in divergent decisions.[1193] On the one hand, the manufacturer

---

[1191] The Code certainly supports this interpretation. It draws a clear distinction between remedies and warranties. *See, e.g.*, U.C.C. § 2-719, Official Comment 3, recognizing that although remedies may not be limited in an unconscionable manner, the seller remains free to disclaim warranties. Furthermore, a mere promise to repair and replace defective goods does not satisfy the definition of express warranty under U.C.C. § 2-313; it is not an affir-mation of fact or promise *which relates to the goods* nor is it a description of the goods.

[1192] Under this view the buyer may have a longer period in which to bring suit than if the limitations period began running at the time the buyer discovered or should have dis-covered the defect. For example, if the defect is discovered on May 1, but the seller does not refuse to repair or replace until July 1, the limitations period would not begin to run until July 1. *See* Hull v. Moore's Mobile Stebra, Inc., 214 A.D.2d 923, 625 N.Y.S.2d 710, 28 UCCR2d 211 (1995).

[1193] For cases holding that the proper time to determine tender of delivery is the time of tender from the manufacturer to the retailer, *see* Wilson v. Class, 605 A.2d 907, 17 UCCR2d 1166 (Del. Super. Ct. 1992); American Alloy Steel, Inc. v. Armco, Inc., 777 S.W.2d 173, 10 UCCR2d 861 (Tex. Ct. App. 1989); Rissew v. Yamaha Motor Co., Ltd., 129 Misc. 2d

has a number of cogent arguments that the proper date of tender for purposes of section 2-725 is the date of its tender to the retail seller. First, the manufacturer's position is consistent with the theory underlying section 2-318. This section permits the buyer to sue the manufacturer as a third-party beneficiary *of the contract between the manufacturer and the retailer.* The buyer's cause of action against the manufacturer derives from this contract, and it should be the date of tender this under contract that governs the limitations period. Second, the manufacturer can argue that permitting the buyer to use the date of tender under the contract between the buyer and the retail seller has the potential to make the manufacturer liable for a lengthy and uncertain period. This result undercuts both policies behind statutes of limitations: to provide certainty and a reasonable period of repose. Finally, a cause of action against the retail seller remains available to the buyer for the full four-year period from the retail seller's tender of delivery to the buyer.

The buyer, however, has no opportunity to become aware of the defect until he receives the goods, which may be months or years after the retail seller has received the goods from the manufacturer. In fact, it is possible that the entire four-year limitations period for suit against the manufacturer may have already passed by the time the buyer receives the goods. Furthermore, the buyer's cause of action against the retailer may be insufficient to protect the buyer. The retailer, for example, may be bankrupt or may have otherwise gone out of business. Or, the retailer may have not provided any express warranties of its own and disclaimed implied warranties. Also, manufacturers are likely to be aware of how long their products are likely to remain on the retailer's shelf before sale and, therefore, the uncertainty problem is not great. Finally, manufacturers can expressly provide for a shorter limitations period in their contract with the retailer to reduce the length of potential liability.

The prestigious New York Court of Appeals took the seller's side in *Heller v. Suzuki Motor Corp.*[1194] Reversing a lower court decision in favor of the buyer, the court said that the purpose of the four-year limitations period is to provide a definite, but reasonable, period of repose consistent with modern business recordkeeping procedure. According to the court:

317, 493 N.Y.S.2d 78, 41 UCCR 1740 (1985), *modified & aff'd,* 129 A.D.2d 94, 515 N.Y.S.2d 352 (1987). For cases holding that the time of tender should be measured from the time the goods are delivered to the ultimate buyer, *see* Berry v. G.D. Searle & Co., 56 Ill. 2d 548, 309 N.E.2d 550, 14 UCCR 346 (1974); Commercial Truck & Trailer Sales, Inc. v. McCampbell, 580 S.W.2d 765, 26 UCCR 340 (Tenn. 1979); Patterson v. Her Majesty Indus., Inc., 450 F. Supp. 425, 23 UCCR 1198 (E.D. Pa. 1978).

[1194] 64 N.Y.2d 407, 477 N.E.2d 434, 40 UCCR 917 (1985).

This purpose is frustrated, however, and the period of exposure to liability becomes unpredictable if the cause of action accrues at the date
of sale to [the ultimate buyer] because the product may have left the
hands of remote third parties such as the manufacturer or the distributor
years earlier. If the product is resold, as it was here, the limitations
period may be extended even longer. Thus, our interpretation is consistent with the purpose for the tender of delivery rule . . . and by the
general rule that the function of the Statute of Limitations is repose.[1195]

Two other factors may have also played a part in the court's decision.
First, the buyer had suffered the injury only fifteen months after the tender
of delivery by the manufacturer to the retailer, and therefore had almost
three years in which to sue the manufacturer. Further, the three-year statute
of limitations for strict products liability actions also appears to have been
available to the buyer, which would not begin to run until the date of injury.

On balance, the New York Court of Appeals was probably correct.
Even though there are forceful arguments on both sides, the fundamental
purpose of a statute of limitations is to assure a potential defendant that
after a specified period, it no longer faces possible liability. This purpose
would be significantly undercut by a rule permitting the buyer four years
from the retailer's tender of delivery to sue the manufacturer. In fact, such
a rule might prompt sellers to explicitly provide a shorter limitations period
than would be applicable under the Code, to the detriment of buyers.

The conflicting cases described above generally involve an attempt by
the buyer to rely upon the manufacturer's implied warranty of merchantability.[1196] There should be no question, however, that when the buyer is suing
on the basis of an express warranty made directly to the buyer by the manufacturer, the time of tender of delivery should be the time the buyer receives
the goods. As explained in an earlier section of this text,[1197] a warranty from
the manufacturer to the consumer creates a direct relationship between the
buyer and the manufacturer. The buyer's suit is not derived from the manufacturer's contract with the retailer. Where the manufacturer has made an
express promise directly to the buyer, the buyer should have the full four-

---

[1195] *Id.* at 412, 477 N.E.2d at 437, 40 UCCR at 920.

[1196] *See, e.g.*, American Alloy Steel, Inc. v. Armco, Inc., 777 S.W.2d 173, 10 UCCR2d
861 (Tex. Ct. App. 1989); Commercial Truck & Trailer Sales, Inc. v. McCampbell, 580
S.W.2d 765, 26 UCCR 340 (Tenn. 1979); Lecates v. Hertrich Pontiac Buick Co., 515 A.2d
163, 2 UCCR2d 865 (Del. Super. Ct. 1986).

[1197] *See* § 4.09[E], *supra*.

year statute of limitations from the time it receives the goods to enforce that promise.[1198]

[C] Tolling of the Statute

Regardless of when the cause of action accrues, section 2-725(4) provides that the Code does not alter the prior law of the jurisdiction on the tolling, or suspending, of the statute of limitations.[1199] Buyers have not had an easy time convincing courts that the statute of limitations should be tolled. Although many buyers have argued that the statute of limitations should be tolled during the period that the attempts at repair are being made, this argument has almost never succeeded.[1200] The assertion that the statute should be tolled as a result of the seller's assurances of repair has enjoyed somewhat greater success,[1201] although other cases hold that the seller's mere assurances of cure, without more, are insufficient to toll the statute.[1202] When the seller, however, makes a specific effort through assurances of repair or replacement to dissuade the buyer from filing a lawsuit within the limitations period, the statute of limitations will likely be tolled.[1203]

[1198] The cases appear consistent with this analysis, although the issue is not always explicitly addressed. *See* Paskell v. Nobility Homes, Inc., 871 S.W.2d 481, 24 UCCR2d 537 (Tenn. 1994); Poppenheimer v. Bluff City Motor Homes, 658 S.W.2d 106, 38 UCCR 167 (Tenn. Ct. App. 1983).

[1199] U.C.C. § 2-725(4) provides:

> This section does not alter the law on tolling of the statute of limitations nor does it apply to causes of action which have accrued before this Act became effective.

[1200] *See* Ranker v. Skyline Corp., 342 Pa. Super. 510, 493 A.2d 706, 41 UCCR 476 (1985); Triangle Underwriters, Inc. v. Honeywell, Inc., 604 F.2d 737, 26 UCCR 1162 (2d Cir. 1979); Zahler v. Star Steel Supply Co., 50 Mich. App. 386, 213 N.W.2d 269, 13 UCCR 1043 (1973). *But see* Daughtry v. Jet Aeration Co., 18 Wash. App. 155, 566 P.2d 1267, 22 UCCR 81 (Wash. Ct. App. 1977) (statute was tolled during the period that the seller was attempting to remedy the defects in the goods).

[1201] *See* Colorado-Ute Elec. Ass'n, Inc. v. Envortech Corp., 524 F. Supp. 1152, 33 UCCR 965 (D. Colo. 1981); Laurita v. International Harvester, 32 D.&C. 3d 563, 41 UCCR 133 (Pa. C.P. 1983) ("repair estoppel" tolling statute established when seller expressly represents that repairs will be made which will cure the defect).

[1202] *See* Pako Corp. v. Thomas, 855 S.W.2d 215, 22 UCCR2d 198 (Tex. Ct. App. 1993); Kemp v. Bell-View, Inc., 179 Ga. App. 577, 346 S.E.2d 923, 2 UCCR 2d 178 (1986); Ludwig v. Ford Motor Co., 510 N.E.2d 691, 5 UCCR2d 361 (Ind. Ct. App. 1987); Ontario Hydro v. Zallea Sys., Inc., 569 F. Supp. 1261, 36 UCCR 1222 (D. Del. 1983); Dynaco Corp. v. KLA Instruments Corp., 200 B.R. 750, 30 UCCR2d 839 (Bankr. D.N.H. 1996).

[1203] *See* City of Bedford v. James Leffel & Co., 558 F.2d 216, 21 UCCR 1332 (4th Cir. 1977).

Buyers have usually been successful in arguing that the statute is tolled when the seller is guilty of fraudulently concealing the buyer's cause of action.[1204] Somewhat surprisingly, however, the cases uniformly hold that the seller's silence concerning a known defect is not sufficient to toll the statute; an active act of concealment is required.[1205]

[D] Warranty and Strict Tort

A second issue that has created great confusion is the applicable statute of limitations when warranty and tort causes of action overlap. As we described in detail earlier,[1206] the rise of strict products liability has created many situations in which the facts may create a cause of action for the buyer in both warranty and tort. Although the statute of limitations for tort is generally shorter than the four years provided by section 2-725,[1207] the tort statute of limitations usually does not begin to run until the time that the defect is, or reasonably should have been, discovered. As a result, the period for bringing a tort action may be shorter or longer than the applicable period under the Code, depending upon when the defect was discovered or should have been discovered.

In some states, the problem has been resolved by legislation, which generally establishes a single statute of limitations for all personal injury claims, regardless of the theory under which they are brought.[1208] When the subject has been left to the courts, however, they have often unnecessarily complicated the issue. The obvious approach to the issue is that, unless the legislature has established otherwise, the plaintiff should have the benefit of both the warranty and tort statute of limitations, assuming that the plaintiff can satisfy the requirements for establishing a cause of action under each theory. That is, if the plaintiff's facts establish both a warranty and tort cause of action, the tort count should be examined under the relevant tort statute

---

[1204] *See, e.g.,* Trust Co. Bank v. Union Circulation Co., 241 Ga. 343, 245 S.E.2d 297 (1978); Ludwig v. Ford Motor Co., 510 N.E.2d 691, 5 UCCR2d 361 (Ind. Ct. App. 1987); Holstad v. Southwestern Porcelain, Inc., 421 N.W.2d 371, 5 UCCR2d 912 (Minn. Ct. App. 1988).

[1205] *See* Tomes v. Chrysler Corp., 60 Ill. App. 3d 707, 377 N.E. 224, 24 UCCR 156 (Ill. App. Ct. 1978); Ludwig v. Ford Motor Co., 510 N.E.2d 691, 5 UCCR2d 361 (Ind. Ct. App. 1987); Lecates v. Hertrich Pontiac Buick Co., 515 A.2d 163, 2 UCCR2d 865 (Del. Super. Ct. 1986).

[1206] *See* § 4.06[B][5], *supra.*

[1207] *See, e.g.,* Ala. Code § 6-5-502 (1996) (one year); Kan. Stat. Ann. § 60-512 (1994) (three years).

[1208] *See, e.g.,* Mass. Ann. Laws ch. 260 §§ 2A, 4 (Law. Co-op 1992); Colo. Rev. Stat. Ann. § 13-80-103 (Bradford 1987); Conn. Gen. Stat. Ann. § 52-584 (West 1991).

of limitations and the warranty count should be considered under section 2-725. Warranty and strict products liability are separate causes of action which, despite their substantive similarities,[1209] have many differences as well. For example, privity is not a concern with strict tort, notice of breach is only required in a warranty suit, only warranties are subject to disclaimer, and the existence of a "defect" is not necessarily required for breach of warranty. If state legislatures have determined that certain facts give rise to both torts and breaches of contract, there is no reason to refuse to apply the respective tort and contract statutes of limitations to each count. If a plaintiff can establish facts permitting recovery under both theories, and is barred by the Code statute of limitations, the plaintiff should be permitted to proceed in strict tort. Conversely, if the tort suit is barred by the limitations period, but the facts also establish a breach of warranty, the plaintiff should have the benefit of section 2-725.

Unfortunately, although many courts have adopted this position,[1210] many others have not. Some courts have held that the nature of the injury should determine the applicable statute of limitations rather than the form of the plaintiff's action.[1211] In particular, a number of courts have held that when the suit is for personal injury, the tort statute of limitations applies, even if all of the elements to establish breach of warranty are properly pled.[1212] This result is wrong. There is no reason to apply a single statute of limitations to two distinct claims simply because the same injury has resulted. While the plaintiff, of course, should not receive a double recovery

---

[1209] *See* §§ 4.06[B][4] and 4.06[B][5], *supra*.

[1210] *See, e.g.,* Spring Motors Distribs., Inc., v. Ford Motor Co., 191 N.J. Super. 22, 465 A.2d 530, 37 UCCR 62 (1983); Weinstein v. General Motors Corp., 51 A.D.2d 335, 381 N.Y.S.2d 283, 19 UCCR 143 (1976); Parish v. B.F. Goodrich Co., 395 Mich. 271, 235 N.W.2d 570, 18 UCCR 414 (1975); Romano v. Westinghouse Elec. Co., 114 R.I. 451, 336 A.2d 555, 17 UCCR 128 (1975); Fernandez v. Char-Li-John, 888 P.2d 471, 26 UCCR2d 1152 (N. Mex. Ct. App. 1994); Simmons v. Albany Boys Club, Inc., 80 Misc. 19, 362 N.Y.S.2d 113, 16 UCCR 427 (1974).

[1211] *See, e.g.,* Southgate Community Sch. Dist. v. West Side Constr. Co., 398 Mich. 72, 247 N.W.2d 884, 20 UCCR 1202 (1976); Davidson Lumber Sales, Inc. v. Bonneville Inv., Inc., 794 P.2d 11, 13 UCCR2d 415 (Utah 1990); Bly v. Otis Elevator Co., 713 F.2d 1040, 36 UCCR 1569 (4th Cir. 1983).

[1212] *See* Taylor v. Ford Motor Co., 185 W. Va. 518, 408 S.E.2d 270, 15 UCCR2d 905 (1991); Grey v. Bradford-White Corp., 581 F. Supp. 725, 38 UCCR 886 (D. Kan. 1984); Parish v. B.F. Goodrich Co., 395 Mich. 271, 235 N.W.2d 570, 18 UCCR 414 (1975); Frazen v. Deere & Co., 334 N.W.2d 730, 36 UCCR 870 (Iowa 1983); Simmons v. Clemco Indus., 368 So. 2d 509, 25 UCCR 1088 (Ala. 1979); Ouellette v. Sturm, Ruger, & Co., Inc., 466 A.2d 478 (Me. 1983); Grey v. Bradford-White Corp., 581 F. Supp. 725, 38 UCCR 886 (D. Kan. 1984).

for the same injury, if he or she establishes both claims, there is no reason the plaintiff should not have the benefit of the applicable statute of limitations for any claim that the plaintiff is able to establish. There is no doubt that the Code's warranty provisions apply to personal injuries resulting from a breach of warranty[1213] and, unless the legislature clearly establishes a contrary rule, there is no reason to refuse to apply the Code's statute of limitations in these cases.

A recent case catalogs the reasons for choosing a single statute of limitations where personal injury occurs, and none of the reasons are persuasive. In *Taylor v. Ford Motor Co.*,[1214] the court chose to apply the tort statute of limitations despite the fact that the plaintiff had pled a warranty theory to recover for personal injuries. The court offered four justifications for its decision that the same statute of limitations should apply to a personal injury suit, regardless of the theory offered by the plaintiff: (1) when multiple theories are used by a plaintiff for a single injury, it is desirable to have a uniform period of limitations; (2) the Code statute of limitations does not permit the plaintiff to take advantage of the discovery rule; (3) the Code permits the statute of limitations to be reduced by agreement; and (4) the Code's implied warranties do not extend to future performance and, therefore, begin to run at tender of delivery.

The first of these "reasons" is nothing more than a conclusion; the court simply says it is desirable to have a single statute of limitations when personal injury results without offering any reasons why this is so. Of the remaining justifications, reasons (2) and (4) are essentially the same; the tort statute of limitations allows the plaintiff to take advantage of the discovery rule. If the court, however, permits the plaintiff to have the benefit of *both* statutes of limitation (assuming the facts justify both tort and warranty theories), the discovery rule would be available to the plaintiff under the tort statute. Further, because the tort statute is usually shorter than section 2-725, the discovery rule is not always an advantage to the plaintiff. In fact, in *Taylor*, the plaintiff's suit was dismissed under the tort statute but could have been brought under section 2-725. Finally, reason (3), similar to reasons (2) and (4), is an advantage to plaintiffs only if the court has already

---

[1213] *See, e.g.*, U.C.C. § 2-715(2)(b) which includes as consequential damages for breach of warranty "injury to person or property proximately resulting from breach of warranty"; U.C.C. § 2-318, Alternative A, which permits recovery for breach of warranty by a third-party beneficiary of a warranty, who suffers personal injury. *See* Torres v. Northwest Eng'g, 946 P.2d 760, 34 UCCR2d 273 (Wash. 1997).

[1214] 185 W. Va. 518, 408 S.E.2d 270, 15 UCCR2d 905 (1991).

decided that a single statute of limitations is desirable for personal injury claims and feels it must choose either the tort or Code statute.

In deciding which statute is applicable, other courts have focused not so much on the nature of the injury but on whether the plaintiff and defendant are in contractual privity. A number of courts have held that when the parties are not in privity, section 2-725 does not apply.[1215] Some of these decisions are explicable on the basis that a cause of action in warranty was not available because of the lack of privity.[1216] Therefore, the only applicable statute of limitations was the tort statute or some non-Code contract statute. There are other cases, however, where a warranty cause of action was available to the plaintiff despite the lack of privity, and the courts nonetheless refused to apply section 2-725.[1217] These cases should not be followed. A third-party beneficiary or person not in privity with the seller occupies the same position as the buyer and should be subject to (and have the benefit of) the Code's statute of limitations.

§ 4.12   DEFENSES TO LIABILITY: STRICT TORT AND WARRANTY COMPARED

[A]   General

Because of the overlap between strict tort and warranty liability, issues concerning defenses to each of these theories arise frequently. Many of these issues have been covered in previous sections of this work. For example, the extent to which a seller can rely on a lack of privity to defeat a claim for injury from a defective product has been treated elsewhere.[1218] We also concluded earlier that privity is not a problem either in warranty or strict tort where personal injury results, whereas privity of contract is usually required where the sole harm is economic.[1219] Similarly, differences in the

---

[1215] *See, e.g.,* Williams v. Fulmer, 695 S.W.2d 411, 41 UCCR 795 (Ky. 1985); Plouffe v. Goodyear Tire & Rubber Co., 118 R.I. 288, 373 A.2d 492 (1977); Lee v. Wright Tool & Forge Co., 48 Ohio. App. 2d 148, 356 N.E.2d 303, 20 UCCR 645 (Ohio Ct. App. 1975).

[1216] *See, e.g.,* Williams v. Fulmer, 695 S.W.2d 411, 41 UCCR 795 (Ky. 1985); Fisher v. Graco, Inc., 81 A.D.2d 209, 440 N.Y.S.2d 380, 31 UCCR 873 (1981); Teel v. American Steel Foundries, 529 F. Supp. 337, 33 UCCR 42 (E.D. Mo. 1981).

[1217] *See* Southgate Community Sch. Dist. v. West Side Constr. Co., 399 Mich. 72, 247 N.W.2d 884, 20 UCCR 1202 (1976); Leid v. Volkswagen of Am., Inc., 575 F.2d 1175, 27 UCCR 1197 (6th Cir. 1978).

[1218] *See* § 4.09, *supra.*

[1219] Privity of contract is usually not required, even when the harm is solely economic, when a nonprivity seller has made an express warranty to the suing buyer. *Id.*

application of the statute of limitations between warranty and tort were also discussed in previous sections.[1220]

Additional defenses to warranty liability have also been dealt with in preceding sections, but have not been directly compared to strict tort. For example, we discussed the effect of a failure to give notice of breach and concluded that a failure to give notice under section 2-607 would generally defeat any recovery in warranty.[1221] In strict tort, however, courts have generally found that it is unnecessary for a buyer to give notice of breach.[1222]

Section 4.07 described the seller's ability to disclaim liability for breach of warranty and limit the buyer's remedies or damages. The Code provides that in most cases, a seller can successfully disclaim liability for breach of warranty, subject to the limitations of the Magnuson-Moss Federal Warranty Act and some state consumer-protection legislation.[1223] Sellers may also limit the buyer's remedies, including the exclusion of consequential damages. In strict tort, however, sellers are generally unable to limit or disclaim liability for personal injury or property damage caused by a product defect.[1224] The only exception is a line of cases in which both parties are commercial entities who have intentionally bargained to restrict liability for product defects.[1225] Courts, however, are uniform in refusing to permit sellers to disclaim their liability in strict tort to ordinary consumers.

Defenses relating to the buyer's conduct, however, with the exception of product misuse,[1226] have not been discussed. These defenses fall into three categories: proximate cause, contributory/comparative negligence, and assumption of the risk. These defenses are sometimes difficult to distinguish

---

[1220] *See* § 4.11, *supra.*

[1221] *See* § 4.10, *supra.*

[1222] *See* Vandermark v. Ford Motor Co., 61 Cal. 2d 256, 391 P.2d 168, 37 Cal. Rptr. 896 (1964); Elliot v. Lachance, 109 N.H. 481, 256 A.2d 153, 6 UCCR 1051 (1969); Dippel v. Sciano, 37 Wis. 2d 443, 155 N.W.2d 55, 4 UCCR 1033 (1967); Restatement (Second) of Torts § 402A, cmt. n (1965).

[1223] *See* § 9.02, *infra.*

[1224] *See* Weiner v. Mount Airy Lodge, Inc., 719 F. Supp. 342 (M.D. Pa. 1989); Sipari v. Villa Olivia Country Club, 63 Ill. App. 3d 985, 380 N.E.2d 819, 20 Ill. Dec. 610 (1978); Henningsen v. Bloomfield Motors, Inc., 32 N.J. 358, 161 A.2d 69 (1960); Restatement (Second) of Torts § 402A, cmt. n (1965).

[1225] *See* Keystone Aeronautics Corp. v. R.J. Engstrom Corp., 499 F.2d 146, 14 UCCR 1087 (3d Cir. 1974); Appalachian Ins. Co. v. McDonnell Douglas Corp., 214 Cal. App. 3d 1, 262 Cal. Rptr. 716 (1989); K-Lines, Inc. v. Roberts Motor Co., 273 Or. 242, 541 P.2d 1378 (1975).

[1226] *See* § 4.06[B][3], *supra.*

from each other and often overlap.[1227] This section briefly describes the application of these defenses to both warranty and strict tort liability.

[B]   Proximate Cause

Ever since the famous case of *Palsgraf v. Long Island R.R.*,[1228] a defendant is liable in tort only if his or her wrongful act (or omission) was the proximate cause of the injury. In a number of places, the Code and its Comments make it clear that the concept of proximate cause applies to breach of warranty as well. Comment 13 to section 2-314 states in part:

> In an action based on breach of warranty, it is of course necessary to show not only the existence of a warranty but the fact that the warranty was broken and that the breach of the warranty was the proximate cause of the loss sustained. In such action an affirmative showing by the seller that the loss resulted from some action or event following his own delivery of the goods can operate as a defense.

Cases dealing with proximate cause under the Code are not plentiful; however, there is no indication in the Code or cases that the concept has a different meaning in warranty cases from its meaning in tort.[1229] A number of cases in which proximate cause has been an issue involve the intervening acts of third persons. For example, in *Falcon Tankers, Inc. v. Litton Systems, Inc.*,[1230] a buyer purchased expansion joints from a seller. The joints failed, and the buyer purchased replacement joints from another seller. These joints also failed, and the buyer sought to hold the original seller liable for the consequential damages caused by the failure of the replacement joints. The court held that the failure of the original joints was not the proximate cause of the consequential damages caused by the failure of the replacements. The failure of the replacement joints was not foreseeable and, despite the fact that the replacement joints would not have been

---

[1227] *Compare* Brooks v. Dietz, 218 Kan. 698, 545 P.2d 1104 (1976) (voluntarily and unreasonably encountering a known danger is assumption of risk) *with* Buttrick v. Arthur Lessard & Sons, Inc., 110 N.H. 36, 260 A.2d 111 (1969) (voluntarily and unreasonably encountering a known danger is contributory negligence).

[1228] 248 N.Y. 339, 162 N.E. 99 (1928).

[1229] *See* Klages v. General Ordnance Equip. Corp., 240 Pa. Super. 356, 367 A.2d 304, 19 UCCR 22 (1976) (court applies same standard for proximate cause in tort and under U.C.C. § 2-715).

[1230] 355 A.2d 898, 19 UCCR 434 (Del. Super. Ct. 1976).

necessary had the original joints not failed, the failure of the replacement joints was sufficient to break the chain of causation.[1231]

In *Migerobe, Inc. v. Certina USA, Inc.*,[1232] however, a seller was held liable for a buyer's lost profits when the seller failed to deliver watches to the buyer. The watches were to be resold as a "loss leader" by the buyer—the losses on the watches hopefully to be recovered by the profits on other sales to customers lured into the store by the price of the watches. The court held that the seller's failure to deliver the watches was the proximate cause of the loss of collateral sales, and this loss was foreseeable because the seller knew that the watches were going to be sold as a loss leader.

A more questionable result occurred in *Garavalia v. Heat Controller, Inc.*[1233] In this case, a defect in an air conditioner caused it to blow out only uncooled air. As a result, a 71-year-old man died of hyperthermia when the temperature in his residence reached 96 degrees Fahrenheit. The court found that the buyer may not have fully understood that the air conditioner had ceased functioning or may have believed that the operation of the blower alone was adequate to ventilate his house, and therefore refrained from taking remedial action. Further, because of his age or disability, there may not have been adequate remedial measures available. Consequently, despite a strong dissent, the court refused to hold, as a matter of law, that the air conditioner's failure was not the proximate cause of the buyer's death.

The *Garavalia* case is indicative of situations where the defense of proximate cause and the defenses of contributory or comparative negligence overlap. The seller of the air conditioner might well have argued that the actions of the decedent in failing to take action to ameliorate the effects of the broken air conditioner constituted contributory (or comparative) negligence, in addition to breaking the chain of causation. Certainly, the Comments to the Code strongly suggest that buyer misconduct of the sort that would constitute contributory negligence in a tort context is, at least, relevant to the issue of proximate cause in a Code context. Comment 13 to section 2-314 provides:

> Action by the buyer following an examination of the goods which ought to have indicated the defect complained of can be shown as a matter bearing on whether the breach itself was the cause of the injury.

[1231] *But see* Klages v. General Ordnance Equip. Co., 240 Pa. Super. 356, 367 A.2d 304, 19 UCCR 22 (Pa. Super. Ct. 1976) (failure of mace was the proximate cause of the plaintiff's being shot in the head by thief; act by thief did not break the chain of causation).

[1232] 924 F.2d 1330, 14 UCCR2d 59 (5th Cir. 1991).

[1233] 212 Ill. App. 3d 381, 570 N.E.2d 1227, 156 Ill. Dec. 505, 15 UCCR 2d 503 (1991).

A similar indication that the buyer's actions may affect proximate cause is found in comment 5 to section 2-715:

> Subsection (2)(b) states the usual rule as to breach of warranty, allowing recovery for injuries "proximately" resulting from the breach. Where the injury involved follows the use of the goods without discovery of the defect causing the damage, the question of "proximate" cause turns on whether it was reasonable for the buyer to use the goods without such inspection as would have revealed the defects. If it was not reasonable for him to do so, or if he did in fact discover the defect prior to his use, the injury would not proximately result from the breach of warranty.

The latter quotation illustrates the congruity between the defense of proximate cause and the defenses of contributory/comparative negligence and assumption of the risk. The unreasonable failure to discover a danger posed by another's conduct is the classic case of contributory negligence.[1234] Similarly, the use of defective goods after the discovery of a defect may very well constitute assumption of the risk.[1235]

The overlap between the defense of contributory negligence and the defense of proximate cause was dealt with explicitly by the Texas Supreme Court in the case of *Signal Oil & Gas Co. v. Universal Oil Products.*[1236] In this case, a buyer sued a seller for damage resulting from a fire allegedly caused by a defect in an "isomax reactor change heater." The buyer's complaint alleged both negligence and breach of warranty. The seller successfully argued that the buyer was contributorily negligent in failing to shut down the heater before the fire. Because Texas had not adopted a comparative negligence scheme at the time of the accident,[1237] recovery by the buyer in negligence was completely barred by the buyer's contributory negligence.

The court said that there were three possible approaches it could take in assessing the effect of the buyer's conduct on the warranty cause of

---

[1234] *See* Wooten v. White Trucks, 514 F.2d 634 (5th Cir. 1975); Cronin v. J.B.E. Olson Corp., 8 Cal. 3d 121, 501 P.2d 1153, 104 Cal. Rptr. 433 (1972); Stephan v. Sears, Roebuck & Co., 110 N.H. 248, 266 A.2d 855, 7 UCCR 1318 (1970); Henderson v. Ford Motor Co., 519 S.W.2d 87 (Tex. 1974); Restatement (Second) of Torts § 466 (1965). *See also* Restatement (Second) of Torts § 402A, cmt. n ("Contributory negligence of the plaintiff is not a defense [to strict products liability] when such negligence consists merely in a failure to discover the defect in the product, or to guard against the possibility of its existence").

[1235] *See* § 4.12[C], *infra.*

[1236] 572 S.W.2d 370, 24 UCCR 555 (Tex. 1978).

[1237] Texas later adopted a comparative negligence regime. *See* Tex. Civ. Prac. & Rem. Code Ann. §§ 33.001–33.017 (West 1986).

action: (1) contributory negligence has no effect on warranty recovery, although assumption of the risk is a defense; (2) both contributory negligence and assumption of the risk are defenses to a breach of warranty action; (3) neither assumption of the risk nor contributory negligence are defenses in warranty, but both are relevant to the issue of proximate cause. The court adopted the third approach, stating that Comment 5 to section 2-715 "clearly indicates that the buyer's conduct may affect his recovery . . . under an implied warranty cause of action."[1238] Instead of finding the buyer's conduct to be an absolute bar, as the lower court had done, the court sent the case back to the lower court to determine the respective percentages of the "concurrent proximate causes" of the buyer's and seller's conduct. In this manner, the court adopted, in warranty cases, a form of comparative fault that the legislature had not yet adopted in tort cases. Further, the *Signal* case and the Code Comments indicate that, on the same facts, proximate cause may be a defense in a jurisdiction that does not permit a contributory negligence defense.

[C]   Contributory/Comparative Negligence

The comments to the Restatement (Second) of Torts, section 402A, make it clear that traditional contributory negligence is inapplicable to products liability cases:

> Contributory negligence of the plaintiff is not a defense when such negligence consists merely in a failure to discover the defect in the product, or to guard against the possibility of its existence.[1239]

Courts have generally followed the direction of this Comment and have held that conduct described in the Comment does not bar recovery by the plaintiff in strict tort.[1240] Occasionally, however, some courts have permitted contributory negligence as a defense in strict tort.[1241]

[1238] U.C.C. § 2-715, Official Comment 5.

[1239] Restatement (Second) of Torts § 402A, cmt. n (1965).

[1240] *See, e.g.*, Gregory v. White Truck & Equip. Co., 163 Ind. App. 240, 323 N.E.2d 280, 16 UCCR 644 (1975); Busch v. Busch Constr., Inc., 262 N.W.2d 377 (Minn. 1977); Wallace v. Owens-Ill., Inc., 300 S.C. 518, 389 S.E.2d 155, 11 UCCR2d 835 (1989); Henderson v. Ford Motor Co., 519 S.W.2d 87 (Tex. 1974).

[1241] *See, e.g.*, Stevens v. Kanematsu-Gosho Co., 494 F.2d 367 (1st Cir. 1974); Wallner v. Kitchens of Sara Lee, Inc., 419 F.2d 1028 (7th Cir. 1969); Caterpillar Tractor Co. v. Ford, 406 So. 2d 854 (Ala. 1981); Denton v. Bachtold Bros., Inc., 8 Ill. App. 3d 1038, 291 N.E.2d 229 (1972).

Many courts have similarly held that contributory negligence is not a defense to a breach of warranty action under section 2-314.[1242] Usually, they have done so on the basis that implied warranty suits involving property damage or personal injury are sufficiently similar to strict products-liability actions that the same rules should apply to both actions. Even courts that prohibit contributory negligence as a defense, however, often allow defendants the opportunity to use the plaintiff's conduct to show a lack of proximate cause.[1243] A few courts have explicitly permitted contributory negligence to act as a defense to a breach of implied warranty action.[1244]

The traditional rule that a plaintiff's contributory negligence acted as a complete bar to recovery for negligence has been replaced in virtually every jurisdiction by the principle of comparative negligence. In most states this has occurred by legislative enactment,[1245] although in others it has resulted from court action.[1246] Inevitably, the question has arisen as to how comparative negligence principles apply in strict tort and warranty actions.

Unlike contributory negligence, states have generally applied comparative negligence to strict products liability.[1247] In some cases, this is a result of the statutory scheme that makes comparative negligence applicable to strict tort cases.[1248] In other states, courts have applied comparative negligence to strict products liability without explicit legislative direction.[1249]

[1242] *See, e.g.,* Murphy v. Eaton, Yale & Towne, Inc., 444 F.2d 317, 9 UCCR 805 (6th Cir. 1971); Reibold v. Simon Aerials, Inc., 859 F. Supp. 193, 24 UCCR2d 496 (E.D. Va. 1994); Bronson v. Club Comanche, Inc., 286 F. Supp. 21, 5 UCCR 694 (D.V.I. 1968); Wallace v. Owens-Ill., Inc., 300 S.C. 518, 389 S.E.2d 155, 11 UCCR2d 835 (Ct. App. 1989).

[1243] *See, e.g.,* Ford Motor Co. v. Lee, 137 Ga. App. 486, 224 S.E.2d 168, 18 UCCR 1184 (1976), *aff'd in part and rev'd in part,* 237 Ga. 554, 229 S.E.2d 379 (1976); McNeely v. Harrison, 138 Ga. App. 310, 226 S.E.2d 112 (1976).

[1244] *See* Westerman v. Sears, Roebuck & Co., 577 F.2d 873, 24 UCCR 1141 (5th Cir. 1978); Gillespie v. American Motors Corp., 69 N.C. App. 531, 317 S.E.2d 32, 39 UCCR 869 (1984).

[1245] *See, e.g.,* Del. Code Ann. tit. 10, § 8132 (Supp. 1994); Kan. Stat. Ann. § 60-258a (Supp. 1996); Ohio Rev. Code Ann. § 2315.19 (Baldwin 1994); S.D. Codified Laws Ann. § 20-9-2 (1995); Wis. Stat. Ann. § 895.045 (West Supp. 1995).

[1246] Sun Valley Airlines, Inc. v. Avco-Lycoming Corp., 411 F. Supp. 598 (D. Idaho 1976); Li v. Yellow Cab Co., 13 Cal. 3d 804, 532 P.2d 1226, 119 Cal. Rptr. 858 (1975); Busch v. Busch Constr., Inc., 262 N.W.2d 377 (Minn. 1977); Dippel v. Sciano, 37 Wis. 2d 443, 155 N.W.2d 55, 4 UCCR 1033 (1967).

[1247] Some early cases, however, refused to extend comparative negligence to strict products liability cases. *See, e.g.,* Murray v. Fairbanks Morse, 610 F.2d 149 (3d Cir. 1979); Melia v. Ford Motor Co., 534 F.2d 795 (8th Cir. 1976); Kirkland v. General Motors Corp., 521 P.2d 1353 (Okla. 1974); General Motors Corp. v. Hopkins, 548 S.W.2d 344 (Tex. 1977).

[1248] *See, e.g.,* Neb. Rev. Stat. § 25-21 (1995); Wyo. Stat. § 1-1-109 (Supp. 1995).

[1249] *See, e.g.,* Rodrigues v. Ripley Indus., Inc., 507 F.2d 782 (1st Cir. 1974); Seim v.

Initially, as in the case of strict tort, judges were reluctant to extend comparative negligence to implied warranty actions. Comparative negligence was viewed as a defense applicable to tort actions, not contract actions.[1250] More recent cases, however, have generally extended comparative fault principles to implied warranty actions as well as strict tort,[1251] although there are cases to the contrary.[1252] Even in states that do not apply comparative negligence directly, comparative fault principles have been applied through notions of proximate cause.[1253]

[D] Assumption of the Risk

While Comment n to section 402A of the Restatement (Second) of Torts, as discussed previously,[1254] generally precludes the defense of contributory negligence to a strict products-liability claim, the same Comment explicitly sanctions one type of contributory behavior as a defense:

> [T]he form of contributory negligence which consists in voluntarily and unreasonably proceeding to encounter a known danger, and commonly passes under the name of assumption of risk, is a defense under this Section as in other cases of strict liability. If the user discovers the defect and is aware of the danger, and nevertheless proceeds unreasonably to make use of the product and is injured by it, he is barred from recovery.[1255]

The assumption of the risk defense under section 402A of the Restatement (Second) of Torts has both objective and subjective components. In order to

---

Garavalia, 306 N.W.2d 806 (Minn. 1981); Hao v. Owens-Ill., Inc., 69 Haw. 231, 738 P.2d 416 (1987); Sun Valley Airlines v. Avco-Lycoming Corp., 411 F. Supp. 598 (D. Idaho 1976).

[1250] *See* Karl v. Bryant Air Conditioning Co., 705 F.2d 164, 35 UCCR 1494 (6th Cir. 1983).

[1251] *See, e.g.,* Coulter v. American Bakeries Co., 530 So. 2d 1009, 7 UCCR2d 49 (Fla. Ct. App. 1981); Wolfe v. Ford Motor Co., 386 Mass. 95, 434 N.E.2d 1008, 33 UCCR 850 (1982). *See generally* Note, "Use of the Comparative Negligence Doctrine in Warranty Actions," 45 Ohio St. L.J. 763 (1984).

[1252] *See, e.g.,* Little Rock Elec. Contractors, Inc. v. Okonite Co., 29 Ark. 399, 744 S.W.2d 381, 5 UCCR2d 978 (1988); Fernandes v. Union Bookbinding Co., 400 Mass. 27, 507 N.E.2d 728, 5 UCCR2d 959 (1987).

[1253] *See* Signal Oil & Gas Co. v. Universal Oil Prods., 572 S.W.2d 320, 24 UCCR 555 (Tex. 1978) (relying on Comment 5 to section 2-715, court applied principle of comparative causation). *See also* Uniform Comparative Fault Act, 12 U.L.A. 1 (1996) (applying comparative fault principles to warranty actions).

[1254] *See* § 4.12[C], *supra.*

[1255] Restatement (Second) of Torts § 402A, cmt. n (1965).

establish the defense, the seller must show that the user or consumer was unreasonable in using the goods with knowledge of the danger presented by the defect. If, despite discovery of the defect, the user was nonetheless reasonable in continuing to use the goods, the defense will fail.[1256] In addition, the seller must establish two subjective elements: that the user had (1) actual knowledge of the defect and the danger it presented, and (2) voluntarily proceeded to use the goods.[1257]

Courts have generally followed the guidance of the Restatement section 402A and held that assumption of the risk is a defense in a strict products-liability case if these elements are established.[1258] The development of comparative fault, however, has complicated the picture. Some states apply comparative-fault principles only to contributory negligence and continue to treat assumption of the risk as a complete defense.[1259] Many states, however, apply comparative-fault principles to both contributory negligence and assumption of the risk.[1260] Some states retain the rules of the Restatement section 402A: contributory negligence is no defense while assumption of risk is a complete defense.[1261] There are other permutations as well.[1262]

[1256] See, e.g., Cremeans v. Willmar Henderson Mfg. Co., 57 Ohio St. 3d 145, 566 N.E.2d 1203 (1991). A few courts have held that it is not necessary to show that continued use of the goods was unreasonable in order to establish the defense. See Yarborough v. Phipps, 285 So. 2d 788 (Miss. 1973); Henderson v. Ford Motor Co., 519 S.W.2d 87 (Tex. 1974).

[1257] See Green v. Edmands Co., 639 F.2d 286 (5th Cir. 1981); Suter v. San Angelo Foundry & Mach. Co., 81 N.J. 150, 406 A.2d 140 (1979); Cremeans v. Willmar Henderson Mfg. Co., 57 Ohio St. 3d 145, 566 N.E.2d 1203 (1991).

[1258] See, e.g., Westerman v. Sears, Roebuck & Co., 577 F.2d 873, 24 UCCR 1141 (5th Cir. 1978); Phillips v. Allen, 427 F. Supp. 876, 21 UCCR 74 (W.D. Pa. 1977); Gregory v. White Truck & Equip. Co., 163 Ind. App. 240, 323 N.E.2d 280, 16 UCCR 644 (1975); Monsanto Co. v. Logisticon, Inc., 763 S.W.2d 371, 9 UCCR2d 934 (Mo. Ct. App. 1989). Cf. Suter v. Angelo Foundry & Mach. Co., 81 N.J. 150, 406 A.2d 140 (1979) (assumption of risk defense not available when an employee is harmed while engaged in an assigned task). See generally Note, "Assumption of Risk and Strict Products Liability," 95 Harv. L. Rev. 872 (1982).

[1259] See Scherebeck v. Sterling Drug, Inc., 291 F. Supp. 368 (E.D. Ark. 1968); Otto v. Hendry, 132 Ga. App. 598, 208 S.E.2d 611 (1974); Rickey v. Boden, 421 A.2d 539 (R.I. 1980).

[1260] See Franco v. Zingarelli, 72 A.D.2d 211, 424 N.Y.S.2d 185 (1980); Blair v. Mount Hood Meadows Dev. Corp., 291 Or. 293, 630 P.2d 827 (1981); Meese v. Brigham Young Univ., 639 P.2d 720 (Utah 1981).

[1261] See Lust v. Clark Equip. Co., 792 F.2d 436, 1 UCCR2d 697 (4th Cir. 1986).

[1262] Scoggins v. Jude, 419 A.2d 999 (1980) (merging unreasonable assumption of risk into contributory negligence and leaving reasonable assumption of risk as separate defense); Thompson v. Weaver, 277 Or. 299, 560 P.2d 620 (1977) (implied assumption of risk is abolished while express assumption of risk is a valid defense).

The applicability of the defense of assumption of risk in implied warranty actions is, if anything, even more complex than in strict products liability. For the most part, the evolution of the law in the area of implied warranty has paralleled the development in strict liability. As a general proposition, assumption of the risk is a defense in implied warranty actions.[1263] In some cases, however, it is a complete defense,[1264] while in others, comparative-fault principles are applied.[1265]

The issue is further complicated by the suggestion in Comment 5 to section 2-715 that assumption of the risk, as defined by the Restatement of Torts (Second), is to be treated as an element of proximate cause for purposes of warranty actions.[1266] A number of cases have held that facts that would establish assumption of the risk are relevant to the issue of proximate cause, and may be used to reduce the plaintiff's damages.[1267]

[E] Conclusion

The preceding discussion is intended only as the most general of road maps; the scale of miles is large, and the level of detail small. Relying on this discussion for anything more is an invitation to malpractice. Each jurisdiction must be carefully researched and evaluated; the law in many jurisdictions is a complex mixture of statutory and case law and continues to develop. Nonetheless, even the most undetailed map can serve to orient the traveler new to the territory. The authors hope that the discussion has served this purpose.

[1263] *See, e.g.,* Phillips v. Allen, 427 F. Supp. 876, 21 UCCR 74 (W.D. Pa. 1977); Barry v. Stop & Shop Companies, Inc., 24 Mass. App. Ct. 224, 507 N.E.2d 1062 (1987); Monsanto Co. v. Logisticon, Inc., 763 S.W.2d 341, 9 UCCR2d 934 (Mo. Ct. App. 1989).

[1264] *See* Hensley v. Sherman Car Wash Equip. Co., 33 Colo. App. 279, 520 P.2d 146, 14 UCCR 940 (1974); Gregory v. White Truck & Equip. Co., 163 Ind. App. 240, 323 N.E.2d 280, 16 UCCR 644 (1975).

[1265] *See* Larson v. Pacesetter Sys., Inc., 74 Haw. 1, 837 P.2d 1273, 20 UCCR2d 877 (1992).

[1266] Comment 5 to U.C.C. § 2-715 states, in part, that "if the plaintiff discovered the defect before use . . . the injury would not proximately result from the breach of warranty."

[1267] *See* Frazer v. A.F. Munsterman, Inc., 123 Ill. 2d 245, 527 N.E.2d 1248, 123 Ill. Dec. 473, 7 UCCR2d 121 (1988); Signal Oil & Gas Co. v. Universal Oil Prods., 572 S.W.2d 320, 24 UCCR 555 (Tex. 1978). *See also* § 4.12[B], *supra.*

CHAPTER 5
PERFORMANCE OF THE SALES CONTRACT

§ 5.01 INTRODUCTION

Section 2-301 sets out the general performance obligations of the parties to a contract for the sale of goods:

> The obligation of the seller is to transfer and deliver and that of the buyer is to accept and pay in accordance with the contract.

The obligations of both parties are to be determined "in accordance with the contract."[1] The parties may determine the time, place, and method of delivery as well as when the buyer must accept the goods and pay the price. For example, the contract may require that the seller deliver the goods "F.O.B. seller's tank car, Pacific Coast."[2] Or, the parties may agree that the buyer must pay cash on delivery of the goods—or the buyer may be given a period of time after delivery to pay the price.[3] In general, the terms of the parties' agreement determine the scope of their obligations.

There will be instances in which the parties will have said nothing about certain aspects of their delivery or payment obligations. The seller may have agreed to deliver 10,000 pairs of shoes at a stated price, but nothing was said as to when delivery was to be made or whether delivery was to be made at the seller's or buyer's place of business. Or, the parties may have said nothing about whether the buyer was to pay in cash or by check, or whether the buyer was to have a period after delivery in which to pay the price. In most cases, the Code supplies such terms in the absence of explicit agreement of the parties.[4] In other cases, usage of trade, course of dealing, or course of performance supply the missing terms.[5] Finally, general contract law can be called upon to fill in the gaps.

Unless the parties have otherwise agreed, tender of payment by the buyer and tender of delivery by the seller are concurrent conditions:

> Tender of delivery is a condition to the buyer's duty to accept the goods and, unless otherwise agreed, to his duty to pay for them. Tender entitles the seller to acceptance of the goods and to payment according to the contract.[6]

---

[1] U.C.C. § 2-301.

[2] For the obligations required by such a contract, see § 5.02[A], *infra*.

[3] *See* § 5.05[A], *infra*.

[4] *Id.*

[5] The Code requires that courts give due consideration to usage of trade, course of dealing, and course of performance in interpreting the parties' obligations in accordance with the contract. U.C.C. § 2-301, Official Comment; *see also* U.C.C. §§ 1-205, 2-208.

[6] U.C.C. § 2-507(1).

Unless otherwise agreed tender of payment is a condition to the seller's duty to tender and complete any delivery.[7]

The practical implication of tender of payment and delivery as concurrent conditions is that the seller is not in default, even though the date set for delivery has gone by, unless the buyer has tendered the price. Conversely, the buyer is not in default, even though the date set for payment has passed, unless the seller has tendered the goods. The parties can, of course, change the order of performance by agreement. For example, the seller can agree to extend credit to the buyer, in which case the seller would be required to deliver the goods to avoid default even though there has been no tender of payment.

I.   PERFORMANCE OBLIGATIONS OF THE SELLER

§ 5.02   WARRANTY AND TENDER OBLIGATIONS OF THE SELLER

The seller's basic obligation is to transfer and deliver the goods in accordance with the contract.[8] That is, the seller must transfer and deliver the goods that he promised to the buyer, and he is to deliver those goods at the time and place agreed upon. In addition, those goods must *conform* to the terms of the contract.

The conformity of the goods to the warranties of title and quality were discussed in previous sections of this text.[9] If the goods do not conform to the warranties of title and quality, the seller has failed to perform his basic obligation to deliver goods in accordance with the contract and—assuming the buyer has made a proper tender or tender by the buyer is excused—the seller will be liable for breach. If the goods do conform to the warranties of title and quality, the buyer will be obligated to accept the goods and pay

---

[7] U.C.C. § 2-511.

[8] U.C.C. § 2-301 provides:

The obligation of the seller is to transfer and deliver and that of the buyer is to accept and pay in accordance with the contract.

There is a minor syntactic difficulty with this section. Do the words "in accordance with the contract" modify only the buyer's obligation to pay or do they also modify the seller's obligation to transfer and deliver? The only answer that makes sense is that the words modify both parties' obligations. The idea that the contract controls all of the parties' obligations is central to Article 2, and there is no reason why the seller's transfer and delivery obligations should not be controlled by the contract of the parties.

[9] *See* Chapter 4, *infra*.

according to the contract, *so long as the seller's tender was otherwise in accordance with the contract.* It is these tender obligations that are the subject of this section.

Tender by the seller requires:

> [T]hat the seller put and hold conforming goods at the buyer's disposition and give the buyer any notification reasonably necessary to enable him to take delivery.[10]

Thus, tender is performed by two acts: (1) putting and holding conforming goods at the buyer's disposition and (2) giving the buyer a notification that will enable the buyer to take delivery. The manner, time, and place of tender are governed by the parties' agreement and the provisions of Article 2.[11] When the contract does not deal explicitly with these issues, they are governed by (1) usage of trade, course of dealing, and course of performance; or (2) by the Article 2 "gap fillers" discussed previously in this text.[12] Furthermore, according to section 2-503(1):

> (a) tender must be at a reasonable hour, and if it is of goods [as opposed to documents] they must be kept available for the period reasonably necessary to enable the buyer to take possession; but
> (b) unless otherwise agreed, the buyer must furnish facilities reasonably suited to the receipt of the goods.

Thus, for example, if a buyer contracted to purchase a new automobile from a dealer, the dealer would normally tender by ensuring that the automobile conformed to the contract, placing the automobile on the lot,[13] holding it for the buyer's disposition, and giving the buyer notice that she could come and pick it up.

When the buyer and the seller are separated by a considerable distance so that the goods must be shipped by an independent transporter (e.g., railroad, ship, truck, or airline), the seller's tender obligations become more complicated. Consider the following example:

---

[10] U.C.C. § 2-503(1). The Code definition of tender relaxes the requirement of some common-law cases that held that the seller had to attempt to physically hand the goods to the buyer. *See* Aetna Ins. Co. v. Maryland Cast Stone Co., 254 Md. 109, 253 A.2d 872, 6 UCCR 661 (1969).

[11] U.C.C. § 2-503(1).

[12] *See* § 3.14, *supra.*

[13] In this case, the place of tender, unless the contract stipulated otherwise, would be the seller's place of business. U.C.C. § 2-308(a).

Buyer, located in Memphis, Tennessee, sends a purchase order for 500 tires to Seller, located in Akron, Ohio. Seller would like to sell the tires, but cannot deliver them to Tennessee. Buyer wants the tires but cannot pick them up in Akron. Furthermore, Seller does not want to release possession of the tires until the price has been paid, and Buyer does not want to pay the price until he is assured possession of the tires.

Seller's tender in this case will be accomplished through some intermediary—probably by train or truck. The seller will turn the goods over to the intermediary, make some provision for paying the freight charges, and receive a receipt for the goods called a "bill of lading."[14]

A bill of lading is, however, more than a receipt for the goods. A bill of lading is also a document of title,[15] and a *negotiable* bill of lading evidences that the holder of the bill is entitled to the goods it covers.[16] The bill of lading also represents a contract between the carrier and the shipper of the goods. It deals with such things as liability for loss, the obligation to pay freight charges, the right of the carrier to sell unclaimed goods, and conditions on claims.

A bill of lading is "negotiable" (i.e., the holder of the bill has a right to the goods) in only two instances: (1) if, by its terms, the goods are to be delivered to *bearer* or to *the order of* a named person; or (2) where recognized in overseas trade, if the bill runs to a named person or assigns. In all other instances, the bill is nonnegotiable and does not entitle a person to the goods.[17] If, in the preceding example, Seller had taken a negotiable bill of lading from the carrier, the carrier would be obligated to deliver the tires

---

[14] U.C.C. § 1-201(6). *See* Globekirk, Ltd. v. E.D.&F. Man "Coffee" Ltd., 123 Misc. 2d 902, 474 N.Y.S.2d 388, 38 UCCR 894 (Sup. Ct. 1984).

[15] *See* U.C.C. § 1-201(15).

[16] The definition of "holder" is contained in U.C.C. § 1-201(20). Documents of title are covered in Article 7 of the Code. Rights acquired by due negotiation of a negotiable document of title include title to the goods. *See* U.C.C. §§ 7-502, 7-503. Warranties on negotiation and transfer are covered by U.C.C. § 7-507.

Only intrastate shipments are covered by Article 7 of the Code. If the goods must cross state lines to reach their destination, the bill is governed by the Federal Bills of Lading Act, 49 U.S.C. §§ 81 *et seq.* (1976). If the goods cross water, the bill may be governed by several federal laws, including the Shipping Act, 46 U.S.C. §§ 801 *et seq.* (1976); the Intercostal Shipping Act, 46 U.S.C. §§ 843 *et seq.* (1976); and the Carriage of Goods at Sea Act, 46 U.S.C. §§ 1300 *et seq.* (1976). There is little difference between the provisions of Article 7 and the enumerated acts.

[17] The typical uniform order bill of lading (negotiable) contains the clause "consigned to the order of" and is printed on yellow paper. The typical uniform straight bill of lading (nonnegotiable) states simply "consigned to," and is printed on white paper.

to any holder of the bill of lading.[18] Seller can have Buyer's name entered on the bill as the consignee, or Seller could have its own name entered as consignee and indorse the bill to the Buyer. In either case, the Buyer would be entitled to the goods when they arrive in Memphis and can secure their possession by delivering the bill of lading to the carrier in Memphis.

How Seller tenders the goods in this example depends on the terms of the agreement between the Seller and the Buyer. Undoubtedly, the contract would contain provisions concerning delivery and would have created either a "shipment" or a "destination" contract. The seller's method of tender under each of these is considered next.

[A] Performance Obligations in Shipment and Destination Contracts

The authorization to send the goods by carrier may be found in trade usage, course of performance, course of dealing, or the terms of the contract itself. In this respect, the fact that the parties are located in distant cities is often sufficient to authorize shipment by the seller. Thus, in the example, the seller of tires would undoubtedly be authorized to ship the tires to the Memphis buyer by carrier and to use a bill of lading in connection with that shipment.

Contracts that require or authorize the seller to ship the goods are divided by the Code into two groups: shipment contracts and destination contracts. In a *shipment* contract, the seller tenders delivery at the point of shipment, and risk of loss passes to the buyer when the goods are duly delivered to the carrier.[19] In a *destination* contract, the seller tenders delivery at the stated destination, and risk of loss passes to the buyer when the goods are tendered there so as to enable the buyer to take delivery.[20] It is therefore important in all contracts calling for delivery by carrier to determine whether the seller is required to deliver the goods at a particular destination or whether the contract is satisfied by the seller's making a contract to ship the goods and delivering them to the carrier.

Whether a shipment or destination contract is involved depends on the agreement of the parties. If the parties have stated their intention, that intention will control. If the intention is not stated, then a court can look to the custom in the trade and the course of dealing and course of performance of the parties, or it can imply a term from other circumstances. Finally,

---

[18] U.C.C. §§ 7-301(1), 7-403. *See also* Consolidated Packing Co. v. Capitol Packing Co., 389 F.2d 505 (1st Cir. 1968).

[19] U.C.C. § 2-509(1)(a). Risk of loss is discussed in § 6.05, *infra*.

[20] U.C.C. § 2-509(1)(b).

Comment 5 of section 2-503 creates a presumption in favor of shipment contracts.[21]

Sometimes the parties use "shorthand" terms to convey whether a shipment or destination contract is involved. Often they do so through the use of "F.O.B." (which means "free on board") or "F.A.S." (which means "free along side") terms. When the term is "F.O.B. [the place of shipment]" the contract is a shipment contract, and the seller's tender obligations are those that accompany shipment contracts.[22] When the term used is "F.O.B. the [place of destination]" the contract is a destination contract and the seller must comply with the tender obligations of destination contracts.[23] A term "F.A.S. [seller's port or dock]" is a shipment contract,[24] as are C.I.F. and C.&F. contracts.[25]

[1]   Tender in a Shipment Contract

In a shipment contract, the seller tenders at the point of shipment and, if the tender is proper, the risk of loss passes to the buyer when the goods are delivered to the carrier.[26] The seller, however, is tendering at a point distant from the buyer; typically, the buyer has no one present to ensure that the goods will be given proper care during shipment or that the bill of lading will be forwarded promptly so that the buyer can obtain the goods from the carrier when they arrive in the buyer's city. Thus, the seller in a shipment contract ought to be required to take reasonable precautions to protect the buyer's interest in the goods when they are in transit.

The Code accomplishes this though its tender requirements in shipment contracts. The general Code section on the manner of the seller's tender of delivery (section 2-503) provides that the seller must comply with section 2-504 in all shipment contracts. Section 2-504 provides:

> Where the seller is required or authorized to send the goods to the buyer and the contract does not require him to deliver them to a particular destination, then unless otherwise agreed he must

---

[21] U.C.C. § 2-503, Official Comment 5. This Comment says that shipment contracts are normal and destination contracts are variant. Specific agreement or commercial understanding is necessary to create a destination contract. *See* Eberhard Mfg. Co. v. Brown, 61 Mich. App. 268, 232 N.W.2d 378, 17 UCCR 978 (1975).

[22] U.C.C. § 2-319(1)(a).

[23] U.C.C. § 2-319(1)(b).

[24] U.C.C. § 2-319(2).

[25] *See* Ladex Corp. v. Transportes Aereos Nacionales, S.A., 476 So. 2d 763, 42 UCCR 133 (Fla. Ct. App. 1985); U.C.C. § 2-320.

[26] Risk of loss is dealt with in greater detail in § 6.05, *infra. See* Electric Regulator Corp. v. Sterling Extruder Corp., 280 F. Supp. 550, 4 UCCR 1025 (D. Conn. 1968).

(a) put the goods in the possession of such a carrier and make such a contract for their transportation as may be reasonable having regard to the nature of the goods and other circumstances of the case; and

(b) obtain and promptly deliver or tender in due form any document necessary to enable the buyer to obtain possession of the goods or otherwise required by the agreement or by usage of trade: and

(c) promptly notify the buyer of the shipment.

Failure to notify the buyer under paragraph (c) or to make a proper contract under paragraph (a) is a ground for rejection only if material delay or loss ensues.

Thus, the seller's performance obligations under a shipment contract extend beyond simply delivering conforming goods to the carrier. The choice of the type of carrier (and even the carrier itself) must be reasonable.[27] If the type of goods involved requires prompt delivery, sending by railroad or by truck rather than airplane may be an improper tender if material loss or delay occurs. Furthermore, failure to require a refrigerator car for frozen foods[28] or failure to declare the full value of the goods would be a failure of proper tender.

Prompt notification of the shipment must be given in all cases, whether or not it is expressly called for in the contract.[29] This notification in credit shipments comes most often through the invoice; in documentary sales, it comes through delivery of the documents. Once again, the failure to notify is a ground for rejection only if material loss or delay ensues.[30] The Comments indicate, however, that the parties may contractually make prompt notification an express ground for rejection even though the buyer suffers *no* loss.[31]

---

[27] *See* Larsen v. A.C. Carpenter, Inc., 620 F. Supp. 1084, 2 UCCR2d 433 (E.D.N.Y. 1985) (seller has a duty to secure a vessel that will refrigerate and safely carry perishable potatoes even though a refrigerated carrier was not expressly contracted for).

[28] *Id.*

[29] *See* Rheinberg-Kellerei Gmbh. v. Vineyard Wine Co., 53 N.C. App. 560, 281 S.E.2d 425, 32 UCCR 96 (1981) (requirement of notification must be construed as taking into consideration the need of the buyer to be informed of the shipment in sufficient time to take action to protect himself from the risk of damage to or loss of the goods while in transit).

[30] The Code does not expressly state that the loss or delay must result from the failure to notify. If tender is otherwise proper, however, the risk of loss should not shift back to the seller in a shipment contract simply because the seller has failed in its duty of notification when that failure has nothing to do with the loss. Therefore, a requirement that the failure in notification *cause* the loss should be implied.

[31] U.C.C. § 2-504, Official Comment 5.

The final requirement in a shipment contract is that the seller tender the documents necessary for the buyer to obtain possession of the goods.[32] This completes the buyer's protection because, with the documents, he can obtain the goods from the carrier or, in the event of loss, proceed against the carrier under the contract of shipment.[33] The seller who has complied with these provisions of section 2-504 has a cause of action against the buyer if the buyer refuses to accept the goods and pay their price.[34]

[2] Tender in a Destination Contract

The second type of delivery contract is a destination contract. In a destination contract, the seller is obligated to tender conforming goods at the point of destination. Because the goods must conform to the contract at the time they are tendered, it usually makes no difference to the buyer how the goods were transported from the place of shipment or whether a reasonable contract was made with any carrier that might be involved. If the goods in fact conform when they reach their destination, the buyer has received what he contracted for; if they do not conform, the buyer may reject the goods. In either event, the buyer is protected against losses or delays that occur during shipment. Therefore, the Code need not (and does not) contain provisions for a destination contract that protect the buyer as to the kind of carrier selected or the nature of the contract made with that carrier. The normal tender requirements discussed previously protect the buyer in a destination contract.[35]

There are some destination contracts that involve documents. The Code makes it clear that the necessary documents must be tendered to the buyer as part of the seller's obligations. Two examples are described in the Code: the first is the documentary sale in which the contract expressly requires the seller to deliver documents;[36] the second is the situation in which the goods are in the possession of a bailee and are to be delivered without being moved.[37] In the latter case, the seller performs by tendering either a nego-

---

[32] U.C.C. § 2-504(b).

[33] U.C.C. § 7-301(1).

[34] *See* Permalum Window & Awning Mfg. Co. v. Permalum Window Mfg. Corp., 412 S.W.2d 863, 4 UCCR 194 (Ky. Ct. App. 1967).

[35] *See* § 5.02[A], *supra*.

[36] U.C.C. § 2-503(5). Documentary sales are those in which documents are required, not just authorized.

[37] U.C.C. § 2-503(4).

tiable document of title covering the goods or an acknowledgment by the bailee of the buyer's right to possession of the goods.[38]

[3] Use of a Sight Draft or Letter of Credit

Returning to the example involving the sale of tires,[39] if we assume that the seller shipped the tires "F.O.B. Akron," we would have a shipment contract, with the seller's performance obligations being measured by the seller's tender at the point of shipment. Therefore, the seller would be required to put 500 conforming tires into the possession of a carrier, make a reasonable contract for their delivery to the buyer, obtain a bill of lading from the carrier, deliver the bill to the buyer, and promptly notify the buyer that the goods have been shipped.[40] When the seller has performed these acts, he has tendered the goods, obligating the buyer to accept and pay in accordance with the contract.

If the seller had agreed to extend credit to the buyer, the endorsed bill of lading could be sent directly to the buyer so that it could pick up the tires in Memphis by surrendering the bill of lading. The seller would invoice the buyer and would collect the price at the time provided in the contract. If the seller does not want to surrender possession of the tires until the price has been paid, however, this will not suffice. The seller could collect the price in advance, but what if the buyer does not want to pay the price until it gets the bill of lading entitling it to the goods? The seller could send an agent to Memphis to deliver the bill of lading and collect the price, or the buyer could send an agent to Akron to pay the price and collect the bill of lading, but this is unlikely to be efficient. Fortunately, business people have worked out a method of solving this problem without leaving their respective locations.

The seller takes the bill of lading to an Akron bank and draws a draft on the buyer. A draft is similar to a check, except that this draft will be drawn on the buyer instead of on a bank.[41] The draft will order the buyer to pay the purchase price for the tires (assume $12,000) to the order of the seller's bank. The draft will look something like this:

---

[38] *Id.*

[39] Section 5.02, *supra.*

[40] U.C.C. § 2-504. The bill of lading is prima facie evidence of its authenticity and genuineness and of facts stated in the document by the carrier. U.C.C. § 1-202.

[41] Negotiable drafts and checks are covered in Articles 3 and 4 of the Code. Both are defined in U.C.C. § 3-104.

$12,000   Akron, Ohio, March 15, 1997

AT SIGHT pay to the order of Akron First Bank

Twelve thousand dollars and no/100

Bill of lading attached

To: Buyer Company

Through: First Memphis Bank

Raymond E. Snyder, Jr.
for Seller Corp.

The words "at sight" tell the buyer that payment is to be made when the draft is presented.

The seller is now ready to complete the transaction. The seller indorses the bill of lading to the buyer (or it could be indorsed to "bearer" as well). The seller attaches the indorsed bill to the draft and leaves both with Akron First Bank. Akron First Bank indorses the draft and sends both the draft and the bill of lading to First Memphis Bank (as noted on the draft). When these documents arrive in Memphis, the buyer is notified and can go to First Memphis Bank, pay the draft, and pick up the bill of lading. If the goods have not already arrived, the carrier will call the buyer when the goods arrive, the buyer will deliver the indorsed bill of lading to the carrier, and receive the goods. The $12,000, through various bank credits, is credited to the account of the seller in the Akron bank. The goals of both the buyer and the seller have been accomplished: the seller was able to retain control of the goods through the bill of lading until the price was paid, and the buyer did not have to pay the price until he was assured that he could obtain possession of the goods.

A sight draft affords the seller considerable financial protection. It does not, however, protect the seller if the buyer changes his mind and decides he no longer wants the goods. While a seller may have a cause of action against the buyer for breach in such a situation, the seller does not sell goods to obtain lawsuits, especially suits that may have to be conducted in a distant state with attendant litigation costs. A seller who wants more assurance of payment than is given by a sight draft can demand a letter of credit before shipping the goods. While a detailed discussion of letters of credit is beyond the scope of this text,[42] a short description will suffice to show how it affords the seller greater protection than a sight draft.

A seller who wants to be paid before shipping the goods could demand payment in advance by the buyer. For example, payment in advance (or a signed credit card authorization) is generally required by most mail-order houses. However, the buyer may not be interested in extending the seller credit by paying in advance. The buyer and the seller could use a third-party escrow arrangement, but this is likely to be a cumbersome and inefficient solution. Instead, parties in this situation have relied on the letter of credit. Although letters of credit are most frequently used in international sales,[43] they are used domestically as well. A letter of credit is a letter written by a bank to a "beneficiary," in this case, the seller. The letter contains a promise by the bank either to pay or accept drafts presented by the seller on the buyer when those drafts are accompanied by documents of title under the conditions specified in the letter. The letter of credit originates in a bank selected by the buyer, whose account has been charged with the amount of the letter or who has otherwise paid the bank for the issuance of the letter. The letter is forwarded to a bank in the seller's city, which notifies the seller of its receipt of the credit. Upon surrender of the documents of title, the seller is entitled to payment from the issuing bank.

The seller receives greater protection with the letter of credit than with the sight draft[44] because, upon surrender of the documents of title, the issuer becomes liable to the seller for the amount of the draft—up to the amount of the letter. Thus, the seller has obtained the credit not only of the buyer, but also of the issuing bank.

---

[42] Letters of credit are dealt with in Article 5 of the Code.

[43] In international sales, the Uniform Customs and Practice for Documentary Credits (UCP 500) may govern the contract. Most of its provisions are similar to those of Article 5 of the U.C.C.

[44] A letter of credit may be revocable or irrevocable, although the Code provides that a letter of credit is always irrevocable unless otherwise agreed. U.C.C. §§ 2-325(3), 5-106(a). The latter type is the only one that gives the seller complete protection from the buyer's change of mind. Section 5-106(b) provides that "after a letter of credit is issued, rights and obligations of a beneficiary, applicant, confirmer, and issuer are not affected by an amendment or cancellation to which that person has not consented except to the extent the letter of credit provides that it is revocable or that the issuer may amend or cancel the letter of credit without that consent." This means, in effect, that unless the letter provides otherwise, upon issuance of the letter neither the buyer nor the issuing bank can withdraw, amend, or cancel the credit.

§ 5.03   THE PERFECT TENDER RULE

In most other kinds of contracts, the performance obligations of one party are triggered by the *substantial* performance of the promise of the other contracting party.[45] Full performance is not required in order to hold the other party to contractual duties; substantial performance will suffice.[46] The Code, however, adopts the traditional rule with respect to the sale of goods, present in the Uniform Sales Act:[47] "if the goods or their tender of delivery fail *in any respect* to conform to the contract," the buyer may, among other courses of action, reject all of the goods.[48] Both the goods and the tender must conform precisely to the contract; a failure to conform in any respect is a basis for rejecting the seller's tender.[49] A rejection of the goods, if uncured or uncurable, entitles the buyer to cancel the contract, receive a return of his consideration, and collect damages for the seller's nonperformance.[50]

The majority of cases decided under the Code adhere to the perfect tender rule.[51] There has, however, been substantial scholarly criticism of the

---

[45] *See* Arthur L. Corbin, Corbin on Contracts § 700, at 653; II E. Allan Farnsworth, Farnsworth on Contracts § 8.1 at 343 (1990); Restatement (Second) of Contracts § 237 (1981).

[46] Jacob & Youngs, Inc. v. Kent, 230 N.Y. 239, 129 N.E. 889 (1921). In the event of substantial, but less than complete, performance, the injured party has a right to collect damages for the breach, but is not discharged from its contractual duties. Restatement (Second) of Contracts § 235 & cmt. b (1981).

[47] Mitsubishi Goshi Kaisha v. J. Aron & Co., 16 F.2d 185 (2d Cir. 1926); Goldenberg v. Cutler, 189 A.D. 489, 178 N.Y.S. 522 (App. Div. 1919); Uniform Sales Act § 69(d), 1A U.L.A. 294–295 (1950) (repealed 1962).

[48] U.C.C. § 2-601 (emphasis added).

[49] *See* Gregory M. Travalio, "The UCC's Three 'R's': Rejection, Revocation and (the Seller's) Right to Cure," 53 U. Cin. L. Rev. 931, 937 (1984).

[50] *See* § 7.03[C] for a discussion of the buyer's rejection remedy.

[51] *See, e.g.*, Marlowe v. Argentine Naval Comm'n, 808 F.2d 120, 2 UCCR2d 1226 (D.C. Cir. 1986); Intermeat, Inc. v. American Poultry Inc., 575 F.2d 1017, 23 UCCR 925 (2d Cir. 1978) ("no doubt perfect tender rule applies to measure the buyer's right of initial rejection"); Moulton Cavity & Mold, Inc. v. Lyn-Flex Indus., Inc., 396 A.2d 1024, 25 UCCR 1026 (Me. 1979) (section 2-601 represents continuation of perfect tender rule); Ramirez v. Autosport, 440 A.2d 1345, 33 UCCR 134 (N.J. 1982); Jakowski v. Carole Chevrolet, Inc., 180 N.J. Super. 122, 433 A.2d 841, 31 UCCR 1615 (1981) (degree of non-conformity is irrelevant is assessing the buyer's right to reject); Colonial Dodge v. Miller, 322 N.W.2d 549, 34 UCCR 123 (Mich. Ct. App. 1982); DeJesus v. Cat Auto Tech Corp., 161 Misc. 2d 723, 615 N.Y.S.2d 236, 23 UCCR2d 755 (N.Y. Civ. Ct. 1994); Printing Ctr. of Tex., Inc. v. Supermind Publishing Co., 669 S.W.2d 779, 39 UCCR 127 (Tex. App. 1984) (conformity does not mean substantial performance; it means complete performance); Midwest Mobile

perfect tender rule,[52] including by Karl Llewellyn (principal drafter of Article 2) himself.[53] This criticism has not gone unnoticed, and a small number of cases explicitly question the perfect tender rule, even to the point of abandoning it.[54] Other commentators have suggested that the actual application by the courts of the perfect tender rule, and the various exceptions to it, have, in the words of one commentator, "so eroded the perfect tender rule that the law would be little changed if 2-601 gave the right to reject only upon 'substantial' non-conformity."[55] Neither of these critiques is well founded.

The primary criticism of the perfect tender rule is that it opens the door to opportunism on the part of the buyer.[56] Should the buyer decide that he doesn't want the goods, he need merely find a slight defect in the goods or the tender and he can thrust the goods back on the seller. The usual example offered is where the market price of the goods has dropped between the time of the contract and the time of delivery and the buyer can now get the goods more cheaply elsewhere.

This criticism is misguided for at least two reasons. First, a review of the cases does not reveal that the world is replete with opportunistic buyers. There are very few cases in which sellers have accused buyers of rejecting for opportunistic reasons, and even fewer where buyers actually appear to

---

Diagnostic Imaging, L.L.C. v. Dynamics Corp., 965 F. Supp. 1003, 33 UCCR2d 453 (W.D. Mich. 1997).

[52] *See* John A. Sebert, Jr., "Rejection, Revocation, and Cure Under Article 2 of the Uniform Commercial Code: Some Modest Proposals," 84 Nw. U. L. Rev. 375, 422–425 (1990); Ellen A. Peters, "Remedies for Breach of Contract Relating to the Sale of Goods Under the Uniform Commercial Code: A Roadmap for Article Two," 73 Yale L.J. 199, 215

[53] K.N. Llewellyn, "On Warranty of Quality and Society," 37 Colum. L. Rev. 341, 389 (1937).

[54] *See* McKenzie v. Alla-Ohio Coals, Inc., 29 UCCR 852 (D.D.C. 1979); D.P. Technology Corp. v. Sherwood Tool, Inc., 751 F. Supp. 1038, 13 UCCR2d 686 (D. Conn. 1990). *See also* National Fleet Supply, Inc. v. Fairchild, 36 UCCR 480 (Ind. Ct. App. 1983) (court says in dicta in footnote that it is generally understood that rejection is not available where the goods or delivery fail in some small respect); Oral-X Corp. v. Farnham Cos., Inc., 931 F.2d 667, 16 UCCR2d 111 (10th Cir. 1991) (court applies substantial performance standard without discussion).

[55] James J. White & Robert S. Summers, Uniform Commercial Code 301 (4th ed. 1995). *See also* Ellen A. Peters, "Remedies for Breach of Contract Under the Uniform Commercial Code: A Roadmap for Article 2," 73 Yale L.J. 199, 206 (1963). *But see* William H. Lawrence, "The Prematurely Reported Demise of the Perfect Tender Rule," 35 Kan. L. Rev. 557, 559–573 (1987).

[56] *See, e.g.*, 1 James J. White & Robert S. Summers, Uniform Commercial Code § 8.3 at 442 (4th ed. 1995); Sebert, *supra* note 51, at 385.

be doing so. As the critics have pointed out,[57] even in those cases in which courts have explicitly upheld the perfect tender rule, the defects upon which the buyers' rejections are premised are usually substantial. While the incentive to opportunism cannot be completely discounted,[58] there is scant evidence in the cases that it is a problem of any significance.

Second, and perhaps more important, at least some of the qualifications to the perfect tender rule built into the Code militate strongly against this kind of opportunism. Although they are discussed in greater detail in a subsequent section of the text,[59] usage of trade, course of dealing, and course of performance limit the buyer's ability to reject for inconsequential defects, as does the seller's right to cure under section 2-508. While somewhat more questionable,[60] the obligation of good faith under the Code might also directly control opportunism by the buyer.

On the other hand, the perfect tender rule serves some salutary purposes. First, it provides a degree of certainty that the "substantial performance" rule does not.[61] Whether performance is substantial or not is typically a question of fact.[62] Therefore, except at the margins, court decisions offer little guidance as to when performance is substantial. Further, the appropriate standard for determining when performance is "substantial" is itself unclear. The Restatement of Contracts, for example, simply provides a list of "circumstances" that it says are "significant" in determining whether a breach is material, without any guidance as to their relative importance or how they are to be balanced.[63] Under the perfect tender rule, the buyer is not required to guess whether a rejection of the goods for a defect will turn the tables and cause the buyer to be liable to the seller in damages for material breach.[64]

---

[57] *See* 1 James J. White & Robert S. Summers, Uniform Commercial Code, § 8.3 at 441 (4th ed. 1995).

[58] *See* T.W. Oil, Inc. v. Consolidated Edison Co., 57 N.Y.2d 574, 457 N.Y.S.2d 458, 443 N.E.2d 932, 35 UCCR 12 (1982); Neumiller Farms, Inc. v. Cornett, 368 So. 2d 272, 26 UCCR 61 (Ala. 1979).

[59] *See* § 5.03[E], *infra*.

[60] *See* § 5.03[D], *infra*.

[61] *See* William H. Lawrence, "Appropriate Standards for a Buyer's Refusal to Keep Goods Tendered by a Seller," 35 Wm. & Mary L. Rev. 1635, 1640–1649 (1994). *See also* II E. Allan Farnsworth, Farnsworth on Contracts, § 8.12 at 416 (1990) ("Plainly, a test as flexible as substantial performance sacrifices predictability to achieve justice").

[62] II E. Allan Farnsworth, Farnsworth on Contracts, § 8.12 (1990).

[63] Restatement (Second) of Contracts § 241 (1979). Whether a breach is material is the mirror image of whether the performance is substantial. If a breach is material, the performance is not substantial.

[64] *See* Lawrence, *supra* note 60, at 1641–1643.

Further, the perfect tender rule provides the buyer with the leverage to ensure that the buyer receives what it was promised under the contract. Under the present rule, the burden of proof with respect to defects is on the seller until the buyer has accepted the goods. Thus, if a buyer rejects the goods, the seller has the burden of proving that the goods were conforming. Under section 2-607(4), however, the burden of proof to establish breach shifts to the buyer after acceptance of the goods.[65] If the perfect tender rule were abolished, if a defect did not amount to a failure to render substantial performance, the buyer would have no choice but to accept the goods or breach by rejecting them. This would have the effect of always placing the burden of proof of a defect on the buyer, because rejection would be unavailable as a means of placing this burden on the seller. The Code places the burden of proof on the seller prior to acceptance for a reason: if a defect is found prior to acceptance, it probably existed before the goods were delivered to the buyer, and the seller should have the burden of proving the contrary. It is unfair to place the burden of defects, even insubstantial ones, on the buyer from the time the goods are first delivered to him. Further, placing this burden on the buyer might also give the seller an incentive to shave costs. The seller might deliberately choose to provide substantially conforming, but not perfectly conforming, goods in the expectation that the buyer will not be able to prove the full extent of its damages or that the buyer will decide that it is not worth the time and expense to do so.[66]

The second critique of the perfect tender rule is similarly flawed. One prong of this critique is that the courts have not applied the perfect tender rule with the strictness required by the rule.[67] Instead, through factual and doctrinal manipulation, courts have *sub silentio* applied the standard of material breach, and this standard should be openly recognized and accepted. Thus, according to the critics, even in those cases in which the perfect tender rule is accepted by the courts, the defects have been substantial enough to justify rejection under the traditional contract standard. The second prong of the critique is that the exceptions to the perfect tender rule have so qualified it that it does not function much differently from a "substantial performance" rule.

---

[65] U.C.C. § 607(4).

[66] *See* Francis A. Miniter, "Buyer's Right of Rejection: A Quarter Century Under the Uniform Commercial Code and Recent International Developments," 13 Ga. L. Rev. 805, 825–826 (1979); Lawrence, *supra* note 60, at 1649.

[67] See 1 James J. White & Robert S. Summers, Uniform Commercial Code § 8.3 at 441 (4th ed. 1995); Robert A. Hillman, "Keeping the Deal Together After Material Breach— Common Law Mitigation Rules, the UCC, and the Restatement (Second) of Contracts," 47 Colo. L. Rev. 553, 589 (1976); Sebert, *supra* note 51, at 384–385.

The response to the first prong is that it is not factually accurate, and may be irrelevant as well. Although the number of cases is small, courts have upheld rejections for defects that are less than substantial. For example, in *Colonial Dodge, Inc. v. Miller*,[68] the court upheld the rejection of a new car because it was not equipped with a spare tire. Tires were in short supply and the invoice for the car indicated that the spare tire would be delivered later. Certainly, the criteria of the Restatement (Second of Contracts),[69] suggest that the temporary absence of a spare tire in a new car that was otherwise perfect is not a material breach.[70] In *Marlowe v. Argentine Naval Commission*,[71] the court upheld a rejection of airplanes that had been purchased by the buyer when they arrived six days late. There was no showing that this short delay was a substantial breach, and the court said that it was following the perfect tender rule in permitting the rejection. Other cases also present at least a reasonable argument that the defect did not rise to the level of material breach.[72]

Perhaps more important, however, is that the evidence that is generally offered in support of this critique is that most of the cases in which courts

---

[68] 34 UCCR 123 (Mich. App. 1982).

[69] In determining whether a failure to render or to offer performance is material, the following circumstances are significant:

> (a) The extent to which the injured party will be deprived of the benefit which he reasonably expected;
> (b) The extent to which the injured party can be adequately compensated for the part of that benefit of which he will be deprived;
> (c) The extent to which the party failing to perform or to offer to perform will suffer forfeiture;
> (d) The likelihood that the party failing to perform or to offer to perform will cure his failure, taking account of all the circumstances including any reasonable assurances;
> (e) The extent to which the behavior of the party failing to perform or to offer to perform comports with standards of good faith and fair dealing.

Restatement (Second) of Contracts § 241 (1979).

[70] The court said that the buyer drove long distances and had paid for high-quality tires. These facts, however, should not be determinative. The short distances for which spare tires are generally used until a damaged tire is repaired or replaced, and the relative inexpensiveness of a tire that could be used as a spare until the promised spare arrived, both suggest that the breach was not material.

[71] 808 F.2d 120, 2 UCCR2d 1226 (D.C. Cir. 1986).

[72] *See* DeJesus v. Cat Auto Tech Corp., 161 Misc. 2d 723, 615 N.Y.S.2d 236, 23 UCCR2d 755 (N.Y. Civ. Ct. 1994) (court allowed rejection of printed gift certificates when decorative border was missing and color on some was almost imperceptibly outside border); Jakowski v. Carole Chevrolet, Inc., 180 N.J. Super. 122, 433 A.2d 841, 31 UCCR 1615 (1981) (car delivered without undercoating).

have applied the perfect tender rule have, in fact, involved substantial defects.[73] This, of course, proves very little. In none of these cases is it suggested that the court would refuse to apply the rule if the defect were, in fact, not material. Far more persuasive evidence in support of this criticism of the perfect tender rule would be examples in which courts have circumvented the perfect tender rule, despite their stated adherence to it, to preclude rejection for minor defects. Yet the critics do not provide this more convincing evidence.[74] The reasons for which this evidence is lacking are simple. First, it is unlikely that most cases involving less than material defects end up in court, particularly on appeal. In cases where the defects are minor, the seller will probably be able to exercise its right to cure and provide the buyer with conforming goods.[75] In the alternative, the seller will simply retake possession of the goods and dispose of them elsewhere. Finally, the buyer may be sufficiently satisfied with the goods that it does not attempt to reject them, despite their non-conformity, especially if the seller is willing to make some adjustment in the price. The bottom line is that the smaller the defect, the less likely the case will end up in court in the first place.[76]

As to the second prong of the critique—the suggestion that the recognized exceptions have swallowed the rule—the answer is that this is simply not true. While the exceptions qualify and limit the rule in significant ways, the rule still retains a significant scope of operation. Although a full understanding of this must await a discussion of the various qualifications to the perfect tender rule,[77] none of the exceptions seriously impinge on the buyer's initial right to reject goods when the goods are non-conforming. First, while installment contracts are not subject to the perfect tender rule,[78]

---

[73] James J. White & Robert S. Summers, Uniform Commercial Code § 8.3 at 441 (4th ed. 1995) ("Of the reported Code cases on rejection, none that we have found actually grants rejection on what could fairly be called an insubstantial non-conformity, despite language in some cases allowing such rejection").

[74] Professors White and Summers, for example, do not cite a single case for the proposition that courts have denied rejection for insubstantial defects by manipulating the procedural requirements for rejection.

[75] See § 5.03[B], infra.

[76] Even if courts do not apply the perfect tender rule with the rigor that its name suggests, it still may have an effect on conduct. If sellers perceive that buyers have the right to reject for nonmaterial defects, they will not contest such a rejection. Regardless of how the courts actually apply the rule, if the perception among sellers is that buyers can reject for nonmaterial defects, sellers will act accordingly. Even when there is a risk that a court will apply the rule with more rigor than the substantial performance rule, sellers will be more cautious in contesting a rejection.

[77] See §§ 5.03[A] to 5.03[E], infra.

[78] See § 5.03[C], infra.

in actual commerce, installment contracts seem to be the exception rather than the rule.[79] Second, while the seller may have a right under section 2-508 to cure a non-conforming tender, this does not render the buyer's initial rejection wrongful, nor does it mean that the rejection will not stand in the event the seller cannot or will not cure.[80] Finally, the limitations on the perfect tender rule found in section 2-504 are both limited in scope and do not apply to defects in the quality of the goods.[81]

[A] Acceptance

A major limitation on the buyer's right to reject is that rejection is only available as a remedy up to the time the buyer has accepted the goods.[82] Once the buyer accepts the goods, the only way the buyer can lawfully thrust the goods back on the seller is through the remedy of revocation of acceptance, which imposes both greater procedural and substantive burdens on the buyer.[83] A thorough discussion of acceptance can be found in § 7.03[D] of this volume.

[B] The Seller's Right to Cure

Another limitation on the seller's obligation to make a perfect tender as a condition to the buyer's obligation to accept and pay for the goods, is the seller's right to cure a defective tender. Cure is allowed by section 2-508 in two situations:

> (1) Where any tender or delivery by the seller is rejected because non-conforming and the time for performance has not yet expired, the seller may seasonably notify the buyer of his intention to cure and may then within the contract time make a conforming delivery.
> (2) Where the buyer rejects a non-conforming tender which the seller had reasonable grounds to believe would be acceptable with or without money allowance the seller may if he seasonably notifies the buyer have a further reasonable time to substitute a conforming tender.

In one sense, section 2-508 does not limit the seller's obligation to deliver or tender conforming goods. Even when the seller cures, the seller

---

[79] No authority is cited for this proposition other than common sense and experience and the relatively small number of reported cases dealing with installment contracts.

[80] *See* § 5.03[B], *infra.*

[81] *See* § 5.03[E], *infra.*

[82] U.C.C. §§ 2-602, 2-606.

[83] *See* § 7.03[E], *infra.*

must eventually either "make a conforming delivery" or "substitute a conforming tender."[84] Section 2-508, however, allows sellers in some situations to make a second delivery or tender when the seller learns that the first delivery was non-conforming. In these situations, the perfect tender need not be made the first time but must be made at some later date. Only in this sense does section 2-508 act as a limitation on the seller's obligation to deliver conforming goods.

The right to cure permitted by subsection (1) to section 2-508 is not novel to the Code; pre-Code law recognized the right of a seller to correct a tender if the seller did so prior to the contract time for delivery.[85] This rule is fair to the seller and causes no harm to the buyer. When a seller has made an early delivery, that fact alone ought not to prevent the seller from withdrawing that delivery if it turns out to be non-conforming and tendering conforming goods on or before the date set for delivery in the contract. A typical example is a contract to deliver a certain model refrigerator, "aqua green in color," on or before March 1. On February 20, the seller delivers a refrigerator, but when he uncrates it in the buyer's home, he notices that the one he put on the truck was beige in color. If the seller immediately tells the buyer that he is taking the beige refrigerator back to the store and will have the aqua green model delivered before March 1, the cure requirements of section 2-508(1) will be met. The seasonable notice protects the buyer, and the early mistake ought not to prevent the seller from performing within the time specified in the contract.[86]

The right to cure under section 2-508(1) is dependent upon seasonable notice. If the goods are of a kind that the buyer needs on the date specified, and the early non-conforming tender could cause the buyer reasonably to believe that conforming goods will not be forthcoming from the seller, the buyer should have the right to make an alternative contract to fill his needs and should not have to speculate as to whether he will receive conforming goods from the seller on the date specified in the contract. If the buyer has

---

[84] "Cure" in an installment contract may require only a delivery of goods that substantially conform to the contract. See § 5.03[C], infra.

[85] Lowinson v. Newman, 201 A.D. 266, 194 N.Y.S. 253 (App. Div. 1922); Portfolio v. Rubin, 196 A.D. 316, 187 N.Y.S. 302 (App. Div. 1961). See William D. Hawkland, "Curing an Improper Tender of Title to Chattels: Past, Present and Commercial Code," 46 Minn. L. Rev. 697 (1962).

[86] See Robertson Mfg. Co. v. Jefferson Tile Co., 5 UCCR 119 (N.Y. Sup. Ct. 1968). Comment 1 to U.C.C. § 2-508(1) states that cure can occur even though the buyer has returned the goods and received a refund of the price. A mutual recission would prevent such a cure, but the buyer's unilateral rejection would not. See Lowinson v. Newman, 201 A.D. 266, 194 N.Y.S. 253 (App. Div. 1922).

made a substitute contract before receiving notice of cure from the seller, and it was reasonable for the buyer to do so, the seller's notice would not be "seasonable." Whether a seller's notice of cure is seasonable should depend on the goal of facilitating early cure, whether the buyer has altered his position prior to notice, and on whether it was reasonable for the buyer to do so.[87]

Section 2-508(1) has generated little controversy and virtually no litigation.[88] The same cannot be said of section 2-508(2). Cure under this section has prompted a significant amount of comment and controversy,[89] and a fair number of cases. This is because this section presents ideas not found in pre-Code law[90] and because there are a number of ambiguities in the section. This book deals in detail with three issues that arise under section 2-508(2): when does a seller have reasonable grounds to believe a non-conforming tender would be acceptable; when has a seller effected a "cure" under section 2-508; and can a seller cure when a buyer revokes acceptance of the goods.

[1] Reasonable Grounds to Believe

Under certain circumstances, section 2-508(2) permits a seller a further reasonable time *after* the time of delivery specified in the contract to cure a non-conformity. Like section 2-508(1), this right is conditioned on seasonable notice to the buyer. It is, however, also conditioned upon the seller's having "reasonable grounds to believe [the tender] would be acceptable with or without money allowance."[91] Deciding when "reasonable grounds" for the seller's belief exist is an issue upon which the cases and commentary are badly split.

The problem can be illustrated by the following hypotheticals:

---

[87] *See* Bartus v. Riccardi, 55 Misc. 2d 3, 284 N.Y.S.2d 222 (City Ct. 1967) (court upholds notice of cure because buyer had not altered his position when the seller provided notice).

[88] *But see* Uchitel v. F.R. Tripler & Co., 107 Misc. 2d 312, 434 N.Y.S.2d 77, 30 UCCR 933 (App. Div. 1980); Traynos v. Walters, 342 F. Supp. 455, 10 UCCR 965 (M.D. Pa. 1972).

[89] *See, e.g.,* 1 James J. White & Robert S. Summers, Uniform Commercial Code § 8.5 at 468 (4th ed. 1995); Travalio, *supra* note 49; William H. Lawrence, "Cure Under Article 2 of the Uniform Commercial Code: Practices and Prescriptions," 21 U.C.C.L.J. 138 (1988); Michael A. Schmitt & David Frisch, "The Perfect Tender Rule—An 'Acceptable' Interpretation," 13 U. Tol. L. Rev. 1375 (1982).

[90] Under pre-Code law, if a seller did not make a conforming tender within the period required by the contract, the buyer could rescind the contract and the seller had no right to cure. *See* Norrington v. Wright, 115 U.S. 188 (1885).

[91] U.C.C. § 2-508(2).

Case 1. A seller and buyer entered into a contract for the sale of a new color television of a specified make and model. Between the time of the making of the contract and the date set for delivery, the manufacturer introduced a new model of the set ordered. The seller, knowing the new model was not the one ordered by the buyer, but reasonably believing that the buyer would prefer the improved model, delivers the new model to the buyer for the original price. The buyer may reject the tender because it does not conform to the contract. If the buyer rejects, does the seller have a reasonable time beyond the contract date to cure his non-conforming tender?

Case 2. Assume the same contract as in *Case 1.* Unlike *Case 1,* the seller delivers the proper make and model. When delivered to the buyer, it was packed in a sealed box in the condition in which it was received by the seller from the manufacturer. Although the seller believed that the delivered set was conforming, it was in fact defective: all pictures were bright red, and no amount of adjustment in the home would correct the defect. Does the seller have a reasonable time beyond the contract time to correct the non-conforming tender?

Case 1 is relatively easy. While the seller knew that his tender did not conform to the agreement of the parties, he reasonably believed that his non-conforming tender would be acceptable to this particular buyer. Comment 2 to section 2-508 indicates that the purpose of section 2-508(2) is to avoid injustice when the seller is met with a "surprise" rejection.[92] If we assume that there was no reason for the seller to think that this buyer would not be equally satisfied (or more so) with the newer model, this appears to be precisely the kind of case with which section 2-508(2) was intended to deal.[93]

Case 2, however, is not so easily resolved. In *Case 2,* the seller was unaware of the non-conformity prior to rejection. Does this ignorance of the non-conformity prevent the seller from curing under section 2-508? That is, can section 2-508 afford the seller an opportunity to cure in cases other than when the seller is aware of the non-conformity at the time of tender and nonetheless believes it will be acceptable (*Case 1*)? Or, alternatively, is the scope of section 2-508(2) broader than the relatively infrequent situation in which the seller knowingly delivers non-conforming goods?

The cases and commentary suggest several approaches to this problem. The first is that section 2-508(2) is available only when a seller is aware at

---

[92] U.C.C. § 2-508(2), Official Comment 2.

[93] *See* Bartus v. Riccardi, 55 Misc. 2d 3, 284 N.Y.S.2d 222 (City Ct. 1967) (seller had further reasonable time to cure when buyer rejected newer, improved model of hearing aid because it gave him headaches).

the time of tender that the goods are non-conforming but nonetheless has reasonable grounds to believe that the buyer will accept them.[94] Thus, relief would be available for the seller in *Case 1*, but not *Case 2*.

Several arguments, both textual and policy, support this position. First, the phrase "with or without money allowance" in section 2-508 suggests the seller's awareness of the defect at the time of tender. Unless the seller has knowledge of the defect, the seller would have no reason to consider a money allowance.[95] Second, the Code Comments suggest this reading. Official Comment 2, in discussing the requirement that the seller have reasonable grounds to believe the tender is acceptable, indicates that these grounds can be based upon prior course of dealing, usage of trade, or course of performance.[96] These factors only support a seller's reasonable belief that tender will be acceptable when the seller is aware of the defect. For example, a prior course of dealing may give a seller reasonable grounds to believe that a tender, which the seller knows contains small defects, is acceptable because the buyer has accepted such goods in the past. This past experience is irrelevant, however, if the seller is unaware of the defect at the time of tender. Finally, a broader reading of section 2-508(2) that would cover *Case 2* has the potential for extending the time for performance in a great many contracts by some uncertain reasonable time, contrary to the general obligations of the seller to deliver according to the terms of the contract.

There are also powerful arguments against this position. First, the arguments presented above based on the text and comments are suggestive rather than conclusive.[97] The discussion of usage of trade, course of dealing, and course of performance in Comment 2 is only an *example* of a case in which section 2-508(2) might operate; nothing in the Comment suggests that it might not operate in other circumstances as well. Also, as some cases have noted, a broad right to cure seems a suitable counterpart to the harshness of the perfect tender rule.[98] Finally, this approach often leads to inef-

---

[94] *See* Meads v. Davis, 22 N.C. App. 479, 206 S.E.2d 868 (1974). *See also* Robert J. Nordstrom, The Law of Sales § 320 (1970).

[95] The phrase would not, however, be superfluous, even if this interpretation is rejected. Alternative readings of section 2-508(2), to be discussed subsequently, would allow cure in both *Case 1* and *Case 2*. Under these interpretations, the language "with or without money allowance" is still meaningful in cases where the seller *did* have knowledge of the defect at the time of tender.

[96] U.C.C. § 2-508, Official Comment 2.

[97] *See supra* note 50.

[98] *See* Midwest Mobile Diagnostic Imaging, L.L.C. v. Dynamics Corp. of Am., 965 F. Supp. 1033 (W.D. Mich. 1997); Leitchfeld Dev. Corp. v. Clark, 757 S.W.2d 207, 7 UCCR2d 1092 (Ky. Ct. App. 1988); Uchitel v. F.R. Tripler Co., 127 Misc. 2d 310, 434 N.Y.S.2d 77, 30 UCCR 933 (Sup. Ct. 1980); Sebert, *supra* note 51 at 381; Lawrence, *supra* note 60, at 1668–1686.

ficient and inequitable results. In some cases, the seller is denied the opportunity to cure even if he would have had reasonable grounds to believe the tender would be acceptable *had he known of the defect*. If the defect is small, a seller aware of the defect might offer a money allowance in conjunction with the goods, which he would reasonably believe the buyer would accept. It seems unfair to deny the seller the opportunity to cure because he was ignorant of the defect when he would have had the opportunity to cure had he been aware of it.

Further, preventing the seller from curing will result in the seller undergoing the costs of finding a new customer and redisposing of the goods, and thus unnecessarily expending resources that could have been saved by requiring the buyer to accept the goods. Although the parties might bargain to this result in any event, the costs of this process are likely to be significant.[99] Also, if properly limited, the right to cure in section 2-508(2) will not result in unjustifiably extending the time for performance. Finally, case law supporting this limited approach is extremely scant.[100]

A second approach that would alleviate some of the harshness to sellers of the interpretation discussed previously has been suggested by Professors Schmitt and Frisch.[101] They suggest that knowledge of a defect be "imputed" to the seller in deciding whether the seller had reasonable grounds to believe that the tender would be acceptable.[102] If, charged with knowledge of the non-conformity, the seller would nonetheless reasonably believe his tender would be acceptable to the buyer, with or without a money allowance, the seller will have the benefit of section 2-508(2). Schmitt and Frisch assert that this interpretation avoids the inequities to the seller of the first interpretation without providing a right of cure that is too broad.[103]

This interpretation, however, has no support in the text of section 2-508; there is nothing to suggest that knowledge of a defect is to be imputed to the seller. There is also no basis in the Comments for this interpretation,[104]

---

[99] For a full development of this argument, *see* Travalio, *supra* note 49, at 948–941.

[100] The only case that firmly supports this interpretation is Meads v. Davis, 22 N.C. App. 479, 206 S.E.2d 868, 15 UCCR 40 (1974).

[101] Schmitt & Frisch, *supra* note 88.

[102] Schmitt & Frisch, *supra* note 88, at 1395.

[103] *Id.*

[104] Schmitt and Frisch argue that their interpretation is supported by the Comments to U.C.C. § 2-508 and cite the portion of Comment 2 stating that "[t]he seller is charged with commercial knowledge of any factors in a particular sales situation which require him to comply strictly with his obligations under the contract." It is hard to see how this Comment supports their thesis. The Comment speaks in terms of a "particular" sales situation, not *every* sales situation. The quoted language reflects the unusual or atypical situation, not the usual sales transaction. This is made clear by the full sentence in Comment 2, rather than the portion of the sentence cited by Schmitt and Frisch: "The seller is charged with com-

and the cases are devoid of support for this position.[105]

More important, the approach of Frisch and Schmitt would still preclude cure in cases where it would be both fair and efficient to permit the seller to cure. If the seller, despite reasonable and prudent business behavior, was unaware of a defect that he is now willing and able to correct in a timely manner, he should not be deprived of the right to cure solely because he would not have believed the tender to be acceptable had he known of the defect. The attendant costs of retrieving and disposing of the goods, or bargaining with the buyer to permit cure, should not depend on what the seller would have believed had he been aware of the defect.[106] The nature of the defect should affect the seller's right to cure only if the buyer, because of the nature of the defect, is reasonably wary of the reliability of a substitute product. The courts, however, have developed the doctrine of "shaken faith" to deal with this particular problem in a more narrow way than Schmitt and Frisch, while more generally preserving a seller's right to cure.[107]

A third interpretation of section 2-508(2) has been forcefully articulated by Professors White and Summers.[108] They argue that a seller can have reasonable grounds to believe his tender will be acceptable, despite a nonconformity, in two instances: (1) when a seller has knowledge of the defect, but nonetheless reasonably believes his tender will be acceptable to the buyer, and (2) when the seller is ignorant of the defect despite his good faith and prudent business behavior.[109] Unlike Schmitt and Frisch, White and Summers would impute knowledge of the defect to the seller only when the seller, in the exercise of reasonable and prudent business behavior, should have discovered the defect. Thus, White and Summers would allow for cure in both *Cases 1* and *2*, assuming in *Case 2* that the seller had acted reasonably and prudently.

---

mercial knowledge of any factors in a particular sales situation which require him to comply strictly with his obligation under the contract, as, for example, strict conformity of documents in an overseas transaction or the sale of precision parts or chemicals for use in manufacture." U.C.C. § 2-508(2). Neither of these examples suggest that knowledge of a defect is to be imputed to sellers in all cases. *See* Travalio, *supra* note 49, at 945–946.

[105] Arguably, the case of McKenzie v. Alla-Ohio Coals, Inc., 29 UCCR 852 (D.D.C. 1979) supports the interpretation of Schmitt and Frisch. The court does impute knowledge of a defect to a seller who was ignorant of the defect at the time of tender. However, the knowledge of the defect was imputed by the court only after it decided that a reasonable selller would have been aware of the defect. There is no suggestion that the court would impute such knowledge in all cases, as Schmitt and Frisch suggest.

[106] For a full exposition of this argument, *see* Travalio, *supra* note 49, at 948–952.

[107] *See* § 5.03[B][2], *infra*.

[108] 1 James J. White & Robert S. Summers, Uniform Commercial Code § 8-3 (4th ed. 1995).

[109] *Id.* § 8-5, at 470–472.

The approach of Professors White and Summers is the approach that has been most frequently used by the courts, either explicitly or implicitly. In a much-cited early Code case, *Wilson v. Scampoli*,[110] the approach adopted by the court mirrored that advocated by White and Summers. In *Wilson,* the buyer purchased a new color television from a retailer. Upon operation, it was discovered that the television had a reddish tinge, which the retailer's serviceman could not eliminate at the buyer's home. When the serviceman said that he would have to take the set back to the shop to determine the nature of the defect, the buyer refused, saying that she wanted a new set. Shortly thereafter, the buyer demanded her money back, a demand that was refused by the seller. The buyer then brought an action for the return of her money. In deciding whether the seller had a right to cure the defect in the television under section 2-508(2), the court concluded that the seller had reasonable grounds to believe that the tender would be acceptable. It reasoned that: "a retail dealer would certainly expect and have reasonable grounds to believe that merchandise like color television sets, new and delivered as crated from the factory, would be acceptable as delivered."[111] The court neither required prior knowledge of the defect by the seller nor imputed knowledge of the defect to the seller.

The New York Court of Appeals, in *T.W. Oil, Inc. v. Consolidated Edison Co.,*[112] explicitly rejected the first interpretation of section 2-508(2) and adopted the approach of White and Summers. In this case, the seller purchased a cargo of fuel oil that was certified to have a 0.5 percent sulfur content. While the oil was still at sea, the seller contracted to sell the oil to the buyer. The contract included a provision that the sulfur content of the oil would not exceed 0.5 percent, although the buyer could use oil with a sulfur content up to 1 percent. Delivery was to take place no later than January 30. On January 25, the oil was delivered to the buyer, and the buyer discovered that it had a sulfur content of 1 percent. As a result, the buyer rejected the oil. The seller first offered a price reduction equal to the market difference between 0.5 percent oil and 1 percent oil. The buyer refused this offer, and the seller then promised to deliver conforming oil by February 28. This offer was also refused by the buyer, which insisted that it would take the oil only at the prevailing market price, which was 25 percent below the contract price. The seller refused to sell at this price, and sold the oil elsewhere on the market at the prevailing market price. It then sought damages from the buyer equal to the difference between the contract price and market price.

---

[110] 228 A.2d 848, 4 UCCR 178 (D.C. 1967).

[111] *Id.* at 849, 4 UCCR at 180.

[112] 57 N.Y.2d 574, 443 N.E.2d 932, 457 N.Y.S.2d 458, 35 UCCR 12 (1982).

The seller argued that after rejection of the oil by the buyer, it had a right to cure under section 2-508(2), which the buyer improperly refused. The buyer, however, argued that section 2-508(2) was limited to cases in which the seller *knew* of the non-conformity at the time of tender, and nonetheless reasonably believed the buyer would accept the goods. The court rejected this argument, saying that the focus should be on the reasonableness of the seller's belief rather than on the seller's knowledge or lack of knowledge of the defect. A seller, said the court, can have reasonable grounds to believe a tender wi'l be acceptable despite ignorance of a defect. The seller had a refinery certificate indicating that the oil met the contract's terms,[113] and the seller knew that the buyer could use oil up to 1 percent sulfur content. Under these circumstances, the court held that the seller, despite its ignorance of the defect, had reasonable grounds to believe the goods would be acceptable. Other cases also support the interpretation of Professors White and Summers.[114]

The interpretation advocated by White and Summers has been the subject of scholarly criticism.[115] The thrust of this criticism is that it derogates too greatly from the contractual obligations that the seller has freely undertaken and that it encourages sloppy business practices. For a number of reasons, these criticisms are not well founded. First, even under a broad interpretation of section 2-508(2), sellers remain ultimately responsible for delivering "conforming goods," which is precisely what the buyer bargained for. And, to the extent that section 2-508(2) extends the time for performance, it does so only for an additional *reasonable time*. The urgency of the buyer's need for the goods is a critical factor in determining whether cure occurs within a reasonable time.[116] If the buyer does not get the goods at

---

[113] The refinery certificate indicated that the oil had a sulfur content of 0.52 percent, but there was unimpeached testimony that 0.5 percent and 0.52 percent were trade equivalents.

[114] *See, e.g.*, T&S Brass & Bronze Works, Inc. v. Pic-Air, Inc., 790 F2.d 1098, 1 UCCR2d 433 (4th Cir. 1986) (court finds that seller had reasonable grounds to believe that goods were acceptable because prior shipments were conforming); Ramirez v. Autosport, 88 N.J. 277, 440 A.2d 1345, 33 UCCR 134 (1982).

[115] Schmitt & Frisch, *supra* note 88, at 1378; George I. Wallach, "The Buyer's Right to Return Unsatisfactory Goods—The Uniform Commercial Code Remedies of Rejection and Revocation of Acceptance," 20 Washburn L.J. 20, 28 (1980).

[116] *See* Ramirez v. Autosport, 88 N.J. 277, 440 A.2d 1345, 33 UCCR 134 (1982) (determination of what constitutes a further reasonable time depends, in part, on inconvenience to the buyer); Robertson Mfg. Co. v. Jefferson Tile Co., 5 UCCR 119 (N.Y. Sup. Ct. 1968) (refusal to allow cure unjustified because buyer could not show delay would result in hardship); Miniter, *supra* note 65 (buyer's requirements will probably determine length of reasonable time).

the time she needs them, she has not received the substantial benefit of her bargain and should not have to accept the goods.

Equally important, the approach advocated by White and Summers does not permit cure by *all* sellers who deliver goods in ignorance of a defect. The seller must be ignorant of the defect *despite the seller's good faith and prudent business behavior.*[117] Before a seller has a right to rely upon section 2-508(2), the seller's ignorance of the defect must have been reasonable under all of the circumstances.[118] Thus, the approach is expressly conditioned on the prudent business behavior of the seller, which would, by definition, exclude cases in which "shoddy" practices are the cause of the seller's ignorance of the defect.

[2]   A "Conforming Tender"

A number of cases have considered the issue of whether a seller's offer of a substitute performance constitutes a sufficient "cure" under section 2-508 to allow a seller to overcome a buyer's rejection. Most frequently, these cases have involved attempts by a seller to repair goods rather than replace them,[119] or to replace the defective goods with nonidentical substitutes.[120] The issue also involves whether a money allowance, such as a reduction in price, can be an effective cure.

Section 2-508(2) requires that the seller cure by "substituting a conforming tender."[121] Section 2-106(2) states that "[g]oods or conduct including any part of a performance are 'conforming' or conform to the contract when they are in accordance with the obligations under the contract."[122] Thus, in order to have the benefit of section 2-508, the seller must deliver goods that are in accordance with the obligations under the contract—

---

[117] 1 James J. White & Robert S. Summers, Uniform Commercial Code § 8-5, at 470 (4th ed. 1995).

[118] A seller's ignorance of the defect is reasonable only if the costs of discovering the defect are greater than the costs of cure if the defect turns out to exist. This provides the seller with the incentive to choose the least costly alternative. In a competitive market, this benefits buyers generally, because the lower costs should result in lower prices to the buyer. For a full explanation, *see* Travalio, *supra* note 49, at 952.

[119] *See, e.g.,* Worldwide RV Sales & Serv., Inc. v. Brooks, 534 N.E.2d 1132, 8 UCCR2d 386 (Ind. Ct. App. 1989); Bayne v. Nall Motors, Inc., 12 UCCR 1137 (Iowa Dist. Ct. 1973); Rozmus v. Thompson's Lincoln Mercury, Inc., 209 Pa. Super 120, 224 A.2d 782, 3 UCCR 1225 (1966).

[120] *See, e.g.,* David Tunick, Inc. v. Kornfeld, 838 F. Supp. 848, 22 UCCR2d 417 (S.D.N.Y. 1993); Bowen v. Foust, 925 S.W.2d 211, 29 UCCR2d 825 (Mo. Ct. App. 1996).

[121] U.C.C. § 2-508(2).

[122] U.C.C. § 2-106(2).

anything less will not do.[123] This means, at a minimum, the seller must deliver goods that do not breach any implied or express warranties. Thus, if a seller, in an attempt to cure, delivers goods that are not fit for their ordinary purpose or would not pass without objection in the trade under the contract description, the cure will not be effective. More important, however, for the goods to conform to the contract, sellers must also deliver goods that do not breach any *express* warranties, and it is this requirement that imposes the most significant limitation on the seller's right to cure. If a seller has represented that a product is "new," for example, the seller does not deliver goods in accordance with his obligations under the contract unless he ultimately delivers "new" goods.

This interpretation of section 2-508(2) does not mean, however, that a seller will be required to provide replacement goods in all circumstances, or that cure can never be accomplished by repair. Repair is permissible when it results in the goods conforming to the contract, including all express and implied warranties. Thus, in cases involving "new" goods, cure results when the goods are "as good as new." The content of the warranty of "newness" is determined in the same way as any other term of the contract—by the standard of the reasonable person under the circumstances.[124]

An example of an effective cure by repair is *Rozmus v. Thompson's Lincoln Mercury Co.*[125] In this case, the buyer of a new car was driving the car away from the lot when he noticed smoke coming from the car's exhaust pipe and heard a loud thumping noise. He returned the car immediately, demanding either return of his money or a new car. The problem was discovered to be two loose engine mounting bolts, which were tightened in a matter of minutes and which completely resolved the problems. The facts of the case provide an instance where reasonable people would consider the car, after repairs, to be "as good as new" and therefore conforming to all express and implied warranties.[126]

Courts have generally done a good job of determining whether a proffered cure is effective under section 2-508(2), although they have not always

---

[123] Some courts have simply overlooked the fact that "conforming" is a term defined in the Code in deciding whether a cure was sufficient. *See, e.g.*, Marine Mart, Inc. v. Pierce, 252 Ark. 601, 480 S.W.2d 133, 10 UCCR 124 (1972); Pavesi v. Ford Motor Co., 155 N.J. Super. 373, 382 A.2d 954, 23 UCCR 929 (1978).

[124] *See* Travalio, *supra* note 49 at 957.

[125] 209 Pa. Super. 120, 224 A.2d 782, 3 UCCR 1025 (1966).

[126] The case was actually decided in the seller's favor on the basis of whether the buyer had grounds for revocation of acceptance. However, given the short time period involved prior to the car's return, the buyer's action should have been characterized as a rejection, rather than revocation of acceptance. *See* §§ 7.03[C], 7.03[E], *infra*. In any event, the facts of the case are simply offered as an example of an effective cure by repairing the goods.

done so by reference to the Code's definition of "conforming," using the analysis suggested.[127] In *Worldwide RV Sales & Service, Inc. v. Brooks*,[128] the buyer ordered a custom van for $39,000. The van that was ordered was supposed to have two air conditioners, one in the front and one in the back. The van that was delivered had one air conditioner in the center. The dealer offered to move the one in the center to the front and place another one in the back. This, however, would leave a hole in the center of the van's roof. The customer refused this offer, a refusal that the court upheld.

In properly focusing on the requirement that the seller can cure only by providing conforming goods, the court in *Bowen v, Faust*[129] refused to allow the seller to cure by substituting equipment that was not fully compatible with existing equipment. In doing so, the court said that even if the substitute equipment was flawless, it was not an effective cure unless it conformed to the contract. Other cases have similarly permitted a buyer's rejection to stand when the seller's proposed cure could not reasonably be described as the provision of conforming goods.[130]

Even if conforming goods are provided, however, there is still the possibility that the buyer will be left in worse shape than if the contract had been performed properly the first time. The buyer may have suffered some damage as a result of the goods not being available at the time promised under the contract. If this is the case (despite the seller providing the goods within a "further reasonable time"), these damages should be recoverable under section 2-714, which allows for the recovery of damages that result in the ordinary course of events from any non-conformity of tender.[131] However, even if there are no damages caused by the delay and the goods are conforming, the buyer may have "insecurity costs" in the form of increased apprehensiveness or anxiety about the particular item of goods purchased or the brand of goods in general. This harm would generally not be recoverable, either because it is too speculative[132] or because it constitutes com-

---

[127] *See* Travalio, *supra* note 49 at 976–984.

[128] 534 N.E.2d 1132, 8 UCCR2d 386 (Ind. Ct. App. 1989).

[129] 925 S.W.2d 211, 29 UCCR2d 825 (Mo. Ct. App. 1996).

[130] *See* David Tunick, Inc. v. Kornfeld, 838 F. Supp. 848, 22 UCCR2d 417 (S.D.N.Y. 1993) (substitution of another Picasso print for a forgery); Central Dist. Alarm, Inc. v. Hal-Tuc, Inc., 886 S.W.2d 210, 25 UCCR 58 (Mo. Ct. App. 1994) (substitution of used JVC VCR for new Javelin VCR). *See also* Wilson v. Scampoli, 228 A.2d 848, 4 UCCR 178 (D.C. 1967) (buyer is not required to "accept patchwork goods or substantially repaired articles in lieu of flawless merchandise").

[131] U.C.C. § 2-714(1).

[132] *See* 5 Arthur L. Corbin, Corbin on Contracts § 1.22, at 135–147 (1964); III E. Allan Farnsworth, Farnsworth on Contracts § 12.14 (1990).

pensation for mental distress, which is generally not recoverable for breach of contract.[133] To deal with this problem, the courts have developed the doctrine of "shaken faith."

The doctrine originated in the case of *Zabriskie Chevrolet, Inc. v. Smith*,[134] which involved the sale of a new car. After taking possession of the car, the buyer experienced severe difficulties on the way home from the dealership. The car would operate only in "low-low" gear and it made peculiar noises. The buyer demanded a replacement vehicle, but the seller refused the demand and replaced the car's transmission with one taken from an automobile on the showroom floor. The buyer refused to take the car in its repaired condition, and stopped payment on the his check. The dealer sued the buyer for the balance of the purchase price.

The seller argued that it had a right to cure the non-conforming goods, which the seller said that it had done by replacing the defective transmission. The court found that the replacement of the transmission with a substituted transmission "not from the factory and of unknown lineage" was not an effective cure:

> For a majority of people, the purchase of a new car is a major investment, rationalized by the peace of mind that flows from its dependability and safety. Once their faith is shaken, the vehicle loses not only its real value in their eyes, but becomes an instrument whose integrity is substantially impaired and whose operation is fraught with apprehension.[135]

The shaken-faith doctrine has become fairly well-established in the extant case law. In *Zabriskie,* the buyer's faith was shaken in the product because the replacement transmission was "not from the factory and of unknown lineage." The buyer remained apprehensive about the product because he could not be sure that the replacement part would function as effectively as a "new" transmission. In *Bayne v. Nall Motors*, Inc.,[136] the cause of the buyer's shaken faith was somewhat different. In this case, the entire rear end of a new car "locked up" after 406 miles because the rear axle housing had not been lubricated at the factory. The buyer demanded a new car. Instead, the seller replaced the entire differential (except for one axle) and asserted that the defect had been cured. Although the car ran fine as repaired, the court found that the seller had not cured the non-conformity.

---

[133] Restatement (Second) of Contracts § 353 (1981); III E. Allan Farnsworth, Farnsworth on Contracts § 12.17 (1990).

[134] 99 N.J. Super. 441, 240 A.2d 195, 5 UCCR 30 (1968).

[135] *Id.* at 458, 240 A.2d at 205, 5 UCCR at 42.

[136] 12 UCCR 1137 (Iowa Dist. Ct. (1973).

The court found that the possibility of damage to other parts of the vehicle still existed as a result of the heat generated by the lack of lubrication and the sudden stop when the differential froze. Because the purchaser was subjected to the uncertainty of possible damage to other major parts of the vehicle, it was not the same as a similar automobile that had not experienced the same internal impact. In *Bayne*, the cause of the buyer's shaken faith was not concern about the replacement part itself, but other damage the original non-conformity may have caused.[137]

The shaken-faith doctrine does not permit a buyer to refuse a proffered cure merely by asserting that his or her faith in the product has been shaken. Rather the buyer must prove that his or her faith in the product is *reasonably* shaken. It is an objective test that requires the buyer to show that a reasonable person would have continuing insecurities about the product after the seller's "cure."[138]

The issue of whether the seller's proposed cure is "conforming" and the issue of whether the buyer's faith has been shaken are closely related. In *Bayne*, for example, the buyer's insecurity resulted from a reasonable concern that the freezing of the differential may have damaged other parts of the automobile. Rather than asking whether the buyer's faith in the product has been shaken, the question could be phrased as whether a car that has suffered that kind of incident is "conforming" (i.e., "as good as new") when only the differential is replaced. On the other hand, the two issues are not necessarily congruent. For example, if a brand new replacement is tendered, it is difficult for the buyer to argue that the goods are not "conforming," since they are precisely the goods called for by the contract. The buyer may nonetheless be concerned that the defect represents a problem with the product line rather than the individual product and may want to purchase another brand entirely. Similarly, when an item has been repaired in a way that makes it "as good as new," the buyer might still believe that the defect is only a precursor of further defects. Should the doctrine of shaken faith apply only when, because of the nature of the seller's cure, the goods themselves cannot reasonably be described as "conforming," or should it also apply in cases where the goods themselves are conforming but the buyer's faith is nonetheless reasonably shaken?

---

[137] *See also* Champion Ford Sales, Inc. v. Levine, 433 A.2d 1218, 32 UCCR 108 (Md. Spec. Ct. App. 1981) (rebuilt engine not effective replacement for new factory engine); Gappelberg v. Landrum, 654 S.W.2d 549, 37 UCCR 1563 (Tex. App. 1983) (court did not require buyer to take new TV as replacement for defective one and said that shaken faith is best reason not to permit cure after revocation of acceptance).

[138] *See* Welch v. Fitzgerald-Hicks Dodge, Inc., 121 N.H. 358, 420 A.2d 144, 31 UCCR 1336 (1981).

Applying the shaken-faith doctrine in cases in which the seller replaces defective goods with a new product or a repair that will make the product "as good as new" raises two possible concerns. The first is that the shaken-faith doctrine, interpreted this way, will make it too easy for buyers to avoid offers of cure by sellers. The second is that there is no support for the shaken-faith doctrine in the Code or the Comments; section 2-508 requires only that the seller substitute a "conforming tender." So long as the seller does all that section 2-508 requires, a proposed cure should not be subject to further qualifications.

Despite the fact that there is no textual support in the Code for the idea of "shaken faith," it should be applicable in the preceding situations. The key to understanding this conclusion is twofold. First, the buyer's faith in the product must be *objectively* shaken. If the buyer's fears concerning the product, even after a complete replacement, are not reasonable, the seller's cure will be effective if the seller has provided conforming goods. Thus, the idea of shaken faith does not undermine a seller's right to cure. Unless a new replacement product will nonetheless leave the buyer with continuing *reasonable* fears about the product, the cure will be effective.

Second, the basis for the shaken-faith doctrine lies in the drafters' conceptions of the terms "contract" and "bargain." The Code defines "contract" as the total legal obligation that results from the parties' agreement.[139] In turn, "agreement" means "the bargain of the parties in fact as found in their language or by implication from other circumstances."[140] It is this notion of the contract as the bargain-in-fact of the parties that justifies a broad application of the shaken-faith doctrine. The bargain of the parties in fact is made up of their reasonable expectations in light of all of the circumstances surrounding the deal.[141] These reasonable expectations include receiving goods with which the buyer can feel reasonably secure and whose continued use is not "fraught with apprehension." In order to cure a nonconformity, the seller must deliver goods that produce a degree of security reasonably equivalent to the degree of security that would have resulted had the original product been defect-free. Only then will the buyer have received goods that are in accord with the bargain-in-fact of the parties, and thus in conformity with the seller's obligations under the contract.

The cases do not resolve the question of whether the shaken-faith doctrine applies to cases in which the goods offered as a cure by the seller

---

[139] U.C.C. § 1-201(11).

[140] U.C.C. § 1-201(3).

[141] *See* John E. Murray, Jr., " 'Basis of the Bargain': Transcending Classical Concepts," 66 Minn. L. Rev. 283, 317–318 (1982).

conform to the contract in the narrow sense that they are physically indistinguishable from the goods that were promised, but where the prior defect or defects created reasonable insecurity on the part of the buyer in the product or product line. A couple of cases, however, support the broad concept of shaken faith advocated here,[142] and no case has definitively held that the concept cannot apply despite the seller's tender of a replacement product.[143]

[3] Cure Following Acceptance

By its terms, section 2-508 does not apply after acceptance.[144] The language of the section permits a seller to cure only if that a buyer *rejects* a non-conforming tender, and a buyer cannot reject once it has accepted the goods.[145] Despite the fact, however, that section 2-508 by its terms applies only before acceptance, courts have struggled with whether a seller might also have a post-acceptance right of cure. In part, this issue turns on a buyer's right to revoke acceptance under section 2-608.

A detailed discussion of revocation of acceptance must await a later chapter.[146] An introduction to section 2-608, however, is necessary to understand fully the parameters of a seller's right to cure. Section 2-608(1) provides:

> The buyer may revoke his acceptance of a lot or commercial unit whose non-conformity substantially impairs its value to him if he has accepted it
> (a) on the reasonable assumption that its non-conformity would be cured and it has not been seasonably cured; or

---

[142] *See* Durfee v. Rod Baxter Imports, Inc., 262 N.W.2d 349, 22 UCCR 945 (Minn. 1977) (repair and replacement warranty not sufficient to overcome shaken faith): Gappelberg v. Landrum, 666 S.W.2d 88 (Tex. 1984) (buyer permitted to refuse seller's offer of new replacement TV because of shaken faith).

[143] A couple of cases offer marginal support for the proposition that cure can always be effected by a replacement. *See* Champion Ford Sales, Inc. v. Levine, 49 Md. App. 547, 433 A.2d 1218, 32 UCCR 108 (1981); Asciolla v. Manter Oldsmobile-Pontiac, Inc., 117 N.H. 85, 370 A.2d 270, 21 UCCR 112 (1977). Both of these cases involved repairs that the courts said were ineffective to cure the non-conformities, and the courts in both cases indicated that cure could be effected by tendering replacement vehicles. In neither case, however, was there any indication that the buyer would not have been satisfied with a replacement. In fact, in *Asciolla*, the buyer had requested a replacement. Therefore, neither case provides much support for the idea that a replacement is *always* a satisfactory cure.

[144] *See* U.C.C. § 2-508 (section applies when a buyer rejects a non-conforming tender).

[145] *See* § 5.03[A], *supra.*

[146] *See* § 7.03[E], *infra.*

   (b) without discovery of such non-conformity if his acceptance
was reasonably induced either by the difficulty of discovery before acceptance or by the seller's assurances.

Subsection (a) assumes that the buyer has implicitly agreed to permit the
seller to cure as a condition of accepting the goods,[147] and thus necessarily
contemplates cure occurring after acceptance. If the seller does not seasonably cure the non-conformity, the buyer is permitted to revoke acceptance
of the goods, assuming the other requirements for revocation of acceptance
have been met.[148]
   Subsection (b) makes no mention of a seller's cure, and applies in cases
in which the non-conformity is not discovered until after the buyer has
accepted the goods.[149] Because of the failure to mention cure in section 2-
608, and the language limiting section 2-508 to rejection, many courts and
commentators have concluded that there is no right of cure after acceptance
except under subsection (a).[150]

---

   [147] Commentators agree that subsection (a) applies only in the event that the buyer is
aware of the non-conformity prior to acceptance, and agrees to accept the goods, rather than
rejecting them, only on the reasonable assumption that the seller will cure the non-
conformity. *See, e.g.,* Travalio, *supra* note 49 at 976 n.243; Lawrence, *supra* note 60 at 1682.
Although most courts have correctly applied the subsection, *see, e.g.,* American Honda Motor
Co. v. Boyd, 475 So. 2d 835, 41 UCCR 410 (Ala. 1985); Hollingsworth v. Software House,
Inc., 32 Ohio App. 3d 61, 513 N.E.2d 1372, 4 UCCR2d 1400 (1986); Henery v. Robinson,
834 P.2d 1091, 18 UCCR2d 1121 (Wash. Ct. App. 1992), some have applied the section in
cases in which the buyer did not discover the defect until after acceptance, or when the
buyer never accepted the goods. *See* Jackson v. Rocky Mountain Datsun, Inc., 693 P.2d 391,
39 UCCR 885 (Colo. Ct. App. 1984); Palmisciano v. Tarbox Motors, Inc., 39 UCCR 146
(R.I. Super. 1984). *See also* Stridiron v. I.C., Inc., 578 F. Supp. 997, 37 UCCR 1568 (D.V.I.
1984) (court applies subsection (a) without discussion of whether non-conformity discovered
before or after acceptance).
   [148] *See, e.g.,* City Nat'l Bank of Charleston v. Wells, 181 W. Va. 763, 384 S.E.2d 374,
10 UCCR2d 798 (1989); Henery v. Robinson, 834 P.2d 1091, 18 UCCR2d 1121 (Wash. Ct.
App. 1992).
   [149] It has been argued that U.C.C. § 2-608(3) grants the seller a right to cure even when
the defect is not discovered until after acceptance. The argument is that because a buyer
who revokes acceptance "has the same rights and duties with regard to the goods" as one
who rejects, the buyer has the same "duty" to permit the seller to cure that would accrue
under section 2-508 had the buyer rejected the goods instead of having revoked his acceptance. *See* Note, "U.C.C. Section 2-508: Seller's Right to Cure Non-Conforming Goods," 6
Rut.-Cam. L.J. 387, 414 (1974). This argument relies upon a strained reading of section
2-608(3) and has been suggested, in dicta, in only one case. *See* David Tunick, Inc. v.
Kornfeld, 838 F. Supp. 848, 22 UCCR2d 417 (S.D.N.Y 1993); Travalio, *supra* note 49 at
977 n.247.
   [150] *See, e.g., Lawrence, supra* note 60 at 1681–1685; American Honda Motor Co. v. Boyd,

As others have recognized, however, refusing to permit cure after acceptance has the potential to undercut substantially the policies underlying section 2-508.[151] By immediately accepting the goods,[152] the buyer could intentionally avoid the right of the seller to cure, with the resulting inefficiency and unfairness described earlier.[153] In addition, there is no reason to permit a seller to cure when the defects are easily discoverable but to preclude cure when they are more difficult to discover and therefore not likely to be uncovered until after acceptance. In fact, tender of a non-conforming product is, in a certain sense, more excusable when the nature of the defect is not obvious. Also, if the goods have been in the hands of the buyer a longer time, they will often have depreciated significantly in value and the buyer will sometimes have enjoyed considerable use of them. Further, there is a greater likelihood that the price of the goods will have fallen between the time of the contract and the time of revocation than during the shorter time between the contract and rejection,[154] which would both provide an incentive to the buyer to revoke in bad faith and increase the difficulty to the seller of disposing of the goods.

---

475 So. 2d 835, 41 UCCR 410 (Ala. 1985); Preston Motor Co., Inc. v. Palomares, 650 P.2d 1227, 34 UCCR 1184 (Ariz. Ct. App. 1982); U.S. Roofing, Inc. v. Credit Alliance Corp., 228 Cal. App. 3d 143, 279 Cal. Rptr. 533, 14 UCCR2d 746 (1991); Jensen v. Seigel Mobile Homes Group, 105 Idaho 189, 668 P.2d 65, 35 UCCR 804 (1983); Asciolla v. Manter Oldsmobile Pontiac, Inc., 117 N.H. 85, 370 A.2d 270, 21 UCCR 112 (1977); Pavesi v. Ford Motor Co., 155 N.J. Super. 373, 382 A.2d 954, 23 UCCR 929 (App. Div. 1978); Gappelberg v. Landrum, 654 S.W.2d 549, 37 UCCR 1563 (Tex. App. 1983); Kesner v. Lancaster, 378 S.E.2d 649, 9 UCCR2d 122 (W. Va. 1989); City Nat'l Bank of Charleston v. Wells, 384 S.E.2d 374, 10 UCCR2d 798 (W. Va. 1989).

[151] See Travalio, *supra* note 49 at 976–984; Sebert, *supra* note 51 at 392–393; Web Press Servs. Corp. v. New London Motors, Inc., 203 Conn. 342, 525 A.2d 57, 3 UCCR2d 1386 (1987); North River Homes, Inc. v. Bosarge, 17 UCCR2d 120 (Miss. 1992); Fitzner Pontiac-Buick-Cadillac, Inc. v. Smith, 523 So. 2d 324 (Miss. 1988).

[152] When acceptance occurs is at least partially within the control of the buyer. Under U.C.C. § 2-606(1)(c), acceptance can occur when the buyer does any act inconsistent with the seller's ownership. Such an act might consist of the buyer's simply using the goods after discovery of the defect. See Linscott v. Smith, 587 P.2d 1271, 25 UCCR 1329 (Kan. Ct. App. 1978); Fablock Mills, Inc. v. Cocker Mach. & Foundry Co., 120 N.J. Super. 350, 294 A.2d 62, 11 UCCR 59 (1972).

[153] See § 5.03[B][1], *supra*.

[154] Personal computers provide a good example of this. Revocation can often occur long after the goods have been delivered. See, e.g., Conte v. Dwan Lincoln-Mercury, Inc., 172 Conn. 112, 374 A.2d 144, 20 UCCR 899 (1976) (buyer permitted to revoke acceptance more than fourteen months after sale). If the goods consist of a personal computer, there is little doubt that in today's market, the cost (and value) of such a computer will have dropped significantly.

Courts have accepted these arguments, either implicitly or explicitly, and incorporated a right to cure after acceptance in a number of ways. In *Fitzner Pontiac-Buick-Cadillac, Inc. v. Smith*,[155] the Mississippi Supreme Court permitted a seller to cure after acceptance by drawing an analogy to section 2-508 and concluding that a right to cure after acceptance furthered the policies of section 2-608 on revocation of acceptance.[156] In *Web Press Services Corp. v. New London Motors, Inc.*,[157] the court ignored the limiting language of section 2-508 and used the section to permit the seller a right to cure following acceptance. Other cases have simply assumed that the seller has some right to cure non-conformities after acceptance.[158]

Other courts have incorporated a right to cure following acceptance in an indirect way. These courts have seized upon the requirement of substantial impairment in section 2-608 to give sellers at least a limited right to cure. Beginning with the case of *Rozmus v. Thompson's Lincoln-Mercury*,[159] a number of courts have considered the seller's willingness and ability to cure a non-conformity in determining whether the non-conformity substantially impairs the value of the goods to the buyer.[160] The court in *Rozmus*, in language that has been quoted in later cases,[161] said that a buyer cannot revoke for "trivial defects or *defects that can be easily corrected.*"[162] Presumably, the "defects that can be easily corrected" are those that, in the absence of correction, would constitute a substantial impairment of value; otherwise there would be no right to revoke acceptance in the first instance.

A seller's right to cure after revocation is subject to a number of limitations. First, the cure must be accomplished within a reasonable time. Even those courts that have permitted a seller to cure after acceptance have said

---

[155] 523 So. 2d 324, 6 UCCR2d 396 (Miss. 1988).

[156] A number of other Mississippi cases have used the same analysis to find a right to cure after acceptance. Rester v. Morrow, 491 So. 2d 204, 1 UCCR2d 751 (Miss. 1986); Guerdon Indus., Inc. v. Gentry, 531 So. 2d 1202, 7 UCCR2d 67 (Miss. 1988); Tucker v. Aqua Yacht Harbor Corp., 749 F. Supp. 142, 13 UCCR2d 382 (N.D. Miss. 1990); North River Homes, Inc. v. Bosarge, 594 So. 2d 1153, 17 UCCR2d 121 (Miss. 1992).

[157] 203 Conn. 342, 525 A.2d 57, 3 UCCR2d 1386 (1987).

[158] *See, e.g.*, Sierra Diesel Injection Serv., Inc. v. Burroughs Corp., 651 F. Supp. 1371, 3 UCCR2d 538 (D. Nev. 1987) (court assumes that seller has right to cure after acceptance).

[159] 209 Pa. Super. 120, 224 A.2d 782, 3 UCCR 1025 (1966).

[160] *See, e.g.*, Page v. Dobbs Mobile Bay, Inc., 599 So. 2d 38, 18 UCCR2d 720 (Ala. Ct. App. 1992); Jackson v. Rocky Mountain Datsun, Inc., 693 P.2d 391, 39 UCCR 885 (Colo. Ct. App. 1984).

[161] Pratt v. Winnebago Indus. Inc., 463 F. Supp. 709, 26 UCCR 68 (W.D. Pa. 1979); Conte v. Dwan Lincoln-Mercury, Inc., 374 A.2d 144, 20 UCCR 899 (Conn. 1976); Champion Ford Sales, Inc. v. Levine, 49 Md. App. 547, 433 A.2d 1218, 32 UCCR 108 (1981).

[162] 209 Pa. Super. at 124, 224 A.2d at 784, 3 UCCR at 1027.

that a seller does not have the right to tinker with the goods indefinitely in order to make them conforming.[163] If the seller has already had a reasonable time to attempt to cure the non-conformities prior to the buyer's revocation of acceptance and has been unsuccessful,[164] the seller should not be allowed additional time to cure simply because the buyer has been patient prior to exercising the remedy of revocation. The reasonable time to cure non-conformities should be measured from the time that the seller becomes aware of the non-conformities, not from the time that the buyer attempts to revoke his acceptance.

Second, the value of the goods to the buyer following cure must no longer be substantially impaired. If the goods, after cure, are "conforming," according to the objective test described earlier,[165] the cure is effective to prevent revocation of acceptance by the buyer. If the goods are not conforming, but their value to the buyer is no longer substantially impaired, the cure should also be effective to prevent revocation of acceptance,[166] although the buyer retains a right to damages for any remaining non-conformity.[167] If, following the seller's attempt to cure, the value of the goods remains substantially impaired, the buyer may then revoke his acceptance of the goods.

[C] Installment Contracts

Installment contracts are another exception to the perfect tender rule. In an installment contract, the buyer may have an obligation to accept and pay for the goods despite the seller's tender of less than complete performance. The failure to perform completely is, of course, a breach for which the seller is liable in damages; in that sense a "perfect tender" is still required by the Code. Nevertheless, something short of a perfect tender obligates the buyer to accept the goods and pay their price (less damages); in

---

[163] *See, e.g.*, Guerdon Indus., Inc. v. Gentry, 531 So. 2d 1202, 7 UCCR2d 67 (Miss. 1988); Rester v. Morrow, 491 So. 2d 204, 1 UCCR2d 751 (Miss. 1986).

[164] *See, e.g.*, Rester v. Morrow, 491 So. 2d 204, 1 UCCR2d 751 (Miss. 1986); Oberg v. Phillips, 615 P.2d 1022, 29 UCCR 846 (Okla. Ct. App. 1980); Welsh v. Fitzgerald-Hicks Dodge, Inc., 430 A.2d 144, 32 UCCR 1336 (N.H. 1981).

[165] *See* § 5.03, *supra*.

[166] One commentator has strenuously objected to this conclusion on the grounds that it gives the buyer less than the buyer bargained for (i.e., conforming goods). *See* Lawrence, *supra* note 60 at 1681–1684. However, the essence of the "substantial impairment" criterion for revocation of acceptance is that after acceptance, the buyer must retain non-conforming goods so long as their value to him is not substantially impaired. Whether the impairment of value is initially "insubstantial" or becomes insubstantial only after the seller's cure should make no difference as to whether a buyer should be permitted to revoke acceptance.

[167] *See* U.C.C. § 2-714 (giving the buyer a right to damages for accepted goods).

that sense the "perfect tender" rule is relaxed by the Code with respect to installment contracts.

An installment contract is one "which requires or authorizes the delivery of goods in separate lots to be separately accepted, even though the contract contains a clause 'each delivery is a separate contract' or its equivalent."[168] It is important to note that the definition of an installment contract does not *require* the seller to deliver in installments; it need only *authorize* the seller to do so. Further, this authorization does not have to be explicit; it can be implied from the circumstances of the transaction.[169]

The Code divides a seller's defective performance under an installment contract into two categories: those that involve a defect in the *required* documents and those that involve other defects. The first kind of defect, defects in required documents, is considered subsequently. The second category—all other defects—requires further subdivision: those defects that do not substantially impair the value of an installment, and those that do substantially impair the value of an installment.[170] Those non-conformities that do not substantially impair the value of an installment give the buyer no right to reject the goods. In such cases, the seller is not obligated to make a perfect tender to avoid a rejection by the buyer, and the buyer is obligated to accept and pay for the goods, minus damages for any harm suffered by the buyer because of the defective tender.

Even when the defect does cause a substantial impairment in the value to the buyer of an installment, the buyer is not necessarily entitled to reject the installment. Section 2-612(2) allows rejection if the defect cannot be cured. If the defect can be cured, and the seller gives the buyer adequate assurance of cure, the buyer must accept the defective installment despite its substantially impaired value. If the seller then fails to cure, the buyer may revoke its acceptance of the installment.

There is some difficulty in determining the meaning of "cure" as used in section 2-612, and, in particular, the relationship between cure in section 2-612 and the seller's right to cure in section 2-508.[171] First, how does one tell whether a defect is curable for purposes of section 2-612(2)? The logical

---

[168] U.C.C. § 2-612(1).

[169] U.C.C. § 2-612, Official Comment 1; Traynor v. Walters, 342 F. Supp. 455, 10 UCCR 965 (M.D. Pa. 1972).

[170] The statutory langauge provides that the "buyer may reject any installment which is non-conforming if the non-conformity substantially impairs the value of that installment and cannot be cured or if the non-conformity is a defect in the required documents; but if the non-conformity does not fall within subsection (3) and the seller gives adequate assurance of its cure the buyer must accept that installment." U.C.C. § 2-612(2).

[171] *See* § 5.03[B], *supra.*

place to look would be section 2-508, which describes a seller's right to cure a defective tender. If, for example, section 2-508 governs cure under section 2-612, then subsection (2) of section 2-508 requires that the seller have reasonable grounds, at the time of tender, to believe that the goods would be acceptable to the buyer. If the seller does not have reasonable grounds to believe that the goods would be acceptable and the defect substantially impairs the value of an installment, the non-conformity cannot be cured, and the buyer can reject the installment. Furthermore, section 2-508 requires that the buyer make a "conforming delivery"[172] or substitute a "conforming tender."[173] If this criterion were applied to a cure under section 2-612(2), it would be insufficient for the seller to correct the delivery of an installment so that it substantially conforms to the contract; his cure would have to result in a perfect tender.

The assumption that section 2-508 provides the template for cure under section 2-612(2) should not be accepted too readily, however. First, there is no mention of section 2-508 in either the text of section 2-612 or its Comments.[174] In addition, section 2-508 is not listed in the cross-references to section 2-612. Also, Comment 5 to section 2-612 indicates that a defective delivery can often be cured by a money allowance against the price, which is something less than the conforming delivery or tender called for by section 2-508.

These discrepancies have caused a number of commentators to conclude that section 2-508 is inapplicable to installment contracts and should not determine the seller's cure rights in an installment contract.[175] Instead, the right to cure in section 2-612 is independent of section 2-508 and should be interpreted in light of the differences between installment and single delivery contracts. The drafters of the Code clearly expressed the importance of preserving the ongoing relationship inherent in an installment contract.[176] For this purpose, they made a policy choice that in an installment contract, a rejection is justified only in the event that a non-conformity results in a substantial impairment of value. If the seller delivers non-conforming goods that do not result in a substantial impairment to the value of the installment,

---

[172] U.C.C. § 2-508(1).

[173] U.C.C. § 2-508(2).

[174] Comments 5 and 6 to U.C.C. § 2-612, which deal with the curability of defects, give no indication that section 2-508 defines the seller's cure rights for purposes of section 2-612.

[175] *See* Travalio, *supra* note 49 at 1000–1001; Lawrence, *supra* note 60 at 1687.

[176] *See* Proceedings of the Larger Editorial Board, 28 A.L.I. Proc. 191–192 (1951) (remarks of Professors Llewellyn and Braucher). *See also* Midwest Mobile Diagnostic Imaging, L.L.C. v. Dynamics Corp., 965 F. Supp. 1003, 33 UCCR2d 453 (W.D. Mich. 1997).

the buyer must accept the goods and seek recovery in damages. If, however, the seller delivers a non-conforming installment that *does* cause a substantial impairment in the value of the installment, adopting the standards for cure in section 2-508 would require the seller to deliver fully conforming goods in order to avoid rejection. There is no reason to believe that requiring a perfect tender to cure a defective installment would be any less disruptive to the parties' on-going relationship than requiring a perfect tender in the first instance.[177] In fact, Comment 5 to section 2-612 implies the opposite. Therefore, a seller should not have to make a perfect tender in order to cure a defective installment under section 2-612, but merely to offer a cure that will make the buyer's loss of value insubstantial. Any further loss can be recovered through an allowance by the seller or, if necessary, through an action for money damages.[178] An offer by a seller to provide a fair and reasonable adjustment that will reduce the consequences of the defect to the point where they no longer cause a substantial impairment of value should be an effective cure under section 2-612 despite the fact that section 2-508 would require more.

On the other hand, a court may want to require that a seller have reasonable grounds at the time of tender to believe the tender would be acceptable to the buyer before the seller is entitled to cure under section 2-612(2).[179] Adopting this requirement from section 2-508 would not seem to interfere with the policies of section 2-612.[180]

The Code rules discussed thus far apply only to rejection of a defective *installment*. Under section 2-612, the fact that a buyer can reject a defective installment does not necessarily entitle the buyer to cancel the contract. Section 2-612(3) says that a buyer can cancel the contract only "[w]henever non-conformity or default with respect to one or more installments substantially impairs the value of the whole contract."[181] A substantial impairment

---

[177] *See* Lawrence, *supra* note 60 at 1689.

[178] Arkla Energy Resources v. Roye Realty & Developing, Inc., 22 UCCR2d 155 (10th Cir. 1993) (citing Travalio, *supra* note 49 at 1001–1002).

[179] U.C.C. § 2-508(2). *See* § 5.03[B][2], *supra*.

[180] Comment 5 to U.C.C. § 2-612 can provide some guidance in defining the parameters of the seller's cure rights under section 2-612. It suggests, for example, that deficiencies in quantity can sometimes be cured by partial rejection and that cure often can be effected by a money allowance.

[181] The full text of U.C.C. § 2-612 provides:

> Whenever non-conformity or default with respect to one or more installments impairs the value of the whole contract there is a breach of the whole. But the aggrieved party reinstates the contract if he accepts a non-conforming installment without seasonably notifying of cancellation or if he brings an action with respect only to past installments or demands performance as to future installments.

of the value of the whole contract may result from a defect in a single installment or it may be cumulative.[182] Whether there is a substantial impairment in the value of the whole contract is a question of fact,[183] and should take into account factors similar to those used in deciding generally whether a breach of contract is material.[184] The buyer should not be able to declare a breach of the whole contract solely because the seller's failure to deliver one or more installments makes it unlikely that further deliveries will be forthcoming. If the probability of obtaining future deliveries reasonably concerns the buyer, he should demand adequate assurance of performance (section 2-609), and only if he fails to get the assurance may he cancel future performances under an installment contract.[185]

Subsection (3) to section 2-612 permits a buyer to cancel a contract when a breach substantially impairs the value of the contract as a whole. Unlike subsection (2), subsection (3) does not premise cancellation on the inability of the seller to cure the defect. This would suggest that sellers have no right to cure defects that justify cancellation under subsection 2-612(3).

---

[182] *See* Continental Forest Prods., Inc. v. White Lumber Sales, Inc., 474 P.2d 1, 8 UCCR 178 (Or. 1970); Cherwell-Ralli, Inc. v. Rytman Grain Co., 433 A.2d 984, 29 UCCR 513 (Conn. 1980); Plotnick v. Pennsylvania Smelting & Ref. Co., 194 F.2d 859 (2d Cir. 1952) (pre-Code law).

[183] *See* Holiday Mfg. Co. v. B.A.F.S. Sys., Inc., 380 F. Supp. 1096, 15 UCCR 820 (D. Neb. 1974); Midwest Mobile Diagnostic Imaging, L.L.C. v. Dynamics Corp., 965 F. Supp. 1003, 33 UCCR2d 453 (W.D. Mich. 1997).

[184] *See* II E. Allan Farnsworth, Farnsworth on Contracts § 8.18 at 442 (1990) (doctrine of material breach is simply the converse of the doctrine of substantial performance); Burroughs Corp. v. United States, 634 F.2d 516, 30 UCCR 526 (U.S. Ct. Cl. 1980) (equating substantial impairment and material breach). The Restatement (Second) of Contracts § 241 lists the following factors that are significant in determining whether a breach is material:

> (a) the extent to which the injured party will be deprived of the benefit which he reasonably expected;
> (b) the extent to which the injured party can be adequately compensated for the part of that benefit of which he will be deprived;
> (c) the extent to which the party failing to perform or to offer to perform will suffer forfeiture:
> (d) the likelihood that the party failing to perform or to offer to perform will cure his failure, taking account of all the circumstances including any reasonable assurances:
> (e) the extent to which the behavior of the party failing to perform or to offer to perform comports with standards of good faith and fair dealing.

[185] U.C.C. § 2-612, Official Comment 6. On the other hand, if the non-conformities themselves are sufficient to be a breach of the whole contract, resort to section 2-609 on adequate assurance of performance is not required. *See* Cherwell-Ralli, Inc. v. Rytman Grain Co., 433 A.2d 984, 29 UCCR 513 (Conn. 1980) (if buyer's conduct in and of itself constitutes a substantial impairment of the value of the whole contract, resort to section 2-609 not required).

Further, there is no indication in the Comments to section 2-612 that a seller has a right to cure a defect that justifies cancellation of an installment contract. This is in contrast to the discussion in Comment 5 of the right to cure a non-conformity in an individual installment. Finally, there is an implication in the language of subsection (2) that a seller does not have the right to cure non-conformities that fall within subsection (3). Subsection (2) says that a buyer must accept an installment if the seller gives assurances of cure *and* if the non-conformity does not fall within subsection (3).

There are suggestions, however, in the few cases that are relevant, that a seller has at least a limited right of cure, even when the non-conformities constitute a breach of the whole. A number of cases suggest that the willingness and ability of the seller to quickly cure a non-conformity is a factor in determining whether a non-conformity is a substantial impairment of the value of the whole contract.[186] For example, in *Holiday Mfg. Co. v. B.A.S.F. Systems, Inc.,*[187] while acknowledging that subsection (3) contains no requirement that the non-conformity be "non-curable," the court took into account the fact that the seller promptly and adequately cured all defects in deciding whether there was a substantial impairment of the contract.

Although section 2-612(3) does not indicate that a seller has a right to cure a non-conforming installment that causes a breach of the whole contract, section 2-508 might directly apply to give the seller such a right. A number of courts have applied subsection (1) of section 2-508 to installment contracts and permitted cure by the seller if the time for performance has not yet passed.[188] There are, however, no cases that have yet decided whether the more important subsection (2) of section 2-508 can be used by a seller

---

[186] *See* Holiday Mfg. Co. v. B.A.S.F. Sys., Inc., 380 F. Supp. 1096, 15 UCCR 820 (1974) (although section 2-612(3) does not contain a requirement that the defect cannot be cured, ability of seller to cure defects was evidence that defects were not a substantial impairment); Plastic Moldings Corp. v. Park Sherman Co., 606 F.2d 117, 27 UCCR 407 (6th Cir. 1979) (assurance of cure is a factor in determining whether there is substantial impairment of whole contract); Bodine Sewer, Inc. v. Eastern Ill. Precast, Inc., 143 Ill. App. 3d 920, 493 N.E.2d 705, 1 UCCR2d 1480 (1986) (seller's willingness to cure is a factor in determining whether there is a substantial impairment of whole contract); United States ex rel. Whitaker's Inc. of Sumter v. C.B.C. Enters., Inc., 820 F. Supp. 242, 22 UCCR2d 501 (E.D. Va. 1993) (seller's unwillingness to cure non-conformities in first installment was a factor in deciding non-conformities substantially impaired value of whole contract).

[187] 380 F. Supp. 1096, 15 UCCR 820 (1974).

[188] Traynor v. Walters, 10 UCCR 965 (M.D. Pa. 1972); Bodine Sewer, Inc. v. Eastern Ill. Precast, Inc., 143 Ill. App. 3d 920, 493 N.E.2d 705, 1 UCCR2d 1480 (Ill. App. Ct. 1986). *See also* Arkla Energy Resources v. Roye Realty & Developing, Inc., 22 UCCR2d 155 (10th Cir. 1993) (court applies U.C.C. § 2-508 in determining whether seller's offer was effective cure of non-conformity in installment contract).

in an installment contract to prevent cancellation of the contract by the buyer. Section 2-508, by its terms, is not limited to single-delivery contracts, and could, therefore, provide basis for cure even though section 2-612(3) does not. Furthermore, given the drafters' expressed preference for preserving the parties' ongoing relationship in installment contracts, there is a strong reason to permit a seller to cure even if the non-conformity is a breach of the whole contract, assuming the seller is willing and able to do so quickly and with minor inconvenience to the buyer.

[D] The Obligation of Good Faith

It has been suggested in the cases and commentary that the Code's obligation of good faith imposes limits on the buyer's ability to reject goods for minor non-conformities.[189] Section 1-203 says that: "[e]very contract or duty within this Act imposes an obligation of good faith in its performance or enforcement."[190] "Good faith" is defined in section 1-201(19) as "honesty in fact in the conduct or transaction concerned."[191] A few cases have held or suggested that if a rejection, which purports to be based upon minor non-conformities in the tender or goods, is in reality based upon falling prices for the goods or some other extraneous reason, the rejection is not "honest in fact" and is impermissible under the Code.[192] In addition, section 2-103(1)(b) says that "good faith" in the case of a merchant means both honesty in fact "and the observance of reasonable commercial standards of fair dealing in the trade." This section suggests that if a rejection contravenes reasonable commercial standards of fair dealing, it would be in bad faith.[193]

There are very few cases, however, that actually *hold* that the obligation of good faith places limits on the perfect tender rule. In a number of cases, the language suggesting that good faith limits the perfect tender rule is, at best, dicta.[194] In another case often used to support a good-faith limitation,

---

[189] *See* Lawrence, *supra* note 54 at 557–573; 1 James J. White & Robert S. Summers, Uniform Commercial Code § 8-3, at 440–441 (4th ed. 1995).

[190] U.C.C. § 1-203.

[191] U.C.C. § 1-201(19).

[192] *See* George E. Warren Corp. v. Olco Oil Co. & Universal Terminals, Ltd., 1988 WL 47350 (N.D.N.Y. 1988); Oil Country Specialists, Ltd. v. Phillipp Bros., Inc., 762 S.W.2d 170 (Tex. App. 1988); Alden Press, Inc. v. Block & Co., 173 Ill. App. 3d 251, 527 N.E.2d 489, 7 UCCR2d 78 (1988).

[193] *See* Alden Press, Inc. v. Block & Co., Inc., 173 Ill. App. 3d 251, 527 N.E.2d 489, 7 UCCR2d 78 (1988).

[194] *See, e.g.*, Alden Press, Inc. v. Block & Co., 173 Ill. App. 3d 251, 527 N.E.2d 489, 7 UCCR2d 78 (1988) (court upholds finding that goods conformed to contract; comments about good faith dicta); D.P. Technology Corp. v. Sherwood Tool, Inc., 751 F. Supp. 1038,

the contract contained a condition of satisfaction, and the court held that the buyer must use good faith in determining whether the condition of satisfaction had been met. Thus, the perfect tender rule was not at issue in the case.[195] In two other cases, the courts applied the good-faith standard to a rejection, but determined that the rejection was not in bad faith.[196] In only one case has a court, in a very confused opinion, appeared to hold a rejection to be in bad faith.[197] Thus, despite the suggestion of some commentators,[198] the cases do not clearly establish that the Code's obligation of good faith limits the perfect tender rule.[199]

Application of the Code's good-faith obligation to the perfect tender rule presents a number of difficulties. First, proving the buyer's subjective state of mind is costly and prone to error.[200] Simply because the market in the goods is falling does not mean that the buyer would otherwise be satisfied with the goods. Also, in many cases the buyer's motivations are mixed; he is not entirely satisfied with the goods, but also wants to reject because of a falling market.[201] Also, as previously mentioned, the Article 1 obligation of good faith is "honesty in fact." If the buyer candidly admits that his rejection is motivated by a falling market, how can it be said that the buyer is not "honest in fact"?[202]

In addition, it is not clear that requiring a rejection to be in "good faith" is necessary to protect the seller. The cases have generally liberally

---

13 UCCR2d 686 (D. Conn. 1990) (court holds that Connecticut requires substantial non-conformity); T.W. Oil, Inc. v. Consolidated Edison Co. of N.Y., Inc., 57 N.Y.2d 574, 457 N.Y.S.2d 458, 443 N.E.2d 932, 35 UCCR 12 (N.Y. 1982) (court holds that seller was denied right to cure non-conformity).

[195] Neumiller Farms, Inc. v. Cornett, 368 So. 2d 272, 26 UCCR 61 (Ala. 1979).

[196] George E. Warren Corp. v. Olco Oil Co., WL 47350 (N.D.N.Y. 1988); Printing Ctr. of Tex., Inc. v. Supermind Publishing Co., 669 S.W.2d 779, 39 UCCR 127 (Tex. App. 1984).

[197] Oil Country Specialists, Ltd. v. Phillipp Bros., 762 S.W.2d 170 (Tex. App. 1988).

[198] *See, e.g.,* Lawrence, *supra* note 54 at 570–573; 1 James J. White & Robert S. Summers, Uniform Commercial Code § 8-3, at 440–441 (4th ed. 1995).

[199] *Cf.* Bellsouth Telesensor v. Information Sys. & Networks Corp., 65 F.3d 166 (4th Cir. 1995) (court excludes evidence of motive in revocation of acceptance).

[200] *See* Schwartz, "Cure and Revocation for Quality Defects: The Utility of Bargains," 16 B.C. Indus. & Comm. L. Rev. 543, 545 (1975).

[201] It is not clear what the test of bad faith would be in this circumstance. What, for example, should happen if neither the non-conformity nor the falling market would itself have been sufficient to motivate the buyer to reject the goods, but in combination, they are sufficient to cause the buyer to reject? Is it sufficient for the seller to show that "but for" the falling market the buyer would not have rejected, or should the seller have to show that the non-conformity played no part in the buyer's decision to reject?

[202] *See* Travalio, *supra* note 49 at 968. *But see* Robert S. Summers, " 'Good Faith' in General Contract Law and the Sales Provisions of the Uniform Commercial Code," 54 Va. L. Rev. 195, 205–206 (1968) (arguing that conduct that is not misleading may constitute bad faith).

interpreted the seller's right to cure under section 2-508.[203] If a buyer rejects goods for minor non-conformities, the seller usually has a right to cure the non-conformities and thus force the buyer to accept the goods.[204]

Some of these difficulties appear to be resolved by the application of Article 2's definition of "good faith." Section 2-103 states that in the case of a merchant, "good faith" means honesty in fact *and* the observance of reasonable commercial standards of fair dealing in the trade. Thus, it could be argued that if a merchant buyer rejects, not because of a minor non-conformity but because of a falling market, the buyer would not be observing reasonable commercial standards of fair dealing. However, the Article 2 definition of "good faith" appears to apply *only* when the term "good faith" actually appears in a section of Article 2.[205] That is, the Article 2 definition does not redefine the overarching obligation of good faith contained in section 1-203, but instead applies only to those sections in Article 2 in which the term "good faith" is expressly used. Therefore, only the Article 1 definition of "good faith" as "honesty in fact" is a potential limitation on the right of rejection.

The Code's good-faith obligation is not well suited to deal with rejections based upon a falling market. Instead, the drafters included an expanded right of cure to compensate for the rigors of the perfect tender rule. A seller who innocently delivers non-conforming goods generally has the right to cure regardless of the buyer's motivation in rejecting the goods. Trade usages also limit the ability of the buyer to reject goods with only slight non-conformities.[206] There is insufficient reason to engage in the difficult and uncertain process of determining the buyer's "true" motivation in rejecting non-conforming goods, and therefore good faith should not limit the buyer's right of rejection.

[E] Other Limitations on the Perfect Tender Rule

The Code contains a number of other limitations on the perfect tender rule, although some of them are not accurately characterized as "limita-

---

[203] *See* § 5.03[B] *supra.*

[204] *See* T.W. Oil v. Consolidated Edison Co. of N.Y., 57 N.Y.2d 574, 457 N.Y.S.2d 458, 443 N.E.2d 932, 35 UCCR 12 (1982). It is also not clear why the cases and commentators impose a good faith limitation only on the buyer's right to reject for *minor* non-conformities, not for substantial non-conformities. If motivation for a rejection is the crucial element in determining whether a rejection is justified, there is no reason why this should not be the case whether the non-conformity is minor or substantial. A rejection because of a falling market is no more "honest in fact" when the non-conformity is substantial than when it is minor, if the falling market rather than the non-conformity is the true reason for the rejection.

[205] *See* Summers, *supra* note 201 at 212–223.

[206] *See* § 5.03[E] *infra.*

tions." Usage of trade, course of dealing, and course of performance may limit a buyer's right to reject in a number of ways. They may do so directly, as for example, when a usage exists in an industry that minor non-conformities will be settled by money allowance rather than through rejection. These concepts may also serve, however, to make goods that might appear at first glance to be non-conforming actually conform to the contract. For example, there may be a usage of trade that a certain number of rotten apples in a bushel do not make the bushel of apples non-conforming.

Sections 2-504 and 2-614 place further limits on the perfect tender rule. Section 2-504 applies when a seller is required or authorized to send the goods to the buyer and the seller does not assume the risk of loss during shipment.[207] Section 2-504 requires that the seller in such a contract do three things: put the goods in the possession of the carrier and make a reasonable shipment contract; deliver or tender any documents required for the buyer to take possession of the goods; and promptly notify the buyer of the shipment. Under section 2-504, a failure to make a proper shipment contract or promptly notify the buyer of shipment is a ground for rejection only if *material* delay or loss ensues. Section 2-614 provides that a buyer may not reject delivery if an agreed-upon type of carrier or manner of delivery becomes commercially impracticable as long as a commercially reasonable substitute is available.[208]

§ 5.04   EXCUSE FROM PERFORMANCE

[A]   General

The Code contains three sections that state the general principles that relieve the seller from full performance of its contractual obligations. These principles are embodied in the common law of contracts in the doctrines of impossibility, impracticability, and implied conditions.[209] The most accurate way of describing these principles is to say that they are all intended to deal

---

[207] Such contracts are called "shipment" contracts. Contracts in which the seller is required to assume the risk of delivering the goods to a particular destination are called "destination" contracts. *See* U.C.C. § 2-504, Official Comment 1.

[208] There were a number of pre-Code cases in which a buyer in a falling market was allowed to escape from a sales contract because the goods were not delivered by the agreed-upon carrier or did not originate at the designated place. *See, e.g.*, Filley v. Pope, 115 U.S. 213 (1885); National Bank of Commerce of Norfolk v. Lamborn, 2 F.2d 23 (4th Cir. 1924).

[209] *See* American Trading & Prod. Corp. v. Shell Int'l Marine, Ltd., 453 F.2d 939 (2d Cir. 1972).

with the allocation of risks that the parties have not expressly allocated in their agreement.

The necessity for the doctrine of excuse is created by two things: the imprecision of language and the fact that people are not omniscient. For example, words chosen in a contract may be absolute and unconditional, and yet this may not be what the parties truly "intend." Further, the parties may actually intend an obligation to be unconditional within an assumed or foreseeable set of circumstances, and yet have formed no intention with respect to that obligation if the assumed set of circumstances does not exist or if an unforeseeable event occurs. Stated another way, the law of excuse deals with situations in which the parties have intended to allocate a risk in a contract in a particular way but have not adequately or clearly expressed that allocation, and also when they had no intention with respect to the allocation of that risk at all.

The task of deciding how risks were allocated by the parties' agreement is one of the more difficult problems that courts face. If the court, after applying appropriate interpretive principles, believes that the parties objectively intended to place responsibility for the occurrence or nonoccurrence of an event on one of the parties, that objective intention ought to prevail. For example, the parties may have, during the course of negotiations, considered providing an excuse for the event that occurred or for similar occurrences and rejected that alternative. Or, there may be a course of dealing, course of performance, or usage of trade that indicates that the parties intended to allocate a risk in a particular way.[210] Often, however, the court is confronted with a lack of evidence of the parties' objective intention— generally because the parties did not consider the problem at the time they entered into the contract. In this situation, there is no escape from the fact that the court's decision as to where the loss should fall is a policy determination. The result can be clothed in language of "implied intent," impossibility, or impracticability, but these expressions are shorthand methods of stating that one party or the other ought to assume responsibility for the events that occurred or did not occur.[211]

Three sections of the Code apply these ideas to contracts for the sale of goods. The first section deals with casualty to identified goods,[212] the

---

[210] *See* Columbia Nitrogen Corp. v. Royster Co., 451 F.2d 3, 9 UCCR 977 (4th Cir. 1971).

[211] *See* E. Allan Farnsworth, "Disputes Over Omissions in Contracts," 68 Colum. L. Rev. 860, 861–62 (1968); Sheldon W. Halpern, "Application of the Doctrine of Commercial Impracticability: Searching for 'The Wisdom of Solomon,' " 135 U. Pa. L. Rev. 1123, 1128 (1987).

[212] U.C.C. § 2-613; *see also* § 5.04[B], *supra*.

second deals with substitute performance,[213] and the third, and by far most important of the three, deals with excuse because of a failure of presupposed conditions.[214] Each is discussed in the following sections of this text.

[B] Casualty to Identified Goods

Section 2-613 incorporates into the Code a doctrine applicable to the law of contracts[215] but attempts to make results under the doctrine more predictable than they were at common law. Section 2-613 provides:

> Where the contract requires for its performance goods identified when the contract is made, and the goods suffer casualty without fault of either party before the risk of loss passes to the buyer, or in a proper case under a "no arrival, no sale" (Section 2-324) then
> (a) if the loss is total the contract is avoided; and
> (b) if the loss is partial or the goods have so deteriorated as no longer to conform to the contract, the buyer may nevertheless demand inspection and at his option either treat the contract as avoided or accept the goods with due allowance from the contract price for the deterioration or the deficiency in quantity but without further right against the seller.

This section contains several conditions that must be satisfied before the relief in subsections (a) and (b) is available to the seller. These conditions vary depending upon whether the contract is a "no arrival, no sale" contract.

The "no arrival, no sale" term is sometimes used in overseas destination contracts, often when the seller is reselling goods that have been shipped by another. Whenever the term is used, the seller, unless the parties have otherwise agreed, "must properly ship conforming goods and if they arrive by any means he must tender them on arrival but he assumes no obligation that the goods will arrive unless he has caused the non-arrival."[216] Therefore, under a "no arrival, no sale" term, the seller is in default if it either ships non-conforming goods or causes their nonarrival, but if the goods are lost during shipment, the seller is not liable to the buyer for

---

[213] U.C.C. § 2-614; *see also* § 5.04[C], *supra*.

[214] U.C.C. § 2-615; *see also* § 5.04[D], *supra*.

[215] *See* Taylor v. Caldwell, 3 Best & S. 826, 122 Eng. Rep. 309 (K.B. 1863). In this case, a hired hall was destroyed after the execution of the contract but before the date set for performance. The lessor was excused from performance because the fire made performance "impossible."

[216] U.C.C. § 2-324(a).

breach. If goods under such a contract are partially lost, if they have deteriorated so that they no longer conform, or if they arrive late, the buyer is entitled to the relief provided for by subsection (b) of section 2-613.[217]

Section 2-613 provides for avoidance or partial avoidance of some contracts that do not contain a "no arrival, no sale" term. The circumstances under which section 2-613 is applicable are limited, however, and roughly coincide with the common-law doctrine of impossibility as first explicated in the famous case of *Taylor v. Caldwell*.[218] The conditions under which it is applicable are:

1. The goods must be "identified" when the contract is made. Section 2-501 defines when identification occurs, and perhaps the closest synonym for "identified" is "specified." If, at the time of the contract, the goods that are the subject matter of the contract have been singled out or "specified" (such as that particular refrigerator and no other), the first condition of section 2-613 has been met.[219] As Comment 1 to section 2-613 points out, the section is applicable only when the continued existence of goods is presupposed by the agreement. Thus, section 2-613 does not apply in cases where, at the time of the contract, the parties cannot point to *specific* goods as the subject matter of the contract.[220]

2. The contract must "require" that the identified goods be delivered in performance of the contract. The section has no application to the usual contract for the sale of goods in which the seller is not required to deliver a particular item of goods but may deliver any goods fitting a generic contract description. The first two conditions should be read together to under-

---

[217] In theory, the seller would also be entitled to the relief in subsection (a), but because total avoidance is part of the meaning of a "no arrival, no sale" contract, there is no reason to rely on subsection (a).

[218] 3 Best & S. 826, 122 Eng. Rep. 309 (K.B. 1863).

[219] *See, e.g.*, Bunge Corp. v. Recker, 519 F.2d 449, 17 UCCR 400 (8th Cir. 1975); Bender & Sons, Inc. v. Crown Recreation, Inc., 548 F. Supp. 1018, 34 UCCR 1587 (E.D.N.Y. 1982) (combat boots not identified at the time contract was made). The drafters also intended to include cases in which the goods were already destroyed at the time of contracting without the knowledge of either party. U.C.C. § 2-613, Official Comment 2.

[220] U.C.C. § 2-615 might, however, apply in these cases, as where, for example, a specially manufactured machine is constructed subsequent to the contract, and then is destroyed prior to the risk of loss passing to the buyer. *See* § 5.04[D], *supra*. Such goods would be "future goods," and, under section 2-501, identification with respect to future goods does not occur until the goods are "shipped, marked, or otherwise designated by the seller as goods to which the contract refers." U.C.C. § 2-501(1)(b). Because identification would not occur in such a case until after the contract was made, section 2-613 would not, by its terms, be applicable.

stand the limited scope of section 2-613; the contract must obligate the seller to deliver a specific item or items and none other.[221]

3. The goods must suffer casualty.

4. The casualty must be suffered without the fault of either party. The inference from this requirement is that if the buyer is at fault, he will remain obligated to purchase, but if the seller is at fault, he will remain obligated to deliver.[222] One court has said that the seller has the burden of establishing that the loss was not the fault of the seller before section 2-613 is available.[223]

5. The risk of loss must not have passed to the buyer. If the risk of loss has passed to the buyer, the section has no application, and the contract is not partially or wholly avoided by any casualty to the goods.[224]

Although most of the requirements are relatively straightforward and there has been little litigation involving section 2-613, the requirement that the contract require for its performance goods that have been identified to the contract can be troublesome, as illustrated by the case of *Emery v. Weed*.[225] In this case, the buyer contracted to purchase a Chevrolet Pacer Corvette from the seller. The automobile was on the seller's showroom floor at the time of the contract and was the only Corvette Pacer, of the 6,500 manufactured, that had been allocated to the seller. Between the time of the contract and the time of delivery, two unfortunate things happened: the buyer died, and the car was stolen from the seller's lot. When the buyer's father sought to cancel the contract and receive back the $12,229.90 downpayment that his son had made, the seller refused the refund and offered to replace the Pacer Corvette with another obtained from another dealer. The father refused the offer and sued to recover the purchase price.

---

[221] *See, e.g.*, Dreyfus Co. v. Royster Co., 501 F. Supp. 1169, 31 UCCR 1366 (E.D. Ark. 1980) (contract did not require the delivery of any particular soybeans); Valley Forge Flag Co. v. New York Dowel & Moulding Import Co., 90 Misc. 2d 414, 395 N.Y.S.2d 138, 21 UCCR 1320 (Civ. Ct. 1977) (U.C.C. § 2-613 does not apply to "fungible goods"; there must be a meeting of the minds as to the particular goods to be bought and sold).

[222] *See* Beal v. Griffin, 849 P.2d 118, 21 UCCR2d 244 (Idaho Ct. App. 1993); Carlson v. Nelson, 204 Neb. 765, 285 N.W.2d 505, 28 UCCR 80 (1979) (citing the predecessor to this text).

[223] *See* Carlson v. Nelson, 204 Neb. 765, 285 N.W.2d 505, 28 UCCR 80 (1979) (citing the predecessor to this text).

[224] *See* Salinas v. Flores, 583 S.W.2d 813, 26 UCCR 1159 (Tex. App. 1979). In this case, the court held that in the sale of a "patch" of watermelons, the risk of loss passed to the buyer at the time of the contract.

[225] 494 A.2d 438, 41 UCCR 115 (Pa. Super. Ct. 1985).

The buyer claimed that under section 2-613, the contract was avoided because the car, having never been recovered, was a total loss. The seller claimed that 2-613 was inapplicable because the contract did not require the delivery of the particular Chevrolet Pacer Corvette. The seller said that all Pacer Corvettes were identical, and that the contract merely required the delivery of a new Pacer Corvette, something that it had offered to do; according to the seller, the contract did not *require* the delivery of the Pacer Corvette that had been identified on the showroom floor. With little discussion, the court held that the contract did require the delivery of the particular Corvette from the showroom floor, and therefore, section 2-613 was applicable. The court appeared to rely on the fact that the contract specified the Corvette by serial number, and the car had been removed from the showroom floor prior to being stolen. The court rejected any argument that the goods had to be unique to be covered by section 2-613; all that was required was that the contract required for its performance the Pacer Corvette identified when the contract was made.

The court was probably correct in its conclusion that section 2-613 was applicable to the contract. However, the circumstances that the written contract identified the automobile by serial number and that it was removed to the back lot do not *necessarily* establish the applicability of section 2-613. Although these facts establish that the car was identified at the time of the contract, they do not establish the additional prerequisite that the contract *required* the delivery of the identified vehicle. It is certainly possible that the Corvette was identified at the time of the contract, and yet the parties intended that the delivery of any Pacer Corvette would satisfy the seller's obligations under the contract. There is no avoiding the sometimes difficult factual inquiry into whether the parties objectively intended that the seller could satisfy its contractual obligations *only* by delivery of the particular car identified at the time of the contract.

Assuming that section 2-613 is applicable, if the loss is total, the contract is "avoided." The seller is not obligated to deliver, and, as illustrated by *Emery*, the buyer is not obligated to pay. Neither party is in default for the failure to perform. If the loss is partial, the contract is wholly avoided only if the buyer so chooses. The buyer is given the right to inspect the goods to decide whether to accept them or to avoid the entire contract. If the buyer decides to accept, "due allowance" is to be made from the contract price. On some occasions, the computation of this allowance will be mechanical—as where a specific portion of the goods has been destroyed but the remaining portion has not been harmed. In other cases, as when there is only one good that is damaged or when the deterioration affects all of the goods, it may be difficult to determine what constitutes a "due allowance." This does not, however, seem to have been a problem thus far with section 2-316, probably because the buyer retains the right to completely avoid the contract if an allowance offered by the seller is insufficient.[226]

[C]   Substitute Performance

Another excuse provision that has seen very little litigation is section 2-614. The section has been briefly described previously,[227] and applies in limited circumstances. Some contracts for the sale of goods contain an agreement as to the berthing, loading, or unloading facilities that are to be used in the performance of the seller's obligations. Others may contain a provision as to the type of carrier or manner of delivery to be used by the seller. These provisions become part of the seller's contractual obligations, and the perfect tender rule would normally require that the seller fully comply with them before the buyer becomes obligated to accept and pay for the goods. Section 2-614, however, provides a limited excuse from complying with these provisions when it becomes impracticable to do so. Section 2-614(1) provides:

> Where without fault of either party the agreed berthing, loading, or unloading facilities fail or an agreed type of carrier becomes unavailable or the agreed manner of delivery otherwise becomes commercially impracticable but a commercially reasonable substitute is available, such substitute performance must be tendered and accepted.

This subsection does not apply if all that is involved is a seller who has found that the agreed facilities, carrier, or manner of delivery has become financially burdensome. The facility must "fail"; the carrier must become "unavailable"; the manner of delivery must become "commercially impracticable."[228] When any of these tests is met and a commercially reason-

---

[226] It is possible, however, that the buyer may need the goods, even in their deteriorated form, and the seller is unwilling to give what the buyer considers to be a "due allowance." Under U.C.C. § 2-613, the buyer has the right to the goods and also has the right to a "due allowance" for their damaged condition. Under these conditions, the leverage of avoiding the contract may be insufficient to convince the seller to satisfy the buyer's demands for allowance, and the buyer may have to sue and have the court determine the amount of the allowance.

[227] *See* § 5.04[B], *supra.*

[228] *See* Camden Iron & Metal, Inc. v. Bomar Resources, Inc., 719 F. Supp. 297, 12 UCCR2d 398 (D.N.J. 1989) (condition of ship rendered ability to load "commercially impracticable" when condition was extreme deviation from foreseeable contingencies).

able substitute is available, that substitute must be tendered and accepted.[229] It is the seller's obligation to tender the reasonable substitute (assuming one is available) and if the seller does not, the seller will be in breach if the goods are not delivered in accordance with the contract.[230] The failure of the seller to attempt to find a commercially reasonable substitute may deprive the seller of the excuse as well.[231]

Section 2-614 does not provide an excuse when the party seeking excuse has caused the problem. For example, in *S&S, Inc. v. Meyer*[232] the court held that a grain dealer was not entitled to the protection of section 2-614 when the dealer's criminal indictment and loss of license necessitated an assignment of the contract and a change in the delivery arrangements. Also, the availability and consequences of an excuse under section 2-614 can be modified by agreement of the parties. In *Jon-T Chemicals, Inc. v. Freeport Chemical Co.*,[233] the court held that a *force majeure* clause in a contract excused the seller from its obligation to deliver the goods when the agreed method of transportation (rail) became unavailable without regard to whether the seller had looked for and tendered a commercially reasonable substitute.

[D] Excuse by Failure of Presupposed Conditions

By far the most significant excuse section in Article 2 is section 2-615. It is broader in scope and more general in application than either section 2-613 or section 2-614. The ideas it seeks to capture are difficult to state in terms of a general rule, and the drafters may have been better advised to simply permit the common-law doctrines of mistake, impossibility (as expanded by courts to include impracticability),[234] and frustration of purpose to operate through section 1-103. It is questionable whether the section adds anything to these concepts as they have developed over the years, and it is unlikely that the section has altered the result that would otherwise have occurred in very many, if any, cases.

Section 2-615 provides:

---

[229] If a commercially reasonable substitute is not available, the seller is excused from performing if the facts bring the case within U.C.C. § 2-615. *See* § 5.04[D], *infra*.

[230] *See* Caruso-Rinella-Battaglia Co., Inc. v. Delano Corp. of Am., 1966 WL 8971, 3 UCCR 863 (U.S. Dept. Agric. 1966).

[231] *See* Nova Springs Coop. Co. v. Brandan, 247 N.W.2d 744, 20 UCCR 909 (Iowa 1976).

[232] 478 N.W.2d 857, 17 UCCR2d 137 (Iowa Ct. App. 1991).

[233] 704 F.2d 1412, 36 UCCR 154 (5th Cir. 1983).

[234] The doctrine of commercial impracticability appears to be traceable to Mineral Park Land Co. v. Howard, 172 Cal. 289, 156 P. 458 (1916).

Except so far as a seller may have assumed a greater obligation and subject to the preceding section on substituted performance:

(a) Delay in delivery or non-delivery in whole or part by a seller who complies with paragraphs (b) and (c) is not a breach of his duty under a contract for sale if performance as agreed has been made impracticable by the occurrence of a contingency the non-occurrence of which was a basic assumption on which the contract was made or by compliance in good faith with any applicable foreign or domestic governmental regulation or order whether or not it later proves to be invalid.

(b) Where the causes mentioned in paragraph (a) affect only a part of the seller's capacity to perform, he must allocate production and deliveries among his customers but may at his option include regular customers not then under contract as well as his own requirements for further manufacture. He may so allocate in any manner which is fair and reasonable.

(c) The seller must notify the buyer seasonably that there will be a delay or non-delivery and, when allocation is required under paragraph (b), of the estimated quota thus made available for the buyer.

The central thrust of section 2-615 is found in subsection (a). The section sets out three basic criteria for excuse: (1) a contingency must occur; (2) the nonoccurrence of the contingency must have been a basic assumption on which the contract was made; and (3) the occurrence of the contingency has made performance impracticable. Alternatively, the seller will also be excused if performance has been made impracticable by a government regulation or order.

Section 2-615 is made necessary by the realization that the language that parties use in their agreements sometimes inartfully or incompletely states the risks that each party has assumed. For example, a buyer, by entering into a fixed-price contract for the future delivery of goods, may intend to assume the risk that at the time of delivery the price of the goods will decline. Conversely, the seller in the same contract may be willing to supply those goods at a fixed price, realizing that there is a risk that he could sell the goods at the time of delivery to another buyer at a higher price. The language of the parties' agreement simply says that the buyer agrees to buy the goods and the seller agrees to sell them and deliver them at a particular time, with no qualifications or exceptions. Nevertheless, the obligations of the parties may have rested on certain assumptions that were never expressed, or perhaps never consciously considered. For example, the parties may have assumed that a flood would not occur, making timely delivery of shoes impossible.[235] Or they may not have anticipated that one of the worst

---

[235] *See* SCA Int'l, Inc. v. Garfield & Rosen, Inc., 337 F. Supp. 246, 10 UCCR 1062 (D. Mass. 1971).

droughts on record would occur causing the seller's source of peanuts to dry up.[236] If these assumptions turn out to be incorrect and events occur that the parties assumed would not occur, enforcing the contract as stated in the parties' words may result in a contract to which the parties never agreed.

While the theory behind section 2-615 might be easy to state, however, it has proven extremely difficult to apply. The law reviews are filled with articles suggesting how section 2-615 should be properly applied.[237] The fundamental problem is that simply because the parties entered into the contract on the basis of certain shared assumptions it is not necessarily the case that the seller (or the buyer)[238] should be relieved of its obligations if the assumptions turn out to be incorrect. For example, it may be evident from their negotiations or otherwise that the parties actually intended that the seller take the risk that the assumption was mistaken.[239] And, even when the intentions of the parties cannot be ascertained, there must be some reason to believe that it is better to condition the seller's obligation on the failed assumption rather than require performance notwithstanding the occurrence of the unanticipated contingency. After all, excusing the seller from performance may result in great harm to the buyer, who may have planned its

---

[236] *See* Alimenta (U.S.A.), Inc. v. Cargill, Inc., 861 F.2d 650, 7 UCCR2d 1100 (11th Cir. 1988).

[237] *See, e.g.*, P.J.M. Declercq, "Modern Analysis of the Legal Effect of Force Majeure Clauses in Situations of Commercial Impracticability," 15 J.L. & Com. 213 (1995); Halpern, *supra* note 210; Alan J. Sykes, "The Doctrine of Commercial Impracticability in a Second-Best World," 19 J. Legal Stud. 43 (1990); Stephen Walt, "Expectations, Loss Distribution and Commercial Impracticability," 24 Ind. L.J. 65 (1990); Stephen G. York, "Re: The Impracticability of the U.C.C.," 29 Duq. L. Rev. 221 (1991).

[238] By its terms, U.C.C. § 2-615 only provides an excuse to the seller. On the other hand, Comment 9 suggests that when it is reasonable to assume that the buyer's obligation was conditioned upon a definite and specific venture or assumption, the "reason" of section 2-615 would apply to buyers as well. Furthermore, even without this direction, the excuse of commercial impracticability is sufficiently well established in the common law to be available to buyers under section 1-103. *See* Restatement (Second) of Contracts § 261 (1981). The cases have uniformly permitted a buyer to plead commercial impracticability. *See, e.g.*, Sabine Corp. v. Org. W., Inc., 725 F. Supp. 1157, 11 UCCR2d 83 (W.D. Okla. 1989); Lawrence v. Elmore Bean Warehouse, Inc., 702 P.2d 930, 41 UCCR 358 (Idaho 1985); Northern Ill. Gas Co. v. Energy Coop., Inc., 122 Ill. App. 3d 940, 461 N.E.2d 1049, 38 UCCR 1222 (1984); Power Eng'g & Mfg., Ltd. v. King Int'l, 501 N.W.2d 490, 23 UCCR2d 382 (Iowa 1993). As with sellers, their claims are rarely successful.

[239] As is the case throughout this text, we are speaking of the *objective* intentions of the parties. A seller may not have subjectively intended to bear the risk of a certain contingency, but if the reasonable understanding of the seller's acts and words is that the seller has assumed this risk, he will be deemed to have done so. *See* Restatement of Contracts (Second) § 201 (1981).

activities on having a long-term supply of goods available at a particular price.[240]

[1] Basic Assumption

For an assumption to justify excusing the seller from its contract, the assumption must be one that is shared by both parties.[241] In addition, while the parties may have shared many assumptions about the conditions likely to exist at the time of performance, for an assumption to excuse the seller it must be *basic*. While it is not clear what the drafters meant by a "basic" assumption, the cases establish that a primary ingredient is whether the event that the parties assumed would not occur was foreseeable. It is a rare case where the issue of foreseeability is not central to the court's decision as to whether a contingency should excuse the seller from responsibility for performance under section 2-615. A significant number of cases have either stated or suggested that proving that the contingency was unforeseeable is indispensable to establishing an excuse under section 2-615.[242] In almost all other cases, it is either the primary factor or the sole factor addressed by

---

[240] *See, e.g.,* Florida Power & Light Co. v. Westinghouse Elec. Corp., 517 F. Supp. 440, 31 UCCR 930 (E.D. Va. 1981); Missouri Pub. Serv. Co. v. Peabody Coal Co., 583 S.W.2d 721, 27 UCCR 103 (Mo. Ct. App. 1979).

[241] For example, in Power Eng'g & Mfg., Ltd. v. King Int'l, 501 N.W.2d 490, 23 UCCR2d 382 (Iowa 1993), the buyer contracted to buy goods from the seller for resale to Iraq. When the Gulf War broke out and economic sanctions were imposed upon Iraq, the buyer could no longer sell the goods to Iraq and sought to be excused from the contract. The court held that since the seller had never been told that the buyer intended to sell the goods to Iraq, there was no shared assumption that Iraq would be available as a customer for resale of the goods.

[242] *See, e.g.,* Cliffstar Corp. v. Riverbend Prods., Inc., 750 F. Supp. 81, 13 UCCR2d 392 (W.D.N.Y. 1990) (whether a contingency was a basic assumption "hinges on" whether it was foreseeable); Eastern Air Lines, Inc. v. Gulf Oil Corp., 415 F. Supp. 429, 19 UCCR 721 (S.D. Fla. 1975) (if a contingency is foreseeable, it and its consequences are taken outside the scope of U.C.C. § 2-615); Northern Ill. Gas Co. v. Energy Coop., Inc., 122 Ill. App. 3d 940, 461 N.E.2d 1049, 38 UCCR 1222 (1984) (question of whether the occurrence of an event was a basic contract assumption is a question of foreseeability); Alamance County Bd. of Educ. v. Bobby Murray Chevrolet, Inc., 121 N.C. App. 222, 465 S.E.2d 306, 28 UCCR2d 1220 (1996) (failure of seller to provide for a foreseeable contingency precludes application of section 2-615); Heat Exchangers, Inc. v. Map Constr. Corp., 34 Md. App. 679, 368 A.2d 1088, 21 UCCR 123 (1977) (foreseeability of lack of supplies makes section 2-615 inapplicable). *See also* Roy v. Stephen Pontiac-Cadillac, Inc., 15 Conn. App. 101, 543 A.2d 775, 7 UCCR2d 1507 (1988) (applicability of defense of commercial impracticability turns largely on foreseeability); Canusa Corp. v. A&R Lobosco, Inc., 986 F. Supp. 723, 35 UCCR2d 73 (E.D.N.Y. 1997).

the court in making its decision as to whether the nonoccurrence of a contingency was a basic assumption of the contract.[243]

The Comments to section 2-615 also point to the central importance of foreseeability. In fact, Comment 1 to section 2-615 supports those courts that have decided that the lack of foreseeability of the intervening event is an essential element of excuse under the section:

> This section excuses a seller from timely delivery of goods contracted for, where his performance has become commercially impracticable because of *unforeseen* supervening circumstances not within the contemplation of the parties at the time of contracting.[244]

Comment 6 is similar to Comment 1 in its emphasis on foreseeability:

> Thus the exemptions of [section 2-615] do not apply when the contingency in question is sufficiently foreshadowed at the time of contracting to be included among the business risks which are fairly to be regarded as part of the dickered terms, either consciously or as a matter of reasonable, commercial interpretation from the circumstances.[245]

Other Comments point in a similar direction.[246]

---

[243] *See, e.g.*, Arabian Score v. Lasman Arabian Ltd., 814 F.2d 529, 3 UCCR2d 590 (8th Cir. 1987); Waldinger Corp. v. CRS Group Eng'rs, Inc., 775 F.2d 781, 42 UCCR 172 (7th Cir. 1985); Bernina Distribs., Inc. v. Bernina Sewing Mach. Co., 646 F.2d 434, 31 UCCR 461 (10th Cir. 1981); Bende & Sons, Inc. v. Crown Recreation, Inc., 548 F. Supp. 1018, 34 UCCR 1587 (E.D.N.Y. 1982); Florida Power & Light Co. v. Westinghouse Elec. Corp. (In re Westinghouse Elec. Corp. Uranium Contracts), 517 F. Supp. 440, 31 UCCR 930 (E.D. Va. 1981); Iowa Elec. Light & Power Co. v. Atlas Corp., 467 F. Supp. 129, 23 UCCR 1171 (N.D. Iowa 1978); Sunflower Elec. Coop., Inc. v. Tomlinson Oil Co., 638 P.2d 963, 32 UCCR 1462 (Kan. Ct. App. 1981); Missouri Pub. Serv. Co. v. Peabody Coal Co., 583 S.W.2d 721, 27 UCCR 103 (Mo. Ct. App. 1979); Helms Constr. & Dev. Co. v. State *ex rel.* Dept. of Highways, 97 Nev. 500, 634 P.2d 1224, 32 UCCR 859 (1981); Maple Farms, Inc. v. City Sch. Dist. of Elmira, 76 Misc. 2d 1080, 352 N.Y.S.2d 784, 14 UCCR 722 (Sup. Ct. 1974); Westech Eng'g, Inc. v. Clearwater Constructors, Inc., 835 S.W.2d 190, 20 UCCR2d 36 (Tex. App. 1992); Syrovy v. Alpine Resources, Inc., 68 Wash. App. 35, 841 P.2d 1279, 19 UCCR2d 995 (1992); Canusa Corp. v. A&R Lobosco, Inc., 986 F. Supp. 723, 35 UCCR2d 73 (E.D.N.Y. 1997).

[244] U.C.C. § 2-615, Official Comment 1 (emphasis added).

[245] U.C.C. § 2-615, Official Comment 6.

[246] For example, Comment 4 states that, "[i]ncreased cost alone does not excuse performance unless the rise in cost is due to some unforeseen contingency which alters the essential nature of performance."

This emphasis on foreseeability is understandable. As a number of cases have explicitly recognized, if an event that may make performance impracticable is known or should be known to the seller at the time of contracting, and yet the seller accepts an obligation that is not conditioned upon the nonoccurence of that event, there is at least an inference raised that the seller is undertaking to perform whether the contingency occurs or not.[247] A buyer who receives the unqualified promise of the seller to provide goods, despite the apparent possibility of an event that may make the seller's performance impracticable, is generally reasonable in believing that the seller has not conditioned performance on the nonoccurrence of the event.

A number of notable section 2-615 cases resulted from the economic effects of the Arab oil embargo of the 1970s. In these cases, the oil embargo and the creation of OPEC caused the cost of the seller's performance to increase, sometimes dramatically, and the seller sought relief from a fixed-price, long-term contract. For example, in *Missouri Public Service Co. v. Peabody Coal Co.*,[248] the seller agreed in December 1967 to provide the utility buyer's requirements for coal for a period of ten years. During the negotiations, the seller sought a price escalator based upon the consumer price index (CPI). This escalator was rejected by the buyer, and the parties agreed on a price escalator based upon the Industrial Commodities Index (ICI). The ICI was largely a function of material production costs. The contract was profitable for the first few years, but thereafter production costs for the coal began to outpace the ICI, and by 1974, the disparity had become so great that the seller requested a modification of the price-adjustment index. The buyer refused to modify the price-adjustment features, but did offer a $1.00-per-ton increase in the base price, which was refused by the seller. The seller then sought relief from the contract under section 2-615, claiming that both the failure of the ICI to track actual inflation in production costs and the Arab oil embargo were events, the nonoccurence of which were basic to the contract and which had rendered performance impracticable.

The court's analysis revolved entirely around whether these events were foreseeable at the time of the contract.[249] It held that both the lack of con-

---

[247] *See* Eastern Air Lines, Inc. v. McDonnell Douglas Corp., 532 F.2d 957, 19 UCCR 353 (5th Cir. 1976); Eastern Air Lines, Inc. v. Gulf Oil Corp., 415 F. Supp. 429, 19 UCCR 721 (S.D. Fla. 1975); Roy v. Stephen Pontiac-Cadillac, Inc., 15 Conn. App. 101, 543 A.2d 775, 7 UCCR2d 1507 (1988).

[248] 583 S.W.2d 721, 27 UCCR 103 (Mo. Ct. App. 1979).

[249] As the court put it: "Central to this concept [excuse under 2-615] is that the doctrine may be applicable upon the occurrence of a supervening, unforeseen event not within the

gruity between production costs and the ICI and the Arab oil boycott were foreseeable and, therefore, that the seller was not entitled to excuse from performance. The court said that the factors that made up the ICI were known to the seller and that both parties were skilled and experienced in making these kind of judgments. Thus, a divergence between production costs and the ICI was foreseeable. Similarly, because the possibility of a boycott by the Arab countries was "common knowledge and had been thoroughly discussed and recognized for many years by our government, media economists, and business,"[250] it, too, was foreseeable.[251]

With one notable exception,[252] sellers in other cases in which excuse was premised, at least in part, upon an increase in the cost of supplies caused by the Arab oil embargo met a similar fate, with the courts holding that the embargo was foreseeable and, therefore, not a contingency that would satisfy section 2-615.[253]

The difficulties encountered by the nuclear power industry in the 1970s and 1980s also contributed a number of cases in which sellers claimed excuse as a result of dramatic increases in their costs and in which the court's primary focus was the foreseeability of the problems that the entire industry would encounter. *Iowa Electric Light & Power v. Atlas Corp.*[254] involved the agreement by a seller to provide "yellowcake" uranium to a utility for operation of the utility's nuclear power facilities. During a four-year period of the contract, the seller's costs increased seven-fold, causing millions of dollars in losses. The seller blamed the dramatic rise in its costs on a number of factors: (1) large increases in expenditures to meet environmental and safety regulations; (2) the Arab oil embargo and the OPEC

---

reasonable contemplation of the parties at the time the contract was made." 583 S.W.2d at 725–726, 27 UCCR at 110.

[250] 583 S.W.2d at 728, 27 UCCR at 113.

[251] One wonders, if the boycott was so foreseeable, why the United States was so ill-prepared when it occurred.

[252] Aluminum Co. of Am. v. Essex Group, Inc., 499 F. Supp. 53, 29 UCCR 1 (W.D. Pa. 1980). The result in this case is at least partially explainable by the timing of the contract. As the court pointed out, the contract in this case was concluded in 1967; thus, it antedated the 1971 OPEC price increase and the Arab oil boycott by a number of years. In most of the other boycott-related cases, the contract was concluded much closer to the time of the oil price increase and boycott when these events were presumably more foreseeable.

[253] *See, e.g.,* Eastern Air Lines, Inc. v. Gulf Oil Corp., 415 F. Supp. 429, 19 UCCR 721 (S.D. Fla. 1975) (contract to sell jet fuel); Publicker Indus. Inc. v. Union Carbide Corp., 17 UCCR 989 (E.D. Pa. 1975) (contract to sell ethanol); Helms Constr. & Dev. Co. v. State, 97 Nev. 500, 634 P.2d 1224, 32 UCCR 859 (1981) (contract to pave highways with asphalt).

[254] 467 F. Supp. 129, 23 UCCR 1171 (N.D. Iowa 1978).

cartel; (3) an increase in the cost of chemicals and equipment; (4) the significant inflation in wages in the industry; and (5) certain developments in the uranium market. Because of these events, the seller claimed that its costs had climbed to the point that continued performance of the contract was impracticable, and it sought relief under section 2-615.

The court's focus was on the foreseeability of the price increase and the events that caused it.[255] In an opinion that is not entirely unsympathetic to the seller, the court nonetheless held that the seller had not established that the events were sufficiently unforeseeable to justify excuse under section 2-615:

> While some of these phenomena may have been unforeseen, and certainly the total impact was not contemplated by either party during contract negotiations, the evidence in this case shows that prior to the contract being signed there was good reason to anticipate rising costs and drastically increased expenditures for environmental and safety equipment and procedures. . . . It would be unfair to expect Atlas to have prophesied the magnitude of the increases complained of, but it is not clear that it was not in a position to protect itself contractually from some of the risks which would drive the price of yellowcake up and consequently affect the cost of production.[256]

Thus, the court held that the seller had not established an excuse under section 2-615, at least in the absence of proof as to what share of the total increase was assignable to unforeseen conditions.[257]

---

[255] According to the court:

> Where the risk of substantially increased costs is not allocated by the contract, § 2-615 comes into play and the court looks to the foreseeability of the conditions claimed as a basis for excuse and the nature of the burden to determine if the occurrence or occurrences make performance commercially impracticable.

467 F. Supp. at 134, 23 UCCR at 1177.

[256] *Id.* at 134–135, 23 UCCR at 1178.

[257] *Id.* at 135, 23 UCCR at 1178. On a later motion to amend the court's opinion, the court gave the seller the opportunity to demonstrate which costs were the result of unforeseeable events. 25 UCCR 163 (N.D. Iowa 1978). The seller's attempt was completely unsuccessful. The court held that (1) the cost increases from the events that the seller claimed were unforeseeable were not sufficient to justify excuse; (2) while the events that caused the price increase may have been somewhat unforeseeable, the seller was in a better position to anticipate them and guard against them than the buyer; and (3) the seller was better able to bear the risk than the buyer, and did in fact, successfully spread the risk through highly profitable subsequent contracts that took advantage of some of the same events that had made the contract with the buyer unprofitable.

While the emphasis on foreseeability is understandable, the quotation in the previous paragraph illustrates at least one of the difficulties that the standard presents. Events are not "foreseeable" or "unforeseeable"; they are *more* or *less* foreseeable. A bright line separating foreseeable events from unforeseeable events does not accord with our everyday reality. It is perfectly sensible and consistent with our common understanding to say that the stock market crash of 1929 was less foreseeable than the stock market crash of 1987 which, in turn, was less foreseeable than the "correction" of 1997. At what point an event becomes sufficiently unforeseeable to merit an excuse is the crux of the problem, not simplistically deciding whether an event is foreseeable or unforeseeable.

Even acknowledging that in common understanding events are more or less foreseeable does not explain what the idea of foreseeability is intended to capture. In the context of the foreseeability of damages for breach, Professor Patrick Atiyah has put it well:

> There does seem to be an air of unreality about the foreseeability test. . . . In one sense, everything that happens according to the laws of the physical universe, and in so far as they are known (and they after all are pretty well known today) virtually any result is predictable from a base which presupposes knowledge of the original breach of contract.[258]

Atiyah's point is that so long as events behave according to our common understanding of cause and effect, we can theoretically anticipate virtually any event. For example, it is certainly foreseeable that a major earthquake ("the big one") might strike the west coast of the United States in the near future. The preconditions for such an event seem present and appear widely known.[259] Many scientists have predicted such an event,[260] and many agree that it could occur at any time. It would certainly seem odd in the face of this knowledge to say that if the "big one" occurred, it would be an unforeseeable event.

On the other hand, it does not seem at all unlikely that if a severe earthquake occurs in California, disrupting communication and transportation facilities, courts will find the performance of many contracts excused

---

[258] Patrick Atiyah, An Introduction to the Law of Contract 467–468 (5th ed. 1995).

[259] The California legislature declared in 1979 that "[b]ecause of the generally acknowledged fact that California will experience moderate to severe earthquakes in the foreseeable future, increased efforts to reduce earthquake hazards should be encouraged and supported." Cal. Health and Safety Code § 19160(a) (West 1984).

[260] *See, e.g.*, Budiansky, "A Chilling Dress Rehearsal for Calamity," U.S. News & World Rep., Oct. 12, 1987.

under section 2-615.[261] There is a sense in which the earthquake in the example above might be said to be unforeseeable and which might justify an excuse under section 2-615. The possibility of an earthquake is not something that would occur to most parties negotiating a short-term sales contract,[262] and it would not seem unusual to describe the event, should it occur tomorrow, as unexpected or unanticipated. The entire concept of foreseeability is, at best, however, imprecise and vague.[263]

We nonetheless feel that in the context of some transactions, performance should not reasonably be expected if certain events occur that render performance impracticable. This is the fundamental idea behind excuse and is only imperfectly captured in the idea of foreseeability. The inadequacy of foreseeability has led some courts and commentators to suggest, while not abandoning foreseeability entirely, that reliance solely on the concept of foreseeability is misplaced. In one of a number of cases involving the closure of the Suez canal in 1956, the court in *Transatlantic Financing Corp. v. United States*[264] considered the question of whether the closure of the canal provided an excuse for shippers who had expected to use the canal to transport goods from Europe or the United States to the Middle East or Asia. In *Transatlantic Financing*, when the canal was closed, the shipper transported the goods around the Cape of Good Hope and sought a quantum meruit recovery for the extra cost involved in delivering the goods, claiming that commercial impracticability had excused it from its original contract to deliver the goods.

Judge Wright, writing for the court, said that three requirements were necessary for a defense of impracticability:

> First, a contingency—something unexpected—must have occurred. Second, the risk of the unexpected occurrence must not have been allocated

---

[261] *See* Alimenta (U.S.A.), Inc. v. Cargill, Inc., 861 F.2d 650, 7 UCCR2d 1100 (11th Cir. 1988) (drought); Alimenta (U.S.A.), Inc. v. Gibbs Nathaniel (Canada) Ltd., 802 F.2d 1362, 2 UCCR2d 490 (11th Cir. 1986) (drought); SCA Int'l, Inc. v. Garfield & Rosen, Inc., 337 F. Supp. 246, 10 UCCR 1062 (D. Mass. 1971) (flood).

[262] However, the possibility of an earthquake might occur to the parties negotiating a long-term contract. This is not because the event is more or less "foreseeable," but because it is more likely to disrupt the contract.

[263] In the context of consequential damages, Professor Dan Dobbs had this to say about foreseeability:

> The test of foreseeability has little or no meaning. The idea is so readily subject to expansion or contraction that it becomes in fact merely a technical way in which judges can state their conclusion.

Dan B. Dobbs, Law of Remedies § 12.3 (1973).

[264] 363 F.2d 312, 3 UCCR 401 (D.C. Cir. 1966).

either by agreement of custom. Finally, occurrence of the contingency must have rendered performance commercially impracticable.[265]

Although Judge Wright said that before an excuse could be granted an "unexpected" contingency was necessary, he expressly refused to require that the contingency be "unforeseeable." According to the court's analysis, a party's apparently unconditional obligation might nonetheless be implicitly conditioned on the nonoccurence of a contingency even if the contingency was foreseeable:

> Foreseeability or even recognition of a risk does not necessarily prove its allocation [citations omitted]. Parties to a contract are not always able to provide for all the possibilities of which they are aware, sometimes because they cannot agree, often simply because they are too busy.

Judge Wright's sentiment has been echoed in some subsequent cases,[266] although there appear to be no cases in which a court has explicitly found an event to be foreseeable while at the same time excusing the seller from performance. In addition, Judge Wright's opinion did not offer much in the way of an alternative to foreseeability as a basis to resolve these cases. In fact, despite his disclaimer, foreseeability was the focus of Judge Wright's opinion and a principal reason he decided the case against the shipper.

In a seminal article,[267] Professor (now U.S. Court of Appeals Judge) Richard Posner and Professor Andrew Rosenfield posited a view that the risk of a contingency should be allocated to the party that is better able to bear that risk. A party may be better able to bear the risk because that party can more efficiently distribute the risk, more cheaply prevent the risky event from occurring, or more cheaply insure against it. The assumption is that had the parties expressly allocated the risk, they would have allocated it to the party who could bear it most cheaply.

Although this approach has received extensive commentary in the scholarly literature,[268] it has received scant attention in the cases, even

---

[265] *Id.* at 315, 3 UCCR at 403.

[266] *See* Cliffstar Corp. v. Riverbend Prods., Inc. 750 F. Supp. 81, 13 UCCR2d 392 (W.D.N.Y. 1990); Golsen v. Ong Western, Inc., 756 P.2d 1209, 5 UCCR2d 605 (Okla. 1988); Robberson Steel, Inc. v. J.D. Abrams, Inc., 582 S.W.2d 558, 27 UCCR 114 (Tex. App. 1979).

[267] Richard A. Posner & Andrew M. Rosenfield, "Impossibility and Related Doctrines in Contract Law: An Economic Analysis," 6 J. Leg. Stud. 83 (1977).

[268] *See, e.g.,* John Elofson, "The Dilemma of Changed Circumstances in Contract Law: An Economic Analysis of the Foreseeability and Superior Risk Bearer Tests," 30 Colum. J.L. & Soc. Probs. 1 (1996); Robert L. Flores, "Risk of Loss in Sales: A Missing Chapter in History of the U.C.C.: Through Llewellyn to Williston and a Bit Beyond," 27 Pac. L.J.

though some courts have implicitly used the approach as a component of their analysis.[269] In fact, while giving lip service to this approach, Judge Posner effectively ignored it in the case of *Northern Indiana Public Service Co. v. Carbon County Coal Co.*[270] In deciding whether a seller of coal who had agreed to a twenty-year fixed-price contract should be excused on impracticability grounds, Judge Posner simply (and simplistically) said that the fact that the contract was a fixed-price contract was sufficient evidence that the parties intended to place the risk on the seller and it was therefore unnecessary to inquire further.

The "better risk-bearer" approach is a useful contribution in a number of ways. First, it provides insight into how the parties might have *actually intended* to allocate the risk. That is, the parties may have actually intended that the seller, whose obligation to deliver is unqualified in the contract, bear the risk, and the fact that the seller can bear the risk more cheaply is evidence of this intention. In other words, economic analysis provides a window into the parties' actual, albeit implicit, intention as to the risk. Also, because in most cases it is impossible to determine whether the parties had an actual intent as to risk allocation, this approach provides an answer that is probably consistent with their intent if it does exist. Finally, the "better risk-bearer" approach may provide an incentive to the better risk-bearer in contracts to take economically efficient steps either to insure against a risk or to take precautions to prevent the risky event from occurring.

The reason the approach has not received a better reception in the cases is that it suffers from some serious defects. First, and most important, is the capacity of the courts to determine *ex post* who is the better risk-bearer.[271] Hindsight may appear to be a benefit, but courts must still consider and resolve such difficult (and therefore costly) factual issues as which party was the more risk averse and to what degree, what various insurance options were available to both parties and their relative costs and benefits, and the precautions that each party could have taken to avoid the risk and their costs.[272] Thus, it may be very difficult to predict in advance which party will be determined by a court to be the better risk-bearer. This uncertainty

---

161 (1996); Halpern, *supra* note 210; Andrew Kull, "Mistake, Frustration, and the Windfall Principle of Contract Remedies," 43 Hastings L.J. 1 (1991).

[269] For example, in the *Transatlantic* case discussed previously, Judge Wright decided against the shipper in part because the shipper was no less able to insure against the contingency's occurrence than the government and probably was in a better position to do so.

[270] 799 F.2d 265, 1 UCCR2d 1505 (7th Cir. 1986).

[271] *See* Halpern, *supra* note 210, at 1159–1165.

[272] *See* Robert A. Hillman, "An Analysis of the Cessation of Contractual Relations," 68 Cornell L. Rev. 617, 626–627 (1983).

will, in turn, decrease the security of contracts generally (because of the uncertainty as to whether performance will ultimately be required), and decrease the value of the approach as an incentive to efficient behavior.

Second, it is possible that parties may not have chosen, in the context of a particular transaction, to allocate a risk to the cheaper risk-bearer. Although this generally is not the case, there are plausible scenarios where it might occur. For example, a party may accept the risk of an event that the other party could bear less expensively in order to foster good will and a long-term relationship.[273] Or a party may be willing to assume a risk as compensation or in gratitude for past concessions or behavior.

Third, many of the cases involve events which neither party contemplated. Because neither foresaw the risk, neither paid the other to bear it; it was simply not seen as a cost to the contract for which one party would have to compensate the other. Therefore, to allocate the risk to the better risk-bearer is forcing a cost upon it for which it was not paid and giving the other party a benefit for which it has not paid. While this would also be true if the risk were allocated to the other party, it may in some circumstances be fairer to allocate the risk to the party better able to bear the *loss* (as opposed to the risk) of an event that was truly outside of the parties expectations even though that party was not the cheaper risk-bearer *ex ante*.

Other approaches have been suggested to resolve the problem of excuse. For example, "relational" theorists have argued that the entire concept of excuse should be replaced by a more flexible approach that would give judges significant powers to make adjustments in the rights and duties of the parties in long-term contracts to account for unanticipated events.[274] According to these commentators, such contracts should be viewed as joint ventures or partnerships in which compromise and modification is both necessary and expected. When the parties cannot accomplish this themselves, courts should be able to make the appropriate adjustments in the interests of the continuing relationship. As with the economic approach, however, with one possible exception,[275] this approach has been ignored by the courts;

---

[273] *See* Robert A. Hillman, The Richness of Contract Law 227–228 (1997). Of course, viewed in the long term, this behavior might be "efficient." However, the broader the context required to determine who was the most efficient risk-bearer, the more difficult the court's task becomes.

[274] *See* Victor P. Goldberg, "Price Adjustments in Long Term Contracts," 1985 Wis. L. Rev. 527; Halpern, *supra* note 210, at 1171–75 and authorities cited therein.

[275] Aluminum Co. of Am. v. Essex Group, Inc., 499 F. Supp. 53, 29 UCCR 1 (W.D. Pa. 1980). Although the court does not discuss the relational theorists or the approach they suggest, the complex price-adjustment formula that the judge imposed on the parties and his interest in the continued viability of the contract suggest a relational approach.

it suffers from some of the same problems of judicial capacity as the economic approach.[276]

Thus, the concept of foreseeability remains the principal tool for resolving these cases. Despite its vague and elastic nature, it is unlikely to be replaced as the primary focus in deciding whether a party has satisfied the requirements of section 2-615. This does not mean that the insights suggested by legal academics and by Judge Wright in the *Transatlantic* case should be ignored. There is nothing inconsistent with relying on both foreseeability *and* some of the tools that alternative approaches suggest. Perhaps over time a clearer synthesis will emerge.

[2] Impracticability

Section 2-615 not only requires that a contingency occur that the parties assumed would not occur, but that the occurrence of the contingency must make performance commercially impracticable. While it is clear that the drafters did not require physical impossibility as a pre-condition for excuse,[277] little else about the drafters' intentions is clear concerning the standard of impracticability. Comment 4 to section 2-615 deals with the issue and begins by stating that "[i]ncreased cost alone does not excuse performance unless the rise in cost is due to some unforeseen contingency which alters the essential nature of performance."[278] This tells us that the nonoccurence of a cost increase is not by itself a basic assumption of the contract and, therefore, it is not grounds for excuse if a cost increase occurs. The Comment, however, continues:

> Neither is a rise or collapse in the market in itself a justification, for that is exactly the type of business risk which business contracts made at fixed prices are intended to cover. But a severe shortage of raw materials or of supplies due to a contingency such as war, embargo, local crop failure, unforeseen shutdown of major sources of supply or the like, which either causes a marked increase in cost or altogether prevents the seller from securing supplies necessary to his performance is within the contemplation of this section.[279]

It is hard to know what to make of this Comment. It states that a rise in the market that causes the seller's costs to go up is "in itself" not a basis for

---

[276] *See* Halpern, *supra* note 210, at 1173.
[277] U.C.C. § 2-615, Official Comment 3.
[278] U.C.C. § 2-615, Official Comment 4.
[279] *Id.*

excuse. What the drafters intended, however, by the quoted language is impossible to discern, because markets never rise or fall "in themselves." They may rise or fall for a variety of reasons, but they never simply rise or fall without cause. The second sentence then suggests that if the seller's cost increase (i.e., a rise in the market) is caused by a shortage of raw materials or supplies due to an unforeseen contingency, it *is* within section 2-615. But Comment does not tell us what other reasons (if any) for an increase in a seller's costs might be a basis for excuse; for example, do increased environmental compliance costs or increased energy costs qualify? And, except for the single direction that the increase must be "marked," there is no indication how severe the increase in the seller's costs must be before performance will be "commercially impracticable."

It has been left to the courts to work out the meaning of "commercial impracticability" and the standard most have applied provides precious little solace to those seeking excuse. It is clear that the standard of commercially impracticability is not met simply because a contingency makes performance more burdensome than the parties expected.[280] Furthermore, the fact that the seller will suffer a loss, even a large loss, on the contract is not sufficient to render performance of the contract impracticable.[281] The consequences on performance must be so "severe"[282] as to change the essential nature of performance.[283]

Virtually no courts have excused a seller from performance whose costs have less than doubled from what were anticipated. In *Louisiana Power & Light Co. v. Allegheny Ludlum*,[284] the seller's costs of some raw materials had increased as much as 185 percent and its total costs had increased 38

---

[280]*See* Transatlantic Fin. Corp. v. United States, 363 F.2d 312, 3 UCCR 401 (D.C. Cir. 1966).

[281] *See, e.g.*, Louisiana Power & Light Co. v. Allegheny Ludlum Indus., Inc., 517 F. Supp. 1319, 32 UCCR 847 (E.D. La. 1981) (loss of $428,500); Aluminum Co. of Am. v. Essex Group, Inc., 499 F. Supp. 53, 29 UCCR 1 (W.D. Pa. 1980) (possible losses of $60 million); Missouri Pub. Serv. Co. v. Peabody Coal Co., 583 S.W.2d 721, 27 UCCR 103 (Mo. Ct. App. 1979); Iowa Elec. Light & Power Co. v. Atlas Corp., 467 F. Supp. 129, 23 UCCR 1171 (N.D. Iowa 1978) (actual losses of $1.8 million and projected losses of $4 million); Lawrence v. Elmore Bean Warehouse, Inc., 702 P.2d 930, 41 UCCR 358 (Idaho Ct. App. 1985) (price for beans dropped 40 percent); Maple Farms Inc. v. City School Dist. of Elmira, 76 Misc. 2d 1080, 352 N.Y.S.2d 784, 14 UCCR 722 (Sup. Ct. 1974) (loss of $7,350 on contract to deliver milk to school district).

[282] *See* Upsher-Smith Labs., Inc. v. Mylan Labs., Inc., 944 F. Supp. 1411, 31 UCCR2d 698 (D. Minn. 1996); Mishara Constr. Co. v. Trans-Mixed Concrete Corp., 310 N.E.2d 363, 14 UCCR 556 (Mass. 1974).

[283] Publicker Indus., Inc. v. Union Carbide Corp., 17 UCCR 989 (E.D. Pa. 1975).

[284] 517 F. Supp. 1319, 32 UCCR 847 (E.D. 1981).

percent, resulting in a loss on the contract of about a half a million dollars. The court found that this did not approach the level of severity necessary to render performance commercially impracticable. Similarly, a 52 percent increase in costs was insufficient in *Iowa Electric Light & Power v. Atlas Corp*,[285] even though losses of almost $6 million would result.[286] An even greater increase was deemed insufficient in *Publicker Industries, Inc. v. Union Carbide Corp*.[287] In this case, the seller's cost for goods during a three-year contract climbed from 21.1¢ per gallon to 37.2¢ per gallon, while its resale price under the contract was fixed at 26.5¢. Despite that fact that this would result in continuing and substantial losses, the court said that anything less than a 100 percent increase in costs would generally not suffice for a claim of commercial impracticability.

The most interesting issue that has surfaced in connection with whether performance has been rendered commercially impracticable is whether the court's focus should be solely on the contract at issue or whether other aspects of the seller's business should play a part in the analysis. Other factors might include the seller's size, its profitability, other contracts the seller might have with the buyer and others, the relationship of the contract at issue to the seller's total business, and others. To date, the courts are split on how to approach the problem. In *Aluminum Co. of America v. Essex Group*,[288] ALCOA entered into a contract with Essex to process raw alumina provided by Essex into aluminum, which it would then return to Essex for processing into aluminum wire, which Essex then sold. The contract was to run from 1967 to 1983, with Essex having the option to extend it until 1988. With Alan Greenspan (present chairman of the Federal Reserve Board) advising ALCOA, the parties agreed to a complex price-escalation clause. One index was chosen to reflect increases in ALCOA's labor costs, and the Wholesale Price Index-Industrial Commodities (WPI-IC) was selected to reflect nonlabor production costs. Historical data showed that the WPI-IC had fairly closely tracked ALCOA's nonlabor production costs in the past, and Greenspan approved of its use for this purpose. Essex agreed to these escalators, but demanded a cap on the price escalation to which ALCOA agreed.

Beginning in the early 1970s, ALCOA's nonlabor production costs began increasingly to outpace the WPI-IC, resulting in decreased profits and

---

[285] 467 F. Supp. 129, 23 UCCR 171 (N.D. Iowa 1978).

[286] *See also* Lawrence v. Elmore Bean Warehouse, Inc., 702 P.2d 930, 41 UCCR 358 (Mass. 1985) (cost increase of 40 percent insufficient).

[287] 17 UCCR 989 (E.D. Pa. 1975).

[288] 499 F. Supp. 53, 29 UCCR 1 (W.D. Pa. 1980).

huge prospective losses over the twenty-year period of the contract. The variation between ALCOA's costs and the WPI-IC were due primarily to the soaring cost of energy resulting from the Arab oil boycott and the prices fixed by the OPEC cartel. In addition, passage of environmental controls had also driven up ALCOA's production costs to a greater extent than reflected in the WPI-IC. ALCOA sought relief from the contract.

In granting ALCOA partial relief from the contract, the court focused entirely upon the particular contract at issue. In finding that the losses on the contract justified a finding of commercial impracticability, the court focused exclusively on the increase in ALCOA's costs of performing this particular contract and the absolute magnitude of the loss that continued performance would cause. It did not take into consideration ALCOA's ability to absorb the loss (either at the time of the contract or the time of the suit), the relationship of the loss to ALCOA's assets, its profitability during the contract period or other extrinsic facts.[289] Based upon this narrow view, ALCOA was granted a partial excuse.[290]

The court in *Iowa Electric Light & Power Co. v. Atlas Corp.*[291] took a slightly broader view of what information is relevant to an impracticability defense. The facts of the case are described in a previous section,[292] and involved the agreement by Atlas to sell "yellowcake" uranium to Iowa Light & Power for the operation of Iowa Light's nuclear power plants. The cost of producing uranium jumped dramatically, and total losses on the contract were projected to be close to $6 million. In deciding whether Atlas deserved to be excused from the contract, the court said that for purposes of deciding whether performance was impracticable, the contract should normally stand alone. Factors such as the overall corporate financial condition should generally be ignored. The market price for yellowcake, however, had climbed even more dramatically than the cost of production, and Atlas had subsequently entered into a series of contracts with other utilities that were very profitable. The court said that the contract in question was one of a series of contracts to provide yellowcake to various utilities, and it considered the impact of this contract in relation to the group of contracts as a whole in deciding whether Atlas should be excused from performing.[293]

---

[289] For a similar case, *see* Alimenta (U.S.A.), Inc. v. Cargill, Inc., 861 F.2d 650, 7 UCCR2d 1100 (11th Cir. 1988) (court says that net sales, net worth, and size of seller are irrelevant to a claim of commercial impracticability).

[290] *See* § 5.04[D][4], *infra.*

[291] 467 F. Supp. 179, 23 UCCR 1171 (N.D. Iowa 1978).

[292] *See* § 5.04[D][1], *supra.*

[293] 467 F. Supp. at 136, 23 UCCR at 1180–81. On a motion to amend the opinion, the court further remarked that Atlas managed to successfully spread the risk of loss through

At the other end of the spectrum is the decision in *Missouri Public Service Co. v. Peabody Coal Co.*,[294] the facts of which were also described previously.[295] The seller in this case had argued that in deciding whether its performance should be considered impracticable, only the contract at issue should be considered and that the seller's overall financial condition, its experience in the production of coal, its available reserves, and other factors apart from the contract should be ignored. The court strongly disagreed with the seller and said that these factors were directly related to the issue of impracticability:

> A commercial, governmental or business trend affecting a contract's value which would be foreseeable to a party with wide experience and knowledge in the field and, perhaps, not to a party with less; a loss to a party with vast resources and ample supply of raw materials to perform a bad bargain would be less harmful than to a party without them; and, the application of the doctrine and the equitable principles inherent therein might call for relief in one instance and not another based upon these factors, and others, outside the strict confines of the contract itself.[296]

It is not surprising that when the court considered these factors, Peabody Coal did not merit an excuse from performance.

As a general matter, the approach of the *Missouri* case is better. In deciding how much risk to accept, a party is not simply concerned with the consequences of contingencies relevant only to that particular contract. If a company is diversified, it may be willing to accept more risk on a particular contract than if the company's business is concentrated in a narrow industry. Similarly, it might be willing to accept the risk that a contingency might make a particular contract unprofitable if that same contingency is likely to make other contracts or other operations more profitable.[297] Or, very simply,

---

these highly profitable contracts. It said that although the increased cost of production altered Atlas's expectations with respect to this particular contract, it could (and did) take advantage of the inflated market price to effectively spread the loss among other buyers. 25 UCCR at 168. For a court taking a similar approach, *see* Florida Power & Light Co. v. Westinghouse Elec. Corp. (Westinghouse I), 517 F. Supp. 440, 31 UCCR 930 (E.D. Va. 1981). In this case, the court looked at a contract to provide uranium fuel as part of an "entire package" of contracts between Westinghouse and Florida Power & Light in connection with Florida's nuclear power production, some of which were quite profitable.

[294] 583 S.W.2d 721, 27 UCCR 103 (Mo. Ct. App. 1979).

[295] *See* § 5.04[D][1], *supra.*

[296] 583 S.W.2d at 726, 27 UCCR at 111.

[297] *See* Eastern Air Lines, Inc. v. Gulf Oil Corp., 451 F. Supp. 429, 19 UCCR 721 (S.D Fla. 1975).

a large company with large assets may simply be more willing to take risks than a smaller company with more of its total worth at stake in a particular contract. Thus, consideration of these facts is necessary in order to decide both whether a party may have *impliedly* assumed the risk under the contract or, if it did not, whether it should nonetheless be allocated the risk. Evaluation of these factors is required to decide whether the cost of performance has reached the point where it has such severe consequences on the party as to make performance, from an equitable standpoint, impracticable. On the other hand, this does not mean that the larger, more diverse, company should automatically lose on a claim of excuse. There may be many reasons that a party may or may not have assumed a risk in addition to the factors mentioned.

The ALCOA case is one in which the refusal of the court to look outside the contract was almost certainly wrong. The very factors that had made its contract with Essex unprofitable, especially the oil crisis of the early 1970s, dramatically increased the demand for aluminum (because of its light weight), and ALCOA was experiencing years of unprecedented profitability as a result.[298] It may very well be the case that ALCOA was willing to take the risk from the beginning that an increase in the cost of some of its production factors would outstrip the WPI-IC, knowing that an increase in the cost of these factors would also drive up demand for the very product that ALCOA produced. In any event, even if this were not the case, ALCOA was certainly the better risk-bearer of this contingency.

[3] Agreement of the Parties

Section 2-615 begins with the words, "Except so far as the seller may have assumed a greater obligation." These introductory words indicate that the seller is free to bear the risk of a contingency that might otherwise constitute an excuse. Comment 8 to section 2-615 expands upon the quoted language and says:

> The provisions of this section are made subject to assumption of greater liability by agreement and such agreement is to be found not only in the expressed terms of the contract but in the circumstances surrounding the contract.[299]

From this it is clear that the section is not intended to supplant the parties' freedom of contract or their ability to define the scope of the risk assumed

---

[298] Additional facts behind the *ALCOA* case were graciously provided by Professor Howard Marvel of the Department of Economics, The Ohio State University.

[299] U.C.C. § 2-615, Official Comment 8.

by each.[300] Furthermore, the parameters of the risks assumed, and whether those risks extend beyond the risks that would be assumed if section 2-615 were permitted to operate freely, is to be determined not only from the language of the parties' contract but from circumstances from which an allocation of risks can be inferred.

Courts have heeded the drafters' direction that the section should not be interpreted to impair the parties' freedom to allocate the risks of performance and have not allowed excuses in cases where, but for the parties' contract or the surrounding circumstances, an excuse would have otherwise been available under section 2-615. For example, the contract in *Swift Textiles, Inc. v. Lawson*[301] provided that "if for any reasons except those [in the *force majeure* clause] the seller fails to make shipment or delivery within the time specified in the contract, the buyer . . . may buy in the open market cotton equal to that contracted for . . . the market difference to be adjusted between the buyer and seller, with one quarter cent per pound penalty against the seller." When the seller asked the court to be excused from performance under section 2-615, the court said that the seller had assumed a greater obligation in the contract than section 2-615 might otherwise impose by accepting the language in the contract making the seller responsible for nondelivery *for any reason* other than those in the *force majeure* clause.[302]

Another example of how parties can expand liability by contract, even when performance becomes literally *impossible,* is *Sunflower Electric Cooperative, Inc v. Tomlinson Oil Co., Inc.*[303] In this case, the seller agreed to provide the buyer with natural gas from a particular field, and to provide a minimum amount to the buyer from the field. When it turned out that the field did not have the reserves necessary to supply the minimum amount, the seller claimed an excuse under section 2-615. The seller claimed that the parties had agreed on a particular source of supply and that the lack of reserves from that source, which the seller claimed was unforeseeable given

---

[300] Comment 8, however, does go on to say that, "[g]enerally, express agreements as to exemptions designed to enlarge upon or supplant the provisions of this section are to be read in the light of mercantile sense and reason, for this section itself sets up the commercial standard for normal and reasonable interpretation and provides a minimum beyond which the agreement cannot go." Presumably, this would prevent boilerplate clauses that attempt to prevent any excuse from performance regardless of the contingency or its effect.

[301] 135 Ga. App. 799, 219 S.E.2d 167, 18 UCCR 115 (1975).

[302] For a similar case, *see* Gold Kist, Inc. v. Stokes, 138 Ga. App. 482, 226 S.E.2d 268, 19 UCCR 1131 (1976) (contract expressly imposed liability on seller even for reasons beyond seller's control).

[303] 638 P.2d 963, 32 UCCR 1462 (Kan. Ct. App. 1981).

the information at hand, had made performance impossible. Comment 5 to section 2-615 says that "[i]n the case of failure of production by an agreed source for causes beyond the seller's control, the seller, if possible, should be excused since production by an agreed source is without more a basic assumption of the contract." The Comment seemed to support the seller's argument.

The court found that the parties had, in fact, agreed upon an exclusive source of supply (the particular field) and that the lack of reserves had made performance literally impossible. Nonetheless, the court held against the seller. The court also said that a reasonable interpretation of the contract showed that the seller had assumed the risk of literal impossibility of performance. The contract stated that natural gas was a "valuable and depleting natural resource" and that "the availability of gas to [the] Buyer is the essence of this Agreement." The court found that this language was a significant indication, along with the fact that gas reserves are "inherently unknown," that the seller had assumed the risk that reserves would be insufficient despite the fact that the parties had agreed that the gas would come from a single source. The fact that the buyer had spent large sums constructing pipeline in reliance upon the contract also indicated to the court that the seller had assumed the risk of insufficient reserves.[304]

Although the Code does not explicitly so provide, the parties can also enlarge the circumstances that will provide an excuse. For example, a number of cases have held that events encompassed by a *force majeure* clause do not necessarily have to be unforeseeable in order to provide an excuse for nonperformance.[305] This is in keeping with the philosophy of section 2-615 that the primary source for allocation of risk is the contract of the parties.

[4] Consequences of Excuse

Under section 2-615, an excuse may be total or partial. If the contingency makes it impracticable for the seller to perform any part of the con-

---

[304] *See also* Scullin Steel Co. v. Paccar, Inc., 708 S.W.2d 756, 1 UCCR2d 1172 (Mo. Ct. App. 1986) (where contract to supply material to make railroad cars was deemed by the parties to be "non-cancelable" and seller had invested substantial sums to improve plant in order to fulfill the contract, buyer was not excused from performance despite the complete collapse of the railroad car market); Cliffstar Corp. v. Riverbend Prods., Inc., 750 F. Supp. 81, 13 UCCR2d 392 (W.D.N.Y. 1990) ("time is of the essence" clause indicates an assumption of greater obligation and precludes application of U.C.C. § 2-615).

[305] *See, e.g.*, PPG Indus., Inc. v. Shell Oil Co., 919 F.2d 17, 13 UCCR2d 390 (5th Cir. 1990); Sabine Corp. v. Ong W. Corp., 725 F. Supp. 1157, 11 UCCR2d 83 (W.D. Okla. 1989).

tract, the seller is excused from performance and is not liable to the buyer for breach. In addition, because the seller has not performed, the buyer is likewise excused without liability. So, for example, if the seller's crops are completely destroyed and performance is excused under section 2-615, neither party has any further obligation to the other. It may be, however, that the contingency affects only a part of the seller's capacity to perform the contract. In addition, the seller may have other contracts for its goods as well as other potential customers. In these circumstances, the seller must allocate its remaining goods among its customers. Under the Code, the seller can make this allocation in any manner that is fair and reasonable and can include regular customers in the allocation, even though they are not under contract at the time of the contingency.[306] Also, there is no obligation that each customer receive any particular portion of the seller's goods; so long as the allocation is fair and reasonable, one customer may receive a greater portion than another customer. The seller, however, is generally not permitted to profit from the impracticability by entering into new contracts to sell the goods at higher prices if the excusing event causes prices to rise. This unfairly reduces the share of the goods that can be allocated to already existing lower-priced contracts. Comment 11 says that when prices have advanced, the seller must exercise "real care" in making allocations, and in cases of doubt should favor customers already under contract.[307] Also, although the Code does not say so specifically, the seller must deliver his production to one buyer if this is the only buyer or customer that he has at the time of the intervening impracticability.[308]

Cases involving issues of allocation are rare, in large part because parties are so rarely successful in establishing an excuse under section 2-615, and the results of the cases are unremarkable. In *Chemetron Corp. v. McLouth Steel Co.*,[309] the seller contracted to deliver oxygen and nitrogen to the buyer for the buyer's use in manufacturing steel. When a series of explosions affected the seller's ability to perform the contract, the seller delivered only about one-third of the buyer's requirements, while at the same time providing its own steel mill with 100 percent of its requirements. The

---

[306] Comment 11 says that subsections (a) and (b) of U.C.C. § 2-615 "explicitly permit in any proration a fair and reasonable attention to the needs of regular customers who are probably relying on spot orders for supplies." *See* Terry v. Atlantic Richfield Co., 72 Cal. App. 3d 962, 140 Cal. Rptr. 510, 22 UCCR 669 (1977) (allocation is fair and reasonable if it is fair and reasonable to customers as a whole).

[307] U.C.C. § 2-615, Official Comment 11.

[308] In effect, the requirement of apportionment is merely a specific example of the application of the general doctrine of good faith in the performance of contracts. *See* U.C.C. § 1-203.

[309] 381 F. Supp. 245, 15 UCCR 832 (N.D. Ill. 1974).

court said that this allocation could not be considered fair and reasonable under section 2-615(b).

The court in *Cosden Oil & Chemical Co. v. Karl O. Helm Aktienge-sellschaft*[310] held that the failure to make a fair and reasonable allocation deprives the seller of excuse under section 2-615. A buyer who has been deprived of a fair and reasonable allocation can sue for damages for the *entire* contract amount, not simply the amount a fair and reasonable allocation would have given to the buyer. The court said that this rule was necessary to provide sufficient incentive to the seller to allocate its goods fairly. Thus, under *Cosden,* if the buyer and seller have a contract for 1,000 widgets, and a fair and reasonable allocation to the buyer would be 100 widgets, the buyer can sue for nondelivery of the entire 1,000 widgets if the seller refuses to deliver the 100 widgets.

Finally, the court in *Olson v. Spitzer*[311] held that the allocation provision of section 2-615 does not apply to only one item. When the seller of a combine was unable after diligent effort to obtain promised attachments for the combine buyer, the court held that the seller was excused from performance. The court further held that section 2-615(b) imposed no obligation upon the seller to make a "modified offer" to the buyer, because there was only one combine and thus there was no issue of allocation. Although the court did not consider the question, the Code's good-faith obligation might be the basis for requiring the seller to make a reasonable substitute offer even if section 2-615(b) is inapplicable.

Subsection (c) of section 2-615 requires the seller to notify the buyer seasonably that there will be a delay in delivery or a nondelivery and of any estimated quota that will be made available to the buyer. Section 2-616 gives the buyer a reasonable time, not to exceed thirty days, to give the seller written notice as to whether the buyer will terminate the contract or modify the contract by agreeing to take his available quota in substitution for the promised performance. If the buyer does not give this notice, the contract lapses with respect to the deliveries affected. This procedure provides considerable certainty for the parties who face a disruption resulting from the failure of a presupposed condition.

In addition to the allocation process described above, Comment 6 suggests that in some cases something less than a complete excuse might be appropriate under section 2-615:

> In situations in which neither sense nor justice is served by either answer when the issue is posed in flat terms of "excuse" or "no excuse," ad-

---

[310] 736 F.2d 1064, 38 UCCR 1645 (5th Cir. 1984).
[311] 257 N.W.2d 459, 22 UCCR 677 (S.D. 1977).

justment under the various provisions of this Article is necessary, especially the sections on good faith, on insecurity and assurance and on the reading of all provisions in light of their purposes, and the general policy of this Act to use equitable principles in furtherance of commercial standards and good faith.

The meaning of this Comment is by no means clear. It could mean that the Code's obligation of good faith and its policy of using equitable principles to further reasonable commercial standards sometimes imposes upon the parties an obligation to modify or "adjust" their contractual obligations in the event of an unforeseen contingency, even if the contingency and its effects do not rise to the level of a complete excuse. That is, there may be some obligation on the part of the buyer to agree to a contract modification even when the seller has not satisfied the requirements for excuse. Alternatively, the Comment may impose upon the seller an obligation to propose a reasonable modification even when the seller has satisfied the requirements for excuse.[312] Finally, it could be a direction to the courts to feel free to impose their own "adjustments" on the parties' contracts when neither requiring full performance or granting a complete excuse makes "sense nor justice."

Whatever the Comment means, it has largely been ignored by the courts. Buyers have not been required to agree to proposals for modification when the seller has not satisfied the requirements for an excuse under section 2-615. Conversely, sellers have not been required, outside of the allocation required by section 2-615, to propose adjustments to buyers when the requirements for an excuse are present.[313] With one famous (or infamous) exception, courts have not taken the Comment as an invitation to judicially modify contracts.

The exception is the case of *Aluminum Co. of America v. Essex Group.*[314] The facts of the case have been described previously.[315] After a laborious analysis of ALCOA's claims of mistake, commercial impracticability, and frustration of purpose, the court decided that ALCOA had sufficiently satisfied the requirements of these doctrines to be excused from its contractual obligations. It did not, however, grant ALCOA a complete excuse from its duty to provide Essex with aluminum for the remaining eight years of the contract. Instead, the judge crafted a very complicated alternative price schedule, which he proceeded, by order, to impose upon the

---

[312] *But see* Olsen v. Spitzer, 257 N.W.2d 459, 22 UCCR 677 (S.D. 1977).

[313] *Id.*

[314] 499 F. Supp. 53, 29 UCCR 1 (W.D. Pa. 1980).

[315] *See* § 5.04[D][2], *supra.*

parties. The judge's purpose in the schedule was to devise a price formula that would substantially reduce ALCOA's losses, while also preserving the value of the contract to Essex. The judge, in effect, created a brand new eight-year contract.

The court's resolution received a wealth of scholarly commentary, both laudatory[316] and critical.[317] The critics have emphasized a number of points: the inability of judges, often with little business experience, to create contracts that would remotely resemble those that the parties might themselves agree to,[318] the uncertainty created in the firmness of contractual obligations, and even the strategic "game-playing" that it might introduce into contract negotiations.[319] Those applauding the judge's remedy point out its fairness and the fact that the contractual relationship between the partes is maintained.[320]

The arguments of both sides have some validity. Judges should be hesitant to create binding obligations in areas where they may have little expertise or experience. On the other hand, judges have long filled in gaps in commercial contracts, and what should happen in the event of a contingency that the parties never anticipated is nothing more than a "gap" in the contract. Furthermore, the judge can, to some extent, rely on the parties to provide him or her with the expertise to craft a sensible solution. Also, unless the flexibility in remedy makes judges more inclined to grant excuses in the first place, there is little to fear with regard to the security of contracts. Sometimes a fair and reasonable solution that protects at least some of the value to the contract to both parties will be apparent, and the risk of error will be manageable. In this situation, a judge should be willing to impose a commercially reasonable solution.

Unfortunately, the drafters did not go further and consider another problem: how losses ought to be apportioned following a casualty or impracticability that excuses the seller's further performance. Suppose, for example, that the buyer had made a downpayment and that none of the goods

---

[316] *See, e.g.*, Richard E. Speidel, "The New Spirit of Contract," 2 J.L. & Com. 193 (1982); Leon E. Trakman, "Winner Take Some: Loss Sharing and Commercial Impracticability," 69 Minn. L. Rev. 471 (1985).

[317] The most critical commentary was probably that of Professor Dawson, who described the decision as "grotesque." John P. Dawson, "Judicial Revision of Frustrated Contracts: The United States," 64 B.U. L. Rev. 1, 26 (1984). *See also* James J. White & Robert S. Summers, Uniform Commercial Code 182 (4th ed. 1995).

[318] *See* Dawson, *supra* note 316, at 37.

[319] *See* White & Summers, *supra* note 54, at 182.

[320] *See, e.g.*, Richard E. Speidel, "Court-Imposed Price Adjustments Under Long-Term Supply Contracts," 76 Nw. U. L. Rev. 369 (1981).

had been delivered at the time of the intervening casualty or impracticability. Although the seller is excused from performance and the buyer cannot, therefore, sue for breach, can the buyer recover his downpayment? The answer must certainly be "yes." While the Code says nothing about this problem, principles of restitution and unjust enrichment would require the return of the buyer's downpayment. This right to restitution is explicitly recognized in the Restatement (Second) of Contracts § 272 and was the pre-Code rule as well.[321] These rules are undoubtedly incorporated into the Code through section 1-103 as principles of law and equity.

Unfortunately, other damage problems occur when a party is excused from performance. A seller who is excused might have nonetheless expended considerable sums in manufacturing or securing the goods. Alternatively, the buyer may have relied on the contract with the seller and spent money in anticipation of receiving the goods. The drafters said nothing about how to apportion losses following intervening casualty or impracticability, and restitutionary principles are of no assistance when the loss has not resulted in a benefit to the other party.

Section 272(2) of the Restatement (Second) of Contracts deals explicitly with this issue. This section permits the court in the case of excuse for impracticability or frustration of purpose to "grant relief on such terms as justice requires including protection of the parties' reliance interests."[322] Thus, the court could allow a seller to keep a portion of a buyer's deposit to reflect the seller's costs expended on the contract prior to the excusing event, or could permit the seller an excuse only upon condition that the seller reimburse the buyer for all or a portion of the buyer's out-of-pocket costs spent in reliance on the contract. In the absence of any direction in the Code, courts should be willing to apply contract law generally in this area, and in particular the rule of the Restatement Section 272.

[5] Governmental Regulation

In addition to the occurrence of a contingency whose nonoccurence was a basic assumption of the contract, section 2-615 also excuses a seller when performance becomes impracticable because of "compliance in good

---

[321] *See, e.g.*, Cochrane v. Forbes, 257 Mass. 135, 153 N.E. 566 (1926); Panto v. Kentucky Distilleries & Warehouse Co., 215 A.D. 511, 214 N.Y.S. 19 (App. Div. 1926). Other cases are collected in E.H. Schopfloches, Annotation, "Right to Recover Consideration Paid or Performed Upon Contract, Performance of Which by Other Party is Excused by Reason of Supervening Impossibility," 144 A.L.R. 1317 (1943).

[322] Restatement (Second) of Contracts § 272(2) (1981).

faith with any applicable foreign or domestic governmental regulation or order whether or not it later proves to be invalid."

Because the language of the section does not require that the governmental regulation be a "basic assumption" on which the contract was made, it is not clear whether the strict foreseeability requirement that the courts apply in other contexts applies in the case of a governmental regulation.

Comment 10 suggests that foreseeability remains important, at least so far as the foreseeability of the regulation supports an inference that the seller actually assumed the risk of the regulation. It says that "governmental interference cannot excuse unless it truly "supervenes" in such a manner as to be beyond the seller's assumption of risk. A number of cases have refused to permit an excuse on the basis of compliance with a governmental regulation because, at least in part, the regulation was foreseeable.[323] As a general matter, it appears that the courts have treated governmental regulations little differently from other contingencies.

[6] Conclusion

As mentioned previously, judges have been very stingy in granting excuses to parties under section 2-615. Only a dozen or so appellate decisions have granted a party an excuse under section 2-615. There are a number of reasons for this paucity of cases permitting excuse. First, most courts treat the question of impracticability as a question of fact.[324] As a result, the total number of appellate cases is relatively small. Second, in many cases in which a party might be deserving of an excuse, the parties probably work out suitable modifications to the contract or simply cancel the contract without litigating the issue of excuse. There is no reason to assume that parties to contracts are unreasonable or unfair people, and when unexpected events occur that truly make performance impracticable, most people are probably willing to make reasonable adjustments. Third, some judges have expressed

---

[323] See, e.g., Neal Cooper Grain Co. v. Texas Gulf Sulphur Co., 508 F.2d 283, 16 UCCR 7 (7th Cir. 1974); Sabine Corp. v. Ong W., Inc., 725 F. Supp. 1157, 11 UCCR2d 83 (W.D. Okla. 1989); see also Iowa Elec. Light & Power Co. v. Atlas Corp., 467 F. Supp. 129, 23 UCCR 1171 (N.D. Iowa 1978) (seller should have foreseen dramatic increase in costs for compliance with governmental health and safety regulations).

[324] See, e.g., Alimenta (U.S.A.), Inc. v. Cargill, Inc., 861 F.2d 650, 7 UCCR2d 1100 (11th Cir. 1988); Michigan Bean Co. v. Senn, 93 Mich. App. 440, 287 N.W.2d 257, 28 UCCR 625 (1979); Glassner v. Northwest Lustre Craft Co., 39 Or. App. 175, 591 P.2d 419, 26 UCCR 416 (1979); Meuse-Rhine-Ijssel Cattle Breeders of Canada, Ltd. v. Y-Tex Corp., 590 P.2d 1306, 26 UCCR 292 (Wyo. 1979). But see Butler Mfg. Co. v. Americold Corp., 850 F. Supp. 952, 23 UCCR2d 428 (D. Kan. 1994) (question of impracticability is for the court).

concern that the uncertainty created by a liberal rule for excuse would increase the volume of litigation.[325] Finally, judges are rightly concerned with the effect that granting excuse too liberally may have on the security of contracts. If there is a serious risk that a party's obligation, which appears unconditional on its face, might later be modified or excused, parties might feel compelled to expend additional resources explicitly negotiating all possible contingencies or otherwise investing in costly security against nonperformance (such as third-party insurance). Because courts have been so reluctant to grant excuses under section 2-615, the number of cases has decreased from a sizeable number in the 1970s and early 1980s to a mere handful today. Despite the more liberal language of the Code, we have not moved far from the literal impossibility required by *Taylor v. Caldwell* more than a hundred years ago.

II.   PERFORMANCE OBLIGATIONS OF THE BUYER

§ 5.05   BUYER'S OBLIGATIONS AND RIGHTS GENERALLY

The buyer's method of tender and his performance obligations are not as complicated as those of the seller. The seller has promised to deliver a given quantity of goods of a certain quality. Deciding whether the seller has performed opens questions of warranties as well as how the goods must be tendered to the buyer. Disclaimers, limitations of remedies, installment contracts, the right to cure, the distinction between shipment and destination contracts, and excuse from performance are all important in deciding whether the seller has tendered and whether the seller has performed its obligations.

The buyer, on the other hand, has normally agreed to but one thing—to pay the price at a specified time and place. There are, on occasion, problems of interpreting that agreement—problems of deciding how much the buyer promised to pay for the goods or when the buyer agreed to make the payment—but these problems do not arise as frequently and are generally

---

[325] *See, e.g.,* Lawrence v. Elmore Bean Warehouse, Inc., 702 P.2d 930, 41 UCCR 358 (Idaho Ct. App. 1985) in which the court stated:

> The tough stance we are taking in this case is in view of the fact that virtually all contracts which are based upon a fixed price could be subject to modification if a change in the market price would occur. Interpreting the law as appellants suggest would invite countless suits by speculators in the market as well as by persons merely disappointed in their bargains.

930 P.2d at 933, 41 UCCR at 362.

not as complicated as those involving whether goods measure up to their warranted quality and whether the seller's tender conformed to the parties' contract.

In discussing the performance obligations of the buyer, we will consider two questions:

1. What acts must the buyer perform in order to obligate the seller to perform its part of the sales agreement?

2. What obligations does the buyer have once the seller has properly tendered conforming goods?

The first question is directed toward determining the necessary conditions precedent to the buyer's obtaining a cause of action against the seller. If the seller's obligations are conditioned on the prior or concurrent performance of some act by the buyer, failure of the buyer to perform that act prevents the seller's obligation from arising, and the seller will not be in default. The second question assumes that the seller has performed the necessary conditions and that the buyer is, therefore, required to perform his obligations to prevent a default.

[A] Tender of the Price

The buyer's tender obligations can be introduced through the following hypothetical fact pattern:

> A seller and buyer agreed to the sale and purchase of a television set for a total price of $425. The agreement was reached and a writing signed on July 1. The seller agreed to deliver the set to the buyer's home on July 5. Nothing was said about the terms of payment and no custom, course of performance, or course of dealing indicated that the buyer was to be extended credit in paying the price. Assume that, as of July 6, the seller has not delivered the set and the buyer has made no effort to hand $425 in cash to the seller.

The Code's beginning point in analyzing the hypothetical is section 2-511:

> Unless otherwise agreed tender of payment is a condition to the seller's duty to tender and complete any delivery.[326]

Before the seller has a *duty* to deliver the goods, the buyer must have tendered payment or there must be an agreement that the buyer need not tender

---

[326] U.C.C. § 2-511.

payment in order to be entitled to delivery of the goods.[327] If neither has occurred, the seller has no duty to deliver the goods, and his failure to deliver—even though July 5 has come and gone—is not a default.

Has the buyer tendered payment? It does not appear so from the facts given. "Tender" of payment is the offer of payment with the present willingness and ability to make payment.[328] The buyer appears to have made no offer of any payment to the seller, nor do we know whether the buyer is willing or able to make payment. The buyer's tender obligations are discussed in detail in the remainder of this section.

How much must be tendered? The Code requires that "payment" must be tendered. A tender of a portion of the price—even 99 percent—is not sufficient, unless the parties' agreement permits tender of less than the full price.[329] Unless credit has been extended, the buyer obligates the seller to deliver the goods only by tendering the entire price.

What must be tendered? Section 2-511(2) defines what the buyer must tender:

> Tender of payment is sufficient when made by any means or in any manner current in the ordinary course of business unless the seller demands payment in legal tender and gives any extension of time reasonably necessary to procure it.[330]

Thus, the buyer need not tender cash; payment may be tendered by any means that is acceptable in the ordinary course of business. A check is generally sufficient as a tender of payment,[331] and a bank draft may be

---

[327] *See* Hope's Architectural Prods., Inc. v. Lundy's Constr., Inc., 781 F. Supp. 711, 16 UCCR2d 1059 (D. Kan. 1991) (seller who never tendered delivery had no right to demand payment); Ross Cattle Co. v. Lewis, 415 So. 2d 1029, 34 UCCR 913 (Miss. 1982) (tender of delivery must be made by seller to activate the buyer's duty to accept and pay for the goods).

[328] *See* Crowder v. Aurora Coop. Elevator Co., 223 Neb. 704, 393 N.W.2d 250, 2 UCCR2d 1292 (Neb. 1986) (tender contemplates an offer coupled with a present ability to fulfill all conditions resting in the tendering party); Cohn v. Fisher, 118 N.J. Super. 286, 287 A.2d 222, 10 UCCR 373 (1972) (tender occurs when party is ready, willing, and able to close the deal at the time and place of delivery).

[329] *See* Aero Consulting Corp. v. Cessna Aircraft Co., 867 F. Supp. 1480, 27 UCCR2d 337 (D. Kan. 1994) (tender of purchase price minus commission is not sufficient when contract calls for payment of the full price); Spikes v. Bauer, 626 P.2d 816, 31 UCCR 498 (Kan. Ct. App. 1981) (tender of $24 per ton for hay insufficient for tender when contract called for $27 per ton).

[330] U.C.C. § 2-511(2).

[331] Comment 4 to U.C.C. § 2-511 states in part that the taking of a seemingly solvent party's check is commercially normal and proper.

sufficient as well. In *Modern Aero Sales, Inc. v. Winger Research, Inc.*,[332] the buyer of an airplane sent payment to the seller by means of a bank draft payable when the seller delivered certain documentation to the bank. The seller claimed that the draft was not a tender of payment and, therefore, did not activate the seller's duty to deliver the plane. The court disagreed, and said that such draft was an accepted (in fact typical) method of payment in the business of selling airplanes. The court further said that it was irrelevant whether the seller had knowledge of this practice so long as it was normal in the business that was the subject of the contract.[333]

The seller, however, may demand payment in legal tender, even if the buyer offers payment in a manner current in the ordinary course of business. If the seller does so, the seller must give the buyer an extension of time reasonably needed to procure the cash.[334] Failure to grant the extension means that the original tender of the buyer is sufficient and the seller is obligated to deliver the goods.[335]

When and where must the tender be made? Unless the contract provides otherwise, payment is due at the time and place at which the buyer is to *receive* the goods—which is often, but not necessarily, the same as the place of delivery.[336] The only exception (in reality, not an exception but merely a case in which the contract provides otherwise) is for documentary sales— that is, sales in which the buyer has agreed to pay the price against documents of title. In all other cases, unless the contract provides otherwise, payment is due at the time and place at which the buyer is to receive the goods. The place the buyer is to receive the goods is determined by the contract. In the absence of an express or implied term in the contract, the Code supplies the place the buyer is to receive the goods.[337] Thus, if the buyer had agreed to pick up the television set at the seller's place of business, tender of payment would require the buyer to go to the seller's place of business during working hours on July 5 and there tender payment for the full amount of the price.

---

[332] 486 S.W.2d 135, 11 UCCR 986 (Tex. App. 1972).

[333] *See also* Penny v. Kelley, 528 S.W.2d 330, 18 UCCR 454 (Tex. App. 1975) (assignment of note to bank without indorsement of instrument itself not a manner within the ordinary course of business).

[334] *See* Silver v. Sloop Silver Cloud, 259 F. Supp. 187, 3 UCCR 971 (S.D.N.Y. 1966); Chrysler Credit Corp. v. Barnes, 191 S.E.2d 121, 11 UCCR 327 (Ga. Ct. App. 1972).

[335] Silver v. Sloop Silver Cloud, 259 F. Supp. 187, 3 UCCR 971 (S.D.N.Y. 1966).

[336] In shipment contracts, the place of delivery is the place where the goods are delivered to the carrier. *See* U.C.C. § 2-504. This, however, is not the place where the buyer is to receive the goods.

[337] *See* U.C.C. § 2-308(a) (unless otherwise agreed the place for delivery is the seller's place of business).

How may tender be made if the seller is not present at the time and place for tender? The facts in the hypothetical indicate that the seller was to deliver the goods to the buyer's home and it is there that tender must be made. How can the buyer tender payment when the seller is not present? The Code does not prescribe what a buyer is to do in this situation. Generally, however, the law requires only that a party show that he was present at the time and place that he was to perform, and was ready, willing, and able to make payment.[338] Therefore, it may well be that the buyer in the opening hypothetical *did* make the necessary tender to obligate the seller to deliver the television set. Whether the buyer was present at home at the time of delivery and was ready, willing, and able to make payment requires a further examination of the facts, but if tender was made by the buyer, the failure of the seller to deliver is a default for which the seller may be held liable in damages.

The parties may agree that tender of payment is not necessary to entitle the buyer to delivery of the goods.[339] If the seller in the hypothetical expressly agreed to extend credit to the buyer, or there were a basis to imply such a term,[340] then the seller would almost certainly be liable for failing to deliver the goods. The seller's duty to deliver is determined by the agreement; if the goods are to be delivered on the basis of the buyer's credit, the seller is obligated to deliver the goods even though the buyer has made no payment, and the seller's failure to deliver the goods is a breach.

[B] The Buyer's Obligations Rights and Obligations Upon Seller's Tender

Until the seller has made a proper tender of conforming goods, the buyer has no obligation to perform. Once the seller has properly tendered conforming goods, the buyer's basic obligations are stated in section 2-507(1):

> Tender of delivery is a condition to the buyer's duty to accept the goods and, unless otherwise agreed, to his duty to pay for them. Tender entitles

---

[338] *See, e.g.*, Cohn v. Fisher, 118 N.J. Super. 286, 287 A.2d 222, 10 UCCR 373 (1972); Catlin v. Jones, 52 Or. 337, 97 P. 546 (1908).

[339] *See* In re Automated Bookbinding Servs., Inc., 336 F. Supp. 1128, 10 UCCR 209 (D. Md. 1972) (seller was required to assemble machine, put it in running order, and train operator before payment was required); Berube v. Mobile Home Sales & Serv., 28 N.C. App. 160, 220 S.E.2d 636, 18 UCCR 668 (1975) (tender of payment is not required to activate seller's duty of delivery when contract required seller to "set-up" trailer upon payment of deposit only).

[340] For example, through course of dealing, course of performance, or usage of trade. *See* U.C.C. §§ 1-205, 2-208.

the seller to acceptance of the goods and to payment according to the contract.[341]

Under this section, when the seller makes a proper tender of conforming goods, the buyer must accept the goods. However, before the buyer is required to accept the goods, and often before the buyer is required to pay the price, the buyer has a right to inspect the goods.[342] Once the goods have been accepted, the seller is entitled to recover the price of the goods as stated in the contract, and the seller is not obligated to retake them if the buyer later changes his mind and wants to return the goods.[343] The obligation to accept the goods has another consequence as well. If the buyer fails to accept a proper tender of conforming goods, the buyer has "wrongfully rejected" the goods under section 2-703. The seller may then recover damages for nonacceptance.[344]

Once proper tender has been made, the buyer is also obligated to pay the price "according to the contract." This language covers any arrangement between the parties for the payment of the price, whether arising out of express language or usage of trade, course of performance, or course of dealing. For example, the agreement may give the buyer a period of credit, allow him to receive the goods after accepting a time draft, provide for payment against a sight draft, or contain some combination of these methods of payment. Absent an agreement, the Code fills out the payment term in the manner already discussed in the section dealing with the buyer's tender.[345] Unless the contract provides otherwise, the buyer is required to pay the entire price, by any means or in any manner current in the ordinary course of business, at the time and place the buyer is to receive the goods.[346]

Much of the litigation concerning the buyer's obligations upon tender by the seller has involved sections 2-507(2) and 2-511(3). Section 2-507(2) makes the buyer's rights to retain or dispose of the goods conditional on payment where payment is due and demanded on delivery. Consistent with

---

[341] U.C.C. § 2-507(1).

[342] The right to inspect the goods before payment is lost in documentary sales. U.C.C. §§ 2-512, 2-513; *see also* § 5.06, *infra*.

[343] Once acceptance has occurred, the buyer can return the goods only if the buyer justifiably revokes acceptance. Revocation of acceptance requires a non-conformity in the goods that substantially impairs their value to the buyer. *See* § 7.03[E], *infra*. If the goods are conforming, there can be no revocation of acceptance, and the buyer must pay the price of the goods.

[344] Until there has been acceptance, the seller is generally not able to recover the price, although there are some circumstances in which the price is allowed even when there has been no acceptance. *See* U.C.C. § 2-709; § 7.08[E], *infra*.

[345] *See* § 5.05[A], *supra*.

[346] *Id.*

Comment 4 to section 2-507, this provision has been interpreted by most courts to mean that when payment is due upon delivery and not made, the seller has a right to reclaim the goods from the buyer.[347] Section 2-511(3) states that payment by check is conditional and is defeated as between the parties by dishonor of the check on due presentments. Most,[348] but not all,[349] courts have interpreted this as a "sister" provision to section 2-507(2) and held that the seller has a right to reclaim the goods upon dishonor of the buyer's check.[350]

A number of cases have involved the question of how long the seller's reclamation right survives under these two provisions. Prior to 1990, courts held, by analogy to section 2-702,[351] that the right of reclamation under section 2-507 lasts only ten days from the time of delivery of the goods to the buyer, despite the lack of any such limit in the statute.[352] A contrary direction that there is no specific time limit to the reclamation right was added to Comment 3 to section 2-507 in 1990 by the Permanent Editorial Board. Further, the majority of courts have also attached a similar time limitation to reclamation of goods by a seller under section 2-511(3).[353] A few courts have held that the Code does not impose a ten-day time limitation

---

[347] *See, e.g.,* In re Helms Veneer Corp., 287 F. Supp. 840, 5 UCCR 977 (W.D. Va. 1968); Citizens Bank of Roseville v. Taggart, 191 Cal. Rptr. 729, 143 Cal. App. 3d 318, 36 UCCR 529 (1983). Comment 2 to U.C.C. § 2-507 states that section 507(2) "codifies the cash seller's right of reclamation which is in the nature of a lien."

[348] *See, e.g.,* Ranchers & Farmers Livestock Auction Co. v. Honey, 38 Colo. App. 69, 552 P.2d 313, 29 UCCR 1337 (1976); Hardick v. Hill, 403 So. 2d 1125, 32 UCCR 547 (Fla. Dist. Ct. App. 1981); Lawrence v. Graham, 29 Md. App. 472, 349 A.2d 271, 18 UCCR 657 (1974); Peck v. Augustin Bros., 203 Neb. 574, 279 N.W.2d 397, 26 UCCR 889 (1979).

[349] *See* In re Fairfield Elevator Co., 14 UCCR 96 (Bankr. S.D. Iowa 1973).

[350] Unlike Comment 2 to U.C.C. § 2-507, neither the text nor the Comments to section 2-511 specifically give the seller a right to reclaim the goods if a check given by the buyer in payment is dishonored.

[351] *See* § 7.07[C], *infra.*

[352] *See, e.g.,* Szabo v. Vinton Motors, Inc., 630 F.2d 1, 29 UCCR 737 (1st Cir. 1980); Stowers v. Mahon, 510 F.2d 139, 16 UCCR 577 (5th Cir. 1975); In re Kirk Kabinets, Inc., 15 UCCR 746 (Bankr. M.D. Ga. 1974); In re Helms Veneer Corp., 287 F. Supp. 840, 5 UCCR 977 (W.D. Va. 1968); First Nat'l Bank of Ariz. v. Carbajal, 645 P.2d 778, 33 UCCR 1523 (Ariz. 1982); B. Milligan Contracting Inc. v. Andrew R. Mancini Assocs., Inc., 174 A.D.2d 136, 578 N.Y.S.2d 931, 17 UCCR2d 117 (App. Div. 1992).

[353] *See* Holiday Rambler Corp. v. First Nat'l Bank & Trust Co. of Great Bend, Kan., 723 F.2d 1449, 37 UCCR 1553 (10th Cir. 1983); Szabo v. Vinton Motors, Inc., 630 F.2d 1, 29 UCCR 737 (1st Cir. 1980); Stowers v. Mahon, 510 F.2d 139, 16 UCCR 577 (5th Cir. 1975); Catalina Yachts v. Old Colony Bank & Trust Co. of Middlesex County, 497 F. Supp. 1227, 32 UCCR 241 (D. Mass. 1980); In re Kirk Kabinets, Inc., 15 UCCR 746 (Bankr. M.D. Ga. 1974).

on the exercise of the seller's reclamation rights under these sections, and have criticized the majority rule as giving insufficient protection to the seller.[354] It remains to be seen whether the change in Comment 3 will prompt courts not to impose a ten-day limit under section 2-507.[355]

A frequent issue also arising with respect to the seller's right to reclaim the goods under these sections is the relative priority of the seller who attempts to exercise his right to reclaim the goods upon nonpayment or the dishonor of a check and an intervening secured creditor of a buyer. For example, assume that the seller delivers goods to the buyer for the buyer's inventory, and the buyer pays with a check. Assume further that a secured creditor has a perfected "floating lien" covering all of the buyer's inventory. When the check is dishonored and the seller attempts to reclaim the goods, can the secured creditor assert a prior right to the goods if there is a default of the buyer's obligation to the secured creditor? This basic scenario, with minor variations, has occurred in a substantial number of cases.[356]

In jurisdictions that place a ten-day limitation on the seller's reclamation rights, if the seller attempts to reclaim the goods more than ten days following delivery, the secured creditor wins, and the seller simply becomes another unsecured creditor.[357] If the seller attempts to exercise his right to reclaim the goods within the ten-day period, or if the court does not impose the ten-day restriction on the seller, the law is less clear. The reasoning of most of the cases, however, suggests that even in this case, the secured creditor would win. This is because most courts consider a secured creditor to be a good-faith purchaser for value, and the Comments to both sections

---

[354] *See, e.g.*, Burk v. Emmick, 637 F.2d 1172, 29 UCCR 1489 (8th Cir. 1980) (only limit on reclamation right is reasonableness); Citizens Bank of Roseville v. Taggart, 191 Cal. Rptr. 729, 143 Cal. App. 3d 318, 36 UCCR 529 (1983). In *Citizens Bank of Roseville*, the court said that in the case of a dishonored check, the seller is unlikely to become aware that the check has been dishonored until close to the expiration or after the expiration of the ten-day period.

[355] For a more complete discussion of this issue, *see* § 7.07[D] *infra*.

[356] *See, e.g.*, Holiday Rambler Corp. v. First Nat'l Bank & Trust Co. of Great Bend, Kan., 723 F.2d 1449, 37 UCCR 1553 (10th Cir. 1983); Stowers v. Mahon, 576 F.2d 1238, 18 UCCR 545 (5th Cir. 1976); Holiday Rambler Corp. v. Morris, 32 UCCR 1222 (D. Kan. 1981); First Nat'l Bank of Ariz. v. Carbajal, 132 Ariz. 315, 645 P.2d 830, 32 UCCR 817 (Ct. App. 1982); Guy Martin Buick, Inc. v. Colorado Springs Nat'l Bank, 184 Colo. 166, 519 P.2d 354, 14 UCCR 40 (1974); Hardick v. Hill, 403 So. 2d 1125, 32 UCCR 547 (Fla. Dist. Ct. App. 1981); R&P Lumber Co. v. First Nat'l Bank of Atlanta, 147 Ga. App. 762, 250 S.E.2d 505, 25 UCCR 1033 (1978); Evans Prods. Co. v. Jorgensen, 145 Or. 362, 421 P.2d 978, 3 UCCR 1099 (1966); Stumbo v. Paul B. Hult Lumber Co., 251 Or. 20, 444 P.2d 564, 5 UCCR 753 (1968).

[357] *See* In re Helms Veneer Corp., 287 F. Supp. 840, 5 UCCR 977 (W.D. Va. 1968).

2-507 and 2-511 indicate that the seller's reclamation rights are subject to the rights of good-faith purchasers.[358] According to these courts, the seller's reclamation right is not a security interest and is therefore not entitled to any priority.[359] Under this rationale, the seller loses even as against an *unperfected* security interest.[360] Only if the secured creditor has notice at the time the security interest attaches that the buyer has not paid the seller in accordance with the contract or has paid with a dishonored check does the seller win, because the creditor would no longer be a good-faith purchaser.[361]

A few courts have held that the seller's reclamation right is superior to a secured creditor's interest so long as the seller attempts to reclaim the goods within the ten-day period.[362] In one case, the court said that a security interest cannot attach during this period because the debtor does not have rights in the collateral until the reclamation period has expired.[363] This reasoning is clearly erroneous because the buyer has the right to possession of the goods until the seller exercises his reclamation right. In another case, the court held that the reclamation right is superior to a security interest that

---

[358] *See* First Nat'l Bank of Ariz. v. Carbajal, 132 Ariz. 315, 645 P.2d 830, 32 UCCR 817 (Ct. App. 1981); B&P Lumber Co. v. First Nat'l Bank of Atlanta, 147 Ga. App. 762, 250 S.E.2d 505, 25 UCCR 1033 (1978); Genesee Merchants Bank & Trust Co. v. Trucker Motors Sales, 143 Mich. App. 339, 372 N.W.2d 546, 42 UCCR 150 (1985); Stumbo v. Paul B. Hult Lumber Co., 251 Or. 20, 444 P.2d 564, 5 UCCR 753 (1968). *See also* Robert Weed Plywood Corp. v. Downs, 18 UCCR 384 (Bankr. N.D. Ind. 1975) (seller's reclamation right subordinate to trustee in bankruptcy even if attempt to reclaim the goods is exercised within ten days).

[359] *See* First Nat'l Bank of Ariz. v. Carbajal, 132 Ariz. 315, 645 P.2d 830, 32 UCCR 817 (Ct. App. 1981); Guy Martin Buick, Inc. v. Colorado Springs Nat'l Bank, 184 Colo. 166, 519 P.2d 354, 14 UCCR 40 (1974).

[360] *See* First Nat'l Bank of Ariz. v. Carbajal, 132 Ariz. 315, 645 P.2d 830, 32 UCCR 817 (Ct. App. 1981); Guy Martin Buick, Inc. v. Colorado Springs Nat'l Bank, 184 Colo. 166, 519 P.2d 354, 14 UCCR 40 (1974).

[361] *See* Ranchers & Farmers Livestock Auction Co. v. Honey, 38 Colo. App. 69, 552 P.2d 313, 19 UCCR 1337 (1976) (seller's reclamation right under U.C.C. § 2-511(3) superior to that of purchaser who had notice of seller's claim). Furthermore, if the security interest does not attach until after the seller has attempted to reclaim the goods, the seller's reclamation right will prevail. *See also* Chapman Parts Warehouse, Inc. v. Gudesian, 609 S.W2d 317, 30 UCCR 940 (Tex. App. 1980). For a more complete discussion of this issue, *see* § 7.07[G], *infra*.

[362] *See* Holiday Rambler Corp. v. First Nat'l Bank & Trust Co. of Great Bend, Kan., 723 F.2d 1449, 37 UCCR 1553 (10th Cir. 1983); Chicago Limousine Serv., Inc. v. Hartigan Cadillac, Inc., 191 Ill. App. 3d 886, 548 N.E.2d 386, 10 UCCR2d 1418 (1989) (during ten-day period reclamation right not subject to secured creditor's claims).

[363] Holiday Rambler Corp. v. First Nat'l Bank & Trust Co. of Great Bend, Kan., 723 F.2d 1449, 37 UCCR 1553 (10th Cir. 1983).

is *unperfected* at the time the seller attempts to reclaim the goods.[364] The court held that the seller's reclamation right is *similar* to a security interest and is perfected when the seller attempts to reclaim the goods. If the secured creditor's interest is not perfected at the time, the seller will be permitted to reclaim the goods.

§ 5.06   BUYER'S RIGHT OF INSPECTION

Although, in the absence of an agreement to the contrary, the buyer is obligated to pay the price and accept the goods if the seller tenders conforming goods, the buyer is accorded the right to inspect the goods prior to either paying the price or accepting the goods. The Code does not require the buyer to contract expressly for the right to inspect the goods before payment or acceptance, but rather grants the buyer this right unless the contract provides otherwise. Even if the contract requires the buyer to *pay* for the goods prior to inspection, the buyer is not obligated to *accept* the goods prior to their inspection.[365] The principal Code section dealing with the buyer's right to inspect the goods is section 2-513, which provides in subsection (1):

> Unless otherwise agreed and subject to subsection (3), where goods are tendered or delivered or identified to the contract for sale, the buyer has a right before payment or acceptance to inspect them at any reasonable place and time and in any reasonable manner. When the seller is required or authorized to send the goods to the buyer, the inspection may be after their arrival.

The buyer's right to inspect the goods is a *condition* to the buyer's obligation to accept the goods and pay the price.[366] That is, the buyer is not

---

[364] Hardick v. Hill, 403 So. 2d 1125, 32 UCCR 547 (Fla. Dist. Ct. App. 1981).

[365] U.C.C. § 2-512(2).

[366] *See* Ledford v. Cowan, 496 So. 2d 64, 2 UCCR2d 903 (Ala. Civ. App. 1986) (buyer of used auto not liable for price when seller refused to permit the buyer to inspect prior to payment). The buyer's right to inspect could be interpreted only as a *promise* and not as a condition of the buyer's duty of payment and acceptance. Under this construction, the seller's failure to allow the buyer to inspect would be a default entitling the buyer to damages, but would not prevent the buyer's obligation to pay the price from arising, provided that the goods were conforming. This interpretation should be rejected on the basis of the discussion that follows in the text. Furthermore, such an interpretation would substantially undercut the purpose of the buyer's inspection right: to give the buyer some assurance that what has been delivered to him conforms to the contract before he parts with his money.

in breach if the buyer refuses to accept the goods or pay the price prior to inspection. If the seller refuses to allow the buyer the right to inspect the goods prior to payment or acceptance, and, as a result, the buyer rejects the goods, the seller is in breach and may be held liable for damages. This is made clear by Comment 2 to section 2-503:

> [W]here the seller is demanding payment on delivery he must first allow the buyer to inspect the goods in order to avoid impairing his tender unless the contract for sale is on C.I.F., C.O.D., cash against documents or similar terms negating the privilege of inspection before payment.[367]

According to this Comment, the failure to allow inspection *impairs the seller's tender*. If tender is improper, the buyer may reject the goods and refuse to pay the price.[368] Also, because the buyer's rejection is rightful, the buyer can hold the seller liable for any damages suffered as a result of the failure to properly tender conforming goods.[369]

[A]   Time, Place, and Manner of Inspection

The Code does not attempt to detail the time, place, and manner of inspection. Instead, it properly leaves these matters to a case-by-case determination under the general mandate that the buyer has a right to inspect "at any reasonable place and time and in any reasonable manner."[370] Because of the variety of goods that can be the subject of sale, this was as specific as the drafters could, or should, have been. Some goods can be inspected on the loading dock by casual observation; others may require a test run in the factory or chemical analysis in the laboratory. So long as the buyer selects a place, time, and manner of inspection that are reasonable, the buyer may withhold acceptance and payment until the inspection is completed.

[1]   Place of Inspection

As mentioned in the preceding paragraph, the basic rule is that the buyer has the right to inspect at any reasonable place. In one instance, however, the Code does not leave the question open as to whether a particular place is reasonable; when the seller is required or authorized to send

---

[367] U.C.C. § 2-503, Official Comment 2.

[368] *See* § 5.03, *supra*.

[369] *See* U.C.C. § 2-711(1). The buyer may, of course, waive the condition by not exercising his right of inspection. The Code does not require the buyer to inspect; it only says that the buyer has a "right" to do so.

[370] U.C.C. § 2-513(1).

the goods to the buyer, the inspection may be after their arrival.[371] Thus, if a seller agrees to ship machines by carrier to the buyer's city, the buyer may inspect the machines after they have arrived at the destination prescribed in the shipping contract; the buyer has no obligation to inspect them before they are given to the carrier or before the carrier has shipped them.[372]

In fact, even when the buyer takes control of the goods prior to arrival at their ultimate destination, a reasonable place to inspect may nonetheless be at their ultimate destination. For example, in *D.C. Leathers, Inc. v. Gelmart Industries, Inc.*,[373] the seller agreed to sell to the buyer leather palms for incorporation into knit gloves that the buyer made in Manila, the Phillippines. The seller transported the leather palms in sealed boxes to the buyer's warehouse in New York for shipment by the buyer to Manila. When the palms arrived in Manila, they were found to be defective and were rejected by the buyer. The seller argued that a reasonable place for inspection was the buyer's warehouse in New York rather than Manila. The court disagreed and said that the seller was aware that the ultimate destination for the goods was Manila and that the buyer's warehouse was merely a temporary receiving point that had no inspection facilities. Furthermore, it was not a practice in the industry to open sealed boxes to inspect such goods prior to their arrival at the place at which they were to be used. Therefore, the buyer was justified in inspecting the goods in Manila.[374]

The ability of the buyer to inspect at the place of arrival is not lost simply because the risk of loss may be on the buyer during shipment. For example, a buyer may order machines under an F.O.B. seller's point contract which, assuming that the seller makes a proper tender at the place of shipment, places the risk on the buyer if the goods are lost in transit.[375] Nevertheless, the Code adopts the sensible position that the buyer need not have someone inspect those goods at the time they are delivered to the carrier but may await their arrival. A contrary rule would effectively deny the right

---

[371] U.C.C. § 2-513(1).

[372] This is not to say that the buyer could not select a place other than the place of arrival so long as the other location was reasonable. The Code language is that inspection *may* be made after arrival. *See* the pre-Code case of Phoenix Iron & Steel Co. v. Wilkoff Co., 253 F. 165 (6th Cir. 1918).

[373] 125 A.D.2d 738, 509 N.Y.S.2d 161, 2 UCCR2d 1305 (App. Div. 1986).

[374] *See also* EPN-Delaval, S.A. v. Inter-Equip, Inc., 542 F. Supp. 238, 34 UCCR 130 (S.D. Tex. 1982). In this case, the court held that the place of arrival was buyer's plant in Mexico despite the fact that delivery under the contract was to take place in Laredo, Texas. Although the buyer's forwarding agent was in Texas, he lacked the expertise to discover the defect, and was not charged with inspecting the goods.

[375] *See* § 6.05[A][1], *infra.*

of inspection to many buyers because they do not have agents at the point of shipment.[376]

[2] Time of Inspection

The buyer has a reasonable time in which to inspect the goods once they arrive at the place for inspection. A reasonable time to inspect the goods can vary considerably depending upon the nature of the contract and the goods as well as the practices in the particular trade. In *Hammel v. Skyline Dodge, Inc.,*[377] the court found that a buyer who was a dealer in used cars had a sufficient opportunity to inspect a car the day that it was delivered to the buyer, and had therefore accepted the car despite the buyer's failure to discover substantial defects.[378] On the other hand, in *GNP Commodities, Inc. v. Walsh Hefferman Co.,*[379] the court held that a two-month delay between the time the buyer took control of the goods (pork bellies) and the buyer's inspection was reasonable when the goods remained in the same warehouse following purchase in which they were located prior to the sale. Further, a trade usage existed permitting inspection to be delayed until the buyer was prepared to resell the goods. Similarly, in *Buckeye Trophy, Inc. v. Southern Bowling & Billiard Supply Co.,*[380] the court held that it was a question for the jury whether a 65-day delay between the arrival of specially designed marble for awards and the inspection of the marble was reasonable when the buyer's business was seasonal, the goods were not perishable nor subject to market fluctuations, and inspection in the trade was not customarily made of similar goods until they were actually used by the buyer.

---

[376] *See* HCI Chems. (USA), Inc. v. Henkel KgaA, 966 F.2d 1018, 18 UCCR2d 436 (4th Cir. 1992) (buyer had the right to inspect shipment of sodium cyanide in New York even though goods were delivered "FOB Chile."); T.J. Stevenson & Co. v. 81,193 Bags of Flour, 629 F.2d 338, 30 UCCR 865 (4th Cir. 1980) (point of arrival in Bolivia was reasonable place to inspect goods despite "F.A.S. Mobile, Ala." term).

When the goods are lost after the risk of loss has passed to the buyer, the buyer cannot use his right of inspection to defeat an action by the seller for the price. The Code's policy in placing the risk of loss on a buyer following proper tender in a shipment contract is based upon the commercial decision that from that point in time the buyer ought to bear the risk that the goods might be lost. "Risk of loss" means that if the goods are lost, the buyer is nevertheless obligated to perform the contract—to pay the price for the goods. The right of inspection cannot be used to upset this specific assignment by the Code of the risk of loss.

[377] 589 P.2d 73, 26 UCCR 46 (Colo. Ct. App. 1978).

[378] *See also* Michael M. Berlin & Co. v. Whiting Mfg., Inc., 5 UCCR 357 (N.Y. Sup. Ct. 1968) (reasonable time to inspect passed when buyer did not inspect steel until thirteen weeks after delivery and inspection of thickness of steel could have been done easily and with minimum of effort).

[379] 95 Ill. App. 3d 966, 420 N.E.2d 659, 31 UCCR 1342 (1981).

[380] 3 Ohio App. 3d 32, 443 N.E.2d 1043, 35 UCCR 140 (1982).

The reasonable time to inspect does not begin until the seller has tendered the goods to the buyer.[381] Thus, the fact that the buyer had a chance to inspect the goods prior to the contract does not satisfy the buyer's right to inspect under section 2-513.[382] The parties may agree on the length of time within which the buyer is allowed to inspect so long as the time selected is not "manifestly unreasonable."[383]

[3] Manner of Inspection

The buyer is entitled only to make a "reasonable" inspection. As with the time for inspection, whether the manner of inspection is reasonable is a function of the nature of the goods, the nature of the buyer's business, the usages in the trade of the parties, and other relevant circumstances of the contract. The purpose of the buyer's right to inspect is to determine whether the goods conform to the contract,[384] and this is obviously more easily done with respect to some goods than with others. It is much easier to determine, for example, whether a box of pencils conforms to the contract than whether a mainframe computer is conforming. The parties can explicitly agree on the details of the buyer's inspection rights and, unless manifestly unreasonable, such agreements control.[385] If a method chosen for inspection becomes impracticable, the buyer is required (and entitled) to inspect in some other reasonable manner, unless the manner chosen in the contract was an indispensable condition to the contract.[386]

[B] Payment Without Inspection

The statutory rule that the buyer has a right to inspect goods before payment or acceptance is subject to the introductory phrase: "Unless oth-

---

[381] *See* Performance Motors, Inc. v. Allen, 280 N.C. 385, 186 S.E.2d 162, 10 UCCR 568 (1972) (tender not completed under contract until mobile home was set up on blocks and reasonable time to inspect did not begin until then); Davis v. Vintage Enters., Inc., 23 N.C. App. 581, 209 S.E.2d 824, 15 UCCR 1066 (1974) (holding similar to *Performance Motors*).

[382] *See* E.L.E.S.C.O. v. Northern States Power Co., 370 N.W.2d 700, 41 UCCR 414 (Minn. Ct. App. 1985).

[383] U.C.C. § 1-204(1). *See also* Wilson Trading Corp. v. David Ferguson, Ltd., 23 N.Y.2d 398, 297 N.Y.S.2d 108, 244 N.E.2d 685, 5 UCCR 1213 (1968).

[384] Comment 2 to U.C.C. § 2-612 provides that "[i]nspection under this section is an inspection in a manner reasonable for detecting defects in goods whose surface appearance is satisfactory." The rights of inspection under sections 2-612 and 2-613 are correlative. *See* U.C.C. § 2-612, Official Comment 6.

[385] *See, e.g.*, Lawner v. Engelbach, 249 A.2d 295, 5 UCCR 1236 (Pa. 1969) (parties agreed that appraisal of diamond was part of inspection).

[386] U.C.C. § 2-513(4).

erwise agreed and subject to subsection (3)." Subsection (3) lists types of contracts in which the buyer is obligated to pay without inspection.[387] Each of these types of contracts is one in which the parties normally understand that payment of the price must precede inspection and can be considered as specific examples of the general proposition that parties may, by agreement, vary the rules provided by the Code.

There are cases when it is reasonable for the seller to require payment before inspection. Consider, for example, the seller who has an order from an overseas buyer but who fears that the buyer will misuse the right of inspection before payment to make false claims as to the conformity of the goods. The distance between the seller and the buyer may be such that it is inconvenient and expensive to determine the validity of the buyer's claims. The seller may be willing to sell the goods to this buyer but only if the buyer will pay in advance or on arrival of the necessary documents and, if the goods turn out to be non-conforming, seek a recovery of the purchase price.

A common way of accomplishing the seller's purpose is through a "C.I.F." or "C.&F." contract. The use of these terms means, in the case of a C.I.F. contract, that the quoted price includes the cost of goods, insurance, and freight, [388] and in the case of a C.&F. contract, that the price includes the cost of goods and freight. In addition, the Code further provides:

> Under the term C.I.F. or C.&F. contracts unless otherwise agreed the buyer must make payment against tender of the required documents and the seller may not tender nor the buyer demand delivery of the goods in substitution for the documents.[389]

C.I.F. and C.&F. contracts are examples of contracts in which the buyer has agreed to pay against documents and has lost the right of inspection before payment—but not before acceptance.

---

[387] It is possible, although it would be an extremely odd case, in which the parties agree that the buyer must accept the goods without having the right to inspect them first. In fact, U.C.C. § 2-606, in describing those acts by the buyer that constitute acceptance, requires in subsections (a) and (b) that a reasonable opportunity to inspect the goods precede acceptance. Only if acceptance occurs under subsection (c)—through an act inconsistent with the seller's ownership—is a reasonable opportunity to inspect not required. Comment 1 to section 2-513 suggests that the only time the buyer must accept the goods before inspection is when the sale is of "this thing"; however, even here the buyer is entitled to the "thing" bought, and if the seller delivers a different "thing," the buyer can reject. Therefore, it is a safe conclusion that the buyer always has the right to inspect before acceptance.

[388] U.C.C. § 2-320(1).

[389] U.C.C. § 2-320(4).

There are other sales in which the seller may require payment before inspection. The seller may accomplish this with a C.O.D. contract,[390] or by a contract providing for payment *against* documents.[391] The latter agreement is often called a documentary sale and should not be confused with an agreement in which the seller is simply authorized or required to ship with documents, but the contract does not obligate the buyer to pay upon proper tender of the documents. Unless the contract *requires* the buyer to pay against documents, the buyer may inspect the goods before payment even though the seller uses documents of title to complete the sale.[392] In addition, the buyer is permitted to inspect the goods even in a sale against documents "when the contract requires payment only after the goods are to become available for inspection."[393]

When the contract requires payment before inspection, the buyer's obligation to pay before inspection is not excused by the fact that the goods are not conforming, even if the goods arrive prior to or concurrently with the documents.[394] Section 2-512(1) states this rule with two exceptions:

> Where the contract requires payment before inspection non-conformity of the goods does not excuse the buyer from so making payment unless
> > (a) the non-conformity appears without inspection; or
> > (b) despite tender of the required documents the circumstances would justify injunction against honor under the provisions of this Act (Section 5-109(b)).

The reference in subsection (b) to section 5-109 deals with a defect in the documents sufficient to obtain an injunction against the honor of a letter of credit. Subsection (a) applies when a non-conformity "appears without inspection." This refers to such situations, for example, as the C.O.D. china which, when delivered, rattles in such a manner as to indicate that the contents have been shattered. In these cases, the buyer is not obligated to pay

---

[390] *See* Gragg Farms & Nursery v. Kelly Green Landscaping, 81 Ohio Misc. 2d 34, 674 N.E.2d 785, 32 UCCR2d 1119 (Ohio Mun. Ct. 1996).

[391] C.I.F. and C.&F. contracts are contracts that require payment against documents. However, the parties can require payment against documents without engaging in a C.I.F or C.&F. contract.

[392] *See* U.C.C. § 2-513(3).

[393] U.C.C. § 2-513(3)(b). The fact that the goods happen to arrive before the documents does not satisfy this condition, however. It is only when *the contract* between the parties delays payment until the goods arrive that the buyer has the right to inspect before payment.

[394] U.C.C. § 2-512(1).

for the goods even though the buyer has agreed to do so without inspection.[395]

[C] Expenses of Inspection

The Code deals expressly with the problem of which party bears the expenses of inspection:

> Expenses of inspection must be borne by the buyer but may be recovered from the seller if the goods do not conform and are rejected.[396]

The buyer may not shift the cost of inspection to the seller if the buyer decides to accept non-conforming goods; the goods must be non-conforming *and* rejected before the seller is required to pay the cost of inspection.[397]

---

[395] Shaking the package enough to hear the rattles is a kind of "inspection." Even looking at a crushed box could qualify as an "inspection." Nevertheless, the drafters meant to excuse the buyer from his payment obligation in situations in which the apparent non-conformity "is evident in the mere process of taking delivery." U.C.C. § 2-512, Official Comment 3.

[396] U.C.C. § 2-513(2).

[397] The contract can, however, expressly provide that the seller bears the cost of inspection if the goods are non-conforming but nonetheless accepted, or even if the goods are conforming. U.C.C. § 2-513, Official Comment 4.

Although U.C.C. § 2-513(2) permits recovery of the costs of inspection only if the goods are *rejected*, they should also be recoverable if the buyer justifiably revokes acceptance. Section 2-608 says that a buyer who justifiably revokes acceptance has the same rights and duties with regard to the goods involved as if he had rejected them. Although this section expressly applies only to rights and duties with regard to the *goods*, it suggests that a buyer who has justifiably revoked acceptance should be placed in the same position as a buyer who has rejected. Even more convincing is Comment 1 to section 2-715, which suggests that the same incidental expenses (including those associated with inspection) are recoverable when a buyer justifiably revokes acceptance as when the buyer rejects.

CHAPTER 6

TITLE, IDENTIFICATION, AND RISK OF LOSS

§ 6.01   TITLE UNDER THE CODE

One of the hallmarks of pre-Code sales law was its emphasis on the concept of title. Writing in the late 1930s, Professor Karl Llewellyn (who became the Chief Reporter for the Code) put it this way: "The approach of prevailing Sales doctrine, before or apart from the [Uniform Sales] Act and in it, is this: Unless cogent reason be shown to the contrary, the location of Title will govern every point which it can be made to govern. It will govern, between the parties, risk, action for the price, the applicable law in an interstate transaction, the place and time for measuring damages, the power to defeat the other party's interest, or to replevy, or to reject; it will govern, as against outsiders, leviability, rights against tort-feasors, infraction of criminal statutes about sales, incidence of taxation, power to insure."[1]

There were many difficulties with a legal system that attempted to solve sales problems through a search for an all-pervading title. People do not care one whit where title, as such, is located. They want to know if the law will protect their possession of goods and whether an insurance company can be compelled to pay if those goods are destroyed. Buyers are interested in remedies against defaulting sellers, and sellers are interested in remedies against defaulting buyers. Both want to know who bears the risk of loss if goods are destroyed in transit, and manufacturers have a financial concern as to whether they must pay a property tax on goods still in their possession but subject to a contract for sale on the tax date. These are the problems that worry people, and the only time they become concerned about "title" is when their lawyer tells them that the answer to their problems turns on who has the title to the goods involved.

Nevertheless, title might have been a satisfactory method of solving legal problems if there had been some objective method of determining its location. But title to goods has neither form nor substance. It is a concept created by lawyers, and its location is wherever lawyers place it.[2] Some judges were astute enough to realize that a question of who ought to pay a

---

[1] Karl N. Llewellyn, Through Title to Contract and a Bit Beyond, 3 Law: A Century of Progress 80, 87 (1937).

[2] Under the Uniform Sales Act the location of title was a matter of intent. Uniform Sales Act §§ 18–19. The same rule existed at common law. The difficulty was that parties often had no intent at all about the location of title because they did not think in terms of title. *See* Cadillac Mach. Co. v. Mitchell-Diggins Iron Co., 205 Mich. 107, 171 N.W. 479 (1919); George Boiko & Co. v. Atlantic Woolen Mills, Inc., 195 App. Div. 207, 186 N.Y.S. 624 (1921), *aff'd mem.*, 234 N.Y. 583, 138 N.E. 455 (1922). Another difficulty arose out of the courts' willingness to ignore express statements of intent. *See* Low v. Pew, 108 Mass. 347 (1871).

tax involved policy considerations different from those involved in a risk-of-loss problem, and these judges manipulated the title concept to produce sensible results in the cases before them. Other judges, however, slavishly followed title precedents from cases presenting problems strikingly different from the problems before them and reached indefensible results. Thus, the single-title concept of sales produced uneven results and obstructed careful analysis.[3] Further, the concept was too simplistic to cope adequately with the increasingly complex and sophisticated practices that the commercial community was developing.

At the urging of Professor Llewellyn and other scholars, the drafters of the Code discarded the notion that the principal method of solving sales problems should turn on the search for a single (or, as Llewellyn called it, a "lump") title. The Code's approach can be summarized thus: specific problems are identified and solutions to those problems are established without reference to who has title or the time a title might have passed from seller to buyer.[4] According to the Comment to section 2-101, "The purpose is to avoid making practical issues between practical men turn upon the location of an intangible something, the passing of which no man can prove by evidence and to substitute for such abstraction proof of words and actions of a tangible character."[5]

Section 2-401 is Article 2's title provision, and its first two sentences tell much of the story:

> Each provision of this Article with regard to the rights, obligations and the remedies of the seller, the buyer, purchasers or other third parties applies irrespective of title to the goods, except where the provision refers to such title. Insofar as situations are not covered by the other provisions of this Article and matters concerning title become material the following rules apply: [then follows a series of rules which are summarized in the next section of this text].

The result is the reversal of pre-Code law. Title is no longer the primary tool for solving sales problems. Instead, Article 2 provides solutions through

---

[3] *See* Note, "The Effect of Prepayment Upon the Buyer's Right to Goods," 37 Colum. L. Rev. 630, 634 (1937).

[4] Article 9 takes a similar approach to title. Its section 9-202 is captioned "Title to Collateral Immaterial" and provides:

> Each provision of this Article with regard to rights, obligations and remedies applies whether title to collateral is in the secured party or in the debtor.

[5] U.C.C. § 2-101, Comment.

a series of "if . . . then . . ." sections: if such-and-such facts occur, then the solution is so-and-so. Title's role has been reduced to that of a bit player—governing only problems not provided for in Article 2 and situations where Article 2 makes specific reference to title.

There are few specific references to title in Article 2.[6] Section 2-106(1) refers to title in defining a "sale"; section 2-312 deals with a seller's warranty of title; sections 2-326 and 2-327 refer to title in connection with sale on approval and sale or return; section 2-403 provides that a purchaser acquires its transferor's title and, in some circumstances (entrustment and a transferor with voidable title) may acquire a better title than its transferor had; section 2-501(2) refers to title in connection with a seller's insurable interest in goods; and section 2-722 mentions title in connection with suits against third parties for injury to the goods. In applying these sections, it may become necessary to decide whether the buyer or the seller had title to the goods at a particular time. In applying other Article 2 sections, inquiries as to who had title will be unnecessary and usually unhelpful.

§ 6.02   RULES ON PASSAGE OF TITLE

As § 6.01 has pointed out, Article 2's title rules are only bit players in the solution of sales problems. Courts, however, use them for other purposes, such as determining whether the buyer or the seller is liable for a personal-property tax on the goods. The rules, which are contained in section 2-401, deal with the passage of title from seller to buyer. That is, they operate in a two-party world, and have little or nothing to say about any ownership interests that third parties may have in the goods. And they are written against the background assumption that, as between the parties, title starts out in the seller and at some point during the life of a contract of sale passes to the buyer. The section 2-401 rules can be summarized in the following manner:

Rule 1. Title cannot pass before the goods are identified to the contract.[7] Identification is covered in section 2-501 and is discussed *infra* in § 6.03. It is on identification that the buyer first obtains an ownership interest in the goods. Often this ownership interest, which section 2-501 calls "a special property and an insurable interest," is small—far short of title. But

---

[6] A number of Article 2 sections refer to "documents of title," which are defined in U.C.C. § 1-201(15) to include warehouse receipts, bills of lading, and the like, and which are the subject matter of Article 7. But these are not references to title in the sense intended in the first sentence of U.C.C. § 2-401.

[7] U.C.C. § 2-401(1).

until identification occurs and this special property is created, there can be no passage of title.

Under section 2-501, identification cannot occur until the goods "exist."[8] Once the goods exist, the parties may "explicitly" agree as to when identification occurs and, if they do so, their agreement will control. In the absence of explicit agreement, section 2-501(1) provides that identification occurs:

> (a) when the contract is made if it is for the sale of goods already existing and identified;
>
> (b) if the contract is for the sale of future goods[9] other than those described in paragraph (c) [which deals with contracts for the sale of certain unborn young of animals and unplanted crops], when goods are shipped, marked or otherwise designated by the seller as goods to which the contract refers.

It is often easy to apply these rules and, when it is not, effect should be given to the Comment 2 admonition: "In view of the limited effect given to identification by this Article, the general policy is to resolve all doubts in favor of identification."

The first title rule thus becomes: title cannot pass from the seller to the buyer until the goods exist and are identified to the contract. Section 2-401 states this rule in absolute terms, following it with other title rules that are subject to modification by explicit agreement of the parties. It therefore appears that the drafters of the Code meant to invalidate agreements that title would pass before identification.[10] Notice that this first title rule does not state that title does pass to the buyer the moment existing goods are identified; it only prevents passage of title before identification. Once the goods have been identified, other title rules control when and where title passes.

Rule 2. Unless it is otherwise explicitly agreed, identification gives the buyer a "special property" in the goods.[11] This section 2-401 title rule tracks the language and the thought of the first sentence of section 2-501(1): "The

---

[8] U.C.C. §§ 2-501(1), 2-106(2).

[9] "Future goods" are goods that are not both existing and identified. U.C.C. § 2-105(2). Thus, title to existing goods that are not "identified" when the contract is made cannot pass to the buyer until the goods are "designated" by the seller as the goods to which the contract refers. Whether title passes at the moment of designation depends upon the application of the other title rules discussed in this section of the text.

[10] *See* the final sentence of U.C.C. § 2-401(1) and U.C.C. § 2-105(2). In terms of U.C.C. § 1-102(3), these subsections "otherwise provide" and thus prevent variation by agreement.

[11] U.C.C. § 2-401(1).

buyer obtains a special property and an insurable interest in goods by identification of existing goods as goods to which the contract refers." The term "special property" is not defined, but, as it is used in both sections 2-401 and 2-501, it is plainly an interest that is different from, and smaller than, "title." Absent explicit agreement otherwise, identification automatically gives the buyer this limited special property. In some situations, the buyer obtains more—obtains title on identification, but this is not automatic. Whether and when it occurs will depend on other title rules.

Rule 3. Any retention or reservation of title by the seller in goods that have been shipped or delivered to the buyer is limited to a reservation of a security interest.[12] This oft-cited rule is basically a scope provision; it delineates one of the boundaries between Article 2 and Article 9.[13] Article 9 establishes a comprehensive scheme for the regulation of security interests in personal property (including goods). It is designed to cover seller security interests as well as lender security interests. That is, it is designed to cover the security-interest aspects of a transaction in which a seller sells and delivers goods on credit and, by agreement with the buyer, retains a security interest in the sold goods to secure the buyer's obligation to pay the price.[14] It is designed to apply without regard to the language in which the security agreement is couched. The fact that title-retention or conditional-sale language is used should not, and does not, exempt a security interest from Article 9 coverage.[15] Thus, the primary effect of the third title rule is to subject to the coverage of Article 9 (to treat as Article 9 security interests) any property interests that the buyer has allowed the seller to retain in goods that have been shipped or delivered.

Rule 4. Subject to the three rules set out above and subject to Article 9, title passes from the seller to the buyer in any manner and on any conditions explicitly agreed on by the parties.[16] The agreement must be explicit and will not be implied from the intention of the parties. It need not, however, be found in the same document as the other terms of the contract of sale; if the title agreement is written in some other document to which reference is made by the sales contract, this reference is sufficient to satisfy the requirements of the fourth title rule.

---

[12] *Id.*

[13] The rule is restated in the second sentence of U.C.C. § 1-201(37), as a part of the definition of "security interest," and so finds its way into U.C.C. § 9-102, the principal Article 9 scope provision.

[14] Article 2 covers the sale-of-goods aspects of this transaction.

[15] *See* Comment 1 to U.C.C. § 9-102.

[16] U.C.C. § 2-401(1).

Rule 5. When there is no explicit agreement and when delivery involves moving the goods, title passes to the buyer at the time and place the seller completes its performance with reference to physical delivery of the goods.[17] In a shipment contract, this is at the point of shipment, even though the buyer will not receive the goods until they reach their destination,[18] while in a destination contract, it will be at the point of destination.[19]

Rule 6. When there is no explicit agreement, and when delivery is to be made without moving the goods, section 2-401(3) provides:

> (a)   if the seller is to deliver a document of title, title passes at the same time when and the place where he delivers such documents; or
>
> (b)   if the goods are at the time of contracting already identified and no documents are to be delivered, title passes at the time and place of contracting.

Comment 4 to 2-401 explains the drafters' intention with respect to both the fifth and sixth rules:

> The factual situations in subsections (2) and (3) upon which passage of title turns actually base the test upon the time when the seller has finally committed himself in regard to specific goods. Thus in a "shipment" contract he commits himself by the act of making the shipment. If shipment is not contemplated subsection (3) turns on the seller's final commitment, i.e. the delivery of documents or making of the contract.

These are the six basic title rules. There are gaps and inconsistencies. Fortunately, not many commercial law problems turn on a determination of title, and most of the inconsistencies remain of academic interest only. However, the job that the drafters did is probably better than could be expected with such a nebulous concept as title to goods.[20] The principal ideas that emerge from section 2-401 are that title cannot pass from seller to buyer until goods "exist," and that, once the goods do exist, title is to pass at the time the seller commits the goods to the contract. This principle may aid in

---

[17] U.C.C. § 2-401(2). Title passes at this time and place even though the seller has retained a security interest in the goods, and even though a document of title is to be delivered at a different time or place.

[18] U.C.C. § 2-401(2)(a).

[19] U.C.C. § 2-402(2)(b).

[20] The proposed revisions to Article 2, in § 2-501, preserve the present title rules without significant change. The American Law Institute, Uniform Commercial Code Revised Article 2 Sales, Council Draft No. 4 (December 1, 1998) (hereinafter Council Draft).

reaching solutions in those cases that fall between sections of the Code and in those cases covered by two inconsistent sections.

Rule 7. Subsection 2-401(4) provides an additional title rule to deal with rejections and revocations of acceptance:

> A rejection or other refusal by the buyer to receive or retain the goods, whether or not justified, or a justified revocation of acceptance revests title to the goods in the seller. Such revesting occurs by operation of law and is not a "sale."

This revesting rule is triggered by any rejection, whether rightful or wrongful, but only by "justified" revocations of acceptance. Thus, a buyer who has accepted the goods delivered cannot by unilateral action revest title in the seller unless his revocation of acceptance meets the Code tests for a justified or rightful revocation.

§ 6.03 IDENTIFICATION

As has been seen, Article 2 has abandoned the title approach to sales problems that prevailed under prior law. No longer are most important questions resolved on the basis of which party, as between buyer and seller, had "title" to the goods at a particular moment. With rare exceptions, Article 2's provisions make no reference to title and apply without regard to title and whether it resided in the buyer or in the seller.[21] It is nevertheless true that when we think of contracts of sale, we think of the ownership of the goods passing from the seller to the buyer—at least if both parties perform. In fact, section 2-106(1) defines a "sale" as "the passing of title from the seller to the buyer for a price." But, for Article 2 purposes, ownership need not, and frequently does not, pass all at one time, as a single or lump title. Instead, the incidents of ownership are often divided between the seller and the buyer. The buyer, for example, may have a "special property" in the goods while the risk of their loss remains on the seller. And the seller may retain a security interest in the goods after their risk has passed to the buyer.

The two ideas just mentioned—that, in sales, ownership starts out in the seller and at some point passes to the buyer, and that the passage often occurs in steps rather than all at once—are part of the background against which section 2-501 is written. Under the Article 2 and section 2-501 scheme of things, all of the incidents of ownership reside in the seller until "identification." When the goods are identified as the goods to which the contract refers, the buyer obtains a "special property" in them. This is the

---

[21] *See* § 6.01, *supra.*

buyer's first (in the sense of earliest in time) property right in the goods, and it is usually a very limited interest, much more limited than the interest that the buyer received under the old law when title passed. Typically, the risk of loss and most other incidents of ownership remains with the seller for some time after identification.

Although identification plays a minor role in Article 2,[22] several sections use identification as a precondition (one of a number of preconditions) to a right of one of the parties. Thus, section 2-502 conditions the buyer's right to the goods on the seller's insolvency on: (1) the buyer's having an identification special property in the goods; (2) the buyer's having paid some or all of the price; (3) the buyer's keeping good a tender of any unpaid portion of the price; and (4) the seller's becoming insolvent within ten days after receipt of the first installment on the price.

Section 2-510(3) conditions the seller's right to treat the risk of loss as resting on the buyer on: (1) the goods' identification to the contract; (2) the buyer's default; and (3) a deficiency in the seller's effective insurance coverage. Section 2-716(3) makes similar use of identification in connection with a buyer's right to replevin. And section 2-722 makes use of identification in its provisions on who can sue third parties for injury to the goods.

Section 2-501(1) describes *when* identification occurs—when the buyer gets a special property and insurable interest in the goods. It begins by requiring that the goods be "existing." The Code does not define "existing," but common understanding can usually be relied on to determine whether particular goods exist at particular times. Difficult cases can often be resolved by the second statutory requirement: the goods must be identified as the goods to which the contract refers.[23] This requirement can be gleaned from section 2-501(1) and is expressly stated in section 2-105(2), which makes it clear that no property interest in goods can pass from seller to buyer until the goods are both existing and identified. Section 2-105(2) defines as "future goods" those goods that are not both existing and identified.

Section 2-501(1) goes on to provide some rules for when identification occurs. First, once the goods exist, identification of them can be made "at any time and in any manner explicitly agreed to by the parties." In the absence of explicit agreement, identification occurs:

> (a) when the contract is made if it is for the sale of goods already existing and identified;

---

[22] *See* Comment 2 to U.C.C. § 2-501.

[23] As U.C.C. § 2-501(10) provides, goods can be identified, and the buyer can obtain a special property in them even though they are nonconforming.

    (b)   if the contract is for the sale of future goods other than those described in paragraph (c), when the goods are shipped, marked, or otherwise designated by the seller as goods to which the contract refers;

    (c)   when the crops are planted or otherwise become growing crops or the young are conceived if the contract is for the sale of unborn young to be born within twelve months after contracting or for the sale of crops to be harvested within twelve months or the next normal harvest season after contracting whichever is longer.

These provisions can be easily applied in many situations. Assuming no explicit agreement as to when identification occurs, section 2-501(1)(a) causes identification to occur at contract formation when the contract is for the sale of a unique item, a particular used car, the contents of a particular warehouse, or other goods that exist and are identified, at contract formation, as those to which the contract refers. When the contract is for the sale of future goods, such as 100,000 tons of coal that the seller does not own at contract formation but expects to acquire, or a printing press that the seller expects to manufacture after contract formation, and there is no explicit agreement, section 2-501(1)(b) will cause identification to occur at the earliest point that the goods are tagged to the contract by the seller.[24]

Comment 5 to section 2-501 notes that shares in fungible bulks, such as grain in elevators or oil in storage tanks, can be sold. If the bulk is identified at contract formation, identification of the share can occur then as well.[25] The Comment 2 statement that, "[i]n view of the limited effect given to identification by this Article, the general policy is to resolve all doubts in favor of identification" may be particularly applicable to contracts for the sale of shares in bulks and other complicated situations.[26]

Subsection 2-501(1)(c) addresses some agricultural situations and states identification times for certain crops and unborn young of animals.[27] As with sections 2-501(1)(a) and 2-501(1)(b), it applies only in the absence of explicit agreement. For crops that are to be harvested within twelve months after contract formation, or within the next normal harvest season after contract formation if this is longer than twelve months, section 2-501(1)(c)

---

[24] *See* In re Quality Processing, Inc., 9 F.3d 1360, 22 UCCR2d 525 (8th Cir. 1993).

[25] *See* U.C.C. § 2-105(4).

[26] *See* Martin Marietta Corp. v. New Jersey Nat'l Bank, 612 F.2d 745, 27 UCCR 1153 (3d Cir. 1979).

[27] The U.C.C. § 2-105(1) definition of goods specifically includes "the unborn young of animals and growing crops."

provides that identification occurs when the crops are planted or otherwise become growing crops. Although it does not expressly say so, section 2-501(1)(c) appears to apply only to crops that have not been planted (or have otherwise become growing) at contract formation. For crops growing at contract formation, identification presumably occurs when the contract is formed, at least if they are to be harvested within twelve months or the next normal harvest season. Section 2-501(1)(c) plainly does not apply to crops that are to be harvested more than twelve months or after the next normal harvest season after contract formation. For them, identification probably occurs when the crops are designated by the seller as those to which the contract refers. The provision for unborn young of animals is similar; it expressly provides that identification occurs when the young are conceived if they are to be born within twelve months after contract formation. The identification of unborn young which have already been conceived at contract formation occurs then, at least if they are to be born within twelve months after contract formation. And the identification of unborn young which are to be born more than twelve months after contract formation presumably occurs when they are designated by the seller as the goods to which the contract refers.

§ 6.04   INSURABLE INTEREST

The doctrine of insurable interest grew up as, and remains, a part of insurance law. It rests in significant part on the idea—often referred to as the "principle of indemnity"—that an insurance contract should not confer a benefit greater in value than the loss suffered by the insured. Underlying policies include policies against wagering, against the deliberate destruction of property for the purpose of reaping a profitable insurance benefit, and against frauds on insurance companies. Insurance companies are the enforcers of the doctrine, and they enforce it by denying coverage when their insureds lack insurable interests. An insurer of goods that were destroyed could, for example, deny coverage (refuse to pay even though the event insured against had occurred) on the ground that its insured had no insurable interest in the goods. That is, the insurance company could deny coverage if the insured had no relationship to the goods, or such a tenuous relationship that the destruction of the goods did not cause it to suffer a loss.[28]

Buyers and sellers normally have sufficient relationship to the contract goods to merit insurable interests in the goods. They need to be able to

---

[28] For a comprehensive discussion of the insurable-interest doctrine, *see* Robert E. Keeton & Alan I. Widiss, Insurance Law 134–78 (1988).

obtain insurance policies covering the goods, insurance policies which, in the event of a casualty to the goods, can be enforced against the insurance companies that issued the policies. It is against this background that Article 2, in section 2-501, makes provision for buyers' and sellers' insurable interests.

Section 2-501 contains three subsections, each of which deals with insurable interest. First, section 2-501(1) addresses the buyer's insurable interest, and provides that a buyer obtains an insurable interest (and a "special property") in the goods on identification. What has been said about identification in the preceding section of this text is of obvious relevance in this connection. Second, section 2-501(2) addresses the seller's insurable interest, providing that a seller "retains an insurable interest in goods so long as title to or any security interest in the goods remains in him." This text's discussion of section 2-401's provisions on title is relevant in this connection. Because sellers frequently have title or a security interest (or both) for appreciable periods after identification, Article 2 recognizes the possibility of the parties having concurrent insurable interests.[29] This means, among other things, that both parties can have insurable interests although only one of them has the risk of loss.[30] Third, section 2-501(3) makes it clear that the Code is not the only source of buyers' and sellers' insurable interests; either party or both parties can have insurable interests under non-Code law:

> Nothing in this section impairs any insurable interest recognized under any other statute or rule of law.

Sections 2-501(1) and 2-501(2) provide the parties with insurable interests in most of the situations where they need such interests. Section 2-501(3) will probably cover the remaining situations where insurable interests are needed. Subsection (3) has considerable breadth; it recognizes non-Code law—particularly insurance law—to the extent that it gives one or both of the parties insurable interests. In light of this broad reference to

---

[29] *See, e.g.*, Hayward v. Postma, 31 Mich. App. 720, 188 N.W.2d 31, 9 UCCR 379 (1971).

[30] A party may have reason to insure and to enforce the insurance policy against the insurer even though it does not bear the risk of loss. Consider, for example, the situation of a seller that has delivered goods to its buyer on secured credit (the buyer's promise to pay being secured by a security interest in the goods). Assume that the delivery passed the risk of loss to the buyer under U.C.C. § 2-509. The seller may nevertheless want to insure the goods so that it can recover from a collectible insurance company if the goods are destroyed. Note that, if the insurance company pays the insured seller in such circumstances, it would be subrogated to the seller's rights against the buyer.

non-Code law, the importance of the section 2-501(1) and section 2-501 (2) provisions on Article 2 might well be questioned. The whole matter could have been left to insurance law. There has, however, been relatively little reported litigation about insurable-interest problems in sales cases, and the proposed revisions to Article 2 retain the current provisions without significant change.[31]

§ 6.05   RISK OF LOSS

Goods can be destroyed. Goods can be lost. Goods can be stolen. A customer who has "bought" a fur coat may ask the retailer to alter the coat's length. Suppose that before the customer picks up the coat, the coat is stolen from the retailer's store. Which party bears the risk of loss of the coat? Is the answer the same if, two weeks before the theft, the retailer had told the customer that the coat was ready to be picked up? Does it matter whether the customer has paid for the coat—with cash, a check, or a credit card?

The same retailer may have ordered fifty fur coats from a furrier in a distant city, F.O.B. the furrier's city. Suppose that the furrier shipped the coats and that, while they were in transit, they and the truck carrying them were destroyed by fire. Which party bears the risk of loss of the coats? Is the answer the same if the furrier had agreed to pay the shipping costs? If the coats were to be shipped F.O.B. the retailer's city? These examples suggest some of the many situations in which the parties to a contract of sale may be concerned about which of them bears the risk of the loss that occurred.

The Code contains two sections applicable to this problem. The first deals with the risk of loss in absence of breach;[32] the second considers the effect of breach on risk of loss.[33] Each section contains multiple subsections. There is, however, one principle, albeit a negative principle, that applies to all risk-of-loss problems. This principle is summarized in one sentence from the Comments:

> The underlying theory of these sections on risk of loss is the adoption of the contractual approach rather than an arbitrary shifting of the risk with the "property" in the goods.[34]

No longer is the question of title important in determining whether a buyer or a seller bears the risk of loss. It is true that the person with title may

---

[31] *See* Council Draft 2 § 2-502.

[32] U.C.C. § 2-509.

[33] U.C.C. § 2-510.

[34] U.C.C. § 2-509, Comment 1.

incidentally bear the risk that the goods may be destroyed or lost; but the seller may have title and the buyer the risk, or the seller may have the risk and the buyer the title.

Before the contract is formed, the risk that the goods may be lost or destroyed is on the seller. If the seller is a retailer or wholesaler, the seller bears the risk while the goods are on its shelves and before it has agreed to sell them to the buyer. If the seller is a manufacturer, the seller bears the risk as the goods come off the production line and before there is a contract for their sale. After the contract has been fully performed (without breach by either party) and the goods have been placed in the possession of the buyer, the buyer bears the risk. The risk thus shifts from seller to buyer at some time during the life of the contract, at least if the seller is not in breach. Determining the moment when this shift occurs is important to the parties so that they will know which of them ought to insure against loss and so that disputes between them following casualty to the goods can be speedily resolved.

Section 2-509 deals with risk of loss in the absence of breach. It assumes that the risk of loss is on the seller until some event occurs to pass that risk to the buyer. Rather than stating some all-inclusive single rule applicable to every situation, section 2-509 lists three types of situations and establishes for each the time when the risk of loss passes to the buyer:[35]

1. *Situations in which the contract requires or authorizes the seller to ship the goods by carrier.* Such contracts may be either shipment or destination contracts.[36]

2. *Situations in which the goods are held by a bailee and are to be delivered without being moved.* Typically, this type of case involves goods held by a warehouseman that are being sold to the buyer without removal from the warehouse. Often a negotiable warehouse receipt is transferred by the seller to the buyer, but the receipt may be nonnegotiable, or the arrangement may be less formal with no receipt having been issued by the bailee.

3. *Situations different from those described in items 1 and 2.* This residuary group includes contracts under which the buyer is to pick up the goods at the seller's place of business or residence as well as those in which the seller is to deliver the goods to the buyer by some means other than by "carrier."

---

[35] If the goods are destroyed or lost before the risk of their loss has passed to the buyer, the seller will be required to supply further conforming goods or be in default unless the circumstances are such that the seller can be excused from its obligation under U.C.C. § 2-613 or § 2-615.

[36] *See* § 5.02[A], *supra.*

Each of these three situations involves its own policy considerations as to when the risk of loss ought to pass; consequently, a separate rule is stated for each. These rules are outlined in the following sections of this text, but two exceptions should be noted. First, the parties may agree as to which is to bear the risk of loss.[37] They may agree to something completely different from the applicable section 2-509 rule, or they may make only a slight modification of the rule. The parties must, however, "agree" before this exception is applicable. A printed clause hidden in a maze of boilerplate raises familiar problems as to whether there has in fact been an agreement. Second, in a sale on approval, the seller bears the risk of loss until the goods are accepted by the buyer.[38]

Section 2-510 deals with the effect that a breach has on risk of loss. It covers three situations. The first is that in which the seller's tender so fails to conform to the contract that the buyer has the right to reject. The second is that in which the buyer has accepted the goods but has later rightfully revoked its acceptance. Both of these are situations in which the seller is in default. The third situation dealt with by section 2-510 involves a buyer's breach: that in which the buyer has repudiated or otherwise defaulted after the goods have been identified but before their risk has passed to the buyer. Once again different commercial policies are involved in each of these situations and different rules are stated by the Code.

[A] Goods Shipped by Carrier

The first of section 2-509's rules on the passage of the risk of loss in the absence of breach involves those situations in which the goods are to be shipped by carrier. "Carrier" is not defined in Article 2, but the context requires a party independent of both the seller and the buyer—a railroad, an airline, a trucking company, or the like.[39] The rule is contained in section 2-509 and is as follows:

> (1) Where the contract requires or authorizes the seller to ship the goods by carrier
> > (a) if it does not require him to deliver them at a particular destination, the risk of loss passes to the buyer when the goods are duly delivered to the carrier even though the shipment is under reservation (Section 2-501); but

---

[37] U.C.C. § 2-509(4).

[38] U.C.C. §§ 2-509(4), 2-327(1)(a).

[39] La Casse v. Blaustein, 93 Misc. 2d 572, 403 N.Y.S.2d 440, 23 UCCR 907 (1978) treats the U.S. Postal Service as a carrier for U.C.C. § 2-509(1) purposes.

(b)   if it does require him to deliver them at a particular destination and the goods are there duly tendered while in the possession of the carrier, the risk of loss passes to the buyer when the goods are there duly so tendered as to enable the buyer to take delivery.

This section applies both when the contract "requires" and when it "authorizes" the seller to ship the goods by carrier. Absent agreement to the contrary, authorization to ship by carrier can be implied in most sales contracts when the seller and buyer are located at any distance from each other, and is a part of all sales contracts containing an F.O.B., C.I.F., or like term.[40]

[1]   Shipment Contracts

Section 2-509(1)(a) deals with shipment contracts, such as contracts containing F.O.B. seller's point terms. It states the following risk-of-loss rule for such contracts: if the seller duly delivers the goods to the carrier, the risk of loss passes to the buyer on delivery to the carrier. Later loss or damage to those goods usually leaves the buyer liable for the price.[41] However, the loss or damage of those goods must have occurred "within a commercially reasonable time after risk of their loss has passed to the buyer."[42] This latter requirement is found in section 2-709, the section dealing with the seller's action for the price, and its relation to risk of loss is puzzling. If the risk has passed to the buyer, why must the loss occur within a "commercially reasonable time" in order to make the buyer liable for the agreed price of the goods? Suppose, for example, that the buyer and seller entered into a shipment contract, that the seller duly delivered conforming goods to the carrier, but that the carrier wrongfully held the goods for more than a commercially reasonable time before the goods were lost in transit. The risk passed to the buyer on delivery to the carrier, but does the buyer escape price liability because the loss did not occur within a commercially reasonable time after the delivery? If so, the risk of loss has effectively been shifted back to the seller by section 2-709 in spite of section 2-509—except in those cases in which the buyer paid in advance of the shipment.

Other sections of the Code indicate that the price section (section 2-709) ought not be read to change the risk of loss in the supposed situation.

---

[40] *See* U.C.C. §§ 2-319–2-322. The references in these sections to "risk" reinforce the rules of U.C.C. § 2-509(1) and sometimes make them more explicit.

[41] *See, e.g.,* Montana Seeds, Inc. v. Holiday, 178 Mont. 119, 582 P.2d 1223, 24 UCCR 884 (1978) and Ninth St. E., Ltd. v. Harrison, 5 Conn. Cir. Ct. 597, 259 A.2d 772, 7 UCCR 171 (1968).

[42] U.C.C. § 2-709(1)(a); § 7.08[E], *infra.*

Section 2-507 provides that tender of delivery "is a condition to the buyer's duty to accept the goods and, unless otherwise agreed, to his duty to pay for them. Tender entitles the seller to acceptance of the goods and to payment according to the contract." Section 2-709 was not meant to take this right to payment from the seller when a third party (the carrier) has defaulted on its obligations. The carrier's default ought to extend the "reasonable time" requirement of section 2-709, and the buyer ought to continue to bear the risk of loss and to be liable for the price. The buyer's action is against the carrier.

The purpose of the "commercially reasonable time" language of section 2-709 can be gleaned from the history of the section. The 1952 version of section 2-709 contained no reference to a "commercially reasonable time" but simply provided that the seller could recover the price when the goods had been lost or damaged after risk of their loss had passed to the buyer. The New York Law Revision Commission objected, because this version of the statute provided "no limit on the time during which seller may hold goods at buyer's risk."[43] The type of situation that troubled the Commissioners was one in which the risk of loss had passed to the buyer but in which the seller was still *holding* the goods at the time of the casualty. Both destination and shipment contracts can provide examples. In a destination contract involving a delivery by carrier, the risk of loss passes on a proper tender by the carrier; in a shipment contract involving delivery by a carrier, the risk of loss passes on a proper delivery to the carrier. In either event, the buyer's wrongful refusal to accept the goods leaves the goods with the carrier, subject to the seller's orders. The Commissioners did not believe that the buyer ought to bear the risk of loss of those goods forever. Only if casualty occurred to the goods within a commercially reasonable time after the wrongful refusal to accept should the buyer be liable for their price; otherwise, the loss ought to fall on the seller—the party with control over the goods.

In response to the Commission's criticism, the drafters inserted the "commercially reasonable time" language in sections 2-709 and 2-510(3). There was no objection as to how the 1952 rule operated when the goods had been lost while in the control of a carrier; the concern was about those situations in which the seller retained control after the risk had shifted to the buyer. However, the addition of the time limitation to section 2-709 (rather than dealing with the problem exclusively in the risk of loss sections) could produce cases like the one set out above: that is, one in which the seller in a shipment contract had duly delivered goods to a carrier, the carrier

---

[43] New York Law Revision Comm'n, 1955 Report (vol. 1) 489.

had held the goods for a commercially unreasonable time without shipping them to the buyer, and the goods were then destroyed by some casualty. In such a situation, the risk of loss would have passed to the buyer on delivery to the carrier, but the seller would not be able to recover the price under a literal application of the language of section 2-709. Fortunately such cases are rare; however, when they do arise, the court should take account of how the section 2-709 time limitation became a part of the Code and apply that limitation only when the seller had control of the goods following passage of the risk of loss to the buyer.

The principal problem under section 2-509(1)(a) is that of determining the meaning of the words "duly delivered." This much is clear; until delivery to the carrier, the risk of loss in a shipment contract remains with the seller; and even on delivery to the carrier, the risk does not pass to the buyer unless the goods have been *duly* delivered. The difficulty comes in detailing the requirements that change a plain delivery into a due delivery. These words are not defined, but appear to carry with them some notion that the seller's delivery to the carrier must conform to the contract with the buyer. If the contract called for a refrigerator, the delivery to the carrier of a water softener ought not place on the buyer the risk that the softener would be lost in transit. Likewise, if the contract required air shipment, delivery to a trucking company ought not transfer the risk of loss.

The Comments support this construction by suggesting that the word "duly" was used to incorporate into section 2-509 the tender requirements of a shipment contract.[44] Under those requirements the seller must (1) put the goods in the possession of such a carrier as is reasonable; (2) make a reasonable contract for their transportation; (3) obtain and promptly deliver or tender the necessary documents; and (4) promptly notify the buyer of the shipment.[45] Certainly if the seller does these four things and, in addition,

---

[44] U.C.C. § 2-509, Comment 2.

[45] U.C.C. § 2-504. For a case of failure to make a reasonable contract with the carrier (and thus of failure to shift the risk to the buyer), see La Casse v. Blaustein, 93 Misc. 2d 572, 403 N.Y.S.2d 440, 23 UCCR 907 (1978), in which the seller placed the "theft-tempting" label "calculators" on the goods' packaging and insured the goods for less than 10 percent of their price. In this connection, note that Comment 3 to U.C.C. § 2-504 states that "[i]t is an improper contract under paragraph (a) for the seller to agree with the carrier to a limited valuation below the true value and thus cut off the buyer's opportunity to recover from the carrier in the event of loss, when the risk of shipment is placed on the buyer." *But see* Cook Specialty Co. v. Schrlock, 772 F. Supp. 1532, 16 UCCR2d 360 (E.D. Pa. 1991), which holds that the seller did not violate its reasonable-contract obligation by failing "to ensure that a carrier has sufficient insurance to cover a particular potential loss, in which case the carrier is still liable to the buyer."

Failure of the seller to notify the buyer of the shipment until after the ship sailed and

makes certain that the goods involved conform to the contract, there has been a due delivery, and the risk has shifted to the buyer. The problem centers on how much short of this ideal performance a seller can fall and still satisfy section 2-509(1)(a).

The initial temptation is to state flatly that any default by the seller removes the case from section 2-509 (after all, the section is captioned: "Risk of Loss in the Absence of Breach") and prevents the risk from passing on delivery to the carrier. This may, however, be reading too much into the single word "duly." It may be that the scheme of the Code allows something short of perfect performance by the seller to satisfy the delivery to a carrier requirements of section 2-509. For example, section 2-510(1) provides:

> Where a tender of delivery of goods so fails to conform to the contract as to give a right of rejection the risk of their loss remains on the seller until cure or acceptance.

The implication of this section is that some nonconformities do not prevent the risk of loss from shifting to the buyer. It is only a nonconformity that gives the buyer a right of rejection that keeps the risk of loss on the seller. The delivery of the water softener in place of the refrigerator or the selection of truck transportation in place of an agreed-upon air shipment would give the buyer the right to reject. However, if the buyer-seller contract had been an installment contract and the nonconforming goods delivered to the carrier did not *substantially* impair the value of that installment to the buyer, the buyer could not reject, and the risk of loss would shift to the buyer in spite of the seller's breach. Thus, the word "duly" does not always carry with it a requirement of a perfect tender, but only of a tender that is sufficient to require the buyer to accept the goods on their arrival.[46]

[2] Destination Contracts

The second type of contract covered by section 2-509(1) is the destination contract. When the seller is required to deliver goods at their destination, their risk does not shift on delivery to a carrier but only when the

---

sunk (thus depriving the buyer of the opportunity to insure the goods while in transit) prevented the risk from shifting in Rheinberg-Kellerei Gmbh v. Vineyard Wine Co., Inc., 53 N.C. App. 560, 281 S.E.2d 425, 32 UCCR 96 (1981).

[46] Thus, the broad language of the opinion in William F. Wilke, Inc. v. Cummins Diesel Engines, Inc., 252 Md. 611, 250 A.2d 886, 6 UCCR 45 (1969), should be limited to the facts of that case—a contract calling for the delivery of a single item. For a discussion of when the buyer may reject, *see* §§ 7.03[C] & 7.03[D], *infra*.

goods are duly tendered at the point of destination so "as to enable the buyer to take delivery." Once again the Code uses the word "duly." The meaning here is the same as that discussed previously; the tender must be such as requires the buyer to accept the goods. This necessitates looking at: (1) the agreement between the parties to determine the quality of the goods ordered and any contractual limitations on the privilege of rejection; (2) at the goods delivered to determine whether they conform to the contract (or, in the case of deliveries under an installment contract, whether they substantially conform); and (3) the mechanics of the tender. This last requirement would make section 2-503 applicable in determining whether the risk of loss had been shifted to the buyer. The carrier's tender in a destination contract must be at a reasonable hour and be kept open for a period of time reasonably necessary for the buyer to take possession. In addition, any necessary documents must have been delivered by the seller.

The resulting patterns under both types of contract (shipment and destination) are similar. The seller begins with the risk of loss. The risk shifts to the buyer at the moment when the seller takes such action as is needed to place on the buyer the duty of accepting the goods. If the buyer wrongfully refuses those goods and returns them to the control of the seller, the seller effectively regains the risk after a commercially reasonable time.

[B] Goods Held by a Bailee to Be Delivered Without Being Moved

There are some sales in which the goods bought and sold are in the possession of a bailee and the sale is completed without moving the goods. As an example, grain stored in a warehouse may be sold, and the contract of sale fully performed by both parties—the seller giving the buyer control over the grain and the buyer paying the price—all without moving the grain. The buyer may later (after the contract of sale has been fully performed) remove the grain from the warehouse. Alternatively, the buyer may resell the grain (say to a purchaser that plans to leave the grain in the warehouse for some time before removing it and milling it into flour) in the same way that it bought it—without moving the goods. In sales of this kind, it does not make commercial sense to keep the risk of loss on the seller until it has "delivered" the goods to the buyer or until the buyer has "received" the goods. Some earlier time must be chosen to shift the risk—else the seller could continue to bear the risk long after the buyer had been given control over the goods and paid for them.

The Code's key to risk of loss in these situations lies in the concept of control of the goods. The warehouseman of grain would most probably have issued some receipt to show that it had stored the grain for the owner and would deliver it according to certain terms. Such a receipt is a document of title under the Code.[47] If the receipt is negotiable,[48] the bailee's obligation is to deliver the goods to the holder of the document.[49] Thus, with a negotiable document, control over the goods is locked up in the document and can be transferred by delivery of the document. If the receipt is nonnegotiable, the bailee's obligation is to deliver the goods to the person to whom delivery is to be made by the terms of the document or in accordance with written instructions under the document. Thus, with a nonnegotiable document, possession of the document gives less assurance of entitlement to the goods, and a buyer of the document will need to give notice to the bailee to firm up its rights.[50] Therefore, when the bailee has issued a document of title covering the goods, control of the document of title (plus a reasonable time to check with the bailee if the document is nonnegotiable) is a sufficient control of the goods to shift the risk to the buyer.

There are situations, however, in which the bailee has not issued a document of title. A racing car may be stored at a garage; a yacht may be docked for the winter at a marina; or a horse may be stabled on a farm in Kentucky. The arrangement between the owners of these goods and their bailees may have been informal with no document of any kind having been issued by the bailees. Nevertheless, the owner of the car, yacht, or horse ought to be able to sell without requiring the buyer to take immediate possession. The new owner may want to leave the car in the garage, the yacht in the marina, or the horse on the farm—being satisfied to have the bailee become its (rather than the former owner's) bailee. Control is again the key factor. When the buyer has converted the seller's bailee into the buyer's bailee, the buyer has control over the goods and the risk of their loss ought to shift.[51]

The ideas just developed on the passage of the risk of loss are those on which section 2-509(2) is based. It provides:

---

[47] U.C.C. § 1-201(15). *See also* the definitions in U.C.C. § 7-102.

[48] U.C.C. § 7-104 distinguishes negotiable documents of title from nonnegotiable documents. A document is negotiable "if by its terms the goods are to be delivered to bearer or to the order of a named person" or "where recognized in overseas trade, if it runs to a named person or assigns." Any other document is nonnegotiable.

[49] U.C.C. §§ 7-403, 7-502.

[50] U.C.C. §§ 2-403, 7-504(2). *See* Procter & Gamble Distrib. Co. v. Lawrence Am. Field Warehousing Corp., 16 N.Y.2d 344, 213 N.E.2d 873, 3 UCCR 157 (1965).

[51] *See, e.g.*, Whately v. Tetrault, 29 Mass. App. Dec. 112, 5 UCCR 838 (1964), where the risk of loss in goods sold while in the possession of a bailee shifted to the buyer when the bailee was made aware of the buyer's right to possession of the goods and made arrangements for the buyer's agent to pick up the goods.

(2) Where the goods are held by a bailee to be delivered without being moved, the risk of loss passes to the buyer
   (a) on his receipt of a negotiable document of title covering the goods; or
   (b) on acknowledgement by the bailee of the buyer's right to possession of the goods; or
   (c) after his receipt of a non-negotiable document of title or other written direction to deliver, as provided in subsection 4(b) of Section 2-503.

The seller's performance obligations under a contract for the sale of goods held by a bailee (to be delivered without being moved) are related to section 2-509(2)'s provisions on the shifting of the risk of loss. The performance problem centers on what the seller must do to trigger the buyer's obligation to accept the goods and to pay for them according to the terms of the contract. The required performance is a unilateral act on the part of the seller—usually a tender of goods or documents, or both. Tender is provided for in section 2-504, subsection (4) of which deals with tender when the goods are held by a bailee to be delivered without being moved. If the buyer refuses the seller's conforming tender, the buyer is in default and is liable to the seller for that default. But whether the buyer should bear the risk of loss of the goods following a wrongful rejection is a different problem. Because the placement of the risk is usually based on some type of control over the goods, the unilateral tender by the seller is not sufficient to shift the risk. Thus, although a buyer may be liable in damages for a wrongful rejection, later destruction of those goods could be at the seller's risk.

The Code's rules on the passing of the risk of loss in some specific situations in which the goods are held by a bailee and are to be delivered without being moved as follows:

1. *Negotiable documents.* If the goods are covered by a negotiable document of title, the seller can and should tender performance by *tendering* the negotiable document.[52] But under section 2-509(2)(a) the risk of loss shifts to the buyer only on his *receipt* of the document. "Receipt" carries with it the idea that the buyer has taken physical possession of the document;[53] thus, if the buyer refuses the seller's tender, the goods in the pos-

---

[52] U.C.C. § 2-503(4)(a).
[53] *Cf.* U.C.C. § 2-103(1)(c).

session of the bailee remain at the seller's risk.[54] Tender begins the delivery, which is not complete until receipt.[55]

2. *Nonnegotiable documents.* Tender of a nonnegotiable document is a sufficient tender of performance "unless the buyer seasonably objects."[56] If the buyer does object, the seller must find some other way to perform— such as by obtaining and tendering a negotiable document or by procuring the bailee's acknowledgment of the buyer's right to the goods.

The receipt of a nonnegotiable document does not shift the risk to the buyer. The reason for this rule is that the buyer, although it holds the non-negotiable document, can lose its rights to creditors of the seller, to certain purchasers from the seller, or to the bailee itself.[57] The buyer is protected against such third parties only from the time it gives notice to the bailee. Risk of loss, therefore, remains on the seller until the buyer has had a reasonable time to present the nonnegotiable document to the bailee, and a refusal to honor the document defeats the tender.[58]

3. *No documents involved.* When the bailee holds goods for which no documents have been issued and the seller wants to sell those goods without moving them, the seller can perform in one of two ways. It can either (1) deliver to the buyer a writing that directs the bailee to deliver the goods to the buyer, or (2) procure from the bailee an acknowledgment that the buyer is entitled to the goods. If the seller chooses the first method of performance, tender and risk of loss are determined by the same rules as if a nonnegotiable document had been involved.[59] If the seller chooses the second method of performance, tender is accomplished by procuring the acknowledgment of the bailee,[60] and risk of loss passes "on acknowledgment by the bailee of the buyer's right to possession of the goods."[61]

---

[54] A wrongful rejection by the buyer triggers U.C.C. § 2-510(3) and enables the seller to treat the risk of loss as resting on the buyer for a commercially reasonable time if and to the extent that there is a deficiency in the seller's effective insurance coverage. U.C.C. § 2-510(3) is discussed in § 6.06[B], *infra.*

[55] U.C.C. § 2-509, Comment 4.

[56] U.C.C. § 2-503(4)(b).

[57] U.C.C. § 7-504(2).

[58] This is provided by the "after his receipt of a non-negotiable document of title . . . as provided in subsection (4)(b) of Section 2-503" language of U.C.C. § 2-509(2)(c) and by the following U.C.C. § 2-503(4)(b) language: "but risk of loss of the goods . . . remains on the seller until the buyer has had a reasonable time to present the document . . . and a refusal by the bailee to honor the document . . . defeats the tender."

[59] U.C.C. §§ 2-509(2)(c), 2-503(4)(b).

[60] U.C.C. § 2-503(4)(a).

[61] U.C.C. § 2-509(2)(b).

In most situations, these rules work without difficulty. If the buyer is given a writing that directs the bailee to hold or deliver the goods on the buyer's order, the buyer has a reasonable time to present that writing—and the risk of loss will not shift until that time has expired. If the seller procures the bailee's acknowledgment that the goods are being held for the buyer, the buyer has immediate control over the goods and risk passes at that time. Must the bailee's acknowledgment be made to the buyer, or would an acknowledgment to the seller be sufficient to shift the risk? The Code does not expressly answer this question, but the policies underlying section 2-509(2) suggest that the acknowledgment must be made to the buyer, and it has been so held.[62] The proposed revisions to Article 2 expressly codify the requirement that the acknowledgment be made to the buyer.[63]

[C] Other Cases

Subsection 2-509(3) contains the residuary risk-of-loss rules—rules for those situations in which there has been no breach triggering section 2-510, in which there is no section 2-509(4) agreement by the parties allocating risk, in which the seller was neither authorized nor required to ship the goods by carrier, and in which the goods were not held by a bailee to be delivered without being moved. These residuary rules are stated in these words:

> In any case not within subsection (1) or (2), the risk of loss passes to the buyer on his receipt of the goods if the seller is a merchant; otherwise the risk passes to the buyer on tender of delivery.[64]

The merchant rule conforms to the general Code policy of placing the risk on the party who has control of the goods at the time of their loss. Risk does not pass until the buyer has *received* the goods. But the nonmerchant seller can shift the risk even though it retains control of the goods, because the risk passes when the nonmerchant seller *tenders* delivery. The policy reason for distinguishing merchant sellers from nonmerchant sellers is suggested by Comment 3 to section 2-509: merchant sellers can be expected to insure goods in their possession.

The difference in the two rules can be easily illustrated. Suppose that a buyer agreed to purchase a used automobile and to pay the price and to

---

[62] Jason's Foods, Inc. v. Peter Eckrich & Sons, Inc., 774 F.2d 214, 41 UCCR 1287 (7th Cir. 1985).

[63] Council Draft § 2-612(b)(3)(B).

[64] U.C.C. § 2-509(3).

take delivery as soon as the seller had the brakes relined. The seller had the work done, telephoned the buyer, and told him that he could pick up the automobile at his convenience. Before the buyer took possession, the automobile was destroyed by a fire in the seller's garage. If the seller was a merchant, the risk of loss problem would turn on whether the buyer had received the goods; because section 2-103(1)(c) defines "receipt" of goods as "taking physical possession," and because the buyer had not taken physical possession of the automobile, the risk would remain on the seller.[65] If, however, the seller was not a merchant, the risk problem would center on whether the seller had tendered delivery. Had he put and held conforming goods at the buyer's disposition and given the appropriate notice? If so, the risk would be on the buyer.

Showing that a seller has tendered delivery requires a showing (1) that the goods were conforming, (2) that they were put and held "at the buyer's disposition," and (3) that the seller gave the buyer whatever notice was reasonably necessary to enable the buyer to take delivery.[66] There are difficulties in reading these requirements into the Code section on risk of loss. The contents of the notice (or the contents of the notice plus the prior understandings of the parties) must let the buyer know where the goods are held so that the buyer can go there and take delivery; otherwise the notice would not reasonably "enable him to take delivery." That much is clear, but when the goods are destroyed before the buyer takes delivery, does the notice requirement also include a time factor? Must the notice be given long enough before the casualty so that the buyer had a reasonable time to take delivery of the goods before their destruction? Further, what is the meaning of the phrase, "at the buyer's disposition?" Are goods held at the buyer's disposition if the contract requires the buyer to perform some act (such as paying the price) as a condition precedent to obtaining delivery, or must the tender be unconditional? Certainly the tender need not be unconditional when the problem is whether the acts of the seller were sufficient to place the buyer in default—and the Comments recognize this[67]—but this conclusion does not necessarily control the answer to the risk-of-loss problem. Ought the risk of loss shift even though the buyer must perform some act before he can obtain delivery? The answers to these questions cannot be found in specific Code language; they will turn on how courts feel about

---

[65] *See* Galbraith v. American Motorhome Corp., 14 Wash. App. 754, 545 P.2d 561, 18 UCCR 914 (1976).

[66] U.C.C. § 2-503(1).

[67] U.C.C. § 2-503, Comment 2.

placing the risk on a party who does not have control of goods which suffer destruction.[68]

Returning to the residuary rule for merchant sellers: Risk of loss passes to the buyer on its receipt of the goods. Usually the application of this rule will cause few complications. Suppose that a buyer made a contract with a retail seller of sewing machines to purchase a specific floor-model sewing machine. The buyer would have an insurable interest in that sewing machine at the moment the contract was made but the risk of its loss would remain with the seller until the buyer's receipt of the machine—"receipt" meaning the buyer's taking physical possession of the machine.[69] If the sewing machine was destroyed while still in the seller's store or while on the seller's truck en route to the buyer's home, the seller would bear the loss.[70] Likewise, if a buyer had agreed to purchase a diamond ring from a jeweler but had left the ring to be engraved, the risk would not pass to the buyer even though the price had been paid, the engraving had been completed, and the buyer had been notified that she could pick up the ring.[71] Neither the buyer of the sewing machine nor the buyer of the ring had as yet taken physical possession of the goods. Holding the ring for the purpose of deciding whether to purchase or admiring a purchase already made (but with the intention of returning the goods to the retail seller for further modification) does not amount to a "receipt" for the purposes of the Code's risk-of-loss rules. The Code shifts the risk of loss when a merchant-seller loses control of the goods—at that moment of time when the buyer has physical possession of the goods *as a buyer.*

The merchant-seller rule of section 2-509(3)—that risk passes on the buyer's receipt of the goods—applies to sales to merchants as well as to sales to consumers. In other words, the buyer's merchant or nonmerchant status is irrelevant to the application of the rule. Of course, a substantial number of merchant-to-merchant sales are governed by subsection (1) of section 2-509 because the contract will authorize or require the seller to ship the goods by carrier. But when the merchant buyer is to pick the goods up at the merchant seller's place of business, or when the merchant seller is to use its own truck to deliver the goods to the merchant buyer's place of business, section 2-509(3) applies, and the risk does not shift until the buyer's receipt of the goods.

---

[68] *See* Martin v. Melland's, Inc., 283 N.W.2d 76, 27 UCCR 94 (N.D. 1979).

[69] U.C.C. § 2-103(1)(c).

[70] Delivery on the seller's truck is not a shipment by "carrier." § 6.05[A] *supra.*

[71] U.C.C. § 2-509, Comment 3.

A merchant seller holding goods at its buyer's disposition when the goods suffered a casualty might be tempted to argue that section 2-509(2) applied to its situation—that it was not only the seller but also a bailee, and that the risk passed to the buyer on its acknowledgment of the buyer's right to possession,[72] that is, before the casualty. Such arguments should generally be rejected. "Bailee," as used in section 2-509(2) means a third-party bailee, not the buyer, and particularly not the seller.[73] Further, if it is contemplated that the buyer will pick up the goods, it is doubtful that they are to be "delivered without being moved." Save in rare situations when, by a clear agreement, the seller is made the buyer's bailee after the sale contract has been performed, section 2-509(3) and its rule that risk passes on the buyer's receipt of the goods should govern such cases.

Two problems with section 2-509(3) remain for discussion. First, as has been seen, receipt of the goods (the controlling event for merchant sellers) is defined to mean "taking physical possession of them."[74] Usually the moment that the buyer takes possession can be readily determined. She will place the item in her hand and walk out of the store; she will get into her new automobile and drive away; or she will have the seller deliver and place the item in her home or place of business. In these cases the buyer's "possession" is clear. Unfortunately, however, there has been a great deal of common-law litigation over the meaning of "possession." Inevitably, there are arguments over whether the purchaser from a merchant seller had taken possession of the goods before they were destroyed. The seller's delivery man, not finding the buyer at home, may leave the goods (for example, the sewing machine) on the buyer's front porch or with a neighbor. Has the buyer taken physical possession of such goods? Does it make a difference if the porch is enclosed or open, whether the buyer lives in an apartment or a single residence, whether the delivery man was following a common practice of the seller in leaving the goods with someone other than the buyer, or whether the buyer was informed of the location of the goods? Answers to these questions are not easy, and common-law decisions on the meaning of "possession" in cases involving larceny, title, or conversion afford little aid in reaching satisfactory answers.[75] Here the problem is whether risk of loss should shift to the buyer; perhaps the Code's concept of control of the goods is the best guide that can be given in solving difficult cases.

---

[72] U.C.C. § 2-509(2)(b).
[73] See Martin v. Melland's, Inc., 283 N.W.2d 76, 27 UCCR 94 (N.D. 1979).
[74] U.C.C. § 2-103(1)(c).
[75] See Burke Shartel, "Meanings of Possession," 16 Minn. L. Rev. 611 (1932).

Second, the residuary risk-of-loss rules of section 2-509(3) distinguish between the merchant seller and the nonmerchant seller. Usually this distinction is not hard to make. The manufacturer who sells goods it has manufactured is a merchant for that sale; the wholesaler and retailer selling goods of the kind they normally sell are merchants for those sales. There will, however, be troublesome cases in which it is difficult to determine whether a particular seller falls within section 2-104(1)'s definition of merchant. For example, a manufacturer selling an old machine that it had long used in its factory is not selling goods of the kind in which it "deals." To make such a seller a merchant (and to keep the risk of loss from shifting until the buyer has received the machine), a court would have to conclude that the manufacturer (or its agent) is, by its occupation, holding itself out "as having knowledge or skill peculiar to the practices or goods involved."[76] Concluding that every seller that has made business use of the goods it is selling is a merchant with respect to the *goods* would cause difficulty with other Code sections, but an emphasis on the *practice* of insuring goods can be employed to expand the number of sellers falling within the "merchant" definition for risk-of-loss purposes. Most business sellers do, by their occupations as people in business, hold themselves out as having knowledge about the practices of caring for and insuring goods and thus can be considered "merchants" for section 2-509(3) purposes even though the goods sold are not of the kind in which they usually deal. In view of the underlying Code policy of placing the risk on the party in control of the goods unless there is good reason to do otherwise, close cases should be resolved in favor of finding the seller to be a merchant.

Although the proposed revisions to Article 2 continues much of the current law on risk of loss in cases of goods shipped by carrier and goods held by a bailee to be delivered without being moved, it proposes a major change with respect to other cases. It would pass the risk on the buyer's receipt of the goods without regard to the seller's status as a merchant. In other words, it would abolish the rule that when the seller is a nonmerchant, the risk passes on tender of delivery.[77]

§ 6.06   EFFECT OF BREACH ON RISK OF LOSS

Section 2-509, which has just been considered, deals with risk of loss in the absence of breach. Section 2-510 deals with the effect of breach on

---

[76] U.C.C. § 2-104(1).
[77] Council Draft § 2-612(b)(1).

the risk of loss. Its first two subsections are concerned with certain breaches by sellers, and its third subsection is concerned with the effect of certain buyers' breaches. We begin with the sellers' breaches.

[A]   Effect of Seller's Breach

Subsection (4) of section 2-509 provides that the section 2-509 risk-of-loss rules are subject to the section 2-510 provisions on the effect of breach. Subsections (1) and (2) of section 2-510 specify the effects of certain sellers' breaches:

> (1) Where a tender or delivery of goods so fails to conform to the contract as to give a right of rejection the risk of their loss remains on the seller until cure or acceptance.
>
> (2) Where the buyer rightfully revokes acceptance he may to the extent of any deficiency in his effective insurance coverage treat the risk of loss as having rested on the seller from the beginning.

When the buyer has a right to reject. When nonconforming goods are tendered or delivered by the seller, the buyer may in some instances reject the goods. Other portions of this text develop the instances in which rejection is allowed.[78] For example, if the contract calls for a single delivery of goods and if no other limitation on rejection is applicable, the buyer may reject for any nonconformity in the goods or tender of delivery.[79] On the other hand, if the contract calls for delivery of the goods in installments, the buyer may not reject an installment unless the nonconformity substantially impairs the value of that installment and cannot be cured.[80] It is only when the nonconformity is sufficient to give the buyer the privilege of rejection that section 2-510(1) leaves the risk of loss on the seller.

When the contract requires or authorizes the seller to ship the goods by carrier, section 2-510(1) restates the risk-of-loss rule obtained from section 2-509(1). In a shipment contract the risk passes when the goods are *duly* delivered to the carrier; in a destination contract the risk passes when the goods are *duly* tendered to the buyer.[81] To pass muster under this section 2-509(1) "duly" standard, the delivery or tender must sufficiently comply

---

[78] §§ 7.03[C] and 7.03[D], *infra*.

[79] U.C.C. § 2-601.

[80] U.C.C. § 2-612.

[81] U.C.C. § 2-509(1).

with the contract that it prevents the buyer from rightfully rejecting the goods.

U.C.C. § 2-510(1) does, however, limit the operation of the section 2-509(3)'s merchant-seller rule—that the risk passes when the buyer receives the goods. A buyer may receive goods (that is, take physical possession of them)[82] and still have the right to reject them.[83] An inspection by a buyer of goods in his possession may prove that the goods were nonconforming—or, in the case of an installment contract, substantially nonconforming. So long as the buyer has the right of rejection, section 2-510(1) keeps the risk of loss on the seller.[84] Even though the buyer has control of the goods, the buyer does not have their risk if they were so nonconforming as to give it the right to reject them. Only cure or acceptance of such goods will shift their risk to the buyer.

When the buyer has rightfully revoked acceptance. Under the "until cure or acceptance" language of section 2-510(1), acceptance of goods that are nonconforming and that could have been rejected shifts their risk to the buyer. This fits with the rule that acceptance precludes rejection.[85] Once goods have been accepted, the buyer no longer has a right of rejection and can no longer use section 2-510(1) to keep the risk of loss on the seller. In limited instances, however, a buyer may revoke its acceptance.[86] Revocation of acceptance is discussed in another portion of this text[87] and that discussion is not repeated here. It is sufficient at this juncture to note that the effect of a successful revocation of acceptance is similar to that of a rightful rejection: the nonconforming goods are thrown back on the seller, and the buyer has the same rights and duties with regard to the goods as if it had rejected them.[88]

The Code, however, draws a risk-of-loss distinction between rejection cases (which are handled by the just discussed section 2-510(1)) and revocation cases (which are handled by section 2-510(2)). As has been seen, the risk passes to the buyer when it accepts nonconforming goods. If the buyer

---

[82] U.C.C. § 2-103(1)(c).

[83] §§ 7.03[C] and 7.03[D], *infra*; Zabriskie Chevrolet, Inc. v. Smith, 99 N.J. Super. 441, 240 A.2d 195, 5 UCCR 30 (1968); Jakowski v. Carole Chevrolet, Inc., 180 N.J. Super 122, 433 A.2d 841, 31 UCCR 1615 (1981).

[84] *See* William F. Wilke, Inc. v. Cummins Diesel Engines, Inc., 252 Md. 611, 250 A.2d 886, 6 UCCR 45(1969).

[85] U.C.C. § 2-607(2).

[86] *See* U.C.C. § 2-608.

[87] § 7.03[E], *infra*.

[88] U.C.C. § 2-608.

thereafter rightfully revokes its acceptance, section 2-510(2) authorizes it to treat the risk of loss as having rested on the seller from the beginning of the transaction[89]—but only to the extent of any deficiency in the buyer's effective insurance coverage. The operation of this rule is illustrated by the following hypothetical case:

Suppose a buyer had paid the full price—$10,000—for goods that it had accepted without discovering their substantial nonconformity and under circumstances that made it difficult to discover the nonconformity. Thereafter, the buyer discovered the defect and rightfully revoked its acceptance, giving timely notice to the seller. Before the seller could remove the goods from the buyer's possession, the goods were destroyed by a fire. The buyer's insurance coverage on the goods was $6,000. The buyer may treat the risk of loss to the extent of $4,000 as having rested on the seller from the beginning of this transaction.[90] Because, to the extent that the buyer's insurance coverage is deficient, section 2-510(2) treats the risk of loss as having rested on the seller, the seller's insurance carrier would have no subrogation rights against the buyer for any amounts that it paid the seller on account of the loss.[91]

The rules of sections 2-510(1) and 2-510(2) are subject to the criticism that they place the risk of loss on the seller in circumstances where the seller does not possess or control the goods and is unlikely to insure them. The justification, of course, is that the seller is in breach. But, at least in section

---

[89] The retroactive aspect of the "treat the risk of loss as having rested on the seller from the beginning" language of U.C.C. § 2-510(2) has limited effect. U.C.C. § 2-608(2) provides that revocation of acceptance must occur "before any substantial change in condition of the goods which is not caused by their own defects." Usually, the event that causes the goods to be lost or destroyed—the fire, theft, or the like—is not caused by a defect in the goods. When this is so, the buyer will be unable rightfully to revoke its acceptance after the casualty because of the substantial change in the condition of the goods wrought by the casualty. The upshot is that U.C.C. § 2-510(2) will almost always apply to losses that occur *after* the revocation. It will apply to losses that occurred before the revocation only if they were caused by defects in the goods, and those are the only situations where the retroactive aspect of the "treat the risk of loss as having rested on the seller from the beginning" language will have bite.

[90] If the buyer had not paid the price, it would probably be unable to recover from its insurer (because it could not show a loss). In these circumstances, the seller should not be able to recover the price from the buyer. Because, to the extent that the buyer lacks effective insurance coverage, the risk of loss rests on the seller, the seller cannot recover the price under the "lost or damaged" portion of U.C.C. § 2-709(1)(a). The seller might argue that he is entitled to the price because the goods were "accepted." Assuming, however, that the buyer's revocation of acceptance was rightful, this argument should be rejected. § 7.08[E], *infra*.

[91] U.C.C. § 2-510, Comment 3.

2-510(1) situations, the breach may be a minor one, and, in all cases, it may be wholly unrelated to the event that caused the goods to be destroyed or lost.

Criticisms of this nature have led the drafters of the proposed revisions to Article 2 to suggest major changes. First, the proposed revisions pass the risk from the seller to the buyer regardless of the conformity of the goods to the contract unless the nonconformity causes loss or damage to the goods.[92] Second, the risk will pass back from buyer to seller on the buyer's rightful and effective rejection or revocation of acceptance.[93] Third, the proposed revisions to Article 2 allocate the risk of loss without regard to insurance coverage—that is, they eliminate language and ideas like present section 2-510(2)'s "to the extent of any deficiency in his effective insurance coverage."

[B]   Effect of Buyer's Breach

The effect of a default by the buyer is covered in section 2-510(3):

> Where the buyer as to conforming goods already identified to the contract for sale repudiates or is otherwise in breach before the risk of their loss has passed to him, the seller may to the extent of any deficiency in his effective insurance coverage treat the risk of loss as resting on the buyer for a commercially reasonable time.

Several conditions must be met before this section is applicable. First, the goods must be *conforming*—that is, they must be "in accordance with the obligations under the contract."[94] Any nonconformity, whether minor or substantial, prevents the seller from using section 2-510(3). The impact of this requirement can be exemplified through the installment contract where a buyer can reject a defective tender only if the nonconformity substantially impairs the value of that installment and cannot be cured.[95] In situations in which the nonconformity is not great enough to allow the installment-contract buyer to reject, the nonconformity would nevertheless operate to keep the entire risk on the seller even though the buyer had repudiated or was otherwise in breach.

Second, the goods must be *identified* to the contract. The seller cannot transfer any of the loss to the buyer simply by showing that a warehouse

---

[92] Council Draft §§ 2-612(b) and 2-612(c)(2).
[93] Council Draft § 2-612(c)(1).
[94] U.C.C. § 2-106(2).
[95] U.C.C. § 2-612.

full of goods was destroyed and, had it not been for this casualty, some of those goods would have been used to fill the buyer's order. The goods must have been existing and identified at the time of the contract or they must have been marked or otherwise designated by the seller as the goods to which the contract with the buyer refers.[96]

Third, the goods must have been *already* identified to the contract. This is a time reference: at the moment some event occurs, the goods must have been "already" identified. The difficulty arises in determining the precise event referred to by the word "already." Several constructions are possible,[97] but only two are probable: the goods must have been "already" identified (1) when the buyer defaulted or (2) when the loss occurred. The choice between these two constructions assumes importance depending on the sequence in which the three events (breach, identification, and loss) occur. Those three factors can be combined in six sequences:

Case 1: Identification	Breach	Loss
Case 2: Identification	Loss	Breach
Case 3: Breach	Identification	Loss
Case 4: Breach	Loss	Identification
Case 5: Loss	Breach	Identification
Case 6: Loss	Identification	Breach

Because Cases 4 through 6 assume that identification occurred after the loss, they will be disregarded. Section 2-510(3) requires conforming goods to be identified, and goods which have suffered casualty are not "conforming."

Case 1 causes no difficulty with the "already identified" portion of section 2-510(3). Under that Case, the identification occurred before both the breach and the loss; thus the goods were already identified at both critical times. In this respect, Case 2 is like Case 1, but the result of shifting some of the loss to the Case 2 buyer is strange and probably not anticipated by the drafters. Adding dates to Case 2 produces this situation: assume a contract that called for delivery by the seller on June 15; on June 10, the seller identified goods to the contract by marking them with the buyer's name; two days later, the seller's warehouse and the identified goods were destroyed by fire; on June 14, the buyer, not knowing of the fire, called the

---

[96] U.C.C. § 2-501; § 6.03, *supra*.

[97] For example, one construction of U.C.C. § 2-510(3) might be that the goods must be identified before their risk of loss passes to the buyer. This construction has been rejected because identification in some form is always required before risk of loss passes. The reference in U.C.C. § 2-510(3) to the time risk of loss passes is connected with the buyer's breach—not with identification.

seller and repudiated his order. One reading of section 2-510(3) would place the risk of loss on the buyer to the extent of any deficiency in the seller's insurance coverage. The goods were conforming when identified, they were "already" identified at the time of loss and breach, and the risk had not passed to the buyer. This reading should be rejected because the loss occurred before the buyer did anything to justify shifting any portion of the loss to him. Perhaps the best statutory method of reaching this conclusion is to emphasize that section 2-510(3) allows the seller to treat the risk as on the buyer "for a commercially reasonable time," and to hold that this time begins to run with the buyer's breach.[98] Because, in Case 2, the goods were already destroyed at the time of breach, their risk is determined without reference to section 2-510(3).

Case 3 causes difficulties of construction. Here, the buyer defaulted, and the seller followed by identifying goods to the contract. Those goods were later lost through some casualty. Were these goods "already" identified so that this requirement of section 2-510(3) is satisfied? Restating a question already asked: must the identification precede the breach or is it sufficient if it precedes the loss?

There are good commercial reasons for identification following breach. The seller may be interested in taking advantage of its resale remedy or in pursuing its suit for full price.[99] If the word "already" refers to the time of breach, the Case 3 seller will not be able to treat any of the risk as having rested on the buyer even though that seller was following Code procedures to obtain a remedy. Some authorities have assumed that the Case 3 seller is protected by section 2-510(3),[100] and their position is strengthened by the fact that the risk rests on the buyer for only a "commercially reasonable time." The seller could not identify goods after breach and keep the risk on the buyer for an unduly long period of time, but (goes this argument) the seller can identify goods after breach and place a part of the risk on the buyer for a commercially reasonable time.

Nevertheless, the syntax of section 2-510(3) favors the reading that the goods must have been "already" identified at the time of breach. Loss is not referred to in section 2-510(3); breach is specifically mentioned. The connection between identification and breach is clearly made by the statutory

---

[98] *See* Multiplastics, Inc. v. Arch Indus., Inc., 166 Conn. 280, 348 A.2d 618, 14 UCCR 573 (1974), in which thirty-three days elapsed between the buyer's breach and the destruction of the goods, and the court held that this was a commercially reasonable time for the seller to treat the risk of loss as resting on the buyer.

[99] U.C.C. §§ 2-706, 2-709.

[100] New York Law Revision Comm'n, 1955 Report (vol. 1) 498 (Case No. 4). This argument is supported by U.C.C. § 2-704.

language. Further, if the reference is to identification at the time of loss, there was no reason to include the word "already." Conforming goods cannot be identified following casualty and, on the assumption that something was meant by the inclusion of that word, the only probable meaning is that the goods must have been identified at the time of breach.[101]

As a fourth condition to the application of section 2-510(3), the breach must occur *before the risk of loss has passed to the buyer*. If the risk has passed under any of the branches of section 2-509, the buyer's later breach does not trigger section 2-510(3) and operates to return some of the risk to the seller's insurance carrier.

When these four conditions are met, the seller may, to the extent of any deficiency in its effective insurance coverage, treat the risk as resting on the buyer for a commercially reasonable time. The limitation of the time is understandable. The seller will have control of the goods (if they have been received by the buyer, the risk will have passed) and ought not be able to keep all or some of the risk on the buyer for an unduly long period of time.

Section 2-510(3) is complicated by its reference to a deficiency in the seller's effective insurance coverage. A return to Case 1, with some added facts, illustrates the complexities. Suppose that a contract calls for delivery of goods on June 15. On June 1, the buyer paid $5,000 on a total contract price of $12,000, with the balance to be paid on delivery. On June 10, the seller identified the goods to the contract; on June 12, the buyer repudiated; and on June 14, the goods were destroyed. Section 2-510(3) places the risk on the buyer "to the extent of any deficiency in his [the seller's] effective insurance coverage." If the seller had no insurance, the buyer would bear the entire risk and would, under section 2-709(1)(a), be liable for the unpaid $7,000 of the price.[102] If the seller had $12,000 of effective insurance, the buyer would bear none of the risk—and under principles of restitution, ought to be able to recover its $5,000 downpayment. If the seller has only $7,000 of effective coverage, $5,000 of the risk would rest on the buyer, and the buyer would presumably be unable to recover its downpayment but would have no further price liability. To the extent that the seller's insurer covers the loss, it is the drafters' intention, expressed in Comment 3 to 2-510, that the insurer bear the loss and be unable to shift it to the buyer by subrogation.

---

[101] The proposed revisions to Article 2 would clarify the situation by requiring that the goods be identified "when the buyer repudiates or is otherwise in breach" and giving the buyer the risk of loss "for a commercially reasonable time after the breach or repudiation." Council Draft § 2-612(c)(3).

[102] *See* Multiplastics, Inc. v. Arch Indus., Inc., 166 Conn. 280, 348 A.2d 618, 14 UCCR 573 (1974).

As with sections 2-510(1) and 2-510(2), section 2-510(3) is based on the thought that it is appropriate to allocate some of the risk of loss to the "contract breaker" simply because it is a contract breaker. It is subject to criticisms similar to those leveled against sections 2-510(1) and 2-510(2). It can operate to place the risk on the buyer when the buyer does not possess or control the goods and is unlikely to insure them, and it can do this even though the buyer's default in no way caused, or was related to, the casualty that the goods suffered. Nevertheless, the proposed revisions to Article 2 retain the basic thrust of section 2-510(3). In fact, they would impose a greater quantum of risk on defaulting buyers because of their elimination of the "to the extent of any deficiency in [the seller's] effective insurance coverage" language.[103]

---

[103] Section 2-612(3)(c) of the proposed revisions to Article 2 provides:

If conforming goods are identified to the contract when the buyer repudiates or is otherwise in breach and the risk of loss has not otherwise passed to the buyer, the buyer has the risk of loss for those goods for a commercially reasonable time after the breach or repudiation.

Council Draft § 2-612(3)(c).

CHAPTER 7

REMEDIES

I. INTRODUCTION

§ 7.01 PROTECTED INTERESTS ON BREACH OF CONTRACT

The Anglo-American law of contract remedies focuses on the party aggrieved by a breach. It seeks to compensate that party for its loss.[1] The law usually does not seek to punish the defaulting party—or to deter breach—except insofar as compensation of the aggrieved party for its loss incidentally and necessarily involves punishment and deterrence of the defaulter.[2] In its remedial provisions, the Code incorporates and continues this focus on compensation rather than on punishment or deterrence.[3]

It has become customary to identify and compensate the aggrieved party's loss in terms of three interests: the expectation, reliance, and restitution interests.[4] The Restatement (Second) of Contracts provides the following general description of these interests:

> § 344. Purposes of Remedies
> Judicial remedies under the rules stated in this Restatement serve to protect one or more of the following interests of a promisee:
>
> (a) his "expectation interest," which is his interest in having the benefit of his bargain by being put in as good a position as he would have been in had the contract been performed,
>
> (b) his "reliance interest," which is his interest in being reimbursed for loss caused by reliance on the contract by being put in as good a position as he would have been in had the contract not been made, or
>
> (c) his "restitution interest," which is his interest in having restored to him any benefit that he has conferred on the other party.

Brief discussions and examples of the three interests in the sale-of-goods context follow:

(a) The expectation interest. When parties enter into an agreement for the purchase and sale of goods, certain hopes—or expectations—are created by their respective promises. Most fundamentally, the buyer expects to receive the goods and the seller expects to receive the price. If the agreement is also a contract, and if one of the parties defaults, these expectations

---

[1] Compensation is usually provided by way of money damages, but specific relief (for example, entitling a buyer to obtain the specific goods promised by defaulting seller) is sometimes allowed.

[2] *See* Restatement of Contracts (Second), Introductory Note to Chapter 16.

[3] *See, e.g.,* U.C.C. § 1-106(1).

[4] These interests were first comprehensively discussed in L.L. Fuller & William R. Perdue, "The Reliance Interest in Contract Damages: 1," 46 Yale L.J. 52 (1936).

can receive judicial protection. A seller who has delivered the goods may be entitled to an action for their price; a buyer who has failed to receive the goods from its seller may be entitled to recover the difference between the cost of substitute goods and the contract price. Article 2 provides these and (for other factual patterns) other expectation-interest damage formulas. The common theme in protecting the expectation interest is awarding the aggrieved party the gain that it expected to, and would have, made had the contract been performed.

(b) The reliance interest. Parties frequently spend money or take other action in reliance on the contracts that they have made. And breach can destroy all or part of the value of their reliance. When this occurs, the aggrieved party is often entitled to compensation for its wasted reliance expenditures. For example, suppose that, after entering into a contract to purchase a pair of panda bears, a zoo employs (for a fee) an advertising agency to prepare and print mailing leaflets advertising the acquisition of the bears and a "grand opening" on a particular date on which the bears will first be exhibited. And suppose that the seller thereafter repudiates its promise to deliver the bears. In these circumstances, the words "reliance interest" describe the fee that the zoo has paid to the advertising agency, and the zoo—contending that the seller's default has rendered this expenditure worthless to it—may be able to recover the fee from the seller.[5] Among the questions relevant to the recovery of the fee are whether the seller, at the time of contracting, had reason to foresee this kind of reliance and whether the zoo could have avoided the waste of the leaflet fee by obtaining substitute bears from another seller in time for the grand opening.[6]

(c) The restitution interest. The action that a party takes in reliance on a contract may confer a benefit on the other party. For example, a buyer of goods may make a downpayment on the price weeks or months before the date on which the seller has promised delivery. If, in breach of its promise, the seller refuses to deliver, the buyer will, of course, want to recover its downpayment. In these circumstances, the words "restitution interest" describe the downpayment, and the buyer will be able to recover it. Allowing

---

[5] It is difficult to think of expenses incurred before contract formation as expenses incurred in reliance on a contract, and such expenses are generally not recoverable. Chicago Coliseum Club v. Dempsey, 265 Ill. App. 542 (1932). *But see* Anglia Television Ltd. v. Reed [1971] 3 All E.R. 690 (Court of Appeal, 1971). The kind of reliance that is generally protected is that which occurs between contract formation and breach, and which is reasonable, foreseeable, and of no value to the aggrieved party. Expenses incurred after breach are generally not thought of as reliance expenses, but may be recoverable as incidental damages. *See infra* § 7.04[F][1].

[6] *See* U.C.C. § 2-715(2)(a).

a defaulting seller to retain a completely unearned downpayment would involve obvious unjust enrichment.

The three interests present claims of different strengths. A restitution claim is the strongest, involving as it does both (1) a loss the aggrieved party has incurred in reliance on the contract, placing the aggrieved party in a worse position than it occupied before the contract was made, and (2) the fact that the aggrieved party's loss went into the contract breaker's pocket (i.e., it benefited the contract breaker).

A reliance claim is, in a sense, only half as strong. There is an out-of-pocket reliance loss to the aggrieved party but no corresponding benefit to—or enrichment of—the contract breaker. In a reliance-interest situation, rather than going into the contract breaker's pocket, the aggrieved party's loss goes out the window, or into the hands of some third party, like the advertising agency in the panda bears–zoo example.

The expectation interest presents the weakest claim. A party can have a good expectation-interest claim even though the contract and its breach have not made it worse off than it was before contract formation. Protection of the expectation interest measures the aggrieved party's loss not in terms of regression from its pre-contract position, but in terms of loss of anticipated gain (i.e., failure to progress to the position promised by the contract breaker).

Nevertheless, Code remedial thinking, like general Anglo-American contract remedial thinking, begins with the protection of the expectation interest. Section 1-106(1) makes this clear:

> The remedies provided by this Act shall be liberally administered to the end that the aggrieved party may be put in as good a position as if the other party had fully performed but neither consequential or special nor penal damages may be had except as specially provided in this Act or by other rule of law.

Among the reasons for beginning with the expectation interest is the fact that its protection—placing the aggrieved party in the position that performance would have done—invites parties to rely on contracts and protects (at least to the extent that performance would have done so) their various acts and forbearances[7] in reliance even in circumstances when these might be

---

[7] A common kind of forbearance in reliance on a contract is the passing up of opportunities to make another contract. For example, a buyer that has contracted to buy goods from X may, relying on X to perform and thus satisfy the buyer's need for the kind of goods involved, fail to make a contract with Y or Z for like goods. This kind of negative reliance—what one did *not* do because one had a contract with X—though often real, is likely to be

difficult or impossible to prove.[8]

Frequently, aggrieved parties seek the protection of two or all three of the interests at the same time. Often, this is required if the aggrieved party is to be placed in the position that performance would have done. This can be illustrated in terms of the panda bears–zoo example. Suppose that the contract price—the price that the zoo agreed to pay the contract-breaking seller for the bears—was $100,000. Suppose further that, before the seller's repudiation, the zoo (1) paid the seller $20,000 of this price as a downpayment and (2) paid an advertising agency $5,000 for leaflets advertising a grand opening on a particular date. Finally, suppose that the zoo, after canvassing the market and bargaining carefully, succeeded in obtaining substitute pandas for $125,000, but too late for the originally scheduled grand opening. If the aggrieved zoo is to be put in the position performance would have done, it needs to recover $50,000. $20,000 of this—the recovery of the zoo's downpayment—protects its restitution interest. $5,000—the amount paid for the leaflets that the seller's repudiation rendered worthless—protects its wasted reliance expenditure.[9] $25,000—the difference between the $125,000 cost of cover (buying the substitute bears) and the $100,000 contract price—protects its pure expectation interest—that is, it gives the zoo the benefit of its favorable bargain. Obviously, protection of the pure expectation interest alone—allowing only a $25,000 recovery—would leave the aggrieved zoo far short of the position it would have occupied had the contract been performed. On these facts, placing the zoo in that position requires the compensation of its restitution and reliance losses along with its expected gain. Given different facts, the Code works with the interests in different ways.

In its discussion of Code remedies, the remainder of this chapter refers from time to time to the parties' expectation, reliance, and restitution interests, using these words in the senses previously outlined.

---

very hard to prove. The law, by protecting the buyer's expectation interest, provides a kind of compensation for this kind of reliance without requiring its proof.

[8] For a thoughtful discussion of why contract law begins with the protection of the expectation interest, *see* L.L. Fuller & William R. Perdue, "The Reliance Interest in Contract Damages: 1," 46 Yale L.J. 52, 57–66 (1936).

[9] Whenever an aggrieved party seeks to recover both a reliance and an expectation loss, a court must take care to avoid overcompensating the plaintiff—that is, putting it in a better position than performance would have done. The difficulties that this can involve are discussed in L.L. Fuller & William R. Perdue, "The Reliance Interest in Contract Damages: 1," 46 Yale L.J. 52, 80–84 (1936) and *infra* § 704[F][1].

§ 7.02   OVERVIEW OF ARTICLE 2's REMEDIAL STRUCTURE

Part 7 of Article 2 contains twenty-five sections dealing with the remedies available to the parties to a sales transaction. These provisions interlock with the rest of the Article, particularly with Part 6 (Breach, Repudiation and Excuse). While there are a number of sections that apply to both buyers' and sellers' remedies, the structure of Article 2 is such that it usually provides for buyers' remedies in one section or set of sections and for sellers' remedies in a separate section or set of sections.

The Article's remedial provisions are organized in terms of (1) the major types of default that a contract breaker can commit, (2) the courses of action that the aggrieved party may follow in response to a breach, and (3) the remedies, monetary or specific, available to the aggrieved party. The overriding remedial goal is protecting the aggrieved party's expectation interest—placing it in the position performance would have done.[10]

For example, consider the Code's provisions for buyers' remedies. Three important ways in which a seller may default are by (1) repudiating its promise to sell, (2) failing to deliver the goods, or (3) making a nonconforming tender—such as a late tender or a tender of nonconforming goods. The Code provides for all three types of default and for the seller's insolvency[11] as well. If the seller's default is a nonconforming tender, the Code moves on to consider the buyer's responsive courses of action: either (1) thrusting the goods back on the seller by way of rejection[12] or revocation of acceptance,[13] or (2) accepting[14] and retaining the goods. The Code then provides remedies designed to protect the buyer's expectation interest, both in cases where the buyer ends up without the goods (cases of a seller's repudiation or failure to deliver or of a buyer's rightful rejection or revocation of acceptance)[15] and in cases where the buyer retains the goods, even though they or their tender are nonconforming.[16] The monetary remedies available to an aggrieved buyer who either fails to receive the goods or successfully thrusts them back on the seller include the avoidance of any obligation to pay the price for the goods and damages measured by (1) the cost at which substitute goods are purchased minus the contract price[17] or

---

[10] U.C.C. § 1-106 and *supra* § 7.01.
[11] U.C.C. § 2-502.
[12] U.C.C. § 2-602.
[13] U.C.C. § 2-608.
[14] U.C.C. § 2-606.
[15] U.C.C. §§ 2-711, 2-712, 2-713, 2-715, 2-716.
[16] U.C.C. §§ 2-714, 2-715.
[17] U.C.C. § 2-712.

(2) the market price of the goods minus the contract price.[18] The damages recoverable by an aggrieved buyer who retains the goods are generally measured by the value of the goods promised minus the value of the goods accepted.[19] Incidental and consequential damages are available in proper cases both when the goods end up in the buyer's hands and when they do not.[20]

The treatment of the sellers' remedies is analogous. A buyer may default in various ways, including: (1) repudiating its promise to buy; (2) failing to make a payment due on or before delivery; (3) wrongfully thrusting the goods back on the seller, by way of a wrongful rejection or wrongful revocation of acceptance; or (4) failing to make a payment due after delivery. If the buyer's default occurs before the seller has completed delivery, the seller is usually able to respond by withholding delivery;[21] in some situations, the seller may be able to reclaim goods that have already been delivered.[22] The Code also provides remedies designed to protect the seller's expectation interest, both in cases where the seller retains or reclaims the goods[23] and in cases where the buyer ends up with the goods.[24] When the buyer ends up with the goods, the aggrieved seller will be entitled to an action for their price.[25] When the aggrieved seller ends up with the goods, the measure of its compensation will depend on the course of action the seller has followed and on the circumstances. If the seller has made a proper resale, it may recover the contract price minus what it received on the resale.[26] Alternatively, the seller may recover the contract price minus the market price of the goods.[27] If the contract-minus-market measure is inadequate to place the aggrieved seller in the position performance would have done, the seller may recover its lost profit.[28] If the goods cannot be sold at a reasonable price, the seller may recover the full price, delivering the goods to the buyer when it does so.[29] As with buyers' remedies, the seller's remedies are designed to place the seller in the position as performance.

---

[18] U.C.C. § 2-713.
[19] U.C.C. § 2-714.
[20] U.C.C. § 2-715.
[21] U.C.C. §§ 2-703, 2-705.
[22] U.C.C. §§ 2-507, 2-702.
[23] U.C.C. §§ 2-703, 2-704, 2-706, 2-708, 2-709, 2-710.
[24] U.C.C. §§ 2-709, 2-710.
[25] U.C.C. § 2-709.
[26] U.C.C. § 2-706.
[27] U.C.C. § 2-708(1).
[28] U.C.C. § 2-708(2).
[29] U.C.C. § 2-709.

The remedial provisions of the proposed revisions to Article 2 are designed with the same protection-of-the-expectation-interest in mind. Although they are structured differently[30] and are frequently couched in different language, the new provisions preserve much of the substance of the current Article. There is, however, a shift in emphasis away from rules and toward looser general principles, and there are a number of specific changes of importance. This chapter deals with the remedies available under the current Article 2, making occasional references to changes that would be wrought by the proposed revisions to Article 2. The general scheme of the chapter involves, first, an analysis of the buyer's remedies on default of the seller, and, second, an analysis of the seller's remedies on default of the buyer.

II. SELLER IN DEFAULT

§ 7.03 THE BUYER'S COURSES OF ACTION

[A] The Code's Approach to Buyer's Remedies

The Code contains several sections devoted to an aggrieved buyer's remedies. In summary, these sections allow an aggrieved buyer to select an appropriate remedy from the following:

1. Recover as much of the price as it has paid.[31]
2. In cases where the seller has retained the goods or had them thrust back on it, recover damages measured by either market price minus contract price[32] or the cost of "cover" (the cost at which substitute goods are actually purchased) minus contract price.[33]
3. In cases where the buyer has accepted and retained goods, recover damages measured by the difference between the seller's promised performance and the performance received.[34]

---

[30] For example, Part 8 (titled "Remedies") of the proposed revisions is divided into three subparts. Subpart B (sections 2-815 through 2-822) provides for sellers' remedies and subpart C (sections 2-823 through 2-829) provides for buyers' remedies. The subpart B and C sellers' and buyers' remedies are subject to the general remedial provisions set out in subpart A ("In General"). Subpart A includes sections 2-801 through 2-814 and deals with such matters as avoidable consequences or mitigation, incidental and consequential damages, specific performance, liquidated damages, contractual limitations of remedies, and limitation of actions.

[31] U.C.C. § 2-711.

[32] U.C.C. § 2-713.

[33] U.C.C. § 2-712.

[34] U.C.C. § 2-714.

4. Recover incidental and consequential damages.[35]
5. In a proper case, obtain the promised goods through specific performance or replevin.[36]
6. In some situations in which the seller becomes insolvent, recover the goods by tendering performance.[37]

In many circumstances, an aggrieved buyer would need to select more than one of the listed remedies to obtain full protection of its expectation interest. For example, a particular buyer may need to recover its downpayment plus the difference between the cost of cover and the contract price plus incidental and consequential damages if it is to attain as good a position as if the contract had been performed. In addition, remedies not specifically mentioned in the Code may be available to an aggrieved buyer through the Code's adoption of general principles of law and equity.[38]

Each Code remedy has its own specific conditions, and these are discussed in later sections. Before moving to this detailed discussion, however, two observations may make the Code's approach to remedies more understandable.

First, in most situations, a buyer's remedy takes the form of money damages. Although there are instances in which an aggrieved buyer can obtain the goods themselves (through specific performance, replevin, or on the seller's insolvency), the buyer's usual remedy is a money substitute for the goods. In this regard, the Code follows the general approach of the Anglo-American common law—that money damages are the standard remedy and that specific relief is a supplemental and unusual remedy that is available only when money damages prove inadequate.

This is plainly not the only possible, or the only workable, remedial scheme. In civil-law countries, specific performance is the standard remedy for aggrieved buyers, and it is the preferred remedy under the United Nations Convention on Contracts for International Sale of Goods (CISG). Much can be, and much has been, said for and against both approaches. In recent years, scholars have employed economic analysis in arguing both for[39] and

---

[35] U.C.C. § 2-715.
[36] U.C.C. § 2-716.
[37] U.C.C. § 2-502.
[38] U.C.C. § 1-103.
[39] *See, e.g.*, Alan Schwartz, "The Case for Specific Performance," 89 Yale L.J. 271 (1979); Thomas S. Ulen, "The Efficiency of Specific Performance: Toward a Unified Theory of Contract Remedies," 83 Mich. L. Rev. 341 (1984).

against[40] the general availability of specific performance. Whatever the merits of this interesting theoretical debate, money damages are in fact the Code's standard remedy, with specific relief available only in exceptional cases. The proposed revisions to Article 2 would continue this approach, but with one major change. It would allow specific performance in cases where the parties had expressly agreed to that remedy in their contract.[41]

The second observation is that, under the Code's remedial scheme, the availability of a remedy or set of remedies to a buyer depends on the course of action which that buyer has followed. For this reason, an appreciation of the Code's remedial sections requires an understanding of the various courses of action open to a buyer. This involves:

1. An analysis of the particular default committed by the seller.
2. Understanding the meaning and impact of "rejection" and "acceptance" and the buyer's choice between them.
3. Knowing when and how acceptance can be revoked.
4. Understanding the consequences of the buyer's retention of nonconforming goods.

These matters are discussed in the following sections of the text.

[B] Types of Defaults by Sellers

The Code provides expressly for three types of sellers' defaults: the first occurs when the seller repudiates its promise before the date set for performance; the second occurs when there has been no repudiation but the seller fails to deliver the goods; and the third occurs when the seller delivers the goods but they or their tender do not conform to the contract.[42] When the seller has repudiated or failed to make a delivery, the buyer may proceed directly to a remedy. Because the seller knows or should know that it has repudiated or failed to make delivery, the Code does not require the buyer to reject, give a notice,[43] or follow any other particular course of action before filing suit.

---

[40] *See, e.g.*, Anthony T. Kronman, "Specific Performance," 45 U. Chi. L. Rev. 351 (1978); Edward Yorio, "In Defense of Money Damages for Breach of Contract," 82 Colum. L. Rev. 1365 (1982); R. Posner, Economic Analysis of Law 130–132 (4th ed. 1992).

[41] The American Law Institute, Uniform Commercial Code, Revised Article 2. Sales, Council Draft No. 4, December 1, 1998 (hereinafter "Council Draft").

[42] U.C.C. §§ 2-711, 2-714.

[43] Chemetron Corp. v. McLouth Steel Corp., 381 F. Supp. 245, 15 UCCR 832 (N.D. Ill. 1974); Eastern Air Lines, Inc. v. McDonnel Douglas Corp., 532 F.2d 957, 19 UCCR 353 (5th Cir. 1976). The § 2-607(3)(a) notice is only required with respect to *accepted* goods.

The nonconforming tender is the type of seller's default that interposes course-of-action requirements that the buyer must follow before proceeding to a remedy. The seller may not know that its tender did not conform to the contract, and it should be alerted to the buyer's claims. Perhaps the nonconformity can be cured.[44] In any event, the Code requires that the buyer take certain action if it intends to seek a remedy for a nonconforming tender. The action the buyer must take is not burdensome, but it does give the seller some protection.

[C] Rejection of the Goods

When a seller tenders nonconforming goods, the buyer has a choice: it may accept the goods or it may reject them. The Code does not define either "rejection" or "acceptance," but the basic meaning and function of the terms can be gleaned from a reading of Parts 6 and 7 of Article 2. Rejection involves the buyer's thrusting goods which the seller has tendered back on the seller. It is a self-help action, not something that is done in court. When a buyer rejects and does so effectively and rightfully, it avoids any obligation to pay for the rejected goods and earns the right to pursue other remedies as well.[45] Acceptance—also an out-of-court self-help action—involves the buyer's retention of tendered goods. Unless effectively revoked, acceptance obligates the buyer to pay for the accepted goods at the contract price[46] and has other consequences that are detailed in the following section.

A single-delivery contract involves section 2-601's perfect tender rule; the buyer may rightfully reject "if the goods or the tender of delivery fail in any respect to conform to the contract."[47] With an installment contract, the buyer may rightfully reject an installment only if the nonconformity "substantially impairs the value of that installment and cannot be cured or if the nonconformity is a defect in the required documents" or if the default with respect to one installment impairs the value of the whole contract.[48]

Commercial units. Rejection must be exercised in terms of commercial units. Section 2-105(6) defines a commercial unit as "such a unit of goods as by commercial usage is a single whole for purposes of sale and division

---

[44] *See* U.C.C. § 2-508.
[45] U.C.C. § 2-711.
[46] U.C.C. § 2-607(1).
[47] *See* § 5.03 *supra.*
[48] U.C.C. § 2-612. *See* § 5.03[A][3] *supra.*

of which materially impairs its character or value on the market or in use."[49] When a seller's nonconforming tender includes more than one commercial unit, the buyer may reject the whole, accept the whole, or reject one or more commercial units and accept the rest.[50] In other words, the buyer may break up a tender, rejecting some commercial units and accepting others. What the buyer may not do is break up a commercial unit for purposes of rejection, as by rejecting that part of the unit that does not conform and accepting the remainder of the unit that does conform. By definition, the breakup of a commercial unit impairs the value of the unit. A buyer who attempts such a breakup is treated as having accepted the entire commercial unit.[51] Circumstances under which it is difficult to identify a commercial unit obviously call for care and caution on the part of buyers. Buyers would be well advised to resolve doubts against themselves and either reject the whole or reject in terms of expansively defined commercial units.

Timeliness. If the buyer decides to reject the goods, it must do so promptly—"within a reasonable time after their delivery or tender"—and the rejection will be "ineffective unless the buyer seasonably notifies the seller."[52] There are at least two good reasons for requiring promptness and notice to the seller: (1) early rejection and notice often enhance the seller's ability to cure, thus enabling some transactions to go forward without breach, and (2) even when there is no cure, prompt rejection and notice help the seller to recover the goods before they have depreciated, become obsolete, or otherwise declined in value, thus minimizing loss.

The drafters have chosen to couch the promptness requirement in flexible language—"within a reasonable time" and "seasonably"—rather than in hard-edged terms such as "within ten days after tender or delivery." While this choice creates some uncertainty (and perhaps fosters litigation), it has the advantages of recognizing that the facts of cases differ widely and of enabling the trier of fact[53] to reach a just result under the facts of the par-

---

[49] U.C.C. § 2-105(6) goes on to provide that "A commercial unit may be a single article (as a machine) or set of articles (as a suite of furniture or an assortment of sizes) or a quantity (as a bale, gross, or carload) or any other unit treated in use or in the relevant market as a single whole."

[50] U.C.C. § 2-601.

[51] U.C.C. § 2-606(2).

[52] U.C.C. § 2-602(1).

[53] Courts usually treat the questions whether rejection and notice of it are timely as questions of fact. Sometimes, however, the facts are so clear (the rejection notice is so prompt, or so late), that courts are able to decide these questions as matters of law, in effect directing verdicts on them. Lynx, Inc. v. Ordnance Prods., Inc., 273 Md. 1, 327 A.2d 502, 15 UCCR 1040 (1974).

ticular case before it. Section 1-204 offers some help on the meanings of "reasonable time" and "seasonably." First, section 1-204 provides that whenever the Code requires an action to be taken within a reasonable time, the parties may fix "any time which is not manifestly unreasonable" by agreement. Second, it says that an action is taken "seasonably" when the action is taken "at or within the time agreed or if no time is agreed at or within a reasonable time." Finally, and least helpfully, section 1-204 states that a reasonable time for taking an action "depends on the nature, purpose and circumstances of such action."

The uncertainty in the reasonableness standard argues for expressly covering the time of rejection in the parties' agreement. Courts should, and generally do, follow the mandate of section 1-204(1) and enforce a "not manifestly unreasonable" agreement requiring rejection to occur within a specified time, or giving the buyer a specified time to inspect, or otherwise expressly bearing on the time for rejection.[54] In cases where there is no such provision and the reasonableness standard must be applied, courts seem to be influenced by the difficulty of discovering the defect in the goods (the more difficult this is, the longer the period likely to be allowed for rejection), the perishability of the goods (the more perishable they are, the shorter the period likely to be allowed for rejection), and the seller's efforts to cure or the parties' negotiations about the defect (rejection unlikely to be required during such efforts or negotiations). For example, when the tendered goods consisted of an expensive race horse with a broken leg, readily discoverable by a veterinarian, both the ease of discovering the defect and the fact that the horse might sustain further injury argued for a short (less than twenty-four hours after delivery) rejection period.[55] Conversely, when the goods consisted of truck chassis frames, whose nonconformity was not readily recognizable and that were not perishable or subject to rapid price fluctuations, the question whether a rejection more than two months after delivery was within a reasonable time was held to be one for the jury.[56] When a new car is sold to a consumer, the difficulties of inspection and discovery of defects are such that the buyer may drive the car for more than the traditional "spin around the block" before losing the ability to reject.[57] And a buyer

---

[54] *See* Texpor Traders, Inc. v. Trust Co. Bank, 720 F. Supp. 1100, 10 UCCR2d 1227 (S.D.N.Y. 1989).

[55] Miron v. Yonkers Raceway, Inc. 400 F.2d 112, 5 UCCR 673 (2d Cir. 1968).

[56] Sherkate Sahami Khass Rapol v. Henry R. Jahn & Son, Inc., 701 F.2d 1049, 35 UCCR 790 (2d Cir. 1983).

[57] Zabriskie Chevrolet, Inc. v. Smith, 99 N.J. Super. 441, 240 A.2d 195, 5 UCCR 30 (1968).

may reasonably delay exercising its right to reject while the seller is attempting to cure the defect.[58]

Content of notice. The buyer's notice, if it is to accomplish an effective rejection, must not only be timely; it must also inform the seller that the buyer is refusing to accept the goods. Notices that do no more than say that the goods are nonconforming and that the buyer considers the seller responsible for the damages have been held ineffective to create rejections.[59] Although they presumably satisfy the section 2-607(3)(a) notice-of-breach requirement and thus preserve the buyer's ability to recover under section 2-714 for breach in regard to accepted goods, such notices fail to inform the seller that the buyer is refusing the goods—is thrusting them back on the seller.

The Code does not require that rejection notices be in writing; oral notices can be effective. There are, however, obvious evidentiary reasons for giving written notice or a prompt written confirmation of an oral notice, and careful business people and lawyers will do so. They will also state the discoverable defects that cause them to reject. In some circumstances, section 2-605(1) makes this imperative. First, it precludes a buyer from relying on an unstated defect that was ascertainable by reasonable inspection "where the seller could have cured it if stated seasonably." Second, if both parties are merchants, section 2-605(1) allows the seller, after rejection, to make a request in writing for "a full and final written statement of all defects on which the buyer proposes to rely." If the seller makes such a request, the buyer will be precluded from relying on any unstated defects that were ascertainable by reasonable inspection.[60] Where it applies, section 2-605(1) provides for a broad preclusion: the buyer may not rely on the unstated defect "to justify rejection *or to establish breach*," meaning that the precluded buyer must not only retain the goods and pay for them at the contract price, but that it cannot recover any damages resulting from the goods' defects.

Distinction between ineffective and wrongful rejection. Subsection (1) of section 2-602 refers to "ineffective" rejections. Subsection (3) speaks of "wrongfully" rejected goods. It is important to distinguish between the two

---

[58] Latham & Assocs., Inc. v. William Raveis Real Estate, Inc., 218 Conn. 297, 589 A.2d 337, 14 UCCR2d 394 (1991).

[59] HCI Chems. (USA), Inc. v. Henkel KGaA, 966 F.2d 1018, 18 UCCR2d 436 (5th Cir. 1992); CMI Corp. v. Leemar Steel Co., Inc., 733 F.2d 1410, 38 UCCR 798 (10th Cir. 1984).

[60] Subsection (2) of 2-605 states another preclusion: "Payment against documents made without reservation or rights precludes recovery of the payment for defects apparent on the face of the documents."

words and ideas.[61] An ineffective rejection (for example, one that is not timely made, or of which notice is not given seasonably)[62] does not operate to thrust the goods back on the seller. On the contrary, in circumstances where the buyer has had a reasonable opportunity to inspect, it becomes an acceptance. Section 2-606(1)(b) so states:

> (1) Acceptance of goods occurs when the buyer . . .
>　　(b) fails to make an effective rejection (subsection (1) of Section 2-602), but such acceptance does not occur until the buyer has had a reasonable opportunity to inspect them.

Under section 2-607 an acceptance triggers the buyer's obligation to pay the contract price and precludes rejection. The upshot is that, even when rejection is justified by the nonconformity of the goods or the tender, a buyer that fails to reject effectively will (unless it can and does revoke its acceptance) end up retaining the goods, paying their price, and, at best, recovering damages because of the nonconformity under section 2-714.

An effective rejection—one that is timely made and properly noticed—can be either rightful or wrongful. It will be rightful if there is a nonconformity of the goods or the tender that justifies it under section 2-601 or section 2-612, and wrongful if there is no such justifying nonconformity. In either case—whether rightful or wrongful—an *effective* rejection thrusts the goods back on the seller and avoids the buyer's obligation to pay the price. If rightful, the rejection also entitles the buyer to recover damages measured by either the cost of cover or the market price less the contract price[63]— that is, to have its (the aggrieved buyer's) expectation interest protected. If wrongful, however, the rejection is a material breach by the buyer that entitles the seller to recover damages measured by the contract price less either the resale price or the market price or, in a proper case, by the seller's lost profit[64]—that is, to have its (the aggrieved seller's) expectation interest protected.

In short, the adjectives "rightful" and "wrongful," as used in the Code to modify "rejection," are relevant to the question of who is in material

---

[61] Integrated Circuits Unlimited, Inc. v. E. F. Johnson Co., 691 F. Supp. 630, 7 UCCR2d 1478 (E.D.N.Y. 1988) contains an excellent discussion of the difference between wrongful and ineffective rejections.

[62] Other examples of ineffective rejections include those in which the notice does not tell the seller that the buyer is refusing the goods and those in which the notice runs afoul of section 2-605(1)'s defect particularization requirements.

[63] U.C.C. §§ 2-711, 2-712, 2-713.

[64] U.C.C. §§ 2-703, 2-706, 2-708(1), 2-708(2).

breach, the buyer or the seller. The adjectives "effective" and "ineffective" are unrelated to the question of who is in breach; they deal with the success or failure of the buyer's attempted course of action, its effort to thrust the goods back on the seller (whether rightful or wrongful). If an attempt to reject is ineffective, an acceptance usually results.

Rights and duties after rejection. Four Code provisions—sections 2-602(2), 2-603, 2-604, and 2-711(3)—deal with a buyer's rights and duties after a rightful rejection.[65] Under section 2-602(3), wrongful rejections are treated as breaches by the buyer that open the seller's remedies under section 2-703.

Subsection 2-602(2) sets forth the most basic provisions dealing with a rightfully rejecting buyer's rights and duties. Consistent with the idea that rejection is a thrusting of goods back on the seller, a post-rejection exercise of ownership by such a buyer is wrongful as against the seller. If the buyer has taken physical possession of the goods before rejection, it must hold them with reasonable care at the seller's disposition for a time sufficient to permit the seller to remove them. Subsection 2-602(2) expressly refers to sections 2-604 and 2-711(3), which add to a buyer's post-rejection rights, and to section 2-603, which imposes certain post-rejection duties on a merchant buyer. Section 2-711(3) gives a rightfully rejecting buyer "a security interest in goods in his possession or control for any payments made on their price and any expenses reasonably incurred in their inspection, receipt, transportation, care, and custody." A buyer with such a security interest may enforce it by holding the goods or by foreclosure sale. That is, to the extent of its security interest, the buyer need not hold the goods at the seller's disposition but may rightfully exercise the ownership rights of a secured party over them. It is noteworthy that the section 2-711(3) security interest exists only to the extent that the buyer has made a payment on the price or incurred one or more of the listed handling expenses; it does not secure the damages that the buyer has suffered because of the seller's nonconforming tender.[66]

---

[65] U.C.C. § 2-711(3) is expressly conditioned on "rightful" rejection (or justifiable revocation of acceptance). Sections 2-602, 2-603, and 2-604 all include the word "rightful" in their captions, making it a part of the legislation via section 1-109. Further, Comment 3 to section 2-603 states that the section "applies only to rightful rejection by the buyer," and points out that subsection (3) deals with wrongful rejections, treating them as breaches which open sellers' remedies. Specifically, subsection (3) provides:

> (3) The seller's rights with respect to goods wrongfully rejected are governed by the provisions of this Article on Seller's remedies in general (Section 2-703).

[66] U.C.C. § 2-711, Comment 2.

As has been noted, section 2-602(2)(b) requires a rejecting buyer that has taken possession of the goods to hold them at the seller's disposition. Section 2-604 deals with situations in which the seller fails to remove the goods or to instruct the buyer concerning their disposition. In such cases, it gives the buyer certain salvage options: storing the goods for the seller's account; reshipping them to the seller; or selling them for the sellers's account, with reimbursement for its expenses. It provides that such action is not acceptance or conversion.

Section 2-604 is subject to section 2-603, which, when the seller has no agent or place of business at the market of rejection, imposes two duties on rejecting buyers who have possession or control of the goods and who are merchants.[67] The first of these merchant duties is (subject to any section 2-711(3) security interest) to follow reasonable instructions received from the seller with respect to the goods. Instructions are not reasonable if, on demand, indemnity for expenses is not forthcoming. The second duty concerns goods that are "perishable or threaten to decline in value speedily." In the absence of instructions, a merchant buyer must make reasonable efforts to sell such goods for the seller's account.[68] The point, as expressed in Comment 1, is to give the merchant buyer the duty of making "reasonable efforts to effect a salvage sale where the value of the goods is threatened and the seller's instructions do not arrive in time to prevent serious loss."

The same duties and options apply to a buyer who has revoked acceptance. Section 2-608(3) provides: "A buyer who so revokes has the same rights and duties with respect to the goods as if he had rejected them."

[D] Acceptance of the Goods

The alternative to rejecting tendered goods is accepting them.[69] When goods are tendered to a buyer, the buyer must either reject (thrust the goods back on the seller) or accept (retain the goods). Whereas rejection requires the buyer to act—to give a timely notice to the seller—acceptance can and frequently does occur through the buyer's inaction.[70]

---

[67] "Merchant" is defined in U.C.C. § 2-104(1).

[68] Subsection (2) deals with reimbursement for expenses, and subsection (3) provides that a buyer's good-faith conduct under section 2-603 is neither acceptance nor conversion nor the basis of an action for damages.

[69] The Code concepts of rejection, acceptance, and revocation of acceptance are inextricably related. This subsection on acceptance should be read in conjunction with the preceding subsection on rejection and the following subsection on revocation of acceptance.

[70] The buyer's failure to give a timely rejection notice amounts to an acceptance. U.C.C. § 2-606(1)(b).

When acceptance occurs. Section 2-606(1) sets out three ways in which a buyer may accept goods:

(1) Acceptance occurs when the buyer
  (a)   after a reasonable opportunity to inspect the goods signifies to the seller that the goods are conforming or that he will take or retain them in spite of their nonconformity; or
  (b)   fails to make an effective rejection (subsection (1) of Section 2-602), but such acceptance does not occur until the buyer has had a reasonable opportunity to inspect them; or
  (c)   does any act inconsistent with the seller's ownership; but if such act is wrongful as against the seller it is an acceptance only if ratified by him.

Under section 2-606(1)(a) the buyer's signification to the seller either that the goods conform to the contract or that the buyer will retain them even though they do not conform is an acceptance, but only if the signification occurs after the buyer has had a reasonable opportunity to inspect the goods. The required signification can be made in various ways. The buyer's agreeing to buy identified goods, taking possession of goods, or making whole or partial payment for goods are all circumstances that tend to establish an indication to the seller that the buyer will retain the goods, but none of these circumstances is conclusive.[71] And if these circumstances or other words or conduct on the part of the buyer do in fact amount to an indication that it will retain the goods, this signification will constitute an acceptance only if it occurs after the buyer has had a reasonable opportunity to inspect the goods.[72]

---

[71] *See* U.C.C. § 2-606, Comment 3.

[72] The frequently cited case of Zabriskie Chevrolet, Inc. v. Smith, 99 N.J. Super. 441, 240 A.2d 195, 5 UCCR 30 (1968), discusses a buyer's reasonable opportunity to inspect in connection with the acceptance of a new car:

It is clear that the buyer does not accept goods until he has had a "reasonable opportunity to inspect." Defendant sought to purchase a new car. . . . Plaintiff contends that defendant had "reasonable opportunity to inspect" by the privilege to take the car for a typical "spin around the block" before signing the purchase order. If by this contention plaintiff equates a spin around the block with "reasonable opportunity to inspect," the contention is illusory and unrealistic. To the layman, the complicated mechanisms of today's automobiles are a complete mystery. . . . Consequently, the first few miles of driving become even more significant to the excited new car buyer. This is the buyer's first reasonable opportunity to enjoy his new vehicle to see if it conforms to what it was represented to be and whether he is getting what he bargained for.

See also Capitol Dodge Sales, Inc. v. Northern Concrete Pipe, Inc., 131 Mich. App. 149,

Section 2-606(1)(b)'s provision that acceptance occurs when the buyer, having had a reasonable opportunity to inspect, fails to make an effective rejection is the hardest working and most important of section 2-606(1)'s three when-acceptance-occurs provisions. Read in conjunction with section 2-602(1), to which it expressly refers, this provision says that if the buyer waits more than a reasonable time after delivery or tender to give a rejection notice and a reasonable opportunity to inspect has passed, the buyer will be treated as having accepted. Thus, a section 2-606(1)(b) acceptance can occur without any signification, exercise of ownership, or other action on the buyer's part. The mere failure to give a seasonable rejection notice is sufficient. The material in the preceding subsection on the timeliness and content of rejection notices is relevant in this connection. And it bears emphasis that there will be no section 2-606(1)(b) lapse-of-time acceptance until the buyer has had a reasonable opportunity to inspect the goods.

Section 2-606(1)(c) provides that acceptance occurs when the buyer "does any act inconsistent with the seller's ownership." Because of the generality of the word and the idea of "ownership," this subsection is puzzling and difficult to apply. There is no need to cope with these difficulties in situations where acceptance has occurred under either section 2-606(1)(a) or section 2-606(1)(b). But the question of what acts of the buyer are sufficiently inconsistent with the seller's ownership to constitute acceptances must be confronted in situations where there has been no section 2-606(1)(a) retention signification or no section 2-606(1)(b) failure to give seasonable notice of rejection.

Although section 2-606(1)(c) does not expressly reserve a reasonable opportunity to inspect to the buyer, the words and policies of other Code provisions, particularly sections 2-606(1)(a) and 2-606(1)(b), should preclude interpreting section 2-606(1)(c) to treat the buyer's taking possession of tendered goods and proceeding to inspect them as acts sufficiently inconsistent with the seller's ownership (or with the buyer's right to reject) to constitute acceptance. The provision requires something more than possession and inspection. The "more" would seem to be a use or other treatment of the goods that is inconsistent with reasonable inspection or with the buyer's exercise of its right to reject. For example, a use of the goods that significantly alters them before the buyer attempts to inspect should amount to a section 2-606(1)(c) acceptance. So should most uses of the goods after the buyer has discovered, or should have discovered, a rejection defect. In addition, unnecessary use after a rejection decision has been made or a

---

346 N.W.2d 535, 38 UCCR 114 (1983). Section 5.06, *supra*, contains a comprehensive discussion of the buyer's right of inspection.

rejection notice given presents a strong case for the application to section 2-606(1)(c).[73] By calling for an "unreasonable act inconsistent with the seller's ownership or the buyer's claim of rejection or revocation of acceptance,"[74] the proposed revisions to Article 2 better articulate the probable meaning of present section 2-606(1)(c). Under both the current Article 2 and the proposed revisions, a buyer's inconsistent act becomes an acceptance only if the seller ratifies it.

The effects of acceptance. Section 2-607 states most of the effects of acceptance. First, acceptance requires the buyer to pay for the goods at the rate provided for in the contract.[75] If the accepted goods and their tender conform to the contract, the seller is entitled to the full contract price. Even if the goods or their tender are nonconforming, the accepting buyer's liability starts with the contract price (rather than with the value of the goods), but in this case the buyer may deduct from the contract price whatever damages it has suffered because of the nonconformity.[76]

Second, acceptance precludes rejection. A buyer that has accepted goods cannot thrust them back on the seller under section 2-602. Such a buyer may be able to thrust the accepted goods back on the seller, but the means will be section 2-608—revocation of acceptance—rather than section 2-602 and rejection. Revocation of acceptance, which will be treated in the section to follow, differs from rejection in that it requires a nonconformity of some magnitude—one that "substantially" impairs the value of the goods to the buyer.[77] Further, there can be no revocation if the buyer knew of the nonconformity when it accepted the goods unless the buyer accepted on the reasonable assumption that the nonconformity would be cured and it has not been seasonably cured.[78] The upshot is, at least in terms of the language and theory of Article 2, and often in practice as well, that it is more difficult for a buyer to thrust goods back on the seller and avoid liability for their price by way of revocation of acceptance than by way of rejection.

---

[73] In some circumstances, it is not possible or reasonable to stop using goods immediately on discovering a defect or making a rejection decision. Continued usage that is necessary or reasonable should not produce an acceptance. *See infra* § 7.03[E] for discussion of continued usage in connection with revocation of acceptance.

[74] Council Draft § 2-706(a)(4).

[75] U.C.C. § 2-607(1).

[76] U.C.C. § 2-714 allows an accepting buyer who has given the notification required by section 2-607(3) to recover damages resulting from nonconformity of goods or tender. Section 2-717 allows the buyer to subtract such damages from the contract price.

[77] U.C.C. § 2-608(1).

[78] U.C.C. §§ 2-607(2), 2-608(1)(a).

Third, acceptance shifts to the buyer the burden of proof with respect to defects in the goods.[79] When a buyer effectively rejects, the burden is on the seller to establish that the goods and tender conformed to the contract (making the rejection wrongful and a breach by the buyer). But after a buyer has accepted, the buyer, not the seller, will have the burden with respect to defects in the goods and tender. A buyer that has accepted must carry that burden to justify either its revocation of acceptance or its right to damages based on a nonconformity with respect to retained goods.

Fourth, acceptance changes the kind of notice that a buyer must give to a seller to establish breach and may change the time at which notice must be given.[80] As has been seen, a rejection notice, which is by nature a pre-acceptance notice, must inform the seller that the buyer is thrusting the goods back on the seller. It must be given within a reasonable time after delivery or tender.[81] As is shown in § 7.03[E], a revocation-of-acceptance notice must also inform the seller that the buyer is thrusting the goods back on the seller. It must be given within a reasonable time after the buyer discovers or should have discovered the ground for revocation and before any substantial change in the condition of the goods not caused by their own defects.[82] Subsection 2-607(3)(a) provides for a third kind of notice:

> (3) Where a tender has been accepted
>   (a) the buyer must within a reasonable time after he discovers or should have discovered any breach notify the seller of breach or be barred from any remedy. . . .

The section 2-607(3)(a) notice, which is by nature a post-acceptance notice, need not, and normally will not, attempt to thrust goods back on the seller. To the extent that it does so, it becomes an attempt to revoke acceptance and subject to section 2-608 as well as to section 2-607.

The section 2-607(3)(a) notice is usually used (and required) in situations where the buyer is retaining accepted goods but seeking damages because of a nonconformity in the goods or their tender. What the buyer that has accepted and will be retaining goods must do, on pain of being barred from any remedy,[83] is give the seller a timely notice "of breach." The idea,

---

[79] U.C.C. § 2-607(4).

[80] Compare U.C.C. § 2-607 (3)(a) with U.C.C. §§ 2-602(1) and 2-608(2).

[81] U.C.C. § 2-602(1).

[82] U.C.C. § 2-608(2).

[83] Subsection 2-608(c)(1) of the proposed revisions to Article 2 substantially softens the effect of a failure to give notice. It provides that "a failure to give notice bars the buyer from a remedy only to the extent that the seller establishes that it was prejudiced by the failure." Council Draft § 2-608(c)(1).

as expressed in Comment 4 to section 2-607, is that the buyer "must let the seller know that the transaction is still troublesome and must be watched." As long as the contents of the notice (which the Code does not require to be in writing) accomplish this, the notice should be sufficient to preserve the accepting buyer's rights. Section 4.10 of this text contains a comprehensive discussion of the Section 2-607(3)(a) notice requirement.

Still another consequence of acceptance involves the statute of frauds. To the extent that goods have been both received[84] and accepted, a contract is enforceable even though there is no signed writing.[85]

[E] Revoking Acceptance of the Goods

In some circumstances, a buyer that has accepted nonconforming goods may be able to thrust those goods back on the seller. The Code's term for this course of action is "revocation of acceptance."

Revocation of acceptance resembles rejection in that, if it is effective and rightful, the goods are treated as the seller's, and the buyer does not have to pay their price.[86] Revocation differs from rejection in that it occurs after acceptance[87] and is subject to more conditions and consequently available in fewer circumstances.[88] In single-delivery contracts, rejection is available for *any* nonconformity of the goods or their tender. Revocation, however, is available to a buyer only if the nonconformity in an accepted lot[89] or commercial unit[90] "substantially impairs its value to him" and if the buyer accepted

    (a)   on the reasonable assumption that the non-conformity would be cured and it has not been seasonably cured; or

---

[84] U.C.C. § 2-103(10(c) defines the "receipt" of goods as "taking physical possession of them."

[85] U.C.C. § 2-201(3)(c). *See* § 3.01[C][4], *supra*.

[86] If a revocation is effective but wrongful, the buyer may remain liable for the price. *See infra* § 7.08[E], where this situation is discussed.

[87] Under U.C.C. § 2-607(2), acceptance precludes rejection.

[88] Compare U.C.C. § 2-601, which provides that the buyer may reject if the goods or their tender "fail in any respect to conform to the contract" (the perfect tender rule), with section 2-608, which, along with section 2-607(2), sets out the various conditions to revocation of acceptance.

[89] "Lot" is defined in U.C.C. § 2-105(5).

[90] "Commercial Unit" is defined in U.C.C. § 2-105(6). The discussion of commercial units in connection with rejection (§ 7.03[C], *supra*) is relevant here.

(b)   without discovery of such non-conformity if his acceptance was reasonably induced either by the difficulty of discovery before acceptance or by the seller's assurances.[91]

Thus, there can be no rightful revocation of acceptance for a defect in the goods that impairs their value to the buyer, but only insubstantially; revocation requires a "substantial" impairment. Further, even if there is a defect that substantially impairs the value of the goods to the buyer, there can be no rightful revocation if the buyer knew of the defect when it accepted—unless it accepted on the reasonable assumption that the defect would be cured and it has not been seasonably cured. Finally, if the buyer accepted without knowledge of a substantially impairing defect, it will nevertheless be barred from revocation if it should have discovered the defect before accepting.[92] In statutory terms, such a buyer is barred from revocation unless "acceptance was reasonably induced either by the difficulty of discovery before acceptance or by the seller's assurances."

The drafters had good reasons for making revocation of acceptance more difficult than rejection. By definition, revocation occurs after the buyer has accepted the goods. It almost always occurs after the buyer has taken possession of the goods, and often long afterward. During the interval between acceptance and revocation, the buyer is likely to use (and perhaps misuse) the goods, and they are likely to depreciate in value. Further, in many situations, revocation comes as an upsetting surprise to the seller, who, having delivered the goods and received payment, will for some time have regarded the transaction as closed. Consequently, and especially in situations where the buyer has had the goods for some time, it makes sense to condition rightful revocation on a substantial impairment in value to the buyer and on the justifiability of the buyer's failure to have made an earlier rejection.

Like rejection, revocation of acceptance is ineffective "until the buyer notifies the seller of it."[93] The notice must be of "it"—that is, of revocation of acceptance. Thus, the buyer must do more than simply tell the seller that the goods are defective; it must inform the seller that the goods are being returned.[94]

The power to revoke acceptance, like the power to reject, is lost if the necessary notice is not timely given. To accomplish an effective revocation

---

[91] U.C.C. § 2-608(1).

[92] Hummel v. Skyline Dodge, Inc., 41 Colo. App 572, 589 P.2d 73, 26 UCCR 46 (1978).

[93] U.C.C. § 2-608(2).

[94] International Commodities Export Corp. v. North Pacific Lumber Co., 764 F. Supp. 608, 15 uCCR2d 825 (D. Or. 1991).

of acceptance, a buyer must give notice "within a reasonable time after the buyer discovers or should have discovered the ground for it [revocation of acceptance] and before any substantial change in condition of the goods which is not caused by their own defects."[95] Comment 4 to section 2-608 elaborates on the time for giving revocation notice and notes that it should generally extend beyond the time for giving section 2-607(3)(a) notice of breach:

> Subsection (2) requires notification of revocation of acceptance within a reasonable time after discovery of the grounds for such revocation. Since this remedy will be generally resorted to only after attempts at adjustment have failed, the reasonable time period should extend in most cases beyond the time in which notification of breach must be given, beyond the time for discovery of non-conformity after acceptance and beyond the time for rejection after tender.

Delay in notification of revocation is especially justified where the buyer is "in constant communication with the seller regarding nonconformity of the goods, and 'the seller makes repeated assurances that the defect or nonconformity will be cured and attempts to do so.' "[96]

Substantial impairment. Perhaps the most important condition to rightful revocation of acceptance is a nonconformity that "substantially impairs" the value of the goods to the buyer.[97] A trivial nonconformity from what the seller has promised in the contract obviously falls short of substantial impairment and does not justify revocation. The same is true of a nonconformity that can be and is fully cured by repair. But where the nonconformity is significant, the seller's efforts to repair are unsuccessful or unduly prolonged, and the buyer's faith in the goods is shaken, courts have held that revocation of acceptance is justified.

Fortin v. Ox-Bow Marina, Inc.,[98] a case involving a power boat with a number of defects, including an engine that overheated and a marine toilet that malfunctioned, is illustrative. Noting that substantial impairment was a

---

[95] U.C.C. § 2-608(2). The requirement that the buyer give notice "within a reasonable time after" a specified event has been discussed in § 7.03[C] with respect to rejection notices (U.C.C. § 2-602(1)) and in § 7.03[D] with respect to section 2-607(3)(a) notices of breach. Those discussions, and particularly the portions of them that deal with the uncertainty that inheres in the reasonableness standard and with the possibility of providing for a more definite notice period by agreement have relevance to revocation of acceptance notices.

[96] Fortin v. Ox-Bow Marina, Inc., 408 Mass. 310, 318, 557 N.E.2d 1157, 1163, 12 UCCR2d 691, 698 (1990).

[97] U.C.C. § 2-608(1).

[98] 408 Mass. 310, 557 N.E.2d 1157, 12 UCCR2d 691 (1990).

question for the trier of fact, the Massachusetts Supreme Judicial Court sustained the trial court's finding that it existed, and summarized the relevant case law in the following terms:

> Most courts read this test as an objective, or common sense, determination that the impaired value of the goods to the buyer was substantial as opposed to trivial, or easily fixed, given his subjective needs. [Citations omitted.] The evaluation is made in light of the "totality of circumstances" of each particular case, including the number of deficiencies and type of nonconformity and the time and inconvenience spent in downtime and attempts at repair. [Citations omitted.] Thus, it has been said that, in the proper circumstances, even cosmetic or minor defects that go unrepaired despite a number of complaints or attempts at repair, [citations omitted] or remaining minor defects after an earlier, serious problem has been repaired, [citations omitted] or defects which do not totally prevent the buyer from using the goods, but circumscribe that use or warrant unusual or excessive maintenance actions in order to use, [citations omitted] can substantially impair the goods' value to the buyer. Experiencing in a major investment a series of defects, even if some have been cured and others are curable, can shake a buyer's faith in the goods, at which point "the item not only loses its real value in the buyer's eyes, but also becomes an article whose integrity has been substantially impaired and whose operation is fraught with apprehension. [Citations omitted.][99]

The statutory standard is a nonconformity that substantially impairs the value of the goods "to him,"[100] that is, to the buyer. Courts have treated this language as creating both a subjective and an objective test: subjective in the sense that value impairment is to be tested in terms of the needs and circumstances of the particular buyer, even if the seller did not know of them at the time of contracting, and objective in the sense that the buyer's personal belief that the value of the goods is substantially impaired is not controlling. The trier of fact must make an objective determination that the value of the goods to the particular buyer, not to a fair average buyer, is in fact substantially impaired.[101] In cases in which consumers bought and expected to receive new cars—that is, cars that could be confidently relied upon for years—defects (such as ice in the transmission and a grinding

---

[99] Id. at 316–317, 557 N.E.2d at 1162, 12 UCCR2d at 697.

[100] U.C.C. § 2-608(1).

[101] Asciolla v. Manter Oldsmobile-Pontiac, Inc., 117 N.H. 85, 370 A.2d 270, 21 UCCR 112 (1977); Capitol Cadillac Olds, Inc. v. Roberts, 813 S.W.2d 287, 15 uCCR2d 1221 (Ky. Sup. Ct. 1991).

noise) that were sufficient to shake the faith of the buyers in the integrity of their vehicles were held to substantially impair value and justify revocation.[102]

Rights and duties after revocation. Subsection 2-608(3) provides that a buyer that revokes acceptance "has the same rights and duties with regard to the goods involved as if he had rejected them." A rejecting buyer's rights and duties were discussed earlier, and that discussion is relevant here. The fundamental idea is that both rejection and revocation involve thrusting the goods back on the seller—treating them as the seller's goods. Accordingly, a rightfully revoking buyer is under a duty to hold the goods involved at the seller's disposition and to refrain from exercising ownership over them.[103] This situation is altered if the revoking buyer has paid some or all of the price or has incurred certain expenses in connection with the goods. In such circumstances, section 2-711(3) gives the revoking buyer a security interest in the goods. A buyer with a security interest must still treat the goods as the seller's—except to the extent of its security interest, which it may enforce—by holding the goods or by sale foreclosure.

Nowhere does the Code expressly authorize a revoking buyer (with or without a section 2-711(3) security interest) to use the goods after it has given notice of revocation. On the contrary, it can be argued that use following a revocation should be treated as an acceptance (a second one) which, because made with knowledge of the revocation nonconformity and not on the assumption that it will be cured, cannot be revoked.[104] In many situations, however, courts have held that post-revocation use of the goods by the buyer did not vitiate revocation. The focus has been on the "reasonableness" of the use. Factors such as the seller's failure to retake possession of the goods or to instruct the buyer as to their disposition after revocation, the buyer's lack of funds and consequent inability to obtain substitute goods, and the seller's continued assurances and efforts to repair the goods after revocation tend to make post-revocation use reasonable.[105] On the other hand, when a revoking buyer, which has the means to do so, fails to search for and obtain replacement goods expeditiously, but instead continues to use the goods after revoking acceptance, the use has been determined to be

---

[102] *Id.*

[103] U.C.C. § 2-602(2).

[104] *See* U.C.C. §§ 2-606(1)(c), 2-607(2), and 2-608(1); Waltz v. Chevrolet Motor Div., 307 A.2d 815, 12 UCCR 874 (Del. Super. 1973).

[105] *See* McCullough v. Bill Swad Chrysler-Plymouth, Inc., 5 Ohio St. 3d 181, 449 N.E.2d 1289, 36 UCCR 513 (1983) (a case in which the buyer's use of a car for seventeen months and 23,000 miles after giving notice or revocation was held reasonable and consequently did not vitiate the revocation).

unreasonable. Some courts have held that in this case the revocation is ineffective.[106]

Cure after revocation. As has been discussed previously,[107] section 2-508 of the Code gives the seller the right to cure nonconforming tenders in certain circumstances. Section 2-508 grants the right to cure "[w]here any tender of delivery by the seller *is rejected*" and "[w]here the buyer *rejects.*"[108] It does not expressly grant the right to cure where the buyer revokes acceptance, and neither does section 2-608. This has led some courts to conclude that there is no right to cure after revocation.[109] Other cases and some commentators, making both statutory and policy arguments, have found a right to cure after some revocations.[110]

The proposed revisions to Article 2 take the latter approach. Section 2-709 expressly provides for cure after revocation as well as after rejection. Under the draft revisions, post-revocation cure is available only when the buyer accepted without discovering the nonconformity; it is not available when the buyer accepted on the reasonable assumption that the nonconformity would be cured and it has not been seasonably cured.[111] This distinction is sound. When the buyer has relied on the seller to cure, and the seller has failed to cure within a reasonable time, and this very failure has given rise to the buyer's right to revoke, the seller has no claim to a further cure opportunity after revocation, and the buyer has strong fairness and efficiency objections to the granting of additional time. When, on the other hand, the buyer's right to revoke arises out of the post-acceptance discovery of a nonconformity of which the buyer and seller were previously unaware, affording the seller a post-revocation opportunity to cure usually makes commercial sense.

---

[106] L.S. Heath & Son, Inc. v. AT&T Info. Sys., Inc., 9 F.3d 561, 22 UCCR2d 27 (7th Cir. 1993).

[107] *See* § 5.03[B][2], *supra.*

[108] U.C.C. §§ 2-508(1) and 2-508(2) (emphasis added).

[109] Gappelberg v. Landrum, 666 S.W.2d 88 (Tex. Sup. Ct. 1984); City Nat'l Bank of Charleston v. Wells, 181 W. Va. 763, 384 S.E.2d 374, 10 UCCR2d 798 (1989).

[110] Tucker v. Aqua Yacht Harbor Corp., 749 F. Supp. 142, 13 U.C.C.R 382 (N.D. Miss. 1990); Howard Foss, "The Seller's Right to Cure When the Buyer Revokes Acceptance: Erase the Line in the Sand," 16 S.U. Ill. L.J. 1 (1991); Gregory M. Travalio, "The U.C.C.'s Three 'R's': Rejection, Revocation and (The Seller's) Right to Cure," 53 U. Cinn. L. Rev. 931 (1984).

[111] Sections 2-709 and 2-708 of the Council Draft.

[F]   Retention of the Goods

A buyer with a right to reject or to revoke acceptance may nevertheless elect to retain nonconforming goods in spite of their nonconformity. Alternatively, such a buyer may attempt to reject or revoke acceptance but do so tardily or otherwise ineffectively, and consequently be required to retain the goods. A retaining buyer must pay for the goods at the contract rate, but may be able to deduct from the contract price the damages it has suffered because of the nonconformity of the goods or tender.[112] Before the buyer can deduct damages from the price or recover damages from the seller, it must give notice of breach under section 2-607(3)(a).

[G]   Summary of the Buyer's Courses of Action

The preceding subsections have presented the buyer's courses of action when it receives nonconforming goods or a nonconforming tender. The buyer may first choose between rejection and acceptance. If it rejects effectively, the goods are treated as belonging to the seller, and the buyer has no obligation to pay their price. If it accepts, the buyer may have a further choice between keeping the goods and revoking acceptance. If the buyer effectively revokes, the goods are treated as belonging to the seller and the buyer's obligation to pay the price is avoided—just as with rejection. If, either by choice or by inadvertently failing to make an effective rejection or revocation, the buyer retains the goods, it must pay for them at the contract rate. A retaining buyer, however, may be able to recover damages caused by the nonconformity of the goods or tender.

The requirement of seasonable notice runs throughout the process. To accomplish an effective rejection or revocation of acceptance, the buyer must seasonably notify the seller that it is thrusting the goods back on the seller. Even in situations where the buyer has accepted the goods and intends to retain them, it must notify the seller of any breach or be barred from any remedy.[113]

§ 7.04   THE BUYER'S MONETARY RECOVERIES

[A]   Recovery of the Purchase Price Paid

When, because of a material breach by the seller, the buyer fails to receive the goods or effectively thrusts them back on the seller, the buyer

---

[112] U.C.C. §§ 2-607(1), 2-714, 2-715, 2-717.
[113] U.C.C. § 2-607(3)(a).

ought not have to pay the price, in whole or in part. Because the buyer has not received the agreed-upon exchange, an essential condition to its duty to pay has not occurred. The seller has not earned the price and would be unjustly enriched by payment. To the extent that the buyer has already paid—has made an advance or downpayment—it should be able to recover the payment from the seller. Allowing such a recovery both returns to the buyer money that it spent in reliance on the broken contract and disgorges an unearned gain from the contract-breaking seller. In other words, such a recovery protects the buyer's restitution interest.[114]

In section 2-711, Article 2 codifies the fundamental contract principles outlined in the preceding paragraph with respect to an aggrieved buyer's recovery of the price paid. Section 2-711(1) provides, among other things, for recovery of whatever portion of the price has been paid when one of four triggering events occurs:

> Where [1] the seller fails to make delivery or [2] repudiates or [3] the buyer rightfully rejects or [4] justifiably revokes acceptance . . . the buyer may cancel and whether or not he has done so may *in addition to recovering so much of the price as has been paid.* [Numbers and emphasis supplied.]

Each of section 2-711(1)'s four triggering events involves a situation in which the buyer, because of the seller's breach, ends up without the goods. In the case of the first two triggering events—failure to deliver and repudiation by the seller—the buyer never received the goods. In the case of the last two—rightful rejection and justifiable revocation of acceptance—the seller has either retaken the goods or has a right to do so. The defaulting seller cannot be entitled to both the goods and payment for them. To the extent that it has received payment, it must return the money to the aggrieved buyer.

When the buyer receives and retains the goods, none of the section 2-711(1) triggering events occurs. A retaining buyer will consequently be unable to recover any payments it has made on the price, even though the goods do not conform to the contract. This makes remedial sense. The aggrieved buyer would be overcompensated—that is, put in a better position than it would have occupied had the seller fully performed—if it were allowed to (1) retain the goods, (2) avoid payment for them, and (3) recover the damages that it has suffered because of the nonconformity of the goods

---

[114] *See* the discussion of the restitution interest in § 7.01, *supra*.

(which, if it has given the necessary notice,[115] it will be able to do under section 2-714).[116]

When one of section 2-711's triggering events occurs—that is, when the defaulting seller and not the buyer ends up with the goods—the right to recover the price paid is only one of the monetary remedial rights available to the buyer. In addition to recovering whatever portion of the price it has paid (having its restitution interest protected), the aggrieved buyer may recover damages measured by the difference between the cost of cover and the contract price[117] or between the market price and the contract price,[118] together with any incidental or consequential damages it has suffered[119]— that is, the aggrieved buyer may have its expectation and reliance interests protected as well.[120]

[B] "Cover" Damages

Code remedial thinking, like general contract remedial thinking, begins with the protection of the expectation interest—with an effort to place the party aggrieved by a breach in the position it would have occupied had the other party performed insofar as this can be accomplished with a money-damage remedy.[121] It is often possible to measure some or all of the aggrieved party's expectation-interest loss by comparing the value (to the aggrieved party) of the promised performance with the contract price.[122] In recognition of this circumstance, the law—both common and statutory law—has developed some damage formulas. These formulas involve the subtraction of one monetary amount from another to produce damages (which damages are sometimes referred to as "difference-money" damages).

For example, consider a services contract subject to the common law— in particular, a building contract—in which a builder promises an owner to build a garage on the owner's land according to certain plans and specifications for a price of $10,000. If the builder repudiates before beginning

---

[115] U.C.C. § 2-607(3)(a).

[116] U.C.C. § 2-717 allows a retaining buyer to offset its section 2-714 nonconformity damages against any unpaid portion of the contract price.

[117] U.C.C. § 2-712.

[118] U.C.C. § 2-713.

[119] U.C.C. § 2-715.

[120] *See* the discussion of the expectation and reliance interest in § 7.01, *supra*.

[121] U.C.C. § 1-106. The proposed revisions to Article 2 takes the same track, providing in section 2-803(a) that "In accordance with Section 1-106, the remedies provided in this article must be liberally administered with the purpose of placing the aggrieved party in as good a position as if the other party had fully performed." Council Draft § 2-803.

[122] *See* Restatement of Contracts (Second), § 347.

work and before the owner has made any payments on the price, the aggrieved owner's expectation loss can be measured by the formula of reasonable cost of construction minus contract price.[123] If it will cost the aggrieved owner $12,000 to get another builder to build the garage, the owner can recover $2,000 from the defaulting builder. When added to the $10,000 unpaid contract price that remains in the owner's pocket, this $2,000 will enable the owner to get the garage it was promised at the price it was promised. In other words, it will put the aggrieved owner in approximately the same economic position that performance would have done. A difference-money damage formula may also be used to measure the builder's loss if it is the owner which repudiates the contract. If the owner repudiates, the damage formula will be the unpaid contract price ($10,000) minus the amount that the builder could reasonably save by not doing the work.[124] If the builder's savable costs were $9,000, this formula would produce a recovery of $1,000, which is the gain or expectancy that the builder would have realized through performance.

Article 2 codifies several difference-money damage formulas—each aimed at protecting the aggrieved party's expectation interest in particular circumstances. For a buyer who, because of the seller's default, ends up without the promised goods and with the contract price, there are two formulas, which are alternatives to each other. These are (1) the cost of cover—that is, the actual price at which substitute goods are purchased—minus the contract price (section 2-712) and (2) the market price minus the contract price (section 2-713). For a buyer that receives and retains goods but is aggrieved because the goods are of a lesser quality than the seller promised, there is the formula of value of the goods as warranted minus the value of the goods actually received (section 2-714(2)). For a seller that, because of the buyer's default, ends up without the promised contract price and with the goods, there are three difference-money formulas. The first two (alternatives to each other) are (1) the contract price minus the price obtained on resale (section 2-706) and (2) the contract price minus the market price (section 2-708(1)). When the section 2-708(1) contract-minus-market measure is inadequate to put the aggrieved seller in as good a position as performance, section 2-708(2) provides that the seller may recover its profit. Although in section 2-708(2) the subtraction equation is implicit rather than express, profit recoveries also involve a difference-money damage formula, that of contract price minus savable costs.

---

[123] *See* Restatement of Contracts (First), § 346(1).
[124] *See* Restatement of Contracts (First) § 346(2).

Sellers' difference-money damage recoveries are considered in § 7.08. The discussion now turns specifically to buyers' difference-money recoveries and particularly to section 2-712 and its cost of cover minus contract price.

Section 2-712 is activated by one of section 2-711(1)'s triggering events—that is, when a buyer ends up without promised goods because the seller has failed to deliver the goods or has repudiated, or because the buyer has rightfully rejected or revoked its acceptance. In such circumstances, section 2-712 protects the aggrieved buyer's expectation interest by subtracting the contract price from the price that the buyer actually and reasonably pays for substitute goods. Suppose a contract for the purchase and sale of a particular tractor for $30,000, and suppose that the seller repudiates before the buyer has made any payments on the price. If the buyer, acting reasonably, pays $35,000 to obtain a substitute tractor from a third party, section 2-712 allows the buyer to recover the $5,000 difference between the $30,000 contract price and the $35,000 "cost of cover." Awarding the buyer $5,000 in damages enables it to obtain the substitute tractor at a net cost of $30,000 and thus puts the buyer in the position it would have occupied had the seller performed.

Provision for cover damages was one of the innovations wrought by the Code. Under previous law, including the Uniform Sales Act, aggrieved buyers who ended up without the goods could recover the market price of the goods minus the contract price.[125] Section 2-713, which is discussed in § 7.04[C], provides for a similar recovery. The Code's innovation was to add cover price minus contract price as an alternative measure of recovery. Thus, the Code allows a buyer, buys substitute goods in a manner that qualifies as a section 2-712 cover purchase to use the amount it actually paid for substitute goods rather than the market price as a baseline for measuring its damages.

Aggrieved buyers will frequently have good reason to prefer the cover-minus-contract measure of damages over the market-minus-contract measure. First, prices actually paid are usually much easier to prove than hypothetical market prices. More important, a buyer that makes a cover purchase will not, or, at least, should not, be second-guessed by a decision that although it paid more than the market price for the substitute goods, it can nevertheless recover only the difference between the market price and the contract price, thus ending up short of full compensation—that is, short of the position in which performance would have placed it. Such a buyer should receive the difference between what it actually paid and the contract price, and thus be fully compensated.

---

[125] Uniform Sales Act § 67.

Although it has great advantages, allowing the use of an actual transaction as a baseline for measuring the buyer's damages could lead to unfairness to the defaulting seller if there were no restrictions on the buyer's cover recovery. It would not be fair to allow the buyer to measure its damages by any actual purchase price, no matter how extravagant or how much motivated by a desire to run up damages. Accordingly, section 2-712 imposes reasonableness, good-faith, and other limitations on the kind of purchase that will qualify as a cover purchase. Specifically, it provides as follows:

> § 2-712. "Cover"; Buyer's Procurement of Substitute Goods.
> (1) After a breach within the preceding section the buyer may "cover" by making in good faith and without unreasonable delay any reasonable purchase of or contract to purchase goods in substitution for those due from the seller.
> (2) The buyer may recover from the seller as damages the difference between the cost of cover and the contract price together with any incidental or consequential damages as hereinafter defined (Section 2-715), but less expenses saved in consequence of the seller's breach.
> (3) Failure of the buyer to effect cover within this section does not bar him from any other remedy.

Elements of a cover purchase. Subsection (1) defines a "cover" purchase—one whose price will qualify as a baseline for measuring the buyer's damages. It imposes five requirements: (1) there must be a seller's breach "within the preceding section"—that is, the buyer must end up without the goods because one of section 2-711(1)'s four triggering events has occurred; (2) the buyer's purchase must be made "in good faith"; (3) the buyer's purchase must be made "without unreasonable delay"; (4) the buyer's purchase must be "reasonable"; and (5) the buyer's purchase must be of goods "in substitution for those due from the seller."

The first requirement—that one of section 2-711(1)'s triggering events has occurred—is fundamentally a requirement that, because of the seller's breach, the buyer end up without the goods. This is the only situation in which the cover-minus-contract damage formula (or the market-price-minus-contract-price formula of section 2-713) makes sense in terms of the overriding goal of protecting the buyer's expectation interest. The protection of the expectation interest of a buyer that does not have the goods requires a remedy that will enable the buyer to get the goods or their value at the contract price, and the cover-minus-contract-price measure of damages is directly aimed at this result.[126] On the other hand, the protection of the

---

[126] *See* U.C.C. § 2-712, Comment 1.

expectation interest of a buyer that receives and retains the goods but that is aggrieved because the goods are of a lesser quality than promised or because they were delivered late or otherwise out of compliance with the seller's promises, requires a different measure of damages.

The second requirement is that the buyer's purchase be made "in good faith." "Good faith" is defined in section 1-201(19) as "honesty in fact." This definition applies to all Code articles except to the extent that it is modified in individual articles. It creates a subjective test. Was the buyer acting honestly when it paid $10,000 for goods in substitution for those due from the defaulting seller? In most cases, the answer is "Yes," because buyers usually act with subjective honesty with regard to paying as low a price as possible when they buy things. In a cover situation, however, a buyer might act dishonestly by paying an unduly high price for the purpose of building up a damage claim against the seller or to convey a gift-like benefit (to be paid for by the seller) on a favored supplier of the substitute goods. In rare cases like these, the buyer's subjective dishonesty prevents its purchase from qualifying as a cover.

The good-faith requirement has a greater impact when the covering buyer is a merchant, as defined in section 2-104(1). This is because section 2-103(1)(b) contains a more expansive definition of good faith in the case of merchants in Article 2. For them, the definition is "honesty in fact and the observance of reasonable commercial standards of fair dealing in the trade." Thus, a merchant buyer that covers must not only be subjectively honest, it must also pass the objective test of observing reasonable commercial standards of fair dealing. If fair commercial practices require checking prices with a number of suppliers before making the substitute purchase, those practices must be followed if the buyer is to be allowed to take advantage of the section 2-712 measure of recovery. On the other hand, if, because of the buyer's immediate need for the goods, commercial standards are satisfied by checking with only one supplier, that should meet the good-faith requirement.

Closely related to the good-faith requirement is the requirement that the substitute purchase be "reasonable." The reasonableness requirement adds an objective test to the subjective "honesty in fact" good-faith standard for nonmerchants and overlaps the "reasonable commercial standards of fair dealing" part of the good-faith standard for merchants. The basic idea is one of mitigation of damages: an aggrieved buyer should do what is reasonable to minimize the consequences of its seller's default. If it does not do so, but instead buys substitute goods at an unreasonably high price—one appreciably above the prevailing market price and for which it can offer no satisfactory explanation—it will not be able to use that price to measure its damages. This kind of policing on reasonableness grounds is necessary but should not be carried too far, lest the cover remedy—that is, basing damages on the price actually paid for substitute goods, be denied the significant role the drafters envisaged for it. Comment 2 to section 2-712 suggests the appropriate balance:

> The test of proper cover is whether at the time and place the buyer acted in good faith and in a reasonable manner, and it is immaterial that hindsight may later prove that the method of cover used was not the cheapest or most effective.[127]

Another closely related requirement is that the substitute purchase be made "without unreasonable delay." The thought is that the buyer should not wait too long after the relevant triggering event—after the seller has repudiated or failed to deliver, or the buyer has rejected or revoked acceptance.[128] How long is too long varies with the circumstances. Quoting Comment 2's statement that "cover 'without unreasonable delay' is not intended to limit the time necessary for [the buyer] to look around and decide as to how he may best effect cover," the New Jersey Supreme Court held that four months after revocation of acceptance did not amount to an unreasonable delay for a buyer of an expensive speedboat.[129] On the other hand, when the goods involved are corn or beans, and there is a well-organized market that is easily accessible to a merchant buyer, the allowable time in which to effect cover is likely to be brief. One court has said that it expires on the day of an unequivocal repudiation.[130] In a volatile market, however,

---

[127] Despite this Comment exhortation, hindsight inevitably plays a role in the decision of some cases. Purchases made at more than what is later shown to have been the market price are often attacked on reasonableness and good-faith grounds. And in cases where there are significant discrepancies that cannot be explained by the buyer's need to act quickly or otherwise, such attacks are likely to succeed.

[128] Doubt as to whether a triggering event has occurred—if, for example, it is unclear that the seller has repudiated, or if the seller has missed its promised delivery date but has assured the buyer that it will deliver—should postpone the commencement of the unreasonable delay period. *See* Erie Casein Co. v. Anric Corp., 217 Ill. App. 3d 602, 577 N.E.2d 892, 15 UCCR2d 1240 (1991), *app. denied,* 142 Ill. 2d 653, 584 N.E.2d 128 (1991).

[129] Meshinsky v. Nichols Yacht Sales, Inc., 110 N.J. 464, 541 A.2d 1063, 6 UCCR2d 1144 (1988).

[130] Oloffson v. Coomer, 11 Ill. App. 3d 918, 296 N.E.2d 871, 12 UCCR 1082 (1973). *See also* Trinidad Bean & Elevator Co. v. Frosh, 494 N.W.2d 347, 20 UCCR2d 462 (Neb. App. 1992).

waiting to see if high prices will fall may be reasonable and not invalidate a cover.[131]

The final requirement for a cover purchase is that it be of goods "in substitution for those due from the seller." This, like the other requirements, should be interpreted in light of the overriding purpose of protecting the buyer's expectation interest without penalizing the seller.[132] Except in unusual circumstances, it would be inconsistent with this purpose to allow a buyer who has been promised goods of modest size and limited features (for example, a compact and modestly equipped Chevrolet), to base his damages on the purchase price of a larger, luxuriously appointed model (for example, a full-size,"loaded" Cadillac).[133] On the other hand, a buyer who (at a price higher than the contract price) purchased a speedboat that was less powerful and had ten percent fewer features than the promised boat should be, and was, able to use the price paid for the lesser boat to measure his damages.[134] As Comment 2 points out, there is no requirement that the cover goods be identical with the goods promised by the seller; goods that are "commercially usable as reasonable substitutes under the circumstances of the particular case" will suffice.[135] What is "commercially usable as a reasonable substitute" will depend, in significant part, on what is available to the buyer in time to meet its needs.[136]

Not only may the cover goods differ from the promised goods, so may the terms of the cover contract differ from the terms of the broken contract. Section 2-712(1) expressly recognizes both a "purchase" and a "contract to purchase"—suggesting that the delivery dates of the broken contract and of the cover contract may be significantly different. Comment 2 says that, as long as they are "reasonable," credit and delivery terms may differ. Differences between the two contracts frequently require adjustments in the damages recoverable, sometimes under section 2-712(2)'s "less expenses saved in consequence of the seller's breach," sometimes under section 2-715(1)'s

---

[131] *See* Dura-Wood Treating Co. v. Century Forest Indus., Inc., 675 F.2d 745, 33 UCCR 1201 (5th Cir. 1982).

[132] *See* U.C.C. § 1-106(1).

[133] *See* Martella v. Woods, 715 F.2d 410, 36 UCCR 1200 (8th Cir. 1983).

[134] Meshinsky v. Nichols Yacht Sales, Inc., 110 N.J. 464, 541 A.2d 1063, 6 UCCR2d 1144 (1988).

[135] Although it gives it a new number (section 2-725), the proposed revisions to Article 2 make few significant changes to what is now section 2-712. One of its changes is to add the adjective "comparable," so that under the new section a cover purchase must be of "comparable goods to substitute for those due from the seller." It is doubtful that this will work any substantive change in the law.

[136] *See* In re Lifeguard Indus., Inc. 42 B.R. 734, 39 UCCR 1268 (Bankr. S.D. Ohio 1983).

provision for incidental damages (which include "any commercially reasonable charges, expenses or commissions in connection with effecting cover"), and sometimes simply to produce damages that compensate but do not penalize.[137] Buyers have even been allowed to cover by manufacturing substitute goods themselves, when this was reasonable and made compensatory sense.[138] The fundamental question is whether, under all the circumstances, the purported cover affords a fair basis for compensating the buyer for the loss caused by the seller's breach. If it does, it should qualify as a purchase of, or contract to purchase, goods in substitution for those due from the seller.

When all of the section 2-712(1) requirements are satisfied, the buyer's basic recovery is the cost of cover minus the contract price (plus, under section 2-711, any amounts paid down by the buyer). Thus, if a contract provided for the sale of a tractor for $27,000, the seller repudiated, and the buyer covered (complying with all the requirements of section 2-712(1)) at a cost of $30,200, the buyer's basic recovery would be $3,200—and this even though the market price of the tractor was later found to have been only $29,500. If the buyer had made a $700 downpayment on the tractor, its recovery would be increased to $3,900. This recovery might then be further adjusted in accordance with section 2-712(2)'s provisions that incidental (section 2-715(1)) and consequential (section 2-715(2)) damages be added and "expenses saved in consequence of the seller's breach" be subtracted. For example, expenses incurred in effecting cover—say, $25 in long distance telephone charges—would be added as incidental damages, producing a recovery of $3,925. And if the seller's repudiation caused the buyer to be without a needed tractor for three days, the buyer might be able to add the profits it lost because of the absence of the tractor—say, $750—as consequential damages, producing a recovery of $4,675.[139] If the buyer realized a savings because of the breach—if, for example, the broken contract called for the buyer's picking up the tractor at a distant point (something that would have cost the buyer $200) and the cover-contract seller delivered

---

[137] See Productora e Importadora de Papel S.A. de C.V. v. Fleming, 376 Mass. 826, 383 N.E.2d 1129, 25 UCCR 729 (1978).

[138] Dura-Wood Treating Co. v. Century Forest Indus., Inc., 675 F.2d 745, 33 UCCR 1201 (5th Cir. 1982), cert. denied, 459 U.S. 865, 103 S. Ct. 144, 74 L. Ed. 2d 122 (1982).

[139] The buyer's ability to add these lost profits as U.C.C. § 2-715(2) consequential damages would depend on (1) whether the seller at the time of contracting had reason to know that the buyer needed the tractor to earn profits and (2) whether the buyer could reasonably have prevented the loss of the profits—for example, by covering more promptly or by renting a substitute tractor (in which case the rental cost might be recovered as consequential damages).

the substitute tractor to the buyer's place of business—the $200 savings should be deducted as an expense "saved in consequence of the seller's breach," producing a recovery of $4,475.

Identifying cover purchases. When a situation is like the preceding in that the purchase is an unusual one for the buyer (assume that our hypothetical buyer buys a new tractor no more frequently than once every four or five years), there is unlikely to be much difficulty in identifying the purchase that should be tested against section 2-712(1) to see whether it qualifies as a cover. In other situations, however, there can be difficulty. As part of their normal operations, many merchant buyers repeatedly purchase the goods they need from two or more suppliers. For example, a brewery may be more or less constantly in the market for barley, hops, bottles, and cans. Suppose that one seller repudiates its contract to deliver 25,000 bushels of barley, and within the two-week period following the repudiation, the brewery makes two different barley purchases, one at a per-bushel price above the broken-contract price and the other at a price below the broken-contract price. And suppose that making two such purchases during a two-week period was usual for the brewery. The difficult question of which, if either, of these two purchases effected cover will probably be left to the trier of fact.[140] There is no easy or mechanical way for the trier of fact to answer this question.[141] Rather, the purchases should be examined in light of the reasonableness, good-faith, and goods-in-substitution requirements of section 2-712(1), and in light of the overriding goal of placing the aggrieved buyer in the position that performance would have done without penalizing the seller.[142]

Relationship between section 2-712's cover remedy and section 2-713's market-price remedy. Subsection (3) of section 2-712 provides that "[f]ailure of the buyer to effect cover does not bar him from any other remedy." Comment 3 explains that this provision "expresses the policy that cover is not a mandatory remedy for the buyer. The buyer is always free to choose between cover and damages for non-delivery under the next section." It is thus clear that cover is an optional remedy and that buyers that do not effect

---

[140] *See* Commonwealth Edison Co. v. Allied Chem. Nuclear Prods., Inc., 684 F. Supp. 1434, 6 UCCR2d 434 (N.D. Ill. 1988).

[141] While an aggrieved seller must, under U.C.C. §§ 2-706(3) and 2-706(4), give a defaulting buyer notice of a resale if it is to be able to use the resale price as a baseline for calculating its damages, there is no analogous requirement that an aggrieved buyer give notice of a cover purchase.

[142] *See* Milwaukee Valve Co., Inc. v. Milwaukee Brass Mfg., Inc., 107 Wis. 2d 164, 319 N.W.2d 885, 34 UCCR 15 (Wisc. Ct. App. 1982); Farmer's Union Co-op Co. v. Flamme Bros., 196 Neb. 699, 245 N.W.2d 464, 20 UCCR 77(1976).

cover may use section 2-713's market-minus-contract remedy. Nonetheless, some qualifications are in order.

First, despite the language of section 2-712(3), there is a way in which failure to cover can bar a buyer from another remedy—specifically, from the recovery of consequential damages. An aggrieved buyer is subject to the general principle of avoidable consequences: it cannot recover damages that it could reasonably have avoided. This principle is expressly linked to cover in section 2-715(2)(a)'s provision for consequential damages:

> (2) Consequential damages resulting from the seller's breach include
>
> > (a)   any loss resulting from general or particular requirements and needs of which the seller at the time of contracting had reason to know and *which could not be reasonably prevented by cover or otherwise. . . .* [Emphasis supplied.]

Thus, in situations in which procuring substitute goods by cover or in some other way is a reasonable way for an aggrieved buyer to avoid losing profits or suffering other losses, a failure to do so can bar the buyer from recovering such profits or other losses as consequential damages.

Second, a buyer who has made a purchase that qualifies as a cover under section 2-712(1) cannot ignore the section 2-712 cover-minus-contract remedy and opt instead for the section 2-713 market-minus-contract remedy. At least, it cannot do so if, in the circumstances, the 2-713 remedy would place it in a better position than performance would have done. This would be the case if the buyer had managed to cover at less than the market price. In such circumstances, courts have refused to allow recovery under section 2-713.[143] Comment 5 to section 2-713 supports this result:

> The present section provides a remedy which is completely alternative to cover under the preceding section and *applies only when and to the extent that the buyer has not covered.* [Emphasis added.]

Although a buyer that covers is generally foreclosed from using section 2-713, buyers that make replacement purchases that fail to qualify as section 2-712(1) covers (because they are too long delayed, are otherwise unreasonable, or involve goods or terms that are too different from those of the broken contract to be "substitutes") are barred from section 2-712 and must

---

[143] Commonwealth Edison Co. v. Allied Chem. Nuclear Prods., Inc., 684 F. Supp. 1434, 6 UCCR2d 434 (N.D. Ill. 1988); Cosden Oil & Chem. Co. v. Karl O. Helm Aktiengesellschaft, 736 F.2d 1064, 38 UCCR 1645 (5th Cir. 1984).

find their relief in section 2-713. For example, consider a contract for the purchase and sale of a commercial quantity of large eggs for $10,000. Suppose that, on the seller's failure to deliver, the buyer buys a like quantity of extra-large eggs for $12,500, and does so in circumstances where large eggs are available on the market for $11,000. The buyer's purchase should not qualify as a cover because it was of better or more goods rather than of goods "in substitution for those due from the seller." It would not be fair to the seller to allow the buyer to use the $12,500 figure to measure its damages. On the other hand, the buyer was, and should be, free to act as it did, and there is no reason to deprive it of any remedy. It can recover $1,000 under section 2-713's market-minus-contract formula.

[C] Market-Minus-Contract Damages

Section 2-713 is captioned "Buyer's Damages for Non-delivery or Repudiation" and provides:

> (1) Subject to the provisions of this Article with respect to proof of market price (Section 2-723), the measure of damages for non-delivery or repudiation by the seller is the difference between the market price at the time the buyer learned of the breach and the contract price together with any incidental and consequential damages provided in this Article (Section 2-715), but less expenses saved in consequence of the seller's breach.
>
> (2) Market price is to be determined as of the place for tender or, in cases of rejection after arrival or revocation of acceptance, as of the place of arrival.

Both the section caption and the language of section 2-713(1) refer to only two kinds of seller's breach: nondelivery and repudiation. Nevertheless, the section also applies to cases in which the seller neither repudiated nor failed to deliver but in which the buyer rightfully rejected or revoked acceptance.[144] The clear Code policy of treating the market-minus-contract remedy as an alternative to the cover remedy[145] as well as the language of sections 2-711(1) and 2-713(2) compel this conclusion. Section 2-711(1)

---

[144] Gawlick v. American Bldrs. Supply, Inc. 86 N.M. 77, 519 P.2d313, 13 UCCR 1031 (N.M. Ct. App. 1974) (revocation of acceptance); Welken v. Conley, 252 N.W.2d 311, 21 UCCR 1304 (N.D. 1977) (revocation of acceptance); Traynor v. Walters, 342 F. Supp. 455, 10 UCCR 965 (M.D. Pa. 1972) (rejection).

[145] Comment 5 to U.C.C. § 2-713 states that "[t]he present section provides a remedy which is completely alternative to cover under the preceding section and applies only when and to the extent that the buyer has not covered."

lists four triggering events (the seller's failure to make delivery or repudi-ation and the buyer's rightful rejection or justifiable revocation of accep-tance) and provides that, when any one of these events occurs, the buyer may, among other things, "recover damages for non-delivery as provided in this Article (2-713)." And section 2-713(2) provides a place for measuring damages "in cases of rejection after arrival or revocation of acceptance." Thus, the statutory word "non-delivery," as used in section 2-713, should be read to include cases in which the buyer rightfully thrusts goods back on the seller as well as cases in which the seller wholly fails to deliver.

The operation of section 2-713 can be illustrated by a hypothetical. Suppose that in March Buyer and Seller formed a contract for the purchase and sale of a quantity of industrial diamonds at a price of $100,000, delivery to be made to Buyer's plant on August 1, and suppose that Seller failed to deliver the diamonds. As has been seen, Buyer could cover under section 2-712 by making a reasonable purchase of substitute diamonds.[146] If Buyer did so, it could measure its damages by the difference between its cost of cover and the $100,000 contract price. But suppose that Buyer did not buy any diamonds to replace those due from Seller, or that it bought in a way that did not qualify as a section 2-712(1) cover purchase. In such circum-stances, Buyer could, under section 2-713, recover the difference between the market price of the promised diamonds (the market price at the time Buyer learned of the breach—here on August 1, the day delivery was due and not made—at the place for tender—here Buyer's plant) and the $100,000 contract price. If the market price on August 1 at Buyer's plant was $110,000, Buyer could recover $10,000. It could also recover any in-cidental and consequential damages it suffered, but it would have to subtract from the recovery any expenses that seller's breach enabled it to save. The basic justification for the $10,000 market-price-minus-contract-price recov-ery is that Seller's breach deprived Buyer of a favorable bargain, specifically a $10,000 expected gain. Had Seller performed rather than defaulted, Buyer would have acquired goods worth $110,000 for $100,000. The market-minus-contract formula thus provides a way of protecting the buyer's ex-pectation interest.

Some commentators question the previous statement—that the market-minus-contract formula is aimed at the protection of the buyer's expectation interest—and contend that it can best be understood as a kind of statutory liquidated-damages provision.[147] The authors disagree and believe that both

---

[146] See § 7.04[B], Supra.

[147] J. White & R. Summers, Uniform Commercial Code § 6-4 (4th ed. 1995); Ellen A. Peters, "Remedies for Breach of Contracts Relating to the Sale of Goods Under the Uniform Commercial Code: A Roadmap for Article Two," 73 Yale L.J. 199, 259 (1963).

the major policy behind the formula and its usual effect is the protection of the expectation interest, but the authors readily concede that the section 2-713 formula does not protect the buyer's expectation interest as precisely or reliably as does section 2-712's cover-minus-contract formula. The principal reason why this is so is that when the buyer does not replace the promised goods with a cover purchase and thus ends up in a different position from that promised by the seller, translating the buyer's lost expectancy into a specific sum of money is inherently difficult; more difficult than in a situation where the buyer has covered and thus more or less attained the physical position promised by the seller. Of necessity, if the law aims at protection of the expectation interest, it must employ judgment and imagination to determine what the buyer's economic position would have been had the seller performed. Section 2-713 does this on the basis of a theoretical market price (which the aggrieved buyer almost certainly did not pay).

Market price. The Code does not define "market price." The term's meaning can, however, be derived from general, largely pre-Code, law. The "market price" contemplated is the price that a willing buyer would have paid and that a willing seller would have accepted in a theoretical market.[148] For goods such as corn, wheat, cotton, and other agricultural commodities that are fungible and are sold daily on markets that approximate the economist's "perfect" market (a market characterized by numerous buyers and sellers that have complete information and freedom of entry and departure), market price is usually easy to determine and controversial only within narrow limits. But many goods have few, if any, precise duplicates and are sold in markets involving limited numbers of participants who function on the basis of imperfect information. Establishing market prices for such goods, which include most specially manufactured goods, unique goods, and many used goods, can be difficult and controversial.

Often, goods have both a retail and a wholesale market price, and the two are significantly different. In these circumstances, the market price that is relevant to protecting the aggrieved buyer's expectation interest—the price in the market available to the buyer for the purchase of substitute goods—should be used.[149] Generally, this is the price in the market of the broken contract.[150] Thus, a consumer buyer who has agreed to buy a used car at a

---

[148] Standard Oil Co. v. Southern Pac. Co., 268 U.S. 146, 45 S. Ct. 465, 69 L. Ed. 890 (1925); C. McCormick, Damages § 44 (1935).

[149] *See* the discussion in Illinois Cent. R.R. v. Crail, 281 U.S. 57, 50 S. Ct. 180, 74 L. Ed. 699 (1930).

[150] Comment 2 to U.C.C. § 2-713 calls for comparing the contract price with the market price "in the same branch of trade." In this connection, *see* Cargill, Inc. v. Fickbohm, 252 N.W.2d 739, 21 UCCR 1226 (Iowa 1977).

retail price and who seeks a section 2-713 remedy because of the dealer-seller's nondelivery should be able to use the retail market price as a baseline for measuring damages.

The Code specifies the time ("when the buyer learned of the breach"[151]) and the place ("as of the place for tender or, in cases of rejection after arrival or revocation of acceptance as of the place of arrival"[152]) for determining the market price. According to Comment 1 to section 2-713, the statutory goal is to choose "the market in which the buyer would have obtained cover had he sought that relief." Section 2-723(2) provides some needed leeway:

> If evidence of a price prevailing at the times or places described in this Article is not readily available the price prevailing within any reasonable time before or after the time described or at any other place which in commercial judgment or under usage of trade would serve as a reasonable substitute for the one described may be used, making any proper allowance for the cost of transporting the goods to or from such other place.

Market price is frequently proved by proving the price for comparable goods. Expert testimony is frequently used, with the experts sometimes being the parties' employees who handled the transaction.[153]

Cases in which the market-minus-contract measure would place the buyer in a better position than performance would have done. Suppose that a dealer that has a contract to buy raisins at $.30 a pound enters into a second contract to resell the raisins at $.32 a pound. Suppose further that the relevant market price for raisins is $.40 at the time the dealer's seller defaults by failing to deliver. If the aggrieved dealer does not cover but instead seeks damages under section 2-713, may it recover the $.10 difference between the market price and the contract price, or is it limited to the $.02 profit that it would have made on resale had the seller performed? In most cases, the answer should be that the aggrieved dealer is not limited to its resale profit but may recover the larger market-minus-contract differential. The reason is that the aggrieved dealer must either perform its resale contract (for example, by using raisins from its inventory, which it could otherwise have sold at the $.40 market price) or break the contract and be liable to its buyer for damages. In such cases, the market-minus-contract

---

[151] U.C.C. § 2-713(1).

[152] U.C.C. § 2-713(2).

[153] *See* Chappell Chevrolet, Inc. v. Strickland, 4 Ark. App. 108, 628 S.W.2d 25, 33 UCCR 1327 (1982).

measure does reasonable job of protecting the aggrieved buyer's expectation interest. But suppose that the dealer delivers no raisins to its buyer and that the buyer, without compensation, releases the dealer from its obligation to deliver. In such circumstances, where events that occurred after the seller's default indicate that the dealer's loss through breach was *in fact* no more than the $.02 spread it would have been on resale, some courts have limited recovery to that amount.[154]

What is involved in these cases, and in analogous situations, is a tension between a convenient formula—the market-minus-contract differential—and the fundamental compensation principle of protecting the aggrieved party's expectation interest. This tension is resolved in favor of the market-minus-contract formula in most cases.[155] This is partly because section 2-713 is couched in mandatory terms ("the measure of damages for nondelivery or repudiation by the seller *is* the difference between the market price . . . and the contract price" [emphasis added]), partly because this formula provides an expeditious and efficient way to resolve controversies, and partly because, in the substantial majority of cases to which it is addressed, the formula, applied thoughtfully, does a reasonable job of compensating the aggrieved buyer in terms of its expectation interest. The burden of escaping the formula should be on the defaulting seller, and it is usually a heavy burden. However, when a seller can and does prove that, because of the particular facts of the case, the application of the market-minus-contract measure would significantly overcompensate the buyer—would place it in a considerably better position than performance would have done—it will have a good chance of escaping the formula and limiting damages to a lesser amount.[156]

---

[154] *See, e.g.*, H-W-H Cattle Co. v. Schroeder, 767 F.2d 437, 41 UCCR 832 (8th Cir. 1985); Allied Canners & Packers, Inc. v. Victor Packing Co., 162 Cal. App. 3d 905, 209 Cal. Rptr. 60, 39 UCCR 1567 (1984). The *Allied Canners & Packers* analysis was rejected in Tongish v. Thomas, 251 Kan. 728, 840 P.2d 471, 20 UCCR2d 936 (1992). *See also* KGM Harvesting Co. v. Fresh Network, 36 Cal. App. 4th 376, 42 Cal. Rptr. 2d 286, 26 UCCR2d 1028 (1995); Robert E. Scott, "The Case for Market Damages: Revisiting the Lost Profits Puzzle," 57 U. Chi. L. Rev. 1155 (1990); Eric C. Schneider, "UCC Section 2-713: A Defense of Buyers' Expectancy Damages," 22 Cal. W. L. Rev. 233 (1986).

[155] *See* Texpat Energy, Inc. v. Murphy Oil USA, Inc., 45 F.3d IIII, 25 UCCR2d 759 (7th Cir. 1995).

[156] *See* Allied Canners & Packers, Inc. v. Victor Packing Co., 162 Cal. App. 3d 905, 209 Cal. Rptr. 60, 39 UCCR 1567 (1984).

[D] Damages on Repudiation

As has been seen, a buyer cannot make use of either section 2-712's cover damage remedy or section 2-713's market damage remedy unless one of four triggering events—repudiation or failure to deliver on the seller's part, or rightful rejection or revocation on the buyer's part—has occurred.[157] Repudiation cases have given rise to more legal problems and argumentation than have cases resulting from the other triggering events. This is partly because of the inherent complexity of the repudiation situation and partly because of some weaknesses in the Article 2 language dealing with repudiations. The situation can, perhaps, be most easily explored in terms of a hypothetical.

Suppose that in May, an Arkansas merchant that buys lumber and mills it into whiskey barrel staves (Seller) agreed to sell 300,000 white oak staves at a price of $45 per thousand to a Chicago barrel manufacturer (Buyer), delivering the staves in December. Suppose, further, that on July 1, Seller sent Buyer a letter saying that the market prices of lumber and staves were rising and demanding that the contract price be increased to $60 per thousand.[158] On receiving the letter (on July 5), Buyer inquired about its rights.

One problem facing Buyer is that of determining whether Seller has repudiated the contract. The Code does not define "repudiation," but, instead, apparently relies on the general law of contracts for the meaning of the term. Section 250 of the Restatement (Second) of Contracts offers a definition, which, in the context of the current factual pattern, amounts to a statement by a party that it will not or cannot perform.[159] Has Seller made

---

[157] *See* § 7.04[A], *supra*.

[158] This factual pattern has been suggested by Reliance Cooperage Corp. v. Treat, 195 F.2d 977 (8th Cir. 1952).

[159] The full text of the black letter of § 250 of the Restatement (Second) of Contracts is as follows:

§ 250. When a Statement or an Act is a Repudiation
A repudiation is
(a) a statement by the obligor to the obligee indicating that the obligor will commit a breach that would of itself give the obligee a claim for damages for total breach under § 243, or
(b) a voluntary affirmative act which renders the obligor unable or apparently unable to perform without such a breach.

Some of the language of Comment 1 to U.C.C. § 2-610 indicates that the Code's drafters had a similar view of repudiation:

anticipatory repudiation centers upon an overt communication of intention or an action which renders performance impossible or demonstrates a clear determi-

such a statement? Comment 2 to section 2-610 of the Code is instructive. It states that "a demand . . . for more than the contract calls for in the way of counter-performance is not itself a repudiation. . . . However, when under a fair reading it amounts to a statement of intention not to perform except on conditions which go beyond the contract, it becomes a repudiation." Even after careful consideration, Buyer is likely to remain in doubt as to whether, under a "fair reading," Seller's statement has crossed the line and has become a repudiation. And Buyer's problem is far from unusual. Ambiguous statements that are neither clear-cut renunciations of the seller's duties nor simple appeals to the buyer's conscience for added money are common. Sellers who do not want to default but who, in rising markets, are faced with losses they believe their buyers ought to share, frequently make demands or firm requests in the hope that they will produce agreements to price increases.

Such a request or demand can place a buyer in an awkward position. Suppose that Buyer in the hypothetical (1) is unwilling to agree to the requested price increase, (2) needs the promised goods or a substitute for them, and (3) cannot be sure whether Seller's statement amounts to a repudiation. In such circumstances, Buyer takes a risk if it "covers"; it may later learn that Seller has not repudiated and thus end up with both the contract staves and the "cover" staves—that is, with twice the quantity needed. Still, there is an obvious risk in not covering: if Seller has in fact repudiated and consequently fails to deliver in December, failing to cover may leave Buyer without any staves to meet its needs.

The Code gives partial relief to a party that, like Buyer, faces an ambiguous statement from the other contracting party. Section 2-609 states the general rule that a "contract for sale imposes an obligation on each party that the other's expectation of receiving due performance shall not be impaired." Buyer, faced with a possible repudiation, has had its expectation of receiving delivery "impaired."[160] Section 2-609 continues:

---

nation not to continue with performance.

In Section 2-712(b), the proposed revisions to Article 2 offer a definition of repudiation which, as Comment 3 points out, is based on § 250 of the Restatement (Second) of Contracts:

Repudiation includes language that one party will not or cannot make a performance still due under the contract or voluntary affirmative conduct that reasonably appears to the other party to make a future performance impossible.

Council Draft § 2-712.

[160] Likewise, a seller that finds that its buyer's financial position makes it doubtful that payment will be made as promised has had its expectation of receiving payment "impaired." Thus, section 2-609 applies to both buyers and sellers. Comment 1 to U.C.C. § 2-609.

When reasonable grounds for insecurity arise with respect to the performance of either party the other may in writing demand adequate assurance of due performance and until he receives such assurance may if commercially reasonable suspend any performance for which he has not already received the agreed return.[161]

A party may invoke section 2-609 only when *reasonable* grounds for insecurity arise; it may not demand assurance on a whim. Thus, Buyer (in the hypothetical) still faces a factual question, that of determining whether Seller's demand for a price increase gives Buyer reasonable grounds for feeling insecure about Seller's ultimate delivery. It is possible for Buyer to believe that it has reasonable grounds for insecurity and to act accordingly, only to be told by a later reviewing court that there were no reasonable grounds.[162] But the risk of predicting wrongly on the question of whether the seller's demand for a price increase gave the buyer reasonable grounds for *insecurity* seems significantly smaller than the risk of predicting wrongly on the question of whether the seller's demand amounted to a repudiation— that is, a total *breach*. If the buyer demands adequate assurance of due performance, it should be entitled to the benefit of the doubt on the question of the existence of reasonable grounds for insecurity, because the seller could easily resolve the matter by responding that it will perform according to the contract.[163]

If, as is likely, Buyer is correct that Seller's demand creates reasonable grounds for insecurity, Buyer's invocation of section 2-609 is rightful. Section 2-609 enables Buyer to (1) demand adequate assurance of due performance and (2) suspend any performance for which it has not already received the agreed return until it receives the assurance. Thus, if the contract called for Buyer to make a $5,000 downpayment on the price of the staves on August 1 (with Buyer not to receive delivery of the staves until December), Buyer could suspend payment of the $5,000 until it received "adequate

---

[161] U.C.C. § 2-609(1). The basic idea and some of the language of section 2-609 has been incorporated into the Restatement (Second) of Contracts for application to contracts generally, not just to contracts for the sale of goods. *See* Restatement § 251. With some minor stylistic changes, the proposed revisions to Article 2 retain section 2-609, renumbering it section 2-711.

[162] BAII Banking Corp. v. UPG, Inc., 985 F.2d 685, 20 UCCR2d 155 (2nd Cir. 1993); SPS Indus., Inc. v. Atlantic Steel Co., 186 Ga. App. 94, 366 S.E.2d 410, 6 UCCR2d 122 (1988); Cherwell-Rali, Inc. v. Rytman Grain Co., Inc., 180 Conn. 714, 433 A.2d 984, 29 UCCR 513 (1980).

[163] Marine Towing, Inc. v. Panama Canal Co., 730 F.2d 1197, 38 UCCR 490 (5th Cir. 1984), *cert. denied*, 469 U.S. 1037 (1984); Turntables, Inc. v. Gestetner, 52 A.2d 776, 382 N.Y.5.2d 798, 19 UCCR 131 (1976).

assurance of due performance." There can, of course, be factual questions and disputes about what amounts to "adequate assurance."[164] Comment 4 to section 2-609 provides some guidance in this connection.

Suppose that Seller makes no response to Buyer's justified demand for adequate assurance, or that Seller's response is a further and more insistent demand for a price increase and that this does not constitute an adequate assurance. In these circumstances, subsection (4) of section 2-609 comes into play. It provides:

> (4) After receipt of a justified demand failure to provide within a reasonable time not exceeding thirty days such assurance of due performance as is adequate under the circumstances of the particular case is a repudiation of the contract.

Thus, if Seller's failure to provide an adequate assurance continues for more than a reasonable time (which reasonable time cannot exceed thirty days), the troublesome ambiguity will be cleared up and Buyer can reliably treat Seller as having repudiated.

Subsection 2-609(4) is not a simple provision. To use it successfully, Buyer must be able to predict accurately that a court to which the matter is later presented will give affirmative answers to three factual questions: (1) Did Seller's demand for a price increase give Buyer "reasonable grounds for insecurity"?; (2) Did Seller fail to provide "adequate assurance of due performance"?; and (3) Did Seller's failure persist for more than "a reasonable time"? Despite the possibility that any or all of these questions may be contested, section 2-609(4) remains a very useful provision that often enables parties in Buyer's situation to clear up ambiguities.

Reaching a correct conclusion that Seller has repudiated—either because of the unambiguous nature of Seller's initial statement or via a justifiable invocation of section 2-609—solves one legal problem for Buyer but can lead to other perplexing problems. As has been seen, a seller's repudiation is a triggering event that opens either the section 2-712 cover remedy or the section 2-713 market-price remedy. Covering can present practical and legal problems involving the application of section 2-712(1). The alternative course of proceeding to a market-minus-contract remedy leads directly to difficult problems of Code interpretation on the question of *when* the market price of the goods is to be measured. These are explored in terms of the Buyer-Seller whiskey-barrel-stave contract.

---

[164] *See, e.g.,* In re Lone Star Indus, Inc., 776 F. Supp. 206, 16 UCCR2d 301 (D. Md. 1991).

Suppose that, through the proper use of section 2-609, Buyer determines that Seller has repudiated its promise to deliver staves and that this repudiation occurred when the section 2-609(4) reasonable time expired on August 1. Suppose further that Buyer makes no substitute purchase of staves. As of what date is the market price of staves to be measured for purposes of fixing Buyer's section 2-713 damages? The provisions of the Code afford bases for arguing for various dates and particularly for the following three: (1) the date of the repudiation—August 1; (2) a commercially reasonable time after the repudiation—say, September 1; and (3) the time fixed for performance in the contract—December 31. The selection of the date has practical importance in any situation where there is significant change in the market price. In the hypothetical, suppose a rising market, with staves selling at $60 a thousand on August 1, $70 a thousand on September 1, and $100 a thousand on December 31. Given these facts, measuring market price at the time of repudiation would produce a recovery of $4,500—($60 − $45) × 300; measuring it a commercially reasonable time after the repudiation would produce a $7,500 recovery—($70 − $45) × 300; and measuring it at the time of performance would produce a $16,500 recovery—($100 − $45) × 300.

The statutory argument for using the date of the repudiation focuses on the language of section 2-713: "the measure of damages for non-delivery or repudiation by the seller is the difference between the market price *at the time the buyer learned of the breach* and the contract price" [emphasis added]. Quite simply, a repudiation is a breach, and the buyer will learn of the breach when he learns of the repudiation. There may be some difficulties in determining when a repudiation has occurred, but once that has been decided, the time for measuring market price is fixed.

The trouble with this clear and simple interpretation arises when reference is made to other Code sections. Section 2-713 opens by referring to section 2-723, subsection (1) of which provides:

> (1) If an action based on an anticipatory repudiation comes to trial before the time for performance with respect to some or all of the goods, any damages based on market price (Section 2-708 or Section 2-713) shall be determined according to the price of such good prevailing at the time when the aggrieved party learned of the repudiation.

This provision would seem to contain a negative implication: if the case is tried *after* the date fixed for performance (probably the more common situation, given the docket delay that exists in most courts), market price is to be measured at some time other than when the aggrieved party learned of the repudiation. Further, measuring market price at the time fixed for performance accords with most pre-Code repudiation cases,[165] and it can be argued that the various Code provisions dealing with repudiation do not furnish a clear basis for changing this established law. The choice of the date for performance as the measuring point can be further buttressed by reference to section 2-708(1). This section deals, among other things, with the seller's market-price damages when the buyer repudiates, and selects the "market price at the time and place for tender." Arguably, in accordance with section 2-723(1), buyers' and sellers' market-price damages for repudiation should be measured as of like times, and particularly as of the time for performance in cases tried after that time.

The picture is further complicated by section 2-610, which is captioned "Anticipatory Repudiation," and provides as follows:

> When either party repudiates the contract with respect to a performance not yet due the loss of which will substantially impair the value of the contract to the other, the aggrieved party may
>
> (a) for a commercially reasonable time await performance by the repudiating party; or
>
> (b) resort to any remedy for breach (Section 2-703 or Section 2-711), even though he has notified the repudiating party that he would await the latter's performance and has urged retraction; and
>
> (c) in either case suspend his own performance or proceed in accordance with the provisions of this Article on the seller's right to identify goods to the contract notwithstanding breach or to salvage unfinished goods (Section 2-704).

Under this section, the aggrieved party may treat a repudiation as final and may immediately resort to a remedy, but it is not required to do so. Alternatively, it may await performance for a commercially reasonable time. This privilege of waiting for a commercially reasonable time creates a conflict with section 2-713's "learned of the breach" date for measuring market price. If prices are rising (as they may well be when the seller has repudiated), it makes no sense to tell a buyer that it may await performance in spite of a repudiation but that, if it does so and performance is not forthcoming, damages will be measured in terms of the market price at the time the buyer learned of the repudiation, not as of the end of the awaiting-

---

[165] *See, e.g.,* McJunkin Corp. v. North Carolina Natural Gas Corp., 300 F.2d 794 (4th Cir. 1961), *cert. denied,* 371 U.S. 830, 83 S. Ct. 43, 9 L. Ed. 2d 68 (1962); Reliance Cooperage Co. v. Treat, 195 F.2d 977 (8th Cir. 1952); Compania Engraw Commercial & Indus. S.A. v. Schenley Distillers Corp., 181 F.2d 876 (9th Cir. 1950). Pre-Code cases are collected in Comment, "A Suggested Revision of the Contract Doctrine of Anticipatory Repudiation," 64 Yale. L.J. 85, 91–99 (1954).

performance period. Such a rule would effectively destroy the privilege of awaiting performance for a commercially reasonable time.

Section 2-610 also conflicts with the proposition that market damages should be measured as of the time fixed for performance. It allows a buyer aggrieved by a repudiation to await performance "for a commercially reasonable time," and, at least by implication, for no longer.[166] In many circumstances, a commercially reasonable time will have expired well before the performance date arrives. If, however, damages are based on the performance-date market price, the privilege to await performance would, as a practical matter, be extended until that date.

Section 2-610 pushes for measuring damages in terms of the market price that obtains when a commercially reasonable time for awaiting performance runs. There are, however, at least two problems with this. First, it does not fit well with the language of section 2-713—that damages are to be measured in terms of the market price "at the time when the buyer *learned* of the breach"[167] It is linguistically awkward to think of a buyer "learning" of a breach not when it learns of the repudiation, but afterwards, at the point when a commercially reasonable time for awaiting performance expires. Second, there usually are uncertainties, sometimes about when the repudiation occurred and the commercially reasonable time began to run, and almost always about the length of the commercially reasonable time itself. It would be useful to have a more definite time for measuring market price.

The Code thus presents multiple possible answers to the question of when to measure the buyer's market-price damages for repudiation by a seller. Apparently, the drafters either neglected to consider the question or considered it on different occasions and resolved it differently each time. In any event, their work product left the matter in substantial doubt and open

---

[166] Comment 1 to U.C.C. § 2-610 is express on the point that an aggrieved party may suffer adverse consequences if it awaits performance for more than a commercially reasonable time. It states that such a party "cannot recover resulting damages which he should have avoided." Thus, a buyer that awaits performance and does not make a substitute purchase until after more than a commercially reasonable time has run cannot recover any consequential damages which could have been avoided by making a substitute purchase at the end of a commercially reasonable time. It is also probable that the too-long awaiting buyer's purchase will fail to qualify as a section 2-712 cover because it was not made "without unreasonable delay."

[167] U.C.C. § 2-713 (emphasis added).

to various arguments. The arguments have been made in the law reviews and treatises[168] and in the courts.[169]

The weight of decisional authority, both in rationale and result, favors measuring the buyer's damages in terms of the market price that obtained a commercially reasonable time after the buyer learned of the repudiation.[170] The thoughtful opinion in *Cosden Oil & Chemical Co. v. Karl O. Helm Aktiengesellschaft*[171] justifies this reading of the Code and result in a number of ways, and particularly in light of the relationship between the section 2-712 cover remedy and the section 2-713 market-price remedy:

> Allowing the aggrieved buyer a commercially reasonable time, however, provides him with an opportunity to investigate his cover possibilities in a rising market without fear that, if he is unsuccessful in obtaining cover, he will be relegated to a market-contract damage remedy measured at the time of repudiation. The Code supports this view. While cover is the preferred remedy, the Code clearly provides the option to seek damages. . . . When a buyer chooses not to cover, the market is measured at the time he could have covered—a reasonable time after repudiation. . . .
>
> Persuasive arguments exist for interpreting "learned of the breach" to mean "time of performance," consistent with the pre-Code rule. . . . If this was the intention of the Code drafters, however, phrases in § 2-610 and § 2-712 lose their meaning. If buyer is entitled to market-contract damages measured at the time of performance, it is difficult to explain why the anticipatory repudiation section limits him to a commercially reasonable time to await performance. See § 2-610 comment 1. Similarly, in a rising market, no reason would exist for requiring the

---

[168] *See, e.g.*, Robert Childres, "Buyer's Remedies; The Danger of Section 2-713," 72 Nw. U. L. Rev. 837 (1978); Thomas H. Jackson, " 'Anticipatory Repudiation' and the Temporal Element of Contract Law: An Economic Inquiry into Contract Damages in Cases of Prospective Nonperformance," 31 Stan. L. Rev. 69 (1978); John A. Sebert, Jr., "Remedies Under Article Two of the Uniform Commercial Code: An Agenda for Review," 130 U. Pa. L. Rev. 360, 372–380 (1981); J. White & R. Summers, Uniform Commercial Code § 6-7 (4th ed. 1995).

[169] *See, e.g.*, Oloffson v. Coomer, 11 Ill. App. 3d 918, 296 N.E.2d 871, 12 UCCR 1082 (1973); Cargill, Inc. v. Stafford, 553 F.2d 1222, 21 UCCR 707 (10th Cir. 1977); First Nat'l Bank of Chicago v. Jefferson Mortgage Co., 576 F.2d 479, 23 UCCR 1282 (3d Cir. 1978); Cosden Oil & Chem. Co. v. Karl O. Helm Aktiengesellschaft, 736 F.2d 1064, 38 UCCR 1645 (5th Cir. 1984).

[170] In terms of the whiskey barrel stave hypothetical, this would be the $70 per thousand market price prevailing on September 1.

[171] 736 F.2d 1064, 38 UCCR 1645 (5th Cir. 1984).

buyer to act "without unreasonable delay" when he needs to cover following an anticipatory repudiation. See § 2-712(1). . . .

In light of the Code's persistent theme of commercial reasonableness, the prominence of cover as a remedy, and the time given an aggrieved buyer to await performance and to investigate cover before
selecting his remedy, we agree with the district court that "learned of
the breach" incorporates 2-610's commercially reasonable time.

Clarification of the Code repudiation provisions dealing with the date
for measurement of a buyer's market-price damages was an obvious agenda
item for the drafters of the proposed revisions to Article 2, as was the policy
question of what date the clarified provisions should select. After considerable debate,[172] the drafters of the revisions have opted to follow the weight
of interpretative authority under the current Code and to measure damages
as of the end of a commercially reasonable time after repudiation. Specifically, section 2-826(a)(2) provides:

In the case of a repudiation . . . , the measure of damages is the market
price of comparable goods at the time when a commercially reasonable
period after the buyer learned of the breach has expired . . . less the
contract price. The commercially reasonable time includes the time for
awaiting performance . . . and any further commercially reasonable time
needed for the buyer to obtain substitute performance.[173]

In the Comments, the drafters state that new section 2-826(a)(2) is "designed
to approximate the time in which the buyer would have engaged in a cover
transaction."[174]

---

[172] The "Study Group" appointed by the Code's Permanent Editorial Board to study the
revision of Article 2 was divided on the matter, with a majority favoring the agreed time for
performance and a minority favoring a commercially reasonable time after the buyer learned
of the repudiation. PEB Study Group Report 224–226 (1990). The American Bar Association
appointed a "Task Force" to appraise the PEB Study Group's Report, and this task force
disagreed with the majority of the study group, recommending instead that "in anticipatory
repudiation cases, the market price for measuring damages be determined at the time and
place that the seller agreed to tender delivery *only* if the buyer can demonstrate a valid
reason for not having covered. If the buyer could reasonably have covered following the
repudiation, however, the market price should be measured at the time and place the buyer
should reasonably have covered." [Emphasis in original.] ABA Task Force Report, reprinted
in 16 Del. J. Corp. L. 981, 1231 (1991). The drafters of the revised Article and their advisors
continued to debate the matter and tried various approaches to it.

[173] Section 2-821(a)(2) of the proposed revisions makes similar provision for measuring
a seller's market-price damages after a buyer's repudiation. *See* Council Draft § 2-821.

[174] Comment 3 Council Draft. § 2-826.

[E] Damages When Goods Are Retained

As has been seen, sections 2-711, 2-712, and 2-713 provide the measure of damages when the seller has defaulted and the buyer ends up without the goods, either because it did not receive them or because, having received them, it thrust them back on the seller via a rightful rejection or justifiable revocation of acceptance. Section 2-714 provides the measure of damages in cases where the seller has defaulted and the buyer receives and retains the goods in spite of the seller's default.[175] The two situations are significantly different from a remedial standpoint. In the first, the buyer, being without the goods, is entitled to a return of any part of the purchase price that it has paid and to the protection of its expectation interest. In the second, the buyer is again entitled to the protection of its expectation interest, but its monetary recovery should reflect the fact that, despite the seller's default, the buyer's assets have been increased and the seller's decreased by the value of the retained goods.

Section 2-714 provides as follows:

(1) Where the buyer has accepted goods and given notification (subsection 3 of Section 2-607) he may recover as damages for any nonconformity of tender the loss resulting in the ordinary course of events from the seller's breach as determined in any manner which is reasonable.

(2) The measure of damages for breach of warranty is the difference at the time and place of acceptance between the value of the goods accepted and the value they would have had if they had been as warranted, unless special circumstances show proximate damages of a different amount.

(3) In a proper case any incidental and consequential damages under the next section may also be recovered.

---

[175] Although U.C.C. § 2-714 does not refer to the buyer's retention of the goods and is somewhat misleadingly captioned "Buyer's Damages for Breach in Regard to Accepted Goods," it nevertheless applies only to retained goods. That is, it does not apply to situations in which goods were accepted and later returned to the seller by means of justifiable revocations of acceptance. *See* Comment 1, which says: "This section deals with the remedies available to the buyer after the goods have been accepted and the time for revocation of acceptance has gone by." *See also* GNP Commodities, Inc. v. Walsh Hefferman Co., 95 Ill. App. 3d 966, 420 N.E.2d 659, 31 UCCR 1342 (1981). The proposed revisions to Article 2 covers the revocation-of-acceptance point expressly, providing in its section 2-827 (the analogue of current section 2-714) a recovery for a buyer "that has accepted goods and not justifiably revoked acceptance."

The relationship between subsections (1) and (2) is not entirely clear. In providing for damages "for *any* non-conformity of tender" [emphasis supplied], subsection (1) would seem to deal with both (a) seller defaults on performance obligations that are not covered by the Code's warranty sections (sections 2-312 through 2-315)—late delivery, for example—and (b) breach-of-warranty defaults. Subsection (2) expressly provides for "the measure of damages for breach of warranty," and thus has nothing to say about late delivery and similar defaults. But breach-of-warranty defaults seem to be covered by both subsections (1) and (2). Indeed, Comment 2 expressly states that subsection (1) covers both breaches of warranty and other failures of the seller to perform according to its contract obligations. The upshot is that one looks to subsection (1) for nonconformities of tender that are not breaches of warranty but that either subsection can be applied in breach-of-warranty cases. This means that there are two different statutory escape routes from subsection (2)'s money-damage formula for breach of warranty: one via the concluding subsection (2) clause ("unless special circumstances show proximate damages of a different amount")[176] and the other through subsection (1)—treating the breach of warranty as a nonconformity of tender and determining damages "in any manner which is reasonable."[177]

The 2-714(2) formula. The application of section 2-714(2)'s value-the-goods-would-have-had-if-they-had-been-as-warranted minus the-value-of-the-goods-accepted formula can be illustrated by the following examples:

Case 1. Seller sold Buyer an automobile warranting that it was "in all respects as good as new." Buyer paid the $15,000 purchase price in full and took delivery of the car. Buyer later discovered that the car had been wrecked before it was sold to him, and even though repaired, was not "as good as new." Buyer nevertheless retained the car and, after giving an ap-

---

[176] Gem Jewelers, Inc. v. Dykman, 160 A.D.2d 1069, 553 N.Y.S.2d 890, 12 UCCR2d 721 (1990); R.W. Murray Co. v. Shatterproof Glass Corp., 758 F.2d 266, 40 UCCR 1283 (8th Cir. 1985).

[177] *See* Happy Dock Trading Co., Ltd. v. Agro-Indus., Inc., 602 F. Supp. 986, 41 UCCR 1718 (S.D.N.Y. 1984). *But see* Richmond Riders Courier Serv., Inc. v. Dreelin Cellular Sys., Inc. 12 UCCR2d 719 (Va. Cir. Ct. 1990).

The proposed revisions to Article 2 continues U.C.C. § 2-714 (renumbered section 2-827) without major change. It does, however, modify the wording of subsection (2) so that it reads "A [rather than the current "the"] measure of damages for breach of *a* warranty *of quality.*" This clarifies one of the intentions of the present section: that the subsection (2) difference-money formula is intended as only "a" measure of damages for breach of warranty, not as the sole or exclusive measure. It also limits the formula to breaches of warranties "of quality," meaning that damages for breaches of warranties of title are to be determined under subsection (1)—that is, "in any manner that is reasonable."

propriate section 2-607(3)(a) notice, sued Seller for damages. Buyer proved that, had the car been as warranted, it would have had a value equal to its $15,000 purchase price and that, in its delivered condition, it had a value of only $12,000.[178] In these circumstances, the 2-714(2) formula will produce a recovery of $3,000. Had Buyer discovered the breach of warranty before he paid for the car, he would still be liable for the $15,000 price,[179] but would be entitled to deduct his $3,000 damages, paying Seller only $12,000.[180]

Case 2. Assume the facts of Case 1 with one change. Assume that Buyer succeeded in proving that, if the car had been as warranted, it would have been worth $16,000—$1,000 more than the $15,000 price. In other words, assume that Buyer proved that he had a favorable bargain. Had Seller delivered conforming goods, Buyer's assets would have been increased by $1,000, because he would have acquired goods worth that much more than the price he was obligated to pay. In these circumstances, the section 2-714(2) formula will produce a recovery of $4,000.[181] This will result in Buyer's paying a net of $11,000 for goods worth $12,000. Here, the Buyer's expectation interest can be thought of as having two parts: (1) his interest in receiving goods of the quality promised and (2) his interest in buying the goods at the favorable price for which he bargained. The section 2-714(2) formula protects both parts of the Buyer's expectation interest.

Case 3. Assume the facts of Case 1 with one change. Now assume that the parties' proofs showed that Seller had a favorable bargain—that the car as warranted had a value of only $14,000. Had Seller delivered a conforming car, her assets would have been increased by $1,000 since she would have received $15,000 for a car worth only $14,000. Had Seller delivered conforming goods, she would have been entitled to this $1,000 gain—that is, to have her expectation interest protected. But, instead of performing, Seller delivered nonconforming goods. She is a party in default and, under general principles of contract law, does not deserve to have her expectation interest protected. In this connection, note that, had Buyer rejected or revoked his acceptance and thus thrust the goods back on Seller, Buyer's obligation to

---

[178] For a case dealing with the proof of U.C.C. § 2-714(2) difference-money damages when the amounts involved were relatively modest, *see* Burrus v. Itek Corp., 46 Ill. App. 3d 350, 360 N.E.2d 1168, 21 UCCR 1009 (1977). *See also* Schroeder v. Barth, Inc. 969 F.2d 421, 18 UCCR2d 781 (7th Cir. 1992).

[179] U.C.C. § 2-607(1).

[180] U.C.C. § 2-717.

[181] *See* K & C, Inc. v. Westinghouse Elec. Corp., 437 Pa. 303, 263 A.2d 390, 7 UCCR 679 (1970).

pay for the goods would be totally extinguished,[182] thus depriving Seller of her expected gain. But, anomalously, the application of the section 2-714(2) formula protects Seller's expectation interest, or at least her interest in receiving $1,000 more than the goods she delivered were worth. Here the formula is value-as-warranted ($14,000) minus value-as-delivered ($12,000), producing damages of $2,000. This will leave Seller with a net of $13,000 for goods worth only $12,000.

Although a mechanical reading of the Code[183] will protect the $1,000 favorable-bargain portion of Seller's expectation interest in Case 3, the authors believe that such a reading should be rejected. This can be accomplished by treating Case 3 and similar cases as "special circumstances" within the final clause of section 2-714(2), by determining damages in a "manner which is reasonable" under section 2-714(1), or by invoking general principles of compensatory damages in accordance with 1-106.

Damages under 2-714(1). When the buyer retains goods following a seller's default that is not a breach of warranty but rather a late delivery or other nonconforming tender, section 2-714(2) does not apply, and the buyer must look to section 2-714(1) to recover "the loss resulting in the ordinary course of events from the seller's breach as determined in any manner which is reasonable." This is, and needs to be, a general provision. Its application can involve considerable complexity.

Consider the case of *Fertico Belgium, S.A. v. Phosphate Chemicals Export Association, Inc.*[184] This case involved a contract for the sale of fertilizer from an American exporter to a Belgian dealer. As the defendant seller knew at the time of contract formation, the plaintiff buyer needed timely delivery of the fertilizer to Belgium because it had already obligated itself to make prompt delivery to a third-party buyer (a unit of the government of Iraq) after bagging the fertilizer. When the seller told the buyer that it would be late in delivering both of the installments of fertilizer called for by the contract, the buyer made a substitute purchase (of a quantity equal to both installments) at a price $700,000 above the contract price and used this purchase to fulfill its contractual obligations to its Iraqi customer. The buyer cancelled the contract with respect to the second installment but took delivery of the first (one month late) because, via a letter of credit, it had

---

[182] U.C.C. § 2-711(1).

[183] The difficulty is that the Code begins by giving the seller the *contract price* of goods accepted, U.C.C. § 2-607(1), and then deducts damages from the contract price, U.C.C. § 2-717. This works well for most seller-default cases (consider Cases 1 and 2 in the text), but not for the relatively rare case in which the contract price gives the seller a gain, a gain which, because of its default, the seller has not earned (Case 3).

[184] 70 N.Y.2d 76, 510 N.E.2d 334, 3 UCCR2d 1812 (1987).

already paid for that installment. Three months after receiving this install-ment, the buyer resold it for $454,000 more than the buyer-seller contract price.

On these facts, the buyer succeeded in recovering the $700,000 differ-ence between its cost of cover and the contract price. Insofar as the cover purchase was a substitute for the rejected second installment, section 2-712 applies. But insofar as the cover purchase was a substitute for the late de-livered but accepted first installment, the case is, as the New York Court of Appeals recognized,[185] a section 2-714(1) case. The buyer, having accepted the goods, is recovering for a late-delivery nonconformity of tender, its "loss resulting in the ordinary course of events from the seller's breach as deter-mined in any manner which is reasonable."[186] In the circumstances, the difference between the cost of the substitute or cover purchase and the con-tract price is a reasonable way to determine the buyer's loss.

When, in an unusual case like *Fertico*, an argument is made for the application, under section 2-714(1), of the cover-minus-contract formula to a retained goods situation, questions concerning the retained goods—what the buyer did with them and the effect they and their use should have on the determination of the buyer's damages—are almost certain to arise. On the *Fertico* facts, the majority of the Court of Appeals held, over a vigorous dissent, that the $454,000 profit that the buyer made on the resale of the retained first installment should not be offset against its cover dam-ages. The court noted that the buyer was a fertilizer trader, engaged in the business of pursuing profits of this nature, and might well have made this profit even if the seller had fully performed by delivering all of the goods on time. What is involved is the idea of an expansible profit maker, an idea that will be considered in greater detail in connection with sellers' damages and section 2-708(2).[187] In this context, the crucial inquiry should be whether it was the seller's breach and all of its attendant circumstances, including the buyer's retention of the goods from the seller, that enabled the buyer to make a profit on their resale (in which case the profit ought to offset the buyer's damages) or whether the buyer had ability to acquire like goods from other sources and could have made a like profit even if the seller had fully performed (in which case the profit should have no effect on the buyer's damages). This can obviously involve difficult factual questions, and much may turn on the allocation of the burden of proof. On facts like those

---

[185] 70 N.Y.2d at 84, 510 N.E.2d at 338, 3 UCCR 2d at 1817.

[186] U.C.C. § 2-714(1).

[187] *See* § 7.08[D], *infra*.

of *Fertico*, we would place the burden on the defendant, because it is trying to reduce the plaintiff's recovery.[188]

A buyer entitled to a remedy under either section 2-714(1) or section 2-714(2) can also use section 2-714(3) and recover whatever incidental and consequential damages section 2-715 provides in the circumstances. Such additional damages are the subject of § 7.04[F].

[F] Additional Damages

The difference-money damage formulas that have been examined in the preceding four subsections are all aimed at the protection of the aggrieved buyer's expectation interest—that is, at placing the buyer in the financial position it would have occupied had the seller performed. In many situations, however, these formulas do not, by themselves, achieve this goal; additional damages are required.

For example, a buyer that rightfully rejects nonconforming goods and then covers often needs to recover, in addition to the difference between the price it paid for the substitute goods and the contract price, the expenses (other than the price) it incurred in effecting cover and also the expenses it incurred in receiving, inspecting, and rejecting the promised goods. That is, it will need to recover those expenses if its expectation interest is to be fully protected. Similarly, a buyer planning to use the contract goods in collateral transactions, and is prevented from doing so by the seller's nondelivery breach, may need to recover the profits it would have made on the collateral transactions. Likewise, a buyer that has spent money in reliance on the contract—for example, to build a building to house the promised goods—may need to recover its expenditures to the extent that the seller's nondelivery breach rendered them useless. And a buyer who suffers property damage or personal injury because of a breach-of-warranty defect in the goods will need to recover for such damage or injury.

The Code usually applies either the label "incidental" or the label "consequential" to the needed additional damages and provides for them in section 2-715. Sections 2-712, 2-713, and 2-714 all expressly refer to section 2-715 and provide that the buyer may recover incidental and consequential damages in addition to the general changes provided for in the sections themselves. We now turn to the needed additional damages, considering them under separate headings.

---

[188] *See* J. White & R. Summers, Uniform Commercial Code § 6-3 (4th ed. 1995).

[1] Incidental Damages

Section 2-715(1) provides:

> Incidental damages resulting from the seller's breach include expenses
> reasonably incurred in the inspection, receipt, transportation and care
> and custody of goods rightfully rejected, any commercially reasonable
> charges, expenses, or commissions in connection with effecting cover
> and any other reasonable expense incident to the delay or other
> breach.[189]

This provision is less than a full-fledged definition of incidental damages. It states that "[i]ncidental damages . . . include" several kinds of
expenses, but, as Comment 1 to section 2-715 points out, "[t]he incidental
damages listed are not intended to be exhaustive but are merely illustrative
of the typical kinds of incidental damages."[190] The closest the statutory
language comes to a general definition is in its beginning and ending
phrases: "Incidental damages resulting from the seller's breach" and "reasonable expense incident to the delay or other breach." The first of these
phrases is the broader—broad enough to include losses incurred in reliance
on the contract generally—while the second may be read as limited to expenses incurred after a breach and "incident" to the buyer's coping with the
breach. The examples of incidental damages listed in the statute all involve
expenses incurred after a seller's breach, and decided cases dealing with
incidental damages focus on post-breach expenses.

For example, a buyer of an airplane who revoked his acceptance because of a breach of warranty recovered the payments he had made on the
purchase price under section 2-711 plus, as incidental damages under section
2-715(1), his expenses in repairing the airplane and storing and preserving

---

[189] The proposed revisions to Article 2 provide for incidental damages in a section (section
2-805) that is applicable to both sellers' and buyers' breaches. It thus combines current
section 2-715(1) (on buyers' incidental damages) and current section 2-710 (on sellers' incidental damages) into a single section.

[190] One difficulty with the language of U.C.C. § 2-715(1) is that the first portion of the
sentence mentions only cases of rightful rejection. It is, however, apparent from the references to incidental damages in U.C.C. §§ 2-712, 2-713, and 2-714(3) and from the first
sentence of Comment 1 to U.C.C. § 2-715, that the section's provision for incidental damages applies also to cases of nondelivery, repudiation, justifiable revocation of acceptance,
and retention of goods in spite of a nonconforming tender.

it while holding it for the seller.[191] Likewise, a buyer of a racehorse who revoked acceptance because the horse did not conform to the seller's warranties recovered the purchase price paid and, in addition, the cost of caring for and feeding the horse from the date the horse was delivered to the buyer until the date the horse was returned to the seller.[192] In both cases, reimbursement for the post-breach expenses in question was necessary to compensate the buyer in terms of its expectation interest. If the buyer were left to bear the costs of maintaining and caring for the goods, it would, to that extent, end up paying for the seller's default and correspondingly short of the position in which the promised performance would have placed it.[193]

Reliance damages. Expenses that the buyer incurs in reliance on a contract—expenses incurred after contract formation but before breach—can be said not to be "incident" to the breach. This may lead a court to the conclusion that such expenses do not qualify as incidental damages within the meaning of section 2-715(1).[194] If not incidental damages, such pre-breach reliance expenditures may be recoverable in proper cases as conse-

---

[191] Lanners v. Whitney, 247 Or. 243, 428 P.2d 398, 4 UCCR 369 (1967). It is noteworthy that this case involves a coupling of a recovery of the purchase price under U.C.C. § 2-711(1) with the recovery of incidental damages under U.C.C § 2-715(1). Unlike U.C.C. §§ 2-712, 2-713, and 2-714, U.C.C. § 2-711 contains no reference to section 2-715. This, however, was an oversight on the part of the drafters and has not prevented courts from allowing the recovery of the purchase price together with incidental damages. This result can be justified either on grounds of common sense or by noting that, in addition to U.C.C. § 2-711, either U.C.C. § 2-712 or U.C.C. § 2-713 applied (although itself producing no recovery because there was no proof that the cost of cover or market price exceeded the contract price), which expressly refer to U.C.C. § 2-715.

[192] Grandi v. LeSage, 74 N.M. 799, 399 P.2d 285, 2 UCCR 455 (1965).

[193] Both the current Article 2 and the proposed revisions include expenses reasonably incurred in the inspection and receipt of the contract goods in their lists of incidental damages. Allowing the recovery of such expenses in addition to difference-money damages under U.C.C. §§ 2-712, 2-713, or 2-714(2) may overcompensate the aggrieved buyer, however. Awarding the difference between the cost of cover and the contract price, for example, gives the buyer the money equivalent of the promised performance. Awarding, in addition, some of the necessary costs involved in obtaining the promised performance—specifically the costs of inspection and receipt—may amount to giving a kind of double recovery—that is, compensating the buyer twice for the same loss and thus putting it in a better position than performance would have done. The other items on the statutory lists of incidental damages are not subject to this criticism. All of them involve costs of coping with a breach—that is, costs the buyer did not need to incur to obtain the promised performance, but that were imposed on it by the breach.

[194] The Minnesota Court of Appeals did just this in International Fin. Servs., Inc. v. Franz, 515 N.W.2d 379, 23 UCCR2d 1078 (Minn. Ct. App. 1994), and the Minnesota Supreme Court affirmed on this point (although reversing on another point), 534 N.W.2d 261, 26 UCCR2d 1137 (Minn. 1995).

quential damages under section 2-715(2)(a), which permits recovery of "any loss resulting from general or particular requirements and needs [of the buyer]." In cases in which the buyer retains the goods, they may be recoverable under section 2-714(1)'s "loss resulting in the ordinary course of events from the seller's breach as determined in any manner which is reasonable." Or they may be recoverable under section 1-106's prescription that remedies be liberally administered with a view toward protecting the aggrieved party's expectation interest.

Whatever the statutory category, the achievement of the goal of placing the aggrieved party in the same position as performance requires the recovery of reliance damages in many circumstances. Often the statutory classification has no effect on case outcome. In some situations, however, it may be result determinative. For example, choosing the consequential-damages category triggers the foreseeability requirement of section 2-715(2)(a) (to be discussed in § 7.04[F][2]). If a reliance loss falls under section 2-715(2)(a) and the defendant seller had no reason to know, at the time of contracting, of the requirements or needs of the buyer that led to the reliance, the loss is not recoverable.[195] Further, foreseeability aside, if the contract contains an effective exclusion of consequential damages, classifying reliance damages as consequential prevents their recovery in circumstances where they might be recoverable if otherwise classified.[196]

Whichever statutory category is appropriate, in responding to efforts to recover reliance damages, courts must take care to avoid overcompensation. A buyer is often willing to incur certain expenses to obtain the seller's performance. To the extent that the buyer receives that performance or its equivalent in money, it is not also entitled to an award for the expenses that it incurred. Awarding this additional sum would place the buyer in a better financial position than it would have enjoyed had the seller performed the contract. This idea can be illustrated by the following cases:

Case 1. A Kentucky buyer contracted with a Texas seller for ten tank cars of oil at a specified price per gallon, F.O.B. the seller's Texas refinery, the buyer to send its tank cars to pick up the oil. The buyer sent its tank cars to the Texas refinery at a cost of $2,900, only to be told that the seller would not deliver the oil. The market price of the kind of oil involved had increased since contract formation so that, at the time and place for delivery,

---

[195] *See* Bockman Printing & Services, Inc. v. Baldwin-Gregg, Inc., 213 Ill. App. 3d 516, 572 N.E.2d 1094, 15 UCCR2d 490 (1991).

[196] *See* Caroline Co. v. Oxmoor Cntr., 40 UCCR 1728 (Ky. Ct. App. 1985); American Elec. Power Co. v. Westinghouse Elec. Corp., 418 F. Supp. 435, 19 UCCR 1009 (S.D.N.Y. 1976).

it exceeded the contract price by $10,000 for the quantity involved. In these circumstances, the buyer can recover $10,000 under the market-minus-contract formula of section 2-713. Is the buyer also entitled to the $2,900 spent in reliance on the contract?

Even if it is conceded that the expenditure of $2,900 was in all respects reasonable and in reliance on the contract, an attempt by the buyer to collect this sum in addition to the $10,000 should fail. The buyer was willing to spend the $2,900 to get the oil. If the seller had not defaulted, the buyer would have had to spend this money before it could reap any benefit from the contract. Because the section 2-713 damage formula has given the buyer the money equivalent of the seller's performance (the assumption being that by adding the market-minus-contract difference money to the unpaid contract price, the buyer could have obtained a substitute for the promised oil at the time and place fixed for delivery at the same net cost it would have paid had the seller performed), awarding the buyer the $2,900 as well would overcompensate it (put it in a better financial position than performance would have done).[197] Indeed, had the seller repudiated before the buyer spent any money to send the tank cars to Texas, the buyer might have been able to have purchased substitute oil at a closer location and thus have saved some or all of the $2,900. If so, the expenses saved (or that were saveable) should be deducted from the buyer's $10,000 recovery.[198] The controlling principle is that the damage award should place the buyer in the financial position it would have occupied had the seller performed, but not in a better financial position.

The Case 1 buyer's $10,000 recovery under section 2-713 can be thought of as having two parts. First, it compensates the buyer for its $2,900 reliance loss. Second, it compensates the buyer for its loss of a net gain of $7,100 (which the seller's performance would have given it). Plainly, the buyer should not be allowed to recover its $2,900 reliance loss twice, which would be the result if it were allowed to recover both the $2,900 and the $10,000 figures. But there is no reason why the buyer could not choose to recover only its $2,900 reliance loss (less than the $10,000 recovery the law would allow it). The buyer might make this choice if it foresaw difficulty in proving market price and thus its expectation interest. This kind of situation—where a buyer seeks to have only its reliance loss protected—deserves further exploration. Consider:

---

[197] *See* Globe Ref. C. v. Landa Cotton Oil Co., 190 U.S. 540, 23 S. Ct. 754, 47 L. Ed. 1171 (1903).

[198] *See* U.C.C. §§ 2-712(2) and 2-713(1), both of which include the phrase "less expenses saved in consequence of the seller's breach"; 5 A. Corbin, Contracts § 1038 (1964).

Case 2. During World War II, a buyer agreed to purchase four machines for refining old rubber. The seller was late in delivering two of the refiners, not tendering them until after the end of the war. The pre-Code court treated this default as one that entitled the buyer to return all four refiners to the seller. In reliance on the contract, the buyer had built foundations for the refiners in its factory at a cost of $3,000. These foundations were worthless to the buyer, and it sought to recover their $3,000 cost from the seller.[199] The buyer was probably willing to forgo any claim for lost profits because the end of the war made it difficult to prove with certainty what, if any, profits would have been made from the rubber refiners.

Did the buyer suffer a loss when the refiners were not delivered as promised? It did only if, and to the extent that, its use of the refiners would have benefited it financially—would have enabled it to reap a net profit from the venture or, at the least, to recoup some or all of its $3,000 reliance expenditure. In these circumstances, the court concluded that the buyer could recover the $3,000 "subject to the Seller's privilege to deduct from that amount any sum which upon a further hearing it can prove would have been the Buyer's loss upon the contract, had the 'refiners' been delivered on or before May 1, 1945."[200] The Restatement (Second) of Contracts restates the principle involved in the following manner:

---

[199] L. Albert & Son v. Armstrong Rubber Co., 178 F.2d 182 (2d Cir. 1949) (L. Hand, J.).

[200] It is noteworthy that the buyer was allowed to have its reliance interest protected as an alternative to having its expectation interest protected. Had the buyer been able to prove expectation damages—say a $10,000 difference between the market price of the rejected refiners and their contract price—it ought not have been allowed to recover both this difference and the $3,000 it spent on foundations for the refiners. Allowing this—a $13,000 recovery—would have placed it in a better financial position than performance would have done.

In the recent case of International Fin. Servs., Inc. v. Franz, 534 N.W.2d 261, 26 UCCR2d 1137 (Minn. 1995), the Minnesota Supreme Court struggled with an aggrieved buyer's efforts to have both its expectation and reliance interests protected. The case involved the sale of a photoplotter system for $276,000. The court upheld findings of a breach of the implied warranty of merchantability and $216,000 in difference-in-value damages under section 2-714(2) (value-of-the-goods-warranted minus value-of-the-defective-goods-accepted) and thus gave the buyer the money equivalent of performance. The buyer also sought recovery of (1) its expenditures in building a "clean room" (one closely controlled for temperature and humidity) to house the system adequately and (2) its costs in financing the purchase (the buyer had defaulted on its obligations to its financer, and the financer had repossessed the system). The court classified the clean-room construction costs as "direct" damages under section 2-714(1)'s "loss resulting in the ordinary course of events from the seller's breach as determined in any manner which is reasonable," and allowed their recovery except to the extent that the clean room had value despite the breach—that is, it had general

§ 349. Damages Based on Reliance Interest

As an alternative to [recovering damages based on his expectation interest], the injured party has a right to damages based on his reliance interest, including expenditures made in preparation for performance or in performance, less any loss the party in breach can prove with reasonable certainty the injured party would have suffered had the contract been performed.

[2] Consequential Damages

Section 2-715(2) provides:

Consequential damages resulting from the seller's breach include

  (a) any loss resulting from general or particular requirements and needs of which the seller at the time of contracting had reason to know and which could not reasonably be prevented by cover or otherwise; and
  (b) injury to person or property resulting from any breach of warranty.

The damages allowed by subsection (a) include various kinds of losses, usually economic in nature, while the damages allowed by subsection (b) are limited to personal injury and property damage (other than to the contract goods themselves) proximately caused by a breach of warranty. Subsection (a) damages are generally thought of as contractual in nature, and subsection (b) damages are often considered to be tortious in nature. We treat the two kinds of damages separately.

---

value for housing high technology equipment.

In doing this, the court seems to have overcompensated the buyer, in effect allowing it to recover part of the cost of the clean room twice, as part of the money equivalent of performance and directly.

The court saw the issue of overcompensation with regard to the financing costs and treated them differently, denying recovery and giving two separate reasons. First, it classified these costs as consequential damages and denied recovery because consequential damages had been effectively excluded in the agreement. Second, it agreed with the intermediate appellate court that allowing recovery of the financing costs plus the difference-in-value damages would result in overcompensation, granting the buyer both the money equivalent of performance and a return of some of its costs in securing that performance.

For a thoughtful discussion of the difficulties involved with possible overcompensation when a plaintiff seeks the protection of both its reliance and expectation interests, *see* L.L. Fuller & William R. Perdue, "The Reliance Interest in Contract Damages: 1," 46 Yale L.J. 52, 80–84 (1936).

Subsection (a) damages. Most of the ideas underlying 2-715(2)(a) had their Anglo-American origins in the famous case of *Hadley v. Baxendale.*[201] In granting a new trial to the defendant on the ground that the trial judge had misdirected the jury on the question of damages, Baron Alderson stated:

> Now we think the proper rule in such a case as the present is this: Where two parties have made a contract which one of them has broken, the damages which the other party ought to receive in respect of such breach of contract should be such as may fairly and reasonably be considered either arising naturally, i.e., according to the usual course of things, from such breach of contract itself, or such as may reasonably be supposed to have been in the contemplation of both parties, at the time they made the contract, as the probable result of the breach of it.[202]

Writers have disagreed on whether Baron Alderson stated one or two rules of damages. But the appraisal of the above statement that is probably the most accurate is that it does not state any "rule" of damages. In a sense, all damages are "natural" once all the facts are known. If a court wants to hold a defaulting party liable for a particular loss suffered by the aggrieved party, it can find a way to link a chain of causation between the breach and the loss. In another sense, no damages are "natural," because the question of whether a particular loss *arose* from a breach of contract cannot be answered by the laws of nature, the physical order of the universe, or demonstrable rules of cause and effect. Many events combined to form a factual pattern; one of the events was the loss that the injured party suffered and another was the default or failure to provide the promised performance. How can it be determined that the loss arose out of the breach as opposed to one or more of the other events involved?[203] Further, as to the second part of Baron Alderson's pronouncement, most parties probably contemplate performance, not breach, when they enter into contracts. When they do contemplate breach and say something about the measure of recovery, they often raise difficult questions about distinguishing liquidated-damages clauses from penalty clauses. Thus, the search for contemplated damages usually leads only to fiction: what damages the parties would have contemplated had they thought about breach of the contract involved.[204]

---

[201] 9 Ex. 341, 156 Eng. Rep. 145 (1854).

[202] *Id.* at 354, 156 Eng. Rep. at 151.

[203] Felix S. Cohen, "Field Theory and Judicial Logic," 59 Yale L.J. 238, 251–252 (1950). Other excellent discussions include B. Cardozo, Paradoxes of Legal Science 83–85 (1928) and J. Wigmore, The Science of Judicial Proof 236–239 (3d ed. 1937).

[204] *See* Kerr Steamship Co. v. Radio Corp. of Am., 245 N.Y. 284, 157 N.E. 140 (1927) (Cardozo, J.).

The primary achievement of the court in *Hadley v. Baxendale* was not that of stating an immutable rule of damages, but that of granting judges significant control over juries in the determination of contract damages. Only seven years earlier, in 1847, the same Court of Exchequer had approved an award for the same kind of breach (late delivery by a carrier) and against the same defendant involved in *Hadley* on the ground that it was up to the jury rather than to the trial judge to determine what damages were "reasonable."[205] *Hadley* changed this approach; no longer were jurors to be "chancellors"[206] with regard to contract damages. Their awards were to be measured against judicially created standards: what judges thought were appropriate recoveries under the facts presented. The "normal" or "general" measure of recovery (for example, market price minus unpaid contract price) was always considered fair and was described by Baron Alderson as damages which arose "naturally." Recovery that went beyond general damages was fair and appropriate only if the defaulter, at the time of contracting, was alerted to the particular needs of the aggrieved party that led to the special loss. Supposedly, a defaulter that was so alerted could have protected itself by a special term in the agreement; not having done so, it cannot complain when required to pay the special damages.

Notice, however, that Baron Alderson did not require the parties to bargain about damages. Indeed, *Hadley* does not even require that damages, to be recoverable, must either (1) have in fact arisen naturally or (2) have in fact been in the contemplation of the parties. It is sufficient if the damages were either (1) such "as may fairly and reasonably be considered" as arising naturally or (2) such "as may reasonably be supposed" to have been in the contemplation of the parties. Special damages (consequential damages under the Code) need not be bargained about, agreed upon, or consciously considered to be recoverable.

Nevertheless, some courts have misread *Hadley v. Baxendale* as conditioning the recovery of special damages on an agreement, express or implied, concerning those damages.[207] The Code rejects this reading of *Hadley*. The statutory language requires only that the seller have reason to know at the time of contracting of the general or particular needs of the buyer that led to the loss. Two ideas are important here. First, the seller's actual knowl-

---

[205] Black v. Baxendale, 1 Ex. 410, 154 Eng. Rep. 174 (1847).

[206] Hixt v. Goats, 1 Rolle 257, 81 Eng. Rep. 472 (K.B. 1615).

[207] Pre-Code cases include Globe Ref. Co. v. Landa Cotton Oil Co., 190 U.S. 540, 23 S. Ct. 754, 47 L. Ed. 1171 (1903); Lampkins v. Int'l Harvester Co., 207 Ark. 637, 182 S.W.2d 203 (1944); California Press Mfg. Co. v. Stafford Packing Co., 192 Cal. 479, 221 P. 345 (1923); Sward v. Nash, 230 Minn. 100, 40 N.W.2d 828 (1950).

edge of the buyer's requirements and needs is not controlling; the seller can be liable even if it lacked actual knowledge; the test is one of reason to know. Second, the Code does not require the seller to have reason to know of the particular items of damage claimed by the buyer or the precise amount of the loss.[208] The test is less exacting. Recovery turns on the seller's reason to know the facts of the buyer's general or particular requirements and needs. If the seller had reason to know of these facts at the time of contracting (not the time of breach), the buyer may recover consequential damages even though no implied agreement by the seller to pay those damages can be found.[209]

An important consequence of testing the recoverability of consequential damages in terms of the seller's reason to know of the buyer's needs and requirements is that lost profits can frequently be recovered. If the seller, at the time of contract formation, had reason to know that the buyer was engaged in a business and was purchasing the goods for use in that business, the buyer should be able to recover the profits that the seller's breach caused it to lose.[210] That is, there should be no foreseeability impediment to the

---

[208] However, if the amount of the loss is so large that it could not reasonably have been anticipated, only that amount which could have been foreseen is recoverable. *See* Victoria Laundry v. (Windsor) Ltd. v. Newman Indus. Ltd. [1949] 2 K.B. 528; E. Allan Farnsworth, Contracts 825 (3d ed. 1999).

[209] The language of U.C.C. § 2-715 is reinforced by the Comments on this point. Comment 2 states that "[t]he 'tacit agreement' test for the recovery of consequential damages is rejected." Comment 3 adds that "the seller is liable for consequential damages in all cases where he had reason to know of the buyer's general or particular requirements at the time of contracting." The Pennsylvania Supreme Court nevertheless misread U.C.C. § 2-715(2)(a) and held that "[a]nticipated profits are not recoverable unless within the contemplation of the parties when the contract was made." Keystone Diesel Engine Co. v. Irwin, 411 Pa. 222, 191 A.2d 376, 1 UCCR 184 (1963). Fourteen years later, in R.I. Lampus Co. v. Neville Cement Prods. Corp., 474 Pa. 199, 378 A.2d 288, 22 UCCR 1172 (1977), it changed its mind, and said "[t]hat § 2-715(2) does not condition recovery of consequential damages upon a 'tacit agreement' of the parties now appears correct to us. All that is required is that the seller *have reason to know* the buyer's needs and requirements." [Emphasis in original.]

[210] *See, e.g.*, Lewis v. Mobil Oil Corp., 438 F.2d 500, 8 UCCR 625 (8th Cir. 1971), in which the court observed:

Where a seller provides goods to a maufacturing enterprise with knowledge that they are to be used in the manufacturing process, it is reasonable to assume that he should know that defective goods will cause a disruption of production, and loss of profits is a natural consequence of such disruption. Hence, loss of profits should be recoverable under those circumstances. Here, the defendant seller knew that the oil it was supplying was to be used in the operation of the sawmill. It also knew that a defective oil would cause the sawmill equipment to operate improperly. It is a natural consequence of the failure of the equipment to function that production would be curtailed and loss of profits would follow. 438 F.2d at

buyer's recovery of lost profits; the doctrines of certainty and avoidable consequences (about which more in the next two paragraphs) may, however, present impediments. The lost profits that can be recovered may take various forms. In *AM/PM Franchise Association v. Atlantic Richfield Co.*,[211] the court described some of these forms in the context of franchisee buyers of defective gasoline (from a refiner franchisor). The buyers were in the business of reselling the gasoline at retail and also operating mini-markets, in which they sold various other items. The court allowed these buyers to recover as consequential damages three different kinds of lost profits: (1) "lost primary profits" —profits that would have been earned on gasoline sales during the contract period had the gasoline not been defective but were not earned because the gasoline-buying public, aware of the defect, reduced the volume of its gasoline purchases from the plaintiffs; (2) "lost secondary profits"—another loss of volume and consequent loss of profits, but on mini-market items other than gasoline (items not purchased from the defendant seller), the loss of volume resulting from the buying public's reduced patronage of the plaintiffs; and (3) loss of prospective profits or loss of good will—loss of patronage and profits in the future—that is, after the deliveries of defective gasoline had ceased, occasioned by the fact that the defective gasoline had caused customers to become disgruntled with the plaintiffs.

Section 2-715(2)(a) not only codifies something of *Hadley v. Baxendale*'s foreseeability limitation on recoverable special damages; it also codifies—in its "which could not reasonably be prevented by cover or otherwise" language—something of the common-law doctrine of mitigation or avoidable consequences. Based on the policy of encouraging aggrieved parties to attempt to avoid loss, this is a doctrine that "damages are not recoverable for loss that the injured party could have avoided without undue risk, burden, or humiliation."[212] Thus, an aggrieved buyer that seeks to recover lost profits will be prevented from doing so to the extent that the defendant seller proves that the buyer could reasonably (in Restatement terms, "without undue risk, burden, or humiliation") have avoided the loss of the profits.[213] While the burden of proving damages, including consequential

---

510–511, 8 UCCR at 641.

[211] 26 Pa. 110, 584 A.2d 915, 14 UCCR2d 11 (1990).

[212] Restatement (Second) of Contracts, § 350(1) (1981).

[213] *See* Gerwin v. Southeastern Cal. Ass'n of Seventh Day Adventists, 14 Cal. App. 3d 209, 92 Cal. Rptr. 111, 8 UCCR 643 (1971), in which the court stated:

> [P]laintiff did not cover. But it does not follow that he was thereby precluded from recovering consequential damages. Plaintiff was unable to purchase substitute items because of their unavailability at prices within his financial ability.

damages, rests on the plaintiff buyer, the burden of proof with regard to mitigation or avoidability is generally placed on the defendant seller.[214] To defeat or diminish the buyer's recovery, the seller must prove that the buyer could have reasonably avoided the loss of profits by covering—that is, by purchasing substitute goods—or by some other means, such as repairing the defective goods[215] or ceasing to use them.

The common-law requirement of certainty—that "[d]amages are not recoverable for loss beyond an amount that the evidence permits to be established with reasonable certainty"[216]—furnishes another important limitation on the recoverability of consequential damages, particularly lost profits. Despite the fact that there is no express reference to the certainty principle in the statutory language,[217] Code cases have denied the recovery of lost profits in situations where the plaintiff could not or did not lay an adequate evidentary foundation for them.[218] It is considered unfair to the defendant to allow the trier of fact to speculate about the amount of the plaintiff's loss, and, to the extent that the evidence allows no more than speculation, the judge should control the jury and prevent it from awarding damages. To the extent, however, that the evidence enables the trier of fact to find that the plaintiff has lost profits with reasonable (not precise or mathematical) certainty, they may be recovered.[219] Doubts are generally resolved against the defaulter, but only to the extent that the evidence removes

---

Ordinarily a duty to mitigate does not require an injured party to take measures which are unreasonable or impractical or which require expenditures disproportionate to the loss sought to be avoided or which are beyond his financial means. [Citations omitted.] That principle should govern in determining whether a buyer acted reasonably in failing to cover or otherwise mitigate his losses.

[214] Federal Signal Corp. v. Safety Factors, Inc., 125 Wash. 2d 413, 886 P.2d 172, 25 UCCR2d 765 (1994).

[215] Id.

[216] Restatement (Second) of Contracts § 352 (1981).

[217] There is a reference in Comment 4 to U.C.C. § 2-715:

The burden of proving the extent of loss incurred by way of consequential damage is on the buyer, but the section on liberal administration of remedies rejects any doctrine of certainty which requires almost mathematical precision in the proof of loss. Loss may be determined in any manner which is reasonable under the circumstances.

[218] See, e.g., Gerwin v. Southeastern Cal. Ass'n of Seventh Day Adventists, 14 Cal. App. 3d 209, 92 Cal. Rptr. 111, 8 UCCR 643 (1971); B.B. Walker Co. v. Ashland Chem. Co., 474 F. Supp. 651, 34 UCCR 561 (M.D.N.C. 1979).

[219] See Cambridge Plating Co., Inc. v. Napco, Inc. 85 F.3d752, 30 UCCR2d 815 (1st Cir. 1996); American Road Equip. Co. v. Extrusions, Inc. 29 F.3d 341, 24 UCCR2d 905 (8th Cir. 1994).

the matter from the realm of speculation. In some circumstances, the fact and approximate amount of the profits the plaintiff buyer lost because of the breach can be convincingly established by evidence of the profits it was earning before the breach.[220] Where such evidence is unavailable (for example, where the plaintiff's venture is a new one), the recovery of lost profits is more difficult.[221] The loss may, nevertheless, sometimes "be established with reasonable certainty with the aid of expert testimony, economic and financial data, market surveys and analyses, business records of similar enterprises, and the like."[222]

In combining the general damages provided for in sections 2-711 through 2-714 with the special damages of section 2-715(2)(a), courts should take care to avoid overcompensation. The plaintiff should not be compensated twice for the same loss or otherwise placed in a better financial position than performance would have done.

Subsection (b) damages. In addition to the subsection (a) damages discussed above, consequential damages also include subsection (b)'s "injury to person or property proximately resulting from any breach of warranty." This provision has its primary use in accident and other "products liability" cases. In these cases, plaintiffs frequently have multiple theories of recovery available to them, including a Code warranty theory and one or more theories (such as negligence and strict liability) based on the common law of torts. Since the adoption of the Code, the tort theories have become increasingly important and are now playing the leading roles in most jurisdictions.[223]

Subsection (b) concerns only breach-of-warranty cases and physical, as opposed to economic, injuries resulting from them. Unlike subsection (a), it does not condition recovery on foreseeability. Its requirement is that the injury *proximately* result from a breach of warranty. As is the case with foreseeability and *Hadley v. Baxendale*,[224] this requirement falls short of stating a rule that can be mechanically applied. Distinctions between the proximate and the remote effects of a breach can be drawn only on a case-by-case basis. Definitions of proximateness have been attempted, a common one being that a proximate cause is that cause which, in the natural and

---

[220] *See* Cates v. Morgan Portable Buildng Corp., 755 F.3d 87, 25 UCCR 1060 (7th Cir. 1979).

[221] *See* El Fredo Pizza, Inc. Roto-Flex Oven Co., 199 Neb. 697, 261 N.W.2d 358, 23 UCCR 342 (1978).

[222] Restatement (Second) of Contracts, § 352, cmt. b. (1981). *See also* In re Merritt Logan, Inc., 901 F.2d 349, 12 UCCR2d 421 (3d Cir. 1990).

[223] *See* § 4.06[B][5], *supra.*

[224] *See* § 7.04[F], *Supra.*

continuous sequence, unbroken by any efficient intervening cause, produced the injury, and without which the injury would not have occurred.[225] Through such flexible words as "natural," "unbroken," "efficient," and "produces," this statement enables courts to limit or expand recoverable damages in accordance with the facts of the cases before them and their notions of appropriate policy. A more straightforward way of speaking is to rename proximate cause "legal cause," as the Restatement (Second) of Torts has done. The label "legal" tends to eliminate the idea that a mechanical test is involved and to make clear that the problem is one of policy. Given the facts of the particular case, ought the seller that has defaulted on its warranty be held liable to the buyer (or to some third person) for the injuries suffered?[226]

[G] Deduction of Damages From Price

When a buyer accepts goods it becomes liable for their price.[227] If the goods are nonconforming, the buyer, in some instances, can revoke its acceptance and terminate its price liability.[228] There are, however, situations in which a buyer that has accepted nonconforming goods is unable or unwilling to revoke its acceptance and retains the goods despite their defects. Such a buyer remains liable for the price, but, if it has given notice in accordance with section 2-607(3)(a), it has a claim against the seller for the damages it has suffered because of the nonconformity.[229] The Code (in section 2-717) gives the buyer the privilege of deducting its damages from any balance owing on the price:

> The buyer on notifying the seller of his intention to do so may deduct all or any part of the damages resulting from any breach of the contract from any part of the price still due under the same contract.

This section allows the buyer to deduct its damages for *any* breach. Thus, the breach may involve the quality of the goods, their title, their tender, or any other provision of the contract between the buyer and the seller. The default, however, must be on the *same* contract as the one on

---

[225] *See, e.g.,* Roller v. Indep. Silo Co., 242 Iowa 1277, 49 N.W.2d 838 (1951); Michalka v. Great No. Paper Co., 151 Me. 98, 116 A.2d 139 (1955); Burr v. Clark, 20 Wash. 2d 149, 190 P.2d 769 (1948).

[226] For a greater discussion of proximate cause, *see* § 4.12[B], *supra.*

[227] U.C.C. § 2-607(1).

[228] *See* §§ 7.03[E] and 7.04[D], *supra.*

[229] *See* §§ 7.04[E] and 7.04[F], *supra.*

which the buyer has a price liability from which it is making the deduction.[230] In other words, a buyer cannot use section 2-717 to set off its damages arising out of the seller's breach of Contract *A* against its price liability to the same seller on Contract *B*. The buyer must also notify the seller of its intention to deduct the damages from the price. A deduction without the required notice may destroy the buyer's right to use the seller's breach as a defense to the seller's action for the price,[231] or it may give the seller reasonable grounds for insecurity and thus justify a demand by the seller for adequate assurance of due performance under section 2-609.[232] The required notice, like most Code notices, may be informal.[233]

When, in a situation involving only one contract, a buyer has accepted goods and given appropriate notices of breach (section 2-607(3)(a)) and of intention to deduct damages from the price (section 2-717), the seller should be unable to recover the price until the buyer's damage claim has been adjudicated and can be set off against the price. When, however, the buyer's damage claim arises out of a different contract from the one under which the seller is claiming the price, section 2-717 does not apply, and will not enable the buyer to block the seller's recovery of the price. In such a two-contract situation, applicable procedural rules generally allow a buyer that is sued for the price under one contract to counterclaim for its damages under the second contract. But the seller's judgment for the price need not be delayed until the buyer's counterclaim for damages under a different contract has been adjudicated.[234]

[H] Security Interest in the Goods

Article 2 leaves most buyers' claims for damages arising out of sellers' defaults unsecured. This is generally true in both breach-of-warranty and nondelivery cases. If, after accepting and paying for goods, the buyer is personally injured or damaged economically because the goods do not conform to the seller's warranties, the buyer's damage claims under sections 2-714 and 2-715 are unsecured claims against the seller. Similarly, a buyer

---

[230] *See* C. R. Bard, Inc. v. Medical Elecs. Corp., 529 F. Supp. 1382, 33 UCCR 26 (D. Mass. 1982) and Echo, Inc. v. Whitson Co., Inc., 52 F.3d 702, 26 UCCR2d 356 (7th Cir. 1995), in which distributorship agreements, on the one hand, and purchase agreements thereunder, on the other hand, were treated as separate contracts for purposes of U.C.C. § 2-717.

[231] Gutor Int'l AG v. Raymond Packer Co., Inc., 493 F.2d 938, 14 UCCR 567 (1st Cir. 1974).

[232] U.C.C. § 2-717, Comment 2.

[233] *Id.*

[234] Artmark Assocs., Inc. v. Allied Tube & Conduit Corp., 32 UCCR 454 (N.D. Ill. 1981).

that fails to receive the goods it was promised because the seller failed to deliver or repudiated has an unsecured claim for difference-money damages under section 2-712 or section 2-713, a possible unsecured claim for incidental and consequential damages under section 2-715, and an unsecured claim for whatever portion of the price it has paid under section 2-711(1).[235]

There are, however, limited circumstances in which Article 2 provides security for buyers' damage claims. One situation has been discussed in § 7.04[G]. When a buyer that has accepted goods and not paid for them (and that consequently owes the seller their price) has suffered damages because of the seller's default on the same contract, section 2-717 grants a right to set off the damages against the price. In effect, this right of setoff allows whatever portion of the price is unpaid and still in the buyer's pocket to serve as security for the buyer's damages.

Another limited circumstance involves cases of rightful rejection or revocation of acceptance. For them, section 2-711(3) provides as follows:

> On rightful rejection or justifiable revocation of acceptance a buyer has a security interest in goods in his possession or control for any payments made on their price and any expenses reasonably incurred in their inspection, receipt, transportation, care and custody and may hold such goods or resell them in like manner as an aggrieved seller (Section 2-706).[236]

This provision deals with situations in which the buyer has received the goods but is rightfully and effectively thrusting them back on the seller, thus destroying price obligations and earning a right to a return of any portion of the price that has been paid.[237] In such cases, the statute gives a buyer that has paid all or part of the price or has incurred certain other expenses a security interest in the goods. The security interest is possessory. It applies only to goods in the buyer's possession or control.[238] The obligations that it secures are limited. It does not secure the buyer's right to have its expectation interest protected under sections 2-712, 2-713, or 2-715;[239] it secures only the buyer's right to the return of whatever payments have been made on the price and certain other expenses incurred by the

---

[235] *See* In re DeNicola, 92 B.R. 267, 8 UCCR2d 1032 (Bankr. S.D. Ohio 1988).

[236] The Article 2 makes no significant changes in this security-interest provision. *See* proposed revisions to Council Draft § 2-829(b).

[237] U.C.C. § 2-711(1).

[238] *See* Furlong v. Alpha Chi Omega Sorority, 73 Ohio Misc. 2d 26, 657 N.E.2d 866, 28 UCCR2d 1194 (Mun. Ct. 1993).

[239] U.C.C. § 2-711, Comment 2.

buyer ("any expenses reasonably incurred in [the goods'] inspection, receipt, transportation, care and custody").

The section 2-711(3) security interest empowers the buyer to hold the goods as security for its payments and expenses or to foreclose by selling them in accordance with the provisions of section 2-706.[240] It consequently modifies a rejecting or revoking buyer's duties to hold the goods for the seller under section 2-602 and section 2-603; that is, a rejecting or revoking buyer that has paid something on the price or has incurred some of the designated expenses, and that consequently has a section 2-711(3) security interest, will have significantly different section 2-602 and section 2-603 duties than will a rejecting or revoking buyer that, because it has made no payments and incurred no expenses, has no security interest.

The security interest created by section 2-711(3) arises by operation of law.[241] No agreement, written or oral, is needed. And no filing is required for perfection.[242] Although the interest is subject to the provisions of Article 9, Article 2 governs the enforcement rights of the buyer-secured party.[243]

When a seller's solvency is in doubt, a buyer may want to order its conduct with a view toward maximizing its security. Consider a buyer who has paid something on the price to a seller of doubtful collectibility and discovers that it has a right to reject. Such a buyer can either (1) reject and hold the goods as security for what it has paid plus whatever designated section 2-711(3) expenses it has incurred or (2) retain the goods and use section 2-717 to set off its damages under sections 2-714 and 2-715 against the portion of the price that has not been paid. Which course is more advantageous to the buyer turns on factual matters, such as how much of the price it has paid, the value of the goods, and the amount of its damages, and on the legal circumstance that, while section 2-711(3) will enable it to secure only its downpayment and the designated expenses, section 2-717 will enable it to secure (by way of setoff against the unpaid portion of the price) all of the damages it has suffered because of the seller's breach of the contract in question.

---

[240] If the sale brings more than the amounts secured by the security interest, the buyer must turn the excess over to the seller. U.C.C. § 2-706(6).

[241] U.C.C. § 9-113, Comment 2.

[242] U.C.C. § 9-113.

[243] *Id.*

§ 7.05   THE BUYER'S RIGHT TO THE GOODS

Under the Code, an aggrieved buyer's usual remedy is a money judgment.[244] There are, however, limited circumstances in which recovery of the
goods is provided for. Under section 2-716(1), a buyer may be able to obtain
specific performance of the seller's promise to deliver the goods where they
are "unique" or where the court finds that "other proper circumstances"
exist. Under section 2-716(3), a buyer may replevy goods identified to the
contract in circumstances in which it is unable to cover or where the seller
has shipped the goods under reservation and the buyer has satisfied or tendered satisfaction of the security interest in them. Further, under section 2-
502, a buyer that has paid all or part of price of goods that have been
identified to the contract can recover them from a seller that became insolvent within ten days after it received the first installment on the price. These
rights to the goods are discussed in §§ 7.04[A] through 7.05[C].

[A]   Specific Performance

Section 2-716(1) describes in one short sentence the circumstances in
which a buyer may obtain specific performance:

> Specific performance may be decreed where the goods are unique or in
> other proper circumstances.

There is another sentence in the section on what the equitable decree may
contain ("terms and conditions as to payment of the price, damages, or other
relief as the court may deem just"),[245] but that is all that the text of the
statute says with regard to specific performance. The Comments say a good
deal more, including that "this Article seeks to further a more liberal attitude
than some courts have shown in connection with the specific performance
of contracts of sale" and "[i]n view of this Article's emphasis on the commercial feasibility of replacement, a new concept of what are 'unique' goods
is introduced under this section."[246]

The chosen statutory language seems at odds with, or at the least,
inadequate to accomplish the ambitious intention expressed in the Comments—that of significantly expanding the circumstances in which specific
performance is available. The decided cases generally bear this out. Under

---

[244] Scholars have debated and continue to debate the relative merits of damage remedies
versus specific remedies. *See* § 7.03[A], *supra*.

[245] U.C.C. § 2-716(2).

[246] U.C.C. § 2-716, Comments 1 and 2.

the Code, specific performance has continued to be an uncommon remedy, with money damages doing most of the work.

When goods are "unique" in the sense that there are no others like them, a clear case for specific performance is presented. Family heirlooms and original works of art are examples. When goods are rare and consequently difficult to replace on the market, courts have divided on whether the statutory words "unique" and "other proper circumstances" call for specific performance. A "Tayana 37" cruising yacht to be manufactured in Taiwan in accordance with blueprints and a "customizing narration statement" approved by the buyer has been held to be "undeniably unique."[247] And "other proper circumstances" have been found where the goods were a Corvette automobile (one of 6,000 manufactured to commemorate the selection of the Corvette as the pace car for the Indianapolis 500).[248] On the other hand, specific performance and replevin were denied in the case of an agreement to purchase a 19-year-old Corvette.[249] And in *Klein v. Pepsico, Inc.*,[250] the Fourth Circuit reversed a District Judge's grant of specific performance to the buyer of a used Gulfstream G-II corporate jet at a price of $4.6 million. Despite the facts that few G-II's were available and that cover would be expensive and difficult, the Court of Appeals found "no room" for specific performance. The court observed that "Virginia's adoption of the Uniform Commercial Code does not abrogate the maxim that specific performance is inappropriate where damages are recoverable and adequate." It found that "money damages would clearly be adequate in this case," and noted that "price increases alone are no reason to order specific performance."

---

[247] Fast v. Southern Offshore Yachts, 587 F. Supp. 1354, 38 UCCR 1569 (D. Conn. 1984).

[248] Sedmak v. Charlie's Chevrolet, Inc., 622 S.W.2d 694, 31 UCCR 851 (Mo. App. 1981). The court observed that the "Pace Car . . . was not unique in the traditional legal sense. It was not an heirloom or, arguably, not one of a kind. . . . Admittedly, 6,000 Pace Cars were produced by Chevrolet. However, as the record reflects, this is limited production. In addition, only one of these cars was available to each dealer, and only a limited number were equipped with the specific options ordered by plaintiffs. . . . The sticker price for the car was $14,284.21. Yet Charlie's received offers from individuals in Hawaii and Florida to buy the Pace Car for $24,000.00 and $28,000.00 respectively. . . . [T]he location and size of these offers demonstrated this limited edition was in short supply and great demand. . . . This case was a 'proper circumstance' for ordering specific performance."

[249] Scholl v. Hartzell, 20 Pa. D&C 3d 304, 33 UCCR 951 (1981). "Although a 1962 Corvette automobile may be considered by many to be a collector's item, the court fails to find that it is of the 'unique' goods contemplated by § 2-716. Moreover, plaintiff has not alleged in his complaint that he has been unable to cover as provided in § 2-716."

[250] 845 F.2d 76, 6 UCCR2d 728 (4th Cir. 1988).

While money damages could provide effective relief in a single-delivery situation like *Klein* (especially because a substitute for the goods could be obtained, market price was provable, and the defendant (Pepsico) was obviously collectible), they are less likely to meet the aggrieved buyer's needs (or the needs of its customers) in contracts that call for multiple or continuing performances. In such circumstances, specific performance or an injunction against the seller's breach may provide a better remedy, and courts may consequently be moved to find "uniqueness" or "other proper circumstances" and grant it. For example, in *Eastern Air Lines, Inc. v. Gulf Oil Corp.*,[251] the court granted specific performance of a contract to supply Eastern Air Lines' requirements for jet fuel at a number of airports, observing that "[i]f Gulf were to cease to supply this fuel, the result would be chaos and irreparable damage." And in *Colorado-Ute Electric Association, Inc. v. Envirotech Corp.*,[252] the court granted specific performance of express and implied warranties. That is, it ordered that the defendant seller make the precipitator that it had installed at the buyer utility's generating station operate so as to remove the warranted quantities of pollutants. The court was influenced by the "uncertainty" of the damages that the utility would suffer over the lengthy life of the equipment and by the "irreparable" harm it would suffer if the plant were shut down for air-quality violations.

The upshot is that specific performance has continued to be an unusual, rather than a standard, remedy under the Code. Predicting when courts will exercise their discretion to grant it can be difficult. One must go beyond the statutory language—"where the goods are unique or in other proper circumstances"—to the cases that have worked with that language. And in some circumstances, they speak cryptically and inconsistently. Perhaps the most useful generalization that can be attempted is that a grant of specific performance becomes more likely to the extent that the buyer establishes its relative advantage over money damages in protecting its expectation interest in the circumstances, and, conversely, less likely to the extent that the seller establishes that money damages can provide relief that is reasonably adequate and certain.

[B] Replevin

In its subsections (1) and (2), section 2-716 provides for specific performance; in its subsection (3), it provides another remedy that a buyer may use to obtain the contracted-for goods: replevin. Under section 2-716(3), a

---

[251] 415 F. Supp. 429, 19 UCCR 721 (S.D. Fla. 1975).
[252] 524 F. Supp. 1152, 33 UCCR 965 (D. Colo. 1981).

buyer may replevy goods only if they have been identified to the contract *and* if:

1. The buyer is unable to cover after making reasonable efforts to do so, or
2. The circumstances reasonably indicate that efforts to cover will be unavailing, or
3. The goods have been shipped under reservation and the buyer has satisfied or tendered satisfaction of the security interest in them.[253]

The first requirement for replevin is that the goods must have been identified to the contract. This requirement significantly limits the scope and importance of the replevin remedy. If the goods are unidentified, the buyer can obtain them only by specific performance; replevin is unavailable. Identification is covered in section 2-501;[254] it cannot occur until the goods are both existing and identified.[255] This means that replevin is unavailable in situations where the seller was to manufacture the goods but has not done so and in situations where, although the goods exist, they have not been designated as the goods to which the contract refers.

When a contract calls for goods already existing and identified—for example, a contract for the sale of a particular antique clock—identification occurs at the time of contract formation.[256] In such circumstances, replevin will lie if cover is unavailable. But in most such circumstances, specific performance would also lie on grounds of uniqueness or other proper circumstances. The upshot is that replevin has not been, and does not promise to be, an extensively used or important Article 2 remedy.

[C] Insolvency of the Seller

Suppose that the buyer has paid all or a significant part of the price before delivery and that the seller defaults on its promise to furnish the goods. The buyer may, of course, obtain a judgment for the amount it has paid,[257] plus the damages it suffers because of the seller's default. If the seller is collectible, such a money judgment will often afford satisfactory compensation to the buyer. But suppose the seller is insolvent and contemplates filing a petition in bankruptcy. A money judgment against such a seller is likely to be worth only a small fraction of its face amount, if that.

---

[253] *See* U.C.C. § 2-505.

[254] *See* § 5.04[B], *supra.*

[255] U.C.C. § 2-105(2).

[256] U.C.C. § 2-501(1)(a). Identification is discussed in § 6.03, *supra.*

[257] U.C.C. § 2-711(1).

A prepaying buyer whose seller is insolvent will consequently prefer—strongly prefer—a remedy which gives it the goods (on its completion of the payment of the price).

In very limited circumstances, section 2-502 provides for such a remedy:

> (1) Subject to subsection (2) and even though the goods have not been shipped a buyer who has paid a part or all of the price of goods in which he has a special property under the provisions of the immediately preceding section may on making and keeping good a tender of any unpaid portion of their price recover them from the seller if the seller becomes insolvent within ten days after receipt of the first installment on their price.
>
> (2) If the identification creating his special property has been made by the buyer he acquires the right to recover the goods only if they conform to the contract for sale.

There are multiple reasons why section 2-502 has helped, and will help, few buyers. First, it is available only with respect to goods in which the buyer has a special property under section 2-501.[258] That is, like its section 2-716(3) cousin replevin, section 2-502 applies only to goods that have been identified to the contract of sale.[259] Unfortunately, the section does not say *when* the identification which gives the buyer a special property in the goods must occur. The statutory language is: "a buyer who has paid a part or all of the price of goods in which he has a special property . . . may . . . recover them from the seller." Must the goods have been identified at the time the buyer paid a part or all of the price, at the time the seller became insolvent, at the time the buyer tendered the remainder of the purchase price, or at the time of trial? The most likely interpretation is that the goods must have been identified at the time of the tender of the balance of the price, but this is far from clear. The overriding point, however, concerns not the time of identification, but the fact that it must occur if section 2-502 is to be triggered; in the many cases where it has not occurred, section 2-502 will be unavailable.[260]

A second major limiting factor is that section 2-502 allows the buyer to recover the goods only "if the seller becomes insolvent within ten days

---

[258] *See* § 5.04[B], *supra.*

[259] *See* § 7.05[B], *supra.*

[260] In re Koreag, Controle et Revision S.A., 961 F.2d341, 17 UCCR2d 341 (2d Cir. 1992); In re Energy Cooperative, Inc., 700 F. Supp 929, 7 UCCR2d 1469 (N.D. Ill. 1988); In re CSY Yacht Corp., 42 B.R. 619, 39 UCCR 879 (Bankr. M.D. Fla. 1984).

after receipt of the first installment on their price." A showing that the seller was insolvent when the first installment was paid does not suffice, but instead defeats the buyer's use of section 2-502. What the buyer must show is that the seller was solvent when it received the first installment on the price and then became insolvent within ten days thereafter.[261] Trying to prove the particular day on which a business or other person became insolvent[262] is likely to be a foolhardy venture. Save in cases of financial catastrophe (for example, a major uninsured fire or other casualty loss), the slide from solvency to insolvency is a gradual process, and it is unlikely that anyone could carry the burden of proving that the transition occurred on a precise day or within a precise ten-day period. In other words, section 2-502's ten-day provision is enough, by itself, to make the section unavailable to most buyers who have paid part or all of the price to an insolvent seller.

Third, even in the rare situation where it can be proved that the goods were identified and that the seller, while solvent when it received the first price installment, became insolvent within ten days thereafter, the buyer may well fail if the seller is in bankruptcy. The reason is that the policies and provisions of the Bankruptcy Code—federal law—preempt and defeat section 2-502. One of bankruptcy's primary objectives is equality of distribution among unsecured creditors. Except to the extent the Bankruptcy Code provides otherwise, unsecured creditors are to share equally in the bankruptcy estate—each receiving the same percentage dividend, whether ten cents, two cents, or nothing, on every dollar of debt that it was owed. Section 2-502 runs counter to this objective, as can the specific performance and replevin provisions of section 2-716.

A buyer that is aggrieved by its seller's default is a creditor of the seller. If the seller is in bankruptcy and the buyer seeks or is given a monetary remedy, the buyer can easily be treated like the other creditors of the bankrupt seller—afforded the same (say) five-cents-on-the-dollar distribution. But if the buyer reaches the goods specifically, it may achieve much better treatment than the other creditors—recovering all or nearly all of its

---

[261] *See* In re Giles World Mktg., Inc., 29 B.R. 523, 36 UCCR 475 (Barkr. D. Mass 1983).
[262] U.C.C. § 1-201(23) offers the following definition of insolvency:

> A person is "insolvent" who either has ceased to pay his debts in the ordinary course of business or cannot pay his debts as they become due or is insolvent within the meaning of the federal bankruptcy law.

The bankruptcy definition of insolvency, which can be found in section 101(32) of the Bankruptcy Code, looks not at whether a debtor is paying, or is able to pay its debts but at its balance sheet. Under the bankruptcy definition, a debtor is insolvent if its debts are greater than its assets, valued fairly.

loss. Thus, when a section 2-502 buyer makes a downpayment, it extends credit to its seller. If it is allowed, via section 2-502, to recover the contract goods on completing payment of the price, it may well be recouping its entire downpayment or more in the value of the goods, and this while other creditors of the bankrupt seller are realizing only pennies on the dollar.

A seller's trustee in bankruptcy could base an attack on section 2-502 on various Bankrutcy Code provisions, including section 545 on statutory liens, section 544 on the trustee's rights as a hypothetical lien creditor and the successor to the rights of actual unsecured creditors, section 547 on preferences, and section 365 on executory contracts. A similar attack, though probably without reliance on section 545, could be made on efforts to recover goods from a bankrupt seller under the specific performance and replevin provisions of section 2-716 if the specific recovery would treat the buyer more favorably than other creditors.[263] With respect to prepaying buyers, the trustee could also point to section 507(a)(6), which gives an individual who has made a downpayment on consumer goods or services that she has not received a sixth priority of up to $1,800. The trustee's argument would be that, at least with respect to goods, there would be no need for such a priority if the prepaying buyer had an effective right to recover the goods specifically from the bankruptcy estate.

In its section 2-824, the proposed revisions to Article 2 would significantly broaden section 2-502. It would give the prepaying buyer a right to recover identified goods whenever the seller repudiates or fails to deliver as required, wholly without regard to the seller's solvency or insolvency.[264] Many buyers who are blocked by the ten-day insolvency provision of the current section could use the new section. Increased usage would lead to more collisions with sellers' trustees in bankruptcy and, probably, to adjudication of the bankruptcy issues.

---

[263] For discussions of the potential conflict between Code provisions allowing buyers to recover goods specifically and bankruptcy policies, *see* Frank R. Kennedy, "The Trustee in Bankruptcy Under the Uniform Commercial Code: Some Problems Suggested by Articles 2 and 9," 14 Rutgers L. Rev. 518, 556–559 (1960); Morris G. Shanker, "Bankruptcy and Article 2 of the Uniform Commercial Code," 40 J. Nat'l Conf. Referees in Bankr. 37, 43–44 (1966); Nathan Levy, Jr., "Impact of the New Bankruptcy Code on Article 2 Sales," 14 UCC L.J. 307, 336–338 (1982); In re Tennecomp Sys., Inc., 12 B.R. 729, 31 UCCR 1307 (Bankr. E.D. Tenn. 1981).

[264] Council Draft 2-824.

III.   BUYER IN DEFAULT

§ 7.06   THE SELLER'S COURSE OF ACTION

[A]   Remedial Interests of the Seller

Buyers can default on their contractual obligations at various times and in various ways. The type of remedy that will be available and helpful to an aggrieved seller will vary with, and turn largely on, the nature of the buyer's default. For example, a seller that has not delivered the goods at the time of its buyer's default may want to withhold delivery and to do so without committing a breach. In addition, the seller may want damages measured by the losses resulting from the buyer's default. If the buyer's default thrusts the goods back on the seller (by way of wrongful rejection or wrongful revocation of acceptance), the seller will want to recover damages for its losses. And if the defaulting buyer is retaining delivered goods, the seller may want to pursue an action for the price, or it may want to reclaim the goods.

The remedies that Article 2 affords sellers are, in the main, money-damage remedies. When the defaulting buyer is collectible, the aggrieved seller may not need to look any further. But when the defaulting buyer is uncollectible, the seller may have a strong interest in retaining or reclaiming the goods. This is likely to affect third parties, such as purchasers from the buyer, creditors of the buyer, and representatives of those creditors—such as the buyer's trustee in bankruptcy. Section 7.07 of this text explores a seller's Article 2 rights against third parties. As it shows, these rights are limited. It is Article 9 rather than Article 2 that provides the means—perfected security interests—by which sellers may obtain broad protection against the claims of creditors of, and purchasers from, their buyers.

[B]   Index of the Seller's Remedies

Section 2-703 indexes several, but not all, of the remedies that the Code provides to aggrieved sellers. It is roughly analogous to section 2-711 which indexes some of the buyer's major remedies.[265]

Triggering events. The remedies listed in section 2-703 are open to a seller whose buyer has done one or more of four things: (1) wrongfully rejected the goods; (2) wrongfully revoked its acceptance of the goods; (3) failed to make a payment that was due on or before delivery of the goods;

---

[265] U.C.C. § 2-711 is considered in § 7.04[A], *supra.*

and (4) repudiated with respect to a part or the whole of the contract involved. Questions raised by three of these triggering events (wrongful rejection, wrongful revocation, and repudiation) have already been considered.[266] The distinction between ineffective rejections and revocations (rejections and revocations that are too long delayed or inadequately noticed and consequently do not succeed in thrusting the goods back on the seller), and rejections and revocations that are effective but wrongful (because the goods and their tender conform to the contract), is discussed in § 7.03[C].[267] Section 2-703 is triggered by rejections and revocations that are effective but wrongful.

Article 2 does not define "repudiation." Rather, as has been discussed,[268] one must look to the common law of contracts[269] for a definition. In the section 2-703 context, "repudiation" would seem to mean a statement or voluntary action by the buyer indicating that the buyer will not or cannot accept the goods or pay the price as required by the contract. Additionally, it would seem that section 2-703 is referring to anticipatory repudiations— that is, to repudiations that occur before the buyer has taken the goods.[270] As has been noted,[271] it can be difficult to determine whether a repudiation has occurred. In doubtful circumstances, a seller can use its section 2-609 right to adequate assurance of performance to clarify the situation.[272]

Section 2-703 thus indexes the seller's remedies for situations in which the aggrieved seller, and not the defaulting buyer, ends up with the goods. In some section 2-703 situations, the seller has delivered or tendered delivery, and the buyer has effectively, but wrongfully, thrust the goods back on the seller. In other section 2-703 situations, the buyer has failed to make a required payment or repudiated before the seller had completed delivery, thus entitling the seller to retain the goods. Not surprisingly, the various

---

[266] See §§ 7.03[C], 7.03[E], and 7.04[D], supra.

[267] Integrated Circuits Unlimited, Inc. v. E. F. Johnson Co., 691 F. Supp. 630, 7 UCCR2d 1478 (E.D.N.Y. 1988), contains a good discussion of the distinction between ineffective and wrongful rejections and of the remedial consequences of the distinction.

[268] Section 7.04[D], supra.

[269] The common-law idea of repudiation is epitomized in section 250 of the Restatement (Second) of Contracts, which is quoted in § 7.04[D], n.151, supra.

[270] This is strongly suggested by the remedies listed in U.C.C. § 2-703. All of them can be relevant to a repudiation made by a buyer before it has taken the goods. Only one of the listed remedies—the action for the price—has relevance to a repudiation made by a buyer after it has taken the goods and failed to make an effective rejection or revocation.

[271] See § 7.04[D], supra.

[272] Id.

money-damage remedies that are indexed in section 2-703 all take the value of the goods remaining in the aggrieved seller's hands into account.[273]

Remedies. The remedies that section 2-703 indexes deal with four subjects. The first two remedies listed, labelled (a) and (b) in the statute and covering withholding delivery of the goods and stopping delivery by a carrier or other bailee as provided in section 2-705, deal with the seller's right to maintain *control over the goods.* The third (labelled (c)) deals with *goods that were not identified to the contract at the time of the buyer's default* and, through section 2-704, provides the seller certain options with respect to such goods, so that the seller can proceed to one of the money-damage remedies that follow. The next two, labeled (d) and (e), provide *money-damage remedies*—four of them. The last, labeled (f), deals with *cancellation* of the contract.[274]

The four money-damage remedies indexed are provided for in sections 2-706, 2-708(1), 2-708(2), and 2-709. A seller described in section 2-703 can resell the goods in a way that complies with section 2-706 and recover the difference between the contract price and the resale price. Alternatively, the seller may recover the difference between the contract price and the market price under section 2-708(1). If the section 2-708(1) measure is inadequate to protect the seller's expectation interest, the seller may recover its lost profit under section 2-708(2). And, "in a proper case," the seller can recover the price under 2-709.

Comment 1 to section 2-703 notes that the Code rejects the doctrine of election of remedies and observes that the section 2-703 remedies are "essentially cumulative in nature." It adds that "[w]hether the pursuit of one remedy bars another depends entirely on the facts of the individual case." Frequently, the recovery of money damages under one of the section 2-703 money-damage provisions will bar the recovery of money damages under another. A seller, for example, cannot recover both contract-minus-resale damages under section 2-706 and lost-profit damages under section 2-708(2), or both contract-minus-market damages under section 2-708(1) and the price under section 2-709.

Section 2-703 does not index all of the Code sections that provide remedies to aggrieved sellers. A number of unmentioned (in section 2-703)

---

[273] As is pointed out at the end of this section, a careful reading of U.C.C. § 2-703 suggests that it indexes and leads to an action for the price only in the situation (covered by section 2-709(1)(b)) where the goods remain in the seller's hands but are unsaleable at a reasonable price. Section 2-703 does not apply to the situation (covered by section 2-709(1)(a)) where the buyer has received and retained the goods but has not paid for them.

[274] "Cancellation" is defined in U.C.C. § 2-106(4). *See also* U.C.C. § 2-720.

sections are relevant to a seller's control over the goods, and are considered subsequently. Further, if section 2-703 is read carefully, it leads to section 2-709 and an action for the price only in limited circumstances. As has been pointed out, the triggering events that make section 2-703 available describe situations in which the aggrieved seller ends up with the goods. A seller who has retained the goods can occasionally, but only occasionally, recover their price. Under section 2-709(1)(b), a retaining seller can recover the price of goods that cannot, with reasonable effort, be sold at a reasonable price.[275] In such circumstances, payment of the judgment for the price entitles the buyer to the goods. This kind of situation—goods in the aggrieved seller's hands and unsalable at a reasonable price—is the "proper case" for an action for the price referred to in section 2-703(e). The much more common action-for-the-price situation—where the buyer has the goods and has not paid the price when it became due (section 2-709(1)(a))—is not indexed in section 2-703. In it, the more common situation, where the seller has delivered the goods and not been paid, the seller proceeds directly through section 2-709(1)(a), receiving neither help nor hinderance from section 2-703.

§ 7.07 THE SELLER'S CONTROL OF THE GOODS

[A] Withholding Delivery

If the buyer commits one of section 2-703's four triggering events (wrongfully rejects or revokes acceptance, fails to make a payment due on or before delivery, or repudiates), the seller may withhold delivery of the goods, and its refusal to deliver does not constitute a default. The following factual patterns illustrate and explore this proposition.

Case 1. Suppose that on August 1, Seller agreed in writing to sell a computer to Buyer for $2,500. The terms of the writing (which was signed by both parties) called for payment of the price in cash and delivery of the computer on August 15. On August 16, Buyer demanded the computer even

---

[275] In Lipsey Motors v. Karp Motors, Inc., 194 Ga. App. 15, 389 S.E.2d 537, 11 UCCR2d 799 (1989), the court read U.C.C. § 2-703 to allow an action for the price because the goods had been wrongfully rejected even though the rejection effectively thrust the goods back on the seller and even though the goods (automobiles) appeared to be resalable at reasonable prices. We disagree. We believe that the section 2-703(e) words "in a proper case" mean a case in which an action for the price is provided for in section 2-709. Section 2-709 allows an action for the price of goods that have been effectively thrust back on the seller only under the circumstances described in section 2-709(1)(b), where the goods cannot, with reasonable effort, be resold at a reasonable price.

though it had paid no part of the price. Is Seller in default because it did not deliver the computer on August 15?

Common sense suggests a "No" answer, and our law agrees. Section 2-703 provides that "[w]here the buyer . . . fails to make a payment due on or before delivery . . . then with respect to any goods directly affected . . . the aggrieved seller may (a) withhold delivery of such goods." Because Buyer has not made a payment due on or before delivery, Seller's retention of the goods was rightful. Section 2-511(1) provides the same answer; because it was not otherwise agreed, Buyer's tender of payment was a condition precedent to Seller's duty to tender delivery; because Buyer tendered no payment, Seller's obligation to tender delivery was not triggered. This has been our law since 1773, when Lord Mansfield decided *Kingston v. Preston.*[276] When a contract of sale contains no credit term, modern law—first the common law, now the Code—presumes a barrelhead exchange. The seller may withhold delivery until the buyer tenders the price, and, conversely, the buyer may withhold payment until the seller tenders delivery.[277] If, however, the parties have agreed to credit, the situation changes. Consider:

Case 2. Assume the facts of Case 1 except assume that the contract required delivery by Seller on or before August 15 and allowed Buyer thirty days after delivery to pay the price. Is Seller in default for his failure to deliver the computer on August 15?

Section 2-703 does not allow Seller to withhold delivery because none of its triggering events has occurred. Nor does section 2-511(1) allow Seller to withhold delivery; by providing that Buyer was to have a thirty-day credit period, the Case 2 parties have "otherwise agreed"—that is, they have agreed out of the section 2-511(1) provision that Seller's duty to deliver is conditioned on Buyer's tender of payment. Therefore, on the facts of Case 2, Seller is in default for failing to deliver.

There is, of course, usually a reason why a seller who has promised to deliver goods on credit refuses to do so. Some reasons, such as spite or the fact that the seller has misjudged the market and agreed to too low a contract price, do nothing to excuse the seller's nondelivery, leaving the seller in breach and opening buyer's remedies against the seller.[278] If, on the other hand, the buyer has repudiated, section 2-703 expressly authorizes the seller to withhold delivery. Furthermore, if the seller refuses delivery because the goods have been destroyed before the risk of their loss has passed to the

---

[276] 2 Doug. 679, 99 Eng. Rep. 437 (K.B. 1773).

[277] U.C.C. § 2-511(1) and 2-507(1).

[278] U.C.C. § 2-711.

buyer or because of a transportation strike, the refusal may be wholly or partially excused. When and to what extent an excuse for a reason of this sort is recognized has already been discussed,[279] and that discussion is not repeated here. Suffice it to say that to the extent the seller's nondelivery is excused, it does not constitute a default.

Another reason why a seller that has promised to sell on credit might want to withhold delivery is that it has come to doubt its buyer's ability to pay. Consider:

Case 3. On August 1, Buyer and Seller entered into a written agreement for the purchase and sale of a computer for $2,500, delivery to be made on August 15 with payment due thirty days after delivery. On August 10, Seller discovered that Buyer was insolvent. May Seller rightfully withhold delivery of the computer on August 15?

The risk that an insolvent buyer will not pay and will prove uncollectible is obviously greater than the like risk with a solvent buyer. Consequently, requiring delivery from a seller that agreed to sell on credit believing that its buyer was solvent but that has since learned that its buyer is insolvent amounts to requiring the seller to run a greater risk than it planned to assume. This circumstance argues for allowing the seller to withhold delivery—so that it may avoid trading its goods for an uncollectible judgment or a claim in bankruptcy. On the other hand, the seller has agreed to run a credit risk, the buyer has not yet defaulted, and the contract may be important to the buyer. The Code, like the prior law, attempts to deal with this situation in a way that accommodates the interests of both parties. In section 2-702(1), it declines to give the seller a complete authorization to withhold delivery, but does authorize a conversion of the credit term to a cash-on-delivery term:

> Where the seller discovers the buyer to be insolvent he may refuse delivery except for cash including payment for all goods theretofore delivered under the contract, and stop delivery under this Article (Section 2-705).

Thus, while Seller in Case 3 may not completely refuse delivery, it may refuse delivery unless Buyer pays cash.[280] If Buyer pays cash, Buyer is entitled to the computer. If Buyer does not pay cash, Buyer will (because Seller has rightfully used section 2-702(1) to convert the contract's payment term from credit to cash on delivery) be in default under section 2-703's

---

[279] Section 5.04, *supra.*

[280] *See* In re National Sugar Refining Co., 27 B.R. 565, 35 UCCR 821 (S.D.N.Y. 1983).

"fails to make a payment due on or before delivery" language. Consequently, Seller may, in addition to retaining the goods, select an appropriate monetary remedy (with the obvious risk that the damages will prove to be uncollectible).

Section 2-702(1) authorizes a seller that has discovered that the buyer is insolvent to refuse delivery "except for cash including payment for all goods theretofore delivered under the contract." Thus, if an installment contract is involved and the seller has delivered several items on credit before discovering the buyer's insolvency, the seller may withhold delivery of the remaining item or items unless the buyer pays cash not only for them but also for the items already received. This right is limited to goods delivered under *the* contract; a refusal to deliver goods unless the buyer pays for goods delivered under other contracts between the parties is not authorized by section 2-702(1).[281]

There are two "time" problems with section 2-702(1). First, it does not state *when* the seller must have discovered the insolvency. Consider a seller that discovered that the buyer was insolvent before contract formation but nevertheless agreed to sell on credit. Should section 2-702(1) be read as allowing such a seller to change its mind about credit and refuse delivery except for cash? The answer ought to be "No"; such a seller, having knowingly accepted the risks of extending credit to an insolvent, should be obligated to deliver on credit.[282]

A second section 2-702(1) time difficulty lies in determining *when* the buyer is obligated to pay the price in cash. Suppose that between contract formation and the agreed-on delivery date, a seller discovers that the buyer

---

[281] This requires distinguishing multiple-delivery or installment contracts from separate contracts. U.C.C. § 2-612(1)'s provision that contracts that require or authorize delivery in separate lots are installment contracts even though they contain clauses saying that each delivery is a separate contract is relevant in this connection, and will cause many agreements to produce installment contracts rather than separate contracts. Agreements reached at different times (Agreement 1 in February, Agreement 2 in April, for example) will generally produce separate contracts, but it will sometimes be appropriate to treat a later agreement as a modification of an earlier one, leading to a single contract. For a case finding an installment contract rather than a number of separate contracts, *see* Cassidy Podell Lynch, Inc. v. Snydergeneral Corp., 944 F.2d 1131, 15 UCCR2d 1225 (3d Cir. 1991).

[282] In some circumstances, as when the seller's credit risks have significantly increased because the buyer's financial situation has deteriorated between contract formation and the date delivery is due—that is, when the buyer has sunk deeper into insolvency during this period—the seller may need some relief, and U.C.C. § 2-609 may provide it. The buyer's financial deterioration may give the seller reasonable grounds for insecurity and enable it to suspend its performance—that is, refuse delivery—until it receives adequate assurance of performance, which adequate assurance might be payment in cash.

is insolvent. May it demand that the buyer pay in cash on the scheduled delivery date and cancel the contract if the buyer does not do so?[283] The usual answer ought to be "No." Under the terms of the contract, the buyer had until the end of the credit period to acquire the cash to pay the price. In most circumstances, the delivery before payment was for the buyer's benefit. While it makes sense to enable the seller to refuse delivery except for cash, there is no need to require that the cash be paid before it was promised. Indeed, doing so would seem not only unnecessary, but also unfair to the buyer. While this—enabling the buyer to postpone the delivery date until the end of the credit period—should be the usual answer, there are circumstances under which the nature of the goods (if, for example, they are perishable and subject to rapid deterioration) or of the transaction re-quires an early delivery. The Code's good-faith[284] and reasonable-time[285] gap-filling provisions should provide the needed flexibility.

Section 2-702(1) allows a seller that has agreed to sell on credit to withhold delivery only when it discovers that the buyer is *insolvent.* Insol-vency is defined in section 1-201(23):

> A person is "insolvent" who either has ceased to pay his debts in the ordinary course of business or cannot pay his debts as they become due or is insolvent within the meaning of the federal bankruptcy law.

The Bankruptcy Code defines insolvency in balance-sheet terms as a finan-cial condition in which the sum of a debtor's debts is greater than the fair value of its assets.[286] Thus the Code's definition of insolvency is broad; it treats as insolvent both people with negative net worths (regardless of whether they are paying their debts in the ordinary course) and people with positive net worths who are not paying their debts.[287] Despite the definition's breadth, however, there are many circumstances in which a seller will want to use section 2-702(1) but is uncertain that it can prove that the buyer is insolvent. Consider:

---

[283] U.C.C. § 2-703 allows a seller to cancel when, *inter alia*, the buyer fails to make a payment due on delivery.

[284] U.C.C. §§ 1-203, 2-103(1)(b).

[285] U.C.C. §§ 2-309(1), 1-204(2).

[286] Section 101(32) of the Bankruptcy Code (11 U.S.C. § 101(32) (1994)).

[287] It can be argued that, for U.C.C. § 2-702(1) purposes, the Code definition of insolvency is too broad—that the inclusion of the bankruptcy balance-sheet definition can enable sellers to refuse delivery except for cash in circumstances where they neither need nor deserve that right—where, for example, the buyer, although having a negative net worth, has a strong payment record and cash flow.

Case 4. On August 1, Buyer and Seller entered into a written agreement for the purchase and sale of a computer for $2,500, delivery to be made on August 15, with payment due thirty days after delivery. On August 10, Seller heard rumors that Buyer was not paying its debts as they matured. Is Seller obligated to deliver the computer on August 15?

If the rumors accurately reflect Buyer's financial condition, Seller may refuse to deliver except for cash; if the rumors are inaccurate, and Buyer is in fact solvent, Seller's refusal to honor the agreed-on credit term on the basis of section 2-702(1) would be unjustified and would place Seller in breach.[288] In doubtful circumstances like these, Seller may be well advised to make use of section 2-609. Seller could claim that the rumors gave it "reasonable grounds for insecurity." Whether such grounds existed would be a question of fact, and Seller would need to be able to establish that they did. This would, however, be a lighter burden for Seller to carry than would the proof of insolvency. Assuming that the rumors did give Seller reasonable grounds for insecurity, Seller could in writing demand "adequate assurance of due performance," and, "if commercially reasonable," suspend delivery until it received adequate assurance. There might, of course, be factual questions about what on Buyer's part constituted adequate assurance of performance. Nevertheless, and despite the multiple and sometimes difficult factual questions that it raises, section 2-609 often proves helpful to a credit seller that is concerned about its buyer's ability to pay but is uncertain that it can prove insolvency.

[B]   Stopping Delivery

On some occasions, a seller does not learn of the buyer's insolvency or pre-delivery default until after placing the goods in the possession of a carrier or other bailee. Such a seller may want to stop the carrier or other bailee from turning the goods over to the buyer. This problem is covered in section 2-705. The three subsections of this section deal with (1) the scope of the seller's right to stop delivery; (2) the termination of this right; and (3) the rights and duties of the carrier or other bailee upon receiving the stop order.

Scope of the right. The seller may stop any delivery when it discovers the buyer to be insolvent.[289] The seller may stop delivery of carload, truck-

---

[288] U.C.C. § 2-711.

[289] The parenthetical reference to U.C.C. § 2-702 suggests that the seller has a right to stop delivery because of the buyer's insolvency only in cases where withholding delivery except for cash would be justified under section 2-702(1). Thus, a seller that has received full payment for the goods in question and for all other goods previously delivered under the same contract should not be able to stop delivery because the buyer is insolvent.

load, planeload or larger shipments "when the buyer repudiates or fails to make a payment due before delivery or if for any other reason the seller has a right to withhold or reclaim the goods."[290] The Code does not detail the other reasons that could give the seller a right to withhold the goods. One such reason may arise under section 2-609, which (among other things) allows a seller with reasonable grounds for insecurity to suspend a perform-ance such as a delivery (if doing so is commercially reasonable) until it receives adequate assurance of due performance by the buyer.[291] Section 2-705 makes a number of attempts to accommodate the interests of the three parties (seller, buyer, and carrier or other bailee[292]) involved in a stoppage situation. One of these attempts can be seen in subsection (1)'s limitation of the right to stop delivery in noninsolvency situations to large shipments—this with a view toward lessening the burdens that stoppage places on car-riers.[293]

Termination of seller's right. The seller's right to stop delivery contin-ues until (1) the buyer receives the goods; (2) a bailee other than a carrier acknowledges to the buyer that it is holding the goods for the buyer; (3) a carrier makes such acknowledgment to the buyer by reshipment or as a warehouseman; or (4) a negotiable document of title covering the goods is negotiated to the buyer.[294] Although section 2-705(2) addresses the seller's rights as against the buyer, part of it—specifically, the last three events that terminate the seller's right to stop delivery—seems to rest, at least in part, on the protection of the carrier or other bailee. If the seller could regain possession of the goods after the carrier or other bailee had indicated to the buyer that it was holding the goods for the buyer, or after the buyer became the holder of a negotiable document covering the goods, the carrier or other bailee might be liable to the buyer.[295]

The reason that receipt of the goods by the buyer terminates the seller's right to stop delivery is obvious; as its caption indicates, section 2-705 deals with stopping delivery while the goods are "in transit" or otherwise in the

---

[290] U.C.C. § 2-705(1). For a provision on the possible succession of a financing agency to the seller's right to stop delivery, see U.C.C. § 2-506(1).

[291] *See* U.C.C. § 2-705, Comment 1.

[292] For a case dealing with the scope of the "other bailee" statutory language, *see* Donegal Steel Foundry, Inc. v. Accurate Prods. Co., 516 F.2d 583, 16 UCCR 1270 (3d Cir. 1975).

[293] U.C.C. § 2-705, Comment 1. The proposed revisions to Article 2, in its section 2-818(b), eliminates the large-shipment limitation, the drafters considering it "out of date in light of changing shipping methods and practices which now allow individual tracking of goods in shipment." Comment 3 to Council Draft section 2-818.

[294] U.C.C. § 2-705(2).

[295] *See* U.C.C. §§ 7-301, 7-403, 7-502, 7-504.

possession of a bailee; once the buyer has received the goods, delivery has been made, and there is nothing left to "stop."[296] The Code defines receipt of goods as "taking physical possession of them."[297] The precise moment when this has occurred is difficult to determine in some situations, especially with bulky goods. The courts must do their best to determine whether the buyer has "possession"; they are helped by the Code's emphasis on *physical* possession. Telephone calls or letters to the buyer stating that the goods are available at the freight yard or airport do not amount to receipt by the buyer.[298]

Sellers that would have had rights to stop delivery against their buyers had the buyers not filed petitions in bankruptcy have succeeded in stopping delivery against the bankruptcy estates of the buyers. Courts have found support for this result in section 546(c) of the Bankruptcy Code.[299]

Rights and duties of the carrier or other bailee. The basic rights and duties of the bailee are set out in parts (a) and (b) of subsection 2-705(3):

(a) To stop delivery the seller must so notify as to enable the bailee by reasonable diligence to prevent delivery of the goods.

(b) After such notification the bailee must hold and deliver the goods according to the directions of the seller but the seller is liable to the bailee for any ensuing charges or damages.

Parts (c) and (d) of section 2-705(3) consider the rights and duties of a bailee that has issued a document of title for the goods. If the document is negotiable, the bailee is not required to obey a stop order until surrender of the document.[300] If the issuing bailee is a carrier and the document is a nonnegotiable bill of lading, the carrier is not required to obey a stop order given by anyone other than the consignor.[301] Thus, a carrier is under no duty to recognize a stop order from a person who is a stranger to the carrier's contract.[302] A seller who is a stranger to the carrier's contract may never-

---

[296] Stumbo v. Paul B. Hult Lumber Co., 251 Or. 20, 444 P.2d 564, 5 UCCR 753 (1968).

[297] U.C.C. § 2-103(1)(c).

[298] *See* Ceres, Inc. v. Alci Metal & Ore Co., 451 F. Supp. 921, 24 UCCR 140 (N.D. Ill. 1978); In re Marin Motor Oil, Inc., 740 F.2d 220, 38 UCCR 1425 (3d Cir. 1984); In re Brio Petroleum, Inc., 800 F.2d 469, 2 UCCR2d 159 (5th Cir. 1986); In re Morrison Indus., L.P., 175 B.R. 5, 25 UCCR2d 737 (Bankr. W.D.N.Y. 1994).

[299] 11 U.S.C. § 546(c) (1994). *See* In re National Sugar Refining Co., 27 B.R. 565, 35 UCCR 821 (Bankr. S.D.N.Y. 1983); In re Morrison Indus., L.P., 175 B.R. 5, 25 UCCR2d 737 (Bankr. W.D.N.Y. 1994).

[300] U.C.C. § 2-705(3)(c).

[301] U.C.C. § 2-705(3)(d). *See* U.C.C. § 7-102(1)(c) for a definition of "consignor."

[302] U.C.C. § 2-705, Comment 2.

theless have, as against the buyer, a right (under section 2-705(1) and 2-705(2)) to stop delivery. Suppose that in these circumstances the carrier honors the seller's stop order even though it is not obligated to do so. As Comment 2 says, the fact that the carrier was not obligated to stop should not give the buyer cause to complain about what was, as between seller and buyer, a rightful stoppage. Furthermore, a carrier that honors a seller's stop order is entitled to indemnification from the seller for any ensuing charges or damages.[303]

Section 2-707(2) provides, *inter alia*, that a "person in the position of a seller" (defined in 2-707(1)) "may as provided in this Article withhold or stop delivery (Section 2-705)." In applying this section, weight should be given to the statutory words "as provided in this Article" and to the parenthetical reference to section 2-705. A person in the position of a seller should be able to stop delivery in the circumstances in which section 2-705 would enable a seller to stop delivery, and not otherwise.

[C] Reclamation of the Goods

Whatever opportunities a seller may have had to withhold or stop delivery evaporate on the buyer's receipt of the goods. If the buyer's receipt is accompanied or followed by acceptance, the buyer becomes obligated to pay the contract price of the goods[304]—that is, the buyer becomes obligated to pay that part of the price that has not already been paid as it becomes due. In these circumstances, the seller's standard remedy is a section 2-709(1)(a) action for the price. If the buyer is collectible, this will normally serve the seller well. But if the buyer is uncollectible or of doubtful collectibility, the seller may want to reclaim the goods that it has delivered.

The Code allows reclamation in limited circumstances. Sections 2-507(2) and 2-511 provide for it in certain cash-sale situations, and section 2-702(2) provides for it in certain credit-sale situations. These provisions are explored in §§ 7.07[D] and 7.07[E]. The point that bears present emphasis is that they deal with exceptional circumstances; the action for the price (and not reclamation of the goods) is the standard remedy that the Code affords an unpaid seller whose buyer has the goods.[305]

---

[303] U.C.C. §§ 2-705(3)(b) and 7-504(4); Comments 1 and 2 to U.C.C. § 2-705.

[304] U.C.C. § 2-607(1).

[305] A weak statutory argument for a general right of reclamation can be based on U.C.C. § 2-703. This would involve a torturing of the statutory words "repudiates" and "cancel." It would treat a buyer's failure to make a payment due after delivery as a repudiation, and thus an event that triggered section 2-703. And it would treat a "cancellation" (U.C.C. § 2-106(4)) as entitling the seller to goods delivered under the contract. This argument should be rejected.

There are both historical and policy reasons why reclamation is not an as-of-right or matter-of-course remedy for an unpaid seller. The major policy concern is that a seller seeking reclamation is almost always competing not only with the buyer but also with a third party, such as a purchaser from, or creditor of, the buyer. To allow reclamation is to allow the seller to achieve an advantage or priority over the affected third party or parties. Consequently, reclamation should be allowed only in circumstances where there is good reason for it—that is, when the seller's equities are particularly strong. Further, a right of reclamation works in many ways like an Article 9 security interest. To afford it generally to unpaid sellers would be to grant them unbargained-for and undeserved security interests; security interests that were not publicly noticed and thus secret from many competitors.

While reclamation inflicts much of its bite on third parties, we begin with a consideration of its availability against the buyer. This for the reason that the right of reclamation arises (or does not arise) because of the situation between buyer and seller. If no right arises against the buyer, there will be no right that can be asserted against third parties.[306]

[D] Reclamation From the Buyer—Cash Sales

One reason why an unpaid seller is not generally allowed to reclaim the goods is because its position is not distinguishable from that of the buyer's other creditors. The buyer is indebted to many creditors, including this seller, and this seller ought not obtain a greater share of the buyer's assets simply because it can trace the goods that it sold to the buyer. If, however, the seller did not rely on the buyer's unsecured credit, the seller can be distinguished from the other creditors and may be able to reclaim the goods.

There are several situations in which an unpaid seller's position is different from that of the buyer's other unsecured creditors. It is obviously different when the seller has obtained and perfected an Article 9 security interest in the sold goods. A second situation in which it is different arises when the buyer has defrauded the seller into selling on credit—when, for example, the buyer misrepresents its identity or solvency. A third situation arises when a seller delivers goods on the strength of what it believed to be a cash payment—only to discover that the required payment was not in fact made. It is to this third situation that we now turn.

---

[306] The converse of this statement is not true; as will be seen, the fact that a seller has a right of reclamation against the buyer does not necessarily mean that the right can be asserted against a third party.

A buyer may acquire a seller's goods in exchange for counterfeit money or in exchange for goods to which the buyer had no title. More commonly, however, the cash-sale-gone-sour situation arises when the buyer pays by check and the check is dishonored (the usual reason being that the buyer had insufficient funds on deposit to cover it). The hypothetical sellers have trusted their buyers' credit in only a limited sense: they believed that their buyers would deliver genuine money, goods to which they had title, or checks that would be paid on presentment. This trust in a buyer's integrity, though a kind of "credit," is different from the type of credit extended by the buyer's other unsecured creditors that trusted the buyer's promise to pay in the future.

The Code recognizes the difference between cash and credit sales by providing in section 2-507(2):

> Where payment is due and demanded on the delivery to the buyer of goods or documents of title, his right as against the seller to retain or dispose of them is conditional on his making the payment due.

Thus, a cash buyer that does not pay has no right to retain the goods.[307] And section 2-511(3) provides that "payment by check is conditional and is defeated as between the parties by dishonor of the check on due presentment." Accordingly, a seller that delivers goods against a check which bounces has a right to reclaim the goods from the buyer.[308] This will not be the seller's only right. Alternatively, it could sue the buyer for the price (section 2-709(1)(a)), or, since it is the holder of a dishonored check, for the amount of the check.[309] In short, the cash seller that took a bad check can seek either the price or the goods.

Section 2-507(2) gives the seller the right to reclaim the goods only "[w]here payment is due and demanded on delivery." Payment must be both due and demanded. If payment is not due on delivery (because the contract contains a valid credit term), the seller has no right to demand payment then. A seller that demands payment against delivery when it is not due makes a nonconforming tender and commits a breach.[310] If payment is due but not demanded—that is, if a seller that was entitled to cash on delivery delivers the goods without demanding or receiving the cash, the cash aspect of the transaction has been waived and a credit sale substituted.[311]

---

[307] *See* Burk v. Emmrick, 637 F.2d 1172, 29 UCCR 1489 (8th Cir. 1980).

[308] *See* Szabo v. Vinton Motors, Inc. 630 F.2d 1, 29 UCCR 737 (1st Cir. 1980).

[309] U.C.C. §§ 3-414, 3-301.

[310] U.C.C. §§ 2-301, 2-711.

[311] In re Morken, 182 B.R. 1007, 28 UCCR2d 855 (Bankr. D. Minn. 1995); In re Julien Co., 44 F.3d 426, 26 UCCR2d 117 (6th Cir. 1995).

The original version of Comment 3 to section 2-507 asserted that "The provision of this Article for a ten day limit within which the seller may reclaim goods delivered on credit to an insolvent buyer is also applicable here." The reference was to section 2-702(2), which provides that "[w]here the seller discovers that the buyer has received goods on credit while insolvent he may reclaim the goods upon demand made within ten days after the receipt." Although there was no statutory basis for transporting the ten-day provision from section 2-702(2) (which deals with credit sales to an insolvent) to section 2-507(2) (which deals with cash sales), most courts followed the Comment and barred cash sellers whose payment checks were dishonored from reclamation unless reclamation was demanded within ten days after the buyer's receipt of the goods.[312] In *Burk v. Emmick*,[313] the Eighth Circuit disagreed and held that a reasonableness standard governed. In 1990, in its Commentary No. 1, the Permanent Editorial Board for the Uniform Commercial Code agreed with *Burk* and amended Comment 3 by deleting the reference to section 2-702(2)'s ten-day provision and adding, *inter alia*, the following language:

> There is no specific time limit for a cash seller to exercise its right of reclamation. However, the right will be defeated by delay causing prejudice to the buyer, waiver, estoppel, or ratification of the buyer's right to retain possession. Common law rules and precedents governing such principles are applicable (Section 1-103).

The approach taken in the revised Comment is sounder than the original approach, both because it better conforms to the language of the statute and because an absolute ten-day period was unfair to the cash seller, which typically does not learn of its right or need to reclaim the goods until the buyer's payment check has been returned to it dishonored.

[E] Reclamation From the Buyer—Credit Sales

The standard remedy for a seller that delivers goods on open or unsecured credit is an action for the price.[314] There is no general right to reclaim the goods on the buyer's nonpayment. A seller that wants to be able to reclaim whenever its credit buyer does not pay should obtain an Article 9 security interest in the goods. Although Article 2 provides no general right of reclamation to unsecured credit sellers, however, it does allow them to

---

[312] *See, e.g.,* Szabo v. Vinton Motors, Inc., 630 F.2d 1, 29 UCCR 737 (1st Cir. 1980).
[313] 637 F.2d 1172, 29 UCCR 1489 (8th Cir. 1980).
[314] U.C.C. § 2-709(1)(a).

reclaim in certain limited circumstances. These circumstances are set forth in section 2-702(2):

> Where the seller discovers that the buyer has received goods on credit while insolvent he may reclaim the goods upon demand made within ten days after the receipt, but if misrepresentation of solvency has been made to the particular seller in writing within three months before delivery the ten day limitation does not apply. Except as provided in this subsection the seller may not base a right to reclaim goods on the buyer's fraudulent or innocent misrepresentation of solvency or of intent to pay.

The subsection's second sentence suggests the thought that underlies it, and Comment 2 to section 2-702 articulates that thought: "Subsection (2) takes as its base line the proposition that any receipt of goods by an insolvent buyer amounts to a tacit business misrepresentation of solvency."

Section 2-702(2) is conditioned on the buyer's insolvency; it allows reclamation only when "the buyer has received goods on credit while insolvent." The Code's definition of insolvency and the difficulties that may be encountered in establishing that insolvency exists have been discussed in § 7.07[A],[315] and that discussion is not repeated here. Section 2-702(2) is also conditioned on the seller's demanding reclamation within ten days after the buyer's receipt of the goods, save in situations where there has been a written misrepresentation of solvency within the three months before delivery.

The ten-day provision significantly limits the circumstances in which reclamation is available. In many situations, the event that triggers the seller's investigation and discovery that the buyer is insolvent will be the buyer's nonpayment. When this is so and when the agreed credit period is thirty days or some other period longer than ten days, as it often is, the seller does not learn of the buyer's insolvency and of the need to reclaim until after the running of the ten-day period will have barred reclamation. There will, of course, be earlier discoveries of buyer insolvency—discoveries that enable sellers to make timely demands and thus obtain rights to reclaim. And there will be situations in which it will be important to identify, with precision, the day on which the ten-day period runs. The statutory words that describe it are "within ten days after the receipt." If they are applied literally and carefully, as they should be, the ten-day period begins on the day *after receipt*—that is, on the day after the buyer receives

---

[315] *See also* the discussion of UCC § 2-502 in § 7.05[C], *supra*.

or takes physical possession of,[316] the goods (not on the day after the goods are shipped),[317] and ends *within* ten days thereafter—that is, at the end of the tenth day after receipt. For example, if the buyer received the goods on October 1, the period should begin to run on October 2 and end at the end of the day on October 11. This method of calculating the ten-day period may be modified if the state involved has a day-counting statutory provision that provides otherwise—for example, one that calls for excluding the last day from the count if it falls on a Sunday or legal holiday.

A seller that fails to make a demand for reclamation within the ten-day period may nevertheless reclaim if the buyer (1) received the goods on credit while insolvent and (2) made a written misrepresentation of solvency to the particular seller within three months before delivery of the goods. Comment 2 to section 2-702 elaborates and, in doing so, goes beyond the statutory language in imposing restrictions on reclamation: "To fall within the exception [to the ten-day period] the statement of solvency must be in writing, *addressed* to the particular seller, and *dated* within three months of the delivery." [Emphasis added.] The "addressed" and "dated" requirements cannot be found in the language of the statute. The Ninth Circuit has refused to follow the "dated" Comment requirement, adhering to the language of the statute instead.[318]

The upshot is that a seller that has delivered goods to an insolvent buyer may reclaim the goods from the buyer if the seller makes a demand for reclamation within ten days after the buyer received the goods, or, in circumstances in which the buyer has made a written misrepresentation of solvency to the seller within three months before the delivery, if it demands reclamation within a reasonable time. When a seller seeks reclamation, however, its right against the buyer is typically only the starting point. The more serious contest is usually between the seller and a third party, such as a lien creditor of the buyer, the buyer's trustee in bankruptcy, or a purchaser from the buyer. It is to this seller-third party contest that we now turn.

---

[316] U.C.C. § 2-103(1)(c).

[317] In re Maloney Enters., Inc., 37 B.R. 290, 38 UCCR 498 (Bankr. E.D. Ky. 1983).

[318] In re Bel Air Carpets, Inc., 452 F.2d 1210, 9 UCCR 1313 (9th Cir. 1971) holds that the written misrepresentation of solvency need not be "dated" within three months before delivery; even though dated earlier, a financial statement delivered to the seller within three months before delivery and (falsely) represented to be accurate when delivered, enables the seller to escape section 2-702(2)'s ten-day limitation on reclamation.

[F] Reclamation From Lien Creditors of the Buyer and From the Buyer's Trustee in Bankruptcy

The reclamation-from-a-lien-creditor situation can be easily illustrated. Suppose that Seller *A* sold a computer to Buyer in exchange for Buyer's check and that the check was dishonored on presentment, and that Seller *B* sold a copier to Buyer on credit and five days thereafter discovered that Buyer had been insolvent when it received the copier. Both sellers made immediate demands for reclamation. Under these circumstances, Seller *A* has a section 2-507(2) right to reclaim the computer from Buyer, and Seller *B* has a section 2-702(2) right to reclaim the copier from Buyer. Suppose, however, that when they sought to reclaim, both sellers were opposed not by Buyer, but by Judgment Creditor, which had an unsatisfied judgment against Buyer and which had levied on the computer and copier three days after they were delivered to Buyer. Can the sellers successfully reclaim from their buyer's lien creditor?[319]

The Code does not expressly answer this question, either for cash sellers or credit sellers. Its express provisions deal with the clash between reclaiming sellers and *purchasers* from the buyer. Subsection 2-702(3) subjects a credit seller's section 2-702(2) right to reclaim to the section 2-403 rights of purchasers. And section 2-403(1)(b) and 2-403(1)(c) refer to the rights of purchasers against cash sellers. But lien creditors are not purchasers,[320] and there is no clear Code provision that deals with their rights against reclaiming sellers.[321] In the face of this Code silence, most of the few courts that have addressed the question have resorted to pre-Code law. In a number of states, this favored the reclaiming seller over a lien creditor, and the courts consequently used it to allow reclamation.[322] Where, however, pre-Code law

---

[319] Judgment Creditor qualifies as a lien creditor as defined in U.C.C. § 9-301(3):

A "lien creditor" means a creditor who has acquired a lien on the property involved by attachment, levy, or the like.

[320] "Purchaser" is defined in U.C.C. §§ 1-201(32) and 1-201(33) as someone who takes in a "voluntary transaction creating an interest in property." Lien creditors do not qualify because they obtain their property interests by seizure or the like—that is, in transactions that are anything but voluntary on the part of the debtors whose property is being taken.

[321] There is a reference to lien creditors in U.C.C. § 2-403(4), and there was another reference to them in the pre-1966 official text of U.C.C. § 2-702(3), but neither provision resolved or directly addressed the question of priority between a reclaiming seller and a lien creditor.

[322] In re Mel Golde Shoes, Inc., 403 F.2d 658, 5 UCCR 1147 (6th Cir. 1968) (credit seller reclamation); In re Federal's, Inc. v. Matsushita Elec. Corp. of Am., 553 F.2d 509, 21 UCCR 689 (6th Cir. 1977) (credit seller reclamation).

favored the lien creditor, it has been used to deny reclamation.[323] Rather than resorting to pre-Code law, courts might, and we think should, treat the language of the Code as controlling, and interpret it as allowing reclamation against a lien creditor. In section 2-507(2) and section 2-702(2), the Code grants reclamation rights to sellers; in sections 2-702(3) and 2-403, it allows certain purchasers to trump these rights; nowhere does it allow a lien creditor to trump them. In these circumstances, the Code's silence ought to be interpreted as allowing section 2-507(2) and section 2-702(2) reclaiming sellers to exercise their rights against lien creditors.[324]

While priority contests between reclaiming sellers and actual lien creditors are relatively rare, the result to be reached in such contests used to be of considerable importance, because it controlled the result that would be reached in the much more frequent contests between reclaiming sellers and their buyers' trustees in bankruptcy. Both the old Bankruptcy Act and the current Bankruptcy Code, in their "strongarm" clauses,[325] give the trustee the rights of hypothetical lien creditors. Unlike its predecessor, however, the Bankruptcy Code contains a provision, section 546(c), that directly addresses the rights of reclaiming sellers against trustees in bankruptcy. Since 1979, when the Bankruptcy Code became effective, this provision has largely, if not entirely, governed the question of priority between a reclaiming seller and the buyer's trustee in bankruptcy, and has done so without reference to the rights of a lien creditor.

Section 546(c) of the Bankruptcy Code provides:

> (c) Except as provided in subsection (d) of this section, the rights and powers of a trustee under sections 544(a), 545, 547, and 549 of this title are subject to any statutory or common-law right of a seller of goods that has sold goods to the debtor, in the ordinary course of such seller's business, to reclaim such goods if the debtor has received such goods while insolvent, but—
>> (1) such a seller may not reclaim such goods unless such seller demands in writing reclamation of such goods—
>>> (A) before 10 days after receipt of such goods by the debtor; or

---

[323] In re Kravitz, 278 F.2d 820, 1 UCCR 159 (3d Cir. 1960) (credit seller reclamation).

[324] The Permanent Editorial Board's 1966 amendment, which deleted the reference to lien creditors from U.C.C. § 2-702(3), strongly supports this argument.

[325] Section 70c of the old Bankruptcy Act; section 544(a)(1) of the current Bankruptcy Code (11 U.S.C. § 544(a)(1)(1994)).

(B) if such 10-day period expires after the commencement of the case, before 20 days after receipt of such goods
by the debtor; and

(2) the court may deny reclamation to a seller with such a
right of reclamation that has made such a demand only if the
court—

(A) grants the claim of such a seller priority as a claim
of a kind specified in section 503(b) of this title; or

(B) secures such claim by a lien.

This provision poses a number of interpretation questions, and the
courts have supplied at least tentative answers to most of them. First,
section 546(c) does not grant or create a right of reclamation. To reclaim
from its buyer's trustee in bankruptcy, a seller must have a nonbankruptcy
statutory or common-law right of reclamation.[326] Thus, a seller subject to
Article 2 must have either a section 2-507(2) cash seller's right of reclamation or a section 2-702(2) credit seller's right of reclamation; if the seller
fails to qualify under one of these Code provisions, it will be unable to
reclaim from its buyer's trustee in bankruptcy. Second, influenced by the
"such-a-seller-may-not-reclaim-any-such-goods-unless" language of section
546(c)(1), most courts have read section 546(c) as exclusive—as providing
the only avenue by which a seller can reclaim from a trustee.[327] Because
section 546(c) subjects reclamation from a trustee to conditions that are
different from and additional to those imposed by sections 2-507(2) and 2-
702(2), this means that to reclaim in bankruptcy, a seller must satisfy both
the Code's requirements and those of section 546(c).[328]

Section 546(c) restricts bankruptcy reclamation in four ways that sections 2-507 and 2-702(2) do not. First, it makes reclamation available only
to sellers that have sold the goods involved in the ordinary course of their
businesses.[329] While casual sellers may have Code rights of reclamation,
only those in the business of selling goods of the kind may have bankruptcy
rights of reclamation. Second, section 546(c) conditions bankruptcy reclamation on the buyer's receipt of the goods "while insolvent." This requirement changes the rules for cash sellers more than for credit sellers. It means
that a section 2-507 cash seller that could reclaim outside bankruptcy simply

---

[326] In re Video King of Ill., Inc., 100 B.R. 1008 (Bankr. N.D. Ill. 1989); In re Morken,
182 B.R. 1007, 28 UCCR2d 855 (Bankr. D. Minn. 1995).

[327] In re Julien Co., 44 F.3d 426, 26 UCCR2d 117 (6th Cir. 1995).

[328] For a general treatment of section 546(c) of the Bankruptcy Code, *see* 2 D. Epstein,
S. Nickles & J. White, Bankruptcy 143–159 (1992).

[329] In re GIC Gov't Secs., 64 B.R. 161, 2 UCCR2d 603 (Bankr. M.D. Fla. 1986).

because the buyer's check bounced, may reclaim in bankruptcy only if, in addition, the buyer was insolvent when it received the goods. Further, for both cash and credit sellers, the controlling insolvency definition is the Bankruptcy Code's balance-sheet definition[330] and not the Uniform Commercial Code's broader definition.[331] Third, the reclaiming seller must demand reclamation within ten days after the buyer's receipt of the goods (extended to twenty days if the petition in bankruptcy is filed within ten days). This goes beyond Article 2 by imposing a ten-day demand requirement on cash sellers and on credit sellers that have received written misrepresentations of solvency within three months before delivery.[332] Finally, and most important, unlike the section 2-702(2) demand, bankruptcy's ten-day reclamation demand must be "in writing."

The upshot is that sellers' Code rights of reclamation are both recognized and curtailed in bankruptcy. To reclaim in bankruptcy, a seller must (1) qualify under either section 2-507(2) or section 2-702(2), (2) have sold the goods involved in the ordinary course of business, (3) to a buyer that received them while insolvent in the bankruptcy sense, and make a (4) written demand for reclamation (5) within the period specified in section 546(c)(1).

[G] Reclamation From Purchasers From, and Secured Creditors of, the Buyer—Section 2-403's Protection of Good-Faith Purchasers

Article 2's protection of the good-faith purchaser is contained in section 2-403, a section that deals generally with the question of what title is transferred to purchasers. Section 2-403 governs a reclaiming seller's rights against a purchaser from the buyer, and covers a number of other matters as well. It could have been considered at various other places in this text, but discussion has been delayed to this point so that it may be presented against a broad background.

Section 2-403 states four transfer-of-title rules. These are:

Rule 1. A purchaser acquires all of the title that its transferor had or had power to transfer. The statutory words—"purchaser" and "transferor"—have considerably greater reach than the words "buyer" and "seller" would have. "Purchase" is defined as a "voluntary transaction cre-

---

[330] 11 U.S.C. § 101(32) (1994).

[331] U.C.C. § 1-201(23).

[332] In re Energy Co-op., Inc., 700 F. Supp. 929, 7 UCCR2d 1469 (N.D. Ill. 1988).

ating an interest in property."[333] Donees[334] and Article 9 secured parties[335] are thus purchasers as, of course, are buyers. On the other hand, persons that do not take in voluntary transactions but rather obtain property rights by seizure or the like (such as lien creditors) are not purchasers and must look to sources other than section 2-403 for their rights.[336]

The operation of this first section 2-403 rule with respect to sales transactions can be summarized as follows. Whatever ownership interest the transferor had passes to the purchaser. If the transferor had "title" to the goods, its purchaser receives that title. If the transferor owned a fractional interest or life estate or any other limited interest in the goods, its purchaser acquires that fractional share, life estate, or other limited interest.

Rule 2. A purchaser who takes from a transferor who has "void title"— that is, no title or ownership interest whatsoever—acquires no title or ownership interest. In other words, the purchaser gets no more than the nothing that the transferor had. This rule is implicit rather than expressly articulated in section 2-403. An important example of its operation involves a transferor who has stolen the goods or purchased them from a thief. Such a transferor has no title, and its purchaser consequently receives no title.[337]

The fact that a purchaser from a thief receives no title is not affected by the purchaser's good faith. Even if the purchaser paid the thief value, had no knowledge or notice that the goods were stolen, and acted in complete good faith, the purchaser acquires no title because its thief-seller had none to give.[338] In such a case, the true owner can reclaim the goods from the purchaser or maintain an action in conversion against the purchaser.[339]

Rule 3. The parties may agree that the purchaser is to receive less title than its transferor holds—that is, they may agree that the transferor is transferring only a limited interest in the goods. If they have so agreed, only the limited interest will pass. For example, one who pledges goods or otherwise

---

[333] U.C.C. § 1-201(32).

[334] The Berkeley, Inc. v. Brettler, 354 Mass. 24, 234 N.E.2d 742, 5 UCCR 222 (1968); Rogers v. Rogers, 271 Md. 603, 319 A.2d 119, 14 UCCR 1211 (1974).

[335] General Elec. Credit Corp. v. Tidwell Indus., Inc., 115 Ariz. 362, 565 P.2d 868, 21 UCCR 1188 (1977); Liqui*Lawn Corp. v. The Andersons, 21 Ohio St. 3d 145, 509 N.E.2d 1236, 3 UCCR2d 2009 (1987).

[336] National Shawmut Bank of Boston v. Vera, 352 Mass. 11, 223 N.E.2d 515, 4 UCCR 1 (1967); In re Interstate Stores, Inc., 830 F.2d 16, 5 UCCR2d 161 (2d Cir. 1987).

[337] Marvin v. Connelly, 272 S.C. 425, 252 S.E.2d 562, 26 UCCR 370 (1979); Candela v. Port Motors, Inc., 617 N.Y.S.2d 49, 25 UCCR2d 681 (App. Div. 1994).

[338] Schrier v. Home Indemn. Co., 273 A.2d 248, 8 UCCR 688 (D.C. App. 1971); Textile Supplies, Inc. v. Garrett, 687 F.2d 123, 34 UCCR 900 (5th Cir. 1982).

[339] *Id.*

grants an interest in them to secure an obligation, transfers only that interest (which the Code calls a "security interest" and provides for in Article 9). Rules 1, 2, and 3 all derive from the first sentence of section 2-403: "A purchaser of goods acquires all title which his transferor had or had power to transfer except that a purchaser of a limited interest acquires rights only to the extent of the interest purchased."

Rule 4. A person who has "voidable title" has the power to transfer a good title to a good-faith purchaser for value. This important and complicated rule enables a seller to transfer more title or ownership interest than it had. Like Rule 2, its operation always involves at least three people, which, for convenience, can be labeled the true owner, the transferor, and the bona fide purchaser.

The true owner (who is often a seller with a right to reclaim the goods) and the bona fide purchaser are typically innocent, and the transferor is typically a wrongdoer of one sort or another. When Rule 4 operates, the transferor has, by definition, a flawed title, one that the true owner has the right to avoid. Yet, for policy reasons, the Code, like the law that preceded it, gives the transferor the power (not the right) to transfer a good title to a bona fide purchaser. What our law is doing is making a choice between the true owner and the bona fide purchaser—deciding which of these two generally innocent parties has the weaker ownership claim to the goods. In a Rule 4 or voidable-title situation, the law's decision is that the true owner should bear the loss, whereas in a Rule 2 or void-title situation, it is the bona fide purchaser who bears the loss.

Voidable title is an old and flexible concept, and section 2-403 does not attempt a full-fledged definition of it. The second sentence of section 2-403(1)—"A person with voidable title has power to transfer a good title to a good faith purchaser for value"—should be read in light of pre-Code notions of voidable title. It should also be read in light of the third sentence of section 2-403(1), which deals with four transaction-of-purchase situations, and in light of sections 2-403(2) and 2-403(3), which deal with entrusting. The following text addresses transactions of purchase and entrusting separately.

[1] Transactions of Purchase

The third sentence of section 2-403(1) is difficult to read, both because it refers back to and incorporates the second sentence, and because it deals with two separate purchases and uses the word "purchaser" to refer to two different persons. First, it refers to the person this text has called the "transferor," as a "purchaser." Second, by reference to "good faith purchaser for value," it refers to the person this text has called the "bona fide purchaser." Paraphrased in terms of this text's labels, the third sentence of 2-403(1) provides that when the true owner delivers goods to the transferor "under a transaction of purchase" (first purchase), the transferor has the power to transfer a good title to a bona fide purchaser (second purchase), and this even though, as between the true owner and the transferor, the true owner has the right to avoid the transferor's title for one of the reasons specified in subparagraphs (a) through (d).

For the third sentence of 2-403(1) to operate, the true owner must have delivered the goods to the transferor in "a transaction of purchase"—that is, a "voluntary transaction creating an interest in property."[340] Under most circumstances, a like transaction of purchase is also an essential element in voidable title under the second sentence of section 2-403(1). A thief obviously does not take in a voluntary transaction and thus obtains no power to transfer a good title. While bailees and lessees obtain possession in voluntary transactions, it is only possession and not a purchaser's ownership interest that they obtain. Save in entrustment situations or other special circumstances, they consequently lack the power to transfer the bailor's or lessor's title to a bona fide purchaser.[341]

The application of section 2-403(1) to the situations of reclaiming sellers is reasonably straightforward. First, consider a credit seller that has delivered goods to an insolvent buyer and made a reclamation demand within ten days after their receipt, thus obtaining a section 2-702(2) right of reclamation. Such a seller has plainly delivered the goods under a transaction of purchase, and the buyer's title is plainly voidable; by reclaiming, the seller can avoid it. In these circumstances, the second sentence of section 2-403(1) operates and empowers the buyer to pass a good title to a good-faith purchaser for value. Thus, if the buyer sells the goods to such a purchaser before the seller has reclaimed them, the seller's right to reclaim will be cut off.[342] As between the seller and the good faith purchaser for value, the seller bears the loss.

The situation of a cash seller—one to which payment, although due and demanded on delivery, has not been made, thus giving the seller a section 2-507(2) right to reclaim—is similar. Again the buyer has voidable

---

[340] U.C.C. § 1-201(32).

[341] Towe Farms, Inc. v. Central Iowa Prod. Credit Ass'n, 528 F. Supp. 500, 32 UCCR 1431 (S.D. Iowa 1981); Alamo Rent-a-Car, Inc. v. Williamson Cadillac Co., 613 So. 2d 517, 19 UCCR2d 1080 (Fla. App. 1993); Kimberly & European Diamonds, Inc. v. Burbank, 864 F.2d 363, 34 UCCR 104 (6th Cir. 1982); Evergreen Marine Corp. v. Six Consignments of Frozen Scallops, 4 F.3d 90, 21 UCCR2d 502 (1st Cir. 1993).

[342] See In re Coast Trading Co., Inc. 744 F.2d 686, 39 UCCR 753 (9th Cir. 1984).

title and the consequent power, under the second sentence of section 2-403(1), to transfer good title to a good-faith purchaser for value (which purchaser will take free of the seller's right to reclaim).[343] Further, lest anyone miss the point, the cash seller's vulnerability to a good-faith purchaser is expressly covered in clauses (b) and (c) of the third sentence of section 2-403(1).

The four lettered clauses of the third sentence of section 2-403(1) are worthy of note. Each describes a situation in which a seller—a deliverer under a transaction of purchase—is deemed a better candidate for the loss than a good-faith purchaser for value. Clause (a) deals with the situation in which the seller is victimized by an imposture. It applies when a frauder, by impersonating a financially responsible person, has induced the seller to deliver goods to him. In such circumstances, the defrauded seller has a common-law right to avoid the frauder's title to the goods. But if the frauder sells to a good-faith purchaser for value, such purchaser will obtain a good title—that is, take free of the defrauded seller's right to reclaim the goods, and free of a claim in conversion.[344] As has been mentioned, clauses (b) and (c) deal with the section 2-507(2) reclamation situation. A cash seller that takes a check in exchange for goods can reclaim the goods if the check is dishonored.[345] That is, it can reclaim them from its buyer, but, because of section 2-403(1), the seller cannot reclaim from a person who has, in good faith and for value purchased them from the buyer. Clause (d) deals with situations in which a frauder, by one or another species of fraud, induces a seller to deliver goods to him under a transaction of purchase. The seller's voluntary delivery of the goods with the intent of passing a property interest makes it a candidate for the loss and calls for the application of the voidable-title rule rather than the void-title rule, even though the criminal law labels the fraud larcenous.

A seller's rights to reclaim goods under section 2-507(2) or section 2-702(2), or because it has otherwise been defrauded do not die as against every transferee from the buyer. To prevail over a seller with a right to reclaim, a transferee from the buyer must show (1) that it is a purchaser, (2) that it purchased in good faith, and (3) that it gave value.[346] Each of these terms is defined. A *purchaser* is a person who takes by "sale, discount, negotiation, pledge, lien, issue or re-issue, gift or any other voluntary trans-

---

[343] In re Samuels & Co., Inc. 526 F.2d 1238, 18 UCCR 545 (5th Cir. 1976).

[344] The defrauded seller will, of course, have rights against the frauder.

[345] U.C.C. §§ 2-507(2) and 2-511(3); *see* § 7.07[D], *supra*.

[346] *See* Shacket v. Roger Smith Aircraft Sales, Inc. 497 F. Supp. 1262, 30 UCCR 148 (N.D. Ill. 1980).

action creating an interest in property."[347] *Good faith* means "honesty in fact";[348] additionally, to be in good faith, a merchant[349] must observe "reasonable commercial standards of fair dealing in the trade."[350] A purchaser takes for *value* if, *inter alia*, it takes "as security for or in total or partial satisfaction of a pre-existing claim," or "in return for any consideration sufficient to support a simple contract."[351] As has been pointed out,[352] lien creditors—those who obtain their property rights by judicial process, levy or the like—do not take in voluntary transactions and so do not qualify as purchasers. Thus, a judgment creditor's levy on goods to which the judgment debtor held only voidable title does not convert the voidable title into a good title.[353] Donees are purchasers, but, having given no value, they take only the title that their donors had. There is no requirement that the value a purchaser pays be equivalent to the market value of the goods, but the purchaser's good faith may be called into question if it is significantly lower.[354]

Because an Article 9 secured party acquires its security interest by grant from its debtor (that is, in a voluntary transaction), it qualifies as a purchaser. Under section 2-403(1), a secured party that acts in good faith may consequently acquire a good title even though its debtor—the grantor of its security interest—had only a voidable title; at least, it may do so to the extent of the security interest (a limited interest) that it purchases. For sake of illustration, suppose that Bank loaned money to Merchant and that Merchant secured its promise to repay by granting Bank a security interest in its (Merchant's) inventory, then owned and thereafter acquired. Suppose, further, that six months after Bank obtained its security interest, Merchant bought goods from Seller, took delivery, and added the goods to its inventory. And suppose that Merchant paid Seller with a check that subsequently bounced, giving Seller a section 2-507(2) right to reclaim the goods. Although it is good against Merchant, Seller's right of reclamation will most likely be subject to Bank's security interest. Bank has obtained its security interest as a purchaser and has paid value (its loan) for it. Although Bank

---

[347] U.C.C. §§ 1-201(32), 1-201(33).

[348] U.C.C. § 1-201(19).

[349] U.C.C. § 2-104(1).

[350] U.C.C. § 2-103(1)(b).

[351] U.C.C. § 1-201(44).

[352] § 7.07[F], *supra*.

[353] *See* National Shawmut Bank of Boston v. Vera, 352 Mass. 11, 223 N.E.2d 515, 4 UCCR 1 (1967); Mazer v. Williams Bros. Co., 461 Pa. 587, 337 A.2d 559, 17 UCCR 225 (1975); In re PFA Farmers Market Ass'n, 583 F.2d 992, 24 UCCR 1176 (8th Cir. 1978).

[354] Hollis v. Chamberlain, 243 Ark. 201, 419 S.W.2d 116, 4 UCCR 716 (1967).

obtained its interest in the goods Seller wants to reclaim under an after-acquired property clause, the interest has nevertheless been voluntarily granted by Merchant (provided for in the after-acquired property clause of the security agreement that Merchant signed), and, since it has been taken "as security for . . . a pre-existing claim," it has been taken for value, as value is defined in section 1-201(44). If Bank has acted in good faith, its interest will prevail over Seller's right to reclaim. That is, if Bank asserts its security interest, by foreclosure or in Merchant's bankruptcy, and if it needs the goods that Seller seeks to reclaim as collateral for its loan, Seller will be unable to reclaim. The courts so hold.[355] If, however, a secured party obtains its interest in bad faith, a reclaiming seller can prevail over it.[356]

[2] Entrusting

Under section 2-403(1), as has just been shown, a person that delivers goods in a transaction of purchase puts its ownership claims to the goods at risk; if the transaction-of-purchase transferee sells the goods to a good-faith purchaser for value, such claims will be lost. Subsections (2) and (3) of section 2-403 address another kind of delivery—different from delivery in a transaction of purchase—that also puts the deliverer's ownership claims at risk. Under subsections (2) and (3), a person who *entrusts* goods to a merchant which deals in goods of the kind also risks its ownership claims to the goods, even though the entrustment involves no intention to pass ownership rights from entruster to entrustee—even though, for example, it was a mere bailment. Specifically, subsections (2) and (3) provide:

> (2) Any entrusting of possession of goods to a merchant who deals in goods of that kind gives him power to transfer all rights of the entruster to a buyer in ordinary course of business.
> (3) "Entrusting" includes any delivery and any acquiescence in retention of possession regardless of any condition expressed between the parties to the delivery or acquiescence and regardless of whether the procurement of the entrusting or the possessor's disposition of the goods have been such as to be larcenous under the criminal law.

---

[355] In re Samuels & Co., 510 F.2d 139, 16 UCCR 577 (5th Cir. 1975), *rev'd,* 526 F.2d 1238, 18 UCCR 545 (5th Cir. 1976), *cert. denied sub nom.* Stowers v. Mahon, 429 U.S. 834, 97 S. Ct. 98, 50 L. Ed. 2d 99 (1976); General Elec. Credit Corp. v. Tidwell Indus., Inc., 115 Ariz. 362, 565 P.2d 868, 21 UCCR 1188 (1977); Guy Martin Buick, Inc. v. Colorado Springs Nat'l Bank, 184 Colo. 166, 519 P.2d 354, 14 UCCR 40 (1974); Swets Motor Sales, Inc. v. Pruisner, 236 N.W.2d 299, 18 UCCR 371 (Iowa 1975).

[356] *See* Iola State Bank v. Bolan, 679 P.2d 720, 38 UCCR 755 (Kan. 1984); Dick Hatfield Chevrolet, Inc. v. Bob Watson Motors, Inc., 708 P.2d 494, 42 UCCR 144 (Kan. 1985).

To illustrate the operation of these provisions, suppose that Owner boarded valuable ostriches with Bailee. Bailee, who charged Owner a monthly fee, both boarded and sold exotic animals (selling them frequently enough to be considered a merchant dealing in goods of the kind). Without any consent or authorization by Owner, Bailee sold the ostriches to Buyer. Buyer paid Bailee $75,000, bought in good faith, and without knowledge that the sale violated Owner's rights, thus qualifying as a "buyer in ordinary course of business," as that term is defined in section 1-201(9).[357] In circumstances like these, Buyer acquired Owner's rights in the ostriches.[358] The ground for this result is estoppel. By voluntarily entrusting possession of ostriches to an ostrich merchant, the entruster, as it should realize, has clothed the merchant with indicia of ownership. This is a "minus" for the entruster, and, where the buyer prevails, there is also a "plus" for it; it will have bought in the ordinary way from a merchant in the business of selling goods of the kind.

Entrusting can spring from various motivations and take various forms. For example, the purpose of the entruster's delivery to the merchant may be to enable the merchant to sell the goods for the entruster.[359] Or the entruster's purpose may be to have the goods repaired (with the merchant being in the business of selling as well as repairing goods of the kind).[360] Or the entruster may buy goods from a dealer and, for one reason or another, leave them in the dealer's hands.[361] If the merchant deals in goods of the kind, all of these situations fit within section 2-403(3)'s broad definition of entrusting. In all of them, the entruster has given the merchant the power to pass the entruster's ownership rights in the goods to a buyer in the ordinary course from the merchant.

---

[357] U.C.C. § 1-201(9) provides:

> "Buyer in ordinary course of business" means a person who in good faith and without knowledge that the sale to him is in violation of the ownership rights or security interest of a third party in the goods buys in ordinary course from a person in the business of selling goods of that kind but does not include a pawnbroker. All persons who sell minerals or the like (including oil and gas) at wellhead or minehead shall be deemed to be persons in the business of selling goods of that kind. "Buying" may be for cash or by exchange of other property or on secured or unsecured credit and includes receiving goods or documents of title under a pre-existing contract of sale but does not include a transfer in bulk or as security for or in total or partial satisfaction of a money debt.

[358] Pregner v. Baker, 542 N.W.2d 805, 28 UCCR2d 835 (Iowa 1995).
[359] Medico Leasing Co. v. Smith, 457 P.2d 548, 6 UCCR 786 (Okla. 1969).
[360] Litchfield v. Dueitt, 245 So. 2d 190, 9 UCCR 244 (Miss. 1971).
[361] Simson v. Moon, 137 Ga. App. 82, 222 S.E.2d 873, 18 UCCR 1191 (1975).

In some situations, sections 2-403(1) and 2-403(2) overlap; the goods have been both transferred in a section 2-403(1) transaction of purchase and entrusted to a merchant under section 2-403(2), and the purchaser can qualify as both a subsection (1) good-faith purchaser for value and a subsection (2) buyer in ordinary course of business. In other situations, only subsection (1) will help the purchaser; there being no subsection (2) entrusting, because the person to which the goods are delivered and which sells them is not a merchant who deals in goods of the kind. In such cases, the ultimate purchaser can prevail only if it can show that its seller took in a transaction of purchase or otherwise obtained voidable title. In other situations, only subsection (2) helps the purchaser; as in the ostrich hypothetical, there is no transaction of purchase but rather a bailment, lease, delivery for repair, or other nonpurchase entrusting to a merchant that deals in goods of the kind. In such cases, only a "buyer in ordinary course" can prevail.

It is harder to qualify as a "buyer in ordinary course" than as a "good-faith purchaser for value." Even though Article 9 secured parties are purchasers for value and often act in good faith, it is probably impossible for a secured party to qualify as a buyer in ordinary course. First, there is the final clause of section 1-201(9), which excludes one who takes "as security for . . . a money debt." This plainly excludes secured lenders who take their security interests to secure preexisting money debts, as under after-acquired property clauses. Other secured parties are probably excluded because (1) although "purchasers," they are not "buyers,"[362] and (2) they do not take "in ordinary course." The upshot is that one who entrusts goods otherwise than in a transaction of purchase should not lose its rights to the entrustee's secured party.[363]

Finally, even a buyer in ordinary course that establishes a section 2-403(2) entrusting to its seller acquires only the rights of the entruster. If the entruster was a thief, having no title, the buyer in ordinary course acquires only the entrusting thief's lack of title and is subject to the claims of the true owner.[364] If the entruster had a voidable title, section 2-403(2) gives the

---

[362] *See* U.C.C. § 2-103(1)(a), which defines "buyer" as a person who buys or contracts to buy goods, and U.C.C. § 2-102, which excludes sales intended to operate only as security transactions from the coverage of Article 2.

[363] In re Sitkin Smelting & Refining, Inc., 639 F.2d 1213, 30 UCCR 1566 (5th Cir. 1981).

[364] If the entrusted goods are collateral under an Article 9 security interest, and if the entruster is the debtor, the entrusting enables the merchant to pass the debtor's rights—its equity in the goods—to a buyer in ordinary course. But, assuming that the secured party has not, by acquiescence or otherwise, entrusted the goods to the merchant, its rights—its security interest—should not pass under U.C.C. § 2-403(2). When, however, the secured party has entrusted the goods, it has been held that section 2-403(2) gives the merchant the power

buyer in ordinary course only a voidable title. But in the voidable-title situation, the second sentence of section 2-403(1) can perhaps be read to give the buyer in ordinary course a good title.

[H] Reclamation of Substitute Assets

A cash seller that has a section 2-507(2) right to reclaim sold goods from its buyer will, under section 2-403(1), lose its claim to the goods if the buyer sells them to a good-faith purchaser for value. A credit seller with a section 2-702(2) right to reclaim will suffer the same fate if its buyer sells to such a purchaser. And an owner that has entrusted goods to a merchant dealing in goods of the kind under circumstances entitling the owner to reclaim the goods from the merchant will, under section 2-403(2), be unable to reclaim them from a buyer in ordinary course from the merchant. The question to which we now turn is whether, although they have lost their rights to reclaim their goods because the goods have been purchased, sellers and entrusters can reclaim the assets given in exchange for the goods.

To pose the question in terms of a hypothetical, suppose that Seller sells a boat to Buyer, with Buyer paying on delivery with a check. Buyer's check bounces, giving Seller a section 2-507(2) right to reclaim the boat from Buyer. But, when Seller demands the return of the boat from Buyer, Seller learns that Buyer has sold the boat to Purchaser, who took in good faith and paid with her own check. Having lost the boat to Purchaser under section 2-403(1), may Seller reclaim the proceeds of the boat—Purchaser's check—from Buyer? Seller is plainly entitled to recover the agreed price of the boat from Buyer,[365] but Seller's claim for the price is an unsecured general claim, not a claim to any specific asset. If Buyer is insolvent, Seller's claim for the price may consequently be worth only pennies on the dollar, if that. If Buyer is insolvent, Seller will be strongly interested in having an interest in a specific asset, the asset that Buyer received in exchange for the boat to which Seller had a claim—here, Purchaser's check.

The Code does not expressly address the question posed—whether a seller's right of reclamation can reach beyond the goods involved to their proceeds—to assets exchanged for them. Seller in the hypothetical might argue that, under section 1-103, the law of restitution supplements the Code

---

to transfer the secured party's rights to a buyer in ordinary course even though Article 9—specifically 9-307(1)—would not enable the buyer in ordinary course to prime the security interest (because it had been granted by someone other than the merchant). Executive Fin. Servs., Inc. v. Pagel, 238 Kan. 809, 715 P.2d 381, 42 UCCR 1185 (1986).

[365] Seller has a U.C.C. § 2-709(1)(a) action for the price of the boat and an Article 3 action against Buyer as the drawer of a dishonored check.

and entitles him to reach Purchaser's check by way of constructive trust or equitable lien. Some courts have accepted arguments of this sort,[366] but others have rejected them and limited reclamation rights to the goods involved.[367] The latter idea—that the right of reclamation does not reach proceeds—has hardened into something approaching a rule in the situation in which the seller will have the greatest need for the proceeds—where the buyer is in bankruptcy.[368]

§ 7.08   THE SELLER'S MONETARY RECOVERIES

[A]   Resale Damages

When at least one of section 2-703's four triggering events (wrongful rejection, wrongful revocation of acceptance, failure to make a payment due on or before delivery, or repudiation) occurs, the seller may cancel and thus avoid liability for failing to deliver the goods.[369] The seller may then retain the goods or sell them to another buyer. If the seller sells to another buyer, and does so in accordance with the requirements of section 2-706, it may recover from the defaulting buyer damages measured by the difference between the contract price and the resale price together with section 2-710 incidental damages but less expenses saved in consequence of the buyer's breach.[370]

The section 2-706 contract-price-less-resale-price measure of recovery is designed to protect the seller's expectation interest—to place it in the financial position it would have occupied had the buyer taken and paid for the goods in accordance with the contract.[371] When the buyer wrongfully thrusts the goods back on the seller or (by repudiation or failure to make a payment due on or before delivery) indicates that it will not take or pay for them, the seller "loses" the contract price but "gains" the goods. In these circumstances, the financial loss that the seller suffers can often be measured

---

[366] Greater Louisville Auto Auction, Inc. v. Ogle Buick, Inc., 387 S.W.2d 17, 2 UCCR 344 (Ky. 1965); United States v. Westside Bank, 732 F.2d 1258, 38 UCCR 705 (5th Cir. 1984).

[367] In re Coast Trading, Inc., 744 F.2d 686, 39 UCCR 753 (9th Cir. 1984); In re Landy Beef Co., 30 B.R. 19, 36 UCCR 855 (Bankr. D. Mass. 1983). *See* In re Rawson Food Serv., Inc., 846 F.2d 1343, 6 UCCR2d 128 (11th Cir. 1988).

[368] *Id.*

[369] Section 7.06[B], *supra.*

[370] U.C.C. § 2-706(1). *See* Harlow & Jones, Inc. v. Advance Steel Co., 424 F. Supp. 770, 21 UCCR 410 (E.D. Mich. 1976); Modern Machinery v. Flathead County, 202 Mont. 140, 656 P.2d 206, 36 UCCR 395 (1982).

[371] Section 7.01, *supra.*

by the difference between the contract price (the price that the defaulting buyer promised to pay) and the price for which the seller resells the goods. If the contract price was $34,000 and the seller was able to, and did, resell for only $30,000, the buyer's breach has cost the seller the $4,000 difference. That is, the seller needs a $4,000 recovery if its expectation interest is to be protected—if it is to be placed in the financial position it would have occupied had the buyer performed. Sometimes this difference-money recovery will need to be adjusted by adding additional expenses that the buyer's default caused the seller to incur or by subtracting expenses that the buyer's default enabled the seller to save, all to the end of placing the aggrieved seller in the financial position that performance would have done.[372] And sometimes the section 2-706(1) contract-price-less-resale-price formula proves inadequate to measure the seller's expectation loss, because the seller could have made the second sale even if the buyer had performed. In these circumstances, the aggrieved seller should not elect section 2-706 damages, but should instead seek damages under section 2-708(2).[373]

The section 2-706(1) contract-price-less-resale-price measure of recovery and the section 2-708(1) contract-price-less-market-price measure of recovery[374] are alternatives. Each is designed to protect the seller's expectation interest, and, once a buyer has committed a section 2-703 default, the aggrieved seller can recover under either, but not both. Resale damages under section 2-706(1) are measured by an actual transaction—the seller's resale—while market damages under section 2-708(1) are measured by a hypothetical market price: what a willing buyer would have paid a willing seller.[375] For this reason, sellers frequently prefer resale damages to market damages (as buyers frequently prefer section 2-712 cover damages to section 2-713 market damages). It is easier to prove the concrete—the price at which the goods were actually resold—than to prove the abstract—their market price. And the price actually received on resale measures the seller's loss more reliably than does the market price (which market price the seller did not actually receive).

A seller using section 2-706 (like a buyer using section 2-712) exercises some post-breach control over the amount of its recovery. Usually the seller is interested (self-interested) in getting the best possible price for the goods

---

[372] U.C.C. §§ 1-106, 2-706(1), 2-710. *See* Intermeat, Inc. v. American Poultry, Inc., 575 F.2d 1017, 23 UCCR 925 (2nd Cir. 1978); Gray v. West, 608 S.W.2d 771, 31 UCCR 568 (Tex. Civ. App. 1980).

[373] Section 7.08[D], *infra*.

[374] Section 7.08[B], *infra*.

[375] *See* § 7.04[C] *supra*.

it is reselling, and not in selling them at a low price in order to build up its damage recovery from the buyer. Money obtained on resale is money in hand and immediately spendable, while the recovery of damages may require an expensive lawsuit and considerable delay and the judgment ultimately obtained may turn out to be uncollectible. Although the seller's self-interest usually produces a good resale price and thus protects the buyer, the Code nevertheless polices the seller's resale. To use the actual resale price to measure its damage recovery, a seller must comply with section 2-706(1) and section 2-706(2) and with whichever of section 2-706(3) or section 2-706(4), whichever is applicable.

The principal requirements are that the resale must be made in good faith,[376] that "every aspect of the sale including the method, manner, time, place, and terms must be commercially reasonable,"[377] that the resale must be "reasonably identified as referring to the broken contract,"[378] and that the seller give the buyer appropriate notice.[379] The statute assumes that some resales are "private" (they are provided for in subsection (3)) and that others are "public" (they are provided for in subsection (4)). Although there is no definition of either a public or a private sale, the basic meaning of the terms—that a public sale is an auction and that all non-auction sales are private sales—can be gleaned from the statutory provisions governing the two kinds of sales and from the Comments, particularly Comment 4.

The seller must give the buyer reasonable[380] notice of both kinds of sales. The purpose of the notice is to enable the buyer to police the sale, the goal being the realization of a good price. For a public sale, the notice must inform the buyer of the "time and place"[381] of the contemplated resale. This kind of notice is particularly suited to an auction, where the goods are to be put up and sold at 2:00 P.M. on Thursday afternoon, and unsuited to a non-auction or negotiated sale, where the goods are to be sold whenever

---

[376] U.C.C. § 2-706(1). Most sellers recovering under section 2-706 are merchants, and so the applicable good-faith standard is usually that set forth in U.C.C. § 2-103(1)(b) and not the less arduous U.C.C. § 1-201(19) standard. *See* Coast Trading Co. v. Cudahy Co., 592 F.2d 1074, 25 UCCR 1037 (9th Cir. 1978); Meadowbrook Nat'l Bank v. Markos, 3 UCCR 854 (N.Y. Sup. Ct. 1966).

[377] U.C.C. § 2-706(2). *See* McMillan v. Menser Material & Equipment Co., Inc., 260 Ark. 422, 541 S.W.2d 911, 20 UCCR 110 (1976); Sharp Elecs. Corp. v. Lodgistix, Inc., 802 F-Supp 370, 19 UCCR2d 772 (D. Kan. 1992).

[378] U.C.C. § 2-706(2).

[379] U.C.C. §§ 2-706(3), 2-706(4).

[380] In this context, the statutory word "reasonable" refers primarily the length of time between the notice and the sale. The idea is to give the buyer an adequate opportunity to protect itself. *See* U.C.C. § 2-706, Comment 8.

[381] U.C.C. § 2-706(4)(b).

a suitable deal can be reached with a buyer. Accordingly, the requirement for private sales is reasonable notification of "intention to resell."[382] In the course of its regulation of public sales, subsection (4) provides that "the seller may buy." This is appropriate for a commercially reasonable auction, where having the seller participate as a bidder cannot hurt and may help the buyer,[383] but would be inappropriate for a private sale, as it would have the seller negotiating the price with itself. The choice between a public or auction resale and a private resale, like every other aspect of the resale, must be commercially reasonable.

The overriding requirements for a section 2-706 resale are good faith and commercial reasonableness. Article 9 of the Code imposes similar requirements on a secured party which has repossessed collateral from its debtor and is selling it to obtain money to apply to the secured debt. In fact, sections 9-504(3) and 2-706(2) use identical language in requiring that "every aspect" of the sale "including the method, manner, time, place and terms must be commercially reasonable." As a consequence, courts working with section 2-706 sometimes look to the large volume of section 9-504 litigation for guidance on questions of commercial reasonableness.[384]

Difficulties in applying section 2-706 sometimes arise when the goods involved are fungible and the seller, being in the business of selling goods of the kind, makes multiple sales after the buyer's default.[385] Which of the several sales can the seller use to measure section 2-706 damages? The statute seems to allow the seller to choose by identifying the sale that refers to the broken contract[386] but the identification must be reasonable and in accordance with good faith. Delayed sales may not be reasonable. If the market price of the goods involved is fluctuating, the only sale which can qualify under section 2-706 may be one made shortly after the buyer's default.[387]

---

[382] U.C.C. § 2-706(3).

[383] U.C.C. § 2-706, Comment 9.

[384] *See, e.g.*, Larsen Leasing, Inc. v. Thiele, Inc., 749 F. Supp. 821, 13 UCCR2d 407 (W.D. Mich. 1990), in which the court supported its holding that the U.C.C. § 2-706 reseller has the burden of proving that it has sold in a commercially reasonable manner by looking to section 9-504 cases placing the commercial-reasonableness burden of proof on the foreclosing secured party. For an excellent discussion of commercial reasonableness in the Article 9 context, *see* II Grant Gilmore, Security Interests in Personal Property § 44.5 (1965).

[385] In some fungible-goods circumstances, the buyer's breach costs the seller a profit. When this is the case, the seller should seek damages under U.C.C. § 2-708(2) and not under section 2-706.

[386] U.C.C. § 2-706(2).

[387] *See* Apex Oil Co. v. Belcher Co. of New York, Inc., 855 F.2d 997, 6 UCCR2d 1025 (2d Cir. 1988).

When a resale qualifies for section 2-706 damages, the second sentence of section 2-706(1) provides the damage formula: the contract price less the resale price plus section 2-710 incidental damages but less any expenses that the seller saves because of the buyer's breach. In some circumstances, this formula, applied literally, compensates the seller in terms of its expectation interest without penalizing the buyer. In other circumstances, regard for the fundamental compensation principles epitomized in section 1-106 requires adjustment of the formula. Consider the following hypotheticals.

Case 1. Seller agreed to sell and Buyer to buy goods for a contract price of $50,000. Buyer, having paid nothing on the purchase price, committed one of the section 2-703 triggering events. Seller elected to resell the goods and did so in compliance with section 2-706. Seller obtained only $45,000 on the resale, had $1,000 in incidental damages in connection with the resale, and saved $500 in transportation costs because of the buyer's breach.

Seller's Case 1 damages can be computed under section 2-706 without difficulty. Seller is entitled to the contract price ($50,000) less the amount received on resale ($45,000), or $5,000. To this amount the incidental damages of $1,000 must be added, and the savings of $500 must be subtracted. The result is section 2-706 damages of $5,500. This recovery puts Seller in the financial position it would have occupied had Buyer performed and paid the $50,000 contract price. It is not every case, however, that can be so easily handled.

Case 2. Assume the facts of Case 1 except assume that Buyer made a $3,000 downpayment on the price before defaulting.

In these circumstances, a literal application of the 2-706(1) formula overcompensates Seller. The formula is the *contract* price less the resale price. Because the *contract* price was $50,000, a literal application of the formula produces exactly the same damages in Case 2 as were obtained in Case 1: $5,500. But in Case 2, Seller begins its quest for damages with Buyer's $3,000 downpayment in its pocket, and a $5,500 recovery consequently overcompensates it—puts it in a better financial position than performance would have done—by the amount of the downpayment. Had Buyer performed, Seller would have received $50,000 for the goods and the costs it agreed to incur; a literal application of the section 2-706 formula would, once Seller's extra costs or incidental damages and savings are factored in, give Seller $53,000 for the goods and the costs it agreed to incur.

The recovery in Case 2 can be brought into line with common-law and section 1-106 compensation principles by a judicial insertion of the word "unpaid" before the words "contract price" in section 2-706(1). This gives Buyer credit for its downpayment. Specifically, it recasts the recovery in

Case 2 as follows: from the unpaid contract price ($47,000) subtract the resale price ($45,000), add the incidental damages ($1,000), and subtract the savings ($500). This produces a recovery of $2,500, and thus differs from the Case 1 recovery by the $3,000 amount of Buyer's downpayment. Note that the judicial insertion of the word "unpaid" has no effect on the Case 1 recovery; because there was no downpayment in Case 1, the unpaid contract price and the contract price are the same ($50,000).

The fundamental compensation policy of putting the aggrieved party in the financial position that it would have occupied on performance and not in a better position justifies reading the section 2-706(1) damage formula in unpaid contract-price terms. So do comparisons of section 2-706 with other Code damage formulas, particularly those dealing with a buyer's cover damages and with a seller's market-price damages, where prepayments on the contract price are expressly factored into the statutory recoveries. In the cover situation, the aggrieved buyer recovers the difference between the cost of cover and the contract price under section 2-712(2) and, in addition, recovers "so much of the price as has been paid" under section 2-711(1). In the seller's market-price damages situation, the section 2-708(1) formula is "the difference between the market price at the time and place for tender and the *unpaid* contract price together with any incidental damages provided in this Article (Section 2-710), but less expenses saved in consequence of the buyer's breach."[388] The comparison with section 2-708(1) is persuasive. In many respects, the contract-price-minus-resale-price measure of section 2-706 and the contract-price-minus-market-price measure of section 2-708(1) are alternatives. The former is designed to protect the seller's expectation interest in terms of a specific resale price; the latter is designed to protect the same expectation interest in terms of a legal and economic construct: the market price. It makes no sense, and the drafters could not have intended, to take prepayments on the purchase price into account in one situation and not in the other. Thus, the word "unpaid" should be read into section 2-706(1) so that the seller's recovery is limited to compensation for loss.

The section 2-706(1) formula can also cause difficulties when the goods are resold for more than the unpaid contract price. Such situations are rare, but occasionally occur.

Case 3. Seller agreed to sell and Buyer to buy goods for a contract price of $50,000. Buyer, having paid nothing on the contract price, committed one of the section 2-703 triggering events. Seller elected to resell the goods and did so in compliance with section 2-706. Seller obtained $57,000

---

[388] Emphasis supplied.

on the resale, had $1,000 in incidental damages in connection with the resale, and saved nothing because of the buyer's breach.

In these circumstances, Seller could argue that it is entitled to recover damages (specifically $1,000) by focusing on two portions of section 2-706. The first is subsection (6) which states that the seller is not accountable to the buyer for any *profit* made on the resale. Seller's point would be that this provision entitles it to keep the entire $7,000 profit (the amount by which the resale price exceeded the contract price). Seller would also focus on the subsection (1) formula, which allows the recovery of loss on resale (which in Case 3 would be zero) "together with" incidental damages ($1,000 in Case 3). Seller could thus contend that it is entitled to recover $1,000.

Seller's argument should be rejected. Recovery from Buyer aside, the unusual circumstances of Case 3 have placed Seller in a better financial position ($6,000 better) than it would have occupied had Buyer performed. Subsection (6) properly allows Seller to retain the fruits of its fortunate (vis-à-vis the contract price) resale. Buyer, having defaulted, has not earned a right to share in Seller's good fortune. But allowing Seller to go beyond retaining the net profit that Buyer's breach made possible and also obtain money damages would penalize Buyer. Seller's good fortune has more than protected its expectation interest. On the facts of Case 3, the compensation principle does not support an award of money damages, which would place Seller still further ahead of its expected position. Because Buyer's breach has not caused Seller a loss but has rather done Seller a financial favor, Buyer should be liable for nothing more than nominal damages. In circumstances like these, section 2-706(6) should be read as protecting the seller's net rather than gross profit, and section 2-706(1) should be read as allowing the recovery of incidental damages only to the extent that they are needed to protect the seller's expectation interest.

When the buyer commits a section 2-703 triggering event and the seller resells but, for one reason or another—a defective notice, inadequate advertising, or something else about the resale that is commercially unreasonable—fails to comply with the requirements of section 2-706, the seller will be unable to use the resale price and section 2-706 to measure its damages. The seller may, however, be able to move to section 2-708(1) (which is considered in § 7.08[B]) and use the market price to measure its damages.[389]

[B] Contract-Minus-Market Damages

Section 2-708(1) provides for the seller's traditional contract-price-minus-market-price measure of damages:

---

[389] *See* Wolpert v. Foster, 254 N.W.2d 348, 21 UCCR 516 (Minn. 1977).

> Subject to subsection (2) and to the provisions of this Article with re-
> spect to proof of market price (Section 2-723), the measure of damages
> for non-acceptance or repudiation by the buyer is the difference between
> the market price at the time and place for tender and the unpaid contract
> price together with any incidental damages provided in this Article (Sec-
> tion 2-710), but less expenses saved in consequence of the buyer's
> breach.

Section 2-703(e) opens section 2-708 remedies—the contract-minus-market remedy of section 2-708(1) and the lost-profit remedy of section 2-708(2)—whenever the buyer commits at least one of four triggering defaults (wrongfully rejects, wrongfully revokes acceptance, fails to make a payment due on or before delivery, or repudiates). Section 2-708 does not directly refer to these triggering events (it differs from section 2-706 in this regard), but rather states "the measure of damages for non-acceptance or repudiation by the buyer." The term "non-acceptance" is undefined, but would seem to include, and should be read as including, three of section 2-703's triggering events: wrongful rejection, wrongful revocation of acceptance, and failure to make a payment due on or before delivery.[390] Thus, section 2-708 is available when one of the section 2-703 triggering events has occurred—that is, it is available under the same conditions that section 2-706 is available: when the buyer has committed a material breach and the seller has the goods, having either retained them or had them thrust back upon it. The following hypotheticals illustrate the operation of section 2-708(1):

Case 1. Seller agreed to sell and Buyer to buy a valuable antique chest for $18,000. The agreement provided that Buyer would come to Seller's store and pick up the chest on March 1, paying the $18,000 price when it did so. Buyer, however, changed its mind, and, on March 1, informed Seller that it would not take or pay for the chest.

Under these circumstances (a rejection and a failure to make a payment due on or before delivery), Seller could resell the chest and, if it complied with the requirements of section 2-706, recover the difference between the contract price and the resale price, as discussed in § 7.08[A]. There is, how-ever, no requirement that an aggrieved seller resell under section 2-706. Seller could decide to retain the chest, or sell it to an employee or a valued customer at a bargain price. The Code allows an aggrieved seller to forgo the section 2-706 resale remedy and recover instead under section 2-708(1)'s contract-price-minus-market-price measure.

---

[390] *See* Dehahn v. Innes, 356 A.2d 711, UCCR 407 (Me. 1976).

The section 2-708(1) contract-minus-market formula, like the section 2-706 contract-minus-resale formula, is aimed at the protection of the aggrieved seller's expectation interest—at placing the seller in or near the financial position it would have occupied had the buyer performed. The buyer's performance would have given the seller the contract price in exchange for the goods. When the buyer refused to accept and pay, the seller lost the contract price but was able to retain the goods. If the retained goods are "worth" the contract price, the buyer's breach has not injured the seller, and the seller's recovery will be limited to nominal damages. If the goods are "worth" less than the contract price, the buyer's breach has placed the seller in a less advantageous financial position than it would have enjoyed had the buyer performed. Section 2-708(1) recognizes these circumstances and provides a measure of damages equal to the contract price (actually the unpaid contract price) less the market price of the retained goods.[391] Thus, if Seller in Case 1 could prove that the market price of the chest ("at the time and place for tender"—here March 1 at Seller's store) was $16,000, its basic damage recovery would be $2,000 (the $18,000 contract price minus the $16,000 market price). This basic recovery is subject to adjustment by adding any section 2-710 incidental damages Seller suffered and subtracting any expenses it saved in consequence of Buyer's breach.

Proving market price—what a willing buyer would have paid a willing seller[392]—is sometimes easy. Where the goods are bushels of wheat, bales of cotton, or other widely traded agricultural commodities, it is normally easy to show what buyers paid sellers for commercially identical goods at the time and place fixed by section 2-708(1), and the opportunity for argument will typically be narrowly confined. Where, however, the goods are unique, as in Case 1, it is difficult to establish market price, and resort must be had to sales of comparable items and perhaps to expert appraisals.[393] There is a wide spectrum between these poles, including standard manufactured goods, used goods, and specially manufactured goods.[394] Section 2-

---

[391] See Klockner, Inc. v. Federal Wire Mill Corp., 663 F.2d 1370, 32 UCCR 1097 (7th Cir. 1981); Bache & Co. v. International Controls Corp., 339 F. Supp. 341, 10 UCCR 248 (S.D.N.Y. 1972); Madsen v. Murray & Sons Co., Inc., 743 P.2d 1212, 5 UCCR2d 99 (Utah 1987); Smyers v. Quartz Works Corp., 880 F. Supp. 1425, 27 UCCR2d 142 (D. Kan. 1995).

[392] See § 7.04[C], *supra*, where the meaning of market price and problems in determining market price are discussed in connection with a buyer's UCC § 2-713 market-minus-contract remedy.

[393] See Cole v. Melvin, 441 F. Supp. 193, 22 UCCR 1154 (D.S.D. 1997).

[394] For a discussion of the market price of used aircraft and spare parts inventory, *see* Northwest Airlines, Inc. v. Flight Trails, 3 F.3d 292, 24 UCCR2d 94 (8th Cir. 1993).

723(2) provides some needed leeway; when evidence of the market price prevailing at the time and place specified by section 2-708(1) is not readily available, proof of market prices and other times and places that can serve as commercially reasonable substitutes may be offered.[395]

In situations where proof of market price is difficult, expensive, or open to dispute, section 2-708(1) presents problems for sellers and for the compensation principle. In such situations, the provision often proves an imprecise tool for putting an aggrieved seller in the financial position it would have occupied had the buyer performed.

Difficulties in achieving compensation can also result from the section 2-708(1) mandate to measure damages in terms of the market price "at the time and place for tender." In some situations, this provision works well and produces damages that protect the seller's expectation interest and approximate the damages that would have obtained had the seller resold under section 2-706. Case 1 affords an example. There, the place for tender was the seller's place, the goods were at that place at the time of the buyer's default, and the buyer's default and the seller's learning of it occurred at the time for tender. In such circumstances, a resale, had there been one, probably would have occurred at the seller's place, and not more than a commercially reasonable time after the time for tender. But consider some different circumstances:

Case 2. Seller and Buyer, located 200 miles apart, agreed to the purchase and sale of a new machine for $25,000, F.O.B. Seller's city, Seller to ship by June 1. On May 30, Seller shipped a conforming machine. The machine arrived in Buyer's city on June 2, and, on June 6, after inspecting it, Buyer rejected—wrongfully. Assume that Seller did not resell the machine under section 2-706 and that Buyer's wrongful rejection did not cause Seller to lose a profit and thus did not open section 2-708(2).

Here there are problems with measuring damages in terms of the market price at the "time and place for tender." First, what is the time "for" tender? The last day on which tender could be made in conformance with the contract—June 1? Or the earlier day on which tender was actually made—May 30? More important, why measure damages at the time for tender in a situation where the seller learns of the breach and gets his first opportunity to deal with it at a different time—here the June 6 date of rejection?[396] Still more important, why the place for tender—the seller's

---

[395] *Id.*

[396] Similar and perhaps greater difficulties with U.C.C. § 2-708(1)'s time for tender may arise when the buyer repudiates. They are considered in the next subsection of this text.

point in a shipment contract situation like this[397]—when the goods are hundreds (or perhaps thousands) of miles away at the buyer's point when the seller learns of the default? In situations like Case 2, a seller electing to resell under section 2-706 would often do so at the goods' location—the buyer's point—and obviously cannot do so until after learning of the seller's rejection. The buyer's point and the time of the rejection consequently seem better points for measuring market price and the seller's loss.[398]

Although the drafters' choice of the "time and place for tender" as the point for determining market price is subject to criticism, it often has little or no adverse effect. For many goods, the market price does not fluctuate rapidly and is pretty much the same at various locations. A literal application of the section 2-708(1) formulation results in significant over- or undercompensation in a few cases, but only in a few cases. In those cases, courts may deal with the problem by employing expanded ideas of "incidental damages," "expenses saved in consequence of the buyer's breach," or "market price" itself, or by appeal to the overriding compensation principle expressed in section 1-106. And well-advised sellers can deal with the problem by reselling under section 2-706.

The section 2-708(1) formula calls for the subtraction of the market price from the *unpaid* contract price, and thus gives the defaulting buyer credit for any payments it has made on the price. In so doing, it avoids the pitfall into which section 2-706 fell, which is discussed in § 7.08[A]. As with section 2-706, however, questions can arise in connection with section 2-708(1)'s "together with any incidental damages" language. Consider:

Case 3. Seller agreed to sell and Buyer to buy a new machine for $25,000. Buyer made a $2,000 downpayment at the time of contract formation. Later, Buyer wrongfully rejected Seller's proper tender. The market price at the time and place for tender was $24,000. Seller incurred $750 in incidental damages and saved $200 in consequence of Buyer's breach.

The basic section 2-708(1) formula of unpaid contract price (here $23,000) minus market price (here $24,000) yields a zero recovery. Because Seller holds Buyer's $2,000 downpayment, Buyer's default has not placed Seller in a worse financial position than Seller would have occupied had Buyer performed. But Seller might nevertheless argue that it is entitled to

---

[397] U.C.C. §§ 2-319(1)(a), 2-503(2), 2-504, 2-509(1)(a).

[398] In the analogous situation of a buyer's market-minus-contract damages, U.C.C. § 2-713 calls for using market price "at the time the buyer learned of the breach" and "as of the place for tender or, in cases of rejection after arrival or revocation of acceptance, as of the place of arrival." This formulation seems better adapted to placing the aggrieved party in the financial position that performance would have done than the U.C.C. § 2-708(1) formulation, and it is puzzling why the drafters did not incorporate it into section 2-708(1).

recover its incidental damages less the expenses it saved because of Buyer's breach. Seller would base its argument on the statutory language, contending that it is entitled to recover the unpaid contract price minus the market price (here zero) "together with" its incidental damages of $750, less the $200 of expenses that it saved, or a total of $550. On facts like those of Case 3, Seller's argument should be rejected. Buyer's $2,000 downpayment covers—in fact, more than covers—both (1) the $1,000 difference between the contract price and the market price and (2) the $550 of incidental damages less expenses saved that Seller is claiming. Buyer's downpayment has thus placed Seller in a better financial position than performance would have done. In such circumstances, Seller has no need for a recovery, and granting it one would violate section 1-106's compensation principle.

A further overcompensation problem can arise when a seller both resells the contract goods and seeks to recover under section 2-708(1). Consider:

Case 4. Seller, a wheat farmer, agreed to sell its crop of 10,000 bushels to Buyer for $65,000. Seller made a proper tender, and Buyer wrongfully rejected. At the time and place for tender, the market price was $60,000. Two weeks later, Seller resold the wheat for $64,000. Seller then sued Buyer for section 2-708(1) damages, praying for the $5,000 difference between the $65,000 unpaid contract price and the $60,000 market price.

Buyer's predictable response will be that Seller is entitled to be placed in the financial position that performance would have done but not in a better position. Because Seller has realized $64,000 by reselling, it needs only the $1,000 difference between the contract price and the resale price; awarding it the larger ($5,000) difference between the contract price and the market price would overcompensate Seller, placing it $4,000 ahead of the financial position it would have occupied had Buyer performed.[399]

Neither the Code nor its Comments provide a clear answer to the dispute between Seller and Buyer over the appropriate measure of damages. But the approach proposed by Professors White and Summers[400] and approved in *Tesoro Petroleum Corp. v. Holborn Oil Co.*[401] is sound and should

---

[399] The problem of overcompensation posed by this hypothetical is likely to arise only in limited circumstances, and primarily when, as in the hypothetical, the goods are fungible and actively traded so that their market prices fluctuate rapidly and can be readily proved. If the goods were of a different sort—say a used bulldozer—it would be difficult for a seller to prove a market price that was significantly lower than the resale price. An argument open to the buyer in such a situation would be that the resale price was good evidence of the market price.

[400] J. White & R. Summers, Uniform Commercial Code § 7-7 (4th ed. 1995).

[401] 145 Misc. 2d 715, 547 N.Y.S.2d 1012, 10 UCCR2d 814 (1989).

be followed. This would allow a seller that is aggrieved because its buyer has committed one of the four section 2-703 triggering events to recover contract-minus-market damages under section 2-708(1), and to do so even though it has resold the contract goods, *unless* the buyer carries the burden of proving that, because of the advantageous resale, this measure would overcompensate the seller—would place it in a better financial position than performance would have done. By carrying this burden, the buyer could limit the seller's recovery to the difference between the contract price and the resale price ($1,000 in Case 4). The aim of, and justification for, this approach is, of course, fidelity to the compensation principle.

The burden that we are suggesting for the buyer is a heavy one. To keep a seller from recovering under section 2-708(1), the buyer would have to show that (1) the seller resold the contract goods, (2) realized a price higher than the market price on which it seeks to base a section 2-708(1) recovery, and (3) could not have made the "resale" but for the buyer's breach. If the seller could have performed the contract with the buyer and also made the sale which the buyer now labels a resale (if, for example, the goods are fungible and readily available, like bushels of wheat, and if the seller is a trader that frequently enters the market to buy and sell, and not a farmer selling its crop as in Case 4), the supposed "resale" is not a substitute for the broken-contract sale. It is instead a transaction that is unrelated to the breach and to the seller's loss. In such circumstances, the seller should be able to recover damages under section 2-708(1), or, perhaps, a lost profit under section 2-708(2).

In most cases in which this problem arises, the resale does not qualify as a section 2-706 resale because the seller will not have given the buyer the requisite notice, and, perhaps for other reasons as well. Because the seller has not complied with section 2-706, it is "relegated"[402] to section 2-708(1). In other cases the resale will comply with the requirements of section 2-706. Regardless of whether the resale qualifies under section 2-706, the buyer may want to try to show that the section 2-708(1) measure will overcompensate the seller and that the seller can be adequately compensated in terms of the resale price. Buyers making this election will be shouldering heavy burdens. The cases in which they can carry them and limit sellers to damages based on resale prices are likely to be few.

---

[402] Comment 2 to U.C.C. § 2-706 states that "[f]ailure to act properly under this section deprives the seller of the measure of damages here provided and *relegates* him to that provided in Section 2-708." [Emphasis supplied.]

[C] Damages on Repudiation

Many of the problems facing a seller aggrieved by a buyer's repudiation have already been discussed.[403] They were presented in connection with a buyer's action on repudiation by the seller. Because the general Code sections on repudiation (sections 2-610 and 2-611) and the Code section on proof of market price when a repudiation case comes to trial before the date set for performance (section 2-723) apply irrespective of which party is the repudiator, many of the ideas already explored have direct application when the buyer repudiates. These ideas are:

First, there is the problem of determining whether and when a buyer has repudiated. This problem is both definitional and factual. The Code does not define repudiation, but this text has concluded that the term is used in the sense of an anticipatory repudiation under the law of contracts.[404] Thus, a buyer's repudiation would be a statement or act made or done before the buyer has received the seller's performance, indicating that the buyer will not or cannot perform its contractual obligations.[405] It is often difficult to determine, as a matter of fact, whether the words or actions of the buyer amount to a repudiation, or whether they are only strong requests for a contract modification—such as a lowering of the price—the buyer remaining willing to perform according to the contract, albeit reluctantly, if the request is denied. Sometimes the seller can clear up the ambiguity by using section 2-609.[406] Even if the buyer's words or actions do not amount to a repudiation, they may give the seller "reasonable grounds for insecurity." If they do, the seller may demand "adequate assurance of due performance," and, if commercially reasonable and if the buyer has not already paid, suspend its performance—the delivery of the goods—until it receives adequate assurance. Further, the buyer's failure, after a justified demand, to provide adequate assurance within a reasonable time (which reasonable time cannot exceed thirty days) is, by force of section 2-609(4), a repudiation of the contract, opening section 2-703 and the remedies to which it leads. If, on the other hand, the buyer furnishes assurance which, in the circumstances,

---

[403] Section 7.04[D], *supra*.

[404] *Id.*

[405] *See* § 250 of the Restatement (Second) of Contracts and Comment 1 to U.C.C. § 2-610.

[406] The use of U.C.C. § 2-609 in this context is discussed in § 7.04[D] of this text.

is adequate, there is no repudiation, and both parties remain obligated under the contract.[407]

If, after a buyer's repudiation (whether clear on its face from the beginning or arising out of the buyer's failure to provide adequate assurance within a reasonable time), the seller seeks damages based on market price under section 2-708(1), it will encounter statutory difficulties concerning the date as of which the market price is to be determined. As has been discussed in § 7.08[B], section 2-708(1) provides that the relevant market price is the market price at the time for tender. Thus, if the contract called for delivery on August 1 and the buyer repudiated on May 1, the important market price (according to section 2-708(1)) is the August 1 market price.

But section 2-610(a) complicates matters by allowing the aggrieved seller to await the repudiating buyer's performance for a commercially reasonable time, implying that a seller that waits longer will be unable to hold the buyer responsible for damages caused by a decline in market price after the expiration of the commercially reasonable time. If section 2-610(a) is to be given effect, it would seem that damages should be calculated in terms of the market price at the end of a commercially reasonable time after the repudiation.

Section 2-723(1) further complicates the situation by providing:

> If an action based on anticipatory repudiation comes to trial before the time of performance with respect to some or all of the goods, any damages based on market price (Section 2-708 or Section 2-713) shall be determined according to the price of such goods prevailing when the aggrieved party learned of the repudiation.

Thus, the Code presents several answers to the problem of when market price is to be ascertained for purposes of measuring a seller's repudiation damages. Section 2-708(1) selects the time for tender; section 2-610(a) suggests that the important date is the date on which a commercially reasonable time following the repudiation terminates (often well before the time for tender); and section 2-723 states that, when trial occurs before the performance date, the important date is the date on which the seller learned of the repudiation.

A similar problem arises when the seller repudiates and the buyer seeks market-price damages under section 2-713. This is discussed in § 7.04[D]

---

[407] For cases dealing with a seller's use of U.C.C. § 2-609, *see* Scott v. Crown, 765 P.2d 1043, 7 UCCR2d 464 (Colo. Ct. App. 1988); Smyers v. Quartz Works Corp., 880 F. Supp. 1425, 27 UCCR2d 142 (D. Kan. 1995); S&S, Inc. v. Meyer, 478 N.W.2d 857, 17 UCCR2d 137 (Iowa Ct. App. 1991).

of this text. The conclusions reached there are relevant here. The different approaches taken in different Code sections appear to be the result of oversight rather than design. The difficulties they create ought to be resolved in accordance with the Code's fundamental remedial policies. The Code's treatment of resale as the seller's primary remedy, its emphasis on compensation as the goal of all remedies, and its regard for commercial practices push toward measuring a seller's market-price repudiation damages as of the date when the seller could be expected to resell—that is, at the end of a commercially reasonable time after the seller learns of the repudiation.

[D] Recovery of Lost Profits

Damages measured by either the section 2-706 contract-minus-resale formula or the section 2-708(1) contract-minus-market formula are insufficient to compensate—that is, to protect the expectation interests of—a number of sellers. Consider the situation of lost-volume sellers,[408] sellers that have the capacity either to purchase or to manufacture more goods than they can sell. In many circumstances, a buyer's wrongful refusal to take contract goods from such a seller (whether by way of wrongful rejection, wrongful revocation of acceptance, or repudiation), does not make a substitute transaction (such as a resale or a realization of the market value of the goods) available to the seller. The seller had the goods, or the ability to get the goods, to make another sale even if the buyer had performed. When this is so—when no additional transaction is made possible by the buyer's breach—none of the seller's additional transactions functions as a substitute for the contract that the buyer has broken. No additional transaction is relevant to the measurement of the seller's lost expectancy—to placing the seller in the financial position that performance would have done. Rather than losing the difference between a favorable broken contract and a less favorable substitute transaction made possible by the buyer's breach, a lost-volume seller may lose an entire transaction, and whatever gain or profit it would have realized on that transaction. The fact that such a seller engaged in additional transactions and made profits on them does not compensate it or substitute for the lost transaction, because the seller could have engaged in the additional transactions even if the buyer had performed. These ab-

---

[408] The term "lost-volume seller" appears to have been coined by Professor Robert J. Harris in his article, "A Radical Restatement of the Law of Seller's Damages: Sales Act and Commercial Code Results Compared," 18 Stan. L. Rev. 66 (1965), an article that has played a leading role in shaping thinking about, and results under, U.C.C. § 2-708(2).

stractly stated observations can, perhaps, be best grasped in terms of an illustration. Consider:

Case 1. Retailer contracted to sell a new personal computer to Consumer for $1,500, Consumer to take delivery and pay for the computer three days after contract formation. Consumer changed his mind about the purchase and wrongfully rejected the computer. The computer involved was a popular model that was generally being sold at retail for $1,500, both by Retailer and by Retailer's competitors. During the week following Consumer's breach, Retailer sold the computer whose corrugated carton it had tagged with Consumer's name to another customer, for $1,500. During the same week, Retailer also sold fourteen other identical computers, all in corrugated cartons, to fourteen other customers, each of whom paid $1,500. Retailer then purchased thirty other identical computers from the manufacturer, and proceeded to sell them for $1,500 each.

In Case 1, as in many situations involving mass produced goods that are widely distributed, the market price, the resale price, and the contract price are one and the same: $1,500. A consequence is that both the section 2-706 contract-minus-resale formula and the section 2-708(1) contract-minus-market formula will yield zero, or nominal-damage recoveries. Yet Retailer has had a more significant loss. Had Consumer performed, Retailer would have earned a profit on the Consumer transaction. It is true that Retailer earned profits on the other sales it made, but these are not relevant to its loss of the Consumer profit, as Retailer would have earned them even if Consumer had performed. If Retailer is to be placed in the financial position that it would have occupied had Consumer performed, it needs to recover the profit that Consumer's performance would have given it.

In seeking to recover the profit that it needs, Retailer should proceed under section 2-708(2). Although the wording of this subsection poses a number of problems, it can and has been read to protect the expectation interests of lost-volume sellers like Retailer. Specifically, it provides:

> (2) If the measure of damages provided in subsection (1) is inadequate to put the seller in as good a position as performance would have done then the measure of damages is the profit (including reasonable overhead) which the seller would have made from full performance by the buyer, together with any incidental damages provided in this Article (Section 2-710), due allowance for costs reasonably incurred and due credit for payments or proceeds of resale.

"Profit" is not defined,[409] but has and should be read to mean contract price less cost to the seller—"cost" meaning variable costs—the costs that would have been incurred to perform the broken contract.[410] To illustrate, recall the facts of Case 1 and suppose that Retailer paid the manufacturer $1,200 for the computer that Consumer agreed to buy for $1,500. These facts suggest that Retailer has lost a profit of $300 ($1,500 − $1,200). However, adjustment may be required because Retailer may have other variable costs. Suppose, for example, that the $1,200 that Retailer paid for the computer was not a delivered price, but a price at the manufacturer's plant and that Retailer had also expended $25 to transport the computer to its store. In these circumstances Retailer's variable costs would not be $1,200, but rather $1,225. Thus Retailer's lost profit would not be $300, but $275.

The only costs that should be subtracted from the contract price to determine lost profit are variable costs—costs that the seller saved, or could reasonably have saved, by not performing the broken contract. The seller's fixed costs of doing business—costs that do not vary with the number of sales made (such as real estate taxes, heating, lighting, and cooling costs, administrative salaries, and the like)—are not to be deducted. Such fixed costs are commonly referred to as "overhead," and section 2-708(2) expressly provides that the seller's recoverable profit is to include "reasonable overhead." That is, the recoverable profit is a gross profit rather than a net

---

[409] Comment 2 to U.C.C. § 2-708 suggests the meaning of profit in a lost-volume situations like Case 1:

> [Subsection 2-708(2)] permits the recovery of lost profits in all appropriate cases, which would include all standard priced goods. The normal measure there would be list price less cost to the dealer or list price less manufacturing cost to the manufacturer.

While not as clear or precise as they might be, these two Comment sentences provide significant evidence of the drafters' intention. The references to "all standard priced goods" and to dealers and manufacturers suggest that the drafters intended to provide lost-profit recoveries to retailers and wholesalers that can procure more goods than they can sell and to manufacturers that have the capacity to manufacture more goods than they can profitably sell. The "normal measure" of lost-profit damages for such sellers is the contract price (the apparent meaning of "list price") less the price paid for the goods (for a dealer) or the cost of their manufacture (for a manufacturer).

[410] This meaning should be given to "profit" because it is the meaning that will enable the Code to work its underlying purpose of putting the aggrieved seller in the financial position that performance would have done.

833

profit. This makes compensatory sense, as has been clearly articulated in *Vitex Manufacturing Corp., Ltd. v. Caribtex Corp.*:[411]

> [N]ormally, in a claim for lost profits, overhead should be treated as a part of gross profits and recoverable as damages, and should not be considered as part of the seller's costs. A number of cases hold that since overhead expenses are not affected by the performance of the particular contract, there should be no need to deduct them in computing lost profits. . . . The theory of these cases is that the seller is entitled to recover losses incurred and gains prevented in excess of savings made possible . . . ; since overhead is fixed and nonperformance of the contract produced no overhead cost savings, no deduction from profits should result. . . .
>
> It is true that successful businessmen must set their prices at sufficient levels to recoup all their expenses, including overhead, and to gain profits. Thus, the price the businessman should charge on each transaction could be thought of as that price necessary to yield a pro rata portion of the company's fixed overhead, the direct costs associated with production, and a "clear" profit. Doubtless this type of calculation is used by businessmen and their accountants. . . . However, because it is useful for planning purposes to allocate a portion of overhead to each transaction, it does not follow that this allocate share should be considered a cost factor in the computation of lost profits on individual transactions.
>
> By the very nature of this allocation process, as the number of transactions over which overhead can be spread becomes smaller, each transaction must bear a greater portion or allocate share of fixed overhead cost. Suppose a company has fixed overhead of $10,000 and engages in five similar transactions; then the receipts of each transaction would bear $2,000 of overhead expense. If the company is now forced to spread this $10,000 over only four transactions, then the overhead expense per transaction will rise to $2,500, significantly reducing the profitability of the remaining four transactions.

Although it points toward the proper result—that the seller's section 2-708(2) recovery should be of gross rather than net profit—the statutory language "(including reasonable overhead)" can be read to create needless

---

[411] 377 F.2d 795, 4 UCCR 182 (3d Cir. 1967). *See also* Jericho Sash & Door Co., Inc. v. Building Erectors, Inc., 362 Mass 871, 286 N.E.2d 343, 10 UCCR 1377 (1972); Rogerson Aircraft Corp. v. Fairchild Industries, Inc., 632 F. Supp. 1494, 1 UCCR2d 1572 (C.D. Cal. 1986); Teradyne, Inc. v. Teledyne Indus., Inc., 676 F.2d 865, 33 UCCR 1669 (1st Cir. 1982); Leingang v. City of Mandan Weed Board, 468 N.W.2d 397 (N.D. 1991); Kearsarge Computer, Inc. v. Acme Stable Co., 116 N.H. 705, 366 A.2d 467 (1976).

complexity. In particular, it can, but should not, be read to require that the seller begin by showing its net profit on the broken contract (subtracting overhead in doing so) and then prove the subtracted overhead so that it may be added back to determine the damages the seller may recover. Because, as *Vitex* has so clearly pointed out, the allocation of overhead to particular transactions is nothing other than an accountant's or business person's construct that is useful for planning and pricing purposes, it need not be expressly addressed in determining the lost profits that the seller is entitled to recover. Those profits can be determined by subtracting the seller's variable costs from the contract price. When this is done, overhead will automatically and properly be recovered.[412]

The statutory reference to "reasonable" overhead is puzzling. Suppose the seller's overhead is "unreasonably" high. This means that the seller will make a smaller net profit than it would have made had its overhead been lower. The seller, nevertheless, should recover its net profit if it is to be "placed in as good a position as performance would have done," and to recover its full net profit it also needs to recover its actual overhead, even if that overhead is higher than that of similarly situated sellers.[413] To limit the overhead portion of the hypothetical seller's recovery to less than actual overhead—to overhead that would have been "reasonable" (whatever that means)—would necessarily leave the seller in a position short of performance, and thus fail to protect its expectation interest fully.

Suppose, alternatively, that the seller's overhead is "unreasonably" low. This means that the seller will make a greater net profit than it would have made had its overhead been higher. Again, the seller deserves to be "placed in as good a position as performance would have done," and this requires recovery of the lost net profit plus actual overhead. Allowing this hypothetical seller to recover its net profit plus "reasonable" (higher than actual) overhead would put it in a better position than performance would have done, and thus overcompensate it. Perhaps all the drafters meant by "reasonable" overhead was to limit the seller's overhead recovery to costs that

---

[412] Jericho Sash & Door Co., Inc. v. Building Erectors, Inc., 362 Mass. 871, 286 N.E. 2d 343, 10 UCCR 1377(1972).

[413] If the seller has incurred "overhead" expenses (*e.g.*, utility or labor costs) that it could reasonably have saved as a result of the buyer's breach, these expenses should be deducted from the seller's recovery. This is because if the expenses should reasonably have been saved as a result of the buyer's breach, they should be considered variable costs, not overhead for purposes of 2-708(2).

can be reasonably classified as overhead—as fixed rather than variable costs.[414]

The section 2-708(2) statutory language calls for adjusting the seller's lost profits recovery in four ways: "together with [1] any incidental damages provided in this Article (2-710), due allowance for [2] costs reasonably incurred and due credit for [3] payments or [4] proceeds of resale." Two of these, the addition of section 2-710 incidental damages to the seller's lost profits recovery and crediting the buyer with any payments on the price that it has made, are straightforward and should cause little difficulty.

The third, "due allowance for costs reasonably incurred," deserves explanation. This text has proposed that a lost-volume seller's lost profit be determined by subtracting the seller's variable costs from the contract price. Thus, in Case 1, Retailer's lost profit would be the $1,500 contract price of the computer less its $1,200 cost and the $25 expense of transporting it to Retailer's store, or $275. But now suppose that there was another expense involved in the transaction: that in exchange for the $1,500 price, Retailer had agreed not only to sell the computer but also to deliver it to Consumer's house (a service costing $30). Suppose, further, that Consumer defaulted, say repudiated, before Retailer spent the $30 on delivery, thus enabling Retailer to save this cost. In these circumstances, placing Retailer in the position that performance would have done calls for a $245 recovery. Had Consumer performed, Retailer would have realized a profit of $245 (the $1,500 contract price less (1) the $1,200 cost of the computer, (2) the $25 expense of transporting the computer to Retailer's store, and (3) the $30 expense of transporting it to Consumer's house). Note that the three costs that are subtracted from the contract price are not only variable costs, they are also saveable costs. Retailer saves the cost of the computer and the cost of transporting it to Retailer's store because it can use these costs in making another sale. Retailer saves the cost of transporting the computer to Consumer's house because Consumer's early breach enabled Retailer to avoid spending that money.

Now suppose that Consumer did not repudiate before Retailer delivered the computer to Consumer's house; suppose, instead, that Consumer wrongfully rejected when the delivery was made—after Retailer had expended $30 in making the delivery. Now placing Retailer in the position that performance would have done calls for a $275 recovery. Retailer needs to recover both its $245 profit on the transaction and its $30 in wasted, non-

---

[414] The suggestion in Comment 2 to U.C.C. § 2-708(2) that the measure of recovery for a lost volume seller is contract price less variable costs saved supports this interpretation of "reasonable."

saveable variable costs. The "due allowance for costs reasonably incurred" statutory language is directed at such wasted, nonsaveable costs. The protection of the seller's expectation interest requires their recovery. But care must be taken in applying the statutory language and the underlying principles to particular facts, lest either over- or undercompensation result.

The fourth adjusting factor, "due credit for . . . proceeds of resale," makes no sense when applied to a lost-volume situation such as Case 1. If Consumer is given credit for the $1,500 that Retailer receives when it resells the computer intended for Consumer, Retailer's lost profit recovery will be wiped out and replaced by a nominal-damages recovery, leaving Retailer significantly short of the position it would have enjoyed had Consumer performed. The courts have consequently decided that "due credit for . . . proceeds of resale" is not to be applied to lost-volume situations such as Case 1, but rather to situations in which a manufacturing or assembling seller resells partially completed goods after its buyer repudiates, as is illustrated in Case 2, discussed later in this section. Thus, in *Teradyne, Inc. v. Teledyne Industries, Inc.*,[415] the First Circuit observed that:

> [I]t is universally agreed that in a case where after the buyer's default a seller resells the goods, the proceeds of the resale are not to be credited to the buyer if the seller is a lost volume seller—that is, one who had there been no breach by the buyer, could and would have had the benefit of both the original contract and the resale contract.

Although many of the problems inherent in the language of section 2-708(2) have been judicially resolved,[416] the section remains difficult to apply. The facts of lost-volume cases vary widely, and few are as simple as those of Case 1. The calculation and adjustment of the profit that the seller has lost so as to achieve full compensation, and not overcompensation, frequently require careful thought. Arguments frequently arise as to whether the seller has in fact lost a profit—whether it deserves to recover under section 2-708(2) rather than section 2-708(1).

Some cases are plain. When the goods involved are unique, when the seller's supply of the goods (and ability to obtain more of them) is limited, or when the seller is a manufacturer operating at full capacity (has more customers than it can profitably supply), the buyer's section 2-703 breach

---

[415] 676 F.2d 865, 33 UCCR 1669 (1st Cir. 1982).

[416] *See, e.g.*, Neri v. Retail Marine Corp., 30 N.Y.2d 393, 334 N.Y.S.2d 165, 285 N.E.2d 311, 10 UCCR 950 (1972); Famous Knitwear Corp. v. Drug Fair, Inc., 493 F.2d 251, 14 UCCR 415 (4th Cir. 1974); Teradyne, Inc. v. Teledyne Indus., Inc., 676 F.2d 865, 33 UCCR 1669 (1st Cir. 1982).

will make a resale possible. In such circumstances, section 2-706 or section 2-708(1) will be adequate to protect the seller's expectation interest, and section 2-708(2) is not triggered. Other cases are more difficult. Suppose that Dealer (a new car dealer) has or can acquire more cars than it can sell. And suppose that Dealer has contracted to sell a new car to Buyer. The car involved was the only one of the particular model, color, and accessory package that Dealer had in stock, and it would take Dealer three weeks to obtain a duplicate from the manufacturer or from another dealer. Buyer repudiated, and on the next day Dealer sold the car that Buyer had agreed to buy to Purchaser. Purchaser bought only because (1) the car that Buyer had agreed to buy was precisely what Purchaser wanted and (2) it was in stock and immediately available. Had that car not been on Dealer's lot, Purchaser would have continued to shop and would have purchased a car from another dealer. In these circumstances, Dealer, although able to obtain more goods than it can sell, has not lost a sale because of Buyer's breach; but for Buyer's breach, Dealer could not have sold to Purchaser. Difference-money damages, under section 2-706 or section 2-708(1) are consequently adequate to compensate Dealer.

While it is easy to state, hypothetically, that Purchaser would not have purchased but for the fact that Buyer's breach made a particular car available at a particular time, proving this (or its opposite) is another matter. An important section 2-708(2) question is what burden of proof the plaintiff seller must carry to establish the right to a lost-volume, lost-profit recovery and to shift to the defendant buyer the burden of showing that there has in fact been no loss of a profit. The Seventh Circuit has considered the allocation of the burden of proof in connection with economics-based arguments[417] that lost-profit recoveries can result in overcompensation:

> Courts awarding lost profits to a lost volume seller have focused on whether the seller had the capacity to supply the breached units in addition to what it actually sold. In reality, however, the relevant questions include, not only whether the seller could have produced the breached units in addition to its actual volume, but also whether it would have been profitable for the seller to produce both units. Goetz & Scott,

---

[417] Some of the leading law review articles that have brought economic analysis to bear on U.C.C. § 2-708(2) and related matters are Charles J. Goetz & Robert E. Scott, "Measuring Seller's Damages: The Lost Profits Puzzle," 31 Stan. L. Rev. 323 (1979); Robert E. Scott, "The Case for Market Damages: Revisiting the Lost Profits Puzzle," 57 U. Chi. L. Rev. 1155 (1990); Victor P. Goldberg, "An Economic Analysis of the Lost Volume Retail Seller," 57 S. Cal. L. Rev. 283 (1984); and Robert Cooter & Melvin Aron Eisenberg, "Damages for Breach of Contract," 73 Cal. L. Rev. 1432 (1985).

Measuring Sellers' Damages: The Lost Profits Puzzle, 31 Stan. L. Rev. 323, 332-33, 346-47 (1979). As one commentator has noted, under

> the economic law of diminishing returns or increasing marginal costs[,] . . . as a seller's volume increases, then a point will inevitably be reached where the cost of selling each additional item diminishes the incremental return to the seller and eventually makes it entirely unprofitable to conclude the next sale.

Shanker, [The Case for a Literal Reading of UCC Section 2-708(2) (One Profit for the Reseller), 24 Case W. Res. L. Rev. 697, 705 (1973)]. Thus, under some conditions, awarding a lost volume seller its presumed lost profit will result in overcompensating the seller, and § 2-708(2) would not take effect because the damage formula provided in § 2-708(1) does place the seller in as good a position as if the buyer had performed. Therefore, on remand, [plaintiff seller] must establish, not only that it had the capacity to produce the breached unit in addition to the unit resold, but also that it would have been profitable for it to have produced and sold both. [Plaintiff seller] carries the burden of establishing these facts because the burden of proof is generally on the party claiming injury to establish the amount of its damages; especially in a case such as this, the plaintiff has easiest access to the relevant data.[418]

In apportioning the burden of proof in lost-volume cases, courts should exercise care lest they impose such heavy burdens on plaintiff sellers that they read section 2-708(2) out of the Code. There is particular risk in this connection where economic data is involved, as this is often difficult and expensive to prove. There is a good deal to be said for requiring a seller to lay only a foundational case for a lost profit and its amount and then shifting the burden to the defendant buyer to prove that, in the circumstances, the seller has not lost a profit or has lost less than the profit claimed. And it should be remembered that, even in circumstances where the seller has lost no net profit, its loss of a transaction is nevertheless harmful, if, and to the extent that, the transaction would have contributed to the defrayal of overhead.

Now consider a different kind of lost-profit situation:

Case 2. For a price of $285,000, Manufacturer agreed to design and manufacture some office furniture for Buyer's executive suite. The furniture was to be designed in accordance with some rough sketches that Buyer provided, and was to be unusual (i.e., custom-made for Buyer). Manufac-

---

[418] R. E. Davis Chem. Corp. v. Diasonics, Inc., 826 F.2d 678, 4 UCCR2d 369 (1987).

turer did the design work (which Buyer approved) at a cost of $20,000, spent $40,000 for the wood (solid walnut), and began to sand and saw the wood. At this point, Buyer repudiated. Exercising reasonable commercial judgment,[419] Manufacturer decided to cease production and sold the wood for $30,000 (the work that it had done before the repudiation having diminished the value of the wood to other buyers). Manufacturer then sued Buyer for damages. In circumstances like these, neither section 2-706 (which contemplates the difference between the contract price and the resale price of the goods contracted for—that is, the completed goods) nor section 2-708(1) (which contemplates the difference between the contract price and the market price of the completed goods) is well designed to measure Manufacturer's loss, for the reason that the goods were never completed. In such a situation, which is sometimes labeled that of a "components" seller,[420] section 2-708(2) can be employed to place the seller in the financial position that performance would have done.

Suppose that Manufacturer proves that, had it completed the furniture, its variable costs would have been $200,000. In so doing, Manufacturer has established that its profit on the transaction would have been $85,000 (contract price ($285,000) less variable costs ($200,000) = profit ($85,000)). If this is adjusted as provided for in section 2-708(2), by adding the costs which Manufacturer has reasonably incurred ($20,000 for the design work and $40,000 for the wood, or $60,000) and by subtracting the proceeds of resale (the $30,000 obtained for the wood), a total recovery of $115,000 is produced (profit, including overhead, of $85,000 plus due allowance for $60,000 in costs reasonably incurred and less due credit for $30,000 in proceeds of resale). This amount plus, perhaps, some section 2-710 incidental damages, and less any payments that Buyer has made on the price, will compensate Manufacturer for both its wasted expenditures and its lost profit and thus put Manufacturer in the financial position that performance would have done.[421]

---

[419] See U.C.C. § 2-704, which is discussed in § 7.08[F], infra, in terms of this factual pattern and variations of it.

[420] The term appears to have been coined by Professor Harris in his "A Radical Restatement of the Law of Seller's Damages: Sales Act and Commercial Code Results Compared," 18 Stan. L. Rev. 66 (1965).

[421] The same dollar result and the same protection of the seller's expectation interest could be achieved under UCC § 2-706, but more awkwardly. Under section 2-706, the formula would be contract price ($285,000) less resale price (here $30,000, the salvage resale of the wood) or $255,000 less "expenses saved in consequence of the buyer's breach," with the unexpended $140,000 of Manufacturer's variable costs being the expenses saved.

The statutory "due credit for . . . proceeds of resale," which did not work at all in lost-volume situations, works well in components situations and was apparently designed for them. It is noteworthy that Case 2's Manufacturer would not have qualified for a lost-profit recovery if it had completed manufacture of the furniture. The furniture was custom-made for Buyer and would not have been available for resale if Buyer had performed. In other words, the resale of the completed furniture would operate as a substitute for the breached contract. Had Manufacturer finished the furniture, difference-money damages under section 2-706 or section 2-708(1) would have been adequate to protect its expectation interest.[422] Thus, a components seller need not show that it lost volume to merit a lost-profit recovery. If, however, a buyer's breach enables a seller to make a profit which it could not otherwise have made, that profit ought to mitigate or reduce the damages that the seller could otherwise recover.[423] Thus, if Manufacturer had been operating at full capacity, and if Buyer's repudiation (coupled with Manufacturer's cessation of work on the Buyer job) had enabled Manufacturer to make another sale, a sale it could not have made had Buyer performed, the profit Manufacturer made on the additional sale ought to reduce Manufacturer's recovery. From a remedial standpoint, Manufacturer's situation is the same as that of a full-time employee who, having been discharged in breach of an employment contract, uses the time that has been freed to take another job. The earnings of the job made available by the employer's breach of the employment contract mitigate the damages which the employer must pay. Similarly, sale profits made available only because of a buyer's breach should mitigate the damages that the buyer must pay.[424]

By its terms, section 2-708(2) makes a lost-profit recovery available only when the contract-minus-market measure of section 2-708(1) is inadequate to protect the seller's expectation interest. The drafters' apparent assumption was that a seller's lost profit would, in most circumstances, be

---

[422] To see that this is so, suppose that Manufacturer completed the furniture (at a cost of $200,000) and resold it under U.C.C. § 2-706 for $220,000. Manufacturer could recover the $285,000 contract price less the $220,000 resale price or $65,000 under section 2-706. This plus the $220,000 realized on the resale would compensate Manufacturer for both its outlays of $200,000 and its profit of $85,000.

When a buyer repudiates, the question of whether a seller situated like Manufacturer should (1) cease work and salvage the components it has on hand or (2) complete the job and resell the finished goods is governed by U.C.C. § 2-704 and is discussed in § 7.08[F], *infra*.

[423] *See* USX Corp. v. Union Pac Resource Co., 753 S.W.2d 845, 7 UCCR2d 100 (Tex. Ct. Civ. App. 1988).

[424] *See* § 350 of the Restatement (Second) of Contracts and its comment c.

greater than the contract-minus-market differential. In some situations, however, the contract-minus-market differential is greater than a seller's lost profit, an aggrieved seller will predictably seek damages under either section 2-708(1) or section 2-706. In most cases, there will be no problem with this. But what of the rare case where the contract-minus-market measure overcompensates the seller—puts it in a better financial position than performance would have done? Can the buyer limit the seller to a smaller lost-profit recovery? In *Nobs Chemical, USA, Inc. v. Koppers Co., Inc.*,[425] the Fifth Circuit answered that the buyer could do so. The case involved an agreement by Koppers to buy 1,000 tons of cumene (an additive to motor fuel) from Nobs for $540,000.[426] Nobs was operating as a trader or jobber, and had a contractual right, but not a contractual obligation, to acquire the cumene for $445,000—meaning that it expected to realize a profit of $95,000 on the transaction. Koppers repudiated before Nobs had acquired the cumene and at a time when the cumene's market price had dropped to $250,000. Nobs consequently declined to acquire the cumene and sued Koppers for damages under section 2-708(1)—that is, for the $290,000 difference between the $540,000 contract price and the $250,000 market price. Both the trial court and the affirming Fifth Circuit refused to award these damages and instead limited Nobs to its $95,000 lost profit. The rationale was that, on the facts of the case, the smaller lost-profit recovery placed the seller in the financial position it would have occupied on full performance while the section 2-708(1) contract-minus-market measure would have substantially overcompensated the seller.

The language and structure of the Code, which treat the section 2-708(1) contract-minus-market measure as the standard, automatically available remedy, and the section 2-708(2) lost-profit measure as unusual and available only when section 2-708(1) is inadequate to compensate the seller, gave the court difficulty. But the court's result is fully justified under the compensation principle articulated in section 1-106, and we approve it. It is noteworthy, however, that while the result makes sense on the *Nobs* facts, it will not make sense in many situations. Suppose, for example, that Nobs had acquired the cumene at a cost of $445,000 before Koppers repudiated. Then, Nobs would need to dispose of the cumene on the market, and, to be placed in the position that performance would have done, it would need to recover under section 2-708(1) or section 2-706, even though the recovery

---

[425] 616 F.2d 212, 28 UCCR 1039 (5th Cir. 1980), *reh'g denied*, 618 F.2d 1389 (5th Cir. 1980).

[426] In the interests of brevity, this text's exposition of the *Nobs Chemical* case both simplifies and clarifies the facts of that case.

is much greater than its lost profit. In the circumstances now supposed, Nobs would have a reliance loss (the difference between its acquisition cost of $445,000 and the market price of $250,000) as well as a lost profit of $95,000, and compensation would call for a recovery of both (a recovery which either section 2-706 or section 2-708(1) would provide). Alternatively, suppose that, while Nobs had not actually acquired the cumene at the time of Koppers' repudiation, it was then contractually obligated to acquire it at a price of $445,000. Again, Nobs would have lost the difference between the $540,000 contract price and the $250,000 market price.

[E] Recovery of the Price

An action for the price—the contract price—of the goods is not the seller's standard remedy under the Code. On the contrary, it is provided for only in limited circumstances: when the buyer has failed to pay the price as it becomes due *and* (1) the buyer has accepted the goods, (2) the goods have been lost or damaged after the risk of their loss has passed to the buyer, *or* (3) the goods are not resaleable at a reasonable price.[427]

The more usual monetary remedies for an aggrieved seller are those that have just been considered (sections 2-706, 2-708(1), and 2-708(2)), and all of them lead to recoveries that are significantly less than the full contract price. Under section 2-706, the seller's recovery is the difference between the contract price and the resale price; under section 2-708(1), it is the difference between the contract price and the market price; and under section 2-708(2) it is the seller's lost profit (i.e., the price less the seller's variable costs). When section 2-706, 2-708(1), or 2-708(2) applies, the goods remain in the seller's hands, and, in assessing the damages that the buyer must pay, the buyer is in effect credited for their value. This means that the aggrieved seller and not the defaulting buyer is left with the problem of disposing of the goods on the market.

An action for the price is the equivalent of an action for specific performance against the buyer. If broadly available, it would have a "cramdown" effect, figuratively enabling sellers to cram unwanted goods down defaulting buyers' throats, leaving the buyers with the problem of disposing of the goods. The Code's policy is·otherwise. It is based in part on Anglo-American law's aversion to the compulsion of specific remedies when monetary damages can achieve compensation. It is also based on the fact that sellers are usually better positioned to dispose of goods than buyers. Sellers

---

[427] U.C.C. § 2-709(1).

typically have sales forces, contacts, and expertise in disposing of the kinds of goods that they sell.

The seller's action for the price is provided for in section 2-709. Subsection (1) of this section begins by conditioning the seller's recovery of the price on the occurrence of a triggering event—the buyer's failure "to pay the price as it becomes due"—and goes on to allow recovery of the price in any of three different situations:

> When the buyer fails to pay the price as it becomes due, the seller may recover, together with any incidental damages under the next section, the price
>
> (a) [first situation] of goods accepted or [second situation] of conforming goods lost or damaged within a commercially reasonable time after risk of their loss has passed to the buyer; and
>
> (b) [third situation] of goods identified to the contract if the seller is unable after reasonable effort to resell them at a reasonable price or the circumstances reasonably indicate that such effort will be unavailing.

Goods accepted. The first of these situations—the buyer's having accepted the goods and not paid for them at the promised time—is the most common situation for a price recovery. The seller has tendered the goods, and the buyer has accepted them (as acceptance is defined in section 2-606).[428] That is, the seller has performed, and, by its performance, it has earned the buyer's promised performance.[429] When, as is often the case, the buyer has not only accepted but is also retaining and using the goods, the seller's entitlement to a price recovery seems obvious. The buyer, having the goods, ought to pay for them when its promise to do so matures.[430]

---

[428] Acceptance is considered in § 7.03[D], *supra.*

[429] Note that the first part of U.C.C. § 2-709(1)(a) tracks U.C.C. § 2-607(1): "The buyer must pay at the contract rate for any goods accepted."

[430] Actions for the price under the first part of UCC § 2-709(1)(a) most frequently arise in situations where sellers have delivered goods on credit. Suppose, for example, a contract that calls for payment of the full price thirty days after delivery. In such circumstances, the seller's action for the price becomes available when the thirty-day credit period runs. Suppose, alternatively, a contract that calls for payment in three monthly installments. If the contract contains an acceleration clause, the buyer's failure to pay the first installment when it becomes due enables the seller to accelerate the maturity of the remaining installments and sue for the full price. If the contract contains no acceleration clause, the situation is not so clear. The common-law approach would allow the seller to sue for past-due installments, but not for those not yet due. *See* E. Allan Farnsworth, Contracts 593–594 (3d ed. 1999). One case, however, has held that U.C.C. § 2-709 changes this common-law approach and

The price that the first part of section 2-709(1)(a) entitles the seller to recover is the contract price. As has been discussed, however, the buyer, in appropriate circumstances, can reduce this, because the performance the seller rendered fell short of the performance promised. Thus, if the buyer has accepted nonconforming goods and has given the seller the notice required by section 2-607(3), the buyer will be entitled to damages under section 2-714 on accepted goods and may deduct those damages from its price obligation under section 2-717.[431]

If the buyer does not accept the goods but rather rejects[432] them and does so effectively, the seller cannot recover the price under the first part of section 2-709(1)(a). If the rejection is rightful, the buyer will not be in default and consequently will not be liable to the seller for any damages (the seller will instead be liable to the buyer).[433] If the rejection is wrongful but effective,[434] the buyer will be in default but will have succeeded in thrusting the goods back on the seller, remitting the seller to a less-than-price recovery under section 2-706 or section 2-708.

Suppose that the buyer accepts but then proceeds to revoke its acceptance.[435] Must it still pay the price because it "accepted" the goods? If the revocation was both effective and rightful, the answer is plainly "No." Although the acceptance bound the buyer to pay the contract price,[436] its effective and rightful revocation thrusts the goods back on the seller and avoids the buyer's price obligation. For a revocation of acceptance to be rightful, there must, among other things, be a nonconformity that substantially impairs the value of the goods to the buyer;[437] that is, the seller must be in substantial default. Being in such default and having the goods, the seller does not deserve to recover the price. On the contrary, the seller's default opens the buyer's remedies under section 2-711, and one of those remedies is "recovering so much of the price as has been paid."[438] It would,

---

allows a seller to sue for the entire price of accepted goods on the buyer's missing of a single installment (even though the contract does not contain an acceleration clause). Gantry Constr. Co., Inc. v. American Pipe & Constr. Co., Inc., 49 Cal. App. 3d 186, 122 Cal. Rptr. 834, 17 UCCR 1218 (1975).

[431] *See* the discussion of these matters in §§ 7.03[D], 7.04[E] and 7.04[G], *supra*.

[432] Rejection is covered in U.C.C. § 2-602 and discussed in § 7.03[C], *supra*.

[433] *See* U.C.C. §§ 2-711, 2-712, 2-713, 2-715.

[434] The difference between ineffective and wrongful rejections is discussed in § 7.03[C], *supra*.

[435] Revocation of acceptance is provided for in UCC § 2-608 and discussed in § 7.03[E], *supra*.

[436] U.C.C. § 2-607(1).

[437] U.C.C. § 2-608(1).

[438] U.C.C. § 2-711(1).

of course, make no sense to allow the seller to recover the price under section 2-709 only to return it immediately to the buyer under section 2-711.[439]

If the buyer's revocation was ineffective—if, for example, the buyer delayed too long in giving the seller the required notice[440]—the buyer's acceptance remains intact and so does the buyer's liability for the price. The buyer has failed in its effort to thrust the goods back on the seller.

The most difficult case is that in which the buyer's revocation is effective but wrongful (wrongful, for example, because the nonconformity of the goods did not substantially impair their value to the buyer). An argument can be made that the Code contemplates relieving a wrongfully revoking buyer of liability for the price just as it relieves a wrongfully rejecting buyer of that liability—remitting the aggrieved seller to a section 2-706 or section 2-708 remedy in both situations. Subsection (3) of section 2-709 can be read as supporting that argument.[441] On the other hand, it can be argued that a wrongful revocation does not destroy an acceptance—that it is different from a wrongful rejection, which, under sections 2-606 and 2-602, prevents an acceptance from occurring. Buyers that have accepted goods and have no rightful basis for revoking their acceptances often seem good candidates for price liability. They frequently have used (or perhaps misused) the goods for some time before wrongfully revoking their acceptances. In such circumstances, a seller that rebuffs its buyer's effort wrongfully to revoke may have a good chance at a price recovery.

Suppose that the buyer ineffectively or wrongfully revokes its acceptance, and that the seller, having a right to the price and no obligation to

---

[439] Comment 5 to U.C.C. § 2-709 supports this analysis:

"Goods accepted" by the buyer under subsection (1)(a) include only goods as to which there has been no justified revocation of acceptance, for such a revocation means that there has been a default by the seller which bars his rights under this section.

[440] *See* U.C.C. § 2-608(2) and the discussion in §§ 7.03[C] and 7.03[E], *supra.*
[441] U.C.C. § 2-709(3) provides:

(3) After the buyer has *wrongfully* rejected or *revoked acceptance* of the goods or has failed to make a payment due or has repudiated (Section 2-610), a seller who is held not entitled to the price under this section shall nevertheless be awarded damages for non-acceptance under the preceding section. [Emphasis supplied.]

This can be read as treating a wrongful revocation as a kind of non-acceptance, meaning that there is no price liability under the "goods accepted" language of section 2-709(1)(a).

take the goods back,[442] nevertheless does so. Does this conduct by the seller destroy its right to recover the price? It may be argued that it does—that the seller now has the goods, that the buyer deserves credit for their value, and that section 2-706 or section 2-708 (both of which provide such credit) will adequately and appropriately compensate the seller. But at least one case allowed the seller to recover the price even though it had taken possession of the goods after the buyer's wrongful and ineffective revocation, observing that, under section 2-709(2), the buyer would be entitled to either (1) a credit against the price for the net proceeds of resale if the seller resold or (2) the goods themselves on payment of the price judgment if the seller had not resold.[443]

The Code is not clear on whether a seller can recover the price from a buyer that wrongfully revokes its acceptance, but the question is not of great importance. Whether the seller's recovery is a price recovery under section 2-709 or a recovery under section 2-706 or section 2-708, compensation sufficient to protect the seller's expectation interest can be provided.

Goods lost or damaged after the risk of loss has passed to the buyer. The second part of section 2-709(1)(a) allows the seller to recover the price "of conforming goods lost or damaged within a commercially reasonable time after risk of their loss has passed to the buyer." This fits with the Code's provisions on risk of loss (sections 2-509 and 2-510)[444] and is designed to effectuate some of their provisions—in particular, those that, in specified circumstances, pass the risk of loss to the buyer before it has accepted or taken possession of the goods. An effective allocation of the risk of loss to the buyer requires that the buyer be obligated to pay for goods that are stolen, destroyed, or otherwise lost. Without such an obligation to pay, the allocation of the risk to the buyer would operate only to the extent that the buyer had paid before the loss.

These ideas and the working of the second part of section 2-709(1)(a) can be hypothetically illustrated. Suppose that Seller in San Francisco agreed to sell goods to Buyer in Boston and that the contract was a shipment contract, with the risk of the goods' loss passing from Seller to Buyer when the goods were duly delivered to the carrier in San Francisco.[445] Seller duly delivered the goods to the carrier, an air freight company, and the goods

---

[442] The seller would plainly have no obligation to take the goods back if the revocation were ineffective, and would arguably have no such obligation if the revocation were effective but wrongful.

[443] Akron Brick & Block Co. v. Moniz Eng'g Co., Inc., 365 Mass. 92, 310 N.E.2d 128, 14 UCCR 563 (1974).

[444] U.C.C. §§ 2-509 and 2-510 are considered in §§ 6.05[A] and 6.05[B], *supra.*

[445] *See* U.C.C. §§ 2-504 and 2-509(1)(a).

were destroyed when the airplane crashed while en route from San Francisco to Boston. In these circumstances, the second part of section 2-709(1)(a) enables Seller to recover the price from Buyer.[446] Buyer must pay even though it never received the goods. If it were otherwise, the risk of loss would not have been effectively allocated to Buyer.[447]

Subsection 2-709(1)(a) allows the seller to recover the price of lost or damaged goods only if the loss or damage occurred "within a commercially reasonable time after" the risk of loss has passed to the buyer. The quoted words, which are more fully discussed in the portion of this text which deals with risk of loss,[448] were added to the Code in response to a criticism by the New York Law Revision Commission.[449] The type of case that troubled the Commission was that in which the risk of loss had passed to the buyer but the seller was *holding* the goods at the time of the casualty. For example, suppose that the parties made a shipment contract, that the seller duly shipped the goods (thus passing their risk to the buyer), and that, on the goods' arrival, the buyer wrongfully rejected them, leaving them with the carrier and subject to the seller's orders. In these and similar circumstances in which the seller is given *control* over the goods after the risk has passed and before the casualty, the Commission did not believe that the risk of loss ought to remain on the buyer forever, but that it ought to shift back to the seller after a commercially reasonable time. Unfortunately, however, the statutory words "within a commercially reasonable time after risk . . . of loss has passed to the buyer" are not expressly limited to situations in which the seller has had control over the goods for more than a commercially reasonable time before the casualty occurs. Courts ought to so limit them and thus give effect to the underlying intent. For example, the risk ought not revert to the seller in a shipment-contract situation in which the seller duly ships (thus passing the risk, control over the goods, and the right to hold the carrier for its defaults to the buyer), the carrier delays delivery to the buyer for more than a commercially reasonable time, and then the casualty occurs.

---

[446] *See* Ninth St. E., Ltd. v. Harrison, 5 Conn. Cir. 597, 259 A.2d 772, 7 UCCR 171 (1968); Montana Seeds, Inc. v. Holliday, 178 Mont. 119, 582 P.2d 1223, 24 UCCR 884 (1978); Forest Nursery Co. v. I.W.S., Inc., 141 Misc. 2d 661, 534 N.Y.S.2d 86; 8 UCCR2d 923 (1988). For an action-for-the-price case where the risk had passed to the buyer under U.C.C. § 2-509(1)(b), *see* Rheinberg Kellerei GmbH v. Brooksfield Nat'l Bank of Commerce Bank, 901 F.2d 481, 11 UCCR2d 1214 (5th Cir. 1990).

[447] Buyer may not be the ultimate bearer of the loss. It may have the benefit of insurance coverage or a right to recover from the carrier.

[448] Section 6.05[A], *supra.*

[449] 1955 N.Y. Law Rev. Comm'n (Vol. 1) 489.

Identified goods that are not resaleable at a reasonable price. Section 2-709(1)(b) allows price recoveries in situations in which the goods remain with the seller but are nearly worthless. Goods that are custom-made for the buyer and have only a salvage or junk value to anyone else are examples.[450]

If the goods have been identified to the contract,[451] and "if the seller is unable after reasonable effort to resell them at a reasonable price or the circumstances reasonably indicate that such effort will be unavailing," the seller may recover the price, and subsection (2) is triggered. It provides:

> (2) Where the seller sues for the price he must hold for the buyer any goods which have been identified to the contract and which are still in his control except that if resale becomes possible he may resell them at any time prior to collection of the judgment. The net proceeds of any resale must be credited to the buyer and payment of the judgment entitles him to any goods not resold.

A price recovery under section 2-709(1)(b) can thus result in cramming unwanted goods down the buyer's throat. Although this is a bad idea in most circumstances, it makes sense when the goods have scant resale value—when the seller, even with its sales force and marketing expertise, cannot sell them for a reasonable price.

While the purpose and sense of sections 2-709(1)(b) and 2-709(2) are clear enough, courts have not applied the provisions with consistency. Subsection (1)(b) calls for factual judgments about resalability—the judgments to be made in accordance with a reasonableness standard (the word "reasonable" is used twice and the word "reasonably" once). This has led to varying results.[452] If it were always borne in mind that the choice is between a price remedy (meaning that the buyer must take and dispose of the goods) and a remedy under section 2-706 or section 2-708 (with the seller disposing of the goods), results might be more predictable and justifiable. If there is a market, other than a salvage or scrap market, on which the seller can resell

---

[450] *See* Walter Balfour & Co. v. Lizza & Sons, Inc., 6 UCCR 649 (N.Y. Sup. 1969); Weisz Graphics Div. of Fred B. Johnson Co., Inc. v. Peck Indus., Inc., 304 S.C. 101, 403 S.E.2d 146, 15 UCCR2d 80 (S.C. App. 1991).

[451] Identification to the contract is provided for in U.C.C. § 2-501 and discussed in § 6.03, *supra*.

[452] *See, e.g.*, Great W. Sugar Co. v. Pennant Prods., 748 P.2d 1359, 4 UCCR2d 1080 (Colo. App. 1987); Royal Jones & Assocs., Inc. v. First Thermal Sys., Inc., 566 So. 2d 853, 14 UCCR2d 131 (Fla. App. 1990); Ludwig, Inc. v. Tobey, 28 Mass. App. Dec. 6, 5 UCCR 832 (1964); Karen v. Cane, 152 Misc. 2d 639, 578 N.Y.S.2d 85, 16 UCCR2d 1088 (Civ. Ct. 1991); In re Narragansett Clothing Co., 138 B.R. 354, 17 UCCR2d 786 (Bankr. R.I. 1992); Cole v. Melvin, 441 F. Supp. 193, 22 UCCR 1154 (D.S.D. 1977).

the goods (albeit at a price substantially lower than the contract price), it usually makes sense to treat the price on that market as a reasonable price, thereby imposing the burden of disposing of the goods on the seller. If, however, there is only a salvage market or its like, a price recovery should lie, leaving it to the buyer to dispose of the goods.

[F] Recovery When Goods Were Not Identified at Time of Buyer's Default

Section 2-704 is addressed, at least primarily, to situations in which sellers have contracted to manufacture or assemble goods for buyers and the buyers have anticipatorily repudiated their promises to buy. The hypothetical posed in § 7.08[D] to illustrate a "components" seller's lost-profit recovery (there labeled Case 2) can also be employed to illustrate the meaning and operation of section 2-704. Let us again consider it:

For a promised price of $285,000, Manufacturer agreed to design and manufacture some office furniture for Buyer's executive suite. The furniture was to be designed in accordance with some rough sketches that Buyer provided and was to be unusual—custom-made for Buyer. Manufacturer did the design work (which Buyer approved) at a cost of $20,000, spent $40,000 for the wood (solid walnut), and began to sand and saw the wood. At this point, Buyer repudiated.

In these circumstances, what may and what should the aggrieved seller—Manufacturer—do? Complete the manufacture of the furniture and seek a remedy based on the completed goods? Or cease work and sell the wood for what it can get (perhaps only salvage value) and seek a remedy on that basis? Section 2-704 (particularly its subsection (2)) offers both leeway and guidance:

> (2) Where the goods are unfinished an aggrieved seller may in the exercise of reasonable commercial judgment for the purpose of avoiding loss and of effective realization either complete the manufacture and wholly identify the goods to the contract or cease manufacture and resell for scrap or salvage value or proceed in any other reasonable manner.

If Manufacturer ceases work and sells the wood for its salvage value of $30,000, Manufacturer's most likely remedy will be its lost profit.[453] (This is discussed in § 7.08[D].) If Manufacturer's total variable costs, had it completed the furniture, would have been $200,000, performance would have

---

[453] See Bead Chain Mfg. Co. v. Saxton Prods., Inc., 183 Conn. 266, 439 A.2d 314, 31 UCCR 91 (1981).

earned it an $85,000 profit, and Buyer's repudiation has caused it to lose this profit. To this $85,000, the section 2-708(2) formula adds the "costs reasonably incurred" by Manufacturer—here, the $20,000 spent on the design and the $40,000 spent for the wood, or a total of $60,000—and subtract the "proceeds of resale" received by Manufacturer—here, the $30,000 obtained for the wood, thus yielding a total recovery of $115,000. This will place Manufacturer in the financial position that performance would have done.[454]

If, on Buyer's repudiation, Manufacturer does not stop work but rather completes the furniture, its most likely remedy will be under section 2-706: the $285,000 contract price less the resale price or whatever Manufacturer receives on an appropriate resale of the completed furniture. Thus, if Manufacturer succeeds in reselling the completed furniture for $220,000, its recovery would be $65,000 (plus incidental damages under section 2-710), but if Manufacturer is able to obtain only $140,000 for the completed furniture, its recovery would be $145,000 (plus incidental damages).

Suppose that Manufacturer does complete and resell the furniture for $140,000. May it recover the $145,000 difference between the contract price and the resale price even though those damages are $30,000 more than the $115,000 (a lost profit of $85,000 plus $60,000 in costs reasonably incurred less $30,000 in proceeds of resale) that Manufacturer would have lost had it ceased work? Or should Manufacturer be limited to $115,000, on the ground that, by stopping and salvaging, it could have avoided losing more than this?[455]

Comment 2 to 2-704 addresses questions of this sort:

> [T]he seller is given express power to complete manufacture or procurement of goods for the contract unless the exercise of reasonable commercial judgment as to the facts as they appear at the time he learns of the breach makes it clear that such action will result in a material increase in damages. The burden is on the buyer to show the commer-

---

[454] The same dollar result (and the same protection of Manufacturer's expectation interest) could be achieved, albeit more awkwardly, under section 2-706. Here, the formula would be the $285,000 contract price less the $30,000 resale price of the wood or $255,000 less "expenses saved in consequence of the buyer's breach"—with the $140,000 in variable costs that were not expended being the expenses saved.

[455] The same kind of problem can arise where, on the buyer's repudiation, the seller ceases work. For example, suppose that Manufacturer ceased work and in so doing lost $115,000. May it recover that amount if completion would have enabled it to resell for $220,000— that is, if the market price for the completed goods would have been $220,000—and would thus have limited its loss to $65,000?

cially unreasonable nature of the seller's action in completing manufacture.

This Comment allows the aggrieved seller considerable leeway. First, its conduct is to be judged on the basis of the facts as they appeared to it at the time of the buyer's repudiation and not by hindsight. Second, the buyer bears the burden of proving that the seller did not employ commercially reasonable judgment in acting as it did.[456] Third, this is a heavy burden; to carry it the buyer needs to show that commercially reasonable judgment on the basis of the apparent facts at the time of the repudiation made it "clear" that the course the seller followed would result in a "material" increase in damages. Comment 2 perhaps goes a bit beyond the language of the statute, but it can be justified on the basis of the same fundamental mitigation-of-damages or avoidable-consequences principles that support section 2-704(2) itself. As articulated in section 350 of the Restatement (Second) of Contracts, these principles are:

> (1) Except as stated in Subsection (2), damages are not recoverable for loss that the injured party could have avoided without undue risk, burden, or humiliation.
> (2) The injured party is not precluded from recovery by the Rule stated in Subsection (1) to the extent that he has made reasonable but unsuccessful efforts to avoid loss.[457]

It is usually difficult for a repudiating buyer to show that the course of action the seller followed after the breach not only failed to avoid loss but also was unreasonable—did not accord with "the exercise of reasonable commercial judgment for the purposes of avoiding loss and of effective realization." Buyer in the hypothetical could attempt to marshal the necessary evidence, but this would not be easy.

---

[456] For a case placing this burden on the buyer, *see* Young v. Frank's Nursery and Crafts, Inc., 58 Ohio St. 3d 242, 569 N.E.2d 1034, 14 UCCR2d 463 (1991), *reh'g denied*, 60 Ohio St. 3d 705, 573 N.E.2d 673 (1991).

[457] Comment h to Restatement (Second) of Contracts § 350 explicitly refers to U.C.C. § 2-704(2):

Sometimes the injured party makes efforts to avoid loss but fails to do so. The rule stated in Subsection (2) protects the injured party in that situation if the efforts were reasonable. If, for example, a seller who is to manufacture goods for a buyer decides, on repudiation by the buyer, "in the exercise of reasonable commercial judgment for the purpose of avoiding loss" to complete manufacture of the goods, he is protected under Uniform Commercial Code § 2-704(2) even if it later appears that he could have better avoided loss by stopping manufacture.

Subsection 2-704(2) deals with factually complicated situations and calls for careful inquiry about both (1) the seller's actual conduct following the buyer's repudiation and (2) an alternative, unfollowed course of action that the buyer contends would have mitigated damages. As to both, the focus should be primarily on what "the exercise of reasonable commercial judgment for the purpose of avoiding loss and of effective realization" told the seller to do at the time for action. For an appreciation of the potential complexity, return to the hypothetical, in which Manufacturer has completed manufacture and resold for $140,000—producing section 2-706 damages of $145,000. To challenge these damages, Buyer might try to show that completion was unreasonable—that Manufacturer's commercial judgment should have told it that stoppage would have produced a lesser loss—that had it stopped, it would have lost only an $85,000 profit and $30,000 in unsalvageable costs. Manufacturer might resist in a number of ways. It might, for example, contest Buyer's profit and salvage figures (note that both are would-have-been figures—what would have been had a different course been followed). Or Manufacturer might try to show that it reasonably anticipated a much lesser loss from the course it followed, that at the time it decided to complete, it reasonably expected sell the completed furniture for $220,000 or more.

Cessation and salvage sale of components and completion are not the only two courses open to an aggrieved seller situated like Manufacturer. Section 2-704(2) also authorizes proceeding "in any other reasonable manner." For example, Manufacturer might decide to stop manufacture but not to sell the wood that it had acquired for the Buyer job, instead retaining that wood for use on another project. Or it might decide to "complete" manufacture, but of furniture different from that designed for Buyer because the altered furniture would be easier to sell at a good price. In such situations, courts should be flexible with a view toward compensating the aggrieved seller for its loss, unless and to the extent that, in the exercise of reasonable commercial judgment, it should have avoided that loss.

[G] Incidental and Consequential Damages and Expenses Saved

Incidental damages. Sections 2-706, 2-708(1), 2-708(2), and 2-709 provide the basic monetary damages for sellers: contract-minus-resale, contract-minus-market, lost profit, and price. Each section contains the words "together with any incidental damages provided in this Article (Section 2-710)" or their equivalent and thus provides for the supplementation of basic damages with incidental damages. Section 2-710 does not so much define incidental damages as list examples of them and suggest their nature. It provides:

> Incidental damages to an aggrieved seller include any commercially rea-
> sonable charges, expenses or commissions incurred in stopping delivery,
> in the transportation, care and custody of goods after the buyer's breach,
> in connection with return or resale of the goods or otherwise resulting
> from the breach.

Clear incidental damages situations are those in which the seller incurs extra
expenses because of, and after, the buyer's default. One example is reasonable expenses incurred in conducting a proper section 2-706 resale.[458] If the
seller is to be placed in the financial position that performance would have
done, it is necessary that such expenses be recovered. They are not covered
by section 2-706's basic measure ("the difference between the resale price
and the contract price"), but rather by the following "together with any
incidental damages" language and by section 2-710's "expenses or commissions incurred . . . in connection with . . . resale of the goods." Other
examples are reasonable expenses incurred in caring for the goods between
wrongful rejection and resale,[459] and necessary post-breach transportation
expenses incurred by the seller.[460] Again, the full protection of the seller's
expectation interest requires the recovery of such expenses.

One kind of loss that results from the buyer's breach—the reasonable
attorney's fees that the seller pays to recover its damages—is generally not
recoverable as incidental damages or otherwise.[461] This is because the Code
is an American statute and under the "American rule" victorious litigants
do not recover their attorney's fees. At least they do not do so in the absence
of an enforceable agreement specifically providing for attorney's fees. To
this extent, they are left short of full compensation.

Consequential damages. In section 2-715, Article 2 makes both
incidental and consequential damages available to aggrieved buyers.[462] For
sellers, however, there is no provision for consequential damages; section
2-710 provides only for incidental damages. The reason for this different
treatment possibly lies in the nature of the parties' promised performances
and potential defaults. Sellers promise to deliver conforming goods. When

---

[458] *See* Peoria Harbor Marina v. McGlasson, 105 Ill. App. 3d 723, 61 Ill. Dec. 431, 434
N.E.2d 768, 33 UCCR 448 (1982).

[459] *See* Cole v. Melvin, 441 F. Supp. 193, 22 UCCR 1154 (D.S.D. 1977).

[460] *See* Ernst Steel Corp. v. Horn Constr. Div., Halliburton Co., 104 A.D.2d 55, 481
N.Y.S.2d 833, 40 UCCR 145 (1984).

[461] *See* Brownie's Army & Navy Store, Inc. v. E. J. Burke, Jr., Inc., 72 A.D.2d 171, 424
N.Y.S.2d 800, 28 UCCR 90 (1980); Great W. Sugar Co. v. Mrs. Alison's Cookie Co., 563
F. Supp. 430, 36 UCCR 164 (E.D. Mo. 1983).

[462] Buyers' incidental and consequential damages are considered in §§ 7.04[F][1] and
7.04[F][2], *supra.*

they fail to deliver, deliver late, or deliver defective goods, their buyers can suffer significant consequential damages by way of business disruption, personal injury, or property damage. Buyers, on the other hand, promise payment, and their defaults usually resolve into depriving their sellers of money, either for a time or entirely. "Consequential" losses resulting from the deprivation of funds are neither so frequent nor so obvious as consequential losses resulting from the deprivation of goods or from defective goods. Further, nonpaying debtors frequently are protected from substantial liability for consequential damages because they had no reason to foresee the damages at the time of contract formation, or because their creditors could have avoided all or a large part of the losses.

For whatever reason, the Code contains no express provision for sellers' consequential damages. This has led a number of courts to say that such damages may not be recovered.[463] Decisions to this effect frequently rest on section 1-106's provision that "neither consequential or special nor penal damages may be had except as specifically provided in this Act or by other rule of law" and on the observation that even though the drafters provided consequential damages for buyers, they did not do so for sellers. Another approach is possible. Section 1-106 does not bar the recovery of consequential damages, even though not provided for in the Code, if the recovery of such damages is provided for by "other rule of law." Further, section 1-103 allows the common law to supplement the Code except to the extent that the common law has been displaced by particular Code provisions. Under the common law, particularly as that law is restated in section 347 of the Restatement (Second) of Contracts, a party injured by a contract breach is entitled to damages based on its expectation interest, including damages for both incidental and consequential losses. On this basis, at least one court has approved a seller's recovery of consequential damages.[464]

To the extent that current law allows sellers to recover incidental damages but bars them from recovering consequential damages, the distinction between incidental and consequential damages becomes important and something of a battleground.[465] The argument often concerns interest: either

---

[463] *See, e.g.*, Nobs Chem., USA, Inc. v. Koppers, Co., Inc., 616 F.2d 212, 28 UCCR 1039 (5th Cir. 1980); Sprague v. Sumitomo Forestry Co., Ltd., 104 Wash. 2d 751, 709 P.2d 1200, 42 UCCR 202 (1985).

[464] Associated Metals & Minerals Corp. v. Sharon Steel Corp., 590 F. Supp. 18, 39 UCCR 892 (S.D.N.Y. 1983), *aff'd*, 742 F.2d 1431 (2d Cir. 1983).

[465] For cases considering the distinction between incidental and consequential damages, *see* Petroleo Brasilerio, S.A., Petrobras v. Ameropan Oil Corp., 372 F. Supp. 503, 14 UCCR 661 (E.D.N.Y. 1974) and Afram Export Corp. v. Metallurgiki Halyps, S.A., 772 F.2d 1358, 41 UCCR 1709 (7th Cir. 1985) (Posner, J.—employing economic analysis).

the seller's cost of borrowing the funds of which the buyer's breach deprived it during the period of the deprivation or the loss by the seller of the opportunity to earn interest during the period of the deprivation.

The proposed revisions to Article 2 would clarify the situation and smooth the seller's road to full compensation. The proposed revisions to sections 2-804 and 2-806 would allow sellers, as well as buyers, to recover consequential damages.[466]

Expenses saved. The damage formulas of sections 2-706 and 2-708(1) both contain the language "but less expenses saved in consequence of the buyer's breach." Although sections 2-708(2) and 2-709 do not contain this language, the same idea applies to lost-profit and price recoveries.[467] The idea is that expressed in section 347(c) of the Restatement (Second) of Contracts, that a party injured by a contract breach is entitled to damages measured by his expectation interest "less . . . any cost or other loss that he has avoided by not having to perform."[468] Examples of expenses saved include transportation costs to the buyer's city that the seller had agreed to bear but saved because of the buyer's repudiation, sales commissions to the extent that they are saved because of the buyer's breach, and the costs of providing promised services that the seller avoided because of the breach.

IV.   LIQUIDATED DAMAGES AND PENALTIES

§ 7.09   LIQUIDATED DAMAGES

As this text has repeatedly pointed out, the Code's scheme of monetary damages, for both aggrieved buyers and aggrieved sellers, follows common-law principles, particularly the principles of compensating the aggrieved party in terms of its expectation interest and of rarely doing more than this. Section 1-106(1) makes this clear:

---

[466] *See* Comment 1 to Council Draft § 2-806.

[467] Copymate Mktg., Ltd. v. Modern Merchandising, Inc., 34 Wash. App. 330, 660 P.2d 332, 36 UCCR 161 (1983) (lost-profit recovery); Walter Balfour & Co., Inc. v. Lizza & Sons, Inc., 6 UCCR 649 (N.Y. Sup. Ct. 1969) (price recovery); Continental-Wirt Elecs. Corp. v. Sprague Elec. Co., 329 F. Supp. 959, 9 UCCR 1049 (E.D. Pa. 1971) (price recovery). *But see* Beco, Inc. v. Minnechaug Golf Course, Inc., 5 Conn. Cir. Ct. 444, 256 A.2d 522, 6 UCCR 910 (1968) (price recovery).

[468] For a fuller development of this idea, *see* Comment d and Illustrations 5–11 to Restatement (Second) of Contracts § 347. The proposed revisions to Article 2 will deal with expenses saved by providing in § 2-804, a general provision applicable to breaches by both buyers and sellers, that recoveries are to be "less expenses and costs avoided as a result of the breach."

The remedies provided by this Act shall be liberally administered to the end that the aggrieved party may be put in as good a position as if the other party had fully performed but neither consequential or special nor penal damages may be had except as specifically provided in this Act or by other rule of law.

In accordance with their belief that damages should be compensatory and no more than compensatory, common-law courts have long limited parties' freedom to agree on the amount of damages to be paid on breach. They have carefully scrutinized agreed-damages clauses and have declined to enforce such clauses when they produced damage amounts significantly larger than those that common-law compensatory damage principles would produce. Article 2 continues in this tradition, but it does grant parties to sales contracts a bit more freedom to agree on damages than obtained before its enactment.

Article 2's test for agreed-damages clauses is set forth in section 2-718(1):

Damages for breach by either party may be liquidated in the agreement but only at an amount which is reasonable in light of the anticipated or actual harm caused by the breach, the difficulties of proof of loss, and the inconvenience or nonfeasibility of otherwise obtaining an adequate remedy. A term fixing unreasonably large liquidated damages is void as a penalty.

This provision follows the traditional law on agreed-damages clauses in a number of ways. First, its labels are traditional; clauses that pass muster and are enforced are called "liquidated-damages clauses," while clauses that are found to be unenforceable are termed "penalty clauses." Second, a clause that is found to be a penalty clause and unenforceable does not contaminate the remainder of the contract. The remainder—provisions dealing with the goods, delivery, price, time for payment, and the like—will be enforced, and, the agreed-damages clause having failed, remedy will be had in accordance with the applicable Code provisions. Third, the test for enforceability (the reasonableness of the amount agreed upon in the light of three factors: (1) the anticipated or actual harm caused by the breach, (2) the difficulties of proof of loss, and (3) the inconvenience or nonfeasibility of otherwise obtaining an adequate remedy) is, in the main, traditional.[469]

---

[469] Compare the U.C.C. § 2-718(1) factors with those articulated by the Supreme Court of Errors of Connecticut in 1914: "The damages to be anticipated as resulting from the breach must be uncertain in amount or difficult to prove; (2) there must have been an intent

857

Section 2-718(1)'s most significant departure from prior law lies in its provision that the amount agreed upon may be tested for reasonableness by comparing it to either (1) the harm anticipated at contract formation or (2) the harm actually suffered. Under pre-Code formulations of the law, only the anticipated harm was available for comparison; reasonableness in light of the actual harm suffered would not save a clause that stated an amount unreasonable in light of the anticipated harm. By making both anticipated and actual harm available for comparison, Article 2 provides for the enforcement of some—though probably only a few—agreed-damages clauses that would previously have been unenforceable. It is important to read section 2-718(1) carefully in this connection, so that the drafters' intent may be effectuated. Their idea was to make more agreed-damages clauses enforceable. Courts should enforce a clause if the amount it stipulates is reasonable in light of *either* the anticipated harm or the actual harm.[470] They should not insist that a clause pass muster in terms of both the anticipated and the actual harm. The Restatement (Second) of Contracts, which was promulgated in 1979, tracks Article 2's innovation, and thus would allow agreed-damage clauses to be enforced in non-Code, common-law situations if their amounts are reasonable in light of either anticipated or actual harm.[471]

The distinction between an enforceable liquidated-damages clause and an unenforceable penalty clause is to be made by the court as a matter of law, and it can be difficult.[472] Subsection 2-718(1)'s second sentence—"A term fixing unreasonably large liquidated damages is void as a penalty"—raises questions. Does this sentence merely state the consequences for a clause that fails to pass one of the tests of the first sentence, or does it state a separate and additional test? *Equitable Lumber Corp. v. I.P.A. Land Development Corp.*,[473] the first important case interpreting section 2-718(1), treats it as stating a separate and additional test—meaning that even if a

---

on the part of the parties to liquidate them in advance; and (3) the amount stipulated must be a reasonable one—that is to say, not greatly disproportioned to the presumable loss or injury." Banta v. Stamford Motor Co., 89 Conn. 51, 92 A. 665 (1914).

[470] Equitable Lumber Corp. v. I.P.A. Land Dev. Corp., 38 N.Y.2d 516, 344 N.E.2d 391, 18 UCCR 273 (1976). *But see* California & Hawaiian Sugar Co. v. Sun Ship, Inc., 794 F.2d 1433, I UCCR2d 1211 (1986).

[471] Section 356 Restatement (Second) of Contracts; Comment b and Illustrations 3 & 4 thereto.

[472] Lake River Corp. v. Carborundum Co., 769 F.2d 1284 (7th Cir. 1985) (Posner, J.— the opinion considers policy arguments for and against the enforcement of agreed-damages clauses).

[473] 38 N.Y.2d 516, 344 N.E.2d 391, 18 UCCR 273 (1976).

clause passes under the first sentence, it can be invalidated under the general and open-ended language of the second. Further, the second sentence refers only to "unreasonably large" liquidated damages and so inevitably raises the question of what happens to a term fixing unreasonably small liquidated damages. Comment 1 responds that "[a]n unreasonably small amount would be subject to similar criticism and might be stricken under the section on unconscionable contracts or clauses."

As this Comment sentence indicates, section 2-718(1) is not the only Code provision, and the liquidated-damages-vs.-penalty-clause doctrine is not the only legal doctrine that may be applied to agreement clauses dealing with damage amounts. There are also section 2-302 on unconscionability and section 2-719 on contractual modification or limitation of remedy. Whether a clause is classified as a section 2-718(1) agreed-damages clause or a section 2-719 modification-or-limitation-of-remedy clause can be result determinative. Thus, a party wishing to draft and enforce a clause providing for a small-dollar recovery would do well to try to do so within section 2-719 (and to try to avoid the pitfalls of sections 2-302 and 2-718(1)). Parties can also sometimes use section 2-719 to add a recovery not provided for by law and thus increase the burden on the contract breaker; for example, in jurisdictions and circumstances that so permit, they may provide for the recovery of attorney's fees. Clauses that simply provide for the recovery of reasonable attorney's fees do not trigger section 2-718(1). But clauses that go further and fix the dollar or percentage amount of the attorney's fees will be scrutinized under 2-718(1).[474]

Problems can also arise in distinguishing between promises of alternative performances and a promise of a particular performance accompanied by an agreed-damage clause to be applied if the promisor defaults. In the latter situation, the liquidated-damages-penalty-clause tests of section 2-718(1) are to be applied, but, in the former, there is no agreed-damages clause, and remedy should be had as provided by law.[475] Consider, for example, "take-or-pay" contracts—contracts in which pipeline companies agree to buy natural gas from producers for multiyear periods, promising either (1) to take (and pay for) a specified quantity each year or (2) to pay for that quantity even though not taken, reserving the right to take it in subsequent years. Pipeline-company buyers have sometimes repudiated such contracts and argued that the contracts were contracts to buy accompanied by agreed-damages clauses that are unenforceable under the section 2-718(1)

---

[474] *Id.*

[475] For a general discussion of alternative contracts, *see* 5 Arthur L. Corbin, Contracts §§ 1079–1087 (1964).

tests. The courts have generally rejected such arguments and treated take-or-pay contracts as contracts promising alternative performances, with the buyer promisor having the right to chose which performance to render.[476]

§ 7.10   PENALTIES

Punitive or penal damages differ from compensatory damages in that they are not designed to compensate for loss but rather to punish or deter conduct considered particularly reprehensible. As has been seen, section 1-106(1) states the Code-wide policy of compensating for loss, and of doing so in terms of the aggrieved party's expectation interest. The section adds, among other things, that no penal damages may be recovered "except as specifically provided in this Act or by other rule of law." While other parts of the Code contain occasional punitive-damages provisions,[477] there are none in Article 2.[478] On the contrary, the Article 2 damage provisions are designed to compensate and to do no more than compensate. Consequently, buyers and sellers of goods may obtain punitive damages only when they are provided for "by other rule of law"—that is, by non-Code law which has not been displaced by the Code.[479]

Punitive damages are frequently sought in Article 2 cases, but rarely recovered. Although the relevant non-Code law varies from state to state, the usual rule that punitive damages will not be awarded for breach of contract[480] is generally applied to contracts for the sale of goods.[481] Thus,

---

[476] Universal Resources Corp. v. Panhandle E. Pipe Line Co., 813 F.2d 77, 3 UCCR2d 988 (5th Cir. 1987); Resources Inv. Corp. v. Enron Corp., 669 F. Supp. 1038, 5 UCCR2d 616 (D. Colo. 1987).

[477] *See, e.g.,* U.C.C. §§ 9-404(1) and 9-507(1).

[478] U.C.C. § 2-718(2)(b), which is discussed in § 7.13 *infra*, may be considered penal in the sense that it can result in overcompensation, but it is not penal in the sense of calling for a plaintiff's recovery; all it does is deny restitution of the amount it specifies.

[479] *See* U.C.C. § 1-103.

[480] *See* section 355 of the Restatement (Second) of Contracts, which provides:

Punitive damages are not recoverable for a breach of contract unless the conduct constituting the breach is also a tort for which punitive damages are recoverable.

[481] *See, e.g.,* Cancun Adventure Tours, Inc. v. Underwater Designer Co., 862 F.2d 1044, 8 UCCR2d 1035 (4th Cir. 1989) (no punitive damages for a seller's breach of warranty under Virginia law unless the elements of an independent, willful tort are established); Computerized Radiological Servs. v. Syntex Corp., 595 F. Supp. 1495, 40 UCCR 49 (E.D.N.Y. 1984) ("Neither California nor New York courts would award punitive damages for a mere breach of warranty, absent evidence that the conduct constituting the breach was so malicious or morally culpable that it constituted a tort in and of itself."); Fedders Corp. v. Boatright, 493 So.2d 301, 1 UCCR2d 1452 (Miss. 1986).

in most states, a seller that does nothing worse than breach a warranty is not liable for punitive damages. If, however, the conduct constituting the breach is also tortious (e.g., the seller has committed a fraud as well as a breach of contract) and if, under applicable non-Code law, punitive damages are available for the tort in question, punitive damages may be awarded.[482] Punitive-damage questions can thus be answered only by reference to the governing non-Code law.

V. PROTECTION OF CONTRACT BREAKER'S RESTITUTION INTEREST

§ 7.11 INTRODUCTION

The primary focus of Article 2's remedial provisions is on the protection of the aggrieved party's expectation interest. A party that is in default has not earned and will not receive such protection. But there is good reason to protect a contract breaker's restitution interest to the extent that this can be done while protecting the aggrieved party's expectation interest. Doing so avoids overcompensation of the aggrieved party and so accords with our law's fundamental compensation principles and with the Code's section 1-106(1) articulation of those principles.

Article 2 affords full protection to the restitution interests of sellers that, although in substantial default, have partially performed contracts of sale. It is, however, less generous to defaulting buyers and sometimes impairs their restitution interests to a greater extent than the protection of the aggrieved sellers' expectation interests requires. To these matters we now turn.

§ 7.12 SELLER'S RESTITUTION INTEREST WHEN SELLER IS IN DEFAULT

As has been explained elsewhere,[483] Article 2 allows a seller to recover the price of goods that the buyer accepts and retains and does this even though the seller is in substantial default. Section 2-607(1) requires the buyer to pay at the contract rate for accepted goods, and section 2-709(1)(a) provides the seller with an action for the price of accepted goods. A rightful and effective revocation of acceptance can destroy the seller's right to the

---

[482] See, e.g., Seaton v. Lawson Chevrolet-Mazda, Inc, 821 S.W.2d 137, 16 UCCR2d 1070 (Tenn. 1991) (punitive damages allowed against a car dealer that had fraudulently misrepresented the car); Z.D. Howard Co. v. Cartwright, 537 P.2d 345, 17 UCCR 123 (Okla. 1975).

[483] Sections 7.03[D] and 7.08[E], supra.

price,[484] but if the buyer does not revoke but rather retains the goods, it must pay for them at the contract rate.

The buyer is, of course, entitled to compensation for whatever harm it has suffered because of the seller's default. If the accepted goods or their tender do not conform to the contract, and if the buyer gives the notice required by section 2-607(3)(a), the buyer may recover the loss it suffered because of the nonconformity.[485] The buyer may also recover for nondelivery defaults with respect to other installments provided for in the same contract.[486] Under section 2-717, the buyer may set off its damages against its accepted-goods price obligation.[487] The result is that the aggrieved buyer may have damages that protect its expectation interest (i.e., place it in the financial position that performance would have done) and that, after this is done, the defaulting seller may have its restitution interest protected and may recover for goods that the buyer accepted and do so in terms of the contract price.

§ 7.13 BUYER'S RESTITUTION INTEREST WHEN BUYER IS IN DEFAULT

A buyer that wrongfully refuses to accept or to pay for tendered goods is liable to its seller in damages. Those damages are computed under formulas designed to compensate the seller for the financial losses that were suffered by reason of the breach. No amount is added to punish the buyer for its failure to perform or to serve as a warning to others who may be contemplating default; nor is any amount added because the court believes sellers have some damages that are hard to prove. Indeed, unless the seller can prove its damages without resort to speculation, the buyer will be required to pay only nominal damages.[488]

These principles can become strangely muddled, however, when the buyer has made a downpayment before defaulting. If the downpayment approximately equals (or exceeds) the seller's damages, the seller is usually willing to retain the payment and forgo any damage action against the buyer. If the payment exceeds the seller's damages by any significant amount, however, the buyer will most likely be interested in securing a partial return of what it paid. This is the fact that caused many common-law courts dif-

---

[484] Sections 7.03[E], 7.04[A], and 7.08[E], *supra*.

[485] U.C.C. § 2-714, discussed in § 7.04[E], *supra*.

[486] *See* U.C.C. §§ 2-608, 2-711, 2-712, 2-713, 2-715.

[487] U.C.C. § 2-717 is considered in § 7.04[G], *supra*.

[488] The bases for the statements made in this textual paragraph were developed in §§ 7.08[A]–7.08[E], *supra*.

ficulty: the defaulting buyer was initiating legal action. How could it use its own "neglect" as a basis for a cause of action?

There are many answers to this question. The same common-law courts had no difficulty in awarding a defaulting seller damages based upon the benefits it transferred to an aggrieved buyer. Certainly the buyer's neglect calls for compensation, but the fact that this buyer has made a downpayment does not call for punishment (whereas a buyer that had made no downpayment would escape punishment and be required only to compensate its seller). Probably the best answer to the question posed is that the buyer is not using its neglect as a basis of suit. It is bringing the action for the benefits it transferred to the seller. It is suing for the value of those benefits not because of, but in spite of, its neglect. The defaulting buyer should be made to compensate the seller for losses arising out of the default (including full protection of the seller's expectation interest), but the existence of a prepayment ought not be used as a reason to punish the buyer for default.

These general ideas may be explored in terms of the following hypothetical:

Seller agreed to sell and Buyer to buy goods at an agreed price of $5,000. Buyer prepaid $2,000 and defaulted by committing one of the acts listed in section 2-703. Seller resold the goods for $4,200, incurring no incidental damages and saving no expenses because of the breach. The agreement contained no liquidated-damage clause.

What the answer *ought* to be is not hard to state. The seller is entitled to the contract price for these goods; at the moment it has received $6,200 on a $5,000 contract, $2,000 from the defaulting buyer and $4,200 from the resale; thus, the buyer should be entitled to a return of $1,200. This compensates the seller (i.e., leaves it in the financial position where performance would have put it) without punishing the buyer. Had the seller also incurred $200 in incidental damages, the $200 should be subtracted from the $1,200 to be returned to the buyer.

Although some common-law cases reached this result,[489] the majority refused to grant the defaulting buyer any recovery,[490] often with colorful

---

[489] *See, e.g.,* Amtorg Trading Corp. v. Michie Printing Press & Mfg. Co., 206 F.2d 103 (2d Cir. 1953); Michigan Yacht & Power Co. v. Busch, 143 F. 929 (6th Cir. 1906); Foster v. Warner, 42 Idaho 729, 249 P. 771 (1926); Stewart v. Moss, 30 Wash. 2d 535, 192 P.2d 362 (1948).

[490] *See, e.g.,* Tomboy Gold & Copper Co. v. Marks, 185 Cal. 336, 197 P. 94 (1921) (*but compare* Freedman v. Rector, Wardens & Vestrymen, 37 Cal. 2d 16, 230 P.2d 629 (1951)); Thach v. Durham, 120 Colo. 253, 108 P.2d 1159 (1949); Reitano v. Fote, 50 So. 2d 873 (Fla. 1951); Notti v. Clark, 133 Mont. 263, 322 P.2d 112 (1958). *See generally* Corman, "Restitution for Benefits Conferred by Party in Default Under Sales Contract," 34 Texas L.

language about the impact that an allowance of restitution would have on the commercial world.[491] The Code rejected the majority common-law position and took a long step toward the protection of defaulting buyers' restitution interests. In the complicated and difficult language of section 2-718(2) and 2-718(3), it stopped short of full protection, however:

(2) Where the seller justifiably withholds delivery of goods because of the buyer's breach, the buyer is entitled to restitution of any amount by which the sum of his payments exceeds

(a) the terms to which the seller is entitled by virtue of terms liquidating the seller's damages in accordance with subsection (1), or

(b) in the absence of such terms, twenty per cent of the value of the total performance for which the buyer is obligated under the contract or $500, whichever is smaller.

(3) The buyer's right to restitution under subsection (2) is subject to offset to the extent that the seller establishes

(a) a right to recover damages under the provisions of this Article other than subsection (1), and

(b) the amount or value of any benefits received by the buyer directly or indirectly by reason of the contract.

The application of sections 2-718(2) and 2-718(3) to the foregoing hypothetical allows the buyer to recover some of its prepayment, but there is opportunity for argument as to the amount. Because there was no liquidated-damage clause, the buyer is, under section 2-718(2)(b), "entitled to restitution" in the amount of its $2,000 prepayment less (1) the statutory 20 percent of the total price or (2) $500, whichever is smaller.[492] The $500 is the smaller amount; thus, section 2-718(2)(b) entitles the hypothetical buyer to restitution in the amount of $1,500.

Rev. 582 (1956); Talbott, "Restitution for the Defaulting Buyer," 9 W. Res. L. Rev. 445 (1958). Annot., 11 A.L.R.2d 701 (1950).

[491] Dlujge v. Whiteson, 292 Pa. 334, 141 A. 230 (1928); Nels v. O'Brien, 12 Wash. 358, 41 P. 59 (1895).

[492] It is possible to read U.C.C. § 2-718(2)(b) as placing the maximum deduction at 20 percent of $500. This reading has been rejected because this amount would be fixed at $100 and, had the drafters intended a fixed amount to be the maximum recovery, it is likely that they would have stated that amount as a figure, not as a percentage.

Subsection (3) adds, however, that the "right to restitution under subsection (2)"—(the $1,500?)—is "subject to offset" to the extent of the seller's damages and the buyer's benefits. If some of the goods had been delivered to the buyer, the benefit measured by the contract price would be deducted from the $1,500. None were delivered in the hypothetical; therefore, our only concern is with the seller's damages.

If there had been no downpayment, it would be clear that the seller had suffered damages. The buyer had promised to pay $5,000 for the goods. Its default left the seller without the $5,000 and with goods worth only $4,200. In these circumstances, the seller would be entitled to recover $800 under section 2-706 or section 2-708(1). Section 2-718(3)(a) can be read as allowing the seller to set off this $800 against the buyer's section 2-718(2)(b) $1,500 "right to restitution"—meaning that the buyer can obtain restitution of only $700. This reading of the statute gives effect to its structure and language, but it is troublesome from a policy standpoint. It diminishes the buyer's restitutionary recovery both by a compensatory amount ($800) and a penal amount ($500) in circumstances in which the argument for a penalty is, at best, weak.

In *Neri v. Retail Marine Corp.*,[493] the New York Court of Appeals read sections 2-718(2) and 2-718(3) differently. There, the buyer agreed to buy a boat for $12,587, paid $4,250 down, and then repudiated. The buyer sued to recover his downpayment, and the seller counterclaimed for damages. The court found the seller entitled to $2,579 in section 2-708(2) lost-profit damages and $674 in section 2-710 incidental damages—a total of $3,253. It then held the buyer entitled to recover his downpayment less only this $3,253 in damages—that is, it made no $500 deduction from the buyer's restitutionary recovery. It instead read sections 2-718(2)(b) and 2-718(3)(a) as establishing "alternative right[s] to offset in favor of the seller." Thus, in the court's view, a seller can reduce a defaulting buyer's restitutionary recovery by either (1) its actual damages or (2) the 2-718(2)(b) statutory 20 percent or $500, but it cannot do both.

From a policy standpoint, there is much to be said for the *Neri* court's reading of the statute. Treating the section 2-718(2)(b) 20 percent or $500 penal amount and the seller's actual damages as alternatives minimizes the impact of the penal provision. Whenever a seller has suffered substantial damages, it will, as a matter of self-interest, opt to reduce the down paying buyer's restitutionary recovery by those damages, rather than by the penal amount. Thus, the penal provision has no effect in substantial-damage situations. Further, even if the seller has suffered no damages at all, the $500

---

[493] 30 N.Y.2d 393, 285 N.E.2d 311, 10 UCCR 950 (1972).

upper limit on the penal provision means that it will have scant practical importance in large transactions.

In small transactions, especially those involving consumer buyers, the penal provision can have impact. However, its impact is limited to 20 percent of the total price if the total price is less than $2,500, or to $500 if the total price exceeds $2,500. Further, if the *Neri* approach of treating the penal provision and the seller's actual damages as alternatives is followed, it will have impact only when, and to the extent that, the penal amount exceeds the seller's actual damages. Thus, the section 2-718(2)(b) deviation from the compensation principle is relatively modest. It is nevertheless unfortunate. The proposed revisions to Article 2 makes a desirable reform by dropping the penal provision entirely.[494] Under the new Article, defaulting sellers and defaulting buyers that seek restitution will be treated in parallel fashion, both parties being entitled to full restitution after the aggrieved party's expectation interest has been protected.

---

[494] *See* Council Draft § 2-809 and its Comment 2.

CHAPTER 8

FEDERAL REGULATION OF SALES

§ 8.01   INTRODUCTION

The regulation of the sale of goods used to be almost entirely within the province of the states, and this remains true with respect to transactions between commercial entities. Consumer transactions, however, are another matter. The past three decades have seen an explosion of federal legislation and regulation that impact in one way or another on consumer sales. Much of this legislation, while related to consumer sales, is beyond the scope of this treatise.[1] This chapter, however, considers two provisions of federal law that directly affect consumer sales: The Magnuson-Moss Federal Warranty Act,[2] and the FTC Rule on the Preservation of Defenses.[3]

§ 8.02   THE MAGNUSON-MOSS FEDERAL WARRANTY ACT

[A]   Overview of the Act

The Magnuson-Moss Federal Warranty Act (the Act) was enacted by Congress in 1975. Congress believed that consumers were confused and misled by the bewildering array of warranties accompanying products in the marketplace. In many cases, these "warranties" gave very little protection to the consumer, while simultaneously stripping him or her of the assurances of product quality that the law otherwise provides.[4] The widespread use of "legalese," and fine print warranty disclaimers and remedy limitations, often deceived consumers into believing that the seller (or, more likely, the manufacturer) had guaranteed the product against defects when, in fact, the purported warranty made the sale largely devoid of any promises of product quality. Moreover, in many cases the warranty document was not received until after the sale had been consummated; for example, the warranty was often found in the glove compartment of the new car or in the box containing the new stereo. Finally, consumers were frequently required to endure a time-consuming, lengthy, and expensive process in order to receive the limited coverage to which they were entitled under the warranty.

---

[1] *See, e.g.*, The Truth-in-Lending Act, 15 U.S.C. §§ 1601–1667e (1996); Fair Debt Collection Practices Act, 15 U.S.C. §§ 1692–1692m (1996); Fair Credit Reporting Act, 15 U.S.C. §§ 1681–1681t (1996); Motor Vehicle Information and Cost Savings Act, Title IV, 15 U.S.C. §§ 1981–1991 (1996); Consumer Product Safety Act, 15 U.S.C. §§ 2051–2083 (1996).

[2] 15 U.S.C. §§ 2301–2312 (1996).

[3] 16 C.F.R. § 433 (1996).

[4] For example, most written warranties disclaimed the implied warranty of merchantability. For a discussion of the implied warranty of merchantability, *see* § 4.07[C], *supra*.

Congress reacted to these problems with a statutory scheme that contains little substantive regulation of warranty content, although the substantive regulation of warranty terms that is present has had a significant impact.[5] Rather, the Act and its accompanying regulations attempt primarily to standardize the manner in which warranty terms are disclosed, and to ensure that consumers are made aware of warranty terms prior to the sale. The hope of Congress was that this standardization would remove, at least in part, the dizzying array of terms and complex language that was then present in warranties. In addition, Congress believed that standard terminology and disclosure would better enable consumers to compare the warranty coverage of various sellers, thus promoting competition that would lead to enhanced warranty coverage. Ironically, the few provisions that substantively regulate warranty terms and provide the consumer with enhanced remedies have had a much greater impact than the much more voluminous sections that regulate the form, rather than the content, of warranties.

[B]   Scope and Coverage of the Act

The definitions in the Act are very important and largely determine its scope and coverage. With one very important exception,[6] the Act deals only with "written warranties" of "consumer products." A "written warranty" is defined by the Act as follows:

> (A) any written affirmation of fact or written promise made in connection with the sale of a consumer product by a supplier to a buyer which relates to the nature of the material or workmanship and affirms or promises that such material or workmanship is defect free or will meet a specified level of performance over a specified period of time, or
> (B) any undertaking in writing in connection with the sale by a supplier of a consumer product to refund, repair, replace, or take other remedial action with respect to such product in the event that such product fails to meet the specifications set forth in the undertaking, which written affirmation, promise, or undertaking becomes part of the basis of the bargain between a supplier and a buyer for purposes other than resale of such product.[7]

---

[5] *See* § 4.07, *supra.*

[6] The exception is section 108 of the Act dealing with disclaimers of implied warranties.

[7] 15 U.S.C. § 2301(6) (1996).

The definition of "written warranty" limits the application of Magnuson-Moss to the *sale* of *consumer products*.[8] The Act does not cover the *lease* of consumer products,[9] nor does it cover the sale of services.[10] Also, the definition of "written warranty" in Magnuson-Moss is both similar to and different from the definition of "express warranty" in the Code.[11] Although there is considerable overlap, in some ways a written warranty is narrower than an express warranty. Most obvious, a written warranty must be, in fact, *written*, while an express warranty can be oral. In addition, a written warranty under Magnuson-Moss must "relate to the nature of the material or workmanship" and "affirm or promise that the material or workmanship is defect free or will meet a specified level of performance over a specified period of time." An express warranty, on the other hand, can be a description of the goods, or an affirmation of fact or promise related to the goods; the description, affirmation of fact, or promise does not have to relate to material or workmanship. For example, a promise that a car has a "new" engine, even if made in writing, would not be a written warranty under Magnuson-Moss, but would clearly be an express warranty under the Code. Or, to take an example from the governing regulations,[12] an energy efficiency rating is probably an express warranty, but not a written warranty because it does not promise a specified level of performance over a specified period of time.[13] Furthermore, a Magnuson-Moss written warranty cannot consist of a sample or model.

On the other hand, the Magnuson-Moss definition of written warranty is, in other ways, broader than the Code's definition of express warranty. Subsection (B) includes within the definition of written warranty an "undertaking" by the supplier to perform remedial action (e.g., refund, repair

---

[8] 15 U.S.C. § 2301(1) (1996). In addition, the definition of "implied warranty" in the Act is limited to implied warranties arising under state law "in connection with the *sale* by a supplier of a consumer product." Magnuson-Moss Act § 101(7), 15 U.S.C. § 2301(7) (1996).

[9] *See* Sellers v. Frank Griffin AMC Jeep, Inc., 526 So. 2d 147 (Fla. Dist. Ct. App. 1988); Barco Auto Leasing Corp. v. PSI Cosmetics, Inc., 125 Misc. 2d 68, 478 N.Y.S.2d 505 (N.Y. Civ. Ct. 1984). *But see* Henderson v. Benson-Hartman Motors, Inc., 33 Pa. D.&C. 3d 6, 41 UCCR 782 (Pa. Ct. C.P. 1983) (Magnuson-Moss Act applies to lease with most of the characteristics of a sale).

[10] *See* 16 C.F.R. § 700.1(h) (1996).

[11] *See* § 4.05, *supra*.

[12] 16 C.F.R. § 700.3(a) (1996).

[13] *See also* Skelton v. General Motors Corp., 660 F.2d 311 (7th Cir. 1981) *cert. denied*, 456 U.S. 974 (1982) (description of automobile component not written warranty under Magnuson-Moss Act); Motor Homes of Am., Inc. v. O'Donnell, 440 So. 2d 422 (Fla. Dist. Ct. App. 1983) (brochure describing motor home not written warranty).

or replacement) if the product fails to meet the specifications set forth in the undertaking. Unlike subsection (A), this provision does not require that the undertaking relate to the material or workmanship of the goods or meet a specified level of performance; presumably any promise by the supplier to perform some remedial action would be a sufficient "undertaking." Such promises are unlikely to be express warranties under the Code because they do not relate to the goods themselves.

The difference between written warranties and express warranties is aptly illustrated by the case of *Ventura v. Ford Motor Co.*[14] In this case, the buyer purchased a new automobile from a dealer. In the purchase contract, the dealer disclaimed all implied warranties. The contract also provided that the dealer would "promptly perform and fulfill all terms and conditions of the owner service policy" of the manufacturer, Ford Motor Co. When the buyer sued both the dealer and the manufacturer, the court properly held that the dealer's contract with the buyer included an undertaking sufficient to constitute a written warranty under section 101(6)(B) of Magnuson-Moss. As a result, the dealer's attempted disclaimer was invalid, because the Act precludes sellers who make written warranties from disclaiming implied warranties.[15] The provision in the dealer's contract to perform the manufacturer's warranty obligations, found by the court to be a written warranty under Magnuson-Moss, would almost certainly not have qualified as an express warranty under the Code.[16]

Magnuson-Moss is also limited to written warranties of "consumer products," and only suppliers or other warrantors of "consumer products" are covered by the Act. The definition of "consumer product," does not, however, look to the *actual* use of the product in a particular case but, rather, the *ordinary* use of the product, and is defined as:

> [A]ny tangible personal property which is distributed in commerce and which is normally used for personal, family, or household purposes.[17]

The regulations supplementing the Act provide further guidance:

> The Act applies to written warranties on tangible personal property which is normally used for personal, family, or household purposes. . . . This means that a product is a "consumer product" if the use of that

---

[14] 180 N.J. Super. 45, 433 A.2d 801, 32 UCCR 57 (1981).

[15] *See* § 8.02[G], *infra.*

[16] This is because the provision made no affirmations of fact or promises relating to the goods nor was it a description of the goods.

[17] Magnuson-Moss Act § 101(1), 15 U.S.C. § 2301(1) (1996).

type of product is not uncommon. The percentage of sales or the use to which a product is put by any individual buyer is not determinative. For example, products such as automobiles and typewriters which are used for both personal and commercial purposes come within the definition of consumer product. Where it is unclear whether a particular product is covered under the definition of consumer product, any ambiguity will be resolved in favor of coverage.[18]

Because the definition focuses on the *normal* use of a product, the fact that the particular buyer uses the product for personal, family, or household purposes does not make it a consumer product if it is not normally used for these purposes.[19]

Agricultural products are generally not covered by Magnuson-Moss except for those agricultural products normally used for personal or household gardening.[20] Separate items of equipment attached to real property, such as air conditioners, furnaces, and water heaters, are "consumer products" even though they would be considered fixtures under state law.[21] Items such as wiring, plumbing, and ducts that are integral parts of a structure, however, are not considered to be "consumer products,"[22] although when these and similar items are sold over the counter, they are consumer products.[23]

There have not been many cases that have considered whether a product is a "consumer product" and most of these have been easy calls.[24] A couple of courts, despite the clear direction of the statute, have applied an individual-use test to determine whether the item is a "consumer product." For example, in *Balser v. Cessna Aircraft Co.,*[25] the court had to decide whether a general aviation airplane was a "consumer product." In refusing to grant the seller's motion to dismiss the buyer's Magnuson-Moss complaint, the court said that the determination of whether the aircraft was a consumer product was a factual question that could not be decided on a motion to

---

[18] 16 C.F.R. § 700.1(a) (1996).

[19] *See* Crume v. Ford Motor Co., 60 Or. App. 224, 653 P.2d 564, 35 UCCR 144 (1982) (flatbed truck).

[20] 16 C.F.R. § 700.1(b) (1996).

[21] 16 C.F.R. § 700.1(c) (1996).

[22] 16 C.F.R. § 700.1(d) (1996).

[23] 16 C.F.R. § 700.1(e) (1996).

[24] *See, e.g.,* Ismael v. Goodman Toyota, 106 N.C. App. 421, 417 S.E.2d 290 (N.C. Ct. App. 1992) (automobile is consumer product); Business Modeling Techniques, Inc. v. General Motors Corp., 123 Misc. 2d 605, 474 N.Y.S.2d 258 (N.Y. Sup. Ct. 1984) (automobile); Walsh v. Ford Motor Credit Co., 113 Misc. 2d 546, 449 N.Y.S.2d 556 (N.Y. Sup. Ct. 1982) (tractor trailer not consumer product).

[25] 512 F. Supp. 1217 (N.D. Ga. 1981).

dismiss. Further, the opinion suggested that this factual issue depended upon the actual use of the product by the buyer, not the normal use.[26] In *Richards v. General Motors Corp.*,[27] the Alabama Court of Appeals held that a trial court determination that a pickup truck was not a "consumer product" was not incorrect in view of evidence that the buyer had used the truck to haul produce to market and to pull a cattle trailer, and had deducted it as a business expense on a federal income tax return. Had the court correctly analyzed the issue, it would have determined that the use of a pickup truck for personal, family or household purposes was a normal use (not uncommon) for this product, regardless of the buyer's actual use, and therefore the pickup was a consumer product.

For reasons that will shortly become apparent,[28] the term "supplier," as used in the Act, is also important. According to the Act, a "supplier" is "any person engaged in the business of making a consumer product directly or indirectly available to consumers."[29] The term is not coterminous with "seller," and includes manufacturers, distributors, and other who "indirectly" make a product available to consumers.

[C]   Disclosure Provisions of the Act

As mentioned previously, an important purpose of the Act is to standardize the manner in which warranty terms are disclosed to consumers to better enable them to compare the warranties of various sellers. The statute and implementing regulations attempt to accomplish this in two related ways:

1. All written warranties on products costing more than $10 must be labeled as either a "full (statement of duration) warranty" or "limited warranty." A product with a "full" warranty is required to contain certain substantive terms.

2. The terms and conditions of written warranties on products costing more than $15 must be "fully and conspicuously" disclosed in "simple and readily understood language." Certain items must be included in the written warranty and disclosed in a particular manner.

---

[26] The court relied upon cases interpreting other statutes dealing with consumer products that had held that the determination of whether an item was a "consumer product" was based upon its actual use by the consumer. The court rejected an earlier FTC interpretation that had specifically excluded general aviation aircraft from the definition of consumer product.

[27] 461 So. 2d 825 (Ala. Civ. App. 1984).

[28] *See* § 8.02[G][3], *infra.*

[29] Magnuson-Moss Act § 101(4), 15 U.S.C. § 2301(4) (1996).

[1] "Full" and "Limited" Warranties

Section 103 of the Act requires that all written warranties on consumer products costing more than $10 be clearly and conspicuously designated as either "full (statement of duration)" warranties or "limited" warranties.[30] These are the only designations permitted unless an exemption is granted by FTC rule.[31] The intent behind this section was to encourage suppliers to offer "full" warranties rather the suffer the ignominy of admitting in conspicuous form that their warranty coverage was "limited." Unfortunately, a quick trip to the local department store provides convincing evidence of the excessive optimism of the drafters—the market is hardly overrun by full warranties.

For those few warrantors who choose to offer full warranties, the warranty must meet the federal minimum standards for full warranties detailed in section 104 of the Act.[32] Simply by designating the warranty as a "full (statement of duration) warranty" the warrantor is obligated to meet these minimum standards, whether or not they are actually expressed in the written warranty itself. The warrantor must provide a remedy within a reasonable time and without charge if the product fails to conform to the warranty.[33] To "remedy" the product, the warrantor must repair the product or provide a replacement or refund, although the warrantor may elect the refund alternative only if (1) it is unable to provide a replacement and repair is not commercially practicable or cannot be made in a timely fashion, or (2) the customer is willing to accept a refund. Also, under a full warranty, the remedy must be provided "without charge." The term "without charge" means that that consumer cannot be assessed for any costs the warrantor incurs in remedying the product.[34]

The warrantor giving a full warranty cannot impose any duty, other than notification, on the consumer as a condition to securing a remedy under the warranty unless the warrantor can demonstrate in a rule-making or en-

---

[30] Magnuson-Moss Act § 103(a), 15 U.S.C. § 2303(a) (1996).

[31] 15 U.S.C. § 2303(c) (1995). The FTC has not exercised this rule-making authority. *See* FTC v. Virginia Homes Mfg. Corp., 509 F. Supp. 51 (D. Md. 1981), *aff'd,* 661 F.2d 920 (4th Cir. 1981) (warranty titled "Manufacturer's Warranty and Limitation of Remedy" is violation of Magnuson-Moss Act).

[32] 15 U.S.C. § 2304 (1996).

[33] 15 U.S.C. § 2304(a)(1) (1996).

[34] 15 U.S.C. § 2304(c) (1996). The Act, however, does not require the warrantor to compensate the consumer for "incidental expenses," unless these expenses were incurred because the remedy was not made available within a reasonable time or because the warrantor imposed an unreasonable duty upon the consumer as a condition of securing the remedy. *Id.* Neither the Act nor the regulations define "incidental expenses." It is possible that these refer to "incidental damages" as defined in U.C.C. § 2-715(1). *See* § 7.04[F], *infra.*

forcement proceeding that the duty is reasonable.[35] The FTC, by rule, has determined that requiring consumer to return a warranty registration card in order to be entitled to the benefits of the warranty is *per se* unreasonable.[36]

Perhaps the reason that more suppliers have not offered full warranties can be found in section 104(a)(2) of the Act. In conjunction with section 108, this provision precludes a supplier who gives a full warranty from either disclaiming implied warranties or limiting their duration. A supplier who offers a "limited" warranty, on the other hand, while also unable to disclaim implied warranties,[37] may limit the duration of implied warranties to the duration of the written warranty.[38] As a result, if the supplier's full warranty is of relatively short duration, implied warranties may extend far beyond the duration of the full written warranty. And, while a supplier who gives a full warranty may exclude or limit consequential damages, the supplier must do so in clear and conspicuous language on the face of the warranty.[39] Although neither "conspicuous" nor "consequential damages" are defined in the Act, given the drafters' familiarity with the U.C.C.,[40] these terms should be given the same meaning as they have under the Code.[41]

There are no "minimum standards" for limited warranties; the only substantive restriction is that a supplier making a limited written warranty cannot disclaim implied warranties. A supplier making a limited warranty can, however, limit the duration of implied warranties to the duration of the written warranty, if the limitation is conscionable, set forth in clear and

---

[35] The warrantor may also require that the consumer make the product available free and clear of liens or other encumbrances. Magnuson-Moss Act § 104(b)(2), 15 U.S.C. § 2304(b)(2) (1996).

[36] 16 C.F.R. § 700.7 (1996). In 1980, the FTC proposed a detailed rule describing unreasonable consumer duties, but it has not been promulgated. *See* 45 Fed. Reg. 37,386 (1980).

[37] Magnuson-Moss Act § 108(a), 15 U.S.C. § 2308(a) (1996).

[38] *Id.* at § 108(b), 15 U.S.C. § 2308(b) (1996).

[39] 15 U.S.C. § 2308(6) (1996).

[40] H.R. Rep. No. 1107, 93d Cong., 2d Sess. 4 (1994), reprinted in 1974 U.S.S.C.A.N. 7702, 7706 ("Warranties are currently governed by common law and the Uniform Commercial Code. . . . In the jurisdictions where it is in effect, it generally controls the rights of parties in commercial transactions and it is commonly accepted as today's law of sales.").

[41] The phrase "on the face of the warranty" is defined in 16 C.F.R. § 701.1(I) (1996) as:

(1) Where the warranty is single sheet with printing on both sides of the sheet or where the warranty is comprised of more than one sheet, the page on which the warranty text begins;

(2) Where the warranty is included as part of a larger document, such as a use and care manual, the page in such document on which the warranty text begins.

unmistakable language, and prominently displayed on the face of the warranty.[42]

It is not clear what it means to limit the duration of an implied warranty to the duration of the written warranty. A written warranty of a specific duration may be drafted in a number of ways. The warranty may require only that the defect *exist* during the warranty period. Somewhat more restrictively, it may require that the defect *become apparent* during the warranty period. Even more restrictively, the warranty may require that the consumer *notify* the supplier during the warranty period. Finally, the written warranty may be ambiguous as to what must occur during the warranty period for the buyer to be entitled to coverage.[43] Presumably, the drafters of Magnuson-Moss intended that if a supplier limits the duration of implied warranties to the duration of the written warranty, the same durational conditions will apply to implied warranties as apply to the written warranty. For example, if the written warranty requires that the defect *appear* within ninety days of the sale to be covered by the written warranty, any defect the buyer claims is a breach of the implied warranty of merchantability must also appear within ninety days. Similarly, if the written warranty requires that *notice of the defect be given* to the seller within ninety days of the sale for the defect to be covered by the written warranty, then notice of breach of the implied warranty of merchantability must also be given within the same period.

This inability to disclaim implied warranties once a written warranty is given is perhaps the most significant substantive change in the law wrought by Magnuson-Moss. Prior to Magnuson-Moss, suppliers would disclaim implied warranties in their written warranties as a matter of course.[44] Because most manufacturers of consumer products—at least those costing more than a minimal price—provide written warranties with their products, the practice of routinely disclaiming implied warranties is no longer available. If *no* written warranty is given by a supplier, however, the supplier remains free under Magnuson-Moss to disclaim implied warranties entirely. Such disclaimers must, however, be consistent with state law, including section 2-316 of the Code.[45]

---

[42] 15 U.S.C. § 2308(6) (1996). It is the authors' experience that most suppliers do, in fact, limit the duration of implied warranties to the length of the limited written warranty.

[43] An example of an ambiguous warranty would be a warranty "against defects in material and workmanship for a period of one year."

[44] H.R. Rep. No. 1107, 93d Cong., 2d Sess. 4 (1994), reprinted in 1974 U.S.C.C.A.N. 7702, 7706 ("For the paper operated to take away from the consumer the implied warranties of merchantability and fitness arising by operation of law leaving little in its stead.").

[45] *See* § 4.07[C], *supra.*

[2] Disclosure Requirements

Section 102(a) of Magnuson-Moss[46] authorizes the FTC to make rules governing the disclosure of terms in written warranties. In 1975, the FTC promulgated disclosure rules, which are codified in 16 C.F.R. Part 701. All written warranties, both full and limited, on consumer products[47] actually costing the consumer more than $15 must comply with the Act's disclosure requirements.[48]

The required disclosures must be made in a single document in simple and readily understood language. The following items must be disclosed:

1. The identity of the party or parties to whom the warranty extends if the warranty is limited to persons other than every consumer owner during the term of the warranty. Thus, if a warranty is limited to the original purchaser, this must be disclosed.
2. The products, parts, characteristics, components, or properties covered by the warranty.
3. A statement of what the warrantor will do in the event of a defect, malfunction, or failure to conform to the written warranty, including those items that warrantor will pay for or provide and, when necessary for clarification, those items that the warrantor will not pay for or provide.
4. The time when warranty coverage commences, if different from the purchase date, and the duration of the warranty.
5. A step-by-step explanation of the procedure to be followed to obtain performance of the warranty obligations, including the names and addresses (or toll-free telephone number) of those responsible for performing warranty service.
6. Information on available informal dispute settlement mechanisms.[49]
7. Any limitations on the duration of implied warranties, accompanied by the statement: "Some states do not allow limitations on how long an implied warranty lasts, so the above limitation may not apply to you." As mentioned previously, limitations on the

---

[46] 15 U.S.C. § 2302(a) (1996).

[47] For purposes of Part 701 only, products that are purchased solely for commercial or industrial use are excluded from the definition of "consumer product" even if they "normally" are used for personal, family, or household purposes. *See* § 8.02[B], *supra.*

[48] Section 102(e) of the Act, authorizing the FTC to make rules governing the disclosure of warranty terms, set a threshold of $5. The FTC raised the minimum amount to $15. 16 C.F.R. § 701.3(a) (1996).

[49] *See* § 8.02[E], *infra.*

duration of implied warranties are not permitted when a "full (statement of duration) warranty" is given.

8. Any exclusions or limitations on relief, such as exclusions of incidental or consequential damages, accompanied by the statement: "Some states do not allow the exclusion or limitation of incidental or consequential damages, so the above exclusion may not apply to you."[50]

9. The following statement verbatim: "This warranty gives you specific legal rights, and you may also have other rights which vary from state to state."

The FTC has enforced these provisions in a number of actions. For example, in *In re George's Radio and Television Co.*,[51] the FTC found that a warranty failed to comply with the Act's disclosure provisions in at least three ways: (1) the designation "George's extended limited warranty" did not comply with the warranty designation provisions of the Act;[52] (2) the warranty failed to specify certain items that were excluded from the warranty; and (3) the warranty did not specify that it took effect at the date of delivery, not the date of sale. In *FTC v. Virginia Homes Manufacturing Corp.*[53] the court found, among other defects, that a warranty on a mobile home did not specify the manner in which the consumer could obtain warranty performance. In order to remedy the violations, the FTC ordered the company to notify past customers of their rights under the Act.

[D] Pre-Sale Availability

Section 102 of Magnuson-Moss mandates that the FTC prescribe rules requiring that the terms of written warranties be made available to the consumer prior to the sale of the product. This section was prompted by concerns that consumers were not receiving information about the coverage of suppliers' warranties until after the sale was consummated—often not until the product was taken home and its package or carton opened. Shortly after the passage of the Act, the FTC promulgated rules regarding the pre-sale availability of warranties. These rules were too inflexible and were amended in 1987. The present rules are codified in 16 C.F.R. Part 702. The major provisions of the rules will be discussed briefly.

---

[50] The statements in items (7) and (8) above may be combined. 16 C.F.R. § 701.3(8) (1996).

[51] 94 FTC 1135 (1979).

[52] *See* § 8.02[C], *supra.*

[53] 509 F. Supp. 51 (D. Md.), *aff'd,* 661 F.2d 920 (4th Cir. 1981).

The rules apply to all consumer products costing more than $15.[54] They impose obligations upon both *sellers* (those who sell the consumer product directly to the consumer)[55] and *warrantors* (those who actually make a written warranty to the consumer).[56] Sellers of products that have written warranties are required by the rule to make the warranties available to consumers prior to the sale in one of two ways: (1) the seller can display the warranty in close proximity to the warranted product; or (2) the seller can furnish the warranty to the consumer upon request.[57] If the latter method is chosen, the seller must place signs in prominent locations informing consumers of the availability of warranties upon request.[58]

Warrantors (generally manufacturers) must provide sellers with the warranty materials necessary for the sellers to comply with their obligations. This can be done in one of four ways: (1) providing to the seller a copy of the written warranty with every warranted consumer product; (2) providing a tag, sign, sticker, label, decal, or other attachment to the product containing the text of the warranty; (3) printing or attaching the text of the warranty on any package, carton, or container normally used for display purposes; or (4) providing a notice, sign or poster disclosing the text of the warranty.[59] If options (3) or (4) are chosen, a copy of the warranty must accompany each warranted product.

With respect to catalog or mail-order sales, a seller can comply with the rules by clearly and conspicuously disclosing either the full text of the warranty, or disclosing that the warranty can be obtained free upon specific written request and providing an address from which it can be obtained.[60] In either case, the required information must be provided in close conjunc-

---

[54] As in 16 C.F.R. Part 701, the definition of "consumer product" for purposes of Part 702 is narrowed somewhat from the definition contained in the Act itself. *See* § 8.02[C][2] note 47, *supra.*

[55] 16 C.F.R. § 702.1(e) (1996).

[56] 16 C.F.R. § 702.1(d) (1996).

[57] 16 C.F.R. § 702.3(a) (1996).

[58] *See* Montgomery Ward & Co. v. FTC, 691 F.2d 1322 (9th Cir. 1982). In this case the Court of Appeals for the Ninth Circuit overturned an FTC ruling that required Montgomery Ward to have a sign in each department indicating the location where warranty binders were kept. (Under the prior regulation, one option for the seller to comply with the pre-sale availability rules was to keep a "warranty binder" with copies of the warranties of warranted products.) The court held that the rule (now superseded) required that signs advising of the location of warranty binders were only required to be displayed in prominent locations in the store, and that signs in each department were not required. *See* 16 C.F.R. § 702.3(a)(1)(ii)(B) (1985).

[59] 16 C.F.R. § 702.3(b)(I) (1996).

[60] 16 C.F.R. § 702.3(c)(2)(I) (1996).

tion with the warranted product or in an information section of the catalog that clearly references (including the page number) a description of the warranted product. If the product is sold door-to-door, the seller must, prior to consummating the sale, disclose the fact that the sales representative has copies of warranties for the products being offered for sale and that they are available to the buyer for inspection.[61] This information must be provided both orally and in any sales literature.

[E] Informal Dispute Settlement Mechanisms

Section 110 requires the FTC to promulgate rules establishing informal dispute settlement mechanisms.[62] This provision was intended to encourage the fair and expeditious settlement of consumer disputes. The FTC has prescribed the rules governing these procedures in 16 C.F.R. Part 703. If a warrantor creates a procedure that complies with these rules, it can require that the consumer resort to that procedure prior to instituting a private suit.[63]

The rules governing these procedures are lengthy and complex. They are not explored in this text. It suffices to say that, except in the automobile industry, few warrantors have created informal dispute settlement mechanisms.

[F] Tie-in Prohibition

Section 102(c) of the Act prohibits the tying of warranty coverage to the consumer's use of any other article or service identified by brand, trade, or corporate name.[64] For example, a provision such as "this warranty is void if service is performed by anyone other than an authorized 'ABC' dealer and all replacement parts must be genuine 'ABC' parts" violates the Act.[65] Only if the article or service is provided to the consumer free of charge is a tie-in permissible. Thus, for example, a warranty may provide that all repairs must be done by an authorized representative if all parts and labor are provided without charge. The prohibition is subject to waiver by the FTC if the warrantor satisfies the FTC that (1) the warranted product will

---

[61] 16 C.F.R. § 702.3(d)(2) (1996).

[62] 15 U.S.C. § 2310(a)(1) (1996).

[63] 15 U.S.C. § 2310(a)(3) (1996).

[64] 15 U.S.C. § 2302(c) (1996).

[65] This example is taken from the regulations. *See* 16 C.F.R. § 700.10(c) (1996). The Regulations do not preclude a warrantor from expressly excluding liability for defects or damage *caused* by the use of unauthorized products or services or from denying liability when a defect or damage is caused by the unauthorized products or services. *Id.*

function properly only if the tied product or service is used, and (2) that the waiver is in the public interest. No waivers have been granted to date.

[G] Private Rights of Action

[1] Introduction

By far the most significant aspect of Magnuson-Moss is the private right of action created by section 110(d)(1) of the Act.[66] This section provides that:

> Subject to subsections (a)(3) and (e) of this section, a consumer who is damaged by the failure of a supplier, warrantor, or service contractor to comply with any obligation under this [Act], or under a written warranty, implied warranty, or service contract, may bring suit for damages and other legal and equitable relief.[67]

The Act provides a private cause of action in three instances: (1) violation of the Act itself; (2) breach of a written warranty or service contract; and (3) breach of implied warranty. In all cases, however, only actual damages are recoverable (with perhaps attorney's fees);[68] there are no provisions for statutory or punitive damages in Magnuson-Moss such as exist in some other federal consumer-protection statutes.[69]

[2] Written Warranty

The Act provides a federal cause of action for breach of a written warranty as defined by the Act. As discussed earlier,[70] the definition of "written warranty" in Magnuson-Moss and the concept of an express warranty under the Code are not coextensive. As a result, a Magnuson-Moss cause of action may exist for breach of a *written* warranty, although no

---

[66] 15 U.S.C. § 2310(d)(1) (1996).

[67] *Id.*

[68] *See* § 8.02[G][3], *infra.*

[69] *See, e.g.*, The-Truth-in-Lending Act § 130(a)(2)(A)(I), 15 U.S.C. § 2310(d)(1) (1995) (statutory damages); Fair Debt Collection Practices Act § 813(a)(2)(A), 15 U.S.C. § 1692k(2)(A) (1995) (statutory damages); Fair Credit Reporting Act § 616(2), 15 U.S.C. § 1681(n)(2) (1995) (punitive damages for willful noncompliance); Equal Credit Opportunity Act § 706(b), 15 U.S.C. § 1691(e)(6) (1995) (punitive damages up to $10,000 per aggrieved applicant). Although not explicitly authorized by the Act, some cases suggest that if punitive damages are available for breach of warranty under state law, they will also be available under Magnuson-Moss. *See* § 8.02[I][2], *infra.*

[70] *See* § 8.02[B], *supra.*

express warranty has been created under the Code.[71] Conversely, there are many cases in which a cause of action would exist under the Code for breach of express warranty, but where no Magnuson-Moss claim exists—for example, when a warranty is oral rather than in writing.

[3] Implied Warranty

Section 110(d)(1) also allows a consumer to recover damages for the failure of a supplier, warrantor, or service contractor to comply with an implied warranty. The inclusion of the term "supplier" in this provision is important. A "supplier" is "any person engaged in the business of making a consumer product directly or indirectly available to consumers."[72] A person can be a "supplier" without having provided any written warranty; a person who provides a written warranty is a "warrantor," under the Act. Consequently, section 110 creates a potential Magnuson-Moss cause of action for breach of implied warranty against a supplier even though the supplier has made no written warranty.

The existence of an implied warranty for purposes of Magnuson-Moss is determined by state law. Section 101(7) defines "implied warranty" as "an implied warranty arising under state law . . . in connection with the sale by a supplier of a consumer product."[73] This definition has a number of important consequences, some of which will be discussed in later sections. First, if implied warranties have been successfully disclaimed under state law, there is no Magnuson-Moss cause of action for their breach.[74] Because of the disclaimer, the implied warranty does not "arise" under state law, and there is, therefore, no Magnuson-Moss implied warranty to enforce.[75] Second, if lack of privity would bar recovery for breach of implied warranty under state law, most, but not all, courts hold that recovery is also barred under Magnuson-Moss.[76] Although an implied warranty may have "arisen" in the transaction with respect to some persons, it does not "arise" for purposes of Magnuson-Moss if lack of privity would bar its enforcement by the particular plaintiff under state law.

---

[71] *See, e.g.,* Ventura v. Ford Motor Corp., 180 N.J. Super. 45, 433 A.2d 801 (N.J. Super. Ct. App. Div. 1981); Freeman v. Hubco Leasing, Inc., 253 Ga. 698, 324 S.E.2d 462 (1985); Skelton v. General Motors Corp., 660 F.2d 311 (7th Cir. 1981), *cert. denied,* 456 U.S. 974 (1982); Motor Homes of Am., Inc. v. O'Donnell, 440 So. 2d 422 (Fla. Dist. Ct. App. 1983).

[72] 15 U.S.C. § 2301(4) (1996).

[73] Magnuson-Moss Act § 101(7), 15 U.S.C. § 2301(7) (1996).

[74] *See* Freeman v. Hubco Leasing, Inc., 253 Ga. 698, 324 S.E.2d 462 (1985).

[75] If a disclaimer is ineffective under state law, however, it will be equally ineffective under Magnuson-Moss. 15 U.S.C. § 2308(c) (1996).

[76] *See* § 8.02[H] *infra.*

Despite the fact that most aspects of a Magnuson-Moss cause of action for breach of implied warranties are governed by state law, including damages,[77] there are still potential benefits in suing under Magnuson-Moss for breach of implied warranty. One court has held that a consumer is not required to give notice of breach under U.C.C. § 2-607(3) to sue for breach of implied warranty under Magnuson-Moss.[78] In addition, if the amount in controversy exceeds $50,000, the case can be brought in federal court without the necessity for diversity.[79] Much more important, section 110(d)(2) permits a consumer who prevails in a private action to recover attorney's fees, unless the court finds that an award of attorney's fees would be inappropriate.[80]

The provision permitting recovery of attorneys' fees is of critical importance. Although the amount in controversy must be $50,000 or more for federal court jurisdiction, the state courts are given jurisdiction over Magnuson-Moss claims without regard to the amount in controversy.[81] As a result, in most routine consumer cases in which a claim for breach of implied warranty under the Code is made in state court, there will be grounds for a Magnuson-Moss claim as well. Because attorneys' fees are based upon the actual time expended,[82] consumers are much more willing to bring warranty cases involving modest amounts than would otherwise be the case, and attorneys are much more willing to take these cases.

Most courts have granted attorney's fees to prevailing plaintiffs, although there are cases where they have been denied.[83] In a number of cases, the attorney's fees have approached or exceeded the plaintiff's total recovery.[84] Some courts, however, have reduced the attorney's fees from actual

---

[77] *See* § 8.02[I][1], *infra*.

[78] Mendelson v. General Motors Corp., 105 Misc. 2d 346, 432 N.Y.S.2d 132 (N.Y. Sup. Ct. 1980).

[79] 15 U.S.C. § 2310(d)(3)(B) (1996).

[80] 15 U.S.C. § 2310(d)(2) (1996).

[81] 15 U.S.C. § 2310(d)(1)(A) (1996).

[82] 15 U.S.C. § 2310(d)(2) (1996).

[83] *See, e.g.,* Trost v. Porreco Motors, Inc., 297 Pa. Super. 393, 443 A.2d 1179 (1982); Hibbs v. Jeep Corp., 666 S.W.2d 792, 38 UCCR 1257 (Mo. Ct. App. 1984), *cert. denied*, 469 U.S. 853 (1984); Carl v. Spickler Enters., Ltd., 165 Wis. 2d 611, 478 N.W.2d 48 (Wisc. Ct. App. 1991).

[84] *See, e.g.,* Universal Motors v. Waldock, 719 P.2d 254, 1 UCCR2d 704 (Alaska 1986) (attorney's fees of more than $36,000 awarded on damage recovery of less than $18,000); Fleetwood Motor Homes v. McGehee, 182 Ga. App. 151, 355 S.E.2d 73 (Ga. Ct. App. 1987) ($15,000 in attorney's fees awarded on $1,500 recovery); Volkswagen of Am., Inc. v. Harrell, 431 So. 2d 156, 36 UCCR 553 (Ala. 1983) (affirmed award of attorney's fees of more than $8,000 on judgment of $10,000); Ventura v. Ford Motor Corp., 180 N.J. Super. 45, 433 A.2d

time expended to account for the small amount in damages recovered by the plaintiff,[85] or to adjust for the fact that the plaintiff had prevailed on only a portion of her claims.[86] Courts have allowed recovery of attorney's fees without apportionment between Magnuson-Moss and other causes of action where the Magnuson-Moss claims and the other claims are closely related, even though the other causes of action do not provide for attorney's fees.[87]

[4] Violation of Magnuson-Moss

In addition to permitting recovery for breach of written warranties (including service contracts) and implied warranties, section 110 also allows recovery for "the failure of a supplier, warrantor, or service contractor to comply with any obligation under this chapter."[88] Consequently, if a consumer can prove that he or she was damaged by a violation of any obligation imposed by the Act, the consumer can recover those damages in a private action. "Obligations" under the Act might consist of the disclosure rules, the pre-sale availability rules, or, more problematically, the proscription against deceptive warranties contained in section 110(c).[89] As previously mentioned, however, there is no provision for statutory damages in the Mag-

---

801 (N.J. Super. Ct. App. Div. 1981) (affirmed attorney's fee of $5,000 on $7,000 recovery); Samuels v. American Motor Sales Corp., 969 F.2d 573 (7th Cir. 1992) (affirmed attorney's fee of $11,000 on $14,000 recovery).

[85] See Carl v. Spickler Enters., Ltd., 478 N.W.2d 48 (Wisc. Ct. App. 1991) (court denied $40,000 attorney's fee when damage recovery was only $3,000); Hanks v. Pandolfo, 38 Conn. Supp. 447, 450 A.2d 1167 (Conn. Super. Ct. 1982) (court reduced requested attorney's fees of $2,825 to $450 based upon small amount at issue in case).

[86] See Mercedes-Benz of N. Am., Inc. v. Norman Gershman's Things to Wear, Inc., 596 A.2d 1358, 16 UCCR2d 1076 (Del. 1991) (court reduced claim for attorney's fees by 40 percent to account for time attributable to unsuccessful claims). See also Samuels v. American Motors Sales Corp., 969 F.2d 573 (7th Cir. 1992) (attorney's fee claim reduced from $38,000 to $11,000 for the attorney's inefficient and dilatory manner of prosecuting case).

[87] See Drouin v. Fleetwood Enters., 163 Cal. App. 3d 486, 209 Cal. Rptr. 623 (Cal. Ct. App. 1985); King v. Taylor Chrysler-Plymouth, Inc., 184 Mich. App. 204, 457 N.W.2d 42, 12 UCCR2d 686 (Mich. Ct. App. 1990) (court appeared to allow recovery of attorney's fees without apportionment for time expended on both Magnuson-Moss claims and claims under U.C.C. and Michigan Consumer Protection Act).

[88] 15 U.S.C. § 2310(d)(1) (1995).

[89] Recovery for a deceptive warranty in a private action is problematic because the proscription against deceptive warranties is contained in a provision giving the Attorney General and the FTC the authority to bring an action to restrain warrantors from making deceptive warranties. Thus, there is some question whether this is an "obligation" for which the Act provides a private right of action.

nuson-Moss Act. Consequently, a consumer must show actual damage to recover for violation of one of these provisions.[90] In most cases, this is difficult, which explains why very few Magnuson-Moss actions have been brought for violations other than a failure to comply with written or implied warranties.

[H] Privity

As discussed earlier,[91] lack of privity may be a bar to a breach of warranty action under the Code, especially when the buyer suffers solely economic harm. The extent to which Magnuson-Moss allows recovery notwithstanding the privity restrictions of state law is a matter of controversy, especially with regard to "vertical" privity.[92]

[1] Horizontal Privity

Section 110 permits a "consumer" damaged by the failure to comply with a written warranty, implied warranty, or service contract to sue under the Act.[93] The term "consumer" is defined as:

> [A] buyer (other than for purposes of resale) of any consumer product, any person to whom such product is transferred during the duration of an implied or written warranty (or service contract) applicable to the product, and any other person who is entitled by the terms of such warranty (or service contract) or under applicable State law to enforce . . . the obligations of the warranty (or service contract).[94]

With respect to owners subsequent to the original consumer purchaser, Magnuson-Moss appears to eliminate horizontal privity requirements. The definition of "consumer" includes any person to whom the product is transferred during the duration of an implied or written warranty. Thus, so long as the warranty has not expired, any subsequent transferee is entitled to enforce the warranty regardless of the lack of horizontal privity.

This conclusion, however, is subject to a number of qualifications. First, there is nothing in the Act to prevent a supplier who provides a limited warranty from expressly limiting the warranty to the original purchaser. For example, although a limited warranty might have a one-year duration, the

---

[90] *See* Gates v. Chrysler Corp., 397 So. 2d 1187 (Fla. Dist. Ct. App. 1981).

[91] *See* § 4.09, *supra*.

[92] *See* § 4.09[A], *supra*, for a general discussion of vertical privity.

[93] 15 U.S.C. § 2310(d)(1) (1995).

[94] 15 U.S.C. § 2301(3) (1995).

warranty might also provide that coverage ceases if the product is transferred prior to the expiration of the one-year warranty. If the supplier offers a full warranty, the supplier cannot limit coverage to the original purchaser in this manner.[95] The duration of a full warranty, however, can be coextensive with the original buyer's ownership. For example, a supplier could offer a full warranty on a muffler "for as long as you own your car."[96]

Second, it is not clear whether the expansive definition of "consumer" has any effect on horizontal privity when the cause of action is based on an implied warranty rather than a written warranty. The definition of "implied warranty" as previously discussed,[97] is an implied warranty "arising under State law."[98] With respect to vertical privity, the majority of courts have held that an implied warranty does not "arise" under state law if lack of privity prevents its enforcement by a plaintiff.[99] The same reasoning can be applied to horizontal privity, which would preclude enforcement of an implied warranty under Magnuson-Moss if state horizontal privity rules bar its enforcement under the Code.[100] Further, a supplier offering a written warranty that is limited to the original purchaser may also expressly limit implied warranties in the same manner so long as the limitation otherwise complies with section 108 of the Act. Finally, the Act should have no effect with respect to plaintiffs who are not subsequent *transferees* of the product. To the extent to which the Act's definition of "consumer" expands horizontal privity, the expansion encompasses only transferees from the original consumer purchaser, not others who happen to be damaged by the breach of warranty.

[2] Vertical Privity

It is not clear whether Magnuson-Moss permits a suit by a consumer against a supplier (e.g., a manufacturer) that would otherwise be barred by the absence of vertical privity. If a *written* warranty is provided by a manufacturer directly to the consumer, there is no doubt that Magnuson-Moss permits a suit by the consumer directly against the manufacturer for breach of the written warranty without regard to privity. Section 110(d)(1) permits a suit by a consumer against a warrantor who fails to comply with a written

---

[95] Magnuson-Moss Act § 104(b)(4), 15 U.S.C. § 2304(b)(4) (1996).

[96] 16 C.F.R. § 700.6(b) (1996).

[97] *See* § 8.02[G][3], *supra.*

[98] 15 U.S.C. § 2301(7) (1996).

[99] *See* § 8.02[H][2], *infra.*

[100] The Senate Report on Magnuson-Moss supports this interpretation. *See* S. Rep. No. 151, 93d Cong., 1st Sess. 21 (1973).

warranty, and the term "warrantor" is defined by the Act as "any supplier or other person who gives or offers to give a written warranty or who is or may be obligated under an implied warranty."[101] Once a supplier—defined as anyone who makes a consumer product *directly or indirectly* available to consumers[102]—makes a written warranty to a consumer, the supplier becomes a "warrantor" and is subject to suit by a consumer under section 110.[103] As previously described, however,[104] vertical privity is rarely a bar to the enforcement of an express warranty under the Code when the manufacturer makes the express warranty directly to the consumer. As a result, Magnuson-Moss does not add much, if anything, in this regard.

The issue is considerably more difficult with respect to implied warranties. The courts are split as to whether Magnuson-Moss abrogates the requirement of vertical privity with respect to implied warranties, although the larger number of jurisdictions hold that it does not.[105] The argument that lack of vertical privity is not a bar to Magnuson-Moss claims is premised on the Act's definitions. Section 110 permits suits against "suppliers" who fail to comply with implied warranties. The term "supplier" includes all those who "*directly or indirectly*" make a consumer product available to consumers, thus including manufacturers. Ergo, the Act permits suits against manufacturers by consumers based upon implied warranties.[106]

Furthermore, the Act defines "warrantor" as "any supplier or other person who gives or offers to give a written warranty or who is or may be obligated under an implied warranty."[107] Under this definition, warrantors

---

[101] 15 U.S.C. § 2310(d)(1) (1996).

[102] 15 U.S.C. § 2301(4) (1996).

[103] *See* Abraham v. Volkswagen of Am., Inc., 795 F.2d 238, 248, 1 UCCR2d 681, 687 (2d Cir. 1986).

[104] *See* § 4.09[E], *supra.*

[105] For those cases that hold that Magnuson-Moss abrogates any requirement for vertical privity, *see* Ventura v. Ford Motor Co., 180 N.J. Super. 45, 433 A.2d 801, 32 UCCR 57 (N.H. Super. Ct. App. Div. 1981); Szajna v. General Motors Corp., 115 Ill. 2d 294, 503 N.E.2d 760, 2 UCCR2d 1268 (1986); Rothe v. Maloney Cadillac, Inc., 119 Ill. 2d 288, 518 N.E.2d 1028 (1988). For those holding that state law regarding vertical privity applies to Magnuson-Moss suits, *see* Abraham v. Volkswagen of Am., Inc., 795 F.2d 238 (2d Cir. 1986); Feinstein v. Firestone Tire & Rubber Co., 535 F. Supp. 595 (S.D.N.Y. 1982); Mendelson v. General Motors Corp., 105 Misc. 2d 346, 432 N.Y.S.2d 132 (N.Y. Sup. Ct. 1980); Walsh v. Ford Motor Co., 588 F. Supp. 1513 (D.D.C. 1984), *rev'd on other grounds,* 807 F.2d 1000 (D.C. Cir. 1986).

[106] This assumes, of course, that the supplier has not disclaimed implied warranties. As mentioned previously, however, if a supplier makes a written warranty to the consumer, the supplier cannot disclaim implied warranties. Magnuson-Moss Act § 108(a), 15 U.S.C. § 2308(a) (1996).

[107] 15 U.S.C. § 2301(5) (1995).

may be suppliers, who, in turn, can be manufacturers or other remote parties. Since section 110(d) permits suits by consumers against warrantors, if a warrantor has not disclaimed implied warranties,[108] the warrantor should be subject to suit without regard to privity. These arguments have met with success in a number of cases.[109]

Counterarguments are based on both the text of the Act and its legislative history. Magnuson-Moss defines an "implied warranty" as one "arising under State law."[110] If applicable state law does not extend the implied warranty to a remote plaintiff, then, with respect to that plaintiff at least, the implied warranty has not "arisen."[111] And, because there is no implied warranty to enforce under these circumstances, section 110 is of no help to a remote plaintiff.[112]

In addition, the legislative history is fairly convincing that Congress did not intend to abrogate state privity law. After a detailed discussion of the legislative history of the Act, the court in *Abraham v. Volkswagen of America, Inc.*[113] quoted the Senate Report on this issue:

> It is not the intent of the Committee to alter in any way the manner in which implied warranties are created under the Uniform Commercial Code. For instance, an implied warranty of fitness for a particular purpose which might be created by an installing supplier is not, in many instances, enforceable by the consumer against the manufacturing supplier. The Committee does not intend to alter currently existing state law on these subjects.[114]

Although the quoted passage mentions the implied warranty of fitness for a particular purpose, and not the warranty of merchantability (which would be the typical basis for an implied warranty suit against a manufacturer),

---

[108] If the supplier has made a written warranty, it cannot disclaim implied warranties. *See* § 8.02[C][1], *supra*.

[109] *See, e.g.*, Ventura v. Ford Motor Corp., 180 N.J. Super. 45, 433 A.2d 801 (N.J. Super. Ct. App. Div. 1981).

[110] 15 U.S.C. § 2301(7) (1996).

[111] As one court metaphorically put it: "If state law requires vertical privity to enforce an implied warranty and there is none, then, like a yeastless souffle, the warranty does not arise." Feinstein v. Firestone Tire & Rubber Co., 535 F. Supp. 595, 603 n.13 (S.D.N.Y. 1982).

[112] The counterargument to this argument is that, unless disclaimed, the implied warranty has arisen; the only issue is to whom it extends.

[113] 795 F.2d 238, 1 UCCR2d 681 (2d Cir. 1986).

[114] S. Rep. No. 151, 93d Cong., 1st Sess. 21 (1973) *quoted at* 795 F.2d 238 at 248, 1 UCCR2d at 688.

the report is a strong indication that Congress did not intend any alteration of state law with regard to privity. There is no contrary indication to be found anywhere in the legislative history, and no basis for believing that the limitations imposed by state privity rules were of concern to Congress in promulgating the legislation. One would assume that if Congress had intended to abrogate privity requirements in the Act it would have done so more clearly. Consequently, it is the authors' view that the better cases are those, such as *Abraham*, that apply state privity rules to Magnuson-Moss claims based upon implied warranty.

A provision somewhat related to the issue of privity is section 110(f) which provides that:

> [O]nly the warrantor actually making a written affirmation of fact, promise, or undertaking shall be deemed to have created a written warranty, and any rights arising thereunder may be enforced under this section only against such warrantor and no other person.[115]

This provision is intended to preclude liability under a written warranty for retailers and distributors who do nothing more than distribute a product covered by a written warranty given by the manufacturer.[116] If, however, the retailer or distributor also makes written representations of its own that qualify as "written warranties," the retailer or distributor also becomes a "warrantor" and is independently liable for those representations under the Act. Furthermore, the regulations provide that if a supplier, under state law, is deemed to have "adopted" the written warranty of another, then the adopting supplier also becomes a "warrantor" for purposes of the Act.[117]

[I]   Remedies

Prior to bringing any action under Magnuson-Moss, the consumer must give the seller a reasonable opportunity to cure the defect.[118] The Act does not define "a reasonable opportunity to cure," and it is not clear to what extent that the seller's right to cure under Magnuson-Moss differs from that in section 2-508 of the Code.[119] A seller has a right to cure under the Code only before the buyer accepts the goods.[120] There is no similar limitation in

---

[115] 15 U.S.C. § 2310(f) (1996).
[116] *See* 16 C.F.R. § 700.4 (1996).
[117] 16 C.F.R. § 700.4 (1996).
[118] Magnuson-Moss Act § 110(s), 15 U.S.C. § 2310(e) (1996).
[119] *See* Cosman v. Ford Motor Co., 674 N.E.2d 61, 33 UCCR2d 118 (Ill. App. Ct. 1996).
[120] U.C.C. § 2-508.

Magnuson-Moss, and courts have extended the seller's right to cure after the buyer's acceptance of the goods.[121] Furthermore, the Code requires that, in order to cure, the seller must substitute "a conforming tender."[122] The concept of cure under Magnuson-Moss may be broader. One court has described "cure" for purposes of Magnuson-Moss as "repair, replacement, or refund."[123] This interpretation is consistent with the definition of "remedy" under Magnuson-Moss. Courts have generally held that whether the buyer has given the seller a reasonable opportunity to cure is a question of fact,[124] although some cases have held that the buyer must give the seller more than one attempt at cure before bringing an action under the Act.[125]

[1] Compensatory Damages

The rule of thumb is that damages recoverable under Magnuson-Moss are those that would be recoverable under state law for breach of warranty under the Code.[126] Generally, this means that sections 2-712 through 2-715 of the Code, with some qualifications, govern the buyer's recovery for breach of Magnuson-Moss. Thus, for example, a buyer who is entitled to recover damages for breach of warranty under section 2-714 of the Code, measured by the difference between the value of the goods as warranted and the value of the goods as accepted, enjoys the same recovery under Magnuson-Moss.[127] In addition, consequential and incidental damages caused by the breach of warranty are also recoverable under Magnuson-Moss.[128]

---

[121] *See, e.g.*, Ventura v. Ford Motor Corp., 180 N.J. Super. 45, 433 A.2d 801 (N.J. Super. Ct. App. Div. 1981); Champion Ford Sales, Inc. v. Levine, 49 Md. App. 547, 433 A.2d 1218 (Md. Ct. Spec. App. 1981); Royal Lincoln-Mercury Sales, Inc. v. Wallace, 415 So. 2d 1024 (Miss. 1982); Fleetwood Motor Homes of Pa., Inc. v. McGehee, 182 Ga. App. 151, 355 S.E.2d 73 (Ga. Ct. App. 1987).

[122] U.C.C. § 2-508.

[123] Gorman v. Saf-T-Mate, Inc., 513 F. Supp. 1028, 1034 (N.D. Ind. 1981).

[124] *See* Royal Lincoln-Mercury Sales, Inc. v. Wallace, 415 So. 2d 1024 (Miss. 1982); Gilbert v. Astro Lincoln-Mercury, Inc., 496 So. 2d 987 (Fla. Dist. Ct. App. 1986); Laiosa v. Camelot AMC/Jeep Ltd., 113 A.D.2d 145, 495 N.Y.S.2d 285 (N.Y. App. Div. 1985).

[125] *See* Olmstead v. General Motors Corp., Inc., 500 A.2d 615, 42 UCCR 439 (Del. Super. Ct. 1985); Sepulveda v. American Motor Sales Corp., 521 N.Y.S.2d 387 (N.Y. Civ. Ct. 1987).

[126] H.R. Rep. No. 1107, 93th Cong., 2d Sess. 4 (1974), reprinted in 1974 U.S.C.C.A.N. 7702, 7704. *See* MacKenzie v. Chrysler Corp., 607 F.2d 1162 (5th Cir. 1979); Novosel v. Northway Car Corp., 460 F. Supp. 541, 25 UCCR 137 (N.D.N.Y. 1978).

[127] U.C.C. § 2-714(2). *See* § 7.04[E], *supra.*

[128] *See* Universal Motors, Inc. v. Waldock, 719 P.2d 254 (Alaska 1986) (incidental damages); Volkswagen of Am., Inc. v. Harrell, 431 So. 2d 156 (Ala. 1983) (both incidental and consequential damages); Volkswagen of Am., Inc. v. Novak, 418 So. 2d 801 (Miss. 1982) (both).

Section 111(b)(2) of the Act provides an exception of uncertain dimension to the recovery of consequential damages:

Nothing in this chapter (other than sections 108 and 104(a)(2) and (4) of this title) shall (A) affect the liability of, or impose liability on, any person for personal injury, or (B) supersede any provision of State law regarding consequential damages for injury to the person or other injury.

There is no doubt that this provision prevents a Magnuson-Moss cause of action for personal injury damages resulting from a breach of warranty.[129] The difficult question is the effect of the parenthetical reference to sections 108 and 104(a)(2) and 104(a)(4). The issue is simple: was this reference intended to create a Magnuson-Moss cause of action for personal injury if a supplier violated section 108 or sections 104(a)(2) or 104(a)(4)?

The problem can be simply illustrated. Assume that a supplier has offered a written warranty and at the same time disclaimed implied warranties. As we have seen,[130] section 108 prohibits a supplier who has given a consumer a written warranty from disclaiming implied warranties. If a consumer is later injured by a defect in the supplier's product, does the consumer have a Magnuson-Moss cause of action for the personal injury as a result of the supplier's violation of section 108? If so, the consumer may receive attorney's fees and may not be subject to all of the defenses that might exist for a breach of warranty action under the Code, such as a failure to give notice of breach.[131]

A number of early cases suggested in dicta that the answer was "yes"; the intent of the parenthetical in section 111 was to exclude a violation of sections 108 and 104(a)(2) and 104(a)(4) from the general prohibition of a Magnuson-Moss cause of action for personal injury.[132] In 1986, a federal district court in Arkansas in *Hughes, v. Segal Enterprises, Inc.*[133] squarely faced the issue. It held that a violation of one of the substantive provisions of the Act mentioned in section 111 did create a Magnuson-Moss cause of

---

[129] *See, e.g.,* Voelkel v. General Motors Corp., 846 F. Supp. 1468, *aff'd,* 43 F.3d 1484 (D. Kan. 1994); Boelens v. Redman Homes, Inc., 748 F.2d 1058 (5th Cir. 1984), *aff'd on reh'g,* 759 F.2d 504 (5th Cir. 1985); Washington v. Otasco, Inc., 603 F. Supp. 1295 (N.D. Miss. 1985); Bush v. American Motors Sales Corp., 575 F. Supp. 1581 (D. Colo. 1984); Gorman v. Saf-T-Mate, Inc., 513 F. Supp. 1028 (N.D. Ind. 1981).

[130] *See* § 8.02[C][1], *supra.*

[131] *See* § 4.10, *supra.*

[132] Gorman v. Saf-T-Mate, Inc., 513 F. Supp. 1028 (N.D. Ind. 1981); Bush v. American Motor Sales Corp., 575 F. Supp. 1581 (D. Colo. 1984); Boelens v. Redman Homes, Inc., 748 F.2d 1058 (5th Cir. 1984), *aff'd on reh'g,* 759 F.2d 504 (5th Cir. 1985).

[133] 627 F. Supp. 1231 (W.D. Ark. 1986).

action for personal injury. In *Hughes,* the supplier had not conspicuously labeled a warranty form as either "full" or "limited." Although this failure, standing alone, was not a violation of any of the sections referred to in section 111,[134] the failure to label the warranty as either "full" or "limited" caused the court to treat the warranty as a full warranty. As a result, the warranty limitations and disclaimers were in violation of section 108, and its inconspicuous exclusion of consequential damages violated section 104(a)(3).[135] As a result of these violations, the court held that the plaintiffs had properly asserted a Magnuson-Moss cause of action for personal injury and allowed the case to proceed as a class action in federal court.[136]

The authors believe that the *Hughes* case was wrongly decided. Section 111 was intended to preclude a Magnuson-Moss cause of action for personal injury under all circumstances. The parenthetical reference to sections 108 and 104 in section 111 was intended only to ensure consistency between these sections and section 111. Sections 108 and 104(a)(2) and 104(a)(3) invalidate certain exclusions and limitations for the purposes of Magnuson-Moss and state law. For example, section 108 invalidates disclaimers of implied warranties when a supplier gives a written warranty. Consequently, a consumer may have a cause of action for personal injury *under state law* that the consumer would not have had *but for* Magnuson-Moss. The parenthetical references in section 111(b)(c) were meant to ensure that when a cause of action exists for personal injury under state law solely because of sections 108 or 104, section 111 would not be interpreted to preclude recovery of the personal injury damages in the *state* cause of action. There is no indication, however, in the legislative history that section 111 was intended to create a Magnuson-Moss cause of action for personal injury when a substantive violation of section 108 or 104(a)(2) or 104(a)(3) was involved. Moreover, the drafters recognized at the time the Act was passed that because of the rise of strict tort liability, adequate remedies existed under state

---

[134] Although it did violate section 103 of the Act.

[135] Courts have uniformly held that the reference to Act section 104(a)(4) in section 111 was intended to refer to section 104(a)(3). Otherwise the exclusion makes little sense. *See* Voelkel v. General Motors Corp., 846 F. Supp. 1468 (D. Kan. 1994); Gorman v. Saf-T-Mate, 513 F. Supp. 1028 (N.D. Ind. 1981); Hughes v. Segal Enters., Inc., 627 F. Supp. 1231 (W.D. Ark. 1986).

[136] Section 110(d)(1)(B) of the Act grants federal court jurisdiction over Magnuson-Moss claims. Section 110(d)(3), however, limits this jurisdiction to cases in which the amount in controversy exceeds $50,000. Class actions are limited to cases in which the total amount in controversy exceeds $50,000, the number of named plaintiffs is 100 or more, and the amount of each individual claim is greater than $25. Magnuson-Moss Act §§ 110(d)(3)(A)–110(d)(3)(C), 15 U.S.C. §§ 2310(d)(3)(A)–2310(d)(3)(C) (1996).

law for personal injuries caused by defective products. There is no reason
to believe that the drafters were interested in carving out in section 111
three exceptions to the exclusion of personal injury damages. They were,
however, interested in ensuring that all portions of the Act were consistent;
that if the Act invalidated a disclaimer for purposes of state law, the inval-
idation applied to personal injury claims brought under state law as well as
claims for other damages.

[2] Punitive Damages

A number of cases have dealt with the recovery of punitive damages
under Magnuson-Moss. Punitive damages are not mentioned in Magnuson-
Moss; the Act merely gives plaintiffs the right to sue "for damages and
other legal and equitable relief."[137] It has been argued that this provision
creates a federal right to punitive damages,[138] but this assertion has been
uniformly rejected.[139] Instead, courts apply state law, which generally does
not award punitive damages for breach or warranty or breach of contract.[140]

[3] Other Equitable Relief

In addition to damages, the Act also authorizes the court to award
"other legal and equitable relief."[141] Whether this provision authorizes the
court to grant equitable relief in circumstances in which it might not be
available under state law is not clear. One federal court has suggested that
injunctive relief might be available under Magnuson-Moss, but dismissed
the case because the plaintiff failed to meet the $50,000 requirement for
federal court jurisdiction.[142] Another case, *Sadat v. American Motors
Corp.*,[143] clearly decided that the availability of equitable relief was to be
determined by whether the relief prayed for would be available under state
law. This holding suggests that equitable relief, particularly injunctive relief,
will rarely be available in a private suit because it will be difficult to estab-

---

[137] Magnuson-Moss Act § 110(d)(1) (1996).

[138] *See* Walsh v. Ford Motor Co., 627 F. Supp. 1519 (D.D.C. 1986).

[139] *Id.* at 1524; Schafer v. Chrysler Corp., 544 F. Supp. 182 (N.D. Ind. 1982); Lieb v.
American Motors Corp., 538 F. Supp. 127 (S.D.N.Y. 1982).

[140] *See, e.g.*, Simmons v. Taylor Childre Chevrolet-Pontiac, Inc., 629 F. Supp. 1030 (M.D.
Ga. 1986); Boelens v. Redman Homes, Inc., 748 F.2d 1058 (5th Cir. 1984); Novosel v.
Northway Motor Car Corp., 460 F. Supp. 541 (N.D.N.Y. 1978); Schafer v. Chrysler Corp.,
544 F. Supp. 182 (N.D. Ind. 1982).

[141] 15 U.S.C. § 2310(d)(1) (1996).

[142] Lieb v. American Motors Co., 538 F. Supp. 127, 134 (S.D.N.Y. 1982).

[143] 104 Ill. 2d 105, 470 N.E.2d 997 (1984).

lish that money damages are an inadequate remedy for breach of warranty in a typical consumer action under Magnuson-Moss. Other nondamage remedies, however, such as rescission (revocation of acceptance under the Code),[144] that are routinely available under state law for breach of warranty should also be available under Magnuson-Moss.

[J] Conclusion

This chapter has not attempted to deal comprehensively with the Magnuson-Moss Act. The Act also contains sections dealing with service contracts,[145] the designation of representatives to perform warranty service,[146] jurisdiction,[147] and public enforcement.[148] We have tried, however, to address the most important provisions of the Act in some detail because attorneys are only now becoming aware of the potential advantages it can bestow on a consumer who has suffered from a breach of warranty. The most important of these, by far, are the grant of attorney's fees and the inability of a supplier who makes a written warranty from disclaiming implied warranties. The section allowing the recovery of attorney's fees permits claims to be brought that would otherwise be uneconomical to bring as private actions. Because most consumer products of any value now come with written warranties, the provision disallowing disclaimers of implied warranties precludes the previous practice of providing a written "warranty" (appropriately gilt-edged) that actually gave the buyer next to nothing in the way of coverage for product defects. Magnuson-Moss has undoubtedly not met its drafters' expectations in all respects: most warranties are "limited" rather than "full," the pre-sale availability rules do not appear to have accomplished much, and the rule on informal dispute resolution mechanisms has had little impact outside the automobile industry. On the other hand, there is little doubt that the Act has provided an additional arrow in the consumer's quiver to deal with suppliers who fail to keep their promises.

§ 8.03 THE FTC RULE CONCERNING THE PRESERVATION OF CONSUMERS' CLAIMS AND DEFENSES

In 1976, the FTC promulgated a regulation called the Rule on the Preservation of Consumers' Claims and Defenses,[149] otherwise known as the

---

[144] *See* § 7.03[E], *supra.*
[145] 15 U.S.C. § 2306 (1996).
[146] 15 U.S.C. § 2307 (1996).
[147] 15 U.S.C. § 2310(d) (1996).
[148] 15 U.S.C. § 2310(c) (1996).
[149] 16 C.F.R. § 433 (1996).

"holder rule." The rule mandates that sellers,[150] in consumer credit contracts (i.e., installment sales contracts and promissory notes), provide notice to future contract holders that the holders are subject to all the claims and defenses the consumer could assert against the seller.[151] The notice must also be included in loan agreements involving lenders that are closely tied to the seller, such as with lenders to whom sellers refer customers or when there is a common control or other business agreement or arrangement between the lender and seller.

---

[150] A "seller" is defined as a "person who, in the ordinary course of business, sells or leases goods or services to a consumer." 16 C.F.R. § 433.1(b) (1996). The FTC rule excludes credit card issuers. 16 C.F.R. § 433.1(c) (1996). Credit card issuers are, however, made subject to the claims (other than tort claims) and defenses of consumer card holders through § 170 of the Truth-in-Lending Act, 15 U.S.C. § 1666i (1996), although there are some exceptions to this liability. The liability of a credit card issuer for claims and defenses against the seller is limited to the amount of credit outstanding with respect to the transaction at the time the credit card holder first notifies the card issuer or the seller of the claim or defense. 15 U.S.C. § 1666i(b) (1996).

[151] 16 C.F.R. § 433.2 (1996) provides:

In connection with any sale or lease of goods or services to consumers, in or affecting commerce as "commerce" is defined in the Federal Trade Commission Act, it is an unfair or deceptive act or practice within the meaning of section 5 of that Act for a seller, directly or indirectly, to:

(a) Take or receive a consumer credit contract which fails to contain the following provision in at least ten point, bold face, type:

NOTICE
ANY HOLDER OF THIS CONSUMER CREDIT CONTRACT IS SUBJECT TO ALL CLAIMS AND DEFENSES WHICH THE DEBTOR COULD ASSERT AGAINST THE SELLER OF GOODS OR SERVICES OBTAINED PURSUANT HERETO OR WITH THE PROCEEDS HEREOF. RECOVERY HEREUNDER BY THE DEBTOR SHALL NOT EXCEED AMOUNTS PAID BY THE DEBTOR HEREUNDER.

or,

(b) Accept, as full or partial payment for such sale or lease, the proceeds of any purchase money loan (as purchase money loan is defined herein), unless any consumer credit contract made in connection with such purchase money loan contains the following provision in at least ten point, bold face, type:

NOTICE
ANY HOLDER OF THIS CONSUMER CREDIT CONTRACT IS SUBJECT TO ALL CLAIMS AND DEFENSES WHICH THE DEBTOR COULD ASSERT AGAINST THE SELLER OF GOODS OR SERVICES OBTAINED WITH THE PROCEEDS HEREOF. RECOVERY HEREUNDER BY THE DEBTOR SHALL NOT EXCEED AMOUNTS PAID BY THE DEBTOR HEREUNDER.

The rule was promulgated in response to a very common practice. Consumers would often execute installment sales contracts, usually with accompanying negotiable promissory notes, in order to finance the purchase of goods from the seller. The seller would immediately assign the note, and perhaps the installment sales contract as well, to another party, frequently a lending institution, at a cash discount. If the goods proved defective and the seller was unable or unwilling to respond to the buyer's complaints, the buyer would cease making payments on the installment contract or note. The buyer would then be sued by the assignee (holder) of the contract or note, and the buyer would attempt to assert the defect in the goods as a defense or setoff in the holder's claim.

In such cases, the buyer was generally met with two arguments. First, if the instrument held by the assignee was "negotiable" under applicable law,[152] the holder of the instrument could claim under the holder-in-due-course rule[153] that the holder was not subject to the defenses and claims that the consumer had against the seller. Second, even if the assignee had not received a negotiable instrument (such as a negotiable promissory note) from the seller, the installment contract often contained a "waiver of defense" clause in which the consumer agreed not to assert claims or defenses that it might have against the seller against subsequent holders of the contract.

The FTC rule is intended to prevent the "cut-off" of consumer defenses by these devices. When the notice required by the rule is included in the credit contract,[154] the assignee of the contract, such as a bank or finance company, is subject to all of the claims and defenses that the consumer could assert against the seller. A consumer may assert fraud,[155] breach of

---

[152] U.C.C. § 3-104 defines a "negotiable instrument."

[153] U.C.C. § 3-305 states:

> To the extent that a holder is a holder in due course he takes the instrument free from:
> (1) all claims to it on the part of any person; and
> (2) all defenses of any party to the instrument with whom the holder has not dealt.

[154] The Rule requires that a seller put the notice in any "consumer credit contract," which is defined as "[a]ny instrument which evidences or embodies a debt arising from a 'Purchase Money Loan' transaction or a 'financed sale' as defined in paragraphs (d) and (e)." 16 C.F.R. § 433.1(I)(1996). A "financed sale" is defined by reference to the Truth-in-Lending Act. 16 C.F.R. § 433.1(e)(1996).

[155] See Armstrong v. Edelson, 718 F. Supp. 1372 (N.D. Ill. 1989); Tinker v. DeMaria Porsche Audi, Inc., 459 So. 2d 487 (Fla. Dist. Ct. App. 1984).

warranty under the U.C.C.,[156] or violation of a state[157] or federal statute.[158] In fact, if state law permits the recovery of attorney's fees, the consumer may be able to recover them from the assignee in addition to actual damages.[159]

The notice must also be included in loan documents when loans to consumers are made by lenders that are closely tied to the seller and the proceeds are used to finance the sale. This includes lenders to whom sellers refer[160] customers or where there is an "affiliation" between the seller and lender, defined as "common control, contract, or business arrangement" between the lender and seller.[161] If a referral or affiliation relationship exists and the seller has reason to know that the proceeds came from an affiliated lender,[162] the seller cannot accept the loan proceeds as payment for the goods or services unless the loan documents contain the required notice.

---

[156] *See* Thomas v. Ford Motor Credit Co., 48 Md. App. 617, 429 A.2d 277 (1981).

[157] *See* Home Sav. Ass'n v. Guerra, 733 S.W.2d 134 (Tex. 1987).

[158] *See, e.g.*, Motor Vehicle Mfrs. of U.S., Inc. v. Abrams, 899 F.2d 1315 (2d Cir. 1990); Armstrong v. Edelson, 718 F. Supp. 1372 (N.D. Ill. 1989); Maberry v. Said, 911 F. Supp. 1343 (D. Kan. 1995).

[159] *See* De La Fuente v. Home Sav. Ass'n, 669 S.W.2d 137 (Tex. Ct. App. 1984) (attorney's fees constitute a "claim" if permitted under state law). *But see* Hardeman v. Wheels, Inc., 56 Ohio App. 3d 142 (Ohio Ct. App. 1988) (attorney's fees and punitive or treble damages not recoverable).

[160] For a referral relationship to exist, the seller and lender must be working together so that the seller directs borrowers to the lender. For example, if the seller suggests several different lenders to a consumer in order to help the consumer, there is no referral relationship, even if the lender is aware that the seller is doing this. Nor is there a referral relationship if a seller, without the lender's knowledge, simply suggests a lender as a possible source of financing. On the other hand, if a seller repeatedly calls a lender to determine whether the lender would loan money to consumers, a referral relationship exists. The seller need not refer the *particular* consumer to the lender to fall within the rule as long as the seller generally refers consumers to a particular creditor. *See* Preservation of Consumers' Claims and Defenses—Statement of Enforcement Policy on Trade Regulation Rule, 6 (CCH) Consumer Credit Guide, ¶ 10,191 at 59,325 (1992).

[161] 16 C.F.R. § 433.1(f) (1996) defines "contract" as "[a]ny oral or written agreement, formal or informal, between a creditor and a seller, which contemplates or provides for cooperative or concerted activity in connection with the sale of goods or services to consumers or the financing thereof." 16 C.F.R. 4331(g) defines "business arrangement" as "[a]ny understanding, procedure, course of dealing, or arrangement, formal or informal, between a creditor and a seller, in connection with the sale of goods or services to consumers or the financing thereof." Facts suggesting an affiliation relationship between the seller and the lender include the lender's loan applications being available at the seller's place of business, the seller's preparation of the loan documents for the lender, referral by the lender to the seller, joint advertising of the lender and the seller, and participation by the lender in the seller's sales efforts. 41 Fed. Reg. 34,594-34,596 (1996).

[162] *See* Staff Guidelines, 41 Fed. Reg. 20,024 (May 14, 1976), which establish the "reason to know" standard.

The rule makes it an unfair or deceptive trade practice under the FTC Act for the seller, directly or indirectly, to take or receive a contract or promissory note, or to accept proceeds from a referred or affiliated lender, if the contract or promissory note does not contain the required notice of preservation of claims defenses.[163] The FTC Act, however, does not provide for a private right of action.[164] Moreover, the rule provides that it is a violation of the Act for the *seller* to receive a contract that violates the rule or receive proceeds from a loan that violates the rule; it imposes no liability on the *lender or assignee* of a contract or loan that is in violation of the rule. Thus, only the seller may be sanctioned by the FTC for violation of the rule.

The effect of the rule is indirect; it makes an assignee or lender subject to the consumer's claims and defenses only because the required notice removes the holder-in-due-course defense and invalidates a "waiver of defense" clause. If the notice is omitted, is the consumer prevented from asserting claims and defenses against an assignee or lender, assuming that the holder-in-due-course defense would otherwise apply or the contract contains a waiver of defense clause? Courts have used a variety of devices to avoid this result. At least one court has held that language required by the rule is an implied term of the instrument, thus subjecting the creditor to the claims and defenses that the consumer may assert against the seller even when the required notice is absent.[165] Others have said that if an assignee takes the instrument with knowledge that it should have contained the required notice, the assignee is not acting in good faith[166] and therefore cannot qualify as a holder in due course,[167] or qualify as a protected party under a waiver-of-defense clause.[168]

In addition, even though the FTC Act does not permit a private right of action, when the required notice is not present the consumer is likely to be able to reach both the seller and the assignee or affiliated lender in a private action through state anti-deception legislation. If a state's anti-

---

[163] The prohibition applies to "any sale or lease of goods or services to consumers in or affecting commerce." 16 C.F.R. § 433.2 (1996).

[164] *See* Holloway v. Bristol-Myers Corp., 485 F.2d 986 (D.C. Cir. 1973); Sandoe Pharmaceuticals Corp. v. Richardson-Gicks, Inc., 902 F.2d 222 (3d Cir. 1990).

[165] Xerographic Supplies Corp. v. Hertz Commercial Leasing Corp., 386 So. 2d 299 (Fla. Dist. Ct. App. 1980).

[166] *See, e.g.,* Beakers Trust v. Beltway Inv., 865 F. Supp. 1186, 26 UCCR2d 776 (E.D. Va. 1994). *See also* U.C.C. § 3-103(a)(4). Under this provision, the good faith of the creditor would be judged by the objective standard of "the observance of reasonable commercial standards of fair dealing."

[167] U.C.C. § 3-302(a)(2).

[168] U.C.C. § 9-206(1).

deception statute has language similar to the FTC Act, as many do, there is a good case for liability against the seller, and perhaps the assignee and affiliated lender.[169] In addition, many state anti-deception statutes direct the courts to consider rules, decisions, and interpretations of the FTC Act in determining which practices should be deemed to violate the state statutes.[170] Further, many states have enacted Retail Installment Sales Acts (RISAs) or other statutes that explicitly negate the application of the holder-in-due-course rule in consumer installment contracts and expressly invalidate waiver-of-defense clauses.[171] Virtually all state anti-deception legislation and Retail Installment Sales Acts provide a private cause of action for violation.

The availability of state law, especially RISAs, may be important for another reason as well. The notice required by the Rule, even if included, only provides limited relief to the consumer. The Rule subjects the holder of the installment contract to the consumer's claims and defenses, but permits the consumer an affirmative recovery against the assignee of the contract only up to the amount that the consumer has paid on the contract. Thus, the consumer may assert a product defect as a defense to further payment (assuming it is a defense under applicable state law) and also recover affirmative damages (e.g., for breach of warranty under U.C.C. § 2-714), but only up to the amount that the consumer has paid on the contract. Affirmative damages that exceed these amounts must be sought against the seller. If, however, there is a state law, such as a RISA, that directly invalidates the holder-in-due-course defense or a waiver-of-defense clause, the consumer often is able to recover additional affirmative damages against the holder of the contract.[172]

---

[169] *See* Greenfield, Consumer Law: A Guide for Those Who Represent Sellers, Lenders, and Consumers, § 14.4.4 (1995).

[170] *See, e.g.*, Ohio Rev. Code Ann. § 1345.02(c) (Anderson 1998).

[171] *See, e.g.*, Ohio Rev. Code Ann. § 1317.14 (Anderson 1998); Md. Commercial Law Code Ann. §§ 12-628, 14-1302 (1996).

[172] Staff Guidelines, 41 Fed. Reg. 20,023. *See* Chrysler Credit Corp. v. Copley, 189 W. Va. 90, 428 S.E.2d 313 (1993); De La Fuente v. Home Sav. Ass'n, 669 S.W.2d 137 (Tex. Ct. App. 1984).

CHAPTER 9

STATE REGULATION OF CONSUMER SALES

§ 9.01 INTRODUCTION

During the past three decades, the treatment of consumers has diverged from that of commercial parties in the law of sales. Prior to the 1960s, with a few exceptions such as legislation regulating small loans, consumer sales were largely governed by the same laws as other sales in the marketplace. Although the Uniform Commercial Code provides, in a few places, special rules for consumers,[1] and a number of provisions in Article 2 of the Code apply only "between merchants," the Code generally does not distinguish between consumer sales and other sales of goods.[2] During the decade of the 1960s, however, a movement began to treat consumer sales as a distinct category of transactions requiring special treatment and different legal rules. This trend accelerated in the 1970s, and though the momentum slowed somewhat in the 1980s and the 1990s, states continue to pass legislation regulating such things as "lemon" vehicles[3] and consumer leases.[4]

Much of this consumer-protection legislation supplements the rules provided by the Code.[5] Some statutes, however, provide a governing rule for consumer transactions contrary to the rule that would otherwise control under the Code.[6] Taken together, a voluminous and comprehensive body of law now exists governing consumer sales with which the practitioner of commercial law must be familiar. The purpose of this chapter is not to explore in detail all of the state legislation impacting upon consumer sales. The length of this text does not permit comprehensive treatment of the

---

[1] *See* U.C.C. § 2-207(2) (additional terms treated differently when parties are merchants); U.C.C. § 2-719(3) (limitation on consequential damages for personal injury is unconscionable when contract is for consumer goods).

[2] This may change. One of the most controversial issues that has arisen with respect to the proposed revisions to Article 2 is the extent to which special rules should govern consumer sales. The most recent draft of the revisions distinguish between consumer sales and commercial sales in a number of ways, some of which are fundamental. *See* The American Law Institute, Uniform Commercial Code Revised Article 2. Sales, Proposed Final Draft, May 1, 1999.

[3] *See, e.g.,* Ohio Rev. Code Ann. §§ 1345.01–1345.07 (Anderson 1998).

[4] *See, e.g.,* Ohio Rev. Code Ann. §§ 1351.01–1351.09 (Anderson 1998).

[5] *See, e.g.,* Uniform Consumer Sales Practices Act § 4 (prohibiting unconscionable acts or practices by a supplier in connection with a consumer transaction); Consumer Product Safety Act, 15 U.S.C. § 2063(d) (1996) (giving the seller time to cure a substantial product hazard); Uniform Consumer Credit Act § 5.112 (creditor may take possession of collateral although only with judicial process).

[6] *See, e.g.,* Ohio Retail Installment Sales Act, Ohio Rev. Code Ann. § 1317.031 (Anderson 1998) (exempting consumer installment sales contracts from the holder-in-due-course doctrine of section 3-305 of the U.C.C.); Magnuson-Moss Warranty Act, 15 U.S.C. § 2308(a) (1996) (suppliers who provide written warranties cannot disclaim implied warranties).

subject, and in any event, there already exist excellent texts on the general subject of consumer law.[7] Rather, the purpose is to acquaint the student and practitioner with the state consumer-protection legislation most closely related to the subject matter of Article 2 of the Code. This chapter deals with two examples of consumer sales regulation: statutes regulating unfair and deceptive practices, and state "lemon laws."

Because of space limitations, much of this chapter is necessarily general in nature. We will not attempt to catalog all of the often subtle differences, both in legislation and in court decisions, among the fifty states. Although the legislation in these areas is state-specific, it is surprisingly uniform in many ways. This is largely the result of the adoption by many states, with minor modifications, of uniform legislation promulgated by various organizations.[8] Consequently, many citations are to uniform legislation or to the state laws with which the authors are most familiar. In some cases, states have chosen from among two or three different "models" or general approaches to subjects, and these are described. Occasionally, we will note where one state (or a small group of states) has radically departed from the path taken by most. The purpose of this chapter is to provide a general orientation to state consumer laws regulating the sale of goods, and the practitioner is reminded that it is no substitute for a detailed inquiry into his or her own state's law.

§ 9.02   STATE REGULATION OF UNFAIR AND DECEPTIVE PRACTICES

Federal legislation protecting the consumer has existed since 1938, when Congress amended the FTC Act to prevent the "unfair or deceptive acts or practices"[9] of unscrupulous merchants. The FTC Act suffered from

---

[7] *See, e.g.,* Michael Greenfield, Consumer Law: A Guide for Those Who Represent Sellers, Lenders, and Consumers, § 3.1 (Little, Brown 1995) (hereinafter cited as Greenfield); Dee Pridgen, Consumer Protection and the Law (Clark-Boardman 1986). *See also* various publications of the National Consumer Law Center, Boston, Massachusetts, on specific areas of consumer law.

[8] *See, e.g.,* Uniform Deceptive Trade Practices Act drafted in 1966 by the National Conference of Commissioners on Uniform State Laws (NCCUSL); Uniform Trade Practices and Consumer Protection Law promulgated by the FTC and the Council of State Governments in 1967 and amended in 1970; Uniform Consumer Sales Practices Act adopted in 1971 by NCCUSL and the ABA.

[9] The FTC Act was originally passed in 1914 and prohibited "unfair methods of competition." Federal Trade Commission Act, Pub. L. No. 203, 38 Stat. 717 (1914). The Supreme Court held in FTC v. Raladam Co., 283 U.S. 643 (1931) that this language required the FTC to show injury to a competitor from a method of competition; injury to consumers

a number of serious limitations, however, the most serious of which was that the Act provided no private right of action to consumers.[10] The sole enforcement power lay with the FTC. The ability of the FTC to deal with deceptive or unfair practices that affected only a small number of consumers (perhaps only one) was very limited. As a result, during the 1960s, a number of uniform laws, modeled to a greater or lesser extent on the FTC Act, were promulgated and adopted in various forms by the states. Although the titles and terminology of these statutes are not always the same,[11] they broadly prohibit the same kind of conduct which the FTC Act proscribes, and virtually all contain at least a limited private right of action.[12]

[A] Scope and Coverage

Most of these statutes are limited in one manner or another, to consumer transactions. Many define a "consumer" transaction as one that is for "personal, family, or household" purposes,[13] a definition similar to that used in many federal consumer-protection statutes.[14] Recently, however, a number of states, either by legislation or judicial decision, have broadened the scope of these statutes to cover at least some transactions that would not typically

---

alone was not sufficient. In 1938, Congress amended the Act to include "unfair or deceptive acts or practices." Wheeler-Lea Amendment, Pub. L. No. 75-447 § 3, 52 Stat. 111 (1938). *See* Greenfield, *supra* note 7.

[10] Greenfield at § 3.2 and cases cited therein.

[11] Some of the variations include Deceptive Trade Practices Acts, Consumer Sales Practices Acts, Unfair Trade Practices Acts, and Deceptive and Unfair Trade Practices Acts.

[12] *See, e.g.,* Uniform Consumer Sales Practices Act § 11; Ohio Rev. Code Ann. § 1345.09 (Anderson 1998); Cal. Civ. Code § 1780 (West 1998); Fla. Stat. Ann. § 501.207 (West 1997); Tex. Bus. & Com. Code Ann. § 17.50 (West Supp. 1998). States that do not provide at least a limited private cause of action (a few by judicial interpretation) are Arizona, Arkansas, Iowa, and North Dakota.

[13] *See, e.g.,* Ohio Rev. Code Ann. § 1345.01(A) (Anderson 1998) (consumer transaction is one "to an individual for purposes that are primarily personal, family or household"); Va. Code Ann. § 59.1-198 (Michie 1992) (consumer transaction is one "to be used primarily for personal, family, or household purposes"); W. Va. Code § 46A-6-102 (1996) (consumer transaction is "for a personal, family, household, or agricultural purpose"); Wyo. Stat. § 40-12-102 (1997) (consumer transaction is "for purposes that are primarily personal, family, or household").

[14] *See, e.g.,* The Truth-in-Lending Act, 15 U.S.C. § 1602(h) (1996); Fair Debt Collection Practices Act, 15 U.S.C. § 1692(a)(5) (1995); Magnuson-Moss Act, 15 U.S.C. § 2301(1) (1996).

be thought of as consumer transactions.[15] For example, in at least three states, the statutory definition of "consumer" explicitly includes entities other than individuals, such as corporations and partnerships.[16] In addition, some courts have judicially expanded the coverage of the statute to include transactions by non-individuals.[17] A few statutes are not limited in coverage to consumers.[18]

Even when a statute is limited to transactions for "personal, family, or household purposes" (or contains some similar limitation), there is disagreement on whether the focus is on the purpose of the *particular* transaction or on the *usual* purpose of the product or service involved in the transaction. For example, should a dentist who purchases a television set for her waiting room be covered by the statute? If we focus on the usual use of the product, the law is applicable; however, in this particular case the television is not used for personal, family, or household purposes. Conversely, is an individual who purchases a copying machine for her personal use at home protected? It is probably still true that the normal or usual use for a copier is not for personal, family, or household purposes but rather for business use. It so happens, however, that in this particular case the copier is being used for personal purposes. Does the statute apply?

---

[15] *See, e.g.,* W. Va. Code § 46A-6-102 (1996) (agricultural use); Meyer v. Diesel Equip. Co., Inc., 1 Kan. App. 574, 570 P.2d 1374 (1977) (professional driver bought a part for his truck); Valley Forge Towers S. Condominium v. Ron-Ike Foam Insulators, Inc., 393 Pa. Super. 339, 574 A.2d 641 (1990), *aff'd,* 529 Pa. 512, 605 A.2d 798 (1992) (condominium association had a contractor fix a leaky roof).

[16] Fla. Stat. Ann. § 501.203(7) (West 1997) (consumer means "an individual; child, by and through its parent or legal guardian; firm; association; joint venture; partnership; estate; trust; business trust; syndicate; fiduciary; corporation; or any other group or combination"); Ill. Ann. Stat. Ch. 815, ¶ 505/1(c) (Smith-Hurd 1993) (consumer means "any person," which includes "any natural person or his legal representative, partnership, corporation (foreign or domestic), company, trust, business entity or association, and any agent, employee, salesman, partner, officer, director, member, stockholder, associate, trustee, or *cestui que trust* thereof"); Tex. Bus. & Com. Code Ann. § 17.45(4) (West 1987) (consumer means "an individual, partnership, corporation, this state, or a subdivision or agency of this state").

[17] *See, e.g.,* Catallo Assoc., Inc. v. MacDonald & Goren, P.C., 465 N.W.2d 28 (Mich. Ct. App. 1990) (law firm protected as "person" under the Act); Valley Forge Towers S. Condominium v. Ron-Ike Foam Insulators, Inc., 393 Pa. Super. 339, 574 A.2d 641 (1990) (condominium association protected as "person" under the Act); John Labatt Ltd. v. Molson Breweries, 853 F. Supp. 965 (E.D. Mich. 1994) (beer manufacturer had standing to sue as a "person" under the act); Hundred E. Credit Corp. v. Erie Schuster Corp., 212 N.J. Super. 350, 515 A.2d 246 (1986) (business entity can be a "consumer" under the act).

[18] Ill. Ann. Stat. Ch. 815, ¶ 505/1 (c) (Smith-Hurd 1993) (applies to any natural person); Tenn. Code Ann. § 47-18-102(2) (1995) (applies to any natural person); Tex. Bus. & Com. Code Ann. § 17.45(10) (West 1987) (applies to business consumers).

When the language of a particular statute is clear on this point then the statute governs. Some statutes, however, are not clear, and the courts have reached different conclusions. Some courts have held that the focus should be on the typical or normal use of the product.[19] Most courts, however, have held that coverage depends on the actual purpose of the individual transaction, rather than the typical purpose of the product.[20]

In most states, for the statute to apply, the seller must be in the business of selling the goods or service that is the subject of the transaction.[21] Thus, a sale by an individual of her used car to another individual would normally not be covered by most statutes. Even when the seller is in the business of selling goods or services, if the subject matter of the transaction is something other than the goods or services the seller normally sells, the transaction may not be covered.[22]

Most legislation covers both goods and services.[23] In virtually all states, however, certain transactions or suppliers are explicitly exempted. These exemptions differ substantially from state to state. Many of the statutes, for example, exempt businesses that are already subject to extensive state regulation such as public utilities, financial institutions, and insurance companies.[24] Also expressly exempted by many statutes are certain professionals such as physicians, attorneys, and dentists.[25] In some cases, coverage of

---

[19] *See, e.g.,* Searle v. Exley Express, Inc., 278 Or. 535, 564 P.2d 1054 (1977); Miller v. Hubbard-Wray Co., Inc., 53 Or. App. 531, 633 P.2d 1 (1981).

[20] *See, e.g.,* Valley Forge Towers S. Condominium v. Ron-Ike Foam Insulators, Inc., 393 Pa. Super. 339, 574 A.2d 641 (1990), *aff'd,* 529 Pa. 512, 605 A.2d 798 (1992); Heindel v. Southside Chrysler-Plymouth, Inc., 476 So. 2d 266 (Fla. Dist. Ct. App. 1985); Linthicum v. Archambault, 379 Mass. 381, 398 N.E.2d 482 (1979); Commercial Credit Equip. Corp. v. Carter, 516 P.2d 767, 13 UCCR 1212 (Wash. 1973).

[21] *See, e.g.,* Ohio Rev. Code Ann. § 1345.01(C) (Anderson 1998); Utah Code Ann. § 13-11-3(6) (1996); Va. Code Ann. § 59.1-198(2) (Michie 1992); Vt. Stat. Ann. tit. 9, § 2451a(c) (1993). *But see* Singleton v. Pennington, 568 S.W.2d 367 (Tex. Ct. Civ. App. 1977) (Deceptive Trade Practices Act applies to nonmerchant seller of boat).

[22] *See* Wolverton v. Stanwood, 278 Or. 341, 563 P.2d 1203 (1977), *reh'g denied,* 278 P.2d 709, 565 P.2d 755 (1977) (transaction must be at least indirectly connected to ordinary business of seller).

[23] *See, e.g.,* Uniform Consumer Sales Practices Act § 2(1), 7A U.L.A. 234 (1985); Ohio Rev. Code Ann. § 1345.01(A) (Anderson 1998).

[24] *See, e.g.,* Mich. Comp. Laws Ann. § 445.904(2) (West Supp. 1998); Mo. Ann. Stat. § 407.020(2) (West 1990 & Supp. 1998); Ohio Rev. Code Ann. § 1345.01(9) (Anderson 1998); Va. Code Ann. § 59.1-199(D) (Michie Supp. 1997).

[25] *See, e.g.,* Md. Code Ann., Com. Law § 13-104(1) (1990) (exempting accountants, architects, clergymen, engineers, attorneys, veterinarians, doctors, and dentists); Ohio Rev. Code Ann. § 1345.01(A) (Anderson 1998) (exempting physicians, accountants, attorneys, dentists and veterinarians).

professionals is not clear from the statute, and court decisions go both ways.[26] Some courts have also held that professionals are not covered when engaging in "core" aspects of their professions, but are within the statute when engaging in the "business" aspects of their professions.[27]

Some statutes expressly include real estate transactions,[28] while others explicitly exempt them.[29] In many cases, however, the statute is not clear, and there have been numerous court decisions interpreting various state provisions. In many of these cases, the statute covers "goods" and "services," and the issue is whether real estate transactions fall within these terms. If "goods" are defined in the same way as the term is defined by the U.C.C., real estate transactions should not be included.[30] Some courts have nonetheless included real estate transactions within the definition of goods and services.[31] Other courts have found to the contrary, holding that real estate transactions are not included within the definitions of these terms.[32] Although the argument has been made that a *lease* of residential real estate should be considered within the ambit of the statute, even if the *sale* of residential real estate is not, one court has specifically rejected this argument.[33] A few states' statutes explicitly include leases of residential real estate as covered transactions.[34]

---

[26] *See, e.g.,* Rousseau v. Eshleman, 519 A.2d 243 (N.H. 1986) (attorney not covered); Heslin v. Connecticut Law Clinic of Trantolo & Trantolo, 190 Conn. 510, 461 A.2d 938 (1983) (attorneys covered); White Budd Van Ness Partnership v. Major-Gladys Drive Joint Venture, 798 S.W.2d 805 (Tex. Ct. App. 1990) (architects covered); Investigators, Inc. v. Harvey, 53 Or. App. 586, 633 P.2d 6 (1981) (dentists covered); Gatten v. Merzi, 370 Pa. Super. 148, 579 A.2d 974 (1990) (physicians not covered).

[27] *See, e.g.,* Short v. Demopolis, 103 Wash. 2d 52, 691 P.2d 163 (1984).

[28] Mo. Ann. Stat. § 407.010 (Vernon 1990); Or. Rev. Stat. § 646.605 (1988).

[29] Md. Code Ann., Com. Law § 13-104(1) (1990).

[30] The Uniform Commercial Code defines "goods" as "all things . . . which are moveable at the time of identification to the contract." U.C.C. § 2-105(1) (1996). *See* § 2.03[B], *supra.*

[31] *See, e.g.,* Gabriel v. O'Hara, 368 Pa. Super. 383, 534 A.2d 488 (1987); People *ex rel.* MacFarlane v. Alpert Corp., 660 P.2d 1295 (Colo. Ct. App. 1983); Warren v. LeMay, 142 Ill. App. 3d 550, 491 N.E.2d 464 (1986).

[32] *See, e.g.,* Heritage Hills, Ltd. v. Deacon, 49 Ohio St. 3d 80, 551 N.E.2d 125 (1990); Lauria v. Wright, 805 S.W.2d 344 (Mo. Ct. App. 1991); State of Alaska v. First Nat'l Bank of Anchorage, 660 P.2d 406 (Alaska 1982); Owens v. Curtis, 432 A.2d 737 (D.C. Cir. 1981).

[33] Heritage Hills, Ltd. v. Deacon, 49 Ohio St. 3d 80, 551 N.E.2d 125 (1990).

[34] *See, e.g.,* Conn. Gen. Stat. Ann. § 42-110a (West 1992); Mass. Ann. Laws ch. 93A (Law. Co-op. 1994); Mich. Comp. Laws Ann. § 445.902 (West 1989); Pa. Stat. Ann. tit. 73, § 201-9.2 (1993 & Supp. 1998).

[B]   Substantive Coverage of Deceptive Trade Practices Acts

Statutes dealing with unfair and deceptive trade practices vary in structure;[35] most consist of general prohibitions against deceptive, unfair, or unconscionable conduct followed by a list of specific prohibitions.[36] Obviously, this chapter cannot catalog all of the practices that have been found to violate legislation protecting consumers against unfair or deceptive acts. Such a compilation, in varying detail, can be found in other sources.[37] Instead, this portion of the text has three purposes: (1) to broadly categorize the conduct that has been found to violate these laws, (2) to discuss a few general principles regarding the application of these laws, and (3) to contrast the substantive coverage of these laws with the law of warranty under the Code.

The first category of conduct to which anti-deception legislation applies consists of misrepresentations or other deceptive conduct that would induce a consumer to enter into a contract. This conduct can either be an affirmative misrepresentation or an omission.[38] Further, the deception does not have to be express; it can be implied as well.[39] Although such conduct is similar to common-law fraud, there are critical differences between common-law fraud and the application of anti-deception legislation. Perhaps most important, the courts are virtually unanimous in holding that "scienter"—intent to

---

[35] *See* Greenfield, *supra* note 7 at § 4.1. Professor Greenfield divides "anti-deception" statutes into three general categories: (1) "Little FTC-Acts," modeled after the federal FTC Act, which broadly prohibit unfair or deceptive practices, sometimes followed by a list of specific prohibitions; (2) legislation modeled on the Uniform Unfair and Deceptive Trade Practices Act containing a list of specific prohibitions, which sometimes also contains a more general prohibition against "unfair or deceptive conduct"; and (3) consumer fraud statutes prohibiting deception, fraud, misrepresentation, and similar conduct, which may also proscribe unfair or unconscionable practices. Obviously, there is much overlap between these categories.

[36] *See, e.g.*, Ohio Rev. Code Ann. § 1345.02(B) (Anderson 1998) (generally prohibiting unfair and deceptive acts and then providing ten nonexclusive specific prohibitions) and § 1345.03(B) (Anderson 1998) (generally prohibiting unconscionable acts and then providing seven nonexclusive specific prohibitions).

[37] *See, e.g.*, National Consumer Law Center, Unfair and Deceptive Acts and Practices, Chapter 5 (3d ed. 1991); Dee Pridgen, Consumer Protection and the Law, Chapter 3 (1986).

[38] *See* Winton v. Johnson & Dix Fuel Corp., 147 Vt. 236, 515 A.2d 371 (1986) (affirmative misrepresentation); Duhl v. Nash Realty, Inc., 102 Ill. App. 3d 483, 429 N.E.2d 1267 (1981) (affirmative misrepresentation); Sanders v. Francis, 277 Or. 593, 561 P.2d 1003 (1977) (omission); McRae v. Bolstad, 101 Wash. 2d 161, 676 P.2d 496 (1984) (omission).

[39] 39 *See* Madsen v. Western Am. Mortgage Co., 694 P.2d 1228 (Ariz. Ct. App. 1985); Marshall v. Citicorp Mortgage, Inc., 601 So. 2d 669 (La. Ct. App. 1992); Golt v. Phillips, 308 Md. 1, 517 A.2d 328 (1986); State of Wash. v. Burlison, 38 Wash. App. 487, 685 P.2d 1115 (1984).

deceive—is not necessary to prove a deceptive act.[40] Thus, if the seller represents that the goods have qualities or characteristics that they do not have,[41] the seller has violated the statute even if the seller honestly, and even reasonably, believes that he is telling the truth about the product.[42]

Other elements of common-law deceit, or fraud, have also been eliminated from many of these statutes. For example, many statutory provisions or court decisions have either abolished or relaxed the requirement of common-law deceit that the plaintiff must reasonably rely on the deceptive conduct of the defendant. In some cases, the requirement that the plaintiff must rely on the defendant's conduct has been eliminated entirely,[43] although the consumer must still prove that the deception caused the injury for the consumer to recover actual damages.[44] Similar to cases under the FTC Act, courts have also permitted both enforcement by the state[45] and by consumers[46] without proof of actual deception, so long as a capacity to deceive is shown, although there is authority to the contrary.[47] In other cases, courts have not required that a consumer's reliance be reasonable,[48] justifying this result on the basis that the statutes are designed to protect the weak and

---

[40] See, e.g., Chern v. Bank of Am., 15 Cal. 3d 866, 544 P.2d 1310 (1976); Regency Nissan, Inc. v. Taylor, 194 Ga. App. 645, 39 S.E.2d 467 (1990); Richardson Ford Sales, Inc. v. Johnson, 676 P.2d 1344, 38 UCCR 390 (N.M. Ct. App. 1984); Smith v. Baldwin, 611 S.W.2d 611 (Tex. 1980).

[41] See Ohio Rev. Code Ann. §§ 1345.02(1) and 1345.02(2) (Anderson 1998).

[42] See Truex v. Ocean Dodge, Inc., 219 N.J. Super. 44, 529 A.2d 1017 (N.J. Super. Ct. App. Div. 1987); Forbes v. Par Ten Group, Inc., 99 N.C. App. 587, 394 S.E.2d 643 (1990); Miller v. Soliz, 648 S.W.2d 734 (Tex. Ct. App. 1983); Winton v. Johnson & Dix Fuel Corp., 515 A.2d 371 (Vt. 1986).

[43] See Hinchliffe v. American Motors Corp., 184 Conn. 607, 440 A.2d 810 (1981); Stephenson v. Capano Dev., Inc., 462 A.2d 1069 (Del. 1983); State of Md. v. Andrews, 73 Md. App. 80, 533 A.2d 282 (1987); Sanders v. Francis, 277 Or. 593, 561 P.2d 1003 (1977).

[44] As is discussed subsequently, however, consumers may be able to recover statutory damages, even in the absence of actual damages. See § 9.02[C], infra.

[45] See State of Alaska v. O'Neill Investigations, Inc., 609 P.2d 520 (Alaska 1980); State of Kan. ex rel. Sanborn v. Koscot Interplanetary, Inc., 212 Kan. 668, 512 P.2d 416 (1973); Kugler v. Romain, 58 N.J. 522, 279 A.2d 640 (1971); State of Wash. v. Ralph William's N.W. Chrysler Plymouth, Inc., 87 Wash. 2d 298, 553 P.2d 423 (1976).

[46] See Fletcher v. Security Pac. Nat'l Bank, 23 Cal. 3d 442, 591 P.2d 51 (1979); Claybourne v. Imsland, 414 N.W.2d 449 (Minn. Ct. App. 1987); Blackwell v. Dorosko, 383 S.E.2d 670 (N.C. Ct. App. 1989); Inman v. Ken Hyatt Chrysler Plymouth, Inc., 294 S.C. 240, 363 S.E.2d 691 (1988).

[47] See, e.g., Parks v. Macro-Dynamics, Inc., 121 Ariz. 517, 591 P.2d 1005 (1979); State of Iowa ex rel. Turner v. Limbrecht, 246 N.W.2d 330 (Iowa 1976); Tri-West Constr. Co. v. Hernandez, 43 Or. App. 961, 607 P.2d 1375 (1979).

[48] See Peery v. Hansen, 120 Ariz. 266, 585 P.2d 574 (Ariz. Ct. App. 1978); Sanders v. Francis, 277 Or. 593, 561 P.2d 1003 (1977).

credulous.[49] Finally, courts have not interpreted the statutes to include the requirement of materiality necessary for common-law fraud.[50]

In some cases, however, one or more of these elements is explicitly required by the statute, and in that case, the element will, of course, have to be proved.[51] In addition, when unconscionability or unfairness (as opposed to deception) is at issue, a case can often be made that some element of intent, or knowledge, is necessary, if only by implication. For example, under the Ohio Consumer Sales Practices Act, it is a violation for a supplier to commit an unconscionable act or practice.[52] This general prohibition is followed by seven examples of circumstances describing unconscionable conduct.[53] All of the examples involve knowing conduct on the part of the supplier.[54] Furthermore, the very concept of unconscionability suggests intentional or knowing conduct.

---

[49] *See* Madsen v. Western Am. Mortgage Co., 694 P.2d 1228 (Ariz. Ct. App. 1985); Guggenheimer v. Ginzburg, 43 N.Y.2d 268, 372 N.E.2d 17, 401 N.Y.S.2d 182 (1977); De Santis v. Sears, Roebuck & Co., 543 N.Y.S.2d 228 (N.Y. App. Div. 1989); Chrysler-Plymouth City, Inc. v. Guerrero, 620 S.W.2d 700, 32 UCCR 433 (Tex. Civ. App. 1981).

[50] *See* Jim Walter Homes, Inc. v. Castillo, 616 S.W.2d 630 (Tex. Civ. App. 1981).

[51] *See, e.g.,* Ill. Ann. Stat. Ch. 815, ¶ 505/2 (Smith-Hurd 1993) (plaintiff must prove that there was a material fact and an intent on the defendant's part that others rely on the unfair or deceptive act).

[52] Ohio Rev. Code Ann. § 1345.03(A) (Anderson 1998).

[53] Ohio Rev. Code Ann. § 1345.03(B) (Anderson 1998).

[54] Ohio Rev. Code Ann. §§ 1345.03(B)(1)-(7) (Anderson 1998) states:

(B) In determining whether an act or practice is unconscionable, the following circumstances shall be taken into consideration:

(1) Whether the supplier has knowingly taken advantage of the inability of the consumer reasonably to protect his interests because of his physical or mental infirmities, ignorance, illiteracy, or inability to understand the language of an agreement;

(2) Whether the supplier knew at the time the consumer transaction was entered into that the price was substantially in excess of the price at which similar property or services were readily obtainable in similar consumer transactions by like consumers;

(3) Whether the supplier knew at the time the consumer transaction was entered into of the inability of the consumer to receive a substantial benefit from the subject of the consumer transaction;

(4) Whether the supplier knew at the time the consumer transaction was entered into that there was no reasonable probability of payment of the obligation in full by the consumer;

(5) Whether the supplier required the consumer to enter into a consumer transaction on terms the supplier knew were substantially one-sided in favor of the supplier;

(6) Whether the supplier knowingly made a misleading statement of opinion

These statutes also often regulate the substantive fairness of the terms of the contract between the consumer and the supplier, or the fairness of the bargaining process apart from deception. Some statutes simply prohibit "unfair" conduct in general terms, often expressly referring to orders, rules, guides, and court interpretations of the FTC Act to provide further substance to the prohibition.[55] Some of these statutes also have an additional section dealing with unconscionable conduct.[56] These provisions may proscribe such things as excessive price, one-sided terms, knowingly taking advantage of a consumer's illiteracy or inability to understand the language of the contract, or contracting with knowledge that there was no reasonable likelihood that the consumer could pay the obligation resulting from the agreement.[57]

"Unfair" conduct proscribed by the statutes has taken many forms, although courts frequently rely on FTC decisions and policy statements.[58] High pressure sales techniques or coercive conduct,[59] intentional and unjus-

---

on which the consumer was likely to rely to his detriment;

(7) Whether the supplier has, without justification, refused to make a refund in cash or by check for a returned item that was purchased with cash or by check, unless the supplier had conspicuously posted in the establishment at the time of the sale a sign stating the suppliers's refund policy.

[55] *See, e.g.,* Conn. Gen. Stat. Ann. § 42-110b(c) (West Supp. 1993); Ill. Ann. Stat. ch. 815, ¶ 505/2 (Smith-Hurd 1993); Md. Code Ann., Com. Law § 13-105 (1990); Mass. Ann. Laws ch. 93A, § 2(b) (Law. Co-op. 1994).

[56] *See, e.g.,* Uniform Consumer Sales Practices Act § 4, 7A U.L.A. 241 (1985); Ohio Rev. Code Ann. § 1345.03 (Anderson 1998).

[57] These examples are all taken from the Uniform Consumer Sales Practices Act § 4, 7A U.L.A. 241 (1985).

[58] The landmark case on the FTC's unfairness jurisdiction is FTC v. Sperry & Hutchinson Co., 405 U.S. 233 (1972). The most recent policy statement of the FTC's unfairness jurisdiction is set forth in a letter of December 17, 1980, from the FTC to the Consumer Subcommittee of the Senate Committee on Commerce, Science and Transportation. Reauthorization of the Federal Trade Commission Before the Senate Comm. on Commerce, Science and Transportation, 97th Cong., 2d Sess. 23 (1982).

[59] *See, e.g.,* Monroe Medical Clinic, Inc. v. Hospital Corp. of Am., 522 So. 2d 1362 (La. Ct. App. 1988) (petition alleging that hospital corporation was influencing patients' choices and decisions toward favored health care providers through unethical and oppressive uses of economic advantage stated a cause of action against the hospital corporation for unfair trade practices); Bertassi v. Allstate Ins. Co., 402 Mass. 366, 522 N.E.2d 949 (1988) (insurer committed an unfair trade practice by insisting that the insured execute a trust agreement protecting the insurer's alleged subrogation rights as a condition precedent to payment of underinsurance benefits); Wilder v. Squires, 315 S.E.2d 63 (N.C. Ct. App. 1984) (seller who threatened potential home buyer with the loss of his deposit unless he accepted the seller's financing, committed an unfair trade practice).

tified breaches of contract,[60] and excessively high prices or lease terms[61] have all been found to be unfair practices. There is obviously considerable overlap between unfair practices and unconscionable practices.[62]

The third category of conduct proscribed by anti-deception statutes is conduct that is collateral to the contract itself. This category includes such things as coercive collection practices,[63] bringing suit in a distant forum,[64] unfair or deceptive repossession or foreclosure actions,[65] and the use of

---

[60] *See, e.g.,* State *ex rel.* Guste v. Orkin Exterminating Co., 528 So. 2d 198 (La. Ct. App. 1988) (exterminator's increase of fixed renewal fees was a breach of contract that constituted an unfair trade practice); Wasserman v. Agnastopoulos, 22 Mass. App. 672, 497 N.E.2d 19 (1986) (lessor committed an unfair trade practice by breaching his sale agreement); Leal v. Furniture Barn, Inc., 571 S.W.2d 864 (Tex. 1978) (seller committed an unfair trade practice when he told buyers that if they did not pay a stated sum by a certain date they would forfeit all prior payments although there was no provision authorizing the forfeiture in the contracts).

[61] *See, e.g.,* Murphy v. McNamara, 36 Conn. Supp. 183, 416 A.2d 170 (Conn. Super. Ct. 1979) (contract between buyer and seller of a television set that required the buyer to pay more than two-and-one-half times the regular retail price of the set for an extension of credit was an unfair trade practice); Kugler v. Romain, 58 N.J. 522, 279 A.2d 640 (1971) (seller committed unfair practice where price for a set of educational materials was about two-and-one-half times the reasonable market value, and the materials had little or no educational value for children in the age group and socioeconomic position the seller represented would be benefitted by it).

[62] *See* Kugler v. Romain, 58 N.J. 522, 279 A.2d 640 (1971); Lane v. Fabert, 178 Ill. App. 3d 698, 533 N.E.2d 546 (1989).

[63] *See, e.g.,* State v. O'Neill Investigations, Inc., 609 P.2d 520 (Alaska 1980) (threats to debtors that failure to pay would result in immediate arrest or filing of a criminal complaint and using simulated legal documents or collection forms when no legal action is contemplated is an unfair trade practice); Tillquist v. Ford Motor Credit Co., 714 F. Supp. 607 (D. Conn. 1989) (harassment of debtor by contacting debtor and debtor's family members concerning late payments was an unfair trade practice); People of Ill. *ex rel.* Daley v. Datacom Sys. Corp., 176 Ill. App. 3d 697, 531 N.E.2d 839 (1988) (allegations that debt collection agency trying to collect delinquent parking fines for the city, demanded higher amounts than the assessed fines, used the city seal and insignia, and negotiated and deposited checks payable to the city were sufficient to state a cause of action for unfair trade practices).

[64] *See, e.g.,* Barquis v. Merchants Collection Assn. of Oakland, Inc., 7 Cal. 3d 94, 496 P.2d 817 (Cal. 1972); Bank of New Orleans & Trust Co. v. Phillips, 415 So. 2d 973 (La. Ct. App. 1982); Schubach v. Household Fin. Corp., 375 Mass. 133, 376 N.E.2d 140 (1978).

[65] *See, e.g.,* Cook v. Spillers, 574 So. 2d 464 (La. Ct. App. 1991) (car buyer did not consent to seller's repossession of his car without resort to legal process and thus it was an unfair trade practice); Hanner v. Classic Auto Body Inc., 10 Mass. App. 121, 406 N.E.2d 686 (Mass. Ct. App. 1980) (repairman's unauthorized towing of car in attempt to collect repair bills was an unfair trade practice); Flenniken v. Longview Bank & Trust Co., 661 S.W.2d 705 (Tex. 1983) (bank committed an unfair trade practice by an unconscionable foreclosure of the property owner's home).

confession of judgment clauses.[66] Anti-deception statutes are particularly important in regulating collection practices of creditors that would constitute violations of the Federal Fair Debt Collection Practices Act if the collector was a third-party debt collector rather than the creditor.[67]

There is a close relationship between anti-deception legislation and warranty law under the Code. Much of the legislation proscribes conduct that would also constitute a breach of warranty under the Code. For example, the Uniform Consumer Sales Practices Act lists the following among those acts considered to be unfair or deceptive:

- That the subject of a consumer transaction has sponsorship, approval, performance characteristics, accessories, uses, or benefits it does not have.[68]

- That the subject of a consumer transaction is of a particular standard, quality, grade, style or model, if it is not.[69]

- That the subject of a consumer transaction is new, or unused, if it is not, or that the subject of a consumer transaction has been used to an extent that is materially different from the fact.[70]

Each of these circumstances is likely to involve an express warranty under the Code (i.e., an affirmation of fact or promise relating to the goods or a description of the goods).[71] Because intent to deceive is generally not required to prove a violation of an anti-deception statute, a supplier's breach of warranty often is a violation of the anti-deception statute as well.[72] Some courts balk at this conclusion when the seller's conduct involves a purely

---

[66] *See* S.D. Codified Laws Ann. § 37-24-5.5 (1994).

[67] The Federal Fair Debt Collection Practices Act (FDCPA) regulates debt collection practices in some detail. It proscribes both unfair and deceptive debt collection practices in general terms, and also has fairly lengthy "laundry lists" of specific prohibitions. Fair Debt Collection Practices Act, §§ 806–808, 15 U.S.C. §§ 1692d–1692f (1996). The FDCPA generally applies, however, only to third-party debt collectors. *Id.* at § 803(6), 15 U.S.C. § 1692a(6) (1996). These practices are subject to anti-deception legislation because most of the statutes apply to practices that occur before, during, or after the sales transaction itself. *See, e.g.,* Ohio Rev. Code Ann. §§ 1345.02, 1345.03 (Anderson 1998).

[68] Uniform Consumer Sales Practices Act § 3(b)(1), 7A U.L.A. 237 (1985).

[69] *Id.* § 3(b)(2).

[70] *Id.* § 3(b)(3).

[71] *See* U.C.C. § 2-313.

[72] *See* Wood v. General Motors Corp., 673 F. Supp. 1108 (D. Mass. 1987); Mikos v. Chrysler Corp., 158 Mich. App. 781, 404 N.W.2d 783 (1987); Adams v. Grant, 292 S.C. 581, 358 S.E.2d 142 (S.C. Ct. App. 1986); Gupta v. Ritter Homes, Inc., 646 S.W.2d 168 (Tex. 1983).

unintentional breach of warranty, and require something more.[73] For example, some courts have required that the seller know of the breach and not disclose it to the buyer,[74] or that the seller intentionally refuse to comply with its warranty obligations.[75] Whether a breach of warranty also violates an anti-deception statute may depend on whether the statute consists solely of a general prohibition of unfair and deceptive acts, or whether there are specific prohibitions that suggest that a breach of warranty is a violation without regard to knowledge or intent. Frequently, however, a breach of warranty, even unintentional, gives rise to a claim under an anti-deception statute, with the attendant potential for recovering statutory damages and attorney's fees, which would normally be unavailable in a breach of warranty action under the Code. In some states, certain breaches of warranty are explicitly prohibited by regulations promulgated under the anti-deception legislation.[76]

In addition, there are certain defenses that may not be available to a seller under an anti-deception statute that are available in a breach of warranty suit. For example, notice of breach[77] is generally not necessary if suit is brought under an anti-deception statute. Also, the statute of limitations may not begin to run until the supplier's act was or should have been discovered,[78] while the Code's statute of limitations generally begins to run upon delivery of the goods.[79] Further, most anti-deception statutes create liability without regard to privity,[80] which means that recovery may be available in cases of purely economic loss that would otherwise have been unavailable under the Code because of lack of privity.[81]

Anti-deception statutes may remove another frequently used defense from the seller's arsenal: the parol evidence rule. Many warranty claims are

---

[73] *See, e.g.,* Sharpe v. General Motors Corp., 401 S.E.2d 328 (Ga. Ct. App. 1991); Suminski v. Maine Appliance Warehouse, Inc., 602 A.2d 1173 (Me. 1992).

[74] *See, e.g.,* Gour v. Daray Motor Co., Inc., 373 So. 2d 571 (La. Ct. App. 1979); Homsi v. C.H. Babb Co., Inc., 10 Mass. App. Ct. 474, 409 N.E.2d 219 (1980).

[75] *See, e.g.* State *ex rel.* Webster v. Milbourn, 759 S.W.2d 862 (Mo. Ct. App. 1988); HOW Ins. Co. v. Patriot Fin. Serv. of Tex., Inc., 786 S.W.2d 533 (Tex. Ct. App. 1990).

[76] *See* Greenfield § 4.3.3 at 1878 n.55 and regulations cited therein.

[77] *See* § 4.10, *supra.*

[78] *See* Ala. Code § 8-19-14 (1993); Tex. Bus. & Com. Code Ann. § 17.565 (West 1987).

[79] *See* § 4.11, *supra.*

[80] *See, e.g.,* Ohio Rev. Code Ann. § 1345.01(C) (Anderson 1998) which defines "supplier" as "a seller, lessor, assignor, franchisor, or other person engaged in the business of effecting or soliciting consumer transactions, whether or not he deals directly with the consumer."

[81] *See* § 4.09[D], *supra.*

prevented from reaching the factfinder because of the parol evidence rule.[82] In the typical case, the buyer claims that the seller made an oral representation not included in the written contract, and the seller relies on the parol evidence rule to prevent evidence of the oral representation from being admitted.[83] This argument is often successful, particularly when the writing contains a "merger" clause stating that the writing contains the entire contract between the parties.[84] A number of courts, however, have held that the parol evidence rule does not apply to an allegation of a violation of an anti-deception statute.[85]

This result, if properly limited, is correct. If the claim that there has been a violation of an anti-deception statute does not depend upon the terms of the contract, then the parol evidence rule is inapplicable. For example, if the consumer has been induced to enter into the contract as a result of deceptive statements by a seller, there may be liability under the act whether or not the deceptive statements are excluded from the contract under the parol evidence rule.[86] If, however, liability under the anti-deception statute depends upon the terms of the contract, then it is appropriate to apply the parol evidence rule to first determine those terms. Even in this case, the judge should consider all available evidence of the objective intentions of the parties, including evidence of alleged prior statements, in deciding whether the parties intended the prior statements to survive the writing.[87] In many consumer cases, proper application of the parol evidence rule will result in evidence of the prior statements being admitted. The widespread

---

[82] *See, e.g.,* Shore Line Properties, Inc. v. Deer-O-Paints & Chems., Ltd., 24 Ariz. App. 331, 538 P.2d 760 (1975); Jordan v. Doonan Truck & Equip., Inc., 220 Kan. 431, 552 P.2d 881 (1976); Ace, Inc. v. Maynard, 108 N.C. App. 241, 423 S.E.2d 504 (1992); Apple Valley Red-E-Mix, Inc. v. Mills-Winfield Eng'g Sales, Inc., 436 N.W.2d 121 (Minn. Ct. App. 1989).

[83] *See* § 3.15, *supra.*

[84] *See* § 3.15[C], *supra.*

[85] *See, e.g.,* Coble v. Richardson Corp. of Greensboro, 71 N.C. App. 511, 322 S.E.2d 817 (1984); Teague Motor Co. v. Rowton, 84 Or. App. 72, 733 P.2d 93 (1987); Weitzel v. Barnes, 691 S.W.2d 598 (Tex. 1985); Brown Found. Repair & Consulting, Inc. v. McGuire, 711 S.W.2d 349 (Tex. Ct. App. 1986).

[86] *See* Greenfield § 4.3.3.2 at 189. Further, violation of an anti-deception statute may result from conduct that doesn't involve a prior statement at all.

[87] *See* E. Allan Farnsworth, Farnsworth on Contracts § 7.3 at 432 (3d ed. 1999) (the intention of the parties under the parol evidence rule is determined from all the circumstances, including their language and other conduct, just as intention is determined for any other purpose).

acceptance of this position[88] should remove a major obstacle to the ability of consumers to recover for oral representations made by sellers.

[C]   Enforcement

Almost all anti-deception legislation provides for both public and private enforcement. The state attorney general is generally responsible for public enforcement. Most statutes provide for injunctive relief (cease and desist orders)[89] and grant the attorney general broad investigatory powers.[90] They may also provide for civil penalties[91] and even criminal sanctions,[92] and allow the attorney general to order restitution to injured consumers.[93] In a few states, the attorney general has the power to recover damages on behalf of consumers.[94] Most statutes also permit the attorney general to promulgate regulations pursuant to the statute.[95] These regulations have the force of law, the violation of which constitutes a violation of the anti-deception statute.

The real force behind most anti-deception statutes lies in the private remedies the statutes provide. Most anti-deception statutes explicitly grant

---

[88] There are, however, some cases that apply the parol evidence rule to anti-deception legislation to bar evidence of oral representations that vary the terms of a written contract. *See, e.g.,* Filmlife, Inc. v. Mal "Z" Ena, Inc., 251 N.J. Super. 570, 598 A.2d 1234 (N.Y. App. Div. 1991).

[89] *See, e.g.,* Fla. Stat. Ann. § 501.208 (West 1997); Md. Code Ann., Com. Law §§ 13-403, 13-406 (1990 & Supp. 1997); Tenn. Code Ann. § 47-18-108 (1995).

[90] *See, e.g.,* Ohio Rev. Code Ann. § 1345.06 (Anderson 1998), permitting the attorney general to subpoena witnesses, to require the production of documents or other material, to examine under oath, and to terminate an investigation upon the assurance by the supplier of voluntary compliance.

[91] *See, e.g.,* Ala. Code § 8-19-8 (1993); Fla. Stat. Ann. § 501.2075 (West Supp. 1997); Md. Code Ann., Com. Law § 13-410 (Supp. 1997).

[92] *See, e.g.,* Md. Code Ann., Com. Law § 13-411 (1990).

[93] *See* Ala. Code § 8-19-8(b) (1993); S.C. Code Ann. § 39-5-50(b) (Law. Co-op. 1985); Tex. Bus. & Com. Code Ann. § 17.50(b) (West Supp. 1998).

[94] *See* Commonwealth of Ky. *ex rel.* Beshear v. ABAC Pest Control, Inc., 621 S.W.2d 705 (Ky. Ct. App. 1981); Celebreze v. Hughes, 18 Ohio St. 3d 71, 479 N.E.2d 886 (1985).

[95] *See, e.g.,* Ohio Rev. Code Ann. § 1345.05(B)(2) (Anderson 1998); Or. Rev. Stat. § 646.608(4) (1988 & Supp. 1996); S.C. Code Ann. § 39-5-80 (Law. Co-op. 1985); S.D. Codified Laws Ann. § 37-24-14 (1994). In Ohio, for example, the attorney general has made extensive use of this power, and has adopted rules dealing with exclusions and limitations in advertising, bait advertising, use of the word "free," repairs and services, prizes, deposits, new for used, failure to deliver and substitution of goods or services, substantiation of claims in advertising, direct solicitations, price comparisons, car repairs and services, insulation, car rust inhibitors, advertisement and sales of cars, and distress sales. Ohio Admin. Code §§ 109: 4-3-02—109:4-3-18.

a cause of action to an injured consumer, and, when they do not, courts have implied a private right of action.[96] Virtually all of the states give an injured consumer the right to recover actual damages caused by a violation. In calculating actual damages, consumers should be entitled to at least the same measure of damages that is recoverable under the Code for breach of warranty. Thus, consumers should be entitled to the benefit of their bargain—the difference in value between what they expected to receive and what they, in fact, received.[97] This difference should generally be measured by the cost of repairing the goods or otherwise making them conform to the standard the buyer was led to expect,[98] although a couple of courts have been unwilling to allow recovery of the cost of repair when it greatly exceeded the difference in value measured by the market.[99]

Courts usually permit the recovery of consequential and incidental damages as well. These damages might include lost wages,[100] the cost of replacement transportation,[101] and the interest paid on a loan taken out to buy the goods.[102] The law is mixed on whether damages for mental anguish can be recovered. Some courts have permitted the recovery of these damages when personal injury resulted from the violation,[103] and others have permitted recovery of these damages when the violation was willful or malicious.[104] At least one court has held that damages for mental anguish may be recovered even if no other damages have been suffered.[105] Others courts, however, have held that damages for mental suffering are not recoverable

---

[96] *See, e.g.,* Sellinger v. Freeway Mobile Home Sales, Inc., 110 Ariz. 573, 521 P.2d 1119 (1974) (implying a private right of action under Ariz. Rev. Stat. Ann. § 44-1521 *et seq.* (1994); Young v. Joyce, 351 A.2d 857 (Del. 1975) (implying a private right of action under Del. Code Ann. tit. 6 § 2511 (1993).

[97] *See* U.C.C. § 2-714(2); § 7.04[C], *supra.*

[98] *See* Deltona Corp. v. Jannotti, 392 So. 2d 976 (Fla. Ct. App. 1981); Young v. Joyce, 351 A.2d 857 (Del. 1975); Smith v. Baldwin, 611 S.W.2d 611 (Tex. 1980).

[99] *See* Guest v. Phillips Petroleum Co., 981 F.2d 218 (5th Cir. 1993) (court refused to allow $84,000 cost of moving house to nondangerous site; buyer was allowed $44,000, the value of the house).

[100] *See* Metro Ford Truck Sales, Inc. v. Davis, 709 S.W.2d 785 (Tex. Ct. App. 1986).

[101] *See* Burgess Constr. Co. v. Hancock, 514 P.2d 236 (Alaska 1973); Town E. Ford Sales, Inc. v. Gray, 730 S.W.2d 796 (Tex. Ct. App. 1987); Bob Robertson, Inc. v. Webster, 679 S.W.2d 683 (Tex. Ct. App. 1984).

[102] *See* Gent v. Collinsville Volkswagen, Inc., 116 Ill. App. 3d 496, 451 N.E.2d 1385 (1983); Smith v. Baldwin, 611 S.W.2d 611 (Tex. 1980).

[103] *See* Pope v. Rollins Protective Serv. Co., 703 F.2d 197 (5th Cir. 1983).

[104] Vercher v. Ford Motor Co., 527 So. 2d 995 (La. Ct. App. 1988); West v. Carter, 712 S.W.2d 569 (Tex. Ct. App. 1986).

[105] Dan Boone Mitsubishi, Inc. v. Ebrom, 830 S.W.2d 334 (Tex. Ct. App. 1992).

for violation of the state's anti-deception statute.[106] When the statute designates the damages that may be recovered and mental suffering is not included, one court has held that mental suffering damages may not be recovered.[107]

Most anti-deception statutes further provide for statutory damages, multiple damages, or punitive damages, or some combination of the three. A substantial number of states have provisions for statutory damages that are recoverable even in the absence of proof of actual damages. The amount available ranges from $25 in Massachusetts[108] to as much as $5,000 in Kansas.[109] In most states, anti-deception statutes provide for statutory damages in the range of $100–$200.[110] Although the statutes are sometimes ambiguous,[111] statutory damages are generally held to be available for each violation of the anti-deception statute.[112]

In addition, roughly half of the statutes provide for multiple damages if certain circumstances are present. For example, in Ohio, actual damages may be trebled when the violation is either (1) a violation of a rule promulgated by the attorney general prior to the transaction, or (2) an act or practice that has already been determined by a court of the state to violate the statute and that was committed after the court decision in the prior case was made available by the attorney general for public inspection.[113] Other states require a showing that the supplier's conduct was intentional,[114] know-

---

[106] *See, e.g.*, McCormick Piano & Organ Co., Inc. v. Geiger, 412 N.E.2d 842 (Ind. Ct. App. 1980); Keyes v. Bollinger, 31 Wash. App. 286, 640 P.2d 1077 (1982).

[107] In re Bryant, 111 B.R. 474 (E.D. Pa. 1990) (recovery for emotional distress is not allowed under the Pennsylvania Unfair and Deceptive Acts and Practices statute because it does not fall within the description of actual damages as "any certain loss of money or property").

[108] Mass. Ann. Laws ch. 93A, § 9(3) (Law. Co-op. 1994).

[109] Kan. Stat. Ann. §§ 50-634, 50-636(a) (1994).

[110] *See, e.g.*, Ala. Code § 8-19-10(a)(1) (1993) ($100); Ohio Rev. Code Ann. § 1345.09(B) (Anderson 1998) ($200); Or. Rev. Stat. § 646.638(1) (Supp. 1996) ($200); R.I. Gen. Laws § 6-13.1-5.2(a) (1992) ($200); W. Va. Code § 46A-6-106(1) (1996) (Anderson 1998) ($200).

[111] *See* Ohio Rev. Code Ann. § 1345.09(B) (Anderson 1998).

[112] *See, e.g.*, Arsenault v. Realty Funding Corp., 184 B.R. 864, 874 (Bankr. D.N.H.) (allowing recovery of $200 for each of thirty-six separate violations of the New Hampshire consumer protection statute).

[113] Ohio Rev. Code Ann. § 1345.09(B) (Anderson 1998).

[114] Ga. Code Ann. § 10-1-392 (Supp. 1998); Vmark Software, Inc. v. EMC Corp., 37 Mass. App. 610, 642 N.E.2d 587 (1994).

ing,[115] or willful[116] before multiple damages are available. Even when intent or knowledge is required, the plaintiff is usually required only to show that the act or practice in question was done intentionally, not that the supplier intended to violate the act or that the supplier knew his conduct violated the act.[117] Unlike statutory damages, before multiple damages can be awarded, the consumer must have suffered actual damages.[118] Further, only actual damages may be multiplied, not an award of statutory damages.[119]

The statutes of a number of states expressly permit the recovery of punitive damages.[120] Courts in a number of other states have permitted the recovery of punitive damages in the absence of explicit authorization,[121] although others have refused to grant punitive damages when the statute authorizes multiple damages. Unless the statute prescribes otherwise, punitive damages are generally awarded for conduct that would merit a similar award in a common-law cause of action such as fraud.[122]

Most anti-deception statutes also permit the recovery of attorney's fees by a prevailing plaintiff. Because most consumer cases do not involve large sums of money, lawyers have been traditionally reluctant to pursue them. Billing clients on an hourly basis would often result in a fee that exceeded the likely recovery, and billing them on a contingent fee basis would generally result in a fee too low to compensate the lawyer for her time. Recognizing this, some states have made an award of attorney's fees

---

[115] Tex. Bus. & Com. Code Ann. § 17.50(b)(1) (Supp. 1998); Leatherman v. Miller's Mut. Fire Ins. Co. of Tex., 297 So. 2d 540 (La. Ct. App. 1974); Martin v. McKee Realtors, Inc., 663 S.W.2d 446 (Tex. 1984).

[116] Brown v. LeClair, 20 Mass. App. 976, 482 N.E.2d 870 (1985); Payne v. Holiday Towers, Inc., 321 S.E.2d 179 (S.C. Ct. App. 1984).

[117] Computer Sys. Eng'g, Inc. v. Quantel Corp., 571 F. Supp. 1365 (D. Mass. 1983), aff'd, 740 F.2d 59 (1st Cir. 1984); Shawmut Community Bank v. Zagami, 30 Mass. App. 371, 568 N.E.2d 1163 (1991).

[118] Faris v. Model's Guild, 297 So. 2d 536 (La. Ct. App. 1974); Schafer v. Conner, 805 S.W.2d 554 (Tex. Ct. App. 1991).

[119] See, e.g., Ohio Rev. Code Ann. § 1345.09(B) (Anderson 1998) (permitting in certain circumstances the trebling of "actual damages); Colo. Rev. Stat. § 6-1-113 (1997) (mandating in certain circumstances the trebling of "actual damages").

[120] See National Consumer Law Center, Unfair and Deceptive Act and Practices § 8.2.5.1 at 428 (3d ed. 1991).

[121] Byers v. Santiam Ford, Inc., 281 Or. 411, 574 P.2d 1122 (1978); Bruntaeger v. Zeller, 147 Vt. 247, 515 A.2d 123 (Vt. 1986).

[122] See National Consumer Law Center, Unfair and Deceptive Acts and Practices (3d ed. 1991) § 8.2.5.1 at 429.

mandatory,[123] although in others an award of attorney's fees is discretionary with the court.[124] Courts have varied substantially in their generosity to plaintiffs in calculating an award of attorney's fees.[125]

[D]   Conclusion

As stated previously, this portion of the text is intended merely to alert the practitioner and student to the presence of state anti-deception laws and the substantial impact they have on consumer transactions. Many issues are only touched on and others are ignored entirely. It should be clear, however, that a lawyer cannot be considered well versed in the law of sales without an appreciation of consumer anti-deception legislation. To the attorney considering a case, what first appears as a breach of warranty action with modest damages may be a case in which the availability of multiple or punitive damages presents the potential for recovering a handsome sum on behalf of the client. Moreover, the ability to recover attorney's fees may make it worthwhile for the attorney to invest time and resources in a meritorious case that the attorney would, for economic reasons, be otherwise unable to take. It is rare that when a consumer has received less in a transaction than she legitimately expects that a plausible case cannot be made under most anti-deception statutes,[126] and lawyers ignore these statutes at their extreme peril.

---

[123] *See, e.g.,* Cal. Civ. Code § 1780(d) (West 1998); S.C. Code Ann. § 39-5-140(a) (Law Co-op. 1985); Moore v. Goodyear Tire & Rubber Co., 364 So. 2d 630 (La. Ct. App. 1978); Shands v. Castrovinci, 115 Wis. 2d 352, 340 N.W.2d 506 (1983).

[124] *See, e.g.,* Kleidon v. Rizza Chevrolet, Inc., 173 Ill. App. 3d 116, 527 N.E.2d 374 (1988); Beaulieu v. Dorsey, 562 A.2d 678 (Me. 1989); James v. Thermal Master, Inc., 55 Ohio App. 3d 51, 562 N.E.2d 917 (1988).

[125] *Compare* Beaulieu v. Dorsey, 562 A.2d 678 (Me. 1989) ($18,000 in attorney's fees awarded) *with* Carpenter v. Discount Motors, Inc., 652 S.W.2d 716 (Mo. Ct. App. 1983) ($0 in attorney's fees awarded).

[126] Lawyers should be aware, however, that the statute of limitations for bringing such actions is likely to be far shorter than the four years provided by the Code. *See, e.g.,* Ohio Rev. Code Ann. § 1345.10(C) (Anderson 1998) (action must be brought within two years after the occurrence of the violation); Tenn. Code Ann. § 47-18-110 (1995) (action must be brought within one year from the discovery of the violation); Tex. Bus. & Com. Code Ann. § 17.565 (West 1987) (action must be brought within two years after the occurrence of the violation or after it should have been discovered); Utah Code Ann. § 13-11-19 (1996) (action must be brought within two years after the occurrence of the violation).

§ 9.03   STATE "LEMON LAWS"

[A]   Introduction

During the past ten to fifteen years, virtually all states have passed so-called lemon laws. These laws were passed in reaction to the widespread perception that purchasers of new cars,[127] which did not conform to the manufacturers' warranties were denied effective recourse by the limitations on remedies contained in these same warranties. The archetypal case involves the proverbial "lemon" automobile; the gleaming new car that barely makes it out of the showroom before problems begin popping up with more frequency than prairie dogs on the western plain. The first few complaints may be resolved amicably, but when the dealer is unable to fix the defects or prevent more from occurring, the frustrated owner finally demands a replacement vehicle or her money back. These requests are adamantly refused by both the dealer and the manufacturer, and the consumer is referred to a provision in the warranty documents stating that repair and replacement of defective parts is her exclusive remedy.[128] According to the dealer and manufacturer, the buyer has no choice but to wait patiently while the dealer tinkers indefinitely with the vehicle in a futile attempt to transform the proverbial sow's ear into a silk purse.

It was never really this bad. As explained previously in this text,[129] if an exclusive remedy fails of its essential purpose, the full panoply of Code remedies is available to an aggrieved buyer. One of these remedies is revocation of acceptance, which permits the buyer to return the goods to the seller and recover the price paid for them.[130] By the time that most legislatures got around to passing lemon laws, courts had generally decided that if a seller could not make an automobile conform to express and implied warranties within a reasonable time, the exclusive repair and replacement remedy had failed in its essential purpose. Once this occurred, the buyer could, in fact, get her refund or replacement.[131]

---

[127] The lemon laws of most states deal only with the sale of new cars. A small number of states have also passed similar statutes dealing with the sale of used motor vehicles. *See, e.g.,* Minn. Stat. Ann. § 325F.662 (West 1995); R.I. Gen. Laws § 31-5.4 (1995).

[128] *See* § 4.08, *supra.*

[129] *See* § 4.08[D], *supra.*

[130] *See* U.C.C. § 2-608.

[131] Stutts v. Green Ford, Inc., 47 N.C. App. 503, 267 S.E.2d 919, 29 UCCR 1241 (1980); Goddard v. General Motors Corp., 60 Ohio St. 2d 41, 396 N.E.2d 761, 27 UCCR 973 (1979); Murray v. Holiday Rambler, Inc., 83 Wis. 2d 406, 265 N.W.2d 513, 24 UCCR 52 (1978).

In some ways, however, the lemon laws are marginal improvements to the Code. The most significant advance is that they permit the buyer to return the car to the *manufacturer* if certain criteria are satisfied. In contrast, many states have refused to permit buyers to revoke acceptance against manufacturers, limiting the buyer to revocation against the immediate seller.[132] In addition, most statutes provide the manufacturer (or his representative) with a specified number of attempts at repair, usually three or four for the same nonconformity, after which the buyer can definitely return the vehicle for a refund or replacement.[133] These provisions lend a element of certainty to the buyer's rights; under the Code, the seller is entitled to a "reasonable" number of repair attempts before an exclusive repair remedy fails and the buyer is entitled to revoke acceptance. In many situations, however, the relief provided by the lemon laws merely duplicates that which is also available under the Code, and in some ways, proceeding under the Code is more advantageous to buyers.[134]

[B] Scope of Coverage

As previously mentioned, most lemon laws cover only "new" motor vehicles. Some statutes contain a definition of "new,"[135] while others do not.[136] In most cases, whether or not the statute contains a definition, the question is whether the original title has been issued on the vehicle. If the original title has not been issued, the vehicle is "new." Thus, demonstrators

---

[132] *See* § 7.03[E], *supra*.

[133] *See, e.g.,* Ky. Rev. Stat. Ann. § 367.842(3)(a) (Michie 1996) (four repair attempts for the same nonconformity); Minn. Stat. Ann. § 325F.665(3)(b) (West 1995) (four repair attempts for the same nonconformity); Ohio Rev. Code Ann. § 1345.73(A) (Anderson 1998) (three repair attempts for the same nonconformity; eight repair attempts total). For a more detailed description, *see* § 9.03[F], *infra*.

[134] For example, a number of statutes make resort to an alternative dispute resolution mechanism mandatory before the buyer can seek a refund or replacement. *See, e.g.,* Ky. Rev. Stat. Ann. § 367.865 (Michie 1996); Minn. Stat. Ann. § 325F.665(6) (West 1995); Ohio Rev. Code Ann. § 1345.77 (Anderson 1998).

[135] *See, e.g.,* Ky. Rev. Stat. Ann. § 367.841(4) (Michie 1996) which defines "new motor vehicle" as follows: "a motor vehicle which has been finally and completely assembled and is in the possession of a manufacturer, factory branch, distributor, wholesaler or an authorized motor vehicle dealer operating under a valid sales and service agreement, franchise or contract for the sale of such vehicle granted by the manufacturer, factory branch, distributor or wholesaler which is, in fact, new and on which the original title has never been issued."

[136] *See, e.g.,* N.M. Stat. Ann. § 57-16A-3 (1997); Ohio Rev. Code Ann. § 1345.71 (Anderson 1998).

are "new" vehicles, even though they have accumulated substantial mileage, and some statutes expressly include demonstrators within their coverage.[137]

Occasionally, vehicles are sold for very short periods and then returned to the dealer, often in exchange for another vehicle that the purchaser has decided he or she prefers. Although the original title will have been transferred, the manufacturer's warranty will not have expired when a subsequent buyer purchases the vehicle from the dealer and will often have a considerable period to run. Unless precluded by the statute, courts should be flexible in deciding whether a vehicle qualifies for the protection of the lemon law statute under these circumstances. If the time of previous ownership was very short, the extent of previous use was minor, and the great majority of time remains on the manufacturer's warranty, the vehicle should be treated as "new" for purposes of the lemon law.[138] The purpose of the lemon laws is to ensure that manufacturers honor their warranties and buyers have the ability to secure a refund or replacement if the vehicle turns out to be a lemon. The intervening ownership by the dealer of a few days or even a few weeks should not be permitted to defeat this salutary purpose.

Many of the statutes apply only to motor vehicles purchased by "consumers."[139] Other statutes appear to apply more broadly, covering "buyers"[140] or "purchasers."[141] Even when the statute applies only to purchases by "consumers," the scope of coverage may vary dramatically, depending upon the statutory definition of "consumer" and the interpretation of the term by the courts. A number of statutes define a "consumer" as one who purchases a vehicle primarily for personal, family, or household purposes.[142] These statutes appear to focus on the *actual use* of the vehicle,[143] as opposed to its normal or typical use. Other statutes, however, suggest that the *normal* use of the vehicle, rather than its actual use, governs whether the vehicle

---

[137] *See, e.g.,* Ga. Code Ann. § 10-1-782(11) (1997); Miss. Code Ann. § 63-17-155(f) (1997); Chrysler Motors Corp. v. Flowers, 116 Wash. 2d 208, 803 P.2d 314 (1991).

[138] *See* Britton v. Bill Anselmi Pontiac-Buick-GMC, Inc., 786 P.2d 855 (Wyo. 1990) ("new" vehicle is one on which manufacturer's original warranty has not expired or on which a new car warranty is given).

[139] *See, e.g.,* Ga. Code Ann. § 10-1-782(3) (1997); Miss. Code Ann. § 63-17-155(c) (1997); Ohio Rev. Code Ann. § 1345.71(A) (Anderson 1998); W. Va. Code § 46A-6A-2(1) (1995).

[140] *See, e.g.,* Idaho Code § 48-902(1) (Supp. 1996); Ind. Code Ann. § 24-5-13-8 (West 1995); Ky. Rev. Stat. Ann. § 367.841(1) (Michie/Bobbs-Merrill 1996).

[141] *See, e.g.,* Pa. Stat. Ann. tit. 73 § 1952 (1993).

[142] *See, e.g.,* Ga. Code Ann. § 10-1-782(3) (1997); W. Va. Code § 46A-6A-2(1) (1995).

[143] *See* S.D. Codified Laws § 32-6D-1(1) (Michie Supp. 1996).

has been purchased by a consumer.[144] In Minnesota, a person is a consumer if he or she uses the vehicle for personal, family, or household purposes at least 40 percent of the time.[145] Still other statutes include no explicit requirement in the definition of "consumer" that the vehicle be used (or normally used) for personal, family, or household purposes.[146]

Almost all of the statutes cover subsequent purchasers from the original retail buyer so long as the vehicle has not been resold to a dealer in the interim. Typically, lemon laws cover all consumers to whom a vehicle is transferred during the duration of the manufacturer's warranty as well as any other person entitled by the warranty to enforce its terms.[147] Thus, if Anne purchases a new car from a dealer with a three-year, 36,000-mile warranty and, within this period, Anne sells the vehicle to Bob who then sells it to Charlie, Charlie has the benefit of the statute for as long as the warranty remains in force.[148] If Anne sells to a dealer, however, who then sells to Bob, the lemon law is generally not applicable, because the car is no longer considered "new."[149] Even in this case, however, Bob has the benefit of the warranty coverage itself.

Whether a particular lemon law covers *leased* vehicles usually depends on the specific language of the statute. Many lemon laws expressly include leased vehicles.[150] Even when leased vehicles are not expressly included in the statute, the language of the lemon law can often be interpreted to include them. For example, because lemon laws generally cover all persons entitled to enforce the manufacturer's warranty, courts have allowed lessees to use the lemon laws if the lessee receives a manufacturer's warranty with the lease.[151]

Coverage under most lemon laws is restricted in one of four ways by the place of purchase or the place of registration of the vehicle. Some lemon laws apply only to vehicles registered in that state.[152] Other apply only to

---

[144] *See, e.g.,* N.M. Stat. Ann. § 57-16A-2C (1997) ("'consumer' means the purchaser . . . of a new motor vehicle normally used for personal, family, or household purposes").

[145] Minn. Stat. Ann. § 325F.665(1)(a) (West 1995).

[146] *See, e.g.,* Ohio Rev. Code Ann. § 1345.71(A) (Anderson 1998).

[147] *See, e.g.,* N.J. Stat. Ann. § 56:12-30 (West Supp. 1996).

[148] Or for the period otherwise established in the lemon law. *See* § 9.03[C], *infra.*

[149] As suggested earlier, however, if Anne's period of ownership is very short, the auto should still be considered new when resold by the dealer.

[150] *See, e.g.,* Ga. Code Ann. § 10-1-782(3) (1997); N.J. Stat. Ann. § 56:12-30 (West Supp. 1996).

[151] *See* Pertuset v. Ford Motor Co., 96 Ohio App. 3d 777, 645 N.E.2d 1329 (1994); Potente v. Peugeot Motors of Am., Inc., 62 Ohio Misc. 2d 335, 598 N.E.2d 907 (Ct. C.P. 1991).

[152] *See, e.g.,* Ky. Rev. Stat. Ann. § 367.841(3) (Michie 1996).

vehicles purchased in that state.[153] A number require only that the vehicle be purchased *or* registered in the state.[154] The most restrictive statutes require that the vehicle be *both* sold and registered in the state.[155]

Most states' lemon laws are directed only toward the manufacturer, not the dealer. Although the dealer may be liable under some other theory, such as fraud, misrepresentation, or breach of warranty under the Code or Magnuson-Moss, dealers generally have no liability under the lemon laws. Manufacturers, of course, may delegate their repair responsibilities to their authorized dealers, as they inevitably do, but the ultimate responsibility for compliance with the lemon laws remains on the manufacturer.

[C] Period of Coverage

The period of coverage varies greatly from state to state. A common practice is to cover defects that arise[156] within the period of the manufacturer's warranty or within a period of time (usually between one and two years) designated in the statute. In some cases, it is the *earlier* of these two periods,[157] while other states give the consumer the benefit of whichever period is longer.[158] Some states provide a period of coverage that is entirely independent of the manufacturer's warranty. For example, New Jersey's lemon law covers defects arising within the first two years or 18,000 miles after delivery, whichever comes first, without regard to the period of the manufacturer's warranty.[159] Presumably, unless the statute specifically pro-

---

[153] *See, e.g.*, Miss. Code Ann. § 63-17-155(f) (1997); W. Va. Code § 46A-6A-2(4) (1995).

[154] *See, e.g.*, Del. Code Ann. tit. 6, § 5001(5) (1993); Ga. Code Ann. § 10-1-782(11) (1997); N.J. Stat. Ann. § 56:12-30 (West Supp. 1996).

[155] *See, e.g.*, N.M. Stat. Ann. § 57-16A-2F (1997) (definition of "motor vehicle").

[156] Under the terms of most statutes, the defect must not only arise within the statutory period, but the manufacturer, or its agent, must be given notice of the defect within the period. *See, e.g.*, Minn. Stat. Ann. § 325F.665(2) (West 1995); Miss. Code Ann. § 63-17-158 (1997); Ohio Rev. Code Ann. § 1345.72 (Anderson 1998); W. Va. Code § 46A-6A-3 (1995).

[157] *See, e.g.*, Minn. Stat. Ann. § 325F.665 2 (West 1995) (two years or period of warranty, whichever is earlier); Miss. Code Ann. § 63-17-157 (1997) (one year or period of warranty, whichever is earlier); N.M. Stat. Ann. § 57-16A-3A (1997) (one year or period of warranty, whichever is earlier).

[158] *See, e.g.*, W. Va. Code § 46A-6A-3 (1995) (one year or period of warranty, whichever is longer).

[159] N.J. Stat. Ann. § 56:12-31 (West Supp. 1996). In addition, *see* Ga. Code Ann. § 10-1-782(9) (1997) (one year or 12,000 miles, whichever comes first); Ind. Code Ann. § 24-5-13-7 (West 1995) (eighteen months or 18,000 miles, whichever comes first).

vides otherwise, the consumer is required to pay for repairs for defects arising outside the period of the express warranty.[160]

[D] Defects Covered

Lemon laws generally provide two types of protection to consumers: (1) they require the manufacturer to correct defects that are covered by the manufacturer's warranty and that occur within the time period designated in the lemon law, and (2) they permit the buyer to secure a refund or replacement if the manufacturer cannot remedy the defects after a certain number of attempts.[161] The provisions permitting the buyer to obtain a refund or replacement usually do not cover all defects that result in a breach of the manufacturer's express warranty. Typically, defects must be "substantial" before the buyer will be allowed a refund or replacement because the manufacturer has failed to repair them.[162] Most statutes do not define when a defect is "substantial."[163] Because the remedy provided by lemon laws is similar to the revocation-of-acceptance remedy in section 2-608 of the Uniform Commercial Code, the body of law that has accumulated under section 2-608[164] should be an effective guide in determining whether a defect is substantial.

[E] Covered Vehicles

Vehicles that are covered by lemon laws vary from state to state. Coverage is often restricted to "motor vehicles" or "passenger vehicles," which are then defined by reference to a separate statute.[165] Typically excluded

---

[160] The New Jersey lemon law makes this explicit. N.J. Stat. Ann. § 56:12-31 (West Supp. 1996). *But see* People *ex rel.* Abrams v. Ford Motor Co., 133 Misc. 2d 828, 510 N.Y.S.2d 425 (Sup. Ct. 1986), *affd,* 74 N.Y.2d 495, 548 N.E.2d 906 (1989) ($100 deductible in warranty not applicable to repairs required under lemon law).

[161] *See* Miss. Code Ann. § 63-17-153 (1997) (Declaration of Purpose).

[162] *But see* Miss. Code Ann. § 63-17-159 (1997) (nonconformity must merely be one that "impairs the use, market value, or safety" of the vehicle).

[163] *But see* Ga. Code Ann. § 10-1-782(20) (1997). "Substantial impair" means "to render the new motor vehicle unreliable, or unsafe for ordinary use, or to diminish the resale value of the new motor vehicle more than a meaningful amount below the average resale value for comparable motor vehicles."

[164] *See* § 7.03[E], *supra.*

[165] *See, e.g.,* Ohio Rev. Code Ann. § 1345.71(D) (Anderson 1998).

from coverage are motorcycles,[166] farm vehicles such as tractors,[167] conversion vans,[168] and motor homes (or the nonmotorized portions thereof).[169] In addition, trucks over 10,000 pounds gross weight are excluded from a coverage by a number of states.[170]

[F] Number of Repair Attempts Permitted

Virtually all lemon laws permit the buyer to return the vehicle for a replacement or refund only after the seller has made a "reasonable" number of attempts to repair a specific nonconformity. In almost all cases, the statutes create an explicit presumption that either three or four unsuccessful attempts at remedying the same substantial nonconformity is a reasonable number of attempts. Most statutes are not clear as to whether this presumption is one of fact or law.[171] It is, however, logical to assume that the various legislatures intend a presumption of fact. Otherwise, they could have dispensed with the language of presumption and have simply provided that after a certain number of attempts at repair, the buyer may return the vehicle. One statute, however, makes it explicit that the presumption is one of law.[172] Some states require that the buyer notify the manufacturer after the requisite number of unsuccessful attempts at repair have been made and give the manufacturer one last attempt to cure the defect before an action can be brought under the statute.[173]

In addition, many states also permit the buyer to return the vehicle if, as a result of repairs, it is unusable by the buyer for a specified cumulative period, whether or not the same nonconformity is involved. These provisions

---

[166] *See, e.g.,* Del. Code Ann. tit. 6 § 5001(5) (1993); Ky. Rev. Stat. Ann. § 367.841(3) (Michie 1996); Miss. Code Ann. § 63-17-155(f) (1997).

[167] *See, e.g.,* Alaska Stat. § 45.45.360(6) (Michie 1994); Ky. Rev. Stat. Ann. § 367.841(3) (Michie 1996).

[168] *See, e.g.,* Ind. Code Ann. § 24-5-13-5 (West 1995); Ky. Rev. Stat. Ann. § 367.841(3) (Michie 1996).

[169] *See, e.g.,* Del. Code Ann. tit. 6 § 5001(5) (1993); Ky. Rev. Stat. Ann. § 367.841(3) (Michie 1996); N.J. Stat. Ann. § 56:12-30 (West Supp. 1996).

[170] *See, e.g.,* Fla. Stat. Ann. § 681.102(11) (West Supp. 1996); Ga. Code Ann. § 10-1-782(11) (1997); Ind. Code Ann. § 24-5-13-5 (West 1995); N.M. Stat. Ann. § 57-16A-3F (1997).

[171] *But see* Ibrahim v. Ford Motor Co., 214 Cal. App. 3d 878, 263 Cal. Rptr. 64, 10 UCCR2d 117 (1990) (presumption is rebuttable).

[172] Ga. Code Ann. § 10-1-784(b) (1997). For a case reaching a similar result, *see* Ayer v. Ford Motor Co., 200 Mich. App. 337, 503 N.W.2d 767 (1993).

[173] *See, e.g.,* Ga. Code Ann. § 10-1-784(a)(1) (1997); N.J. Stat. Ann. § 56:12-33 (West Supp. 1996); W. Va. Code § 46A-6A-5 (1995).

are intended to deal with the situation in which the manufacturer corrects (after one or two attempts) each defect as it occurs, but the vehicle contains nothing but defects. The period in which the vehicle must be out of commission may vary from as few as fifteen days to as many as thirty days.[174] Ohio has an additional provision permitting the manufacturer no more than eight cumulative repair attempts during the period of lemon law coverage.[175]

Some states have additional provisions dealing with defects that present significant safety risks. For example, in a number of states, a manufacturer is permitted only one unsuccessful attempt at remedying a nonconformity that is likely to cause death or serious bodily injury.[176] A few statutes have special provisions dealing with defects in brakes or steering.[177]

[G] Informal Dispute-Resolution Mechanisms

Most lemon laws contain provisions providing for alternative dispute resolution of lemon law claims. These provisions vary considerably. In some states, resort to the informal dispute-resolution mechanism (IDSM) is optional before suit can be brought,[178] although in the majority of states, recourse to the alternative dispute mechanism is mandatory prior to suit.[179] Frequently, lemon laws provide that if the manufacturer has established an IDSM that meets or exceeds the requirements under the Maugnuson-Moss Federal Warranty Act, the IDSM will be adequate under the lemon law.[180] Often, the law requires that the state attorney general certify the IDSM as

---

[174] Depending upon the statute these may be business or calendar days. *See* Miss. Code Ann. § 63-17-159(3)(b) (1997) (fifteen working days); N.J. Stat. Ann. § 56:12-33 (West Supp. 1996) (twenty calendar days); Ga. Code Ann. § 10-1-784(b)(4) (1987) (thirty calendar days; Ohio Rev. Code Ann. § 1345.73 (Anderson 1998) (thirty calendar days); N.M. Stat. Ann. § 57-16A-3C(2) (1997) (thirty business days).

[175] Ohio Rev. Code Ann. § 1345.73(C) (Anderson 1998).

[176] *See, e.g.,* Ohio Rev. Code Ann. § 1345.73(D) (Anderson 1998); W. Va. Code § 46A-6A-5(6) (1995).

[177] Minn. Stat. Ann. § 325F.665, Subd. 3(c) (1996).

[178] *See, e.g.,* N.H. Rev. Stat. Ann. § 357-D:4 (1995); N.J. Stat. Ann. § 56:12-36 (West Supp. 1996); N.Y. Gen. Bus. Law § 198-a(9) (McKinney 1988).

[179] *See, e.g.,* Ga. Code Ann. § 10-1-786(c) (1997); Ky. Rev. Stat. Ann. § 367.865 (Michie 1996); Minn. Stat. Ann. § 325F.665(6) (West 1995).

[180] Some lemon laws *require* that the manufacturer establish an IDSM that is sufficient under the Magnuson-Moss Federal Warranty Act. Since the creation of an IDSM by the manufacturer is voluntary under Magnuson-Moss, some manufacturers have argued that this requirement is preempted by Magnuson-Moss. This argument has not been successful. *See* Motor Vehicle Mfrs. Ass'n v. Abrams, 889 F.2d 1315 (2d Cir. 1990), *cert. denied,* 499 U.S. 912 (1991); Automobile Importers of Am., Inc. v. Minnesota, 871 F.2d 717 (8th Cir.), *cert. denied,* 493 U.S. 872 (1989).

in compliance with the requirements of Magnuson-Moss,[181] and sometimes lemon laws add additional requirements to those of Magnuson-Moss before certification can be obtained.[182] Occasionally, the law establishes entirely separate standards for lemon law IDSMs,[183] and some states have created IDSMs run by the state attorney general rather than the manufacturer.[184] A few states, such as New Jersey,[185] allow the consumer to choose between a state-run arbitration board and the manufacturer's IDSM.[186] In most cases, either party may appeal an adverse result from an IDSM, and appeals are usually heard by the trial court *de novo*. In some states, however, the manufacturer's right of appeal is more limited than that of the consumer.[187]

[H] Remedies Available

As mentioned previously, the motivating force behind the passage of lemon laws was to provide the consumer with a new car or a refund when the facts established that the consumer had been stuck with a "lemon." Thus, the primary remedy under these laws is the replacement of the lemon with a comparable new vehicle or the refund of the consumer's purchase price. Under most statutes, the consumer has the option of choosing a replacement or refund. Some states, however, require the manufacturer to provide a replacement vehicle or give the manufacturer the option to choose between a replacement or refund.[188]

If the consumer chooses a refund, the manufacturer is generally required to reimburse the consumer for "incidental" or "collateral" charges. These charges usually include sales tax, license and registration fees, transportation charges, dealer-preparation expenses, and similar charges. In addition, the various statutes require that the consumer be reimbursed for any trade-in allowance given by the dealer. Whether finance charges are recoverable is a matter of some disagreement. Some statutes specifically permit

---

[181] *See, e.g,* Del. Code Ann. tit. 6, § 5007 (Supp. 1994).

[182] *Id.*

[183] Conn. Gen. Stat. § 42-181 (1997); Del. Code Ann., tit. 6 § 5007 (Supp. 1994); Ga. Code Ann. § 10-1-787 (1997).

[184] *See* Ohio Rev. Code Ann. § 1345.77 (Anderson 1998).

[185] N.J. Stat. Ann. § 56:12-39 (West Supp. 1996).

[186] Vermont has a similar provision in its lemon law. Vt. Stat. Ann. tit. 9, § 4173(c) (1997).

[187] *See* Minn. Stat. Ann. § 325F.665(7) (West 1995); N.J. Stat. Ann. § 56:12-37d (West Supp. 1996).

[188] The remedies under most lemon laws are cumulative with remedies that the consumer may have under statutes or the common law. Thus, if the consumer can establish a basis for revocation of acceptance under the U.C.C., the consumer may obtain a refund despite the fact that the lemon law provides only for a replacement. *See* § 7.03[E], *supra.*

their recovery,[189] while others expressly exclude them.[190] Many statutes, however, are silent on the issue, but allow the consumer to recover such things as "all other reasonable charges"[191] or all "collateral charges"[192] or "related purchase costs"[193] incurred in connection with the purchase of the vehicle. When this is the case, these statutes should be interpreted to include finance charges, because the goal should be to put the consumer in the same position as if he or she had not purchased the vehicle.[194] Such charges would be recoverable under the U.C.C. pursuant to a revocation-of-acceptance remedy,[195] and should be equally available if a refund is sought under the lemon law.

Various statutes also expressly permit the recovery of other damages. For example, the West Virginia lemon law allows recovery of damages "for loss of use, annoyance or inconvenience resulting from the non-conformity" including the cost of reasonable replacement transportation during any period the vehicle is out of service.[196] Significantly, most lemon laws permit a consumer to recover attorney's fees from the manufacturer if it is necessary for the consumer to bring a lawsuit to enforce the provisions of the statute.[197] Even if the statute does not explicitly provide for attorney's fees, they may be recoverable in a concurrent cause of action, such as violation of the state's deceptive practices act or the Magnuson-Moss Federal Warranty Act.

The majority of state lemon laws provide that the relief available under the lemon law is in addition to that available under other state and federal law. Thus, in most jurisdictions, a consumer often can couple a claim under the lemon law with a claim for breach of warranty under the Uniform Commercial Code, a claim for violation of the Magnuson-Moss Federal Warranty Act, and perhaps a claim for violation of the state's deceptive trade practices

---

[189] *See, e.g.,* Ala. Code Ann. § 8-20A-2(b)(3) (1993); Ind. Code Ann. § 24-5-13-11(c)(3) (West 1995).

[190] *See* Ga. Code Ann. § 10-1-782(2) (1997).

[191] *See* W. Va. Code § 46A-6A-4(b)(1) (1995).

[192] *See, e.g.,* Ga. Code Ann. § 10-1-784(a)(4) (1997).

[193] *See* Del. Code Ann. tit. 6, § 5003(c) (1993).

[194] A number of recent cases have permitted a buyer to recover finance charges under these circumstances. *See* Baker v. Chrysler Corp., 9 F.3d 1539 (E.D. Pa. 1993); Hughes v. Chrysler Motors Corp., 188 Wis. 2d 1, 523 N.W.2d 197 (Ct. App. 1994).

[195] *See* U.C.C. § 2-711.

[196] W. Va. Code § 46A-6A-4(b)(3) (1995).

[197] *See, e.g.,* Del. Code Ann. tit. 6, § 5005 (1993); Minn. Stat. Ann. § 325F.665(9) (West 1995); N.J. Stat. Ann. § 56:12-42 (West Supp. 1996); W. Va. Code § 46A-6A-4(4) (1995). In some cases the manufacturer is also entitled to recover attorney's fees if the court finds that the buyer's cause of action was frivolous or brought in bad faith. *See, e.g.,* Del. Code Ann. tit. 6 § 5005 (1993); N.M. Stat. Ann. § 57-16A-9 (1997).

act or consumer sales practices act. In a few states, however, buyers using the state's lemon law are expressly precluded from relying on other causes of action, especially those arising under the Code.[198]

[I] Conclusion

Lemon laws are probably less important today than during the period in which they were initially passed. As a result of competitive pressures, especially from overseas, the quality of automobiles (and other motor vehicles) has improved dramatically during the past ten to fifteen years. Moreover, car manufacturers and dealers are much more willing to "make things right" than they were when the "Big Three" dominated the market. Finally, as mentioned previously, the development of the law under sections 2-719 and 2-608 of the U.C.C. has made it simpler for buyers to obtain a refund or replacement under the Code if they are stuck with a "lemon."[199]

State lemon laws vary widely. This short section has attempted to describe provisions common to many of the statutes and to illustrate how lemon laws impact on rights and remedies available under the Code. Practitioners, however, should carefully consult the lemon law in their individual states because differences between the laws can often be subtle.

---

[198] *See* N.M. Stat. Ann. § 57-16A-5 (1997).
[199] *See* § 9.03[A], *supra.*

CHAPTER 10

THE CONVENTION ON CONTRACTS FOR INTERNATIONAL SALE OF GOODS

§ 10.01   BACKGROUND

[A]   Introduction

The Convention on Contracts for International Sale of Goods (the CISG) was adopted by representatives of 62 countries in April of 1980. The CISG entered into force in the United States on January 1, 1988, and, as of July 1997, has been ratified by forty-eight States (countries).[1]

This text does not purport to present a detailed review of the 101 Articles comprising the CISG. For those who need more detailed treatment of the CISG, we point out that the CISG has been the subject of many articles and texts, along with a growing number of court decisions. We recommend Professor John Honnold's *Uniform Law for International Sales Under the 1980 United Nations Convention* (2d ed. 1991) as an excellent and readable text, filled with illustrations.

[B]   Tests for Application of the CISG

Before the CISG applies, four tests must be met:[2] (1) there must be a contract; (2) the contract must be for a sale; (3) the sale must be of goods; and (4) the parties must have places of business in different States (countries), both of which must have ratified the CISG.[3]

§ 10.02   COVERAGE OF THE CISG

[A]   The Contract

[1]   The Offer: General

The CISG approaches formation of contracts from the basis of offer and acceptance. In many cases, there is no question as to whether a com-

---

[1] The CISG is reproduced in the Appendix to 15 U.S.C.A. There have been few U.S. cases considering the CISG as of the date this chapter was written. There have been several articles and decisions from foreign courts. *See* Review of the Convention on Contracts for the International Sale of Goods (CISG) (edited by Cornell Int. L.J. 1995).

[2] The nationality of the parties is specifically excluded as a test for determining whether the CISG is applicable to a transaction, as is the civil or commercial character of the parties or of the contract. Article 1(3) of the CISG. All references herein to "Articles" are references to Articles of the CISG.

[3] Article 2 of the CISG contains a second test for application: when the choice-of-law rules for a transaction would lead to the law of a country that had ratified the Convention. The United States reserved against this test; thus, it is not a part of the CISG ratified by the Senate.

munication is, or is not, an "offer." A letter that is addressed to a specific person and states, "I will sell you 100,000 bushels of potatoes for $6.00 a bushel, for delivery next Tuesday" is an offer. But a brochure, mailed to a number of people and stating, "I have 100,000 bushels of potatoes for which I am asking $6.00 per bushel," is not an offer. On occasion, however, a communication falls between these extremes. To aid in solving those situations, the CISG adopts the general common-law view in two subsections of Article 14.

[2]   The Offer: Communications to One or More Specific Persons

A proposal for concluding a contract addressed to one or more specific persons constitutes an offer if it is sufficiently definite and indicates the intention of the offeror to be bound in case of acceptance.[4]

There are two requirements: definiteness and "intention" to be bound. As far as intention is concerned, an actual intent is not required; the proposal need only indicate that intention. The "to be bound" language could be read to mean that the offeror must indicate that he is thinking in terms of contract law. This is not required, any more than it has been under common-law cases. A better way to read those words is: "if it is sufficiently definite and indicates the intention of the offeror *to have a deal* in case of acceptance." A proposal is "sufficiently definite" if the proposal: (1) indicates the goods and (2) expressly or implicitly fixes or makes provision for determining the quantity and the price.[5]

A later Article provides that, if a contract has been concluded without expressly or impliedly fixing a price, the price will be the price generally charged for such goods under comparable circumstances in the relevant trade.[6]

[3]   The Offer: Communications to the Public

A proposal other than one addressed to one or more specific persons is to be considered merely as an invitation to make offers, unless the contrary is clearly indicated by the person making the proposal.[7]

---

[4] Article 14(1).

[5] *Id.*

[6] Article 55, discussed subsequently. *See* § 10.03[C][4].

[7] Article 14(2).

The result of these rules is that, at least in a common law country, most of the familiar commercial principles are applicable to determine whether an offer has been made.

[4]   The Acceptance: Unconditional Assent

Article 18 provides that an acceptance can occur either by words or conduct indicating assent to the offer. Thus, a timely response to the offer (set out above) that says, "I agree to buy the 100,000 bushels of potatoes for $6.00 a bushel," is an acceptance. So, too, should be a response, "I will be by on Tuesday to pick up the potatoes." Then, as a caution, the CISG adds: "Silence or inactivity does not in itself amount to acceptance."[8] This sentence should carry into the CISG the common law notion that an offeror cannot force a contract on the offeree by making silence into assent, but the "not in itself" implies that silence may become an acceptance if the offeror, because of additional circumstances, could reasonably have so understood.

[5]   The Acceptance: Assent Plus Additions

All legal systems have had problems developing rules applicable to the transaction in which the parties agree as to the goods and the price but exchange forms containing different terms. The typical case involves the buyer's purchase order (complete with terms protecting the buyer) sent to an overseas seller who responds with an acknowledgment (complete with terms protecting the seller) purporting to accept the purchase order. The transaction may abort, or the goods may be shipped and accepted (or rejected) by the buyer. In the ensuing dispute, if the purchase order controls, the buyer wins; if the acknowledgment controls, the seller wins. Which form controls?

The CISG's answer is Article 19. That Article sets out three rules that should produce the following results:

> (1)   If the reply does not purport to accept the principal terms of the offer, there is no contract, the offer has been rejected, and the deal is off—pending further negotiations.
> (2)   If the reply purports to accept the offer[9] but contains additional or different terms from the offer, and:

---

[8] Article 18. This Article also allows acceptance by conduct. *Cf.* U.CC. § 2-206.

[9] That is, a reply that indicates that the offeree wants to sell (or to buy) the goods described in the offer.

(a) If those additional or different terms do not *materially* alter the terms of the offer, a contract has been formed containing the terms of the offer with the modifications stated in the reply—unless the offeror has, without undue delay, objected to the reply; or

(b) If those additional or different terms materially alter the terms of the offer, no contract has been formed by the documents.

The CISG then states that any additional or different terms that relate, among other things, to any of the following are *material* alterations: (1) the price; (2) the payment; (3) the quality and quantity of the goods; (4) the place and time of delivery; (5) the extent of one party's liability to the other; or (6) the settlement of disputes.

The result of these rules is that the offeror should read what comes back and respond, whether or not the changes are material. If the changes are not material, Rule 2(a) makes them a part of the contract unless there is an objection. If the changes are material and Article 19 is applied literally, the same result will follow if the buyer accepts the goods when shipped.[10]

[6] Moment of Contract

The Uniform Commercial Code places almost no emphasis on when a contract comes into existence. "An agreement sufficient to constitute a contract for sale may be found even though the moment of its making is undetermined."[11] Not so with the CISG. An elaborate sequence is established in Articles 15–24.

Rule 1. An offer becomes effective when it reaches the offeree.

Rule 2. An acceptance becomes effective at the moment indication of assent reaches the offeror,[12] contrary to the "mailbox rule" in the United States.

Rule 3. A contract is formed when the acceptance becomes effective.

---

[10] *See* J. Honnold, Uniform Law for International Sales 236–239 (2d ed. 1991), for an argument that the solution could be based on the gap-filling provisions of the CISG. *See* Article 18(1), which can be used to support either Professor Honnold's argument or the position stated in the text.

[11] U.C.C. § 2-204(2).

[12] A reply (to an offer) that contains only immaterial alterations of the offer is an "acceptance" under Article 19(2), unless the offeror objects without undue delay. Absent objection, a contract would be formed when the reply, with its immaterial alterations, reached the offeror. A reply that contains material alterations is not an acceptance. Article 19(1). Therefore, there would be no contract when that reply reached the offeror even though the reply contained an "indication of assent."

Rule 4. An offer may be revoked, unless it is made irrevocable, if the revocation reaches the offeree before the offeree has dispatched an acceptance.[13]

Rule 5. An acceptance may be withdrawn if the withdrawal reaches the offeror before or at the same time as the acceptance.[14] The posted acceptance can be withdrawn if the withdrawal is timely.

Rule 6. An offer becomes irrevocable if: (1) the offer indicates, by stating a fixed time for acceptance "or otherwise," that it is irrevocable;[15] or (2) it was reasonable for the offeree to rely on the offer, and he did in fact rely.[16]

Rule 7. An irrevocable offer is terminated when a rejection (from the offeree) reaches the offeror.[17] Thus, a May 1 offer that states that it will remain open until May 15 is terminated if, on May 6, the offeree delivers a rejection of the offer. An attempt on May 10 to accept comes too late.

Rule 8. An acceptance is not effective unless it reaches the offeror within the time fixed in the offer or, if no time is fixed, within a reasonable time, considering the facts.[18]

Rule 9. If the offer, the practices between the parties, or trade usage allows acceptance by an act (such as shipping the goods or paying the price) without notice to the offeror, acceptance is effective at the moment the act is performed, provided the act is performed within the period of time stated in the prior paragraph.[19]

Rule 10. "An oral offer must be accepted immediately unless the circumstances indicate otherwise."[20] This elliptical statement must mean that the offer "dies" if not accepted immediately. Thus, the offeree's telephone call an hour later which purports to accept the offer is not effective, unless

---

[13] Article 16(1).

[14] Article 22.

[15] Article 16(2)(a). There is no stated time limit during which the offeror may make his offer irrevocable. The "or otherwise" language makes it clear that an offer may become irrevocable even though it does not explicitly state that it is irrevocable for a fixed time. J. Honnold, Uniform Law for International Sales 207–208 (2d ed. 1991). Does every offer imply that it will be irrevocable for at least long enough for the offeree to respond?

[16] Article 16(2)(b). Recall that an indication of assent must reach the offeree within a reasonable time. Article 18(2). An offer supported by consideration should also be irrevocable under common-law principles.

[17] Article 17. Under common-law principles, an offer supported by consideration would not be terminated by a rejection unless the rejection is followed by reliance or a novation. *See* Restatement (Second) Contracts § 37 (1981).

[18] Article 18(2).

[19] Article 18(3).

[20] Article 18(2).

the circumstances of the offer indicate that the offeree had at least an hour to make up his mind.

Rule 11. In determining the period of time an offeree has to accept an offer, the CISG establishes rules that depend on whether the offer was by telegram, letter, or instantaneous communication.[21] Official holidays and nonbusiness days are included in calculating the period of time; however, if the acceptance cannot be delivered because of a holiday or nonbusiness day of the offeror, the period is extended to the first business day thereafter.[22]

Rule 12. A late acceptance becomes a contract in two instances:

> (1) If the writing containing a late acceptance shows that the delay was caused by the means of transmission (e.g., a letter delayed in the mails), the late-arriving acceptance is effective unless the offeror informs the offeree that he considers the offer as having lapsed.[23]

> (2) In those cases in which a delay in transmission is not apparent, the late-arriving acceptance becomes a contract only if, without delay, the offeror gives notice of his acceptance.[24]

Rule 13. An acceptance "reaches" the addressee when given orally or delivered to his place of business or mailing address, or, if he does not have a place of business or mailing address, to his habitual residence.[25]

[7] Freedom of Contract

The CISG provides the parties with considerable freedom of contract. Because sales of consumer goods are excepted from application of the CISG, the drafters did not include provisions providing special treatment for consumers. Thus, most rights and obligations are subject to negotiation, and any agreement between the parties may limit (or expand) their rights and obligations.[26]

Although the approach of the CISG is similar to the U.C.C., the "good-faith" requirement is more pervasive in the U.C.C. than in the CISG. The reference to good faith in the CISG occurs in Article 7 and provides that, in "the interpretation of this Convention," regard is to be had to "the observance of good faith in international trade." No reference is made to the need for good faith in the formation or performance of a contract for the

---

[21] Article 20(1).
[22] Article 20(2).
[23] Article 21(2).
[24] Article 21(1).
[25] Article 24.
[26] Article 6.

sale of goods. Nevertheless, notions of good faith will find their way into CISG decisions.

[B]   The Sale

[1]   Meaning of "Sale"

The CISG does not define "sale," but by inference from other Articles, it is clear that "sale" includes the passing of title from the seller to the buyer. A contract that does not effect the passing of title ought not be within the CISG. Thus, a distribution agreement that required minimum purchases but did not identify the goods to be sold by type, date, or price is not a "sale" within the CISG.[27] The purchase orders and acknowledgments exchanged pursuant to the distribution agreement could qualify as a sale. This leaves open such questions as to whether consignments, leases, barters, three-corner trades, and security agreements will be brought into CISG coverage, by analogy.

[C]   The Goods

[1]   Meaning of "Goods"

There is no definition of "goods" in the CISG. The U.C.C. defines goods as things that are movable at the time of identification to the contract,[28] and, because both the CISG and the U.C.C. deal with items of commerce, the same meaning will undoubtedly be given to the CISG. Contracts in which the furnishing of labor or services is the "preponderant part" of the obligation of the seller are exempted from coverage.[29] Goods to be manufactured or produced are within the CISG, unless the buyer has undertaken to supply a substantial portion of the materials. In such a case, the "seller" is providing services for the buyer's materials.

[2]   Exclusions From Coverage

1. *Certain sales.* The most notable exclusion from CISG coverage is consumer goods. This exclusion allowed the drafters to emphasize freedom

---

[27] Helen Kaminski Pty. Ltd. v. Marketing Australian Prods., Inc., 1997 U.S. Dist. LEXIS (S.D.N.Y.) 10630.

[28] U.C.C. § 2-105(1). Money in which the price is paid, investment securities, and things in action are excluded.

[29] Article 3(2). A contract solely for services is not governed by the CISG. Oberlandesgericht Köln, Regional Ct. of App. Cologne (Case 19 U 282/93 UNILEX E. 1994–21, p. 355).

of contract in determining the rights and duties of the parties.[30] The other exemptions are sales: by auction; on execution or otherwise by authority of law; of stocks, shares, investment securities, negotiable instruments, or money; of ships, vessels, hovercraft, or aircraft; and of electricity.

2. *Effect on title*. The CISG excludes the effect the contract may have on the property (title) to the goods sold.[31] Claims and disputes involving a good faith purchaser are not governed by the CISG but are left to applicable domestic law.

3. *Death or injury*. The CISG also excludes liability for death or personal injury caused by the goods.[32] This removes product-liability problems that result in death or personal injury from CISG coverage, but it does not remove property damage or economic loss. If a buyer purchases a defective machine from a seller and that machine catches fire and burns the buyer's building, the exclusion set out above would not remove the transaction from CISG coverage.

4. *Exclusion or modification by the parties*. Article 6 allows the parties (1) to exclude the entire CISG from the contract or (2), subject to Article 12, to derogate from, or vary the effect of, any of its provisions.[33] The right to vary the effect of provisions of the CISG grants the parties broad freedom of contract, a grant that could be given once certain transactions (such as consumer sales) were exempted from the CISG's coverage. If the parties do not want a certain Article to apply or if they want to modify that Article, they may do so by their contract. All of which means that lawyers must be familiar with the CISG so they can determine whether it should be varied by the contract.

If the CISG is to be excluded, the contract provision should be something more than the typical choice-of-law clause, but should specifically mention the CISG:

---

[30] *See* Article 2. The exemption for consumer goods is as follows: "goods bought for personal, family or household use, unless the seller, at any time before conclusion [formation] of the contract, neither knew nor ought to have known that the goods were bought for any such use." The "unless" clause covers those cases in which the seller is selling goods that can be used for either commercial or personal use. As to these goods, the seller's knowledge or what the seller should have known becomes pivotal. Such a seller should require the buyer to state the use for which the goods are intended, as could be done through the checking of a box on the order form.

[31] Article 4(b).

[32] Article 5. The producer of the goods sold through retailers should not be liable to the ultimate buyer under provisions of the CISG, because the CISG "governs only the formation of the contract and the rights and obligations *of the seller and the buyer* arising from such a contract." Article 4.

[33] Article 6.

The rights and obligations of the parties to this agreement are to be governed by the law of [Ohio], without reference to [Ohio's] choice-of-law rules, and not by the 1980 United Nations Convention on Contracts for the International Sale of Goods.[34]

The privilege of the parties to derogate from, or to vary the effect of, any of the provisions of the CISG is a broad privilege, subject to but one exception. Article 12 allows an adopting country ("Contracting State" under the CISG) to declare that certain provisions of the CISG that eliminated the need for a writing or other formal requirements are not applicable when any party has his place of business in the adopting country.

[D]   The Parties

[1]   Place-of-Business Requirement

The CISG applies only if the parties to a contract have places of business in different countries.[35] Thus, the CISG, if not excluded by the contract, applies to a transaction in which a retailer with its only place of business Paris, France, orders 1,000 dresses from a manufacturer with its only place of business in New York. And it applies irrespective of the point that title and risk of loss pass to the buyer. There are, however, problems with the place-of-business test.

First, a "place of business" is not a defined term. The existence of corporate headquarters, a sales or purchasing office, a factory, or a substantial warehouse operation should qualify as a "place of business." The more troublesome question is whether some contact less than that will suffice.

Second, suppose a buyer of dresses visits the office of the New York manufacturer of dresses and, while in the office, orders 1,000 dresses. Suppose that, as a matter of fact, the buyer had only one office, and, unknown to the seller, that office was located in Paris, France. Does the CISG apply? To answer this situation, the drafters included Article 1(2):

The fact that the parties have their places of business in different States is to be disregarded whenever this fact does not appear either from the

---

[34] In Oberlandesgericht Düsseldorf (Case 17 U 73/93 UNILEX E. 1993-21, p. 261), the Regional Court of Appeals for Düsseldorf held that, under the German Civil Code, the law of Indiana applied to the contract and that the CISG was a part of the law of Indiana; thus, the "provisions of [the CISG] apply to the contractual matters of the parties." A similar result was reached in Oberlandesgericht Frankfurt a Main, Regional Ct. of App. Frankfurt (Case 5 U 261/90 UNILEX E. 1991, p. 5), applying the CISG through a choice-of-law reference to French law.

[35] Referred to as "States" in the CISG.

contract or from the dealings between, or from information disclosed by, the parties at any time before the conclusion [formation] of the contract.

Based on the facts stated above, the CISG would not apply to the contract. But suppose the buyer spoke with a French accent or gave the seller a card listing the buyer as an importer. Or suppose the seller knows that the buyer is a commission agent, acting for foreign and local principals. Does the CISG apply, or do the parties have to look to conflict of laws rules for the applicable law? These questions, and others that may arise will be answered on a case-by-case basis, using the flexibility of the CISG to reach sensible results.[36]

Finally, the CISG has two tidying-up rules. The first provides a guideline for those cases in which a party has more than one place of business. Suppose that the seller has places of business in France and the United States; the buyer has a place of business in the United States only. The CISG provides this answer:

> If a party has more than one place of business, the place of business is that which has the closest relationship to the contract and its performance, having regard to the circumstances known to or contemplated by the parties at any time before or at the conclusion [formation] of the contract.[37]

The other rule seeks to solve the problem when a party has no place of business by referring to the party's "habitual residence."[38]

---

[36] Flexibility in a statute allows courts to reach sensible results in specific cases. There are differences, however, with flexibility in treaties. For example: (1) a treaty is not easily amended to reverse the result of court decisions; (2) some countries adopting a treaty do not report decisions or give them much, if any, weight—thus, decisions cannot be relied upon; and (3) it will be difficult to discover reported decisions in other countries.

[37] Article 10(a). Another application of this Article and the Article mentioned in the following footnote is to determine whether the CISG is applicable if one place of business of a party is in a country that has approved the CISG, and another of its places of business is in a country that has not approved the CISG.

The reference to circumstances known to the parties could raise evidentiary problems that would be treated differently by different court systems. For example, how is the parol-evidence rule treated in countries placing an even greater reliance (than does the United States) on the written word?

[38] Article 10(b).

[2]   The Sale Must Be Between the Parties

A contract for the sale of goods between *ABC* Co. and *XYZ* Co. (both with their place of business in the United States) does not come within the CISG even though *XYZ* Co. is a subsidiary of a company with its place of business in Germany. The *parties* to the contract do not have places of business in countries which have adopted the CISG.

§ 10.03   OBLIGATIONS OF THE PARTIES

[A]   Provisions Applicable to Buyers and Sellers

[1]   Fundamental Breach

The CISG contemplates two kinds of defaults—those that are "fundamental" and those that are not. More remedies (including avoidance of the contract) are available to a party if the other party has committed a fundamental breach than if the default is less than fundamental. It is tempting to equate a "fundamental" breach under the CISG with a "material" breach under common law. There is, however, a difference.

The CISG defines a "fundamental breach" as one that results in substantially depriving a party of what that party is entitled to expect under the contract, "unless the party in breach did not foresee and a reasonable person of the same kind in the same circumstances would not have foreseen such a result."[39] If there was no substantial deprivation[40] *or* if the foreseeability of the result test is not met, there is no fundamental breach.

Cure may prevent a default from becoming "fundamental." As is discussed subsequently,[41] the CISG provides for a right to cure until the delivery date[42] and, under certain circumstances, after the delivery date.[43] If the contract called for the delivery of a machine and the machine was delivered with a defective part, cure may prevent the default from substantially depriving the buyer of what he was entitled to expect from the contract.[44] An offer of refund or price adjustment may also prevent a default from becoming "fundamental."[45]

---

[39] Article 25.

[40] Bundesgerichtshof (BGH) (Case VIII ZR 51/95 E. 1996 p. 549).

[41] Section 10.03[B][9], *infra*.

[42] Article 37.

[43] Article 48.

[44] J. Honnold, Uniform Law for International Sales 375–377 (2d ed. 1991).

[45] *Id*. at 214–215.

This discussion has been limited to the meaning of a fundamental breach—the breach that allows a party to avoid the contract. The remedies for breach are discussed under the sections dealing with remedies. However, any breach—no matter how trivial—allows a party to recover damages.

[2] Modification and Termination

No consideration is needed to modify or terminate an agreement.[46]

[3] No Oral Modification Clauses

Few lawyers can draft a contract or a form without adding that the document cannot be modified orally. Both the U.C.C. and the CISG pay lip service to the enforceability of such a provision, creating a private statute of frauds, but both provide a large loophole. The U.C.C. talks in terms of waiver;[47] the CISG in terms of reliance: "However, a party may be precluded by his conduct from asserting such a provision to the extent that the other party has relied on that conduct."[48]

[4] Notice of Avoidance

The U.C.C. requires notice of rejection[49] and notice of revocation of acceptance,[50] which permit a buyer to "avoid" the contract in the event of a breach by the seller. Earlier drafts of a proposed international uniform sales law[51] gave a party the right to avoid a contract without notice to the defaulting party. This provision was altered in the CISG so that a "declaration of avoidance is effective only if made by notice to the other party."[52]

---

[46] Article 29(1). The language of this Article is broader than the statement in the text: "A contract may be modified or terminated by the mere agreement of the parties." However, courts do not enforce a modification (or termination) just because the parties *agreed*. If that agreement resulted from duress or fraud, the courts will find a way to hold that the "agreement" did not amount to a modification. Thus, the text statement is probably the more accurate way of expressing, to a U.C.C. lawyer, the principle in this Article. *Cf.* U.C.C. § 2-209. Termination agreements are normally supported by consideration because both parties have given up rights.

[47] U.C.C. § 2-209(4).

[48] Article 29(2). There is no indication that the reliance must be reasonable.

[49] U.C.C. § 2-602(1).

[50] U.C.C. § 2-608(2). *See also* U.C.C. § 2-607(3); after acceptance, the failure by buyer to give timely notice to the seller bars the buyer from any remedy.

[51] 1968 Hague Convention on Sales. The draft is referred to as the "ULIS."

[52] Article 26. *See* Articles 81–84.

There are other notice requirements in chapters dealing with specific obligations of the parties. These are discussed in their appropriate places.

[5] Transmission Errors

Several CISG Articles require notice be given to a party, as, for example, the requirement of notice of avoidance.[53] Article 27 of the CISG provides that, "if any notice, request or other communication is given or made by a party *in accordance with this Part* and by means appropriate in the circumstances," a delay or error in transmission (or in its failure to arrive) does not deprive the party giving the notice of the right to rely on the communication.

Article 27 (included in Part III of the CISG) does not apply to notice requirements under other Parts of the CISG. Thus, the Part II rule that an acceptance is not effective if it does not "reach" the offeree within a stated time is not affected by Article 27.

Several Articles in Part III modify Article 27 and require receipt of the notice. Before relying on Article 27, the type of notice or communication involved must be checked against the CISG to determine whether an exception applies and receipt of the notice is required.[54]

[6] Grant of Specific Performance

The CISG provides specific performance as the general remedy for the nondefaulting party.[55] As a concession to common-law countries, Article 28 provides that "a court is not bound to enter a judgment of specific performance unless the court would do so under its own law in respect of similar contracts of sale not governed by this Convention."[56]

[B] Obligations of the Seller

[1] Introduction

The seller has three basic obligations: (1) to deliver the goods; (2) to hand over documents relating to the goods; and (3) to transfer the title to

---

[53] *See* § 10.04[B][4].

[54] *See, e.g.,* Articles 47(2), 48(4), 63(2), 65, and 79(4).

[55] Article 46(1) for the nondefaulting buyer and Article 62 for the nondefaulting seller.

[56] The reference to "its own law" does not include a reference to choice-of-law rules. J. Honnold, Uniform Law for International Sales 272–277 (2d ed. 1991).

the goods—all as required by the contract and by the CISG.[57] Thus, both the contract between the parties and the terms of the CISG are important in determining the obligations of the seller.

[2] Time of Delivery

Three CISG rules determine when delivery must be made.

Rule 1: If the contract fixes a date ("June 15, 2000") or if a date can be determined from the contract ("two weeks after production begins"), the goods must be delivered on that date.[58]

Rule 2: If a period of time is fixed by the contract ("between June 15 and June 30, 2000") or if a period of time can be determined from the contract ("any time within one month after production begins"), the goods must be delivered at any time during that period, unless the circumstances indicate that the buyer is to choose a date.[59] In the latter case, we assume that this puts the contract under Rule 1, but the CISG is silent as to what happens.

Rule 3: In any other case, the goods must be delivered within a reasonable time after the conclusion (formation) of the contract.[60]

[3] How to Make Delivery

With contracts involving carriers—the most common situation in international sales—delivery is made by "handing the goods over to the first carrier for transmission to the buyer."[61] The "handing over" also requires the seller to make such contract with the carrier as is appropriate and according to the usual terms for such transportation.[62] This entails selecting the appropriate type of carrier and route, submitting proper bills of lading, obtaining insurance (if the seller's obligation), and providing for care of the goods in transit. If the seller is not to provide the insurance, the seller must, at the buyer's request, provide all available information necessary to enable the buyer to obtain insurance.[63] If the goods are not clearly identified to the

---

[57] Article 30.

[58] Article 33(1).

[59] Article 33(2).

[60] Article 33(3).

[61] Article 31(a). *See* § 10.05[A], *infra. See* Article 67. The concept of "handing" the goods to a carrier indicates that this Article does not apply when the seller is delivering the goods by its own trucks.

[62] Article 32(2).

[63] Article 32(3).

contract (by markings on the goods, shipping documents, or otherwise) when handed over to the carrier, the seller must give the buyer notice of the consignment, specifying the goods.[64] Failure to comply with these requirements could affect the risk of loss.

In situations not involving either the carriage of goods or a seller who is bound to deliver to a specific location, delivery is to be made (1) in the case of specific goods, or goods to be drawn from a specific stock of goods, or goods to be manufactured, and, at the time of the contract formation, the parties [the buyer (?)] knew that the goods were at, or were to be manufactured at, a particular place—delivery is to be made by placing the goods at the buyer's disposal at that place;[65] and (2) in other cases, delivery is made by placing the goods at the buyer's place of business, to be determined as of the time of the formation of the contract.[66]

[4] Delivery of Documents

Many international sales involve the delivery of documents, often with a letter of credit supplied by the buyer. When the seller is bound to deliver documents relating to the goods, he must hand them over at the time and place and in the form required by the contract.[67] The same Article provides a right to cure nonconforming documents when the cure does not cause the buyer unreasonable expense or unreasonable inconvenience. The cure provisions discussed in § 10.03[B][9] are broad enough to allow cure in defective documents under the terms stated there.

[5] Conformity of the Goods

The seller must deliver goods which are of the quantity, quality and description required by the contract and which are contained or packaged in the manner required by the contract.[68]

The CISG test of conformity is to determine what is "required by the contract." This language should carry most of the express warranty ideas familiar to U.C.C. attorneys. However, when the above-quoted quality test is combined with the CISG rule as to when a contract is formed ("A contract

---

[64] Article 32(1).

[65] Article 31(b).

[66] Article 31(c).

[67] Article 34.

[68] Article 35(1). For early deliveries and over-deliveries, *see* § 10.04[13].

is concluded at the moment an acceptance of an offer becomes effective"[69]), apparently the seller's brochures, advertisements, and statements not known to the buyer at, or prior to, the moment of contract would not become a part of the contract. One hope for the buyer is:

> A contract may be modified or terminated by the mere agreement of the parties.[70]

The buyer's argument would have to be that, after the moment of contract, he saw the brochure or advertisement or heard about the statement and, in reliance thereon, did not seek to return the goods. The buyer could reasonably argue that the brochure or advertisement was analogous to a post-contract modification proposal by the seller that was accepted by the conduct (reliance) of the buyer.

The CISG continues the seller's obligations by providing four quality tests. The goods do not "conform" unless the goods:

(1)   Are fit for the purposes for which goods of the same description would ordinarily be used (roughly, the merchantability warranty of the U.C.C.);[71]

(2)   Are fit for any particular purpose expressly or impliedly made known to the seller at the time of the formation of the contract, unless the circumstances show that the buyer did not rely, or that it was unreasonable for the buyer to rely, on the seller's skill and judgment (roughly, the particular purpose warranty of the U.C.C.);

(3)   Possess the qualities of any sample or model of the goods (one of the express warranties under the U.C.C.); and·

(4)   Are contained or packaged in the manner usual for such goods or, where there is no such manner, in a manner adequate to preserve and protect the goods[72] (one of the U.C.C. tests for merchantability).

The Article listing these four qualities begins with "Except where the parties have agreed otherwise." Thus, any of the four required qualities of the goods and their packaging may be changed by contract.[73] The Article

---

[69] Article 23.

[70] Article 29(1).

[71] The German Federal Court of Appeals has held that, absent special circumstances, conformity of the goods is to be measured by the standards of the seller's country. Bundesgerichtshof (BGH), German Fed. Ct. of App. (Case VII ZR 159/94 UNILEX 1995-9 p. 441).

[72] Article 35(2).

[73] This carries the U.C.C.'s idea of disclaimers, but without the prescribed protective language of U.C.C. § 2-316.

concludes with the statement that, if the buyer knew or could not have been unaware of the lack of conformity, the seller is not liable for a default of the applicable standard set out above.[74]

[6] Disclaimers

The CISG does not have an Article restricting the use of disclaimers in contracts for the sale of goods. To the contrary, it provides the parties with broad freedom to make their own contract. The restraint on this freedom may be found in Article 4(a) which excludes the "validity" of the contract from coverage. While disclaimers ought not be considered provisions going to the contract's validity, unconscionability might. Thus, the U.C.C. rules as to unconscionability may find application to a commercial international sale.[75] Other local rules may also limit the principles discussed above.[76]

[7] Time of Conformity

Suppose that a seller has warranted that a machine sold to the buyer will produce 1,000 fillups (whatever those may be) per hour. At what point in time must that machine be able to produce those 1,000 fillups per hour?

The answer of the CISG, subject to an exception, is that the lack of conformity must exist "at the time when the risk passes to the buyer, even though the lack of conformity becomes apparent only after that time."[77] Thus, the buyer must show that the machine would not have produced 1,000 fillups per hour at the time the risk shifted to the buyer—for example, when the machine was delivered to the first carrier. The one exception is contained in Article 36(2):

> The seller is also liable for any lack of conformity which occurs after the time indicated in the preceding paragraph and which is due to a breach of any of his obligations, including a breach of any guarantee that for a period of time the goods will remain fit for their ordinary purpose or for some particular purpose or will retain specified qualities or characteristics.

---

[74] Article 35(3). The CISG contains Articles that use such language as "knows," "ought to have known," and "could not have been unaware." In theory, these are gradations of what might be learned by an inspection of the goods. There is, however, little practical difference between the second and the third.

[75] U.C.C. § 2-302.

[76] *See* J. Honnold, Uniform Law for International Sales 309–318 (1991) for other examples.

[77] Article 36(1).

If this exception is limited to its guarantee language, there is no problem with the idea expressed. If the seller says that, given proper care and maintenance, the machine will produce those 1,000 fillups per hour for the first year after installation, the time for testing conformity should be (and is) extended. The problem is created because extension of the time for measuring conformity is not limited to guarantees of product quality. A guarantee is stated as an example of the broader language: "which is due to a breach of any of his obligations." Until there are decisions interpreting what those words include, sellers should state, in writing, the time for testing conformity. For example: "Seller warrants that the goods will be free from defects in material and workmanship *at the time the risk of loss passes to the buyer*."

[8] Effect of Specifications

If a contract provides that the buyer is to furnish specifications of the goods and he does not do so within the time stated (or a reasonable time if no time is stated), the seller may establish the specifications and notify the buyer. If the buyer does not respond timely, the specifications established by the seller are binding.[78]

[9] The Seller's Right to Cure

Under Article 37, a seller may cure a nonconforming tender *up to the date set for delivery*, provided that the cure "does not cause the buyer unreasonable inconvenience or unreasonable expense."[79] Under Article 48, the seller may, even after the delivery date, "remedy at his own expense any failure to perform his obligations, if he can do so without unreasonable delay and without causing the buyer unreasonable inconvenience or uncertainty of reimbursement by the seller of expenses advanced by the buyer."[80] The buyer retains any right to damages provided in the CISG. Article 37, however, must be read in connection with the CISG's notion that parties should have additional time to perform their obligations, including the right

---

[78] Article 65.

[79] Article 37. "For example, the buyer should be able to reject a proposal to repair a machine in its place in the buyer's assembly line when that would seriously interfere with assembly operations; in these circumstances only a prompt replacement of the machine might be permitted." J. Honnold, Uniform Law for International Sales 323 (1991).

[80] The Article 48 cure provision is subject to Article 49, which gives a buyer the right to avoid the contract.

of a seller to remedy nonconforming goods after the performance date, subject to some limitations.[81]

The CISG does not deal expressly with the question of whether the cure tender must conform 100 percent to the contract. Suppose that the fillup-producing machine delivered by the seller would produce only 10 fillups per hour, when the contract called for 1,000 fillups per hour. Such a default would undoubtedly be fundamental, allowing the buyer to avoid the contract, absent cure. Suppose that the seller then "cured" by delivering a second machine that produced 999 fillups per hour. Could the buyer avoid the contract and reject the second machine? If we assume that the second machine could not have been rejected if it had been the subject of the first delivery, we then have the question: must the cure tender conform 100 percent to the contract? The answer will come on a case-by-case basis, with emphasis on the delay in delivery, the number of attempts to cure, the needs of the buyer, and the degree of nonconformity. However, it seems safe to predict that a 100 percent perfect cure is not required.

[10] Examination and Notice by the Buyer

The CISG requires the buyer to examine (inspect) the goods within as short a period as is practicable under the circumstances. In a carriage contract, the examination may be deferred until the goods arrive at their destination, including the destination of redispatched goods if the seller knew or ought to have known that the goods would be redispatched.[82]

Stating this idea as a *requirement*[83] is strange. Failure by the buyer to examine creates no cause of action in the seller. What is meant is that, if the buyer fails to give certain notices to the seller (notices that normally follow examination), some of the buyer's rights are lost. Failure to give notice prevents the buyer from avoiding the contract[84] or requiring the seller to repair the goods.[85] Article 39 spells out the most dramatic impact of the failure of timely notice: the buyer loses his right to rely on a claim of nonconformity unless he gives notice "specifying the nature of the lack of conformity" within a reasonable time after discovery or after he should have

---

[81] Article 48(1).

[82] Article 38.

[83] The CISG language is that the "buyer *must* examine the goods, or cause them to be examined within as short a period as is practicable in the circumstances." Article 38(1). Oberlandesgericht Düsseldorf, Regional Ct. of App. Düsseldorf (Case 17 U 82/92 1993-2, p. 127).

[84] Article 26.

[85] Article 46(3).

discovered the nonconformity[86] (which an examination would, in most cases, have revealed), or, in any event, within two years after the date on which the goods were handed over to the buyer—unless the contractual guarantee extends the time.[87] The "handed over" language extends the time beyond the date the risk of loss is normally shifted in overseas shipments.

Article 40 contains an exception to the examination and notice requirements. It will most certainly be used by many buyers who do not examine promptly or who fail to give timely notice.

> The seller is not entitled to rely on the provisions of articles 38 and 39 if the lack of conformity relates to facts of which he knew or could not have been unaware and which he did not disclose to the buyer.[88]

[11] Third-Party Claims

Article 4 states that the CISG does not apply to the effect that the contract may have on the property (title) in the goods sold. Thus, protection of good-faith purchasers is left to local law. Nevertheless, the CISG does have provisions dealing with some title concepts.

First, the seller must deliver goods free from any right or claim (other than industrial or intellectual property rights and claims, discussed in the following paragraph) of a third party, unless the buyer has agreed to take the goods subject to such right or claim. The CISG is not clear as to whether the claim must be a valid claim before the seller is in default of this "warranty."

Second, the seller must deliver goods free from any third-party industrial or intellectual property right or claim (a) *of which the seller is aware or could not have been unaware* at the time of contract formation, and (b) the right or claim is based on the law of the country:

(1) Where the property is resold or used, or, in any other case, where the buyer has a place of business, provided that the parties contemplated (at the time of contract formation) that the goods would be resold or used in that country, or

(2) In other cases, where the buyer has his place of business.[89]

---

[86] Landgericht Munchen (Case: 17 HKO 3726/89 1989-2, p. 5).

[87] If the buyer had a "reasonable excuse" for the failure to give notice, the buyer may nevertheless recover damages, except for lost profits. Article 44. *Cf.* U.C.C. § 2-607(3), which does not contain the "reasonable excuse" language. Because Article 44 refers to Article 39(1) and not Article 39(2), the "reasonable excuse" does not affect the two-year limitation on notice.

[88] For the notice requirement in cases involving third-party claims, *see* § 10.03[B][11].

[89] Article 42(1). *Cf.* U.C.C. § 2-312(3).

Thus, if an Ohio seller sells 10,000 fillups to a Paris buyer who takes those fillups to Germany for resale only to find that the sale in Germany infringed a German patent, the seller would be in default of his obligations under this Article only if the parties contemplated a resale in Germany.[90]

The title obligations of the seller are subject to two exceptions. These are those situations in which (1) the buyer knew or could not have been unaware of the right or claim;[91] or (2) the right or claim resulted from the seller's compliance with specifications furnished by the buyer.[92]

There is a third point that might be viewed as an additional exception to the seller's title obligation, but is more properly classified as a condition to recovery. Unless the buyer gives the seller notice, specifying the nature of the third party's right or claim, within a reasonable time after the buyer became aware, or ought to have become aware, of the right or claim, the buyer loses his right to claim a title defect—unless the seller knew of the right or claim and was aware of its nature.[93]

[C]   Obligations of the Buyer

[1]   Introduction

The buyer is obligated to pay the price and take delivery as required by the contract and the CISG.[94]

[2]   Payment of the Price

So far as the price obligation is concerned, the buyer must take such steps and comply with such formalities as may be required under the contract and any laws and regulations to enable payment.[95] If permission of some governmental authority is needed to make the payment, it is the buyer's obligation to obtain that permission.

The price is due at the time fixed by the contract and the CISG, without demand from the seller.[96] If the contract is silent as to the time of payment, the price is due when the seller places either the goods or documents in the

---

[90] The "awareness" test must also be met. As to the seller's right to cure third-party claims, *see* J. Honnold, Uniform Law for International Sales 323 (2d ed. 1991).
323.

[91] Article 42(2)(a). *Cf.* U.C.C. § 2-312(2) for a narrower exclusion.

[92] Article 42(2)(b).

[93] Article 43(1). If the buyer had a "reasonable excuse" for the failure to give notice, the buyer may nevertheless recover damages, except for his lost profits. Article 44.

[94] Article 54.

[95] Article 54.

[96] Article 59.

buyer's control.[97] As might be expected, the seller may make the payment of the price a condition to the delivery of documents.

[3] Place of Payment

The place of payment may be set by contract, but if the contract does not spell out the place:

(1) If payment is to be made against the handing over of the goods or documents, the place of payment is to be the place where the goods or documents are handed over to the buyer.

(2) Otherwise, the payment is to be made at the seller's place of business, and the seller must pay for any increased costs of the buyer caused by a change in the seller's place of business after the formation of the contract.[98]

[4] Contracts That Do Not Fix the Price

Article 55 provides the rules when the contract does not fix the price:

> Where a contract has been validly concluded but does not expressly or implicitly fix or make provision for determining the price, the parties are considered, in the absence of any indication to the contrary, to have impliedly made reference to the price generally charged at the time of the conclusion [formation] of the contract for such goods sold under comparable circumstances in the trade concerned.

If the price is set based on the weight of the goods, net weight is to be used "in case of doubt."[99] One point that Article 55 makes clear is that it is not the seller's price that controls; it is the price generally charged under comparable circumstances in the trade concerned. There is, however, a problem in reading Article 55 in connection with Article 14.

---

[97] Article 58(1). This provision is inconsistent with Article 58(3), which allows the buyer an opportunity to examine the goods before he is liable to pay the price. The inconsistency will not affect many international sales because Article 58(1) begins with "If the buyer is not bound to pay the price at any other specific time" and Article 58(3) ends with "unless the procedures for delivery or payment agreed upon by the parties are inconsistent with his having such an opportunity [to examine before payment]." Many export sales are by letter of credit, with payment due on delivery of documents. That procedure eliminates the operation of Article 58(3). However, in the case in which nothing is said about the time of payment, these two sections are inconsistent.

[98] Article 57.

[99] Article 56.

Article 14 states that an offer is sufficiently definite if it indicates the goods "and expressly or implicitly fixes or makes provision for determining the quantity and the price." From Article 14, we learn that, before a proposal can become the basis for forming a contract, it must fix the price, either expressly or implicitly. From Article 55, we learn that a contract can be concluded even though no price has been fixed, either expressly or implicitly. These Articles appear inconsistent.

The difference may be more apparent than real. Article 14 deals with the offer. An offer that does not fix or make provision for the price is not sufficiently definite to become a contract upon "acceptance." But once the contract has been "validly concluded," Article 55 supplies the price term. The contract can be validly concluded if the parties go on after the exchange of documents and treat the transaction as a contract as, for example, if the seller ships and the buyer accepts the goods. These two Articles require further interpretation by the courts.

[5] Delivery Obligations of the Buyer

As far as delivery is concerned, the CISG provides that the buyer must (1) do all acts reasonably expected to enable the seller to make delivery and (2) take over (possession of) the goods.[100] The obligation to take delivery is important in overseas contracts. Failure to take delivery can increase demurrage charges for the seller. Also, as is pointed out subsequently, a failure to take delivery is a breach of contract and a basis for shifting the risk of the loss of the goods.[101]

§ 10.04   REMEDIES FOR BREACH OF CONTRACT

[A]   Provisions Applicable to Buyers and Sellers

[1]   Introduction

Rather than providing one group of principles for buyers and another group for sellers, the CISG contains four Articles that state compensation principles applicable to both the buyer and the seller. These principles, set out subsequently, are treated in greater detail in the discussion of the remedies of the buyer and seller.

---

[100] Article 60.
[101] Article 69.

[2] Damages

Article 74 states the basic measure of damages for both parties: the loss the party suffered, including lost profits, as a consequence of the default. Those damages "may not exceed the loss which the party in breach foresaw or ought to have foreseen at the time of the conclusion [formation] of the contract, in light of the facts and matters of which he then knew or ought to have known, as a possible consequence of the breach of contract."[102] This, of course, is the familiar test of *Hadley v. Baxendale*.[103] The difficulty in applying this test literally is that most businesspeople do not foresee any kind of loss when they enter into contracts. This issue is further discussed in § 5.04[D][1].

[3] Cover and Resale

If a CISG contract has been avoided[104] and, within a reasonable time and in a reasonable manner after avoidance, the buyer has purchased replacement goods or the seller has resold the goods, the party claiming damages may recover the difference between the contract price and the price in the substitute transaction, as well as any further damages recoverable under Article 74.[105] This is a sensible approach to damages—to allow a party to enter into a substitute transaction with some assurance that the loss on that transaction will measure the recovery. In many civil-law countries, this is the preferred measure of damages. It is similar to the cover and resale remedies of the U.C.C.[106] Troublesome factual issues that surround any test of reasonableness still remain. For disputes arising in U.S. courts, U.C.C. decisions should be helpful in deciding what is "reasonable."

[4] Current Price as a Measure of Recovery

If the contract has been avoided[107] and no substitute transaction was entered into, the nondefaulting party may recover the difference between the contract price and the "current price" at the time of avoidance, as well as any further damages recoverable under Article 74, unless the party retained the goods.[108] In the latter event, the current price (from which the contract

---

[102] *Cf.* Article 25, discussed *supra*.

[103] 9 Ex. 341, 156 Eng. Rep. 145 (1854).

[104] *See* § 10.06[B].

[105] Article 75. Although the Article refers to "contract price," the only sensible application is to use the *unpaid* contract price.

[106] U.C.C. § 2-706 (seller); U.C.C. § 2-712 (buyer).

[107] Sections 10.04[B][4], 10.04[C][3], and 10.09[A].

[108] Article 76(1). *See* § 10.03[B][9] for discussion of lost profits.

price is subtracted) is determined as of the time of the "taking over" of the goods.

The place at which the current price is to be determined is the place where delivery of the goods should have been made (in most overseas shipments, where the goods are handed over to the first carrier),[109] with a proviso that if there is no current price at that place, a reasonable substitute can be used.[110]

[5] Mitigation

Article 77 requires a party relying on a default to take such measures as are reasonable in the circumstances to mitigate the loss, including a claim for lost profits, resulting from the default. This principle is inartfuly stated in terms of a duty (*"must* take such measures") even though the nondefaulting party has no right against the defaulting party if those measures are not taken. Any supposed language problem is corrected by the next sentence.

> If he fails to take such measures, the party in breach may claim a reduction in damages in the amount by which the loss should have been mitigated.

Because of the way this sentence is written ("the party in breach may claim a reduction"), the defaulting party should bear the burden of proof as to whether the damages could have been mitigated and, if so, the amount of the reduction.

[B] Buyer's Remedies

[1] Introduction

Article 45 lists the buyer's remedies on default by the seller. The buyer may exercise the rights provided in Articles 46 to 52 and claim damages as provided in Articles 74 to 77. The same Article adds that no period of grace is to be granted to a seller when the buyer resorts to a remedy for default and that the right to *damages* is not precluded by the exercise of any other remedy. Some remedies are, however, precluded by the exercise of a remedy that is inconsistent with other remedies.

This section discusses, first, those remedies that rest on situations in which the buyer has refused to accept the goods because of a default by the

---

[109] Article 31.

[110] Article 76(2). In most cases involving international sales, the place of tender and the place where delivery is to be made are the same. *See* Article 31.

seller: rejection, avoidance, cover, and restitution. The second group of sections deals with remedies designed to require the seller to deliver the goods as required by the contract: specific performance, delivery of substitute goods, repair, and reduction of the price. The third group examines the buyer's monetary recoveries: damages and mitigation. Finally, a section is included to show the CISG's treatment of early deliveries and over-deliveries.

Before presenting the buyer's remedies, it is necessary to examine the CISG's provision on the buyer's privilege to extend the time in which the seller has to perform his obligations. The exercise of this privilege may affect the remedy available.

[2] Additional Time to Perform

Article 47(1) has an impact on the buyer's remedies by providing that the "buyer may fix an additional period of time of reasonable length for performance by the seller of his obligations." Why would a buyer give a seller additional time to perform? Why not treat the failure to deliver as a breach and proceed to the buyer's remedies? The most obvious reason is that most buyers want performance, not a lawsuit. However, no statute or treaty is needed to inform the parties that they can work out their own problems if they so desire.

There is another reason why a buyer might want to give the seller additional time to perform. Suppose that the seller did not deliver goods by the date called for in the contract. Should the buyer be able to avoid the contract because he has not received the goods on the appointed date? He can if the delay amounts to a fundamental breach, but time is not always of the essence in the sale of goods. Thus, the CISG provides for the buyer's fixing an additional time of reasonable length, and, if delivery is not made within that time (or if the seller declares that he will not deliver the goods within the period fixed by the buyer),[111] the buyer may then avoid the contract.[112] At this point, the buyer knows that he is no longer obligated to pay the price and that he may pursue his avoidance remedies.

The language of Article 47(1) is broad enough to apply to another type of case—that in which the buyer received nonconforming goods. In such a case, the buyer may fix an additional time for performance, but it does not follow that a failure by the seller to deliver conforming goods gives the

---

[111] Article 47(2).
[112] Article 49(1).

buyer a right to avoid the contract. Such a buyer may avoid the contract only if the nonconformity amounts to a fundamental breach.[113]

The fact that the buyer has fixed an additional period of time for the seller's performance does not deprive the buyer of any damage claim—even if the seller performs during that period.[114] The granting of additional time by the buyer does not convert late performance into performance within the contract.[115]

[3] Rejection

The U.C.C. concept of rejection and revocation of acceptance is treated through "avoidance." "Rejection" is, however, mentioned in Article 86 in the sense of refusing to keep the goods, which is another result of avoiding the contract.

Article 86(1) provides that a buyer who has *received* the goods and intends to reject them under a right granted by the contract or the CISG must take such steps to preserve them as are reasonable under the circumstances. This Article applies only if the buyer has *received* the goods. If the goods were shipped by a negotiable bill of lading "to the order of the Seller" and if the seller has not endorsed the bill of lading to the buyer, the buyer has not *received* the goods and has no obligation to preserve the goods under Article 86(1). If, however, the bill of lading had been for delivery "to the Buyer," the buyer has *received* the goods when they reached the buyer, and Article 86(1) is applicable.

Article 86(1) allows the buyer to retain the goods until he has been reimbursed for his "reasonable expenses" by the seller. This allows the buyer to keep possession until the seller has paid the buyer the reasonable preservation expenses. The question left open is whether the term "expenses" includes any partial payments made by the buyer to the seller. Granting that right to the buyer does not take much license with the language of the CISG, especially when combined with the principle that the nondefaulting party should not be damaged by the default.[116]

Article 86(2) requires the rejecting buyer to take possession of the goods on behalf of the seller if the goods have been *placed at his disposal*

---

[113] Article 49(1)(a). Article 49(1)(b) is not applicable because that subsection is limited to nondelivery. *Cf.* § 10.03[B][9].

[114] Article 47(2).

[115] The transaction between the parties may amount to an accord. Article 29. The notices must be analyzed to determine whether the buyer has fixed a time for performance or has agreed to a new delivery date as the contract date.

[116] Article 74.

at their destination.[117] Goods may be placed at the disposal of the buyer even though he has not "received" them. The idea is that it is preferable for the buyer to be obligated to preserve the goods than to require a remote seller to assume that duty. There are, however, notable exceptions to the Article 86(2) duty. The buyer need not take possession if (1) the buyer must pay the price to obtain possession (as he would with a bill of lading and sight draft calling for payment in exchange for the bill of lading); (2) the buyer can obtain possession only with unreasonable inconvenience or expense; or (3) if the seller (or his authorized agent) is present at the point of delivery.

[4] Avoidance of the Contract

Article 49 deals with the right of a buyer to avoid the contract. Avoidance, however, is not a remedy in the sense that specific performance and damages are remedies. Instead, avoidance is a decision made by the buyer that opens and closes certain remedies for the buyer and affects certain rights and obligations of the seller.

The buyer may elect to "avoid" the contract in two instances: first, if the default by the seller is "fundamental";[118] or, second, in the case of a nondelivery, if the seller either does not deliver the goods within the extended time properly fixed by the buyer or states that the seller will make no delivery within that time period.[119] In either event, the default must be substantial; trivial defaults do not allow the international transaction to be terminated.

One result of avoidance is that it releases both parties from their contractual obligations, subject to any damages that may be due.[120] Thus, the buyer who avoids the contract cannot pursue specific performance but retains his claim to damages. The buyer, faced with an Article 49(1) default by his seller, must be careful not to avoid a contract the buyer wants to enforce.

The buyer's right to avoid a contract will be lost unless the buyer gives notice to the seller within a reasonable time.[121] The commencement of the

---

[117] Such a buyer assumes the rights and obligations of a buyer under Article 86(1).

[118] Article 49(1)(a). A fundamental breach is defined in Article 25.

[119] Article 49(1)(b). Can the failure to deliver, in and of itself, be a fundamental breach that allows avoidance, or must the additional period be fixed and not met? The way the Article is constructed indicates that avoidance is available for a nondelivery only if the additional time period is fixed by the buyer, but the history of the Article indicates that, given the right set of facts, the failure to deliver can be a fundamental breach. J. Honnold, Uniform Laws for International Sales 368–372, 382–385 (1991).

[120] Article 81.

[121] Bundesgerichtshof (BGH), German Fed. Ct. of App. (Case VIII ZR 18/94 UNILEX D. 1995-6, p. 427).

reasonable time period varies depending on whether a late delivery or some other default gave rise to the right of avoidance.[122]

[5] The Substitute Purchase

A buyer that has avoided a contract and, within a reasonable time and in a reasonable manner after avoidance, has purchased replacement goods may recover the difference between the contract price and the price in the substitute transaction, "as well as any further damages recoverable under Article 74."[123] This is a sensible approach to damages—to allow a party to enter into a substitute transaction with some assurance that the loss on that transaction will measure the recovery. In many civil law countries, this is the preferred measure of damages. It is similar to the cover remedy of the U.C.C.,[124] but leaves open the same problem that the U.C.C. left open.

Suppose that the seller agreed to sell 10,000 fillups to the buyer for $20,000. At the time set for delivery, the fillups had a market value of $25,000. The seller failed to deliver. The buyer was able to purchase 10,000 fillups for $22,000. Is the cover measure mandatory once the buyer has purchased substitute goods (thus limiting the buyer to $2,000), or may the buyer ignore that measure and recover the $5,000 under the general damage rules? The answer is not clear under either the U.C.C. or the CISG. However, the reference in Article 74 to "loss" rather than to market price suggests that the CISG will be read to take the sensible approach and allow only the $2,000.

There is also the factual problem of whether the purchase was "in replacement" of the contract with the seller or whether the buyer was fulfilling normal requirements. This factual issue cannot be solved by any treaty or statute.[125]

[6] Restitution

A buyer may elect to "avoid" a contract under the conditions stated in Article 49. One effect of a proper avoidance is to give the buyer a right of restitution.[126] Restitution seeks to "unwind" a transaction—to put the parties back to where they were financially before the contract was formed. Specific

---

[122] Article 49(2). *See also* Article 39.

[123] Article 75. Although the Article refers to "contract price," the only sensible application is to use the *unpaid* contract price.

[124] U.C.C. § 2-712.

[125] For a complete treatment of this issue in the context of the U.C.C., *see* § 7.04[B], *supra*.

[126] Article 81(2).

performance and damages remedies, however, seek to place the nondefaulting party in the financial position he would have found himself if the contract had been performed. A buyer who is entitled to and seeks some type of restitution remedy is entitled to a return of any portion of the price paid, plus interest, and must return any goods received under the contract,[127] but the buyer is precluded from protection of his expectation interest.

[7]　Specific Performance

Article 46(1) sets out the general rule for buyers:

> The buyer may require performance by the seller of his obligations unless the buyer has resorted to a remedy which is inconsistent with this requirement.

The principle of requiring performance rests on civil-law notions. The opening thought is broad, covering the *obligations* of the seller, without limiting the right just to the goods. The right could extend to title defects and to required documents.

This principle is subject to at least two limitations. One has been discussed. This remedy need not be given if the court would not grant specific performance under its internal laws in respect of similar contracts not governed by the CISG.[128] Thus, a U.S. court would award specific performance only in those limited instances provided by U.C.C. § 2-716.[129] However, unless this remedy is excluded from the contract, a foreign court may grant specific performance against a U.S. seller.

The second limitation arises from the "unless" proviso. Performance will not be given if the buyer has resorted to an inconsistent remedy. A declaration by the buyer that the contract has been avoided under Article 49 should be an inconsistent remedy.[130] The problem is to determine whether the actions of the buyer have amounted to an avoidance rather than an attempt to spur performance.

---

[127] *Id.*

[128] Article 28.

[129] "Specific performance may be granted where the goods are unique or in other proper circumstances." U.C.C. § 2-716, discussed in § 7.05[A], *supra*.

[130] Article 81(1). Avoidance "releases both parties from their obligations" under the contract.

[8] Delivery of Substitute Goods

If the seller has delivered nonconforming goods, the buyer may require the seller to deliver substitute goods.[131] The right to demand substitute goods is a limited right. First, the buyer must give the Article 39 notice. Second, the lack of conformity must constitute a fundamental breach; the seller ought not be required to provide substitute goods for a minor breach.[132] Third, the buyer must have requested substitute goods with the Article 39 notice or within a reasonable time thereafter.[133] Fourth, because this is a type of specific performance, the right to substitute goods should be lost if the buyer has resorted to an inconsistent remedy under Article 46(1). Finally, a court that does not normally grant specific performance could refuse to grant this remedy.[134]

The CISG does not state whether the substitute goods must conform 100 percent to the contract. The implication, however, is that, if the substitute goods are sufficient to prevent the default from being "fundamental," the buyer does not have a right to demand an additional substitution or to avoid the contract. The buyer is left with his other remedies, including a damage recovery.

[9] Repair

If nonconforming goods are delivered, the buyer may require that the nonconformity be repaired by the seller, if repair is not unreasonable and if proper notice is given.[135] This remedy is available even if the default was not fundamental. The repair request must be made in conjunction with the Article 39 notice or within a reasonable time thereafter.

[10] Reduction of Price

One remedy of the buyer for nonconforming goods is stated in these words: "the buyer may reduce the price in the same proportion as the value that the goods actually delivered had at the time of delivery bears to the

---

[131] Article 46(2).

[132] If a part of a shipment is nonconforming, a buyer should be allowed to demand substitute goods for the nonconforming goods as long as the other conditions of this Article have been met.

[133] Article 46(2). There is no good business reason for requiring the delivery of substitute goods for a minor breach.

[134] Article 28.

[135] Article 46(3).

value that conforming goods would have had at that time."[136] This approach to a buyer's remedies originated in Roman law and can still be found in the codes of many civil law countries, but the reduction is usually computed as of the time of contract formation, not the time of delivery, as now provided in the CISG.[137]

Assume a contract for the sale of fillups at a price of $20,000 for 10,000 first-grade fillups. The seller delivered 10,000 second-grade fillups, which the buyer accepted. At the time of delivery, first-grade fillups were selling for $2.50 each, and second-grade fillups were selling for $2.00 each. If the buyer elects this remedy, the price of the second-grade fillups would be $16,000 (determined by dividing the value of the goods received by the value conforming goods would have had—$20,000 divided by $25,000 or 80 percent in this case—and multiplying the result by the contract price), and the buyer will have paid $16,000 for second-grade fillups worth $20,000.

This remedy has limited value. Damages would have produced at least $5,000 to the buyer. If the buyer needed the second-grade fillups, he may be willing to accept a portion of his expectation interest rather than pursuing his remedies or, if the seller is excused from damages,[138] the price reduction formula may be acceptable to the buyer.

[11] Damages

The general damage rule is set out in Article 74 and is discussed in § 10.04[A][2], subject to mitigation principles discussed in § 10.04[A][5]. If one item out of 10,000 ordered by the buyer is not delivered, Article 74 provides a remedy. Subject to a foreseeability test, those damages equal the loss suffered, including lost profits.

In *Delchi Carrier SpA v. Rotorex Corp.*,[139] the court found that the seller's default was "fundamental" and granted the buyer its lost profits, determined by deducting *variable*—but not its *fixed*—costs from the average sale price of the goods. "In the absence of a specific provision in the CISG for calculating lost profits, the district court was correct to use the standard formula employed by most American courts and to deduct only variable costs from sales revenue to arrive at a figure for lost profits."[140] The court

---

[136] Article 50.

[137] The 1978 draft of the CISG used the contract formation date to compute the reduction-in-price damages. This was changed in the 1980 draft to use the delivery date as the base from which to compute the damages.

[138] Article 79.

[139] 71 F.3d 1024 (2d Cir. 1995).

[140] *Id.* at 1030.

also granted the plaintiff buyer its incidental damages incurred following the seller's default.

[12] Mitigation

The CISG provides that if the nondefaulting party could mitigate his loss by taking reasonable measures, the defaulting party may claim a reduction by the amount by which the loss could have been mitigated.[141] This Article can be used by sellers in an attempt to reduce the buyers' claimed damages. Whether they will be successful depends on the facts of each situation.

[13] Early Deliveries; Over-Deliveries

The remedies section concludes with two further rules:

1. The buyer may refuse (or take) a delivery which occurs before the date set for delivery.[142]
2. The buyer may accept an over-delivery or refuse to take the excess, but the buyer must pay for the goods accepted at the contract rate.[143]

On occasion, it may be difficult (or impossible) to refuse to take the "excess" without refusing to take the entire delivery—as, for example, when the goods are shipped under a bill of lading with a sight draft for the entire shipment.

[C] Seller's Remedies

[1] Introduction

Article 61 begins with a list of the available remedies, in a manner similar to the U.C.C. The same Article adds that the choice of a *damage* remedy is not precluded by the exercise of any other remedy and that no period of grace is to be granted to a buyer when the seller resorts to a remedy for default. Some remedies are, however, precluded by the exercise of a remedy that is inconsistent with other remedies.

This section discusses, first, those remedies in which the seller wishes to terminate rights under the contract: avoidance and restitution. It then deals with the remedy designed to require the buyer to take delivery and pay the

---

[141] Article 77. *See* discussion in § 10.04[A][5].
[142] Article 52(1).
[143] Article 52(2).

price. Finally, it examines the seller's monetary recoveries: damages; use of current price to measure damages; substitute sale; and mitigation. Finally a section is included to show the effect of the buyer's furnishing specifications.

Before presenting the seller's remedies, it is necessary to examine the CISG's provision on the seller's privilege to extend the time the buyer has to perform his obligations. The exercise of this privilege may affect the remedy available.

[2] Additional Time to Perform

As discussed in connection with the buyer's remedies,[144] the first approach of the CISG is to allow the parties to set an additional time for performance. The seller may fix an additional time of reasonable length for the buyer to perform—that is, to take delivery or to pay the price.[145] If the seller does so, the seller cannot resort to any remedy during the additional time period unless the buyer notifies the seller that there will be no further performance.[146] There is, however, no provision that allows the buyer to set an additional time for payment. A late payment will bear interest,[147] but if payment is a concurrent condition or a condition precedent to delivery, the seller could refuse to make delivery, at least until the additional time for payment set by the seller has expired.

[3] Avoidance of the Contract

The seller may declare a contract "avoided" if the buyer's default amounts to a "fundamental breach"[148] or if the buyer either (1) does not, within the additional time fixed by the seller, pay the price or take delivery of the goods or (2) declares that he will not do so within the period fixed by the seller.[149]

One result of avoidance is that it releases both parties from their contractual obligations, subject to any damages that may be due.[150] Thus, the

---

[144] Section 10.04[B][2].

[145] Article 63(1).

[146] Article 63(2). But the seller is not deprived of a remedy for damages caused by late performance.

[147] Article 78.

[148] Article 64(1)(a). Fundamental breach is defined in Article 25.

[149] Article 64(1)(b). Failing to obtain a required letter of credit or the necessary government approval would be a "failure to pay the price." Article 54. The notice could be given to a buyer who has paid the price but not taken delivery. Cases of that type are rare. The buyer's protection would lie with the length of time required for the notice. Article 63(1). Also, a seller who avoided such a contract would have to return the price.

[150] Article 81.

seller who avoids the contract retains his claim to damages and restitution, but forfeits rights to compel performance. In that sense, avoidance is similar to a seller's remedies under U.C.C. § 2-703.

In those cases in which the buyer has paid the price, the seller loses the right to avoid the contract unless notice is given to the buyer within the times stated in Article 64(2). Those time limits take account of the fact that the seller might not have learned of his right to avoid the contract until a considerable time after the goods were delivered to the carrier for shipment to the seller.

[4] Restitution

One effect of avoidance is to give the avoiding party a right of restitution. When applied to sellers, the result may be different from the result under the U.C.C.

Article 81(2) provides that, when a contract has been avoided, the party that has performed wholly or in part may claim restitution of whatever that party "has supplied or paid under the contract." The typical seller case would be one in which the seller has supplied goods on credit. If the buyer failed to make the required payment, the seller could avoid the contract because of the buyer's fundamental breach.

One way to read Article 81(2) is that such a seller may reclaim goods sold on credit (on the theory that it was the goods that were "supplied"), rather than becoming a general creditor.[151] Whether such a remedy has any practical importance is difficult to evaluate because it has its greatest impact when the buyer is unable—not just unwilling—to pay the price (for example, when he is in some form of bankruptcy proceedings), and the seller is subject to the rights of other creditors, a matter that is left to local law.

Another way to read Article 81(2) is that the seller would be entitled to the value of what he supplied, not the goods delivered.

[5] Action for the Price

The U.C.C. provides for a price action only under limited circumstances;[152] except for specially manufactured goods, it makes no provision for requiring a buyer to take delivery of goods that the buyer agreed to purchase but now does not want. The CISG provision is as follows (Article 62):

---

[151] Such a result would be contrary to that of the U.C.C. under which the unpaid seller (who has not retained a security interest) is limited to a claim for the price.

[152] U.C.C. § 2-709.

The seller may require the buyer to pay the price, take delivery or perform his other obligations, unless the seller has resorted to a remedy
which is inconsistent with the requirement.

This abbreviated treatment of the price remedy and the reference to
requiring a buyer to take delivery is the result of viewing specific performance as the basic remedy for parties. Clearly, if the buyer has accepted
conforming goods and retained them, the buyer is liable for the price. Article
62 goes further and states that the seller may require the buyer to take
delivery *and* pay the purchase price. There are, however, other rules that
may cause a seller to select a more appropriate remedy.

For example, Article 85 provides that if the buyer delays in taking
delivery or paying the price (when payment is to be made concurrently with
the delivery of the goods), the "seller must take such steps as are reasonable
in the circumstances to preserve them [the goods]. He is entitled to retain
them until he has been reimbursed his reasonable expenses by the buyer."
Article 88 allows the seller to sell the goods if there has been an unreasonable delay in taking delivery or in paying the price, provided that reasonable
notice is given the buyer.[153] This may be a more attractive remedy than
trying to force the goods on an unwilling buyer.

Also, there are several principles that prevent a common-law court from
forcing a CISG buyer to take and pay for goods the buyer does not want.
One such principle is found in Article 28: if one party is entitled to "require
performance" of an obligation, a court is not bound to enter a judgment for
specific performance if it would not do so under local law. In the United
States, this would mean that a seller could recover the price only under the
limited instances detailed in U.C.C. § 2-709, although a foreign court could
grant an Article 62 recovery against a U.S. buyer. There are also limitations
found in the CISG. These limitations (in Articles 85 and 88) on the price
remedy, when combined with principles of mitigation,[154] indicate that the
seller ought not rely on recovering the price in most instances when the
buyer is in default and the seller has possession of the goods.

---

[153] The seller may also warehouse the goods at the buyer's expense if the expense is not
unreasonable. Article 87.

[154] Article 77, discussed below. Usually the goods can be resold by the seller, mitigating
his loss. The effect, at least in a U.S. court, is that the seller will be able to recover the price
under the conditions contained in U.C.C. § 2-709.

[6] Damages

The general principles of damages discussed previously are applicable to a damage action by the seller.[155] These principles are contained in Articles 74 through 77.

The seller is entitled to recover his losses, including lost profits in an appropriate case.[156] Those damages are limited by the test of foreseeability—presumably only for so-called indirect or consequential damages. The normal measure of recovery—contract price minus market or current price—is presumed foreseeable.

This basic rule is applicable to all defaults no matter how minor, subject to mitigation principles set out below. If the default is serious enough to allow for avoidance and the seller has avoided the contract, the CISG provides two additional remedies for the nondefaulting seller. The first provides for the use of the current price in measuring damages; the second applies when the seller has made a substitute sale.

[7] Damages Based on Current Price

If the contract has been avoided and no substitute transaction was entered into, the nondefaulting party—in this case, the seller—may recover the difference between the contract price and the "current price at the time of avoidance as well as any further damages recoverable under Article 74," unless the buyer has retained the goods.[157] In the latter event, the current price (from which the contract price is subtracted) is determined as of the time of the "taking over" of the goods.

The place at which the current price is to be determined is the place where delivery of the goods should have been made (in most overseas shipments, the place where the goods are handed over to the first carrier),[158] with a proviso that if there is no current price at that place, a reasonable substitute can be used.[159]

---

[155] Section 10.04[A][2].

[156] Article 74.

[157] Article 76(1). The time and place for measuring the current (market) price under the U.C.C. is the time and place for tender. U.C.C. § 2-708.

[158] Article 31, discussed previously.

[159] Article 76(2). In most cases involving international sales, the place of tender and the place where delivery is to be made will be the same. *See* Article 31.

[8] Substitute Sale

A seller that has avoided a contract and has, within a reasonable time and in a reasonable manner after avoidance, resold the goods may recover the difference between the contract price and the price in the substitute transaction, "as well as any further damages recoverable under Article 74."[160] This is a sensible approach to damages: allowing a seller to enter into a substitute transaction with some assurance that the loss on that transaction will measure his recovery. In many civil-law countries, this is the preferred measure of damages. It is similar to the resale remedy of the U.C.C.,[161] but leaves open the same problem that the U.C.C. left open.

Suppose that the seller agreed to sell 10,000 fillups to the buyer for $20,000. At the time set for delivery, the fillups had a market value of $15,000. The buyer wrongfully refused to accept delivery. The seller was able to sell 10,000 fillups for $18,000. Is the resale measure mandatory once the seller has sold the fillups (thus limiting the seller to $2,000), or may the seller ignore that measure and recover the $5,000 under the general damage rules? The answer is not clear under the U.C.C. or the CISG. However, the reference in Article 74 to "loss" rather than to market price suggests that the CISG will be read to take the sensible approach and allow only the $2,000.

There is also the factual problem of whether the seller was a "lost volume" seller (i.e., whether the sale to the second buyer would have taken place even if the first buyer had not breached). A full discussion of this problem in the context of the U.C.C. can be found at § 7.08[D].

[9] Mitigation

The CISG provides that if the nondefaulting party could mitigate its loss by taking reasonable measures, the defaulting party may claim a reduction by the amount by which the loss could have been mitigated.[162] This Article will be used by buyers in an attempt to reduce the sellers' claimed damages. Whether they will be successful will depend on the facts of each situation.

---

[160] Article 75. Although the Article refers to "contract price," the only sensible application is to use the *unpaid* contract price.

[161] U.C.C. § 2-706, discussed in § 7.08[A], *supra*.

[162] Article 77. For a discussion of the mitigation problems under the U.C.C., when the buyer's default occurs before the goods have been identified to the contract, see § 7.08[F], *supra*.

[10] Supplying Specifications

If a buyer is to supply specifications but fails to do so, the seller may supply those specifications, thus giving the promises the certainty they might otherwise lack.[163] Before the seller's specifications become binding, the buyer must have received the details thereof and must have failed to respond within a reasonable time fixed by the seller.

A manufacturer that decides to supply specifications should consider whether the goods would be resalable if the buyer refuses to take delivery. Manufacturing goods that a buyer does not want and that are unique may cause a court to hold that the loss was one that the seller should have mitigated by not manufacturing those goods.

§ 10.05   RISK OF LOSS

[A]   General Principles

In international shipments involving experienced buyers and sellers, the risk of loss can often be determined by specific provisions in the contract of sale. That provision controls which party bears the risk of loss even though the CISG Articles on passing of the risk do not expressly state that the contract can change the CISG rules. Article 6 provides the necessary authority for application of the contract provisions.

If the parties have not allocated the risk of loss, Article 66 provides that, once the risk of loss has passed to the buyer, he is not discharged from his obligation to pay the price even though the goods are lost or damaged, unless the loss or damage was *due to* an act or omission of the seller.[164] The meaning of "due to an act or omission of the seller" should cover cases in which the loss results from the seller's sending the goods to the wrong address, packaging them improperly, failing to require refrigeration when refrigeration is necessary to preserve the goods, and those matters covered by U.C.C. § 2-504.

Loss or damage resulting from such events as bad weather, improper handling by the carrier, or the failure of the carrier to follow shipping instructions are not "due to" the seller's acts or omissions. These events will not prevent the risk from being shifted to the buyer.

In some situations, a combination of acts or omissions may cause the loss or damage. Suppose the overseas contract calls for the goods to be

---

[163] Article 65.

[164] The CISG is similar to the U.C.C. in that it frees the passing of the risk of loss from the concept of title.

placed on pallets and covered with shrink-wrap polystyrene. The seller used a substitute for polystyrene and delivered the goods to the first carrier.[165] The carrier misdelivered the goods, and, ten days after the goods should have been delivered to the buyer, heavy rains soaked the goods, making them worthless. If the goods had been wrapped in polystyrene, the goods would not have been damaged. If the goods had been delivered on time, there would have been no loss. Was this damage "due to" an act or omission of the seller?

[B] Neither Party in Default

The normal export sale involves the shipment of goods, F.O.B. (or C.I.F. or similar designation) seller's point, by a common carrier or by a series of common carriers. If the seller in a shipment contract (for example, F.O.B. shipper's point) performs certain stated obligations, the U.C.C. shifts the risk of loss to the buyer upon delivery of the goods to the common carrier.[166] The same rule is followed in the CISG. Once the goods have been identified to the contract,[167] the risk in a shipment contract passes as follows:

> If the contract of sale involves carriage of the goods and the seller is not bound to hand them over at a particular place, the risk passes to the buyer when the goods are handed over to the first carrier for transmission to the buyer in accordance with the contract of sale.[168]

There are a number of sub-rules under the general principle. These include:

1. If the contract requires the goods to be delivered to a carrier at a particular location (as, for example, "ex-ship, Providence, Rhode Island"), the risk passes when the goods are placed in the possession of ("handed over" to) a ship in Providence.[169]

2. If the goods are in transit when they are sold, the risk passes at the time of the formation of the contract, subject to two caveats. First, if the circumstances indicate, the risk can be shifted retroactively to the time the goods were put in possession of the carrier. Second, if the seller knew or ought to have known, at the time of contract formation, that the goods

---

[165] If this is a fundamental breach, Article 70 would apply.

[166] U.C.C. §§ 2-319–2-322, 2-509. U.C.C. § 2-323 deals with the form of bills of lading required in overseas shipments.

[167] Article 67(2).

[168] Article 67(1).

[169] *Id.*

were damaged and did not inform the buyer of that fact, the risk is not shifted to the buyer.[170]

In cases other than those stated above, the risk passes to the buyer when he takes possession of the goods or, if he does not do so, when the goods are placed at his disposal and he fails to take them in breach of contract.[171] Finally, as a caution, the CISG adds that the retention by the seller of documents that control the disposition of the goods does not affect the passage of the risk.[172] Thus, the fact that a buyer has a right of inspection (either by the contract or by Article 58(3) of the CISG) of goods that were lost or damaged in shipment does not prevent the risk of loss from being shifted to the buyer.

[C] Seller in Default

The U.C.C. has one section devoted to the problem of who bears the risk of loss if a party is in default.[173] As far as the seller is concerned, that section provides that if the seller's tender of delivery is so deficient that the buyer could have rejected the goods, the seller bears the risk until the seller cures or the buyer accepts the goods. The CISG arrives at the same place through a different route. Article 70 provides that if the seller has committed a fundamental breach, the sections on risk of loss do not impair the buyer's remedies.

Suppose a seller agreed to sell 10,000 Grade A fillups to the buyer, F.O.B. seller's city. Suppose that the seller shipped 9,999 Grade A fillups and one Grade B fillup. During overseas shipment, all of the fillups were destroyed when the ship on which they were loaded sank in a hurricane.

The risk shifted to buyer when the fillups were delivered to the first common carrier in seller's city, and, assuming that the one Grade B fillup did not amount to a fundamental breach giving the buyer the right to avoid the contract under Article 70, the buyer is liable for the price, less the damages for the one Grade B fillup. The loss at sea was not due to any act or omission of the seller.

Alternatively, suppose that the seller shipped 4,000 Grade A fillups and 6,000 Grade B fillups, and all of the fillups were lost at sea during a hur-

---

[170] Article 68.

[171] Article 69(1). Article 69(2) provides the rule for instances in which the buyer is to take possession at a place other than seller's business.

[172] Article 67(1).

[173] U.C.C. § 2-510; § 6.06[A].

ricane. Under Articles 66 and 67, the risk shifted to the buyer when the fillups were placed on the first common carrier.[174] Assuming that the tender of 60 percent Grade B fillups amounted to a fundamental breach, the buyer can avoid the contract[175] and his obligation to pay the price for any of the fillups. He can also recover any advance payments made.[176] Avoidance of the contract effectively shifts the risk back to the seller.[177]

In both situations, the buyer initially bore the risk of loss. Only if the breach was fundamental and proper notice was given by the buyer within the time limits can he shift that risk back to the seller. The lesson is clear: the buyer should insure the goods and not rely on the possibility that he may be lucky and find a fundamental breach.

The fact that the parties can extend the time for performance also causes a number of risk of loss problems if goods are destroyed or damaged during the additional time period. Attorneys dealing with the CISG should be aware of the risk of loss difficulties if the goods are not shipped on time, perhaps handling the problem by specific contract language.

The U.C.C. contains provisions designed to protect the buyer in the case of sales F.O.B. seller's point. For example, U.C.C. § 2-504 requires such a seller to make a reasonable contract with the carrier (which could include insurance), obtain and deliver documents to the buyer, and notify the buyer of the shipment. These protections are found in the general language of Article 32 of the CISG, previously discussed.[178] Also, the seller need only hand the goods to the carrier "in accordance with the contract of sale."[179]

---

[174] There may be an argument that "the goods" were not shipped when the seller's shipment is nonconforming. However, the manner in which the Articles on risk of loss are written should preclude this argument from being successful.

[175] Proper notice must be given. Article 49(2)(b). The buyer must also comply with Articles 82 and 88, when applicable, or lose the right of avoidance. As a variation of the problem in the text, assume that the goods were not lost at sea but were delivered to the buyer. Thereafter, the goods were destroyed in a fire in the buyer's warehouse. If the buyer can meet the notice deadline, he could avoid the contract even though the loss occurred after the goods were in his possession.

[176] Article 81.

[177] The buyer is not required to shift the risk back to the seller. He could, if desired, retain the risk and sue for damages for the tender of the 6,000 Grade B (rather than Grade A) fillups. In a particular case, that remedy (combined with insurance recovery) may provide a preferable result.

[178] Section 10.03[B][3].

[179] Article 67.

[D] Buyer in Default

The buyer has two obligations under the CISG: to pay for the goods and to take delivery. Failure to make payment in accordance with the contract does not create a risk problem. However, failure to take the goods can create a question of which party bears the risk of loss.

In a contract F.O.B. seller's point, the risk passes at the time of delivery to the first carrier, and failure of the buyer to take delivery when the goods arrive does not change the risk of loss. If, on the other hand, the buyer is to pick up the goods at the seller's place of business, Article 69(1) provides:

> In cases not within articles 67 and 68 [shipment and in transit contracts], the risk passes to the buyer when he takes over the goods, or, if he does not do so in due time, from the time the goods are placed at his disposal and he commits a breach of contract by failing to take delivery.

There will be problems of what is a *due time*, when the goods are placed at the buyer's *disposal*, and when the failure to take the goods amounts to a *breach*. Disposal occurs when the goods are identified to the contract.[180] How this is to be accomplished with fungibles (such as oil in a storage tank) remains to be seen. The concept of identification is contained in Article 67(2). Although the Article is limited in scope, the idea of identification is clear: identification occurs "whether by markings on the goods, by shipping documents, by notice given to the buyer or otherwise." The last two words leave room for disagreement.

§ 10.06   PROVISIONS COMMON TO THE SELLER AND THE BUYER

[A] Anticipatory Breach: Suspension of Performance

The CISG follows the scheme of the U.C.C. in allowing either party to suspend performance if it becomes apparent that the other party will not perform a substantial part of his obligations as a result of either (1) a "serious deficiency" in the ability of the other party to perform or in his creditworthiness or (2) in his conduct in preparing to perform or in performing the contract.[181] In addition, a seller may withhold delivery of dispatched goods under the same conditions.[182] A party that decides to suspend per-

---

[180] Article 69(3).
[181] Article 71(1). *Cf.* U.C.C. § 2-609 and its "reasonable ground for insecurity" language.
[182] Article 71(2).

formance must provide the other party with notice and must resume performance if the other party provides adequate assurance of performance.[183] The CISG does not state what amounts to an adequate assurance. Comment 4 to U.C.C. § 2-609 could be helpful.

One practical problem that is not resolved by the CISG (or the U.C.C.) is the effect that suspension of performance has on the performance date established by the contract, once the suspension has been "lifted." Hopefully, the courts will allow some modification of the performance date when required by the facts of particular cases.[184]

[B]   Anticipatory Breach: Avoidance of the Contract

The right to suspend performance does not automatically allow a party to avoid the contract and proceed with avoidance remedies. Only if one party, prior to the date set for performance, makes it clear that it will commit a fundamental breach may the contract be avoided. If time allows, the aggrieved party that has decided to avoid the contract must give reasonable notice to the other party in order to permit that party to provide adequate assurance of performance. Such notice need not be given if the defaulting party has "declared that he will not perform his obligations."[185]

[C]   Installment Contracts

Installment contracts raise avoidance problems different from those of the single-delivery contract. Suppose that the seller agreed to supply the buyer with 1,000 Grade A fillups each month for twelve months—January through December. The seller made proper deliveries in January and February, but tendered only 500 Grade B fillups in March. (1) May the buyer refuse to accept the March delivery? (2) May the buyer refuse to accept the March delivery and declare the contract avoided for the remaining months? (3) May the buyer refuse to accept the March delivery, declare the contract avoided for the remaining months, and require the seller to take back the goods delivered in January and February? These questions are the subject of Article 73 of the CISG.

As far as the March delivery is concerned, the test is whether the failure "constitutes a fundamental breach with respect to that instalment." If it

---

[183] Article 71(3).

[184] Some help may be found in U.C.C. § 2-611(3) dealing with the retraction of a repudiation.

[185] Article 72.

does—and, under the assumed facts, it would seem that a fundamental breach has occurred so far as the March delivery is concerned—the buyer may "declare the contract avoided with respect to that instalment"[186] and refuse to accept delivery.

Whether the failure to deliver an installment can be used to avoid the future deliveries depends upon whether the failure "gives the other party good grounds to conclude that a fundamental breach of contract will occur with respect to future installments."[187] This is a harder test. The buyer must tie this default to his "good" grounds for believing what will occur in the future.

If the buyer also wants to avoid the contract with respect to the prior deliveries (and return the January and February fillups), he must show that, "by reason of their interdependence," those deliveries could not be used for the purpose contemplated by the parties at the time of contracting.[188] If, for example, all of the 12,000 fillups were needed to complete a project, the interdependence should exist.

Article 73 can also be used by a seller when the buyer has failed to make one or more payments due under the installment contract. The tests are the same as those set out in the foregoing text.

[D] Principles of Damages

The principles applicable to this Section are contained in Articles 74 through 77. They have been discussed in connection with the remedies of the buyer and seller.[189]

§ 10.07 INTEREST

[A] Obligation to Pay Interest

Article 78 provides that a party that fails to pay the price or any other sum that is in arrears is entitled to interest. No rate is specified. Evidently, the damage recoveries do not bear interest under CISG rules unless somehow they can be forced within the phrase "any other sum." Otherwise, local law is used to determine the right to, and the rate of, interest on damage recoveries.

---

[186] Article 73(1).
[187] Article 73(2).
[188] Article 73(3).
[189] Sections 10.04[A][2], 10.04[B][11], and 10.04[C][6].

§ 10.08   EXEMPTIONS

[A]   Introduction

The purpose of a contract is to shift risks. The buyer wants to shift to the seller the risk of a source of supply for the goods; the seller wants to shift to the buyer the risk of a source of disposal of the goods. These risks are exchanged in a contract for the sale and purchase of the goods.

On occasion, some event disrupts the assumptions of one of the parties. The price of raw materials increases dramatically, a strike occurs at the seller's supplier, transportation facilities become unavailable, similar goods become available much more cheaply, and so on. When one of these events occurs, one of the parties would like to claim that (1) the specific event was not a risk which he took and (2) he is no longer obligated to perform under the contract.

The intervening event (a) may make performance by one party *impossible*, as when a laborer dies; (b) may make performance not impossible, but *more difficult* than expected, as when a builder discovers the need to remove several feet of rock rather than clay; or (c) may *frustrate the purpose* of one of the parties, as when the coronation route of the king is changed so that a party who has rented rooms, although he can use the rooms, will no longer see the coronation parade from the rooms. In each of these situations, one party's assumptions have been frustrated. Every legal system must develop principles to decide whether these risks were shifted by the contract.

This problem is dealt with in U.C.C. § 2-615 and, to a lesser extent, U.C.C. §§ 2-613 and 2-614. U.C.C. § 2-615 provides relief when a seller's delivery or nondelivery has been made "impracticable by the occurrence of a contingency the non-occurrence of which was a basic assumption of which the contract was made."[190] The cases, while providing some relief to sellers and buyers, have made it clear that the U.C.C. does not allow dissatisfied sellers and buyers to walk away from contracts.

Relief from unexpected events has been given much more freely in some other legal systems than in the United States. In the extreme, a party to a contract is expected to provide relief to the other party if the deal he made turns out to be especially burdensome. Contracts have not enjoyed the sanctity that the Anglo-American system has given them.

---

[190] The section also deals with compliance with laws whether or not those laws later proved invalid. This issue is discussed in § 5.04[D], *supra*.

[B] Failure by a Party to Perform

This divergence of attitudes became the background for the CISG Section entitled "Exemptions." The tests for relief for a party who does not perform as provided in the contract are set out in Article 79(1). Those tests are:

(1) Was the failure to perform due to an "impediment beyond his control"?

(2) If so, could he reasonably be expected:

    (a) To have taken that impediment into account at the time of contract formation, or

    (b) To have avoided or overcome it or its consequences?

Relief will be granted only if the first question is answered "Yes" and both parts of the second question are answered "No."[191] Terms such as *impediment*,[192] *taken into account*, *avoided*, and *overcome* make the results of this Article impossible to predict. Perhaps the only safe prediction is that they are sufficiently ambiguous so that courts in every country can go on doing what they do under their domestic law.

[C] Failure of Third Party to Perform

The CISG contains other provisions worth noting. The first spells out when a party's failure to perform, which is caused by a third party's failure to perform, is grounds for relief.[193] Several tests must be met. The first test has three parts:

1. The third person must have been engaged to perform some or all *of the contract*. Evidently failure of a general source of supply or means of transportation does not satisfy this test.

2. The party claiming the exemption must meet the requirements of Article 79(1), set out above.

3. The third party would be exempt if Article 79(1) were applied to him.

---

[191] Proper notice must also be given. Article 79(4).

[192] The history of that word's inclusion can be used to indicate that the drafters intended to restrict the cases covered by the Article.

[193] Article 79(2). Evidently, the failure of a third party is not an "impediment" within Article 79(1).

The second is the requirement of notice if a party wants to rely on the exemption.[194] The third is the provision that a party may not rely on the exemption, or any failure to perform, to the extent that its failure was caused by the other party to the contract.[195]

[D] Removal of the Impediment

The traditional Anglo-American approach to relief is to determine whether the intervening event made the entire contract unenforceable.[196] The CISG provides that the "exemption provided by this article has effect for the period during which the impediment exists."[197] When the impediment is removed, the performance must continue. This idea has found its way into many clauses prepared by attorneys.

[E] Restitution Recovery

The final paragraph in Article 79 provides that nothing in the Article "prevents any right other than to claim damages under this Convention." The right to avoid the contract is not impaired, and restitution is available under Articles 81 and 84. The measure of restitutionary relief when the frustrating event occurs midway through the contract—the case in which the seller has delivered a part of the goods prior to the time of the frustrating event—has always been difficult. Suppose the contract called for the delivery of 10,000 fillups for $20,000, delivery to be made in five equal monthly installments, with payment due at the time of the last delivery. The first three deliveries were made, and then the frustrating event occurred. Suppose alternatively that the market price of fillups at the time of delivery for all 10,000 fillups was $2.50 and $1.50. This raises at least the following three questions:

1. Is the seller entitled to any recovery? Article 81(2) allows the seller to "claim restitution."

2. How is that restitution to be measured—by the contract (which has been avoided) or by the market price at the time of delivery? If market price is used and if the market price had decreased to $1.50, the buyer will pay $9,000 for the 6,000 fillups instead of the $12,000 he promised to pay. If market price is used and the price had increased to $2.50, the buyer will

---

[194] Article 79(4).
[195] Article 80.
[196] U.C.C. §§ 2-613, 2-615.
[197] Article 79(3).

have to pay $15,000 for the 6,000 fillups he received. Should the buyer be able to deduct damages of at least $3,000 (and perhaps another $.50 for each of the 4,000 fillups that were not delivered) when technically the seller is not in default and when Article 79 cuts off the right to claim damages?

3. If the buyer paid some or all of the price in advance of shipment, should the buyer be allowed to recover some or all of what he has paid? If so, how is his recovery to be measured?

These questions (which are but a few that could arise) indicate that this Section of the CISG provides only a starting point for the situation it treats. Many of the answers must be determined either by the contract or by reference to applicable domestic law.

§ 10.09 EFFECTS OF AVOIDANCE

[A] Avoidance: General Rules

Avoidance of the contract has been discussed previously at several places in the text. Various rights, obligations, and remedies have been mentioned. Four Articles collect the effects of avoidance, as follows:

1. Avoidance releases both parties from their obligations, subject to any damages due.[198]
2. Avoidance does not affect any arbitration provision.[199]
3. Restitution is available to a party who has partially or wholly performed under the avoided contract.[200] The CISG does not state how the restitution is to be measured. (See the discussion in § 10.08[E].)
4. A buyer must be able to restore the goods in substantially the condition he received them, or he loses his right to avoidance or to claim substitute goods unless the cause:

    (a) was not due to his act or omission;
    (b) was the result of the examination allowed by the CISG; or
    (c) was a sale, consumption, or transformation in the normal course of business before he discovered or ought to have discovered the nonconformity.[201]

---

[198] Article 81(1).
[199] *Id. See* Filanto v. Chilewich Int'l Corp., 789 F. Supp. 1229 (S.D.N.Y. 1992).
[200] Article 81(2).
[201] Article 82.

5. A buyer who loses his right to avoid a contract or to require substitute goods retains his other remedies.[202]

6. A seller who must return the price must pay interest from the date the seller received the payment.[203]

7. A buyer must account for benefits received from the goods if he (a) must make restitution of the goods, (b) avoided the contract under conditions which excuse him from making restitution, or (c) required delivery of substitute goods.

§ 10.10   PRESERVATION OF THE GOODS

[A]   Introduction

The CISG contains four Articles dealing with the preservation of goods. The first requires the seller to preserve the goods if the buyer delays in taking delivery.[204] The second requires the buyer to preserve the goods following rejection.[205] The last two contain general provisions applicable to the party obligated to preserve the goods.

[B]   Preservation by the Seller

Even though the risk of loss has passed to the buyer, the seller has an obligation to take reasonable steps to preserve the goods if (1) the buyer delays in taking delivery or, when payment and delivery are to be made concurrently, the buyer fails to pay the price; and (2) the seller has possession or control of the goods.

Suppose that a seller has shipped goods to an overseas buyer, using a bill of lading (which gave control to the seller) and sight draft. When the goods arrived, the buyer refused to pay the draft and accept delivery of the goods. The buyer bears the risk of loss of the goods, but the seller (having control of the goods through the bill of lading) must take reasonable steps to preserve them. The seller is entitled to his reasonable preservation expenses and may retain the goods until he has been reimbursed by the buyer.

---

[202] Article 83.

[203] Article 84(1). *See also* Article 78. What effect does Article 84(1) have on the meaning of "other sum" in Article 78?

[204] Article 85. This Article is discussed in connection with the buyer's remedies.

[205] Article 86. This Article is discussed in connection with the buyer's remedies. It is assumed that the rejection must be rightful. The Article is conditioned on the exercise of a *right* to reject the goods.

If the seller fails to take the necessary action and the goods deteriorate or demurrage charges increase, that loss is the seller's.[206]

[C]   Preservation by the Buyer

The buyer has a duty to take reasonable steps to preserve the goods if (1) the buyer has received the goods and intends to reject them; or (2) the goods have been placed at the buyer's disposal and he has exercised his right to reject them, *and* the seller does not have a person to take charge of the goods on behalf of the seller at the destination of the goods. In the latter situation, the buyer must take possession of the goods if he can do so without paying the price or without unreasonable inconvenience or expense.

[D]   General Provisions

Additional provisions allow the party who is obligated to preserve the goods (1) to deposit them in a warehouse at the expense of the other party, providing the expense is not unreasonable,[207] or (2) to sell the goods if the other party delays unreasonably in taking possession of them.[208] Reasonable notice of sale is required. If the goods are subject to rapid deterioration (a carload of tomatoes) or preservation requires an unreasonable expense (an elephant), the party obligated to preserve the goods must take reasonable measures to sell them.[209] The reasonable expenses in caring for the goods and selling them may be retained, with any balance going to the other party.[210] There is no indication that a buyer could also retain any part of the price he had paid.

---

[206] The principal reason for these rules on preservation by the seller is the broad right to recover the price, a right that is limited under the U.C.C.

[207] Article 87.

[208] Article 88(1). The same principle is found in U.C.C. § 2-603.

[209] Article 88(2).

[210] Article 88(3).

§ 10.11   FINAL PROVISIONS

[A]   Ministerial Provisions

Articles 89–99 deal with miscellaneous matters such as the right of a country to declare that it will not be bound by (1) Part II or Part III of the CISG;[211] (2) Article 1(1)(b) of the CISG;[212] and (3) Articles that allow enforcement without a writing if local legislation requires a writing.[213] These Articles also allow a country to denounce the CISG.[214]

---

[211] Article 92(1).
[212] Article 95.
[213] Article 96.
[214] Article 101.

LEASES UNDER ARTICLE 2A

§ 11.01 INTRODUCTION

Although this is primarily a text on the law of *sales,* the subject of the leases of personal property cannot be ignored. Leases of goods have become a huge part of the economy. The amount of money represented by leases of goods is in the many billions of dollars.[1]

As discussed in § 2.03[A] of this text, Article 2 of the Code generally does not cover "true" leases of goods. Although section 2-102 makes Article 2 applicable to "transactions in goods," which is broad enough to include leases,[2] many of the most important sections of Article 2 apply only to the "sale" of goods or contracts for the sale of goods.[3] Furthermore, many of the provisions of Article 2 refer to "the buyer" or "the seller" of goods, indicating that these provisions are also intended to apply only to sales of goods and not to other transactions, such as leases.[4]

The failure of Article 2 to deal with leases created two distinct problems.[5] The first was the problem of the credit sale disguised as a lease. This situation occurred when goods were "leased" by one party to another for a period of time and at the end of the period, if the lease payments had been made in a timely manner, the lessee could acquire title from the lessor for a nominal amount, or sometimes for no additional consideration at all. The intent behind this transaction was to allow the "lessor" to easily regain possession if the required periodic payments were not made, without complying with the technicalities of Article 9 dealing with security interests.[6] Also, because there was no passage of title in these cases, there was no "sale" under Article 2.[7] As a result, Article 2 (or at least many of its provisions) did not to apply to the transaction, although, in economic substance, the transaction was little different from a credit sale. Moreover, because of the variety of potential lease terms, it was often hard to distinguish between a disguised sale and a true lease, and a substantial amount of litigation ensued on this issue.

---

[1] It has been estimated that leases of goods generate over $150 billion in revenue a year. *See* Dunne, "U.C.C. Article 2A: An Idea Whose Time Is Overdue," 108 Banking L.J. 419 (1993). *See also* Foreward to 1990 Text of Article 2A (Article 2A will apply to transactions involving billions of dollars annually).

[2] *See* § 2.03[A], *supra.*

[3] Section 2-106 of the Code defines a "sale" as "the passing of title from the buyer to the seller for a price." This would obviously exclude a lease, in which, by definition, title remains in the lessor.

[4] *See* Thomas D. Crandall et al., I Uniform Commercial Code § 2.2.8 (1993).

[5] *See* U.C.C. § 2A-101, Official Comment.

[6] Or, perhaps, without complying with the requirements of other statutes relating to credit sales such as state Retail Installment Sales Acts (RISAs).

[7] U.C.C. § 2-106.

The other problem was the law governing the true lease. Since the original promulgation of the Code, the number of leases of personalty has grown dramatically.[8] This is true both with respect to commercial and consumer leases.[9] Yet because of Article 2's limited scope, the law governing leases of personal property was largely the common law of property and contract. In many situations, there was little reason to treat a lease different from a sale, yet the applicable law might vary substantially.[10] For example, why should the law relating to warranties differ when a person leases a luxury sedan for five years as opposed to when she purchases it outright? Although in some particular circumstances the differences between a lease and a sale might justify the application of different legal rules, in many other situations it did not.

The first of these problems was partially dealt with by the courts through the application of Article 2 to credit sales disguised as leases despite the fact that there was no transfer of title. In some cases, Article 2 could be applied through section 2-102 and its requirement that there need only be a "transaction in goods." In cases where the particular provision of Article 2 made specific reference to a "sale" or "contract of sale," the courts applied Article 2 by analogy,[11] or simply ignored the fact that a "sale" under Article 2 requires the passage of title.[12] The difficulty of drawing the line, however, in the absence of explicit statutory guidance, between a true lease and a disguised sale remained.

As to the second difficulty—the law applicable to a true lease—courts often applied the Code by analogy in cases when it made sense to do so. For example, courts have applied Article 2 to long-term automobile leases.[13] In some instances, however, there was no provision of Article 2 that was

---

[8] *See* Foreword to Article 2A (1987) referring to the "exponential expansion" of the number and scale of personal property leases.

[9] *Id. See also* Bureau of Domestic Commerce, U.S. Dept. of Commerce, Leasing and Rental Industries: Trends and Prospects 7–8 (1976).

[10] *See, e.g.,* Hill v. Bentco Leasing, Inc., 288 Ark. 623, 708 S.W.2d 608, 1 UCCR2d 355 (1986); Advanced Computer Sales, Inc. v. Sizemore, 186 Ga. App. 10, 366 S.E.2d 303, 6 UCCR2d 18 (1988).

[11] *See* § 2.03[A], *supra*; J.L. Teel Co. v. Houston United Sales, Inc., 491 So. 2d 851, 1 UCCR2d 337 (Miss. 1986); Cucchi v. Rollins Protective Servs. Co., 524 Pa. 514, 574 A.2d 565, 11 UCCR2d 737 (1990).

[12] *See* Capital Assocs., Inc. v. Hudgens, 455 So. 2d 651, 39 UCCR 66 (Fla. Dist. Ct. App. 1984); Xerox Corp. v. Hawkes, 475 A.2d 7, 38 UCCR 159 (N.H. 1984).

[13] *See, e.g.,* Hornberger v. General Motors Corp., 929 F. Supp. 884, 30 UCCR2d 483 (E.D. Pa. 1996). The general topic is discussed in more detail in an earlier section of the text. *See* § 2.03[A], *supra*.

applicable in the case of a true lease,[14] and there was no guarantee that the non-Code law would be uniform from jurisdiction to jurisdiction.

This situation was viewed by many as unsatisfactory, and it was this dissatisfaction that ultimately led to Article 2A. Article 2A was first proposed in 1987 and was revised in 1990.[15] Concurrently with the promulgation of Article 2A, a wholesale revision to section 1-201(37), which defines "security interest," was also recommended. In an extraordinarily long and complicated definition of "security interest," the drafters attempted to clarify the distinction between a true lease and a credit sale with an accompanying security interest.

Because leases, especially long-term leases, have many of the characteristics of sales, the drafters of Article 2A drew heavily from Article 2. In many cases, there is little or no substantive difference between particular provisions of Article 2 and their counterparts in Article 2A, and the operative language in Article 2A was sometimes lifted verbatim from Article 2.[16] In other cases, the drafters have adopted important concepts present in Article 2, but have altered the substance of the sales provisions to adapt Article 2A to the economic differences between leases and outright sales.[17] The Official Comments suggest that the case law interpreting the provisions of Article 2, which were carried over to Article 2A, be viewed as persuasive authority.[18] Only rarely did the drafters of Article 2A reject a rule found in Article 2.[19]

Although the drafters concluded that Article 2 "was the appropriate statutory analogue,"[20] the separation of title and possession and the lessor's reversionary interest inherent in a true lease precluded the wholesale application of Article 2. These aspects of a lease often presented problems analogous to those presented by security interests—for example, the potential

---

[14] For example, the remedy provisions of Article 2 are inappropriate to true leases.

[15] A brief history of Article 2A is provided in the Official Comment to section 2A-101. For a comprehensive history of Article 2A, *see* Boss, "The History of Article 2A: A Lesson for the Practitioner and Scholar Alike," 39 Ala. L. Rev. 575 (1988).

[16] *Compare, e.g.*, section 2-313 (express warranties) *with* section 2A-210(express warranties).

[17] The best examples of this phenomenon are found in the sections of Article 2A on Remedies. *Compare, e.g.*, section 2-712 (buyer's cover) with section 2A-518 (cover; substitute goods).

[18] U.C.C. § 2A-101, Official Comment.

[19] *See, e.g.*, U.C.C. § 2A-208 which rejects the rule of section 2-208 that a modification that brings a contract within the statute of frauds requires that the statute be satisfied with respect to the entire contract.

[20] U.C.C. § 2A-101, Official Comment.

conflict between the lessee's interests and creditors of the lessor. In these instances, the drafters borrowed heavily from Article 9.

§ 11.02   SCOPE OF ARTICLE 2A

The scope of Article 2A is defined with deceptive simplicity in section 2A-102: "This Article applies to any transaction, regardless of form, that creates a lease."[21] Article 2A defines a "lease" as "a transfer of the right to possession and use of the goods for a term in return for consideration, but a sale, including a sale on approval or a sale or return, or retention or creation of a security interest is not a lease."[22]

A number of aspects of the definition deserve brief mention, and one requires substantial discussion. First, a lease requires only the transfer of the *right* to use and possession; actual possession is not required. There can be a present lease, for example, even if the actual transfer of possession does not occur until some later time, or the lessor agrees to store the leased goods for the lessee when they are not in use. Second, the transfer of the right to possession must take place for a consideration—that is, gratuitous transfers are not included within the scope of Article 2A and presumably will continue to be governed by the common law of gratuitous bailments.

Third, the definition of "lease" includes only leases of "goods." Unlike many other definitions, however, the definition of "goods" in Article 2 was not adopted verbatim by Article 2A.[23] The definitions, however, are similar, and most of the differences, save one, are of little or no consequence. For example, the definition of "goods" in Article 2 excludes money from the definition only to the extent that it constitutes the price to be paid. If money is treated as a commodity (e.g., the purchase of a rare coin), it is included in the Article 2 definition of goods. Because money *as a commodity* (as opposed to a loan of money) would rarely, if ever, be leased, money is *per se* excluded from the definition of goods in Article 2A.

The Article 2A definition of "goods" also excludes "documents, instruments, accounts, chattel paper, [and] general intangibles," whereas Article 2 simply excludes "things in action."[24] These exclusions, however,

---

[21] U.C.C. § 2A-102.

[22] U.C.C. § 2A-103(j).

[23] Section 2A-103(h) defines "goods" as "all things that are movable at the time of identification to the lease contract, or are fixtures (Section 2A-309), but the term does not include money, documents, instruments, accounts, chattel paper, general intangibles, or minerals or the like, including oil and gas, before extraction. The term also includes the unborn young of animals."

[24] U.C.C. § 2-105(1).

cover essentially the same items.[25] "Goods" under Article 2A also excludes minerals (including oil and gas) until severance, whereas the definition of "goods" in Article 2 includes minerals prior to severance if they are to be severed by the seller.[26] Finally, "fixtures" are included as "goods" under Article 2A and are defined in the same manner as in Article 9,[27] whereas Article 2, on the other hand, does not use the term "fixtures." Instead, Article 2 speaks of "things attached to realty and capable of severance without material harm thereto."[28] The reason for this discrepancy is that Article 2A imposes certain filing requirements upon lessors of fixtures in order for the lessor of the fixture to maintain priority over a conflicting interest in the real estate. These requirements are like those imposed by Article 9 upon those having security interests in fixtures in order to gain priority over conflicting interests.

[A] Sale versus Lease

The definition of "lease" in Article 2A explicitly excludes a "sale." Thus, when title to the goods passes, there is a sale as defined in section 2-106(1), and the transaction is governed by Article 2 and not by Article 2A. If title does not pass, application of Article 2A depends upon whether the transaction is a "true" lease or a secured sale disguised as a lease. Article 2A and the Official Comments make it clear that Article 2A is meant to apply only to "true" leases. The definition of "lease" excludes a transaction creating a security interest.[29] Further, the Official Comments to section 2A-103 state that "[i]f the transaction creates a security interest disguised as a lease, the transaction will be governed by the Article on Secured Transactions."[30] The Comments also suggest that the "sale" portion of a sale/secured transaction that is disguised as a lease is governed by Article 2, notwithstanding that title did not pass to the "lessee."[31]

---

[25] Furthermore, all of the exclusions from Article 2A are defined elsewhere in the Code, and their definitions have created little difficulty to date.

[26] U.C.C. § 2-107(1). There can, however, be no present sale of minerals; prior to severance, a present sale operates only as a contract to sell.

[27] U.C.C. § 2A-309 states that "goods are 'fixtures' when they become so related to particular real estate that an interest in them arises under real estate law." This is the same definition as appears in section 9-313(1)(a).

[28] U.C.C. § 2-107(2). Comment 2 to this section states that reference to "fixtures" was avoided because of "the diverse definitions of the term."

[29] U.C.C. § 2A-103(j).

[30] U.C.C. § 2A-103, Official Comment (j).

[31] See Official Comment (j) to § 2A-103.

Although it is clear from the definition of "lease" and the accompanying Comments that Article 2A is meant to apply only to "true" leases, the definition itself provides no assistance in distinguishing a true lease from a disguised sale with a security interest. To make this distinction, the drafters of Article 2A suggested that section 1-201(37), which defines "security interest," be completely revised in conjunction with the promulgation of Article 2A. Acknowledging that the distinction between a lease and a security interest disguised as a lease was "not clear from the case law,"[32] the drafters hoped that the modification of section 1-201(37) would draw a "brighter line"[33] between the two.

Whatever the amendments to section 1-201(37) accomplish, they certainly do not draw a bright line between a true lease and a sale disguised as a lease. In fact, whether the line is any "brighter" than before as a result of the lengthy and complex definition now present in section 1-201(37) is problematic. It has been suggested that the result of the amendments is that those transactions that were clearly leases under prior law are clearly leases under the revised section 1-201(37); those that were clearly disguised sales remain so; and those that were borderline remain borderline.[34] Many pages could be spent analyzing the changes to section 1-201(37), although in the final analysis, such an effort would probably yield the reader little. Instead, the following analysis focuses only on the essentials.

In describing the difference between a true lease and a sale with a security interest, section 1-201(37) begins by repeating the incantation of the original section that "whether a transaction creates a lease or security interest is determined by the facts of each case."[35] The section goes on to say, however, that if the lessee has an obligation to pay the rent throughout the term of the lease, which is not terminable by the lessee, *and* one of four additional tests is met, the transaction is a security interest *as a matter of law*. The first requirement is simply that the obligation to pay rent must be a continuing obligation throughout the term of the lease that the lessee cannot prematurely terminate. Because a true lease, as well as a security interest, frequently satisfies this requirement, the requirement makes sense only in conjunction with the four additional tests, only one of which must also be satisfied to create a true lease:

1. The term of the lease is equal to or greater than the remaining economic life of the goods; or

---

[32] U.C.C. § 2A-103, Official Comment (j).
[33] *Id.*
[34] Thomas D. Crandall et al., I Uniform Commercial Code § 9.3.3. at 9:18. (1993).
[35] U.C.C. § 1-201(37).

2. The lessee is bound to renew the lease for the remaining economic life of the goods or must become their owner at the end of the lease; or

3. The lessee has the option to renew the lease for the remaining economic life of the goods for no or nominal consideration; or

4. The lessee has the option to become the owner of the goods for no or nominal consideration.

These tests are all means of getting at a single idea: if the "lessor" has no true residual economic interest in the goods following the term of the lease, there is no lease at all; the goods have been effectively transferred to the lessee, and the transaction should be treated as a sale. Each of these "tests," however, represents situations that have given prior law little difficulty. When these facts have been present in a case, courts have almost universally found that a security interest, rather than a true lease, has been created.[36]

Section 1-201(37) then goes on to describe five factors that will not, *without more*, create a security interest:

1. *The rent (reduced to present value) is equal to or greater than the fair market value of the goods at the time the lease is entered into.* This provision merely recognizes the parties' freedom of contract: the fact *alone* that the lessee is willing to pay a greater amount in the present value of the rent than the amount it would cost him to buy the goods on the market is not sufficient to make the transaction a sale and security interest.

2. *The lessee assumes the risk of loss, or agrees to pay taxes, insurance, filing, recording, or registration fees, or agrees to be responsible for service or maintenance costs.* This provision recognizes that a lessee might enjoy an advantage over the lessor in assuming these risks or performing these tasks and might be willing to do so in exchange for lower rent. Again, the provision sanctions the parties' freedom to contract, so long as the lessor maintains a reversionary interest that is likely to be valuable following the term of the lease.

3. *The lessee has an option to renew the lease or to become owner.* The fact that a lease includes a renewal option or an option to purchase the goods does not prevent it from being a true lease. If, however, the lessee is *required* to purchase the goods or to renew the lease throughout the useful life of the goods, there is no true lease. Further, if the lessee has the option

---

[36] *See, e.g.*, United Rental Equip. Co. v. Potts & Callahan Contracting Co., 231 Md. 552, 191 P.2d 570 (1963); Transamerica Leasing Corp. v. Bureau of Revenue, 80 N.M. 48, 450 P.2d 934 (N.M. Ct. App. 1969); Hancock County Bank v. American Fletcher Nat'l Bank & Trust Co., 276 N.E.2d 580, 10 UCCR 490 (Ind. Ct. App. 1971); James Talcott, Inc. v. Franklin Nat'l Bank of Minneapolis, 292 Minn. 277, 194 N.W.2d 775, 10 UCCR 11 (1972).

to purchase the goods or renew the lease for the remaining useful life of the goods for no or for a nominal consideration, a sale and security interest, not a true lease, has been created.

4. *The lessee has the option to renew at a rent that is equal to or greater than the reasonably predictable fair market rent for the term of the renewal at the time the option is to be performed.* The fact that the renewal rent is greater than the predicted fair market rent at the time the option is exercised does not prevent the transaction from being a true lease. As with factor 1, the parties' freedom to contract for the rental price of the goods is protected. The alternative would transform all lease renewals at greater than fair market value into sales and security interests.

5. *The lessee has an option to purchase the goods for a price that is equal to or greater than the reasonably predicted fair market value at the time the option to purchase is to be exercised.* The fact that the option price in a lease exceeds the predicted market value of the goods at the time the option is to be exercised does not prevent the transaction from being a lease; the lessee always has the option of refusing to purchase the goods if the price is too high.

The reason that none of these factors (nor all of them together) is sufficient *alone* to create a disguised sale is that each of them is consistent with the fundamental difference between a sale and a true lease: the retention of a substantial economic interest in the goods by the lessor. In fact, the presence of some of the factors make it *more* likely that the transaction is a true lease rather than a disguised sale.[37]

Even prior to the change in the definition of "security interest" in section 1-201(37), it is unlikely that courts would have found any of these factors *alone* sufficient to create a disguised sale. The problem cases are those that fall between the extremes exemplified by the two sets of factors just described: those cases in which the transaction is not a disguised sale as a matter of law under Set 1, but contains facts in addition to those described in Set 2 that suggest a disguised sale. These are the cases that created difficulty prior to the revisions to section 1-201(37), and the revisions are of little help in resolving them.

For example, what if a four-year lease of an automobile contains a provision permitting the lessee to purchase the car at the end of the lease term for a figure (say $5,000) that appears to be less than a reasonable projection of the fair market value of the car at the time of the exercise of

---

[37] *See* U.C.C.§ 1-201, Official Comment 37: "A fixed price purchase option in a lease does not of itself create a security interest. *This is particularly true* if the fixed price is equal to or greater than the reasonably predictable fair market value of the goods at the time the option is to be performed" (emphasis added).

the option? In addition, the lessee bears the risk of loss, is required to insure against loss or damage, and bears all of the cost of maintaining the vehicle. We know from the third factor in Set 2 above that the fact that the lease contains an option to purchase does not prevent the transaction from being a lease, nor do the other responsibilities of the lessee. Further, because the option price is more than nominal,[38] the transaction is not a sale as a matter of law under Set 1. Still, the option price appears less than economically justified and the duties of the lessee mirror those of an owner. This is precisely the kind of case that troubled the courts under the old law. The new definition of "security interest" is of little help in resolving these cases, and in fact, the Official Comment to section 1-201(37) tells us that such cases will continue to be resolved on a case-by-case basis.

§ 11.03   TYPES OF LEASES

Although, as a general matter, Article 2A applies to all leases of goods, the Article establishes three subcategories of leases. Certain provisions of the Article apply only to one category,[39] while other provisions treat these categories differently.[40] The types of leases are:

---

[38] While it certainly appears on its face that the option price is more than nominal, U.C.C. § 1-201(37)(x) says that additional consideration is nominal "if it is less than the lessee's reasonably predictable cost of performing under the lease agreement if the option is not exercised." This language is subject to various interpretations. It could mean that an option price is nominal if it is less than the lessee's total cost of performing under the lease, assuming the option were not exercised. This cannot be the case, however, because when the goods are subject to depreciation, and the lease is a long-term one, the total lease obligation is often greater than the option price. For example, it would not be unusual in a long-term car lease for the total rental payments to substantially exceed the option price. The same might also be true with computer equipment as well as many other kinds of goods. Alternatively, the language might also mean that an option price is nominal if, at the time of exercise, it is less than the costs of the lessee's *remaining* obligations under the lease. For example, if the option price in the contract is $5,000 and it would cost the lessee $6,000 to fulfill the remaining obligations under the lease (from which it would be relieved if it exercised the option), the option price is nominal. This is probably what the drafters had in mind, although it is still not clear at what time the predicted costs of the lessee's remaining performance is to be determined: the time of contracting or the time of the exercise of the option. This may be important. It may be, in the foregoing example, that viewed at the time of contracting, it was reasonable to assume that it would cost the lessee only $4,000 to perform its remaining duties. Viewed at the time of the exercise of the option, however, a reasonable prediction of the cost of performance, the remaining duties would be $6,000. When examined from the time of contracting, the consideration ($5,000) would not be nominal. When viewed from the time of exercise, the consideration would be nominal.

[39] U.C.C. § 2A-109(2) (applies to consumer leases); U.C.C. § 2A-108(2) (applies to consumer leases); U.C.C. § 2A-407 (applies to finance leases).

[40] *See, e.g.*, U.C.C. §§ 2A-212, 2A-213, 2A-219.

1. consumer leases;
2. finance leases;[41] and
3. all other leases.

[A] Consumer Leases

Similar to Article 2, Article 2A is not designed as a consumer-protection statute. Article 2A, however, does create a special category of consumer leases and provides, in a few circumstances, additional protections for lessees, or restrictions on lessors, when consumer leases are involved.[42] These are discussed in the sections of the text dealing with specific topics.

Section 2A-103(e) defines a "consumer lease" as:

> [A] lease that a lessor regularly engaged in the business of leasing or selling makes to a lessee who is an individual and who takes under the lease primarily for a personal, family, or household purpose [if the total payments to be made under the lease contract, excluding payments for options to renew or buy, do not exceed $_____].

Pursuant to the definition, the lessor in a consumer lease must be regularly engaged in the business of leasing or selling goods. A lessor in a consumer lease, however, does not have to be in the business of *leasing*; a person regularly engaged in the business of *selling* goods can qualify as well, even if he does not regularly lease goods. Further, there is no requirement that the lessor in a consumer lease be regularly engaged in the business of selling or leasing goods *of the kind* leased in the particular transaction.[43] Consequently, for example, if a company that is regularly engaged in the business of selling or leasing computers leases its van to a consumer, the lease would be a consumer lease.

The lessee in a consumer lease must be an individual and must take the leased property primarily for personal, family, or household purposes. The section does not define "primarily"; it is not clear whether the goods must be used for these purposes a majority of the time or whether something more (or perhaps less) is required. Many consumer-protection statutes use similar language,[44] and these statutes will presumably provide some guid-

---

[41] The first two categories are not mutually exclusive (i.e., a lease can be both a finance lease and a consumer lease).

[42] U.C.C. §§ 2A-108(2), 2A-219.

[43] In fact, there is a separate definition for "merchant lessor" in Article 2A that does require the lessor to be a merchant with respect to goods of the kind involved in the lease. U.C.C. § 2A-103(t).

[44] *See, e.g.,* Ohio Rev. Code Ann. § 1345.01 (Anderson 1998); S.D. Codified Laws § 40-12-102(a)(ii) (1997).

ance in determining whether the use of the goods is "primarily" for personal, family, or household purposes. The Official Comments exclude leases that are primarily for agricultural purposes.[45]

Unlike the Magnuson-Moss Federal Warranty Act,[46] the definition of "consumer lease" appears to focus on the lessee's individual purpose in leasing the goods, not on the typical or normal use of such goods. Thus, if a person engaged in real estate sales purchases a car primarily for use in her business but also occasionally uses the car for personal and family purposes, the lease is not a consumer lease. If this provision is interpreted in the same manner as similar language in consumer-protection legislation, the time for determining the consumer's purpose is at the time that the goods are leased.[47] Whether courts will require that the lessor have reason to know of the lessee's purpose remains to be seen.

Under the 1987 version of Article 2A, if the total cumulative amount of rental payments exceeded $25,000, the lease was not a consumer lease. Under the 1990 version, the provision setting a specific dollar limitation is bracketed and the amount is left blank. At the present time, approximately twenty states that have adopted Article 2A retain the $25,000 cap,[48] while a somewhat smaller number have eliminated any cap.[49] Only a few states that have a cap have chosen a figure other than $25,000.[50]

[B] Finance Lease

Article 2A recognizes a type of commercial lease that has become common in today's economy and that has many attributes different from a traditional lease. This lease is a three-party arrangement in which the lessee generally selects the goods directly from a "supplier," with the lessor generally acting only as an intermediary. Through the lease arrangement, the lessor finances the acquisition of the goods for the lessee, but is otherwise uninterested in the goods. In fact, the lessor is sometimes a financial institution that does not regularly deal in goods of the kind leased. The Official Comments describe a finance lease in the following manner:

---

[45] U.C.C. § 2A-103, Official Comment (e).

[46] 15 U.S.C. §§ 2301–2312 (1995). *See* § 8.02, *supra*.

[47] In re Pettit, 18 B.R. 8 (Bankr. E.D. Ark. 1981); Linthicum v. Archambault, 379 Mass. 381, 398 N.E.2d 482 (1979); Commercial Credit Equip. Corp. v. Carter, 516 P.2d 767 (Wash. 1973).

[48] *See, e.g.*, Ariz. Rev. Stat. 47-2A103A(5) (Michie 1997); Ark. Code Ann. § 4-2A-103(1)(e) (1995 Supp.); Colo. Rev. Stat. § 4-2.5-103(1)(e) (1997).

[49] *See, e.g.*, Alaska Stat. § 45.12.103(a)(5) (1997); Del. Code Sec. 2A-103(1)(e) (1997).

[50] *See* Michie's Ala. Code § 7-2A-103(1)(e) (1997) ($100,000); Ill. Comp. Ann. Stat. Ch. 810, ¶ 5/2A-103(1)(c) (LEXIS 1997) ($40,000); Mo. Rev. Stat. § 400.2A-103(1)(e) (1997) ($50,000); Okla. Stat. Ann. tit. 12A, § 2A-103(e) (West 1997 Supp.) ($45,000).

A finance lease is the product of a three party transaction. The supplier manufactures or supplies the goods pursuant to the lessee's specification, perhaps even pursuant to a purchase order, sales agreement, or lease agreement between the supplier and the lessee. After the prospective finance lease is negotiated, a purchase order, sales agreement, or lease agreement is entered into by the lessor (as buyer or prime lessee) or an existing order, agreement or lease is assigned by the lessee to the lessor, and the lessee and lessee then enter into a lease or sublease of the goods.[51]

Although this description of a finance lease is relatively simple, the definition provided in Article 2A is lengthy and complicated. It begins with two requirements that *all* finance leases must satisfy:

1. *The lessor does not select, manufacture, or supply the goods.* This is the crux of a finance lease—the lessee chooses the goods that will be acquired by the lessor. The lessor is an intermediary who neither manufactures the goods nor supplies them from existing inventory. The buyer may have already contracted to purchase the goods from the supplier and then assigns the contract to the lessor, or the buyer may even have an existing lease with the supplier. The requirement that the lessor not select, manufacture or supply the goods does not, however, prevent the lessor from taking possession of the goods; for example, they may be delivered from the supplier to the lessor. Nor does it prevent the lessor from assuming maintenance obligations with respect to the goods.[52] It should also not prevent the lessor from assisting the lessee in locating an appropriate source for the goods or from assisting the lessee in negotiating with the supplier.

2. *The lessor acquires the goods (or the right to their possession and use) in connection with the lease.* This requirement mandates that the lessor's reason for acquiring the goods is to lease them to this particular lessee. In other words, were it not for the fact that the lessee had already selected the goods from the supplier, the lessor would not acquire the goods. This requirement may engender some close cases. For example, what if a lessor acquires the goods in anticipation that a particular lessee will need the goods in the near future, but with no intention to retain them if this prediction is wrong? Article 2A contains no explicit requirement that the finance lease exist prior to the lessor's acquisition of the goods,[53] although the description

---

[51] U.C.C. § 2A-103, Official Comment (g).

[52] *Id.*

[53] In fact, the Code suggests the opposite. One of the ways in which the lease can satisfy the third requirement of section 2A-103(g) is for the lessee to receive a copy of the contract by which the lessor acquired the goods before signing the lease contract. U.C.C. § 2A-103(g)(iii). The necessary implication of this provision is that the lessor can acquire the goods prior to entering into a binding lease with the lessee.

of a finance lease in the Official Comments indicates that the lessor's acquisition of the goods in a finance lease will generally take place after the finance lease is "negotiated."[54] The Comments provide no guidance on what it means for the lessor to acquire the goods "in connection with" the finance lease; they simply state that "the scope of the phrase 'in connection with' is to be developed by the courts, case by case."[55] Because a primary effect of a finance lease is to release the lessor from much of the traditional liability of a lessor, in close cases the question should be resolved by looking to whom the lessee would reasonably expect to answer for product performance, the lessor or the supplier.

To be a finance lease, section 2A-103(g) also requires one of the following:

1. The lessee must receive a copy of the contract by which the lessor acquired the goods prior to signing the lease contract.
2. The lessee's approval of the contract by which the lessor acquired the goods is a condition to the effectiveness of the lease.
3. Before signing the lease contract, the lessee must receive an accurate and complete statement of the promises and warranties given by the supplier to the lessor, including disclaimers of warranty, limitations or modifications of remedy, and liquidated damages.
4. Prior to entering into the lease the lessor must inform the lessee (1) of the identity of the supplier of the goods (unless the lessee directed the lessor to acquire the goods from that supplier); (2) that the lessee is entitled to enforce the promises and warranties provided by the supplier; and (3) that the lessee may communicate with the supplier to obtain an accurate and complete statement of the supplier's promises and warranties. Option (3) is not available if the finance lease is also a consumer lease.

These rights are provided to the lessee to ensure that the lessee is aware, or can easily become aware, of the promises and warranties of the supplier prior to signing the lease. This is necessary because, if the lease is a finance lease, it is the supplier to whom the lessee will have to look for failures in product quality or performance.[56]

It is critical to remember that a finance lease must also be a "true lease" or it is not covered by Article 2A at all. That is, the lessor must retain a valuable reversionary interest. If the lease does not satisfy the criteria

---

[54] *Id.*
[55] *Id.*
[56] *See* § 11.07[E], *infra.*

for a true lease under sections 2A-103(j) and 1-201(37), it will not be governed by Article 2A; it will be treated as disguised sale and governed by Articles 2 and 9.

§ 11.04 FORMATION AND CONSTRUCTION OF THE LEASE CONTRACT

[A] Introduction

Issues relating to the formation and construction of the lease contract are dealt with in Part 2 of Article 2A. For the most part, the provisions in Part 2 are lifted directly from Article 2 with little change in language or substance. Seals are equally inoperative with respect to leases as they are with respect to sales,[57] and the firm-offer[58] and parol evidence[59] provisions of Article 2A are identical in substance to their Article 2 counterparts.

[B] Contract Formation

There is virtually no change in Article 2A in the contract formation rules that appear in sections 2-204 and 2-206 of Article 2; their analogues in Article 2A even bear the same section numbers. The general contract formation rules in section 2-204 are adopted by Article 2A in their entirety. This includes the rule of section 2-204(3), which permits enforcement of a contract so long as the parties intended to contract and the contract provides a reasonably certain basis for an appropriate remedy. Thus, so long as the courts can provide a remedy that they believe will not unduly frustrate the reasonable expectations of the parties, a lease will be enforceable, despite the absence of even material terms.[60]

Section 2A-206, dealing with the manner of offer and acceptance, parallels its counterpart in Article 2 in virtually all respects, save one curious deletion. Like the Article 2 provision, section 2A-206(1) allows acceptance in any manner and by any medium reasonable under the circumstances. Unlike its Article 2 counterpart, however, section 2A-206 does not explicitly permit an offer to be accepted by the shipment[61] of nonconforming goods.[62]

---

[57] U.C.C. § 2A-203.

[58] *See* § 3.05, *supra,* for a discussion of firm offers in a sales context.

[59] U.C.C. § 2A-202.

[60] *See* § 3.03, *supra.*

[61] Section 2-106 looks to section 2-504 to determine whether the offer is one that requires "shipment" by the seller.

[62] Under U.C.C. § 2-206(1)(b), if shipment of the goods is a reasonable means of accepting an offer to buy goods, shipment of nonconforming goods constitutes both an acceptance of the buyer's offer and a breach of contract.

As a result, when shipment of the goods is a reasonable means of accepting an offer to lease goods, shipment of nonconforming goods may not conclude a contract. If shipment under these circumstances does not create a contract, and the seller has not otherwise accepted the buyer's offer, the buyer cannot use the delivery of nonconforming goods as a basis for claiming a breach by the seller.

It is doubtful that the drafters intended this result. More probably, they simply believed that it was sufficiently unlikely that shipment would be a reasonable means of accepting an offer to *lease* (as opposed to buy) goods that it was unnecessary to include a parallel provision to Article 2. If cases arise in which shipment of the goods is a reasonable means of accepting an offer to lease the goods, section 2A-206 should be interpreted to establish a contract through the shipment of nonconforming goods, unless the parties' objective intention is otherwise.

[C] Statute of Frauds

Despite criticism of the Article 2 statute of frauds,[63] Article 2A includes a statute of frauds. Like Article 2, the Article 2A statute of frauds relies on a dollar amount for its application. Under section 2A-201, a lease is not enforceable in the absence of a signed writing unless the total payments under the lease (excluding options to renew or buy) are less than $1,000.

The requirements for a sufficient writing are similar to those in Article 2, although there are some minor differences. Article 2A requires that the writing be sufficient to indicate that a (lease) contract has been made, and that the writing be signed by the person against whom enforcement is sought. A body of case law has developed under Article 2 on the issues of whether a writing is "sufficient to indicate a contract has been made"[64] and whether a writing is "signed"[65] that should be applicable in the context of Article 2A. In addition to these requirements, there are three others:

1. *The writing must describe the leased goods.* A description is sufficient if it "reasonably identifies" the leased goods.[66] There is no parallel

---

[63] *See* § 3.01[E], *supra.*

[64] *See* § 3.01[B], *supra.* The touchstone under U.C.C. § 2-201 as to whether a writing indicates a contract has been made is whether the writing "affords a basis to believe that the offered oral evidence rests on a real transaction." U.C.C. § 2-201, Official Comment 1. This is the appropriate standard for Article 2A as well.

[65] U.C.C. § 1-201(39), which defines a "signature," applies to both Article 2 and Article 2A.

[66] U.C.C. § 2A-201(2). The Comment to Section 2A-201 indicates that the requirement that the lease contract reasonably identify the leased goods was borrowed from sections 9-203(1) and 9-110.

provision in Article 2, although Article 2 implicitly requires that the description at least be sufficient to identify the subject matter of the contract as goods.[67] Parol evidence should be admissible to determine whether a writing "reasonably identifies" the leased goods.[68]

2. *The writing must describe the lease term.* Because the essence of a lease is the transfer of possession for a limited period of time, the drafters felt that the term of the lease was so "essential" that it could not be omitted from the writing.

3. *The writing must state a quantity of goods.* Article 2A does not explicitly state that a sufficient writing must contain a quantity term. Section 2A-201(3) says, however, that a lease contract is not enforceable beyond the quantity of goods stated in the writing. The parallel provision in Article 2 has been interpreted to mean that the writing must state a quantity term,[69] although a quantity of one may sometimes be implied. Subsection (3) to section 2A-201 states that the writing is not insufficient because it incorrectly states a term, but the lease contract is not enforceable beyond the quantity and lease term stated in the writing.

[1]   Statutory Exceptions to the Writing Requirement

Article 2A contains three statutory exceptions to the writing requirement. With minor changes, they parallel the statutory exceptions in section 2-201 of Article 2. They are:

1. *Specially manufactured goods.* Section 2A-201(4)(a) provides that in certain cases, leases for goods that are to be specially manufactured or obtained for the lessee do not have to be evidenced by a writing. The section requires that the goods be specially manufactured *or obtained by* the lessor for the lessee; the lessor does not have to manufacture the goods. The section also requires that the goods not be suitable for lease or sale in the ordinary course of the lessor's business. Even if the goods are not suitable for release in the ordinary course of the lessor's business, if they are suitable for *resale* in the ordinary course of the lessor's business, the exception has not been satisfied. The ordinary course of the lessor's business should not have to include the sale of goods like the leased goods. So long as the goods are

---

[67] U.C.C. § 2-201 requires that the writing be sufficient to indicate that a contract for "sale" has been made. The definition of "sale" in Article 2 is confined to a sale of goods. *See* U.C.C. § 2-106(1).

[68] *See* American Plastic Equip., Inc. v. CBS, Inc., 886 F.2d 521, 9 UCCR2d 848 (2d Cir. 1989) (description in writing of "inactive" molds sufficient to identify subject matter of agreement when supplemented by parol evidence). *See also* J. White & R. Summers, Uniform Commercial Code § 22-3 at 760 (1995) (discussing U.C.C. § 9-110).

[69] *See* § 3.01[B], *supra.*

suitable for sale in the ordinary course of the seller's business, a writing should be required to evidence the contract. Thus, if a lessor, in the ordinary course of business, is likely to be able to sell the goods at a reasonable price without unusual effort or expense, the exception has not been met, and a writing is required. The final requirement of the section is that before notice of the lessee's repudiation of the lease contract is received, and under circumstances that reasonably indicate the goods are for the lessee, the lessor has made either a substantial beginning of the manufacture of the goods or a commitment for their procurement.[70] The purpose of these requirements is that there must to be some reason to believe from the circumstances surrounding the lease that the goods are for the lessee and not someone else.[71]

2. *The party against whom enforcement is sought admits the existence of the lease contract in a pleading, testimony, or otherwise in court.* This exception is taken virtually verbatim from the parallel provision in Article 2.[72] Like its Article 2 counterpart, the lease contract is not enforceable beyond the quantity admitted.

3. *Goods received and accepted by the lessee.* Article 2 contains exceptions for goods received and accepted by the buyer *and* for goods for which payment has been made and accepted. Article 2A incorporates only the first half of the Article 2 exception; it does not exclude from the writing requirement goods for which payment has been made and accepted. According to the Official Comment to section 2A-201, this departure from the Article 2 analogue was made because "[u]nlike a buyer in a sales transaction, the lessee does not tender payment in full for the goods delivered, but only payment for one or more months. It was decided that, as a matter of policy, this act of payment is not a sufficient substitute for the required memorandum."[73]

---

[70] The drafting of U.C.C. § 2A-201(4)(a) is ambiguous in one respect. The section states that the lessor must have made, before the lessee's repudiation, "either a substantial beginning of their manufacture or commitments for their procurement." If the goods are to be manufactured by the lessor, it is clear that the lessor must have made a substantial beginning toward their manufacture. If the goods are to be procured elsewhere by the lessor, however, the provision could mean either (1) that the lessor must have made a substantial beginning toward commitments for the procurement of the goods, or (2) that the lessor must have made commitments for the procurement of the goods. That is, it is not clear whether the words "substantial beginning" apply only to goods to be manufactured by the lessor or apply also to goods to be otherwise procured by the lessor. The authors suggest that the latter interpretation is preferable, if only for the sake of certainty and simplicity.

[71] *See* § 3.01[C][2], *supra.*

[72] *See* § 3.01[C][3], *supra,* for a discussion of the exception in the context of Article 2.

[73] U.C.C. § 2A-201, Official Comment.

If the statute is satisfied by one of the exceptions, section 2A-201(5) provides the lease term for the resulting contract. If there is a writing that specifies a lease term and that is signed by the party against whom enforcement is sought, but that is otherwise insufficient to satisfy the writing requirement (e.g, it fails to indicate that a lease contract has been made or fails to describe the leased goods), the lease term is the term specified in the writing. If a party against whom enforcement is sought admits the lease term, but does not otherwise admit the existence of the lease contract, the lease term is the term admitted. If there is no term in a signed writing and no admission, the lease term is a reasonable term. Unfortunately, Article 2A does not permit the party requesting enforcement the opportunity to prove a term orally agreed upon by the parties even though an exception to the writing requirement has been satisfied.

Article 2A also eliminates a statutory exception present in Article 2. Under certain circumstances, a confirmation signed by the party seeking enforcement of the contract (as opposed to the party against whom enforcement is sought) satisfies the writing requirement of Article 2.[74] This exception was not incorporated in Article 2A because the drafters felt that the number of transactions in which these circumstances would occur was slight.[75]

[2] Nonstatutory exceptions

The application of nonstatutory exceptions to the Article 2 statute of frauds has been thoroughly explored in this text.[76] The primary nonstatutory exception to the Article 2 statute is promissory estoppel, and there exists a plethora of case law going both ways on whether such an exception exists. Section 2A, however, deprives those opposed to a promissory estoppel exception of one argument that can be made with respect to the Article 2 statute. Section 2-201 of Article 2 begins by stating "[e]xcept as otherwise provided in this section" a contract for the sale of goods for a price of $500 or more is not enforceable in the absence of a qualifying writing. Opponents of nonstatutory exceptions to the statute have argued that the quoted language is a clear indication that the *only* exceptions to the statute are those provided in the section (i.e., section 2-201) itself. A number of cases have relied upon this reasoning in rejecting a promissory estoppel exception to

---

[74] U.C.C. § 2-201(2). *See* § 3.01[C][1], *supra.*
[75] *See* U.C.C. § 2A-208, Official Comment.
[76] *See* § 3.01[D], *supra.*

the Article 2 statute of frauds.[77] The quoted language is omitted from section 2A-201. There is no indication in Article 2A or the Comment to section 2A-201 that this omission was intended to encourage a promissory estoppel exception; however, since the original promulgation of Article 2 the Restatement of Contracts (Second) adopted a promissory estoppel exception to the statute of frauds,[78] and the Article 2A drafters must have been aware of this. Permitting a promissory estoppel exception to Article 2A would make it more consistent with general contract law and the majority of cases decided under Article 2.[79]

§ 11.05   MODIFICATION, RESCISSION, AND WAIVER

Section 2A-208 is adapted from section 2-209 of Article 2 and is similar in many ways. For example, both contain provisions eliminating the common law requirement that consideration must support a contract modification.[80] In addition, in almost identical language, both Articles sanction "no oral modification" (N.O.M.) clauses, and both permit their waiver under certain circumstances.[81] Section 2-209 has presented substantial interpretive problems that are thoroughly discussed elsewhere in the text.[82] Despite these difficulties, the drafters of Article 2A decided to let well enough alone and mirror the text of the Article 2 sections, warts and all.

The drafters of Article 2A, however, made one major change from section 2-209. In one of the few instances that the drafters of Article 2A rejected outright a policy choice made in Article 2, they did not include in Article 2A the requirement that if a modification brought a contract within the statute of frauds, the contract had to be evidenced by a writing.[83] Under section 2-209(3), if *A* orally agrees to sell *B* his car for $490, the contract is not required to be in writing because the price is less than $500. If the parties modify the contract to make the price $510, neither party can enforce the contract against the other for any amount unless there is a writing sufficient to satisfy section 2-201 (or unless an exception to the statute is satisfied).

---

[77] *See, e.g.,* Cox v. Cox, 292 Ala. 106, 289 So. 2d 609 (1974); Anderson Constr. Co. v. Lyon Metal Prods., Inc., 370 So. 2d 935 (Miss. 1979); Schwedes v. Romain, 587 P.2d 388 (Mont. 1978); Farmland Serv. Corp. v. Klein, 196 Neb. 538, 244 N.W.2d 86 (1976).

[78] Restatement (Second) of Contracts § 150 (1981).

[79] *See* § 3.01[D], *supra.*

[80] U.C.C. §§ 2-209(1), 2A-208(1).

[81] U.C.C. § 2-209(2), 2-209(4), and § 2A-208(2), 2A-208(3).

[82] *See* § 3.10, *supra.*

[83] *See* U.C.C. § 2-209(3).

Under Article 2A, if the parties have an oral lease agreement in which the total lease payments are $900, the oral lease is enforceable because the total rent is less than $1,000. If they later modify the rent so that the total is now $1,100, a writing is not necessarily required before the lease can be enforced. According to the Official Comment to section 2A-208, the drafters believed it was "unfair to allow an oral modification to make the entire lease contract unenforceable, e.g., if the modification takes it a few dollars over the limit."[84] Although the absence of a writing does not *per se* make such a lease unenforceable, it is not clear that the modified lease *will* be enforceable under Article 2A absent a writing. The Comment says that resolution of the issue is left for the courts based upon the facts of each case. Consequently, the court has the power to enforce the modified contract despite the absence of a writing. On the other hand, if the court decides that it is unfair to enforce the modified contract because of the absence of a qualifying writing, the court is not obliged to do so. Furthermore, it is apparently within the discretion of the court to enforce the *original* contract.[85]

The manner in which the drafters dealt with this very troublesome issue is subject to criticism. It is true that the meaning and application of section 2-209(3) has been the subject of much litigation with disparate results.[86] To drop the provision from Article 2A and leave the entire issue to the courts with no guidance, however, does not help to resolve the difficult issue of the application of the statute of frauds to contract modifications. Courts are apparently free under section 2A-208 to enforce the modified contract, to enforce the original contract, or to refuse to enforce any contract. Which alternative the court should choose is simply left to its determination of what is "fair." Even though all of us are interested in fairness, this hardly provides the kind of guidance necessary for an efficacious business code.

---

[84] U.C.C. § 2-208, Official Comment.

[85] The full text of the Official Comment to section 2A-208 states:

> Section 2-209(3) provides that "the requirements of the statute of frauds section of this Article (Section 2-201) must be satisfied if the contract as modified is within its provisions." This provision was not incorporated as it is unfair to allow an oral modification to make the entire lease contract unenforceable, *e.g.,* if the modification takes it a few dollars over the dollar limit. At the same time, the problem could not be solved by providing that the lease contract would still be enforceable in its pre-modification state (if it then satisfied the statute of frauds) since in some cases that might be worse than no enforcement at all. Resolution of the issue is left to the courts based on the facts of each case.

The fact that the Comment, in the penultimate sentence, states that in *some* cases enforcement of the pre-modification lease may be worse than no enforcement at all, indicates that in other cases, enforcement of the pre-modification lease may be the preferable resolution.

[86] *See* § 3.10[C], *supra.*

§ 11.06   UNCONSCIONABILITY

In some ways the Article 2A provision on unconscionability is much like its Article 2 counterpart, and in other ways it is radically different. The differences center almost entirely on Article 2A's special treatment of consumer leases.

Article 2A's analogue to section 2-302 is section 2A-108. The language of the first subsection directly parallels section 2-302(1) and the substance is unchanged:

> If the court as a matter of law finds a lease or any clause of a lease contract to have been unconscionable at the time it was made that court may refuse to enforce the lease contract, or it may enforce the remainder of the lease contract without the unconscionable clause, or it may so limit the application of any unconscionable clause as to avoid any unconscionable result.[87]

As with the Article 2 section, this section gives the court the option to refuse to enforce the entire contract, to enforce the contract absent the unconscionable clause, or to modify the unconscionable clause so as to make the contract conscionable. In addition, section 2A-108(3) provides similar procedural protections to those provided in section 2-302(2).[88] Finally, under both sections, a finding of unconscionability is a matter of law, not an issue of fact for the jury.

Section 2A-108, however, contains two sections dealing exclusively with consumer leases have no parallel provisions in Article 2. Subsection (2) provides:

> With respect to a consumer lease, if the court as a matter of law finds that a lease contract or any clause of a lease contract has been induced by unconscionable conduct or that unconscionable conduct has occurred in the collection of a claim arising from a lease contract, the court may grant appropriate relief.

This provision permits the court to grant any appropriate relief whenever a lease is *induced* by unconscionable conduct, whether or not any *terms* of the contract are unconscionable. This appears to resolve, in this limited context, the issue arising under Article 2 of whether "substantive" uncon-

---

[87] U.C.C. § 2A-108(1).

[88] That is, parties are afforded a reasonable opportunity to present evidence as to the setting, purpose, and effect of the contract or a clause thereof, or the conduct of a party.

scionability must be present before a court can find a contract or term unconscionable[89] (i.e., whether a term must be substantively unfair regardless of the conduct which induced the contract). According to section 2A-108(2), procedural unconscionability alone is sufficient if the lease is a consumer lease.[90] With respect to leases other than consumer leases, the debate will presumably continue to rage.

Section 2A-108(2) also permits a court to grant appropriate relief if unconscionable conduct has occurred in the collection of a claim arising from a consumer lease contract. Although the Code itself offers no insight as to the kind of conduct this provision contemplates, it would likely include such things as bringing a collection action in a distant forum, harassment and similar conduct of the sort barred by the Fair Debt Collection Practices Act[91] and parallel state statutes, invasion of privacy,[92] and improper use of self-help remedies.[93]

The second departure from the Article 2 unconscionability section is the explicit provision of attorney's fees to a successful lessee claiming unconscionability. Section 2A-108 provides that the court *shall* award reasonable attorney's fees to a successful lessee in a consumer lease; once the court finds unconscionability, it appears to have no discretion in awarding attorney's fees, although the court can control the amount of the fees. The court is also required to award attorney's fees to the lessor, but only if the lessee *knew* her claim of unconscionability was groundless. Because the standard is so high ("groundless") and requires actual knowledge on the part of the lessee, grants of attorney's fees to lessors will be extremely rare.

Despite the breadth of the protections accorded to consumer lessees, it is doubtful that they have much impact. Much of the consumer protection legislation already in place covers the lease of goods to consumers[94] and protects consumers against the same kind of conduct that a court would

---

[89] For a discussion of this issue, *see* § 3.09[B], *supra.*

[90] The Official Comment to section 2A-108 provides, in part: Thus, subsection (2) recognizes that a consumer lease may not itself be unconscionable but that the agreement would never have been entered into if the unconscionable means had not been employed to induce the consumer to agree.

[91] 15 U.S.C. § 1692 (1995).

[92] *See* Brents v. Morgan, 299 S.W. 967 (Ky. Ct. App. 1927).

[93] The Official Comment cites as an illustration the use or threat to use violence in the collection of a claim.

[94] *See, e.g.*, Alabama Deceptive Trade Practices Act § 8-19-3 (Michie 1997) ("sale, buying, and distribution" includes leasing goods to consumers); Ohio Consumer Sales Practices Act, Ohio Rev. Code Ann. § 1345.01(A) (Anderson 1998) ("consumer transaction" includes lease of goods to consumer); Texas Deceptive Trade Practices Act, Tex. Bus. and Com. Code § 17.45(1) (1998) (goods include those "purchased or leased for use").

likely find unconscionable under section 2A-108.[95] In addition, most consumer-protection statutes provide for the recovery of attorney's fees, although in many cases the award under these statutes is discretionary with the court.[96]

§ 11.07   WARRANTIES UNDER ARTICLE 2A

[A]   Introduction

Courts have applied Article 2 warranties to leases of goods for three decades.[97] In doing so, courts often said that they were applying Article 2 warranties "by analogy."[98] There was, however, no assurance that a court would apply the Article 2 warranties to a lease of goods by analogy, and occasionally courts refused to do so.[99] Further, already existing law sometimes governed the lease of goods, which constrained courts from adopting the Article 2 warranties.[100] The drafters of Article 2A concluded that the lease of goods was sufficiently similar to the sale of goods[101] that they adopted the warranties of Article 2 with no substantive changes and only minor changes in verbiage.

[B]   Express Warranties

Express warranties are contained in section 2A-210, which is virtually identical in form and substance to its Article 2 counterpart. Express warranties in lease transactions are created as follows:

a.   Any affirmation of fact or promise made by the lessor to the lessee which relates to the goods and becomes part of the basis of the bargain creates an express warranty that the goods will conform to the affirmation or promise.

---

[95] *See* Ohio Consumer Sales Practices Act, Ohio Rev. Code Ann. § 1345.03(A) (Anderson 1998) (prohibiting unconscionable acts or practices in connection with a consumer transaction).

[96] *See, e.g.*, Alaska Stat. § 45.50.531(g) (1997); Ohio Rev. Code Ann. § 1345.09(F)(2) (Anderson 1998).

[97] *See* Sawyer v. Pioneer Leasing Corp., 428 S.W.2d 46, 5 UCCR 453 (Ark. 1968); Cintrone v. Hertz Truck Leasing & Rental Serv., 212 A.2d 769 (N.J. 1965).

[98] *See* § 2.03[A], *supra*.

[99] *See, e.g.*, Clive v. Prowler Indus. of Md., Inc., 418 A.2d 968 (Del. 1980); Cianfrani v. Kalmar-AC Handling Sys., Inc., 1995 WL 563289 (D.N.J. 1995).

[100] *See* Glenn Dick Equip. Co. v. Galey Constr., Inc., 541 P.2d 1184 (Idaho 1975).

[101] *See* U.C.C. § 2A-210, Official Comment.

   b.   Any description of the goods which is made part of the basis of the bargain creates an express warranty that the goods will conform to the description.

   c.   Any sample or model that is made part of the basis of the bargain creates an express warranty that the whole of the goods will conform to the sample or model.[102]

Express warranties in lease transactions are created by precisely the same kind of expressions or conduct as they are in sales transactions. As a result, issues such as whether a representation is part of the basis of the bargain are sure to arise under Article 2A as they have under Article 2.[103] Further, section 2A-210 also contains an analogue to section 2-313(2), which provides that while formal words such as "warrant" or "guarantee" are unnecessary to create an express warranty, affirmations merely of the value of the goods or a statements purporting to be merely the lessor's opinion or commendation of the goods do not create express warranties. Consequently, the murky line between "puffing" and the creation of express warranties is bound to be an issue under Article 2A.[104]

[C]   Implied Warranties

[1]   Warranties Against Interference and Infringement

Section 2A-211 provides warranties against interference and infringement that are modeled after similar warranties in section 2-312 of Article 2. There are, however, some material differences from Article 2.

First, there is no warranty of title in Article 2A. This merely reflects the fact the lessor retains title in a lease transaction. In addition, section 2A-211 provides an implied warranty of quiet possession not present in Article 2:

> There is in a lease contract a warranty that for the lease term no person holds a claim to or interest in the goods that arose from an act or omission of the lessor, other than a claim by way of infringement or the like, which will interfere with the lessee's enjoyment of its leasehold interest.

The drafters' reason for including a explicit warranty of quiet possession is somewhat curious and is as follows:

---

[102] U.C.C. § 2A-210(1).

[103] For a discussion of this issue in the context of Article 2 express warranties, *see* § 4.05[F], *supra*.

[104] For a discussion of this issue in the context of Article 2, *see* § 4.05[B], *supra*.

> The warranty of quiet possession was abolished with respect to sales of goods [citation omitted]. Section 2A-211(1) reinstates the warranty of quiet possession with respect to leases. Inherent in the nature of the limited interest transferred by the lease—the right to possession and use of the goods—is the need of the lessee for protection greater than that afforded to the buyer.[105]

Although it is true that a warranty of quiet possession is not included in section 2-312 of Article 2, Comment 1 to section 2-312 says that "[d]isturbance of quiet possession, although not mentioned specifically, is one way, among many, in which the breach of the warranty of title may be established." Thus, although the Comment to section 2A-211 describes it as such, the warranty of quiet possession is not "abolished" by section 2-312. Instead, it is *incorporated* into the warranty of title. As a result, it is not clear how the explicit warranty of quiet possession in section 2A-211 affords greater protection to a lessee than section 2-312 affords to a buyer.

One possibility is that the warranty of quiet possession in Article 2A is intended to be broader than that of Article 2. Under the common law, the warranty of quiet possession could be breached by a third-party claim even if the claim was ultimately determined to be invalid, so long as the claim was colorable. This standard has been carried forward in the Article 2 cases.[106] It may be that the drafters of Article 2A intended to impose liability upon a lessor for claims asserted by third parties, even if the claims failed to meet the standard of "colorability." There is a hint in the Comment to section 2A-211 that it was for this reason that the warranty of quiet possession was limited to claims resulting from acts or omissions of the *lessor*:

> Since the scope of the protection is limited to claims or interests that arose from acts or omissions of the lessor, the lessor will be in a position to evaluate the potential cost, certainly a far better position than that enjoyed by the lessee. Further, to the extent the market will allow, the lessor can attempt to pass on the anticipated additional cost to the lessee in the guise of higher rent.

Arguably, the drafters intended the lessor to insure the lessee against damage from all claims, whatever their "colorability," because the lessor would be in a better position to anticipate these claims, particularly because they must arise from his acts or omissions. While this may be true with respect to most colorable claims, it is not clear why the lessor is in a better position to anticipate claims that do not even rise to the minimal level of

---

[105] U.C.C. § 2A-211, Official Comment.

[106] *See* § 4.02[A], *supra.*

colorability. The very lack of any reasonable basis in law or fact for these claims often precludes the lessor from having any better reason to anticipate the claim than anyone else.[107]

It remains to be seen how this section will be interpreted. If courts require that a claim be "colorable" before the warranty of quiet possession is breached, section 2A-211 might actually offer less protection than section 2-312. As mentioned previously, section 2A-211 requires that a claim result from an "act or omission *of the lessor*."[108] An act or omission of the vendor or lessor was not generally required for the breach of the warranty of quiet possession at common law,[109] nor does it appear to be required by section 2-312.

Section 2A-211 also contains a counterpart to section 2-312 (3), which provides a warranty by merchant sellers against infringement of intellectual property rights. Like its Article 2 counterpart, section 2A-211(2) applies only to merchants in goods of the kind involved in the lease. Further, like section 2-312, it provides protection against only "rightful" infringement claims of third parties. Whether this means that a claim must be ultimately determined to be valid to constitute a breach of this warranty has been discussed in connection with section 2-312.[110] This warranty is not given by lessors in finance leases.[111] Section 2A-211 also has an analogue in the Article 2 provision[112] requiring a buyer to hold the seller harmless against infringement claims if the seller supplies the goods pursuant to the buyer's specifications.

[2] Implied Warranties of Merchantability and Fitness

Article 2A provides a warranty of merchantability that is indistinguishable from the parallel provision in Article 2. The six standards for merchantability are exactly the same as those in Article 2,[113] and like section

---

[107] It is true that in some cases the lessor will be in a position to anticipate a "colorless" claim, as when the claimant informs the lessor of the claim prior to the lease of the goods to the lessee.

[108] U.C.C. § 2A-211(1) (emphasis added).

[109] Restatement (Second) of Property § 16.3 (1977).

[110] *See* § 4.03, *supra.*

[111] *See* the discussion of finance leases in § 11.03[B], *supra.*

[112] U.C.C. § 2A-211(3).

[113] "Goods to be merchantable must be at least such as

      (a)   pass without objection in the trade under the contract description; and

      (b)   in the case of fungible goods, are of fair average quality within the

2-314, the warranty of merchantability is given only by lessors who are merchants with respect to goods of the kind involved in the lease transaction. The Article 2A warranty of merchantability, however, is not given by the lessor in a finance lease.

Article 2A also provides an implied warranty of fitness for a particular purpose. As with the warranty of merchantability, the warranty of fitness does not apply to finance leases. In all other respects, it is identical to its Article 2 counterpart.[114] The issues arising under both the warranties of merchantability and fitness are similar to those that have arisen under Article 2 and are discussed elsewhere in the text.[115]

[D]   Exclusion and Modification of Warranties

The provisions of Article 2A relating to the exclusion or modification of warranties are similar to those of Article 2, with some modest changes. Section 2A-214(1), like its Article 2 counterpart,[116] provides that express warranties are not subject to disclaimer, although prior representations may be removed as part of the basis of the bargain and thus not constitute express warranties at all.[117] Express warranties are also made subject to the Article 2A parol-evidence rule.[118]

Section 2A-214(2) permits the exclusion or modification of the warranty of merchantability. As with the parallel provision in Article 2,[119] a

---

description; and
(c)   are fit for the ordinary purposes for which such goods are used; and
(d)   run, within the variations permitted by the agreement, of even kind, quality and quantity within each unit and among all units involved; and
(e)   are adequately contained, packaged, and labeled as the agreement may require; and
(f)   conform to the promises or affirmations of fact made on the container or label if any."

For a discussion of these standards, *see* § 4.06[B][2], *supra.*
[114] The text of U.C.C. § 2A-213 is as follows:

Except in a finance lease, if the lessor at the time the lease contract is made has reason to know of any particular purpose for which the goods are required and that the lessee is relying on the lessor's skills or judgment to select or furnish suitable goods, there is in the lease contract an implied warranty that the goods will be fit for that purpose.
[115] *See* §§ 4.06[B] and 4.06[C], *supra.*
[116] U.C.C. § 2-316(1).
[117] For a discussion of this issue, *see* § 4.05[F], *supra.*
[118] U.C.C. § 2A-214(1).
[119] U.C.C. § 2-316(2).

disclaimer of the warranty of merchantability under this section must mention "merchantability." Unlike the Article 2 provision section 2A-214(2) requires that a disclaimer of merchantability be conspicuous and in writing. Section 2-316(2) does not require a disclaimer of the warranty of merchantability to be in writing and requires only that it be conspicuous if it is, in fact, in writing.

Section 2-316(2) permits the exclusion of the implied warranty of fitness by general language excluding all implied warranties without specific mention of the implied warranty of fitness.[120] Section 2A-214(2) also permits the implied warranty of fitness to be excluded or modified, and like section 2-316(2), section 2A-214(2) does not explicitly require that the implied warranty of fitness be mentioned by name in the disclaimer. Unlike section 2-316, however, the example given in section 2A-214(2) of a qualifying disclaimer of the warranty of fitness is not a general disclaimer, and specifically mentions the warranty of fitness.[121] A disclaimer or modification of the Article 2A warranty of fitness must be in writing and conspicuous.

Article 2A also adopts the substance of section 2-316(3), which permits the exclusion of all implied warranties by the use of such terms as "as is," "with all faults," and "other language that in common understanding" makes plain that there are no implied warranties.[122] Section 2A-214(3), however, requires that such disclaimers be in writing and conspicuous. Article 2 contains no similar requirements and, in the absence of explicit language, courts have differed over whether disclaimers must be conspicuous under section 2-316(3).[123] Section 2A-214 also contains analogues to the provisions of section 2-316(3) that permit disclaimers by course of dealing, course of performance, and usage of trade and that exclude implied warranties for defects that should have been discovered upon the lessee's examination of the goods.[124] Section 2A-214(4) permits the exclusion or modification of a warranty against infringement if the disclaimer is specific, in writing, and conspicuous. The warranty against infringement can also be disclaimed by

---

[120] U.C.C. § 2-316(2) states: "Language to exclude all implied warranties of fitness is sufficient if it states, for example, that 'There are no warranties which extend beyond the description on the face hereof.'"

[121] U.C.C. § 2A-214(2) provides in part: "Language to exclude all implied warranties of fitness is sufficient if it is in writing, is conspicuous and states, for example, 'there is no warranty that the goods will be fit for a particular purpose.'"

[122] U.C.C. § 2A-214(3).

[123] For a discussion of this issue, *see* § 4.07[C][2], *supra*.

[124] Like its Article 2 counterpart, section 2A-214(3)(b) excludes all implied warranties when the lessee has examined the goods as fully as desired *or* when the lessee has refused to examine the goods.

circumstances, including course of dealing, course of performance, and usage of trade, which give the lessee reason to know that the goods are leased subject to the claim of a third party.

[E] Third-Party Beneficiaries of Warranties

As a result of the distinction drawn in Article 2A between finance leases and other leases of goods, there are two sections in Article 2A dealing with third-party beneficiaries of warranties. Section 2A-209 gives the lessee the benefit of all of the promises and warranties given by a supplier to a lessor in a finance lease.[125] The extension of the supplier's promises and warranties to the lessee, however, also includes any disclaimers or limitations of warranties contained in the contract between the supplier and the lessor.[126]

Neither a lessor nor a supplier can prevent the supplier's promises and warranties from passing to the lessee under this section.[127] That is, a supplier's contract with the lessor in a finance lease cannot provide that the supplier's warranties extend only to the lessor and not to the lessee. If the supplier in a finance lease wants to disclaim warranties or limit remedies, the disclaimer or limitation must be equally applicable to the lessor and lessee; in the words of the Official Comment, there can be no "selective discrimination" against the lessee.[128]

Under section 2A-209(3), the supplier and lessor in a finance lease can modify or rescind their supply contract and the modification is effective against the lessee so long as the supplier has not received notice prior to the modification or rescission that the lessee has entered into the finance lease. If such modifications are effective against the lessee (because the supplier did not receive the requisite notice),[129] the lessor is deemed to have assumed the supplier's obligations as they existed prior to the modification and were available to the lessee. Thus, for example, if the lessor and supplier modify their contract to eliminate an express warranty, and the supplier has

---

[125] The section also extends to the lessee the promises and warranties of any third party provided in connection with the supply contract. This would include, for example, promises made by a third party with whom the supplier and the lessor have made arrangements to maintain the goods.

[126] U.C.C. § 2A-209(1).

[127] U.C.C. § 2A-209(1), Official Comment 1.

[128] Id.

[129] If, prior to modification, the supplier does receive notice that the lessee has entered into the finance lease, the original terms of the supply contract can be enforced against the supplier by the lessee.

not at that time received notice that the supply lease has been entered into between the lessee and lessor, the lessee cannot enforce the warranty against the supplier. Assuming, however, that the lessee entered into the supply contract having been apprised of the express warranty,[130] the lessor must assume the obligations of the warranty, which can then be enforced by the lessee against the lessor.

Article 2A also contains a general third-party beneficiary provision that applies to all leases and is analogous to section 2-318. Section 2A-216 contains three alternatives parallel to those in section 2-318, and each is similar in effect to its counterpart.[131] However, two changes should be noted. Alternatives A and B of section 2A-216 state that the section is not intended "to displace principles of law and equity that extend a warranty to or for the benefit of a lessee to other persons." Thus, it is clear that the alternatives are to be read *inclusively*—that is, the section describes only to whom a warranty extends, not, by negative implication, to whom it does not extend. Thus, courts are free to extend privity, including horizontal privity, beyond that stated in the section itself.[132]

The other change from section 2-318 is that each alternative of section 2A-216 explicitly provides that any exclusion, modification, or limitation of warranties or remedies effective against the lessee is also effective against any beneficiary. Although this idea is expressed in the Comment to section 2-318,[133] it is not in the text of section 2-318 itself. The lessor, however, is not free to practice "selective discrimination" against the beneficiary—that is, the lessor cannot provide a warranty to the lessee and at the same time exclude liability to the beneficiaries with respect to the warranty.[134]

§ 11.08   TRANSFERS AND RIGHTS OF CREDITORS

[A]   Introduction

Because leases involve the separation of ownership and possession, there is the potential that third parties will be misled as to the respective

---

[130] It should be remembered that under section 2A-103(g)(iii), the lessee must have the opportunity to become aware of the promises and warranties in the supply contract before executing the lease. Only if the lessor complies with this requirement would the lease qualify as a "finance lease" and the lessor be relieved of its implied warranty obligations pursuant to sections 2A-211 through 2A-213. *See* § 11.03[B], *supra.*

[131] *See* § 4.09, *supra*, for a discussion of U.C.C. § 2-318.

[132] For a thorough discussion of this issue in the context of U.C.C. § 2-318, *see* §§ 4.09[A]–4.09[D], *supra.*

[133] U.C.C. § 2-318, Official Comment 1.

[134] *See* U.C.C. § 2A-216, Official Comment.

rights of the lessor and lessee. For example, the lessee who has possession may purport to sell the goods to a third party who is unaware of the lessor's interest. Or, a creditor of the lessor may attempt to recover possession of the property or otherwise foreclose on it in contravention of the lessee's rights under the lease. Article 9 deals in detail with these, and similar issues, in the context of secured transactions. Because a lease involves a division of property interests similar to the division of interests in secured transactions, it is necessary to have a set of rules dealing with parallel issues. Unfortunately, the rules of Article 2A are almost—but not quite—as complex as those in Article 9.[135]

The following sections do not attempt an exhaustive analysis of the various rules found in Part 3 of Article 2A, which relate to the transfer of leasehold interests and relative priority among various contending parties. The authors' intent is to provide an understanding of the basic structure of Part 3 of Article 2A that is sufficient to enable the reader to comprehend and explore, if necessary, more specific issues.

[B] Enforceability of the Lease Contract Against Third Parties

Part Three of Article 2A begins with the proposition "Except as otherwise provided in this Article, a lease contract is effective and enforceable according to its terms between the parties, against purchasers of the goods, and against creditors of the parties."[136]

As a result of this overarching provision, the interests of the lessor and lessee are given priority over all third parties *unless* the Article provides otherwise. Thus, if the lease is a true lease, and a provision is not present in Article 2A giving priority to a party other than the parties to the lease contract, the lease contract is superior to all other interests.[137] If, however, the "lease" is merely a disguised sale with a security interest, transfer and priority are governed by Article 2 and Article 9, not by Article 2A.

[C] Transfer of Leasehold Interests

Rules relating to the transfer of leasehold interests (including the creation of security interests and involuntary transfers) are found in section 2A-

---

[135] For a thorough discussion of these issues in the context of Article 2A prior to the amendments of 1990, *see* Harris, "The Rights of Creditors Under Article 2A," 39 Ala. L. Rev. 803 (1988).

[136] U.C.C. § 2A-301.

[137] This assumes, of course, that there are no conflicting federal or state laws that supersede U.C.C. § 2A-301.

303 and are somewhat complex. Article 2A accepts the general proposition that, absent a contractual prohibition against transfer, interests created by a lease are freely transferrable. Thus, for example, if the contract does not prohibit it, a lessor can transfer her right to the rent. Similarly, unless precluded by the lease contract, a lessee is free to sell or "sublet" his interest or to grant to another a security interest in his leasehold.

It often happens, however, that the lease prohibits the transfer of an interest, usually that of the lessee, or makes such a transfer, at least without the permission of the other party, an event of default. Even in these cases, Article 2A makes a transfer effective, although it may also be a breach of the lease agreement.[138] This means that while the injured party may be entitled to certain rights and remedies for breach,[139] the transferee is nonetheless entitled to the interest transferred.[140]

In one instance, the transfer of an interest constitutes a breach of the lease agreement even if the lease agreement does not prohibit the transfer or make it an event of default. This is when the transfer "materially impairs the prospect of obtaining return performance by, materially changes the duty of, or materially increases the burden or risk imposed upon the other party to the lease contract."[141] If a transfer is made under these circumstances, the other party may seek damages, or, in the court's discretion, receive an injunction against the transfer.[142] For example, suppose that Able leases a truck to Baker to be used by Baker to haul vegetables on paved roads. The lease does not contain any prohibition against the transfer of interests, nor does it make such transfer an event of default. Baker then proposes to sublease the truck to Charlie, who intends to use the truck to haul dirt and

---

[138] *See* Official Comment 1 to U.C.C. § 2A-303, which provides in part:

> Subsection (2) states a rule, consistent with Section 9-311, that voluntary and involuntary transfers of an interest of a party under the lease contract or of the lessor's residual interest, including by way of the creation and enforcement of a security interest, are effective, notwithstanding a provision in the lease agreement prohibiting the transfer or making the transfer an event of default.

[139] If the transfer is made an event of default under the lease, the lessor is entitled to all the rights and remedies outlined in U.C.C. § 2A-501(2). U.C.C. § 2A-303(5)(a).

[140] However, if a transfer of an interest is prohibited by the lease agreement (as distinguished from simply being an event of default), U.C.C. § 2A-303(5)(b) gives the court the discretion to cancel the lease contract or enjoin the transfer when a damage remedy would be ineffective to adequately protect the injured party. *See* U.C.C. § 2A-303, Official Comment 1. In addition, if the transfer is made an event of default under the lease, the lessor may have the right to repossess the goods. *See* U.C.C. § 2A-525.

[141] U.C.C. § 2A-303(5)(b).

[142] *Id.*

rocks over unpaved roads. Because Charlie's use of the truck would both increase the wear and tear on the truck and increase the risk of damage to the truck, the transfer will likely violate section 2A-303(5).[143]

Conversely, in two instances, provisions in lease agreements that prohibit transfers or make transfers an event of default are generally *not* enforceable. The first instance is a prohibition against the grant of a security interest by either party in its interest in the goods. A provision prohibiting the grant or enforcement of a security interest by the *lessor* in its residuary estate or making it an event of default under the lease is unenforceable. Somewhat more complicated, a provision in a lease prohibiting the *lessee* from granting a security interest in its right to use and possession or making such a grant an event of default is unenforceable, except to the extent that there is an *actual* transfer of the lessee's interest in violation of the lease contract. That is, only if the lessee's grant of the security interest involves the present right to use and possession (i.e., a pledge) or the secured party otherwise takes actual possession (e.g., in the event of the lessee's default under the security agreement), can a lease provision barring security interests or making them an event of default be enforced.[144]

The second instance is the presence of a lease provision that "(i) prohibits the transfer by either party of their right to damages for default of the whole lease contract or makes such a transfer an event of default, or (ii) prohibits the transfer by either party of the right to payment arising from due performance by that party of its entire lease obligation."[145] In effect, this provision makes unenforceable any provision restricting the ability to transfer a right to payment.

---

[143] This analysis assumes that the lease between Able and Charlie does not contain a restriction limiting the use of the truck to hauling vegetables. If it did, the use of the truck by the sublessee to haul dirt and rocks would be in violation of the lease. Official Comment 9 to U.C.C. § 2A-303 further states:

> Relief on the ground of material prejudice when the lease agreement does not prohibit the transfer or make it an event of default should be afforded only in extreme circumstances, considering the fact that the party asserting material prejudice did not insist upon a provision in the lease agreement that would protect against such transfer.

[144] To increase the complexity even further, to the extent that the enforcement of a security interest created by either party involves the actual delegation of a material performance, a provision prohibiting such transfers is enforceable. U.C.C. § 2A-303(3). For example, if the enforcement of a security interest involves the secured party's assuming the lessor's obligation to maintain the goods, a provision prohibiting such transfers or making them an event of default would be enforceable.

[145] U.C.C. § 2A-303(4).

The bottom line is that provisions that restrict the right of the parties to transfer their interests are usually enforceable. Their violation creates a breach of the lease agreement, which may create a right to damages or other remedies, although the transfer itself is effective.[146] The primary exceptions to this are restrictions on the creation by the parties of security interests and the right to receive payment, which are generally not enforceable.

[D]   Delegation of Duties

Article 2A says little about the delegation of a party's performance obligations. Section 2A-303 does provide, however, that the transfer of an interest is considered to be a breach when the transfer of the interest materially impairs the prospect that the other party will receive the performance due under the contract.[147] The implication is that a delegation of duties is impermissible when it materially imperils the likelihood that performance will be forthcoming from the party to whom the obligation has been delegated. This parallels the common law rule.[148] In addition, contractual restrictions on delegation of duties are generally enforceable at common law and presumably remain so under Article 2A. In any event, section 2A-303(7) provides that unless the parties agree to the contrary, a delegation of performance does not relieve the transferor of the duty to perform or from liability for nonperformance.

[E]   Subsequent Leases by the Lessor and Sales or Subleases by the Lessee

Sections 2A-304 and 2A-305 deal with situations in which a subsequent lease by the lessor or sublease by the lessee conflicts with the rights of a third party or the rights of the other party to the lease. The sections are patterned after section 2-403 of Article 2, with some revision.

The foundational rule of both sections is that each party may transfer only the interests it possesses or otherwise has the power to transfer.[149]

---

[146] U.C.C. § 2A-303(8) provides that in a consumer lease, a provision prohibiting the transfer of an interest or making a transfer an event of default must be conspicuous and in writing.

[147] U.C.C. § 2A-303(5)(b).

[148] E. Allan Farnsworth, Farnsworth on Contracts, § 11.10 at 826 (2d ed. 1990). The general common-law rule is that a duty is not delegable if the obligee has a substantial interest in performance by the original promisee.

[149] U.C.C. §§ 2A-304 and 2A-305 contain provisions analogous to those of section 2-403 and give a lessor with voidable title or a lessee with a voidable leasehold interest the power to transfer a good leasehold interest under certain circumstances. Generally, a voidable interest is one that has been obtained by fraudulent practices.

Under section 2A-304, a lessor may lease goods he has already leased, but the lessee under the subsequent lease takes subject to the original lease. Because the lessor possesses only a reversionary interest, he does not have the ability to lease anything other than all, or a portion, of this reversionary interest. Thus, if the lessor leases the goods to Lessee 1 for a period of one year beginning October 1, 1999 and leases the same goods to Lessee 2 for a period of two years beginning the same date, Lessee 2 takes subject to the right of Lessee 1 to use and possession through September 30, 2000.

Similarly, a lessee has the power to transfer only those rights to use and possession that are granted by the lease. Thus, a sublessee takes subject to all restrictions and all obligations of the lessee. For example, if Lessee leases a truck from Lessor for a period of three months and the use of the truck is restricted to hauling vegetables, a sublessee can receive a sublease for no more than three months, and the sublessee's use of the goods is restricted to hauling vegetables.

Both sections contain an exception to the general proposition that a party can only transfer the interest that it has under the existing lease. Under section 2A-304, a lessee who leases goods in the ordinary course of business from a lessor who is a merchant in goods of the kind involved in the lease can take free of an existing lease if the goods were entrusted[150] by the existing lessee to the lessor. The way this operates can be illustrated by a simple example. Assume that Lessor is in the business of selling and leasing new and used lawn and garden equipment. Lessee 1 leases a lawn tractor from Lessor for a period of one year. After three months, Lessee 1 returns the equipment to Lessor for routine maintenance. While the lawn tractor is in the possession of the Lessor, she leases it to Lessee 2. If Lessee 2 is a lessee in the ordinary course of business,[151] he will take free of the existing lease. This exception applies only if the goods are entrusted by the existing lessee to the *lessor,* not to some other person who is a merchant in the goods.

---

[150] "Entrusting" is defined in U.C.C. § 2-403(3): "any delivery and acquiescence in retention of possession regardless of any condition expressed between the parties to the delivery or acquiescence and regardless of whether the procurement of the entrusting or the possessor's disposition of the goods have been such as to be larcenous under the criminal law."

[151] "Lessee in the ordinary course of business" is defined in U.C.C. § 2A-103(o) as:

> a person who in good faith and without knowledge, that the lease to him [or her] is in violation of the ownership rights or security interest or leasehold interest of a third party in the goods, leases in ordinary course from a person in the business of selling or leasing goods of that kind but does not include a pawnbroker.

Section 2A-305 contains a similar exception regarding sales or subleases by lessees. If a lessee who is a merchant in the kind of goods involved in the lease transaction sells or subleases goods entrusted by the lessor to a buyer or lessee in the ordinary course of business, the buyer or lessee in the ordinary course of business takes free, to the extent of the interest transferred, of the lease contract and the lessor's rights to the goods. Thus, assume that Lessor leases a lawn tractor to Lessee for a period of one year. Lessee is a merchant in the business of selling and leasing lawn and garden equipment and sells the lawn tractor to a buyer in the ordinary course of business. The buyer in the ordinary course of business takes all of the lessor's interest transferred (in this case full title) free of the lease contract. If Lessee had simply leased the lawn tractor to Sublessee for a period of two years, the Sublessee would be entitled to the full two years of use and possession free of the lease contract between the Lessor and Lessee.

The analysis in the preceding paragraph assumes that the transfer of possession from the Lessor to the Lessee itself constitutes an "entrusting" under the Code. Although the Code does not explicitly say that the lease constitutes an entrustment, this conclusion is both consistent with the definition of "entrusting" and the policy behind section 2A-305. According to section 2-403(3), "[e]ntrusting includes any delivery and any acquiescence in retention of possession regardless of any condition expressed between the parties to the delivery or acquiescence." A lease easily fits within this definition, and there is no indication in section 2A-305 or the Comment to the section that the lease is not an entrustment. In addition, there would be few, if any, cases in which a lessor would otherwise entrust goods to a lessee who already holds the present right to use and possession of the goods under the lease. Finally, this interpretation is consistent with the policy of sections 2A-304 and 2A-305, which is to protect those who deal in good faith with merchants who appear to possess the interests that they are selling or leasing.

[F] The Rights of Creditors

As a general matter, the rights of the creditors of each party to a lease are subordinate to the interests of the other party. In most cases, no filing is necessary by either party to protect its interest against the creditors of the other party once the lease agreement becomes enforceable. This is true whether the creditor is a secured or unsecured creditor. Thus, a creditor of the lessor cannot generally interfere with the lessee's right to use and possession, and a creditor of the lessee cannot overcome the lessor's reversionary interest. In somewhat summary fashion, the following are the exceptions and qualifications to this general rule.

1. A person who has a statutory or common-law "mechanic's lien" takes priority over the interest of the lessor unless the law establishing the lien provides otherwise.[152]

2. A creditor of the lessor who holds a lien (e.g., a judgment lien) that attached prior to the lease contract takes priority over the lease contract.[153] A "lien," however, does not include a security interest held by a creditor.[154]

3. A creditor of the lessor who holds a security interest in the goods takes priority over the lessee's interest if the lessee (1) did not give value[155] for the lease *and* (2) did not receive delivery of the goods without knowledge of the security interest.[156] Thus, under this provision, the lessee must have knowledge of the security interest at the time of the lease contract and must have given no value for the lease before the security interest will prevail over the lessee's interest.

4. A creditor who holds a security interest in the goods has priority over the lessee's interest if the security interest was perfected before the lease contract became enforceable.[157] However, a lessee in the ordinary course of business takes the leasehold interest free of a security interest even though the security interest is perfected at the time the lease becomes enforceable and the lessee knows of the existence of the security interest.[158]

5. A creditor of a lessor who has possession of goods subject to a lease may treat the lease contract as void if possession by the lessor is fraudulent under any statute or rule of law.[159]

6. A lessor of fixtures is treated in much the same way as the holder of a security interest in fixtures under Article 9.[160] The rules are complicated and fairly detailed and are not discussed in this text.[161]

[1] Accessions

Section 2A-310 deals with goods that become accessions. "Accessions" are goods that are "installed in or affixed to other goods," and the

---

[152] U.C.C. § 2A-306.

[153] U.C.C. § 2A-307(2)(a).

[154] U.C.C. § 2A-103(r).

[155] "Value" is defined in U.C.C. § 1-201(44).

[156] U.C.C. § 2A-307(2)(b).

[157] U.C.C. § 2-307(2)(c).

[158] U.C.C. § 2-307(3).

[159] U.C.C. § 2A-308.

[160] U.C.C. § 2A-309. The section is modeled after section 9-313.

[161] For a thorough and cogent discussion, *see* Thomas D. Crandall et al., I Uniform Commercial Code § 11.7 (1993).

Article 2A provision dealing with accessions is taken from Article 9.[162] An example of an accession is an additional hard drive installed in a computer. Summarized, the rules regarding accessions are as follows:

1. The interests of both the lessor and the lessee in the accession are superior to all other interests in the goods in which the accession is installed or to which it is affixed (the "whole"), if the lease contract is entered into *before* the goods become an accession.[163] Thus, if the lease of the hard drive occurs prior to its installation in the computer, the interests of the lessor and lessee in the hard drive prevail over any interests held by others in the computer, such as the holder of a security interest in the computer.

2. The interests of the lessor and lessee under a lease that is entered into after the goods become an accession are subordinate to all interests in the whole existing at the time the lease contract is made. Consequently, if the lease of the hard drive occurs after it is installed in the computer *and* after the interest in the computer has come into existence, the interest in the computer prevails.

3. The interests of the lessor and lessee under a lease that is entered into at the same time or after the goods become an accession are superior to all interests in the whole acquired after the lease contract. Therefore, if the lease of the hard drive occurs after it is installed in the computer but *before* the interest in the computer comes into existence, the interest of the lessor and lessee of the hard drive prevails.

The sole exceptions to these rules are (1) the interest of a buyer in the ordinary course of business of the whole who acquired the interest after the goods became an accession is superior to the interests of the lessor and lessee, and (2) the interest of a creditor holding a security interest in the whole that was perfected before the lease contract was made is superior to the interests of the lessor and lessee, but only to the extent that the creditor makes advances after the lease contract and without knowledge of the lease contract.[164]

In summary, if the lease contract is entered into *before* the goods become an accession, the interests of the lessor and lessee prevail over those with interests in the whole (with the two possible exceptions noted in the preceding paragraph). If the lease contract is entered into *after* the goods become an accession, whichever is first in time—the lease contract or the interest in the whole—will prevail (with the same two possible exceptions).

---

[162] *See* U.C.C. § 9-314.
[163] U.C.C. § 2A-310(2).
[164] U.C.C. § 2A-310(4).

These rules are provided in summary fashion because the problem of accessions is likely to be of little consequence. Leases of accessions (as opposed to security interests in accessions) are extremely rare.

§ 11.09   IRREVOCABLE PROMISES IN FINANCE LEASES

In general, under the Code and the common law of contracts, the substantial performance of one party is either a condition precedent or a concurrent condition to the performance of the other party. For example, under section 2-507 tender of delivery of the goods by the seller is a condition to the buyer's duty to pay for them. Conversely, tender of payment by the buyer is a condition to the seller's duty to deliver the goods.[165] These rules generally govern Article 2A leases as well. If the lessor does not substantially perform its obligations under the lease, the lessee is not obligated to perform its remaining rent obligations and can cancel the lease.[166] Similarly, if the lessee does not pay the rent when due, the lessor may cancel the lease and recover the leased goods.[167] Section 2A-407, however, provides a rule for performance in certain finance leases that is at odds with the traditional rules of contract.

In nonconsumer finance leases, once the lessee has accepted the goods,[168] the lessee's obligation to pay rent is both irrevocable and independent of the obligations owed to the lessee by the lessor and the supplier. According to section 2A-407(2)(b), this means that the lessee's rent obligation is "not subject to cancellation, termination, modification, repudiation, excuse, or substitution without the consent of the party to whom the promise runs."

---

[165] U.C.C. § 2-511(1).

[166] *See* U.C.C. § 2A-508(1).

[167] *See* U.C.C. §§ 2A-523(1); 2A-525(2).

[168] "Acceptance" of the goods is defined in U.C.C. § 2A-515. The definition in section 2A-515 is slightly modified from its counterpart in section 2-606. Section 2A-515 provides:

> Acceptance of goods occurs after the lessee has had a reasonable opportunity to inspect the goods and
>   (a) the lessee signifies or acts with respect to the goods in a manner that signifies to the lessor or the supplier that the goods are conforming or that the lessee will take or retain them in spite of their nonconformity; or
>   (b) the lessee fails to make an effective rejection of the goods (Section 2A-509(2)).

Section 2A-515 explicitly states that the lessee's acts with respect to the goods may signify acceptance. Section 2-606 simply says that acceptance occurs when the buyer "signifies" to the seller that the goods are conforming or that the buyer will take or retain them in spite of their nonconformity. There is no reference to the buyer's "acts."

Comment 1 to section 2A-407 indicates that this section "extends [to lessors in nonconsumer finance leases] the benefits of the classic 'hell or high water' clause"[169] that is explicit in many finance leases. As described earlier,[170] in a finance lease, implied warranties are not made by a lessor, and the lessor generally makes few, if any, express warranties to the lessee. Instead, the lessee automatically receives the benefit of any express and implied warranties made by the supplier to the lessor.[171] In a finance lease, by definition, the lessor does not select, supply, or manufacture the goods. As a result, the lessor in a finance lease is closer in substance to an independent lender than a true lessor. Consequently, the lessor does not want to bear the risk that the goods will be nonconforming; the lessor has no control over the quality or performance of the goods, and expects these problems to be resolved between the lessee and the supplier.

As with an express "hell or high water clause," section 2A-407 obligates the lessee to continue rental payments despite a breach by the lessor or the supplier. The section does not relieve the lessor from liability for any promises or warranties it has made, nor preclude any action by the lessee against the supplier. If the lessor is in breach of the lease contract, the lessee may seek a damage remedy. After acceptance of the goods, however, the lessee may not stop its rental payments or cancel the contract. If it does so, it will be in breach, entitling the lessor to seek its own remedies.

Section 2A-407 applies only to finance leases that are not consumer leases. Comment 2 to the section suggests that even an *express* "hell or high water" clause in a consumer lease might be subject to an unconscionability attack.[172]

---

[169] U.C.C. § 2A-407, Official Comment 1. As the title suggests, a "hell or high water" clause obligates the lessee to continue to pay rent in virtually all circumstances, including breach by either the lessor or supplier.

[170] Section 11.07[E], *supra.*

[171] *Id.*

[172] Comment 2 to U.C.C. § 2A-407 states, in part:

[T]his section excludes a finance lease that is a consumer lease. That a consumer be obligated to pay notwithstanding defective goods or the like is a principle that is not tenable under case law (Unico v. Owen, 50 N.J. 101, 232 A.2d 405 (1967)), state statute (Unif. Consumer Credit Code § 3.403-.405, 7 U.L.A. 126-31 (1974), or federal statute (15 U.S.C. § 1666i (1982)).

None of the authorities cited in Comment 2 is directly controlling on the issue, however. The *Unico* case dealt with the assignment of a retail installment sales contract to a financing entity closely connected to the seller. The sections of the Uniform Consumer Credit Code (U.C.C.C.) cited in the Comment make card issuers, assignees, and lenders subject to the consumer's claims and defenses in consumer credit sales and leases. Further, the U.C.C.C.

§ 11.10   DEFAULT

[A]   Introduction

The sections dealing with remedies in the event of default are collected in Part Five of Article 2A. They are patterned after the remedies in Article 2 of the Code, although there are significant modifications and additions resulting from the fundamental differences between leases and sales. Unlike a sale of goods, a lease of goods involves a division between title and possession. Also, a lease generally involves continuing obligations on the part of both parties over a finite period of time. Rent is usually paid in installments, and the lessor's obligation to permit the lessee to use and possess the goods continues over the lease period.

These differences between a sale and a lease prompted the drafters to include concepts not present in Article 2 along with the adoption of some principles from Article 9. As with prior sections of this chapter, the emphasis is on the differences between the provisions of Article 2A and those of other Articles. When the provisions are essentially the same, the reader is referred to the relevant sections of the text dealing with Article 2, or in a few cases, to the provisions of Article 9.

[B]   General Provisions

The remedial provisions of Article 2A generally recognize broad freedom of contract. The existence of a default is determined by the lease agreement, as well as the Article,[173] and the parties are, for the most part, free to include rights and remedies for default in addition to those contained in the Article.[174] Consequential damages can be limited or excluded, so long as the provision is not unconscionable,[175] and damages may also be liquidated, so long as the liquidation provision complies with section 2A-504.[176]

---

has been adopted in only seven states. Finally, the provision of the Federal Truth-in-Lending Act cited by the Comment deals only with the assertion of claims and defenses against credit card issuers. Taken together, however, these authorities do broadly support the general principle stated in the Comment.

[173] U.C.C. § 2A-501(1).

[174] U.C.C. § 2A-502(1).

[175] U.C.C. § 2A-502(3). As in Article 2, the limitation or exclusion of consequential damages for injury to the person in the case of consumer goods is *prima facie* unconscionable.

[176] *Id.*

As with Article 2, remedies are usually cumulative, and remedies provided in the lease agreement supplement those in Article 2A, unless the parties expressly agree that a remedy is to be exclusive.[177] If an exclusive remedy fails of its essential purpose, remedy may be had as otherwise provided in Article 2A.[178]

[C] Liquidation of Damages

As with Article 2, Article 2A permits the parties to liquidate damages. The relevant provision of Article 2A is somewhat different, however, from the formulation in Article 2 and from most iterations of the common law. Section 2A-504(1) provides:

> (1) Damages payable by either party for default, or any other act or omission, including indemnity for loss or diminution of anticipated tax benefits or loss or damage to lessor's residual interest, may be liquidated in the lease agreement but only at an amount or by a formula that is reasonable in light of the then anticipated harm caused by the default or other act or omission.

Like its counterpart in Article 2, this section requires that a liquidated damages provision be "reasonable." Unlike Article 2, however, reasonableness is measured only against damages anticipated at the time the liquidated damage provision was agreed to. In this sense, the Article 2A provision is narrower than the Article 2 section, which requires that the liquidated damage provision be reasonable in light of anticipated *or actual* damages.[179] Thus, some liquidated damage provisions that would survive Article 2 because they are reasonable when considered against actual, but not anticipated, damage will not survive Article 2A.

In another way, however, section 2A-504 is broader than its Article 2 counterpart. In addition to being reasonable when considered against anticipated or actual damages, section 2-719 requires that a liquidated damage provision also be measured against the difficulties of proof of loss and the inconvenience or infeasibility of otherwise obtaining an adequate remedy. This prerequisite has been eliminated from Article 2A. The Official Comment indicates that the drafters rejected this requirement in order to maximize the parties' freedom to create their own remedies.[180] The sole

---

[177] U.C.C. § 2A-502(2).

[178] For a discussion of the failure of an exclusive remedy in the context of Article 2, *see* § 4.08[D], *supra*.

[179] U.C.C. § 2-718(1).

[180] U.C.C. § 2A-504, Official Comment.

requirement under section 2A-504 is that the provision be reasonable in light of anticipated harm.[181] If the liquidated damage provision fails this test, the injured party is entitled to use all of the remedial provisions of Article 2A.[182]

[D]   Statute of Limitations

As with Article 2, Article 2A contains a statute of limitations of four years from the time the cause of action accrues.[183] In two ways, however, one of marginal importance and the other more significant, the Article 2A statute is different from its Article 2 counterpart. The change of marginal importance is that section 2A-506 permits the parties to extend, as well as shorten, the statute of limitations by agreement. Section 2-725 of Article 2 permits the parties only to shorten the limitations period.[184] This change is unlikely to be of much significance, because four years is a fairly lengthy statute of limitations that parties, particularly lessors, are unlikely to want to extend. Further, the "discovery rule," adopted by section 2A-506 and described in the following paragraph, makes it even more unlikely that lessors will agree to extend the limitations period.

The more significant change from Article 2 is that a cause of action does not accrue under section 2A-506 until the default was or should have been discovered. Under Article 2, a buyer's cause of action often accrues at the time of sale, whether or not the buyer has discovered or should have discovered the breach, or even whether the breach has yet occurred.[185] This "discovery rule" in Article 2A generally has the effect of extending the time that the statute of limitations begins to run well beyond the time at which the parties entered into the original lease agreement. The section is silent

---

[181] It is probably true, however, that courts will continue to utilize these factors indirectly to the extent that they bear on the reasonability of the parties' forecast of anticipated harm.

[182] U.C.C. § 2A-504(2). If the liquidated damage provision is exclusive, as it often is, the injured party is also entitled to use all of the remedial provisions of Article 2A if the liquidated damage provision "fails of its exclusive purpose." The meaning of this provision is not clear. For certain, it cannot mean that the liquidated damage provision must provide the injured party with the equivalent of performance (i.e., make the injured party whole). The very purpose of a liquidated damage provision is to limit the risk that actual damages will exceed those that might reasonably be anticipated at the time of the contract, and such an interpretation would make liquidated damage provisions superfluous. Rather, it must mean that if the parties anticipate that a liquidated damage provision will enable the injured party to accomplish a specific objective (e.g., to obtain substitute goods), and circumstances such as an unanticipated price rise prevent the injured party from doing so, the injured party will have recourse at least to those remedies of Article 2A that will enable the injured party to receive the benefit originally anticipated by the liquidated damage clause.

[183] U.C.C. § 2-506(1).

[184] U.C.C. § 2-725(1).

[185] See § 4.11[A], supra.

upon whether the parties can alter this provision by agreement. In all like-lihood, courts would, and should, uphold agreements in a commercial con-text that alter, or eliminate, the discovery rule, but changes should generally not be permitted in a consumer context.

[E] Lessee's Remedies

[1] Introduction

Section 2A-508 contains a compilation of the lessee's remedies similar to the compilation of the buyer's remedies in section 2-711. When the lessor fails to deliver the goods, repudiates the lease contract, or when the lessee rightfully rejects the goods or justifiably revokes acceptance of the goods, the lessee's remedies are:

1. cancellation of the contract (section 2A-505(1));
2. recovery of so much of the rent and security as has been paid and is just under the circumstances;[186]
3. purchase or lease of substitute goods (section 2A-518); and
4. recovery of damages for nondelivery (i.e., the market-contract dif-ference) (section 2A-519).

When the lessor's default consists of the failure to deliver the goods or when the lessor repudiates the contract, the lessee may also, in certain cases, recover the goods (section 2A-522) or obtain specific performance or replevin (section 2A-521). The lessee may also resort to any remedy pro-vided in the lease contract[187] or recover damages for breach of warranty (section 2A-519(4)).

[2] Rejection and Revocation of Acceptance

Section 2A-509 provides a lessee with a right of rejection that is iden-tical in substance to the buyer's right of rejection under Article 2:

(1) Subject to the provisions of Section 2A-510 on default in installment lease contracts, if the goods or the tender or delivery fail in any respect

---

[186] Comment 2 to U.C.C. § 2A-508 provides, in part:

[I]n recognition of the fact that a lessee may be able to cancel the lease (revoke acceptance of the goods) after the goods have been in use for a substantial period of time, [the section] does not require that all lease payments made by the lessee be returned upon cancellation. Rather, only such portion as is just of the rent and security payments may be recovered.

[187] U.C.C. § 2A-508(3).

to conform to the lease contract, the lessee may reject or accept the goods or accept any commercial unit or units and reject the rest of the goods.

(2) Rejection of goods is ineffective unless it is within a reasonable time after tender or delivery of the goods and the lessee seasonably notifies the lessor.

As with its Article 2 analogue,[188] section 2A-509 adopts a "perfect tender" rule.[189] Similarly, rejection must occur within a reasonable time after tender or delivery of the goods and the lessee must seasonably notify the lessor of its intention to reject.[190] The reader should refer to the sections of this text on the Article 2 right of rejection for a discussion of these, and other, issues related to rejection.[191]

In section 2A-517, Article 2A also contains an analogue to the Article 2 right to revoke acceptance.[192] The substantive requirements for revocation of acceptance in Article 2A are similar to those in section 2-608. A nonconformity must *substantially* impair the value of the goods to the lessee— that is, a minor nonconformity will not give rise to the revocation remedy, though it might create a cause of action for damages. In addition, the use in Article 2A of the language "substantial impairment *to the lessee*" indicates that the drafters intended the same individualized standard of substantial impairment as under the Article 2 revocation remedy. That is, the standard is one of substantial impairment to this particular lessee, not the average, typical, or even reasonable lessee.[193] Revocation of acceptance must occur within a reasonable time after the lessee discovers or should have discovered the ground for it and before any substantial change in the goods not caused by the nonconformity.[194]

The remaining requirements for revocation in section 2A-517 create a sharp division between finance leases and other leases. Revocation is available to a lessee who has accepted the goods under the following circumstances:

1. *Except in the case of a finance lease*, on the reasonable assumption that the nonconformity would be cured and it has not been seasonably cured;

2. Without discovery of the nonconformity if:

---

[188] U.C.C. § 2-601.

[189] *See* § 5.03, *supra.*

[190] *See* U.C.C. § 2-602(1).

[191] *See* § 7.03[C], *supra.*

[192] U.C.C. § 2A-517.

[193] *See* § 7.03[E], *supra*, for a discussion of this issue in the context of section 2-608.

[194] U.C.C. § 2A-517(4).

    a.   the lessee's acceptance was reasonably induced by the lessor's assurances; or

    b.   *except in the case of a finance lease*, the lessee's acceptance was reasonably induced by the difficulty of discovery of the nonconformity before acceptance.

Thus, under this subsection, a lessee in a non-finance lease is entitled to revoke acceptance in three instances: (1) when the lessee discovers the nonconformity before acceptance but, because of the lessor's assurances or otherwise, the lessee reasonably assumes that the nonconformity will be cured; (2) when the nonconformity is not discovered prior to acceptance and acceptance was reasonably induced by the lessor's assurances that the goods were conforming or that nonconformities would be cured; and (3) when the nonconformity is not discovered before acceptance and acceptance was reasonably induced by the difficulty of discovering the nonconformity before acceptance.

    In the case of a *finance lease*, however, the lessee may revoke aceptance only in the second situation. The lessee in a finance lease cannot rely on the reasonable assumption that a known nonconformity would be cured by the lessor nor upon the difficulty of discovery of a nonconformity unknown at the time of acceptance. As a result, the finance lessee's right of revocation is severely restricted.

    This result is consistent with the nature of a finance lease and with section 2A-407. The finance lessor is there to *finance* the transaction; to act as an intermediary or conduit between the supplier and lessee. The fundamental premise of a finance lease is that the lessee must rely on the supplier, not the lessor, for product quality and performance. Furthermore, the remedy of revocation must be limited in the case of a finance lease to be consistent with the independence and irrevocability of the lessee's promise to pay rent under section 2A-407. Revocation of acceptance terminates the contract; the lessee returns the goods to the lessor, and the lessee is entitled to the same rights he would have upon rejection, which includes the right to cancel the contract to receive and a return of rent and security that has been paid.[195] Under section 2A-407, however, the finance lessor has the right to receive rent payments for the term of the contract notwithstanding a nonconformity

---

[195] The lessee has a right to recover so much of the rent and security as is just under the circumstances. *See* U.C.C. § 2A-508(1)(b). Thus, if the lessee has received a substantial benefit from the use of the goods prior to revocation, the lessor will likely be permitted to keep a portion of the rent paid. This is similar to the setoff generally permitted under section 2-608 for a buyer's use of goods prior to revocation. *See* § 7.03[E], *supra*.

in the goods.[196] Therefore, to ensure consistency, a finance lessee's right to revoke acceptance is extremely limited.[197]

A lessee, except a nonconsumer lessee in a finance lease, may revoke acceptance for defaults by the lessor in the lessor's post-acceptance obligations. As the Official Comments suggest,[198] the lessor may have a continuing obligation to maintain the leased equipment or to supply other goods necessary for the operation of the leased equipment. A failure to comply with these, or similar, obligations that substantially impair the value of the goods to the lessee gives the lessee the right to revoke acceptance of the goods.[199]

The rights of lessee in an installment lease are substantively the same as those of a buyer in an installment sale,[200] and the obligations of a lessee with respect to rejected goods are similar to those of a buyer of goods.[201] For further discussion of these rights and obligations, the reader should consult the sections of this text dealing with the analogous Article 2 provisions.[202]

[3]   The Lessee's Monetary Remedies

[a]   Introduction

The lessee's monetary remedies closely parallel the buyer's remedies under Article 2. Certain changes have been made to incorporate the con-

---

[196] *See* § 11.09, *supra.*

[197] The relationship between U.C.C. §§ 2A-407 and 2A-517 is somewhat confused in the case of a finance lease that is also a consumer lease. The irrevocability and independence of the lessee's rent obligation under section 2A-407 applies only to finance leases that are not consumer leases. Comment 2 to section 2A-407 states that it would be "untenable" to require a consumer, even in a finance lease, to continue to pay rent for defective goods. Yet the restrictions on revocation of acceptance applicable to finance lessees do not distinguish between consumer finance leases and nonconsumer finance leases. Only in subsection (3) to section 2A-517 is a distinction between the two kinds of finance leases drawn, and subsection (3) applies only to a lessor's continuing obligations under the lease, such as maintenance, not to nonconformities in the goods. It is not clear how Article 2 can give the right to a consumer lessee in a finance lease to refuse to pay rent for defective goods while at the same time denying the consumer the right to revoke acceptance except in the most limited circumstances. These sections should be interpreted to permit revocation by a consumer lessee in a finance lease under the same conditions as in a non-finance lease.

[198] U.C.C. § 2A-517, Official Comment 1.

[199] U.C.C. § 2A-517(3).

[200] U.C.C. § 2A-510.

[201] U.C.C. §§ 2A-511, 2A-512.

[202] *See* § 7.03[C], *supra.*

ceptual and practical differences between leases and purchases. First, unlike outright purchases, leases vary in their term, and may vary greatly with respect to other provisions as well (e.g., maintenance obligations, security, use of the goods). As a result, it might be difficult to precisely duplicate the breached lease on the market. Second, leases generally require the payment of rent over time, whereas damages for breach normally, although not always,[203] are payable immediately upon judgment. Therefore, in some situations, the rent due over a long period must be reduced to a present value to permit the payment of damages in a lump sum. These issues are discussed in greater detail in the sections that follow.

[b] Cover

When the lessor fails to deliver the goods called for by the lease, or when the lessee rightfully rejects or justifiably revokes acceptance of the goods, section 2A-518 permits the lessee to lease or purchase substitute goods ("cover"). If the cover is by substitute lease,[204] the lessee may collect from the lessor the difference between the cost of the substitute lease and the cost of the breached lease contract, plus any incidental or consequential damages.[205] In order to avail itself of this remedy, the lessee must have never received the goods or must have rightfully returned them to the seller (i.e., rightfully rejected the goods or justifiably revoked acceptance of them). The lease agreement made in substitution must be "substantially similar" to the original lease agreement and the substitute lease agreement must have been effected in good faith and in a commercially reasonable manner.

"Substantially similar." In order to recover the difference in cost between the original lease and the substitute lease, the substitute lease must be substantially similar to the original lease. "Substantially similar" is not defined in Article 2A, because the drafters felt that fairness would be better served if the issue were considered on a case-by-case basis.[206] The comprehensive Comments following section 2A-518, however, attempt to provide some guidance.

The first step in deciding whether the leases are substantially similar is to compare the goods under the two leases. It is clear that the goods

---

[203] *See* Roesch v. Ryan, 841 F. Supp. 288 (E.D. Mo. 1993); Williams v. Bright, 167 Misc. 2d 179, 637 N.Y.S.2d 915 (N.Y. Sup. Ct. 1995).

[204] If the substitute is procured by purchase, the lessee's damages are measured by the contract/market differential as calculated under section 2A-519. *See* § 11.10[E][3][b], *infra.*

[205] The Article 2 analogue to this provision is section 2-712. For a discussion of section 2-712, *see* § 7.04[B], *supra.*

[206] U.C.C. § 2A-518, Official Comment 3.

leased in substitution do not have to be precisely the same as the goods under the original lease.[207] The analysis should focus on whether the substitute goods are a reasonable substitute in the market and whether they serve essentially the same purpose as the goods the lessee originally agreed to lease. Comment 4 offers a hypothetical to illustrate the proper comparison:

> For example, in a lease of computer equipment the new lease might be for more modern equipment. However, it may be that at the time of the lessor's breach it was not possible to obtain the same type of goods in the market place. Because the lessee's remedy under Section 2A-519 is intended to place the lessee in essentially the same position as if he had covered, if goods similar to those to have been delivered under the original lease are not available, then the computer equipment in this hypothetical should qualify as a commercially reasonable substitute.[208]

The Comments then suggest a number of other factors that should be examined to determine whether the leases are substantially similar. These include the presence of options to purchase or re-lease, the warranties accompanying the leased goods, the services to be provided by the lessor, and the presence of insurance. Again, the requirement is only that the leases be "substantially" similar; some differences in any, or even all, of these items should not defeat the remedy. In fact, the Comments suggest that even if some differences between the leases are substantial, if the differences are easily valued, the damages can be appropriately adjusted. After this adjustment, if remaining differences are not substantial, the leases should be considered substantially similar.[209] For example, if the original lease required the lessee to insure at his own expense, and the substitute lease includes insurance in the rental payment, it would be appropriate to deduct the cost of the insurance from the rent due under the new lease when determining the difference in rental between the two leases.[210]

It is not even necessary that the substitute lease have the same term as the remaining term of the original lease. As long as the terms are commercially comparable and the rent under the new lease can be fairly apportioned to the remaining term of the original lease, the leases will be substantially similar. For example, if Lessee revokes acceptance with eight months remaining on a one-year lease with rent payable at $500 per month, and the

---

[207] *See* Official Comment 6 to section 2A-518.
[208] U.C.C. § 2A-518, Official Comment 4.
[209] U.C.C. § 2A-518, Official Comment 6.
[210] *Id.*

Lessee enters into a substitute one-year lease at $600 per month, the court would be justified in holding the Lessor responsible for $800 (8 × $100)[211] if the leases are otherwise substantially similar.

Assuming that the leases are substantially similar, the Lessee is entitled to the difference between the rent under the substitute lease applicable to the remaining period of the original lease, and the remaining rent due under the original lease, *both reduced to present value.*

"Present value." With a lease, the lessee normally agrees to make periodic payments over a period of time—for example, $500 per month for the lease term. If the lessor defaults by not delivering the goods or by delivering defective goods (and the lessee has rejected or revoked acceptance of those goods), the cover remedy will provide the lessee with damages measured by the difference between the rents under the original and new leases. In a long-term lease, the rent may stretch months or years into the future. If the court were to add the total rent due under each of the leases and give the lessee the difference between the two sums, the lessee may be overcompensated[212] because the lessee would receive an amount that it could invest and on which it could earn an additional return during the term of the lease.[213]

To illustrate the problem, suppose the lessee, *A,* leased a tractor for one year for $500 a month, and the lessor, *B,* failed to deliver the tractor. *A* immediately leased a substitute tractor, under a substantially similar one-year lease, for $600 a month. *A*'s loss is $100 a month for the year or $1200. If *B* were to pay *A* $1200 on the day *B* was to deliver the tractor under the original lease, *A* would be overcompensated because *A* could invest the $1200 at (say) 12 percent, withdraw the $100 each month from the investment, and have a balance of about $84 in the investment account at the end of the year.[214] Recognizing that a dollar paid today is worth more than a dollar paid in the future, section 2A-103 provides:

---

[211] As the next section points out, this example is not entirely accurate because the two rents must be reduced to present value.

[212] *But see* Kaczowski v. Bolubasz, 491 Pa. 561, 421 A.2d 1027 (1980), in which the court decided, for tort purposes, that the discount and inflation rates offset each other so there should be no discount to present value in an award of future damages.

[213] These principles are also applicable to lessors who collect a loss before the time for payment is due. U.C.C. §§ 2A-527, 2A-528, and 2A-529. *See* § 11.10[F], *infra.*

[214] The example may be unrealistic because parties do not ordinarily settle disputes this quickly. Lessors may claim that the tender was conforming and a period of negotiations will ensue. Nevertheless, the principle remains applicable to future payments and will find its use most often in long-term leases. For rent that has already become due at the time of settlement,

"Present value" means the amount as of a date certain of one or more sums payable in the future, discounted to the date certain. The discount is determined by the interest rate specified by the parties if the rate is not manifestly unreasonable at the time the transaction was entered into; otherwise the discount is determined by a commercially reasonable rate that takes into account the facts and circumstances of each case at the time the transaction is entered into.[215]

Determination of the damages in the hypothetical tractor case requires reducing the $100 a month (for 12 months) to present value. Unless the parties have agreed on a discount rate meeting the tests of the above paragraph, there may be a dispute as to the rate. The higher the rate, the less the recovery; the lower the rate, the more the recovery. If we assume a rate of 12 percent and that the rent was due on the first day of the month, the present value of the 12 payments of $100 is $1136.76; if the rent was due on the last day of the month, the present value of those payments is $1125.51. (The difference is caused by the fact that the lessee has an extra 30 (or so) days each month for an investment to earn a return.) The reduction to present value has "saved" the lessor about $63—hardly worth the computation time—but in a multi-year, multi-thousand dollar-a-month lease, the difference can be substantial. Income tax is another factor that should be considered in reduction to present value because the amount received by the lessee may be subject to federal, state, or local income taxes. The impact of taxes varies with each situation; thus, we leave to the accountant the determination of how taxes should affect, if at all, the reduction to present value in a specific case.[216]

Incidental and consequential damages are added to any amount determined by this process. "Incidental" and "consequential" damages are defined in a manner similar to the way these same terms are defined in U.C.C. § 2A-520. For a more detailed discussion of these damages, the reader should consult those sections of the text in which these damages are discussed in relation to the sale of goods.[217] Any "expenses" saved as a result of the breach should be subtracted from the difference between the rental

---

the question of intrest on the past due rent will be involved, which will turn on the lease terms and the local law.

[215] U.C.C. § 2A-103(u).

[216] For example, in a business lease, the extra rent paid by the lessee is deductible. This deduction may (at least partially) offset the tax on the present value paid by the lessee.

[217] See § 7.04[F], supra.

amounts.[218] For example, if the maintenance costs to the lessee will be less under the new lease, they should be deducted from the lessee's recovery.[219] Thus, the formula under section 2A-518 is the present value of the difference between the two rental payments for the remaining term of the original lease *plus* incidental and consequential damages *minus* expenses saved as a result of the breach.

[c] Contract/Market Price Differential

In three instances, the lessee is entitled to a different measure of damages when the lessor fails to deliver the goods or repudiates the contract, or when the lessee rightfully rejects or justifiably revokes acceptance of the goods. This measure is the difference between the rent due under the original lease and the *market* rent for the same lease *plus* incidental and consequential damages *minus* the expenses saved as a result of the breach. The three instances in which this measure is available to the lessee are:

1. When the lessee does not acquire goods in substitution for those promised under the lease contract;
2. When the lessee *purchases* goods in substitution for those promised by the lessor; and
3. When the lessee makes a cover lease that does not comply with section 2A-518.

These are the only three instances in which section 2A-519 specifically permits recovery of the market/contract differential by the lessee. The same issue arises, however, with respect to section 2A-519 that has been previously discussed in connection with its counterpart in Article 2, section 2-713: can the contract-market differential be recovered when a qualifying cover lease has been made under section 2A-518, but when recovery under section 2A-519 would net the lessee greater damages than the cover remedy?[220] For example, assume that the lessee, upon repudiation by the lessor, executes a substantially similar lease for the same rent as the original lease. The market, however, for such leases, is higher (the lessee made an excep-

---

[218] U.C.C. § 2A-518(2).

[219] Although section 2A-518 does not require that either incidental and consequential damages or expenses saved be reduced to present value, in some cases they should be reduced to present value. If an item of incidental damage will not occur until sometime in the future, the lessee should not receive the full amount of the damage in the present. Similarly, if an expense will not be actually saved until sometime in the future, the lessee should not presently have the full expense charged against his recovery.

[220] *See* § 7.04[C], *supra.*

tionally good deal under both leases). Can the lessee recover the difference between the rent under the original lease and the market rent, despite having made a below-market cover lease?

The conclusion should be no different under Article 2A from that under Article 2: if the lessee makes a qualifying cover lease, the lessee should be limited to recovery under section 2A-518. The purpose of the Article 2A remedies, like those of Article 2, is to satisfy the injured party's expectation interest (i.e., to place the injured party in the same position as performance).[221] Permitting a recovery under section 2A-519 that exceeds the lessee's actual loss clearly contravenes this principle.

As with section 2A-518, the rent due under both the original lease and under its market equivalent must be reduced to present value when calculating the contract/market differential. Present value is determined under section 2A-519 as of the date of default.[222] Similarly, incidental and consequential damages must be added and expenses saved as a result of the breach deducted from the lessee's recovery.

[d] Market Rent

In calculating contract/market damages under section 2A-519, market rent is determined under section 2A-507(1):

> Damages based on market rent (Section 2A-519 or 2A-528) are determined according to the rent for use of the goods concerned for a lease term identical to the remaining lease term of the original lease agreement and prevailing at the times specified in Sections 2A-519 and 2A-528.

The market rent, in the first instance, must be for an identical lease term. If, however, evidence of market rent[223] for an identical lease term is not readily available, the court may use:

> the rent prevailing within any reasonable time before or after the time described [in section 2A-519] or at any other place for a different lease term which in commercial judgment or under usage of trade would serve as a reasonable substitute for the one . . . described making any proper

---

[221] U.C.C. § 1-106.

[222] Note that the date of "default" may be different from both the date of breach and the date that the lessee discovers the default. An event of default, or "breach," may not become a "default" under the lease until a period of time (grace period) has passed or a notice has been given. *See* U.C.C. § 2A-519, Official Comment 2.

[223] The market rent for the "substitute lease" must be measured as of the *time* of default (U.C.C. § 2A-507(1), and as of the *place* for tender or arrival (U.C.C. § 2A-519(2)).

allowance for the difference, including the cost of transporting the goods to or from the other place.[224]

While this section permits the court to consider the rent of a lease with a different term, or at a different time or place than would otherwise be applicable under section 2A-519, there is no provision in section 2A-519 for taking account of other differences between the original lease and the comparable market lease. That is, there is no counterpart to the requirement of section 2A-518 that a cover lease need only be "substantially similar" to the original lease. What should be done, for example, if there is evidence of the market rent of a lease that is identical in term, time, and place to the breached lease, but the lease available on the market is different from the original lease with respect to maintenance obligations, and no market evidence of a lease with the same maintenance obligations as the original lease is available? To solve this problem, the concept of substantially similarity in section 2A-518 should be applied to section 2A-519 as well as to section 2A-518. If the maintenance obligations can be easily quantified or if they are not material, the evidence of the market rent should be admissible.

[e] Damages for Accepted Goods

Once the lessee accepts the goods and does not justifiably revoke acceptance, the lessee is required to pay the rental price for the goods.[225] To the extent, however, that a default by the lessor causes damage to the lessee, the lessee is entitled to recover for the loss caused by the default. Section 2A-519(3) permits the recovery of damages that result in the ordinary course of events from the default, determined in a manner that is reasonable, as well as the recovery of incidental and consequential damages, less expenses saved as a result of the default. The provision is similar to section 2-714(1) of Article 2.

Of greater importance, because it is generally the applicable measure when the goods prove defective after acceptance, is section 2A-519(4). This section provides the measure for breach of warranty. Like the parallel section in Article 2,[226] this section measures damages for breach of warranty as the difference between the value of the use of the goods for the lease term as accepted and the value of the use of the goods for the lease term as warranted. Because the value of the goods accrues to the lessee over time,

---

[224] U.C.C. § 2A-507(2).
[225] U.C.C. § 2A-206.
[226] U.C.C. § 2-714(2).

section 2A-519 provides that this difference should be reduced to present value. Incidental and consequential damages are added to this difference and expenses saved by the breach are deducted.[227]

[4]   Other Provisions

A number of other provisions relating to a lessee's remedies were taken directly from Article 2 with no substantive change and are simply mentioned here. Section 2A-521(1) permits the court to grant specific performance when the goods are unique or in other proper circumstances. This is the same language used in section 2-716 and will undoubtedly be interpreted in a similar fashion.[228] Subsection (2) of section 2A-521 permits a decree of specific performance to include any terms and conditions as to the payment of the rent, damages, or other relief that the court deems just. Subsection (3) permits the lessee to replevin the goods or obtain similar relief if the goods have already been identified to the contract and if, after reasonable effort, the lessee is unable to effect cover or the circumstances indicate that such an effort would be futile.

A lessor under Article 2A is permitted a right to cure under the same circumstances as an Article 2 seller.[229] Although there are some interesting issues associated with the right to cure, they are discussed in detail elsewhere in the text[230] and the discussion is not repeated here. Under Article 2A, a lessee is also required to give notice of default within a reasonable time after the lessee discovers or should have discovered the default or be barred from *any* remedy. This provision parallels section 2-607(3) of Article 2.[231]

---

[227] For a discussion of this measure of damages as it relates to the sale of goods, *see* § 7.04[C], *supra*.

[228] *See* § 7.05[A], *supra*.

[229] U.C.C. § 2A-513 provides:

> (1) If any tender or delivery by the lessor or the supplier is rejected because nonconforming and the time for performance has not yet expired, the lessor or the supplier may seasonably notify the lessee of the lessor's or the supplier's intention to cure and may then make a conforming delivery within the time provided in the lease.
> (2) If the lessee rejects a nonconforming tender that the lessor or the supplier had reasonable grounds to believe would be acceptable with or without money allowance, the lessor or the supplier may have a further reasonable time to substitute a conforming tender if he [or she] seasonably notifies the lessee.

[230] *See* § 5.03[A][2], *supra*.

[231] For a discussion of U.C.C. § 2-607(3), *see* § 4.10, *supra*.

[F]   Lessor's Remedies

[1]   Introduction

The lessor's remedies in Article 2A, like those of the lessee, strongly reflect the influence of Article 2. Many of the variations between the lessor's remedies in Article 2A and Article 2 reflect the same fundamental differences between leases and sales discussed in connection with the lessee's remedies.[232]

Section 2A-523(1) introduces the lessor's remedies. This subsection describes the remedies available to the lessor in three circumstances: (1) wrongful rejection or wrongful revocation of acceptance by the lessee; (2) failure by the lessee to make a payment when due; and (3) repudiation of the lease contract. In any of these cases, the lessor may:

1. Cancel the lease contract.
2. Identify unfinished goods to the contract and, if commercially reasonable, either stop manufacture of the goods and dispose of them for salvage or complete the manufacture and sell or lease the finished goods.
3. Withhold delivery of the goods (or stop delivery by any bailee) or take possession of goods previously delivered.
4. Re-lease the goods and recover the difference between the rent under the original lease and the substitute lease.
5. Sell or retain the goods and recover the contract/market difference.
6. In certain circumstances, recover the entire rent on the contract.
7. Exercise any additional remedies provided in the lease.

Like the lessee's remedies, the lessor's remedies are cumulative, unless cumulation would place the lessor in a better position than performance.[233]

All of the remedies described above assume that the lessor either retains possession of the goods or regains possession of the goods after the default. Under section 2A-523(2), if the lessor allows the lessee to maintain possession of the goods, the lessor may recover damages resulting in the ordinary course of events from the lessee's default, including any incidental and consequential damages. For example, if the lessee fails to make a payment when due, the lessor may collect the past-due payment without canceling the contract and recovering the goods.

---

[232] *See* § 11.10[E], *supra.*
[233] U.C.C. § 2A-523, Official Comment 4. *See also* U.C.C. § 1-106.

If the lessee defaults, other than by the three instances described previously, the lessor has two possible courses of action:

1. The lessor may pursue any remedies for the default described in the lease contract;
2. If no remedy is prescribed in the lease contract, the lessor may:

    a. Exercise the remedies provided in section 2A-523(1) if the default substantially impairs the value of the lease contract to the lessor.
    b. If the default does not result in a substantial impairment of the value of the lease contract, collect damages under subsection (2) of 2A-523.

For example, the lessee may have any obligation to maintain the goods under the lease contract. If the lessee defaults in this obligation and the remedy for such a default is provided in the lease, the lessor may use this remedy, including cancellation of the lease. If the failure to maintain the goods is a default, but no remedy is provided in the lease, the lessor may cancel the contract and pursue the remedies in section 2A-523(1) only if the default substantially impairs the value of the lease to the lessor. If the default does not substantially impair the value of the lease, the lessor is relegated to a damage remedy under section 2A-523(2).

[2] Lessor's Right of Repossession

If the lessee defaults on the lease contract, the lessor may choose to repossess the goods if they are in the possession of the lessee. This right of repossession exists except when (1) the default does *not* consist of a wrongful rejection or revocation, a repudiation of the contract, or a failure to make a payment, *and* (2) the default does not result in a substantial impairment of the value of the lease, *and* (3) repossession is not provided in the lease contract as a remedy for the default. If all of these conditions are met, the lessee is entitled to retain possession of the goods, and the lessor is relegated to a damage remedy for the loss caused by the default.

The lessor with a right of repossession is permitted to recover possession of the goods by "self-help," so long as recovery of the goods does not result in a breach of the peace. This provision parallels section 9-503, which permits a secured creditor the right of self-help repossession so long as no breach of the peace occurs. A discussion of the circumstances that constitute a breach of the peace is beyond the scope of this text; there are, however, many good discussions elsewhere.[234] If the lessor chooses not to exercise

---

[234] *See, e.g.*, Thomas D. Crandall et al., III Uniform Commercial Code § 27.9.3 (1993).

self-help, perhaps because he cannot do so without a breach of the peace, he is permitted to recover possession through appropriate court action.

[3] Re-Lease of the Goods

If the lessor has retained possession of the goods or reacquires them through self-help or otherwise, he is permitted under section 2A-527 to re-lease the goods. This remedy is the counterpart of the seller's resale remedy under section 2-706 and mirrors the lessee's cover remedy in section 2A-518. If the lessor complies with the prerequisites in section 2A-527, the lessor is entitled to recover the difference between the rent due under the original lease and the rent under the substitute lease.

To be entitled to a re-lease remedy, the lessor must satisfy three conditions:

1. Disposition of the goods must be by lease, not by sale;
2. The substitute lease must be substantially similar to the original lease; and
3. The substitute lease must be entered into in good faith and in a commercially reasonable manner.

These requirements parallel those of the lessee's cover remedy, and the discussion in the Comments to section 2A-523 is taken virtually verbatim from the Comments to section 2A-518.[235]

If the three conditions are met, the lessor may recover (1) any accrued and unpaid rent due to the lessor under the original lease; (2) the difference between the total rent due under the original lease and the total rent due under the substitute lease for the remaining term of the original lease; and (3) any incidental[236] damages. Any expenses saved as a result of the lessee's default must be deducted from the recovery.

---

[235] For a more detailed discussion of these requirements in connection with the lessee's cover remedy, *see* § 11.10[E][3][b], *supra.*

[236] A seller's incidental damages are described in U.C.C. § 2A-530 as: "[A]ny commercially reasonable charges, expenses, or commissions incurred in stopping delivery, in the transportation, care and custody of goods after the lessee's default, in connection with return or disposition of the goods, or otherwise resulting from the default."

There is no provision in Article 2A permitting a lessor to collect *consequential* damages. This is similar to Article 2, which has makes no provision for the collection of consequential damages by a seller of goods. Any specific allowance to a lessor for consequential damages is probably unnecessary because (1) provision is made in section 2A-528(2) for the recovery of lost profits, which is, by far, the most common consequential harm, (2) the definition of "incidental damages" is broad enough to cover most damages that would result from the lessee's default ("any commercially reasonable charges, expenses, or commissions

Like the lessee's cover remedy, the rentals under the original lease and the substitute lease must both be reduced to present value before the difference is calculated.[237] For example, assume that the lessee repudiates a one-year lease contract prior to the beginning of the lease term. The lease contract called for rental payments of $500 per month. The lessor enters into a substitute lease for the same term with rental payments of $450 per month. The landlord would be entitled to the present value of $50 per month for one year. We leave it to the reader to choose an appropriate discount rate and calculate the proper present value.[238]

[4]   Market/Contract Damages

The lessor also has an analogue to the lessee's right to collect the market/contract differential.[239] Section 2A-528 permits the lessor to recover the difference between the present value of the rent for the remainder of the lease term and the present value of market rent for the remainder of the term. This measure may be used in three instances, analogous to those in which an injured lessee may obtain a similar remedy. They are:

1   when the lessor retains the goods;
2.   when the lessor disposes of the goods through sale; and
3.   when the lessor disposes of the goods through re-lease that does not qualify under section 2A-527.

In addition to collecting the contract/market differential, the lessor may also collect any accrued and unpaid rent as of the date of default if the lessee has never taken possession of the goods, or from the date of repossession[240] if the lessee has taken possession of the goods. The lessor may also collect incidental damages but must subtract any expenses saved as a result of the default.[241]

The market rent is determined as of the date of default or repossession[242] and at the place where the goods are located. Both the original rent

---

. . . otherwise resulting from the default"), and (3) section 2A-523(2) permits the lessor to recover damages for the loss occurring in the ordinary course when the lessor "does not fully . . . obtain a remedy to which the lessor is entitled under subsection (1)." *See* the discussion of recovery of consequential damages by a seller at § 7.04[F][2], *supra.*

[237] For a discussion of present value, *see* § 11.10[E][3][a], *supra.*

[238] For an example in which the authors have done so, *see* § 11.10[E][3][a], *supra.*

[239] *See* § 11.10[E][3][c], *supra.*

[240] Or the date the lessee makes retender of the goods to the lessor if it is earlier than the date of repossession. U.C.C. § 2A-528(1).

[241] U.C.C. § 2A-528(1).

[242] Or the date the lessee retenders the goods, if it is earlier.

and the market rent must be reduced to present value before the difference is calculated. Assume, for example, that the lessee repudiates a one-year lease three months into the lease term and returns the leased goods to the lessor on July 4, 1996. The monthly rental under the lease is $800 per month. Assume further that the market rental on July 4, 1998, for the same lease for the remaining term is $700 per month. The lessor would be entitled to the present value of $100 a month for the balance of the term of the lease, *plus* incidental damages *minus* expenses saved as a result of the default.

A potential problem exists with the current formulation of section 2A-528 that parallels a similar problem discussed previously in connection with section 2A-519.[243] Section 2A-528 appears to contemplate the market rent for an *identical* lease; there is no provision for using the market rent for a substantially similar lease. What should be done where evidence of an identical lease is not available? There is nothing in the section that precludes a court from admitting evidence of the market rent for a similar lease and making whatever adjustments, if any, it feels are appropriate to arrive at the market rent for a lease identical to the original lease. In the absence of available evidence of an identical lease, the evidence of substantially similar leases should be admitted. Otherwise the calculation of market rent is likely to be unduly speculative.

[5] The Lost-Volume Lessor

The problem of the lost-volume seller has been discussed in detail in an earlier section of this text.[244] The same problem arises in connection with a lessor. For example, a lessor of vehicles may have a supply in inventory more than sufficient to satisfy his demand. A lessee may contract to lease a particular vehicle and then, before delivery, repudiate the lease contract. The lessor may then lease the vehicle for the same term to someone else for the same price. It appears at first glance that, except perhaps for incidental damages, the lessor has suffered no damage. The lessor, however, may claim that had the lessee not breached the lease contract, the lessor could have nonetheless leased a vehicle to the second customer and made two profits. If this claim is accurate,[245] both sections 2A-527 (re-lease) and

---

[243] *See* § 11.10[E][3][c], *supra.*

[244] Section 7.08[D], *supra.*

[245] The law and economics literature is replete with discussions of the lost-volume seller and the circumstances under which the foregoing analysis applies. This literature is described in § 7.08[D], *supra.*

2A-528(1) (contract/market difference) will result in no damages and will undercompensate the lessor. This is the lost-volume seller problem in a lease context.

The drafters of section 2A-528 have made allowance for the lost-volume problem in the same manner as provided in Article 2.[246] Section 2A-528(2) provides:

> (2) If the measure of damages provided in subsection (1) is inadequate to put a lessor in as good a position as performance would have, the measure of damages is the present value of the profit, including reasonable overhead, the lessor would have made from full performance by the lessee, together with any incidental damages allowed under Section 2A-530, due allowance for costs reasonably incurred and due credit for payments or proceeds of disposition.

Thus, the lessor is entitled to recover for the profit lost as a result of the lessee's default.[247]

Because the language is similar to the parallel provision in Article 2, some difficulties present in the Article 2 provision continue under Article 2A. For example, the provision that requires "due credit for payments or proceeds of disposition" from the lessor's recovery undermines the rationale permitting recovery of lost-volume profits. If the lessor in the foregoing example must credit the payments received from the second lessee against his recovery, he is entitled to no damages. As they have done with respect to the Article 2 counterpart, courts should ignore this language in the context of a lost-volume lessor and should allow for the recovery of the entire lost profit.[248]

[6] Lessor's Action for the Rent

Analogous to a seller's action for the price,[249] Article 2A provides a lessor an action for the entire rent due under the lease. The lessor's right to collect the entire rent due under the lease when the lessee does not retain possession of the goods, like the seller's action for the price, is very limited. It is available only under the following circumstances:

---

[246] *See* U.C.C. § 2-708(2).

[247] Unlike the parallel provision in Article 2, under section 2A-528, lost profit is reduced to present value. For a discussion of the tricky problems this presents, *see* Thomas Crandall et al. I Uniform Commercial Code § 13.7.4 (1993).

[248] For a more detailed discussion of this problem, *see* § 7.08[D], *supra.*

[249] U.C.C. § 2-709.

1. *If the goods are not repossessed by the lessor or tendered to the lessor by the lessee.* If the lessee tenders the goods to the lessor, even though the lessee does so wrongfully, the lessor must take them back and is not entitled to an action for the rent.[250] This is a departure from Article 2. Under Article 2, once a buyer accepts the goods, unless the buyer is entitled to revoke that acceptance or unless the seller voluntarily retakes possession of the goods, the seller is entitled to the price.[251] Rejection of this rule is implicit in section 2A-529 and made explicit in the Comments.[252]

2. *If conforming goods are lost or damaged within a commercially reasonable time after their risk of loss has passed to the lessee.*

3. *If goods have been identified by the seller to the lease contract and the lessor is unable, after reasonable effort, to dispose of them at a reasonable price, or circumstances indicate that such an effort would be unavailing.*

The second and third circumstances in which the lessor is entitled to the rent parallel provisions in section 2-709.[253]

Under section 2A-529, if a lessor succeeds in an action for the rent, the amount of rent recoverable must be reduced to present value, because the rent recovered would not be payable until some future time. The lessor is also entitled to incidental damages—for example, if the lessor expended funds in a reasonable, but unsuccessful, attempt to dispose of the goods. Any expenses saved as a result of the default, such as expenses the lessor would have been required to expend for maintenance, are deducted from the recovery. A lessor who is successful in recovering the rent must hold the goods at the disposal of the lessee for the remaining term of the lease,[254] and if the lessor disposes of the goods prior to the end of the term of the lease, he must give the lessee an appropriate credit against any judgment collected by the lessor.[255]

---

[250] U.C.C. § 2A-529, Official Comment 1 provides:

> There is no general right in a lessor to recover the full rent from the lessee upon holding the goods for the lessee. If the lessee tenders goods back to the lessor, and the lessor refuses to accept the tender, the lessor will be limited to damages it would have suffered had it taken back the goods.

[251] *See* § 7.08[E], *supra.*

[252] U.C.C. § 2A-529, Official Comment 1.

[253] For a discussion of these requirements in the context of section 2-709, *see* § 7.05[E], *supra.*

[254] U.C.C. § 2A-529(4).

[255] U.C.C. § 2A-529(3).

Because of the requirement that the lessor accept a re-tender of the goods from the lessee, however wrongful the lessee's re-tender, it is unlikely that section 2A-529 will be available very often to a lessor. It is a rare instance in which the lessor would be unable to dispose of the goods by re-leasing them or selling them. It is important, however, to remember that the lease contract itself may provide the landlord with a remedy for the full unpaid rent. Comment 1 to section 2A-529 seems to validate such provisions,[256] although general contract principles of mitigation of damages may preclude their enforcement.[257]

[7] The Lessor's Residual Interest

Article 2A also explicitly permits the lessor to recover damages caused to the lessor's residual interest by the lessee.[258] This simply makes explicit the liability of the lessee for harm to the goods caused by the lessee not contemplated by the lease agreement. It would, of course, not cover wear and tear that would ordinarily occur during the lease term.

§ 11.11 CONCLUSION

Article 2A also contains a number of other provisions that parallel provisions of Article 2. These sections are not discussed, because they present little or nothing that differs from their Article 2 counterparts and are not critical to an understanding of the basic structure of Article 2A. These provisions include sections dealing with the risk of loss,[259] casualty to identified goods,[260] commercial impracticability,[261] adequate assurance of per-

---

[256] Official Comment 1 to U.C.C. § 2A-529 provides that "[a]bsent a lease provision to the contrary" the full amount of unpaid rent (reduced to present value) is only available under the circumstances listed in the section.

[257] *See* E. Allan Farnsworth, I Farnsworth on Contracts, § 12.18 at 295. *See also* Chase Manhattan Bank v. American Nat'l Bank, 889 F. Supp. 123 (S.D.N.Y. 1994); Lake Ridge Academy v. Carney, 613 N.E.2d 183 (Ohio 1993).

[258] Article 2A-532 provides:

In addition to any other recovery permitted by this Article or other law, the lessor may recover from the lessee an amount that will fully compensate the lessor for any loss of or damage to the lessor's residual interest in the goods caused by the default of the lessee.

[259] U.C.C. § 2A-219, 2A-220.
[260] U.C.C. § 2A-221.
[261] U.C.C. §§ 2A-405, 2A-406.

formance,[262] anticipatory repudiation,[263] and remedies upon insolvency.[264] It is not expected that these provisions will be interpreted differently than their Article 2 counterparts, and it is anticipated that they will function in roughly the same manner. If the reader is interested in a discussion of these topics, discussions of the corresponding sections of Article 2 are available elsewhere in this text.

---

[262] U.C.C. § 2A-401.
[263] U.C.C. §§ 2A-402, 2A-403.
[264] U.C.C. § 2A-522.

TABLE OF CASES

E

I

J

W

INDEX

D

M

T